In this dictionary of early music, Graham Strahle has compiled definitions of musical terms in English as used and understood during the Renaissance and Baroque periods. He includes terms relating to instruments, performance, theory and composition and draws entirely from original printed and manuscript sources in Britain in the period 1500–1740. The first group of sources are lexicographic works, mainly general English dictionaries but also Latin, Italian, French and Spanish dictionaries published in England. These give a representation of Continental as well as English musical traditions. The second group of sources are musical treatises, performance and composition books and other musical writings of the time. The dictionary reveals how terms and definitions were understood by musicians of the time, using their own words. Definitions are grouped in chronological order under the relevant headword so that changes in meaning can be easily traced. Graham Strahle's Introduction gives an account of the sources and sketches the development of musical vocabulary up to the Enlightenment period.

This book gives innumerable new insights into music as played and heard in earlier times. It provides an invaluable source for scholar and performer and a wide variety of information for the non-specialist.

An Early Music Dictionary

An Early Music Dictionary

Musical Terms from British Sources, 1500–1740

GRAHAM STRAHLE
Faculty of Music,
The University of Queensland

CAMBRIDGE UNIVERSITY PRESS
Cambridge, New York, Melbourne, Madrid, Cape Town, Singapore, São Paulo, Delhi

Cambridge University Press
The Edinburgh Building, Cambridge CB2 8RU, UK

Published in the United States of America by Cambridge University Press, New York

www.cambridge.org
Information on this title: www.cambridge.org/9780521106900

First published 1995
This digitally printed version 2009

A catalogue record for this publication is available from the British Library

Library of Congress Cataloguing in Publication data

Strahle, Graham.
An Early Music Dictionary : Musical Terms from British
Sources, 1500–1740 / Graham Strahle.
p. cm.
Includes bibliographical references.
ISBN 0 521 41688 4 (hardback)
1. Music – Dictionaries. I. Title.
ML108.S88 1994
780′.9′031–dc20 94–9190 CIP

ISBN 978-0-521-41688-7 hardback
ISBN 978-0-521-10690-0 paperback

Published with assistance from the Australian Academy of the
Humanities

For Catherine

Contents

Acknowledgements

In the long path to this project's completion I have benefited from the help and encouragement of countless friends and colleagues. To all I express my appreciation. I want to give particular thanks to Claude Palisca and Curtis Price for generously giving me the opportunity to carry out intensive work on this project at, respectively, Yale University and King's College, London. Special thanks also go to Stanley Sadie for his support and to John Stevens, John Butt and the late Howard Mayer Brown for their invaluable advice and suggestions during the preparation of the manuscript.

The staff of many libraries contributed their expertise during the bibliographical stages of work and I would like to mention especially the assistance given to me by the staff of the British Library and Yale University's Beinecke Rare Book and Manuscript Library, Sterling Library and Music Library. Acknowledgement also goes to Bart Smith at Special Collections, Newberry Library, Chicago, to Timothy Hobbs, Special Collections, Glasgow University Library, to Gillian Jones, Music Librarian at University of Wales College of Cardiff, and to Susan Woodburn, Special Collections, Barr Smith Library, University of Adelaide.

Financial assistance from the Fulbright Commission and the Australian-American Educational Foundation, and also from the Australian Academy of the Humanities is gratefully acknowledged. For their continual support I am also grateful to David Swale, David Tunley, Andrew McCredie and Mary Cyr, while for advice in the early stages on specific sources my thanks go to James Coover and Peter Walls. In the complex and often difficult process of bringing this project to completion I pay special thanks to Penny Souster and to her colleagues at Cambridge University Press.

Extracts from manuscripts 18. B. xix. (Praise of musicke), Harley 4160 (Musical observations and experiments), Sloane 1388 (Letters addressed to Rev. Holder), and Add. MSS 4388 (Papers Relating to the Writings of Birchensha), 4911 (Art of Mvsic), 4919 (Practicall Theory of Musick), 4923 (Tractatus de Musicâ), 19758 (Ravenscrofts Treatise of Musick), 29429 (Various papers written in the autograph of Dr Pepusch), 32531–7 (North manuscripts on music) and 32549 (Capt. Prencourts rules), are reproduced by permission of the British Library. Extracts from Rawlinson D. 751 (An Essay on Musick, wherein is contain'd the Principles of that Science), folios 2–4 *verso*, are reproduced by permission of the Bodleian Library. Extracts from Osborne Shelves Music Manuscript 3 (Treatise of the Thoro' bass), are reproduced by permission of the Beinecke Rare Book and Manuscript Library.

Introduction

Scope and guide to use

This work gathers together definitions of musical terms from British sources of the sixteenth to early eighteenth centuries. The definitions are arranged under each headword in chronological order to enable changes of meaning to be traced. The sources used fall into two categories: first lexicographic works, mainly general language dictionaries of the time; and secondly musical treatises, composition and performance tutors and other writings on music, both printed and manuscript. All the sources consulted for this Dictionary are listed under 'Primary sources' (pp. 461–7) in the Bibliography.

Coverage is extended to all aspects of music. An 'open window' approach has been adopted so as to include all terminological information relating to music. This yields at times unexpected results for the modern reader but allows the full range of musical vocabulary of this period to be studied. Most information falls within the main fields of theory, composition, genres, instruments and performance; however, much also relates to music's connections with poetry, dance, science, mathematics, religion and mythology. Assembled all together, the size and scope of musical vocabulary of this period is very much larger than one might initially imagine. On the other hand, some terms that the modern reader may associate with this period are notably absent: examples include *drumslade, hurdy-gurdy, orpharion* and *suspension*. Their absence means that none of the sources consulted in this work define these terms. It does not mean that these words were not in use at the time, and a variety of explanations can be put forward including sheer oversight by writers, their over-familiarity at the time, their rarity or adjudged lack of importance, or that they went by different names. As an illustration of the latter, the hurdy-gurdy was called a 'symphony' or 'vielle', and the concept of suspension was understood by the terms 'anticipation', 'postposition', 'resolution' and 'supposition'. In the larger picture, however, the sources testify to an enormous wealth of musical vocabulary that existed in the pre-Classical era, and it becomes very evident that much of it has since undergone radical alteration during the course of musical history. Learning more about this vocabulary represents an important further step towards increasing our knowledge of musical traditions of the past.

The chronological period and sources covered in this Dictionary enable a substantial body of musical terminology from the Renaissance to the late Baroque to be assembled. The resulting picture covers the 240 years prior to the appearance of Grassineau's landmark work, *A Musical Dictionary*, in 1740, being the first large-scale musical dictionary to have been published in England. Since Continental sources have not been included, the Dictionary naturally reflects the British perspective. It should be emphasised, however, that of the more than fifty lexicographic works consulted, around one fifth are romance-language dictionaries, that is Italian-to-English, French-to-English and Spanish-to-English dictionaries compiled and published in England in the later sixteenth and seventeenth centuries. Intended for use by English readers learning foreign languages, they fortuitously include hundreds of foreign musical terms and reveal numerous insights into musical traditions on the Continent. Other non-English dictionaries used are Latin-to-English works; these were the backbone of sixteenth-century lexicography in England and are singularly useful for the period up to 1600. After then the first English-to-English dictionaries began to appear, beginning with Cawdrey's modest little *A Table Alphabeticall* in 1604.

Practical demands and the existence of other reference tools have determined the chronological period covered in this work. Musical terms before 1500 in English literary sources have been documented in Carter's *A Dictionary of Middle English Musical Terms*. At the opposite end of the scale there exists a series of period musical dictionaries beginning with Grassineau's *A Musical Dictionary* (1740, later editions in 1769 and 1784), followed by Tans'ur's *New Musical Dictionary* (1766), an English translation of Rousseau's *Dictionnaire de musique* (1771, second edition 1779), Hoyle's *Dictionarium Musicae, being a complete Dictionary or Treasury of Music* (1770, later editions in 1790 and 1791), and Busby's *Dictionary of Music* (1786).

The two source categories used, lexicographic sources and specialist writings on music, have required different editorial approaches and these can be briefly explained. The first category consists primarily of English and bilingual dictionaries. All material relating to music found in these sources has been extracted and fully reproduced in the Dictionary. This category also includes two forerunners of the modern encyclopedia, Harris's *Lexicon Technicum* (1704) and Chambers's *Cyclopædia: Or, An Universal Dictionary Of Arts and Sciences* (1728); the longer musical articles from these texts are assigned to the Appendix, with appropriate cross-referencing in the main body of the Dictionary. These encyclopedic works, and to a lesser extent the universal dictionaries of Kersey and Bailey, move beyond the mere task of providing definitions and give scholarly accounts of subjects digested from scientific writings of the time. Since it is in numerous cases impossible to draw a line between definitions and more discursive writing, and because it is reasonable to treat these sources with the completeness they deserve, a decision has been made to include in full all their entries relating to music.

The second category of sources, comprising musical treatises, tutors and a range of other writings on music such as scientific, philosophical and religious essays, has been treated differently. The approach has been to concentrate on actual definitions but also to allow for the inclusion of other relevant linguistic information that may occur. By their very nature musical treatises rarely give self-standing definitions of terms and tend rather to deal with terminology as an incidental concern. Interwoven in their discussions may be found accounts of the meaning of terms, their etymologies, and commentaries upon correct versus incorrect usages as perceived by the writer. These have all been deemed relevant and are reproduced in the Dictionary. For this category of sources the present work does not extend coverage to illustrative usages of terms, and in this way it differs in approach from other lexicographic tools such as the OED. The purpose here is limited merely to providing a prescriptive record of how terms were defined in the period that they were used.

The two respective categories of source offer fundamentally different material. Lexicographic sources spread across a greater range of musical terminology but the treatise extracts, as is to be expected, provide fuller and more authoritative coverage of individual terms. In view of this, lexicographic and treatise texts have been kept separate. Where a given headword is represented by both source categories, lexicographic material is presented first and the treatise extracts second, as two separate chronological sequences of text.

Leading each original text entry is an abbreviated citation of the source from which it comes. Full identifying information on each source is given in the Bibliography. Text entries are headed by the date of source, in bold, and name of author in upper case. Titles of lexicographic works are generally not included except where the author is anonymous or multiple works by the same author are cited. For treatises and other writings on music abbreviated titles are always given, as are page or folio numbers before each extract. Manuscript sources are identified by library and other relevant holding information after the title.

Cross-references direct the reader to related headwords and other places where further information on a given term may be found. Where headwords are alphabetically contiguous and share similar meanings, cross-referencing is usually not added. Neither are cross-references added where relationships in meaning between headwords are straightforward and obvious. Some cross-referencing is already present in the original extracts themselves (Chambers is the most thorough) and this is self-explanatory.

The Bibliography is divided into two parts: (1) primary sources, including both sources cited in the entries and sources that were consulted but found not to contain any information that could be incorporated into the Dictionary, and (2) secondary sources.

Source discussion

The relatively late appearance of specialist music dictionaries in England makes for special difficulties when researching into the meaning of terms in the early eighteenth century and before. No dictionary of music was printed in England earlier than James Grassineau's *A Musical Dictionary* of 1740, that is, if we exclude the brief *A Short Explication of such Foreign Words, as are made Use of in Musick Books* of 1724. To obtain a full picture of musical terminology as it existed before the appearance of Grassineau's dictionary, a wide scattering of information needs to be drawn together. Locating all surviving documentation relating to musical terms involves having to confront a potentially immense primary source literature. The present work cannot claim to have located every definition of every term, but the 250 sources used here represent the core literature of the period under consideration. The 52 lexicographic sources include all English-language dictionaries and principal bilingual dictionaries of the period. Later editions of some works are also included where they yield additional important information. The second group of sources, the musical writings, is intended to be a comprehensive list of treatises and composition and performance tutors of the period, although not all were found to furnish usable terminological information (see the Bibliography, pp. 465–7).

In commenting upon the sources, discussions can at best be introductory. Greater coverage is given in this Introduction to lexicographic sources because these are relatively much less known in musicological literature. Early dictionaries offer an assortment of musical information that is essentially unrelated to that in treatises. They relate a level of musical knowledge well removed from the confines of specialised musical scholarship, making them more indicative of popular traditions of music-making of the time. Writers of early dictionaries were compilers of information, and instead of originating their own entries habitually reused definitions in existing dictionaries. An extreme example of the same entry making numerous reappearances in a long string of works occurs with the term *diagram*, whose musical meaning was clearly not grasped by lexicographers until Chambers in 1728. Riddell has commented on this in relation to Bullokar, Cockeram and Blount, showing that their dictionaries uncritically borrow material from previously existing dictionaries, glossaries and wordlists. Indeed he concludes that this tendency persists until Dr Johnson.[1]

In the extracts presented in this Dictionary, such patterns of borrowing are frequently encountered but their extent cannot be hoped to be fully documented. A thorough investigation of reliance between sources would involve comparisons with various English glossaries, such as those identified by Schäfer, and numerous Continental dictionaries of the same period. Furthermore, only by systematically comparing every edition of every known source might all these borrowings be properly traced. Smalley has observed this problem in relation to the sources used in Cotgrave's French-to-English dictionary of 1611: 'it is rash to state categorically that any such term originated in the work of a particular writer, since it is manifestly impossible to investigate every work of the period and the word so designated might be found in almost any uninvestigated work of this time'.[2] This statement equally applies to the present study, and the findings presented here must be understood as being confined exclusively to the sources consulted.

The reader may refer to a number of specialist studies of individual lexicographic works or groups of works listed under 'Secondary sources' in the Bibliography.[3]

Lexicographic sources

The lexicographic sources used here consist of a broad range of dictionaries published in England during the period. They encompass English-to-English, Latin-to-English, Italian-to-English, French-to-English and Spanish-to-English dictionaries, two early encyclopedic works, and one specialist musical dictionary, *A Short Explication of such Foreign Words*, of 1724. Grassineau's more important *A Musical Dictionary* (1740) has not been included because it is a large, integrated work in itself. All material from the sources consulted relating to music is presented irrespective of its length or content. Some bilingual dictionaries, such as Torriano (1659), contain a second, reverse dictionary in which English is put before the Italian (or other language), but these have not been consulted in the present work. Polyglot and etymological dictionaries have been excluded because they represent a separate genre and are limited in their usefulness.

Included in the source list are all first editions of principal lexicographic works published in Britain. Where later editions of a given source are judged to be of special importance these have also been included. Decision on which works and which editions have been selected rests primarily on published research by Starnes, Starnes and Noyes, Stein, Hayashi, Schäffer, Collison, and Tonelli. It must nevertheless be stated that the choice of works to be included is necessarily that of the present author.

The Dictionary may record duplicated information if the same entry appears in more than one source. This occurs only when the respective sources that duplicate an entry are judged historically important, the material is rare, or where such duplications may themselves be important to know. Duplications are not recorded in the case of multiple works by Kersey and Bailey in which entries are numerously repeated in unchanged form. If any entry is found to have been revised, augmented or otherwise varied in substance in a later edition or separate work, the altered entry is given in full. Alterations in the spelling of a headword are also recorded if this occurs.

Lexicographic sources offer widely differing scope of material. Early language dictionaries such as Cawdrey (1604) frequently offer little more than synonyms while later ones may offer extended, scholarly articles. Latin dictionaries tend to present an assortment of biographical, geographical and other information in place of strict definitions. However, regardless of the approach taken in individual dictionaries, all information of a musical nature is included. The sheer breadth of musical terminology offered by early dictionaries is by itself impressive, even if their definitions are not always trustworthy. They provide roughly three times the number of musical terms and definitions than do the treatises, and this shows how important they are in comprehending the full range of musical terminology that existed. While it is true that in many cases the information they provide raises more questions than it answers, early dictionaries present us with a uniquely valuable resource. They can help us build up a more detailed picture of past musical traditions, including instruments, performance practice, and the more panoramic picture of music in society.

The dictionaries of **Cawdrey** (1604), **Bullokar** (1616) and **Cockeram** (1623) are the first English-to-English dictionaries that were published. They follow directly in the tradition of pedagogical Latin-to-English dictionaries of the sixteenth century in that they concentrated on 'hard words', many of them Latin; but where they differ is in their inclusion of unusual English and foreign words. All three derive much of their material from earlier Latin dictionaries, particularly that of Thomas (1587 and later editions). The presence of Latin words in an English dictionary at this time would not have been considered strange since the purpose of English dictionaries was not to record spoken language but to assist in scholarly, classical learning.[4] For example, in Cockeram one finds such archaic Latinisms as *absonant, buccinate* (see under *buccinator*), *cantation, citharize* (*citharist*), *eneatour* (under *aeneator*), *hilarode* (*hilarodus*), *minurize* and *præcantation* (*precantation*). All would appear to derive from either Thomas or other Latin dictionaries then in existence. It has to be said that the number of musical terms in these early English dictionaries is small, amounting to barely a dozen in Cawdrey and rising to fifty-five in Cockeram. These works cannot be relied upon to give up-to-date information or any real indication of spoken vocabulary of the time. Nevertheless, as the first English dictionaries they are historically important and cannot be overlooked: they provided the basis for all other subsequent English dictionaries up to the works of Kersey and Bailey after 1700.

Blount (1656) and **Phillips** (1658), respectively the fourth and fifth English dictionaries to be published, represent a step beyond their predecessors in their inclusion of substantial subject vocabularies from a range of arts and sciences. Among the subjects included, all of which are named on their title pages, is music; this makes both dictionaries of special interest to music scholars today. At the same time, however, the musical vocabularies offered reveal many inkhornisms taken from Latin dictionaries, in some instances by way of Cockeram. Examples are *buccinate, calamist* and *encomium* in Blount's dictionary. This continuing reliance on Latin was an outcome of the still prevalent view that Latin provided a core of scholarly terminology in the English language. Again, this has little if any bearing on English as it was spoken at this time: neither dictionary contains significant vocabularies taken from the vernacular. However, their deference to Latin may in turn have exercised its own influence on the development of English by reinforcing its Latin base.

Thomas Blount's *Glossographia* borrows heavily from the Latin dictionaries of Thomas and Holyoke, and in total his Latin borrowings account for slightly more than half his entries.[5] Nevertheless, the *Glossographia* surpasses the efforts of his predecessors, Bullokar and Cockeram, in scholarship and wealth of material. His is the first English dictionary to feature the terms *canzonet, curranto, opera, recitative, trillo* and *virginal*, all of which terms except for the first were very up to date for the 1650s. A continued though modest expansion of musical vocabulary can be observed through the *Glossographia*'s five editions to 1681. Blount rarely includes biographical entries, but an intriguing exception is the entry '*Alphonso* a famous Musician, who invented a particular way of playing on the Viol, which still retains his name'. This presumably is Alfonso

Ferrabosco the younger; Blount's entry *leero* also refers to this composer.

Edward Phillips's *The New World of English Words* of 1658 was a rival work of comparable size to Blount's, but it is notably different in its inclusion of such peculiarly English musical words as *braied, citrial, doced, kern, ribibble* and *rigols*. The first edition includes terms across a range of forty-one arts and sciences, including theology, philosophy, logic, rhetoric and music. Unlike Blount, Phillips adds names of authorities connected with each subject, and for music he gives Dr Charles Coleman; for the second edition of 1662 Coleman is again cited. For the third and fourth editions of 1671 and 1678 the names of both John Birchensha and Matthew Locke are given, while the fifth edition of 1696 names Locke and Henry Purcell. This invites speculation that Phillips received assistance from these and the many other authorities he names, and in the preface of his first edition Phillips implies that he had actually received such assistance in compiling his dictionary; his wording, however, is ambiguous. Seizing on this very ambiguity, Blount launched an attack on *The New World of English Words* in an essay entitled *A World of Errors* (1673), in which he accused Phillips of falsely promoting the dictionary. Blount was convinced that Phillips, far from having received any assistance, had single-handedly plagiarised his own *Glossographia* by reproducing numerous of its entries. Blount's claim can in fact be supported by a comparison between the two works, and detailed analysis strongly discounts the possibility that Coleman, Birchensha, Locke or Purcell had any part in preparing musical entries for *The New World of English Words*. Evidence shows that Phillips indeed drew heavily on Blount and also to a lesser extent on Bullokar and Cockeram. Further, the fifth edition of his dictionary can be seen to have made use of Furetière's *Dictionnaire universel* of 1690; this is most evident in the entries *capriccio, fantasie, monochord, tierce* and *tone*.[6]

But neither was Blount above appropriating material for his *Glossographia* without acknowledgement. From Cotgrave (1611) he copied out entries such as *mot, motet, serenade, tiercet, vaudevil* and *virelay*. The wording of his intriguing entries on *horse-ballet, opera, recitative,* and *trillo* would appear to indicate indebtedness to a further, unidentified French source.

The most interesting feature of both the Blount and Phillips dictionaries is that they incorporate some material from contemporary musical treatises. Phillips was the first to do this, in the first and third editions of *The New World*: here he extracts definitions from Playford's *An Introduction To the Skill of Mvsick* for the entry on counterpoint. A longer entry on *cliff* in the third edition also comes from Playford.[7] For the third edition of the *Glossographia* Blount draws on Playford's *Introduction* for definitions on *mood* and *syncopation*. Blount also cites Bacon for the entry *diapason* and Mersenne for *psaltery*.

In its seven editions to 1720, Phillips's *The New World* underwent a greater expansion of vocabulary than is the case with Blount. The first six editions see a significant increase in musical entries, from 180 in the first edition to just over twice that in the sixth edition of 1706. Disappointingly, the seventh edition is no more than a reprint of the sixth, but it is the latter, prepared by John **Kersey**, that commands attention because it stands as the most impressive, thorough-going revision of *The New World*. Essentially a new work, it forms an important basis for later English dictionaries by other writers including Nathan Bailey and Kersey himself. Containing some 370 entries relating to music, it relies on Harris's *Lexicon Technicum* for technical terms such as *arsis & thesis, comma, concords, descant* and *mood*. However, Kersey appears to have written his own entries on other technical terms such as *diatonos hypaton, diatonum diatonicum, diezeugmenon nete* and *diezeugmenon paranete*. In undertaking the revision Kersey augmented the wordlist by freely drawing on his own smaller work, *A New English Dictionary* (1702), for more popular words such as *bugle-horn, minnekins* and *twang*.

John **Harris** is another lexicographer who incorporated material from musical treatises. Like Blount and Phillips he evidently knew of Playford's *Introduction* because his lengthy entry on *time* in music is taken directly from that work.[8] As a forerunner of the encyclopedia, the *Lexicon Technicum* makes more use of specialist literature of the time than do other dictionaries of the period. For example Harris draws on a passage from Holder's *Treatise of the Natural Grounds* for his article on *sound*, a passage that was in turn repeated by later dictionary writers; and his definition of *measure* comes out of Christopher Simpson's *The Principles of Practical Mvsick*.[9] Entries of particular interest in Harris include *manner* (probably deriving from a French source), the large entries on the monochord and moods, and the truly enormous entry on *watch-work*, dealing with the subject of mechanical chimes. Surprisingly absent, though, are any entries on a number of core musical terms for this period: *bar, breve* (or 'brief'), *clavichord, degree, dorick, flat, gamut, harp, lute, organ, spinet, viol* and *violin*. Neither was

Harris beyond making the odd mistake, and his entry 'flond' for 'florid descant' is an example of just how fallible were dictionary writers (or copy-editors) of the period. This spurious word was given a life of its own when Kersey in turn repeated it in his revision of Phillips and again in his own *Dictionarium Anglo-Britannicum* of 1708.

Of all the dictionary writers of the period, Ephraim **Chambers** was by far the most extensive in his use of contemporary musical writings. His *Cyclopædia* of 1728, regarded today as an early encyclopedia, was in its time conceived as a dictionary and the full title reads: *Cyclopædia: Or, An Universal Dictionary Of Arts and Sciences*. Its inclusion as a source in the present work reflects the expanding nature of the dictionary genre at this time. With 415 entries relating to music the *Cyclopædia* is a major repository of musical information and certainly deserves separate study. Many of the entries are substantial articles in their own right and are reproduced in full in this work. In the field of dictionary writing Chambers clearly emerges as the most careful scholar and his breadth of musical knowledge is impressive, especially when viewed against the backdrop of the numerous other subjects exhaustively treated in the *Cyclopædia*.

Chambers seems to have made it his business to read as widely as possible from contemporary treatises on all subjects, and his range of reference indicates how very well informed he was with theoretical and philosophical writings on music. He shows a thorough acquaintance with Malcolm's *Treatise of Musick*, citing this source in the entries *chromatic, clef, concord, discord, enharmonic, f, harmony, key, music, note, octave, rattle, rhythm, scale, semitone, sol-faing, song, sound, supposition, synaulia, time* and *tune*. Indeed the suggestion arises that Malcolm may have assisted Chambers in the writing of these musical articles, but no evidence for this exists. Holder is cited in the entries *concord, consonance* and *tune*; Lampe in the entry *cymbal*; Salmon in *clef* and *semitone*; Vossius in *ode, rhythm, verse* and *vocal music*; and Wallis in *monochord*. Chambers also refers liberally to articles on musical topics in the *Philosophical Transactions of the Royal Society*, while for the entry on *opera* he even refers to the *Spectator* newspaper. A strong French influence is felt throughout the *Cyclopædia*, as evidenced by the frequent use of French spellings (for example 'dominante' and 'mediante'). Numerous French writers are cited in his scholarly discussions, including Arbeau, Chauvin, Du Cange and Perrault. Particularly noteworthy is the citing of Mersenne in the entries *antipathy* and *concord*, and Brossard in some thirty entries: *cantata, dialogue, duo, group, imitation, natural, o, part, passage, pathetic music, pedals, perfect, perfidia, phantastic style, research* (after Brossard's *ricercata/recherche*), *resolution, second, semi-diapente, semidiatessaron, serenade, sesqui, sonata, style, tablature, theorbo, trias harmonica, variation, viol* and *violin*. On a less important note Chambers evidently intended to include an extended article on degrees in music, since his own cross-references point to this, but either this was overlooked or the article left out. Unknowingly too, Chambers occasionally duplicates his own material: 'chantry' and 'chauntry' appear as two separate entries.

Consideration of bilingual dictionaries logically begins with the Latin-to-English dictionaries of the sixteenth century, since these are chronologically the first group of lexicographic sources. Primarily intended as tools for reading classical texts, these were scholastic works that additionally functioned as encyclopedic storehouses of knowledge. The earliest source used in the Dictionary is the anonymous *Ortus Vocabulorum* (*Garden of Words*) of 1500, a work compiled from English and Continental Latin glosses that date back to the mid fourteenth century. In its footsteps is the Latin dictionary of the Renaissance scholar and writer Thomas **Elyot** (1538); as a pioneering work of humanist learning in England, it takes as its starting point the classical texts of Plautus, Terence and others, supplemented by the writings of Erasmus. Thomas **Cooper**'s prodigiously large *Thesaurus* of 1565 is a continuation of Elyot's humanist model, and is fleshed out with countless illustrative quotations taken from classical writers; the work is augmented by an innovative appendix of names and places, mostly relating to the ancient world. The Latin dictionary of Thomas **Thomas** (1587) is an almost equally copious volume, and although it contains fewer proper names and illustrative quotations, it surpasses that of Cooper in overall content. It emerges ahead of Cooper as the most authoritative Latin source of the Elizabethan period. Its musical entries number 285, slightly ahead of Cooper's 270, and they are similarly constructed out of classical texts. Thomas gathers detailed musical information on such subjects as the names of notes and strings in the ancient Greek diagram or system, for example *hypate, lichanos, mese, nete, proslambanomenos* and *syzeugmenon*. Of particular interest in both Cooper and Thomas is the way they render into English various terms belonging to antiquity. Thus Cooper's translations of *emelia* (described as a 'pauion' dance), *fidicula* (equated with a lute, rebec or gittern), *monaulos* (recorder), *monochord* (clavichord), *tibia* (shawm, flute or recorder) and *tonarion* (shawm) indirectly shed light on Elizabethan musical traditions. Of similar interest in Thomas are the entries *espineta* (equated with virginals) and *spondiales* (waits). Thomas's work was to exercise greater influence than any other dictionary produced in this period in England, and its impact continued to be felt through the work of English lexicographers well into the next century, most immediately in the foreign-language dictionaries of Percyvall, Florio and Cotgrave.

Foreign-language dictionaries emerged as an important genre at the end of the sixteenth century. These works were written by linguists resident in England, and they grow out of the strong political and cultural links that had been forged between England and neighbouring countries. Approached as musical sources they offer spectacularly large and unexpectedly rich treasure troves of information and, in the case of Florio and Cotgrave, far eclipse quantitatively, at least for musical terms, any English dictionary produced in the seventeenth century. Judged in the context of the sources presented in this Dictionary, much of what Florio and Cotgrave relate is unique, and the fact that they reflect non-English musical traditions adds considerably to their interest. Richard **Percyvall**'s Spanish-to-English dictionary first appeared in 1591 and the revision by Minsheu of 1599 is consulted here. The later edition identifies augmentations to the original wordlist by adding an asterisk before each new headword, and in total contains around 115 musical entries. As with other dictionary writers, both Percyvall and Minsheu made use of existing works, Thomas and Florio being two of their major sources.[10] Interestingly, Percyvall may also have gained some of his vocabulary first-hand from captured sailors of the Spanish Armada.[11]

The earliest Italian-to-English dictionaries are those of John Florio, but predating them by several decades is an interesting glossary in William **Thomas**'s school book of 1550, *Principal rvles of the Italian grammer*. As the title page indicates, it was designed to help readers of Boccaccio, Petrarch and Dante; the fifty-five musical entries are to be seen as an outcome of this purpose. Thus Thomas's entries *ballata, canzona, madriali* and *sonatore* are illustrative of a literary tradition represented by those authors. Far more important than this little glossary, **Florio**'s two works of 1598 and 1611 have long been acknowledged as a valuable source for studying Italian language of the turn-of-century period. His first dictionary, *A Worlde of Wordes* of 1598, contains around 430 entries relating to music, which is considerably more than any dictionary in England to that date. By no means are all the entries original, however: many terms and definitions are borrowed from the Latin dictionary of Thomas. These include *musica, nervo, orchestra, palinodia, pandora, paramese, phtongo, preludio, recantare, salterio, simphonia, simphoniacus, succinare, tetracordo, tibilustri, tonarione,* and probably also the terms *corno, ribecca, salmodia, sampogna, spadico, tara tantara* and *testudo*.

Florio's *Qveen Anna's New World of Words* of 1611 is a revision of the 1598 work and, having been elevated by language scholars to a position above all other dictionaries of the period, was for a long time regarded as one of the great monuments of Renaissance scholarship. Its dedicatee, Anne of Denmark, is believed to have received private tuition in Italian from Florio, who as a teacher was held in high esteem in royal circles. More generally, his revision can be viewed as a product of the close cultural ties between England and Italy that had built up by that time. As his sources, Florio lists 72 names and works, including Boccaccio and Petrarch (although curiously not Dante) together with a 'Dittionário Italiáno ed Inglése' (no such work is known to exist), a 'Dittionário Italiáno e Francése', a 'Dittionário volgáre et Latíno del venúti', and a 'Vocabolário delas dos lengnas, Italiáno & Spagnuólo'. Certainly the impression must be that Florio was well read, since according to his will he possessed a personal library of 340 books written in Italian, French and Spanish.[12] More recent scholarly opinion however, does not attach much credibility to Florio's claims of having consulted 72 works in preparing *Qveen Anna's New World of Words*. In the past rash claims have been made about the amount of original work Florio undertook, and a truer picture takes into account his heavy reliance on Thomas's Latin dictionary for both his 1598 and 1611 works.[13] Florio's Latin derivations include *diagram, diesi, epicitharisma, epistomium, epitaph, epode, hemisphero, pectide, phthongo, profetare, simpsalma, spondeo piede, tibilustri* and *tintinabulo*, most if not all of which derive from Thomas. In spite of this debt, considerable attention must centre on the 520 or so entries relating to music in his dictionary if only because this is the largest number of terms encountered in any source consulted for the present work.

Of prime interest in Florio is the colourful picture of popular music-making he conveys, using earthy language, colloquialisms and even vulgarities of expression, all of which lend a distinctive and consistent flavour to both his works. Dozens of terms relate to musical customs in rural communities, about which little is otherwise known; examples include *barzelletta, contadinella, frottola, girometta, stampinata, strambotto* and *villanata*. Fewer terms illustrate town life, but *cantepolare* deserves attention in view of its mention of the city of London.[14] Florio's material is endlessly fascinating, but caution should be exercised in its interpretation, particularly when chronological inferences are drawn: certain anomalies do emerge. It is curious, for example, that Florio's definition of *toccata* implies that the form was outmoded by 1611: this is contrary to what is known of the toccata in Italy of this time. Florio's work was again revised in 1659, by Giovanni **Torriano**. As part of his very substantial revision, Torriano claims to have made use of a manuscript left by Florio for his own revision of the work, which he did not live to complete.

The earliest French-to-English dictionary to have been published is an anonymous work dating from 1570/71.[15] It furnishes less than three dozen rudimentary musical terms. **Hollyband**, a teacher of French in London, based his considerably larger dictionary of 1593 at least partly on this work, but departed from the usual lexicographical approach of the time by adding into the entries numerous expressions, proverbs and other illustrations of word usage, considerably enhancing the historical value of his dictionary. Randle **Cotgrave** continued this precedent further in *A dictionarie of the French and English tongves* of 1611, an inestimably valuable work which is regarded by linguists today as a major source for the study of Renaissance French language. Cotgrave's dictionary is of even greater interest than Hollyband's for its numerous proverbs relating to music; see for example *clairon* and *coup*. Evidence seems to suggest that he prepared his work singlehandedly, using an extensive range of sources, and, like Florio, he writes in an earthy, humorous style conveying a consistently 'common touch'.[16] A borrower like Florio, Cotgrave derives about three fifths of his material from the 1573 and 1606 editions of Nicot's *Thresor*.[17] Testifying to its credibility among native-born French speakers, Cotgrave's dictionary seems to have received wide acclaim when it appeared in France some years later.[18] It has been supposed that he aimed the work at English students of French classical texts, but he may also have had in mind merchants, tradespeople and artisans working between England and France.[19] For a small proportion of the 300 or so musical entries Cotgrave is indebted to the Latin dictionaries of Cooper and Thomas: see for example the entry *tubilustre*. More surprisingly, he is also indebted to Florio, for example in *epinices* and *phrygie*.[20]

Published anonymously, *A Short Explication Of Such Foreign Words, As are made Use of in Musick Books* of 1724, is believed to have been written by John Christopher **Pepusch**.[21] The product of a leading music scholar of this time, this ninety-four-page work belongs to a unique category among the lexicographic sources represented in the present work. Of its approximately 420 entries, around 88 per cent are Italian, 10 per cent are French, and the remainder Greek and Latin. As any comparison between the two works will readily bear out, Pepusch worked from Brossard's *Dictionaire de Musique* in compiling his *Explication*. Coover has tabulated a series of parallel entries from the *Explication*, the 1705 edition of Brossard, and Grassineau's *A Musical Dictionary* (1740), and it is clear that the *Explication* owes directly to Brossard. This is evident in the entries *adagio, ad libitum, affetto, allegro, allemanda, alto concretante, alto ripieno* and *andante*,[22] to which may be added *aria, arpeggio, basso, bassetto, bombardo, brillante, canzone, capella, chiesa, concertante* and many more. Of particular interest are performance-related terms also borrowed from Brossard, including *discreto, divoto, dolce, gratioso, maestoso, moderato, obligata, piu, pronto, senza, sostenuto, spiccato, timoroso, tutti, uguale, vigoroso* and *vistamente*. Only once does Pepusch appear to use an English source: his definition for the term *syncope* is without doubt taken from Bailey's *An Universal Etymological English Dictionary*, London, 1721. Possibly also the entry *theorba* derives from Kersey's sixth edition of Phillips's *New World* (1706).

This borrowing does not detract from the *Explication's* authoritativeness, however, and the information presented is both reliable and, as far as word usage is concerned, probably also up to date. We read, for example, that the cornet or cornetto is 'now out of Use' and superseded by the hoboy, an instrument that is in turn described as 'very common' and 'well known'. In like vein counterpoint is 'now very little used', the galliard is 'ancient', the guitar is 'now out of Use with us', and the madrigal unfashionable; however, the minuet is commonplace and the violin 'too well known to need any Description'. Intriguingly, we can also gauge from the *Explication* that the saraband had slowed down in tempo by this time. Finally, the popularity of Corelli's music in England is reflected in references to this composer in the entries *da, follia, solo* and *sonata*. The omission of an entry on the minuet is surprising, although an entry *minuetto* is present.

That the *Explication* became the standard work of its kind in England is attested by the number of times it was incorporated into music tutors. Both Peter **Prelleur** and William **Tans'ur** printed versions of it as appendices in their general purpose music tutors, respectively *The Modern Musick-Master* of 1731 and *A Compleat Melody* of 1736 (3rd edition). Another printed source which incorporates a version of the *Explication* is the anonymous and undated *Rules; Or a Short and Compleat Method For attaining to Play a Thorough Bass upon the Harpsicord or Organ. By an Eminent Master.* The *Explication* is there retitled 'A Short Explication of such Italian Words, or Terms, as are made use of in Vocal and Instrumental Musick'.[23] A much later source, outside the range of the present work, is *The Muses Delight* of 1754, which contains 'A Musical Dictionary. Being an Explication of Italian, French, And Other Words, Terms, &c. Made Use of In Musical Compositions'. This is essentially the same as the original *Explication* but contains some additions.

As further evidence of its influence is the fact that the entire contents of the *Explication* were incorporated into the third and subsequent editions of **Bailey**'s *An Universal Etymological English Dictionary* (1726 etc.). Bailey's transcriptions are marred by numerous typographical errors, and in having uncritically added in the *Explication* entries, he unwittingly duplicates many headwords already present. Through Bailey, many of the *Explication*'s entries then found their way into other English dictionaries such as those of **Defoe** and Thomas **Dyche**. The resulting pattern of borrowing can be seen in the extracts presented in this Dictionary.

Musical writings

Theoretical works on music form the backbone of the musical writings consulted in this Dictionary. The aim has been to draw upon all treatises on music, both published and in manuscript, originating in Britain in the period 1500–1740. This includes composition and performance treatises, tutors, philosophical and scientific writings specifically relating to music, histories of music, and a selection of pedagogical works and religious writings that deal with music. A register of known theoretical sources was drawn mainly from Atcherson, Chenette, Cooper, Hughes-Hughes, Kassler and Ruff. Included are a number of Scottish sources: these are 'The Art of Music', British Library Add. MS 4911, *An Introduction To The Knowledge And Practice of the Thoro' Bass* (1717), believed to be written by Alexander Bayne, Alexander Malcolm's *Treatise of Musick* (1721), and Thomas Bruce's *The Common Tunes* (1726). Robert Fludd's *De Templo Musicæ*, part of his vast philosophical work *Utriusque Cosmi Maioris* and published in Oppenheim (1617–24), is included since the author was an Englishman.

Several sources do not easily fall into the category of theoretical writings on music but have nevertheless warranted inclusion. Roger North presents the most thorny problem in this regard. His manuscript writings range discursively across many scientific and philosophical disciplines including music, and in order to deal satisfactorily with North's approach to musical terminology it is necessary to venture considerably further than his best known series of musical essays, the 'Musicall Grammarian' (itself in three extant versions). An attempt has been made to consult all of his manuscripts dealing with music, and except where direct repetition occurs, all relevant text has been reproduced. Religious writings on music by Wither and Bedford also furnish useful, relevant material as do some published sermons of the period.[24] John Newton's pedagogical work *The English Academy* (1677) contains a little-known, extended discussion on music with some definitions of terms, and Puttenham's *The Arte of English Poesie* of 1589 contains valuable accounts of a series of musico-poetic terms (for example *eclogue, elegy, encomium* and *epicedium*). The dance treatises of Weaver and Tomlinson have also been consulted, the former yielding several otherwise little documented musical terms connected with dance (for example *emmelia, hyporchemata* and *prosodion*).

Not to be excluded are English translations that were made of Continental treatises. The following have been consulted for the present work: Alford's 1568 translation of Adrien Le Roy's lute tutor, John Dowland's 1609 translation of Ornithoparcus' *Micrologus*, Lord Brouncker's 1653 translation of Descartes, John Birchensha's 1664 translation of Alsted, John Wallis's 1682 translation of Ptolemy, and an anonymous 1729 translation of Hotteterre Le Romain's flute tutor. One of the most important texts to arrive in England, Rameau's *Traité de l'harmonie* (Paris, 1722), appeared in English translation as *A Treatise of Music*, but the long accepted date of 1737 has now been revised to c.1775–78, placing it outside the period covered in this study.[25]

As mentioned at the start, treatises rarely set out to define terms in the way that dictionaries do. The subject of terminology evokes different responses from different authors since terminological matters impinge on a writer's subject in a multitude of possible ways. Terms may be compared or contrasted, the meanings of terms may receive thorough or passing comment, and descriptions given of various techniques, genres and so forth may in many cases resemble but not truly constitute actual definitions. It must be emphasised that in compiling extracts from musical writings a chief difficulty was a lack of a clear boundary between what in the strictest sense is a definition and what instead may be a description or explanation. The approach taken has been to limit extracts to passages in which a writer sets out to provide a prescriptive account of the meaning of a term. Coverage has been widened in exceptional instances to include accounts of an arguably more descriptive vein where these relate to terms that are rare and otherwise unrepresented. Examples include *In Nomine*, some names of ornaments, and performance practice expressions such as *draw*, *laying* and *clean striking* (found in Thomas Mace's *Musick's Monument*).

Where a writer repeats essentially the same information in different parts of a given treatise, the first, the fullest or the most representative passage is taken. However, where a writer returns to discuss the same term, each time with further elaboration or a different perspective, a full series of extracts is presented; this is notably the case with more complex terms such as key and mode (or 'mood'), both of which receive detailed treatment by Malcolm and North.

In the broader picture, this study identifies the principal figures in the contribution to musical terminology as being Thomas Morley, John Dowland (as translator of Ornithoparcus), Charles Butler, John Playford, Christopher Simpson, Alexander Malcolm and Roger North. Later sections of this Introduction comment on the contribution of these and other writers, and on the development of musical terminology as a recognisable field in theoretical literature of the time.

Interpretation of findings

Up-to-dateness of information

Chronological presentation of extracts reveals how many terms underwent significant changes of meaning during the time frame covered. The dating of extracts offers a useful guide to the shifts in meaning that a given term underwent. Sometimes the dates of the earliest and latest entries may reflect the introduction and disappearance of a term from general currency. However, considerable caution needs to be exercised when making chronological interpretations, especially in the case of lexicographical sources, because it cannot be assumed that a writer is necessarily attempting to record contemporary word use.

Until the early eighteenth century dictionaries in England were mostly limited to collecting 'hard words' that were rarely used or obsolete. The first English dictionaries, by **Cawdrey** (1604), **Bullokar** (1616) and **Cockeram** (1623), follow in the scholarly tradition of earlier Latin dictionaries with a strong bias towards Latin vocabulary. They contain only a small proportion of musical terms that can claim contemporary currency: *accent, anthem, clauicordes* and *dittie* (Cawdrey); *canticke* and *descant* (Cawdrey, second edition, 1609); *antiphon, bugle, burdon, cadence, carol, chantor, consort* and *madrigals* (Bullokar); and *modulate* (Cockeram). More attempts at up-to-dateness can be seen in **Blount** (1656): in addition to other terms already mentioned in his *Glossographia*, he gives *chorus, chromatick, fugue, gammut, lavolta, leero, mean, pastoral, pavin, saraband, theorba*, and in his third edition (1670), *concert*. Other terms were left for **Phillips** to add: *almain, bandore, brawl, chorister, counterpoint, flajulet, galliard, orchester, pandure* and *sagbut* (first edition, 1658); *gittern, guittar, viol* and *violin* (third edition, 1671); *recorder* (fourth edition, 1678); and *canon, cittern, flute, hautboy, lute* and *ritornello* (fifth edition, 1696).

Early dictionary writers were more than anything else word collectors with an eye for the unusual and obscure. The first to make a determined effort to include ordinary, widely used words was John **Kersey** in his small, more popularly conceived *A New English Dictionary* of 1702.[26] Musical terms which had escaped the attention of previous writers and appear for the first time in this work are *ballad, drum, fiddle, jews-harp, jig, kettle-drum, kit, menuet, overture, quaver* (as in shake or trill), *sharp, shalm, sing, song, thorough-bass, tune, violist, voluntary* and *waits*. Other contemporary musical terms included by Kersey are *air, bagpipe, choir, courant, fife, gavot, harpsecord, musician* and *taber*. Kersey's more scholarly efforts were directed towards revising Phillips's *New World*, and for this revision (1706) he added entries on *bassoon, boree, continued bass, crowd, division, flourish* and *spinet*. Other equally well-known terms such as *lesson* and *shake* had to wait three decades until **Dyche** and **Pardon** included them for the first time in their *A New General English Dictionary* of 1737.

If dictionaries were slow to build up a vocabulary of well-known musical terms, they also had a tendency to retain terms long after they had disappeared from use. For example *bandora* still appears in 1730, *cittern* in 1736, and *galliard* receives an entry as late as 1737. Words such as 'madrigal' and 'pavan' continue to occur in dictionaries well into the eighteenth century, long after the musical compositions corresponding to them had died out (*madrigal* still appears in 1737, *pavan* in 1730). Musical treatises offer a better guide on the declining use of terms. For instance the term *ligature* is last defined in a treatise in the year 1662 (Davidson), *long* in 1617–24 (Fludd), *madrigal* in 1636 (Butler), and *pavan* in 1676 (Mace).

Foreign language dictionaries are set apart from other dictionaries in the chronological information they offer. Throughout the seventeenth century, French and Italian dictionaries produced in England contained a much greater proportion of common vocabulary than did English dictionaries. The absence of a filtering mechanism in their case in turn becomes a virtue for the historian. Significant early entries include *madrigal*, appearing for the first time in 1550, *galliard* in 1552, and *haltbois* in 1593 (occurring in Hollyband's definition of *naquaire*). **Florio**'s *A Worlde of Wordes*, 1598, is an early source for *alamana, alto, cadenza, ciaciona, eolio canto* (under *æolian*) and *piano* (as 'cantar piano'). Of course, both the terms and the definitions Florio supplies reflect musical traditions that obtained in Italy, not England; likewise the material given in Hollyband and Cotgrave reflects traditions in France. Just how up to date these writers were is difficult to assess. Their reliance on existing sources has already been discussed, but this only accounts for a small proportion of their material. The extent of their originality cannot be determined until more detailed studies are undertaken.

Instruments

Detailed comment could be given to the hundreds of entries that relate to musical instruments but discussion is limited to an overview of the information on this subject to come out of the early dictionaries. In many cases, early dictionary writers do not adequately identify the instruments they seek to define or describe, leaving the reader in considerable doubt. For example, an *altobasso* is uninformatively given in Florio as 'a certain musical instrument with strings'. Even less helpful is his definition of a *cazzolata*: 'a kind of countrie musicall instrument without strings'. Nevertheless, such information at least alerts us to the existence of a whole range of instruments which are poorly known or unknown today. Sometimes the name of an instrument is the same as another object and where this occurs one may speculate on the shape and overall appearance of that instrument. Thus in Florio a cazzolata also means 'a ladlefull', suggesting a bowl-shaped instrument. Where such contextual information seems relevant and useful it is reproduced in the extracts given in the Dictionary.

Florio's two dictionaries of 1598 and 1611 emerge as the richest source for instruments and the dozens he describes belong to many different types. Instruments of the bagpipe variety include the *ciaramella, manganello, sampogna* and *scacciapensiere*. Reed instruments include the *busciarella* and *chalemie*. These would all appear to be used in outdoor, rustic music-making. Other wind instruments associated with country life in Florio are the *busine* and *cemmalo*; fiddle-type instruments include the *baldosa, cacapensiere, donadello, giga* and *tempella*. As already noted the definitions Florio supplies are sometimes confusing, and he will even refer to the same instrument as simultaneously belonging to the string and wind families. This can be seen in the example '*biumbe*, a kinde of pipe, crowd or fiddle'. Either Florio does this out of ignorance or the name 'biumbe' was used freely at the time in reference to a wide variety of unrelated instruments. The latter would lend further weight to the suggestion that Florio is describing a folk tradition.

One of the most frequently cited instruments in the lexicographic sources is the trumpet, known variously by the names *aes, agnafile, auricalco, bemes, buccina, cauum* and *oricalco*. Terms relating to trumpet sounds and calls, many with military connections, are especially abundant; these include *bellicum, cauum, clang, classicum, levet, strombettare* and *taratantara*.

Chronological information on instruments is rarely given in definitions, but one instrument for which the information given is both specific and probably quite reliable is the guitar. We read in 1671 (Phillips) that this instrument was 'heretofore very much in use among the *Italians* and *French*, and now of late among the *English*'. Some fifty years later, the *Explication* of 1724 describes this instrument as by then obsolete in England.

Among the more unusual instruments to be mentioned in the sources is the *poliphant*, described as a wire-strung instrument resembling a lute. It was, according to Playford's *Introduction to the Skill of Musick*, twelfth edition (1694), an instrument that Queen Elizabeth I used to play. Whether this is the same instrument as the 'polyphon', defined by Thomas Blount in 1656 as 'a musical instrument so called, having many strings, and by consequence several sounds', remains unclear.[27]

Cremona was acknowledged as the most celebrated centre for violin making at least as early as 1678, taken on the basis of the description of that city in Phillips's *New World of English Words*. On the other side of the Alps, the *vingt-quatre violons du Roi* in the French court at Versailles were sufficiently famous for Guy **Miege** to include them as an entry in his 1688 revision of Cotgrave's French dictionary. In the same entry Miege refers to their 'chef' or 'Head-man', having been until a year before Jean-Baptiste Lully. Miege's revision of Cotgrave is also noteworthy for its extended entries, in French, on *manicordion, monocorde, orchestre, saquebute, serpent, sourdine, tambour* and *viole.*

Performance terminology

Terms relating to performance are especially numerous in the sources. Detailed consideration of the history and development of performance terminology in England is given later in this Introduction. Here a survey of the most important sources furnishing performance terms and expressions can be examined. Particularly noteworthy is the wide social spectrum represented by the sources: early dictionaries give valuable information relating to outdoor musical performance and musical traditions belonging to the country.

The *Explication,* believed to have been written by **Pepusch,** carries a high proportion of foreign performance terms; these are mostly Italian but paradoxically come via the Frenchman Brossard. In assembling these terms for the first time in England, Pepusch led to their establishment as the standard performance vocabulary for instrumental music. The *Explication* is to be viewed as the single most important vehicle for the transmission of this vocabulary to England. Performance terms prior to 1724 are encountered in a variety of instrumental tutors. Some examples refer to specific instruments, most particularly the lute. Terms connected with lute playing in **Barley**'s *New Booke of Tabliture* (1596) are *close play, fret* and *strike;* these clearly derive from the English translation of **Le Roy**'s lute tutor published in 1568. **Robinson**'s tutor (1603) offers the interesting term *sympathy,* again in relation to lute playing. **Mace** (1667) is a useful source on graces and ornaments for the lute such as *shake, slide, spinger, sting* and *tut.* For the viol, ornaments such as *backfall, beat, cadent, elevation, plain beat, shake* and *spinger* are explained by **Simpson** in *The Division-Violist* (1659), along with the terms *breaking, diminution* and *division,* all relating to extempore playing on the same instrument. In *The Division-Violist* Simpson is probably the first English writer to employ the expressions *continued ground* and *through bass,* making this tutor historically important in documenting the spread of Baroque performance practice in England.[28]

The English translation of **Hotteterre**'s flute tutor, published in London in 1729, is, like Pepusch's dictionary, another important source for the transmission of performance terminology to England. Terms in this translation include *port de voix* and *pointing,* the latter referring not to fuguing in Purcell's sense, but to the *inégal* method playing of quavers. Other ornaments treated in this translation are *shake, slur* and *beat.* Hotteterre's definitions of *pointing* and *slur* were repeated in the third part of **Prelleur**'s *The Modern Musick-Master* (1731), entitled 'The Newest Method for Learners on the German Flute'.

The foreign language dictionaries of **Florio** and **Cotgrave,** both of 1611, offer information relating to performance of a quite different nature. Their vocabularies reflect musical practices in the wider community as against the schooled manner of playing represented by published tutors. In particular, these dictionaries reveal a rich concentration of expressions relating to the apparently widespread practice, in Italy and France, of 'quavering' in singing, that is, shaking and running divisions. The long list of words associated with this ornamental kind of singing includes *brillante, fioretti, fredonner, fringoter, frizzare, gringoter, increspare la voce, ritornello, roulade, tremante, tremblement, tremulo, trigliare, vibrissation* and *warble.* From the definitions given by Florio and Cotgrave it is also clear that the same ornamental style was applied to instrumental playing. One can theorise that the multiplicity of words relating to ornamental style indicates its wide prevalence in the early Baroque period. Furthermore the definitions themselves, though they refer to music, are not confined to music and cover a range of general meanings. The word *frizzare,* for example, is a verb meaning to spurt or to skip and carries the idea of tart, biting sensations; in music it means quavering on an instrument. The general meanings, in this case, may inform us that the type of quavering was lively, rapid, and possibly made use of dissonant notes. The fact that *frizzare* and other words like it are not strict musical terms but clearly popular expressions probably indicates that ornamental singing was equally a feature of popular traditions as it was of the cultivated manner of singing, as advocated by Caccini. In reproducing the entries for words such as *frizzare* in this Dictionary, general meanings are included where they shed possible additional light on the musical meanings.

The Florio dictionaries provide further insights into singing and playing practices of the improvisatory kind. The expressions *cantacchiare* and *cantare a-recisa* are fascinating because they refer to an untrained, 'natural' singing style more characteristic of folk traditions. By contrast *frifolare* refers to nimble, light-fingered playing on wind instruments and the virginals. In a distinctly humorous vein are *stempellare* and *tempellare*, meaning to fumble and play foolishly on a lute or other string instrument.

Taken as a whole, the lexicographic sources offer an unusually wide picture of musical practices across a range of social settings. To sketch only the broadest picture, musical terms that relate to civic and town life include *carnival, concert, proclamation, ridotta* and *waits*. Those that relate to street music include *ballad, cantepolare, case* (a cant word), *charivaris, floralia, ule* and *vielle*. Terms connected with military affairs include *beat, chamade, march, parley* and *troop*; and those associated with hunting include *bugle, mot, recheat* and *trantrac*. Military and hunting terms with musical references are abundantly represented in lexicographic sources, and all are included despite the fact that in this period trumpet calls of various kinds were not considered part of music in the proper sense. Their inclusion in the Dictionary corresponds to the modern acceptance of music as a social phenomenon, and adds to the total picture of music as played and heard in all levels and groups of sixteenth- and seventeenth-century society. Several cant words and expressions, used by beggars, gypsies and town thieves, also occur in the sources. Those of musical significance in **Bailey**'s *The Universal Etymological English Dictionary* include *blind harper, brother of the string, dismal ditty, kit* and *strowler*.

Forms and genres

On the basis of what the lexicographic sources tell us it is possible to speculate on the origin of the names of various compositional forms of the period. It is interesting to trace how many originated outside music in areas such as poetry and dance, later acquiring musical meanings. An example is the term *carol*, which in the earliest sources of 1550 and 1593 relates only to dance, but by 1598 also refers to a song. A similar instance is *bargaret*, given in 1616 as a dance but subsequently meaning a song or ballad. Some dance terms such as *hay* and *round*, both characterised as country dances, do not have a stated musical connection in the sources, but are included because this connection may be implied.

It is similarly evident that for some poetic terms the earliest dictionaries may not state a musical connection where one probably existed. It is not always clear from the sources whether words such as *hymn, ode* and *song* possessed musical connections, but since these connections may generally be assumed, all entries pertaining to them have been included in the Dictionary.

Definitions of instrumental forms such as the *capriccio, fantasia* and *sonata* are of special interest because they help chart the developmental history of these forms. In the Florio dictionaries the sonata is not yet a recognisable genre, and the definition of 1611 is exceptionally broad in rendering it as 'any sound of Musike'. The first source to characterise sonata unequivocally as an instrumental genre is the *Explication* of 1724, which repeats Brossard's distinction between the two main types, the *da camera* and *da chiesa*. The term *fantasia* (or *fancy*) occurs in the musical sense only rarely in seventeenth-century dictionaries, and in no instance does it refer to the English tradition. Cotgrave mentions it in his French dictionary of 1611 and Torriano refers to the expression 'passa fantasia' in his 1659 revision of Florio. It has already been noted that the entries *fantasie* and *capriccio* in the fifth edition of Phillips's *New World* derive from Furetière's *Dictionnaire universel* of 1690. The first definition of *chaconne* is given by Harris in 1704 and this brings to mind Purcell's 'Chacony', except that Harris is more likely to be using a French source than referring to any English example of this genre.

Music theory

As is to be expected, musical treatises are especially informative on theory terms. A primary role of treatises and tutors was to teach what all such terms meant. The question and answer format in *The Pathway to Musicke* (1596), Morley's *Introdvction*, and even some later tutors such as Gorton's *Catechetical Questions in Musick* (1704), Bruce's *The Common Tunes* (1726) and Tans'ur's *Compleat Melody* (1736), provided a convenient way to explain these terms clearly and succinctly to the student.[29]

Thomas **Morley** was very concerned with the correct use of terms and believed that musicians should take the trouble of properly learning them. He points out in *A Plaine and Easie Introdvction to Practicall Mvsicke*, for example, that the terms *syncopation* and *cadence* are widely, and wrongly, confused[30] and that *dupla* is often misunderstood.[31] He also writes at length about how the terms *mode* and *tune* have been incorrectly treated as synonymous.[32] This contrasts with Dowland's translation of the *Micrologus* by Ornithoparcus, in which *mood* and *tone* are assumed to be largely interchangeable since they both refer to the ancient church modes.[33] Morley shows more care on the subject of terminology than his contemporaries and he was keen to point out how terms were no longer understood in their original meaning. As a learned scholar his definitions do not always reflect current compositional theory or practice. For example, his accounts of *mood, prolation* and *time* are deliberately based on older authorities, and he explains this by saying that 'Those who within these three hundred yeares haue written the Art of Musicke, haue set downe the Moodes otherwise then they eyther haue been or are taught now in England.'[34]

There arises a possibility that Morley started with *The pathway to Musicke*, 1596, in formulating some of his definitions. Certain minor but noticeable similarities can be observed between his definitions and those in that much shorter, anonymous work. Instances are *alteration, augmentation, degree, diminution, dupla, imperfection, proportion, quadrupla, sesquialtera* and *triple*. This is surprising because Morley was very disdainful of *The pathway* and condemned it as a superficial work; he particularly took issue with its definition of the word *diatessaron*.[35]

Learning terms connected with music theory was difficult and problematic for students, according to Thomas **Campion** in his treatise *A New Way of Making Fowre parts in Counter-point*. Campion's particular concern was that important words like *tone* and *note* were uncritically used by musicians and consequently lacked precise meanings. This made it doubly difficult for the student trying to learn these terms. His treatise begins with a long discourse on the need to approach terms with care and precision. The passage, from his Preface, is worth quoting in full:

> There is nothing doth trouble, and disgrace our Traditionall Musition more, then the ambiguity of the termes of Musicke, if he cannot rightly distinguish them, for they make him vncapable of any rationall discourse in the art hee professeth: As if wee say a lesser Third consists of a Tone, and a Semi-tone; here by a Tone is ment a perfect Second, or as they name it a whole note: But if wee aske in what Tone is this or that song made, then by Tone we intend the key which guides and ends the whole song. Likewise the word *Note* is sometime vsed proprely, as when in respect of the forme of it, we name it a round or square Note; in regard of the place we say, a Note in rule or a Note in space; so for the time, we call a Briefe or Sembriefe a long Note, a Crotchet, or Quauer a short note. Sometime the word *Note* is otherwise to be vnderstood, as when it is, *signum pro signato*, the signe for the thing signified: so we say a Sharpe, or flat Note, meaniug [sic] by the word Note, the sound it signifies; also we terme a Note high, or low, in respect of the sound. The word *Note* simply produced, hath yet another signification, as when we say this is a sweet Note, or the Note I like, but not the words, wee then meane by this word Note, the whole tune, putting the part for the whole: But this word *Note* with addition, is yet far otherwise to be vnderstood, as when we say a whole Note, or a halfe Note; wee meane a perfect or imperfect Second, which are not Notes, but the seuerall distances betweene two Notes, the one being double as much as the other; and although this kinde of calling them a whole and a halfe Note, came in first by abusion, yet custome hath made that speech now passable. In my discourse of Musicke, I haue therefore striued to be plaine in my tearmes, without nice and unprofitable distinctions, as that is of *tonus maior*, and *tonus minor*, and such like, whereof there can be made no vse.
>
> (Campion, *New Way of Making Fowre Parts* [1610], *The Preface*)

Campion stops short of defining individual terms in his treatise, and in an altogether contradictory manner he attempts to simplify matters by bringing together as synonymous the terms *key, moode* and *tone*. Whether this only served to further the student's confusion is of course not to be known, but his justification was that all three terms properly related to 'the aire of the song'.[36] **Simpson** was similarly unconcerned with possible differences in meaning between these three terms and chose to treat them all as synonymous.[37] Neither did he wish to make a distinction between *cliff* and *key*.[38]

The picture changes considerably when we trace meanings of the terms *key* and *mode* (or 'mood') in later treatises.[39] In *A Treatise of Musick* (1721), **Malcolm** devotes considerable attention to discussion of the meaning of the word *key*, especially by way of distinctions that may be drawn between this and *mode*. He even proposes that the term *mode* be used to differentiate between the two qualities of thirds in the octave scale.[40] Malcolm's concept of key hinges on the governing role of the fundamental and reflects important new developments in harmonic thinking in the early eighteenth century. His use of the terms *fundamental* and *dominant* is central to this new thinking and parallels Rameau's *Traité de l'harmonie* of 1722; however, Malcolm is different to Rameau in his use of the term *supposition*.[41]

North's understanding of the word *key* is complicated by the fact that he recognised it as having two classes of meaning. He believed that certain words, such as *key*, had gained specialised, technical meanings in scholarly discourse on music while still retaining generalised meanings in common speech. For him this ambiguity could only be resolved by making a clear divide between general and technical usage.[42] More difficult for North was the word *ayre*, because it could be related to both key and melody. His writings characterise *ayre* as a multi-faceted concept, but one ultimately related to general fluency and 'good style'.[43] It is interesting to note that **De La Fond** (1725) connects air with the musical expression of various passions or tempers of the mind, thereby connecting this word with the Baroque doctrine of affections.[44]

Having a legal mind and an obsession with detail, North sought in the 'Musical Grammarian' to clarify the whole area of musical terminology. This is evident from a passage from his 'Theory of Sounds' of 1726:

> Here I must make an apology for borrowing somewhat of the language of the Musitians, & their Gamut, of wch wee have litle els, but Names, to be concerned with in this theory; therefore I pretend not here to explaine it, having another part In designe for that End, Intituled a Musicall Grammar. Now therefore it must be no surprise, If some termes ocurr, without a sufficient vocabulary, but I shall take care, whatever Names are assumed, the things shall be clear enough exprest.
>
> (North, 'Theory of Sounds', BL Add. MS 32535, fol. 105 *verso*)

North is rivalled only by Malcolm in the fastidious attention he directs towards issues of terminology. He seems to have been attracted to the idea that terms of central importance, like *key* and *ayre*, can have no single, fixed meaning and that they depend very much on the context of discussion. At any given time he will pursue one layer or nuance of meaning to the exclusion of others, leading to no single, definitive statement. Throughout his writings North also shows a predilection for playing with words, and this does not always result in clarity when he attempts to establish the meaning of individual terms. The temptation to include various 'Northisms' in the Dictionary has mostly been avoided, although some relating to performance practice have been included because they offer special interest, for example the word *wavee*.[45]

The Restoration era saw a revival of interest in ancient Greek and Latin theoretical terms, especially those relating to the mathematical side of music. This is most apparent in John **Wallis**'s articles in *Philosophical Transactions of the Royal Society*, and in the treatises of **Salmon** (1688), **Holder** (1694) and **Malcolm** (1721). In what appears to have been an attempt to align musical discourse more closely with the mathematical disciplines, these authorities vigorously sought to reinstitute a comprehensive range of Greek terminology relating to scales, intervals and proportions.[46] Examples of the kind of terminology invoked by Wallis are *diatonum ditonum*, *diatonum intensum*, *harmonica*, *hemitone* and *trihemitone*. The new rationalistic thinking forged by this group of scholars followed in the wake of the appearance of three important texts in England, all of them translations: **Brouncker**'s translation of Descartes in 1653, **Birchensha**'s translation of Alsted in 1664 and **Wallis**'s translation of Ptolemy's *Harmonics* in 1682. These translations were a major influence in shaping English music theory in the second half of the seventeenth century; their contribution to theory and terminology has already been studied in detail.[47]

A range of important theory terms and definitions relating to compositional method can be found in **Purcell**'s substantial revision of Playford's *An Introduction To The Skill of Musick* of 1694. He gives these in the section entitled 'A Brief Introduction to the Art of Descant' which replaces the treatise on descant by Campion in earlier editions of that work. The terms defined all relate to fuguing, which by the 1690s must be judged as something of an anachronism, except that they are possibly a reflection of the way music was traditionally taught rather than actual compositional practice as it stood at that time. The fugal terms Purcell defines are *arsin & thesin*, *augmentation*, *canon*, *double descant*, *double fuge*, *fuge*, *imitation*, *recto & retro* and *syncopation*. Each of the definitions Purcell gives is notably clear, concise and straightforward. As a writer he shares nothing with the *musica speculativa* group headed by Wallis but rather belongs to the line of practical, instructive teachers such as Morley and Simpson.

Mythology and music

A feature of many Latin-to-English dictionaries is their biographical entries relating to mythological characters of musical significance. The largest number comes from a 'Dictionarivm Historicum & Poeticum propria locorum & Personarum vocabula breuiter complectens' appended to Cooper's great Latin dictionary of 1565. Entries in this appendix include dozens of musicians and writers on music from the ancient world. **Cockeram**'s English dictionary of 1623 contains a third part 'Treating of Gods and Goddesses, Men and Women ...' and includes a list of 'Men that were Musitians'. In the list are Agathon, Aspendius, Babis (see under Babys), Connas (not to be confused with Connus), Marsyas and Orpheus. Betraying a sense of humour, Cockeram precedes this list of notable musicians with a separate list of 'Men that were Gluttons'. The fourth edition of **Phillips**'s *New World* (1678) contains further biographical entries on musicians, again drawn from antiquity, in one instance borrowing material from Cooper (for the entry on Xenophilus). At the end of the same edition Phillips adds a catalogue of ancient personages who were famous in various arts and sciences including music. A total of thirty-seven musicians are listed, three of whom are women: Cottytto, Megaro and Thymele (since in his catalogue Phillips only lists the names and gives no further information, they have not been included in the Dictionary).

Historical perspective of musical terminology

During the post-Restoration period, when influence exerted by French and Italian music of this time was transforming musical life in England, musical terminology came to the foreground of musical thought. The increasing availability of printed music from abroad, especially from Italy and France, meant that the performance terms that were integral to this music had to be learned by English musicians. Italian and to a lesser extent French performance terms came to represent musical high fashion and spurred production of the first musical dictionaries in England. The adoption of a vocabulary of foreign performance terms by English musicians is particularly significant because it can be seen to have signalled the full introduction of Baroque style in England.

Theoretical terms were a different case. With scholarly musical discourse in the post-Restoration period increasingly aligned to mathematical science, a proliferation of specialised, technical terminology came into existence. On the basis of language alone, musical literature of this period saw a divergence along two increasingly separate lines: philosophical works concerned with the mathematical basis of music and the more utilitarian teaching manuals aimed at helping the ordinary musician. If only as a result of market demands the former risked being sidelined because it failed to satisfy the needs of amateur musicians. It was an Enlightenment reaction against 'dark language' that ultimately brought about the decline of esoteric theoretical terminology in the early part of the eighteenth century.

Performance terminology and Baroque style

For the greater part of the seventeenth century English musicians lacked a standard vocabulary of performance-related terminology. Performance practice issues were seldom discussed in any detail in instrumental tutors, and amongst a number of possible reasons for this may be the absence at the time of a standard vocabulary for codifying performance practice. It could be, too, that the lack of suitable terminology inhibited the reception of Baroque style in England, although there were obviously other factors that contributed to the slow response to musical developments abroad. Certainly, however, the development of such a vocabulary after 1700, and its systematic collection in *A Short Explication* in 1724, seems to have coincided with the fullest phase of the importation of foreign music into England. This suggests that establishing an effective performance vocabulary was the key to developing a performance practice that could serve as the necessary counterpart to the new repertories being introduced.

Many Italian performance terms that later became standardised in England and elsewhere, such as those mentioned above, can be seen to have originated in general language. This is a point of special interest when returning to the Italian dictionaries of John Florio. His definitions may not contain any reference to music, but the essential expressive idea – the *affection* – is present and makes for worthwhile reading. For instance in 1611 **Florio** defines *adagio* as 'at ease, at leasure, faire and softlie, leasurelie', and *presto* as 'quicke, nimble, prompt, ready, fleet, swift, prepared ... Also quickly, out of hand, without delay'. This suggests that these words represented more than simply tempo indications when they were applied to music. The word *presto* finds its way into English-to-English dictionaries of a much later period, but surprisingly this does not initially happen by way of a musical connection. **Cocker**'s *English Dictionary* of 1704 defines *presto* as 'presently, instantly, quickly, a word used by Juglers'. Beyond the mere notion of speed, both these dictionary accounts of *presto* convey an idea of agility, eagerness, effortlessness and sleight of hand. *Adagio*, by contrast, is calm, easy, relaxed and perhaps also slow but not with any sense of weightiness. It is disappointing, then, to find that **Pepusch**'s *Explication* of 1724 renders many such terms only as tempo indications, missing out on the extra expressive dimension they imply. Thus by the word *adagio* 'is signified the slowest Movement in Musick', and *presto* is merely 'Fast or Quick'. It may be surmised, therefore, that the adoption of foreign music and musical practices into England was in some respects carried out superficially, at least at the amateur level, although much further research is needed on this question.

In Italy the newer styles of vocal and instrumental music of the early Baroque, calling for contrasts of tempo, dynamics and expression, and greater emphasis placed on the upper, melodic line, were facilitated by a performance vocabulary of terms such as *adagio, allegro, forte, largo, piano* and *vivace*. In England these terms were slow to appear and an equivalent vocabulary of English words never properly caught on. Quite why this is so remains an intriguing question, but the answer cannot be that changes in dynamics were not used. Thomas **Robinson**'s description of 'passionate play' on the lute in *The Schoole of Mvsicke* (1603) makes this clear:

> Passionate play is to runne some part of the squares in a *Treble* (that is foure and foure) first loud, then soft, and so in a decorum, now louder, now softer, (not in extremitie of either) but as companie of other instruments, or farnesse off giueth occasion.
>
> (Robinson, *The Schoole of Mvsicke* (1603), B ii *verso*)

Thomas **Mace** frequently uses the directions 'Soft' (often abbreviated as 'So:'), 'Loud' (or 'Lo:') in the lute pieces in *Musick's Monument* (1676), and occasionally he also uses 'Away' and 'Drag' in the viol pieces toward the end of the same work.[48] Mace explains what he means by 'Soft and Loud Play':

> [*marginalia*: Soft and Loud Play, a most Excellent Grace.] The next, (which I (*my self*) only call a *Grace*; because no *Master* ever yet (as I can find) directed it, as a *Grace*, but my self) is to Play some part of the *Lesson Loud*, and some part *Soft*; which gives *much more Grace, and Lustre to Play, than any other Grace, whatsoever*: Therefore I commend It, as a *Principal*, and *Chief-Ornamental-Grace* (in its *Proper Place*)
>
> (Mace, *Musick's Monument* (1676), p. 109)

Locke and Purcell wrote indications such as 'brisk', 'quick', 'drag', 'slow', 'soft' and 'loud' in their consort works, most notably in their fantasias which typically consist of successive highly contrasting sections. For his Italianate compositions, however, Purcell chose to use Italian terms. In his trio sonatas of 1683, in which he 'faithfully endeavour'd a just imitation of the most fam'd Italian Masters',[49] indications such as 'piano' and 'forte' are given. As these were generally unfamiliar to English musicians, Purcell was obliged to explain them briefly, even if this showed that his own understanding was less than perfect:

> It remains only that the English Practitioner be enform'd, that he will find a few terms of Art perhaps unusual to him, the chief of which are these following: *Adagio* and *Grave*, which import nothing but a very slow movement: *Presto* [sic] *Largo, Poco Largo*, or *Largo* by it self, a middle movement: *Allegro*, and *Vivace*, a very brisk, swift, or fast movement: *Piano*, soft.
>
> (Purcell, *Sonnata's of III Parts* (1683), 'To the Reader')

Purcell openly admitted that his knowledge of Italian was not good.[50] Even so, his account of the terms *allegro, grave* and *largo* show, as far as can be established from the sources used in this Dictionary, that he was the first English writer to explain these terms.

Earlier than Purcell for several other Italian performance terms is a little-known singing tutor, *Synopsis of Vocal Musick* (1680) by 'A. B.'. Probably an English translation or adaptation of an Italian source,[51] it contains what is possibly the first mention in an English musical source of the indications *adagio, forte, piano* and *presto*:

> The secondary signs of the Tact or Time are certain words used by the *Italians*, and afterwards also of others, to wit, *Adagio*, and *Presto*, signifying, that such a part of a Song where *Adagio* is written, is to be Sung slower, and where *Presto*, swifter.
>
> (A. B., *Synopsis of Vocal Musick* (1680), p. 19)

> *Italians* only, and some that them do follow, do use these two words, *Forte* and *Piano*, signifying that such part of a song must be sung clearer and fuller, under which is written *Forte*, but softer and smaller, under which is written *Piano*.
>
> (*Synopsis of Vocal Musick*, p. 42)

The *Synopsis* is also valuable for performance terms in singing, and these probably offer insight into Italian singing practice of the same period or earlier; its accounts of *exclamation, trillo* and *gruppo* may derive from Caccini's *Le Nuove Musiche*.

A fascinating little tutor, and one that might easily be overlooked except for its short glossary of terms, is the anonymous *Preceptor for the Improved Octave Flageolet* of around 1710. The glossary, titled an 'Explanation of Words Commonly Used in Music', briefly defines a total of twenty-two terms, all of which are performance indications. The terms include *amoroso, crescendo* and *diminuendo*, none of which appear in any other source consulted for the Dictionary. The fact that these terms are all Italian and have no relation to any other known British source, may indicate that the *Preceptor* was also of Italian origin. However, there is no preface or other information that may shed light on this.[52]

The wholesale adoption of Italian performance terms came as the inevitable result of the influx of printed Italian music to England. Italian musical terminology gained favour as a result of Italian music itself gaining favour, and here lies the significance of the *Explication* of 1724. Despite the fact that it is aimed at a relatively unsophisticated readership, this dictionary is the nearest thing to a manifesto of Baroque performance practice in England. Its probable author, John Christopher **Pepusch**, set out to help amateur musicians understand the foreign terms that appeared in printed music from abroad. He believed that a proper understanding of these terms was the first step in gaining an appreciation of the style of this music and the manner of performance it required. In the Preface he writes:

> the understanding of [foreign terms] is very necessary, because a great Part of the Beauty and Agreeableness of Musick, depends upon a right and proper Method and Manner of performing it:

The terms defined by Pepusch, and the definitions he gives, assume the reader has no prior knowledge of foreign languages. Pepusch would have otherwise not included such rudimentary entries as '*Seconda*, or *Seconde*, the Second, or Number Two. Thus, *Violino Secondo*, the Second Violin.' In writing the dictionary Pepusch was clearly not aiming at the musical cognoscenti or professional musicians, who presumably would not have needed such help.

At the end of the *Explication* Pepusch gives a list of printed music for which his dictionary would have catered. The works are instrumental trios, sonatas, solos, airs, 'concertes' and lessons. The many composers include Corelli, Marini, Valentini, Veracini, Vitali, Vivaldi, Schickhardt, Lully, Marais, La Barre and Loeillet. Some works by Pepusch himself are listed, but few English-born composers are represented. Availability of printed Continental music in England must be regarded as the major impetus for Pepusch to have issued his *Explication*. The issuing by John Walsh's publishing firm of Corelli's violin sonatas (Op. 5), coinciding with Handel's arrival in London, would have helped create the need and interest for such a dictionary.

For several further Italian performance terms not given in the *Explication*, a vocal tutor by Giuseppe **Riva** gives some useful accounts. His *Advice to the Composers and Performers of Vocal Musick* was published in London in 1727,[53] and in this Riva refers to the terms *legare* and *staccare* in the singing of graces.[54] He also advocates the practice of singing divisions in operatic arias, describing this as capable of producing a wonderful 'chiaroscuro' effect. Not to let the instrumentalists outshine the singers, however, he expresses misgivings about having too many symphonies in opera productions.[55]

In view of the enormous impact of Italian music in England in the first three decades of the eighteenth century, it is little wonder that Italian musical terminology gained the primacy that it did. Italian musical terms reflected the prestige of Italian music. Even a contemporary English dictionary, **Dyche**'s *A New General English Dictionary* of 1737 (second edition), made a note of this fact. Under its entry *bass* can be read the following:

> As *Italy* has been and still is most noted for the finest Musicians, so most Composers in that Science affect to use their Terms

To conclude, the adoption of a foreign-based musical performance vocabulary, reaching its height in the 1720s, may be viewed as an integral part of England's drive to be included in the international musical culture of the late Baroque.

The Enlightenment trend against jargon

The area of theoretical terminology is complicated by the position of two contrasting currents that were operating simultaneously in the early eighteenth century. One was the movement towards a mathematically-based language, as championed by John Wallis and Alexander Malcolm. The other current was a reaction against this, motivated by a distrust of technical language encroaching into an art that was recognised at this time as very much the domain of amateur musicians. It is the second current which is the subject of discussion here, since this has not been properly addressed before.

A major reason for the decline of the new rationalism in the years following Malcolm's *A Treatise of Musick* (1721) was the adverse reaction provoked by its esoteric language and heavy reliance on Greek terminology. A stark difference in language had emerged between deeply philosophical treatises such as Malcolm's and the ever-proliferating composition and performance tutors that served the more immediate needs of practical musicians. Writers such as De La Fond, North and Tans'ur were conscious of this difference, and their solution, symptomatic of one important Enlightenment trend, was to aim for clarity of language. For them Greek- and Latin-based terminology was 'dark' and 'obscure', and the abstruse dialectic of philosophical tracts only served as an impediment to understanding. **De La Fond** explained that by using plain and direct language, dispensing with unnecessary Greek and Latin words, he hoped to make his treatise the more intelligible:

> I endeavour to write in a *style philosophical, but plain, free, and easy; concise, and yet clear*. I desire to speak the Language of Men, I must repeat it once more, not the Language of an Autor, or Mountebank, that burns with desire of being admired for his affected hard Terms, and learned Obscurities. Those hard *Greek* and *Latin* Terms, have indeed a specious look, and a learned

sound, but are often very imposing. I choose to say *Bass-Viol*, instead of *Chelys*: and *fourth, fifth, sixth, seventh*, and *eighth*; instead of *Diatessaron, Diapente, Hexachordon, Heptachordon*, and *Diapason*, &c. If I am obliged sometimes to make use of any uncommon word, I take particular care really to explain it before I go a step farther. I avoid as much as possible fixing any two, even the least different ideas to the same word. The contrary of this, as insignificant as the thing may appear, confounds the Reader, and is the occasion of most of our *learned wars*.

(De La Fond, *A New System of Music* (1725), pp. xxxvii–xxxviii)

Seeing himself as a reformer in the area of language, even if he was not always true to his own word, De La Fond whimsically proposed the introduction of various new terms to replace existing ones in the interests of greater clarity. These included 'nota' for 'key' and 'notation' or even 'notulation' for 'modulation',[56] but these propositions were less than serious. Nonetheless, his efforts to clear away the obscurities of musical terminology were the major concern of his treatise. Paradoxically, De La Fond's 'new system', revealed as the culmination of his reform process, is the assigning of Latin names – prime, second, terce, quart and so on – to the twelve chromatic notes of the scale.[57] Confident that these names would catch on, De La Fond introduces his new system in a marginalia comment expressed in archetypal Enlightenment phraseology:

That great Veil is removed, and that great part of Music *appears wonderful clear and bright.* (De La Fond, p. 113)

De La Fond believed that foreign musical terms were unnecessary if equivalents already existed in the English language. This is perhaps ironic since he advocated such French-style reforms as using the word 'clef' in preference to the still usual 'cliff', and 'concert' rather than the more usual 'consort'. It is perhaps significant that, as a music teacher in London, he supplemented his income by teaching French and Latin to musicians.[58] This background made him well aware of both the trend among English musicians towards greater literacy in other tongues and the backlash that this in turn provoked:

They say, every Art has its *proper Terms*, and he must not only be ignorant, but vain and arrogant that condemns the use of them. I own, and we must all own, that all Arts should have their proper Terms; and that proper Terms are very proper things: but the business is to know what Terms are proper; for I am afraid many of their proper Terms are very improper ones. I believe all will agree, that if we have words of our own to signify things, we need not affect to borrow words from other Languages to signify the same things, especially when those forein words are no more expressive than our own: and I am sure we had better keep to our own words than substitute in the place of them such forein ones as are not in themselves so elegant nor so significant. But I am afraid it is become a question whether Autors are to teach altogether, or partly teach and partly confound, for the sake of being admir'd?

(De La Fond, pp. lxxi–lxxii)

With De La Fond and also with Turner, as shall be seen later, there emerges a sense of unease towards the gathering momentum by English musicians to adopt foreign practices and terminology. Foreign words represented modernity, which was sufficient for Turner to reject them, but they also presented a barrier that, to infer from De La Fond's remarks, was perceived as an attack on the integrity of the English language itself. This conflict represented a deep-seated liguistic problem of the time. As Görlach has pointed out, 'The craze for foreign terms and puristic reactions to them remained a problem, though to a lesser degree, in the seventeenth and eighteenth centuries.'[59]

A similar Enlightenment concern for clear language and dissatisfaction with jargon is expressed by North and Tans'ur. Their writings further demonstrate how the '*Theoreck*, or *Mathematick-Part*' of music (Tans'ur's words, from his preface) had been worked to such a level of sophistry and contained such a plethora of 'dark' terminology that it completely mystified and alienated ordinary practising musicians. Despite being one who can be criticised for using it himself, **North** disapproved of jargon. He could write for example, regarding ancient music theory, that 'I must confess it is wonderfull to see, w[t] a Jargon of Names there is ffor every Note half Note & diesis ...'[60] A more serious reformist than De La Fond, North intended to explain and clarify 'the language of the Musitians' in a work that was to become his 'Musicall Grammarian', and in the final version of this work he unequivocally stated his position:

For no art is more enveloped in dark diallect, and jargon, then musick is, all which impedimenta I would have removed, that the access to the art and practise may be more recomendable and inviting ...

(North, 'Musicall Grammarian' (1728), fol. 9)

A tireless observer of musical fashion, North was preoccupied with 'newer' kinds of instrumental music, particularly of the Italian sonata mould, and to this end he enthusiastically incorporated into his 'Musicall Grammarian' many performance terms that had gained currency in instrumental, particularly violin playing. It would be unfair to accuse him of using jargon when such terms were at the time very much 'alamode'. Most of North's borrowings were Italianisms, including more unusual ones such as *correnti, stravaganza* and *tremolo.* Although interested in all aspects of musical innovation, North could also be a touch facetious, and this is borne out in his comments concerning the faddish predilection by contemporary musicians for using foreign terms to denote changes of speed and meter.

> then comes presto, away, and If faster, prestissimo, and I wonder they stopp there and doe Not goe on to prestitititissimo
>
> (North, 'Musicall Gramarian' (c.1726), fol. 65 *verso*)

> [*re* 'time keeping':] ... The old marks of comon time quickening, were **c¢Ↄ̸Ↄ̸**. Now it is done by description, as adagio, grave, allegro, presto, prestissimo and for humour andante, ricercata, affectuoso, manireonico, cantabile, and others dayly new, which need not be named nor interpreted ...
>
> (North, 'Musicall Grammarian' (1728), fol. 33 *verso*)

It may be noted that the term 'manireonico' is not defined by any of the sources in the Dictionary (see however the related word *manner*), and this may indicate how subject to the whims of fashion such words were at this time.

North's older contemporary William **Turner** was a conservative who drew a hard line against musical innovations of the day. He was highly critical of the practices of embellishment in violin playing that were then fashionable, and his reactionary views extended to rejecting most foreign terms as extraneous and unnecessary.[61] He viewed with suspicion the need to use Italian terms such as *adagio* and *allegro,* preferring instead the employment of different time-signatures to indicate meter and tempo changes in the music:

> For, if such a Method were put in Practise, there would be no manner of Occasion to write (at the beginning of *Lessons*) the *Italian* Words, *Adagio, Grave, Largo,* &c. (which are put before slow *Movements*) or *Allegro, Presto, Vivace,* &c. (which are applied to swift *Movements*: And which they do in all the *Moods* hitherto spoken of, without Exception) there being Variety sufficient in the different Species of the *Notes* themselves, to shew what *Movement* is slow, and what brisk; without putting our *Pupils,* or our selves, to the Trouble of learning Foreign Languages.
>
> (Turner, *Sound Anatomiz'd* (1724), pp. 26–7)

For the later writer William **Tans'ur**, 'theoreck' music belonged to natural philosophy and its deep secrets could only be unfolded after considerable research into mathematics.[62] One chapter of his tutor, *A Compleat Melody: or, the Harmony of Sion,* is devoted to introducing this subject to the reader, but Tans'ur's conscious aim was to expunge from his discussion all terms that might be regarded as 'cramped'. These he felt only confused the student, and this was sufficient grounds for their rejection:

> *Many* great and obscure Volumnes in Former Ages, have been stuffed so up with so many useless *Scales,* pertaining to the *Rules* of *Composition,* that they really appear to us very Dark; by reason their *Scales* seem more strict than *Musical;* and also writ with so much *Tantology* [sic] to fill up the Volumne, that they drowned all Sence by their multitude of Words; some of which *Scales* would almost puzzel the most profound in our Age, to find out either their Use or Meaning. ¶ I am really of the Opinion, that no *Art* or *Science* ought to be explain'd in an obscure Style; for certainly, the easier the *Explanation* is, the better the Matter is understood. Therefore I shall accommodate the ingenious Practitioner with such plain and easy *Rules* which will be as pleasant as they are useful, omitting all cramp Words or *Terms* ...
>
> (Tans'ur, *A Compleat Melody* (1736), p. 43)

Tans'ur's words indicate that the new rationalism, as represented by Wallis and Malcolm, worked at serious odds with the interests of practical musicians, and had the effect of estranging itself from the broader current of musical change. The driving force behind all change proved to be the dictates and practices of the ordinary musician. By contrast, far from initiating or promulgating change, theorists, teachers and commentators were forced to respond to change, whether negatively or positively.

In summary, it can be seen that the expansion of a performance vocabulary and the reaction against technical language were two simultaneous trends operating in the later seventeenth and early eighteenth centuries. They had the potential to conflict with one another, but the fact that this hardly occurred is a measure of their equal force and finely held balance in English musical thought of the time.

Terminology as a path to historical enquiry

Further interest in the subject of terminology arose out of the emerging scholarly discovery of music from the distant past. Various writers recognised the difficulty of learning about past musical traditions without first investigating the meaning of terms associated with those traditions. Here jargon was not the issue. George Wither and Roger North both believed that unfamiliarity with archaic terms was a major obstacle to appreciating the intricacies of ancient musical art. Although separated by a century, these two writers are remarkable in having arrived at an equally sophisticated understanding of the importance of terminology in historical enquiry.

In attempting to fathom musical practices of the

early Christian church, **Wither** was led to speculate at length on a range of terms that had long since disappeared from use. In his *Preparation to the Psalter* of 1619, he set out to discover the original meaning of the psalms, their manner of performance (see for example his very long discussion of the word 'selah'), and the names and types of instruments that were believed to accompany them (for example the psaltery). However, in searching out these questions, Wither was cognisant of the complex unknowns involved:

> For who is able after so many hundred of yeares, and after so many alterations, both in the *Musicke* it selfe, and the tearmes thereof, to reuiue the forgotten melodie vsed by a Nation that is so much a stranger vnto vs and our Tongue, that we are now to seeke (and likely to be for euer vncertaine) whether many of the words prefixed before these sacred *Odes*, doe signifie somewhat concerning the *Tune*, the *Instrument*, or neither, or both?
>
> (Wither, *A Preparation to the Psalter* (1619), p. 80)

Wither would appear to be the first English writer to accept the essential fluidity in the meaning of musical terms as they exist through history. He was able to see that terms are only labels, having in themselves no intrinsic meaning, and that over time they may be re-applied and redefined as musical traditions themselves change. This may result, for instance, in a given term or notational symbol ('character') coming to refer to something quite different if a break in tradition occurs, presenting a special problem if one's aim is to try to re-establish that lost tradition.

> there is nothing whose losse is more irrecouerable, or whose change is lesse demonstrable, then that of *Musicke*: for it consisteth of inarticulate sounds. And if the tearmes or Characters that express them be not by continuall Tradition deliuered ouer from man to man, with all the helpes of practice to informe the eare what sounds such tearmes or Characters denote; they are no more sufficient in their owne nature to expresse them, then the tract of a Hares foote on the earth ...
>
> (Wither, p. 80)

The context of **North**'s comments on the same problem is different because he is writing in the wake of a revival of interest in ancient Greek music and a debate, led by Vossius in the 1670s, as to its merits in relation to 'modern' music. Yet his views are remarkably similar to Wither's. North was interested in the possibility that, in the absence of artistic 'specimens' surviving from ancient times, more could be learnt of ancient traditions of art, including music, rhetoric, poetry and architecture, by a study of documentation left by its practitioners. He saw the possibility of achieving this understanding, however, as remote. The stumbling block was having to understand terms whose meanings were forever lost, and he believed that no scholar would be able to rediscover these meanings and that no amount of scholarly exegesis could reconstruct them.

> Ancient arts knowne by specimens and not by words ¶ It is the misfortune of all arts of which the use happens to be discontinued, (leaving no reall specimens, which onely can demonstrate what the practise of any such art was, except some dark verball descriptions), and so to fall into the catalogue of the artes deperditæ [lost arts], and be hardly, if ever recoverable, but yet by some cloudy expression found remaining to make work for crittiques, and the world litle the wiser; for arts have peculiar terms, that is a language understood by the professors, and some few els in the time; but in after times when such arts are attempted to be revived, who should make the dictionary, or adapt things to the words used by obsolete authors? It is certein that nothing, but the very things appearing by specimens (if any are left) can doe it; and without such authoritys, become enigmatick.
>
> (North, 'Musicall Grammarian' (1728), fol. 104 *recto–verso*)

North's words stand as wise counsel to the present time when strenuous efforts have been made to recreate performance traditions that have long been dead, including those belonging to North's time. With no surviving, fully preserved 'specimens' and limited notational, textual, iconographical and organological evidence to work on, reconstructions can only be, to use his word, enigmatic. All the same, research into terminology can play its part, and dictionaries – such as the present one – can be constructed from the writings of 'obsolete authors'; after all, it is only from these writings that any certain, undeniable authority can be assumed.

Editorial notes

All extracts faithfully reproduce the text as it occurs in the original sources. Original spellings and punctuation are preserved. Early dictionaries contain frequent typographical and other errors, but no attempt has been made to correct these; instead, editorial comments and insertions are given where necessary in square brackets. Errors are especially numerous in passages in Latin and Greek: where breathings and accents are not supplied for Greek spellings this is because they do not appear in the original.

The Dictionary is set out to facilitate easy reference to multiple definitions found in different sources that are contained under a given headword.

Despite the variety of spellings of headwords in the originals, extracts are grouped together under standardised headwords in bold. It must be stressed that the main headword in bold is used only as a method of organisation and is not part of any original extract.

Early dictionaries often give separate entries for variant spellings of the same word, mainly through oversight. Cotgrave for example, either intentionally or unintentionally, gives three entries for lute: *luc, luth* and *lut*. For convenience all have been subsumed under the one headword *lute*. Where different spellings do not necessarily indicate the same meaning, they are kept separate and instead cross-referenced. An example are the entries *bosinnus, bozina, busine* and *busone*, which all justify being kept separate, although these names are clearly etymologically related.

A number of terms possess more than one musical meaning. These include *acute, air, beat, canon, guide, hold, key, opera, pointing, quaver, ritornello, round, saltarella, set* and *symphony*. In such cases the same headword is repeated to introduce different sets of extracts corresponding to each meaning. Where the extracts do not allow a separation to be made, all extracts are placed together under a single headword (for example *air*).

In a very few, exceptional cases the same extract may be duplicated if it discusses or defines two terms simultaneously. In these cases it will be found under the two relevant headwords. An example is a passage by Morley in which *saltarella* and *galliard* are equally treated.[63]

The wide variety of typography encountered in lexicographic sources by necessity has required a degree of standardisation. The word to be defined may be given in upper case, gothic script or italics to differentiate it from the text of the definition itself. For clarity, however, the Dictionary presents the original headword in italics and the definition in roman type. The earliest source used, the *Ortus Vocabulorum*, makes no typographic distinction between headword and definition, and because this produces ambiguity of interpretation in some instances, the full extract is given in roman.

Capitalisations which head a paragraph in an original text have usually been reduced to lower case. Upper-case letters used for emphasis are uniformly given in lower-case italics.

Editorial ellipses are used when text has been deleted at the beginning, in the middle, or at the end of an extract, but in order to simplify presentation of lexicographic sources they are not included at the ends of entries.

In some cases, where it seems more informative to do so, the alphabetical arrangement of entries has been altered from that found in the original dictionary. In the *Short Explication*, for instance, *alto concertante* occurs under *alto* but has been rearranged here under *concertante*.

In some early dictionaries the headword follows rather than precedes the definition. The Latin dictionaries of Huloet (1552) and Rider (1589) are cases in point. In these the order has been reversed to achieve consistency with the other sources used.

Symbols of abbreviation found in some original texts present difficulties for the modern reader, and where it is judged necessary – as in the case of many Latin-to-English dictionaries – these have been expanded. In the original format of Cawdrey (1604), unusual typographic symbols appear in front of or behind many headwords to indicate Greek or French derivations. These symbols have been similarly expanded.

For *The Principles of Musik*, Charles Butler devised his own unique typography in which a range of unconventional letters serve to abbreviate usual vowel and consonant spellings. These are almost impossible to reproduce, and it would be meaningless to do so, so his text is given in expanded form. Where Butler uses square brackets these are substituted for round brackets.

In *A Plaine and Easie Introdvction* Morley uses a question-and-answer format with master and student alternating in dialogue. In quoting Morley, the Dictionary has omitted stating the speaking person unless the context specifically demands this. Normally the Master is the one who defines and explains musical terms, and this can be assumed unless otherwise indicated.

Notes to the introduction

1. Riddell, 'Reliability of Early English Dictionaries'.
2. Smalley, *Sources of 'A Dictionarie'*, p. 11.
3. Most recommended are the studies by Smalley, *Sources of 'A Dictionarie'*, Starnes, *Renaissance Dictionaries* and 'Florio Reconsidered', Starnes and Noyes, *English Dictionary*, and Stein, *English Dictionary*.
4. Starnes and Noyes, *English Dictionary*, pp. 13–36.
5. *Ibid.*, p. 42.
6. Paper, 'Purcell and *The New World of English Words*', by Graham Strahle at conference 'Performing the Music of Henry Purcell, Oxford University, September 17–20, 1993. Starnes and Noyes also conclude that 'There is no evidence in the text to indicate that specialists did actually make contributions', *English Dictionary*, p. 54.
7. Strahle, 'Purcell and *The New World*'.
8. See pp. 16–17 of Playford, *Breefe introduction*, 1654 edition, although Harris probably used a later edition.
9. See the 1665 edition of Simpson, *Principles of Practical Mvsick*, p. 22. Again, Harris possibly used a later edition of this work.
10. Stein, *English Dictionary*, p. 360.
11. Collison, *History of Foreign-Language Dictionaries*, p. 70.
12. *Dictionary of National Biography*.
13. See Starnes, 'Florio Reconsidered', p. 409 onwards.
14. See the longer entry in the 1659 edition.
15. See Stein, *English Dictionary*, p. 245.
16. Smalley, *Sources of 'A Dictionarie'*, pp. 14–16.
17. *Ibid.*, pp. 41–2.
18. *Ibid.*, p. 34.
19. *Ibid.*, pp. 20, 25–9.
20. Thurston Dart extracted a large number of musical terms from Cotgrave's dictionary and discovered the detailed information this source provides on musical instruments: 'Music and Musical Instruments'.
21. See Kassler, *Science of Music in Britain*, vol. II, p. 1138.
22. Coover, *Music Lexicography*, pp. xix–xxii.
23. See *Rules; Or a Short and Compleat Method*, pp. 9 onwards.
24. For a relatively full list of published sermons dealing with music, the reader may consult *Early English Books*, vol. viii, pp. 6,261–2. The present work only includes a selection of such sermons.
25. This revised dating is in light of publication evidence provided by Humphries and Smith: see Supplement entry 367 in *Music Publishing in the British Isles*, which cites an address concerning the translation by publisher John French.
26. Starnes and Noyes, *English Dictionary*, pp. 69–70.
27. See article 'poliphant' by Ian Harwood, *The New Grove Dictionary of Musical Instruments*, vol. iii, p. 137, and the entry 'polyphon' in *The New Grove Dictionary of Music and Musicians*, vol. xv, p. 70.
28. Simpson, *Division-Violist*, p. 47.
29. The immediate model for didactic dialogue was Zarlino's *Dimostrationi harmoniche* of 1571, and amongst the Classical writers, Cicero's *De oratore*. See Palisca, *Humanism in Italian Renaissance Musical Thought*, p. 9.
30. Morley, *Plaine and Easie Introdvction*, p. 144.
31. *Ibid.*, p. 78.
32. *Ibid.*, Annotations on Part III, n.p.
33. Ornithoparcus, trans. Dowland, p. 36.
34. Morley, *Plaine and Easie Introdvction*, p. 12.
35. *Ibid.*, Annotations on Part II, n.p.
36. Campion, *New Way of Making Fowre parts*, n.p.
37. Simpson, *Division-Violist*, p. 11.
38. Simpson, *Principles of Practical Mvsick*, p. 4.
39. For detailed discussion of these terms see Atcherson, 'Symposium'.
40. Malcolm, *Treatise of Musick*, p. 274.
41. Chenette, 'Music Theory', p. 288.
42. See his discussion of 'key' in Add. MS 32533, 'Musicall Gramarian', fols. 67–8. *North's 'Cursory Notes'*, ed. Chan and Kassler, discusses North's concept of key, p. 275. Chenette, 'Music Theory', sees North's use of 'key' as leading to confusion because he uses it to refer to the lowest note of a perfect accord and also a key centre or governing note: pp. 257, 259.
43. See the entry on 'ayre' in BL Add. MS 32537, fol. 100. See also Chenette, who says that for North 'air' was an 'omnibus word', spanning harmony, melody and rhythm, 'Music Theory' p. 259; see also *North's 'Cursory Notes'*, ed. Chan and Kassler, on this, pp. 280–1.
44. De La Fond, *New System of Music*, p. 3.
45. See North, 'Musicall Grammarian', ed. Chan and Kassler, pp. 279 onwards, for a glossary of Northisms in this work.
46. Chenette discusses the contributions to music theory of these writers in 'Music Theory', pp. 22–4, 31–6, 42–8.
47. *Ibid.*, 36–40.
48. Mace, *Musick's Monument*, e.g. pp. 126 and 257.
49. Purcell, *Sonnata's of III Parts*, 'To the Reader'.
50. *Ibid.*

51. *Synopsis of Vocal Musick* (the author is 'A. B. Philo-Mus.'); this tutor is only known by three copies. Included are three-part psalms and songs 'Composed By English and Italian Authors for the benefit of young Beginners'. There is a definite Italian connection in this work: the only composer named in the Preface is 'Giovanni Giacomo Castoldi de Carrivagio', presumably Gastoldi. The dedication is for an Italian, and is written in Italian. The text of the work, in the form of a series of rules and precepts, reads as a translation but probably adapts parts of an Italian original, of which there is no surviving documentation.
52. The *Preceptor*, was published by C. Gerock. The copy consulted is held in the Library of Congress.
53. An Italian version of the same tutor was also issued in London as *Avviso ai Compositori, ed ai Cantanti*, in 1728.
54. Riva, *Advice to the Composers and Performers of Vocal Musick*, p. 14.
55. *Ibid.*, p. 7.
56. De La Fond, *New System of Music*, p. 80.
57. *Ibid.*, p. 106 onwards; see Chenette, 'Music Theory' on this, p. 211.
58. De La Fond writes on the reverse of the title page: 'N.B. The Autor having hitherto chiefly taught the *Latin* and *French* Tungs, as he now still does; those that shall be pleased to employ him as a Master of *Music*, will have the advantage of improving themselves with him in talking those two Languages.'
59. Görlach, *Introduction to Early Modern English*, p. 165.
60. British Library, Add. MS 32531, fol. 56.
61. Turner, *Sound Anatomiz'd*. In his condemnation of violin flourishing in a concluding essay 'On the Abuse of Musick', Turner condemns violinists who 'quite destroy the Subject of what they play, by their ridiculous out-of-the-way *Flourishes*, which is what we call murdering of *Musick*'; p. 4.
62. Tans'ur, *Compleat Melody*, Preface, n.p.
63. Morley, *Plaine and Easie Introdvction*, p. 181.

How to use this dictionary

The following sample definition illustrates the main features used in the presentation of material in the Dictionary.

air *see* aria, arioso, brawl, camera, cantata, formality, interlude, key, lesson, lyrick, melody, prelude, suit, tenor, trumpet air, tune

1598 FLORIO **It→E** *Aere*, ... Also a tune, a sound, a note, or an ayre of musickle or any ditty. **1611** COTGRAVE Fr→E *Air: m.* ... also, a tune, sownd, or ayre in Musick; **1611** FLORIO It→E *Aere*, ... also a tune or aire of a song or ditty. **1688** MIEGE-COTGRAVE **Fr→E** *Air*, (m.) ... an air, or tune; § *Air nouveau de Musique*, a new Tune, a new Air of Musick. *L'Air que vous venez de chanter est grave & melancolique*, the Tune you sung just now is both grave and melancholy. *Un Air accommodé aux Paroles*, a Tune suitable to the Words. *Un Air bien passionné*, a Tune well humoured. *un Air gai*, a merry Tune. **1702** KERSEY *New Engl. Dict.* (1st edn) An *Air, in* Musick, *&c.* **1706** KERSEY-PHILLIPS (6th edn) *Air* ... also a Tune in Musick; **1728** CHAMBERS *Air*, in Musick, signifies the *Melody*, or the Inflection of a Musical Compostion. See *Melody*.¶
The Word is also used for a Song it self. See *Song*. ...

1597 **MORLEY** ***Plaine and Easie Introduction*** (p. 180) ... these [ballete] and all other kinds of light musicke sauing the *Madrigal* are by a generall name called ayres. **[1610]** CAMPION *Two Bookes of Ayres* (*To the Reader*) These Ayres were for the most part framed at first for one voyce with the Lute, or Violl, but vpon occasion, they haue since beene filled with more parts ... the Treble tunes, which are with vs commonly called Ayres, are but Tenors mounted eight Notes higher ... **1636** BUTLER *Principles of Musick* (p. 86) *Air, or Tone*. In this woord is a large *Metalepsis*. Air, of *Aer*, for *Percussio Aeris, Metonimia est Subjecti: Percussio pro Sono* ... **1676** MACE *Musick's Monument* (p. 129) *Ayres*, are, or should be, of the *same Time*, [as almains] (yet many make *Tripla's*, and call them so;) only they differ from *Allmaines*, by being commonly *Shorter*, and of a more *Quick, and Nimble Performance*. **c.1710** NORTH (draft for) **Musicall Grammarian** BL Add. 32537, f. 100 ... and yet It is not easy to say what Ayre is; it seem's best adumbrated by a good style In vers, or prose;...

headword

cross-references for related entries and further information

abbreviated source citation: date and author

Italian-to-English dictionary

original source entry

French-to-English dictionary

signifies that illustrative phrases, proverbs or sub-category definitions follow in same source

lexicographic sources

paragraph sign: break of paragraph in original text

abbreviated source citation: date, author and title

original source entry

treatises and other musical writings

source title in roman indicates manuscript

manuscript source identification

Abbreviations and symbols

General

p.	page number
n.p.	no pagination
f.	folio number
v	verso
BL	British Library
LC	Library of Congress
MS	manuscript

For lexicographic sources

Fr→E	French-to-English dictionary
It→E	Italian-to-English dictionary
L→E	Latin-to-English dictionary
Sp→E	Spanish-to-English dictionary

(All other lexicographic sources are English-to-English.)

§	signifies the appearance of illustrative usages, phrases, proverbs, compounded forms or subcategories of a given term

For treatises and other musical writings

§	signifies that another extract from the same source follows, dealing with the same headword; followed by page or folio number in brackets
¶	(paragraph symbol) is inserted where a break of paragraph occurs in the original text, or where the text is preceded by a heading, e.g. in Dowland–Ornithoparcus (1609) and North (1728)
CHi	Hill, ed. *Briefe Introduction*
CHo	Hogwood, ed. 'Tudway's History of Music'
C-K CN	Chan and Kassler, eds. *North's 'Cursory Notes'*
C-K MG	Chan and Kassler, eds. *North's 'Musicall Grammarian'*
JWi	Wilson, ed. *Roger North on Music*
TDa	Dart, ed. 'Mary Burwell's Instruction Book'

Original abbreviations and symbols used in lexicographic sources

General

†	usually signifies old or obsolete word (but see specific instances below; note the distinction made between this sign and ‡ in **1688** MIEGE)
*	usually signifies obsolete, archaic word, or one that is growing out of use (note that it can signify an entry not present in the previous edition of a given work, as is the case in **1599** MINSHEU-PERCYVALL and **1659** FLORIO-TORRIANO)
ad., adiect., adject.	adjective
adv.	adverb
ang.	anglicane (i.e. in English)
dim.	diminutive
ex	from
f., fem.	feminine gender
F., Fr.	French
i.	id est, idest (that is)
idem	the same
It., Ital.	Italian
m., masc.	masculine gender
met., by met.	metaphorically, by metaphor

n.	neuter gender
part.	participle
pl., plu.	plural
q.	quasi
q. d.	quasi dicat (as if to say)
sing.	singular
Sp., Span.	Spanish
subst.	substantive
v., vid., vide	see
vel	even, for instance, or

Principal classical authorities cited in Latin–English dictionaries

Apul.	Apuleius
Boet.	Boethius
Bud.	Budæus
Catul.	Catullus
Ci., Cic.	Cicero
Claud.	Claudianus
Colum.	Columella
Enn.	Ennius
Fest.	Festus
Firm.	Firmianus
Flac.	(see Valer. Flac.)
Gell.	Gellius
Horat.	Horace
Isid.	Isidorus
Iun.	Junius
Iuuen.	Juvenal
Lamprid.	Lampridius
Liu.	Livius Andronicus
Lucret.	Lucretius
Martial.	Martial
Non.	Nonus
Quint.	Quintilian
Ouid.	Ovid
Pers.	Persius
Philom.	Philomela
Plat.	Plato
Plaut.	Plautus
Plin.	Pliny
Propert.	Propertius
Sen.	Seneca
Serv.	Servius
Sidon.	Sidonius Apollinaris
Sil.	Silius
Stat.	Statius
Sue.	Suetonius
Terent.	Terence
Tertull.	Tertullian
Tibul.	Tibullus
Valer. Flac.	Valerius Flaccus
Val. Max.	Valerius Maximus
Var.	Varro
Veget.	Vegetius
Virg.	Virgil
Vitruv.	Vitruvius

Abbreviations in specific sources

Early Latin–English dictionaries (**1500** *Ortus Vocabulorum*, **1565** COOPER, **1587** THOMAS)

an^{e}., angl.	anglicane (i.e. in English)
f.g.	femininum genus
f.p.	feminina persona
m.g.	masculinum genus
n.	neuter
n.g.	neutrum genus
q.	qui, qua, quod
verb.	verbum
*	[probably archaic]

1593 HOLLYBAND and **1611** COTGRAVE

f.	feminine gender
m.	masculine gender
com.	common gender

1599 MINSHEU-PERCYVALL

†	[probably old word]
*	new word added by Minsheu, i.e. not present in preceding work (Percyvall's *Bibliotheca Hispanica. Containing a grammar, with a dictionarie in Spanish, English, and Latine*, 1591)

1611 COTGRAVE

Poict., Lang., Gasc., Rab.	Poictevin, Languedoc, Gascoigne, Rabelais

1616 BULLOKAR

*	obsolete: 'Remember also that euery word marked with this marke * is an olde word, onely vsed of some ancient writers, and now growne out of vse.' – (from An Instruction to the Reader)

1650 COTGRAVE-HOWELL

†	'... those words are now absolete [sic], and held pedantic, forc'd or affected' – (from The Epistle Dedicatory)

1659 FLORIO-TORRIANO

*	'signifies, that all such words are not to be found in Mr. *Florio's* last Edition of his Dictionary; or that there is an alteration and addition in their Interpretations: But these Asterismes (by over-sight) in some whole Letters, and very many places, are omitted; Of which the Reader is desired to take notice, and to judge of the Additions in this Dictionary, as upon perusall he shall find just cause and Reason.'

1688 MIEGE

†	'Shews, that the Word is only used in a burlesk, jocose, or comical Sense; or else, that it is not current in any Style, but is either forced, or Provincial, or such as grows out of date.'
‡	'Denotes an obsolete, or antiquated Word, hardly fit to be used in any manner of Style.'
*	signifies that the letter 'h' is to be pronounced as in English
cd.	c'est à dire (that is to say)

1707 *Gloss. Angl. Nova* and BAILEY dictionaries

C. Br.	'Country British'
Ch.	Chaucer
L.	Latin
O.	'Old Word'
O.R.	'Old Records'
Sp.	[probably Spenser]

1708 KERSEY *Dict. Anglo-Brit.*

M.T.	military term

1737 DYCHE-PARDON

(A.)	adjective
(Part.)	participle
(S.)	substantive
(V.)	verb

A

abattuta *see* battuta
1598 FLORIO It→E *Abattuta,* orderly, in proportion, as keeping of time in musicke. **1611** FLORIO It→E *Abattuta,* orderlie, in proportion, as musitians keepe time. **1659** TORRIANO-FLORIO It→E *A-battuta, adv.* orderly, in proportion, as musicians keep and beat due time and measure.

absonant *see* sonante
1500 *Ortus Vocabulorum* L→E Absonare idest discordare. anglice to discorde. inde absonautia [sic]. anglice mysisownyngs. n.p. Absonus idest discordans dissidens. anglice. out of toune. o.s. **1538** ELYOT L→E *Absono, absonaui, absonare,* to discorde or sowne euylle. *Absonus, na, num,* that whiche sowneth nat [sic] wel, or discordeth, or scantly may be herde. § *Absonus uoce,* he y[t] hath an vntunable voice **1565** COOPER L→E *Absonus, penul. cor. Adiectiuum.* That sowneth not well: that discordeth, or disagreeth: vntuneable. § *Homo voce absonus. Ci.* He that hath an vntunable voice. **1587** THOMAS L→E *Absonus, a, um, ab antiquo verbo absono, as, &c.* That soundeth not well: that discordeth, or disagreeth: vntuneable. **1611** FLORIO It→E *Absono,* dissonant, vntuned. **1623** COCKERAM *Absonant.* Vntuneable *Absonant, Discordant.* Disagreeing. **1656** BLOUNT (1st edn) *Absonant, Absonous (absonus)* untuneable, jarring **1676** COLES *Absonant,* or ¶ *Absonus, Latin.* Disagreeing (in sound) **1704** *Cocker's Engl. Dict.* (1st edn) *Absonant,* untunable. **1707** *Gloss. Angl. Nova* (1st edn) *Absonant* (Lat.) is untunable, jarring.

academy
1728 CHAMBERS *Academy, Academia* .... Most Nations have now their *Academies, Russia* not excepted: But, of all Countries, *Italy* bears the Bell in this respect.—We have but few in England.—The only one of Eminence is called by another Name, *viz.* the *Royal Society*: An Account whereof, see under the Article *Royal Society.* ¶ Besides this, however, we have a *Royal Academy* of Music; and another of Painting; establish'd by Letters Patent, and govern'd by their respective Directors.... *Academy of Musick,* is no other than the Managers and Directors of the Opera. See *Opera.*

a cavallo
1598 FLORIO It→E *Acauallo acauallo,* ... Also a march sounded vpon the trumpet. **1611** FLORIO It→E *A cauallo a cauallo,* ... Also a certaine march that trumpetters vse to sound in giuing a suddaine alarum. **1659** TORRIANO-FLORIO It→E *A-cavallo a cavallo,* adv. ... also a certain point of war or march, that Trumpetters sound in giving a sudden alarum.

accanto *see* accino
1500 *Ortus Vocabulorum* L→E Accanto as. angl. to syng nere. a.p. **1552** HULOET L→E *Accanto. as, Accino. is* Syng neare. *Accanto. as, Accino. is* Syng together. *Accanto. as, Cantito. as, freq.* Syng often. **1565** COOPER L→E *Accanto, accantas, accantáui, accantâre. Stat.* To synge by. **1587** THOMAS L→E *Accanto, as, Stat.* To sing by or to.

accent *see* acute, grave, modulation, modulator, modulor, tone
1500 *Ortus Vocabulorum* L→E Accentus us. ui. i. sonus proprie tonus. ryghte redynge. or accente. m.q. **1538** ELYOT L→E *Accento, tare,* to synge often. *Accentus,* an accent or tune, wherby a sillable is pronounced. **1552** HULOET L→E *Accento. as, Cantito. as, freq.* Syng often. *Idem* Syng out and syng aloft. **1565** COOPER L→E *Accentus, huius accentus, m.g. Verbale.* An accent: a tune: the rysynge or fallynge of the voyce. **1587** THOMAS L→E *Accentus, us, m.g. verb. ab Accino, Quint.* An accent, a tune: the rising or falling of the voice. **1604** CAWDREY (1st edn) *accent,* tune, the rising or falling of y[e] voice. **1623** COCKERAM *Accent.* Tune. **1656** BLOUNT (1st edn) *Accent (accentus)* tune, tenor, the rising and falling of the voice **1704** HARRIS *Accent in Musick,* is a Modulation of the Voice, to express the Passions either Naturally or Artificially. **1706** KERSEY-PHILLIPS (6th edn) *Accent,* Tune, Tone, or Tenour; the Rising or Falling of the Voice: *Accent,* in Musick, is a Modulation, or warbling of the Voice, to express the Passions, either naturally or artificially. **1708** KERSEY *Dict. Anglo-Brit.* (1st edn) *Accent,* ... In *Musick,* a warbling of the Voice, to express the Passions. **1728** CHAMBERS *Accent, Accentus* .... The *Accent,* properly, has only to do with high and low.—Tho the modern

Grammarians frequently also use it in respect of loud and soft, long and short; which confounds *Accent* with *Quantity*. See *Quantity*. ¶ The Difference between the two may be conceiv'd from that which we observe between the Beat of a Drum, and the Sound of a Trumpet: the former expresses every thing belonging to loud and soft, and long and short; but, so long as there is a μονοτονια in the Sound, there is nothing like *Accent*.... The spurious Accents answer to the Characters of Time in Musick; as *Crotchets, Quavers*, &c.—The genuine *Accents* answer to the musical Notes, *Sol, fa*, &c. See *Note, &c*.... The *Hebrews* have a Grammatical, a Rhetorical, and a Musical *Accent*; tho the first and last seem, in effect, to be the same; both being comprized under the general Name of *Tonic Accents*, because they give the proper Tone to Syllables: as the Rhetorical *Accents* are said to be *Euphonic*; inasmuch as they tend to make the Pronunciation more sweet and agreeable.... The Use of these Tonic or Grammatical *Accents* has been much controverted; some holding that they distinguish the Sense, while others maintain that they are only intended to regulate the Musick or Singing; alledging, that the *Jews* sing rather than read the Scriptures in their Synagogues. ¶ The Truth seems here to be between the two Opinions; for tho we are inclined to think, that the primary Intention of these *Accents* was to direct the Singing; yet the Singing seems to have been regulated according to the Sense; so that the *Accents* seem not only to guide the Singing, but also to point out the Distinctions.—Tho it must be confess'd, that many of these Distinctions are too subtil and inconsiderable; nor can the modern Writers, or the Editors of old ones, agree in the Matter; some of them making twice as many of these Distinctions as others.... As to the *Greek Accents*, now seen both in the manuscript and printed Books, there has been no less Dispute about their Antiquity and Use, than about those of the *Hebrewes*.—*Isaac Vossius*, in an express Treatise *de Accentibus Græcanicis*, endeavours to prove them of modern Invention; asserting, that antiently they had nothing of this Kind but a few Notes in their Poetry, which were invented by *Aristophanes* the Grammarian, about the Time of *Ptolomy Philopater*; and that these were of musical, rather than grammatical Use, serving as Aids in the singing of their Poems; and very different from those introduced afterwards.... *Accent*, in Musick, is a Modulation of the Voice, to express a Passion. See *Passion*. ¶ Every Bar or Measure is divided into *accented* and *unaccented* Parts. See *Measure*. ¶ The *Accented* Parts are the Principal; being those intended chiefly to move and affect: 'Tis on these the Spirit of the Musick depends. See *Bar*, and *Musick*. ¶ The Beginning and Middle; or the beginning of the first half of the Bass, and the beginning of the latter half thereof, in common Time; and the beginning, or first of the three Notes in triple Time; are always the *accented* Parts of the Measure. See *Time*. ¶ In Common Time, the first and third Crotchet of the Bar are on the *accented* Part of the Measure.—In Triple Time, where the Notes always go by three and three, that which is in the middle of every three is always *unaccented*; the first and last *accented*. But the Accent in the first is so much stronger, that in many Cases the last is accounted as if it had no *Accent*. See *Composition*. ¶ The Harmony is always to be full, and void of Discords in the *accented* Parts of the Measure. See *Harmony*.—In the *unaccented* Parts this is not so necessary; Discords here passing without any great Offence to the Ear. See *Discord, Counterpoint, &c.*

1609 DOWLAND-ORNITHOPARCUS *Micrologvs* (p. 69) *Of the Definition, and Diuision of Accent*. ¶ Wherefore *Accent* (as *Isidorus lib.* 1.*eth. cap*. 17. writeth) is a certaine law, or rule, for the raysing, or low carrying of sillables of each word. Or, it is the Rule of speaking. For that speaking is absurd, which is not by *Accent* graced. And it is called *accent*, because it is *ad Cantum*, that is, close by the song, according to *Isidore*: for as an aduerbe doth determine a Verbe, so doth *accent* determine *Concent*. But because these descriptions doe rather agree with the Grammaticall *accent*, than with the Musicall, I hold it necessary to search out by what means the Ecclesiasticall *accent* may rightly be described. Therefore *accent* (as it belongeth to Church-men) is a melody, pronouncing regularly the syllables of any words, according as the naturall *accent* of them requires... § (pp. 69-70) *Of the Diuision of accent*. ¶ Now it is three-fold, as *Priscian* and *Isidore* witnesse, the *Graue*, the *Acute*, and the *Circumflex*. The *Graue* is that, by which a sillable is carried low: but to speake musically, it is the regular falling with finall words, according to the custome of the Church. Of which there be two sorts. One which doth fall the finall word, or any syllable of it by a fift: and this is properly called *Graue*. Another which doth fall the finall word, or any syllable of it onely by a third, which by the Musitians is called the middle Accent.... An *acute Accent* grammatically, is that, by which the syllable is raised. But musically, it is the regular eleuation of the finall words or syllables according to the custome of the Church. Whereof there are likewise two kinds: one which reduceth the finall syllable or word to the place of his discent, keeping the name of *Acute*. The other, which doth raise the second sillable not to the former place of his discent, but into the next below. Which is also called *Moderate*, because it doth moderately carry a sillable on high .... The *Circumflex* is that, by which a sillable first raised is carried low. For it is, as *Isidore* witnesseth, contrary to the *acute*, for it begins with the *acute*, and ends with the *graue*, vnknowne to Church-men. Yet the Monkes, and especially those of the Cistertian order, haue the *Circumflex accent*, as at the old Cell a Monastery of the same order my selfe haue tried, and I my selfe haue seene many of their bookes in the same place. **1731** PRELLEUR *Modern Musick-Master* (III *re* flute, p. 9) The Accent is a Sound borrowed from the end of some Note to give them a greater expression.

accentor *see* incentor
1708 KERSEY *Dict. Anglo-Brit.* (1st edn) *Accentor*, (L.) he that sings the highest Part or Treble in a Choir, *&c*. **1730** BAILEY *Dict. Britannicum* (1st edn) *Accentor* one of Three Singers in Parts.

accettabolo *see* tabour
1598 FLORIO It→E *Accettabolo*, ... Also a kinde of iustrument [sic] of musicke or pipe. **1611** FLORIO It→E *Accettabolo*, the pan or holownesse wherein the huckle bone turneth. Also a iuglers box. Also a kind of musicall instrument.

accidental *see* fictitious note, musica ficta
1721 MALCOLM *Treatise of Musick* (p. 291) The Two *natural Semitones* of the *diatonick Scale* being betwixt *E F* and *A B* shew that the new Notes fall betwixt the other natural ones as they are set down. These new Notes are called *accidental* or *fictitious*, because they retain the Name of their *Principals* in the *natural System*: And this Name does also very well express their Design and Use; which is not to introduce or serve any new Species of *Melody* distinct from the *diatonick* Kind; ...

accino *see* accanto
1500 *Ortus Vocabulorum* L→E Accinere ciniui, entum. i. simul canere. to sing to gedur. a.t. **1538** ELYOT L→E *Acccinere* [sic], to synge to an instrument, or to synge a parte, as a treble to a tenoure, or a descant to a playne songe. **1552** HULOET L→E *Accino. as* Syng a part. *Accino. is, Accanto. as* Syng vnto. **1565** COOPER L→E *Accino, áccinis, pen. breui, accínui, accentum, accínere. Ex ad & cano compositum.* To synge to an instrument: to synge a parte: as a treble to a tenour, or descant to playne songe. **1587** THOMAS L→E *Accino, is, nui, entum, ex ad & Cano*: To sing to an Instrument: to sing a part, as a treble to a tenour, or descant to a plaine song. **1589** RIDER L→E *Accino.* To Accente, singe tune-ably or prnounce [sic] truely. *Accino, concino.* To sing a part with others. *Accino, procino.* To pronounce in singing

accompaniment *see* solo, vocal
1728 CHAMBERS *Accompanyment* .... The Musick, in Dramatic Performances, should only be a simple *Accompanyment*.—The Organists sometimes apply the Word to several Pipes which they occasionally touch to *accompany* the Treble; as the Drone, Flute, *&c*.

accompany *see* thorough bass
1736 BAILEY *Dict. Britannicum* (2nd edn) To *Accompany a Voice, i.e.* to play to it with proper Instruments.

accord *see* concent, concertare, daccordo, full accord, harmony, symphonio, symphony
1570/71 *Dict. Fr. and Engl.* Fr→E § *Vn son accordant*, a concorde in tune. **1593** HOLLYBAND Fr→E § *Vn son accordant*, a concorde in tune. **1598** FLORIO It→E *Accordare*, ... to tune an instrument. *Accordeuole*, agreeable, to be accorded, tunable. **1599** MINSHEU-PERCYVALL Sp→E **Acordado*, ... tuned, or agreed as in musicke or harmonie. *Acordar, yo Acuerdo*, ... to sound well in harmonie *Acorde*, m. agreement, consenting in opinions, or in musicall harmonie. **1611** COTGRAVE Fr→E *Accordance: f.* An accord, or agreement; a concord, or concordance in musicke. **1611** FLORIO It→E *Accordare*, ... Also to tune an instrument *Accordeuole*, that may be accorded, tunable. **1650** HOWELL-COTGRAVE Fr→E *Accord*: m. also, an accord, or concord in Musicke. *Accordance: f.* ... a concord, or concordance in musicke. **1659** TORRIANO-FLORIO It→E *Accordamento, Accordanza*, an accord, an agreement, an atonement, a tuning. **Accordatore*, a tuner. *Accordevole*, accordable, tunable. **1661** BLOUNT (2nd edn) *Accordance* (Fr.) an accord or agreement; a concord in musick. **1688** MIEGE-COTGRAVE Fr→E *Accordé*, agreed ... tuned. *Accorder*, ... to tune. § *Accorder un Lut, une Tuorbe*, to tune a Lute, or a Theorbo. *Un Lut bien accordé*, a well tuned Lute. **1728** CHAMBERS *Accord*, in

Musick, is more usually call'd *Concord*. See *Concord*. ¶ The Word *Accord* is *French*, form'd according to some, from the Latin *ad cor*; but others, with more probability, derive it from the French *Corde*, a String, or Cord; on account of the agreeable Union between the Sounds of two Strings struck at the same time. See *Chord*. ¶ Whence also some of the Consonances in Musick come to be called *Tetrachord*, *Hexachord*, &c. which are a *fourth*, and a *sixth*. See *Tetrachord*, *&c*. ¶ M. *Carre*, in the Memoirs of the Royal Academy of Sciences, lays down a new general Proposition, of the Proportion which Cylinders are to have, in order to form the *Accords* or Consonances of Musick. And it is this—That the solid Cylinders, whose Sounds yield those *Accords*, are in a triplicate and inverse Ratio of that of the Numbers which express the same *Accords*. ¶ Suppose, *e.g.* two Cylinders, the Diameters of whose Bases and Lengths, are as 3 to 2; 'Tis evident their Solidities will be in the Ratio of 27 to 8, which is the triplicate Ratio of 3 to 2: We say, that the Sounds of those two Cylinders will produce a Fifth, which is express'd by those Numbers; and that the biggest and longest will yield the grave Sound, and the smallest the acute one.—And the like of all others. See *Sound*, *Gravity*, and *Acuteness*. **1730** BAILEY *Dict. Britannicum* (1st edn) *Accord* (in *French Musick*) is the Production, Mixture and Relation of two Sounds, of which the one is Grave, and the other Acute.

c.1710 NORTH (Prendcourt's) Treatise of Continued or thro-base BL Add. 32531, ff. 31-31v [annotation by North:] NB. The accord is a terme of art in Musick, & means the full and standing harmony of Eighte. **c.1726** NORTH Musicall Gramarian BL Add. 32533, f. 68v By Accords are meant the distances of these lettered notes from each other ... **1728** NORTH Musicall Grammarian (*C-K MG* f. 37v) ... Wee shall have much to doe with accords, which word ordinarily means cosounding notes, according to their places in the scale, but more striktly referred to the key note.

acousticks

1737 DYCHE-PARDON (2nd edn) *Acousticks* (S.) the Doctrine or Science of Sound, the Art of making musical Instruments, or such that produce Tones or encrease Sounds;

acroamatick *see* chromatic

1500 *Ortus Vocabulorum* L→E Acroma est cantus. angl. a. songe. n.t. **1552** HULOET L→E *Acroma, Cantio. onis, Cantilena, Cantus, us, Modulamen. is, Modulus. li, Musa, æ, Oda, æ, Psalmodia. æ, Versus* Song. **1587** THOMAS L→E *Acroama, atos, n.g. p.b.* A subtile sentence or lesson requiring much studie and search. also [sic] a musicall harmonie, whereby the gesture of players was commended, and the auditorie delighted: also the person that playeth, and by his gesture delighteth the eie. *Acroamaticus, adiect. p.b. Idem quod auscultatorius. Gell.* **1611** COTGRAVE Fr→E *Acroamatie: f.* Melodie harmonie; *Acroamatique.* Musicall, harmonious, delightsome, pleasing, plausible, to the eare. **1656** BLOUNT (1st edn) *Acroamatick* (*acroamaticus*) ... also musical, harmonious, or delightful to the ear. **1658** PHILLIPS (1st edn) *Acroamatick*, (Greek) one that hearkens attentively to any thing, also harmonious. **1671** PHILLIPS (3rd edn) *Acroamatick, (Greek)* one that hearkens attentively to any thing, whence Acroamatick Notes in *Musick* are such, whose harmony draws a most diligent attention. **1676** COLES *Acroamatick, Greek.* That gives or requires much attention, musical. **1678** PHILLIPS (4th edn) *Acroamatick*, (Greek) requiring great attention, whence Acroamatick Notes in Musick are such, whose harmony draws a most diligent attention.

act *see* choir, chorus, intercino, interlude, intermedia

1728 CHAMBERS *Acts*, in Poetry, are certain Divisions, or principal Parts in a Dramatic Poem .... The antient *Greek* Poets were unacquainted with this Division of a Play into *Acts*; tho their Episodes or Chorus's serv'd almost the same Purpose. See *Episode*, and *Chorus*. **1737** BAILEY *The Univ. Etymolog. Engl. Dict.* (3rd edn, vol. 2) *Acts* (in the *Dramatick*, &c.) are the divisions or principal parts, the intervals between, which are for giving respite both to the actors and spectators, while the actors are changing their habits to represent other characters, or for preparing themselves for other parts, during which time the audience is diverted, with musick, a song, dance, *&c*. ¶ The number of acts in a well concerted play is generally five.

active music *see* harmonic music, music

1609 DOWLAND-ORNITHOPARCUS *Micrologvs* (p. 2) *Actiue Musicke*, which also they call *Practick*, is (as Saint *Austine* [sic] in the first booke of his Musicke writeth) the knowledge of singing well: or according to *Guido* in the beginning of his *Doctrinall*, it is a liberall Science, dispensing the principles of singing truely. *Franchinus* (in the third Chapter of his first Booke of his *Theorick*) doth so define it: It is a knowledge of perfect singing, consisting of *sounds, words,* and *numbers;* which is in like sort two-fold, *Mensurall,* and *Plaine.*

acute *as in pitch, see* accent

1538 ELYOT L→E *Acutus, ta, tum,* sharpe, but in voyce it betokeneth high and small, as a treble. **1552** HULOET L→E *Acutus. a. um* Treble voyced, or shyll [sic] tuned. **1565** COOPER L→E *Acûtus* ... In voyce, high, small, shrill. § *Vox acuta. Ouid.* Small: shrill: highe: a treble. **1587** THOMAS L→E *Acutus, a, um, part.* ... In voice or sound, high, small, shrill. **1589** RIDER L→E *Acutus, ad.* Treble voiced. § *Sonus acutus. Sonus summus. succortrilla, succortilla, succotrilla* [sic], A Treble, a small, or shrill voice. *v.* sing [*see* cano]. **1708** KERSEY *Dict. Anglo-Brit.* (1st edn) *Acute* Sounds, so proportionably order'd as to make a Pleasant Harmony. **1724** [PEPUSCH] *Short Explic. of Foreign Words in Mus. Bks.* (p. 7) *Acuto,* Acute; a Voice or Sound is so called when high or shrill. **1726** BAILEY *An Univ. Etymolog. Engl. Dict.* (3rd edn) *Acuto* (in *Musick Books*) a Voice or Sound is so called when high or shrill. **1728** CHAMBERS *Acute,* in Musick, is understood of a Sound, or Tone which is sharp, or shrill, or high, in respect of some other. See *Sound.* ¶ In this Sense, the Word stands opposed to *Grave.* See *Grave.* ¶ Sounds consider'd as *Acute* and Grave, that is, in the Relation of Gravity and *Acuteness,* constitute what we call *Tune,* the Foundation of all Harmony. See *Tune, Concord,* and *Harmony.* § *Acuteness,* in Musick, *&c.* that which constitutes or denominates a Sound, *&c. acute.* See *Acute.* ¶ There is no such thing as *Acuteness* and *Gravity,* absolutely so called; they are only Relations; so that the same Sound may be either *Acute* or *Grave,* according to that other Sound they refer or are compared to. See *Relation.* ¶ The Degrees of Gravity and *Acuteness,* make so many Tones, or Tunes of a Voice, or Sound. See *Tone, Tune, Voice,* &c.

1721 MALCOLM *Treatise of Musick* (p. 35) ... But commonly when we speak of these Degrees [of highness and lowness], we call them several Degrees of *Acuteness* and *Gravity,* without supposing these Terms to express any fixt and determinate Thing; but it implies some supposed Degree of *Tune,* as a Term to which we tacitely compare several other Degrees; ...

acute *as ornament*

1665 SIMPSON *Division-Viol* (2nd edn, p. 11) There is yet another Plain or Smooth Grace called an *Acute* or *Springer,* which concludes the Sound of a Note more acute, by clapping down another Finger just at the expiring of it.

adagio *see* grave

1724 [PEPUSCH] *Short Explic. of Foreign Words in Mus. Bks.* (p. 7) *Adagio,* or by Way of Abbreviation *Adag°,* or *Ad°,* by which is signified the slowest Movement in Musick, especially if the Word be repeated twice over, as *Adagio, Adagio.* (p. 95) *Adagio,* Very Grave. § (p. 95) *Adagio Adagio,* Extream Grave or Slow. **1726** BAILEY *An Univ. Etymolog. Engl. Dict.* (3rd edn) *Adagio, Adag°, Ad°,* (in *Musick Books*) signifies the slowest Movement in Musick, especially if the Word be repeated twice, as *Adagio, Adagio.* **1728** CHAMBERS *Adagio,* in Musick, one of the Words used by the *Italians,* to denote a Degree or Distinction of Time. See *Time.* ¶ The *Adagio* expresses a slow Time; the slowest of any, except *Grave.* See *Allegro.* ¶ The Triple $\frac{3}{2}$ is ordinarily *Adagio.* See *Triple.* **1735** DEFOE *Adagio,* the slowest Movement of Time in Musick. **1737** DYCHE-PARDON (2nd edn) *Adagio* (A.) slow, grave, solemn; a Term in *Musick,* signifying that Part must be plaid or sung very slow to which it is annexed.

1680 B., A. *Synopsis of Vocal Musick* (p. 19) The secondary signs of the Tact or Time are certain words used by the *Italians,* and afterwards also of others, to wit, *Adagio,* and *Presto,* signifying, that such a part of a Song where *Adagio* is written, is to be Sung slower, and where *Presto,* swifter. **1683** PURCELL *Sonnata's of III Parts* (*To the Reader*) ... It remains only that the English Practitioner be enform'd, that he will find a few terms of Art perhaps unusual to him, the chief of which are these following: *Adagio* and *Grave,* which import nothing but a very slow movement: ... **c.1710** ANON. *Preceptor for Improved Octave Flageolet* ('Explanation of Words', p. 82) *Adagio*—A slow Movement **c.1726** NORTH Musicall Gramarian BL Add. 32533, f. 65v Adagio, w[ch] signifyes very slow, as after running then to fall Into a slow pace. **1728** NORTH Musicall Grammarian (*C-K MG* f. 62v) [*re* 'Elegances of an upper part'] ... And this gives me occasion to hint how needfull it is to reflect back upon the many schematismes I have given of accords, commixtures of keys, and other modes, and ornaments that continually occurr in musick. For out of them may be gathered most of the beautyfull turnes that musick is capable of; which may be managed by a single instrument, as most of the prime masters demonstrate in their illustrious handling [of] a grave strain called an adagio. **1731** PRELLEUR *Modern Musick-Master* (Dictionary, p. 1) *Adagio* or *Adag.°* or *Ad.°*, a Slow, movement, especially if the Word be repeated twice over as, *Adagio Adagio* **1736** TANS'UR *Compleat Melody* (3rd edn, p. 66) *Adagio, Recitativo, Recitatif, Recit*, or *Reo, Moters, Opras* [sic]. (Ital.) Either of those *Terms*, or Words signifies, the slowest Movement in *Time*: Also the gravest *Parts* in Songs, or *Cantata's*; which comes as near as possible to the true Pronunciation of the Words.

ad libitum *see* bene placito, libitum

1724 [PEPUSCH] *Short Explic. of Foreign Words in Mus. Bks.* (p. 7) *Ad Libitum*, if you will, or if you please. **1726** BAILEY *An Univ. Etymolog. Engl. Dict.* (3rd edn) *Ad Libitum* (in *Musick Books*) signifies, If you will, or, If you please.

1736 TANS'UR *Compleat Melody* (3rd edn, p. 71) *Ad Libitum*, or *Libitum*, or *Bene Placito*. (Lat.) signifies, if you please, or if you will.

admetinænia *see* nænia

1565 COOPER L→E **Admetinænia*, A prouerbe, whiche signifieth an heuy or sorrowfull songe, or a lamentable complainte.

admodulate *see* modulate

1623 COCKERAM *Admodulate.* to Sing to

Adrianus

1565 COOPER L→E *Adrianus*, A noble Emperour of Rome, aboute the yere of our Lorde, 119 ... a man of excellent wytte, and dyuers in manners, meruaylouse in learnyng, specially in Mathematicalles. Also in Musicke, keruing, and grauing...

adufe *see* pandera

1599 MINSHEU-PERCYVALL Sp→E † *Adufe*, a timbrell † *Adufero*, or *Aduflero*, a player on a Taber, a player on a timbrell, or one that selleth them.

aegloga *see* eclogue

aeneator *see* buccinator

1538 ELYOT L→E *Aenatores*, blowers in trumpettes. **1552** HULOET L→E *Ænator. ris, buccinator. ris, siticen, tibicen, tibicina, tubicen. tympanista* Trumpetour. **1565** COOPER L→E *Aeneâtor, pen. prod. eneatóris, m.g. Sue.* A trumpetour: a blower in a trumpette. **1587** THOMAS L→E *Aeneator, oris, m.g. Suet.* A Trumpetter: one that soundeth or blowthe [sic] a trumpet. **1623** COCKERAM *Eneatour.* a Trumpetor. **1658** PHILLIPS (1st edn) *Aeneator*, (lat.) a Trumpeter. **1676** COLES *Aeneator, Latin.* Trumpeter.

æolian, æolick *see* mood

1598 FLORIO It→E § *Eolio canto*, a kinde of song or musicke. **1611** FLORIO It→E § *Eolio canto*, a kind of song or musicke. **1659** TORRIANO-FLORIO It→E § *Eolio canto*, a kind of musical song. **1706** KERSEY-PHILLIPS (6th edn) *Æolick Mood*, see *Mood in Musick.* **1728** CHAMBERS *Æolic*, or *Æolian Mode*, in Musick. See *Mode. Eolic*, in Music, one of the Modes of the antient Music. See *Mode.* ¶ The *Æolic* Mode was found fittest for *Lyric* Verses; as having a peculiar Sweetness and Gravity. It was the Sol of *G re Sol ut.* ¶ The *Sub-Æolic*, or *Hypo-Æolic*, had the same Effects with the *Æolic*. It was the *re* of *de Sol re;* and began a Diatessaron lower than its natural authentic Mode. **1730** BAILEY *Dict. Britannicum* (1st edn) *Æolick Mood*, was of an airy, soft and delightful Sound, such as our *Madrigals*, and was useful to allay the Passions, by means of its grateful Variety and melodious Harmony.

1636 BUTLER *Principles of Musik* (p. 2) The *Æolik* Moode is that, which, with its soft pleasing sounds, pacifyeth the Passions of the minde, and with instruments or dittiles [sic] *fa-la's*, in continued discant, delighting the sens, and not intending the minde of the hearer, like Mercuries *Caduceus*, charmeth affections and cares, and so lulleth him sweetely a sleepe. § (p. 4) The *Æolik* [was so called] of *Æolia* (the Kingdom of *Æolus*) whence hee is feined to send his rusling windes: the which dooe heerin resemble this Moode, that they also have a sopiting [sic] faculti. § (pp. 5-6) Of the *Æolik* Moode was that Enchanting Musik of the Harp, provided for King *Saul*, when the evil spirit trubbled him: .... Of this Moode was the Pathetical song of the good Bishop *Flavianus*: .... Of this Moode was that calm Symphoni wherewith *Achilles* appeased his own Passions against *Agamemnon*: .... Of this Moode also was the Pythagorean Evn-song, mentioned by *Quintilian*.

æolipile

1728 CHAMBERS *Æolipile, Æolipila*, a hydraulick Instrument, consisting of a hollow metalline Ball, with a slender Neck or Pipe arising from the same;

which being filled with Water, and thus expos'd to the Fire, produces a vehement Blast of Wind.... *Chauvin* suggests such further Uses of the Æolipile.—1°, He thinks it might be applied instead of Bellows to blow the Fire, where a very intense heat is requir'd. 2°, If a Trumpet, Horn, or other sonorous Instrument were fitted to its Neck, it might be made to yield Musick.

aerisonus

1565 COOPER L→E § *Aere ciere viros. Virg.* with the trumpet to stirre vp men to warre. **1587** THOMAS L→E *Aerisonus, a um, Stat.* That soundeth with the noise of brasse: basons, or such like.

aes

1538 ELYOT L→E *Aes, æris,* is proprely copper or brasse. It is oftentymes taken for money, sometyme for trumpettes. **1552** HULOET L→E *Æs. ris, buccina. æ, lituus. i, tibia. æ, tuba. æ* Trumpet. **1565** COOPER L→E § *Acuta æra. Horat.* Shrill ringyng belles. *Aes Cauum, Id est tuba ærea. Virg.* A trumpette. **1587** THOMAS L→E *Aes, æris, n.g.* Brasse, copper, latten: It is also vsed for monie, a trumpet ...

affect, affections *see* accent, modi melopœiæ, music, organ, song

affetto, affettuoso *see* tendrement

1724 [PEPUSCH] *Short Explic. of Foreign Words in Mus. Bks.* (pp. 7-8) *Affetto,* or *Con Affetto,* or *Affettuoso,* by which Words is signified, that the Musick must be performed in a very moving, tender, or affecting Manner, and therefore not too fast, but rather slow. **1726** BAILEY *An Univ. Etymolog. Engl. Dict.* (3rd edn) *Affetto* (in *Musick Books*) signifies that the Musick must be performed in a very moving, tender, or affecting Manner, and for that reason not too fast but rather slow. *Affettuoso* (in *Musick Books*) signifies the same as *Affetto.* § *Con Affetto* (in *Musick Books*) signifies, that Musick must be performed in a very moving, tender, and affecting manner, and therefore not too fast, but rather slow. **1737** DYCHE-PARDON (2nd edn) *Affetto* or *Affettuoso* (A.) a *Musical* Term, signifying that such a Strain or Air should be played or sung in the tenderest and most moving Manner.

c.1710 ANON. *Preceptor for Improved Octave Flageolet* ('Explanation of Words', p. 82) *Affettusoso*—Tenderly **1731** PRELLEUR *Modern Musick-Master* (Dictionary, p. 1) *Affetto,* in a tender Affecting Manner. *Affectuoso,* very tenderly.

affinal key *see* final, key

1609 DOWLAND-ORNITHOPARCUS *Micrologvs* (p. 27) *Of the Affinal Keyes of Tones.* ¶ The *Keyes* (which we call *Affinall*) be the Letters, which end irregular Songs: whereof according to *Guido, Berno,* and Saint *Gregory,* there be three: Although the *Ambrosians* make more...

afistolar *see* fistula

1599 MINSHEU-PERCYVALL Sp→E **Afistolar,* ... to whistle to pipe.

Agathon *see* agonothet, choragus, revels

1565 COOPER L→E *Agathon,* A certain minstrel, which with his sweete songes exceedingly delited mens eares. **1623** COCKERAM *Agathon,* a wanton Minstrell. **1676** COLES *Agathon,* A wanton fidler.

agnafile *see* aguafile, añafil

1611 COTGRAVE Fr→E *Agnafile.* A kind of Moorish Trumpet. **1650** HOWELL-COTGRAVE Fr→E † *Agnafile.* A kind of Moorish Trumpet.

agones capitolini

1730 BAILEY *Dict. Britannicum* (1st edn) *Agones Capitolini* (among the *Romans*) Festivals held to *Jupiter,* as Protector or Guardian of the Capitol. At this Festival Poems were sung or recited in Honour of him by the Poets.

agonothet *see* Agathon, choragus, revels

1656 BLOUNT (1st edn) *Agonath* or *Agonothete (Agonotheta)* ... a Master of Revels. **1658** PHILLIPS (1st edn) *Agonothert* (Greek) a Master of the Revell's. **1676** COLES *Agonarch* or *Agonothete, Greek.* Master of the Revels. **1708** KERSEY *Dict. Anglo-Brit.* (1st edn) *Agonotheta,* an Overseer at Feasts of Activity, a Master of the Revels.

agreslir la voix

1593 HOLLYBAND Fr→E *Agreslir la voix,* to squeake out, or sing shrill **1611** COTGRAVE Fr→E *Agreslir la voix.* To squeale, or squeake; to sing in a high pitch; to rise in singing.

aguafile *see* agnafile, añafil

1611 COTGRAVE Fr→E *Aguafile: f.* A kind of Moorish Trumpet.

aime-lyre

1611 COTGRAVE Fr→E *Aime-lyre.* Musicall, Harpe-louing, Lyre-affecting.

air *see* aria, arioso, brawl, camera, cantata, formality, interlude, key, lesson, lyrick, melody, prelude, suit, tenor, trumpet air, tune

1598 FLORIO It→E *Aere,* ... Also a tune, a sound, a note, or an ayre of musicke or any ditty. **1611** COTGRAVE Fr→E *Air: m.* ... also, a tune, sownd, or ayre in Musick; **1611** FLORIO It→E *Aere,* ... also a tune or aire of a song or ditty. **1688** MIEGE-COTGRAVE Fr→E *Air,* (m.) ... an air, or tune; § *Air nouveau de Musique,* a new Tune, a new Air of Musick. *L'Air que vous venez de chanter est grave & melancolique,* the Tune you sung just now is both grave and melancholy. *Un Air accommodé aux Paroles,* a Tune suitable to the Words. *Un Air bien passionné,* a Tune well humoured. *un Air gai,* a merry Tune. **1702** KERSEY *New Engl. Dict.* (1st edn) An *Air, in* Musick, *&c.* **1706** KERSEY-PHILLIPS (6th edn) *Air* ... also a Tune in Musick; **1728** CHAMBERS *Air,* in Musick, signifies the *Melody,* or the Inflection of a Musical Composition. See *Melody.* ¶ The Word is also used for a Song it self. See *Song.* **1730** BAILEY *Dict. Britannicum* (1st edn) *Air* (with *Musicians*) signifies the Melody or the Inf[l]ection of a Musical Composition. **1737** DYCHE-PARDON (2nd edn) *Air* (S.) a *Musical* Term, signifying the general Bent or Inclination of the Composition; also a particular Tune played alone, without either a Bass, or any other Part to accompany it.

1597 MORLEY *Plaine and Easie Introdvction* (p. 180) ... these [ballete] and all other kinds of light musicke sauing the *Madrigal* are by a generall name called ayres. **[1610]** CAMPION *Two Bookes of Ayres* (*To the Reader*) These Ayres were for the most part framed at first for one voyce with the Lute, or Violl, but vpon occasion, they haue since beene filled with more parts ... the Treble tunes, which are with vs commonly called Ayres, are but Tenors mounted eight Notes higher ... **1636** BUTLER *Principles of Musik* (p. 86) *Air, or Tone.* In this woord is a large *Metalepsis.* Air, of *Aer,* for *Percussio Aeris, Metonimia est Subjecti: Percussio pro Sono* ... **1676** MACE *Musick's Monument* (p. 129) *Ayres,* are, or should be, of the *same Time,* [as almains] (yet many make *Tripla's,* and call them so;) only they differ from *Allmaines,* by being commonly *Shorter,* and of a more *Quick, and Nimble Performance.* **c.1710** NORTH (draft for) Musicall Grammarian BL Add. 32537, f. 100 ... and yet It is not easy to say what Ayre is; it seem's best adumbrated by a good style In vers, or prose; a sort of musick y[t] seem's to flow from nature, one sound following another as If they were of a family, so as nothing occurs that occasions anyone to say why or what means this: Euery thing proper, & nothing fantasticall, or in y[e] least defective, but as the Thames, In Denham's description, still full but never overflowing. It seems odd to give descriptions, & caracters to a thing so litle understood, as musicall Ayre is; a meer Je ne scay quoy. Nothing is so comon as to hear it say'd It may be good Musick, but there is no aire in it. and so y[e] comendation of musick is ordinarily that there is a great deal of very good aire in it. **c.1715-20** NORTH Essay of Musical Ayre BL Add. 32536, f. 20 ... First as for y[e] word Ayre, it was taken into y[e] language of Harmony from a conceipted Analogy with the flow of a gentle & well tempered air abroad as if that yelded the sound... it is not to be wondered If air in musick be hard to be exprest. But by way of endeavour towards it, I shall first propose a plain Key-Note taken ad libitum, with its full accord; As the Mechanisme, so the Idea, of this sound is distinguisht from that of all other Keys whatever, and this peculiarity of sound is called the Ayre of the Key, And being once heard, dwells so strong in our Minds, that whatever Sounds succeed they must maintain an harmonious relation with y[e] Key or some of the accords of it ... § f. 48 ... the melodious tune comonly Expected from the movement of the upper parts, w[ch] may be obtained divers ways under y[e] same accords, as fancy, or Caprice commonly guides, is no less then any other Quality (and with y[e] vulgar principalls) required. This is what they Call air, or humour ... **1728** NORTH Musicall Grammarian (*C-K MG* f. 59v) [a beginner composer should take a prepared] single base, upon which he may practise by putting thereto one or more parts. And it is not well for himself to be his own carver, but to have his artificially made, for in that, (but more in the upper parts,) there must be what is called ayre; and by that wee understand a timely movement in the gradations of some key, and that not changing, but according to the rules already given.

alamire

1659 TORRIANO-FLORIO It→E *Alamire,* a certain tune or sound in Musick. **1678** PHILLIPS (4th edn) *Alamire,* the lowest Note but one in each of the three Septenaries of the Gamut or Scale of Musick; in the lowest of which Septenaries, or the Base Cliff it answers, to the Greek προσλαμ-βανόμενος **1706** KERSEY-PHILLIPS (6th edn) *A-re* or *A-la-mi-re,* the Name of one of the eight Notes in the Scale of Musick. **1721** BAILEY *An Univ. Etymolog. Engl. Dict.* (1st edn) *A-la-mire,* the lowest Note but one in the 3 *Septenaries* of the *Gamut,* or Scale of Musick. **1728** CHAMBERS *A-La-Mire,* in Musick. See *Note,* and *Gamut. A-re,* or *A-la-mire,* one of the eight Notes in the Scale of Musick. See *Note* and *Scale.* **1737** DYCHE-PARDON (2nd edn) *Are* or *Alamire* (S.) the First of the eight Notes in the common Scale of Musick

alamoi

1611 FLORIO It→E *Alamoi,* a certain sound in Musicke raised aboue others.

alarm *see* a cavallo, beat, bellicum, drum, mensural music, trumpet

1598 FLORIO It→E *Al'arma,* ... Also a march so called, sounded vpon the drum or trumpet. § *Dar al'arma,* a kinde of march sounded vpon the drum and trumpet, to strike vp an alarum. **1604** CAWDREY (1st edn) *alarum,* a sound to the battell. **1611** FLORIO It→E *Alarma,* an alaram in time of war. Also the name of march or warning sounded vpon drum or trumpet. **1659** TORRIANO-FLORIO It→E *All'-arma,* the name of a point of warre sounded upon Drum or Trumpet as a warning unto arms, an Allarum. **1696** PHILLIPS (5th edn) *Alarum,* a Signal given by loud Cries, or the sound of Warlike Instruments, to cause People to take Arms upon the sudden arrival of the Enemy. **1706** KERSEY-PHILLIPS (6th edn) *Alarm* or *Alarum,* a Signal given by loud Cries, or the sound of warlike Instruments, to cause People to take Arms upon the sudden arrival of the Enemy. **1728** CHAMBERS *Alarm,* a Signal given by Shouts, or by Instruments of War, for the Soldiers to take to their Arms, at the unexpected Arrival of an Enemy. ¶ The Word is form'd from the French *à l'arme,* to your Arms. **1737** DYCHE-PARDON (2nd edn) *Alarm* or *Alarum* (S.) the Noise made by a Drum, Trumpet, or Voice, in a sudden and hasty Manner, to signify that Preparation must be made against the Invasion of an Enemy, who has in a Manner come upon us by Surprize, or unexpectedly;

Alcæus

1565 COOPER L→E *Alcæus,* A famous poete, of them, whiche are called *Lyrici,* (because they made songes to the harp) ...

Alcidamas

1565 COOPER L→E *Alcidamas,* A famouse wrestler. Also a philosopher whiche wrate of musike.

alla breve *see* breve

1731 PRELLEUR *Modern Musick-Master* (Dictionary, p. 1) *Alla Breve,* the name of a Movement in Musick whose Barrs consist of two Semibreves or four Minims &c.

allegretto

c.1710 ANON. *Preceptor for Improved Octave Flageolet* ('Explanation of Words', p. 82) *Allegretto*—Quicker than Andantino **1731** PRELLEUR *Modern Musick-Master* (Dictionary, p. 1) *Allegretto,* Pretty Quick.

allegrezza

1598 FLORIO It→E *Allegrezza,* ... Also a marche sounded on trumpet and drum in signe of victorie. **1611** FLORIO It→E *Allegrezza,* ... Also a march sounded on trumpet and drume in signe of victory. **1659** TORRIANO-FLORIO It→E *Allegrezza, Allegraggio, Allegranza, Allegria,* gladnesse, mirth, glee or joy; by *met*: a certain March sounded on Trumpet, Fife or Drum, in signe of Victory and joy.

allegro *see* correnti

1721 BAILEY *An Univ. Etymolog. Engl. Dict.* (1st edn) *Allegro,* a Term in Musick when the Movement is quick. **1724** [PEPUSCH] *Short Explic. of Foreign Words in Mus. Bks.* (pp. 8-9) *Allegro,* or by Way of Abbreviation *All°,* by which Word is signified, that the Musick must be performed in a gay, brisk, lively, and pleasant Manner, yet without Hurry or Precipitation: When the Word *Poco* stands before it, it lessens the Strength of its Signification, and sheweth that the Musick must not be perform'd quite so brisk and gay, as the Word *Allegro* only does require. But when the Word *Piu* stands before it, it does, on the contrary, increase the Strength of its Signification, by requiring the Musick to be perform'd more gay and brisk than the Word *Allegro* only does require. When the Word *Allegro* is repeated twice over, it signifies much the same as the foregoing Words *Piu Allegro.* (p. 95) *Allegro,* Brisk, or Briskly. § (p. 95) *Allegro Assai,* not too Brisk. (p. 9) *Allegro ma non Presto,* is as much as to say, gay, brisk, and lively, yet not too fast or quick. *Piu Allegro,* very Brisk, or more Briskly. **1726** BAILEY *An Univ. Etymolog. Engl. Dict.* (3rd edn) *Allegro* (in *Musick Books*) signifies that the Musick ought to be perform'd in a gay, brisk, lively, and pleasant manner; but yet without hurry or precipitation. ¶ When *Poco* preceeds it, it diminishes the strength of its Signification, and intimates that the Musick must not be perform'd quite so brisk and gay, as the Word *Allegro* standing alone requires: When the Word *Piu* preceeds *Allegro,* it adds to the strength of its Signification, and requires, that the Musick be perform'd more gay and brisk, than the Word *Allegro,* standing by it self requires. ¶ *Allegro, Allegro, i.e.* the Word *Allegro* repeated signifies much the same as *Piu Allegro.* ¶ *Allegro ma non Presto* (in *Musick Books*) signifies gay, brisk, and lively, yet not too fast or quick. **1728** CHAMBERS *Allegro,* in Musick, a Word used by the *Italians* to denote one of the six Distinctions of Time. See *Time.* ¶ *Allegro* expresses a very quick Motion, the quickest of all excepting *Presto.* ¶ The usual six Distinctions succeed each other in the following Order, Grave, Adagio, Largo, Vivace, *Allegro,* and Presto. ¶ It is to be observed, that the Movements of the same Name, as *Adagio* or *Allegro,* are swifter in Triple than in Common Time.—The Triple $\frac{3}{8}$ is usually *Allegro,* or *Vivace;* the Triples $\frac{6}{4}$, $\frac{6}{8}$, $\frac{9}{8}$, $\frac{12}{8}$, are most commonly *Allegro.* See *Triple.* **1735** DEFOE *Allegro,* the quickest Time in Musick. **1737** DYCHE-PARDON (2nd edn) *Allegro* (A.) in *Musick,* shows that the Performance ought to be in a brisk, lively Manner, but not too fast. If *Poco* stands before it, the Musick must be performed in somewhat a slower or graver Manner than single *Allegro* requires; if it be preceeded by *Piu,* the Musick must be somewhat faster than *Allegro,* and then is the quickest of all. In every swift Movement; the Player or Singer must be careful to be distinct, and not hurry himself into Confusion, and his Auditors into Uneasiness, by two much Fire and Precipitancy.

1683 PURCELL *Sonnata's of III Parts (To the Reader)* ... It remains only that the English Practitioner be enform'd, that he will find a few terms of Art perhaps unusual to him, the chief of which are these following: ... *Allegro,* and *Vivace,* a very brisk, swift, or fast movement: ... **c.1710** ANON. *Preceptor for Improved Octave Flageolet* ('Explanation of Words', p. 82) *Allegro*—Faster than Allegretto **c.1715-20** NORTH Essay of Musical Ayre BL Add. 32536, f. 47v ... Intending here Explication onely and not Instruction, but give a short Reprehension to one manner I have met with, wch is a beginning a peice of Musick with ye measure, & devision called, Allegro, wch is to be performed very lively and quick, and much Resembling the unwarrantable Entry of a dancer, who Instead of a Solemne and lofty Movem^t, falls to running about the room to & fro as If he were madd. **c.1726** NORTH Musicall Gramarian BL Add. 32533, f. 65v Allegro, is an Easy light-hearted measure, and Reputed twice as quick as the Adagio ... § f. 143v ... I have observed some celebrated Sonnata-men, begin with what they Call Allegro, and at ye very Entrance, start, & fall a running like madd. § f. 145v The next step in the comon sonnata musick, is from the Grave or adagio, to the Allegro, wch means cheerfull, as freinds when they are well acquainted and meet to be merry; ... **1731** PRELLEUR *Modern Musick-Master* (Dictionary, p. 1) *Allegro* or *All.*^{o} Brisk or Quick especially if ye Word be repeated twice over. **1736** TANS'UR *Compleat Melody* (3rd edn, p. 66) *Allegro, Animatio, Vivace, Vivacemente, Vivumente, Brillante.* (Ital) Either of those *Terms,* denotes one Degree quicker than *Largetto;* and is performed with Life, Spirit, and Vigour; and in good *Time.*

alleluia

1599 MINSHEU-PERCYVALL Sp→E **Aleluya,* of ioy, a hymne or song of ioy. **1688** MIEGE-COTGRAVE Fr→E § *Chanter des Allelujas,* to sing Hallelujahs. **1728** CHAMBERS *Hallelujah,* a Term of Rejoycing, sometimes sung or rehears'd, at the End of Verses on that Occasion. ¶ St. *Jerom* first introduced the Word *Hallelujah* into the Church Service: For a considerable Time it was only used once a Year, in the *Latin* Church, *viz.* at *Easter*: But in the *Greek* Church it was much more frequent. St. *Jerom* mentions its being sung at the Interments of the Dead, which it still continues to be in that Church; also on some Occasions in Lent. ¶ In the Time of *Gregory the Great,* it was appointed to be sung all the Year round in the *Latin* Church, which rais'd some Complaints against that Pope, as giving too much into the *Greek* Way, and introducing the Ceremonies of the Church of *Constantinople* into that of *Rome.* But he excused himself by alledging that this had been the antient Usage at *Rome;* and that it had been brought from *Constantinople* at the Time when the Word *Hallelujah* was first introduced under Pope *Damasus.* ¶ The Word is *Hebrew;* or rather, it is two *Hebrew* Words joyn'd together; one of them הללו, *hallelu,* and the other יה, *ja,* an Abridgment of the Name of God, יהוה, *Jehova.* The first signifies *Laudate,* praise ye; and the other *Dominum,* the Lord. **1737** DYCHE-PARDON (2nd edn) *Hallelujah* (S.) an *Hebrew* Expression frequently used in Psalms and *Jewish* Hymns, from whence it came into the Christian Church, meaning, Praise the Lord...

1736 TANS'UR *Compleat Melody* (3rd edn, p. 72) *Hallelujah*, or *Allelujah*, (Heb.) signifies, praise the Lord, *&c*.

allemande, almain *see* chiarantana, imperfect of the less, lesson, phrygian, sonata, suit, time

1598 FLORIO It→E *Alamana*, a lesson in musicke called an Alemaine. **1611** COTGRAVE Fr→E § *Trois pas, & vn saut*. The Almond, or Alman, leape. **1611** FLORIO It→E *Alamana*, an Almane in musicke. **1658** PHILLIPS (1st edn) An *Almain*, ... (a Term in Musick) being a kinde of aire, which hath a slower time then either *Corant*, or *Saraband* **1676** COLES *Almain*. A German, also a slow aire in Musick. **1696** PHILLIPS (5th edn) *Almain*, ... Also (a term in Musick) being a kind of Air that moves in common Time, yet brisker than a Pavan. **1704** HARRIS *Allemande*, is a kind of grave solemn Musick, where the Measure is full and the Movement slow. **1706** KERSEY-PHILLIPS (6th edn) *Allemande* or *Almain*, a kind of grave solemn Musick, where the Measure is full and the Movement slow. *A[l]main*, ... In *Musick*, a kind of Air that moves in Common Time. **1721** BAILEY *An Univ. Etymolog. Engl. Dict.* (1st edn) *Allemande, Almain*, a kind of grave solid Musick, where the Measure is good, and the Movement slow. *Almain*, (in *Musick*) a certain kind of Air that moves in common Time. **1724** [PEPUSCH] *Short Explic. of Foreign Words in Mus. Bks.* (p. 9) *Allemanda*, is the Name of a certain Air or Tune, always in common time, and in Two Parts or Strains, each Part play'd twice over. **1726** BAILEY *An Univ. Etymolog. Engl. Dict.* (3rd edn) *Allemanda* (in *Musick Books*) is the name of a certain Air or Tune, always in common Time, and in two Parts or Strains, each part play'd twice over. **1728** CHAMBERS *Allemand, Almain*, a kind of grave, solemn Musick, where the Measure is good, and the Movement slow. See *Musick, Song, Measure, &c.* **1730** BAILEY *Dict. Britannicum* (1st edn) *Allemande, Almain*, (with *Musicians*) a sort of grave, solemn Musick, whose Measure is full and moving. *Almain* (in *Musick*) a sort of Air that moves in Common Time. **1737** DYCHE-PARDON (2nd edn) *Allemanda* or *Almand* (S.) a certain Air in Musick, always composed in common Time, and consisting of two Parts or Strains, each of which must be played twice over in a grave Sort of Manner, and yet at the same Time so sprightly as to be diverting to the Ear, of which *Corelli* has given Abundance of fine Examples. *Almain* (S.) ... also an Air or Tune in Musick called also an Almond, &c.

1597 MORLEY *Plaine and Easie Introdvction* (p. 181) The *Alman* is a more heauie daunce then this [the galliard] (fitlie representing the nature of the people, whose name it carieth) so that no extraordinarie motions are vsed in dauncing of it. It is made of strains, somtimes two, sometimes three, and euerie straine is made by foure, but you must marke that the foure of the pauan measure is in *dupla* proportion to the foure of the *Alman* measure, so that as the vsuall Pauane conteineth in a straine the time of sixteene semibreues, so the vsuall *Almaine* containeth the time of eight, and most commonlie in short notes. **1667** SIMPSON *Compendium of Practical Musick* (p. 144) An *Almane* (so called from the Country whence it came, as the former [the galliard] from *Gallia*) ... **1676** MACE *Musick's Monument* (p. 129) *Allmaines*, are *Lessons* very *Ayrey*, and *Lively*; and Generally of Two *Strains*, of the *Common*, or *Plain-Time*. **1728** NORTH Musicall Grammarian (*C-K MG* f. 73v) ... Another sort is the almanda[,] from a more heavy style, [which] is supposed to be [de]rived of the Germans, whose musick is good but very articulate and plaine ... **1731** PRELLEUR *Modern Musick-Master* (Dictionary, p. 1) *Allemanda* is the Name of a Tune always in Common Time. **1736** TANS'UR *Compleat Melody* (3rd edn, p. 66) *Alemand, Gravisonous*, (Ital.) or *Grave*. Either of those *Terms* signifies, one Degree quicker than *Adagio*; and moves mostly in *Common-Time*.

alostendardo

1598 FLORIO It→E *Alostendardo*, the name of a marche vpon the drum and trumpet. **1611** FLORIO It→E *Alostendardo*, a march on drumme or trumpet so called. **1659** TORRIANO-FLORIO It→E *A-lo stendardo*, a point of warre sounded on Drum and Trumpet, so called, because it calleth Souldiers to the Standard, to their Ensigns or Colours.

alpa *see* harp

1598 FLORIO It→E *Alpa, Arpa*, an instrument called a harpe. **1611** FLORIO It→E *Alpa*, an instrument called a harpe.

Alphonso *see* leero

1656 BLOUNT (1st edn) *Alphonso* a famous Musician, who invented a particular way of playing on the Viol, which still retains his name.

alt *see* alto, altus, double

1728 CHAMBERS *Alt*, in Musick. See *Diagram*, and *Scale*; see also *Alto*. ¶ The Word is form'd of the

Latin *altus*, high. **1730** BAILEY *Dict. Britannicum* (1st edn) *Alt* (in *Musick*) high, see *Alto*. **1737** DYCHE-PARDON (2nd edn) *Alt* (A.) in *Musick*, signifies those particular Notes or Parts that are above the common System, or five Lines, shrill, &c.

1654 PLAYFORD *Breefe Intro. to Skill of Musick* (p. 3) Those [notes] above *Ela* are called Notes in *Alt*, as *F fa ut*, and *G sol re ut*, &c. in *Alt*: And those below *Gam-ut* are called *double Notes*, as *Double F fa ut*, *E la mi*, &c. as being *Eights*, or *Diapasons* to those above *Gam-ut* ... **1704** GORTON *Catechetical Questions in Musick* (p. 23) *Q*. What is the meaning of that additional word (in alt?) ¶ *A*. It distinguishes the Notes above from the Notes below, which are of the same name, the word (alt) signifying above. **1724** TURNER *Sound Anatomiz'd* (p. 39) Those *Sounds* above *Ela* are called, in *Alt*, which signifies above; as *Ffaut* in *Alt*, *Gsolreut* in *Alt*, &c. and those below *Gamut*, are called *Double*; as *Double Ffaut*, *Double Elami*, and so on, in the same Order as you see them lie in the *Scale*; ... **1731** PRELLEUR *Modern Musick-Master* (VI, from table facing p. 4) ... the four Notes above the Treble stave are called in alt; and those below the Bass stave are called double; ... **1736** TANS'UR *Compleat Melody* (3rd edn, p. 2) Observe, that all *Notes* that shall ascend above *F faut* in the *Treble*, are called *Notes* in *Alt*; and all *Notes* that descend below *Gamut* in the *Bass*, are called *Double*; as Double *F faut*, *Elami*, *D solre*, &c.

altarnativement

1724 [PEPUSCH] *Short Explic. of Foreign Words in Mus. Bks.* (p. 9) *Altarnativement*, is to play or sing Two Airs by Turns, one after another, several Times over. **1726** BAILEY *An Univ. Etymolog. Engl. Dict.* (3rd edn) *Alternativement* (in *Musick Books*) signifies to play or sing two Airs by turns, one after another, several times over.

alteration *see* prick

after 1517 ANON. Art of Mvsic BL Add. 4911, f. 21v *Alteration in figuris* [after] Joannes de Muris, Is callit ane duplication of the proper valour of any noit aftur ye form of the same, Or It is ane ganimation of ony small noit in respect of the man noit **1596** ANON. *Pathway to Musicke* [D iv] *Of Alteration and vvhat it is.* ¶ It is the doubling of the value of anie note, for the perfection of the number of three. **1597** MORLEY *Plaine and Easie Introdvction* (p. 24) *Phi*. What is *alteration*? ¶ *Ma. It is the doubling of the value of any note for the obsaruation* [sic] *of the odde number* ... so that the note which is to be altered is commonly marked with a pricke of *alteration*. **1609** DOWLAND-ORNITHOPARCUS *Micrologvs* (p. 57) *Alteration* according to *Ioannes de Muris*, is the doubling of a lesser Note in respect of a greater, or (as *Tinctor* saith) it is the doubling of the proper value. Or it is the repetition of one, and the selfe-same Note. And it is called *Alteration*, *Quasi altera actio*, it is another action, to wit: A secundary singing of a Note, for the perfecting of the number of three.

alternation *see* amebean verse, anthem, antiphon, fugue, respond, sing, troper, vocal

alto *see* alt, altus, cantus, contralto, sopralto

1598 FLORIO It→E *Alto*, ... Also a treble in song and musicke. **1611** FLORIO It→E *Alto*, ... Also a treble voice in musike. **1659** TORRIANO-FLORIO It→E **Alto*, high, eminent, aloft; also deep or profound; by *met*: a *counter Alt* or counter Tenor in Musick; **1724** [PEPUSCH] *Short Explic. of Foreign Words in Mus. Bks.* (p. 9) *Alto*, or *Altus*, the Upper or Counter Tenor, and is commonly met with in Musick of several Parts. **1726** BAILEY *An Univ. Etymolog. Engl. Dict.* (3rd edn) *Alto*, *Altus* (in *Musick Books*) signifies the Upper or Counter Tenor, and is commonly met with in Musick of several parts.

1731 PRELLEUR *Modern Musick-Master* (Dictionary, p. 1) *Alto* or *Alto-Viola*, or *Alto-Concertante*, Signify Counter-Tenor.

altobasso

1598 FLORIO It→E *Altabasso*, ... Also a kinde of musicall instrument with strings. **1611** FLORIO It→E *Altobasso*, high and low... Also a certain musical instrument with strings.

altus *see* alt, alto, treble

1737 DYCHE-PARDON (2nd edn) *Altus* or *Alt* (S.) a *Musical* Term, signifying the counter Tenor, or upper Part performed by Men, particularly in vocal Musick, that performed by Boys and Women being called the Treble.

1617-24 FLUDD *Utriusque Cosmi Maioris: De Templo Musicæ* (p. 209) *Altus* est vox acuta, per medios etiam ferè acutos decurrens, sed ita, ut vacua complens omnibus vocibus aptetur.

Ambrosian *see* affinal key, chant, key

1728 CHAMBERS *Ambrosian* .... We also meet with the *Ambrosian* Chant, or *Song*; which was distinguish'd from the *Roman*, in that it was stronger and higher.

early 17th C. ANON. Praise of musicke BL 18. B. xix, f. 4v ... But *Isodore de eccle: offic: lib: I. cap: 6.* will make answere who speaketh of St. *Ambrose*, that he not only made songes himselfe, which were songe in the Churche of *Millan*, and called *Ambrosiani* after his name but also was the first that instituted the singing of *Anthems* in ye Churche after the example of the *Greekes*...

ambubaia

1500 *Ortus Vocabulorum* L→E Ambaia idest tibucina vel symphonistica. a mynstrell. f.p. **1552** HULOET L→E *Ambubaia* Minstrell woman. **1706** KERSEY-PHILLIPS (6th edn) *Ambubaiæ*, (*Lat.*) certain Women of *Syria*, who got their Living at *Rome*, by playing on Musick and other lewd Pranks.

amebean verse

1656 BLOUNT (1st edn) *Amebean Verse (Carmen Amœbæum)* a Song or Verse when one answers another by course, or is sung by turns. **1707** *Gloss. Angl. Nova* (1st edn) *Amebean Verse*, a Song or Verse sung Alternately, or by Turns.

amoroso

c.1710 ANON. *Preceptor for Improved Octave Flageolet* ('Explanation of Words', p. 82) *Amoroso*—Amourously

Amphion *see* lydian

1538 ELYOT L→E *Amphion*, a man, whiche with naturall eloquence, brought rude and wilde people to ciuile forme of lyuynge: and as some do suppose, founde first harmony. **1552** HULOET L→E *Amphion, Rasor. oris.* Ffidler. **1565** COOPER L→E *Amphion*, A man whiche with naturall eloquence, brought rude & wild people to a ciuile forme of liuyng. And (as some suppose) found first harmonie. **1658** PHILLIPS (1st edn) *Amphion*, the son of *Jupiter* and *Antiope*, ... [he] became so rare a Musician, that he was said to build the *Theban* Walls, by playing upon *Mercuries* Harp. **1676** COLES *Amphion*, An Excellent Musician, who built the walls of *Thebes*.

Anacreon *see* lyrick

1565 COOPER L→E *Anacreon*, An olde poete, whiche song to the harpe: he was borne in the town of Ionia, called Teum ...

añafil *see* agnafile, aguafile

1599 MINSHEU-PERCYVALL Sp→E § †*Añafil de Moros*, a Moorish trumpet.

anche *see* languette

1593 HOLLYBAND Fr→E *Anches: f.* a pipe that hath as it were a little tongue or tenon, which minstrels doe put into their holt-bois, which they holde in their mouth. **1611** COTGRAVE Fr→E *Anche: f.* The little pipe, tongue, or tenon, which is in the mouth of a Trumpet, Hoeboy, &c; **1650** HOWELL-COTGRAVE Fr→E † *Anche: f.* The little pipe, or tenon, which is the mouth of a Trumpet, Hoeboy, &c. **1688** MIEGE-COTGRAVE Fr→E *Anche*, (f.) the mouth of a hoboy, or the like;

andante *see* saraband

1724 [PEPUSCH] *Short Explic. of Foreign Words in Mus. Bks.* (pp. 10-11) *Andante*, this Word has Respect chiefly to the Thorough Bass, and signifies, that in playing, the Time must be kept very just and exact, and each Note made very equal and distinct the one from the other. Sometimes you will find the Word *Largo* joyn'd with it, as *Andante Largo*, or *Largo Andante*, which is as much as to say, that though the Musick must be performed slow, yet the Time must be observed very exactly; and the Sound of each Note made very distinct, and separated one from another. **1726** BAILEY *An Univ. Etymolog. Engl. Dict.* (3rd edn) *Andante* (in *Musick Books*) chiefly respects the thorough Base, and signifies, that in playing, the Time must be kept very just and exact, and each Note made very equal and distinct from one to the other. § *Largo andante, Andante largo*, (in *Musick Books*) signifies that though the Musick must be performed slow, yet the Time must be observed very exactly, and the sound of each Note must be very distinct, and separated one from another. **1737** DYCHE-PARDON (2nd edn) *Andante* (S.) a *Musical* Term, signifying, that every Note must be play'd very distinctly, and the Time observed very exactly; and is principally applied to the thorough Base.

c.1710 ANON. *Preceptor for Improved Octave Flageolet* ('Explanation of Words', p. 82) *Andante*—Four Crotchets in a Bar Slow **c.1710** NORTH Short, Easy, & plaine rules BL Add. 32531, f. 18 ... If any one part be Movent [i.e. moving], such as ye Italian's call Andante, wch is a breaking of ye other parts ... **1731** PRELLEUR *Modern Musick-Master* (Dictionary, p. 1) *Andante*, from the Verb *Andare*, to go, Signifies especially in Thorough Basses that all the Notes must be plaid equally and Distinctly. **1736** TANS'UR *Compleat Melody* (3rd edn, p. 67) *Andante*, (Lat.) *Picque, Pointe, Spiccato*, (Ital.) Either of those *Terms*, denote that the *Time* must be kept just and true; and that each *Note* must be made equal and distinct, one from another.

andantino

c.1710 ANON. *Preceptor for Improved Octave Flageolet* ('Explanation of Words', p. 82) *Andantino*—Not so slow as Andante

angelot

1678 PHILLIPS (4th edn) *Angelot, (French)* ... also a sort of Musical Instrument somewhat like a Lute. **1688** MIEGE-COTGRAVE Fr→E *Angelique*, (a fem. Subst.) ... a Musical Instrument, that has somthing of a Teorbo;

anima

1724 [PEPUSCH] *Short Explic. of Foreign Words in Mus. Bks.* (p. 11) *Anima*, or *Animato*, is with Life and Spirit, and is of much the same Signification as the Word *Vivace*, which is a Degree of Movement between *Largo* and *Allegro*. **1726** BAILEY *An Univ. Etymolog. Engl. Dict.* (3rd edn) *Anima, Animato* (in *Musick Books*) signifies with Life and Spirit, and is of much the same Signification with *Vivace*, which is a Degree of Movement between *Largo* and *Allegro*.

animato *see* allegro

answer *see* guide

anthem *see* antiphon, antiphonary, chanter, offertory, oratorio, procession, repeat, responsory, ritornello

1598 FLORIO It→E *Anthema*, an anthem in a church. **1604** CAWDREY (1st edn) *anthem*, song. **1611** COTGRAVE Fr→E *Antienne: f.* An Antem [sic], or supplication. **1611** FLORIO It→E *Anthema*, an Anthem sung in a Church. **1616** BULLOKAR *Antheme*. See *Antiphone*. **1623** COCKERAM *Anthemne*. A Song which Church-men sing by course one after another. **1656** BLOUNT (1st edn) *Anthem*. See *Antiphon*. **1658** PHILLIPS (1st edn) *Anthem*, (Greek) a Divine song, wherein each verse is sung by Church-men in their courses. **1676** COLES *Anthem, Greek*. a Divine song. **1678** PHILLIPS (4th edn) *Anthem*, (Greek q. Ανθυμνος) a Divine Song, wherein each verse is sung by Church-men in their courses. **1688** MIEGE-COTGRAVE Fr→E *Antienne*, (f.) Anthem. § *chanter une Antienne*, to sing an Anthem. **1696** PHILLIPS (5th edn) *Anthem*, a divine Song consisting of Verses sung alternatively by the two opposite Quires, and Chorus's. **1702** KERSEY *New Engl. Dict.* (1st edn) An *Anthem*, or hymn sung in a quire. **1704** *Cocker's Engl. Dict.* (1st edn) *Anthem*, See Antiphone. **1706** KERSEY-PHILLIPS (6th edn) *Anthem*, an Hymn or Spiritual Song sung in Divine Service in several Parts, especially in Cathedral and Collegiate Churches. **1707** *Gloss. Angl. Nova* (1st edn) *Anthem*, a Divine Song sung Alternately by two opposite Quires and Chorus's. **1728** CHAMBERS *Anthem, Antiphona*, a Church-Song, performed in Cathedral, and other Service, by the Choristers, divided for that purpose into two Chorus's, who sing alternately. See *Song, Choir, Chorister, &c.* ¶ The Word was originally used both for Psalms, and Hymns, when thus perform'd. See *Psalm* and *Hymn*. ¶ *Socrates* represents St. *Ignatius* as the Author of this way of singing among the *Greeks*; and St. *Ambrose* among the *Latins*—*Theodoret* attributes it to *Diodorus* and *Flavian*. *Amalarius Fortunatus* has wrote expressly of the Order of *Anthems, de Antiphonarum Ordine*. ¶ At present the Term is used in a somewhat narrower Sense; being applied to certain Passages taken out of the Psalms, *&c.* and accommodated to the particular Solemnity in hand. **1730** BAILEY *Dict. Britannicum* (1st edn) *Anthem* (*Anthema*, Ital. *q.* of ἀνθυμνός, Gr.) a Church Song, performed in a Cathedral, *&c.* by the Choristers, divided into two Chorus's, who sing alternately. **1735** DEFOE *Anthem*, a divine Song or Hymn. **1737** DYCHE-PARDON (2nd edn) *Anthem* (S.) a Hymn or Song performed in a Cathedral, by the Choiristers who are divided into two Chorus's, and sing alternately.

anticipation *see* postposition, resolution

1730 [PEPUSCH] *Short Treatise on Harmony* (p. 36) *Anticipation* in Rising or Ascending, is the bringing in a Note upon the Unaccented Part of the Bar, in such a manner as that it has not yet its right Harmony, but by keeping it On, it becomes Harmony upon the next Accented Part of the Bar, by the other Part's moving one Degree whilst that Note holds On. **1731** [PEPUSCH] *Treatise on Harmony* (2nd edn, p. 47) *Anticipation* is the bringing a Note upon the Unaccented Part of a Barr in such a manner as that it has not yet its right Harmony, but by keeping on, it acquires it upon the next Accented Part of the Barr, the other Part also moving to make that Note Harmony.

Antigenidas

1565 COOPER L→E *Antigenidas*, A mynstrell of Thebes, the scholar of Philoxenus...

antipathy

1728 CHAMBERS *Antipathy* ... the Word stands opposed to *Sympathy.... Mersenne*, in his *Quæst. Comment. in Genes.* gives other more extraordinary Instances; as, that a Drum made of a Wolf-Skin, will break another made of a Sheep-Skin: That Hens will fly at the Sound of a Harp strung with Fox-Gut Strings, *&c. See other Matters relating to this Head, under the Articles Sound, Musick, Tune, Tarantula, &c.*

antiphon *see* anthem, primer, responsory

1500 *Ortus Vocabulorum* L→E Antiphona e. dicit quasi otra psalmum sonans. an antemm. f.p. Antiphonista e. q cantat antiphonas. c.p. **1587** THOMAS L→E *Antiphona, *vox reciproca duobus choris alternatim psallentibus.* **1598** FLORIO It→E *Antifana* [sic], an antheme in the church. **1611** COTGRAVE Fr→E *Antiphones: f.* The reciprocall voyces, aunsweres, or chaunting of two companies that sing by turnes, as in a Quier. *Antiphonnier*: m. The booke of Anthems, (In a Cathedrall Church). **1611** FLORIO It→E *Antiphona*, an anthem sung in a Church. **1616** BULLOKAR *Antiphone.* Any verse or litle sentence, which churchmen do by course sing one after another. **1656** BLOUNT (1st edn) *Antiphone (antiphona)* an *Anthemn*, a kinde of Verse or Sentence, which Church-men sing by course, one singing one verse, and another another. *Vox reciproca duobus choris alternatim psallentibus.* A responsory song. **1658** PHILLIPS (1st edn) *Antiphone*, (Greek) see *Anthem.* **1659** TORRIANO-FLORIO It→E **Antifona*, as *Antiphona, &c.* **Antiphona, Antiphonia*, the reciprocall voices answering one another by two severall quires in a Cathedrall Church, used also for an Anthem sung in Churches. **1678** PHILLIPS (4th edn) *Antiphone*, (Greek) each versicle sung alternately to another by Churchmen in the Quire. **1704** *Cocker's Engl. Dict.* (1st edn) *Antiphone*, a verse sung by Church men, one after another. **1706** KERSEY-PHILLIPS (6th edn) *Antiphone*, a Singing by way of Answers, when one Side of the Choir sings one Verse, and the other another. **1707** *Gloss. Angl. Nova* (1st edn) *Antiphon*, (Gr.) the Answer made by one Choir to another, when a Psalm or Anthem is sung between two. *Eccl.* **1728** CHAMBERS *Antiphone, Antiphonum*, the Answer made by one Choir to another, when the Psalm or Anthem is sung between two. See *Anthem, Choir, &c.* **1730** BAILEY *Dict. Britannicum* (1st edn) *Antiphone* (of Ἀντίφωνα, of ἀντί and φωνή, *Gr.* the Voice) a Singing by way of Answer, when the Choir on one Side answers to the Choir on the other, one singing one Verse and the other another. **1737** DYCHE-PARDON (2nd edn) *Antiphone* (S.) the Answer that one Side of the Choir makes to the other, when the Psalm, or Anthem is sung between them.

antiphonary

1500 *Ortus Vocabulorum* L→E Antiphonarius vel antiphonarium. i. liber antiphonarum. antiphoner. m.s. **1659** TORRIANO-FLORIO It→E **Antiphonario*, a book of Anthems, also he that first begins an Anthem. **1676** COLES *Anthiphonary*, a Booke of ¶ *Anthiphones, Greek.* Anthems. **1708** KERSEY *Dict. Anglo-Brit.* (1st edn) *Antiphonarium*, a Book of Anthems.

antiphonere

1726 BAILEY *An Univ. Etymolog. Engl. Dict.* (3rd edn) *Antiphonere*, a Book of Anthems. *Chauc.*

antiphonia *see* symphony

antistrophe *see* strophe

1706 KERSEY-PHILLIPS (6th edn) *Antistrophe*, ... In ancient Stage-plays it signifies the turning of the *Chorus*, or Choir the contrary way; the *Strophe*, or first Turn of the Singers being on one Side of the Stage, and the *Anti[s]trophe*, or Counter-turn on the other.

anzolo

1598 FLORIO It→E *Anzolo*, the part of the bell whereto the clapper hangeth. **1611** FLORIO It→E *Anzolo*, that part of a bell whereto the clapper hangeth.

apiciosus

1500 *Ortus Vocabulorum* L→E Apiciosus a. um. ballyde. caluus capite. o.s.

apodos

1587 THOMAS L→E *Apodos, p.b.* *The vntimelie crowing of a cock, and such a voice as will neither agree with the quyre, nor with an instrument.

Apollo *see* Celænæ, cithara, harp, Linus, lyre, Marsyas, Mercury, Midas, Muse, Orpheus, pæan, Pandora

1538 ELYOT L→E *Apollo*, whom the gentyles honored for god, referrynge to hym the inuencion of musyke, or poetrie, and of phisike: **1550** THOMAS It→E *Apollo*, the God of musike. **1565** COOPER L→E *Apollo*, called also *Phœbus*, and *Sol*, The sonne of Jupiter and Latonia ... He ouercame y[e] cunning minstrell Marsyas that prouoked him in contention of Musike: and when he had gotten the victory, fleaed him, and for his proude attempte pulled of his skinne. He is counted God of Musick, phisike, poetrie, and shooting: and hath by poetes geuen hym a triple name and power. **1656** BLOUNT (1st edn) *Apollinean (Apollineus)* of or belonging to *Apollo* the God of musick, Physick and Poetry, or to the Sun. **1658** PHILLIPS (1st edn) *Apollo*, the son of *Jupiter* and *Latona*... he was called the God of physick, of Musick and Archery, and guided the Chariot of the day. **1676** COLES *Apollo*, the Sun, God of Physick and Musick. **1730** BAILEY *Dict. Britannicum* (1st edn) *Apollo* was one of the most genteel of the Heathen Gods, of whom they do not relate such filthy Stories as of the other[s]. They make him the God of Wisdom, Physick, Musick, Learning, *&c.* ¶ The Antients represented him as a young Man, without a Beard, and Rays of Light about his Head, having in one Hand a Harp and three Graces, and in the other a Shield and Arrows. **1736** BAILEY *Dict. Britannicum* (2nd edn) *Apollo* ... They make him the god of wisdom, physick, learning, *&c.*

apotome *see* enharmonic

1587 THOMAS L→E *Apotomia, p.b. *Maior pars semitoni, quæ discissio dicipotest.* **1696** PHILLIPS (5th edn) *Apotome*, ... In Music, 'tis the remaining part of a whole Tone, when you take from it a Semitone major. **1704** HARRIS *Apotome*, in Musick, is the difference between the greater and lesser Semitone. **1706** KERSEY-PHILLIPS (6th edn) *Apotome*, ... In *Musick*, it is the Difference between the greater and lesser Semitone, or the remaining part of a whole Tone, when a greater Semitone is taken from it. **1728** CHAMBERS *Apotome*, in Musick, is the Part remaining of an entire Tone, after a greater Semi-tone has been taken from it. See *Tone* and *Semi-tone*. ¶ The Proportion, in numbers, of the *Apotome* is, of 2048 to 2187. See *Degree*. ¶ The *Greeks* thought that the greater Tone could not be divided into two equal Parts; for which reason they called the first part ἀποτομή, and the other λέμμα; in this, imitating *Pythagoras* and *Plato*. ¶ The Word is deriv'd from the *Greek* Verb ἀποτέμνω, *abscindo*, I cut off. **1617-24** FLUDD *Utriusque Cosmi Maioris: De Templo Musicæ* (p. 182) *Apothema* est illud toni spatium, quod dicitur semitonium majus. **1636** BUTLER *Principles of Musik* (p. 23) [marginalia: 'Boet. l. 3. c. 15.'] *Apotome major est quàm quatuor Commata, minor quàm quinq;* ... **1665** SIMPSON *Division-Viol* (2nd edn, p. 13) ... the difference between these two Semitones [lesser and greater] or imperfect Seconds, they call an Apotome. **1667** SIMPSON *Compendium of Practical Musick* (p. 104) ... the *Greater Semitone*; and ... the *Less*. The difference betwixt them is called *Apotome*, which signifies a cutting off. Some Authors call the *Greater Semitone*, *Apotome*; That is (I suppose) because it includes the odd *Comma* which makes that *Apotome*.

appeau

1593 HOLLYBAND Fr→E *Les Appeaux*, the chimes: **1611** COTGRAVE Fr→E *Appeau: m.* ... also, a bird-call; the reed. or little pipe wherewith fowlers call sillie birds to their destruction.

Arbeau, Thoinot *see* dance, galliard, pavan

arcata *see* wavee

after 1695 NORTH untitled notebook BL Add. 32532, f. 8 The Italian's have brought y[e] bow to an high perfection, so y[t] nothing of their playing is so difficult, as the arcata or long bow—with w[ch] they will begin a long Note, clear, without rubb, & draw it forth swelling lowder & lowder, and at y[e] ackme take a slow waiver.

archet *see* bow, fusano

1570/71 *Dict. Fr. and Engl.* Fr→E § *l'Archet d'vn rebec, ou autres tels instruments*, the bowe of a vyoll, or such like instrument. **1593** HOLLYBAND Fr→E *l'Archet d'vn rebec, ou autres tels instruments*, the bowe of a Viole, or such like instrument: *m.* **1611** COTGRAVE Fr→E *Archet: m.* The bow of a Viol, &c. **1688** MIEGE-COTGRAVE Fr→E *Archet*, (m.) the bow of a musical Instrument, &c. § *Crin d'archet*, the hair of a bow.

archetto

1598 FLORIO It→E *Archetto*, a little bowe, a fidling sticke **1611** FLORIO It→E *Archetto*, a little bow, a fidling-sticke.

archlute *see* theorbo

1724 [PEPUSCH] *Short Explic. of Foreign Words in Mus. Bks.* (p. 11) *Arcileuto*, an Arch-Lute, or very long and large Lute, differing but little from the

Theorbo Lute, and is used by the *Italians* for playing a Thorough Bass. **1726** BAILEY *An Univ. Etymolog. Engl. Dict.* (3rd edn) *Arcileuto* (in *Musick Books*) is an Arch-Lute, or a very long and large Lute, differing but a little from the Theorbo Lute, and is what the *Italians* use for playing a thorough Base.

arco *see* bow

1550 THOMAS It→E *Arco*, a bowe. **1598** FLORIO It→E *Arco*, a bowe or an arche. **1611** FLORIO It→E *Arco*, any kind of bow § *Budello d'arco*, a bow-string made of guts. **1724** [PEPUSCH] *Short Explic. of Foreign Words in Mus. Bks.* (p. 11) *Arco*, a Bow, or Fiddle-stick. **1726** BAILEY *An Univ. Etymolog. Engl. Dict.* (3rd edn) *Arco* (in *Musick Books*) a Bow or Fiddle-stick.

arculus

1500 *Ortus Vocabulorum* L→E Archulus est selle. cliselle. siue vielle. **1565** COOPER L→E *Arculus*. A little bow or arch. **1587** THOMAS L→E *Arculus, li, m.g.* *A litle bowe.

a re *see* alamire

Aretinus, Guido *see* gamut, scale

Argon

1587 THOMAS L→E **Argon*, A cunning Harper. **1589** RIDER L→E *Argon, m.* A cunning harper.

argutus

1538 ELYOT L→E *Argutus, ta, tum*, ... Also shryll of voyce. **1552** HULOET L→E *Argutus. a. um, calaster, ra. rum crotalus. a. um, Quærilus. a. um, sonorus. a. um, Vocalis. e* Shyll [sic] of voyce. **1565** COOPER L→E § *Olor argutus. Virg.* Hauing a lowde voyce: singynge. **1587** THOMAS L→E *Argutus, a, um, tior, tissimus, adiect.* ... Shrill of voice or sounde, making a great noise.

aria *see* air

1724 [PEPUSCH] *Short Explic. of Foreign Words in Mus. Bks.* (p. 11) *Aria*, an Air, Song, or Tune. **1726** BAILEY *An Univ. Etymolog. Engl. Dict.* (3rd edn) *Aria* (in *Musick Books*) signifies an Air, Song, or Tune. **1737** DYCHE-PARDON (2nd edn) *Aria* (S.) in *Musick*, is an Air, Song, Tune or Lesson.

1728 NORTH Musicall Grammarian (*C-K MG* f. 73v) There are some other modes, which have pl[ace] between the grave and the allegro. One is tituled, aria, but tho cheerfull enough, d[oes] not come up to the fury of an allegro, and hath this property, that it bears well the attendance of a plain consort base ... **1731** PRELLEUR *Modern Musick-Master* (Dictionary, p. 1) *Aria*, an Aire or Song.

aria da camera *see* camera

arietta

1724 [PEPUSCH] *Short Explic. of Foreign Words in Mus. Bks.* (p. 12) *Arietta*, is a little or short Air, Song, or Tune. **1726** BAILEY *An Univ. Etymolog. Engl. Dict.* (3rd edn) *Arietta* (in *Musick Books*) signifies a little short Air, Song or Tune.

1731 PRELLEUR *Modern Musick-Master* (Dictionary, p. 1) *Arietta*, much the same as *Aria*.

arigot *see* harigot, larigot

1611 COTGRAVE Fr→E *Arigot*... also, a (musicall) Recorder.

Arion

1538 ELYOT L→E *Arion*, a famouse harper, whom the maryners wolde haue throwen into the see, for to haue his money: but he desyryng them to let hym play a songe on his harpe or he dyed, afterwarde lepte into the water, but a dolphyn receyuyng hym on his backe, & brought hym to lande a lyue. **1565** COOPER L→E *Arion*, A famous harper, whom y[e] mariners would haue cast into the sea to have his money: but he desiring them, to lette hym playe a songe on his harpe er he did, afterwarde leapte into the water, and a Dolphyne receiuing hym on his back, brought hym to lande alyue. It is also one of Adrastus chariot horses. **1658** PHILLIPS (1st edn) *Arion*, a famous Musician of the Isle of *Lesbos* **1676** COLES *Arion*, a famous Musician of *Lesbos*. **1678** PHILLIPS (4th edn) *Arion*, a famous Musitian of *Mithymna* in the Isle of *Lesbos* ... he is said to be the first inventor of Dithyrambick verse. **1696** PHILLIPS (5th edn) *Arion*, a famous Musician of *Mythimna* in the Isle of *Lesbos*, who throwing himself into the Sea, was carried by a Dolphin to *Tænarus* a Town of *Laconia*.

arioso

1724 [PEPUSCH] *Short Explic. of Foreign Words in Mus. Bks.* (p. 12) *Ariose*, or *Arioso*, signifies the Movement or Time of a common Air, Song or Tune. **1726** BAILEY *An Univ. Etymolog. Engl. Dict.* (3rd edn) *Ariose, Arioso* (in *Musick Books*) signifies the Movement or Time of a common Air, Song, or Tune.

Aristotle *see* diapason, diesis, exodium, interlude, magade, rattle, symphony

Aristoxenus *see* canon, chromatic, mutation, spissum

1678 PHILLIPS (4th edn) *Aristoxenus*, a Philosopher, Physitian and excellent Musitian of *Tarentum*, who flourished in the time of *Tullus Hostilius*, the Third King of the *Romans*. There are yet remaining some of his musical Works set forth by *Meihomius*; together with some other Works of other ancient Musitians; also an Historian cited by *Plutarch* in his life of *Numa*.

armonia *see* harmony

arpa *see* harp

arpeggio

1724 [PEPUSCH] *Short Explic. of Foreign Words in Mus. Bks.* (p. 12) *Arpeggio*, see the Word *Herpeggio* [sic]. (p. 37) *Harpeggio*, or *Harpeggiato*, is to cause the several Notes or Sounds of an Accord to be heard, not together, but one after another, beginning always with the lowest. **1726** BAILEY *An Univ. Etymolog. Engl. Dict.* (3rd edn) *Arpeggio* (in *Musick Books*) is to cause the several Notes or Sounds of an Accord to be heard, not together but one after another, beginning always with the lowest. *Ital. Harpeggio, Harpeggiato*, (in *Musick Books*) signifies to cause the several Notes or Sounds of an Accord to be heard not together, but one after another, beginning always with the lowest. *Ital.* **1737** DYCHE-PARDON (2nd edn) *Arpeggio* (S.) the Manner of making the several Notes of a Chord in Musick be distinctly heard one after another, by a melodious purling and rolling Motion of the Hand, particularly upon stringed Instruments, always beginning at the Ground, or lowest Note, and rising upwards.

after 1695 NORTH untitled notebook BL Add. 32532, f. 20v ... For wee may say, & not Improperly, that all sound or Key, carry's its harmony with it, that is the Musitian, by his skill & memory supply's it tho not sounding. then be y[e] harmony continued sounding, or touch by touch as y[e] sprinkling of harpish Instrum[ts], vizt, lute Gittarr harpsicord &c, w[ch] y[e] Italians call arpeggiando ... **c.1700** NORTH Capt. Prencourts rules BL Add. 32549, f. 12 When this mark ⌇. is set before three notes set directly aboue another, then those Notes must be broken in going up and downe. It must be done as swift as possible, and this is called Harpeger, that's to say to Imitate the harp; and is called Arpeggio. **c.1710** NORTH Short, Easy, & plaine rules BL Add. 32531, f. 24 [quoting Prendcourt:] When this mark ⌇ is set before 3. notes set directly one above another, then those Notes must be broken In going up and down as swift as possible, & this is called Harpeger, that is to say to Imitate an harp. **c.1715-20** NORTH Essay of Musical Ayre BL Add. 32536, f. 36 ... the Breaking movements serve aptly ffor this designe, but they goe further by a Movem[t] they Call Arpeggio; This is done in Imitation of Instruments that sound by a touch onely, and gaine a Continuance by sprinkling as Harps (whence y[e] term is derived) lutes, Harpsichord, &c. **1728** NORTH Musicall Grammarian (*C-K MG* f. 78) The other sort of devision, which I termed the arpeggio, tho exceeding the comon acceptation of that word, hath much more to be sayd for it becaus it carrys a perfect skill in the ornamentall or figurate composition of harmony. The movement is desultory or by way of breaking, and not onely of the notes of any single part but of the fullest consort that can be composed, and thro the devision may be heard all the concords, commixtures, and passing notes, as if they were all in full action, softness and deminution onely excepted. Examples, and florid ones, of this kind are frequently mett with ... **1736** TANS'UR *Compleat Melody* (3rd edn, p. 68) *Harpiggio, Arpeggio, Harpeggiato*, (Ital.) Either of those Terms signifies to cause several *Sounds*, or *Notes* to be heard one after another, beginning always at the lowest.

arpicordo *see* harpsichord

arsis

1598 FLORIO It→E *Arsis*, the eleuation or lifting vp of the voice in singing. **1611** FLORIO It→E *Arsis*, the raising of a voice in singing. **1659** TORRIANO-FLORIO It→E *Arsis*, the raising of the voice in singing or calling.

1731 PRELLEUR *Modern Musick-Master* (Dictionary, p. 1) *Arsis*, v, Fuga.

arsis & thesis *see* fugue, measure, report, revert

1704 HARRIS *Arsis & Thesis*, are certain Terms in Musical Composition; as where a Point being inverted, is said to move *per Arsin & Thesin*, that is to say, where a Point riseth in one Part, and falls in another, or on the contrary, where it falls in one Part, and riseth in another, whence is produced a very agreeable Variety. **1706** KERSEY-PHILLIPS (6th edn) *Arsis & Thesis*, certain Terms in Musical Composition: Thus a Point being inverted or turned, is said, To move *per Arsin* and *Thesin*, that is to say when a Point rises in one Part, and falls in another; or on the contrary, when it falls in one Part, and rises in another; which occasions a very agreeable Variety. **1728** CHAMBERS *Arsis* and *Thesis*, a Phrase in musical Composition; where a Point being inverted, is said to move *per Arsin & Thesin*; that is, rises in one Part, and falls in another; or, on the contrary, falls in one Part, and rises in another: Whence is produc'd a very agreeable Variety.

1582 *Batman vppon Bartholome* (p. 422) *Arsis* is rearing of voyce, and is the beginning of song. *Thesis* is setting, and is the ende, as *Isid*. saith: and so Song is the bending of the voyce, for some passeth straight as he saith, & is before song. **1597** MORLEY *Plaine and Easie Introdvction* (p. 102) ... Here is also another waie in the tenth, which the maisters call *per arsin & thesin*, that is by rising and falling: for when the higher part ascendeth, the lower part descendeth, and when the lower part ascendeth, the higher parte descendeth, and though I haue here set it downe in the tenth, yet may it be made in anie other distance you please... **1636** BUTLER *Principles of Musik* (p. 24) [marginalia: '*Thesis* & *Arsis*.'] The partes of *Tactus* ar two: (*Thesis* and *Arsis*:) i. the Depression or Fall, and the Elevation or Rise of the Hand. **1667** SIMPSON *Compendium of Practical Musick* (p. 131) Sometimes the Point is Inverted, or moves *per Arsin* and *Thesin* (as they phrase it;) that is, where the Point rises in one Part, it falls in another, and likewise the contrary; which produces a pleasing variety: ... **1694** PURCELL-PLAYFORD *Intro. to Skill of Musick* (12th edn, 'A Brief Introduction to the Art of Descant', n.p.) The fourth manner of Fugeing is called *Per Arsin & Thesin*, which admits of great Variety; and that is, when a Leading Part ascends, the other descends exactly the same Notes. **1736** TANS'UR *Compleat Melody* (3rd edn, p. 71) *Arsin & Thesin*, or *Arsis & Thesis*. (Ital.) a *Part, Point*, or *Fuge*, is said to move so, when one *Point* falls in one *Part*, and the same rises in another *Part*.

articulation *see* shake

artificial sound *see* character, chromatic, scale

1724 TURNER *Sound Anatomiz'd* (p. 6) ... when a *Sound* riseth from its natural Situation, half the Distance (which is called a *Semitone*, or *Half-tone*) between that and the next above it; and *Contraction*, when it falleth in the same Proportion towards the *Sound* below it; such Passages being very frequent, both in *Vocal* and *Instrumental Musick*, and are what we call *artificial*, or *chromatick Sounds*.

arts, factive

1730 BAILEY *Dict. Britannicum* (1st edn) *Factive Arts*, such as leave no external Effect behind them after their Operation, as Piping, Fiddling, Dancing.

arts, liberal

1696 PHILLIPS (5th edn) *Liberal Arts*, are such as are noble and genteel, as Music, Painting, Architecture, Poetry, Navigation, *&c*. **1708** KERSEY *Dict. Anglo-Brit.* (1st edn) *Liberal Arts and Sciences*, such as are noble and genteel, *viz*. Grammar, Rhetorick, Musick, Physick, the Mathematicks, *&c*. **1728** CHAMBERS *Art, Ars* .... The *liberal Arts* are those that are noble, and ingenuous; or which are worthy of being cultivated without any regard to Lucre arising therefrom.—Such are *Poetry, Musick, Painting, Grammar, Rhetorick*, the *military Art, Architecture*, and *Navigation*. § *Liberal Arts*, in opposition to Mechanical *Arts*, are such as depend more on the Labour of the Mind, than on that of the Hand; that consist more in the Speculation than the Operation, and that have a greater Regard to Amusement and Curiosity, than the servile Mechanical Works: Such are Grammar, Rhetoric, Painting, Sculpture, Architecture, Music. The *Liberal Arts* used formerly to be summed up in the following *Latin* Verse. ¶ *Lingua, Tropus, Ratio, Numerous, Tonus, Angulus, Astra*. **1730** BAILEY *Dict. Britannicum* (1st edn) *Liberal Arts*, such as are fit for Gentlemen and Scholars; in opposition to *Mechanical Arts*; such as depend more on the Mind than the Hand; that consist more in *Speculation* than *Operation*, as *Grammar, Rhetorick, Painting, Sculpture, Architecture, Musick*. § *The Liberal Arts* (*Artes Liberales*, L.) are those which are noble and ingenuous, and worthy to be cultivated, without any Regard being had to Lucre or Gain: These are Architecture, Grammar, Military Art, Musick, Navigation, Painting, Poetry, *&c*. **1737** DYCHE-PARDON (2nd edn) *Liberal* (A.) ... those Arts and Sciences that polish the Mind, such as Grammar, Rhetorick, Musick, &c. are called liberal Arts.

Asaph

1565 Cooper L→E *Asaph,* An hebrue woorde, signifyng gatheryng or finishing. Of this name was a singyng man in the house of god, to whom kyng Dauid assigned certaine tytles of his psalmes. **1671** Phillips (3rd edn) *Asaph, (Hebr.* gathering) a famous Musitian among the Jews, and one of the chief of *David's* quire. **1721** Bailey *An Univ. Etymolog. Engl. Dict.* (1st edn) *Asaph,* ... a famous Musician among the antient *Jews.*

asmatographer

1656 Blount (1st edn) *Asmotagraphers* [sic] *(asmatographi)* they who sell or make Songs, or Lessons for any Instruments. **1658** Phillips (1st edn) *Asmotographers* [sic], (Greek) composers of lessons to any instrument. **1676** Coles *Asmatographers, Greek.* Composers of Songs. **1721** Bailey *An Univ. Etymolog. Engl. Dict.* (1st edn) *Asmatographers,* Composers of Songs. *Gr.* **1730** Bailey *Dict. Britannicum* (1st edn) *Asmatography* (of ἄσμα a Song and γράφω, Gr. to write) the Composition of Songs. **1737** Dyche-Pardon (2nd edn) *Asmatographer* (S.) a Composer or Writer of Songs.

Aspendius

1565 Cooper L→E *Aspendius,* A certaine harper. **1623** Cockeram *Aspendius,* a cunning Musitian, who played so softly on his Harpe, that none could heare him but himselfe.

assai *see* men, poco

1724 [Pepusch] *Short Explic. of Foreign Words in Mus. Bks.* (pp. 12-13) *Assai,* this Word is always joyned with some other Word, to lessen or weaken the Strength or Signification of the Words it is joyned with. For example, when it is joyned with either of these Words, *Adagio, Grave,* or *Largo,* which do all Three denote a slow Movement, it signifies that the Musick must not be perform'd so slow as each of those Words would require if alone: But if it be joyned with either of the following Words, *Vivace, Allegro,* or *Presto,* which do all Three denote a quick Movement, then it signifies that the Musick must not be perform'd quite so brisk or quick, as each of these Words if alone does require. **1726** Bailey *An Univ. Etymolog. Engl. Dict.* (3rd edn) *Assai* (in *Musick Books*) is a Word which is always join'd with some other Word, to lessen or weaken the Strength or Signification of the Word it is join'd with: As for Example, When it is join'd with either of the Words *Adagio, Grave,* or *Largo,* all which denote a slow Movement, it signifies, that the Musick must not be perform'd so slow as each of those Words would require if alone; but if it be joined with either of these Words that follow, *Vivace, Allegro,* or *Presto,* all which three denote a quick Movement, then it denotes, that the Musick must not be perform'd quite so brisk or quick as each of those Words, if alone, does require.

1731 Prelleur *Modern Musick-Master* (Dictionary, p. 1) *Asai,* Enough, This Word is often joyned w[th.] *Allegro Adagio Presto* &c **1736** Tans'ur *Compleat Melody* (3rd edn, p. 66) *N.B.* That the Word *Assia* [sic], is often set before another Word, which signifies, that the Movement must not be quite so quick, or quite so slow, as the Word it self directs; as, *Assia, Adagio*: is not quite so slow as *Adagio* it self; *&c.* according as the Words do require.

assa voce *see* counterpoint

1538 Elyot L→E *Voce assa,* with the voyce onely of a manne without any instrument of musyke. § *Assa uoce cantare,* to synge withoute an Instrument. **1552** Huloet L→E *Voce assa, ang.* with the only voyce of a man without instrument of musike § *Assa uoce cantare* Synge withoute an instrumente. **1565** Cooper L→E § *Assa voce cantare. Varro.* To singe only with mans voyce, without any other tunes or sownes ef [sic] instrumentes. **1587** Thomas L→E *Assa vox. Nonius.* That which is pronounced with mans voyce, without anie other tune or sound of instrument. *Vox assa, Iun.* A sound made with the vse of the tongue only, the bare voyce without any musicke therewithall mingled: *also* a voyce or crying, a tune, a saying, speaking, talke

assay *see* chord, incension, nervo, proludium

1706 Kersey-Phillips (6th edn) *Assaying,* a Term us'd by Musicians for a Flourish before they begin to Play. **1737** Dyche-Pardon (2nd edn) *Assay* (V.) ... In *Musick,* the Flourish in the Key, to try whether the Instrument is in Tune, and to put the Hand in a proper Position before the grand Performance begins, is called an Assay.

1736 Tans'ur *Compleat Melody* (3rd edn, p. 68) *Assay* (Ital.) Signifies *Examine, Prove, Try,* &c. and is often set at the Beginning of a Piece of *Musick,* importing that you must try if your *Instrument* be in *Tune*: Or, your *Voice* in the right *Key,* &c.

assembly *see* beat, drum
1721 BAILEY *An Univ. Etymolog. Engl. Dict.* (1st edn) *Assembly,* (among *Military Men*) is the second beat of Drum before the March. **1728** CHAMBERS *Assembly,* is also used in the military Art, for the second Beat of the Drum, before the March. See *Drum.* ¶ On hearing this, the Soldiers strike their Tents, roll them up, and then stand to their Arms. See *March.* ¶ The third Beating is called the *March,* as the first is called the *General.* See *General.* **1730** BAILEY *Dict. Britannicum* (1st edn) *Assembly* (with *Military Men*) is a particular Beat of the Drum or Sound of the Trumpet, and is an Order for the Soldiers to repair to their Colours.

assonadas
1599 MINSHEU-PERCYVALL Sp→E **Assonadas,* f. by soundes, by noises, by tunes, by voices.

assonador
1599 MINSHEU-PERCYVALL Sp→E *Assonador,* m. a tuner, one that setteth tunes.

assonar
1599 MINSHEU-PERCYVALL Sp→E *assonar, yo assueno,* to tune or set a tune, to sound, to sing with.

asymphony
1500 *Ortus Vocabulorum* L→E Asymfomia [sic]. i. consonantia. a corde. f.p. **1565** COOPER L→E *Asymphonia.* Discorde in descante. **1587** THOMAS L→E *Asymphonia, æ, f.g. p.l.* *Discorde in descant **1656** BLOUNT (1st edn) *Asymphony (asymphonia)* a discord in discant, a disagreeing **1676** COLES *Asymphony, Greek.* disagreement (in musick.) **1721** BAILEY *An Univ. Etymolog. Engl. Dict.* (1st edn) *Asymphony,* (Ἀσυμφωνία, *Gr.*) a Disorder in Discant, a Disagreement.

1636 BUTLER *Principles of Musik* (p. 94) [*re* types of instrumental music] ... *Asymphona,* that play but one Part: as the *Cornet.*

atabal *see* pandera, tabour
1599 MINSHEU-PERCYVALL Sp→E † *Atabal,* a drum. Also a round instrument like a kettle without a bayle, vsed in war in times past, and yet among the Spaniards vsed at feasts. *† *Atabalejo,* m a little drum. *Atabalera,* f. a she player on a taber. † *Atabalero,* a drummer, a taberer. **Ataval,* vid *Atabal,* drum. **Atavalero,* v. *Atabalero,* a drummer. **1650** HOWELL-COTGRAVE Fr→E *Atabal.* as *Attabale;* also, a Tymbrell, or little brazen drumme to dance by. *Attabale.* A kinde of brazen drum, used by the Moorish horse-men. **1659** TORRIANO-FLORIO It→E *Ataballo,* a kettle-drum, or brasse-tabouret, that the Moorse use to dance by.

atambor *see* tambour
1599 MINSHEU-PERCYVALL Sp→E † *Atambor,* m. a drummer, a taborer. Also the drum it selfe. **Hatambor,* vide *Atambor,* a drum, a taber.

a tempo giusto *see* tempo giusto

attasto *see* tasto

attone
1704 *Cocker's Engl. Dict.* (1st edn) *Attone,* bring into Consort in Tune, or agreement.

aubade
1593 HOLLYBAND Fr→E *Aubades,* as *donner vne aubade,* such musicke as minstrels doe play at ones window at the breaking of the day, morning music: *f.* **1611** COTGRAVE Fr→E *Aubades.* Morning Musicke; such as fidlers play vnder chamber windowes. **1650** HOWELL-COTGRAVE Fr→E § *Les vieilles gens qui font* [sic] *gambades, à la mort sonnent des aubades; Pro.* **1658** PHILLIPS (1st edn) *Aubades,* (French) songs, or instrumental musick, sung, or play'd under any ones Chamber-window in the morning, from *Aube* the morning. **1676** COLES *Aubades, French.* morning lessons under ones window. **1688** MIEGE-COTGRAVE Fr→E *Aubade,* (f.) from *Aube,* morning-musick (such as Lovers divert their Mistress with, under their Chamber-Windows.) **1706** KERSEY-PHILLIPS (6th edn) *Aubade,* (Fr.) Morning-Musick, such as is play'd at the Dawn of Day, before one's Door, or under one's Window. **1730** BAILEY *Dict. Britannicum* (1st edn) *Aubade,* Morning Musick, such as is play'd at Break of Day, before a Door or Window, a Serenade.

augmentation *see* fugue, note
after 1517 ANON. Art of Mvsic BL Add. 4911, f. 26v *Augmentation quhat is it.* [author] Orniparchus [i.e. Ornithoparcus] dois writ in ye sevvnt chaptur of his bouk of mensurall Musick. It is the moreing of nottis beyond ye just valour. Or it is of any sang in ye notte ... of a plurafitation. **1596** ANON. *Pathway to Musicke* [D ii] *Of Augmentation, and vvhat it is.* ¶ It is the increase of the value of noates, vvhich hapneth vnto them by certain signes or rules, by the common or naturall value of them ... **1597** MORLEY *Plaine and Easie*

Introdvction (pp. 24-5) [marginalia: 'Augmentation'] Of the altering of the Moods proceedeth *augmentation, or diminution, augmentation proceedeth of setting the signe of the more prolation in one parte of the songe onely, and not in others,* and is an increasing of the value of the notes aboue their common and essentiall valor [sic], which commeth to them by signes set before them, or Moodes set ouer them, or numbers set by them. Augmentation by numbers is when proportions of the lesse in æqualitie are set down, meaning that euery note and rest following are so often to be multiplyed in them selues, as the lower number contayneth the higher thus. $\frac{1}{2}$ $\frac{1}{3}$ $\frac{1}{4}$ &c. that is, the *minym* to be a *semibrief,* the *semibriefe* a briefe &c. ... **early 17th C.** RAVENSCROFT Treatise of Musick BL Add. 19758, f. 17v Augmentation is that w[ch] many tymes hapeneth to notes by fygures or certaine rules w[ch] doth just augment the note so much as he is him selfe. **1609** DOWLAND-ORNITHOPARCUS *Micrologvs* (p. 47) ... *Augmentation* is the making of more Notes in a Song: or it is the excrement of some Note. For in it is put a *Minime* for a *Semibreefe;* a *Semibreefe* for a *Breefe;* a *Breefe* for a *Long.... Augmentation* is the contradiction of *Diminution...* **1694** PURCELL-PLAYFORD *Intro. to Skill of Musick* (12th edn, 'A Brief Introduction to the Art of Descant', n.p.) A fifth sort of Fugeing is called *Per Augmentation;* that is, if the Leading Part be *Crotchets, Quavers,* or any other Notes in length, the following Part is augmented, and made as long again as the Leading Part.

aula *see* aulos, choraula, synaulia
1500 *Ortus Vocabulorum* L→E Aule arum. sunt fistule organorum per quas elicit melodia. organe pyppis. f.p. Aule grece dicit cannula vel tibia latine. Aules aulis. et auledus a. pypere qui cuz cannis cantat. scz tybicen. m.t. **1538** ELYOT L→E *Aulæ,* shaulmes or waytes. **1552** HULOET L→E *Aulæ,* Waytes instrumente. **1565** COOPER L→E *Aula.* Is also a pipe or shaulme: **1587** THOMAS L→E *Aula, æ, f.g...* also a pipe or shalme **1589** RIDER L→E *Aula, f. aulos monaulos.* A pipe, or flute. *Aula, melina, f. tonarion, n.* A Shalme.

aulædus *see* aulœdus

auleta
1538 ELYOT L→E *Auleticus,* he that playeth best on a shalme or wayte. **1552** HULOET L→E *Auletes. tis* Piper. *Auleticus* a player vpon the waytes *Auleticus. ci* Player on a shalme or wayte. *Auletris. dos* woman piper. **1565** COOPER L→E *Auletes, pen. prod. m.g. Cicer.* He that plaieth on the flute or shaulme: a piper. *Auleticus, pen. cor. Adiectiuum. vt, auleticus calamus. Plin.* Good to make a pipe of. *Auletris, pen. prod. aulétricis, pen. corr. f.g.* A woman piper. **1587** THOMAS L→E *Auletes, æ, m.g.* He that plaieth on the flute or shalme: a piper. *Auleticus, a, um, Pli.* Good to make a pipe of. *Auletris, idis, f.g.* *A woman that plaieth on the flute, a woman piper. **1589** RIDER L→E *Aulæticus, ad.* Good to to [sic] make a pipe of. **1611** FLORIO It→E *Auleta,* a piper, or plaier on a flute. *Auletica,* piping musicke. **1659** TORRIANO-FLORIO It→E **Auleta,* a piper, or player on a flute. *Auletica,* any piping musike. **1730** BAILEY *Dict. Britannicum* (1st edn) *Auletick* (*auleticus,* L.) belonging to Pipes.

aulex
1500 *Ortus Vocabulorum* L→E Aulex cis a pyper w[t] redis. f.t.

aulœdus *see* minstrel
1500 *Ortus Vocabulorum* L→E Auledus a um. dulcis vt sonus organorum. aulidus idem est. o.s. **1552** HULOET L→E *Aulædas. di, Bardus, di, Choraulis.* Minstrell. **1565** COOPER L→E *Aulœdus, aulœdi, m.g.* A singar: a plaier on the flute: a minstrell. **1587** THOMAS L→E *Aulœdus, di, m.g.* A singer: a player on the flute, a minstrell. **1589** RIDER L→E *Aulædus, aulætes, fistulator, m. aulætris, f. flator* A piper. *Aulædus, m.* A plaier on a flute, or pipe.

aulos *see* aula, monaulos, spondaules, synaulia
1565 COOPER L→E *Aulos, li, m.g.* A pipe or flute. **1587** THOMAS L→E *Aulos, li, m.g.* *A pipe or flute. **1589** RIDER L→E *Aulos, m. fistula, tibia, syrinx, syringa, f.* A Flute.

auricalco
1598 FLORIO It→E *Auricalco, ...* Also taken for a trumpet. **1611** FLORIO It→E *Auricalco,* latten mettall. Also a trumpet. **1659** TORRIANO-FLORIO It→E *Auricalco;* the metall called latten, also a shrill brazen trumpet.

authentic *see* division, ecclesiastic tone, mode, mood, tone, tune
1609 DOWLAND-ORNITHOPARCUS *Micrologvs* (p. 13) We may know the *Tones* by three meanes: by the beginning: the middle: and the end. By the beginning; for a Song rising in the beginning

straight wayes aboue the finall *Key* to a Fift, is *Authenticall* ... By the middle, and first, by the rising; For the Song which toucheth an Eight in the middle, is *Authenticall*: that Song which doth not, is *Plagall*: ... **1664** BIRCHENSHA-ALSTED *Templvm Mvsicvm* (p. 77) ... The Ancients had only four *Moods*, the first, second, third, and fourth: to which now the four final *Voices* do respond. *re. mi. fa. sol.* These four *Moods* the *Grecians* call *Authentic*, and the *Latines herile* or *Clamous*. **1667** SIMPSON *Compendium of Practical Musick* (p. 113) These Moods or Tones had yet another distinction; and that was, *Authentick*, or *Plagal*. This depended upon the dividing of the *Octave* into its 5*th*. and 4*th*. *Authentick* was when the 5*th*. stood in the lower place, according to the Harmonical division of an *Octave*. **1694** HOLDER *Treatise of Natural Grounds* (p. 68) [closes of harmony] which ascend from the Unison, *Gamut*, by Third *Major* (or *Minor*) and Fifth, up to the Octave; are usually called Authentick, as relating principally to the Unison, and best satisfying the Ear to rest upon: The other two, which ascend by the Fonrth [sic] and Sixth *Minor*, (or Major) up to the same Octave, are called Plagal, as more combining with the Octave, seeming to require a more proper base Note, *vzi* [sic]. an Eighth below the Fourth, and therefore not making a good concludi[n]g Close: ...

avena

1565 COOPER L→E § *Angusta auena cantare. Martial.* A small pipe. *Structis auenis cantare. Ouid.* with a pipe made of reedes ioyned together. **1587** THOMAS L→E *Avena, æ, f.g. p.b.* Oates: a pipe made of an oaten strawe. **1589** RIDER L→E *Avena, f.* A pipe made of an oaten strawe.

ayre *see* air

B

b *see* B. C.

1611 COTGRAVE Fr→E The letter, *B*. In Musicke, the Note, or Cliffe, called Befabeemie; **1650** HOWELL-COTGRAVE Fr→E The letter, B. in Musicke, the Note, or Cliffe, called Befabeemy; whence; *De b carre en b mol; Prov.* In discourse, to shift often, idly, and on a suddaine, from one subject unto another. **1724** [PEPUSCH] *Short Explic. of Foreign Words in Mus. Bks.* (p. 14) *B*. This Letter is often made Use of as an Abbreviation of the Word Bass or Basso. ¶ And the Letters *B C* for the Words Basso Continuo. **1726** BAILEY *An Univ. Etymolog. Engl. Dict.* (3rd edn) *B* (in *Musick Books*) is an Abbreviation of the Word *Bass* or *Basso*. ¶ *B.C.* (in *Musick Books*) stand for *Basso-Continuo*. **1730** BAILEY *Dict. Britannicum* (1st edn) *B* (in *Musick Books*) signifies *Bass* or *Basso*. **1737** DYCHE-PARDON (2nd edn) *B* ... In *Musick* Books, B signifies the Bass, or Basso Continuo.

1731 PRELLEUR *Modern Musick-Master* (Dictionary, p. 2) *B*. or *Basso*, the Bass in general.

Babys

1565 COOPER L→E *Babys*, A foolishe mynstrell, Marsyas brother. **1623** COCKERAM *Babis*, a foolish Minstrell.

bacchanals *see* menadi, orgy

1728 CHAMBERS *Bacchanalia*, a Religious Feast in Honour of *Bacchus*, celebrated with much Solemnity among the Antients, particularly the *Athenians* ... The Form and Disposition of the Solemnity depended, at *Athens*, on the Archon, and was at first exceedingly simple, but by degrees became incumber'd with a world of ridiculous Ceremonies, and attended with a world of Dissoluteness and Debauchery ... Men and Women met promiscuously at the Feast, all perfectly naked, except for the Vine-Leaves and Clusters of Grapes which bound their Heads and Hips; here they danced and jump'd tumultuously, and with strange Gesticulations sung Hymns to *Bacchus*, till weary and giddy they tumbled down distracted. **1730** BAILEY *Dict. Britannicum* (1st edn) *Bacchantes, Bacchanals*, the Priestesses and Priests of *Bacchus*, who celebrated his Festivals with Cymbals, Drums, Timbrels, Noise and Shouts, running about in a frantick manner, crowned with Ivy, Vine Twigs, *&c.* and carrying in their Hands a Thyrsis or Staff wreathed with the same Plants, *L.* **1737** DYCHE-PARDON (2nd edn) *Bacchanals* (S.) the drunken and revelling Feasts of the Heathen God *Bacchus*; also the Priests of the Deity who celebrated these Festivals with Cymbals, Drums, &c. making a great Noise and Shouting ...

bacchetta
1598 FLORIO It→E *Bacchetta,* ... Also a drummers sticke. **1611** FLORIO It→E *Bacchetta,* ... Also a drummers sticke. **1659** TORRIANO-FLORIO It→E **Bacchetta,* ... a drumstick

Bacchus *see* bacchanals, chorus, dithyramb, episode, hymen, menadi, orgy, Orpheus, thyasus, tragedy
1730 BAILEY *Dict. Britannicum* (1st edn) *Bacchus,* .... His Priests were either Satyrs or Women, because Women are said to have follow'd him in great Companies to his Travels, crying, singing and dancing continually, and they were called *Bacchanales,* that express Fury and Madness.

bachelor
1730 BAILEY *Dict. Britannicum* (1st edn) *Baccalaureus* (*i.e.* the Berry of a Laurel) a Batchelor of Arts in an University, as of Divinity, Law, Physick and Musick. *Batchelor* ... Hence the Title of *Batchelor of Arts, Divinity, Musick,* &c.

bachyllion
1661 BLOUNT (2nd edn) *Bachyllion,* a song or dance, which seems to take name of *Bachyllus,* a famous *Tragædian* Poet, who devised and practised it; as *Piladion,* of *Pilades,* as notable a Comedian. *Plutarch.* **1676** COLES *Bachyllion,* a song or dance of ¶ *Bachyllus,* a Tragedian.

bacile
1598 FLORIO It→E *Bacile, Bacino,* ... also a kinde of musicall instrument. **1611** FLORIO It→E *Bacile,* a bason. Also a timbrell.

bacino
1611 FLORIO It→E *Bacino,* a bason. Also a timbrell.

backfall *see* beat, forefall, half-fall, plain beat, whole-fall
1659 SIMPSON *Division-Violist* (p. 9) ... The shaked *Backfall* is likewise the same in Nature with the Plain *Backfall,* the difference only a shake of the Finger taken off; which must be done in that wideness whence it was removed... **1676** MACE *Musick's Monument* (p. 90) ... a little *Crook, or Comma, Thus* (‘) which is the Mark of a *Grace,* in Play, which we call a *Back-fall* .... Now, how to perform It, is Thus, *viz.* ¶ If you remember, (according to my *General Rule*) that the precedent *Letter* (ꝺ,) is to remain stopt, till you come to strike *This Letter* (ɼ,) you will find, that the *Back-fall,* will be very *easie* to perform; for, (you are to know that) to make a *Back-fall Right,* you are always to strike the *Precedent Letter,* (which stands upon the *same String*) instead of *That Letter,* which is to be *Back-fall'd*) with your Right Hand, and not at all to strike the Letter It self; yet you must make It sound, by your *Left-Hand Finger,* (so soon as you have struck the *Precedent Note*) by *shaking It from That* (ꝺ,) (*so struck*) into the (ɼ). ¶ This is the *Nature* of all *Back-falls, viz.* They ever partake first, of that Tone, either of a *half Note,* or a *whole Note,* next ascending, (according to the *Aire of the Lesson, or Key.* § (p. 104) A *Back-fall,* is only *Thus; viz.* Let your *Note* be what it will; It must 1*st.* partake of the *Tone of another Note, or Half Note above it,* before it Sound ... **c.1698-c.1703** NORTH Cursory Notes (*C-K CN* p. 222) The back-fall is holding the upper note longer descending then the time, and taking it off with a trill. **c.1710** NORTH (draft for) Musicall Grammarian BL Add. 32537, f. 227v Wee derive from hence also, the famous grace of the back-fall as they call it; that is rising to a note from ye half Note below. **c.1710** NORTH Short, Easy, & plaine rules BL Add. 32531, f. 24 [quoting Prendcourt:] ... when a stroke is set this. ⟍ it is called a back-fall [annotation by North:] NB. That is ye English ...

Bacon, Francis *see* diapason

bagpipe *see* burden, busine, busone, ceramella, chevre, ciaramella, cornemuse, drone, faux-bourdon, gayta, gnaccara, loure, manganello, miskin, musa, musette, naccara, pibole, pithaules, piva, porte-vent, ronfo, sampogna, scacciapensiere, sourdeline, sveglia, utricularius, veze, zaino, zaramella
1589 RIDER L→E A bag-pipe, *v.* pipe [*see* tibia utricularis]. **1702** KERSEY *New Engl. Dict.* (1st edn) A *Bag-pipe.* **1728** CHAMBERS *Bagpipe,* a Musical Instrument of the Wind-kind; chiefly used in Country Places. It consists of two principal Parts: The first a Leathern Bag, which blows up like a Foot-Ball, by means of a Portvent, or little Tube fitted to it, and stopp'd by a Valve. The other Part consists of three Pipes, or Flutes; the first called the Great Pipe, or Drone, and the second the Little one; which pass the Wind out only at Bottom: The third has a Tongue, and is play'd on by compressing the Bag under the Arm, when full, and opening or stopping the Holes, which are eight, with the Fingers. The little Pipe is ordinarily a Foot long,

that play'd on 13 Inches, and the Portvent six. The *Bagpipe* takes in the Compass of three Octaves. **1736** BAILEY *Dict. Britannicum* (2nd edn) *Bag-pipe,* a musical Wind-Instrument. **1737** DYCHE-PARDON (2nd edn) *Bag-pipe* (S.) a musical Instrument of the Wind Kind, much used in *Scotland* and by the Northern People of *England* at Fairs and Country Merry-makings, consisting of two Pipes, a larger and a smaller, and a Pair of Bellows so contriv'd, that each Pipe is filled with Wind by the Bellows, and the large one sounds a donble [sic] Octave, or deep Key Note to the lowest Note of the small one; and this is called the Drone, or holding Note, Descants upon which are plaid upon the small Pipe.

baioccare *see* baylar, chioppare, chrich, vaylar
1611 FLORIO It→E *Baioccare,* to snap, to click or flurt with ones fingers as moresco dancers. **1659** TORRIANO-FLORIO It→E *Baioccare,* to clack, to click, or snap with ones fingers ends, as Canarie-dancers and some barbers doe.

bal *see* ball

balade *see* ballad, canticum, canzona, carmen, precention, refrain
1593 HOLLYBAND Fr→E § *Balades & rondeaux auec leur refrain*: Ballets and ditties with their burden or foote: see *Refrain.* **1611** COTGRAVE Fr→E *Balade.* A ballet. **1658** PHILLIPS (1st edn) *Balade,* (French) a Ballet, or roundelay, also a Dance. **1676** COLES *Balade, French.* ballet, poem; also a dance. **1688** MIEGE-COTGRAVE Fr→E *Balade,* (f.) a Ballad. **1721** BAILEY *An Univ. Etymolog. Engl. Dict.* (1st edn) *Balad,* (*Balade, F.*) a Song. See *Ballad.*

baladin
1593 HOLLYBAND Fr→E *Vn Baladin,* a dancer of galliards: *m. Vn baleur, m*: idem. **1611** COTGRAVE Fr→E *Baladin: m.* A common dauncer of galliards, and other stirring, or liuely Ayres. *Balladin*: A dauncer; *Balladinerie*: f. High, or liuely dauncing, as, of galliards, Corantoes, or Jigges. **1658** PHILLIPS (1st edn) *Balladin,* (French) a dancer of Galliards. **1676** COLES *Balladin, French* Galliard-dancer. **1688** MIEGE-COTGRAVE Fr→E *Baladin,* (m.) a great Dancer, one that is much given to dancing;

baldosa
1598 FLORIO It→E *Baldosa,* ... Also a musicall instrument so called. Also a kinde of countrie daunce. **1611** FLORIO It→E *Baldosa,* bolde, saucie. Also a kind of croud or country fiddle. Also a certain country dance. **1659** TORRIANO-FLORIO It→E *Baldosa,* a kind of croud or countrie fiddle, also a generall dancing under a May-pole, when many countrie-people meet together from divers places.

balet *see* orchestra
1688 MIEGE-COTGRAVE Fr→E *Balet,* (m.) a kind of Dance; a sort of dramatick Poetry.

ball *see* brawl, canto, carnival, horse-ballet, orchestra, pavan, revels, ridotta, Terpsichore
1550 THOMAS It→E *Ballare,* to daunce. *Ballo,* a daunce. **1593** HOLLYBAND Fr→E *Bal, m: ou danse, f:* dauncing, a galliard. **1598** FLORIO It→E *Ballo,* any kinde of dance. **1611** COTGRAVE Fr→E *Bal: m.* A daunce; a dauncing; Reuels, or, a Reuelling. **1611** FLORIO It→E *Ballo,* a ball or any kind of dance. **1688** MIEGE-COTGRAVE Fr→E *Bal,* (m.) a Ball, or solemn Dancing.

ballad *see* balade, ballata, bargaret, cantafavole, canticle, cantilena, cantinbanco, canzona, ditty, precention, rhapsodi, romance, vaudeville, villanella
1702 KERSEY *New Engl. Dict.* (1st edn) A *Ballad, or* song, sung up and down the streets. **1706** KERSEY-PHILLIPS (6th edn) *Ballad,* a common Song sung up and down the Streets. **1708** KERSEY *Dict. Anglo-Brit.* (1st edn) *Ballad,* a common Song sung up and down the Streets. **1721** BAILEY *An Univ. Etymolog. Engl. Dict.* (1st edn) *Ballad,* a Song, commonly sung up and down the Streets. See *Balad.* **1730** BAILEY *Dict. Britannicum* (1st edn) *Ballad, Balad,* (*balad,* Fr.) a Song. **1736** BAILEY *Dict. Britannicum* (2nd edn) *Ballad, Balad,* (*balad,* F. *ballata,* Sp.) a Song. **1737** DYCHE-PARDON (2nd edn) *Ballad* (S.) a Song; but now commonly applied to the meaner Sort, that are sung in the Streets by the Vulgar.

ballade *see* balade, ballata, canto, chanson, chant, charivaris, encomium, epithalamy, joüarre, precention, vaudeville

ballata *see* villanella
1550 THOMAS It→E *Ballata,* a balette. **1598** FLORIO It→E *Ballata,* a ballade, a song, a gigge, a roundelaie. **1611** FLORIO It→E *Ballata,* a ballad or roundlay. **1659** TORRIANO-FLORIO It→E **Ballata, vale Poesia ô canzone, che si canta ballando,* a ballade, a jig, a roundelay.

ballatella
1659 TORRIANO-FLORIO It→E **Ballatella, Ballatina,* a little jig, or Song.

ballet *see* air, balade, bargaret, cançion, Geneva jig, horse-ballet

balletto
1659 TORRIANO-FLORIO It→E *Balletto,* a dance, a ballet, but now used for a Maske.

1597 MORLEY *Plaine and Easie Introdvction* (p. 180) [marginalia: 'Ballette.'] There is also another kind more light than this [i.e. villanelle], which they tearme *Ballete* or daunces, and are songs, which being song to a dittie may likewise be daunced: ...

ballo *see* ball

ballonchio
1598 FLORIO It→E *Ballonchio,* a countrey hopping or morrice dance. *Balloncíuolo,* a merrie country dance. **1611** FLORIO It→E *Ballonchio,* a hand-ball or a foote-ball. Also a country hopping round or morice dance. *Balloncíuolo,* a merry skipping dance. **1659** TORRIANO-FLORIO It→E *Ballonchio, Balloncíuolo,* ... also a merrie countrie dance.

ban *see* banoyement, proclamation
1704 HARRIS *Ban,* is a Proclamation made at the Head of a Body of Troops, or in the several Quarters of the Army, by sound of Trumpet or beat of Drums, either of observing of Martial Discipline, for declaring a New Officer, punishing a Soldier, or the like. **1706** KERSEY-PHILLIPS (6th edn) *Ban, (Fr.)* a Proclamation made at the Head of a Body of Troops, by the sound of Trumpet, or beat of Drum, for the observing of Martial Discipline, for declaring a new Officer, or punishing a Soldier, *&c.* **1721** BAILEY *An Univ. Etymolog. Engl. Dict.* (1st edn) *Ban, (Ban, F.)* a Proclamation made at the Head of a Body of Troops, by the sound of Trumpet, ot [sic] beat of Drum for the Observing of martial Discipline, *&c.* **1728** CHAMBERS *Ban,* or *Bans,* a solemn Proclamation or Publication of any thing, or a publick Edict or Summons ... Some derive the Word from the *British, Ban; Clamor, Noise*: Others from the *German, Ban, Publication* or *Proscription,* because frequently made with Sound of Trumpet; **1730** BAILEY *Dict. Britannicum* (1st edn) *Ban,* a Proclamation made at the Head of an Army or Body of Troops, either by Sound of Trumpet or Beat of Drum, requiring the Observance of Martial Discipline for declaring a new Officer, or for punishing a Soldier. **1737** DYCHE-PARDON (2nd edn) *Ban* (S.) a *Musical* Term for a Proclamation made in an Army by Beat of Drum, Sound of Trumpet, &c. requiring the strict Observance of Discipline, either for the declaring a new Officer, or punishing an Offender.

band
1737 BAILEY *The Univ. Etymolog. Engl. Dict.* (3rd edn, vol. 2) *Band of Musick,* a company or set of musicians, united or selected for the performance of a symphony on any extraordinary occasion. **1737** DYCHE-PARDON (2nd edn) *Band* (S.) ... at Theatres, the Company of *Musicians* are called the *Band of Musick;*

bandora *see* entata, pandora, spinet (espinette organisée)
1599 MINSHEU-PERCYVALL Sp→E **Bandurria,* f. a bandore, a gittarne. **1658** PHILLIPS (1st edn) *Bandore,* (Ital.) a kinde of Musical instrument. **1676** COLES *Bandore, Italian.* a Musick-Instrument. **1678** PHILLIPS (4th edn) *Bandore,* (Ital.) a kind of Musical Instrument from the Greek word πανδῶρα. **1706** KERSEY-PHILLIPS (6th edn) *Bandore,* a kind of Musical Instrument with Strings. **1708** KERSEY *Dict. Anglo-Brit.* (1st edn) *Bandore,* a Musical Instrument. **1721** BAILEY *An Univ. Etymolog. Engl. Dict.* (1st edn) *Bandore, (Pandura, L.* of Πανδοῦρα, *Gr.)* a Musical Instrument. **1730** BAILEY *Dict. Britannicum* (1st edn) *Bandora* (πανδῶρα, Gr.) a kind of musical Instruments with Strings.

bandrol *see* cascata, pendaglio, scatta, soga
1656 BLOUNT (1st edn) *Banderol* or *Bannerolle* (Fr. *Banderolle*) a little flag or streamer ... A Cornet Devise. **1688** MIEGE-COTGRAVE Fr→E *Banderole,* (f.) a streamer; the fringed piece of Silk that hangs on a Trumpet. **1706** KERSEY-PHILLIPS (6th edn) *Bandrol,* a little Flag, or Streamer; also the fringed Silk that hangs on a Trumpet. **1708** KERSEY *Dict. Anglo-Brit.* (1st edn) *Bandrol,* ... also the fringed Silk that hangs on a Trumpet. **1730** BAILEY *Dict. Britannicum* (1st edn) *Bandrol* (*banderol,* F.) ... also the little fringed silk Flag, that hangs on a Trumpet.

banoyement *see* ban, proclamation
1611 COTGRAVE Fr→E *Banoyement: m.* A proclaiming, or publishing, by the sound of Trumpet, &c.

bar *see* double bar, whole time
1678 PHILLIPS (4th edn) *Barre*, ... Also in Musick Bar is a Line drawn perpendicular through the Note Lines, to Bar in by themselves a certain number of Notes comprehending such or such a time. **1728** CHAMBERS *Bars*, in Musick, Strokes drawn perpendicularly a-cross the Lines of a Piece of Musick, including between each two, a certain Quantity or Measure of Time, which is various as the Time of the Musick is triple or common. In common Time, between each two *Bars* is included the Measure of four Crotchets, in triple Time three Crotchets. Their principle Use is to regulate the Beating, or Measure of Time in a Consort. See *Time*. **1737** DYCHE-PARDON (2nd edn) *Bar* (S.) in *Musick*, those Strokes that are drawn across, or downwards, between so many Notes as make up the Measure of Time the Air is prick'd in;

1665 SIMPSON *Principles of Practical Mvsick* (p. 25) ... Here you have every Time or Measure distinguished by Strokes, (together with the spaces betwixt them) are called Bars. **1676** MACE *Musick's Monument* (p. 77) [*re* tablature] The *down-right Stroak*, (or *Bar*, as we call It) shews the *Evenness*, *Sufficiency*, or *Observatiou* [sic], of a *Full Time* ... **1700** ANON. *Compleat Instructor to the Flute* (p. 7) Ther[e] is a stroke Drawn cross the five lines thus and is properly call'd a bar which is to devide one bar from another and to Show you where you ought to beat your foot. **1721** MALCOLM *Treatise of Musick* (p. 394) Every *Song* is actually divided into a certain Number of equal Parts, which we call *Bars* (from a Line that separates them, drawn straight across the Staff ...) or *Measures*, because the Measure of the *Time* is laid upon them, or at least by means of their Subdivisions we are assisting in measuring it; and therefore you have this Word *Measure* used sometime for a *Bar*, and sometime for the *absolute* Quantity of *Time*; ... § (p. 411) A *single Bar* is a Line across the Staff, that separates one *Measure* from another. A *double Bar* is Two parallel Lines across the Staff, which separates the greater Periods or Strains of any particular or *simple Piece*.

barbacane
1593 HOLLYBAND Fr→E *Barbacane*, an instrument of musicke: *f*.

barbitist
1500 *Ortus Vocabulorum* L→E Barbitista q vel q cantat cum barbito. c.p. **1656** BLOUNT (1st edn) *Barbitist (barbitista)* a Lutinist, or one that plays on the Lute. **1658** PHILLIPS (1st edn) *Barbitist*, a Lutinist. **1676** COLES *Barbitist, Greek*. Lutinist.

barbiton, barbitos *see* lyre, magade
1500 *Ortus Vocabulorum* L→E Barbitus. i. cithara: vel instrumentum musicum. m.s. **1538** ELYOT L→E *Barbitos*, an instrument of musyke, whiche I suppose is that, that men call doulsimers. **1552** HULOET L→E *Barbitos*. Double harpe, called a roote. *Barbitos, Sambuca*, Dulcimers or dowble harpe called a roote. **1565** COOPER L→E *Barbitos, masc. gen*. An instrument of musicke, called, as I thynke doulcimers: some thinke it is a kinde of harpe. Some the broder parte of the harpe. **1587** THOMAS L→E *Barbitos, vel Barbitus, m. vel f.g. & Barbitum, ti, n.g. Horat*. An instrument of musick, called of some, Dulcimers: of some a Harpe: of some the broder part of a harpe. **1589** RIDER L→E *Barbitum, barbiton, n barbitus, barbitos m. vel f. testudo, chelys, cithara, f*. A Lute. *Barbitum, n. barbitos, m. sambuca, campona, f*. A Dulcimer. **1598** FLORIO It→E *Barbiton*, a musicall instrument called of some a Dulcimer, and of some an Harpe. **1611** FLORIO It→E *Barbiton*, a musicall instrument called a Dulcimer. **1659** TORRIANO-FLORIO It→E *Barbitono*, a musicall instrument called a Dulcimer.

bargaret
1616 BULLOKAR **Bargaret*. A kind of dance. **1658** PHILLIPS (1st edn) *Bargaret*, (old word) a Sonnet, or Ballet. **1676** COLES *Bargaret, -net, Old word*. a ballet; song or dance. **1704** *Cocker's Engl. Dict.* (1st edn) *Bargaret*, a Song, or Dance. **1708** KERSEY *Dict. Anglo-Brit.* (1st edn) *Bargaret* or *Barganet*, (O.) a Ballad, Song or Dance.

baritone
1609 DOWLAND-ORNITHOPARCUS *Micrologvs* (p. 84) *Of the Baritone*. ¶ The *Bassus*, (or rather *Basis*) is the lowest part of each Song. Or it is an Harmony to be sung with a deepe voyce, which is called *Baritonus*, a *Vari*, which is low, by changing *V* into *B*, because it holdeth the lower part of the Song.

barzelletta
1598 FLORIO It→E *Barzellette*, a kinde of madrigall, song, gigge, or sonnet. **1611** FLORIO It→E *Barzellette*, a kind of country gigges or songs or madrigals. **1659** TORRIANO-FLORIO It→E **Barzellante*, a composer, or singer of Barzelle. **Barzellare*, to compose, or sing, *Barzelle*.

Barzelle, Barzelletto, countrie-songs, jigs, ditties, or round-lays.

bass *see* b, bass descant, bassetto, basso continuo, bassotto, B. C., continuato, continued bass, double bass, natural bass, pistoy bass, supposed bass, thorough bass, through bass

1552 HULOET L→E [no headword given] Syng a base. **1589** RIDER L→E The base, *vide* Musicke. *Basis, f. bassus, succentus, m.* The base in a song. **1598** FLORIO It→E *Basso,* ... Also a base in singing. **1611** FLORIO It→E *Basso,* ... Also a base in singing. **1658** PHILLIPS (1st edn) *Base,* ... also the deepest part in Musick, being the foundation of the rest **1659** TORRIANO-FLORIO It→E *Basso,* ... also a base voice, or instrument **1688** MIEGE-COTGRAVE Fr→E *Basse,* (a fem. Subst.) the base, in Musick; he that sings (or bears) it; § *Il nous faudra trois Voix, un dessus, une haute contre, & une basse,* we shall want three Voices, a treble, a tenor, and a base. *La Basse, l'Instrument de Musique qui fait la basse,* the base Viol. *Toucher la basse,* to play upon the base Viol. **1696** PHILLIPS (5th edn) *Base,* or *Basis,* ... also the deepest part in Musick, being the foundation of the whole Composition: **1702** KERSEY *New Engl. Dict.* (1st edn) The *Bass,* in Musick. **1704** HARRIS *Bass,* in Musick, is the lowest of all the Parts thereof, which serves as a Foundation to the others. **1706** KERSEY-PHILLIPS (6th edn) *Bass,* (in *Musick*) the lowest of all its Parts, which serves as a Foundation to the others. **1724** [PEPUSCH] *Short Explic. of Foreign Words in Mus. Bks.* (p. 14) *Basso,* is the Bass in general; tho' sometimes in Pieces of Musick for several Voices, the Singing Bass is more particularly so called. **1726** BAILEY *An Univ. Etymolog. Engl. Dict.* (3rd edn) *Basso* (in *Musick Books*) generally signifies the Bass; but sometimes in Pieces of Musick for several Voices, the singing Bass is more particularly call'd so. **1728** CHAMBERS *Base,* in Musick, that Part of a Consort which is the most heard, which consists of the gravest, deepest and longest Sounds; or, which is play'd on the largest Pipes, or Strings, of a common Instrument, *viz.* an *Organ,* or *Lute;* or, on Instruments larger than ordinary, for that purpose, as *Bass-Viols, Bassons* or *Bass-Hautboys,* &c. Musicians hold the *Base* the principal Part of a Consort, and the Foundation of the Composition; tho some will have the Treble the chief Part; which others only make a Circumstance, or Ornament. *Counter-Base,* is a *second Base,* where there are several in the same Consort. *Thorough Base,* is the Harmony made by *Bass-Viols,* or *Theorbos,* continuing to play, both while the Voices sing, and the other Instruments perform their Part; and also filling the Intervals when any of those stop. M. *Brossard* observes the *Thorough-Base* to be a Part of the modern Musick; first invented in 1600, by an *Italian,* call'd *Ludovico Viadana.* 'Tis play'd by Cyphers mark'd over the Notes, on the *Organ, Spinette, Harpsichord, Theorbo, Harp,* &c. and frequently, simply, and without Cyphers, on the *Bass-Viol, Basson,* &c. **1737** DYCHE-PARDON (2nd edn) *Bass* (S.) in *Musick,* the deepest or lowest Part, or Tones, from which the several other Parts are composed or built up, as it were, from a Foundation; *Basso* (S.) in *Musick,* is the Bass Part universally; but sometimes 'tis restrain'd in vocal Musick to the Bass Part that is to be sung. As *Italy* has been and still is most noted for the finest Musicians, so most Composers in that Science affect to use their Terms, some of which are, *Basso Concertante,* which is the Bass of the little Chorus; *Basso Continuo,* is the thorough or figured Bass, that goes thro' the whole Performance, playing of Chords, and whatever can make the Harmony full and compleat; *Basso Repieno,* the Bass of the grand Chorus, which comes in now and then to make the Composition more affecting.

1617-24 FLUDD *Utriusque Cosmi Maioris: De Templo Musicæ* (p. 209) *Basis* seu *Bassus* est cantio seu vox infima per gravium sonorum systema inflexa, idéoque gravi virorum voce exprimenda. **1636** BUTLER *Principles of Musik* (p. 41) The Base is so called, becaus it is the *basis* or foundation of the Song, unto which all other Partes bee set: and it is to be sung with a deepe, ful, and pleasing Voice. **1653** ?BROUNCKER *Renatvs Des-Cartes Exc. Comp. of Musick* (p. 51) [*re* composition in four voices] The First and most Grave of all these Voices, is that which Musicians call *Bassus.* This is the chiefe, and ought principally to fill the ears, because all other Voices carry the chiefest respect to the *Basse* ... **1686** ANON. *New and Easie Method to Learn to Sing* (p. 69) In all Tunes or Lessons consisting of Parts, one Part is the *Bass,* (so called, because it is the *Basis,* Foundation, or Ground-work, to the other Part or Parts, and on which the Harmony is built:) ... **1721** MALCOLM *Treatise of Musick* (p. 332) The lowest [part] is called the *Bass, i.e. Basis,* because it is the Foundation of the *Harmony,* and formerly in their *plain Compositions* the *Bass* was first made, tho' 'tis otherwise now; the *Bass-clef* is *f* on the 4*th* Line upward: ... **1724** TURNER *Sound Anatomiz'd* (pp. 38-9) The Reason why the lowest

Part is called the *Base*, and also, why the Uppermost is called the *Treble*, would be impertinent to repeat here, the Words being sufficient to explain themselves; ... It may not be amis to observe to you, that, as the Word *Base* is derived from the *Latin* Word, *Bassus*; (which signifies a *Foundation* or *Basis*) so they generally write *Bass*, instead of *Base*; which is an Abreviation [sic] of the Word *Bassus*, or the *Italian* Word, *Bass*; which has the same Signification. **c.1726** NORTH Musicall Gramarian BL Add. 32533, f. 81 In Consort Musick, The lowest Notes are termed, as they are comonly esteemed, the Base; ... **1728** NORTH Musicall Grammarian (*C-K MG* f. 41) Of proper base notes and consort base notes ¶ It is found that in consort, all accords whatsoever (in truth) have for base the key of the scale, but when intermediates happen [i.e. if concordant notes such as 3ds, 4ths or 5ths are placed below the key note], the lower note of the accord usurps the place of the key; and is termed the base of that accord. **1736** TANS'UR *Compleat Melody* (3rd edn, p. 70) *Bass*, or *Bassus*; Is the Name given to the lowest Part of Musick, which is set at the Bottom, and is the Foundation of all other *Parts*; and is the *Ground work* of all the rest. ¶ *Basso*. (Ital.) Is the proper Name for the *Vocal-Bass*.

bass descant

1597 MORLEY *Plaine and Easie Introdvction* (p. 86) *Phi*. What is *Base descant*? ¶ *Ma*. *It is that kinde of descanting, where your sight of taking and vsing your cordes must be vnder the plainsong.*

basse-contre *see* contrabasso, contre-basse

1611 COTGRAVE Fr→E *Basse-contre*. The base-part in Musicke; also, hee that sings, or beares it. **1688** MIEGE-COTGRAVE Fr→E *Basse contre*, (f.) *Terme de Musique*, Counter-Tenour.

basse-dance

1593 HOLLYBAND Fr→E *Basse-dance*, a dance: *f.* **1611** COTGRAVE Fr→E *Basse-dance: f.* A measure.

bassetto *see* bassotto

1611 FLORIO It→E *Bassetto*, a low base voice or instrument. **1659** TORRIANO-FLORIO It→E **Bassetto*, the dim: of *Basso*, also a low, or mean voice **1724** [PEPUSCH] *Short Explic. of Foreign Words in Mus. Bks*. (pp. 15-16) *Bassetto*, is a Bass Viol, or Bass Violin of the smallest Size, and is so called to distinguish them from those Bass Viols or Violins of a larger Size. **1726** BAILEY *An Univ. Etymolog. Engl. Dict*. (3rd edn) *Bassetto* (in *Musick Books*) signifies a Bass-Viol or Bass-Violin of the smallest Size, and is call'd so to distinguish it from Bass-Viols or Violins of a larger Size. *Ital*.

basso concertante *see* bass, concertante

basso continuo *see* bass, B. C., continuato, continued bass, continuo, figure, thorough bass

1724 [PEPUSCH] *Short Explic. of Foreign Words in Mus. Bks*. (pp. 14-15) *Basso Continuo*, is the Thorough Bass, or Continual Bass, and is commonly distinguished from the other Bases by Figures over the Notes; which Figures are proper only for the Organ, Harpsicord, Spinet, and Theorbo Lute. ¶ *N.B*. A Thorough Bass is not always figured, tho' it ought so to be. **1726** BAILEY *An Univ. Etymolog. Engl. Dict*. (3rd edn) *Basso Continuo* (in *Musick Books*) signifies the thorough Bass, or continual Bass, and is commonly distinguished from the other Bases by Figures over the Notes; which Figures are proper only for the Organ, Harpsicord, Spinet, and Theorbo Lute.

bassoon *see* bombardo, courtaud, curtail, drone, dulcino, fagotto, obligata, tarot

1688 MIEGE-COTGRAVE Fr→E *Basson*, (m.) a kind of musical Instrument. **1706** KERSEY-PHILLIPS (6th edn) *Bassoon*, the Bass Haut-boy; a Musical Instrument. **1721** BAILEY *An Univ. Etymolog. Engl. Dict*. (1st edn) *Bassoon*, (*Basson*, *F*.) a Musical Instrument, the Bass-haut-boy. **1728** CHAMBERS *Basson*, or *Bassoon*, a Musical Instrument of the Wind Kind, serving for the *Base* in Consorts of Musick, Hautboys, *&c*. To make it more portable it divides into two Parts: Its Diameter at Bottom is nine Inches, and its Holes are stopp'd with Keys, *&c*. like large Flutes. **1737** DYCHE-PARDON (2nd edn) *Bassoon* (S.) a Musical Instrument that serves as a Bass to the Hautboy, Flute, and other Wind Instruments.

basso recitante

1724 [PEPUSCH] *Short Explic. of Foreign Words in Mus. Bks*. (p. 15) *Basso Recitante*, the same as Basso Concertante [*see* concertante]. **1726** BAILEY *An Univ. Etymolog. Engl. Dict*. (3rd edn) *Basso Recitante* (in *Musick Books*) signifies the same as *Basso Concertante*. Ital.

basso ripieno *see* bass, ripieno

bassotto *see* bassetto
1611 FLORIO It→E *Bassotto,* a good pleasing base-voice. **1659** TORRIANO-FLORIO It→E *Bassotto,* a good pleasing base voice

bass viol *see* viol

bastarda viola *see* viola bastarda

baterie
1688 MIEGE-COTGRAVE Fr→E *Baterie* (f.) from *Batre,* ... a particular way of playing upon the Guitar, or of beating the Drum; § *Batre au Champ, batre pour marcher où l'on est commandé,* to beat for a march, or expedition. *Batre la caisse,* to beat the drum. *Batre la marche,* to beat the march. *Batre la mesure,* to beat the time.

Battalus
1565 COOPER L→E *Battalus,* The name of an effeminate and wanton mynstrell.

battuta *see* abattuta
1598 FLORIO It→E *Battuta,* a beating, a panting, a keeping of time in musicke. *Battuto,* ... a keeping of time in musicke. **1611** FLORIO It→E *Battuta,* a beating or keeping time in musicke. § *Tenere la battuta,* to keep time in Musike. **1659** TORRIANO-FLORIO It→E **Battuta,* ... also a beating, or keeping of time in musike. § *Fare le battute,* to keep or beat time in Musick. *Osservare le battute,* to keep due time as Musicians do. **1724** [PEPUSCH] *Short Explic. of Foreign Words in Mus. Bks.* (p. 16) *Battuta,* is the Beating or Motion of the Hand or Foot, in keeping or beating of Time. **1726** BAILEY *An Univ. Etymolog. Engl. Dict.* (3rd edn) *Battuta* (among *Musick Masters*) signifies the Beating or Motion of the Hand or Foot in keeping or beating Time. *Ital.*

c.1710 NORTH Short, Easy, & plaine rules BL Add. 32531, f. 20v ... whether it be beaten or not beaten att all, so as ye performers keep to gether, for ye battuta (as ye Itallians call ye Efficacy of ye performers actions) will necessarily distinguish ye measure ...

baulk
c.1726 NORTH Musicall Gramarian BL Add. 32533, f. 103 ... and first of the Baulk, as they terme it, or more properly, disappointm^t. And it is when the Cadence is perfectly formed and Instead of the close, the Base riseth a Note, wch changeth the key ...

baylar *see* baioccare, chioppare, chrich, vaylar
1599 MINSHEU-PERCYVALL Sp→E **Bayladera,* f. a woman dauncer, which danceth & snappeth, or maketh a noise with the fingers. *Baylar,* to daunce and make a snapping noise with the fingers.

B. C. *see* b, bass, basso continuo, continuato, continued bass, continuo
1731 PRELLEUR *Modern Musick-Master* (Dictionary, p. 2) *B.C.* or *Basso-Continuo,* ye Thorough Bass for the Organ, Harpsichord, or Spinnet, &c.

bearing *see* temperament
1698 WALLIS *Letter to Samuel Pepys* (*Philos. Trans.,* 1698, p. 253) [*re* the organ] ... Whereby it comes to pass, that each Pipe doth not express its proper Sound, but very near it, yet somewhat varying from it; Which they call *Bearing.* Which is somewhat of Imperfection in this Noble Instrument, the Top of all.

beat *as military term, see* alarm, assembly, ban, baterie, chamade, general, retreat, troop
1702 KERSEY *New Engl. Dict.* (1st edn) The *Beat* of a Drum. **1706** KERSEY-PHILLIPS (6th edn) § To *Beat an Alarm,* (in the Art of *War*) is to give notice by beat of Drum of some sudden Danger, that all may be in a readiness. To *Beat to Arms,* is for Soldiers that are dispers'd to repair to them: To *Beat a Charge,* a Signal to fall upon the Enemy. ¶ To *Beat the General,* to give notice to the Forces that they are to March. To *Beat a March,* to command them actually to move. To *Beat a Parley,* a Signal to demand some Conference with the Enemy. To *Beat a Retreat,* to draw off from the Enemy. To *Beat the Reveille,* to give leave at break of Day, to come out of Quarters. To *Beat the Tat-too,* to order all to retire to their Quarters. To *Beat the Troop,* to order the Men to repair to their Colours. **1708** KERSEY *Dict. Anglo-Brit.* (1st edn) § To *Beat an Alarm,* (*M.T.*) is to give notice by beat of Drum of some sudden Danger, that all may be in a readiness. To *Beat a Charge,* a Signal to fall upon the Enemy. To *Beat the General,* to give notice to the Forces that they are to March. To *beat the Reveille,* to give leave at break of Day, to come out of Quarters. To *Beat the Tat-too,* to order all to retire to their Quarters. To *Beat the Troop,* to order the Men to repair to their Colours. **1737** BAILEY *The Univ. Etymolog. Engl. Dict.* (3rd edn, vol. 2) *To Beat a march (Military Term)* is to beat a drum to give notice to the soldiers actually to move. **1737** DYCHE-PARDON (2nd edn) *Beat* (V.) ... also to give

Notice by Beat of Drum, of a sudden Danger, or that scattered Soldiers may repair to their Arms and Quarters, is to beat an Alarm, or to Arms; also to signify by different Manners of Sounding a Drum, that the Soldiers are to fall on the Enemy, to retreat before, in, or after an Attack ...

beat *as ornament, see* beat up, plain beat, undershake

1659 SIMPSON *Division-Violist* (p. 9) Graces made with open Shakes are these. A *Beat*; a *Backfall*; an *Elevation*; a *Cadent*; and double *Relish*. The *Beat* is the same in Nature with the *Plain-Beat* or *Rise*; the difference, only a short shake of a Finger, before we fix it upon the Place designed. This, as also the *Plain-Beat*, is commonly made from the *Half-Note*; or distance of one *Frett*... **1676** MACE *Musick's Monument* (p. 105) The *Beate*, is your *Letter* struck; (be it what it will) and so soon as it is struck, that Sound must be *Falsifyed*, always into a *Half Note beneath, by taking up your Finger*, (as if you would *Back-fall the False Note, from that stop'd Letter*) and *strongly, so shaked, to and again*; yet, at last, the same Finger, must *rest down*, in the 1*st*. *True Note*. **1681** B[ANISTER] *Most Pleasant Companion* (p. 6) ... when the Mark is placed on the Line even with the Dot, then you are to lift up that Finger and *Shake*, and lay it down again before you play any other Note, this is called a *Beat* ... **1683** GREETING *Pleasant Companion* (n.p.) *Of the several Graces on the Flagelet* ¶ In the former Example of *Graces*, the Mark or Character of a *Beat* and *Shake* is all one, but in Playing them is this difference: When the Mark is on the same Line even with the *Dot*, then you are to lift up that finger and shake, and lay it down again before you play any other, this is called a *Beat*. But when the Mark stands alone upon any other line underneath the *dot*, then with the finger belonging to that Line on which it is set you must shake, taking it off again before you play any other Note; and this is called a *shake*. **c.1710** NORTH Short, Easy, & plaine rules BL Add. 32531, f. 23v [quoting Prendcourt:] This mark ∞ . I call an undershake for ye movem^t^ is to be made. [annotation by North:] NB. This wee call a beat. **[1729]** HOTTETERRE *Rudiments or Principles of German Flute* (p. 22) The Beat is the hitting once or twice as quick a we can, full on the hole, and as near the Note we beat upon as possible, we ought also to end a Beat with the finger off ... **1731** PRELLEUR *Modern Musick-Master* (V *re* violin, p. 7) *Of the usual Graces*. ¶ The first is call'd a Beat, and is marked thus (+) it proceeds from ye half Note below the Note on which it is made, and must be heard a little before the proper Note is drawn with the Bow ...

beating *in time-keeping, see* battuta, manuductor, stroke, tact, tactus

1721 MALCOLM *Treatise of Musick* (p. 399) Now to keep the *Time* equal, we make use of a Motion of the Hand, or Foot (if the other is employed,) thus; knowing the true *Time* of a *Crotchet*, we shall suppose the *Measure* actually subdivided into 4 *Crotchets* for the first Species, and the half *Measure* will be 2 *Crotchets*, therefore the Hand or Foot being up, if we put it down with the very Beginning of the first Note or *Crotchet*, and then raise it with the Third, and then down with the Beginning of the next *Measure*, this is called *Beating* the *Time*; ...

beating *in tuning*

c.1710 NORTH (draft for) Musicall Grammarian BL Add. 32537, f. 187v ... Now however the pulses are indistinguishable, so as the sence wee haue of tone is continued, yet the coincidences may not be so frequent, but wee may perceiv by modes of ye joynt when they happen, and also the degrees of the approach to and departure from them; wch is that wch in tuning of pipes is called the beating and wallowing of the sound; ...

beat up

c.1715-20 NORTH Essay of Musical Ayre BL Add. 32536, f. 23v ... And first observe that the Semitone under the clave, or ye sharp 7th. of ye Key at the very beginning of sounding is Gracefull, nay a very Grace in ye Catalogue of Graces & is called a beat-up ... **c.1726** NORTH Musicall Gramarian BL Add. 32533, f. 107 The Beat-up is used at the Entrance of the sounding any note, and may be with a short shake or temper, or plain, and is but a Mixing the tone, with that next underneath, leaving ye former in full possession. It may be from a tone or semitone, but most properly the latter; ... **1728** NORTH Musicall Grammarian (*C-K MG* f. 56v) The joyning the key with the half note underneath is good, and called a beat up, becaus that (as I sayd before) is a #3d to the fourth below.

bedon

1570/71 *Dict. Fr. and Engl.* Fr→E *Vn Bedon, ou Tabourin*, a tabberet. **1593** HOLLYBAND Fr→E *Vn Bedon ou Tabourin*, a tabret: *m*. *Bedonner*, to play vpon the drumme. **1611** COTGRAVE Fr→E *Bedon*: *m*. A

Tabret; *Bedonner.* To play vpon a taber. **1688** MIEGE-COTGRAVE FR→E *Bedon,* (m.) *sorte de petit Tambour,* a Tabret, or little Drum.

beemol *see* b molle
1611 COTGRAVE *Bemol.* B flat; (a tearme of Musicke;) *B. mol. B.* flat, in Musicke. **1656** BLOUNT (1st edn) *Beemol* (Fr.) the flat key in Musick. *Bac.* **1658** PHILLIPS (1st edn) *Beemot,* the flat key in musick. **1671** PHILLIPS (3rd edn) *Beemol,* the flat key in Musick. See Cliff [clef]. **1676** COLES *Bee-mol, French.* the Musick flat key. **1688** MIEGE-COTGRAVE FR→E *Bémol,* (m.) *Term de Musique,* a b flat (in Musick.) **1704** *Cocker's Engl. Dict.* (1st edn) *Beemol,* Flat Key in Musick.

bell *see* anzolo, campana, carillon, chime, clapper, cloche, copter, doppio, knell, martello, nola, præcoseralis, sally, sampogna, sance bell, scampanare, sing, soniolo, sonnaille, sonnette, timbestoets, timbre, tintinabulum, toll, tonabulum
1696 PHILLIPS (5th edn) *Bell,* ... Also a noisie Instrument of percussive Music, of cast Metal, hung up in Steeples to call the People to Church, and rung out upon all occasions of mourning and gladness. **1702** KERSEY *New Engl. Dict.* (1st edn) A *Bell,* (in several senses) § An *Alarum-bell.* A *Low-bell.* A *Passing-bell.* A *Bell-sounder.* **1706** KERSEY-PHILLIPS (6th edn) *Bell,* ... Also a well known Musical Instrument hung up in Church-Steeples. **1726** BAILEY *An Univ. Etymolog. Engl. Dict.* (3rd edn) A *Bell* (Bell of Bellan, *Sax.* to make a great Noise or Roar) a loud sounding Instrument or Vessel. **1728** CHAMBERS *Bell* ... [*see* Appendix] **1730** BAILEY *Dict. Britannicum* (1st edn) *Bell* (of bell, bellan, *Sax.* to roar) a musical instrument or loud sounding vessel of metal, well known. *Bells,* are proclaimers of joyful solemnities, and are commonly affixed to Churches, where, besides their use for the service [of] God, by calling people to it, they are by some suppos'd to have a virtue to dispel storms and tempests which some attribute to their breaking the air by their sound; but others will have it to be inherent to their being blessed. They were first ordained to call people together in the year 603. *Bells* (bell, *Sax.*) the first harmonious ring of bells that was completed in *England* was at *Croyland* abbey; for *Turketule,* abbot of that place, having caused a bell of prodigious largeness to be made, which he called *Guthlac; Egel* succeeding him, did about the year 976. add two large ones, called *Bartholomew* and *Bertelin,* and also two mean ones, call'd *Turketule* and *Tolwin,* and also two little ones called *Pega* and *Bega,* being seven, which being made of proportional sizes, made together a most delightful harmony not to be equall'd in the whole kingdom. **1735** DEFOE A *Bell,* a loud sounding Instrument hung in the Steeple of Churches. **1737** BAILEY *The Univ. Etymolog. Engl. Dict.* (3rd edn, vol. 2) *Bells* .... The sound of bells plac'd on a plain may be heard further than those on hills, and those in vallies, farther than on plains, the reason of which is not difficult to be assign'd, because the higher the sonorous body is, the rarer is the medium (*i.e.* the air) and consequently it receives the less impulse, and the vehicle is the less proper to convey it to a distance. ¶ The city of *Nankin* in *China,* has been famous for its bells, one of which is 12 foot high, and computed to weigh 50000 pounds. And at *Pekin,* farther *Le Compte* says, there are seven bells, each of which weighs 120000 pounds; but the sounds of them are very poor, being struck with a wooden clapper. **1737** DYCHE-PARDON (2nd edn) *Bell* (S.) a musical Instrument made of Metal, appropriated to many Uses, and consequently of many Sizes; the larger Sort are hung in the Steeples of Churches, and chimed or rung to call the People to Church, and to celebrate Festivals both religious and civil; those Bells are observed to be heard at the greatest Distance that are rung in a Valley, and that the next farthest are, those placed upon a Plain, and those heard at the least Distance upon a Hill.

bell foundry
1728 CHAMBERS *Bell Foundry, or the Manner of casting Bells.* ¶ What has been hitherto shewn of the Casting of Statues, holds, in proportion, of the Casting of Bells: All that there is particular in these latter, is as follows. ¶ First, then, the Metal is different; there being no Tin in the Metal of Statues; but no less than a Fifth Part in that of Bells. Secondly, the Dimensions of the Mould, or Core, and the Wax of Bells, especially if it be a Ring of several Bells that is to be cast, are not left to Chance, or the Caprice of the Workman; but must be measur'd on a kind of Scale, or Diapason, which gives the Height, Aperture, and Thickness necessary for the several Tones required. ¶ It need not be added, that 'tis on the Wax, that the several Mouldings, and other Ornaments and Inscriptions to be represented in Relievo on the Outside of the Bell, are form'd. ¶ The Clapper, or Tongue, is not properly a part of the Bell, but is furnish'd from other Hands. ¶ In *Europe,* it is usually of Iron, with a large Head at the Extreme,

and is suspended in the Middle of the Bell. In *China* it is only a huge wooden Mallet, struck by Force of Arm against the Bell: Whence they can have but little of that Concordancy so much admi[r]'d in some of our Rings of Bell. The *Chinese* have an extraordinary way of increasing the Sound of their Bells, *viz.* by leaving a Hole under the Canon; which our *Bell Founders* would reckon a Defect. ¶ The Proportions of our Bells differ very much from those of the *Chinese*. In ours, the modern Proportions are to make the Diameter fifteen times the Thickness of the Ledge, and twelve times the Height.

bellicum

1565 COOPER L→E *Bellicum, Substantiuum. Liu.* The sowne of the trumpette warnyng to battayle. **1587** THOMAS L→E *Bellicum, ci, n.g.* The sound of a trumpet, when they blow to the battaile, or alarum. § *Bellicum canere.* To blowe to the battaile: **1589** RIDER L→E *Bellicum, classicum, n.* The sounde of the trumpet when they blowe to the battle, or alarum.

bellows *see* souffler

1737 DYCHE-PARDON (2nd edn) *Bellows* (S.) an Instrument to blow, or convey Wind with ... [such as those] causing the Pipes of an Organ, Bagpipe, &c. to speak, &c.

belly *see* soundboard, table, testudo

1696 PHILLIPS (5th edn) *Belly*, ... the belly of a Lute. **1737** DYCHE-PARDON (2nd edn) *Belly* (S.) ... also the wide or hollow Part of several musical Instruments, as, of Lutes, Violins, &c.

1726-8 NORTH Theory of Sounds BL Add. 32535, f. 148v That part of the Instrument upon wch the tension of the String directly bears, wch is called the belly, and by ye Interposition of the bridg, receives the tremuli from the string ...

bemes

1658 PHILLIPS (1st edn) *Bemes*, (old word) trumpets. **1676** COLES *Bemes, Old word.* trumpets. **1740** BAILEY *An Univ. Etymolog. Engl. Dict.* (9th edn) *Bemes*, Trumpets. *O.*

bene placito *see* ad libitum

1724 [PEPUSCH] *Short Explic. of Foreign Words in Mus. Bks.* (p. 16) *Bene Placito*, if you please, or if you will. **1726** BAILEY *An Univ. Etymolog. Engl. Dict.* (3rd edn) *Bene Placito* (in *Musick Books*) signifies, If you please, or, if you will. *L.*

1731 PRELLEUR *Modern Musick-Master* (Dictionary, p. 1) *Abene Placito*, at pleasure. (Dictionary, p. 2) *Bene Placito*, v. A *Bene Placito*

béquarre *see* b quarre

1611 COTGRAVE *Bequarre*, b, sharpe, (a terme of Musicke.) *B carre.* B sharpe (in Musicke.) § *De b carre en b mol: Prov.* Inconstantly, or uncertainely; from one subject to another. **1688** MIEGE-COTGRAVE Fr→E *Béquarre*, (m.) *Terme de Musique*, a b sharpe (in Musick.)

berlingozzo

1598 FLORIO It→E *Berlingozzo*, ... a dronken song, a threemens song. **1611** FLORIO It→E *Berlingozzo*, a kind of simnel or sugar bread. Also a drunken or three mens song. **1659** TORRIANO-FLORIO It→E *Berlingotto, Berlingozzo*, ... also an alehouse song, or rather a drunken, or three mens song

biffara

1598 FLORIO It→E *Biffara*, a fidle or croude. *Biffaro*, a fidler, a crouder, a minstrell. **1611** FLORIO It→E *Biffara*, a fidle, a croud. *Biffare*, to fidle, to croud. *Biffaro*, a fidler, a minstrell. **1659** TORRIANO-FLORIO It→E *Biffara*, any croud or fiddle *Biffare*, to fiddle. *Biffero*, a Fidler, a Minstrel.

binary measure *see* measure

1728 CHAMBERS *Binary Measure*, in Musick, is that wherein you beat equally, or the Time of Rising is equal to that of Falling. See *Time.* **1730** BAILEY *Dict. Britannicum* (1st edn) *Binary Measure* (in *Musick*) is a measure wherein you beat equally, or the time of rising is equal to that of falling. **1737** DYCHE-PARDON (2nd edn) *Binary Measure* (S.) in *Musick*, that which is beat equally up and down.

binding *see* cadence, syncopation, syncope

binding descant

1597 MORLEY *Plaine and Easie Introdvction* (p. 76) [marginalia: 'Binding descant'] *Phi.* You sing two plainesong notes for one in the descant, which I thought you might not haue done, except at a close. ¶ *Ma.* That is the best kinde of descant, so it bee not too much vsed in one song, and it is commonlie called binding descant ...

[birdsong] *see* cacabo, cantar, cantillo, chanter, chirp, coccism, cuccoueggiare, garrire, gazouiller, gringoter, meditor, minurio, querulous, ramager, record, rossignoler, tintin, tirelire, trutilare, verno, warble

biscantare

1598 FLORIO It→E *Biscantare,* to sing and sing againe. **1611** FLORIO It→E *Biscantare,* to sing and sing againe.

bischero

1550 THOMAS It→E *Bischeri,* the Lute pynnes. **1598** FLORIO It→E *Bisciere,* ... Also a pin or peg of a lute: the key of a virginall. **1611** FLORIO It→E *Bischeri,* lute pins or pegs, virginall keies **1659** TORRIANO-FLORIO It→E *Bischero, Bischeri,* the pins, or peggs of any instrument, namely of a Lute, the keyes, or jacks of Virginals

biumbe

1598 FLORIO It→E *Biumbe,* a kinde of pipe, crowd or fiddle. **1611** FLORIO It→E *Biumbe,* a kind of croud or fidle.

blanche *see* minim

1688 MIEGE-COTGRAVE Fr→E *Blanche (Subst.) Note de Musique qui a une queüe avec un peu de blanc à la tête,* a minum.

blind harper

1737 BAILEY *The Univ. Etymolog. Engl. Dict.* (3rd edn, vol. 2, cant section) *Blind-Harpers,* Canters, who counterfeit Blindness, strowl about with Harps, Fiddles, Bagpipes, *&c.* led by a Dog or Boy. **1737** DYCHE-PARDON (2nd edn) *Blind-harpers* (S.) a canting Name for those Impostors that pretend to be blind, and go about stroling with Fiddles, or pretend to beg, being led by a Boy or a Dog.

blur *see* bombus, clang, grailler

1731 KERSEY *New Engl. Dict.* (3rd edn) To *Blur a Trumpet,* to Sound it harsh. **1736** BAILEY *Dict. Britannicum* (2nd edn) To *Blurr* a *Trumpet,* to make a hoarse jarring Sound.

b mi

1678 PHILLIPS (4th edn) *B. mi,* the third note ascending in each of the three Septenaries of the *Gam ut,* or scale of Musick, and in the lowest cliff answers to the *Greek* ὑπατη ὑπατων in the next to τριτη συνεμμενων, in the highest to τριτη υπερβολαιων **1696** PHILLIPS (5th edn) *B Mi,* the third Note in the scale of Music from Gammut. *B mi* is sharp, and is half a Tone from the Note above it. *B fa* is flat, and is a whole Tone from the Note above it. **1706** KERSEY-PHILLIPS (6th edn) *B-mi,* the third Note in the *Gam-ut,* or Scale of Musick.

b molle *see* beemol, fictitious note, properchant

1597 MORLEY *Plaine and Easie Introdvction* (p. 5) *Phi.* What is *b molle*? ¶ *Ma.* It is a propertie of singing, wherein *fa* must alwaies be song in *b fa* ♮ *mi,* and is when the *vt* is in *F fa vt.* **1667** SIMPSON *Compendium of Practical Musick* (pp. 112-13) From these six Notes, *Vt, Re, Mi, Fa, Sol, La,* did arise three properties of Singing; which they named *B Quarre, B Molle,* and *Properchant* or *Naturall... B Molle* was when they sung *fa* in *B.* **1721** MALCOLM *Treatise of Musick* (p. 567) That what [in former times] they called the Series of *b molle,* was no more than this, That because the *8ve f* had a *4th* above at *b, excessive* by a *Semitone,* and consequently the *8ve b* had a *5th* above as much deficient, therefore this artificial Note *b flat* or ♭, served them to transpose their *Modes* to the Distance of a *4th* or *5th,* above or below; ... therefore to transpose from the Series of *b* natural to *b molle* we ascend a *4th* or descend a *5th;* and contrarily from *b molle* to the other: This is the whole Mystery; but they never speak of the other Transpositions that may be made by other artificial Notes. **1731** PRELLEUR *Modern Musick-Master* ('A Brief History of Musick', p. 11) ... Guido Aretinus finding it absolutely necessary for the Space between *A* and *B* to be divided into two Semitones took in the *Trite Synemenon* of the Greeks and called it *B-molle,* or *B-flat;* and every time this Note was to be used he placed a ♭ befor[e] it to shew that y[e] Voice ought to rise but a Semitone from *A.*

bocciuolo

1598 FLORIO It→E *Bocciuolo,* ... Also that part of a horne, of a cornet or trumpet, which is put to ones mouth to winde or sownde him. **1611** FLORIO It→E *Bocciuolo,* ... Also that part of a horne, of a cornet, or of a trumpet which is put to the mouth. **1659** TORRIANO-FLORIO It→E *Bocciuolo, Bocciolo,* ... also that part of a cornet, of a trumpet, of a horn, of a pipe, or of a flute, or of a sack-but, that is put into the mouth.

Boethius *see* apotome, chroma, chromatic, comma, diaschisma, harmonic music, harmony of the spheres, interval, lyre, mode, music, octochordon, schism, semitone, tune

bombardo
1724 [PEPUSCH] *Short Explic. of Foreign Words in Mus. Bks.* (p. 16) *Bombardo*, is an Instrument of Musick, much the same as our Bassoon, or Bass to a Hautboy. **1726** BAILEY *An Univ. Etymolog. Engl. Dict.* (3rd edn) *Bombardo* (in *Musick Books*) is an Instrument of Musick, much the same as our Bassoon, or Bass to a Hautboy. *Ital.*

bombus *see* blur, clang, grailler, rombo
1706 KERSEY-PHILLIPS (6th edn) *Bombus, (Gr.)* ... the hoarse Sound, or Blur of a Trumpet. **1708** KERSEY *Dict. Anglo-Brit.* (1st edn) *Bombus, (G.)* ... the hoarse Sound, or Blur of a Trumpet.

book of psalms *see* psalter
1619 WITHER *Preparation to the Psalter* (p. 45) *Beda* saith, that those holy Songs [the psalms] are called the Booke of the Soliloquies of *Dauid*: and it is tearmed so, because either *Dauid* speakes alone to God in Spirit and contemplation, or else because hee introduceth Christ speaking alone to God the Father, or because he bringeth in the mysticall body of the faithfull, speaking to the Father, or to their Head & Redeemer. For indeed, there are many things that can be appropriated to none other, but vnto our Sauiour: yea, S. *Augustine* saith, that all and euery part of them doe some way concerne him. ¶ These *Odes* [psalms] are also stiled, The booke of the *Hymns* of *Dauid*, because they are Ioyfull thanksgiuings to bee sung to God for the benefits receiued of him, especially in that worke of our Redemption. But amongst vs at this day, they are vsually called the Booke of the *Psalms*: that is, a holy Booke of *Verses*, or *Songs*, expressing the Mysteries contayned in holy Scriptures, and composed to bee sung to the honour of God, either with the harmony of voyces onely, or with Instruments of Musicke also. For some were principally to be sung, others to bee played and sung ... But this last name we haue receiued Authority for, from our Sauiour Christ and his Apostles, who haue so tearmed it; as is manifest in diuers places of the new Testament: and therefore, as one saith, wee neither according to the custome of the Iewes, call them fiue Bookes, nor simply the *Psalmes* of *Dauid*; but according to the Apostolicall dignity, the Booke of the *Psalmes*.

borée *see* bourrée

bosinnus *see* bozina, busine
1676 COLES *Bosinnus*, a rude wind-instrument.

bouffons *see* interlude, minstrel, opera
1593 HOLLYBAND § *Danser les Bouffons*, to daunce a morris daunce with belles about the legges. **1611** COTGRAVE Fr→E § *Danser les buffons.* To daunce a morris. **1650** HOWELL-COTGRAVE Fr→E § *Danser les buffons.* To dance a morris.

bourdon *see* burden

bourrée *see* motion, repeat
1688 MIEGE-COTGRAVE Fr→E *Bourrée*, (f.) ... a merry kind of Dance. **1706** KERSEY-PHILLIPS (6th edn) *Boree*, a kind of *French* Dance. **1708** KERSEY *Dict. Anglo-Brit.* (1st edn) *Boree*, a kind of *French* Dance. **1724** [PEPUSCH] *Short Explic. of Foreign Words in Mus. Bks.* (p. 16) *Bouree*, is the Name of a *French* Dance, or the Tune or Air belonging thereunto. **1728** CHAMBERS *Boree*, or *Bouree*, a kind of Dance, compos'd of three Steps join'd together with two Motions; and begun with a Crotchet, rising. The first Couplet contains twice four Measures, and the second twice eight. It consists of a balance Step and a Coupee: 'Tis suppos'd to come from *Auvergne*. **1730** BAILEY *Dict. Britannicum* (1st edn) *Boree*, a sort of *French* dance. **1737** DYCHE-PARDON (2nd edn) *Boree* (S.) a Sort of Dance, composed of three Steps joined together with two Motions, and begun with a Crochet [sic] rising; the first Couplet contains four Measures, and the second twice eight; it consists of a Balance, Step, and a Coupee.

bow *see* archet, archetto, arco, arculus, coup, dædala, fiddle stick, fusano, plectrum, wrest
1702 KERSEY *New Engl. Dict.* (1st edn) The *Bow* of a musical instrument. **1731** KERSEY *New Engl. Dict.* (3rd edn) A *Bow*, to shoot Arrows with, or to play upon a Musical Instrument. **1736** BAILEY *Dict. Britannicum* (2nd edn) The *Bow* (or Stick) to play upon a Violin.

boyautier
1688 MIEGE-COTGRAVE Fr→E *Boyautier*, (m.) *Artisan qui fait des Cordes à boyaux*, one that makes strings for musical Instruments, &c.

bozina *see* bosinnus, buccina, busine, busone
1599 MINSHEU-PERCYVALL Sp→E *Bozina*, f. a trumpet, a cornet, a shepherds pipe. *Bozinero*, m. a trumpeter, a piper.

b quarre *see* béquarre, properchant
1597 MORLEY *Plaine and Easie Introdvction* (p. 4) *Phi*. What is *b quarre*? ¶ *Ma*. It is a propertie of singing, wherein *mi* is alwaies song in *b fa* ♮ *mi*, and is alwayes when you sing *vt* in *Gam vt*. **1667** SIMPSON *Compendium of Practical Musick* (p. 112) From these six Notes, *Vt, Re, Mi, Fa, Sol, La*, did arise three properties of Singing; which they named *B Quarre, B Molle*, and *Properchant* or *Naturall*. *B Quarre*, was when they Sung *Mi* in *B*; that Cliff being then made of a Square form thus ♮ and set at the beginning of the Lines ...

braied
1658 PHILLIPS (1st edn) *Brayd*, (old word) to break out. **1676** COLES *Braied, Old word*. blew (with a trumpet, &c.)

brando *see* branle
1611 FLORIO It→E *Brando*, ... Also a french dance called a bransel or braule. **1659** TORRIANO-FLORIO It→E *Brando*, ... also a French dance, called a *Bransle*.

brandon
1688 MIEGE-COTGRAVE Fr→E *Brandon* (m.) a lightening ... the noise of the Trumpet

branle, bransle *see* brando, brawl, tripode
1593 HOLLYBAND Fr→E § *Danser vn bransle*, to daunce: *m*. **1598** FLORIO It→E *Branla*, a french dance called a bransle. **1611** COTGRAVE Fr→E *Bransle: m*. ... a brawle, or daunce, wherein many (men, and women) holding by the hands sometimes in a ring, and otherwhiles at length, moue all together. § *Bransle du bouquet*. The nosegay daunce, or kissing daunce (for there is much kissing in it.) **1688** MIEGE-COTGRAVE Fr→E *Branle*, (m.) motion; brawl, a sort of Dance; **1721** BAILEY *An Univ. Etymolog. Engl. Dict*. (1st edn) *Bransles*, Brawls. *Spencer*.

1597 MORLEY *Plaine and Easie Introdvction* (p. 181) ... Like vnto this [the alman] is the French *bransle* (which they cal *bransle simple*) which goeth somwhat rounder in time then this, otherwise the measure is all one. The *bransle de poictou* or *bransle double* is more quick in time, (as being in a rounde Tripla) but the straine is longer, containing most vsually twelue whole strokes. **1728** NORTH Musicall Grammarian (*C-K MG* f. 135) ... But during the first years of Charles 2d all musick affected by the beau-mond run into the French way, and the rather, becaus at that time the master of the court musick in France, whose name was Babtista (an Itallian Frenchifyed) had influenced the French style by infusing a great portion of the Italian harmony into it; whereby the ayre was exceedingly improved. The manner was theatricall, and the setts of lessons composed, called branles (as I take it) or braules, that is beginning with an entry, and then courants etc.

brawl *see* branle
1658 PHILLIPS (1st edn) *Brawl*, a kind of dance, from the *French* word Bransler, to move gently up and down. **1676** COLES *Brawl, French*. a kind of dance. **1696** PHILLIPS (5th edn) *Brawl*, a kind of Dance, wherewith all Balls are generally begun, wherein the persons dance in a ring, and not forward, continually pulling and shaking one another. **1702** KERSEY *New Engl. Dict*. (1st edn) The *Brawls*, a kind of dance. **1706** KERSEY-PHILLIPS (6th edn) *Brawl*, ... Also a kind of Dance, in which several Persons dance together in a Ring, holding one another by the Hand. **1708** KERSEY *Dict. Anglo-Brit*. (1st edn) *Brawl*, ... Also a kind of Dance, in which several Persons dance together in a Ring. **1721** BAILEY *An Univ. Etymolog. Engl. Dict*. (1st edn) *A Brawl*, ... Also a kind of Dance. **1730** BAILEY *Dict. Britannicum* (1st edn) *Brawl* ... also a dance.

1676 MACE *Musick's Monument* (p. 236) ... observe with what a *Wonderful Swiftness* They now run over their *Brave New Ayres*; and with what *High-Priz'd Noise, viz*. 10, or 20 *Violins*, &c. as I said before, to a *Some-Single-Soul'd Ayre*; it may be of 2 or 3 *Parts*, or some *Coranto, Serabrand*, or *Brawle*, (as the *New-Fashion'd-Word* is) and such like *Stuff*, seldom any other; which is rather fit to make a Mans *Ears Glow*, and fill his *Brains full of Frisks*, &c... **c.1726** NORTH Musicall Gramarian BL Add. 32533, f. 171v But Now to finish this litle History, I must take a New rise from the Restauration of K. Cha. 2. he had lived some considerable time abroad, when the french Musick was In Request, w[ch] consisted of an Entry (perhaps) and then Brawles, as they were called, that is motiue aires, and Dances; ...

breaking *see* andante, arpeggio, diminution, division, flourish, transition

1706 KERSEY-PHILLIPS (6th edn) § *Breaking of a Note*, a Term in *Musick*. See *Transition*.

1659 SIMPSON *Division-Violist* (p. 21) *Breaking the Ground*, is the *dividing its Notes into more diminute Notes*: As for *Example*; a *Semibreve* may be broken, into Two *Minims*, Four *Crochets*, Eight *Quavers*, Sixteen *Semiquavers*, *&c*. § (p. 22) [*re* ways of breaking a ground] Thirdly, when those *Minutes*, are imployed, in making a Transition to the ensuing *Note*; commonly called *Breaking one Note to another*: ... **1667** SIMPSON *Compendium of Practical Musick* (p. 65) One thing yet remains, very necessary (sometimes) in Composition: and that is, to make smooth or sweeten the roughness of a Leap, by a graduall Transition to the Note next following, which is commonly called the *Breaking of a Note*. **1728** NORTH Musicall Grammarian (C-K *MG* f. 47) ... there is a very great difference in the composition upon quick notes, and slow; which gives occasion to distinguish passing, from holding, notes. The latter, as in the foregoing instances, dwelling long on the same tones, require accords to every note, but if they move swift, as in passing, many will fall under one accord, without altering, which is the case of most devisions, and what Mr. Sympson calls breaking of notes on a ground; ...

breve *see* alla breve

1598 FLORIO It→E *Breue*, ... a briefe in musike. **1611** FLORIO It→E *Breue*, ... Also a briefe in Musicke. **1671** PHILLIPS (3rd edn) A *Brief*, or *Breve*, ... Also a term in musick, being such a measure of musical quantity, as contains two stroakes of time down and as many up, and is thus Charactered (ㅍ) **1676** COLES *Brief*, as *Breve*, also two full times (in Musick.) **1706** KERSEY-PHILLIPS (6th edn) *Breve*, ... Also a Musical Note, which in common Time, contains two *Semibreves*, four *Minims*, eight *Crotchets*, &c. **1708** KERSEY *Dict. Anglo-Brit.* (1st edn) *A Brief*, (in *Musick*) is such a Measure of Quantity as contains two Strokes down in beating time, and as many up. **1728** CHAMBERS *Breve*, in Musick, is a Note or Character of Time, form'd like a Square, without any Tail; and equivalent to two *Measures*, or *Minims*. See *Characters of Musick*. **1730** BAILEY *Dict. Britannicum* (1st edn) *Breve* (in *Musick*) a note or character of time in the form of a diamond square, without any tail, and equivalent to two measures or minims. **1737** DYCHE-PARDON (2nd edn) *Breve* (S.) in *Musick*, is a long Note of the Quantity of two Bars, or common Measures, and now commonly wrote with the character O. *Brief* (S.) ... also the Name of a Measure of Time in Musick, which is the longest expressed by a single Note.

after 1517 ANON. Art of Mvsic BL Add. 4911, f. 1v *The brewe* is a figur with one quadrat bodie formit w[t] absence of the virgle. **1609** DOWLAND-ORNITHOPARCUS *Micrologvs* (p. 39) A *Breefe* is a Figure, which hath a body foure-square, and wants a tayle. **1617-24** FLUDD *Utriusque Cosmi Maioris: De Templo Musicæ* (p. 191) *Brevis* est dimidia pars longæ. **1731** PRELLEUR *Modern Musick-Master* (Dictionary, p. 2) *Breve*, is ye Name of a Note which is in value as long as two Semibreve.

bridal *see* marriage music

1706 KERSEY-PHILLIPS (6th edn) *Bridal*, belonging to a Bride; as *A Bridal Bed*, a *Bridal Song*, &c.

bridge *see* chevalet, magade, scagnello

1736 BAILEY *Dict. Britannicum* (2nd edn) *The Bridge* (or Supporter of the Strings) in a Lute, and other String-Instruments.

brillante *see* allegro

1598 FLORIO It→E *Brillante*, sparkling, twinkling, twiling, quauering. *Brillare*, to twinkle, to sparkle, to quauer **1611** FLORIO It→E *Brillante*, ... Also quavering. *Brillare*, to spangle, to twinkle. Also to quauer. **1724** [PEPUSCH] *Short Explic. of Foreign Words in Mus. Bks.* (p. 16) *Brillante*, is to play in a brisk, lively Manner. **1726** BAILEY *An Univ. Etymolog. Engl. Dict.* (3rd edn) *Brillante* (in *Musick Books*) signifies to play in a brisk lively manner.

1731 PRELLEUR *Modern Musick-Master* (Dictionary, p. 2) *Brillante*, Brisk, Airy, Lively, &c.

brother of the string

1737 BAILEY *The Univ. Etymolog. Engl. Dict.* (3rd edn, vol. 2, cant section) *Brother of the String*, a Fidler, or Harper.

buccina *see* aes, bosinnus, bozina, busine

1500 *Ortus Vocabulorum* L→E Buccina e. a trompe. f.p. Buccicen [sic] nis. pe. cor. i. cum buccina canens Buccineus a. um. pti. i. clamor buccine. o.s. Buccino as. i. cum buccina sonare. to blow in a trompe. n.p. Buccinus ni. i. clamor buccine. a trompere **1538** ELYOT L→E *Buccina*, a trumpette. *Buccino, aui, are*, to blowe a trumpette. *Buccinum*, the sowne of a trumpette. **1552** HULOET L→E *Buccino. as, signa dare, uel facere militibus*. Blowe a trumpet in warres. *Buccinum. ni* Sounde of a trumpet, or of. s.

Cornelius shell, or suche like. **1565** COOPER L→E *Buccina. Colum. Var.* A swineheardes horne. *Buccina, pen. corr. Ouid.* A trumpette. *Búccino, búccinas, pen cor. buccinâre. Var.* To blow a trumpette: § *Buccina aerem concipit. Ouid.* The trumpette is blowen or gathereth breath. **1587** THOMAS L→E *Buccina, æ, f.g.* A trumpet vsed in warre: also a cowheards, or swineheards horne. *Buccino, as, Var.* To sound a trumpet, to blowe a horne: to publish or spread abroad. *Buccinum, ni, n.g. Plin.* A trumpet or horne: **1589** RIDER L→E *Buccino Cornicino.* To winde, or blow a Horne. *Buccinum, n. & Buccina, f.* A Horne, or trumpet. § *Buccino clango, tubicino, tuba canere, classico.* To sound a Trumpet. *Signum dare buccina, classicum canere.* To sounde the alarum on the trumpet. **1598** FLORIO It→E *Bucina,* a hornepipe. Also a sordine trumpet. *Bucinare,* ... Also to clange or blow out as a trumpet, ... Also to blow a pipe. **1611** COTGRAVE Fr→E *Buccine: f.* A Cornet, or Trumpet for the warres; **1611** FLORIO It→E *Bucina,* a smale low voice. Also a sordin for a trumpet. Also a horne-pipe. *Bucinamento,* ... Also a clang of a trumpet. *Bucinare,* to clang as a trumpet. Also to pipe. **1650** HOWELL-COTGRAVE Fr→E † *Buccine: f.* A Cornet, or Trumpet for the warres; also, the horne of a cowheard, or swineheard; **1659** TORRIANO-FLORIO It→E *Buccina, bucina,* ... also a sourdin for a trumpet; also a loud sounding Cornet or Horn-pipe *Buccinamento, Buccinata, Bucinamento,* ... also a sounding with a sourdin. *Buccinare, Bucinare,* ... also to sound a trumpet with a sourdin. **1706** KERSEY-PHILLIPS (6th edn) *Buccinum,* a Trumpet, or Horn to blow with; **1728** CHAMBERS *Buccina,* an antient Military, or rather Musical Instrument, used in War. 'Tis usually taken for a kind of Trumpet; which Opinion *Festus* confirms, by defining it a crooked Horn, plaid on like a Trumpet. *Vegetius* also observes, that the *Buccina* was bent into a Circle; in which it differ'd from a Trumpet, *Tuba. Varro* adds, they were call'd Horns, *Cornua,* because originally made of the Horns of Cattel; as is still done among some People. *Servius* seems to say, that they were at first made of Goats Horns: And the Scriptures call the Instrument us'd, both in War and in the Temple, *Keren Jobal,* Rams Horns; and *Saphoroth Haijobelim, Buccinæ,* of Rams. The Musical Instruments us'd in a Military March, are *Buccinæ,* Trumpets, Lituus, Clarions, Cornets, Fifes, Drums, Tymbals, *&c.* which see. The Marine *Buccinæ,* given by Poets and Painters to Tritons and Sea-Gods, are Shells twisted in form of Snails. The Word comes from *Bucca,* Mouth; because plaid on by the Mouth.

1582 *Batman vppon Bartholome* (p. 423) *Bvccina* hath that name, as it were, *Vocina parua,* and is a trumpet of horne, of tree, or of brasse, & was blowen against enimies in old time: ... *Propertius* speaketh heerof, & saith. ¶ *Buccina cogebat priscos, ad Arma Quirites:* ¶ *Buccina* made the old *Quirites* aray themselues, namelye in armour. The voyce of such a trumpet, is called *Buccinum,* as he sayth.

buccinator *see* aeneator, cornicen
1565 COOPER L→E *Buccinâtor, pen. prod. Verbale. Cæs.* A trompettour: **1587** THOMAS L→E *Buccinator, oris, m.g. verb. à buccino.* He that soundeth a trumpet or bloweth a horne, a trumpeter, a publisher, a praiser. **1589** RIDER L→E *Buccinator, tubicen, liticen, buccinus, æneator, classiarus, symphonicus, m.* A trumpeter, he that soundeth the trumpet. **1611** COTGRAVE Fr→E *Buccinateur: m.* A Trumpeter. **1623** COCKERAM *Buccinate.* To blow a trumpet. *Buccinate.* to Blowe a trumpet. **1650** HOWELL-COTGRAVE Fr→E † *Buccinateur: m.* A Trumpeter. **1656** BLOUNT (1st edn) *Buccinate (buccino)* to blow or sound a Trumpet or Horn **1658** PHILLIPS (1st edn) *Buccinate,* (Lat.) to blow a Trumpet. **1676** COLES *Buccinate, Latin.* sound a trumpet. **1706** KERSEY-PHILLIPS (6th edn) *Buccinator, (Lat.)* a Trumpeter, one that sounds a Trumpet, or Winds a Horn; **1707** *Gloss. Angl. Nova* (1st edn) *Buccinate,* (Lat.) to blow a Trumpet. **1730** BAILEY *Dict. Britannicum* (1st edn) *Buccinator* (with *Anatomists*) a round circular muscle of the cheeks ... It is called Buccinator from its forcing out the breath of trumpeters.

bucolick *see* eclogue
1500 *Ortus Vocabulorum* L→E Bucolica orum. i. liber boum. vnde bucolicum carmen. i. pastorale. n.s. **1538** ELYOT L→E § *Bucolicum carmen,* a poeme made of herdmen. **1598** FLORIO It→E *Buccolica,* heardmens songs. **1611** FLORIO It→E *Buccolica,* a heardsmans song. **1656** BLOUNT (1st edn) *Bucolicks (bucolica)* pastoral songs, or songs of Heardsmen. **1658** PHILLIPS (1st edn) *Bucoliks,* (Greek) pastoral songs. **1659** TORRIANO-FLORIO It→E *Buccolica, Bucolica,* a heardsmans tale or song **1676** COLES *Bucolicks, Greek.* pastoral songs. **1678** PHILLIPS (4th edn) *Bucolicks, (Greek)* Pastoral Songs, or Poems, such as Virgils Eclogues, and *Theocritus* his *Idyls.* **1704** HARRIS *Bucolicks,* are Pastoral Songs or Poems, such as the *Eclogues* of *Virgil,* and the *Idyls* of *Theocritus..* **1706** KERSEY-PHILLIPS (6th

edn) *Bucolicks, (Gr.)* Pastoral Songs, or Poems, in which Herdsmen and Country-Swains are represented discoursing together about their Love-intrigues, or other Concerns, such as *Virgil's* Eclogues, and *Theocritus's* Idyls. **1708** KERSEY *Dict. Anglo-Brit.* (1st edn) *Bucolicks, (G.)* Pastoral Songs, or Poems, in which Herdsmen and Country-Swains are represented discoursing together.

bugle *see* cor, cornette, cornetto, cornezuela, cornicello, corno, hutchet

1616 BULLOKAR *Bugle.* The same that buffe is: sometime a blacke horne. **1623** COCKERAM *Bugle.* A little blacke horne. **1702** KERSEY *New Engl. Dict.* (1st edn) A *Bugle-horn.* **1704** *Cocker's Engl. Dict.* (1st edn) *Bugle,* a black horn. **1706** KERSEY-PHILLIPS (6th edn) *Bugle-horn,* a sort of Hunting-horn. **1708** KERSEY *Dict. Anglo-Brit.* (1st edn) *Bugle-horn,* a sort of Hunting-horn. **1721** BAILEY *An Univ. Etymolog. Engl. Dict.* (1st edn) *A Bugle Horn,* (of *Bucula* and *Horn*) a sort of Hunting Horn. **1730** BAILEY *Dict. Britannicum* (1st edn) *Bugle horn* (of *bucula* an heifer, *L.* and horn) a sort of hunting horn. **1737** DYCHE-PARDON (2nd edn) *Bugle* (S.) ... also a hunting Horn.

bunda

1500 *Ortus Vocabulorum* L→E Bunda e. sonus tube vel tympani. f.p. bundus. i. sonus tympani. m.s.

burden *see* contre, faburden, falso bordone, faux-bourdon, filibustacchina, intercalarity, lerelot, lire-liron, mimo subservire, quilio, refrain, refret, reprise, tornello

1550 THOMAS It→E *Bordone,* ... It signifieth also the base in singyng or sound of musike. **1552** HULOET L→E *Burdo. onis* Muset. **1598** FLORIO It→E *Bordone,* ... a tennor or keeping of time in musicke, the burden of any song: ... Also the second base string of any instrument. **1599** MINSHEU-PERCYVALL Sp→E *Bordon,* m. ... Also the great or base string of any instrument. § **Bordon de vihuela,* the great or base string of a viall. **1611** COTGRAVE Fr→E *Bourdon: m.* A Drone ... also, the drone of a Bagpipe; **1611** FLORIO It→E *Berdonali,* ... Also such as keep burdons of songs. *Bordone,* ... Also the burdon of a song, or a tenor and keeping of time in musicke. Also the second base string of any instrument. **1616** BULLOKAR *Burdon.* A deepe base. **1623** COCKERAM *Burden.* a deepe Base. *Burdon.* A deepe base. **1650** HOWELL-COTGRAVE Fr→E *Bourdonneur: m.* ... also, one that playes on a Bag-pipe. **1659** TORRIANO-FLORIO It→E *Bordone,* ... the second base-string of any instrument; also the burden of a song; also the keeping of due time in musick; also the drone of a bag-pipe, or any humming sound or noise § **Tenere il bordone,* to keep the burden of a song, to be still of one mind. **1676** COLES *Burden, French.* a deep base; **1702** KERSEY *New Engl. Dict.* (1st edn) The *Burden* of a song. **1704** *Cocker's Engl. Dict.* (1st edn) *Burden,* a deep base; **1726** BAILEY *An Univ. Etymolog. Engl. Dict.* (3rd edn) *Bourdon,* the Drone of a Bag-pipe. *Ch.* **1728** CHAMBERS *Burden,* the Drone or Base in some Musical Instruments, and the Pipe or Part that plays it; as in an Organ, a Bagpipe, *&c.* See *Drone.* Hence the *Burden* of a Song, *&c.* is that Part repeated at the End of each Stanza. The Word comes from the French *Bourdon,* a Staff; or a Pipe made in form of a Staff, imitating the gross murmurs of Bees or Drones. This is what the Antients call'd, *Proslambanomenos.* **1730** BAILEY *Dict. Britannicum* (1st edn) *Burden* (of *bourden,* Fr. a staff or a pipe in the form of a staff) in some musical instruments the drone or the base, and the pipe that plays it; hence that part of a song that is repeated at the end of every stanza, is called the burden of it. **1736** BAILEY *Dict. Britannicum* (2nd edn) The *Burden* (or Repetition of the latter Part) of a Song. **1737** DYCHE-PARDON (2nd edn) *Burden* or *Burthen* (S.) ... Sometimes it is used for the Theme or Subject upon which a Person writes, or the Chorus of a Song.

busciarella

1598 FLORIO It→E *Busciarella,* a reede, a cane, an oaten pipe. **1611** FLORIO It→E *Busciarella,* a reede, an oaten pipe.

busine *see* bosinnus, bozina, buccina

1593 HOLLYBAND Fr→E *Vne Buisine, f:* a little pipe to play. **1611** COTGRAVE Fr→E *Bouzine: f.* A rusticall Trumpet, or wind-instrument, made of piched barke. *Buisine: f.* A little pipe; *Busine: f.* ... also, a bagpipe; or as *Buzine. Buzine: f.* A bagpipe; or, a clownes trumpet; a clownish instrument, made of pitched barke, and sounding like a trumpet: *Gasc.* also, as *Busine.* **1650** HOWELL-COTGRAVE Fr→E † *Buisine; f.* A little pipe; † *Buysine.* as *Buisine.*

busone *see* bosinnus, bozina, buccina

1611 FLORIO It→E *Busone,* a great hole. Also a certaine winde instrument of Musike. **1659** TORRIANO-FLORIO It→E *Busone,* ... also the Drone of a Bag-pipe.

butta in sella *see* monta in sella, serra serra
1598 FLORIO It→E *Butta in sella,* a charge that trumpetters vse to sounde when they would haue men arme themselues and take horse. **1611** FLORIO It→E *Butta in sella,* a charge that trumpeters sound as a warning to take horse. **1659** TORRIANO-FLORIO It→E *Butta in sella,* a charge that trumpetters sound as a warning to leap into the saddle.

buxum *see* tuba
1565 COOPER L→E *Buxus, f.g. & Buxum, n.g. Virg.* Boxe: the boxe tree: a trumpette or pipe. § *Multifori tibia buxi. Ouid.* A boxen pipe. **1587** THOMAS L→E *Buxum, n.g. vel Buxus, xi, f g. Virg.* a trumpet or pipe

by by *see* falcinine, lallatio, lullaby
1721 BAILEY *An Univ. Etymolog. Engl. Dict.* (1st edn) *By By,* ... commonly Sung by Nurses to cause their Nurslings to fall asleep.

Byrd, William *see* countertenor

C

c
1728 CHAMBERS C .... In Musick, a Capital C denotes the highest Part in a thorough Bass.

cabinet organ
1696 PHILLIPS (5th edn) *Cabinet Organ,* a Portative Organ. **1706** KERSEY-PHILLIPS (6th edn) *Cabinet-organ,* a little Organ, that may be easily carry'd, or remov'd from one Place to another. **1708** KERSEY *Dict. Anglo-Brit.* (1st edn) *Cabinet-organ,* a little Orgau [sic], that may be easily carry'd, or remov'd from one Place to another. **1721** BAILEY *An Univ. Etymolog. Engl. Dict.* (1st edn) *Cabinet Organ,* a small portable organ. **1730** BAILEY *Dict. Britannicum* (1st edn) *Cabinet* [sic], a small portable organ.

cacabo
1587 THOMAS L→E *Cacabo, as, Ovid.* To call or sing like a partrich.

cacapensiere *see* scacciapensiere
1598 FLORIO It→E *Cacapensieri,* a kinde of croude, fiddle or kit. **1611** FLORIO It→E *Cacapensiere,* a kind of country croud or fiddle. Also a lasie thoughtles fellow.

cacophony
1589 RIDER L→E *Cacophonia, asymphonia, f.* A discord in musicke.

cadence *see* baulk, calata, close, double cadence, flying a cadence, half cadence, imperfect cadence, perfect cadence, semicadence, simple
1593 HOLLYBAND Fr→E § *Garder la Cadence en dansant,* to keepe measure in dancing. **1598** FLORIO It→E *Cadenza,* a cadence, a falling, a declining, a low note. **1611** COTGRAVE Fr→E *Cadence: f.* A cadence; a iust falling, round going, of words; a proportionable time, or euen measure, in any action, or sound. **1611** FLORIO It→E *Cadenza,* a cadence, a falling, a low note. **1616** BULLOKAR *Cadence.* The falling of the voice. **1623** COCKERAM *Cadence.* a Falling of the voyce. *Cadence.* The falling of the voyce. **1656** BLOUNT (1st edn) *Cadency, Cadence* (from *Cado*) a just falling, round going of words; a proportionable time or even measure in any action or sound. *Cotgr.* **1658** PHILLIPS (1st edn) *Cadence,* (Lat.) a just falling of the tone in a sentence, a descending of notes in musick. **1688** MIEGE-COTGRAVE Fr→E *Cadence,* (f.) cadence. § *Danser en cadence, observer en dansant la cadence de la Musique,* to mind the cadences of Musick in dancing. **1696** PHILLIPS (5th edn) A *Cadence* in Music, is a kind of Conclusion of the Song or piece of Instrumental Composition, which is made of all the parts in several places of every Piece, and divides it into Members and Periods. **1704** *Cocker's Engl. Dict.* (1st edn) *Cadence,* falling the voice. **1704** HARRIS *Cadence,* or *Close,* in Musick, is a kind of Conclusion of the Tune, which is made of all the Parts together, in divers places of any Key. **1706** KERSEY-PHILLIPS (6th edn) *Cadence,* (Lat.) ... In Musick, *Cadence* or *Close,* is a kind of Conclusion of the Tune which is made of all the Parts together in several Places of any Key. See *Close.* **1708** KERSEY *Dict. Anglo-Brit.* (1st edn) *Cadence, (L.)* ... In Musick, *Cadence* or *Close,* is a kind of Conclusion in the Tune, which is made of all the Parts together in several Places of any Key. **1728** CHAMBERS *Cadence,* according to the antient Musicians, is a Series of a certain Number of Musical Notes, in a certain Interval, which strikes the Ear agreeably; and especially at the Close of a

Song, Stanza, *&c.* A *Cadence* ordinarily consists of three Notes. There are three Kinds of *Cadences*: The principal, or final *Cadence*; usually consisting of a fourth and a fifth to make an *Octave*, as being the most excellent of Consonances: The Entry, or mediate, sometimes call'd the attendant *Cadence*; in regard the final one is always expected: and the dominant, or prevailing *Cadence*; so call'd, as being higher than either of the other: as the Mediate has its Name from its being in the middle, between the Dominant and Final. The modern Musicians make *Cadence* the Relation of two Notes sung together, as *ut* and *re*; and when the last of these Notes is follow'd with two Crotchets, the *Cadence* is said to be double. ¶ *Cadence*, in the modern Musick, may be defin'd, a certain Conclusion of a Song, or of the Parts thereof in divers Places of a Piece; which divide it, as it were, into so many Members or Periods. The *Cadence* is, when the Parts fall and terminate on a Chord or Note; the Ear seeming naturally to expect it. A *Cadence* is either perfect or imperfect: A perfect *Cadence*, is that which consists in two Notes, sung after each other, or by Degrees conjoin'd in each of the two Parts; 'tis call'd perfect, because it satisfies the Ear better than the other. The *Cadence* is imperfect, when its last Measure is not in Octave, nor in Unison, but in a Sixth or Third: As when the Bass, in lieu of descending a Fifth, only descends a Third; or when descending a Fifth, or, which is the same thing, ascending a Fourth, it makes an Octave with the Treble, in the first Measure, and a third Major with the Second: 'Tis call'd Imperfect, because the Ear does not acquiesce in this Conclusion, but expects the Continuation of the Song. The *Cadence* is said to be broke, when the Bass, in lieu of falling a Fifth, which the Ear expects, rises a Second, either Major or Minor. Every *Cadence* is in two Measures: Sometimes it is suspended; in which Case 'tis call'd a Repose, and only consists of one Measure: as when the two Parts stop at the Fifth, without finishing the *Cadence.* ¶ M. *Rousseau* distinguishes two kinds of *Cadence*, with regard to the Bass Viol: A *Cadence* with, and without a Rest. The *Cadence* with a Rest, is when the that stop is omitted. There are also simple *Cadences*, and double ones; the Double ones are various: The more Double are those made on a long Note; the less Double, those on a Short Note. The final *Cadence*, should always be preceded by a double one. The *Cadences* are always to be accommodated to the Character of the Air. The Word comes from *Cadencia*, fall; a *Cadence* being the Fall or Conclusion of a piece of Harmony; proper to terminate either the Whole, or a Part. Some Musicians call a *Shake* a *Cadence*; but that is to confound Terms. From this Musical *Cadence* arises ¶ *Cadences*, in Singing, are the same with Points and Virgula's in Discourse. The Singing-Masters say, the *Cadence* is a Gift of a Master, proper for making the Shakes delicate. When the Voice is harsh, the two Notes whereof the *Cadence* consists, must be struck in the Throat, the one after the other; as also on the Harpsicol, in striking the two Fingers on the two Stops that make the Shake. ¶ *Cadence in Dancing*, when the Steps follow the Notes and Measures of the Music. **1730** Bailey *Dict. Britannicum* (1st edn) *Cadence* (in *Dancing*) is when the steps follow the notes and measures of the musick. *Cadences* (in *Singing*) are the same with Points and *Virgula's* in discourse. **1735** Defoe *Cadence*, a just Fall of a Tune or Voice. **1737** Dyche-Pardon (2nd edn) *Cadence* (S.) ... In *Musick*, it is the proper closing of a Strain or Tune in the several Chords of the Key, proper for the several Parts of the Composition. In *Dancing*, it is when the Steps follow the Notes and Measures of the Musick.

1597 Morley *Plaine and Easie Introdvction* (p. 73) *Phi.* What do you tearme a *Cadence*? ¶ *Ma.* A *Cadence* wee call that, when comming to a close, two notes are bound togither, and the following note descendeth thus: [music] or in any other keye after the same manner. § (p. 144) ... but if your base ascende halfe a note thus, [music] any of the other parts making *Syncopation* (which we abusiuely cal a Cadence) then of force must your *Syncopation* be in that order ... **1636** Butler *Principles of Musik* (p. 66) Most excellent in this kinde [of 'Single Alligation' in which a fourth is bound with a third] is a Cadence: which is an Alligation, whose Binding semitone falleth into the next key alway sharp: of which falling the Cadence hath his name: by which the Harmoni & soom parte of the Ditti inclineth to rest. **1673** Locke *Melothesia* (p. 6) A *Cadence* is a Fall or Binding, wherein, after the taking of a *Discord* or *Discords*, there is a meeting or Closure of *Concords*, as is to be seen in the two *last Notes* of all Strains of *Pavans* or any other grave *Musick*, Vocal or Instrumental; the last of which two *Notes* generally riseth four, or falleth five *Notes* from the former; by which it is known (for the most part) to be a *Cadence*. **1676** Mace *Musick's*

Monument (p. 227) Now *This Cadence*, is as it were the *Summing up, Sweetning, or Compleating* of the *whole Story*, or *Matter foregoing*; or *Period* of some *Sentence Intended*; and indeed is the *very Choicest*, and *Most Satisfactory Delight* in all *Musick*, (nothing so *Sweet* and *Delightful*, as a *Sweet Close* or Cadence. **1682** MATTEIS *False Consonances of Musick* (p. 25) You are to know the Cadens that is when ye Base. skips to a fourth up, or a fifth downe, and giving somtimes a fourth and a third which is this common Cypher. 43... **c.1698-c.1703** NORTH Cursory Notes (*C-K CN* p. 175) ... And for this reason, the chang of key to the 4th below, and returne to the former, is the best conditioned of any. And therefore it is used upon the conclusions or periodicall passages, and is called a cadence. **early 18th C.** NORTH (Prendcourt's) Treatis of Continued or Through Basse BL Add. 32549, f. 27 This cadence takes its Etimology from the word Cado, I feell, becaus comonly the close does fall a fifth below the penultime Note, that does forme ye Close. **c.1710** NORTH (Prendcourt's) Treatise of Continued or thro-base BL Add. 32531, f. 35v [quoting Prendcourt:] This Cadence takes it[s] Etimology from ye word Cado, I fall, becaus comonly ye Close does fall a fifth below the penultime note, that does form ye close. 'tis called a Close becaus It is a jumping together of all ye parts, (or at least of some,) that are to enreute [sic] a piece of Composition. **c.1726** NORTH Musicall Gramarian BL Add. 32533, ff. 77v-78 ... therefore there cannot be a more aggreable change of a Key then when it hath bin shifted to Returne againe. Of wch let this be the example ... where the first change is from G. to its 5th. D. and then returne to .G. againe; this passage of the Key is the most celebrated of any, by ye Name of the Cadence. The masters call the first the preparative the 2d the Cadence Note, and If it goeth no further, then it is a semi-cadence, and the last note is the Key againe and often called ye close Note. this is a just acco of that Comon scheme in Musick called a Cadence. **1730** [PEPUSCH] *Short Treatise on Harmony* (p. 5) A Cadence is in Musick, the same as a Period or full stop is in speaking or writing, that is to say, it is a Termination or Ending either of a Part, or of the whole Piece of Musick; as the full stop is either of one sentence only, or of the whole Speech. § (p. 44) The Cadences that finish or End in the Unison or in the Eighth, are only proper to finish a Full Sentence, and as has been said answer to the full stop in Writing, and therefore are called Final Cadences. **1731** [PEPUSCH] *Treatise on Harmony* (2nd edn, p. 56) The Cadences that finish in the *Unison*, or the *Eighth*, answering to the *Full Stop* in Writing, are the only ones proper to finish a full Sentence, and for that Reason are call'd *Final Cadences*. ¶ All other Cadences are to be used in the Middle of a Piece of Musick, but not at the End of it, and are therefore call'd *Middle Cadences*. **1736** TANS'UR *Compleat Melody* (3rd edn, p. 71) A *Cadence* is the Fall of the *Voice*, or a *Conclusion*, or *Close* made by all *Parts*, in several Places of any *Key*, &c.

cadent *see* elevation

caduceus
1730 BAILEY *Dict. Britannicum* (1st edn) *Caduceus*, the wand or rod that *Apollo* gave to *Mercury*, in exchange for the 7 stringed harp ...

caisse *see* caxa
1611 COTGRAVE Fr→E *Caisse*... also, a drumme;

calamist
1500 *Ortus Vocabulorum* L→E Calamiso as. i. leta cantare n.p. **1656** BLOUNT (1st edn) A *Calamist* (from *calamus*) a Piper or whistler with a reed. *Calamize (calamizo)* to pipe or sing. **1658** PHILLIPS (1st edn) *Calamist*, a Piper upon a reed, from the Latin word *Calamus*. **1676** COLES *Calamist*, a Player upon ¶ *Calamus*

calamus *see* fistula
1538 ELYOT L→E *Calamus*, a rede, or wheate strawe... It is also taken for a pype, or whystell. **1552** HULOET L→E *Calamus, Fistula, Tibia. æ* Whistle. *Calamus, mi, Fistula. æ, Tibia. æ.* Pype. **1565** COOPER L→E *Calamus, cálami, pen. cor.* A reede: a wheaten or oten straw: a pipe or whistle: *Calamus. Virg.* A pipe. § *Aequiparare calamis aliquem. Virg.* To play as well on a pipe. *Arguti calami. Sil.* Loude or shrill pipes. *Terere calamo labellum. Virg.* To play on his pipe. **1587** THOMAS L→E *Calamus, mi, m.g.* A reede: a wheaten or oaten straw ... a pipe or whistle: **1611** COTGRAVE Fr→E *Calame: m.* A cane, reed; wheaten, or oaten straw; pipe, flute; &c. as the Latine *Calamus*. **1676** COLES *Calamus, Latin.* a reed.

1582 *Batman vppon Bartholome* (p. 424) *Calamus* hath ye name of this worde *Calando*, sounding, & is the generall name of pipes. A pipe is called *Fistula*, for voyce commeth thereof: for voice is called *Fos* in Greeke, & send, is *stolia* in Greeke, & so the pipe is called *Fistula*, as it wer sending out voyce or sound.

calastri

1538 Elyot L→E *Calasastri* [sic], boyes whyche doo synge with a shyll [sic] voyce. § *Calastri pueri*, syngynge boyes.

calata

1598 Florio It→E *Calata*, a falling note. **1611** Florio It→E *Calata*, ... Also a falling note. **1659** Torriano-Florio It→E *Calata, Calamento, Calatura, Calo*, ... also a falling note in singing

call *see* chiamamento, mot, raccolta, recheat

1706 Kersey-Phillips (6th edn) *Call*, (in *Hunting*) a Lesson blown upon the Horn to comfort the Hounds: **1708** Kersey *Dict. Anglo-Brit.* (1st edn) *Call*, (in *Hunting*) a Lesson blown upon the Horn to comfort the Hounds: **1728** Chambers *Call*, (in Hunting) is a Lesson blown upon the Horn, to comfort the Hounds. § [entry *hunting*:] ... A Lesson on the Horn to encourage the Hounds, is nam'd a *Call*, or a *Recheat*.—That blown at the Death of a Deer, is call'd the *Mort*. **1731** Kersey *New Engl. Dict.* (3rd edn) *Calls*, or *Bird-Calls*, artificial Pipes, to imitate the Notes of Quails, Partridges, *&c*.

Calliope *see* Muse

1706 Kersey-Phillips (6th edn) *Calliope*, the first of the nine Muses, said to preside over Harmony, Heroick Poetry, and Hymns made in honour of the Gods. **1707** *Gloss. Angl. Nova* (1st edn) *Calliope*, the first of the nine Muses, that presides over Harmony, Heroick Poetry, and Divine Hymns. **1708** Kersey *Dict. Anglo-Brit.* (1st edn) *Calliope*, the first of the Nine Muses, said to preside over Harmony and Heroick Poetry.

1586 Anon. *Praise of Mvsicke* (pp. 52-3) ... therefore they [Pythagoras and others] made 8. peculiar *Muses*, attributing to *Luna* the muse *Clio*: to *Mercurius, Euterpe*: to *Venus, Thalia*: to *Sol, Melpomene*: to *Mars, Terpsichore*: to *Iupiter, Erato*: to *Saturne, Polymnia*, to the firmamant or *cœlum stellatum, Vrania*; and because of eight particular soundes or voices, keeping due proportion and time, must needes arise an harmony or concent, which is made by them all, therefore that sound which al these make is called *Calliope*.

calza

1659 Torriano-Florio It→E **Calza, Calzamento, Calze*, ... also the bag for pipes in country musick.

çamarro *see* zamara

1599 Minsheu-Percyvall Sp→E *† *çamarro*, m. ... Also a kinde of musicall instrument with strings.

camena *see* camœna, carmen

1598 Florio It→E *Camene*, the nine muses. Also a poeticall song. **1611** Florio It→E *Camene*, the nine Muses, or a Poeticall song. **1659** Torriano-Florio It→E *Cameine*, used for the nine Muses, also for Poeticall songs. **Camena* the Goddess of the art of singing. **1688** Davis-Torriano-Florio It→E **Camena*, a Muse, a song, or piece of Poetry.

camera *see* da, sonata

1724 [Pepusch] *Short Explic. of Foreign Words in Mus. Bks.* (p. 17) *Camera*, a Chamber. This Word is often used in the Title Page of Musick Books, to distinguish such Musick as is designed for Chambers, or private Consorts, from such as is designed for Chapels, or great Consorts: Thus *Sonata da Camera*, is Chamber Sonatas; and *Sonata da Chiesa*, is Church or Chapel Sonatas. **1726** Bailey *An Univ. Etymolog. Engl. Dict.* (3rd edn) *Camera* (in the Title of *Musick Books*) denotes such Musick as is design'd for Chambers and private Consorts, in distinction to such as is designed for Chapels and great Consorts. **1730** Bailey *Dict. Britannicum* (1st edn) *Camera* (in the title of *Mus. Books*) signifies chamber-musick, or musick for private consorts, in distinction to musick us'd in chapels and publick consorts. **1737** Dyche-Pardon (2nd edn) *Camera* (S.) is sometimes used for Chamber, and sometimes for Musick designed for a Chamber for private Use;

1728 North Musicall Grammarian (*C-K MG* f. 83) Of sociall musick in consort ¶ The next partition of musicall enterteinement [after 1. solitary] is the sociall or what is called musica di camera; this hath 2 respects, 1. to the performers, and 2. the auditors, for there is a vast difference both in designe and event between these 2 nations. The former I presume to consist of scollars advanced, or as it may be, adept in practise, commixt with some of the musicall profession; but all cheifly delighted in the exercise of difficultys; and in shewing their skill, conceiting themselves envyed for the fine things they are able to performe; ... **1731** Prelleur *Modern Musick-Master* (Dictionary, p. 2) *Camera*, Chamber, as *Arie da Camera*[,] Chamber Aires

camœna *see* camena, carmen
1565 COOPER L→E *Camœna.* A songe. **1587** THOMAS L→E *Camœna, æ, f.g. Plin.* A song, or poetrie.

campana *see* bell, scampanare
1500 *Ortus Vocabulorum* L→E Campana e. a bell. f.p. Campanaria. e. idem est, f.p. Campanarius est ille q facit campanas. **1538** ELYOT L→E *Campana,* a belle. **1550** THOMAS It→E *Campana,* a bell. **1565** COOPER L→E *Campana, næ.* A bell. **1587** THOMAS L→E *Campana, æ, f.g.* *A bell. **1589** RIDER L→E *Compana, f. companum, m.* A Bell. *Campanista.* A bel ringer. **1593** HOLLYBAND Fr→E *Campane,* a Bell: *f.* **1598** FLORIO It→E *Campana,* a bell. *Campanaio,* a bell-ringer, a sexten of a church, or a bell-founder. *Campanaria,* a iangling, or ringing of belles. § *Campana a martello,* to ring the bels backward as they vse in Italy in dangerous times. *Madaglio della campana,* the clapper of a bell. *Sonare le campane,* to ring the bels. *Tocco di campana,* a knock, a stroke, a knell, or peale, or toule vpon the bels. **1599** MINSHEU-PERCYVALL Sp→E *Campanario,* f. ... Also iangling or ringing of bels. **Campañear,* to ring a bell. *Campanero,* m. a bell ringer, a sexten of a church, a bell founder. **1611** COTGRAVE Fr→E *Campane: f.* A bell; *Campanel*: m. A Campanell *Campanelle*: f. as *Campanel*; also, a little tinging bell. § *Tympan d'une campanelle.* The broad-end of a Campanell. **1611** FLORIO It→E *Campana,* a bell. *Campanaio,* a bell-ringer, a sexton of a Church. Also a bel-founder. *Campanaria,* a iangling of belles. *Campaneggiamenti,* ianglings of belles. *Campaneggiare,* to iangle or ring belles. *Campano,* bell-mettle. *Campanuccio,* a meane bell. Also a ring of belles in a steeple. § *Campana a martello,* to ring the belles backeward, or with stones and hammers, as they doe in Italy in dangerous times. *Madaglio della campana,* a Bell-clapper. *Sonare le campane,* to ring the bells. *Tocco di campana,* a knocke, a stroke, a knell, a peale or toule vpon a bell. **1659** TORRIANO-FLORIO It→E *Campana,* any kind of ringing-bell *Campanare, Campaneggiare,* to ring or jangle the bells **Campanaria, Campanamento, Campanata, Campaneggiamento, Campaneria,* any kind of ringing, jangling or tolling of bells, a peale or ring of bells *Campanaro, Campanaio,* a bell-man, a bell-keeper, a bell-ringer, a sexton, a bell-founder. *Campane,* all sortes of bells, also bell-pearles *Campano,* a ringing or jangling of bells for joy or gladness, or in signe of triumph. § *Sonare la campane,* to ring the bells. **Tirare le campane,* to ring the bells. *Tocco di campana,* a knock, a stroke, a knell, a peal or toul upon a bell. **1706** KERSEY-PHILLIPS (6th edn) *Campana,* (Lat.) a Bell. § *Campana bajula,* a small portable Hand-bell, such as were in use among other foppish Ceremonies in the Roman Church, and are still retain'd by Parish-Beadles, Publick Criers, *&c.* **1708** KERSEY *Dict. Anglo-Brit.* (1st edn) *Campana, (L.)* a Bell. § *Campana bajula,* a small Hand-bell, such as were in Use among other foppish Ceremonies in the *Roman* Church, and are still retain'd by Parish-Beadles, publick Criers, *&c.*

campanella
1500 *Ortus Vocabulorum* L→E Campanella est vel campauula [sic]. est diminutiuum. a lytyle belle. f.p. **1550** THOMAS It→E *Campanella,* a littell bell. **1598** FLORIO It→E *Campanella,* a little bell **1611** FLORIO It→E *Campanella,* ... Also any little bell. **1650** HOWELL-COTGRAVE Fr→E *Campanelle: f.* ... also a little tinging bell. **1659** TORRIANO-FLORIO It→E *Campanello, Campanella, Campanino, Campanuccia,* any kind of little bel

campanino
1611 FLORIO It→E *Campanino,* a little bell.

campanology
1736 BAILEY *Dict. Britannicum* (2nd edn) *Campanology* (of *campana,* i.e. a Bell, and λόγος *Gr.* Speech) a treatise concerning the art of casting and ringing of Bells.

campanula
1706 KERSEY-PHILLIPS (6th edn) *Campanula,* a little Bell; **1708** KERSEY *Dict. Anglo-Brit.* (1st edn) *Campanula,* a little Bell;

campinolator
1589 RIDER L→E *Campinolator, m.* A low-beller.

çampoña *see* sampogna

canaries *see* baioccare, castanet, chioppare, chrich, paganina
1598 FLORIO It→E *Canarino,* a daunce called the canarie daunce. **1659** TORRIANO-FLORIO It→E *Canarino,* a Canarie, one that danceth the Canaries **1688** MIEGE-COTGRAVE Fr→E § *Danser les Canaries,* to dance the Canaries.

cançion *see* canzona

1599 MINSHEU-PERCYVALL Sp→E *Cançion*, f. a song, a singing, a sonnet, a canzonet, a ballet, a dittie, a lay, a rundelay, a virelay.

cançionero *see* canzoniere

1599 MINSHEU-PERCYVALL Sp→E *Cancionero*, m. a song-booke, a dittie-booke.

canere

1538 ELYOT L→E *Canere fibi & musis*, to synge or wryte for his owne pleasure, and for theym that doo fauour hym, nothing caring for any other. **1552** HULOET L→E § *canere fidibus, Scire fidibus* Playe on the harpe. **1565** COOPER L→E § *Absurdè canere. Cic.* To singe foolishly, or out of tune. *Ad certos modos canere. Ouid.* By proportion. *Canere ad citharam laudes alicuius. Quintil.* To the harpe. *Canere ad tibiam. Cic.* To singe to the shalme. *Canere fidibus. Cic.* To play on the harpe, or other stringed instrument. *Canere indoctum. Horat.* To synge a rude and vnlearned songe. *Canere sacra. Virg.* To synge hymnes and psalmes to the honour of God. *Canere vota diuis. Virg.* To sing hymnes and prayers. *Cantilenam candem canere. Terent.* To repete one thing: alway to singe one songe. *Celebrare dapes canendo. Ouid.* To set foorth the blanket and make it more solemne with musicke. *Elisa voce canere, vel loqui. Bud.* To fayne in singyng: ... also to speake or singe as one coulde hardely vtter his voyce. *Tibijs canere. Cic.* To play on the flute or pipe.

canna

1587 THOMAS L→E *Canna, æ, f.g.* A cane, or reede: a pipe: **1598** FLORIO It→E *Canna*, ... a flute, a recorder, a pipe to play vpon. **1611** FLORIO It→E *Canna*, ... Also a flute, a pipe or a recorder. **1659** TORRIANO-FLORIO It→E **Canna*, any kinde of cane or hollow reede ... also a flute, a pipe or a recorder

cannamella

1598 FLORIO It→E *Cannamella*, a kinde of musicall instrument or pipe. **1611** FLORIO It→E *Cannamella*, a sugar-cane. Also a kind of musical pipe or recorder.

cannella

1598 FLORIO It→E *Cannella*, a little cane, pipe or reede, a flute, a spigot. **1611** FLORIO It→E *Cannella*, Also a flute or recorder. **1659** TORRIANO-FLORIO It→E **Cannella*; ... flute or recorder

cano *see* occano

1538 ELYOT L→E *Cano, cecini, nere*, to synge, to playe on the shalme or other instrument. **1552** HULOET L→E *Cano. is, Canto. as, Edere cantus, Pango. is. nxi, uel pepigi, Psallo. is. li* Syng. *Cano. is, Præmoderor aris, Pulso. as* Playe on an instrument. **1565** COOPER L→E *Cano, canis, cécini, pen. corr. cantum canere. Plin.* To singe: to play on an instrument: **1587** THOMAS L→E *Canens, part. à Cano, is.* Singing. *Cano, is, cecini, cantum.* To sing, to plaie on an instrument **1589** RIDER L→E *Cano, canto, psallo, pango, panxi, modulor.* To Sing. *Cano, psallo, persono, vt personare cithara.* To plaie vppon, as vppon an instrument.

1636 BUTLER *Principles of Musik* (p. 10) Becaus Singing is the best expressing of Musical sounds; therefore, by a *Synecdoche*, the woord *Cano* (to Sing) is enlarged, and signifyeth commonly, as wel to play on Instruments, as to Sing with voices: ...

canon *as composition, see* catch, fuga ligata, hypodiapente, imitation, recte & retro, resolution, revert, two parts in one

1696 PHILLIPS (5th edn) *Canon*, in Musick, is a short composition of three or more parts, wherein one part leads, and the other follows, in an Eighth before or a Fifth above, or in an unison; so that the same Notes keep a harmonial [sic] distance. **1706** KERSEY-PHILLIPS (6th edn) (Gr.) In *Musick, Canon* is a short Composition of one, or more Parts in which one Part leads, and the other follows: **1728** CHAMBERS *Canon*, in Musick, is a Rule, or Method of determining the Intervals of Notes. See *Interval.* ¶ *Ptolemy*, rejecting the *Aristoxenian* Way of measuring the Intervals in Musick, by the Magnitude of a Tone, (which was suppos'd to be form'd by the Difference between a *Diapente* and a *Diatessaron*) thought that musical Intervals should be distinguish'd, according to the Ratio's or Proportions which the Sounds terminating those Intervals bear to one another, when consider'd according to their degree of Acuteness or Gravity; which, before *Aristoxenus*, was the old *Pythagorean* Way. He therefore made the *Diapason* consist in a double Ratio; the *Diapente* in a Sesquialteral; the *Diatessaron*, in a Sesquitertian, and the Tone it self in a Sesquioctave; and all the other Intervals, according to the Proportion of the Sounds that terminate them: Wherefore, taking the *Canon*, (as 'tis call'd) for a determinate Line of any length, he shews how this *Canon* is to be cut accordingly, so that it may represent the respective Intervals: and this Method answers exactly to Experiment, in the different Lengths of musical Chords. From this *Canon, Ptolemy* and his Followers, have been call'd *Canonici;* as those of *Aristoxenus,* were call'd *Musici.* See *Musick.* **1737** DYCHE-PARDON (2nd edn) *Canon* (S.) ... with the *Musicians,* it is a short Composition, in which one Part leads and another follows;

after 1517 ANON. Art of Mvsic BL Add. 4911, f. 30 *Quhat is ane canone?* It is ane Institutione of noittis or wordis directrit be the arbitar of the compositor schalb and be diuerss signis the augmentation and diminucion of signris. **1609** DOWLAND-ORNITHOPARCUS *Micrologvs* (p. 48) *What a Canon is.* ¶ ... A *Canon* therefore is an imaginarie rule, drawing that part of the Song which is not set downe out of that part, which is set downe. Or it is a Rule, which doth wittily discouer the secrets of a Song. Now we vse *Canons,* either to shew Art, or to make shorter worke, or to try others cunning ... **1636** BUTLER *Principles of Musik* (p. 75) The Canon is *Fuga Epidiapason, seu Octava superiore, post duo Tempora.* **late 17th C.** ANON. Tractatus de Musicâ BL Add. 4923, f. 12 Canon d[r], quando integra cantilena, papt aliquas pausas assumitur ab alterâ parte, vel in unisono, vel in Quartâ, Quintâ, Octavâ &c **1667** SIMPSON *Compendium of Practical Musick* (p. 146) A Canon is a Fuge, so bound up, or restrained, that the following Part or Parts must precisely repeat the same Notes, with the same degrees rising or falling, which were expressed by the Leading Part; and because it is tyed to so strict a Rule, it is thereupon called a *Canon.* **1694** PURCELL-PLAYFORD *Intro. to Skill of Musick* (12th edn, 'A Brief Introduction to the Art of Descant', n.p.) The eighth and noblest sort of Fugeing is *Canon,* the Method of which is to answer exactly Note for Note to the end. **1731** [PEPUSCH] *Treatise on Harmony* (2nd edn, p. 86) A *Canon* is that sort of *Fugue* wherein the several Parts do strictly contain the *same Subject* from the Beginning to the End; that is, that the *Guide* and the *Answers* are throughout the whole Composition exactly *alike.* **1731** PRELLEUR *Modern Musick-Master* (Dictionary, p. 2) *Canon,* or *Canone*[,] a Perpetual Fuge. **1736** TANS'UR *Compleat Melody* (3rd edn, p. 64) A *Canon,* is a *Fuge* or *Point;* so strictly bound up, that the following *Parts* must repeat the very same *Notes* as the *Leading-Parts;* and because the *Musick* is bound up by so strict a *Rule,* it is therefore called *Canon;* which is the *Superlative,* or highest Degree of *Musical Composition.* § (p. 71) A *Canon* (Lat.) is a Piece of *Musick* composed by an exact *Rule,* i[.]e. The following *Parts* repeating the very same *Notes* as the foregoing *Part.*

canon *as part of instrument, see* sommier, soundboard

1593 HOLLYBAND Fr→E § *Canon musical,* the sound boord in Organes. **1611** COTGRAVE Fr→E *Canon: m.* ... also, the sound-boord of an Organ;

canonica musica *see* musica canonica

canonici *see* canon

1552 HULOET L→E *Canonicus* Musician or tryer of musycke. **1565** COOPER L→E *Canonici.* They that trie musike by rules and reason: as *Harmonici,* be they that iudge by delectation of the eare. **1587** THOMAS L→E *Canonici,* *Be those that trie Musick by rules and reason. **1589** RIDER L→E *Canonici, m.* Those that trie musicke by rule and reason.

1721 MALCOLM *Treatise of Musick* (pp. 506-7) Therefore he [Ptolomy] would have Sense and Reason always taken together in all our Judgments, about Sounds, that they may mutually help and confirm one another. And of all the Methods to prove and find the *Ratios* of Sounds, he recommends as the most accurate, this, *viz.* to stretch over a plain Table an evenly well made String, fixt and raised equally at both Ends, over Two immoveable Bridges of Wood, set perpendicularly to the Table, and parallel to each other; betwixt them a Line is to be drawn on the Table, and divided into as many equal Parts as you need, for trying all Manner of *Ratios:* then a moveable Bridge runs betwixt the other Two, which just touches the String, and being set at the several Divisions of the Line, it divides the Chord into any *Ratio* of Parts; whose Sounds are to be compared together, or with the Sound of the Whole. This he calls *Canon Harmonicus.* And those who determined the *Intervals* this Way, were particularly called *Canonici,* and the others by the general Name of *Musici.*

canor *see* nugicanoricrepe

1500 *Ortus Vocabulorum* L→E Canor oris. i. sonus cantus suauis. m.f. Canorus a. um. i. sonorus. i. dulcis suauis. sherll. o.s. **1538** ELYOT L→E *Canor, oris,* melody, lowde. *Canorosus, a, um,* full of melody. **1552** HULOET L→E *Canor. oris, Harmonia. æ, melodia. æ, melos. dis* Melody. *Canor. ris, Symphonia. æ, musica,* Musycke. *Canorosus. a. um,* full of musycke *Canorus. a. um Harmonicus. a. um* Melodious, or full of melody. **1565** COOPER L→E *Canor, canôris, pen. prod. m.g. Quintil.* Melodious singyng. **1587** THOMAS L→E *Canor, oris, m.g. Ouid.* Melodious singing, melodie. *Canorus, a, um.* Lowde or shrill, ringing, melodious, pleasant, sweete. **1589** RIDER L→E § *Canor lyræ.* The tune of the harpe. **1611** COTGRAVE Fr→E *Canore: com.* Shrill, ringing; harmonious, melodious, of a pleasant, or pleasing sound. **1650** HOWELL-COTGRAVE Fr→E † *Canore: com.* Shrill, ringing; harmonious, melodious, of a pleasant, or pleasing sound. **1656** BLOUNT (1st edn) *Canor* (Latin. *Cano*) melody or sweet singing *Canorous (canorus)* loud singing. *Br.* **1658** PHILLIPS (1st edn) *Canorous,* (Lat.) shrill, loud singing. **1704** *Cocker's Engl. Dict.* (1st edn) *Canorous,* loud singing. **1706** KERSEY-PHILLIPS (6th edn) † *Canorous,* (*Lat.*) shrill, loud-singing, high-sounding. **1730** BAILEY *Dict. Britannicum* (1st edn) *Canorous* (*canorus,* L.) shrill, loud singing, high-sounding.

canta

1538 ELYOT L→E *Canta,* olde writers vsed for cantata. **1587** THOMAS L→E *Canta, pro Cantata, Fest.*

cantabile

1611 FLORIO It→E *Cantabile,* that may be sung. *Incantabile,* that cannot be sung. **1659** TORRIANO-FLORIO It→E *Cantabile, Cantevole, Cantativo,* that may be sung, or chanted. **1724** [PEPUSCH] *Short Explic. of Foreign Words in Mus. Bks.* (p. 17) *Cantabile,* is to play in a Kind of Singing or Chanting Manner. **1726** BAILEY *An Univ. Etymolog. Engl. Dict.* (3rd edn) *Cantabile* (in *Musick Books*) signifies to Play in a kind of Chanting or Singing manner. *Ital.*

1736 TANS'UR *Compleat Melody* (3rd edn, p. 67) *Cantabal.* (Ital.) Denotes that you must *Play* in a *Vocal* Manner.

cantacchiare

1598 FLORIO It→E *Cantacchiare,* to sing foolishly. **1611** FLORIO It→E *Cantacchiare,* to sing foolishly. **1659** TORRIANO-FLORIO It→E *Cantacchiare, Canticchiare, Canterellare, Cantocchiare,* to chant it without skill, to sing naturally

cantado

1599 MINSHEU-PERCYVALL Sp→E **Cantado,* m. sung.

cantador *see* cantator

1599 MINSHEU-PERCYVALL Sp→E **Cantador,* m a singer.

cantafavole

1598 FLORIO It→E *Cantafauole,* a singer of ballads or tales **1611** FLORIO It→E *Contafauole* [sic], a mountibanke, or singer of fables. **1659** TORRIANO-FLORIO It→E **Cantafavole, Cantafole, Canta in banco,* ... a singer of fables, idle songs, or idle tales *Contafavole,* as *Cantafavole*

cantante

1599 MINSHEU-PERCYVALL Sp→E **Cantante,* a singer, Vide *Cantor.*

cantar

1599 MINSHEU-PERCYVALL Sp→E *Cantar,* to sing, to chaunt, to chirpe

cantare *see* biscantare, stracantare

1550 THOMAS It→E *Cantare,* to synge. **1565** COOPER L→E § *Adimam cantare seueris. Horat.* I will take syngynge from graue men. *Amicam cantare. Horat.* To singe of his loue. *Amores veteres cantare. Ouid.* To sing songes of olde loue. *Longos soles condere cantando. Virg.* To passe ouer or spend whole dayes in singyng. **1598** FLORIO It→E *Cantare,* to sing, to chaunt **1611** FLORIO It→E *Cantare,* to sing to chante. **1659** TORRIANO-FLORIO It→E *Cantaro,* they sang. § **Cantare a-recisa,* to sing-out without intermission, methode, or order, and skill. *Fare cantare,* to make to sing

cantarella *see* canto, chanterelle, minnekin

1598 FLORIO It→E *Cantarella,* the treble string or minekin of an instrument **1611** FLORIO It→E *Cantarella,* the treble string or minikin of an instrument. **1659** TORRIANO-FLORIO It→E *Cantarella, Canterella,* ... also the treble-string or minikin of any instrument, namely of a Lute

cantaria, canteria *see* chantry

1598 FLORIO It→E *Chanteria,* a chantrie. **1611** FLORIO It→E *Canteria,* a chantery or singing place. **1659** TORRIANO-FLORIO It→E *Canteria,* a singing place or company, a crue of merry lads. **1688** DAVIS-TORRIANO-FLORIO It→E *Cantaria,* a singing place or company, a crue of merry lads.

cantarini

1598 FLORIO It→E *Cantarini,* such as sing threemens songs, common begging singers. **1611** FLORIO It→E *Cantarini,* such as sing three mens songs.

Cantarino, a singer. **1659** TORRIANO-FLORIO It→E *Cantarini*, such as sing catches, or three mens songs. *Cantarino*, a singer, a chanter **1688** DAVIS-TORRIANO-FLORIO It→E *Cantarini*, such as sing catches, or of three parts.

cantata *see* canta

1565 COOPER L→E *Cantâtus, pen. prod. Participium. Stat.* Songe of: praysed: enchanted. **1587** THOMAS L→E *Cantatus, a, um, part. à Cantor, aris, Ouid.* Song of, praised, enchaunted. **1724** [PEPUSCH] *Short Explic. of Foreign Words in Mus. Bks.* (p. 18) *Cantata*, is a Piece of Vocal Musick, for one, two, three, or more Voices, and sometimes with one or more Instruments of Musick, of any Sort or Kind; composed after the Manner of Operas, consisting of Grave Parts and Airs intermixed one with another. **1726** BAILEY *An Univ. Etymolog. Engl. Dict.* (3rd edn) *Cantata* (in *Musick*) is a Piece of Vocal Musick for one, two, three or more Voices, and sometimes with one or more Musical Instruments, of any Sort or Kind; compos'd after the manner of Opera's, consisting of grave Parts and Airs, intermix'd one after another. *Ital.* **1728** CHAMBERS *Cantata*, in Musick, a Song, or Composition, intermix'd with Recitatives, little Airs, and different Motions: ordinarily intended for a single Voice, with a thorough Bass; sometimes for two Violins, or other Instruments. See *Song.* ¶ The *Cantata* passed from *Italy* into *France*, and thence to us: It has something in it extremely fantastical and capricious, and seems only to please by its Novelty. The Word is *Italian*, where it signifies the same thing. **1737** DYCHE-PARDON (2nd edn) *Cantata* (S.) a Song for one or more Voices, with or without Instruments, composed with divers Movements, and in the Stile of an Opera.

1731 PRELLEUR *Modern Musick-Master* (Dictionary, p. 2) *Cantata*, a Song in an Opera Style. **1736** TANS'UR *Compleat Melody* (3rd edn, p. 72) A *Cantata*. (Ital.) is a Piece of *Musick* composed for *Voices*, or *Instruments*, in several *Parts*; being intermixed one with another, like *Opera's*, &c.

cantation

1538 ELYOT L→E *Cantatio*, a syngynge. **1552** HULOET L→E *Cantatio. onis* Singyng. **1565** COOPER L→E *Cantatio. Verbale.* A singyng or inchauntyng. **1587** THOMAS L→E *Cantatio, onis, f.g.* A singing or inchanting. **1589** RIDER L→E *Cantatio, f.* A singing. **1623** COCKERAM *Cantation.* Singing. **1656** BLOUNT (1st edn) *Cantation (cantatio)* singing or enchanting. **1658** PHILLIPS (1st edn) *Cantation*, (lat.) a singing, also an inchanting. **1676** COLES *Cantation, Latin.* a singing, also an enchanting.

cantativo

1611 FLORIO It→E *Cantatiuo*, that may be sung or chaunted.

cantator *see* cantador, percantatrix

1538 ELYOT L→E *Cantator*, a synger. **1550** THOMAS It→E *Cantatore*, the synger. **1552** HULOET L→E *Cantator. ris, uel trix* Singer. **1565** COOPER L→E *Cantâtor, & cantâtrix, penu. prod. alia verbalia. Varro.* A singar. § *Cantator cygnus funeris sui. Martial.* Singyng at his owne death. *Cantatrices choreæ. Claud.* That daunce to a songe. **1587** THOMAS L→E *Cantator, oris, m.g. verb. à canto Mart.* A singer, a chanter. § *Cantator fidibus, Gell.* A minstrell a harper. *Cantatrix, icis, f.g. verb. à Canto, Varr.* A woman singer. **1589** RIDER L→E *Cantator, psaltes, cantor, aulædus, choricanus, paristonus, m.* A singer, or singing man **1598** FLORIO It→E *Cantatore*, a singer, a chanter. **1611** FLORIO It→E *Cantatore*, a singer, a chanter. *Cantatrice*, a chantres or woman singer.

canta-versi

1659 TORRIANO-FLORIO It→E *Canta-versi*, as *Canta-fauole*, also a nice spruce Courtier that sings verses.

cantepolare

1611 FLORIO It→E *Cantepolare*, to sing at ones window. Also to keepe a filthy singing. **1659** TORRIANO-FLORIO It→E *Cantepolare*, as *Cantacchiare*, to sing and chante at ones dore, or window, as poor men do in London.

canteria *see* cantaria

cantes

1538 ELYOT L→E *Canthes*, organ pipes. **1552** HULOET L→E *canthes* Organ pypes **1587** THOMAS L→E *Cantes, f g. plu. num. Fistulæ sunt Organorum.* **1589** RIDER L→E *Cantes, f pl.* Organ pipes.

canticle *see* hymn

1609 CAWDREY (2nd edn) *canticke*, a song. **1611** FLORIO It→E *Cantica*, a canticle. **1656** BLOUNT (1st edn) *Canticle (canticum)* a pleasant song, a ballad, a rime **1658** PHILLIPS (1st edn) *Canticle*, (lat.) a song or ballad. **1659** TORRIANO-FLORIO It→E **Cantica, Cantico*, a canticle, that is, a praising of God singing with the voice, or a book set with musick. **1676** COLES *Canticle, Latin.* Song. **1688** MIEGE-COTGRAVE Fr→E *Cantique,* (m.) a Song, a spiritual Song § *Le Cantique de Salomon,* Solomon's Song. **1702** KERSEY *New Engl. Dict.* (1st edn) The *Canticles, or* song of *Solomon.* **1704** *Cocker's Engl. Dict.* (1st edn) *Canticle,* a pleasant song. **1706** KERSEY-PHILLIPS (6th edn) *Canticles,* (Lat. i.e. Spiritual Songs) one of the Books of Holy Scripture, otherwise call'd *Solomon*'s Song. **1726** BAILEY *An Univ. Etymolog. Engl. Dict.* (3rd edn) *Canticles* (*i.e.* Spiritual Songs) the Book of *Solomon*'s Song. *L.* **1737** DYCHE-PARDON (2nd edn) *Canticles* (S.) holy or divine Songs, which carry a spiritual Meaning in them farther than the bare Words themselves express, such as *Solomon*'s Song in the Bible.

canticum

1500 *Ortus Vocabulorum* L→E Canticum ci. vox cantatium laus. a songe. n.s. **1538** ELYOT L→E *Canticum,* a pleasant or mery songe. **1552** HULOET L→E *Canticum* Pleasaunt songe. *Canticum. ci* Song mery and pleasaunt. **1565** COOPER L→E *Cánticum, pen. cor. Quintil.* A pleasant songe: a balade. § *Cantica obscœna. Quintil.* Baudy songes. **1587** THOMAS L→E *Canticum, ci, n.g.* A pleasaunt song, a Balade. **1589** RIDER L→E *Canticum, carmen, melos, n. melæ. pl.* Balad, or balet.

cantiere

1598 FLORIO It→E *Cantiere,* ... Also a chanter. **1611** FLORIO It→E *Cantiere,* a chanter. **1659** TORRIANO-FLORIO It→E **Cantiere,* a chanter, a singer

cantilena

1500 *Ortus Vocabulorum* L→E Cantilena e. est dulcis cantus carmen. a lyttyll swete sange or a saence. f.p. **1538** ELYOT L→E *Cantilena,* the melody of the songe. **1552** HULOET L→E *Cantilena. æ* Song ouer often repeted. **1565** COOPER L→E *Cantilena, cantilénae, pen. prod. Cic.* A songe: a speeche or tale commonly vsed ... **1587** THOMAS L→E *Cantilena, æ, f.g.* A song, a speech or tale commonlie vsed: **1598** FLORIO It→E *Cantilena,* a ballad, a tale **1611** FLORIO It→E *Cantilena,* a ballad, a flimflam tale. *Cantilenare,* to sing flimflam tales. **1656** BLOUNT (1st edn) *Cantilene (cantilena)* ... a song **1658** PHILLIPS (1st edn) *Cantilene,* (lat.) a tale or song. **1659** TORRIANO-FLORIO It→E *Cantilena;* a ballade, a dittie, or dogrell-tale that may be sung, a jig. *Cantilenare,* to chante and sing idle ballades, or jigs. **1676** COLES *Cantilene, Latin.* a song or tale.

cantillo

1587 THOMAS L→E *Cantillo, as,* *To chirp as birdes doe, and [t]o chaunt as singing men doe. **1589** RIDER L→E *Cantillo.* To sing softly.

cantinbanco

1598 FLORIO It→E *Cantinbanco,* a mountibanke, a ballad-singer. **1611** FLORIO It→E *Cantinbanco,* a mount banke. **1659** TORRIANO-FLORIO It→E *Cant' in banco,* look *Canta-favole.*

cantion

1538 ELYOT L→E *Cantio,* a songe. **1565** COOPER L→E *Cantio, cantiônis. Verbale. Plaut.* A songe: a charme or inchauntmente. § *Cantio lepida & suauis. Plaut.* A pleasant and sweet songe. **1587** THOMAS L→E *Cantio, onis, f.g. verb. à Cano,* A song, a charme or enchantment. **1589** RIDER L→E *Cantio, cantilena, musa, oda, æ, & ode, es, f. cantus, m. canticum, cantamen, Carmen, melos, n. modulus versus, m. camæna, f.* A song. **1656** BLOUNT (1st edn) *Cantion (cantio)* a song or enchantment

cantito

1500 *Ortus Vocabulorum* L→E Cantito as. frequentatiuum de canto as. a.p. **1538** ELYOT L→E *Cantito, aui, are,* to synge often. *Cantito, tare,* to synge often. **1565** COOPER L→E *Cántito, cántitas. pen. corr. cantitâre, Frequentatiuum. Cic.* To singe often. **1587** THOMAS L→E *Cantito, as, frequent. á Canto.* To sing often. **1589** RIDER L→E *Cantito.* To sing often.

cantiuncula

1538 ELYOT L→E *Cantiuncula,* a lytell songe. **1552** HULOET L→E *Cantiuncula. æ* Song of lyght matters. **1565** COOPER L→E *Cantiúncula, penul. corr. Diminutiuum. Cicer.* A songe of light mattiers. **1587** THOMAS L→E *Cantiuncula, æ, f.g. dim.* A song of light matters. **1589** RIDER L→E *Cantiuncula.* A little song.

canto *see* accanto, cantarella, chanterelle, treble

1500 *Ortus Vocabulorum* L→E Canto as. to synge. tor trix & tio. ubale. **1538** ELYOT L→E *Canto, aui, are,* to synge or to charme. **1550** THOMAS It→E *Canto,* the song or armonie. **1565** COOPER L→E *Canto, cantas, cantare, Frequentatiuum. Plin.* To singe: to inchante § *Quotidiano cantu vocam & neruorum, nocturnísque conuiuijs tota vicinitas personat. Cic.* Al that quartier ringeth with syngyng, minstrelsie, and noise of night feastyng & bankettyng. **1587** THOMAS L→E *Canto, as, frequent. á Cano.* To sing, to enchaunt **1598** FLORIO It→E *Canto,* a song, a singing, a sonet, the treble string of an instrument. **1599** MINSHEU-PERCYVALL Sp→E *Canto,* m. a song, singing, a sonnet, the treble string of an instrument, a hymne, a ballade. § *Canto accordado,* a song well sung togither. **1611** FLORIO It→E *Canto,* a song, a sonnet, a canto. Also the treble string of an instrument. **1656** BLOUNT (1st edn) *Canto* (Ital.) a Song or Sonnet **1659** TORRIANO-FLORIO It→E **Canto,* any kind of song, sonnet, *canto, canzonet,* ballade, singing, or chanting ... also the treble, or minikin string of any instrument, also the whole body of a Ball, or Maske, that goeth singing together ... also a part of a poem, also the art or skill in musick. **1702** KERSEY *New Engl. Dict.* (1st edn) A *Canto,* a song, *or* division in a Poem. **1721** BAILEY *An Univ. Etymolog. Engl. Dict.* (1st edn) *Canto,* a Song, *Ital.* Also a Division in any Heroick Poem; as Chapter and Section in Prose. **1724** [PEPUSCH] *Short Explic. of Foreign Words in Mus. Bks.* (p. 18) *Canto,* a Song, or the Treble Part thereof; **1726** BAILEY *An Univ. Etymolog. Engl. Dict.* (3rd edn) *Canto,* a Song, or the Treble Part thereof. *Ital.* **1737** DYCHE-PARDON (2nd edn) *Canto* (S.) ... also in *Musick,* a Song, or the treble Part thereof.

1731 PRELLEUR *Modern Musick-Master* (Dictionary, p. 2) *Canto* the first Treble.

canto fermo

1659 TORRIANO-FLORIO It→E **Canto fermo,* a plain set song or ground to sing or play upon, such as religious men in their quires.

1731 [PEPUSCH] *Treatise on Harmony* (2nd edn, p. 25) What has been said hitherto, has been of the taking *Concords* only, as Accompaniments to every Note of the Key we are in. That is call'd in Italian *Canto Fermo,* and in English *Plain Counterpoint,* as being Note against Note in *Concords* only.

canto figurato

1611 FLORIO It→E *Canto figurato,* a set song. **1659** TORRIANO-FLORIO It→E *Canto figurato,* a song set with all his parts.

1731 [PEPUSCH] *Treatise on Harmony* (2nd edn, p. 26) We will now treat of *Descant,* or *Figurate Counterpoint,* which the *Italians* call *Canto Figurato...*

cantor *see* musician, singer

1565 COOPER L→E *Cantor, & Cantrix, Verbalia. Plaut.* A singyng man or woman. **1587** THOMAS L→E *Cantor, oris, m.g. verb. à Cano.* A singer. a chaunter. *Cantrix, icis, f.g. verb. Plaut.* A woman singer. **1589** RIDER L→E *Cantrix, cantatrix, psaltria. percantatrix, fidicina, f.* A singing wenche. **1598** FLORIO It→E *Cantore,* a chanter, a singer. **1599** MINSHEU-PERCYVALL Sp→E *Cantor,* m. a singer, a chanter. § **Cantor tiple,* a singer of the treble or small. **1611** FLORIO It→E *Cantore,* a chanter, a singer. **1656** BLOUNT (1st edn) *Cantor* (Lat.) a singer or charmer. **1676** COLES *Cantor, Latin.* a singer or Charmer. **1724** [PEPUSCH] *Short Explic. of Foreign Words in Mus. Bks.* (p. 18) *Cantore,* a Singer, or Songster: One that sings.

cantus

1500 *Ortus Vocabulorum* L→E Cantus ti. rote cantus tus. cantica psallit. Cantus us. ui. dicit modulatio voces. a songe **1538** ELYOT L→E *Cantus, tus,* a songe. **1565** COOPER L→E *Cantus, huius cantus.* A songe: a charme § *Accersere cantus lachrymis. Propert.* To make one singe in weepyng. *Bisoris cantus. Virg.* A plaiying vpon two pipes, of sundrye tunes. *Cantus componere. Tibul.* To make songes or balades. *Cantus edere, & cantare, Idem. Cic.* To singe. *Cantus lugubres. Horat.* Sorowfull songes. *Citharæ cantus. Horat.* The tune or melody. *Dare cantus. Virg.* To singe. *Euehere cantu ad sydera. Sil.* To synge ones greate prayse. *Exercere cantus. Virgil.* To singe. *Fundere cantus ex gutture dicitur rana. Cic.* To singe in the throte. *Fundere cantus gutture. Cic.* To singe in the throte. *Pastoralis cantus. Claud.* A sheaperdes songe. *Percrepat lucus cantu symphonie. Cic.* Ringeth with melodie. *Stimulare cantus alicuius. Stat.* To stirre to singe. *Tremulus. Horat.* warbling. **1587** THOMAS L→E *Cantus, us, m.g. verb.* A song or singer, a tune, sound, melodie, or dumpe: a charme: an inchauntment in verses. **1671** PHILLIPS (3rd edn) *Cantus, (Lat.)* that part in Musick, which is called the *Mean* or *Countertenor,* being the highest next the *Altus* or *Treble.* **1676** COLES *Cantus, Latin.* the mean or Counter-tenour in Musick. **1708** KERSEY *Dict. Anglo-Brit.* (1st edn) *Cantus,* (*L.*) Singing: In *Musick,* the Mean or Counter-Tenor. **1721** BAILEY *An Univ. Etymolog. Engl. Dict.* (1st edn) *Cantus,* Singing, a Song. *L. Cantus,* (in *Musick*) the Mean, or Counter-Tenor. **1737** BAILEY *The Univ. Etymolog. Engl. Dict.* (3rd edn, vol. 2) *Cantos* (in *Musick*) is the counter tenor. **1737** DYCHE-PARDON (2nd edn) *Cantus* (S.) in *Musick,* is the Medius, or counter Tenor.

1636 BUTLER *Principles of Musik* (p. 45) But heere one of the upper Partes is necessarily to have a special Melodi aboov the rest: which is called the *Cantus* or Tune: ... **1736** TANS'UR *Compleat Melody*

(3rd edn, p. 70) *Cantus, Medius, Mean, Contra Tenor, Alto, Altus, Haut-Contra, Second Treble.* (Ital.) Either of those are a Name given to the *Middle Part*, being the *Second System*, or *Octave* above the *Bass*.

cañuto

1599 MINSHEU-PERCYVALL Sp→E *Cañuto*, m. a reede to make a pipe, the joints of a cane or reede.

canzona *see* cançion, ciancioni

1550 THOMAS It→E *Canzona*, a songe, or balade. **1598** FLORIO It→E *Canzona, Canzone*, a song, a canzonet, a ballad, a dittie, a laye, a roundelay, a virelaye. *Canzonare*, to sing, to chaunt, to make songs, to write songs and sonets. **1611** FLORIO It→E *Canzona*, as *Canzone*. *Canzonare*, to sing songs or canzonets. Also to make or write songs or sonnets. *Canzone*, a song, a canzonet, a dittie. **1659** TORRIANO-FLORIO It→E *Canzona, Canzone, Conzonetta* [sic], any song, canzonet, or dittie. **1724** [PEPUSCH] *Short Explic. of Foreign Words in Mus. Bks.* (p. 19) *Canzone*, in general signifies a Song or Tune. If this Word is fixed to a Piece of Vocal Musick, it signifies much the same as the Word *Cantata*: But if fixed to a Piece of Instrumental Musick, it then signifies much the same as the Word *Sonata* or *Suonata*. When this Word is found fixed to any Part of a Sonata, it signifies much the same as the Word *Allegro*; for it only denotes that the Movement of the Part to which it is fixed, ought to be after a gay, brisk, or lively Manner. **1726** BAILEY *An Univ. Etymolog. Engl. Dict.* (3rd edn) *Canzone* (in *Musick Books*) in general, signifies only a Song or Tune. *Ital.* *Canzone*, fixed to a Piece of Vocal Musick, signifies much the same as *Cantata*, which see. *Canzone*, fix'd to a Piece of Instrumental Musick, signifies much the same as *Sonata* or *Scionata*. *Canzona*, fix'd to any part of a *Sonata*, signifies much the same as *Allegro*, and only denotes, that the Movement of the Part to which it is fix'd, ought to be after a gay, brisk, lively manner. **1737** DYCHE-PARDON (2nd edn) *Canzone* (S.) a *Musical* Term, and when applied to vocal Musick, means the same with Cantata; and when added to instrumental Musick, means the same with Sonata; and if added to any particular Part of the Composition, is the same with Allegro.

1731 PRELLEUR *Modern Musick-Master* (Dictionary, p. 2) *Canzone* a Song, in general.

canzona a la napolitana *see* neapolitan

canzonet

1656 BLOUNT (1st edn) *Canzonet* (from the It. *Canzonetta*) a song or ditty. **1658** PHILLIPS (1st edn) *Canzonet*, (Ital.) a song or sonnet. **1676** COLES *Canzonet, Italian*. Song, Sonnet. **1708** KERSEY *Dict. Anglo-Brit.* (1st edn) *Canzonet*, (*I*) one of the Divisions of *Italian* Lyrick Poetry, in which every several Stanza answers, both as to the Number and Measure of the Verses. **1726** BAILEY *An Univ. Etymolog. Engl. Dict.* (3rd edn) *Canzonet* (*Canzonetta*, Ital.) a little Song or Tune, *Cantata* or *Sonata*;

1597 MORLEY *Plaine and Easie Introdvction* (p. 180) [marginalia: 'Canzonets'] ... The second degree of grauitie in this light musicke [i.e. after the madrigal] is giuen to Canzonets that is little shorte songs (wherin little arte can be shewed being made in straines, the beginnng [sic] of which is in composition of the musick a counterfet of the *Madrigal*. **1636** BUTLER *Principles of Musik* (p. 8) A Canzonet (as the name importeth) is a les or shorter song of the same Moode [as the madrigal, which exemplifies the ionick or 'chromatic' mood]: whose notes, for the moste parte in Counterpoint, dooe seldom exceede the number of the syllables, beginning and ending together the Lines of each vers, commonly in 4 partes: so that the Canzonet is to the Madrigal, as the Canticle to the Motet.

canzonetta

1550 THOMAS It→E *Canzonetto*, a littell songe. **1611** FLORIO It→E *Canzonetta*, a canzonet or dittie. **1659** TORRIANO-FLORIO It→E *Canzonetta*, dim. of *Canzone*. **1724** [PEPUSCH] *Short Explic. of Foreign Words in Mus. Bks.* (p. 19) *Canzonetta*, is a little Song or Tune, Cantata, or Sonata.

1731 PRELLEUR *Modern Musick-Master* (Dictionary, p. 2) *Canzonetta* ye same as *Camzone* [sic]

canzoniere *see* cançionero

1598 FLORIO It→E *Canzoniere*, a maker or writer, or singer of songs. **1611** FLORIO It→E *Canzoniere*, a maker or singer of songs. Also a booke of songs or sonnets. **1659** TORRIANO-FLORIO It→E *Canzoniere*, a maker or singer of songs, also a book of songs, or canzonets

çapateador

1599 MINSHEU-PERCYVALL Sp→E **çapateador*, m. one that daunceth and claps his hands on his shooes.

capella *see* maestro, Palestrina alla
1659 TORRIANO-FLORIO It→E *Capella,* a chappell, or little Church, an Oratory ... also a meeting of musicians in consort. **1724** [PEPUSCH] *Short Explic. of Foreign Words in Mus. Bks.* (pp. 19-20) *Capella* signifies a Church or Chapel, but more properly the Musick or Musicians belonging thereunto, or the chief Master thereof: Thus *Maestro di Capella,* is Master of the Chapel Musick. Though sometimes by *Maestro di Capella,* is to be understood only a Musick-Master; but then it means one of the first Rank. **1726** BAILEY *An Univ. Etymolog. Engl. Dict.* (3rd edn) *Capella* (in *Musick Books*) signifies the Musick, or Musician, belonging to a Chapel or Church. *Ital.* See *Maestro* di *Capella* in [letter] M.

capiscol
1599 MINSHEU-PERCYVALL Sp→E *Capiscol,* m. a chanter in the quire.

capo *see* da capo
1724 [PEPUSCH] *Short Explic. of Foreign Words in Mus. Bks.* (p. 20) *Capo,* for which see the Words *Da Capo.*

1731 PRELLEUR *Modern Musick-Master* (Dictionary, p. 2) *Capo* v. *Da.*

capriccio
1696 PHILLIPS (5th edn) *Capriccio's* are pieces of Music, Poetry, and Painting, wherein the force of Imagination has better success than observation of the Rules of Art. **1706** KERSEY-PHILLIPS (6th edn) *Caprichio's* are also pieces of Musick, Poetry and Painting, in which the force of Imagination goes beyond the Rules of Art. **1708** KERSEY *Dict. Anglo-Brit.* (1st edn) *Caprichio's* are also pieces of Musick, Poetry, and Painting. **1721** BAILEY *An Univ. Etymolog. Engl. Dict.* (1st edn) *Caprichio, Caprice;* ... Also a particular Piece of Musick, Painting and Poetry. **1730** BAILEY *Dict. Britannicum* (1st edn) *Caprice, Caprichio,* pieces of poetry, painting and musick, where the force of imagination goes beyond the rules of art.

carillon *see* bell, chime
1593 HOLLYBAND Fr→E *Carillon,* a chiming of bels, courfew. *Carrillon, m*: chyming of Bels. *Carrillonner,* to ring bels, and florish therewith. **1598** FLORIO It→E *Cariglionare,* to chime the bels. *Cariglione,* a chime of bels. **1611** COTGRAVE Fr→E *Carillon: m.* A chyming of bels; a knell. *Carillonné: m. ée: f.* Chymed, or knowled. *Carillonner.* To chyme, or knowle, bels. *Carillonneur: m.* A chymer, or knowler, of bels. *Carrillon: m.* A chyming, or knowling of bels. See *Carillon. Carrilloner.* To chyme, or knowle bels; to make a knell. **1611** FLORIO It→E *Cariglionare,* to chime the bells. *Cariglione,* a chime or iangle of bells. **1659** TORRIANO-FLORIO It→E *Cariglionare,* to chime the bells. *Cariglione,* a chime or jangle of bells. **1688** MIEGE-COTGRAVE Fr→E *Carillon,* (m.) a chime, or musick of bells. *Carillonneur,* (m.) a chimer, or knowler of bells. § *Carillonner, faire un carillon de cloches,* to chime, to knowl bells, to make a musick of bells.

Carissimi, Giacomo *see* style

carmen, carmina *see* camena, camœna
1500 *Ortus Vocabulorum* L→E Carmen inis. a dytie... n.t. Carmentis tis. est dea carminum. f.t. Carmineus a. um. ad carmen perti. o.s. Carmino as. to make diteis. n.p. **1565** COOPER L→E *Carmen, cárminis, pen. cor. n.g.* A verse or meter: a balade: a woorke in verses: a charme § *Carmen lachrymosum. Ouid.* A lamentable songe prouoking to weepe. *Carmen vigilatum. Ouid.* A songe or meter made by night. *Carmina concelebrare cantu. Lucret.* To singe songes or balades. *Carmina exequialia. Ouid.* At funeralles. *Carmina gesticulari. Sueton.* To daunce a songe or meter by measures. *Carmina nuptialia. Catull.* Songes at mariage. *Carmina socialia. Ouid.* Songes at mariages. *Carmina socians neruis. Ouid.* Singynge balades to the harpe or lute. *Concordant carmina neruis. Ouid.* Agree to the lute. *Connubiale carmen. Claud.* A mariage songe. *Flebile carmen. Ouid.* A lamentable songe. *Fœdum. Horat.* Ill made. *Fœlicia carmina. Ouid.* Very well made. *Incondita carmina. Liu.* A confuse songe. *Læta carmina. Virg. Lamentabile carmen. Stat. Mansurum carmen. Stat.* That will neuer die. *Medicabile carmen. Valer. Flac.* Comfortable. *Resonantia carmina chordis. Ouid.* Songe to the instrument. *Socialia carmina. Ouid.* Balades at mariage. **1587** THOMAS L→E *Carmen, inis, n.g.* A song, meeter, verse, or poetrie: enchantment or charm: a balade: § *Orthium carmen. Gell.* A kinde of musick in an high tune that Arion vsed when he cast himselfe into the sea. **1589** RIDER L→E *Carmen, canticom.* A Ditty. **1728** CHAMBERS *Carmen,* an antient Term among the *Latins,* us'd, in its general Sense, to signify a *Verse* ... *Pezron* fetches the Original of *Carmen,* from the Celtic *Carm,* the Shout of Joy, or the Verses which the

antient Bards sung, to encourage the Soldiers before the Combat:

carmentali

1688 DAVIS-TORRIANO-FLORIO It→E **Carmentali*, a feast, wherein they used to make verses, and sing in honour of *Carmenta*, *Evander*'s mother.

carmina *see* carmen

carnival *see* opera

1728 CHAMBERS *Carnaval*, or *Carnival*, a Season of Mirth and Rejoicing, observ'd with great Solemnity by the *Italians*, and particularly at Venice. The *Carnaval* Time commences from Twelfth Day, and holds till Lent. ¶ Feasts, Balls, Operas, Concerts of Music, Intrigues, Marriages, *&c.* are chiefly held in *Carnaval* Time. **1730** BAILEY *Dict. Britannicum* (1st edn) *Carnaval* ... a season of mirth and rejoicing observed with great solemnity by the *Italians* and *Venetians*, it commences from XIIth day, and holds till *Lent* feasts, balls, opera's, concerts of musick and intrigues, *&c.* are held in that time.

carol *see* chant, chiarantana, noel, sicinnium, teda

1550 THOMAS It→E *Carola*, a daunce. *Carolare*, to daunce. **1593** HOLLYBAND Fr→E *Carolle*, a kind of daunce: *f. Caroller*, to daunce. **1598** FLORIO It→E *Carola*, a caroll or a song. Also a kinde of dance. *Carolare*, to caroll, to reuell, to sing and dance, to be merie. **1611** COTGRAVE Fr→E *Carolle: f.* A kind of daunce wherein many daunce together; also, a Carroll, or Christmas song. *Caroller*. To daunce, to reuell it; to sing carrols. **1611** FLORIO It→E *Carola*, a song, a caroll. Also a dance. *Carolare*, to caroll, to sing, to reuell. Also to dance and be mery. **1616** BULLOKAR *Carol*. A song: sometime a dance. **1623** COCKERAM *Carol*. A song. **1656** BLOUNT (1st edn) *Caroll*, A Christmas song, or Hymn in honor of our Saviours birth, it comes from *Cantare, i.* to sing, and Rola an interjection expressing joy; for heretofore in the burden of delightful songs, and when men were jocund, they were wont to sing *Rola, Rola*, as sometimes they now do, *Hey down, derry derry*. It was an ancient custom among the Christians in their Feasts, *to bring every one into the midst, and incite him to sing unto God, as well as he could, either out of the Holy Scriptures, or of his own wit and invention*. Tertul. lib. adversus gentes, cap. 39. **1658** PHILLIPS (1st edn) *Caroll*, a Christmasse song, or hymn, sung at Christmasse, in honour of our Saviours birth. **1659** TORRIANO-FLORIO It→E *Carola*, a Caroll-song, also a merrie dance, that follows singing. *Carollare*, to caroll, to sing carols, to dance, to revell and be merry singing togther **1676** COLES *Carol*, a Christmas-song. **1678** PHILLIPS (4th edn) *Caroll, (French Carolle)* a sort of Dance; also a Song or Hymn, sung at Christmas, in honour of our Saviours birth. The properest Etymology. [sic] I find of this word, were it not a little forced, is from the Greek *χαρά. Joy.* **1706** KERSEY-PHILLIPS (6th edn) *Carol*, (Fr.) a kind of Dance: Also an Hymn, or Song sung at Christmas, in honour of our Blessed Saviour's Birth. **1721** BAILEY *An Univ. Etymolog. Engl. Dict.* (1st edn) *Carol, (Carolle, F.* Caꞃl or Ceoꞃl, *Sax.* Rustick, *q.d.* a Rural Song; or of *Καρά, Gr.* Joy) a Song usually sung on one's Birth Day; also a Hymn sung at *Christmas* in honour of the Birth of our Blessed Saviour. To *Carol*, to sing Songs of Joy. *Spen.* **1735** DEFOE *Carol*, a Song usually sung on one's Birth-day; also a Hymn at *Christmas*, in Honour of Christ's Nativity. **1737** DYCHE-PARDON (2nd edn) *Carol* (S.) a Song of Joy or Salutation at a Feast or a Birth-Day, or any publick or private Banquetting or Merriment.

carpea

1598 FLORIO It→E *Carpea*, a kinde of dance vsed among the Grecians. **1611** FLORIO It→E *Carpea*, a dance among the *Grecians*. **1728** CHAMBERS *Carpæa*, a kind of Dance, or military Exercise, in use among the *Athenians* and *Magnesians*, perform'd by two Persons; the one acting a Labourer, the other a Robber. The Labourer, laying by his Arms, goes to sowing and ploughing; still looking warily about him, as if afraid of being surpriz'd: The Robber at length appears, and the Labourer, quitting his Plough, betakes himself to his Arms, and fights in defence of his Oxen. The Whole perform'd to the Sound of Flutes, and in Cadence. ¶ Sometimes the Robber was overcome, and sometimes the Labourer; the Victor's Reward being the Oxen and Plough. The Design of the Exercise, was to teach and accustom the Peasants, to defend themselves against the Attacks of Russians.

cascabel *see* cascavelle, caxa

1599 MINSHEU-PERCYVALL Sp→E *Cascabel*, or *Cascavel*, m. hawkes bels, a rattle or bell such as children play withall. *Cascabellillo*, m. a little bell or rattle, a little hawkes bell.

cascata *see* scatta
1659 TORRIANO-FLORIO It→E *Cascata,* ... also the pennon, or streamer of a trumpet.

cascavelle *see* cascabel
1611 COTGRAVE Fr→E *Cascavelle: f.* A roundelay, or countrey song.

case
1730 BAILEY *Dict. Britannicum* (1st edn) *Case,* a house where thieves, pick-pockets, whores, house-breakers, highway-men, and all the loose, idle furacious crew meet and drink, sing, dance, and revel.

cassettare
1598 FLORIO It→E *Cassettare,* .... Also a kinde of musicall instrument.

castanet *see* Curetes, morisco, naccara, saraband
1598 FLORIO It→E *Castagnette,* little shels, such as they vse that daunce the canaries, to make a noise or sound or clack with their fingers. **1599** MINSHEU-PERCYVALL Sp→E *Castanuelas,* f. the cracking of the fingers, the snapping of the fingers. **1611** COTGRAVE Fr→E *Castagnettes: f.* Finger-knackers, wherewith Players, &c, make a prettie noyse in some kind of daunces. **1611** FLORIO It→E *Castagnette,* little shels vsed of those that dance the canaries to clacke or snap with their fingers. **1658** PHILLIPS (1st edn) *Castanetts,* a certain sort of snappers, which dancers tying about their fingers, keep time with them as they dance; they are so called from their resemblance of a a [sic] Chesnut, called in Latin *Castanea.* **1659** TORRIANO-FLORIO It→E *Castagnette,* little chestnuts, little cockle-shells used of those, that dance the Canaries, to clack, or fip with their finger, called Finger-knackers **1676** COLES *Castanets,* snappers (for dancing) like Chesnuts. **1678** PHILLIPS (4th edn) *Castanets,* a certain sort of Snappers, which Dancers of *Sarabands* tying about their Fingers, keep time with them as they dance; they are so called from their resemblance of a Chesnut, called in Latin *Castanea.* **1688** MIEGE-COTGRAVE Fr→E *Castagnettes,* (f.) castanietto's. § *Jouër des castagnettes,* to play with castanietto's. **1696** PHILLIPS (5th edn) *Castanets,* a certain sort of Snappers, which Dancers of *Sarabrands* tying about their Fingers, keep time with as they dance. **1702** KERSEY *New Engl. Dict.* (1st edn) *Castanets, or* snappers to dance with. **1704** *Cocker's Engl. Dict.* (1st edn) *Castanets,* Snappers like Chesnuts, used in dancing. **1706** KERSEY-PHILLIPS (6th edn) *Castanets, (Fr.)* a sort of Snappers which Dancers of Sarabands tie about their Fingers, to keep time as they Dance. **1708** KERSEY *Dict. Anglo-Brit.* (1st edn) *Castanets,* (*F.*) a sort of Snappers which Dancers tie about their Fingers. **1728** CHAMBERS *Castanets, Castagnettes,* or *Castanettas,* a kind of Musical Instrument, wherewith the *Moors, Spaniards,* and *Bohemians,* accompany their Dances, Sarabands, and Guittarres. It consists of two little round Pieces of Wood dried, and hollow'd in manner of a Spoon, the Concavities whereof are placed on one another fastned to the Thumb, and beat from to time with the Middle Finger, to direct their Motions and Cadences. The *Castagnettes* may beat eight or nine times in the Space of one Measure, or Second of a Minute. **1737** DYCHE-PARDON (2nd edn) *Castanets* (S.) small Instruments of Wood, Ivory, &c. that some Dancers use to play the Tune they dance.

castorio, castorlo
1659 TORRIANO-FLORIO It→E *Castorio,* ... also a kind of musick among the Grecians. **1688** DAVIS-TORRIANO-FLORIO It→E *Castorlo,* ... also a kind of Musick among the Grecians.

castration
1728 CHAMBERS *Castration* .... *Castration* also obtains in *Italy,* where 'tis us'd with a View to preserve the Voice for singing. See *Eunuch.*

castrato *see* eunuch

cat-call
1726-8 NORTH Theory of Sounds BL Add. 32535, ff. 63-63v The metalline voicing, is by a spring plate adapted to a cavity thro wch ye wind is to pass, as half a cilinder or pipe closed at one end, ye thin plate thereto affixed, with a mouth peice, all adjusted to a tube, of wch ye whole is accurately seen in a Comon pipe children play with called a cat-call.

catch *see* cantarini, roundelay, strambotto
1708 KERSEY *Dict. Anglo-Brit.* (1st edn) *Catch,* ... also a short and witty Song. **1737** DYCHE-PARDON (2nd edn) *Catch* (S.) a short, witty or merry Song;

1636 BUTLER *Principles of Musik* (p. 77) A Catch is also a kinde of *Fuga*: when, upon a certain Rest, the Partes dooe follow one an other round in the Unison. In which concise Harmoni, there is much varieti of pleasing Conceipts: the Composers whereof assume unto themselvs a special licence, of breaking, soomtimes, *Priscians* head: in unlawful taking of Discords, and in special Consecution of Unisons and Eights, when they help to the Melodi of a Part. § (p. 81) A Catch. *Fugæ etiam species est, quando voces aliquot, post certum tempus, in Vnisono in orbem canunt, & a fine ad Principium redeunt...* **1667** SIMPSON *Compendium of Practical Musick* (p. 174) ... a Catch or Round: Some call it a Canon in *Vnison;* or a Canon consisting of Periods.

catling

1706 KERSEY-PHILLIPS (6th edn) *Catlings* or *Catlins* are also a sort of small Cat-gut Strings for Musical Instruments. **1708** KERSEY *Dict. Anglo-Brit.* (1st edn) *Catlings* or *Catlins,* a sort of small Cat-gut Strings for musical Instruments. **1721** BAILEY *An Univ. Etymolog. Engl. Dict.* (1st edn) *Catlings,* also small Strings, for Musical Instruments, made of Cat-gut. **1737** DYCHE-PARDON (2nd edn) *Catling* (S.) ... also a small Gut String fit for a *Musical* Instrument.

1610 R. DOWLAND *Varietie of Lute-Lessons* [Dv] ... The best strings of this kinde are double knots ioyned together, and are made at *Bologna* in Lumbardie, and from thence are sent to *Venice*: from which place they are transported to the Martes, and therefore commonly called *Venice* Catlines.

caula *see* tibia (ascaula)

1598 FLORIO It→E *Caula,* a kinde of musicall instrument. **1611** FLORIO It→E *Caula,* a kind of musicall instrument. **1659** TORRIANO-FLORIO It→E *Caula,* a musicall instrument. **1688** DAVIS-TORRIANO-FLORIO It→E *Caula,* a musical instrument, a Sheep-coat, or fold.

cauum *see* aes

1565 COOPER L→E *Cauum, Id est tuba ærea. Virgil.* A trumpette.

cavicchia

1611 FLORIO It→E *Cauicchia,* as *Cauiglia. Cauiglia,* ... Also any peg or pin for any instrument. **1659** TORRIANO-FLORIO It→E *Cavicchia, Cavicchio, Caviglia, Cavigliuola,* any peg ... as the peg of an instrument

caxa *see* caisse, cascabel, sonagliera

1599 MINSHEU-PERCYVALL Sp→E † *Caxa,* f. ... Also a drumme. **Caxabel,* vide *Cascabel,* haukes bels, morris bels.

cazzolata

1598 FLORIO It→E *Cazzolata,* a kind of countrie musicall instrument without strings. **1611** FLORIO It→E *Cazzolata,* a ladle-full. Also a musicall instrument without strings. **1659** TORRIANO-FLORIO It→E *Cazzolata,* a ladlefull, also a certain musicall instrument without strings.

cefaut *see* c-fa-ut-key

Celænæ

1658 PHILLIPS (1st edn) *Celænæ,* a hill in *Asia,* where *Marsyas* is said to have contended with *Apollo* for the mastery upon the Fluit.

celestial music *see* harmony of the spheres

cella

1589 RIDER L→E *cella, f. delubrum, pangitorium* the Quire of a church

cembalo *see* cemmalo, cennamella, clavicembalo, cymbal, gravicembalo

1550 THOMAS It→E *Cembalo,* a tymberell. *Ciembalo,* an instrument of musike, that we call the Claricymballes. **1598** FLORIO It→E *Cembalo,* a cymball, or timbrell. *Ciembalo,* as *Cembalo.* **1611** FLORIO It→E *Cembelliero,* a plaier on Cymbals. *Cembalista,* idem. *Cembalo,* a Cymball or Timbrell. *Ciembalista,* a player on Cymbals. *Ciembalo,* as *Cembalo.* **1659** TORRIANO-FLORIO It→E *Cembalista, Cemballiero,* as *Cimbalista. Cembalo,* a cimball, as *Cimbalo. Ciembalo,* as *Cimbalo.* **1688** DAVIS-TORRIANO-FLORIO It→E *Cembalo,* a Cymbal; as *Cimbalo.*

cemmalo

1611 FLORIO It→E *Cemmalo,* a musicall instrument that country wenches vse to dance and sing vnto. **1659** TORRIANO-FLORIO It→E *Cemmalo, Cemmamella,* a musicall wind instrument, that countrey wenches use to sing and dance unto.

cennamella

1550 THOMAS It→E *Cennamella,* a certein instrument of musike. **1598** FLORIO It→E *Cennamella,* a kinde of musicall instrument. **1611** FLORIO It→E *Cennamella*, as *Cemmalo*.

ceramella *see* ciaramella, zaramella

1598 FLORIO It→E *Ceramela*, a pipe or bagpipe. **1611** FLORIO It→E *Ceramella*, a kind of bag-pipe. **1659** TORRIANO-FLORIO It→E *Ceramella*, as *Ciaramella*.

cetara *see* cithara

1550 THOMAS It→E *Cetera*, and *cetra*, an harpe or a vyale. **1598** FLORIO It→E *Cetara*, *Cetarella*, a citterne, a gitterne, a croud, a kit. *Cetaredo*, a player vpon a citterne or gitterne. *Ceterare*, to play vpon a citterne. **1611** FLORIO It→E *Cetara*, a citterne, a gitterne. *Cetaredo*, a gitterne or citterne-plaier *Cetarella*, a litle citterne or gitterne. *Ceterare*, to play vpon a citerne. *Ceteratoio*, as *Cetaredo*. *Ceteratore*, as *Cetaredo*. *Ceterista*, a gitterne-plaier. **1659** TORRIANO-FLORIO It→E *Cetaredo*, *Ceterista*, a ghittern-player. *Ceterare*, as *Cetare*, a cittern, a ghittern *Ceteratoio*, *Ceteratore*, *Ceterista*, a player upon a ghittern, or cittern. **Cetrare*, to play upon a ghittern.

c-fa-ut-key

1598 FLORIO It→E *Cefaut*, a key in musick. **1611** FLORIO It→E *Cefaut*, a key in musicke. **1659** TORRIANO-FLORIO It→E *Ce-fa-ut*, a key in Musick.

1676 MACE *Musick's Monument* (p. 196) ... *C-fa-ut-Key*, (which is the most *Noble*, *Heroick*, and *Majestical Key*, in the *whole Scale*;) ...

chace *see* fugue

chaconne *see* chichona, ground, lesson, morisco, opera, perfidia, sonata, variation

1598 FLORIO It→E *Ciacione*, ... a flattring song. **1704** HARRIS *Chaconne* (in Musick) is a kind of *Sarabrand* whose Measure is always Triple Time. **1706** KERSEY-PHILLIPS (6th edn) *Chaconne* or *Chacoon*, (*Fr.* in *Musick*) a kind of Saraband-Dance, whose Measure is always triple Time. **1707** *Gloss. Angl. Nova* (1st edn) *Chaconne*, (Fr.) a sort of Dance, whose Measure is ever-Tripla-time. **1721** BAILEY *An Univ. Etymolog. Engl. Dict.* (1st edn) *Chaconne*, *Chacoon*, a sort of Saraband Dance, the Measure of which is always Triple Time. *F.* **1724** [PEPUSCH] *Short Explic. of Foreign Words in Mus. Bks.* (pp. 21-2) *Ciacona*, a Chacoon, a particular Kind of Air, always in Triple Time, containing great Variety of Humour, contrived to a Bass in eight Bars, play'd several Times over; but not so much confin'd as is the Bass of a Ground, but is allow'd to vary every Time to humour the Treble, and sometimes to imitate it. These Airs are commonly play'd in a brisk, lively Manner. **1726** BAILEY *An Univ. Etymolog. Engl. Dict.* (3rd edn) *Ciacona* (in *Musick Books*) a Chacoon, signifies a particular kind of Air always in tripple Time, which contains a great Variety of Humour, contriv'd to a Bass in 8 Bars, play'd several Times over; but so confin'd as is the Bass of a Ground, but is allow'd to vary every Time to humour the Treble, and sometimes to imitate it: It is common to play these Airs in a brisk, lively manner. *Ital.* **1728** CHAMBERS *Chacoon*, or *Chaconde*, a kind of Dance, in the Air of a Saraband, deriv'd from the *Moors*. The Bass always consists of four Notes, which proceed in conjunct Degrees; and whereon they make divers Concords and Couplets with the same Burden. ¶ The Word is form'd of the Italian *Ciacona*, of *Cecone*, a blind Man; this Air being said to be the Invention of a blind Man. **1730** BAILEY *Dict. Britannicum* (1st edn) *Chaconde*, *Chacoon*, (of *ciacona*, Ital.) a sort of dance in the air of a saraband borrowed from the *Moors*. **1737** DYCHE-PARDON (2nd edn) *Chacoon* (S.) in *Musick*, a particular Kind of Air, always in triple Time, composed with great Variety of Humour, contrived to a Bass of eight Bars, play'd several Times over, but not so much confin'd as the Bass of a Ground, Liberty being given to vary each Time to humour the Treble, and sometimes to imitate it: These Airs or Tunes are always play'd in a lively brisk Manner.

1731 PRELLEUR *Modern Musick-Master* (Dictionary, p. 2) *Ciacona* is a Chacoon or Tune. Composed to a ground Bass.

Chæris

1565 COOPER L→E *Chæris*, A foolyshe mynstrell.

chalemie

1593 HOLLYBAND Fr→E *Chalemeler*, to sing with a little pipe made with the stalke of Oates. *Chalemie*, a little pipe. **1611** COTGRAVE Fr→E *Chalemer*. To play on a little pipe. *Chalemelle: f.* A little pipe made of a reed, or of a wheaten, or oaten, straw. *Chalemie: f.* as *Chalemelle*. **1650** HOWELL-COTGRAVE Fr→E † *Chalemeler*. To play on a little pipe. † *Chalemie: f.* as *Chalemelle*.

chalumeau *see* pipe, sourdeline
1593 HOLLYBAND Fr→E *Chalumeau,* a reede, a pipe, stemmes of hearbs: *m.*

chamade, shamade *see* beat, drum
1611 COTGRAVE Fr→E *Chamade: f.* The sounding of Trumpets; a call, or summon by the sound of Trumpets; § *Sonner la chamade.* To sound a parley; **1702** KERSEY *New Engl. Dict.* (1st edn) A *Shamade,* a beat of drum for a parley. **1704** HARRIS *Chamade,* is a Signal made by the Enemy, either by beat of Drum or sound of Trumpet, when they have any Matter to propound; as when they sound or beat a *Parley.* **1706** KERSEY-PHILLIPS (6th edn) *Chamade,* (*Fr.* in the Art of War) a Signal made by the Enemy, by beat of Drum, or Sound of Trumpet, when they have any Matter to propose, which is otherwise call'd a *Parley;* as *The Besieged beat the Chamade and Capitulated. Shamade,* a beat of Drum for a Parley. See *Chamade.* **1707** *Gloss. Angl. Nova* (1st edn) *Chamade,* (Fr.) a Signal by Drum or Trumpet, made by the Enemy for a Parley. **1708** KERSEY *Dict. Anglo-Brit.* (1st edn) *Chamade,* (*F.M.T.*) a Signal made by the Enemy, by Beat of Drum, or Sound of Trumpet. [sic] when they have any Matter to propose. *Shamade,* a beat of Drum for a Parley. **1728** CHAMBERS *Chamade,* in War, a certain Beat of a Drum, or Sound of a Trumpet, which is given the Enemy as a kind of Signal, to inform them of some Proposition to be made to the Commander; either to capitulate, to have leave to bury the Dead, make a Truce, or the like. *Shamade.* See *Chamade.* **1730** BAILEY *Dict. Britannicum* (1st edn) *Chamade* (in *Military Affairs*) a beat of drum or sound of trumpet, which is given the enemy as a kind of signal to inform them concerning some proposition to be made to the commander, either to capitulate, to have leave to bury their dead, or make a truce, *&c. Shamade* (*chamade,* F.) a Beat of Drum for a Parley. **1735** DEFOE *Chamade,* a Signal by Drum or Trumpet, when they have a mind to parley. **1737** DYCHE-PARDON (2nd edn) *Chamade* (S.) a Signal made, or given by the Enemy, sometimes by Drum, sometimes by Trumpet, importing they desire to parley, or come to a Treaty. *Shamade, Chamade* or *Parley* (S.) in *War,* is a Signal made by the Enemy, either by Beat of Drum, or Sound of Trumpet, when they have any Matter to propose; sometimes called a sounding or beating a Parley; at a *Siege,* the Besieger beat the Chamade to have Leave to bury their Dead, the Besieged to capitulate, &c.

chanson
1570/71 *Dict. Fr. and Engl.* Fr→E *Chanson,* a song. **1593** HOLLYBAND Fr→E *Chanson,* a song: *f.* **1611** COTGRAVE Fr→E *Chanson: f.* A Song; Ayre; Ballade; Lay, Roundelay, Virelay; *Chansonneur: m.* A great singer of songs. *Chansonnier: m. ere: f.* Alwaies singing, full of songs. § *Chanson de Ricochet.* A Song, Play, Tale, or Discourse, thats endlesse, and hangs ill together; or, whereof one part confutes, or contradicts, another. *Chanson de Robin.* A merrie, and exemporall song, or fashion of singing, whereto one is euer adding somewhat, or may at pleasure adde what he list; hence, also, any tedious, or endlesse discourse, &c. **1650** HOWELL-COTGRAVE Fr→E § *C'est la chanson du ricochet.* 'Tis an idle, or endlesse taile, or song; a subject whereof one part contradicts, marres, or overthrowes, another. *En vne chanson n'y a qu'un bon mot; Pro.* There is but one good word in a song. **1688** MIEGE-COTGRAVE Fr→E *Chanson,* (f.) a Song. § *Canevas de Chanson. Ce font certaines Notes d'un Maître de Musique qui marquent au Poëte la mesure des Vers de la Chanson qu'il doit faire. Chanson à boire,* a drinking Song. *Chanson Bachique,* a drunken Song. *Chanson gaillarde,* a merry Song. *Chanson lugubre,* a mourneful Song. *Chanter des chansons dissolue,* to sing licencious Songs. *Chanter une jolie chanson,* to sing a pretty Song. *direz vous toujours la même chanson?* will you still harp upon the same string? will you say still the same thing over and over? *Une Chanson falote,* a merry Song. *Une Chanson lugubre,* a moanfull Song. *un faiseur de chansons,* a Ballad-maker.

chansonette
1570/71 *Dict. Fr. and Engl.* Fr→E *Chansonette,* a little song. **1593** HOLLYBAND Fr→E *Chansonnette,* a litle Song: *f.* **1611** COTGRAVE Fr→E *Chansonette: f.* A little song, a prettie aire; a sleight, or light note, or tune. **1688** MIEGE-COTGRAVE Fr→E † *Chansonette,* (f.) a little Song.

chant *see* Ambrosian, plainchant, properchant
1570/71 *Dict. Fr. and Engl.* Fr→E *Chant,* song. **1593** HOLLYBAND Fr→E *Chant,* song: *m.* § *Chant harmonieus,* a sweete melody: *m. vn chant lugubre,* a sorrowfull singing, *com.* **1604** CAWDREY (1st edn) (French) *chaunt,* sing **1611** COTGRAVE Fr→E *Chant: m.* A Song, Ayre; Caroll, Ballade; Lay, Roundelay, Virelay; *Chanté: m. ée: f.* Sung, chaunted; warbled; crowed; resounded; commended, or described in Meeter, or in Verse. *Chantement: m.* A singing, resounding, chaunting; warbling; crowing.

§ *Chant ramage.* Naturall chaunting, rurall singing. *Douceur de chant.* The melodie, or harmonie of tuneable singing. **1650** HOWELL-COTGRAVE Fr→E § *Chant Royal.* A kinde of ancient Poem dedicated to the honour of Jesus Christ, or of his mother; and concluding with some five or six verses, commending, or directed unto, one Prince or other, not formerly mentioned. **1688** MIEGE-COTGRAVE Fr→E *Chant,* (m.) singing; a tune. § † *Un chant melancolique, pour dire un air melancolique,* a melancholy tune. **1702** KERSEY *New Engl. Dict.* (1st edn) To *chant, or* sing. **1706** KERSEY-PHILLIPS (6th edn) To *Chant, (Fr.)* to Sing. **1708** KERSEY *Dict. Anglo-Brit.* (1st edn) To *Chant,* (*F.*) to sing. **1721** BAILEY *An Univ. Etymolog. Engl. Dict.* (1st edn) To *Chant,* (*Chanter, F.* of *Cantare, L.*) to sing. **1728** CHAMBERS *Chant,* or *Chaunt.* See *Song.* ¶ *Chant, Cantus,* is particularly us'd for the Vocal Musick of Churches. ¶ In Church History we meet with divers Kinds of *Chant,* or *Song*: The first is the *Ambrosian,* establish'd by St. *Ambrose.* See *Ambrosian Chant.* ¶ The second the *Gregorian Chant,* introduc'd by Pope *Gregory* the Great, who establish'd Schools of *Chantors,* and corrected the Church Song. ¶ This is still retain'd in the Church under the Name of *Plain Song*: At first it was call'd the *Roman Song.* ¶ The *Plain,* or *Gregorian Chant,* is where the Choir and the People sing in Unison, or all together in the same manner. See *Gregorian Chant.* **1737** BAILEY *The Univ. Etymolog. Engl. Dict.* (3rd edn, vol. 2) *Chant* (*cantus,* L.) the vocal musick of churches. **1737** DYCHE-PARDON (2nd edn) *Chant* (V.) to sing, or divert one's self or others with vocal Musick. *Chant* (S.) the vocal Musick of Churches, which is commonly called plain Song, or that where all the People sing alike.

1706 BEDFORD *Temple Musick* (p. 163) The word *Chant* [in Hebrew] is פורטים and comes from פרט a *Particle,* a *small,* or a *Little Matter.* And therefore in *Musick* the פורטים or *Chanters* did Cut their Notes Short, as we do also in our *Chanting Tunes,* and mad[e] them *Small,* or *Little,* not only like unto that of *David.*

chantepleur

1658 PHILLIPS (1st edn) A *Chantepleur,* (French) he that singeth and weepeth together. **1674** BLOUNT (4th edn) *Chauntepleur* (Fr.) One that sings and weeps in the same breath. **1676** COLES *Chantepleur, French.* he that sings and weeps both together. **1726** BAILEY *An Univ. Etymolog. Engl. Dict.* (3rd edn) *Chantepleure* (of *Chanter,* to sing, and *Pleurer* to weep, *F.*) one that sings and weeps in the same Moment. *Chauc.*

chanter

see cantarini, cantator, cantiere, cantor, capiscol, contrechanter, ordines majores, ordines minores, precentor, primicerius, subchanter

1570/71 *Dict. Fr. and Engl.* Fr→E *Chantement,* singing. *Chanter,* to sing. *Chanteresse,* a woman singer. *Chantonner,* to chaunt. *Chantre,* a singer. **1593** HOLLYBAND Fr→E *Chantement,* singing: *m. Chanter,* to sing. *Chanteresse,* a woman singer: *f. Chantonner,* to chaunt. *Chantre,* a singer: *m.* **1599** MINSHEU-PERCYVALL Sp→E **Chantar,* vide *Cantar,* to sing a part. § *Chantre de yglesia,* m. the chanter in a church, or he that beginneth the tune. **1611** COTGRAVE Fr→E *Chanter.* To sing; resound; chaunt it; warble, as a bird; *Chanter: m.* A singing, or chaunting; *Chanteresse: f.* A Chaunteresse; a woman that sings, or sings much. *Chanteur: m.* A singer, a Chaunter; *Chantre: m.* A chaunter, a singer; also, a Chaunter in a Queere, or Cathedrall Church; § *Chanter l'hymne du Cigne.* To sing, speake, or utter, his last. *Chantez à l'asne il vous fera des pets: Prov.* The ignorant blockhead scornes both Musicke, and the Muses; ... **1616** BULLOKAR *Chantor.* A singer. *Chaunter.* A singer. **1623** COCKERAM *Chantor.* A singer. **1658** PHILLIPS (1st edn) A *Chanter,* he that singeth divine service in a Church, or Chappel. **1676** COLES *Chanter,* a (Church) singer. **1678** PHILLIPS (4th edn) A *Chanter, (Lat. Præcentor)* he that leads or begins in the singing of Divine service in a Church, or Chappel. **1688** MIEGE-COTGRAVE Fr→E *Chanté,* sung. *Chanter,* to sing. *Chanteur,* (m.) a Singer, a singing-man. *Chanteuse,* (f.) a Singer, a singing-woman. *Chantre,* (m.) a Chanter, a Singer (in a Quire.) § *C'est bien chanté,* that's well sung; well said (in an Ironical sense.) *Chanter la Prose,* to sing the Prose. *Chanter sa partie de Musique,* to sing his part in Musick. *Chanter une chanson, en dire l'air,* to sing a Song. *Les François chantent mieux que les Italiens,* the French sing better than the Italians. *Un bon Chanteur,* a good Singer. *Une belle chanteuse,* a fair singer. **1696** PHILLIPS (5th edn) A *Chanter,* he that leads or begins in the singing of Divine Service in a Church or Chappel. Properly the Master of the Quire. **1702** KERSEY *New Engl. Dict.* (1st edn) A *Chanter, or* chief singer in a Cathedral. **1704** *Cocker's Engl. Dict.* (1st edn) *Chantor,* a singer. **1706** KERSEY-PHILLIPS (6th edn) *Chanter,* the chief Singer in a Cathedral Church, or Chappel, the Master of the Quire. **1708** KERSEY *Dict. Anglo-Brit.* (1st edn) *Chanter,* the chief Singer in a Cathedral Church, or Chappel. **1721** BAILEY *An Univ. Etymolog. Engl. Dict.* (1st edn) *Chanter, (Chanteur, F.)* the Chief Singer in a Chappel or Cathedral. **1728** CHAMBERS *Chanter*, or *Chauntor*, a Person who sings in the Choir of a Cathedral. See *Choir, &c.* ¶ All great Chapters have *Chantors* and Chaplains to ease and assist the Canons, and officiate in their Absence.... St. *Gregory* first instituted the Office of *Chantors*, erecting them into a Body, call'd *Schola Cantorum*: tho *Anastasius* seems to attribute their Rise to Pope *Hilary*, who liv'd an hundred Years before *Gregory*. ¶ But the Word grows obsolete in this Sense, and instead thereof we use the Word *Chorister*, or Singing-Man. See *Chorister.* ¶ *Chantor* is us'd, by way of Excellence, for the *Præcentor*, or Master of the Choir; which is one of the first Dignities of the Chapter. ¶ The *Chantor* bears the Cope and the Staff at solemn Festivals; and gives Tune to the rest at the beginning of Psalms and Anthems. See *Præcentor.* ¶ The Antients call'd the *Chantor Primicerius*. See *Primicerius.* ¶ To him formerly belong'd the Direction of the Deacons, and other inferior Ministers. **1735** DEFOE *Chanter*, a Singer in a Chapel or Cathedral. **1737** DYCHE-PARDON (2nd edn) *Chanter* (S.) the principle or chief Singer in a Cathedral, or other Church or Chapel, where a Set of Choiristers or other Singers were kept.

chanterelle *see* cantarella, canto, lute, pinceter
1593 HOLLYBAND Fr→E *Chanterelle*, as *chorde chanterelle*, the singing string, the cord or string of any instrument of musick. **1611** COTGRAVE Fr→E *Chanterelle: f.* The treble, in singing; also, a treble string, or bell; also, a small bell for a chyme. **1688** MIEGE-COTGRAVE Fr→E *Chanterelle*, (f.) the treble string of a Violin, the smallest string of any musical Instrument. ¶ Or thus. As, Eccl. 12. 6. *Les Chanterelles seront abbaissées*, the Daughters of Musick shall be brought low.

chanticleer *see* risvegliatoio
1656 BLOUNT (1st edn) *Chanticleer* (Fr.) one that sings clear **1704** *Cocker's Engl. Dict.* (1st edn) *Chanticleer*, sings cleer, like a Cock.

chantillonner
1611 COTGRAVE Fr→E *Chantillonné: m. ée: f.* Chaunted; sung roundly, or merrily. *Chantillonner.* To chaunt it; to sing roundly, or merrily. **1650** HOWELL-COTGRAVE Fr→E † *Chantillonné: m. ée: f.* Chaunted; sung roundly, or merrily. † *Chantillonner.* To chant it; to sing roundly, or merrily.

chantry *see* cantaria, precentura
1570/71 *Dict. Fr. and Engl.* Fr→E *Chanterie*, Musicke. **1593** HOLLYBAND Fr→E *Chanterie.* Musicke, chantrie: *f.* **1611** COTGRAVE Fr→E *Chanterie: f.* Chaunting, singing; Musicke; also, a Chanterie; the place, degree, or office, of a Chaunter. *Chantrerie.* as *Chanterie.* **1650** HOWELL-COTGRAVE Fr→E † *Chantrerie.* as *Chanterie.* **1661** BLOUNT (2nd edn) *Chanterie* (Fr. from the Lat. *canto*, to sing) was a Chappel (commonly annexed, to some Parochial or Cathedral Church) endowed with lands or other yearly Revenues, for the maintenance of one or more Priests, daily to *sing* Mass for the Souls of the Donors, or such others as they did appoint. 37 *Hen.* 8.4.1. *Edw.* 6.14. Of these *Chanteries*, there were forty seven within St. *Pauls* Church *London*. See Mr. *Fullers Ch. Hist. l.* 6. *f.* 357. **1676** COLES *Chauntry, French.* a church, chappel or quire endowed with maintenance for singers of Divine service. **1688** MIEGE-COTGRAVE Fr→E *Chanterie*, (f.) a singing. § *J'ois une Voix de chanterie*, (Ex. 32. 18.) I heare the Noise of them that sing. **1702** KERSEY *New Engl. Dict.* (1st edn) A *Chantery, or* Chappel where the Service is sung **1704** *Cocker's Engl. Dict.* (1st edn) *Chantery*, a Chappel Erected and endowed with a yearly maintenance, for Priests to sing Mass daily for the Soules of the Founders, and others as they appoint; the Priest so officiating, is called a *Chanting* Priest. **1706** KERSEY-PHILLIPS (6th edn) *Chantry*, a Chappel formerly joyn'd to some Cathedral, or Parish-church, and endow'd with Yearly Revenues, for the Maintenance of one, or more Priests daily to sing Mass for the Souls of the Founders, and others: Of these Chantries there were no less than forty seven within St. *Paul's* Church, *London*. **1707** *Gloss. Angl. Nova* (1st edn) *Chantry*, a Chappel endow'd for the maintaining a Priest or Priests to sing Mass for the Souls of their Founders. **1708** KERSEY *Dict. Anglo-Brit.* (1st edn) *Chantry*, a Chappel formerly joyned to some Cathedral, or Parish-church, and endow'd with yearly Revenues, where Masses were daily sung for the Souls of the Founders and others. **1726** BAILEY *An Univ. Etymolog. Engl. Dict.* (3rd edn) *Chauntry*, a Church or Chapel endow'd with a yearly Revenue for the maintenance of one or more Priests, to sing Mass daily for the Souls of the Donors, and such as they appoint. **1728** CHAMBERS *Chantry*, a Chapel endow'd for the maintaining a Priest, or Priests, to sing Mass for the Souls of the Founders.

Chauntry, or *Chantry*, was antiently a Church, or Chapel endow'd with Lands, or other yearly Revenue, for the Maintenance, formerly, of one or more Priests, daily saying or singing Mass for the Souls of the Donors, and such others as they appointed. **1730** Bailey *Dict. Britannicum* (1st edn) *Chauntry*. See *Chantry*.

chapas

1599 Minsheu-Percyvall Sp→E *Chapas*, f. a cimball. a clapper, rattles, an instrument made with two plates. Also thin plates, spangles. **Chaperia*, f. the working of plates or spangles, rattles, Cymbals, or such like.

character *see* dot, figure, sign

1728 Chambers *Characters* us'd in *Musick*. ¶ *Characters of the Musical Notes, with their Proportions.* [gives table showing large, long, breve, semibreve, minim, crotchet, quaver, semiquaver and demisemiquaver] ¶ *Characters of the artificial Notes.* ¶ ✕ *Character* of a *sharp Note*: This *Character* at the beginning of a Line, or Space, denotes all the Notes in that Line, or Space, to be taken a Semitone higher than in the natural Series. And the same affects all their Octaves, above and below, tho not mark'd. See *Sharp*. ¶ When the *Character* is prefix'd to any particular Note, it shews that Note alone to be a Semitone higher than it would be without such *Character*. ¶ ♭ *Character* of a *flat Note*: This *Character*, at the beginning of a Line, or Space, shews, that all the Notes in that Line, or Space, are to be taken a Semitone lower than in the natural Series; affecting, in like manner, all the Octaves, both above and below. See *Flat*. ¶ When prefix'd to any Note, it shews that Note alone to be a Semitone lower than it wou'd otherwise be. ¶ ♮ *Character* of a *natural Note*. Where, in a Line or Series of artificial Notes, mark'd at the Beginning for either Sharps or Flats, the natural Note happens to be requir'd, it is denoted by this *Character*. ¶ *Characters of Sign'd Clefs.* ¶ 𝄞 *Character* of *Treble Clef.* ¶ 𝄡 *Mean Clef.* ¶ 𝄢 *Bass Clef.* ¶ *Characters of Time*. See *Time*. ¶ 2, or 2/4, or 4/8; *Characters* of *Common*, or *Duple Time*; signifying the Measure of two Crotchets to be equal to two Notes, whereof four make a Semibreve. ¶ C ₵ Ↄ *Characters* that distinguish the Movements in *Common Time*: The first implying *slow*; the second *brisk*; the third *very quick*. ¶ 2/1, 3/2, 3/4, 3/8, 3/16, *Characters* of the *Simple Triple Time*; whose Measure is equal either to three Semibreves, or to three Minims, *&c*. See *Triple*. ¶ 6/4, or 6/8, or 6/16; *Characters* of *mix'd Triple Time*; where the measure is equal to six Crotchets, or six Quavers, *&c*. ¶ 9/4, or 9/8, or 9/16; or 9/1, or 9/2; *Characters* of *compound Triple Time*. ¶ 12/4, or 12/8, or 12/16, or 12/1, or 12/2; *Characters* of the fourth Species of *Triple Time*; call'd, *The Measure of twelve Times*. ¶ *Rests or Pauses of Time*. [gives illustration showing rests for large, long, breve, semibreve, minim, crotchet, quaver, semiquaver and demisemiquaver; shows signs for single bar, double bar, repeat, close, tie and direct]

charivaris

1611 Cotgrave Fr→E *Charivaris: m.* A publicke defamation, or traducing of; a foule noise made, blacke *Santus* rung, to the shame, and disgrace of another; hence, an infamous (or infaming) ballade sung, by an armed troupe, vnder the window of an old dotard married, the dæy before, vnto a young wanton, in mockerie of them both § *Charivaris de poelles*. The carting of an infamous person, graced with the harmonie of tinging kettles, and frying-pan Musicke.

chelys *see* barbiton

1500 *Ortus Vocabulorum* L→E Chelis lis. cythara. a harpe. **1538** Elyot L→E *Chelys*, ... sometyme it is taken for an harpe or lute. **1552** Huloet L→E *chelys, cithara, Fidicen, Lyra*. Harpe. **1565** Cooper L→E *Chelys, fœm. gen. Testudo*. ... also a lute or harpe, because the fyrst lute was made of a Torteise shell. § *Digitis errantibus scindere chelyn. Stat.* To play vpon a lute vnskilfully. *Exuere chelyn. Stat.* To lay downe his lute. *Intendere chelyn. Stat.* To wreste vp the stringes of the lute. *Laxare chelyn. Stat.* To sette downe. **1587** Thomas L→E *Chelys, ys, f.g. Ovid.* A Torteise, also, a lute, or harpe, because the first lute was made of a Torteise shel.

1636 Butler *Principles of Musik* (p. 17) It is recorded by *Homer*, that *Mercuri* finding a Tortois, whose nervs or Chords, being dryed and strained in the Sun, yeelded, with a touch, a pleasing sound, did thereupon make an Instrument like unto it, which, after the name of the Tortois, hee called *Chelys*, (*Testudo*:) and strung it with fowr Strings or Chords of 4 distinct Notes: the lowest *Nete*, the next *Paranete*; the Highest *Hypate*, and the next *Parhypate* ...

chevalet

1593 HOLLYBAND Fr→E Vn *Chevalet*, ... also a parke, or a viol, harpe, or other instrument of musicke: *m.* **1611** COTGRAVE Fr→E *Chevalet: m.* ... also, the Bridge of a Lute, Violl, &c; **1688** MIEGE-COTGRAVE Fr→E *Chevalet*, (m.) ... the bridge of a musical Instrument;

chevre

1611 COTGRAVE Fr→E *Chevre: f.* A she-goat; also a bag-pipe; *Chevrie: f.* A bag-pipe. **1650** HOWELL-COTGRAVE Fr→E † *Chevrie: f.* A Bag-pipe.

chiamamento

1659 TORRIANO-FLORIO It→E *Chiamamento, Chiamata, Chiamatione, Chiamazione, Chiamore*, a call by drum, or trumpet

chiaramella *see* ciaramella

chiarantana *see* chirinzane

1598 FLORIO It→E *Chiaranzana*, a kind of leape, or hopping or dauncing, as the Alman leape. **1611** FLORIO It→E *Chiarantana*, a kinde of Caroll or song full of leapings like a Scotish gigge, some take it for the Almaine-leape. *Chiarantanare*, to dance *Chiarantana*. *Chi[a]ranzana*, as *Chiarantana*. *Chiarentanare*, to dance *Chiarantana*. **1659** TORRIANO-FLORIO It→E *Chiarantana, Chiaranzana*, a kind of song or caroll, unto which the Countrey people dance a full of leapings and jumpings, answering our Scottsh jiggs, some take it for the Alman-leape. *Chiarantare*, to dance, to skip, to jump, or sing to a *Chiarantana*.

chiaretto

1611 FLORIO It→E *Chiaretto*, ... Also a sounding instrument called a Clarion. **1659** TORRIANO-FLORIO It→E *Chiarello, Chiaretto*, ... also a kind of cleere and shrill-sounding instrument, called with us a Clairon.

chiarino *see* clarion

1611 FLORIO It→E *Chiarino*, a clairon [i.e. clarion] of a trumpet.

chiave *see* clef

1598 FLORIO It→E *Chiaue*, ... Also a clif in musike. **1611** FLORIO It→E *Chiaue*, ... Also a cleefe in musike. **1724** [PEPUSCH] *Short Explic. of Foreign Words in Mus. Bks.* (p. 21) *Chiave* is a Cliff, a Term or Character in Musick. **1726** BAILEY *An Univ. Etymolog. Engl. Dict.* (3rd edn) *Chiave* (in *Musick Books*) is Cliff, a Term or Character of Musick. *Ital.* **1736** BAILEY *Dict. Britannicum* (2nd edn) *Chiave* (in *Musick Books*) is a cliff, a term or character of Musick, *Ital.* a *Key*.

chichona *see* chaconne, lesson

1676 MACE *Musick's Monument* (p. 129) *Chichona's*, are only a few *Conceited Humorous Notes*, at the end of a *Suit of Lessons, very Short*, (*viz.*) not many in Number; yet sometimes consists of Two *Strains*, although but of Two *Semibreves in* a *Strain*, and commonly, of a *Grave kind of Humour*.

chiesa *see* sonata, tuono di chiesa

1724 [PEPUSCH] *Short Explic. of Foreign Words in Mus. Bks.* (pp. 20-1) *Chiesa*, a Church or Chapel. This Word is used in the Title Page of some Musick Books, to distinguish the Musick design'd for Churches, from that design'd for Chambers or private Consorts. Thus *Sonata, Musiche*, or *Concerti, &c. da Chiesa*, is Sonatas, Musick, or Concertes, *&c.* for a Church or Chapel: And *Sonata, Musiche*, or *Concerti da Camera*, is Sonatas, Musick, or Concertes, *&c.* for a Chamber or private Consort. **1726** BAILEY *An Univ. Etymolog. Engl. Dict.* (3rd edn) *Chiesa* (in *Musick Books*) is set to distinguish the Musick design'd for Churches, from that design'd for Chambers, or private Consorts; as *Sonata da Chiesa*, is Sonata for the Chapel.

chifle *see* cifello

1599 MINSHEU-PERCYVALL Sp→E † *Chiflar*, to whistle. † *Chifle*, or *Chiflo*, m. a whistle, a piping.

chime *see* appeau, bell, carillon, repicco, vettina, watch-work

1658 PHILLIPS (1st edn) *A Chime* of Bells, a pleasant tune rung upon the Bells. Some say from the Latin word *Cymbalum*. **1702** KERSEY *New Engl. Dict.* (1st edn) A *Chime* of Bells. To *chime* the bells **1706** KERSEY-PHILLIPS (6th edn) *Chime*, a Tune set upon Bells, or in a Clock. **1708** KERSEY *Dict. Anglo-Brit.* (1st edn) *Chime*, a Tune set upon Bells, or in a Clock. **1728** CHAMBERS *Chimes of a Clock* ... [*see* Appendix] **1730** BAILEY *Dict. Britannicum* (1st edn) *Chime* (prob. of *gamme*, F) a tune set upon bells or in a clock; a kind of periodical musick, produced at certain seasons of the day, by a particular *apparatus* added to a clock. To *Chime*, to ring a tune by the spring of a mechanical clock. **1735** DEFOE To *Chime*, to ring Bells in a particular manner.

chioppare *see* baioccare, baylar, chrich, vaylar
1598 FLORIO It→E *Chioppare,* to clack or snap with ones fingers as barbers vse, or such as dance the canaries. **1611** FLORIO It→E *Chioppare,* to clacke or snap, or phip, or click, or lirp with ones fingers as they that dance the Canaries

chipassa
1598 FLORIO It→E *Chipassa,* the name of a galliard. **1611** FLORIO It→E *Chipassa,* the name of a galliard.

chirinzane *see* chiarantana
1659 TORRIANO-FLORIO It→E *Chirinzane,* a kinde of dance.

chironomica saltatio
1565 COOPER L→E *Chironomica saltatio.* The morrisse daunce. **1587** THOMAS L→E *Cheironomica saltatio.* The morrisse daunce. **1589** RIDER L→E *Chironomica saltatio, chironomia, f.* The moris daunce.

chironomus
1538 ELYOT L→E *Chironomus,* a daunser of a moriske. **1565** COOPER L→E *Chironomus, pen. corr. Iuuenal.* He that teacheth one to gesture: or one that daunseth with gesture in a morrisse. **1587** THOMAS L→E *Chironomus, mi, m.g. & Chironomon, ontis, Iuven.* He that teacheth one to gesture, or one that daunceth with gesture in a morreise.

chirp
1706 KERSEY-PHILLIPS (6th edn) To *Chirp,* to sing, warble, or peep, as a Bird does. **1726** BAILEY *An Univ. Etymolog. Engl. Dict.* (3rd edn) To *Chirp,* to make a chirping Noise, to Sing or Warble as a Bird does.

chirrmia
1599 MINSHEU-PERCYVALL Sp→E *† *Chirrmia,* f. an instrument of musicke. *Chirrmias,* f. a kinde of musicall instrument.

chitariglia
1659 TORRIANO-FLORIO It→E **Chitariglia,* a Spanish ghittern.

chitarra *see* cithara
1598 FLORIO It→E *Chitarra,* a gitterne, or such instrument. **1611** FLORIO It→E *Chitarista,* a Gitterne or Cittern-plaier. *Chitarra,* a Gitterne, or Citterne. **1659** TORRIANO-FLORIO It→E *Chitarista,* a ghittern-player. **Chitarra,* a ghittern, a little Lute wanting a base and treble, a ghitarre, an instrument, commonly known by that name.

choir *see* choral, chorister, chorus, quire, quirister, symphonio
1550 THOMAS It→E *Choro,* the queere that is vsed in churches. **1593** HOLLYBAND Fr→E *Choëur,* as *les religieux sont assemblez en leur Choëur,* the Monkes are gathered togither in their quire or priuate place of prayers: or vestrie: *m.* **1598** FLORIO It→E *Choro,* a quire, a companie, a chorus. Also a musicall instrument. *Coro,* ... Also a Quier of a church **1611** COTGRAVE Fr→E *Choëur: m.* The Quire of a Church; also, a round, ring, or troope of singers, or dauncers; or of Auditors, or Spectators of those, or the like Exercises. *Chore: m.* A companie of singers, or dauncers; any number, assembly, or whole companie; as the Chorus between euerie Act in a Tragedie. *Choreal: m. ale: f.* Frequenting, or belonging to, a Queere. *Choriaux: m.* Queeremen, singing men, quirresters. *Corial: m.* A Singing-man, Quire-man, or Quirrester. § *Enfans de choëur.* Quirresters. *Enfant de choëur.* A Quirrester. *Enfant de coeur* [sic]. A Quirester, or singing boy. **1611** FLORIO It→E *Choro,* as *Coro. Coro,* a Quier of a Church, a companie of people gathered close together. Also a Chorus in a Tragedie... Also a kind of musicall instrument. **1650** HOWELL-COTGRAVE Fr→E † *Chore: m.* A company of singers, or dancers; any number, assembly, or whole company; as the Chorus between every Act in a Tragedy. **1659** TORRIANO-FLORIO It→E *Coro, Choro,* a Quire of a Church, also a Chorus in a Tragedie, also a company or consort of people gathered together to sing, or to do any thing else, ... also a certain musicall instrument used in Quires of Churches § *Giovane di choro,* a chorister. **1688** MIEGE-COTGRAVE Fr→E *Chœur,* (m.) Quire, the Quire of a Church; a Company of Players. § *Enfant de Chœur,* a singing-Boy. *Enfans de chœur,* singing Boys. *Maître des Enfans de Choeur,* the Master of the Singing Boys. **1702** KERSEY *New Engl. Dict.* (1st edn) A *Choire, or* quire in a Church. **1706** KERSEY-PHILLIPS (6th edn) *Choir,* the Quire of a Church, that part of it where Divine Service is said, or sung. **1724** [PEPUSCH] *Short Explic. of Foreign Words in Mus. Bks.* (p. 21) *Choro, Choeur,* or *Chorus,* is when all the several Parts of a Piece of Musick perform together, which is commonly at the Conclusion. **1726** BAILEY *An Univ. Etymolog.*

Engl. Dict. (3rd edn) *Choro, Choeur, Chorus* (in *Musick Books*) is when all the several Parts of a Piece of Musick perform together, which is commonly at the Conclusion. *Ital.* **1728** Chambers *Choir*, that part of a Church, Cathedral, *&c.* where the Priests, and *Choristers*, or Singers, are dispos'd. See *Church.* ¶ The *Choir* is distinguish'd from the *Cancel* [sic], or *Sanctuary*, where the Communion is celebrated; as also from the *Nave*, or Body of the Church, where the People assist. ¶ The Patron is said to be oblig'd to repair the *Choir* of a Church; and the Parishioners the Nave. ¶ The *Choir* was not separated from the Nave, till the Time of *Constantine*: From that Time the *Choir* was rail'd in with a Ballustrade, with Curtains drawn over; not to be open'd till after the Consecration. ¶ In the XIIth Century they began to enclose the *Choir* with Walls: But the antient Ballustrades have been since restor'd; out of a View to the Beauty of the Architecture. The Chantor is Master of the *Choir*. See *Chantor.* ¶ In Nunneries, the *Choir* is a large Hall, adjoining to the Body of the Church; separated by a Grate, where the Religious sing the Office. ¶ The Word, according to *Isidore*, is derived *à Coronis circumstantium*; because, antiently, the *Choristers* were dispos'd round the Altar to sing: which is still the manner of building Altars among the *Greeks*. **1737** Dyche-Pardon (2nd edn) *Choir* (S.) that Part of a Church, Cathedral, &c. where the Priests, Choristers or Singers are dispos'd in proper Order to perform their several Offices.

choragus *see* Agathon, agonothet, chorus, revels
1706 Kersey-Phillips (6th edn) *Choragus*, the Master, or Setter forth of Plays; the Leader of the Dance, the Master of the Revels who was to look to the Musick, or to furnish the Attire.

choraico *see* modi melopœiæ, style (stylo choraico)

choral
1656 Blount (1st edn) *Choral (choralis)* belonging to the Chorus or Quire. **1661** Blount (2nd edn) *Choral (choralis)* belonging to the Chorus or Quire. As *Viccars Choral*, mentioned in Act 1649. *ca.* 24. **1696** Phillips (5th edn) *Choral*, a Law term, one that by vertue of the ancient Orders of the Clergy was admitted to serve God in the Quire. **1706** Kersey-Phillips (6th edn) *Choral*, belonging to the Choir of [a] Church; as a *Vicar Choral*, i.e. one that by virtue of any of the Orders of the Clergy, was admitted to sit and serve God in the Quire; of these there were formerly six belonging to St. *Paul's* Cathedral. **1708** Kersey *Dict. Anglo-Brit.* (1st edn) *Choral*, belonging to the Choir of a Church; as a *Vicar Choral*, i.e. one that was admitted to sit and serve God in the Quire.

1736 Tans'ur *Compleat Melody* (3rd edn, p. 62) A *Composition* of *Eight Parts* is commonly called *Choral-Musick*; which is perform'd by two opposite *Quires* (or by, or with *Instruments;*) which *Musick* is said to have two *Basses*, i.e. one *Bass* peculiar to each *Quire*; and also all the three other *Parts* affixed to each *Bass*; and do perform, either with a *single Voice*, or with *two, three* or all four *Parts* together: ... § (p. 70) *Coral-Musick*, is *Musick* sung by turns; by two opposite *Quires*.

choraula *see* aulœdus, fidicen
1500 *Ortus Vocabulorum* L→E Choraula qui ducit choream vel q in choro cum canulis cantat. anglice a leyder of a dannce. Choraules. princeps chori vel q cum canulis & fistulis canit in choro. angl. a chuntter. **1538** Elyot L→E *Choraula*, the crafte to blowe trumpettes, or to playe on shawlmes, or other lyke pypes. *Choraules*, players on the sayde Instrumentes. **1552** Huloet L→E *Choraula*. Crafte musicall. **1565** Cooper L→E *Choraula, vel choraules, huius choraulæ, vel choraulis. Marttial* [sic]. A player on a pype or fluite: a minstrell. **1587** Thomas L→E *Choraules, & Choraula, æ, m.g. Mart.* A player on a pipe or fluite, a minstrell.

chord *as interval, see* common cord, flat cord, interval, sharp cord
1728 Chambers *Chord* is also us'd in Musick, for the Note, or Tone to be touch'd, or sounded; in which Sense, it is applicable to all the Intervals of Musick. See *Concord.* ¶ In this Sense, the Fifth is said to consist of five *Chords*, or Tones. See *Fifth, &c.* **1737** Dyche-Pardon (2nd edn) *Chord* (S.) ... and in *Musick*, ... sometimes it means the striking two or more Sounds together, which give a most grateful Salutation to the Ear.

1676 Mace *Musick's Monument* (p. 225) Those 7 *Keys*, or *Distances*, as they are us'd in *Composition*, go by the name of *Chords, viz.* a *Unison*, *2d. 3d. 4th. 5th. 6th.* and *7th.* And whereas you have heard talk of an *8th. 9th. 10th.* &c. They are but as the very same before *Repeated, viz.* and *Eighth*, is as an *Unison*, the *9th.* as a *2d.* the *10th.* as a *3d.* So that your *Business* will be no more, than to understand the *Right use* of the 7 *Chords*. § (p. 226) You will do well also to avoid the *Consecution* of *Fifths* and *Eighths*; which although they be very *True Chords*, (and indeed the most *Lushious ones*; for which cause They are called the *Perfect Chords*) ... **c.1710** NORTH Short, Easy, & plaine rules BL Add. 32531, f. 24v ... what wee call chords, that is The consonancy's & dissonancys In Musick ... **1731** HOLDER *Treatise of Natural Grounds... revis'd* (p. 159) By *Chords* is meant either *Concords* or *Discords*; by *Semitones* is meant half Notes. **1736** TANS'UR *Compleat Melody* (3rd edn, p. 68) *Chords*, or *Cords*, are the *Names* given to the Musical Sounds made by either *Voice*, or *Strings*; or by *Wind* Artificially: *i.e.* when two or more *Sounds* do Sound together; each *Note* being an *Interval* either *greater* or *lesser* Distance one from another. So these *Distances*, or *Intervals*, are called *Cords* and *Discords*.

chord *as string, see* cord, nervo, string

1552 HULOET L→E *Chorda. æ, Fides. is, Neruia. æ, Neruus, ui*, Stryng for an instrument of musike. **1565** COOPER L→E *Chorda, huius chordæ. Cic.* A stringe of an harpe, lute, or other instrument. § *Chordas vocales impellere pollice. Tibull.* To play on a lute or harpe. *Experiri chordas. Stat.* To assaye or trie whether stringes be in tune. *Habili pollice prætentat chordas. Ouid.* He trieth the stringes with his nimble thumbe. *Impulsas tentauit pollice chordas. Ouidius.* He assayed the stringes. *Mouere chordas pollice. Stat.* To play on the harpe or lute. *Oberrare eadem chorda. Horat.* To harpe alwaie on one strynge. *Prætentare chordas. Oui.* To assay whether they be in tune. *Quarta chorda ad septimam respondet. Varro.* The fourthe strynge agreeth with the seuenth. *Socíanda chordis. Horat. Verses lyrici*, Balades to be songe to the harpe. *Socianda verba chordis. Horat.* Verses or meter to be songe to the harpe. *Tenuis chorda psalterij. Virg.* A small stryng. *Verba socianda chordis. Horat.* To be songe to an instrument. **1587** THOMAS L→E *Chorda, æ, f.g.* A string of an harpe, lute, or other instrument. **1706** KERSEY-PHILLIPS (6th edn) *Chord*, ... Also a Term in Musick. See *Cord*. *Chorda, (Gr.)* ... the String of a Musical Instrument made of a Gut **1728** CHAMBERS *Chords*, or *Cords*, in Musick, are the Strings, or Lines, by whose Vibrations the Sensation of Sound is excited; and by whose Divisions the several Degrees of Tune are determin'd. See *Sound*, and *Tune*. ¶ Some say, they are called *Cords*, or *Chords*, from the *Greek* χορδαί, a Name the Physicians give to the Intestines; in regard, the Strings of Musical Instruments are ordinarily made of Guts: Others are made of Brass or Iron Wire; as those of Spinets, Harpsichords, *&c.* ¶ *Chords* of Gold Wire, in Harpsichords, yield a Sound almost twice as strong as those of Brass: *Chords*, or Strings of Steel, yield a feebler Sound than those of Brass; as being both less heavy, and less ductile. ¶ M. *Perrault* observes, that of late they have invented a way of changing the *Chords*, to render their Sound more strong, without altering the Tone. ¶ The sixth *Chord* of *Bass-Viols*, and the tenth of large *Theorbos*, consist of 50 Threads, or Guts: There are some of them 100 Foot long, twisted and polish'd with *Equisetum*, or Horse-Tail.... See *Monochord*, see also *Tune, Concord, Harmony, &c.* **1731** KERSEY *New Engl. Dict.* (3rd edn) The *Chords*, or Strings of a musical Instrument. **1737** DYCHE-PARDON (2nd edn) *Chord* (S.) ... and in *Musick*, sometimes it means the Strings of the Instruments themselves, by whose Vibrations the Sensation of Sound is excited, and by whose Divisions the several Degrees of Tone are determined;

chorea

1500 *Ortus Vocabulorum* L→E Chorea e. a daunce or sange.

choreuma

1565 COOPER L→E *Choreuma, huius choréumatis, pen. cor. neut. ge. Plato.* A songe when many synge and daunce together. **1587** THOMAS L→E *Choreuma, atis, n.g. Plat.* A song when many sing and daunce togither. **1589** RIDER L→E *Choreuma, n.* A song wherein many sing together.

choreutes

1565 COOPER L→E *Choreutes, tis, m.g. Budæus*, A daunser: a singer: a quier man. **1587** THOMAS L→E *Choreutes, is, m.g. Bud.* A daunser, or a quier man.

choricanus *see* cantator

1500 *Ortus Vocabulorum* L→E Choricanus ni. i. qui canit in choro. a singar in the quere. m.s. Choricista e. idem est. c.p.

choricius

1500 *Ortus Vocabulorum* L→E Choricius ij. idest chorus. m.s.

chorister *see* chanter, clergeon, clerizon, quirister, symphonist

1552 HULOET L→E *Chorista. æ, Symphoniacus puer* Querister. **1589** RIDER L→E *Chorista, symphonista, symphoniacus, puer, choricanus, paraphonista, m.* A Querister. **1598** FLORIO It→E *Chorista,* a querister, or singing boy in a church. **1611** COTGRAVE Fr→E *Choriste: m.* A Chorist; a singing man in a Queere. **1611** FLORIO It→E *Chorista,* a Quirister in a Church. **1658** PHILLIPS (1st edn) *Chorister,* (Greek) a singing-man of a quire. **1676** COLES *Chorister, Greek.* Quirister, singing man or boy. **1696** PHILLIPS (5th edn) *Chorister,* see *Querister* [quirister]. **1702** KERSEY *New Engl. Dict.* (1st edn) A *Chorister, quirister, or* singer in a quire. **1704** *Cocker's Engl. Dict.* (1st edn) *Chorister,* a singing man or boy. **1706** KERSEY-PHILLIPS (6th edn) *Chorister.* See *Quirister.* **1708** KERSEY *Dict. Anglo-Brit.* (1st edn) *Chorister,* a Singing-man or Boy in a Cathedral Church. **1721** BAILEY *An Univ. Etymolog. Engl. Dict.* (1st edn) *Chorister,* (*Choriste, F.* of *Chorista, L.*) a Singing Boy or Man in a Cathedral, a Quersiter. **1728** CHAMBERS *Chorist,* or *Chorister,* a Chantor, or Singer in the Choir. See *Choir.* **1737** DYCHE-PARDON (2nd edn) *Chorister* or *Quirister* (S.) one who sings or performs a Part in the Service of the Choir.

chorocitharista

1538 ELYOT L→E *Chorocitharista,* he that leadethe a daunce, and playeth hym selfe on an instrument. **1552** HULOET L→E *chorocitharista, præsultor, uel trix.* Leder of a daunce. **1565** COOPER L→E *Chorocitharistæ, Qui in choro citharizant. Sueton.* They that play on a harpe in daunsynge with other them selues. **1587** THOMAS L→E *Chorocytharistæ, t.b. Sue.* They that play on a harpe in daunsiug [sic] with other them selues. **1589** RIDER L→E *Chorducharistæ* [sic], *m.* They that play vpon the harpe, dancing with other themselues.

chorodidascalus

1565 COOPER L→E *Chorodidascalus, pen. cor. Magister est chori. Platoni.* The maister of a company of syngers or dauncers.

chorostates

1565 COOPER L→E *Choróstates, pen. cor. Præsentor* [sic] *est chori. Budæus.* The chaunter in a quyer or companie. **1587** THOMAS L→E *Chorostates, Bud.* The chaunter in a quier or companie.

chorulus

1500 *Ortus Vocabulorum* L→E Corulus li. dimi. i. puus chorus. m.s. **1589** RIDER L→E *Chorulus, m.* A little quier.

chorus *see* act, choral, episode, grande, semichoro

1500 *Ortus Vocabulorum* L→E Chorus ri. a qwre or a cramake. in equiuocis. m.s. **1538** ELYOT L→E *Chorus,* the company of players or dauncers. also a quyar. **1552** HULOET L→E *chorus. ri.* Companye of dauncers or players. *Chorus. ri* Quere. **1565** COOPER L→E *Chorus, ri, m. gen. Cic.* A companie of singers or dauncers: § *Chori circulares. Budæus.* A rounde: when men daunce and synge takyng handes rounde. *Virgineus chorus. Ouid.* A companie of maydens syngynge and daunsyng. **1587** THOMAS L→E *Chorus, ri,* A companie of singers or dauncers: **1589** RIDER L→E *Chorus, m.* A company of dauncers. *Chrous* [sic], *m. symphonium, n.* A Quier of singers. **1656** BLOUNT (1st edn) *Chorus* (Lat.) a Company of Singers or Dancers, a Quire. The singing or musick between every Act in a Tragedy or Comedy. In a Comedy there are four Accessory parts. *viz.* 1 The *Argument.* 2 *Prologue.* 3 *Chorus.* 4 *Mimick.* Of all which the Tragedy hath onely the *Chorus.* Of these see more in Mr. *Godwins Anthology.* ch. *de Ludis.* **1658** PHILLIPS (1st edn) *Chorus,* a company of Singers in a quire, also that which is sung or played in a Tragedie or Comedy, between every act. **1659** TORRIANO-FLORIO It→E *Choro,* a Quire, as *Coro* **1676** COLES *Chorus,* a Company of Singers (in a Quire.) **1696** PHILLIPS (5th edn) *Chorus,* several persons singing together in consort, after a Verse of one or more parts; But still the *Chorus* is more full, as consisting of more Voices. **1702** KERSEY *New Engl. Dict.* (1st edn) A *Chorus,* the singing, *or* musick, in a stage-play; also a company of Choristers in a Church. **1704** *Cocker's Engl. Dict.* (1st edn) *Chorus,* a Company of Singers; also distinct lines at the end of any part of a Song or Comedy, *&c.* **1706** KERSEY-PHILLIPS (6th edn) *Chorus,* the Company of Singers and Dancers in a Stage-play, or of Persons Singing together in Consort; a Choir, or Quire. **1707** *Gloss. Angl. Nova* (1st edn) *Chorus,* the Singing or Musick in a Stage Play; also a Company of *Choristers* in a Church. **1726** BAILEY *An Univ. Etymolog. Engl. Dict.* (3rd edn) *Chorus* (Χόρος, Gr.) the Company of Singers and Dancers: Also the Singing or Musick in a Stage-Play: Also a Company of Choristers in a Church; a Choir or Quire. *L.* **1728** CHAMBERS *Chorus,* is Dramatic Poetry, one, or more Persons, present on the Stage during the Representation, and suppos'd to be By-standers thereto, without any particular Share or Interest in the Action. See *Drama.* ¶ Tragedy in its Origin, M. *Dacier* observes, was no more than a single *Chorus*, who trod the Stage alone, and without any other Actors; singing Dithrambics [sic], or Hymns in honour of *Bacchus.* ¶ *Thespis,* to relieve the *Chorus*, added an Actor, who rehears'd the Adventures of some of their Heroes. *Æschylus,* finding a single Person too dry an Entertainment, added a second; and at the same time reduc'd the singing of the *Chorus*, to make more room for the Recitation. ¶ Every thing introduc'd between the four Songs of the *Chorus*, they call'd by the Term *Episode;* and those four Songs made the four Intervals, or Acts of the Piece. See *Episode, Act, &c.* ¶ But when once Tragedy began to be form'd, those Recitatives, or Episodes, which at first were only intended as accessory Parts, to give the *Chorus* a breathing Time, became now the principal Part of the Tragedy: And whereas, before, they were taken from various Subjects, they were now all drawn from one and the same. ¶ The *Chorus,* by degrees, became inserted and incorporated into the Action, to which it was only intended as an Addition or Ornament. Sometimes the *Chorus* was to speak, and then their Chief, whom they call'd *Coryphæus,* spoke in behalf of all the rest: The singing was perform'd by the whole Company; so that when the *Cho[r]yphæus* struck into a Song, the *Chorus* immediately join'd him. See *Coryphæus.* ¶ Besides the four Songs, which made the Division of the Piece, and which were manag'd by the *Chorus*, the *Chorus* sometimes, also, join'd the Actors in the Course of the Representation, with their Plaints and Lamentations; on occasion of any unhappy Accidents that befel 'em. ¶ But the proper Function of the *Chorus*, now that Tragedy was form'd, and that for which it seem'd chiefly retain'd, was to shew the Intervals of the Acts: While the Actors were behind the Scenes, the *Chorus* engag'd the Spectators; their Songs usually turn'd on what was just exhibited; and were not to contain any thing but what was suited to the Subject, and had a natural Connection with it: so that the *Chorus* concurr'd with the Actors for advancing the Action. ¶ 'Tis a Fault observ'd in *Euripides*'s Tragedies, that his *Chorus*'s are detach'd from the Action, and not taken from the same Subject. There were some other Poets, who to save the Pains of composing *Chorus*'s, and adapting them to the Piece, contented themselves with inventing Songs, which had no relation to the Action. These Foreign *Chorus*'s were the less pardonable, as the *Chorus* was esteem'd to act a Part in the Piece; and to represent the Spectators, who were look'd on as interested therein; insomuch that the *Chorus* was not always to be mute, even in the Course of the Acts. ¶ In the modern Tragedies, the *Chorus* is laid aside; and the Fiddles supply its Place. M. *Dacier* looks on this Retrenchment as of ill consequence; and thinks it robs Tragedy of a great part of its Lustre. He adds, that 'tis ridiculous to have a Tragic Action broke, and interrupted by impertinent Flourishes from the Musick Box and to have the Spectators, who are suppos'd to be mov'd by the Representation, become all of a sudden calm and easy, break off at the height of a Passion, and amuse themselves peaceably with a Foreign Entertainment. The Re-establishment of the *Chorus* he judges necessary, not only for the Embellishment and Regularity of the Piece; but also, in regard it was one of its principal Functions, to redress and correct any Extravagancies that might fall from the Mouths of the Actors, when under any violent Passion, by prudent, and virtuous Reflections. ¶ That which occasion'd the Suppression of the *Chorus*, was its being incompatible with certain Complots, and secret Deliberations of the Actors. For 'tis in no wise probable, that such Machinations should be carry'd on in the Eyes of Persons interested in the Action. As the *Chorus*, therefore, never went off the Stage, there seem'd a Necessity of laying it aside, to give the greater Probability to these kind of Intrigues, which require Secrecy. See *Tragedy.* ¶ M. *Dacier* observes, there was a *Chorus*, or *Grex*, also in the antient Comedy; but that too is suppress'd in the new: chiefly because made use of to reprove Vices, by attacking Persons. See *Comedy.* ¶ The *Chorus* in Comedy was at first no more than a single Person, who spoke in the antient Composures for the Stage: The Poets, by degrees, added to him another; then two, afterwards three, and at last more: so that the most antient Comedies had nothing but the *Chorus*, and were only so many Lectures of Virtue. ¶ *To give the Chorus,* among the *Greeks*, was to purchase a Dramatic Piece of the Poet, and defray the Expences of its Representation. ¶ The Person who did this was call'd *Choragus.* At *Athens*, the Charge of *Choragus* was laid on the Archon; at *Rome* on the *Ædiles.* See *Choragus.* ¶ *Chorus* is likewise us'd in Musick, where, at certain Periods of a Song, the whole Company are to join the Singer, in repeating certain Couplets, or Verses. **1736** BAILEY *Dict. Britannicum* (2nd edn) *Chorus* (L. of χόρος, Gr.) the company of singers and dancers in a stage-play, or of persons singing together in consort; a choir or quire; also what is so sung. **1737** DYCHE-PARDON (2nd edn) *Chorus* (S.) that Part of vocal or instrumental Musick, where the Voices or Instruments perform together.

1736 TANS'UR *Compleat Melody* (3rd edn, p. 68) ... *Chorus*, also signifies a Quire, or Company of Singers.

chrich *see* baioccare, baylar, chioppare, vaylar
1598 FLORIO It→E *Chrich*, ... Also a clicking, a snapping or lirping of the fingers, as they vse that dance the canaries.

chrisor
1500 *Ortus Vocabulorum* L→E Chrisor aris. i. fricare. et est proprie musicorum.

chroma *see* colores generum
1587 THOMAS L→E *Chroma. Boet. Modulatio crebritate & solertia modulorum oblectans.* **1589** RIDER L→E *Chroma, n.* Sweete musicke cunningly plaied. **1598** FLORIO It→E *Croma*, ... Also pleasant and delightsome musike with descant, faining or quauering. **1611** FLORIO It→E *Croma*, pleasant and delightsome musike with descant, faining or quauering. **1706** KERSEY-PHILLIPS (6th edn) *Chroma*, (Gr.) ... In *Musick*, the Graceful Way of Singing with Quavers and Trilloes. **1728** CHAMBERS *Chroma*, in Musick. See *Chromatic*.

chromatic *see* acroamatick, artificial sound, genus, molle, pathetic music, scale, species, toniæum
1587 THOMAS L→E § *Chromaticum melos ab antiquis dicebatur vna ex tribus musicæ partibus, quæ ob nimiam mollitem infamiæ nota non caruit.* **1598** FLORIO It→E § *Cromatica musica*, musicke deuided by halfe notes. **1611** FLORIO It→E § *Cromatica musica*, musike deuided by halfe notes. **1656** BLOUNT (1st edn) *Chromatick (chromaticus)* ... pleasant or delightful; as *Chromatick Musick*, pleasant Musick. But *Chromaticum melos ab antiquis dicebatur una ex tribus musicæ partibus, quæ ob nimiam mollitiem infamiæ nota non caruit.* **1658** PHILLIPS (1st edn) *Chromatic*, (Greek) ... also a soft kind of musick, which by the Ancients was taxed of effeminacy. **1659** TORRIANO-FLORIO It→E § *Cromatica-musica*, musicke divided with half notes or descant. **1661** BLOUNT (2nd edn) *Chromatick (chromaticus)* ... pleasant or delightful; as *Chromatick Musick*, composed much of discords to render it more delightful. But *Chromaticum melos ab antiquis dicebatur una ex tribus musicæ partibus, quæ ob nimiam mollitiem infamiæ nota non caruit.* **1671** PHILLIPS (3rd edn) *Chromatick, (Greek)* ... pleasant, delightful; also vulgarly used for *Acroamatic*, see *Acroamatic*. **1676** COLES *Chromatick, Greek.* ... also as *Acroamatick.* **1688** MIEGE-COTGRAVE Fr→E *Chromatique*, Chromatick. § *Musique chromatique*, chromatick Musick, a nice and most exquisite Musick. **1696** PHILLIPS (5th edn) *Chromatick*, in Musick, is the second of those sorts of Musick that abound in Semitones, and has the same proportion with Diatonick Musick as whole Numbers with broken. **1704** HARRIS *Chromatick*, a Term in Musick, being the second of the three kinds, which abounds in Semi-tones, and contains only the least *Diatonical Degrees*. It is recorded in History, that *Timotheus* the *Milesian* first invented this sort of Musick, in the time of *Alexander the Great*, and the *Spartans* banished him by reason that being accustomed only to the *Diatonick* kind, they judged the *Chromatick* to be too soft. **1706** KERSEY-PHILLIPS (6th edn) *Chromaticks*, a pleasant and delightful sort of Musick, which consists in keeping the Intervals close, by an ingenious Artifice so as to make the Melody sweeter and softer. See *Diatonick* and *Enharmoniack*. **1728** CHAMBERS *Chromatic*, in the antient Musick, the second of the *Genera*, or Kinds, into which the Consonant Intervals were subdivided into their concinnous Parts. See *Genus*. ¶ The other two Kinds were, the *Enharmonic*, and the *Diatonic*. See *Enharmonic*, and *Diatonic*. ¶ The *Chromatic* abounds in Semitones: It had its Name, either by reason the *Greeks* mark'd it with the Character of Colour, which they call χρῶμα; or, as *P. Parran* says, because the *Chromatic* Kind is a Medium between the other two, as Colour is between black and white: or because the *Chromatic* Kind varies and embellishes the *Diatonic* Kind, but its Semitones; which have the same Effect in Musick, with the Variety of Colours in Painting. ¶ *Aristoxenus* divides the *Chromatic* Genus into three Species; the *Molle*, *Hemiolion*, and *Tonicum*. *Ptolemy* into *Molle* or *Antiquum*, and *Intensum*. See *Species*. ¶ These Species were also call'd *Chroai*, or Colours of the Genera: the *Molle* express a Progression by small Intervals, the *Intensum* by greater. ¶ The *Chromatic* and *Enharmonic* Kinds, only contain the smallest of the *Diatonic* Degrees; so as they have the same proportion to the *Diatonic*, as Fractions have to Integers. ¶ *Boetius*, and after him *Zarlin*,

attribute the Invention of the *Chromatic* Genus to *Timotheus* a *Milesian*, in the Time of *Alexander* the Great. The *Spartans* banish'd it [from] their City, by reason of its softness. ¶ Mr. *Malcolm* observes, that we are at a loss for what use the Antients could make of these Divisions, and Subdivisions into *Genera* and *Species*. All acknowledg'd the *Diatonic* to be the true Melody; the others seem only humorous Irregularities, calculated to please the Fancy by their novelty and oddness; and were besides so very difficult, that few, if any, are said to have ever practis'd them accurately. See *Musick*. **1730** BAILEY *Dict. Britannicum* (1st edn) *Chromatick Musick*, is a delightful and pleasant sort of musick; but this, by Reason of its wanton measures, was rejected. **1737** DYCHE-PARDON (2nd edn) *Chromatick* (A.) ... also a *Musical* Term, importing such Compositions as abound much in Semitones.

1597 MORLEY *Plaine and Easie Introdvction* (annotations to Part I) *Chromaticum*, is that [kind of music] which riseth by *semitonium minus* (or the lesse halfe note) the greater halfe note, and three halfe notes thus:
1688 SALMON *Proposal to Perform Musick* (p. 15) *Chromatick* Musick is that which ascends and descends gradually by half Notes. I don't mean such as is commonly call'd the half Note in *Diatonick* Musick, the 16th part of the String, the proportion assigned between B and C, between E and F: These are self-subsistent, and reck[o]ned as two compleat Steps, as well as any of the rest. And if we consider the value of their proportions, deserve rather to be reputed three-quarter than half-Notes. **c.1702** ANON. Practicall Theory of Musick BL Add. 4919, f. 4v They [chromatic notes] were so considerable among the ancients that they constituted a particular Species of Musick called the Chromatick; ... **c.1710** NORTH miscellaneous essay BL Add. 32531, f. 56 ... when a Movement is by half Notes, wee call y[e] Musick Cromatick. For in y[e] antiq way that bore y[t] Name, the progression had 2. half Notes together, w[ch] ours has not, and the Italian's call y[e] # mark il Croma. and becaus the composition proves comonly Extravagant & hard such sort of Musick is called cromatick. **1721** MALCOLM *Treatise of Musick* (p. 516) As to the Names of the *Genera* themselves, ... The *Chromatick* was so called, say some, from χρόα *color*, because as Colour is something betwixt Black and White, so the *Chrom.* is a *medium* betwixt the other Two [i.e. the enharmonic and chromatic].

1725 DE LA FOND *New System of Music* (p. 87) ... I must take notice that by *Chromatic Music* is understood, strains proceeding by what has hitherto been called half Notes, the ancient *Greeks* and *Romans* having had no better notion of Notes, than the *Moderns* have had hitherto: and indeed it is a great question, whether their notion of them was not more imperfect still. And as for the term *Chromatic*, it is derived from the Greek *Chroma*, which signified a particular color, by which the Semi-notes were distinguished from the whole Notes. This kind of *Music* proceeded and proceeds now still by their Semi-notes, which is exactly the progression of the *Twelve Notes*. **1728** NORTH Musicall Grammarian (*C-K MG* f. 110) ... The next [scale] is the chromatick, which stepps by 2 semitones, and a trihemitone, or ♭ 3d into the fourth. And from hence our masters call all movement by semitones, chromatick.

chromatic mood *see* ionick

chronometer

1721 MALCOLM *Treatise of Musick* (p. 407) I have spoken a little already of the measuring the *absolute Time*, or determining the *Movement* of a Piece by means of a *Pendulum*, a Vibration of which being applied to any one Note, as a *Crotchet*, the rest might be easily determined by that. Monsieur *Loulie* in his *Elemens, ou Principes de Musique*, proposes for this Purpose a very simple and easy Machine of a *Pendulum*, which he calls a *Chronometer*; ...

church music

c.1714-20 TUDWAY history of music BL Harley 7342 (*CHo* f. 9) ... what we call Church Music, is Artfull Music, compos'd, & perform'd wth great exactnes, to time, or measure, by a Choir of voices, fitted to their severall parts; This was found to raise devotion, by y[e] Harmony resulting therefrom, being in a style, or Air, proper to y[e] solemnity of y[e] service of God in his Church; This is by y[e] Italians therfore, call'd Stilo Ecclesiastico, by us, Church Music; ...

church tone *see* ecclesiastic tone, tone, tuono di chiesa

ciacona *see* chaconne

ciancioni

1550 THOMAS It→E *Ciancioni*, flatteryng songes.

ciaramella *see* ceramella, zaramella
1598 FLORIO It→E *Chiaramella,* a kinde of musicall instrument. *Ciaramella,* a bagpipe. *Ciaramellare,* to play musicke, to fiddle **1611** FLORIO It→E *Chiaramella,* a kind of bag-pipe. *Ciaramella,* a bag-pipe. Also any pratling or babling in merry sort. *Ciaramellare,* to play vpon a bag-pipe. Also to prattle merrily. **1659** TORRIANO-FLORIO It→E *Chiaramella,* as *Ciaramella. Ciaramella, Ciaramiglia,* a merry bag-pipe, by Met. any merie pratling.

Cicero *see* music of the world

cicuticen
1565 COOPER L→E *Cicuta. Virgil.* A pipe made with the holow stalke of a hemlocke, or of a cane. **1587** THOMAS L→E *Cicuta, æ, f.g.* ... Also, a pipe made with the hollow stalke of a hemlocke, or cane. **1589** RIDER L→E *Cicuticen, m. cicuticina, f. Aulex.* A piper on a reed, or cane.

cicutremma *see* cucutremma
1611 FLORIO It→E *Cicutremma,* a country musicall instrument. **1659** TORRIANO-FLORIO It→E *Cicutrema,* a kind of countrey croud or musicall instrument.

cifello *see* chifle, cimbello, suffolo, zuffolo
1598 FLORIO It→E *Cifello,* a piper, a crouder, a whistler. *Ciuffolare,* to whistle. *Ciuffolo,* a whistle. **1611** FLORIO It→E *Cifello,* a piper, a whistler. *Ciuffolare,* to whisse, or whistle. *Ciuffolo,* a whisse, a whistle. **1659** TORRIANO-FLORIO It→E *Cifello,* any kind of whistle. *Cifolare,* to whistle *Cifolo,* a whistle. *Ciuffolare,* to whistle *Ciuffole, Ciuffolerie,* whistlings *Ciuffolo,* a whistle.

cillone
1565 COOPER L→E *Cilones & Cillones, num. m.g.* Minstrels vsynge filthy and vncleane iestures. **1587** THOMAS L→E *Cillones,* and *Cyllones, m.g.* Minstrels vsing filthie and vncleane gestures.

cimbal *see* cymbal

cimbello *see* cifello, zimbello
1598 FLORIO It→E *Cimbello,* a whistle. **1611** FLORIO It→E *Cimbello,* a whisse, or whistle.

cingria
1500 *Ortus Vocabulorum* L→E Cinearea instrumentum musicum. pe. co. f.p. **1538** ELYOT L→E *Cingria,* a shorte pype, hauinge a smalle sownde. **1565** COOPER L→E *Cingria, f.g.* A shorte pipe with a small sounde. **1587** THOMAS L→E *Cingria, æ, f.g.* *A shorte pipe with a small sound. **1589** RIDER L→E *Cingria, f.* A short pipe with a smal sound.

circumflex *see* accent

cistre *see* sistrum

cithara *see* barbiton, cetara, chelys, chitarra, lyre
1500 *Ortus Vocabulorum* L→E Cithara e. a harpe. vel quedam vena. f.p. Citharedus. an harper syngynge with the harpe. m.s. Citharedo. idem est. Cithariso as. to harpe. vel cithara canere. to synge with an harpe. n.p. Citharo as. to harpe. n.p. **1538** ELYOT L→E *Cithara,* a harpe. **1550** THOMAS It→E *Cithara,* a crowde. **1565** COOPER L→E *Cithara, cítharæ, pen. cor. Plin.* An harpe. *Cithara, pro ipsa musica & harmonia. Virg.* Harmony. § *Ad strepitum citharæ. Horat.* At the sounde or tune of. *Cithara imbellis. Horat.* A womanly harpe singyng songes of loue and not of valiant actes. *Cithara omnibus neruis intenta. Quint.* An harpe hauynge all the stringes wrested vp in tune. *Deditus studio citharæ. Horat.* Geuen to learne to play on the harpe. *Imbellis cithara. Hora.* Note meete for martiall prowes, but onely to sing louetoyes. *Molles citharæ modi. Horat.* The pleasant tune and measures of the harpe. *Perfecta cithara. Quint. Laquenta cithara reboant. Lucret.* A harpe made holow like a vaute. *Sciens citharæ. Horat.* Cunnyng in playing on the harpe. **1587** THOMAS L→E *Cithara, æ, f.g.* A harpe: also harmonie. *Virg. Citharœdicus, a, um, Suet.* Belonging to an harp. Pertaining to minstrells. *Citharœdus, di, m.g.* An harper singing to his harpe. **1589** RIDER L→E *Cithara, f. Sistrum.* A Citterne. *Cithara, lyra, f.* A harpe. **1598** FLORIO It→E *Citara,* a gitterne, a citterne, a crowd. *Cithera, Citera,* a citterne, a gitterne, a croude, a kit. **1599** MINSHEU-PERCYVALL Sp→E **Citara,* f. an instrument of musicke called a citterne. **Cithara,* f. idem. **1611** FLORIO It→E *Citara,* a gitterne, a citterne. *Cithara,* a gitterne, a citterne. *Cithera,* a citterne, a gitterne. **1706** KERSEY-PHILLIPS (6th edn) *Cithara, (Gr.)* a Harp, a Cittern, or Guittar: **1728** CHAMBERS *Cythara,* an ancient Musical

Instrument, by some supposed the same with the *Lyra*; at least, a particular Species of the *Lyra*; by others different: Tho its precise Structure does not appear. See *Lyre*. ¶ The Antients describe it as triangular, in form of a *Greek Delta*, Δ: The Poets ascribe the Invention to *Apollo*. **1737** DYCHE-PARDON (2nd edn) *Cythara* (S.) a musical Instrument among the Ancients, of a triangular Form, by some supposed to be the same with the Lyre.

1582 *Batman vppon Bartholome* (p. 424) The Harpe is called *Cithera*, and was first found of *Apollo*, as the Greeks deeme. And the harpe is like to a mans brest, for likewise, as the voyce commeth of the brest, so the notes come of y[e] harp, & hath therefore that name *Cithara*, for the breast is called *Cithara, in Dorica lingua*, & afterward some & some [sic] came foorth many maner instruments therof, & had y[e] name *Cithara*, as y[e] harp & psalterie, and other such & some be foure cornered, and some three cornered: the strings be many, and speciall manner thereof is diuers. **c.1668-71** *Mary Burwell's Instruction Bk. for Lute* (*TDa* p. 9) ... We believe that the word *cythara*, which was an instrument that David commanded us to make use of in praising God, was a kind of lute, which has got his perfection according as the lights of Heaven have spread themselves upon the earth.

citharist *see* chorocitharista, psallocitharist

1500 *Ortus Vocabulorum* L→E Citharista. e. an harper. f.p. Citharistes tes. grece est quidam mons. m.t. **1538** ELYOT L→E *Citharistria*, a woman harper. *Citharizo, aui, are*, to harpe. *Citharœdus*, a harper. **1552** HULOET L→E *citharista, Fidicen, Lyricen, Psaltes. tis* Harper. *citharistria, Fidicina, Lyricina, Psaltria...* the woman harper *citharizo. as, pulsare lyram.* Harpen or playe on the harpe. *citharœdas.* Harper whyche syngeth to hys harpe. **1565** COOPER L→E *Citharísta, citharistæ, m.g. Cic.* An harper that singeth not. *Citharistria, Quæ cithara canit. Terent.* A woman harper. *Citharœdicus, pen. cor. Adiectiuum: vt Citharœdicus habitus. Suet.* A minstrels apparell. *Citharœdus. Cic.* An harper singyng to his harpe. **1587** THOMAS L→E *Citharista, & citharistes, æ, m.g.* A harper that singeth not. *Citharistria, æ, f.g. Terent.* A woman harper. *Cith[a]rizo, as,* *To harpe. *Citharœdicus, a, um, Suet.* Belonging to an harp. Pertaining to minstrells. *Citharœdus, di, m.g.* An harper singing to his harpe. **1589** RIDER L→E *Citharædus, citharædo, m.* a harper that singeth to his harpe *Citharædus, lyricen. Fidicen. Lyristes, m.* An harper. *Citharista, citharistes, m.* A harper that singeth not. *Citharizo, Psallo, pulso, canere fidibus. Citharo.* To Harpe. *Citharœdicus, ad.* Of, or belonging to minstrels. **1598** FLORIO It→E *Citaredo*, a fidler, a musition. *Citharista, Citharello*, one that plaies on such instruments. **1611** FLORIO It→E *Citaredo*, a fidler or gitterne plaier. *Citarista*, as *Citaredo*. *Citharista*, a gitterne-plaier. *Citherista*, a citterne-plaier. **1623** COCKERAM *Citharize.* To play on the harpe. *Cytharize.* to play on a Harpe. **1656** BLOUNT (1st edn) *Cytharist (cytharista)* he that plays on a harp, a Harper. *Citharize (citharizo)* to play on the harp. **1659** TORRIANO-FLORIO It→E *Citaredo, Citarista, Citarizzatore, Citaro*, a fidler, a crouder, a minstrell, a player on a ghittern or cittern *Citarizzare*, to play upon a gittern. § **Citaredica-poesia*, gittern poetry. **1676** COLES *Citharist, Latin.* a Harper. *Citharize*, to Harp. **1688** DAVIS-TORRIANO-FLORIO It→E *Citarizzare*, to play upon a Cittern. § **Citaredica-poesia*, Lyrick Poesia.

citola

1599 MINSHEU-PERCYVALL Sp→E † *Citola*, f. a citterne, the clapper of a mill.

citolero

1599 MINSHEU-PERCYVALL Sp→E † *Citolero*, m. a maker of citternes.

citrial

1658 PHILLIPS (1st edn) *Citriale*, a Cittern, a word used by *Chaucer*. **1676** COLES *Citriale, Old word.* a Cittern, Ghittern, or a dulcimer. **1706** KERSEY-PHILLIPS (6th edn) *Citriale*, a Word us'd by *Chaucer*, for a Cittern, or Guittar. **1708** KERSEY *Dict. Anglo-Brit.* (1st edn) *Citriale*, a Cittern, or Guittar. *Chaucer.* **1721** BAILEY *An Univ. Etymolog. Engl. Dict.* (1st edn) *Citriale*, a Citron or Guittar *Chauc*

cittern *see* cetara, chitarra, cithara, citola, entata, gittern, ribibble, sistrum

1696 PHILLIPS (5th edn) *Cittern*, a Musical Instrument with Wyre Strings. **1702** KERSEY *New Engl. Dict.* (1st edn) A *Cittern*, a musical instrument. **1706** KERSEY-PHILLIPS (6th edn) *Cittern*, a kind of Musical Instrument. **1721** BAILEY *An Univ. Etymolog. Engl. Dict.* (1st edn) *Cittern*, (of *Cithara, L.*) a sort of musical Instrument. **1736** BAILEY *Dict. Britannicum* (2nd edn) *Cittern* (*cistre*,

F. *cetâra*, It. *cítola*, Sp. *cyster*, *Du. citnar*, G. of *cithara*, L.) a kind of musical instrument.

ciuffolo *see* zuffolo

clang *see* blur, bombus, grailler, rombo, taratantara, thremot

1500 *Ortus Vocabulorum* L→E Clango is xi. sonare to make noyse as trumpettes n.t. Clangor oris. a cryenge of trumpetes or bestes. et est irrationabilium. m.t. **1538** Elyot L→E *Clango, xi, gere*, to sowne a trumpette. *Clangor, oris*, the sowne of a trumpet. **1565** Cooper L→E *Clango, clangis, clanxi, clángere*. To sowne a trumpette: *Clangor, clangôris, m.g. Virg*. The sowne of a trumpette: § *Tuba clangens. Valer. Flac*. A trumpet sownynge. **1587** Thomas L→E *Clango, gis, xi, ctum, ere, Val. Flac*. To sounde a trumpet *Clangor, oris, m.g*. The sound of a trumpet **1589** Rider L→E *Clango* To Sound a trumpet § *clangor tubæ*. The sounde of the trumpet. **1598** Florio It→E *Clangore*, a clangor or sounde of a trumpet. **1611** Florio It→E *Clangorare*, to clang as a trumpet *Clangore*, a clang of a trumpet **1656** Blount (1st edn) *Clangor* (Lat.) the sound of a Trumpet **1659** Torriano-Florio It→E *Clangorare*, to clang as a trumpet *Clangore*, the clang of a trumpet **1706** Kersey-Phillips (6th edn) To *Clang*, to sound as a Trumpet does. **1708** Kersey *Dict. Anglo-Brit*. (1st edn) To *Clang*, to sound as a Trumpet does. **1730** Bailey *Dict. Britannicum* (1st edn) A *Clang* (*clangor*, L.) the sound of a trumpet. **1737** Dyche-Pardon (2nd edn) *Clang* (V.) to sound like a strong and shrill Trumpet.

clapper *see* anzolo, bell

1702 Kersey *New Engl. Dict*. (1st edn) The *Clapper* of a bell **1736** Bailey *Dict. Britannicum* (2nd edn) *Clapper* (*Klepel, Du. Kloeppel*, G.) a Hammer or Striker of a Bell. **1737** Dyche-Pardon (2nd edn) *Clapper* (S.) the Tongue or Iron Ringer of a Bell

claricords *see* clavecin, clavecymbal, clavichord, manichord, menacorda, monochord, organetti, rigols, spinet

1656 Blount (1st edn) *Claricords*, instruments so called. **1658** Phillips (1st edn) *Claricord*, or *Clericord*, a kinde of Musical instrument, somewhat like a Cymbal. **1676** Coles *Claricord, cler-*, an instrument somewhat like a cymbal. **1702** Kersey *New Engl. Dict*. (1st edn) *Claricords*, a musical instrument, so call'd. **1706** Kersey-Phillips (6th edn) *Claricords*, a kind of Musical Instrument. **1708** Kersey *Dict. Anglo-Brit*. (1st edn) *Claricords*, a kind of Musical Instrument. **1728** Chambers *Claricord*, or *Manichord*, a Musical Instrument, in form of a Spinett. See *Spinett*. ¶ It has 49 or 50 Stops, and 70 Strings, which bear on five Bridges; the first whereof is the highest, the rest diminishing in proportion. Some of the Strings are in Unison; their Number being greater than that of the Stops. ¶ There are several little Mortaises for passing the Jacks, arm'd with little Brass Hooks, which stop and raise the Chords in lieu of the Feather us'd in Virginals and Spinetts. But what distinguishes it most, is, that the Chords are cover'd with pieces of Cloth, which render the Sound the sweeter; and deaden it so, as that it can't be heard to any considerable distance. ¶ Hence some call it the *dumb Spinett*; whence it comes to be particularly in use among the Nuns, who learn to play, and are unwilling to disturb the Silence of the Dormitory. ¶ The *Claricord* is more antient than either the Spinett or Harpsicord; as is observ'd by *Scaliger*, who only gives it 35 Chords. **1737** Dyche-Pardon (2nd edn) *Clarichord* or *Manichord* (S.) a Musical Instrument in the Form of a Spinnet; it has 49 or 50 Stops, and 70 Strings, which bear on five Bridges, the first being the highest, and the others diminishing in Proportion; some of the Strings are in Unison, their Number being greater than that of the Stops; there are several little Mortises for passing the Jacks, aimed with little Brass Hooks, which stop and raise the Chords in Lieu of the Quill used in Virginals and Spinnets, and the Chords are covered with Pieces of Cloth, which renders the Sound sweeter, and deadens it so that it can be heard but a very small Distance, from whence it is called the Dumb Spinnet, and much used in Nunneries; this Instrument is much older than the Harpsichord or Spinnet.

clarico's *see* gravicembalo

claricymbal *see* cembalo, clavecymbal

clarigols *see* harpsichord

clarion *see* chiaretto, chiarino, tambourine, timburins

1593 Hollyband Fr→E *Clairon*, a horne or trumpet like Corneilis horne: *m*. **1599** Minsheu-Percyvall Sp→E **Clarin*, m. a certaine musicall instrument. *Clarion*, m. an instrument of musicke called a clarion. **1611** Cotgrave Fr→E *Clairon: m*. A

Clarion; a kind of small, strait-mouthed, and shrill-sounding Trumpet, vsed (commonly) as a Treble vnto the ordinarie one. *Claironner*. To sound a Clarion; § *A pain, & oignon trompette, ne clairon: Prov.* Hard fare, poore dyet, course Acates require neither State in the seruing, nor Musicke in the eating; or, the sound of forraine Trumpets is but seldome heard in a poore, and barren State. **1611** FLORIO It→E *Clarino*, a kind of trumpet called a Clairon. **1656** BLOUNT (1st edn) *Clarion* (Fr. *Clairon*) a kind of smal straight mouthed, and shrill sounding Trumpet, used commonly as a treble to the ordinary one. *Min.* **1658** PHILLIPS (1st edn) *Clarion*, a kinde of Trumpet. **1676** COLES *Clarion*, a kind of shrill Trumpet. **1688** MIEGE-COTGRAVE Fr→E *Clairon*, (m.) *sorte d'Instrument à Vent*, Clarion, a sort of Wind-Instrument. **1696** PHILLIPS (5th edn) *Clarion*, a kind of Trumpet, that has a shriller sound than other Trumpets. **1702** KERSEY *New Engl. Dict.* (1st edn) A *Clarion*, a kind of trumpet. **1704** *Cocker's Engl. Dict.* (1st edn) *Clarion*, a shrill Trumpet. **1706** KERSEY-PHILLIPS (6th edn) *Clarion*, a kind of shrill Trumpet: **1708** KERSEY *Dict. Anglo-Brit.* (1st edn) *Clarion*, a kind of shrill Trumpet: **1721** BAILEY *An Univ. Etymolog. Engl. Dict.* (1st edn) *Clarion*, (*Clairon, F. Clario, L.*) a shrill sort of Trumpet. **1724** [PEPUSCH] *Short Explic. of Foreign Words in Mus. Bks.* (p. 22) *Clarino*, a Trumpet, *A doi Clarini*, for two Trumpets. **1728** CHAMBERS *Clarion*, a kind of Trumpet, whose Tube is narrower, and its Tone acuter and shriller than the common Trumpet. See *Trumpet*. ¶ *Nicod* says, the *Clarion*, as now us'd among the *Moors*, and *Portugueze*[,] who borrow'd it from the *Moors*, serv'd antiently for a Treble to several Trumpets, which sounded Tenor and Bass. He adds, that it was only us'd among the Cavalry and the Marines. ¶ *Menage* derives the Word from the Italian *Clarion*, of the Latin *Clarus*, by reason of the Clearness of its Sound. **1736** BAILEY *Dict. Britannicum* (2nd edn) *Clarion* (*clairon*, F. *chiarina*, It. *clarîn*, Sp. of *clario*, L.) a sort of shrill Trumpet. **1737** DYCHE-PARDON (2nd edn) *Clarion* (S.) a Trumpet, whose Tube is narrower, and Tone shriller than the common Trumpets;

clark *see* chorister, clergeau

classicum *see* bellicum, inflatus
1500 *Ortus Vocabulorum* L→E Classarius. i. tubicen et proprie militum. a trumpere. m.s. Classitum classiti. idest cornu vel tuba vel aliud instrumentum causa conuocan defectum. Etiam dicitur signum bellicum vel sonus tube. vel alterius instrumenti bellici. proprie tamen classitum est concentus et concordia omnium instrumentorum insimul sonantium siue sint tube et cornua in bello. siue sint campane. siue etiam homines. anglice a peele of belles. n.s. Classo. as. anglice to trumpe. n.p. Classus si. anglice an horne or a trumpe. m.s. **1538** ELYOT L→E *Classicum*, a peale or noyse of trumpettes, or belles to calle menne togither, or to goo to battaile. *Classicus*, an officer, which with a trumpette or tabore called people together. **1552** HULOET L→E *Classicum, ci* Peale or noyse of belles, trumpet, or such like **1565** COOPER L→E *Classici. Curt.* They that with trumpettes or drumslates call men together. *Clássicum, clássici, pen. corr. Substantiuum. Virg.* A noyse of trumpettes to call to battayle: a trumpette: a larme. § *Aduocare classico ad concionem. Liu.* To assemble by the sound of a trumpette. *Classico facere silentium. Liu.* By sounde of trumpet to will scilence. *Classicus horror. Ouid.* The dreadfull sowne of the trumpet. *Horror classicus nocte diéq; gemit. Oui.* The terrible sowne of the trumpette. *Inflare classica. Virg.* To sownde the trompette. *Martia classica pulsare. Tibul.* To blowe the trumpette. *Matura classica. Lucan.* The sowne of the trumpet when all is readie to battaile. **1587** THOMAS L→E *Classicum, ci, n.g. Virg.* A trumpet, or the sound of a trumpet: a peale, or noise of trumpets, or bells, to call men togither, or to go to warre: a larme [i.e. an alarm]. *Classicus, & classicen, Varr.* He that with trumpet or drumselate calleth men togither. § *Classicum canere, Cæs.* To blow the retraite. **1589** RIDER L→E *Classicum, n.* A Peale, or noise of belles, trumpets, or such like. *Classicus, classicen, m.* He that with a trumpet, or drumslade, calleth the men together. *Classicus, classicen, m.* Hee that calleth men togeather with a drumme.

clausula *see* close

clave *see* clef
1617-24 FLUDD *Utriusque Cosmi Maioris: De Templo Musicæ* (p. 172) *Claves* literæ, quibus cantus quasi reseratur...

clavecin *see* harpsichord
1611 COTGRAVE Fr→E *Clavessins: m.* Claricords, or Claricols. **1688** MIEGE-COTGRAVE Fr→E *Clavecin*, (m.) *Instrument de Musique fort harmonieux*, Claricords, a kind of Musical Instrument. § *Toucher le Clavecin*, to play upon the Clarichords.

clavecymbal *see* clavicembalo, spinet
1656 BLOUNT (1st edn) *Claricymbal*, See *Clavecymbal*. *Clavecymbal (clavecymbalum)* a pair of Virginals, or Claricords; so called, because the strings are wrested up with *Clavis* a key. *Min.* **1658** PHILLIPS (1st edn) *Clavecymbal*, or *Claricymbal*, a kinde of instrument with wire-strings, by some taken for a Harpsical, or Virginal. **1676** COLES *Clavecymbal, Claricy-* an instrument with wire strings, by some an Harpsical or Virginal. **1708** KERSEY *Dict. Anglo-Brit.* (1st edn) *Clavecymbal* or *Clarycymbal*, a kind of Musical Instrument with Wire-strings. **1730** BAILEY *Dict. Britannicum* (1st edn) *Clavecymbal* (*clavio cymbal*, Ital.) an harpsichord.

clave signata *see* signed clef

claveta *see* enclavijado
1599 MINSHEU-PERCYVALL Sp→E **Claveta*, or *Clavija*, f. ... Also pegs or pins to winde vp the stringes of an instrument. *Clavija*, f. the key of virginals, the pin of a lute, any pegge or pin.

clavicembalo *see* clavecymbal, clavichord
1598 FLORIO It→E *Clauicembalo*, a kind of instrument like our rigols or virginals. **1611** FLORIO It→E *Clauicembalo*, an instrument like vigoles [sic]. **1659** TORRIANO-FLORIO It→E *Clavicembalo, Clavicordo*, a kind of musicall instrument like rigols. **1724** [PEPUSCH] *Short Explic. of Foreign Words in Mus. Bks.* (p. 22) *Clave Cimbalo*, a Harpsicord.

clavichord *see* claricords, clavicembalo, regal, rigols, tecla
1598 FLORIO It→E *Clauicordo*, as *Clauicembalo*. **1599** MINSHEU-PERCYVALL Sp→E **Clavicordio*, m. an instrument of musicke called Claricords, or virginals. **1604** CAWDREY (1st edn) (French) *clauicordes*, mirth **1611** FLORIO It→E *Clauicordo*, as *Clauecembalo*.

clavier *see* manichord
1593 HOLLYBAND Fr→E § *Clavier d'vne espinette*, or *orgues*, the keyes of Virgenals or organes. **1611** COTGRAVE Fr→E § *Clavier d'une espinette, &c.* The keyes of, or, a set of keyes for, a paire of Virginals. **1688** MIEGE-COTGRAVE Fr→E *Clavier*, (m.) the Keys of a Musical Instrument (such as Organs, Virginals, Claricords, &c;)

clef *see* b, character, chiave, clave, c sol fa ut clef, f, g, geresol, key, mi-clef, signature, signed clef, tenor clef, treble clef
1611 COTGRAVE Fr→E *Clef: f.* ... also, a Cliff in Musicke; **1670** BLOUNT (3rd edn) *Cliff* ... It is also a term in Musick. In the Gam-ut are conteined three Septenaries of Letters, *viz.* G.A.B.C.D.E.F. These seven Letters are set at the beginning of each Rule and space, and are called the seven Cliffs or Cleaves. **1671** PHILLIPS (3rd edn) *Cliff* or *Cleave*, in Musick (from the Latine word *Clavis*) a Character particularly plac't upon the letter from whence the notes of the song are to be prov'd[;] of these Cliffs or Keys there are only four in use, the first is called F Fa ut, being onely propre [sic] to the Base or lowest part, and is thus markt (𝄢) The 2[d.] is C Sol fa ut Cliff, being Proper to the middle or former parts as the Tenor, or Counter-Tenor and it is thus markt ♯ the 3d. is G *Sol re ut Cliff*, being only proper to the Treble or highest part, and is thus marked on the lowermost line but one (𝄞) the 4th. is called the *B Cliff*, being proper to all parts alike, its property being only to shew when notes are to be sung flatt and when sharp, the *B fa* or *B flatt*, is thus markt (♭) the *B* mi or *B* sharp thus markt ♯ **1676** COLES *Cliff, French.* (key) the whole scale of Musick is divided into 3 Cliffs, Basse, Mean and Treble. **1688** MIEGE-COTGRAVE Fr→E *Clef*, (f.) ... a cliff, in Musick; § *La position de la Clef de Musique*, the setting of a Song in the right Key. **1702** KERSEY *New Engl. Dict.* (1st edn) A *Cliff* in musick. **1704** HARRIS *Cliff*, or *Cleff*, a Term in Musick, signifying a certain Mark from the Position whereof the proper Places of all the other Notes in any Song or Lesson are understood by proving the said Notes from thence according to the Scale of the *Gam-ut*; wherein are contained three Septenaries of Letters, *viz. G, A, B, C, D, E, F*; which seven Letters of the Alphabet set at the beginning of every Rule and Space represents as many *Cliffs*; but of these, Four are only used, and generally placed at the beginning of the Staves of every Lesson either Vocal or Instrumental. ¶ The first is called *F-fa-ut Cliff*, and appropriately only to the *Bass* or lowest Part. ¶ The Second is *C-sol-fa-ut Cliff*, peculiar to the Inner Parts, as the *Tenor* and *Counter-Tenor*. ¶ The Third is *G-sol-re-ut Cliff*, which is only fit for the *Treble* or Highest Part. ¶ The Fourth is the *B-Cliff* or *B-fa-b-mi Cliff* which is proper to all Parts, and serves for the *Flatting* and *Sharping* of *Notes*. **1706** KERSEY-PHILLIPS (6th edn) *Cliff* or *Cleave*, (in *Musick*) is a

certain Character, or Mark from the Seat of which the proper Places of all the other Notes in any Song, or Lesson, are discover'd by proving the said Notes from thence, according to the Scale of the *Gam-ut*, in which are contain'd three Septenaries of Letters, *viz.* G.A.B.C.D.E.F. which seven Letters of the Alphabet set at the beginning of every Rule and Space, serve to express as many *Cliffs*, or Keys: But of these four are only us'd, and generally plac'd at the beginning of the Staves of every Lesson, either Vocal or Instrumental, *viz.* ¶ The first call'd *F-fa-ut*, being only proper for the Bass, or lowest Part, and marked thus 𝄢 The second is *C-sol-fa-ut*, peculiar to the inner, or middle Parts, as the Tenor and Counter-tenor, and known by this Mark 𝄡 The third is *G-sol-re-ut*, which belongs only to the Treble, or highest Part, and is thus mark'd on the lowermost Line but one 𝄞 The fourth is nam'd the *B. cliff*, or *B-fa-be-mi* Cliff, and apply'd to all Parts indifferently; its Property being only to shew, when Notes are to be sung, or play'd Flat, and when Sharp. The *B-fa*, or *B-flat* is distinguished by this Character (♭) and the *B-mi*, or *B Sharp* is thus express'd ♯ **1707** *Gloss. Angl. Nova* (1st edn) *Cliff*, in *Musick*, a Character plac'd on one of the Lines, by which the Places of all the other Notes are known and prov'd. **1721** BAILEY *An Univ. Etymolog. Engl. Dict.* (1st edn) *Clief, Cleave*, (in *Musick*) a Character placed on one of the Lines, by which the places of all the other Notes are known and proved. **1728** CHAMBERS *Clef* ... [*see* Appendix] **1737** DYCHE-PARDON (2nd edn) *Cliff* (S.) the nominating Mark or Character used in Musick, from which the other Notes take their respective Names; for a Note in the same Space or upon the same Line, in different Cliffs, hath different Names. There are commonly 3, *viz.* C. F. G; the G is put upon the 2d Line counting upwards, and is used for the Treble or upper Part; F is used for the Bass or lower Part, and is put upon the 4th Line (counting upwards) of the 5 Lines generally made use of to set the Musick on; C is put indifferently upon any of the Lines, and used oftentimes for the Treble as well as the mean or inner Parts, but not so much latterly as formerly.

1584 BATHE Briefe Intro. to True Art of Music (MS copy, 1st half 16th c., *CHi* p. 3) ... it var nessasrie to knav quhat a cleif is; quhich is nothing else bot a mark of on of these places conteined in the scalle of *gam ut*, quharby it is knaven in q[t] place evrie not standeth: quharof ther be thrie kyndes commonlie vsed ... **1597** MORLEY *Plaine and Easie Introdvction* (p. 3) A *Cliefe* is a charecter [sic] set on a rule at the beginning of a verse, shewing the heigth and lownes of euery note standing on the same verse, or in space (although vse hath taken it for a generall rule neuer to set any cleife in the space except the *b* cleife) and euery space or rule not hauing a cleife set in it, hath one vnderstoode, being only omitted for not pestering the verse, and sauing of labor to the writer: but here it is taken for a letter begining the name of euery keye: and are they which you see here set at the beginning of euery worde.... There be in all seuen cliefes (as I told you before) as A. B. C. D. E. F. G. but in vse in singing there be but foure: that is to saie, the *F fa vt*, which is commonly in the *Basse* or lowest part, being formed or made thus 𝄢. The *C sol fa vt* cliefe which is common to euery part, and is made thus 𝄡. The *G sol re vt* cliefe, which is commonly vsed in the *Treble* or highest part, and is made thus 𝄞. And the *b* cliefe which is comon to euery part, is made thus *b* or thus ♮ the one signifying the halfe note and flatt singing: the other signifying the whole note or sharpe singing. **1654** PLAYFORD *Breefe Intro. to Skill of Musick* (p. 2) These seven Letters of the Alphabet [G, A, B, C, D, E, F] are called the 7 *Cliffs*, or more properly *Cleaves*, the other names or sylables adjoyned to them, the Notes; ... § (pp. 7-8) In the *Gam-ut* (as I said before) is contained three *Septenaries* of Letters, which are G. A. B. C. D. E. F. these 7 Letters are set at the beginning of each *Rule* and *Space*, and are called the seven *Cleaves*; of these seven, foure is onely usuall: the first is the *F fa ut Cleave*, which is only proper to the Basse, or lowest part, and is thus signed or marked 𝄢 The second is the *C sol fa ut*, which is proper to the middle, or inner parts, as Tenor, Counter-Tenor, or Meane, and he is thus signed or marked 𝄡 The third is the *G sol re ut* Cleave, which is only proper to the Treble, or highest, and is signed or marked thus 𝄞 ¶ These three Cleaves are called the three signed Cleaves, because they are alwayes set at the beginning of every line of a Song, or Lesson; for *Cleave* is derived from *Clavis*, which signifies a *Key*, for by this Key the places of all the Notes in the Song are known. ¶ The fourth is the *B Cleaves*, which is proper to all parts, as being of two natures or properties, that is to say, *Flat* and *Sharp*, and doth onely serve for that purpose for the flatting and sharping of Notes, and therefore he is called *B fa, B mi*: the *B fa* signifies *Flat*, the *B mi Sharp*. The *B fa* or *B flat*, is known by this marke ♭ and the *B mi*, which is *sharp* by this ✳. **1655** PLAYFORD *Intro. to Skill of Musick* (2nd edn, 'Art of Setting or Composing of Musick in Parts', n.p.) I will therefore insist upon these seven Letters, which in the *Scale* of Musick are called Cliffes, *(quasi Claves)* or Keyes, for that they open the meaning and nature of the Longs unto us. **1662** [DAVIDSON] *Cantus, Songs and Fancies* (n.p.) Q *What call you a Cliefe, and what a Note?* ¶ A. A Cliefe is a Character set on a Rule at the beginning of a Verse, shewing the height & lownesse of every Note standing on the same Verse, or in space (although use hath taken it for a general Rule never to set any Cliefe in the space except the *b* Cliefe) and every Space, or Rule, not having a Cliefe set in it, hath one understood, being onely omitted for not pestering the Verse, and saving of labour to the Writter [sic]: ... **1665** SIMPSON *Principles of Practical Mvsick* (p. 4) The Common Scale of Musick consists of Eleven Lines and Spaces; each line and space a Letter in it, which Letters are called *Cliffs, Claves,* or *Keys,* because they open to us the meaning of every Song. **1677** NEWTON *English Academy* (pp. 90-1) By these seven Letters of the Alphabet, otherwise called seven *Cliffs* or *Cleaves,* the Scale is divided into Three several Parts of *Musick;* The first and lowest is called the *Base;* the second or middle Part, the *Mean;* the third or highest Part, the *Treble.* **1680** B., A. *Synopsis of Vocal Musick* (p. 34) To discern rightly these seven Degrees of the Scale of Musick, are commonly used the first seven letters of the Alphabet, called Cliffs ... which by their Notes do shew before ones Eyes, the just altitude and profundity of the sound of every Degree. **1686** ANON. *New and Easie Method to Learn to Sing* (p. 2) ... That the Characters at the beginning of the Lines are called *Cliffs* or *Keys,* opening and signifying what Part or Pitch of Voice, *viz. Treble, Mean* or *Bass,* the Notes properly belong to, and also on what Line or Sp[a]ce each of the seven Letters is placed. **1694** PURCELL-PLAYFORD *Intro. to Skill of Musick* (12th edn, n.p.) ... *Cliff* or *Cleave* is derived from *Clavis* a Key, or Guide to understand the *Notes.* **1704** GORTON *Catechetical Questions in Musick* (p. 25) *Q.* Why are they call'd Cliffs? ¶ *A.* From the French Word *Clef,* or from the Lattin Word *Clavis* which signifies a Key also, because they open and let us into the Knowledge of what part it is we are to play. **1721** MALCOLM *Treatise of Musick* (pp. 330-1) Again, tho' every Line and Space may be marked at the Beginning with its Letter, as has been done in former Times; yet, since the Art has been improven, only one Line is marked, by which all the rest are easily known, if we reckon up or down in the Order of the Letters; the Letter marked is called the *Clef* or *Key,* because by it we know the Names of all the other Lines and Spaces, and consequently the true Quantity of every *Degree* and *Interval.* But because every Note in the *Octave* is called a *Key,* tho' in another Sense, this Letter marked is called in a particular Manner the *signed Clef,* because being written on any Line, it not only *signs* or marks that one, but explains all the rest. And to prevent Ambiguity in what follows, by the Word *Clef,* I shall always mean that Letter, which, being marked on any Line, explains all the rest; and by the Word *Key* the principal Note of any Song, in which the Melody closes ... **1722** B., T. *Compleat Musick-Master* (p. 2) Each of these Parts in *Singing* is known by a Character for the *Cliff,* or *Cleave,* from *Clavis* a *Key;* so called, because it openeth, or signifieth to you what Part in *Musick, Viz.* whether *Treble*[,] *Mean,* or *Bass,* the Notes properly belong to... on the lowest Line but one in the *Treble* Part you have this mark 𝄞 which is called (from the Line it stands on) the *Gsolreut* or *Treble Cliff:* The *Tenor Cliff* marked thus 𝄡 is variously placed, but upon what Line soever it stands, the same takes its Denomination from the Letter C, and therefore 'tis call'd the *C faut Cliff:* The *Bass Cliff* stands always upon the uppermost Line but one in the *Bass* Part, call'd *F faut,* from which it is likewise called the *F faut Cliff,* and marked thus 𝄢. **1724** TURNER *Sound Anatomiz'd* (pp. 34-5) ... this *Mark;* 𝄢 which is called a *Cliff* or *Key,* from its opening to us the meaning of any thing, being commonly placed upon the fourth *Line* at the Beginning of each *Staff* ... reckoning from the Bottom upward, and is proper to the *Base,* for which Reason, it is called the *Base Cliff,* or otherwise, the *Ffaut Cliff;* the First, signifying for what *Voice* any *Song* is composed, and the Last, the Names of the Places where the *Notes* lie, according to the Order of the *Scale;* for upon what *Line* soever this *Cliff* may happen to be placed, (it being, upon some Occasions, (but very rarely) placed upon the third *Line*) that Line is called *Ffaut;* and the *Space* between that and the *Line* above it *Gsolreut;* ... **1725** DE LA FOND *New System of Music* (preface, xlix-l) All Practicers have found to their great discouragement, what is call'd a *Clef* in *Music.* The word *Clef,* not *Cliff* nor *Clifft,* as most mistake, is a *French* word which signifies *Key.* Judicious Autors tell us it is impossible to begin a Song or an Air without the *Clef,* as to open a lock without the key: for without the *Clef,* they say, names cannot be given to Notes.

1726 Bruce *Common Tunes* (p. 11) Q. *Why are these signed Cliffs or Cleaves called by the Name* Cliff? ¶ *A*. As before was hinted, they are so called, because they give Opening or Sound, in a regular Manner, to the Tone or Song so prickt or signed at the Beginning thereof; for its proper and native Derivation comes from the Word *clavis*, signifying a *Key*, by which Access is given into any Thing or Place. **c.1726** North Musicall Gramarian BL Add. 32533, f. 49 Cliffs are but marks whereby it is knowne where in y[e] 5. lines some one Note of the Gamut falls, & then all the Rest ascending & descending are given. **1728** North Musicall Grammarian (C-K *MG* f. 23) ... Here the conspic[u]ous marks, 𝄢 , 𝄡 and 𝄞 , are called cliff, being to signifye some one note, as it stands in the five lines (to be extracted for use) and if the place of any one note is knowne[,] all the rest follow one way or other. **1731** Prelleur *Modern Musick-Master* (VI, from table facing p. 4) ... The first Stave contains the Treble and has this mark 𝄞 , (which is called the Treble Cliff) set at the beginning of it; this mark 𝄢 which is called the Bass Cliff is usually at the beginning of the second stave which contains the Bass .... There is also another Cliff besides those two before mentioned which is called the Tenor Cliff. and [sic] is used when the Bass goes high to avoid Ledger lines. this [sic] Cliff is placed upon any of the four lowest lines and is always the middle Cfaut of your Instrument. **1736** Tans'ur *Compleat Melody* (3rd edn, p. 5) *Scholar*. Why are those *Characters* called *Cliffs*? And for what reason can't a *Tune* be pricked down as well without a *Cliff* as with? ¶ *Master*. The Word *Cliff*, *Cleave*, or *Clavis*, is a *Latin* Word, which signifies To *open*, or a *Key* to let into, *&c*. which openeth to us the *Names*, and *Keys* of all Musick; either *Flat*, or *Sharp*.

clef note

1672 Salmon *Vindication of an Essay* (p. 39) ... Musicians did by assigning a certain Note (which they call'd the Cliff-Note) to one Line in a Staff, shew by consequence which five or six Lines they had taken out of the Scale for the use of that part, wherein they were concern'd; ...

clepsiambo

1598 Florio It→E *Clepsiambo*, a kinde of musicall instrument. **1611** Florio It→E *Clepsiambo*, a kind of musicke instrument. **1659** Torriano-Florio It→E **Clepsiambo*, a kind of musicall instrument, that by water-works is made to sound.

clergeau

1611 Cotgrave Fr→E *Clergeau: m.* A pettie Clarke, vnder Clarke, or young Clarke.

clergeon

1611 Cotgrave Fr→E *Clergeon: m.* as *Clergeau*; or, a Singing man, or Quirester, in a Queere.

clerizon

1599 Minsheu-Percyvall Sp→E **Clerizon*, m. youth or boyes that sing in the quire, singing boies, quiristers, boies bred vp to be priests.

cliff *see* clef

clinch *see* strambotto

Clinias

1565 Cooper L→E *Clinias*, A certaine philosopher of Pithagoras secte. Also a Musician.

cloche *see* sonnette

1570/71 *Dict. Fr. and Engl.* Fr→E *Cloche*, a Bell. *Clochette*, a little Bell. **1593** Hollyband Fr→E *Cloche*, a bell; *f*. *Clochette*, a little bell: *f*. **1611** Cotgrave Fr→E *Cloche: f.* A Bell, or Clocke; to ring, or strike; *Clocher: m.* A Bell-sounder. *Clocherie: f.* A ringing, or peale of Bells. *Clochetier: m.* A Bell-sounder. *Clochette: f.* A little Bell; § *Trinqueballer les cloches*. To iangle, or to ring bels vntuneably, and too much. **1650** Howell-Cotgrave Fr→E *Clocher*. ... also, (in some places) to ring, or toll a Bell; to make a bell sound, or strike. § *Cobeter vne cloche*. To toule a Bell; or, to ring it not full out, but so, as it strikes onely the one side. **1688** Miege-Cotgrave Fr→E § *Sonner les Cloches*, to ring the Bells.

close *see* cadence, false close, falso bordone, fin, half cadence, imperfect cadence, neume, stay

1678 Phillips (4th edn) *Close*, in Musick is either the end of a strain, or that place in a Song, where all the parts meet before the end, and marked with a single bar, (and this is an imperfect Close) or the end of a Song marked 𝄐 or thus 𝄑 and this is a perfect Close. **1704** Harris *Close*, in Musick: See *Cadence*. **1708** Kersey *Dict. Anglo-Brit.* (1st edn) In Musick, a *Close* is either the End of a Strain call'd an *Imperfect Close*, or else the End of a Tune, or Lesson, term'd a *Perfect Close.* **1728** Chambers *Close,* in Musick. See *Cadence.* **1737** Dyche-Pardon (2nd edn) *Close* (S.) ... In *Musick,* it is the End of a Strain, or Part of the Air, or the general End of the whole Composition, or at least of such Part of a Movement where the Musick ends in the Key of the Composition.

1609 Dowland-Ornithoparcus *Micrologvs* (p. 84) *Of the formall Closes.* ¶ Being that euery Song is graced with formall *Closes,* we will tell what a *Close* is. Wherfore a *Close* is (as *Tinctor* writes) a little part of a Song, in whose end is found either rest or perfection. Or it is the coniunction of voices (going diuersly) in perfect *Concords.* **1636** Butler *Principles of Musik* (p. 82) [marginalia: 'A *Cloze. Clausula.*'] The Cloze is a Formal meeting of all Partes in Primari Concords, (commonly with a Cadence, and not without soom preparation and propulsion unto it) for the concluding either of the whole Song, or of soom Principal Part thereof. The which, as *Epilogus Oratiouis* [sic] shoolde be sweetest and moste Pathetical: and therefore reqireth moste Art. **early 18th C.** North (Prendcourt's) Treatis of Continued or Through Basse BL Add. 32549, f. 27 ... 'tis called a close becaus it is a jumping together of all y[e] parts, (or a least of some) that are to beaute [i.e. beautify] a peice of Composition. **1721** Malcolm *Treatise of Musick* (p. 269) ... That by a *Close* or *Cadence* is meant a terminating or bringing the *Melody* to a Period or Rest, after which it begins and sets out anew, which is like the finishing of some distinct Purpose in an Oration; ... **1736** Tans'ur *Compleat Melody* (3rd edn, p. 71) A *Perfect-Close,* is when all *Parts* end in the proper and fundamental *Key.* ¶ An *Imperfect Close,* is a *Close* made at the End of several *Strains* but not in the proper Key

close play

1568 Le Roy *Brief and Easye Instrution* (p. 11) ... the knowledge of the saied barre is so necessarie, that hauyng founde out, and exercised the same, thou shalte not neede to remoue, but those fingers whiche thou shalt be forced, whiche we call close or couert plaie, as for the other barres, whiche come straight ouerthwart the lines ... **1596** Barley *New Booke of Tabliture* (n.p.) [*re* the lute] ... I haue here set downe an example at large, and very fit for the purpose [of showing 'barres or lines ... that be drawen by as vnder the letters or passages'], wherein thou shalt not finde anye example better ordered or measured, that thou shalt [not] neede to remooue any of thy fingers from the saide measure, the knowledge of the said barre is so necessarie, that hauing found out and exercised the same, thou shalt not neede but to remooue those fingers which thou shalt be forced, which manner of handling wee call closse or couert play ...

cobbola

1611 Florio It→E *Cobbolare,* to sing country songs or gigges. **1659** Torriano-Florio It→E *Cobbola,* any merrie dittie, countrey-jig or roundelay. *Cobbolare,* to make or sing countrey-jigs or merry ditties.

coccism

1721 Bailey *An Univ. Etymolog. Engl. Dict.* (1st edn) *Coccism,* the old silly Tune like a Cuckasory. *Stillingfl.* **1730** Bailey *Dict. Britannicum* (1st edn) *Coccism,* the old, silly tune of a cuckow.

colachon

1688 Miege-Cotgrave Fr→E *Colachon,* (m.) an Italian Instrument of Musick, much like a Lute, but that the neck of it is something longer.

collabi

1587 Thomas L→E *Collabi, Cæl. Claviculi in cithara aut testudine, quibus intendur & remittunter fides.*

collateral *see* hypermixolydian, mood

1575 Agrippa *Vanitie and vncertaintie of Artes and Sciences* (chap. 17, pp. 28-28v) [*re* the four kinds of music of the ancients, i.e. the phrygian, lydian, dorian and mixolidian] ... There are some whiche haue founde besides these fower measures, others also, as them whiche they call *Collaterall,* that is, *Hypodorius, Hypololydius* [sic], and *Hypophrigius,* that there may be seuen correspondente to so many Planetes: to the whiche *Ptolomeus* added the eighte, called *Hippemixolidius* [sic], the highest of al the other, assigned to the Firmament.

colonna

1598 Florio It→E *Colonna,* ... Also a kinde of pipe like a recorder. **1611** Florio It→E *Colonna,* any columne, or piller. Also a kind of pipe or flute. **1659** Torriano-Florio It→E *Colonna,* ... also a kind of long pipe or flute.

colophony *see* resine
1728 CHAMBERS *Colophony*, a kind of Gum; being only a finer Turpentine, boil'd in Water till it be reduc'd into a solid Consistence.... It is also used by Musicians, to rub the Hairs of the Bow withal; the Effect whereof is, that the Gum cleaning the Hairs, and communicating to 'em a tenacious Quality, prevents their sliding too easily over the Strings; and promotes that trembling which forms the Sound.

colores generum *see* genus
1721 MALCOLM *Treatise of Musick* (pp. 515-16) *Ptolomy* gives an Account of the following 8 Divisions of the *Tetrachord* [being the '*Enharmonium, Chroma Molle* or *Antiquum, Chroma Intensum, Diatonum Molle, Diatonum Tonicum, Diatonicum Ditonicum* or *Pythag., Diatonum Intensum* or *Syntonum Diatonum Æquabile*']; where the Fractions express the *Ratio* betwixt each Sound ... and the next .... These different *Species* were also called the *Colores (Chroai) generum*: *Molle* expresses a Progression by small Intervals, as *Intensum* by greater; the other Names are plain enough. The Two first Intervals of the *Enharmonium*, are called each a *Diesis*; the Third is a *Ditonum*, and particularly the *3d g*. already explained. The Two first of the *Chromatick* are called *Hemitones*, and the Third is *Triemitonium*; and in the *Antiquum* it is the *3d l*. ... The first in the *diatonick* is called *Hemitonium*, and the other Two are *Tones*; particularly the $\frac{243}{256}$ is called *Limma (Pythagoricum;)* ...

colour *see* discolouration
after 1517 ANON. Art of Mvsic BL Add. 4911, f. 46v *Collorat quhat is it*. It is ane fractur or parting of symple noittis in dyvvers figuris mensurall. The quhilk to Name is callit discant. § f. 19v *Colur quhat is it*. It is of principall figuris denigration Of the quhilk ye stentht is so mekith yat fro figuris in thair perfyt quantatie deducit ye thrid part of the valour dois abstract fro Imperfyt ... **early 17th C.** RAVENSCROFT Treatise of Musick BL Add. 19758, f. 16 ... *Coloration*; That is when any perfit notes are made black wch note (as I haue said touching dimunition [sic]) ar diminished by the 3 part by vertue of the coulor. **1609** DOWLAND-ORNITHOPARCUS *Micrologvs* (p. 56) *Of Colour*. ¶ Wherefore *Colour* in this place is nothing, but the fulnes of the Notes: Or, it is the blacking of the principall figures: the force whereof is such, that it takes away the third part of the value from figures placed in their perfect quantitie: and from imperfects sometime it takes away the fourth part, sometimes it makes them of the *Hemiola* proportion.

come sopra *see* repetatur
1724 [PEPUSCH] *Short Explic. of Foreign Words in Mus. Bks.* (p. 22) *Come Sopra*, as above; or the Part above over again: Which Words are used when any foregoing Part is to be repeated. **1726** BAILEY *An Univ. Etymolog. Engl. Dict.* (3rd edn) *Come Sopra* (in *Musick Books*) signifies as above, or the Part above over again; which Words are used, when any foregoing Part is to be repeated. *Ital.*

1731 PRELLEUR *Modern Musick-Master* (Dictionary, p. 2) *Come Sopra*, as above.

comma *see* schism
1704 HARRIS *Comma*, in Musick, is the ninth part of a Tone, or the Interval whereby a Semi-tone or a Perfect Tone exceeds the Imperfect. This Term is used only in Theorical Musick, to shew the exact proportion between Concords. **1706** KERSEY-PHILLIPS (6th edn) (Gr.) In *Musick, Comma*, is the ninth part of a Tone or the Interval whereby a Semi-tone, or a Perfect Tone exceeds the Imperfect: This Term is us'd only in Theorical Musick, to shew the exact Proportion between Concords. **1724** [PEPUSCH] *Short Explic. of Foreign Words in Mus. Bks.* (p. 22) *Comma*, is one of the least Intervals of Musick that the Ear is sensible of. **1728** CHAMBERS *Comma*, in Musick, is the smallest of all the sensible Intervals of Tune. See *Interval*. ¶ The *Comma* is about the tenth Part of a Tone: or, it is the Interval whereby a perfect Semitone surpasses an imperfect one; or a perfect Tone, an imperfect one. See *Tone*. ¶ M. *Sauveur* says, a *Comma* is the Difference between a Tone-major and minor. It is seldom in use, except in the Theory of Musick, to shew the Justness of the Consonances; for in the Practice, the Division is drown'd and lost. Each lesser Tone ordinarily contains ten *Commas*. ¶ *Lancelot* only divides his Tone into nine Parts, or *Commas*; so that according to him, a *Comma* is the ninth Part of a Tone. ¶ The proportion of the greater *Comma* in Numbers, is as 80 to 81; that of the smaller, as 2025 to 2048. See *Tune*. ¶ The Word *Comma* is *Greek* form'd of κόπτω, *seco*, I cut.

1617-24 FLUDD *Utriusque Cosmi Maioris: De Templo Musicæ* (p. 182) *Coma* est spatium, quo sesquioctava proportio major est duabus diesibus, hoc est duobus semitoniis minoribus, vel est spatium, quo 6. sesquioctavæ majores sunt uno Diapason; vel *Coma* est differentia inter semitonium majus & minus, idest, excessus semitonii majoris supra minus. **1636** BUTLER *Principles of Musik* (p. 23) [quoting Boethius:] *Comma est spatium quo major est Sesquioctava proportio duabus Diesibus.* **1667** SIMPSON *Compendium of Practical Musick* (p. 104) Thereupon, is a *Tone*, or whole Note (as we term it) divided into Nine Particles, call'd *Comma's*: ... **1680** B., A. *Synopsis of Vocal Musick* (p. 32) Between the first and second Degree is a lesser Tone, containing nine comma's: between the second and the third is a greater Tone, exceeding the lesser by its tenth part, which tenth part is commonly called a Comma; between the third and fourth is an half greater Tone, commonly called a greater Semitone; ... **1721** MALCOLM *Treatise of Musick* (p. 261) We shall next consider what the Errors of these *false Intervals* are. The Variety, as to the Quantity, of *Intervals* that have the same Number of *Degrees* in the *Scale*, arises ... from the Differences of the Three *Degrees*; and therefore the Differences among *Intervals* of the same Species and Denomination, *i.e.* the Excesses or Defects of the *false* from the *true*, are no other than the Differences of these *Degrees*, viz. 8:81, the Difference of a *t g.* and *t l.* which is particularly called a *Comma* among *Musicians*; ... **1726** JACKSON *Preliminary Discourse to a Scheme* (p. 17) ... the Difference between a greater and lesser Tone, call'd a *Comma*.

commeditor
1500 *Ortus Vocabulorum* L→E Commeditor aris. i. simull modulare. putare vel dulciter cantare. to synge togyder. d.p.

common cord *see* flat cord, sharp cord
1724 TURNER *Sound Anatomiz'd* (p. 11) *The Reason why the* Third *and* Fifth *are called* Common Cords. ¶ But some will be apt to ask, (and with very good Reason) why the *Third* and *Fifth* are mentioned particularly, apart from the other *Concords*? To which, it may be answered, that all *Cadences* Center in those *Cords*; for which Reason they are called *Common-Cords*, as being nearest to the *Base*; ... **1737** LAMPE *Plain and Compendious Method* (pp. 13-14) In the first Place it is to be observed, that the *Interval* of the greater or lesser Third, and that of the Fifth (*not the sharp or flat Fifth*) produce a perfect *Harmony*, and is called a *Common Cord* ...

common time *see* dupla, imperfect of the less, mood, pointing, semibreve time, time, whole time
1708 KERSEY *Dict. Anglo-Brit.* (1st edn) *Common Time*, (in *Musick*) the same as *Duple Time.* **1728** CHAMBERS *Common or Duple Time*, in Musick. See *Time*.

common tune *see* lesson
1676 MACE *Musick's Monument* (p. 129) *Common Tunes*, (so called) are Commonly known by the *Boys, and Common People, Singing Them in the Streets*; and are of either *sort of Time*, of which there are many, very *Excellent*, and *well Contriv'd Pieces, Neat*, and *Spruce Ayre*.

communion *see* choir
1688 MIEGE-COTGRAVE Fr→E § *Post-Communion*, (f.) *sorte de Priere que le Peuple chante aprês la Communion du Prestre*, Post-Communion, a Prayer sung by the People after the Priest's Communion, in the Roman Church.

compass *see* system
1609 DOWLAND-ORNITHOPARCUS *Micrologvs* (p. 11) *Of the Compasses of the Tones.* ¶ The Compasse is nothing else, but a circuite or space allowed by the authoritie of the Musitians to the *Tones* for their rising and falling.

compline *see* primer

composer *see* asmatographer, musurgus
1593 HOLLYBAND Fr→E *Compositeurs*, or *Composeurs en musique ou imprimerie, m*: compositors in musicke or printing. **1611** COTGRAVE Fr→E *Composeur: m.* A composer, poet, writer, maker; a setter in Musicke. **1659** TORRIANO-FLORIO It→E **Componere*, to compose ... also to set musick. *Componitore*, a composer, also a setter in Musike. **1688** MIEGE-COTGRAVE Fr→E *Compositeur*, (m.) ... a setter in Musick. **1706** KERSEY-PHILLIPS (6th edn) To *Compose, (Lat.)* ... In *Musick*, to make or set Tunes, Airs, *&c.* **1737** DYCHE-PARDON (2nd edn) *Compose* (V.) ... In *Musick*, to make Airs, or set Tunes, single or in Parts, for Instruments or Voices.

composition
1658 PHILLIPS (1st edn) *Composition*, (Lat.) a setting together, also a work set forth in any piece of learning, or art. **1707** *Gloss. Angl. Nova* (1st edn) *Composition*, (Lat.) ... also any Treatise, or Piece of

Musick is called a *Composition*. **1721** Bailey *An Univ. Etymolog. Engl. Dict.* (1st edn) *Composition,* (in *Musick*) is a Treatise or piece of Musick. **1724** [Pepusch] *Short Explic. of Foreign Words in Mus. Bks.* (p. 22) *Composizio,* Composition, a Term used n Musick. **1726** Bailey *An Univ. Etymolog. Engl. Dict.* (3rd edn) *Composizio* (in *Musick Books*) signifies Composition. *Ital.* **1728** Chambers *Composition,* in Musick, the Art of disposing musical Sounds into Airs, Songs, *&c.* either in one, or more Parts; to be sung with the Voice, or play'd on Instruments. See *Musick,* and *Song.* ¶ *Zarlin* defines it the Art of joining and combining Concords together, which are the Matter of Musick: But this Definition is too scanty; in regard, Discords are always used with Concords in the *Composition* of Parts. See *Concord,* and *Discord.* ¶ Under *Composition* are comprehended the Rules, first, of *Melody,* or the Art of making a single Part; *i.e.* of contriving and disposing the simple Sounds, so as that their Succession and Progress may be agreeable. See *Melody.* ¶ 2dly, Of *Harmony,* or the Art of disposing and concerting several single Parts so together, that they may make one agreeable Whole. See *Harmony.* ¶ It may be here observ'd, that Melody being chiefly the Business of the Imagination, the Rules of its *Composition* serve only to prescribe certain Limits to it; beyond which, the Imagination, in searching out the Variety and Beauty of Airs, ought not to go: But Harmony, being the Work of Judgment, its Rules are more certain, extensive, and more difficult in practice. ¶ In the Variety and Elegancy of the Melody, the Invention labours a great deal more than the Judgment; so that Method has but little place: but in Harmony 'tis otherwise; the Invention, here, has nothing to do; and the *Composition* is conducted from a nice Observation of the Rules of Harmony, without any Assistance from the Imagination at all. **1730** Bailey *Dict. Britannicum* (1st edn) *Compositio* (in *Musick Books*) composition, *Ital.* **1737** Dyche-Pardon (2nd edn) *Composition* (S.) ... in *Musick,* it is the Piece or Book of Musick made fit for Voices or Instruments;

1721 Malcolm *Treatise of Musick* (pp. 30-1) ... we have the Science [of music] divided into these two general Parts. *First,* The *Knowledge* of the *Materia Musica,* or, how to produce Sounds, in such relations of *Tune* and *Time* as shall be agreeable in *Consonance* or *Succession,* or both... *Second,* How these Principles are to be applied; or, how Sounds, in the Relations that belong to *Musick* (as these are determined in the First Part) may be ordered, and variously put together in *Succession* and *Consonance* so as to answer the End; which Part we rightly call *The Art* of *Composition;* and it is properly the *practical* Part of *Musick.* **1730** [Pepusch] *Short Treatise on Harmony* (p. 1) *Composition* is that Part of Musick, which teaches how to make use of the Concords, and of the Discords, in a proper Manner; so as that the Union of the Parts, shall make Good Harmony.

con

1724 [Pepusch] *Short Explic. of Foreign Words in Mus. Bks.* (pp. 22-3) *Con* is as much as to say with, and is thus used, ¶ *Con Diligenza,* is with Diligence, Care, and Exactitude. ¶ *Con Discretione,* is with Judgment and Discretion. ¶ *Con Dolce Maniera,* is with or after a sweet, and agreeable Manner. ¶ *Con e senza Violini,* is as much as to say, with or without Violins. **1726** Bailey *An Univ. Etymolog. Engl. Dict.* (3rd edn) *Con* (in *Musick Books*) signifies, with. *It.* § *Con Diligenza* (in *Musick Books*) signifies with Diligence, Care, and Exactness. *It.* *Con Discretione* (in *Musick Books*) signifies with Judgment and Discretion. *Ital.* *Con Dolce Maniera* (in *Musick Books*) signifies, after a sweet and agreeable Manner. *Ital.* *Con e Senza Violina* (in *Musick Books*) signifies either with or without Violins. *Ital.*

1731 Prelleur *Modern Musick-Master* (Dictionary, p. 2) *Con,* with as *Con e senza Violins* with and without Violins.

concent *see* concino, harmony, symphony

1500 *Ortus Vocabulorum* L→E Concentum us ui. acorde of a songe m.q. **1538** Elyot L→E *Concento, tare,* to agree in one tune. *Concentus, tus,* a consente, many voyces in one tune, or accorde in musyke. **1552** Huloet L→E *Concento. as, Concinno. is, Simphonio. as,* Agree in one tune. *Concentus, us, ui,* Accord or consent in Musike. *Vide plus in* Consent. **1565** Cooper L→E *Concentus, huius concentus. Virgil.* A consent of many voyces in one: an accorde in musike. § *Seruare concentum. Cic.* To kepe in tune. *Volucres acra mulcent concentibus. Ouid.* Tunes. **1587** Thomas L→E *Concentio, onis, f.g. verb. à Concino.* A consent of manie voices in one, an accorde in musike, concorde, agreement. *Concentor, *qui consonat & concinit canenti.* **1589** Rider L→E *Concentio, concentus, canor, m.* Musicke, or pleasant melody. *Concentio, f.* A concent of many voices in one. *Concentus, m. concentio, f.* A singing in tune. **1598** Florio It→E *Concento,* a consort, or concordance in musick. **1599** MINSHEU-PERCYVALL Sp→E *Concento*, a consent, a consort or concordance in musicke. **1611** FLORIO It→E *Concento*, a consort or concordance, a harmony, a tunable accord. **1656** BLOUNT (1st edn) *Concention (concentio)* a consort of many voyces or instruments in one, an agreement or concord, singing in tune. **1658** PHILLIPS (1st edn) *Consent* [sic], (lat.) a Harmony, or agreement in Musick. **1659** TORRIANO-FLORIO It→E *Concentare*, ... an harmonious consort. *Concento*, a tunable accord, a concordance **1671** PHILLIPS (3rd edn) *Concent, (Lat.)* a harmony, or agreement in Musick. **1688** DAVIS-TORRIANO-FLORIO It→E *Concento*, an harmonious consort, an agreement. **1706** KERSEY-PHILLIPS (6th edn) *Concent*, a Consort of Voices, an Accord, or Agreement of Parts in *Musick*; a Singing in Tune. **1707** *Gloss. Angl. Nova* (1st edn) *Concention*, (Lat.) a Consort of many Voices or Instruments in one. **1721** BAILEY *An Univ. Etymolog. Engl. Dict.* (1st edn) *Concent*, (*Concentus, L.*) a Consort of Voices or Instruments, an Agreement of Parts in Musick.

1635 ANON. Papers rel. to Writings of Birchensha BL Add. 4388, f. 46v *Concentus* est compositio artificiosa *sonorum* secundum harmoniam, rhythmum & symphonium.

concert *see* carnival, chiesa, concerto, consort, overture, part, play, trio

1611 COTGRAVE Fr→E § *Concert de Musique*. A consort of Musicke. **1670** BLOUNT (3rd edn) *Concert* (Fr.) a consort in musick; an agreement. **1688** MIEGE-COTGRAVE Fr→E *Concert*, (m.) consort, harmony: Musick-house; unanimity. *Concerter*, to have a Consort of Musick; to concert, or contrive. § *Aller au Concert*, to go to the Musick-house. *Nous concerterons demain*, to morrow we shall have a consort of Musick. *Un charmant concert de Musique*, a charming consort of Musick. **1728** CHAMBERS *Concert*, or *Concerto*, popularly *Consort*, a Number, or Company of Musicians playing, or singing the same Song, or piece of Musick together. See *Musick*. ¶ The Word *Concert* may be applied where Musick is only Melody, *i.e.* the Performers are all in Unison; but it is more properly, as well as more usually understood of Harmony, or where the Musick consists of divers Parts; as Bass, Tenor, *&c.* See *Melody, Harmony, Part, &c.* **1730** BAILEY *Dict. Britannicum* (1st edn) *Concert, Concerto*, (in *Musick*) a consort, a company of musicians playing or singing the same piece of musick or song at the same time. **1737** DYCHE-PARDON (2nd edn) *Concert* or *Concerto* (S.) when applied to Musick, means the Harmony or Melody arising from the Agreement of the several Parts of the Composition, and is generally spoken of those grand Performances in that Art, that require many Persons or Instruments to perform it;

1725 DE LA FOND *New System of Music* (preface, xii-xiii) As to the word *Concert*, it is certainly more proper than *Consort*; and this upon three very good accounts. *1.* By *Concert* we mean a mixture of musical Voices and Instruments, which seem *to act together in Concert*, or agreement; which *Concert* or agreement is the very soul of what we call a *Concert* of *Music*, and the word it self. *2.* This word is *French*, and signifies this agreement of musical Voices and Instruments: and it must be either ignorance, or inadvertence, that makes them use *Consort* instead of *Concert*. *3.* As it is most improper to fix any two different ideas to the same word, we had better say *Concert*, than *Consort*; for, this last is used to signify a partner for life; in which signification it is not only proper, but very elegant.

concertante *see* necessario, obligata

1724 [PEPUSCH] *Short Explic. of Foreign Words in Mus. Bks.* (p. 23) *Concertante*, are those Parts of a Piece of Musick which play thoroughout the whole, to distinguish them from those which play only in some Parts. § (p. 10) *Alto Concertante*, the Tenor of the Little Chorus, or the Tenor that sings or plays throughout. (p. 15) *Basso Concertante*, the Bass of the little Chorus, or the Bass that plays throughout the whole Piece. (p. 18) *Canto Concertante*, is the Treble of the little Chorus, or the Part, that sings throughout. (p. 79) *Tenore Concertante*, the Tenor playing throughout. **1726** BAILEY *An Univ. Etymolog. Engl. Dict.* (3rd edn) *Concertante* (in *Musick Books*) signifies those Parts of a Piece of Musick that plays [sic] throughout the whole, to distinguish them from those that play only in some Parts. *Ital.* § *Alto Concertante* (in *Musick Books*) signifies the Tenor of the little Chorus, or the Tenor that sings and plays throughout. *Basso Concertante* (in *Musick Books*) signifies the Bass of the little Chorus, or the Bass that plays throughout the whole Piece. *Canto Concertante* (in *Musick Books*) signifies the Treble of the little Chorus, or the Part that sings throughout.

1731 PRELLEUR *Modern Musick-Master* (Dictionary, p. 2) *Basso Concertante*, Bass of the Small Chorus. **1736** TANS'UR *Compleat Melody* (3rd edn, p. 70) *Concertante, Continuo, Continuoto*, or *C. Necessario, Recitante*. (Ital.) Either of those *Terms* signifies, *Continual*; being a Name applied to those *Parts* that move continually, thro' the whole *Composition*. As *Basso Continuoto, Alto Continuoto, Canto Continuo,* &c. which distinguisheth those *Parts* that move continually, from those that move in but some certain Places: Which *Parts* are called *The Parts of the Grand Chorus*.—The *Bass* of these *Parts* are commonly marked with *Figures;* and sometimes set only with *Notes*, thro' the whole *Concerto*, or *Concert*.

concertare *see* conserto

1598 FLORIO It→E *Concertare*, to agree, or tune together, or proportion or accord together, to sing or play in consort. **1611** FLORIO It→E *Concertamento*, as *Concerto*. *Concertare*, ... to agree or tune together, to sing or play in consort. *Disconcertare*, to disagree, to vntune. **1659** TORRIANO-FLORIO It→E *Concertare*, ... to agree and accord together, to consort, to sing, to tune, or play in consort **Concertatamente*, adv. tunably, with accord.

concerto *see* chiesa, concert, conserto, consort, rehearsal, ripieno, sconcerto, symphony, tutti

1598 FLORIO It→E *Concerto*, as *Concento*. **1611** FLORIO It→E *Concerto*, an agreement, an accord, a consort, or concordance. *Disconcerto*, a disagreement in tunes. **1659** TORRIANO-FLORIO It→E *Concerto, Concertamento*, as *Concento*. *Disconcerto*, a discord in tunes. **1724** [PEPUSCH] *Short Explic. of Foreign Words in Mus. Bks.* (p. 23) *Concerto*, a Consort, or a Piece of Musick of several Parts for a Consort. **1726** BAILEY *An Univ. Etymolog. Engl. Dict.* (3rd edn) *Concerto* (in *Musick Books*) signifies a Consort, or a Piece of Musick of several Parts for a Consort. *Ital.*

c.1726 NORTH Musicall Gramarian BL Add. 32533, ff. 150v-151 ... And this puts me In Mind not to let pass, a late manner of full musick called concierto's, or In plain English, consorts, without a word or two; ... they differ litle from comon sonata's, having the like variety's, but pretending to Imploy more Instruments, and to sound fuller. The parts beyond .4. are doubles; but y[e] cheif use of them is to obtain y[e] Grace of soft, and loud, ffor at the soft the apposititious parts are silent and come in at the loud, and after a solo, or clinquant of a part or two, then, Tutti, and all away together. **1731** PRELLEUR *Modern Musick-Master* (Dictionary, p. 2) *Concerto*, signifies properly a Concert. **1736** TANS'UR *Compleat Melody* (3rd edn, p. 70) *Concerto*, (Ital.) or *Consort*, is a Piece of *Musick* composed in several *Parts*.

concerto grosso

1724 [PEPUSCH] *Short Explic. of Foreign Words in Mus. Bks.* (p. 23) *Concerto Grosso*, is the great or grand Chorus of the Consort, or those Places of the Concerto or Consort where all the several Parts perform or play together. **1726** BAILEY *An Univ. Etymolog. Engl. Dict.* (3rd edn) *Concerto Grosso* (in *Musick Books*) signifies the Grand Chorus of the Consort, or those Places of the Consort where all the several Parts perform or play together. *Ital.*

1736 TANS'UR *Compleat Melody* (3rd edn, p. 68) *Concerto Groso, Tutti, Tutto*, or *T. Pieno, Grande*, (Ital.) Either of these Words signifies *Full;* and used when all Parts fall in, and perform together in full Chorus: as *Pieno Choro*, a full Chorus.

concha *see* lituus, luter

1538 ELYOT L→E *Concha*, ... Also a trumpet, as it semethe made of erthe, lyke to suche as the poore men do vse, which haue the fallyng sycknes, and do come from the place in Ducheland, called saint Cornelius. **1565** COOPER L→E *Concha, conchæ. Plin.* Euery shell fish ... also a trumpette, properly made of earth, lyke a Cornelis horne. *Concha, pro Tuba ponitur. Virg.* A trumpet. **1587** THOMAS L→E *Concha, æ, f.g* ... also a trumpet, properlie made of earth, like a Cornelis horne.

concinnous *see* interval, system

1728 CHAMBERS *Concinnous Intervals*, in Musick. Discords are distinguish'd into *Concinnous* and *Inconcinnous* Intervals: The *Concinnous* are such as are fit for Musick, next to, and in Combination with Concords; being neither very agreeable nor disagreeable in themselves; but having a good Effect, as by their opposition they heighten the more essential Principles of Pleasure; or as by their mixture and combination with 'em, they produce a Variety necessary to our being better pleased. See *Harmony*. ¶ The other Discords, that are never used in Musick, are called *Inconcinnous*. See *Discord*. ¶ Systems are also divided into *Concinnous* and *Inconcinnous*. A System is said to be *concinnous*, or *concinnously* divided, when the Parts thereof, consider'd as simple Intervals, are *concinnous;* and are, besides, placed in such an Order, between the Extremes, as that the Succession of Sounds from one Extreme to the other, may have an agreeable Effect. See *System*. ¶ Where the simple Intervals are *inconcinnous*, or ill-disposed between the Extremes, the System is said to be *inconcinnous*. **1730** BAILEY *Dict. Britannicum* (1st edn) *Concinnous Intervals* (in

Musick) are such as are fit for musick, next to and in combination with concords. **1737** DYCHE-PARDON (2nd edn) *Concinnous* (A.) ... also certain Intervals in Musick that produce a Sort of Tone between Concords and Discords.

1694 HOLDER *Treatise of Natural Grounds* (p. 194) Concords are within a limited Number, Discords innumerable. But of them, those here considered, which are (as the *Greeks* termed them) ἐμμελῆ *Concinnous*, apt and usefull in Harmony: Or which, at least, are necessary to be known, as being the Differences and Measures of the other; and helping to discover the reason of Anomalies, found in the Degrees of Instruments tuned by *Hemitones*. § (p. 185) Those [diatonic intervals] which arise from the Differences of Consonant Intervals, are called *Intervalla Concinna*, and properly appertain to Harmony: The rest are necessary to be known, for making and understanding the Scales of Musick. **1721** MALCOLM *Treatise of Musick* (pp. 36-7) *Discords* have a more general and very remarkable Distinction, which is proper to be explained here; they are either *concinnous* or *inconcinnous Intervals*; the *concinnous* are such as are apt or fit for *Musick*, next to and in Combination with *Concords*; and are neither very agreeable nor very disagreeable in themselves; they are such Relations as have a good Effect in *Musick* only as, by their Opposition, they heighten and illustrate the more essential Principles of the Pleasure we seek for; or by their Mixture and Combination with them, they produce a Variety necessary to our being better pleased; and therefore are still called *Discord*, as the Bitterness of some Things may help to set off the Sweetness of others, and yet still be bitter: And therefore in the Definition of *Concord* I have said *always and of themselves agreeable*, because the *concinnous* could have no good Effect without these, which might subsist without the other, tho' less perfectly. The other Degrees of *Discord* that are never chosen in *Musick* come under the Name of *inconcinnous* ... § (p. 40) A most remarkable Distinction of *Systems* is into *concinnous* and *inconcinnous*. How these Words are applied to simple Intervals we have already seen; but to *Systems* they are applied in a twofold Manner, thus, In every *System* that is concinnously divided, the Parts considered as simple Intervals must be *concinnous* in the Sense of Article *Third*; but not only so, they must be placed in a certain Order betwixt the Extremes, that the Succession of Sounds from one Extreme to the other, may be agreeable, and have a good Effect in Practice. An *inconcinnous System* therefore is that where the simple Intervals are *inconcinnous*, or ill disposed betwixt the Extremes.

concino *see* accino

1538 ELYOT L→E *Concinere*, to agre in one song, or one tune. **1565** COOPER L→E *Concino, cóncinis, pen. corr. concínui, concentum, concinere* ... To singe: to agree in one songe or tune: § *Ad fores alicuius concinere. Ouid.* To singe at ones doore. *Concinunt signa & tubæ. Cæs.* The trumpettes sowne or goe. *In modum concinere. Catul.* To singe by measure. *Lyra concinere. Ouid.* To singe to, or play on the harpe. *Modis quibusdam concini. Ouid.* To be songe in measure. *Plectro aliquem concinere. Horat.* To singe ones prayses to an instrument. *Pressis & flebilibus modis concinere. Cic.* To singe leisurely by pauses and with lamentable measures. **1587** THOMAS L→E *Concino, is, ui, entum, ere, ex con & Cano.* To agree or accorde in one song or tune: to signe, to praise, to sounde: **1589** RIDER L→E *Concino, concento, Symphoneo, as.* To Agree in one tune.

concionatorius

1565 COOPER L→E *Concionatórius. Adiectiuum: vt, Concionatoria tibia. Gell.* A pipe or shaulme vsed in assembles.

concord *see* consonance, consonant, imperfect concord, perfect concord, simple, true relation

1500 *Ortus Vocabulorum* L→E Concordatista te. ille qui canit cum cordis. com. p. **1565** COOPER L→E § *Sonus concors. Ouid.* An agreable tune. **1587** THOMAS L→E *Concors, dis, adject.* ... tunable, or musicall. **1589** RIDER L→E *Concors, consors, flexibilis, ad., vt flexibile vocis genus.* Tuneable. **1656** BLOUNT (1st edn) *Concords*, In Musick, which are Perfect or semi-perfect, between the unison and the Diapason, are, the fifth, which is most perfect, the third next, and the sixth which is more harsh, and the fourth which is called *Diatessaron. Bac.* **1658** PHILLIPS (1st edn) *Concord*, (lat.) ... also a perfect Tone in Musick, as an eighth, or a third, *&c.* **1676** COLES *Concord, Latin.* agreement, also (in musick) an agreeing Note as an eight, fifth, &c. **1688** MIEGE-COTGRAVE Fr→E *Concorde*, (f.) concord, union. **1704** *Cocker's Engl. Dict.* (1st edn) *Concord*, ... in Musick an agreeing Note, in perfect Harmony, as the fifth, third, sixth and fourth, *&c.* **1704** HARRIS *Concords*, in Musick, are certain Intervals between Sound, which delight the Ear when heard at the same time. These *Concords* are the Third, Fifth, Sixth, and Eighth, together with their Octaves, as the Tenth, Thirteenth, Fifteenth, *&c.* They are also of two sorts, *viz. Perfect* and *Imperfect: Perfect Concords* are the Fifth and Eighth with all their Octaves: *Imperfect Concords,* are the Third and Sixth with their Octaves. The *Imperfect have yet another distinction, viz.* the Greater and Lesser Third, as also the Greater and Lesser Sixth. Some reckon the Vnison among the *Concords,* but others will not admit it into the number of the Intervals. **1706** KERSEY-PHILLIPS (6th edn) *Concord, ... In Musick, Concords,* are certain Intervals, or Distances between Sounds, which delight the Ear, when heard at the same time: These Concords are the Third, Fifth, Sixth and Eighth, together with their *Octaves,* as the Tenth, Thirteenth, Fifteenth, &c. They are also of two sorts, *viz.* Perfect and Imperfect. ¶ *Perfect Concords,* are the Fifth and Eighth with all their Octaves. *Imperfect Concords,* are the Third and Sixth with their Octaves: The Imperfect ones are likewise distinguish'd into the greater and lesser Third; as also the greater and lesser Sixth. **1728** CHAMBERS *Concord* ... [*see* Appendix] **1730** BAILEY *Dict. Britannicum* (1st edn) § *Compound Concords,* are equal to any 2 or more concords. *Simple Concords,* are those whose extremes are set at a distance, less than the sum of any other 2 concords. **1737** DYCHE-PARDON (2nd edn) *Concord* (S.) ... In *Musick,* if two single Sounds be in such Relation, or have such a Difference as that being sounded together they make a mixed or compound Sound, which pleases the Ear, that Relation is called a Concord.

1597 MORLEY *Plaine and Easie Introdvction* (p. 70) *Phi.* What is a *Concord?* ¶ *Ma. It is a mixt sound compact of diuers voyces, entring with delight in the eare,* and is eyther perfect or vnperfect. **1609** DOWLAND-ORNITHOPARCUS *Micrologvs* (p. 79) *What Concord is.* ¶ ... Consonance (which otherwise we call *Concordance*) is the agreeing of two vnlike Voyces placed together. Or is (as *Tinctor* writeth) the mixture of diuers Sounds, sweetly pleasing the eares. Or according to *Stapulensis lib.* 3. It is the mixture of an high, and lowe sound, comming to the eares sweetly, and vniformely... § (pp. 79-80) Of *Concords* also some be perfect; some imperfect. The perfect are those, which being grounded vpon certaine Proportions, are to be proued by the helpe of numbers. The imperfect, as not being probable, yet placed among the perfects, make an Vnison sound; ... **1636** BUTLER *Principles of Musik* (p. 48) A *Concord* is the mixture of a Grave and Acute sound sweetely falling to the ear.... The sevn Concords ar first an Eight, (which *Glareanus,* for perfection and chiefti [sic], calleth *Consonantiarum Regina*) a Perfect and imperfect Third, a Fowrth, a Fift, a perfect and imperfect Sixt: with their Compounds. Unto these Intervall-concords is added the Unison: ... **1662** [DAVIDSON] *Cantus, Songs and Fancies* (n.p.) Q. *What is a Concord?* ¶ A. It is a mixt sound compact of diverse voices, entring with delight in the eare, and is either perfect, or imperfect ... **1694** HOLDER *Treatise of Natural Grounds* (p. 50) Concords are Harmonic sounds, which being joyned please and delight the Ear; and Discords the Contrary. **early 18th C.** ANON. Essay on Musick BODLEIAN Rawl. D. 751, f. 2 Different sounds which strike the ear at the same time, either are agreable to it, and then they are called *concords* or accords; or disagreable to it, and then they are call'd *discords* or bad accords. **1721** MALCOLM *Treatise of Musick* (p. 36) *Concord* is the Denomination of all these Relations that are always and of themselves agreeable, whether applied in *Succession* or *Consonance* (by which Word I always mean a mere sounding together;) *that is,* If two simple Sounds are in such a Relation, or have such a Difference of *Tune,* that being sounded together they make a Mixture or *compound* Sound which the Ear receives with Pleasure, that is called *Concord;* and whatever Two Sounds make an agreeable Compound; they will always follow other [sic] agreeably. § (p. 38) Some indeed have restrained the Word *Concord* to *Intervals,* making it include a Difference of *Tune;* but it is precarious; for as the Word *Concord* signifies an Agreement of Sounds, 'tis certainly applicable to *Unisons* in the First Degree. ¶ Observe, the Words *Concord* and *Harmony* are of the same Sense, yet they are arbitrarily made different Terms of Art; *Concord* signifies the agreeable Effect of two Sounds in *Consonance; Harmony* is applied to the Agreement of any greater Number of Sounds in *Consonance.* Again *Harmony* always signifies *Consonance,* but *Concord* is applied sometimes also to *Succession,* yet never but when the Terms [intervallic members] can stand agreeably in *Consonance:* ... § (p. 84) ... take this *Definition, viz. That* Concord *is the Result of a frequent Union and Coincidence of the Vibrations of Two sonorous Bodies, and consequently of the undulating Motions of the Air, which being caused by these Vibrations, are like and proportional to them; which Coincidence the more frequent it is with respect to the Number of Vibrations of both Bodies performed in the same Time,* cæteris paribus, *the more perfect is that* Concord, *till the Rarity of the Coincidence in* *respect of one or both the Motions become* Discord. § (pp. 152-3) *Definition.* A *simple Concord* is such, whose Extremes are at a Distance less than the Sum of any Two other *Concords.* A *compound Concord* is equal to Two or more Concords. This in general is agreeable to the common Notion of *simple* and *compound;* but the *Definition* is also taken another Way among the Writers on *Musick;* thus an *Octave* 1:2, and all the lesser *Concords* ... are called *simple* and *original Concords;* and all greater than an *Octave* are called *compound Concords,* because all *Concords* above an *Octave* are composed of, or equal to the Sum of one or more *Octaves,* and some single *Concord* less than an *Octave;* and are ordinarily in Practice called by the Name of that *simple Concord;* ... § (p. 507) Of *Concords.* They [the ancient Greeks] defined this, An Agreement of Two Sounds that makes them, either successively or jointly heard, pleasant to the Ear. **1724** TURNER *Sound Anatomiz'd* (p. 8) ... *Discords* or *Concords,* the latter of which being termed so, as being their Property to please the *Ear* (or rather, the *Fancy*) when managed judiciously; otherwise, a nice *Ear* will be very much offended, false *Concords* not being allowed in *Musick,* any more than in *Grammar.* **1731** [PEPUSCH] *Treatise on Harmony* (2nd edn, p. 1) *Concords,* are those Intervals whose Extreme Notes being sounded together, are agreeable to the Ear. They are Eight in number, *viz.* the *Unison,* the *Octave,* the *Fifth,* the *Fourth,* the *Third major,* the *Third minor,* the *Sixth major,* and the *Sixth minor.* **1736** TANS'UR *Compleat Melody* (3rd edn, p. 1) *Concord,* is when two, three, or more *Sounds* are performed together in *Musical Concordance;* there being the Distance of 3, 5, or 8 *Notes* above another; which when regularly composed together, 'tis called *Harmony;* i.e. *Three in One.* **1740** LAMPE *Art of Musick* (p. 39) *Zarlin* in his harmonical Demonstrations, *R* 2 *D* 1 gives the following Definition of a Concord, *Consonanza propriamente detta, e Mistura ò compositione di Suono grave, & di acuto, la quale suavemente & uniformemente viene all' Udito.* And again in Part 2. Chap xii of his Institutions: *La Consonanza nasce, quando due Suoni, che sono tra lor differenti, senza alcun Suono mezono, si conguingono concordevolmente in un Corpo.*

concordance

after 1517 ANON. Art of Mvsic BL Add. 4911, f. 46v *Concordance quhat is it.* ¶ *Concordance* is ane consonance and mixtur of gravve and scherp soundis sweitly to aeris convement quhilk all one cays and besmes exerce zat **1609** DOWLAND-ORNITHOPARCUS *Micrologvs* (p. 78) ... *Concordance* (as saith *Boêtius*) is the due mingling of two or more voices ... **1617-24** FLUDD *Utriusque Cosmi Maioris: De Templo Musicæ* (p. 210) *Concordantia* est congruens sonorum per intervalla systematis convenientia seu proportio, vel est dissimilium inter se vocum in unum redacta concordia.

conjunction

1609 DOWLAND-ORNITHOPARCUS *Micrologvs* (p. 24) *Of Coniunctions.* ¶ The Coniunct sounds were called by the ancients *Dijuncts* because it is added to songs besides their nature, either to make them more sweet, or to make the *Moodes* more perfect: for thus saith Saint *Bernard:* In euery kinde, where it is meet a flatter sound should be, let there be put a flat in stead of a sharpe; yet couertly, least the Song seeme to take vpon it the likenesse of another *Tone.* Now a *Coniunct* is this, to sing a Voyce in a *Key* which is not in it. Or it is the sodaine changing of a *Tone* into a *Semitone,* or a *semitone* into a *Tone.*... *Coniuncts* are two-fold: that is, Tolerable ones, when a Voyce is sung in a *Key,* wherein it is not, yet is found in his eight: as to sing *Mi* in *A re, La* in *Dsolre.* Intolerable ones, when a Voyce is sung in a *Key* which is not in it, nor in his eight, as to sing *Fa* in *Elami, Mi* in *Ffaut.* Of these *Coniuncts* there be two signes, *viz. b* round and ♮. The first sheweth that the *Coniunct* is in ♮ *dure* places; the second, that it is in *b flat* places. ¶ There be 8. *Coniuncts* most vsuall: although there may be more. The first in a Base, is marked with round *b.* The second in *E* finall, is marked with the same signe. The third is in *Ffaut,* and is marked with ♮. The fourth in a small, is knowne by *b flat.* The fift, in *c* affinall by ♮ *dure.* The sixt, in *e* by *b* round. The seuenth, in *f* by ♮. The eight in *aa* by *b.* There be examples enough to to [sic] be found of these both in plaine and mensurall Songs.

Connas

1565 COOPER L→E *Connas,* A drunken minstrell, that after was a great dooer in the plaies at Olympus in Greece: **1623** COCKERAM *Connas,* a drunken Fidler.

Connus

1565 COOPER L→E *Connus,* Socrates maister in musike.

consecution

1636 BUTLER *Principles of Musik* (pp. 57-8) Consecution is the following of Intervalls, Consonant or Dissonant, upon Concords. In which, skilful Artists have observed divers necessary Cautions, that may bee reduced unto certain brief Rules or Canons. ¶ Consecution of Consonant Intervalls is either Simple or Mixt. ¶ Simple Consecution is of Concords upon Concords of their own kinde.... ¶ Mixt Consecution is of sorts of Concords, variously entermedled, and enterchangeably succeeding one an other... **c.1698-c.1703** NORTH Cursory Notes (*C-K CN* p. 179) This brings it in my way to speak of consecution, of accords. That means the same accord sounding upon removes successively, and masters doe absolutely inhibite it, as to octaves and fifths, as too luscious to goe downe without some acrid in the sauce ... **1736** TANS'UR *Compleat Melody* (3rd edn, p. 72) *Consecution,* is when two, three or more *Cords* of the same kind follows one another; both *Parts* moving the same way; which are taken either between the *Bass* and *Tenor,* or between two of the *upper Parts*: When two, or more *Cords,* either *Thirds, Fourths, Fifths, Sixths, Sevenths,* or *Eighths* are taken together, either rising or falling; it is called a *Consecution* of two, or more; some of which are *Dissallowances,* especially if two *Fifths* or two *Eighths* are taken together, in two *Parts.*

conserto *see* concerto

1598 FLORIO It→E *Consertare,* to reduce to order, forme, tune or proportion. *Conserto,* a consort or vnison in musicke. **1611** FLORIO It→E *Consertare,* as *Concertare. Conserto,* ... Also as *Concerto.* **1659** TORRIANO-FLORIO It→E *Disconsertare,* to jar in tunes.

consonance *see* concord

1538 ELYOT L→E *Consono, nui, are,* to make one sowne togither. Also to accorde or agree. **1552** HULOET L→E *Consonans tis.* Consonaunte or accordaunte. **1565** COOPER L→E *Consono, cónsonas, pen. cor. consonâre. Plaut.* To make sounde together: to accorde, agree, or be like to. **1587** THOMAS L→E *Consonantia, æ, f.g.* The agreeing of voyces. *Consono, as ui, are.* To make sound togither, to ring, to accord, agree *Consonus, a, um.* Of like tune or sound, convenient, agreeable. **1598** FLORIO It→E *Consonantia,* a consonance or agreement in voices or sounds. **1599** MINSHEU-PERCYVALL Sp→E *Consonancia,* f. ... a harmonie or consent either in voices or in sounds **1611** COTGRAVE Fr→E *Consonant.* Consonant, accordant, harmonious, agreeing in sound, consorting with. **1611** FLORIO It→E *Consonanza,* a consonant in sounds. *Consonare,* to agree in voices or tune. **1650** HOWELL-COTGRAVE Fr→E *Consoner.* To accord, consort, agree, or sound, alike **1658** PHILLIPS (1st edn) *Consonant,* (lat.) sounding together, or agreeing; **1659** TORRIANO-FLORIO It→E *Consonante, Consonevole,* consonant, accordant, consorting with, harmonious *Consonanza, Consonevolezza,* accord, good pr[o]portion, concordance, agreemen[t] or consonance in sounds. **Consonare,* to sound together. *Consuonare,* to sound together. **1696** PHILLIPS (5th edn) *Consonance in Musick,* the agreeing of two Sounds, the one deep, the other higher, so proportionably order'd, that they make a pleasing sound to the Ears. **1704** HARRIS *Consonance,* in Musick, is the Agreement of two Sounds, the one *Grave* the other *Acute,* which are compounded together by such a Proportion of each as shall prove agreeable to the Ear. A *Vnison* is the first *Consonance,* an *Eighth* is the Second; the *Fifth* is the Third; and then follows the *Fourth,* and the *Thirds* and *Sixths, major* and *minor.* There are other *Consonances,* which are the Doubles, or other Repetitions of the former. There can be but seven or eight *Simple Consonances,* the *Perfect* ones are the *Vnison,* the *Eighth,* and the *Fifth,* with their Correspondents. **1706** KERSEY-PHILLIPS (6th edn) *Consonance,* ... In *Musick,* the Agreement of *Grave* and *Acute* Sounds, so proportionably order'd as to make a pleasing Harmony. **1707** *Gloss. Angl. Nova* (1st edn) *Consonance,* in Musick, is an agreement of two Sounds, the one *Grave,* and the other *Acute*; compounded by such a Proportion of each, as shall prove agreeable to the Ear. **1724** [PEPUSCH] *Short Explic. of Foreign Words in Mus. Bks.* (p. 23) *Consonante,* all agreeable Intervals in Musick are so called. **1726** BAILEY *An Univ. Etymolog. Engl. Dict.* (3rd edn) *Consonante* (in *Musick*) signifies all agreeable Intervals in Musick. *Ital.* **1728** CHAMBERS *Consonance,* in Musick, is ordinarily used in the same Sense with *Concord, viz.* for the Union or Agreement of two Sounds produced at the same time, the one Grave, the other Acute; which mingling in the Air, in a certain Proportion, occasion an Accord agreeable to the Ear. See *Concord.* ¶ Dr: *Holder,* on this Principle, defines *Consonancy,* 'A Passage of several tunable Sounds thro' the Medium, frequently mixing and uniting in their undulated Motions caused by the well-proportion'd commensurate Vibrations of the sonorous Bodies, and consequently arriving smooth, and sweet, and pleasant to the Ear; as, on the contrary, *Dissonancy,* he maintains to arise from disproportionate Motions of Sounds, not mixing, but jarring and clashing as they pass, and arriving in the Ear grating and offensive.' ¶ Which Notion of a *Consonance,* exactly quadrates with that we have already laid down for a *Concord*. Accordingly, most Authors confound the two together: Tho some of the more Accurate distinguish 'em; making *Consonance* to be what the Word implies, a mere *sounding of two or more Notes together*, or *in the same time*; in contradistinction to the Motion of those Sounds *in Succession*, or one after the other. See *Succession*. ¶ In effect, the two Notions coincide; for two Notes, thus play'd in *consonance*, constitute a Concord; And two Notes that please the Ear in *Consonance*, will likewise please it in Succession. ¶ Notes in *Consonance* constitute *Harmony*, as Notes in Succession *Melody*. See *Harmony*, and *Melody*; see also *Tune*. ¶ In the popular Sense, *Consonances* are either *Simple*, or *Compound*, &c. The most perfect *Consonance* is Unison; tho many, both among the Ancients and Moderns, discard it from the Number of *Consonances*; as conceiving *Consonance* an agreeable Mixture of different Sounds, grave and acute; not a Repetition of the same Sound. See *Unison*. ¶ The second *Consonance* is the Octave, then the Fifth, the Fourth, the Thirds, and the Sixths: The rest are Multiples, or Repetitions of these. See *Octave, &c.* **1737** DYCHE-PARDON (2nd edn) *Consonance* (S.) ... and in *Musick*, the Agreement of a grave and an acute Tone, compounded in such a Proportion as to be musical and agreeable to the Ear;

1609 DOWLAND-ORNITHOPARCUS *Micrologvs* (p. 78) ... Consonance is a mixture of two Sounds, falling into the eares vniformely. **1721** MALCOLM *Treatise of Musick* (pp. 84-5) ... I shall give you Dr. *Holder*'s Definition in his own Words, who has written chiefly on this One Point [concord], as the Title of his Book bears: Says he, "*Consonancy* (the same I call *Concord*) is the Passage of several tunable Sounds through the Medium, frequently mixing and uniting in their undulating Motions caused by the well proportioned commensurate Vibrations of the sonorous Bodies, and consequently arriving smooth and sweet and pleasant to the Ear. On the contrary, *Dissonancy* is from disproportionate Motions of Sounds, not mixing, but jarring and clashing as they pass, and arriving to the Ear harsh and grating and offensive." If the Dr. means by our Pleasure's being a Consequence of the frequent Mixture of Motions, any other Thing than that we find these Things so connected, I do not conceive it; but however he understood this, he has applied his *Definition* to the Preference of *Concord* no further than these Five, 1:2, 2:3, 3:4, 5:4, 5:6. **1740** LAMPE *Art of Musick* (pp. 38-9) ... Euclid says: *Consonantia est Mistio duorum, sonorum acuti Scilicet and gravis.*

consonant *see* concord

1597 MORLEY *Plaine and Easie Introdvction* (p. 70) *Phi.* What is a *perfect consanant* [sic]? ¶ *Ma. It is that which may stand by it selfe, and of it selfe maketh a perfect harmony, without the mixture of any other...* [e.g.] *A third, a Fift, a Sixt, and an eight.* ¶ *Phi.* Which be perfect, and which vnperfect. ¶ *Ma.* Perfect, *an Vnison, a Fift*, and their eights. § (p. 71) Which distances do make vnperfect consonants? A third, a sixt, and their eightes: a tenth, a thirteenth, &c. **c.1668-71** *Mary Burwell's Instruction Bk. for Lute* (*TDa* p. 52) [*re* 'true strokes and false strokes'] The strokes are called 'Consonants': the word *Con* is a Latin word that signifies 'with', and *Sonants* comes from 'sound'; that is, 'consonants', sounding with or together. **1736** TANS'UR *Compleat Melody* (3rd edn, p. 69) *Consonants*, or *Concords*, is a Name applied to all agreeable *Sounds*, or *Intervals*; *viz.* The *Unison*, 3d, 5th, 6th; and their *Octaves*. ¶ In the Compass of every 8th, or *Octave*, there are 12 several Degrees of *Sound*, each Degree having a proper Name from the lowest *Note*, which are called the *Greater*, or *Lesser*, *Perfect*, or *Imperfect*; ...

consone

1609 DOWLAND-ORNITHOPARCUS *Micrologvs* (pp. 78-9) ... Voyces are called some *Vnisons*; some not *Vnisons*... Of not *Vnisons*, some are *æquisons*; some *Consones*; ... *Consones* are those, which yeeld a compound or mingled Sound, *Diapente* and *Diapason diapente*.

consonous

1730 BAILEY *Dict. Britannicum* (1st edn) *Consonous* (*consonus*, L.) of the same tune or sound, agreeing in sound;

consort *see* camera, capella, chorus, concent, concert, concertare, concerto, entertainment, symphony

1616 BULLOKAR *Consort*... a company of Musitions together. **1623** COCKERAM *Consort.* a Companion in musique. *Consort.* A companion, or Musitians together. **1658** PHILLIPS (1st edn) *Consort*, (lat.) ... also a set or company of Musitians. **1676** COLES *Consort*, ... also a company (of Musicians.) **1696** PHILLIPS (5th edn) *Consort, (Lat.)* ... Also a piece of Musick consisting of three or more parts, which is either Instrumental or Vocal. **1702** KERSEY *New Engl. Dict.* (1st edn) A *Consort* of musick. **1704** *Cocker's Engl. Dict.* (1st edn) *Consort,* ... Also a Company of Musicians. **1706** KERSEY-PHILLIPS (6th edn) *Consort,* ... Also the Harmony made by several Voices or Musical Instruments; a Musick-meeting. **1707** *Gloss. Angl. Nova* (1st edn) *Consort,* ... Also a piece of Musick consisting of three or more Parts. **1721** BAILEY *An Univ. Etymolog. Engl. Dict.* (1st edn) *Consort,* (*Consors, L.*) ... Also a piece of Musick consisting of three or more Parts. *F.* **1728** CHAMBERS *Consort,* in Musick. See *Concert.* **1735** DEFOE *Consort* of Musick, a Piece of Musick consisting of several Parts. **1736** BAILEY *Dict. Britannicum* (2nd edn) *Consort better Concert* (*Concert,* F. *Concerto,* It. *Concierto,* Sp. (in *Musick*) a Piece that consists of 3 or more Parts. **1737** DYCHE-PARDON (2nd edn) *Consort* (S.) ... also the Performance of a Piece of Musick, consisting of various Parts.

1736 TANS'UR *Compleat Melody* (3rd edn, p. 70) A *Consort* of *Musick,* is *Three Parts;* and no less.

consort pitch

1721 MALCOLM *Treatise of Musick* (pp. 338-9) [*re* the harpsichord] ... And as to the tuning [of] the Instrument, I shall only add, that there is a certain Pitch to which it is brought, that it may be neither too *high* nor too *low,* for the Accompaniment of other Instruments, and especially for the human Voice, whether in *Unison* or taking a different *Part;* and this is called the *Consort Pitch.*

consort viol *see* viol

contadinella

1598 FLORIO It→E *Contadinelle,* countrie songs, gigs, madrigals or pastorall sonets. **1611** FLORIO It→E *Contadinella,* a yongue or pretty country wench. Also country songes or gigges. **1659** TORRIANO-FLORIO It→E *Contadinella,* a prettie Countrey wench, also a countrey-song or jig.

contemperara

1598 FLORIO It→E *Contemperare,* ... to accord, to tune with. **1611** FLORIO It→E *Contemperara,* ... to accorde or tune with.

continuato *see* bass, basso continuo, B. C., concertante, figure, thorough bass

1724 [PEPUSCH] *Short Explic. of Foreign Words in Mus. Bks.* (p. 24) *Continuato,* is to continue or hold on a Sound or Note in an equal Strength or Manner; or to continue a Movement in an equal Degree of Time all the Way. **1726** BAILEY *An Univ. Etymolog. Engl. Dict.* (3rd edn) *Continuato* (in *Musick Books*) signifies to continue or hold on a Sound or Note in an equal Strength or Manner; or to continue a Movement in an equal Degree of Time all the way. *Ital.*

1736 TANS'UR *Compleat Melody* (3rd edn, p. 68) *Continuoto* [sic]. *Sostenuto. Uguale, Ugualement* (Ital.) Either of those Terms import that you must continue, or hold on a Sound with equal Strength; yet hold their full *Time.*

continued bass *see* bass, basso continuo, B. C., figure, thorough bass

1706 KERSEY-PHILLIPS (6th edn) *Continued Bass,* a Term in *Musick,* the same as *Thorough-bass;* so call'd, because it goes quite thro' the Composition. **1708** KERSEY *Dict. Anglo-Brit.* (1st edn) *Continued Bass,* the same as *Thorough-Bass.* **1728** CHAMBERS *Continued,* or *Thorough Bass,* in Musick, is that which continues to play, constantly; both during the Recitatives, and to sustain the Choir, or Chorus. See *Bass.* **1730** BAILEY *Dict. Britannicum* (1st edn) *Continued Thorough Bass* (in *Musick*) is that which continues to play constantly, both during the recitatives and to sustain the chorus. **1737** DYCHE-PARDON (2nd edn) *Continued* (A.) ... so in *Musick,* the thorough Bass, or that which goes thro', or along with every Part, is called the continued Bass;

continued ground *see* ground

continuo *see* B. C., concertante

1724 [PEPUSCH] *Short Explic. of Foreign Words in Mus. Bks.* (p. 24) *Continuo,* for this see the Words *Basso Continuo.* **1726** BAILEY *An Univ. Etymolog. Engl. Dict.* (3rd edn) *Continuo* (in *Musick Books*) signifies thorough, as *Basso Continuo,* the Continual Base or Thorough Bass. *Ital.*

contra

1726 BRUCE *Common Tunes* (p. 6) ... the fond Fancy and Opinion of some in our Day, who (besides these three principal signed Cliffs, which serve to express the three essential and harmonious Parts of Musick, *viz. F. fa ut, C. sol fa ut,* and *G. sol re ut*) have dream'd of a 4th, *viz. C. sol fa ut,* prickt upon the 3d Rule of the Tone or Song; and this they call by the Name and Title of *Contra.*

contrabasso *see* basse-contre, contre-basse
1598 FLORIO It→E *Contrabasso,* a false base in musick, a counterbase, voice or string of any instrument. **1611** FLORIO It→E *Contrabasso,* a counterbase, be it voice, string or instrument. **1659** TORRIANO-FLORIO It→E *Contra-base,* a counterbase, also the lowest part of a basis. *Contrabasso,* a counterbase, be it voyce, string, or instrument.

contra harmonical proportion *see* harmonic proportion
1730 BAILEY *Dict. Britannicum* (1st edn) *Contra Harmonical Proportion* (in *Musick*) that relation of three terms, wherein the difference of the *first* and *second* is to the difference of the *second* and *third,* as the *third* is to the *first.*

contralto
1598 FLORIO It→E *Contralto,* a counter treble in musicke. **1611** FLORIO It→E *Contralto,* a countertreble in Musicke.

contramezzana *see* mezzana
1611 FLORIO It→E *Contramezzana,* ... Also a counter tenor stringe of an instrument. **1659** TORRIANO-FLORIO It→E *Contramezzana,* ... also a Countertenor.

contrapasso
1659 TORRIANO-FLORIO It→E **Contrapasso,* a counterstep, a counterpace, also a kinde of dance

contrapeso
1659 TORRIANO-FLORIO It→E *Contrapeso,* a counterpoise, also a ground or plain song in Musick.

contrapunto, contrapunctum, contrepoinct *see* counterpoint

contrapunto doppio *see* double descant

contrary motion *see* moto contrario

contra-sovrano
1611 FLORIO It→E *Contrasourano,* a counter treble. **1659** TORRIANO-FLORIO It→E *Contra-sovrano,* a countertreble.

contratempo
1659 TORRIANO-FLORIO It→E **Contra-tempo,* against time, also false time in musick.

contratenor, contretaille, contreteneur *see* countertenor

contre
1611 COTGRAVE Fr→E *Contre.* (Substantiuely, as) *faire le contre.* To second, assist, helpe forward; and (in Musicke) to beare the burden; or sing the Plainesong whereon another descants.

contre-basse *see* basse-contre, contrabasso
1611 COTGRAVE Fr→E *Contre-basse: f.* The Base part in Musicke.

contrechanter
1611 COTGRAVE Fr→E *Contrechanter.* To record in singing; to answer in the same note, or tune.

contrefugue *see* counterfugue

copter
1593 HOLLYBAND Fr→E *Copter,* when the bell doth not ring out, but of one side. **1611** COTGRAVE Fr→E *Copté: m. ée: f.* Tolled, or strucken only on the one side, as a Bell, &c. *Copter.* To toll, or strike only on one side; as a bell, when it is not fully rung out. **1650** HOWELL-COTGRAVE Fr→E † *Copté: m. ée: f.* Tolled, or strucken only on the one side, as a Bell, &c: † *Copter.* To toll, or strike onley on one side; as a Bell, when it is not fully rung out.

cor
1593 HOLLYBAND Fr→E *Vn Cor,* an Hunters horne: *m. Corne,* a horne: *f. Vn Cors,* or *cornet,* a blowing horne: *m.* § *Faire sçavoir, à Cors & à cri,* to make a proclamation with a trumpet. **1611** COTGRAVE Fr→E *Cor: m.* A hunters horne; a Bugle, or Hutchet; *Corner.* To sound a Cornet, to wind a Horne; § *Faire sçavoir, à Cors & à cri,* to make a proclamation with a trumpet. **1688** MIEGE-COTGRAVE Fr→E *Cor* (m.) horn, a Hunters horn; *Corner,* to sound a cornet, to wind a horn. § *Cor de Belier* (Jos. 6. 4.) a Trumpet of Rams-horn. *Donner (sonner) du Cor,* to wind a horn. *Sonner du Cor,* to blow the Horn. *Sonneur de Cor,* a Horn-blower.

coranto *see* correnti, courante, curranto, imperfect of the more, lesson, suit
1598 FLORIO It→E *Coranta, Corranta,* a kinde of French-dance. **1611** FLORIO It→E *Corranta,* a dance so called. **1659** TORRIANO-FLORIO It→E *Corranta,* a

french running dance, and therefore called a Corrante.

1731 PRELLEUR *Modern Musick-Master* (Dictionary, p. 2) *Corente*, a Tune always in Triple Time.

cord *as interval, see* chord, interval

early 18th C. PEPUSCH various papers BL Add. 29429, f. 2 Cords are y[e] Joyning and Playing of Two or more Tones together; and are either Concords or Discords.

cord *as string, see* chord, string

1550 THOMAS It→E *Corda*, a coarde or lute stryng **1565** COOPER L→E § *Discordantia corda. Sil.* Strynges out of tune. **1598** FLORIO It→E *Corde*, strings for instruments. *Incordato*, ... Also tuned, strung, and corded as an instrument. *Incordatura, Incordamento*, ... a tuning, stringing, or cording. § *Corde di minugie*, strings made of guts, as lute strings. **1599** MINSHEU-PERCYVALL Sp→E *Cuerda*, f. a string of an instrument of musicke § *Cuerda, de vihuela*, the string of a violl. **1611** FLORIO It→E *Corde*, all kinds of strings for instruments. *Incordare*, to corde, to string an instrument. *Incordato*, strung or corded as an instrument. **1659** TORRIANO-FLORIO It→E *Corda*, ... also any string for musicall instruments or bows **1688** MIEGE-COTGRAVE Fr→E § *Amortir le son des cordes d'un Instrument de Musique*, to dead the sound of a musical Instrument. *Corde de Lut*, a Lute-string. *Corde de Violon, de Lut*, &c. the string of a Violin, of a Lute, &c. *Corde qui fait un Son agreable*, a String that makes a pleasant sound. *Cordes de leton, ou de boyau, pour des Instrumens de Musique*, wire-strings, or gut-strings, for musical Instruments. *Garnir de cordes un Violon*, to string a Violin. **1704** HARRIS *Cords*, in Musick, properly signifies the Strings of a Harp, Violin, Lute, or any other Musical Instrument: But the Term is also applyed to denote the Sounds which proceed from such Instruments, even from those that have no Strings. **1706** KERSEY-PHILLIPS (6th edn) *Cords* or *Chords*, (in *Musick*) properly signify the Strings of a Harp, Viol, Violin, Lute, or any other Musical Instrument: But the Term is also apply'd to denote the Sounds that proceed from such Instruments, even from those that have no Strings. **1728** CHAMBERS *Cord*, in Geometry, Musick, *&c.* See *Chord*. **1730** BAILEY *Dict. Britannicum* (1st edn) *Cords* (in *Musick* ...) See *Chords*. **1737** DYCHE-PARDON (2nd edn) *Cord* (S.) ... in *Musick*, the Strings of Instruments by the Vibrations, whereof the Sound is occasioned, by whose Divisions the several Sorts of Tones are determined.

1582 *Batman vppon Bartholome* (chap. 134) A string is called *Corda*, and hath that name of *Corde*, the heart: for as the pulse of the heart, is in the brest, so the pulse of the strings is in the harpe.

cordon

1611 COTGRAVE Fr→E § *Cordons d'une trompette*. The cordines, or strings of a Trumpet. **1659** TORRIANO-FLORIO It→E *Cordone*, ... also the Cordins or strings of a Trumpet or horne.

Corelli, Arcangelo *see* allemande, da, fifth, follia, solo, sonata

coretto

1659 TORRIANO-FLORIO It→E *Coretto*, a little quire of singing-men, also a little heart.

corial *see* choir

1611 COTGRAVE Fr→E *Corial: m.* A Singing-man, Quire-man, or Quirrester.

cornabon

1611 COTGRAVE Fr→E *Cornabon*. A musicall Cornet; or such a wreathed instrument: *Rab.*

cornaro *see* corneur

1598 FLORIO It→E *Cornare*, to horne *Cornaro, Corniere*, a horner. **1611** FLORIO It→E *Cornare*, ... Also to wind a horne. *Cornaro*, a horner. **1659** TORRIANO-FLORIO It→E **Cornare*, to winde or blow a horne ... also as *Cornamusare*. *Cornato*, a horner *Cornatore*, a horner, a Cornuter, also a winder of a horn. **Cornatura*, a horning, a cornuting, also the qualitie of horne.

corne *see* cor

cornemuse *see* bagpipe, musette

1550 THOMAS It→E *Cornamusa*, a baggepype. **1593** HOLLYBAND Fr→E *Vne Cornemuse*, a pipe: *f.* **1598** FLORIO It→E *Cornamusa*, a bagpipe or a hornet. *Cornamusare*, to plaie vpon a bagpipe or hornepipe. **1599** MINSHEU-PERCYVALL Sp→E *Cornamusa*, f. a cornamuse, a horne-pipe, a bagpipe. **1611** COTGRAVE Fr→E *Cornemuse: f.* A Bagpipe; *Cornemuseur: m.* A Bagpiper. **1611** FLORIO It→E *Cornamusa*, a bagpipe or a hornet *Cornamusare*, to play vpon a bagpipe or horne pipe. **1658** PHILLIPS (1st edn) *Cornimuse*, (lat.) a kinde of musical in-instrument [sic], which some take for a kind of Bag-pipe. **1659** TORRIANO-FLORIO It→E *Cornamusa*, a bag-pipe, a horne-pipe, a hornet § *Fare cornamusa*, to play the bag-pipe **1676** COLES *Cornimuse, French.* bag-pipe. **1688** MIEGE-COTGRAVE Fr→E *Cornemuse*, (f) *Instrument de Musique*, a Bag-pipe. § *Jouër de la cornemuse*, to play upon the bag-pipe. **1706** KERSEY-PHILLIPS (6th edn) *Cornemuse, (Fr.)* a kind of Bag-pipe, a Musical Instrument. **1726** BAILEY *An Univ. Etymolog. Engl. Dict.* (3rd edn) *Cornmuse* (*Cornemeuse*, F.) a Bag-pipe. *Chauc.*

cornet *see* bozina, buccina, cor, cornabon, cornu, cornuchet, empneusta (under entata), naccherino
1570/71 *Dict. Fr. and Engl.* Fr→E *Corner*, to play on the cornet, to blowe in a horne. *Cornet, ou trompe*, an instrument called a cornet, a horne. **1593** HOLLYBAND Fr→E *Corner*, to play on the cornet, to blowe in a horne. *Cornet, m: ou trompe, f:* an instrument called a cornet, a horne. **1599** MINSHEU-PERCYVALL Sp→E *Corneta*, f. a cornet, an instrument of musicke. **1611** COTGRAVE Fr→E *Cornet: m.* A Cornet, a Trumpe; a little Horne; § *Cornet à bouquin*. A Musicall Cornet. **1688** MIEGE-COTGRAVE Fr→E *Cornet*, (m.) Cornet, a musical Cornet; **1696** PHILLIPS (5th edn) A *Cornet* is also a Musical Wind-Instrument, formerly used in Cathedrals, being the Treble to the Sackbut. **1702** KERSEY *New Engl. Dict.* (1st edn) A *Cornet*, a small shawm; **1706** KERSEY-PHILLIPS (6th edn) *Cornet*, ... Also a kind of Shawm, a Musical Instrument formerly us'd in Cathedrals, being the Treble to the Sackbut: **1708** KERSEY *Dict. Anglo-Brit.* (1st edn) *Cornet*, ... Also a kind of Shawm, a Musical Instrument: **1721** BAILEY *An Univ. Etymolog. Engl. Dict.* (1st edn) *Cornet*, (of *Cornu, L.* a Horn) a sort of musical Instrument made of Horn: **1726** BAILEY *An Univ. Etymolog. Engl. Dict.* (3rd edn) *Cornet* (*Cornetto*, Ital. of *Cornu*, L. a Horn) a sort of Musical Instrument made of Horn, or something like a Hautboy, now out of use: **1728** CHAMBERS *Cornet*, a Horn, or Musical Instrument us'd by the Antients in their Wars. See *Musick*. ¶ *Vegetius* informs us, that the Legions had Trumpets, *Cornets*, and Buccinæ: that when the *Cornets* sounded, only the Ensigns were to march above without the Soldiers, the *Cornet* alone was sounded: as, on the contrary, when the Soldiers were to move without the Ensigns, the Trumpets alone were sounded: That the *Cornets* and *Buccinæ* sounded the Charge and Retreat; and the *Cornets* and Trumpets during the Course of the Battle. **1737** DYCHE-PARDON (2nd edn) *Cornet* (S.) a Horn or musical Instrument used by the Antients in their martial Affairs;

cornette
1593 HOLLYBAND Fr→E *Vne Cornette de chevalliers*, a Cornet or standard of horsemen **1611** COTGRAVE Fr→E *Cornette: f.* A Bugle, Hutchet, or little Horne;

cornettino
1724 [PEPUSCH] *Short Explic. of Foreign Words in Mus. Bks.* (p. 24) *Cornettino*, a small or little Cornet. It is also sometimes used to signify an Octave Trumpet. **1726** BAILEY *An Univ. Etymolog. Engl. Dict.* (3rd edn) *Cornettino*, a small or little Cornet; also an Octave Trumpet. *Ital.*

cornetto
1550 THOMAS It→E *Cornetto*, is a certein instrument called a cornette **1598** FLORIO It→E *Cornettaro*, a cornet maker. Also one that windes a cornet. *Cornetto*, ... Also a cornet or little horne, a bugle **1599** MINSHEU-PERCYVALL Sp→E **Cornetica*, f. a little cornet, an instrument so called. **1611** FLORIO It→E *Cornettaro*, a Cornet-maker or winder. *Cornetto*, a Cornet, a little horn, a bugle **1659** TORRIANO-FLORIO It→E **Cornettaro*, a Cornet-maker, a winder of a Cornet **Cornetti*, the plu: of *Cornetto* **Cornetto*, any little horn, a Cornet, a hutchet, a bugle **1724** [PEPUSCH] *Short Explic. of Foreign Words in Mus. Bks.* (p. 24) *Cornetto*, a Cornet, which is an Instrument of Musick now out of Use, somewhat like a Hoboy.

corneur *see* cornaro
1570/71 *Dict. Fr. and Engl.* Fr→E *Corneur*, a horner. **1593** HOLLYBAND Fr→E *Corneur*, a horner: *m.* **1611** COTGRAVE Fr→E *Corneur: m.* A Horner; a winder of a Horne. *Cornier: m...* Also, a Horner.

cornezuela
1599 MINSHEU-PERCYVALL Sp→E **Cornezuela*, f. a little horne or bugle.

corniccino
1659 TORRIANO-FLORIO It→E *Corniccino*, the dim. of *Corno.*

cornicello
1598 FLORIO It→E *Cornicello*, a little horne, or bugle. **1611** FLORIO It→E *Cornicello*, a litle horne or bugle. **1659** TORRIANO-FLORIO It→E *Cornicello*, the dim. of *Corno.* **1688** DAVIS-TORRIANO-FLORIO It→E **Cornicello*, the *dim*: of *Corno.*

cornicen
1500 *Ortus Vocabulorum* L→E Cornicen inis. qui canit cum cornu. a synger with a horne. m.t. **1538** ELYOT L→E *Cornicen,* a blower in a horne. **1565** COOPER L→E *Córnicen, pen. cor. cornícinis, pen. corr. Iuuenal.* A blower in a horne. **1587** THOMAS L→E *Cornicen, inis, com. g. Iuven.* A blower in ahorne. **1589** RIDER L→E *Cornicen, Buccinator, Cornicularius, m.* A blower of a horne. *Cornicino, cornu inflare.* To blow, or wind a horne.

cornichon
1593 HOLLYBAND Fr→E *Cornichon,* a little horne: *m.* **1611** COTGRAVE Fr→E *Cornichon: m.* A little Horne;

cornicle
1656 BLOUNT (1st edn) *Cornicle (corniculum)* a little horn. **1676** COLES *Cornicle, Latin.* a little horn. **1704** *Cocker's Engl. Dict.* (1st edn) *Cornicle,* a small horn.

corno *see* ward-corn
1550 THOMAS It→E *Corno,* an horne. **1598** FLORIO It→E *Corno,* a horne. Also a kind of brazen instrument like a horn. § *Sonare il corno.* to winde, or sounde a horne. **1611** FLORIO It→E *Corno,* ... Also a kind of brasen instrument like a horne, called a Hornepipe. § *Sonare di corno,* to blow or winde a horne or bugle. *Sonare il corno,* to winde a horne, to blow a horne or bugle. **1659** TORRIANO-FLORIO It→E **Corno,* a kind of horne, a hunters-bugle, or hutchet, a brazen instrument like a horn, called [a] horne-pipe § *Sonare di corno,* to wind or blow a horn or beugle. *Sonare Il corno,* to wind a horn.

cornu *see* buccina
1565 COOPER L→E *Cornua. Varro.* A horne: a trumpet. **1587** THOMAS L→E *Cornu, n.g. indecl. & cornus, Prise. Plurali, cornua, um.* A horne: ... also a trumpet, *Varro.* **1589** RIDER L→E *Cornu, Indecl. Cornum, n. cornus, m.* A Horne **1706** KERSEY-PHILLIPS (6th edn) *Cornu,* the Horn of a Beast, a Cornet, Horn, or Trumpet to blow with. **1708** KERSEY *Dict. Anglo-Brit.* (1st edn) *Cornu,* ... a Cornet, Hornet, or Trumpet to blow with.

cornuchet
1611 COTGRAVE Fr→E *Cornuchet.* A little Cornet. **1650** HOWELL-COTGRAVE Fr→E *Cornucher* [sic]. A little Cornet.

coro *see* choir

correnti
1728 NORTH Musicall Grammarian (*C-K MG* f. 77) But to return to the allegro divisions, they are either correnti, or arpeggianti; the former is when a part takes a carriere thro a whole strain without ceasing, and the other parts favour the action, by short touches in the accords...

Corybant *see* crotalum, Curetes, Cybele, cymbal
1538 ELYOT L→E *Corybantes,* the priestes of the Idoll *Cybeles,* which as madde men waggyng their heedes and daunsynge, playinge on cymbales, ranne about the stretes, prouokyng other to do the semblable. **1565** COOPER L→E *Corybantes,* The priestes of the ydole *Cybele,* whiche as madde men, waggyng their heades and daunsynge, plaiynge on Cimballes, ranne about the streates, prouokyng other to doe the lyke. They fyrst inhabited the mounte Ida in Phrygia, and afterwarde passynge into Crete, tooke for theyr abydynge an hyll, whiche of their olde habitation they called also Ida: where (as poetes feigne) they pryuily nourished Jupiter, when his father Saturne commaunded him to be slaine, and coatinally [sic] played on tymbrelles and drumslades, that the noise of the childe criyng might not be hearde. **1611** COTGRAVE Fr→E *Corybanter.* Madly to run vp and downe, playing on a Cymball, and wagging his head, like one of *Cybeles* Priests; **1656** BLOUNT (1st edn) *Corybants (Corybantes)* Cybeles, or Cybelles Priests, so called from *Corybantus,* one of her first Attendants. ¶ To play the *Coryant,* is to run madly up and down, playing on a Cymbal, and wagging the head, as those Priests were wont to do; **1658** PHILLIPS (1st edn) *Corybantes,* the Priests of *Cybele,* who used to celebrate the Feasts of *Cybele* with dancing and ringing of Cymbals; they were thought to be the same with the *Curetes* and *Idæi Dactyli.* **1678** PHILLIPS (4th edn) *Corybantes,* the Priests of *Cybele,* who used to celebrate the Feasts of *Cybele,* with Dancing and Ringing of Cymbals; they were thought to be the same wih the *Curetes,* and *Idæi Dactyli.* **1728** CHAMBERS *Corybantes,* in Antiquity, Priests of *Cybele,* who danced and caper'd to the Sound of Flutes, and Drums. ¶ *Catullus,* in his Poem call'd *Atys,* gives a beautiful Description of 'em; representing them as Madmen. Accordingly, *Maximus Tyrius* says, that those possess'd with the Spirit of *Corybantes,* as soon as they heard the Sound of a Flute, were seiz'd with an Enthusiasm, and lost the use of their Reason. ¶ Hence, the *Greeks* use the Word κορυβαντιαῖν, *Corybantising,* to signify a Person's being

transported, or possess'd with a Devil. ¶ Some say, the *Corybantes* were all Eunuchs; and that 'tis on this account that *Catullus*, in his *Atys*, always uses feminine Epithets and Relatives. ¶ *Diodorus Siculus* remarks, that *Corybas* Son of *Jason* and *Cybele*, passing into *Phrygia* with his Uncle *Dardanus*, there instituted the Worship of the Mother of the Gods, and gave his own Name to the Priests. *Strabo* relates it as the Opinion of some, that the *Corybantes* are Children of *Jupiter* and *Calliope*, and the same with the *Cabires*. Others say, the Word had its Origin from this, that the *Corybantes* always walk'd dancing, (if the Expression may be allow'd) *quod* κορύπτοντες βαίνοιεν. *Vossius*. **1730** BAILEY *Dict. Britannicum* (1st edn) The *Corybantes* (of κορύπτειν, *Gr.* to wag the head in dancing, or *q.* κρύβαντες of χρυπτω, *Gr.* to hide, of the sounding the tympana to drown the noise of *Jupiter*'s crying being heard by his father *Saturn*) the priests of *Cybele* .... They performed their solemnities with a furious noise of drums, trumpets, beating on brass, and musical instruments.

coryphæus *see* chorus

1728 CHAMBERS *Coryphæus*, in ancient Tragedy, was the Chief or Leader of the Company that compos'd the Chorus. See *Chorus*. **1730** BAILEY *Dict. Britannicum* (1st edn) *Coryphæus* (χορυφαιος, *Gr.*) the chief leader of the company or chorus in the ancient tragedy.

counterfugue *see* fugue

1688 MIEGE-COTGRAVE Fr→E *Contrefugue* (f.) *sorte d'Echo qu'on fait en Musique*, a kind of Eccho in Musick. **1696** PHILLIPS (5th edn) *Counterfugue*, a term in Musick. See *Fugue*. **1704** HARRIS *Counterfugue*, in Musick, is when the *Fugues* proceed contrary to one another. **1706** KERSEY-PHILLIPS (6th edn) *Counter-fugue*, (in *Musick*.) is when the Fugues proceed contrary one to another. **1728** CHAMBERS *Counter-fugue*, in Musick, is when the Fugues proceed contrary to one another. See *Fugue*.

late 17th C. ANON. Tractatus de Musicâ BL Add. 4923, f. 12 *Contra-fuga* est, quando utraq pars proprium punctum assumit, deinde factâ permutatione punctum altorius depotit in eâdem vel diversa clavi. **1736** TANS'UR *Compleat Melody* (3rd edn, p. 71) *Counter-Fuges*, is when two *Fuges*, or *Points* proceed contrary one from another[.]

countering

after 1517 ANON. Art of Mvsic BL Add. 4911, f. 85 *Quhat is countering* ¶ It is ane formall fractione of sympill noittis ... figurativve deducit quhilk be Musitians in plesand sowndis of harmony craftellie is conveyit

counterpart *see* part

1704 HARRIS *Counter-part*, a Term in Musick, only denoting one Part to be opposite to another, as the *Base* is said to be the *Counter-part* of the *Treble*. **1706** KERSEY-PHILLIPS (6th edn) *Counter-part*, ... Also a Term in *Musick*, only importing one Part to be opposite to another; as the Bass is said To be the Counter-part of the *Treble*. **1728** CHAMBERS *Counter-part*, a Part of something opposite to another Part. See *Part*. ¶ Thus, in Musick, the Bass and Treble are two *Counter-parts*, or opposite Parts. *Counter-part*, in Musick, denotes a Part to be opposite to some other; as the Bass is the *Counter-part* of the Treble. See *Part*. **1737** DYCHE-PARDON (2nd edn) *Counter-part*, ... in *Musick*, the Bass and Treble are counter or opposite Parts.

counterpoint *see* canto fermo, canto figurato, harmonia gemina, imitation, point, setting, simple

1599 MINSHEU-PERCYVALL Sp→E **Contrapuntear*, to counterpoint. **Contrapunto*, a counterpoint, pause, or rest in musicke. **1598** FLORIO It→E *Contrapuntare*, to counterpoint. *Contrapunto*, counterpointed. **1611** COTGRAVE Fr→E *Contrepoinct: m.* ... also, a ground, or plainsong (in Musicke.) *Contrepois: m.* a ground, or plaine-song, in Musicke. **1611** FLORIO It→E *Contrapuntare*, ... Also to descant in singing. *Contrapunto*, ... Also a descant in Musicke or singing... Also a lesson of descant. § *Fare contraponti*, to descant in singing, to make counterpoints. **1658** PHILLIPS (1st edn) *Counterpoint*, ... also a Term in Musick, being a composing of parts together by setting points one against another **1659** TORRIANO-FLORIO It→E **Contrapuntare, Contrapunteggiare*, ... also to descant in singing. **Contrapunto*, ... also a plaine-song, a ground or lesson of descant in Musick or singing. § *Fare contraponti*, to make counterpoints, also to descant in musick. **1671** PHILLIPS (3rd edn) *Counterpoint* ... also a Term in Musick *(Lat. Contrapunctum)* being the old manner of composing parts, by setting points or pricks against another, the measure of which points or pricks was according to the words or syllables to which they were applyed, the Notes now in use, being not then found out; and because now a dayes in plain song Musik we set note against note, as they did point against point, hence it is that this kind of Musick doth still retain the name of Counterpoint; **1676** COLES *Counterpoint*, opposition, composing parts (in Musick) by setting point or note against note **1702** KERSEY *New Engl. Dict.* (1st edn) A *Counter-point* in Musick, by setting point, *or* note against note. **1704** *Cocker's Engl. Dict.* (1st edn) *Counter point*, ... composing parts in Musick, by setting point, or Note against Note **1704** HARRIS *Counter-point*, in Musick, is a Term whereby is understood the old manner of composing Parts, before Notes of different Measure were invented; which was, to set Pricks or Points one against another, to denote the several Concords; the Length or Measure of which Points was sung according to the quantity of the Words or Syllables whereto they are apply'd; so that in regard that in composing our Descant we set Note against Note, as the Ancients did Point against Point; the Term *Counter-point* is still retained in these Compositions. **1706** KERSEY-PHILLIPS (6th edn) *Counter-point*, ... In *Musick*, it is the old Method of composing Parts by setting Points or Pricks one against another to express the several Concords, the length or measure of which was according to the Words or Syllables to which they were apply'd; the different Notes now in Use, not being then found out: And because at this Day, in Plain-song *Musick*, we set Note against Note, as the Ancients did Point against Point, thence it is this kind of Composition still retains the Name of *Counter-point*. **1707** *Gloss. Angl. Nova* (1st edn) *Counter-point*, in Musick, is the old manner of composing Parts before Notes of different Measure were invented, which was to set Pricks or Points one against another, to denote the several Concods [sic], the Length or Measure of which Points were sung or play'd according to the Length or Quantity of the Words or Syllables whereunto they were apply'd. **1708** KERSEY *Dict. Anglo-Brit.* (1st edn) *Counter-point*, ... In *Musick*, the old way of composing Parts by setting Points or Notes one against another to express the several Concords. **1724** [PEPUSCH] *Short Explic. of Foreign Words in Mus. Bks.* (p. 24) *Contrapunto*, a Way or Method of composing Musick, called Counterpoint, now very little used. **1726** BAILEY *An Univ. Etymolog. Engl. Dict.* (3rd edn) *Contrapunto* (in *Musick Books*) signifies a Way or Method of composing Musick called *Counterpoint*, now very little in use. *Ital.* **1728** CHAMBERS *Counter-point* ... [*see* Appendix] § *Figurate Counter-point*, in Musick, is that wherein there is a Mixture of Discords along with the Concords. See *Counter-point*. ¶ *Figurative Counter-point* is of two Kinds: That wherein the Discords are introduced occasionally, to serve only as Transitions, from Concord to Concord; and that, wherein the Discord bears a chief Part in the Harmony. See *Discord*. ¶ 'Tis a Rule in Composition, that the Harmony must always be full on the accented Parts of the Bar, or Measure[,] *i.e.* Nothing but Concords are allowed in the Beginning and Middle; or the Beginning of the first half of the Bar, and Beginning of the latter half thereof in common Time; and the Beginning, and first three Notes in triple Time. But upon the unaccented Parts, this is not so necessary: But Discords may transiently pass there without any Offence to the Ear. ¶ This the *French* call *Supposition*, because the transient Discord supposes a Concord immediately to follow it. See *Supposition*. ¶ Where the Discords are used as a solid, and substantial Part of the Harmony, the *Counter-point* is properly called the *Harmony* of *Discords*. See *Harmony of Discords*. **1730** BAILEY *Dict. Britannicum* (1st edn) § *Figurate Counterpoint* (in *Mus.*) that wherein there is a mixture of discords along with the concords. **1737** DYCHE-PARDON (2nd edn) *Counter-point*, a Composition in Musick, perfectly agreeable in all its Parts. It is divided into Simple and Figurative; the Simple is that used at the first introducing of Musick in Parts, wherein the Notes were all of the same Time, and every Note a Concord; the Figurative is that used when this Kind of Musick was brought to a higher Pitch, wherein different Time was introduced, and Discords brought in between the Parts. § Figurate Counterpoint, is where there is a Mixture of Discords along with the Concords; and when the Composer introduces all the ornamental as well as harmonic Parts of Musick, and uses Points, Syncopes, &c. it is called Figurate Descant. **1740** BAILEY *An Univ. Etymolog. Engl. Dict.* (9th edn) *Contrapuntal* (in *Musick Books*) signifies a Way or Method of composing Musick, called *Counterpoint*, now very little in use. *Ital.*

after 1517 ANON. Art of Mvsic BL Add. 4911, f. 46 *Sympill contrapunct quhat is it?* It is ye art of declynyng of cantable soundis for proporcionall dimension and mesur of tym. **1584** BATHE Briefe Intro. to True Art of Music (MS copy, 1st half 16th c., *CHi* p. 19) [*re* composing with concords and discords] The first kynd of vay yat is vsed to be maid, is to mak on concord for evrie not of ye plain song, quhich is called counter poynt, in quhich certain roules ar to be observed, vherof, ye first and cheifest is, yat twa perfect conncordes of on kynd sould not be maid ascending or discending to gieder: ... **1597** Morley *Plaine and Easie Introdvction* (p. 71) The first waie wherein we shew the vse of the cordes, is called Counterpoint: that is, when to a note of the plainsong, there goeth but one note of descant. Therfore when you would sing vpon a plainsong, looke where the first note of it stands, and then *sing another for it which may bee distant from it, three, fiue, or eight notes,* and so foorth with others, but *with a sixt we sildome begin or end.* **1609** Dowland-Ornithoparcus *Micrologvs* (p. 77) *Of the Definition, Diuision, and difference of the names of the Counterpoint.* ¶ *Nicomachus* the Musitian saith, That the Art of *Musicke* was at first so simple, that it consisted of a *Tetrachord.* And was made with the voice *Assa,* that is, one Voyce alone (for *Assa* the Ancients called alone, whereof it is called *Vox assa,* when it is vttered with the mouth, not adding to it other Musicall *Concents,* wherein the praises of the Ancients was sung, as *Phil. Beroaldus* writeth in the Tenth booke of his Commentary vpon *Apuleius.* Yet by the meanes of diuers authors, the *Tetrachord* from foure Cords grew to fifteen. To which the after-ages haue added fiue and sixe Voyces, and more. So that a Song in our times hath not one voyce alone, but fiue, sixe, eight, and sometimes more. For it is euident, that *Ioannes Okeken* did compose a Motet of 36. Voyces. Now that part of Musick which effecteth this, is called of the Musitians, the *Counterpoint.* For a *Counterpoint* generally, is nothing else than the knowledge of finding out of a Song of many parts. Or it is the mother of *Modulation,* or (as *Franchinus lib.* 3. *cap.* 1. writes) it is the Art of bending sounds that may be sung, by proportionable Dimension, and measure of time. For, as the clay is in the hands of the Potter; so is the making of a Song in the hands of the Musitian. Wherefore most men call this Art not the *Counter-point,* but *Composition.* Assigning this difference of names, and saying, that *Composition* is the collection of diuers parts of Harmony by diuers *Concords.* For to compose is to gather together the diuers parts of Harmony by diuers *Concords.* But the *Counter-point* is the sodaine, and vnexpected ordering of a plaine Song by diuers Melodies by chance. Whence *Sortifare* signifies to order a plain Song by certain *Concords* on the sodaine. Now it is called *Counterpoint* (as *Bacchus* saith) as it were a concordant *Concent* of Voyces set one against another, examined by Art. **1636** Butler *Principles of Musik* (p. 89) Counterpoint is when the Notes of all the Partes, beeing of eqal time and number, goe jointly together. If soomtime, by reason of Binding and Disjoyning, the Notes dooe happen to bee od; they ar presently made eevn [sic] again: .... Counterpoint is used in Rhythmical vers, as Psalms in Meeter, and other Tunes, mesured by a set number of syllables: unto which the like number of Notes dooeth answer. § (p. 90) *Counterpoint.* In Latin *Contrapunctum*: so called, becaus, in the beginning, (when there was no varieti of Times and Figures of Notes) they marked out their Songs by Pricks or Points; which, in framing the Partes, they set one against an other: so that *Contrapunctum,* or Counterpoint, is the proper Term for Setting of Plain-song; as Discant (which signifyeth Division in singing) is of Figured Musik. **1655** Playford *Intro. to Skill of Musick* (2nd edn, 'Art of Setting or Composing of Musick in Parts', p. 2) [annotation by Simpson:] *Counterpoint, in Latine* Contra punctum, *was that old maner of composing parts together, by setting points or pricks one against another (as Minims and Sembriefs are set in this following Treatise) the measure of which points or pricks, were sung according to the quantity of the words or Syllables to which they were applyed. (For these Figures* ▭ ▭ ◇ *were not as yet invented.) And, because in plainsong Musique we set Note against Note, as they did point against point, thence it is that this kinde of Musique doth still retaine the name of Counterpoint.* **late 17th C.** Anon. Tractatus de Musicâ BL Add. 4923, f. 12 Contrapunctum est dispositio diversarum prætium in unam Symphoniam con spirantium; est q vel simplex, bel figurata: simplex, q^{d} simpliciter Contrapuntum d^{r}. est quoties tonis Singulis unius prætis respondent sui toni in alijs partibus **1665** Simpson *Principles of Practical Mvsick* (p. 16) In the Infancy of Musick, before Notes or Marks of different measure were invented, Songs were expressed by *Pricks* or *Points;* which being set one against another the Descant was called *Counterpoint,* which name it still retains. **1667** Simpson *Compendium of Practical Musick* (pp. 36-7) Before Notes of different Measure were in use, their way of Composing was, to set Pricks or Points one against another, to denote the Concords; the length or Measure of which Points, was Sung according to the quantity of the Words or Syllables which were applied to them. And because, in composing our Descant, we set Note against Note, as they did Point against Point, from thence it still retains the name of *Counterpoint.* **1721** Malcolm *Treatise of Musick* (pp. 419-20) ... *Observe* also that this Art of *Harmony* has been long known by the Name of *Counterpoint;* which arose from this, That in the Times when *Parts* were first introduced, their *Musick* being so simple that they used no Notes of different Time, that Difference depending upon the Quantity of Syllables of the Words of a Song, they marked their *Concords* by Points set against one another. And as there were no different Notes of Time, so the *Parts* were in every Note made *Concord*: And this afterwards was called *simple* or *plain Counterpoint*, to distinguish it from another Kind, wherein Notes of different Value were used, and *Discords* brought in betwixt the *Parts*, which was called *figurate Counterpoint*.

countertenor *see* cantus, contramezzana, falsetto, haute-contre, mezzana, occentor, occentus, setting

1552 HULOET L→E [no headword given] Syng a contratenor. **1589** RIDER L→E *Contratenor, occentus, m.* The countertenour. **1598** FLORIO It→E *Contratenore*, a countertenor in musike. **1611** COTGRAVE Fr→E *Contretaille: f.* ... also, the Counter-tenor part, in Musicke, and he that sings, or beares, it. *Contreteneur: m.* The Counter-tenor part in Musicke. **1611** FLORIO It→E *Contratenore*, a counter tenor. *Contro*, ... Also a tenor in Musicke. **1676** COLES *Counter-tenour*, against the tenour, a midle part in Musick. **1696** PHILLIPS (5th edn) *Counter-tenor*. See *Cliff*. **1702** KERSEY *New Engl. Dict.* (1st edn) The *Counter-tenor* in musick **1704** *Cocker's Engl. Dict.* (1st edn) *Counter-Tenour*, against the Tenour, a middle part in Musick **1704** HARRIS *Counter-tenor*, one of the mean or middle Parts of Musick, so called as it were opposite to the *Tenor*. **1706** KERSEY-PHILLIPS (6th edn) *Counter-Tenor*, one of the mean, or middle parts of *Musick*, so call'd as it were opposite to the Tenor. **1707** *Gloss. Angl. Nova* (1st edn) *Counter-tenor*, one of the middle Parts of Musick; so call'd, because it is as it were opposed to the *Tenor*. **1708** KERSEY *Dict. Anglo-Brit.* (1st edn) *Counter-Tenor*, one of the mean, or middle Parts of *Musick*. **1724** [PEPUSCH] *Short Explic. of Foreign Words in Mus. Bks.* (p. 24) *Contra Tenor*, Counter Tenor, a Part in Musick. **1726** BAILEY *An Univ. Etymolog. Engl. Dict.* (3rd edn) *Contra Tenor* (in *Musick Books*) stands for *Counter Tenour*, a part in Musick. *Ital.* **1728** CHAMBERS *Counter-tenor*, is one of the mean or middle Parts of Musick; so call'd, as if it were opposite to the Tenor. See *Tenor*. **1737** DYCHE-PARDON (2nd edn) *Counter-Tenor*, one of the mean or middle Parts of Musick, an Opposite to the Tenor.

1617-24 FLUDD *Utriusque Cosmi Maioris: De Templo Musicæ* (p. 210) *Contratenor* est pars media inter Tenorem & Altum. **1636** BUTLER *Principles of Musik* (pp. 41-2) The Countertenor or *Contratenor*, is so called, becaus it answereth the Tenor; thowgh commonly in higher keyz: and therefore is fittest for a man of a sweete shril voice. Which Parte thowgh it have little Melodi by it self; (as consisting much of monotonies) yet in Harmoni it hath the greatest grace: specially when it is sung with a right voice: which is too rare. **c.1714-20** TUDWAY history of music BL Harley 7342 (*CHo* f. 10v) ... Mr Tallis, & Mr Bird, two of ye Queens own Servants, who, it is own'd at this day, set an incomparable Pattern of Church Music, in a style, befitting ye solemnity of ye service; Their compositions, are all in 4 parts, except, some Anthems in five; The adding of this 4th part, gave a wonderfull Harmony, to ye whole Chorus, whereas before, they never aim'd at above 3 parts, for wch there were 3 cliffs establish'd, suited to each part; But these skilfull Artists, finding, there might yet be a higher part, than a Tenor introduc'd, betwixt ye Tenor & Treble; compos'd a 4th part, calling it Contratenor; ...

countertreble *see* contralto, contra-sovrano

country dance *see* baldosa, ballonchio, haydegines, ridda, rigoletto, romanzina, stampinata, villanella, volta

coup

1611 COTGRAVE Fr→E m. § *On ne fait à grands coups douce vielle*: *Prov.* Hard stroakes yeeld but harsh Musicke. Not great, but apt, stroakes make sweet Musicke. Tis not the great (but the apt) stroake that makes the harmonie.

coupée

1728 CHAMBERS *Coupee*, a Motion in Dancing, wherein one Leg is a little bent, and suspended from the Ground; and with the other a Motion is made forwards. ¶ The Word, in the original *French*, signifies a *Cut*.

couplet

1611 COTGRAVE Fr→E § *Couplet de chanson*. A Staffe, or Stanzo of a Poeme, or Song. **1688** MIEGE-COTGRAVE Fr→E *Couplet* (m.) *partie de Poëme*, a Staff of a Song. **1728** CHAMBERS *Couplet*, a Division of an Hymn, an Ode, Song, *&c.* wherein, an equal Number, or an equal Measure of Verses are found in each Part. ¶ In Odes, these Divisions are more ordinarily call'd *Strophes*. See *Strophe*. **1730** BAILEY *Dict. Britannicum* (1st edn) *Couplet*, a division of an hymn, ode, song, *&c.* wherein an equal number or an equal measure of verses are found in each part. **1737** DYCHE-PARDON (2nd edn) *Couplet* (S.) in a Hymn, Song, &c. when an equal Measure, or equal Number of Verses is found in each Division, they are all called Couplets.

courante *see* coranto, curranto, dance, lesson, motion, repeat, sonata, variation, volta
1611 COTGRAVE Fr→E *Courante: f.* A Curranto. **1688** MIEGE-COTGRAVE Fr→E *Courante* (a fem. subst.) Courante, or Couranto (a kind of Dance.) **1702** KERSEY *New Engl. Dict.* (1st edn) A *Courant*, a kind of dance **1706** KERSEY-PHILLIPS (6th edn) *Courant, (Fr.)* a sort of Dance; **1708** KERSEY *Dict. Anglo-Brit.* (1st edn) *Courant*, (*F.*) a sort of Dance; **1728** CHAMBERS *Courant* is also a Term in Musick and Dancing; being used to express both the Time or Air, and the Dance. ¶ With regard to the first, *Courant* or *Currant* is a Piece of Musick in triple Time: The Air of the *Courant* is ordinarily noted in Triples of Minims; the Parts to be repeated twice. It begins and ends, when he who beats the Measure falls his Hand; in contradistinction from the Saraband, which ordinarily ends when the Hand is rais'd. ¶ With regard to Dancing, the *Courant* is the most common of all the Dances practis'd in *England*: It consists, essentially, of a Time, a Step, a Balance, and a Coupee; tho it also admits of other Motions. ¶ Formerly they leap'd their Steps; in which Point, the *Courant* differ'd from the low Dances and Pavades [sic]. There are *simple Courants*, and figur'd *Courants*, all danc'd by two Persons. ¶ The Term is *French*, and properly signifies running. **1736** BAILEY *Dict. Britannicum* (2nd edn) *Courant* (*courante*, F. *corrente*, It. *corriente*, Sp.) a sort of dance; **1737** DYCHE-PARDON (2nd edn) *Courant* ... also a Dance.

course
c.1596 BATHE *Briefe Intro. to skill of Song* [C] [*re* two and three parts in one on a plainsong or ground] Next heere is to be vnderstanded that by this word, Course, is ment the distaunce of that which followeth iust so long after, as the following part resteth to that which goeth beefore, in the plaine Song or ground, as if the following part haue a Semibreefe rest, then the Note of the ground is in the first course, which hath in the same place that which followeth, iust a Semibreefe length after, and that note is in the second course, which hath in the second place that which followeth iust a Semibreefe length after, whether it bee vp or downe, &c.

courtaud *see* curtail
1688 MIEGE-COTGRAVE Fr→E *Courtaut* (m.) a Musical Instrument, like *un Basson*, but somthing lesser. **1706** KERSEY-PHILLIPS (6th edn) *Courtaud, (Fr.)* ... Also a short Bassoon, a Musical Instrument

crecerelle
1570/71 *Dict. Fr. and Engl.* Fr→E *Crecerelle*, A Tymbrell, a rattell. **1593** HOLLYBAND Fr→E *Crecerelle*, a Tymbrell, a Rattle: *f*: a clacke. **1611** COTGRAVE Fr→E *Crecerelle: f.* A Rattle, or Clacke for children to play with;

Cremona
1678 PHILLIPS (4th edn) *Cremona*, a rich and well fortified Town in *Longobardia*, or the Dutchy of *Milan*. The violins made in this place, are accounted the best in the World. **1708** KERSEY *Dict. Anglo-Brit.* (1st edn) *Cremona*, a Town in the Dutchy of *Milan* in *Italy*, noted for the best Violins made there.

crepitaculum *see* rattle, tintinabulum
1500 *Ortus Vocabulorum* L→E Crepitaculum est instru[men]tum quod fit crepitus n.s. Crepitum tus tui. i. sonus. a sownde m. qr **1538** ELYOT L→E *Crepitaculum*, a tymbrell, or other instrument, which being touched with the hand, maketh a sownde. **1552** HULOET L→E *Crepitaculum. li, tympanum. ni* Tymbrell. **1565** COOPER L→E *Crepitáculum, pen. cor. Colum.* A tymbrell or any like instrument made of brasse: a rattle. **1587** THOMAS L→E *Crepitacillum, li, n.g. dim. à Crepitaculo, Lucret. Crepitaculum, li, n.g. Colum.* A timbrell or anie like instrument made of brasse, a rattle. **1598** FLORIO It→E *Crepitacolo*, a shrill timbrell, a rattle for children. **1611** FLORIO It→E *Crepitacolo*, a shrill timbrell. Also a childs rattle. **1659** TORRIANO-FLORIO It→E *Crepitaccolo*, a shrill-sounding timbrell, also a childs rattle.

crescendo
c.1710 ANON. *Preceptor for Improved Octave Flageolet* ('Explanation of Words', p. 82) *Crescendo* —To increase the Sound

crocciola *see* crotchet
1659 TORRIANO-FLORIO It→E **Crocciola, Crocciole*, ... also a crotchet in musick

croche *see* crotchet

croma *see* chroma

crome *see* crotchet, semicrome
1598 FLORIO It→E *Crome,* a crotchet in musike, that is the fourth part of a note. **1611** FLORIO It→E *Crome,* crotchets in musike, that is the fourth part of a note.

crotalum *see* cymbal, rattle, staffa, tambourine
1538 ELYOT L→E *Crotalum,* an instrument, whiche the Egiptians vsed in sacrifice made of .ii. plates, whiche beaten togither, made an harmony. **1565** COOPER L→E *Crotalum, crótali, pen. cor. Virg.* A cymballe: a rattle: an instrument of musike made of two plates beaten together. A rynge of brasse striken with an Iron rodde. **1587** THOMAS L→E *Crotalum, li, n.g.* A cimball, a rattle, an instrument of musike made of two plates, beaten togither, a ring of brasse striken with an iron rodde. **1598** FLORIO It→E *Crotalo,* a musicall instrument, made like a great ring of brasse, and beaten with an iron rod maketh a sweete harmonie. Also a childs rattle or bell. Also a cimball, a gingling rattle or clapper. **1611** FLORIO It→E *Crotalo,* a musicall instrument made like a great ring of brasse, hollow, which beaten with an iron rod maketh sweet harmony. Also a Cimbal or gingling rattle or clapper. Also a childes rattle. **1659** TORRIANO-FLORIO It→E *Crottalo,* a kind of musicall instrument made like a hoope or ring of brass and hollow, which being beaten with an iron-rod, yeildeth a very sweet harmonie, some call it, a cimball or jingling rattle, also a rattle for children to play withall **1728** CHAMBERS *Crotalum,* a kind of *Castagnetta,* or Musical Instrument found on Medals, in the Hands of the Priests of Cybele. See *Corybantes.* ¶ The *Crotalum* differ'd from the *Sistrum;* tho Authors frequently confound the two. It consisted of two little brass Plates, or Rods, which were shook in the Hand, and in striking against each other made a Noise. ¶ It was sometimes also made of a Reed split lengthwise; one Part whereof they struck against the other: and as this made a Noise somewhat like that of a Crane's Bill, they call'd that Bird *Crotalistria, Player on Crotala.* ¶ An Antient, in *Pausanias,* says, that *Hercules* did not kill the Birds of the Lake *Stymphala,* but that he drove them away by playing on *Crotala.* On this footing, the *Crotala* must be exceedingly antient. ¶ *Clemens Alexandrinus* attributes the Invention to the *Sicilians;* and forbids the Use thereof to the Christians, because of the indecent Motions and Gestures that accompany it.

crotalus *see* argutus
1538 ELYOT L→E *Crotalus,* he that hath a sownynge voyce, and a shyll [sic]. **1565** COOPER L→E *Crotalus, li, m.g.* He that hath a sownyng and a shrill voyce. **1587** THOMAS L→E *Crotalus, li, m.g.* *He that hath a shrill and sounding voice.

crotchet *see* crocciola, crome, simpla
1611 COTGRAVE Fr→E *Crochuë: f.* A Quauer in Musicke; **1650** HOWELL-COTGRAVE Fr→E *Crochet: m.* ... also, a Quaver in Musicke; **1656** BLOUNT (1st edn) *Crotchet* (Fr. *Crochet*) a measure of time in Musick, containing in quantity a quarter of a *Sembrief,* or two *Quavers.* **1658** PHILLIPS (1st edn) *Crotchet,* a measure in musick being half a Minim, and a Minim is once down or up **1676** COLES *Crochet,* half a minim **1688** MIEGE-COTGRAVE Fr→E *Croche,* (f.) a crotchet (in Musick.) **1702** KERSEY *New Engl. Dict.* (1st edn) A *Crotchet,* a kind of musical note; **1704** *Cocker's Engl. Dict.* (1st edn) *Crotchet,* a Note in Musick, containing a quarter of a *Semibrief,* or half a Minnum **1704** HARRIS *Crotchet,* a Term in *Musick*: See *Notes* and *Time.* **1706** KERSEY-PHILLIPS (6th edn) *Crotchet,* ... Also a kind of Musical Note, which is half the Measure of a Minim; **1707** *Gloss. Angl. Nova* (1st edn) *Crotchet,* a Measure in Musick, being half a Minum [sic]. **1728** CHAMBERS *Crotchet,* in Musick, one of the Notes, or Characters of Time, mark'd thus equal to half a Minim, and double a Quaver. See *Note,* and *Character.* ¶ 'Tis not each to conceive how this Character comes by the Name *Crotchet*: The Word is apparently borrow'd from the French *Crotchet,* of *Croc,* a Crook or Hook, used by them for what we call the *Quaver,* or half *Crotchet;* by reason of the additional Stroke at [the] bottom, which gives it an Appearance of a Crook. See *Quaver.* ¶ A Dot added to the *Crotchet,* thus increases its Time by half; that is, makes it equal to a *Crotchet* and a half, or to three Quavers. See *Time.*

1609 DOWLAND-ORNITHOPARCUS *Micrologvs* (p. 39) A *Crochet,* is a Figure like a *Minime* in colour varying. **1724** TURNER *Sound Anatomiz'd* (p. 16) The Second [note of duration after the minim] is called a *Crotchet;* marked like the *Minim* with the Head filled up, thus; [note] which being but half the Length of the *Minim*, divides the *Semibreve* into *Four* Parts.

crowd *see* baldosa, biffara, biumbe, cacapensiere, cetara, cicutremma, cithara, cucutremma, donadello, fiddle, giga, kit, naccara, pandora, rebeck, ribecchino, tempella, zaramella, zimbello
1706 KERSEY-PHILLIPS (6th edn) *Crowd*, ... also an old Word for a Fiddler. **1708** KERSEY *Dict. Anglo-Brit.* (1st edn) *Crowd*, ... also an old Word for a Fidler. **1721** BAILEY *An Univ. Etymolog. Engl. Dict.* (1st edn) *Crowd*, (*Crwth, C.Br.*) a Fiddle. **1726** BAILEY *An Univ. Etymolog. Engl. Dict.* (3rd edn) *Croud*, a Fiddle. *O.* **1730** BAILEY *Dict. Britannicum* (1st edn) *Crowd* (*cruth, C. Br.*) ... also an old name for a fiddle. **1737** DYCHE-PARDON (2nd edn) *Crowd* (S.) ... also a Fiddle.

crowder *see* fiddler
1736 BAILEY *Dict. Britannicum* (2nd edn) *Crowder*, an old Country Fidler. *Hudibrass. Crowdero.*

crusma
1565 COOPER L→E *Crusma, huius crúsmatis, n.g. pen. cor. quod alij dicunt cruma. Martial.* A tymbrell whereon maydens playe with their fingers. **1587** THOMAS L→E *Crusma, atis, n.g. Mart.* A timbrel whereon maides play with their fingers. **1589** RIDER L→E *Crusma.* A timbrell whereon maides play with their fingers.

[crwth] *see* crowd

c sol fa ut clef *see* tenor clef
c.1596 BATHE *Briefe Intro. to skill of Song* [B vii *verso*] Heere note, that C. called Csolfavt cleue, is a fift beneth G. called Gsolrevt cleue, and F. called Ffavt cleue, is a fift beneth C. called Csolfavt, Cleue.

cuccoueggiare
1598 FLORIO It→E *Cuccoueggiare*, to sing or play the cuckoe. **1611** FLORIO It→E *Cuccoueggiare*, to sing as a Cuckoe

cucutremma *see* cicutremma
1611 FLORIO It→E *Cucutremma*, a kind of croud or fidle. **1659** TORRIANO-FLORIO It→E *Cucutremma*, a kinde of croud or fiddle.

cuerda *see* cord

curasnetta
1659 TORRIANO-FLORIO It→E *Curasnetta*, an instrument so called

Curetes *see* Corybant, cymbal
1728 CHAMBERS *Curetes*, in Antiquity, a sort of People of the Isle of *Crete*; call'd also *Corybantes*. See *Corybantes*. ¶ *Ovid* says, they arose from a huge Shower of Rain: *Lucian* and *Diodorus Siculus* represent them as very expert in casting of Darts; tho other Authors give 'em no Weapons for Bucklers and Pikes: But all agree in furnishing 'em with Tabours, and Castanetta's; and relate that they used to dance much to the Noise and clashing thereof. **1736** BAILEY *Dict. Britannicum* (2nd edn) *Curetes*, are said to be descended of the *Dactyli*, who were Priests of the Goddess *Vesta*.... To these *Curetes Rhea* is said to have committed the Care of *Jupiter*. To preserve him from his Father *Satnrn* [sic]; and they by Dancing in Armour and clashing their Weapons to the Sound of Pipes, Drums and Cymbals, made such a Noise as drowned the Cry of this infant God.

curranto *see* coranto, courante
1656 BLOUNT (1st edn) *Curranto (ab huc & illuc Currendo*, Fr. *Courante)* a running dance, a French dance, different from what we call a Country dance. **1658** PHILLIPS (1st edn) *Curranto*, (French,) a running French Dance, also a musical Aire of a more than ordinary swift time. **1659** TORRIANO-FLORIO It→E *Corranta*, a french running dance, and therefore called a Corrante. **1670** BLOUNT (3rd edn) *Coranto* (Ital. *Corranta*) a French running Dance; *Curranto* (*ab huc & illuc currendo*, Fr. *Courante*) a running dance, a French dance, different from what we call a Country dance. **1676** COLES *Coranto*, a *French* running dance *Curranto, French.* a running French dance. **1678** PHILLIPS (4th edn) *Curranto*, (French) a running *French* Dance: also a musical Air, which runs in that Mood called the *Imperfect of the More*, consisting of Triple time. **1704** *Cocker's Engl. Dict.* (1st edn) *Coranto*, a *French* dance also Musick, which runs in triple time. **1706** KERSEY-PHILLIPS (6th edn) *Curranto* or *Courant, (Ital. & Fr.)* a running *French* Dance: Also a Musical Air which runs in a Mood call'd the *Imperfect of the more*, consisting of triple Time. **1708** KERSEY *Dict. Anglo-Brit.* (1st edn) *Curranto* or *Courant*, (*I.* & *F.*) a running *French* Dance: Also a Musical Air,

consisting of Triple Time. **1726** BAILEY *An Univ. Etymolog. Engl. Dict.* (3rd edn) *Curranto, Courant,* a running *French* Dance; Also a Musical Air, consisting of tripple Time, call'd *Imperfect of the More.* **1728** CHAMBERS *Currant, Curranto,* a sort of running *French* Dance: Also a Musical Air in triple Time. See *Courant.*

1676 MACE *Musick's Monument* (p. 129) *Corantoes,* are *Lessons* of a *Shorter Cut* [than galliards], and of a *Quicker Triple-Time;* commonly of 2 *Strains,* and full of *Sprightfulness,* and *Vigour, Lively, Brisk,* and *Cheerful.*

curtail *see* courtaud, fagottino, fagotto

1706 KERSEY-PHILLIPS (6th edn) §*Double Curtail,* a kind of Musical Instrument, serving as a Bass to the Haut-bois. **1708** KERSEY *Dict. Anglo-Brit.* (1st edn) § *Double Curtail,* a Musical Instrument. **1726** BAILEY *An Univ. Etymolog. Engl. Dict.* (3rd edn) *Double Curtail,* a Musical Instrument that plays the Bass. **1737** DYCHE-PARDON (2nd edn) *Curtail* (V.) ... also the Name of a Musical Instrument.

cut lute

c.1668-71 *Mary Burwell's Instruction Bk. for Lute* (*TDa* p. 9) [*re* history of the lute] We have that they call 'cut' lutes—that is, when of a great lute they will make a little one, which is done in cutting off something of the breadth and length of every rib, and then joining them together upon a little mould.

Cybele *see* Corybant, crotalum, cymbal

1565 COOPER L→E *Cibéle,* or rather *Cybéle, es,* and after some *Cybelle,* The daughter of Minos, king of Creta: was cast out into the deserte, nourished with beastes, and founde by a woman that kepte sheepe, and by hir nourished: after she became meruayleus fayre and wyse. she [sic] found fyrst the pype and tabour, and cimbals amonge the greekes: **1730** BAILEY *Dict. Britannicum* (1st edn) *Cybele* (according to the *Pagan Theology*) was the wife of *Saturn....* Her priests ... were also called *Corybantes,* and in their celebration of her rites acted the part of *madmen* with their drums, trumpets, and such other instruments, singings, howlings, cutting themselves desperately, and all that they met.... She was extraordinary beautiful, and as she grew to years of understanding, became very famous for her skill in musick .... She afterwards fell in love with a young man named *Atys;* but he not obtaining liberty to marry her, she was got with child by him, for which *Atys* was condemned to die, which caused her to run mad for grief, and leaving her father's court, she ran up and down the country with a pipe and drum in her hand.

cymbal *see* cembalo, chapas, cimbello, crotalum, entata, gnaccara, harpsichord, vielle

1500 *Ortus Vocabulorum* L→E Cimbala & cimbalum. pe. cor. est instrumentum musicum. angl. a tumbrell n.s. **1538** ELYOT L→E *Cymbalum,* an instrument of musike. **1552** HULOET L→E *cymbalum.* Cymball. **1565** COOPER L→E *Cymbalum, cymbali, n.g. pen. cor. Cic.* An instrumente of musicke: a simball. **1587** THOMAS L→E *Cymbalum, li, n.g.* An instrument of musick: a cymball. **1589** RIDER L→E *Cymbalum, crotalum, n.* A cimbal. *Symbalum* [sic], *crotalum, n.* A Simball. **1593** HOLLYBAND Fr→E *Cymbale,* a Cymball: *f.* **1598** FLORIO It→E *Cimbalo,* a Cymball or Timbrell. *Cimbanello,* as *Cimbalo.* **1604** CAWDREY (1st edn) *cymball,* an instrument of musicke, so called. **1611** COTGRAVE Fr→E *Cimbale: f.* A Cymball. Seeke *Cymbale. Cymbale: f.* A Cymball to play on. **1611** FLORIO It→E *Cimbalo,* a Cimball, a Timbrell. *Cimbanello,* a litle Cimball or Timbrell. *Cimbellare,* to play on Cimbals. **1616** BULLOKAR *Cimball.* An old musicall instrument, made in some places of two or mo[re] plates of brasse, which with beating together made a ringing noyse. **1623** COCKERAM *Cimball.* An old musicall instrument made with plates of brasse. **1650** HOWELL-COTGRAVE Fr→E § *Iouër des cymbales. autant que paillarder;* Rab. **1656** BLOUNT (1st edn) *Cymbal (cymbalum)* was a kind of instrument, composed of thin plates of brass, with certain small bars of Iron, fastened and cross billeted in the plates, wherewith they made a great noise. Others think *Cymbals* are bells, which according to the opinion of some, were consecrated to the service of the Church by Pope *Sabinian Caussinus.* **1658** PHILLIPS (1st edn) *Cymbal,* a Musical instrument, made of plates of brasse, resembling a kinde of boat, called *Cymba.* **1659** TORRIANO-FLORIO It→E *Cimbalo, Cimbano, Cimbanello,* a cymball or a timbrell **1676** COLES *Cymbal,* a Musical instrument of brass plates, resembling a small boat. **1688** MIEGE-COTGRAVE Fr→E *Cymbales,* (f.) Cymbals. § *Cymbale qui tinte,* I am become as sounding Brass, or a tinkling Cymbal. *Si je n'ai point de Charité, je suis comme l'Airain qui resonne, & comme la Cymbale qui tinte,* (1 Cor. 13. 1) if I have not Charity, I am become as sounding Brass, and a tinkling Cymbal.

Toucher les Cymbales, to play upon the Cymbals. **1702** KERSEY *New Engl. Dict.* (1st edn) A *Cymbal*, a musical instrument. **1706** KERSEY-PHILLIPS (6th edn) *Cymbal*, a Musical Instrument, anciently made of two hollow Plates of Copper, or Brass, like a Porrenger; but it is now taken for a sort of Wind-musick. **1728** CHAMBERS *Cymbal*, a Musical Instrument, used among the Antients; call'd by the *Greeks* κύμβαλον, and by the Latins *Cymbalum*. ¶ It was of Brass, like our Kettle-Drums; and some think in their Form, but smaller, and its Use different. ¶ *Cassiodorus*, and *Isidore*, call in *Acetabulum*, the Name of a Cup or Cavity of a Bone wherein another is articulated; and *Xenophon* compares it to a Horse's Hoof; whence it must have been hollow; which appears, too, from the Figure of several other Things, denominated from it, as a Bason, Caldron, Goblet, Casque; and even a Shoe, such as those of *Empedocles*, which were of Brass. ¶ In effect, the ancient *Cymbals* appear to have been very different from our Kettle-Drums; and their Use of another Kind: To their exterior Cavity was fasten'd a Handle; whence *Pliny* takes occasion to compare 'em to the upper Part of the Thigh, *Coxendicibus*, and *Rabban* to Phiols. ¶ They were struck against one another, in Cadence, and made a very acute Sound. Their Invention was attributed to *Cybele*; whence their use in Feasts and Sacrifices: Setting aside this Occasion, they were seldom used but by dissolute and effeminate People. ¶ Mr. *Lampe*, who has wrote expressly on the Subject, attributes the Invention to the *Curetes*, or Inhabitants of Mount *Ida* in *Crete*: 'Tis certain, these, as well as the *Corybantes*, or Guards of the Kings of *Crete*; and those of *Rhodes*, and *Samothracia*, were reputed to excel in the Musick of the *Cymbal*. See *Corybantes*. ¶ *Sylburgius* derives the Word κύμβαλον from three several *Greek* Roots, *viz.* from κυφος, *crooked*; from κυπελον, *Cup*; and from φωνή, *Voice*. *Isidore* derives it from *cum*, and *ballematica*, an immodest Dance, used to accompany this Instrument. The real Etymology appears to be from κύμβος, *Cavity*. ¶ The *Jews*, too, had their *Cymbals*, which they called צלצלים, or מצלתים; or at least, Instruments, chiefly that the *Greek*, *Latin*, and *English* Translators render *Cymbals*; for as to their Matter, Form, *&c.* the Criticks are wholly in the dark. ¶ The Modern *Cymbal* is a paltry Instrument, chiefly in use among Vagrants, Gypsies, *&c.* It consists of steel Wire, in a triangular Form, whereon are pass'd five Rings, which are touch'd and shifted along the Triangle with an Iron Rod held in the left Hand, while 'tis supported in the right by a Ring, to give it the freer Motion. ¶ *Durandus* says, that the Monks us'd the Word *Cymbal* for the Bell hung in the Cloister, used to call 'em to the Refectory. **1730** BAILEY *Dict. Britannicum* (1st edn) *Cymbal* (κύμβαλον, Gr.) a musical instrument used among the ancients. **1737** DYCHE-PARDON (2nd edn) *Cymbal* (S.) a musical Instrument made of Brass, like a Kettle Drum, and some think in the same Form, but smaller, and for another Purpose; it was much used by the Ancients.

1721 MALCOLM *Treatise of Musick* (p. 469) ... we hear [in ancient accounts] of the *Tympanum* or *Cymbalum*, of the Nature of our Drum; the *Greeks* gave it the last Name from its Figure, resembling a Boat.

cymbalist

1538 ELYOT L→E *Cybaliste*, they that play vpon cymbals. **1552** HULOET L→E *cymbalistæ*. Cymball players. **1565** COOPER L→E *Cymbalissare. Cassius Hemina*. To play on the cymballes. *Cymbalista, cymbalistæ. Apul.* A player on cymballes. **1587** THOMAS L→E *Cymbalissare, Non.* To play on the Cymballs. *Cymbalista, æ, m.g. Apul.* Which plaieth vpon Cymballs. **1589** RIDER L→E *Cymbalisso*. To plaie on the Cimbals. *Cymbalista, m.* He that plaieth on cimbals. *Symbalista* [sic], *m.* Hee which plaieth on simbals. **1598** FLORIO It→E *Cimbalista*, one that playes vpon a Cymball or Timbrell. **1611** FLORIO It→E *Cimbalista*, a plaier on cimbals or Timbrels. **1656** BLOUNT (1st edn) *Cymbalist (cymbalistes)* he that plays on the Cymbals. **1659** TORRIANO-FLORIO It→E *Cimbalista*, a cymbalist, a player on a cymball or a timbrell. **Cimballizare*, to play on a cymball or timbrell. **1676** COLES *Cymbalist*, he that playes on a ¶ *Cymbal* **1704** *Cocker's Engl. Dict.* (1st edn) *Cymbalist*, a Player on a *Cymbal*, an Instrument of brass plates like a small boat, with small bars of Iron fastened, and cross billeted in the plates, which make a great noise.

cymbalum *see* cymbal

cythara *see* cithara

D

da

1724 [Pepusch] *Short Explic. of Foreign Words in Mus. Bks.* (p. 25) *Da, Dal, Del,* or *Di,* is as much as to say, For or By. Thus, *Da Camera,* for the Chamber. *Dal, Del,* or *Di Arcangelo Corelli,* is by *Arcangelo Corelli.* **1726** Bailey *An Univ. Etymolog. Engl. Dict.* (3rd edn) *Da* (in *Musick Books*) signifies *for* or *by*. *Dal* (in *Musick Books*) signifies *for* or *by*. Ital.

dabuda

1598 Florio It→E *Dabuda,* ... Also a kinde of musicall instrument among shepheards. **1611** Florio It→E *Dabuda,* ... Also a musicall instrument among Shepherds. **1659** Torriano-Florio It→E *Da buda, Dabbuda,* a kind of musicall instrument without fretts, and is plaid upon with two sticks, streaking the strings with them

da capo *see* capo, hold, repeat, rondeau

1724 [Pepusch] *Short Explic. of Foreign Words in Mus. Bks.* (pp. 25-6) *Da Capo,* or by Way of Abbreviation *D C*; which is as much as to say, at the Head, or at the Beginning again. These Letters or Words are commonly met with at the End of Rondeaus, or such other Airs or Tunes as end with the first Part; signifying thereby that the Song or Air must be begun again, and ended with the first Part: And this is done chiefly to save the Trouble of writing the same Thing twice or three Times over. **1726** Bailey *An Univ. Etymolog. Engl. Dict.* (3rd edn) *DC* an Abbreviation of *Da Capo* (in *Musick Books*) are Words commonly met with at the End of Rondeaus, or such Airs or Tunes as end with the first Part, and signifies, at the Head or at the Beginning again, and intimates, that the Song or Air must be begun again, and ended with the first Part.

c.1710 Anon. *Preceptor for Improved Octave Flageolet* ('Explanation of Words', p. 82) *DC* or *Da capo*—Repeat the first strain **1731** Prelleur *Modern Musick-Master* (Dictionary, p. 2) *D.C.* or *Da Capo,* begin again & end with the first Strain. **1736** Tans'ur *Compleat Melody* (3rd edn, p. 71) *Da Capo,* or *D.A* [sic]. (Ital.) is a Word often set at the End of a Piece of Musick that ends with the first *Strain,* which signifies to begin again. These *Tunes* that end so, are commonly called *Rondea's*: The Word *Fin,* or *F,* ought to stand over the last *Note.*

daccordo *see* accord

1598 Florio It→E *Daccordo,* ... accorded, tuned. **1611** Florio It→E *Daccordo,* agreed, accorded, tuned.

dædala

1587 Thomas L→E *Dædala,* *A bow wherewith they play on a kitte or a viole.

dance *see* balade, baldosa, ball, bargaret, basse-dance, bouffons, bourrée, branle, canaries, carol, chaconne, chiarantana, contrapasso, courante, emmelia, galliard, gavotte, gigue, hay, hornpipe, jig, loure, madama d'Orliens, matachin, menuet, morris dance, nizzarda, paganina, pavan, reorgarza, ridda, rigadoon, rigoletto, rodaja, romanzina, roundelay, saltarella, saraband, siciliano, stampita, style (stylo choraico), tinton, tordiglione, triccatina, tripode, villanata, villanella, virelay, volta

1611 Cotgrave Fr→E *Dansement.* A dauncing; hopping, skipping; a motion directed by time, and harmonie. **1688** Miege-Cotgrave Fr→E § *Danser au Violon, ou aux Chansons,* to dance to the Violin, or to Singing. *Danser d'un air degagé,* to have a free way of dancing, to dance handsomly. *Danser d'un bel air,* to dance briskly, bravely. *Danser une Courante, ou une Gigue,* to dance a Courant, or a Jig. **1696** Phillips (5th edn) To *Dance,* to move the Body in Measure and Figure, according to the Tune or Air that is plaid at the same time, for the Delight of the Spectators. **1706** Kersey-Phillips (6th edn) To *Dance,* to move the Body in measure and time, according to the Tune, or Air that is play'd or Sung. **1726** Bailey *An Univ. Etymolog. Engl. Dict.* (3rd edn) § *No longer Pipe no longer Dance.* ¶ This Proverb is a *Reflection* upon the *mercenary* and *ungrateful* Tempers of too many People: and is also a good *memento* of *Prudence,* intimating that *Misfortune* will have few or no Friends; for *ungrateful* and *mercenary* People, tho' they have had twenty good turns done them formerly, will Dance no longer than while the *Musick* of this Proverb obliges them for their Pains; ... **1728** Chambers *Dance,* an agreeable Motion of the Body, adjusted by Art to the Measures or Tune of a Violin, or Voice.... The Ancients had three kinds of *Dances*: The first Grave, call'd *Emmelia*, answering to our *low Dances* and *Pavanes*. The second Gay, call'd *Cordax*; answering to our *Courants, Galliards, Gavots* and *Vaults*. The third, call'd *Siccinnis*, was a Mixture of Gravity and Gayety.... 'Tis not many Years ago, since *Thoinet Arbeau*, a *Dancing*-Master of *Paris*, gave an *Orchesography*, wherein all the Steps and Motions of a *Dance* are writ, or noted down; as the Sounds of a Song are scored in Music. Tho' the famous *Beauchamp* has some Pretensions to be the Inventor of this Secret, and accordingly procured an *Arret* in his Favour. **1737** DYCHE-PARDON (2nd edn) *Dance* (V.) to move the Body regularly, according to the Air of Musick sung or play'd, by Rules of Art;

decachord *see* monochord, psalm, psaltery

1500 *Ortus Vocabulorum* L→E Decacordus a um. i. decem cordarum o.s. **1538** ELYOT L→E *Decachordum*, an instrument with tenne strynges. **1565** COOPER L→E *Decachordum, Instrumentum musicum decem chordas habens*. **1587** THOMAS L→E *Decachordium, dij, n.g.* *An instrument of musicke hauing ten strings. **1589** RIDER L→E *Decachordium, n.* An instrumente having ten stringes. **1598** FLORIO It→E *Decacordo*, an instrument of ten strings. **1604** CAWDREY (1st edn) *decacordon*, (Greeke) an instrument with tenne strings **1611** FLORIO It→E *Decacordo*, an instrument of ten strings. **1656** BLOUNT (1st edn) *D[e]cachord (decachordium)* an instrument with ten strings. **1659** TORRIANO-FLORIO It→E *Deca-cordo*, an instrument of ten strings. **1676** COLES *Decachord, Greek.* an instrument of ten strings **1696** PHILLIPS (5th edn) *Decacordon*, an Instrument of ten Strings. **1706** KERSEY-PHILLIPS (6th edn) *Decachordon, (Gr.)* a Musical Instrument, having ten Strings.

decant

1500 *Ortus Vocabulorum* L→E Decanto as. idest organizando cantare Tor trix et tio verbalis a.p. **1565** COOPER L→E § *Miserabiles decantare elegos. Horat.* To singe or make. **1587** THOMAS L→E *Decanto, as.* To reporte or speake often: to sing or make: **1589** RIDER L→E *Decanto.* To sing the tenor. **1598** FLORIO It→E *Decantare*, to sing out. **1611** FLORIO It→E *Decantare*, to sing **1659** TORRIANO-FLORIO It→E *Decantare*, to sing out **1670** BLOUNT (3rd edn) *Decant (decanto)* to report or speak often, to sing, to enchant. **1676** COLES *Decant, Latin.* report, sing enchant

decantator

1589 RIDER L→E *Decantator, m.* He that singeth the tenor.

decima

1724 [PEPUSCH] *Short Explic. of Foreign Words in Mus. Bks.* (p. 26) *Decima* is the Tenth, or Number Ten. Thus, ¶ *Opera Decima* is the Tenth Opera. ¶ *Undecima*, the Eleventh. ¶ *Duodecima*, the Twelfth...

deformity

1728 CHAMBERS *Deformity*, then, is only the Absence of Beauty, or a Deficiency in the Beauty expected in any Species: Thus bad Music pleases Rusticks, who never heard any better; and the finest Ear is not offended with tuning of Instruments, if it be not too tedious ...

degree *see* note, scale

1596 ANON. *Pathway to Musicke* [C iii] *VVhat is a degree in Musick?* ¶ It is a certaine rate, by the vvhich the value of the principall notes is measured and knowne by a certaine marke. **1597** MORLEY *Plaine and Easie Introdvction* (p. 12) [marginalia: 'The definition of a degree.'] Those who within these three hundred yeares haue written the Art of Musicke, haue set downe the Moodes otherwise then they eyther haue been or are taught now in England.... Those which we now call Moodes, they tearmid degrees of Musick: the definition they gaue thus: a degree is a certayne meane whereby the value of the principall notes is perceaued by some signe set before them, degrees of musicke they made three, *Moode*: *Time* and *Prolation*. **1694** HOLDER *Treatise of Natural Grounds* (pp. 124-5) And these apt and useful Discords, are either Simple uncompounded Intervals, such as immediately follow one another, ascending or descending in the Scale of Music: As *Ut Re Mi.* [sic] *Fa Sol Fa Sol*, and are called Degrees: § (pp. 125-6) Degrees, are uncompounded Intervals, which are found upon 8 Chords and in 7 Spaces, by which an immediate Ascent or Descent is made from the *Unison* to the *Octave* or *Diapason*; and by the same progression to as many *Octaves* as there may be occasion. These are different according to the different Kinds of Music; *viz. Enharmonic, Chromatic*, and *Diatonic*, and the several Colours of the two Later: § (p. 132) ... the Degrees *Diatonic*; which are so called; not because they are all Tones; but because most of them, as many as can be, are such; *viz.* in every *Diapason*, 5 *Tones*, and two *Hemitones*. **1721** MALCOLM *Treatise of Musick* (pp. 222-3) ... we shall make *Experience* the Judge, which approves of those, and those only, with their *Dependents* (besides the *harmonical Intervals*) as Parts of the true *natural System* of *Musick, viz.* whose *Ratios* are 8:9. called a *greater Tone*, 9:10 called a *lesser Tone*, and 15:16 called a *Semitone*: And these are the lesser *Intervals*, particularly called *Degrees*, by which a Sound can move upwards or downwards successively, from one Extreme of any *harmonical Interval* to another, and produce true *Melody*; ...

deltatono

1611 FLORIO It→E *Deltatono*, ... Also a concord of three voices or tunes. **1659** TORRIANO-FLORIO It→E *Delta-tono*, a concord of three tunes or voices

demi-crochue *see* semiquaver

1611 COTGRAVE Fr→E *Demi-crochuë: f.* A semyquauer, in Musicke.

demiditone *see* semiditone

1704 HARRIS *Demi-diton*, a Note in Musick, being the same with *Tierce Minor*: See *Monochord*. **1706** KERSEY-PHILLIPS (6th edn) *Demi-ditone*, a Note in *Musick*, the same with *Tierce Minor*; which See. **1708** KERSEY *Dict. Anglo-Brit.* (1st edn) *Demi-ditone*, a Note in *Musick*.

demiquaver *see* semiquaver

1704 HARRIS *Demi-quaver*, a Note in Musick: See *Notes* and *Time*. **1706** KERSEY-PHILLIPS (6th edn) *Demi-quaver*, a Musical Note; See *Semi-quaver*. **1707** *Gloss. Angl. Nova* (1st edn) *Demi-quaver*; a Note in Musick, half a Semi-quaver. **1708** KERSEY *Dict. Anglo-Brit.* (1st edn) *Demi-quaver*, a Musical Note. **1728** CHAMBERS *Demi-Quaver*, is a Note in Musick; two of which are equal to the Quaver. See *Quaver*, and *Note*.

demisemiquaver

1706 KERSEY-PHILLIPS (6th edn) *Demi-semi-quaver*, the least Note in *Musick*, two of which make a Semi-quaver, four a Quaver, eight a Crotchet, &c.

1721 MALCOLM *Treatise of Musick* (p. 559) ... about the Year 1330 or 1333, says *Kircher*, the famous *Joannes de Muris*, Doctor at *Paris*, invented the different Figures of Notes, which express the *Time*, or Length of every Note, at least their true relative Proportions to one another; ... But anciently they were called, *Maxima, Longa, Brevis, Semibrevis, Minima, Semiminima, Chroma*, (or *Fusa*) *Semichroma*. What we call the *Demisemiquaver* is of modern Addition. **1724** TURNER *Sound Anatomiz'd* (p. 17) The Fifth, and Last [note of duration, after the minim, crotchet and quaver and semiquaver], is called a *Demisemiquaver* or *Demiquaver*; which being but half the Length of the *Semiquaver*, has its Tail turned up with a tripple Stroke, thus; [note symbol] and divides the *Semibreve* into *Two* and *Thirty* Parts.

Demodocus

1538 ELYOT L→E *Demodocus*, the name of a harper i Homer. **1565** COOPER L→E *Demodocus*, The name of an harper, of whom Homere maketh mention.

dervises

1656 BLOUNT (1st edn) *Dervises*, or *Derveeshes*, a kind of Monks, or falsely termed religious persons among the Turks, that turn round with Musick in their divine Service. **1704** *Cocker's Engl. Dict.* (1st edn) *Dervises*, religious *Turks*, that turn round with Musick in their Divine Service. **1728** CHAMBERS *Dervis*, or *Derviches*, a Sort of Monks among the *Turks*, who lead a very austere Life, and profess extream Poverty .... Tuesdays and Fridays they hold Meetings, at which the Superior of the House presides. ¶ One of them plays all the while on a Flute, and the rest dance, turning their Bodies round and round with the greatest Swiftness imaginable. Long Custom to this Exercise from their Youth, has brought them to such pass, that it does not maze, or discompose them at all. This Practice they observe with great Strictness, in Memory of *Mevelava* their Patriarch's turning miraculously round, for the Space of four Days, without any Food, or Refreshment; his Companion *Hamsa* playing all the while of the Flute; after which he fell into an Extasy, and therein receiv'd wonderful Revelations for the Establishment of his Order. They believe the Flute an Instrument consecrated by *Jacob*, and the Shepherds of the Old Testament; by reason they sang the Praises of God thereon. **1730** BAILEY *Dict. Britannicum* (1st edn) *Dervices, Dervises* ... among the *Turks* a sort of monks who profess extreme poverty, and lead a very austere life... They have meetings on *Tuesdays* and *Fridays*, at which the superior of their house is present; at which meetings one of them plays all the while on a flute (which instrument they highly esteem as consecrated by *Jacob* and the Old Testamant shepherds that sung the praises of God upon it) the rest dance, turning their bodies round with an incredible swiftness, having inured themselves to this exercise from their youth: **1737** DYCHE-PARDON (2nd edn) *Dervices* or *Dervises* (S.) a Kind of Monks among the *Turks*, who lead a very austere Life, and profess extream Poverty... they hold Meetings, at which the Superior presides; one of them plays all the while upon a Flute, the rest turning themselves round with incredible Swiftness.

desaccorde *see* discord

descant *see* accino, bass descant, binding descant, canto figurato, chroma, chromatic, colour, contre, counterpoint, diminution, division, double descant, fugue, incentor, in nomine, intonation, motet, quaver, tenor, voluntary

1500 *Ortus Vocabulorum* L→E Discanto as. to synge descant n.p. Discantus ti. descant m.t. **1570/71** *Dict. Fr. and Engl.* Fr→E *Deschant*, descant, sometyme a recantation. *Deschanter*, to descant. **1589** RIDER L→E *Discanto*. To sing Descant. *Discantus, m.* Descante *Discantus, triplex* The treble. *Discentor, m.* He that singeth the treble. *Discino, discento, minurio, minurizo* To sing the treble. **1593** HOLLYBAND Fr→E *Deschant*, descant, sometime a recantation: *m.* *Deschanter*, to descant. **1609** CAWDREY (2nd edn) *descant*, variation of the ground of a song. **1611** COTGRAVE Fr→E *Deschant: m.* Descant (of Musicke;) *Deschante: ée: f.* Descanted; also, recanted. *Deschanter*. To Descant; **1656** BLOUNT (1st edn) *Descant (discanto)* to run division, or variety with the voyce, upon a musical ground, in true measure; to sing off of a ground. **1658** PHILLIPS (1st edn) *Descant*, called in Latin *frequentamentum vocis*, in French *fredon*, is a term in Musick, signifying the answering of quick notes in one part, unto a slower measure in the other part **1659** TORRIANO-FLORIO It→E **Discantare*, to sing descant. **1676** COLES *Descant*, the answering of quick notes in one part to a slower measure in the other **1702** KERSEY *New Engl. Dict.* (1st edn) A *Descant, or* division in musick; To *descant* in musick, *or* discourse; **1704** *Cocker's Engl. Dict.* (1st edn) *Descant*, in Musick, to answer a quick note with a slower **1704** HARRIS *Descant*, in Musick, signifies the Art of Composing in several Parts, and is threefold, *viz. Plain, Figurate,* and *Double.* ¶ *Plain Descant*, is the Ground-work or Foundation of Musical Composition, and consists altogether in the ordinary placing of many Concords. ¶ *Figurate* or *Florid Descant*, is that wherein Discords are concern'd, as well (though not so much) as Concords; and may well be termed the Ornament or Rhetorical part of Musick, in regard that in this are introduced all the Varieties of Points, Figures, Syncopes, diversities of Measures, and whatsoever else is capable of adorning the Composition. ¶ *Double Descant*, is when the Parts are so contrived, that the *Treble* may be made the *Bass*, and on the contrary, the *Bass* the *Treble.* **1706** KERSEY-PHILLIPS (6th edn) *Descant* (in *Musick*) signifies the Art of Composing in several Parts, and is threefold, *viz,* Plain, Figurate and Double. ¶ *Plain Descant* is the Foundation or Groundwork of Musical Composition, and consists altogether in the orderly placing of many Concords. ¶ *Figurate* or *Florid Descant*, is that wherein some Discords are intermix'd with the Concords; so that it may well be Term'd the Rhetorical Part of Musick, in regard that here are brought in all the Variety of Points, *Syncope's*, Figures and whatever else is capable of affording an Ornament to the Composition. ¶ *Double Descant*, is when the Parts are so contriv'd, that the Treble may be made the Bass, and on the contrary the Bass the Treble. To *Descant*, to run descant in *Musick*; **1707** *Gloss. Angl. Nova* (1st edn) *Descant*, in Musick, is to run Division or Variety with the Voice upon a Musical Ground in true Measure **1728** CHAMBERS *Descant*, in Music, the Art of Composing in several Parts. See *Composition.* ¶ *Descant* is three-fold; viz. *Plain, Figurate,* and *Double.* ¶ *Plain Descant*, is the Ground-work, or Foundation of Musical Composition, and consists altogether in the orderly Placing of many Concords; answering to simple *Counter-point.* ¶ *Figurate*, or *Florid Descant*, is that wherein Discords are concern'd as well, tho' not as much, as Concords. This may be well term'd, the Ornamental, or Rhetorical Part of Musick; in Regard that in this are introduced all the Varieties of Points; Figures, Syncopes, Diversities of Measures, and whatsoever else is capable of adorning the Composition. ¶ *Double Descent*, is when the Parts are so contrived, that the Treble may be made the Bass; and on the contrary, the Bass the Treble. See *Harmony, Counter-Point, &c.* **1730** BAILEY *Dict. Britannicum* (1st edn) To *Descant* (in *Musick*) is to run a division or variety, with the instrument or voice. § *Florid Descant* (in *Musick.*) See *Figurate Descant* [entry follows that of 1706 Kersey-Phillips]. **1735** DEFOE To *Descant*, to run a Division with the Voice; **1737** DYCHE-PARDON (2nd edn) *Descant* (V.) ... In *Musick*, 'tis the Art of Composition, and according as 'tis employed is called plain, or figurative: Plain, when it only relates to Counter-point, as in Psalmody; and figurative, when it employs the whole Art and Fancy of the Composer, both as to Air, Measure, and all the other Parts of Composing. ¶ *Double Descant*, is when the Parts are so contrived, that the Bass may be made the Treble, and the Treble the Bass.

after 1517 ANON. Art of Mvsic BL Add. 4911, f. 46v *Discant quhat is it?* ¶ It is ane Melodius consonance of harmony quilk be Numeris artificiall dois mak diuisions and fraction of notte mensurall. Puttand them in dyverss concordis intermixtie fluresing craftelly vpone sympill and mensurall grundis **1596** ANON. *Pathway to Musicke* [E iv *verso*] *A direction for Descant, and vvhat it is.* ¶ It is a song made of diuers voyces, and noates of certaine value. **1597** MORLEY *Plaine and Easie Introdvction* (p. 70) The name of Descant is vsurped of the musitions in diuers significations: some time they take it for the whole harmony of many voyces: others sometime for one of the voyces or partes: & that is, when the whole song is not passing three voyces. Last of all, they take it for singing a part extempore vpon a playnesong, in which sence we commonly vse it: so that when a man talketh of a Descanter, it must be vnderstood of one that can extempore sing a part vpon a playne song. § (annotations to Part II) *The name of descant*) This is the second member of our deuision of practical musicke, which may be properly tearmed *syntactical, poeticall, or effectiue*: ... the word *descant* signifieth in our toung, the forme of setting together of sundry voices or concords for producing of harmony: and a musician if he heare a song sung and mislike it, he will saie the *Descant* is naught. But in this signification it is seldome vsed, and the most common signification which it hath, is the singing *ex tempore* vpon a plain song: in which sence there is none (who hath tasteth the first elements of musicke) but vnderstandeth it. When descant did begin, by whom and where it was inuented is vncertaine, for it is a great controuersie amongst the learned if it were knowne to the antiquitie, or no... **1609** DOWLAND-ORNITHOPARCUS *Micrologvs* (p. 83) The *Discantus* (as *Tinctor* saith) is a Song made of diuers voyces. For it is called *Discantus, Quasi diuersus Cantus*, that is, as it were another Song. By which name the ancients did call euery Mensurall Song. But we, because *Discantus* is a part of a song seuered from the rest, will describe it thus. *Discantus* is the vppermost part of each Song. Or it is an Harmony to be song with a Childs Voyce. **1617-24** FLUDD *Utriusque Cosmi Maioris: De Templo Musicæ* (p. 210) *Discantus* est vox suprema ex sonis peracutis modulatè inflexa, ideóque tenera & puerilis. **1636** BUTLER *Principles of Musik* (p. 90) Discant is, when unto Integral Notes of longer time in one Parte, ar sung eqivalent Particles, or Notes of shorter time, in an other: (as to one Sembrief, 2 Minims, 4 Crochets, or 8 Qavers) the Parts following one an other in Melodious Points, Reported, or Reverted, or bothe; (with other Harmoni interposed) until at the last they meete all together in the Cloze. **1667** SIMPSON *Compendium of Practical Musick* (pp. 110-11) Figurate Descant is that wherein Discords are concerned as well as Concords. And, as we termed Plain Descant (in which was taught the use of the Concords) The Ground-work or Grammar of Musical Composition, so may we as properly nominate This, the Ornament or Rhetorical part of Musick. For, in This are introduced all the varieties of Points, Fuges, Syncope's or Bindings, Diversities of Measures, Intermixtures of discording Sounds; or what else Art and Fancy can exhibit; which, as different Flowers and Figures, do set forth and adorn the Composition; whence it is named *Melothesia florida vel figurata*, Florid or Figurate Descant. **after 1695** NORTH untitled notebook BL Add. 32532, f. 20 Of Descant. ¶ This signifies & mean's, onely the modulation of many part's, In air & harmony. and is that art, wch is the ultimate perfection of a Composer. **c.1726** NORTH Musicall Gramarian BL Add. 32533, f. 155v ... one may observe a practis of more skill then now can Readily be found above ground and that is By the voice to performe an harmonious composition upon a plain song Extempore wch with all other Harmonious Compositions was called Descant ... **1736** TANS'UR *Compleat Melody* (3rd edn, p. 54) The Original of *Composition* is called *Plain-Discant*; which is the *Grammar*, or *Ground-work* of Musical *Composition*: Wherein all *Concords* are orderly taken. *Figurate Discant*, is when *Discords* are admitted into *Harmony*, either by gradual *Transition*, or otherwise taken: Which is the *Ornamental*, or *Rhetorical Part* of *Musick*. § (p. 71) *Plain-Descant*, is the *Ground-work* of *Musical Composition*, where *Concords* are orderly taken. ¶ *Figurate-Descant*, is when *Discords* are concern'd as well as *Concords*, tho' not so much. ¶ *Double-Descant*, is contrived so, that the *Treble* may be made *Bass*, or the *Bass* be made *Treble*, &c.

desentonado *see* destonnement

1599 MINSHEU-PERCYVALL Sp→E *desEntonado*, m. discord in musicke. **desEntonamiento*, m. a being out of tune. *desEntonar*, to sound out of tune.

desesperade *see* disperate
1611 Cotgrave Fr→E *Desesperade: f.* A kind of mournefull song.

dessus *see* haut-dessus
1611 Cotgrave Fr→E *Dessus: m. (substant.) le dessus de;* ... also, the treble part, in Musicke. **1650** Howell-Cotgrave Fr→E § *Faire le dessus.* To sing the treble part; **1688** Miege-Cotgrave Fr→E *Dessus,* (a masc. Subst.) top ... the treble (or upper part) in Musick. § *Chanter le dessus,* to sing the treble part.

destendu *see* rimesso
1593 Hollyband Fr→E *Destendu,* stretched or retched forth: but rather loosened, as the strings of a lute.

destonnement *see* desentonado
1611 Cotgrave Fr→E *Destonnement: m.* A discord, or iarre, in sound; also, a changing of tune. *Destonner.* To change, or alter, a tune; to take it higher, or lower.

dextera *see* tibia

diagram *see* genus, harmonical hand, scale
1587 Thomas L→E *Diagramma, atis, n.g. Vitru.* ... and in musicke it is called a proportion of measures distinguished by certaine notes. **1611** Florio It→E *Diagramma,* ... Also among Musicians a proportion of measures distinguished by certaine notes. **1656** Blount (1st edn) *Diagram (diagramma)* ... And in Musick it is called a proportion of measures distinguished by certain notes. *Rider.* **1658** Phillips (1st edn) *Diagram,* (Greek) ... also a proportion of measures in Musick distinguished by Notes. **1659** Torriano-Florio It→E **Diagramma,* ... also a Geometricall figure drawn in a place among Musicians, It is a proportion of measures distinguished by certain notes. **1676** Coles *Diagram, Greek...* also a proportion of measures in musick. **1702** Kersey *New Engl. Dict.* (1st edn) A *Diagram,* ... also a certain proportion of measures in musick. **1704** *Cocker's Engl. Dict.* (1st edn) *Diagram,* ... also a proportion of measures in Musick. **1706** Kersey-Phillips (6th edn) *Diagram,* ... In *Musick,* a proportion of Measures distinguished by certain Notes. **1728** Chambers *Diagram,* in the ancient Music, was what we call the *Scale,* or *Gammut* in the modern. See *Scale,* and *Gammut.* ¶ The Extent of the *Diagramma,* which they also call'd, *Systema perfectum,* was a *Disdiapason,* or two Octaves in the *Ratio* 1:4. In that Space, they had eighteen Chords, tho' these had not all different Sounds. See *Chord.* ¶ To explain it, they represent to us eighteen Chords, or Strings of an Instrument, as the Lyre, supposed to be tuned according to the Proportions in any of the *Genera,* viz. Diatonic, Enharmonic, or Chromatic. See *Genera, Diatonic, &c.* ¶ As the Lyre was improv'd, and more Chords added to it; so was the *Diagramma*: By such means it came from 4 Chords to 7, then 8, then 10, then 14, and at last 18. See *Lyre.* ¶ To each of these Chords, or Sounds, they gave a particular Name, taken from its Situation in the *Diagramma,* or the Lyre. Their Names, and Order, commencing from the lowest, are as follows: *Proslambanomenos, Hypate-Hypaton, Parhypate-hypaton, Lychanos-Hypaton, Hypate-Meson, Parhypate-Meson, Lychanos-Meson, Mese, Trite-Synem, Trite-Synem-menon, Paranete-Synem-menon, Nete-Synem-menon, Para-Mese, Trite-Diezeugmenon, Paranete-diezeugmenon, Nete-Diezeugmenon, Trite-Hyperbolæon, Paranete-Hyperbolæon, Nete-Hyperbolæon* [i.e. giving a total of 19]. ¶ *Guido Aretine* improved this Scale, or *Diagram,* very greatly. Finding it of too small Extent, he added five more Chords, or Notes to it; lay'd them all down on a Staff of 5 Lines; and instead of the long *Greek* Names abovementioned, names all his Notes by *Gregory*'s seven Letters. See *Note,* and *Gammut.* ¶ The first, or lowest Note of his Scale, he marked Γ, and call'd *Gamma;* whence the whole Scale came to be denominated *Gammut.* **1737** Dyche-Pardon (2nd edn) *Diagram* (S.) ... also the Gamut, in *Musick.*

dialogue *see* opera, pastoral, pause
1724 [Pepusch] *Short Explic. of Foreign Words in Mus. Bks.* (p. 27) *Dialogo,* a Dialogue, a Piece of Musick for two or more Voices or Instruments, which answer one another. **1726** Bailey *An Univ. Etymolog. Engl. Dict.* (3rd edn) *Dialogo* (in *Musick Books*) signifies a piece of Musick for two or more Voices or Instruments, which answer one to another. **1728** Chambers *Dialogue,* in Music, is a Composition for at least two Voices, or two Instruments, which answer each other; and which frequently uniting make a *Trio* with the *Thoro'-Bass.* ¶ There are Abundance of *Dialogues* in the *Italian* Opera's. **1737** Dyche-Pardon (2nd edn) *Dialogue* (S.) ... In *Musick,* 'tis a Composition for two or more Voices or Instruments, which frequently unite, and make a Trio with the Thorough Bass.

diana

1598 FLORIO It→E *Diana,* a kind of march sounded by trumpetters in a morning to their generall and captaine. **1611** COTGRAVE Fr→E § *Sonner la Diane.* Trumpetters to sound in a morning to their Generall, and Captaines. **1611** FLORIO It→E *Diana,* ... Also a march sounded by Trumpeters in a morning to their Generall or Captaine. **1659** TORRIANO-FLORIO It→E **Diana,* ... also the name of a march or point of warre, sounded by trumpeters to their Generall or Captain in a morning at their uprising

diapantono

1598 FLORIO It→E *Diapanton,* a rule or note in musicke. **1599** MINSHEU-PERCYVALL Sp→E **Diapanton,* a note or rule in musicke. **1611** FLORIO It→E *Diapantono,* a rule or note in Musicke. **1659** TORRIANO-FLORIO It→E *Diapontono,* a tone, a tune, a note or a rule in Musick.

diapason

see disdiapason, eighth, octave, semidiapason, tetradiapason, trisdiapason

1500 *Ortus Vocabulorum* L→E Diapason. est cantus constans ex octo sonis. **1538** ELYOT L→E *Diapason,* a concorde in musyke of fiue tunes, and two halfe tunes. **1552** HULOET L→E *Diapason.* Concorde in musycke of fyue tumes [sic] and two halfe tunes. **1565** COOPER L→E *Diapason.* A concorde in musike. **1587** THOMAS L→E *Dia-pason, Plin.* A concorde in Musicke. **1589** RIDER L→E *Diapason.* A concord in musick, ¶ Of 5. notes and 2. half notes, called an eight **1598** FLORIO It→E *Diapason,* a diapason, a concorde in musicke of all parts. **1599** MINSHEU-PERCYVALL Sp→E **Diapason,* a concord in musicke of all parts, a diapason. **1604** CAWDREY (1st edn) *diapason,* (Greeke) a concorde in musick of all parts **1611** COTGRAVE Fr→E *Diapason.* A Diapason, in Musicke; **1611** FLORIO It→E *Diapason,* a diapason or concord in Musicke of all parts. **1616** BULLOKAR *Diapason.* A concord in musicke of all. **1623** COCKERAM *Diapason.* A concord in musicke of all. **1656** BLOUNT (1st edn) *Diapase* or *Diapason* (Gr.) a concord of all in Musick: An eighth. See a further explanation of this in *Lord Bacons Natural Hist. fo.* 30. **1658** PHILLIPS (1st edn) *Diapason,* (Greek) an eight, or the most perfect concord in Musick. **1661** BLOUNT (2nd edn) *Diapase* or *Diapason* (Gr.) a perfect concord of all in Musick: An eighth. See a further explanation of this in *L. Bac. Nat. Hist. fo.* 30. **1676** COLES *Diapase, -son, Greek.* an Eight, the most perfect concord. **1704** *Cocker's Engl. Dict.* (1st edn) *Diapason,* an Eighth Concord in Musick; **1704** HARRIS *Diapason,* a Greek Word signifying a Chord including all Tones, 'tis the same with what we call an *Eighth* or an *Octave,* because there are but seven Tones or Notes, and then the *Eighth* is the same again with the first. *Aristotle* says it was not called *Diocto* as it should have been, because the Ancient Harp, and which hath all the Tones then known, had but 7 Strings. The Terms whereof are as 2 to 1. **1706** KERSEY-PHILLIPS (6th edn) *Diapason* (in *Musick*) a Chord including all Tones, which is the same with what is commonly call'd an *Octave,* or *Eighth,* because there are but Seven Tones Notes, and then the Eighth is the same again with the First: It is the most perfect Concord, and the Terms of it are as Two to One. **1707** *Gloss. Angl. Nova* (1st edn) *Diapason,* (Gr.) a Term in Musick, is an *Octave*; the Terms whereof are as 2 to 1. **1721** BAILEY *An Univ. Etymolog. Engl. Dict.* (1st edn) *Diapason,* (διαπασῶν, *Gr.*) a Term in Musick signifying an Octave. **1724** [PEPUSCH] *Short Explic. of Foreign Words in Mus. Bks.* (p. 27) *Diapason,* is a Term in Musick of much the same Signification as the Word *Octave.* **1728** CHAMBERS *Diapason,* in Music, a Musical Interval, by which most Authors, who have wrote on the Theory of Music, use to express the Octave of the *Greeks*; as they use *Diapente, Diatessaron, Hexachord,* and *Tetrachord,* to express *Fifths, Fourths, Thirds,* and *Sixths.* See *Octave.* ¶ The *Diapason* is the first, and most perfect of the Concords: If consider'd *Diatonically,* by Tones and Semi-Tones, it contains seven Degrees, *viz.* three greater Tones, two lesser Tones, and two greater Semi-tones. See *Degree.* ¶ The Interval of a *Diapason,* that is, the Proportion of its grave Sound to its acute, to *duplicate,* that is, as 2 to 1. See *Interval.* ¶ *Diapason,* among the Musical Instrument-makers, is a Kind of Rule, or Scale, whereby they adjust the Pipes of their Organs, and cut the Holes of their Flutes, Haut-Bois, *&c.* in due Proportion, for performing the Tones, Semi-tones, and Concords just. ¶ A Square being divided into eight equal Parallelograms; the Points wherein a Diagonal intersects all these Parallelograms, express all the usual Intervals in Music: And on this Principle it is, that the *Diapason* is founded. ¶ There is a particular Kind of *Diapason* for Trumpets; serving as a Standard, or Measure, for the different Magnitudes, they must have to perform the four Parts of Music. See *Trumpet.* ¶ There is another for Sack-buts, and Serpents, shewing how far they are to be lengthen'd, or shorten'd, to rise or fall from one Tone or Interval to another. ¶ The Bell-founders have likewise a

Diapason, or Scale, serving to regulate the Size, Thickness, Weight, *&c.* of their Bells. See *Bell-Foundery*. **1737** BAILEY *The Univ. Etymolog. Engl. Dict.* (3rd edn, vol. 2) *Diapason* (of δια and πασῶν, all, *Gr.*) a chord in musick including all tones, and is the same with what is commonly called an octave or eighth; because there is but seven tone notes, and then the eighth is the same again with the first. It is the most perfect concord, and the terms of it are as two to one. **1737** DYCHE-PARDON (2nd edn) *Diapason* (.S [sic]) that Interval in *Musick* called an Octave; those Authors who have wrote on this Science, mean the old Octave of the *Greeks*. It is the first and most perfect Concord; simply considered, it is but one harmonical Interval; but diatonically, it consists of several Degrees, *viz.* three greater Tones, two lesser Tones, and two greater Semitones.

1603 ROBINSON *Schoole of Mvsicke* [B ii] [*re* strings of the lute] Againe if you haue 14. 16. or 18. strings, those bases are called *Diapasones* ... § [N] [*re* rules for singing] First, you shall vnderstand, that all that is to be done in song, is within the compasse of an eight, called a *Diapason*, for what is aboue an eight, is but a repetition of the same notes which you vttered before, in the eight notes of your *Gam-vt*. **1609** DOWLAND-ORNITHOPARCUS *Micrologvs* (p. 19) *Diapason.* ¶ ... It is a distance of one Voyce from another by an eight, consisting of fiue *Tones*, and two lesser *semitones*. **1617-24** FLUDD *Utriusque Cosmi Maioris: De Templo Musicæ* (p. 183) *Diapason* est quædam consonantia composita ex unione Diatessaron & Diapente simul, vel quæ inter duos æquisonos à qualibet litera ad literam consimilem elevatur & ponitur ... **1636** BUTLER *Principles of Musik* (p. 47) *Diapason* is a perfect Eight, conteining a *Diapente*, and a *Diatessaron*; or 5 whole Tones and 2 Hemitones: (i. all the 7 Naturall Sounds or Notes besides the Ground;) or briefly All the 12 Simple Intervalls: (whereof it hath his name) as from *Ut* to *Ut*, from *Re* to *Re*, or from any Note in any Clief to the same Note in the same Clief, in the next Septenari. **1664** BIRCHENSHA-ALSTED *Templvm Mvsicvm* (p. 93) The *Diapente* is the skipping of a Voice from a Voice by a Fifth: called vulgarly *Quadrimode* and *Quinta*. As between *vt sol. re la. mi mi. fa fa.* **1665** SIMPSON *Division-Viol* (2nd edn, p. 14) An Octave is divided into Perfect, called *Diapason*, and Imperfect called *Semediapason*. **1694** HOLDER *Treatise of Natural Grounds* (pp. 52-3) The System of an Eighth, containing seven Intervals, or Spaces, or Degrees, and eight Notes reckoned inclusively, as expressed by eight Chords, is called Diapason, *i.e.* a System of all intermediate Concords ... § (p. 177) ... *Diapason*, being the compleat System, containing all primary Simple *Harmonic* Intervals that are; (and for that reason called *Diapason*;) ... **c.1710** NORTH (draft for) Musicall Grammarian BL Add. 32537, f. 131 [*re* considerations as to the choice of pipes to be used in organs] And of them one is the difference, between a pipe open and stopt, w[ch] organ maker's call diapason's, and are the most usefull pipes y[t] can be Imployed. **1721** MALCOLM *Treatise of Musick* (p. 507) ... and the *Octave* 1:2, which they [the ancient Greeks] called *Dia-pason*; ...

diapasondiaex

1728 CHAMBERS *Diapasondiaex*, in Music, a Kind of compound Concord; whereof there are two Sorts: The greater, which is in the Proportion of 10 to 3; and the less, in that of 16 to 5. See *Concord*. **1730** BAILEY *Dict. Britannicum* (1st edn) *Diapasondiaex* (with *Musicians*) a sort of compound concord, either as 10 to 3, or as 16 to 5. **1737** DYCHE-PARDON (2nd edn) *Diapasondiaex* (S.) in *Musick*, a compound Concord, in Proportion, as 10 to 3, or 16 to 5.

diapason diapente

1728 CHAMBERS *Diapasondiapente*, in Music, a compound Consonance, in the Triple Ratio, or as 3 to 9. See *Concord*. ¶ The *Diapason-diapente* is a Symphony made when the Voice proceeds from the 1st to the 12th Tone. ¶ The Word is properly a Term in the *Greek* Music: We should now call it a *Twelfth*. **1730** BAILEY *Dict. Britannicum* (1st edn) *Diapasondiapente*, a compound consonance in the triple ratio, or as 3 to 9. **1737** DYCHE-PARDON (2nd edn) *Diapasondiapente* (S.) in *Musick*, a compound Consonance, in Ratio, as 3 to 9.

1609 DOWLAND-ORNITHOPARCUS *Micrologvs* (p. 21) *Diapason Diapente.* ¶ Is a consonance of twelue *sounds*, and eleuen *Interuals*, consisting of eight *Tones*, and three *semitones*. The examples of these *Moodes* are verie rarely seene in plaine Song; in mensurall often.

diapason diatessaron

1728 CHAMBERS *Diapasondiatessaron*, in Music, a compound Concord, founded on the Proportion of 8 to 3. ¶ The *Diapason-diatessaron* is a Symphony, wherein the Voice proceeds from its first Tone to its eleventh. This the Moderns would rather call the *Eleventh*. **1730** BAILEY *Dict. Britannicum* (1st edn)

Diapasondiatessaron, a compounded concord, founded on the proportion of 8 to 3. **1737** DYCHE-PARDON (2nd edn) *Diapasondiatessaron* (S.) in *Musick*, a compound Concord, in Ratio, as 8 to 3.

diapason ditone

1728 CHAMBERS *Diapasonditone*, in Music, a Concord, whose Terms are in the Proportion of 10 to 4, or 5 to 2. **1730** BAILEY *Dict. Britannicum* (1st edn) *Diapasonditone*, a concord, the terms of which are in the proportion of 5 to 2. **1737** DYCHE-PARDON (2nd edn) *Diapasonditone* (S.) in *Musick*, a Concord, in Proportion, as 5 to 2.

diapason semiditone *see* semiditone diapason

diapente *see* fifth, hypodiapente, quinta, semidiapente, tonus diapente

1500 *Ortus Vocabulorum* L→E Diapente. cantus constans ex quinque sonis. **1589** RIDER L→E *Diapente*. A concord in musick, ¶ Of 3. notes, & a halfe, called a fift. **1659** TORRIANO-FLORIO It→E *Diapente*, ... in Musick it is one tone and a half. **1661** BLOUNT (2nd edn) *Diapente* (Gr.) a concord in Musick called a fifth. **1671** PHILLIPS (3rd edn) *Diapente*, a certain Chord in Musick vulgarly call'd a fifth: **1704** HARRIS *Diapente*, (an Interval of *Musick*) whose Terms are as 3 to 2. It being the second of the Concords, and makes an *Octave* with the *Diatessaron*; it is otherwise called a *perfect Fifth*. **1706** KERSEY-PHILLIPS (6th edn) *Diapente* (in *Musick*) the second of the Concords, whose Terms are as Three to Two. It is otherwise call'd a *Perfect Fifth*, and makes up an *Octavo* with the *Diatessaron*; **1707** *Gloss. Angl. Nova* (1st edn) *Diapente*, (Gr.) a Term in Musick, its Terms are as 3 to 2. **1721** BAILEY *An Univ. Etymolog. Engl. Dict.* (1st edn) *Diapedesis* [sic], (διαπήδησις, *Gr.*) is a Second of the Concords in Musick, called a *Perfect Fifth*. **1728** CHAMBERS *Diapente*, in the ancient Music, an Interval making the Second of the Concords; and with the *Diatessaron*, and Octave. ¶ This is what in the modern Music we more usually call a *Fifth*. See *Fifth*. ¶ The *Diapente* is a simple Concord; yet if consider'd Diatonically, it contains four Terms, two greater Tones, a lesser Tone, and a greater Semi-tone. The *Diapente* is the greatest Part of the Diapason, or Octave, harmonically divided. It is produced when the Voice passes from its first Tone to its fifth. **1737** DYCHE-PARDON (2nd edn) *Diapente* (S.) ... and in *Musick*, it is usually called a fifth; *diatonically* considered, it consists of two greater Tones, a lesser Tone, and a Semitone, otherwise it is but a simple Concord.

1609 DOWLAND-ORNITHOPARCUS *Micrologvs* (p. 18) *Diapente*. ¶ Is a Consonance of fiue *Voyces*, and 4. *Interuals*, as saith *Boêtius lib*. 1. *cap*. 18. Or it is the leaping of one *Voyce* to another by a fift, consisting of three *Tones*, and a *semitone*. It hath foure kinds in *Boêtius lib*. 4. *cap*. 13. Therefore *Pontifex* cals it the *Quadri-moode Interuall*. The first, is from *vt* to *sol*; the second, from *re* to *la*; the third, from *mi* to *mi*; the fourth, from *fa* to *fa*. **1617-24** FLUDD *Utriusque Cosmi Maioris: De Templo Musicæ* (p. 183) *Diapente* est quædam consonantia, quæ inter duas voces, tres continet tonos cum semitonio intermixtos ... **1636** BUTLER *Principles of Musik* (p. 47) *Diapente* is a perfect Fift, or 3 Tones and a Hemitone: as from *Vt* to *Sol*, from *Re* to *La*, from *Fa* to *Ut*. § (p. 49) ... that which conteineth 5 is called a *Diapente* or a fift. **1665** SIMPSON *Division-Viol* (2nd edn, p. 14) A Fifth is divided into Perfect and Imperfect; the former is called *Diapente*, the later *Semediapente*; a false Fifth.

diaphonicks

1737 DYCHE-PARDON (2nd edn) *Diaphonicks* (S.) that Part of the Science of *Musick* that treats of the Properties of refracted Sounds, as they pass thro' different Mediums.

diaphony

1500 *Ortus Vocabulorum* L→E Diaphonia nie. est dissonantia vocum a dyuerse sownde f.p. Diaphonista diaphoniste. qui facit diaphoniam com. p. **1538** ELYOT L→E *Diaphonia*, a discorde. **1565** COOPER L→E *Diaphonia*. A discorde. **1587** THOMAS L→E *Diaphonia, æ, f.g. Isid.* A discorde. **1598** FLORIO It→E *Diafonia*, a discord. **1611** FLORIO It→E *Diafonia*, discord, iarring. **1656** BLOUNT (1st edn) *Diaphony (diaphonia)* a divers sound, a discord. *Diaphonist (diaphonista)* he that makes divers sounds. **1658** PHILLIPS (1st edn) *Diaphony*, (Greek) a harsh sound, a sound which maketh a discord. **1659** TORRIANO-FLORIO It→E *Diafonia*, a discord or jarring. **1676** COLES *Diaphonist*, he that makes a ¶ *Diaphony*, a discord or harsh sound. **1706** KERSEY-PHILLIPS (6th edn) *Diaphonia* (in *Musick*) a harsh Sound, a Sound that makes a Discord. **1737** DYCHE-PARDON (2nd edn) *Diaphonia* (S.) a musical Term for a disagreeable or harsh Sound, commonly called Discord;

1721 MALCOLM *Treatise of Musick* (p. 508) ... all [ancient Greek writers] agree to call the Discords *Diaphoni*.

diapsalma *see* psalm, selah

1500 *Ortus Vocabulorum* L→E Diaplasma [sic] me. i. diuisio psalmi f.p. Diapsalma e. idem est f.p. **1587** THOMAS L→E *Diapsalma, atis. Heron. Commutatio rythmi, aut vicissitudo canendi.* **1706** KERSEY-PHILLIPS (6th edn) *Diapsalma,* a Pause or change of Note in singing. **1708** KERSEY *Dict. Anglo-Brit.* (1st edn) *Diapsalma,* a Pause or change of Note in singing.

diaschisma *see* schism

1582 *Batman vppon Bartholome* (p. 422) *Diacesma* is a couena[---] space of two voyces, or of mo [sic] according. **1617-24** FLUDD *Utriusque Cosmi Maioris: De Templo Musicæ* (p. 182) *Diaschisma* est dimidium semitonii majoris, id est, Diesis est illud spatium, vel illa toni pars, quæ semitonium minus dicitur. **1636** BUTLER *Principles of Musik* (p. 23) [quoting Boethius:] *Diaschisma est dimidium Diesios.* i. *Semitonii minoris.*

diastaltic

1694 HOLDER *Treatise of Natural Grounds* (pp. 198-9) Lastly, A mixture of these [sharp and flat keys], with a suitable *Rhythmus,* gently fix the Spirits, and compose them in a middle Way: Wherefore the First of these is called by the Greeks *Diastaltic,* Dilating; the second, *Systaltic,* Contracting; the last, *Hesychiastic,* Appeasing.

diastem *see* genus, interval

1728 CHAMBERS *Diastem,* in Musick, a Name the Ancients gave to a simple Interval; in Contra-distinction to a compound Interval, which they call'd a *System.* See *Interval.* ¶ Musicians divide Intervals into two Kinds: One of them [is] call'd *System,* which is to contain at least two Intervals in any Kind of Music whatever; but many, contain more. ¶ The other, call'd *Diastem,* is a mere, or single Interval; The Proper Signification of the *Greek* διάστημα being *Interval.* See *System.* **1730** BAILEY *Dict. Britannicum* (1st edn) *Diastem* (in *Ancient Musick*) a name given to a simple interval, in contradistinction to a compound interval, which they call a *System.*

1694 HOLDER *Treatise of Natural Grounds* (pp. 144-6) I shall only add a word or two concerning their [the Greeks'] Antient use of the Words *Diastem* and *System. Diastem* signifies an Interval or Space; *System* a Conjunction or Composition of Intervals. So that generally speaking, an *Octave,* or any other *System,* might be truly called a *Diastem,* and very frequently used to be so called, where there was no occasion of Distinction. Though a *Tone,* or *Hemitone,* could not be called a *System*: For when they spoke strictly, by a *Diastem* they understood only an Incomposit Degree, whether *Diesis, Hemitone, Tone, Sesquitone,* or *Ditone;* for the two last were sometimes but Degrees, one *Enharmonic,* the other *Chromatic.* By *System* they meant, a Comprehensive Interval, compounded of Degrees, or of less *Systems,* or of both. Thus a *Tone* was a *Diastem,* and *Diatessaron* was a *System,* compounded of Degrees, or of a 3d. and a Degree. *Diapason* was a *System,* compounded of the lesser *Systems,* 4th, and 5th; or 3d. and 6th; or of a Scale of Degrees: and the *Scale* of Notes which they used, was their Greatest, or Perfect *System.* Thus with them, a 3d. *Major,* and a 3d. *Minor,* in the *Diatonic Genus,* were (properly speaking) *Systems;* the former being compounded of two *Tones,* and the latter of three *Hemitones,* or a *Tone* and *Hemitone*: But in the *Enharmonic* Kind, a *Ditone* was not a *System,* but an Incomposit Degree; which, added to two *Dieses,* made up the *Diatessaron*: And in the *Chromatic* Kind, a *Trihemitone* was the like; being only an Incomposit *Diastem,* and not a *System.* **1721** MALCOLM *Treatise of Musick* (p. 252) In Ch. 2. § 1. [p. 39] I have defined a *Diastem,* such an Interval as in Practice is never divided, tho' there may be of these some greater some lesser. To understand the Definition perfectly, take now an *Example* in the *diatonick Scale*: A *Semitone* is less than a *Tone,* and both are *Diastems;* we may raise a *Tone* by *Degrees,* first raising a *Semitone,* and then such a Distance as a *Tone* exceeds a *Semitone,* which we may call another *Semitone, i.e.* from *a* to *b* a *Semitone,* and then from *b* to *c* the Remainder of a *Tone* which is supposed betwixt *a c.* § (p. 510) The *simple Intervals* are called *Diastems,* which are different according to the *Genera* ... § (p. 518) Now, these Parts of the *Diatessaron* are what they called the *Diastems* of the several *Genera,* upon which their Differences depend: Which are called in the *Enharm.* the *Diesis* and *Ditonum;* in the *Chromatick,* the *Hemitonium* and *Triemitonium;* in the *Diaton.* the *Hemitonium* (or *Limma*) and the *Tonus;* but under these general Names, which distinguish the *Genera,* there are several different *Intervals* or *Ratios,* which constitute the *colores generum,* or Species of *Enharm. Chrom.* and *Diatonick,* as we have seen: ...

diastema

1598 FLORIO It→E *Diastema,* a distance or space, a word vsed in musicke. **1611** FLORIO It→E *Diastema,* a distance or space in Musicke. **1659** TORRIANO-FLORIO It→E *Diastasi, Diastema,* a certain distance, space, or pause in musick.

diatessaron *see* fourth, quarte, semidiatessaron

1500 *Ortus Vocabulorum* L→E Diatessaron. idest cantus constans ex quatuor sonis **1552** HULOET L→E *Diatesseron.* Concorde in musycke of eyght tunes. **1589** RIDER L→E *Diatessaron.* A concord in musick, ¶ Of 2. and a halfe called a fourth. **1656** BLOUNT (1st edn) *Diatessaron* (Gr.) ... a fourth in musick. **1658** PHILLIPS (1st edn) *Diatesseron,* (Greek) one of the chief Chords in Musick, called a fourth **1661** BLOUNT (2nd edn) *Diatessaron* (Gr.) ... a concord in Musick called a *Fourth,* whereof there are four in the Scale, which compriseth fifteen strings. **1676** COLES *Diatessaron,* a fourth (in musick,) **1704** *Cocker's Engl. Dict.* (1st edn) *Diatesseron,* a fourth Concord in Musick **1704** HARRIS *Diatessaron,* (a Word used in Musick) signifying an Interval composed of one greater *Tone,* one lesser, and one greater Semi *Tone;* its proportion being as 4 to 3. In Musical Composition it is called a *Perfect Fourth.* **1706** KERSEY-PHILLIPS (6th edn) *Diatessaron* (in *Musick*) a Chord or Interval, consisting of one greater *Tone,* one lesser, and one greater *Semi-tone*: In Musical Composition 'tis call'd a *perfect Fourth,* and its Terms of Proportion are as Four to Three. **1707** *Gloss. Angl. Nova* (1st edn) *Diatessaron,* a word used in Musick, to denote an Interval composed of a greater and a lesser Tone, the Ratio whereof is that of 4 to 3. **1728** CHAMBERS *Diatessaron,* in the ancient Music, was a Concord or harmonical Interval, composed of one greater Tone, one lesser, and one greater Semi-tone; Its Proportion being as 4 to 3. See *Concord.* ¶ In the modern Music, it is call'd a perfect *Fourth.* See *Fourth.* **1737** DYCHE-PARDON (2nd edn) *Diatessaron* (S.) ... but in *Musick,* it is a Concord composed of a greater and a lesser Tone.

1609 DOWLAND-ORNITHOPARCUS *Micrologvs* (p. 18) *Diatessaron.* ¶ In *Boêtius lib.* 1. *cap* 17. It is a *Consonance* of 4. *Voyces,* and 3. *Interuals.* Or it is the leaping from one *Voyce* to another by a Fourth, consisting of two *Tones,* and a lesser *semitone.* It hath three kinds in *Boêtius lib.* 4. *cap.* 13. and in *Pontifex cap.* 8. the first is from *vt* to *fa,* the second from *re* to *sol,* the third from *mi* to *fa.* **1617-24** FLUDD *Utriusque Cosmi Maioris: De Templo Musicæ* (p. 183) *Diatessaron* est consonantia, quæ continet in se Ditonum cum Semitonio ... **1636** BUTLER *Principles of Musik* (p. 47) *Diatessaron* is a Fowre, of 2 Tones and a Hemitone: as from *Ut* to *Fa,* from *Re* to *Sol,* from *Mi* to *La,* &c. § (p. 49) ... That therefore which conteineth 4 is called a *Diatessaron* or a Fourth: ... **1664** BIRCHENSHA-ALSTED *Templvm Mvsicvm* (p. 93) A *Diatessaron* is the leaping from a Voice into a Voice by a fourth. As is between *vt fa. re sol.* and *mi la.* otherwise called a fourth. **1721** MALCOLM *Treatise of Musick* (p. 504) Particularly, he [Aristoxenus] calls *Diatessaron* equal to Two *Tones* and a Half; and taking Two *Tones,* or *Ditonum,* out of *Diatessaron,* the Remainder is the *Hemitonium;* then the Sum of *Tonus* and *Hemitonium* is the *Triemitonium.* § (p. 507) ... *viz.* the *Fourth* 3:4, and *Fifth* 2:3 called [by the ancient Greeks] *Dia-tessaron* and *Diapente* ...

diatonic *see* degree, diagram, genus, natural, scale, species, tone

1598 FLORIO It→E *Diatonico,* a certain concord in musicke, or plaine song betweene two. *Diatono,* D sol re, or G sol re ut. a plaine song betweene two. **1611** FLORIO It→E *Diatonico,* a concord in Musicke or plain song betweene two. *Diatono,* D sol re, or G sol re ut. Also a plaine song betweene two. **1704** HARRIS *Diatonick,* a Term which signifies the Ordinary sort of Musick which proceeds by different Tones, either in ascending or descending; it contains only the two greater and lesser Tones, and the greater Semi-tone. **1706** KERSEY-PHILLIPS (6th edn) *Diatonick,* belonging to plain Song. **1707** *Gloss. Angl. Nova* (1st edn) *Diatonick,* a Term which signifies the ordinary sort of Musick, proceeding by different Tones, either in ascending or descending. **1728** CHAMBERS *Diatonic,* an Epithet given the common Music, as it proceeds by different Tones, or Degrees, both ascending, and descending. See *Music,* and *Genera.* ¶ Authors divide the Sorts of Music into *Diatonic, Chromatic,* and *Enharmonic.* **1737** BAILEY *The Univ. Etymolog. Engl. Dict.* (3rd edn, vol. 2) *Diatonick* (of διά and τόνος, *Gr.*) as diatonick musick, which see [entry follows that of 1730 Bailey below]. **1737** DYCHE-PARDON (2nd edn) *Diatonick* (A.) an Epithet given to the common Musick, as it proceeds by different Tones both ascending and descending. This Kind of Musick allows of but three Degrees, *viz.* the greater and the lesser Tone, and the greater Semitone.

1597 MORLEY *Plaine and Easie Introdvction* (annotations to Part I) *Diatonicum,* is that [kind of music] which is now in vse, & riseth throughout the scale by a whole, not a whole note and a lesse halfe note (a whole note is that which the Latines call *integer tonus*, and is that distance which is betwixt any two notes, exeept [sic] *mi* & *fa*. For betwixt *mi* and *fa* is not a full halfe note, but is lesse than halfe a note by a *comma*: and therfore called the lesse halfe note) in this maner. **early 18th C.** ANON. Essay on Musick BODLEIAN Rawl. D. 751, f. 2v Hitherto the system was purely *diatonick*; that is to say compos'd of tones & semitones ...

diatonic music

1661 BLOUNT (2nd edn) *Diatonick Musick* (*diatonum*) keeps a mean temperature between *Chromatic*, and *Enharmoniac*; and may go for plain Song. **1671** PHILLIPS (3rd edn) *Diatonic* musick, see *Enharmonic*. **1676** COLES *Diatonick musick*, plain-song **1704** *Cocker's Engl. Dict.* (1st edn) *Diatonick Musick* plain Song. **1706** KERSEY-PHILLIPS (6th edn) *Diatonick Musick*, one of the three ancient Methods of Singing, and the most natural, in regard that it makes easy intervals, which render it more plain and familiar than the others; See *Chromatick* and *Enharmonick*. **1721** BAILEY *An Univ. Etymolog. Engl. Dict.* (1st edn) *Diatonick Musick*, one of the 3 ancient Methods of Singing. **1728** CHAMBERS *Diatonic Music* only allows of three Degrees; the greater and lesser Tone, and the greater Semi-tone. See *Tone*, and *Degree*. ¶ Hence *Diatonic Music* appears the most natural, and of Consequence is the most ancient. The *Genus*, or Kind, which makes the Character of the *Diatonic Music*, is call'd the *Diatonic Kind*, or *Genus*. ¶ In the *Diatonic Music* there is a Tone between every two Notes, except between *Mi* and *Fa*, and *Si* and *Ut*, where there is only a greater Semi-tone. See *Scale*. **1730** BAILEY *Dict. Britannicum* (1st edn) *Diatonick Musick*, a Musick proceeding by different Tones, either in ascending or descending: This the Antients admitted.

1721 MALCOLM *Treatise of Musick* (pp. 250-1) This *Scale* [of music or 'Natural Scale'] not only shews us, by what *Degrees* a Voice can move agreeably, but gives us also this *general Rule*, that *Two Degrees* of one Kind ought never to follow other[s] immediately in a progressive Motion upwards or downwards; and that no more than Three *Tones* (whereof the middle is a lesser *Tone*, and the other Two greater *Tones*) can follow other, but a *s.* or some *harmonical Interval* must come next; and every *Song* or *Composition* within this *Rule* is particularly called *diatonick Musick*, from the *Scale* whence this *Rule* arises; and from the Effect we may also call it the only *natural Musick*: ... § (p. 282) ... *Musick* composed under the Limitations of that *Scale* [i.e. the diatonic scale] is called *diatonick Musick*.

diatonic scale *see* diastem, key, natural scale

1667 SIMPSON *Compendium of Practical Musick* (p. 97) The *Diatonick* Scale, is that which rises to a 5*th*. by three *Tones* and a *Semitone*; and from thence to the 8*th*. by two *Tones* and one *Semitone*: ... **1721** MALCOLM *Treatise of Musick* (p. 247) As to the Order in which the *Degrees* of this *Scale* follow, we have this to remark, that if either Series, (*viz*. that with the 3*d l*. or with the 3*d g*.) be continued *in infinitum*, the Two *Semitones* that fall naturally in the Division of the 8*ve*, are always asunder 2 *Tones* and 3 *Tones* alternately, *i.e.* after a *Semitone* come 2 *Tones*, then a *Semitone*, and then 3 *Tones*; and of the Two *Tones* one is a greater and the other a lesser; of the Three, one is lesser in the middle betwixt Two greater. If you continue either Series to a double *Octave*, and mark the *Degrees*, all this will be evident. *Observe* also, that this is the *Scale* which the *Ancients* called the *Diatonick Scale*, because it proceeds by these *Degrees* called *Tones* (whereof there are Five in an 8*ve*) and *Semitones* (whereof there are *Two* in an *Octave*) But we call it also the *Natural Scale*, because its *Degrees* and their Order are the most agreeable and *concinnous*, and preferable, by the Approbation both of Sense and Reason, to all other Divisions that have ever been instituted... I shall always call this, *The Scale of Musick*, without Distinction, as 'tis the only true *natural System*. **1726** JACKSON *Preliminary Discourse to a Scheme* (p. 37) The Diatonick Scale, (which signifies a Scale of Plain Song) is the common Scale now in Use and consists of *seven* Parts, or Intervals of Sound contain'd within an Octave; five of which are distinguish'd by the Name of Tones, Three greater and Two lesser, otherwise expressed by *Major* and *Minor*; and Two Semitones or half Notes; ... **1728** NORTH Musicall Grammarian (*C-K MG* f. 110) The tetrachords, or scales of musicall tones were three ... One of these scales was called the diatonick, and for degrees [upward] hath a semitone, and two tones to come at the fourth...

diatonic system *see* system

1731 PRELLEUR *Modern Musick-Master* ('A Brief History of Musick', p. 7) [*re* ancient Greek music] This is the ancient *Diatonical System*, so call'd by reason of its consisting of none but whole *Tones* and *Semitones major*; according to which any one who has a tollerable good Ear and an Indifferent good voice may tune to a very great nicety by the help of nature only.

diatonos

1706 KERSEY-PHILLIPS (6th edn) *Diatonos Hypaton*, the Musical Note call'd *D-sol-re* *Diatonos Meson* *G-sol-re-ut*.

diatonum

1500 *Ortus Vocabulorum* L→E Diatorium [sic] dicitur genus modorum in musica n.s.

1721 MALCOLM *Treatise of Musick* (p. 516) As to the Names of the *Genera* themselves, ... The *Diatonum*, [was so called by the ancient Greeks] because the *Tones* prevail in it.

diatonum diatonicum *see* colores generum

1706 KERSEY-PHILLIPS (6th edn) *Diatonum Diatonicum*, a kind of Song which proceeds by different Tones, and Semi-tones, either in ascending or descending, being more Natural and less forced than the other sorts of Musick; Plain Song. **1708** KERSEY *Dict. Anglo-Brit.* (1st edn) *Diatonum* or *Diatonicum*, a kind of Song which proceeds by different Tones, and Semi-tones; Plain Song.

diatonum ditonum

1698 WALLIS *Letter to Samuel Pepys* (*Philos. Trans.*, 1698, p. 252) ... And this is what *Ptolemy* calls *Diatonum Ditonum*, (of the *Diatonick* kind with *Two full Tones*.)

diatonum intensum *see* colores generum

1698 WALLIS *Letter to Samuel Pepys* (*Philos. Trans.*, 1698, p. 252) ... *Ptolemy's Diatonum Intensum* (of the *Diatonick* Kind, more *Intense* or Acute than that other.)

diazeutick tone

1721 BAILEY *An Univ. Etymolog. Engl. Dict.* (1st edn) *Diazeutick Tone*, in the Ancient Greek Musick, was that which disjoined two Fourths each on one side of it, and which being join'd to either, made a Fifth. **1728** CHAMBERS *Diazeutic Tone*, in the ancient *Greek* Music, was that which disjoyn'd two Fourths, one on each Side of it, and which being joyn'd to either, made a Fifth. This, in their Music was from *Mese* to *Paramese*; that is, in ours, from A to B: Supposing *Mi* to stand in B *sub Mi*. They allowed to this *Diazeutic Tone*, which is our *La*, *Mi*, the Proportion of 9 to 8, as being the unalterable Difference of *Diapente* and *Diatessaron*.

1721 MALCOLM *Treatise of Musick* (p. 512) ... Thus the Sum of *4th* and *5th* is an *Octave*, and their Difference is a *Tonus*; if therefore to the same Fundamental, suppose *a*, we take a *4th b*, *5th c*, and *8ve d*, then also *b-d* is a *5th*, and *c-d* a *4th*, and *b:c* [sic] is the *Tonus*; which they [the ancient Greeks] called particularly the *Tonus diazeucticus*, because it separates or stands in the Middle betwixt Two *4ths*, one on either Hand, *a-b*, and *c-d*.

diazeuxis

1731 PRELLEUR *Modern Musick-Master* ('A Brief History of Musick', p. 8) [*re* the ancient diatonic system] *Diaseuxis* signifies *Disjunction* or *Seperation* [sic] and is when two *Tetrachords* are not joyned by the same note but both together make an Octave, as it happens in the *Tetrachords*; *Dieseugmenon* and *Meson* ...

diesis *see* enharmonic, feint, sharp

1587 THOMAS L→E *Diesis, Vitru.* The quarter of a tune, or the halfe of halfe a tune. **1589** RIDER L→E *Diesis*. The quarter of a tune. **1598** FLORIO It→E *Diesi, Diepsi*, the quarter of a tune, the halfe of halfe a tune in musicke. **1611** COTGRAVE Fr→E *Diése: f.* A sharpe, in Musicke. **1611** FLORIO It→E *Diesi*, as *Diepsi*. *Diepsi*, the halfe of halfe a tune. **1659** TORRIANO-FLORIO It→E *Diepsi, Diesi*, ... also half of half a tune, the quarter of a tune. **1696** PHILLIPS (5th edn) *Diesis*, a Sharp in Musick marked thus ✖. **1704** HARRIS *Diesis*, in Musick, is the Division of a Tone below a Semi-tone, or an Interval composed of a lesser or Imperfect Semi-tone: so that when Semi-tones are placed where there ought to be Tones or when a Tone is set, where there should be only a Semi-tone, this is called *Diesis*. ¶ *Enharmonical Diesis* is the Difference between the Greater, and the Lesser Semi-tone. ¶ These *Diesis*, are the least sensible Divisions of a Tone, and are mark'd on the Score in form of St. *Andrews* Cross. **1706** KERSEY-PHILLIPS (6th edn) *Diesis* (*Gr.* in *Musick*) is the Division of a Tone below a Semi-tone, or an Interval made up of a lesser or Imperfect Semi-tone: So that when Semi-tones are plac'd where there ought to be Tones; or when a Tone is set, where there should be only a Semi-tone, this is call'd Diesis. **1707** *Gloss. Angl. Nova* (1st edn) *Diesis*, a Term in Musick. **1708** KERSEY *Dict. Anglo-Brit.* (1st edn) § *Enharmonical Diesis*, is the Difference between the greater and the lesser Semitone. **1721** BAILEY *An Univ. Etymolog. Engl. Dict.* (1st edn) *Diesis*, (διεσίς, *Gr.*) a Term in Musick, denoting a Tone below a Semi-tone. § *Diesis Enharmonical*, is the difference between the Greater and the Lesser Semi-tone. **1724** [PEPUSCH] *Short Explic. of Foreign Words in Mus. Bks.* (p. 27) *Diesis*, a Sharp, which is a Character in Musick well known. **1728** CHAMBERS *Diesis*, in Music, a Division of a Tone, lesser than a Semi-tone; or an Interval consisting of a lesser, or imperfect Semi-tone. See *Tone.* ¶ The *Diesis* is the smallest, and softest Change, or Inflexion of the Voice imaginable. It is also call'd a *Feint*, and express'd by a St. *Andrew*'s Cross, or Saltier. ¶ *Aristotle* calls *Dieses* the Elements of Voice, as Letters are those of Discourse. Indeed, *Aristotle*'s *Dieses* were apparently different from ours: And we find *Vitruvius* expressly making the *Diesis* a fourth Part of a Tone. But the *Phythagoreans*, who are held the Inventors of the Name *Diesis*, did not make it so small; they only divided the Tone into two unequal Parts, and call'd the lesser *Diesis*, which we call the lesser Semi-tone; and the greater, which we call the greater Semi-tone, they call'd *Anatome*. See *Semitone.* ¶ But in After-times, when the Tone came to be divided into three and four Parts, the Name *Diesis* was retain'd to them all. And hence those different Accounts we meet withal in Authors, of the Quantity of the *Diesis*. ¶ The *Enharmonical Diesis* is the Difference between a greater, and lesser Semi-tone. ¶ *Dieses* are divided into three Kinds: The *Lesser Enharmonick Diesis*, or *Simple Diesis*, denoted by a single Cross, raises the Note following by two Comma's, or about $\frac{1}{4}$ of a Tone: The *Chromatic*, or *double Diesis*, denoted by a double Cross, raises the following Note by a lesser Semi-tone, or about 4 Comma's; which is the common *Diesis*: The *Greater Enharmonical Diesis*, denoted by a triple Cross, raises the Note by 6, or 7 Comma's, or about $\frac{3}{4}$ of a Tone. None but the *double Diesis* is used in [modern] Music. A Flat is frequently used to take away the *Diesis*, and a *Diesis* to take away a Flat. ¶ When Semi-tones are placed where regular Tones should be; or a Tone where there should be a Semi-tone, it is call'd a *Diesis*, or a *Feint*. **1730** BAILEY *Dict. Britannicum* (1st edn) *Diesises* are the least sensible divisions of a tone, and are marked on the score in the form of St. *Andrew*'s-cross. **1736** BAILEY *Dict. Britannicum* (2nd edn) *Diesis* (in *Musick*) is the division of a tone below a semi-tone, or an interval, consisting of a lower or imperfect semi-tone, *i.e.* the placing of a tone where there ought to be only a semi-tone. **1737** DYCHE-PARDON (2nd edn) *Diesis* (S.) in *Musick*, an Interval consisting of a lesser or Semi-tone.

1582 *Batman vppon Bartholome* (p. 422) *Diesis* is the space of doing of melody, and chaunging out of one sound into another. **1597** MORLEY *Plaine and Easie Introdvction* (annotations to Part I) ... *diesis* is halfe of *Semitonium minus*, whose signe was made thus ✕. **1636** BUTLER *Principles of Musik* (p. 23) *Diesis (inquit Philolaus) est spatium, quo major est Sesquitertia proportio duobus Tonis.* Bothe which hee doeth afterward describe by the number of Comma's. **c.1702** ANON. Practicall Theory of Musick BL Add. 4919, ff. 4v-5 ... learned antiquity descended to a further Division of these [notes of the diatonic and chromatic scales] into quarter Notes which were produced out of the Chromatick half Notes, after the same manner as these were derived from the whole Notes. Which least divisions of all, were called Dieses & constituted the Species of Enharmonick Musick.

diezeugmenon *see* diagram, scale

1706 KERSEY-PHILLIPS (6th edn) *Diezeugmenon nete* (in *Musick*) the Note call'd *E-la-mi*. *Diezeugmenon paranete D-la-sol-re.*

early 18th C. PEPUSCH various papers BL Add. 29429, f. 6 Diezeugmenon, i.e. disjoins (: Tetr:) Diazeuxis, i.e. Disjunction **1731** PRELLEUR *Modern Musick-Master* ('A Brief History of Musick', p. 6) *Explanation of the Names by which the* Greeks *used to Distinguish their Notes....* The next *Tetrachord* is called *Tetracordon Dieseugmenon*, that is to say *Tetrachord of the Separated* by reason of its not being joyned to another at the lowest String as the former is. The lowest String of this *Tetrachord* they called *Paramese* which signifies *near* or *next the Mean*; this answers to *B-fa-b-mi.* ¶ The next was called *Trite Dieseugmenon* or the *third Separated*, & answers to *C-sol-fa-ut* the Tenor Cliff. ¶ The next was called *Paranete Dieseugemenon* or *Dieseugemenon Diatonos* which signifies the *last but one of the Separated*, this Note answers to our *D-la-sol-re*. The highest string of this *Tetrachord* was called *Nete-Dieseugmenon*, i.e. *the last of the Separated*: This Note answers to our *E-la-mi* two Notes above the Tenor Cliff, or two Notes below the Treble Cliff.

diligenza

1736 TANS'UR *Compleat Melody* (3rd edn, p. 67) *Con Diligenza, Discerto* [sic], *Timoroso.* (Ital.) Either of those *Terms*, denote that you must *sing*, or *play* with Care, Diligence, and Exactness.

diminished flat seventh

1731 [PEPUSCH] *Treatise on Harmony* (2nd edn, p. 2) ... the Extreme-flat *Seventh*, otherwise call'd the *Diminish'd-flat Seventh*.

diminished interval

1728 CHAMBERS *Diminish'd Interval*, in Music, is a defective Interval, or an Interval which is short of its just Quantity by a lesser Semi-tone. See *Interval*, and *Semi-tone*. ¶ A *diminish'd Interval* is mark'd with a flat, or a double *Diesis*. **1730** BAILEY *Dict. Britannicum* (1st edn) *Diminished Interval* (in *Musick*) a deficient interval, or one which is short of its just quantity by a lesser semitone.

diminuendo

c.1710 ANON. *Preceptor for Improved Octave Flageolet* ('Explanation of Words', p. 82) *Diminuendo*—To decrease the Sound

diminution *see* division, fugue, group, note

1611 COTGRAVE Fr→E *Diminutions*. Diuision (in Musicke.) **1704** HARRIS *Diminution*, in Musick, is nothing else but the diminishing or abating somewhat of the full Value or Quantity of any *Note*. **1706** KERSEY-PHILLIPS (6th edn) *Diminution*, ... In *Musick* the diminishing or abating somewhat of the full Value or Quantity of any Note. **1728** CHAMBERS *Diminution*, in Music, is when there are a Number of Words, which are to make Tones and several quick Motions in the Space of a Cadence; several Quavers, and Semi-quavers, corresponding to a Crochet [sic], or Minim. **1730** BAILEY *Dict. Britannicum* (1st edn) *Diminution* (with *Musicians*) is when there are a number of words which are to make tones, and several quick motions in the space of a cadence; several quavers and semiquavers corresponding to a crotchet or minim.

after 1517 ANON. Art of Mvsic BL Add. 4911, f. 27 diminucion, as *gafforus*, in his secund bvrik in ye fourten chaptour dois affirme. That it is a precisione of the mid part in mesur noting discrepant fro semidit... **1596** ANON. *Pathway to Musicke* [D ii *verso*] *Of Diminution and vvhat it is.* ¶ It is a certaine decreasing of the naturall value of notes and rests, by certaine signes or canons ... **1597** MORLEY *Plaine and Easie Introdvction* (p. 25) *Diminution is a certaine lessening or decreasing of the essential value of the notes and rests*, by certayne signes or rules, by signes, when you finde a stroke cutting a whole circle or semicircle thus, ⦶ ₵ ⦶ ₵ But when ... a circle or halfe circle is crossed thus ⨂ ⨂ it signifieth diminution of diminution, so that wheras a note of the signe once parted was the halfe of his owne value: here it is but the quarter. By a number added to a cirkle or *semicircle* thus. O2 C 2 ⊙2 C 2. also by proportionate numbers as thus. $\frac{2}{1}$ dupla. $\frac{3}{1}$ tripla $\frac{4}{1}$ quadrupla &c. By a semicircle inuerted thus Ɔ Ɔ and this is the vsuall signe of diminution, diminishing stil the one halfe of the note: but if it be dashed thus, Ɔ Ɔ it is double diminished. **early 17th C.** RAVENSCROFT Treatise of Musick BL Add. 19758, ff. 13-13v *Dimunition* is a certaine decreasinge both of perfit and Imperfit prolation. both of his notes and rests by a certaine figure bnexid [i.e. next] unto him and by that figure hee beareth force ouer all the prolations; ... **1609** DOWLAND-ORNITHOPARCUS *Micrologvs* (p. 48) *Diminution*, which is more truely called *syncopation*, is the varying of Notes of the first quantity, as writeth *Fran. li.* 2. *Pr.* 14. Or it is a certain cutting off of the measure. For as in Grammer we say *sæcla* for *sæcula*, so in Musicke we do curtall the naturall and essentiall measure of the Notes by this *syncopation*. Therefore generally it shall be called *syncopation*, not *Diminution*, because it is a kind of *syncopation*. § (pp. 48-9) *Diminution* (as the Ancients thought) is the taking away of the third part from the measure. But the opinion of the Modernes, is more true and laudable, which make no difference betwixt *Diminution* and *Semiditie*, as *Ioan: Tinctoris*, of all that euer excelled in Musicke the most excellent writer, and *Franchinus Gafforus lib.* 2. *cap.* 14. haue positiuely set downe. ¶ Therefore *Diminution* is the cutting off of the halfe part in the measure, nothing differing from *semiditie*, but that it is found in perfect Signes, and in figures which are to be measured by the number of 3. § (p. 51) *Diminution* is the contradiction of *Augmentation*. **1653** ?BROUNCKER *Renatvs Des-Cartes Exc. Comp. of Musick* (p. 53.) *Diminution*, is when against one Note of one part, are set 2. or 4. or more in another; ... **1659** SIMPSON *Division-Violist* (p. 15) ... *Diminution*: that is, when 2, 3, 4. or more *Notes* of one *Part*, are set against *One Note* of a different Part; ... § (p. 21) *Diminution*, or *Division* to a *Ground*, is the *Concordance* of *quick* and *slow Notes*. § (p. 28) *Descant-Diminution*, or *Division, is That, which maketh another distinct, and concording Part unto the Ground*... **1665** SIMPSON *Division-Viol* (2nd edn, p. 27) *Diminution* or *Division to a Ground*, is the Breaking, either of the *Bass*, or of any higher

Part that is applyable thereto... **1667** SIMPSON *Compendium of Practical Musick* (p. 34) *Diminution* (in this acception) is the lessning or abating something of the full value or quantity of Notes; a thing much used in former times when the *Tripla Moods* were in fashion. **1724** TURNER *Sound Anatomiz'd* (pp. 17-18) ... there are sometimes several *Notes* to be sung in one *Vowel*; (which are called *Diminutions* or *Divisions*) ...

Dionysiodorus

1678 PHILLIPS (4th edn) *Dionysiodorus*, a Flutinist, mentioned by *Pliny*.

direct, director *see* index, mostra

1584 BATHE Briefe Intro. to True Art of Music (MS copy, 1st half 16th c., *CHi* p. 4) ... Then in the end of the lyn or sett, he may see a thing marked thus  which is called a director, Becaus it is alwayes put wpon the rule or space wherin the first of the next lyn or sett standeth, and doth so direct a man, evin as in bookes the word that is lowest upon everye [side] of the leafe doth direct a man to the word nixt following: **c.1596** BATHE *Briefe Intro. to skill of Song* [A v *verso*] ... then in the ende of the set [i.e. stave], hee may see a thing thus 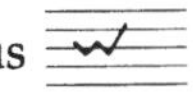 marked, which is called a direct, because it is alwayes put vpon the rule or space wherein the first of the next set standeth, and doth so direct a man, euen as in bookes the word that is lowest vpon euery side of the leafe doth direct a man to the word next following. **1636** BUTLER *Principles of Musik* (p. 38) A Direct in the ende of a line, sheweth where the Note standeth in the beginning of the next line: and is marked thus ⩗/, or thus √. **1665** SIMPSON *Principles of Practical Mvsick* (p. 27) This mark √ which you see at the end of the five Lines, is set to direct us where the first Note of the next five lines doth stand, and is therefore called a *Directer*. **c.1710** NORTH Short, Easy, & plaine rules BL Add. 32531, f. 23v [quoting Prendcourt:] This Signe. ʌʌ/. is called a guid becaus being set at ye End of ye lines or spaces shews you where the first Note of the next staff of ye lines doth begin. [annotation by North:] NB, our Mast^rs call it a direct ... **1721** MALCOLM *Treatise of Musick* (p. 412) A *Direct* is a Mark set at the End of a Staff, especially at the Foot of a Page, upon that Line or Space where the first Note of the next Staff is set. **1724** TURNER *Sound Anatomiz'd* (p. 63) This Mark ⩯ is commonly set at the End of each *Staff*, for the Guide of the *Eye*, in performing any Thing at the first Sight of it, to direct us where the first *Note* of the next *Staff* stands; for which Reason, it is called a *Director*. **1736** TANS'UR *Compleat Melody* (3rd edn, p. 9) A *Direct*, is placed at the End of a *Line*, to direct the Performer to the Place of the first *Note* in the next *Line*.—Either of these Words signifies the same, *viz, Index, Guidon, Monstra*.

dirge *see* elegy, epicedy, epitaph, monody, nænia, obit, threnody

1702 KERSEY *New Engl. Dict.* (1st edn) A *Dirge, or* popish office for the dead; or a lamentation sung at a funeral. **1706** KERSEY-PHILLIPS (6th edn) *Dirge*, ... Also a mournful Ditty or Song of Lamentation sung at a Funeral, from the *Teutonick* Word *Dyrke*, to commend or praise. **1707** *Gloss. Angl. Nova* (1st edn) *Dirge*, a Service for the Dead used by the Roman Catholicks: Also a mournful Ditty, Song, or Lamentation at a Funeral. **1730** BAILEY *Dict. Britannicum* (1st edn) *Dyrge, Dirge*, (as some say, of *dyrken, Teut.* to praise) a mournful ditty or song over the dead, a laudatory song. **1737** DYCHE-PARDON (2nd edn) *Dirge* (S.) a mournful Song sung at the Death of some eminent Person great in Power or Parts; in the Church of *Rome*, it is the Service they use for dead Persons.

discantus *see* descant

discolouration *see* colour

after 1517 ANON. Art of Mvsic BL Add. 4911, f. 18v *Discoloration*. It is ane knawleig and consideration of tua collours. That is to say, quhyt and blak, quhilk ar nistitut to be amange figuris distribut for cognition of perfection and Imperfectionis

discord *see* desentonado, destonnement, diaphony

1538 ELYOT L→E *Discordia*, discorde. **1565** COOPER L→E § *Discordes modi. Stat.* Discordes. *Modi discordes. Stat.* Discordes, or tunes not agreeyng. **1587** THOMAS L→E *Discors, is, adiect* Discordant, agreeing ill togither, vntunable **1589** RIDER L→E *Discors, ad.* Discordant. **1598** FLORIO It→E *Discordare*, to disagree, to vntune *Discordia*, discorde, iarre *Discordo*, a disagreement, a discorde, a iarre **1611** COTGRAVE Fr→E *Desaccord: m.* A iarre, discord, vntuneablenesse; *Desaccordé.* Discordant, iarring, out of tune; *Discord: m.* Discord, iarring *Discordamment.* Jarringly ... without any order, or harmonie. § *Descorder en chantant.* as *Desaccorder.* To iarre. **1611** FLORIO

It→E *Discordare,* ... Also to vnstring or vntune. *Discorde,* discordant, disagreeing. *Discordia,* discord, iarring *Discordo,* a discord, adisagreement [sic] **1650** HOWELL-COTGRAVE Fr→E *Desaccorder.* To discord, or disaccord; to jarre **1659** TORRIANO-FLORIO It→E *Discordare,* to discord, to uncord *Discorde,* discordant. **Discordia, Discordio, Discordo,* discord *Discordioso,* full of discord. **1676** COLES *Discords (in Musick,)* harsh, disagreeing notes. **1688** MIEGE-COTGRAVE Fr→E *Desaccordé,* put out of tune. *Desaccorder,* to put out of tune. † *Discord.* See *Discorde. Discordant,* discordant, jarring, untuneable. *Discorde,* (f.) discord, jarring **1704** HARRIS *Discords,* in Musick, are certain Intervals of Sounds, which being heard at the same time offend the Ear, nevertheless when orderly taken and intermix'd with Concords, they make the best Musick. These *Discords* are the Second, Fourth, and Seventh, with their Octaves; that is to say, all Intervals except those few which precisely terminate the *Concords* are *Discords.* **1706** KERSEY-PHILLIPS (6th edn) *Discords* (in *Musick*) are certain Intervals of Sounds, which being heard at the same Time are harsh and offensive to the Ear; yet when orderly taken and intermix'd with Concords, they make the best Musick. These Discords are the Second, Fourth and Seventh, with their Octaves; that is to say, all Interval except those few which precisely determine the Concords, are *Discords.* **1728** CHAMBERS *Discord* ... [*see* Appendix] **1737** DYCHE-PARDON (2nd edn) *Discord* (S.) ... In *Musick,* if two Sounds so far differ in Tune, as that being sounded together, they compose a Sound that is offensive to the Ear, they are said to make a Discord.

1597 MORLEY *Plaine and Easie Introdvction* (p. 71) *Phi.* What is a *discord?* ¶ *Ma. It is a mixt sound compact of diuers sounds naturallie, offending the eare,* & therfore commonlie excluded from musicke. ¶ *Phi.* Which distances make discord or dissonant sounds? ¶ *Ma.* All such as doe not make concords: as a second, a fourth, a seuenth, and theyr eightes: a ninth, aleuenth [sic], a fourteenth, &c. **1609** DOWLAND-ORNITHOPARCUS *Micrologvs* (p. 79) *Discords* are they whose Sounds mingled together, doe strike the sence vnpleasingly.... A *Discord* (as saith *Boêtius*) is the hard and rough thwarting of two sounds, not mingled with themselues. Or, (as *Tinctor* saith) it is the mixture of diuers sounds, naturally offending the eares ... **1636** BUTLER *Principles of Musik* (p. 48) A *Discord* is a jarring noiz of 2 permixed sounds offending the ear. **1676** MACE *Musick's Monument* (p. 266) Let any 2 *Voices,* endeavour to *Sing* (strongly) together, *Gam-ut,* and *A-re; A-re,* and *B-mi;* or any other 2 of the *Scale,* (next adjoyning) and there will quickly be perceiv'd *That Tormenting Unsufferable Horrour* before mentioned; even such, as a *True Harmonical Ear,* is no more able to endure the noise of, than the cutting of his own *Flesh.* ¶ And This is that we call a *Dischord* in *Musick;* .... There is yet another *Distance,* call'd a *Discord,* viz. the *4th.* but nothing of the *Nature,* or *Kind* with Those other Two; But I use to say) a very *Favourable Discord;* ... **early 18th C.** PEPUSCH various papers BL Add. 29429, f. 2v Discords are those Tones, which, when joint or playd with the Unity, produce a disagreable Sound to ye Ear, and therefore call'd Dissonants; viz the 2^d^, and ye 7. **c.1715-20** NORTH Theory of Sounds BL Add. 32534, f. 38 ... And then the Extreams of coincidence and separation are grosly distinguishable by the beats, and such sounds havving so much more of disagreement then of agreement, are justly termed Discords ... § f. 46v But all this while that wee talk of discords wee are seduced by ye sence In wch that word is taken. For In striktness discord (as hath bin touched) is that sound that gives a strong offence, and makes one at ye hearing of it shrink; but in Regular Musick proper discord is rather to be called out of tune, then discord. **1721** MALCOLM *Treatise of Musick* (p. 36) *Discord* is the Denomination of all the Relations or Differences of *Tune* that have a contrary Effect. **1724** TURNER *Sound Anatomiz'd* (p. 4) ... for as regular *Tones* have a particular Relation to each other, where two or more are joyned together; so, where *Voices* or *Instruments,* or both, are performing together in Consort, they must all move upon the same *Basis,* or there can be no *Harmony,* but a confused Jumble of disturbed *Atoms,* irregularly Jingling, very disagreeably upon the *Ear-drum;* which is, what we call *Discords,* from their disagreeing with one another. § (p. 8) ... the Definition of a *Discord* being a *Sound* which is ungrateful to the *Ear;* § (p. 9) ... the *Second* and *Seventh* only, being properly termed *Discords,* from their jangling with the *Basis.* And even these, when artfully introduced, yield a most agreeable *Harmony,* as well as some others; which may not be improperly termed *Discords,* although it be the *Third, Fourth, Fifth* or *Sixth,* &c. when they are occasionally extended or contracted, according to their Capacity.

discordance *see* absonant

1598 FLORIO It→E *Discordanza,* a discorde, a iarring **1611** COTGRAVE Fr→E *Desaccordant.* Discordant;

Discordant. Discordant, iarring ... most harsh, most vntuneable. **1611** FLORIO It→E *Discordante,* disagreeing, discordant. *Discordanza,* a disagreement, a discorde. **1650** HOWELL-COTGRAVE Fr→E *Desaccordance: f.* A discordance, or disaccording; a squaring, jarring **1656** BLOUNT (1st edn) *Discordant (discordans)* disagreeing, out of tune. **1658** PHILLIPS (1st edn) *Discordance,* (lat.) a disagreement, jarring, or being out of tune; for in Musick those Notes are called discords which make harsh and unpleasing sounds, as seconds, fourths, sevenths, *&c.* **1659** TORRIANO-FLORIO It→E *Discordante,* discordant, jarring. *Discordanza,* discord, jarring. **1688** MIEGE-COTGRAVE Fr→E *Discordant,* discordant, jarring, untuneable. § *Voix discordante,* a jarring Voice. **1696** PHILLIPS (5th edn) *Discordance,* ... Also a being out of Tune; for in Musick those Notes are called *Discords,* which sung or played make harsh and unpleasing Sounds, as Seconds and Sevenths. **1702** KERSEY *New Engl. Dict.* (1st edn) *Discordant,* jarring, *or* untunable. **1706** KERSEY-PHILLIPS (6th edn) *Discordant,* untunable, jarring, as *A discordant Voice.*

after 1517 ANON. Art of Mvsic BL Add. 4911, f. 54v *Discordance* quhat is it. It is ane Mixtur of dyuerss soundis naturally offendent the aeris. To Nam vtherwayis dissonance.

discreto

1724 [PEPUSCH] *Short Explic. of Foreign Words in Mus. Bks.* (p. 27) *Discreto,* or *Con Discretione,* is to play or sing with Care, Moderation, Judgment, and Discretion. **1726** BAILEY *An Univ. Etymolog. Engl. Dict.* (3rd edn) *Discreto* (in *Musick Books*) signifies to Play or Sing with Care, Moderation, Judgment, and Discretion.

1736 TANS'UR *Compleat Melody* (3rd edn, p. 67) *Con Discertone, Moderation.* (Lat.) Either of those *Terms,* denote that you must *sing* or *play* with Discretion, and Adoration.—*Con,* signifies with.

disdiapason *see* diagram, equison

1659 TORRIANO-FLORIO It→E **Disdiapason,* a double diapason. **1704** HARRIS *Disdiapason,* a Term in Musick, denoting a double Eighth or Fifteenth. **1706** KERSEY-PHILLIPS (6th edn) *Disdiapason, (Gr.)* a Term in *Musick,* denoting a double Eighth or Fifteenth. **1728** CHAMBERS *Disdiapason,* in Music, a compound Concord, described by *Fa. Parran* as Quadruple of 4 to 1, or of 8 to 2. See *Concord.* ¶ The *Disdiapason* is produced when the Voice goes from the first Tone to the 15th, and may be call'd a *Fifteenth.* ¶ The Voice ordinarily does not go further than from its first Tone, to the *Disdiapason,* i.e. it does not go beyond the Compass of a double Octave, for the *Disdiapason* is an Octave doubled. See *Octave.* ¶ The Voice may sometimes rise several Tones above a *Disdiapason,* but the Effort or Struggle disfigures it, and makes it false. ¶ The antient Scale, or Diagramma, only extended to a *Disdiapason.* See *Diagramma.* ¶ *Disdiapason-Diapente,* in Music, a Concord in a Sextuple *Ratio* of 1 to 6. ¶ *Disdiapason-Diatessaron,* a compound Concord in the Proportion of 16 to 3. ¶ *Disdiapason-Diton,* a compound Consonance in the Proportion of 10 to 2. ¶ *Disdiapason-Semi-diton,* a compound Concord in the Proportion of 24 to 5. **1730** BAILEY *Dict. Britannicum* (1st edn) *Disdiapason Diapente,* a concord in a sextuple ratio of 1 to 6. *Disdiapason Diatessaron,* a compound concord in the proportion of 16 to 3. *Disdiapason Ditone,* a compound consonance in the proportion of 10 to 2. *Disdiapason Semi-ditone,* a compound concord in the proportion of 24 to 5. **1736** BAILEY *Dict. Britannicum* (2nd edn) *Disdiapason Semi-ditone,* a compound concord in the proportion of 23 to 5. **1737** DYCHE-PARDON (2nd edn) *Disdiapason* (S.) in *Musick,* a compound Concord, having the Ratio of four to one. *Disdiapason diapente,* a Concord in Ratio, as 1 to 6. *Disdiapason diatessaron,* a compound Concord, in Proportion, as 16 to 3. *Disdiapasonditone,* a compound Concord, in Proportion, as 10 to 2. *Disdiapason-semiditone,* a compound Concord, in Proportion, as 24 to 5.

1609 DOWLAND-ORNITHOPARCUS *Micrologvs* (pp. 21-2) *Disdiapason.* ¶ Is an *Interuall* by a Fifteenth, occasioned (as saith *Macrobius*) by a quadruple proportion. Wherein antiquitie sayd we should rest, and goe no further, as *Ambrosius Nolanus* doth proue in the prouerb *Disdiapason,* which is in *Erasmus* that other light of *Germany...* this is the naturall compasse of mans voice, which going aboue this, is rather a squeaking; and going vnder, is rather a humming than a *Voyce:* ... **1680** B., A. *Synopsis of Vocal Musick* (p. 28) ... an eighth once compounded, commonly called a *disdiapason,* a *double eighth, or fifteenth;* and of a twice compounded, which is called a *trisdiapason, a triple eighth or two and twentieth;* and also of a thrice compounded called a *tetradiapason, a quadrula* [sic] *eighth, or nine and twentieth* ... **1736** TANS'UR *Compleat Melody* (3rd edn, p. 69) A *Disdiapasion* is a *Double Octave;* being a 15th (Gr.)

disharmony *see* dissonance

1706 Kersey-Phillips (6th edn) *Disharmony*, want of Harmony, Discord, Jarring. **1708** Kersey *Dict. Anglo-Brit.* (1st edn) *Disharmony, (L.)* Discord, Jarring.

dismal ditty

1737 Bailey *The Univ. Etymolog. Engl. Dict.* (3rd edn, vol. 2, cant section) *Dismal-Ditty*, a Psalm at the Gallows. **1737** Dyche-Pardon (2nd edn) *Dismal Ditty*, a mournful Song, a wretched or bad Composition; also a cant Expression for a Psalm sung by a Criminal at the Gallows.

disperate *see* desesperade

1598 Florio It→E *Disperate*, a kinde of waylefull songs. **1611** Florio It→E *Disperate*, a kind of wailefull songs. **1659** Torriano-Florio It→E **Disperate*, dolefull songs.

dissonance

1500 *Ortus Vocabulorum* L→E Dissono as nui. i. diuersis modis sonare vel discordare. cor so. n.p. Dissonus a um. idest discordans. yll sowndynge o.s. **1552** Huloet L→E *Dissonantia.* Discorde in speache, tune, or voyce. *dissono. as* Discorden in speach, tune, or voyce. **1565** Cooper L→E *Dissonantia, æ, f.g.* Discorde in tunes. **1587** Thomas L→E *Dissonantia, æ, f.g.* *A discorde in tunes and voices. **1589** Rider L→E *Dissonantia, f.* A discordance in tunes, and voices. *Dissonantia, f. dissonus crepitus.* A discorde in tunes and voices *Dissonus, ad.* Dissonant. *Dissonus, dissentaneus, discors, ad.* Vntunable. **1598** Florio It→E *Disonante*, dissonant, disagreeing. *Disonanza*, a dissonance, a discord, or iarre in musicke. *Disonare*, to disaccord, to iarre, to disagree in sounds, to dissent. **1611** Cotgrave Fr→E *Dissonant.* Dissonant; discording, disagreeing, iarring, vntuneable, of different tune from, sounding vnlikely. **1611** Florio It→E *Disonante*, dissonant, disagreeing. *Disonanza*, a dissonance or discord in Musike. *Disonare*, to disaccord, to dissent, to iarre. *Dissonante*, dissonant, disagreeing. *Dissonanza*, a dissonance, a disagreeing. *Dissonare*, to disaccord *Dissono*, dissonant **1616** Bullokar *Dissonant.* Of a contrary sound, not agreeing. **1623** Cockeram *Dissonant.* Disagreeing. **1656** Blount (1st edn) *Dissonance (dissonantia)* a discord in tunes and voyces. **1658** Phillips (1st edn) *Dissonance*, (lat.) a difference in sound, also a disagreement. **1659** Torriano-Florio It→E *Dissono*, dissonant, discord. **1676** Coles *Dissonance, Latin.* disagreement (in sound.) **1696** Phillips (5th edn) *Dissonance*, a discord in Harmony; **1702** Kersey *New Engl. Dict.* (1st edn) A *Dissonance, or* disagreement in sound. *Dissonant, or* jarring. **1704** *Cocker's Engl. Dict.* (1st edn) *Dissonance*, disagreeing in sound. **1704** Harris *Dissonance*, in Musick, is a disagreeable Interval between two Sounds, which being continued together offend the Ear. **1706** Kersey-Phillips (6th edn) *Dissonance* (in *Musick*) a disagreeable Interval between two Sounds, which being continu'd together offend the Ear; a Discord in Tunes or Voices: *Dissonant*, untunable, jarring, disagreeing. **1724** [Pepusch] *Short Explic. of Foreign Words in Mus. Bks.* (p. 27) *Dissonante*, all disagreeable Intervals in Musick are so called. **1726** Bailey *An Univ. Etymolog. Engl. Dict.* (3rd edn) *Dissonante* (in *Musick Books*) signifies all disagreeable Intervals. **1728** Chambers *Dissonance*, or *Discord*, in Music, a false Consonance, or Concord. See *Concord*, and *Consonance.* ¶ A *Dissonance* is properly the Result of a Mixture, or Meeting of two Sounds, which are disagreeable to the Ear: Such are *Ditones, Tritones, False Fifth, Redundant Fourth, Seventh*, &c. ¶ *Dissonances* are used in Music, and have a good Effect therein; tho' it be only by Accident. See *Discord.* **1730** Bailey *Dict. Britannicum* (1st edn) *Dissonant (dissonans,* L.) untunable, jarring, disagreeing. **1737** Dyche-Pardon (2nd edn) *Dissonance* (S.) in *Musick*, a Jarring or Disagreement between Sounds, called a Discord. *Dissonant* (A.) out of Tune, disagreeing with, or differing from.

1596 Anon. *Pathway to Musicke* [F] *VVhat is a Disonant.* ¶ It is a combination of diuers sounds, naturallie offending the eare. **1736** Tans'ur *Compleat Melody* (3rd edn, p. 69) *Dissonants, Disharmony*, (Lat.) or *Discords*; is a *Name* applied to all *jarring Sound*, or all disagreeable Intervals; *viz.* a 2d, a 4th, a 7th, *&c.* and their *Octaves.*

dithyramb *see* Arion, modi melopœiæ

1587 Thomas L→E *Dithyrambus, bi, m.g. s.b. Horat.* A song made in the honour of Bacchus. *hinc Dithyrambicus, a, um, qui Baccho afflatus furit.* **1589** Rider L→E *Dithyrambus.* A song in honour of Bacchus. **1598** Florio It→E *Ditirambo*, a song made in honor of Bacchus. § *Ditirambico poeta*, a Poet singing in praise of Bacchus. **1599** Minsheu-Percyvall Sp→E **Ditirambo*, a song made in honor of Bacchus. **1611** Florio It→E *Ditirambo*, a song in honor of Bacchus. § *Ditirambico poeta*, a poet singing in praise of Bacchus. **1656** Blount (1st edn) *Dithyrambick (dithyrambus)* a kind of verse or song in honor of *Bacchus*. **1658** PHILLIPS (1st edn) *Dithyramb*, (Greek) a kind of Hymne antiently sung in honour of *Bacchus*, also any kind of lusty or jovial Song. **1659** TORRIANO-FLORIO It→E **Ditirambo*, a Song or Hymn in honour of *Bacchus* **1661** BLOUNT (2nd edn) *Dithyramb (dithyrambus)* a kind of Hymn or song in honor of *Bacchus*, who was surnamed *Dithyrambus*; and the Poets, who composed such Hymns, were called *Dithyrambicks*. **1676** COLES *Dithyramb, French.* a jovial song (to Bacchus.) **1678** PHILLIPS (4th edn) *Dithyramb*, (*qu.* δὶς θύρας ἀμείβων) a kind of Hymn, anciently sung in honor of Bacchus; also a kind of lusty or jovial song. **1688** MIEGE-COTGRAVE Fr→E *Ditirambe*, or *Dithyrambe*, (m.) *Hymne en l'honneur du Vin & de Bacchus*, Dithyrambes, a Song in honour of Bacchus. *Ditirambique*, or *Dithyrambique*, Dithyrambick. **1696** PHILLIPS (5th edn) *Dithyramb*, a kind of Hymn, anciently sung in honour of *Bacchus*; also a kind of lusty or jovial Song, full of transport and poetical fury. **1704** *Cocker's Engl. Dict.* (1st edn) *Dithyramb*, a Song in honour of *Bacchus*. **1706** KERSEY-PHILLIPS (6th edn) *Dithyramb* or *Dithyrambus (Gr.)* a kind of Hymn anciently sung in honour of *Bacchus* the God of Wine; a jovial Song full of Transport and Poetical Fury. *Dithyrambick*, belonging to such Composures; as *A Dithyrambick Poet.* **1708** KERSEY *Dict. Anglo-Brit.* (1st edn) *Dithyramb* or *Dithyrambus*, (*G.*) a kind of Hymn anciently sung in honour of *Bacchus*, the God of Wine. **1728** CHAMBERS *Dithyrambus*, in the ancient Poetry, a Hymn in Honour of *Bacchus*, full of Transport, and Poetical Rage. **1737** DYCHE-PARDON (2nd edn) *Dithyrambus* (S.) a Bacchanalian Song, or Poem in Honour of *Bacchus*, in Praise of Wine, and encouraging what is called good Fellowship. *Dithyrambick* (A.) belonging to a Dithyrambus.

ditone *see* demiditone, semiditone, sesquiditonus, third

1589 RIDER L→E *Ditonus.* A concord in musick, ¶ Of 2. notes, or a note and a halfe, called a third note. **1598** FLORIO It→E *Ditono*, hauing or making two sounds or two parts in musicke. **1599** MINSHEU-PERCYVALL Sp→E **Ditono*, hauing two sounds or parts in musicke. **1611** FLORIO It→E *Ditono*, hauing or making two sounds or two parts in musicke. **1696** PHILLIPS (5th edn) *Diton*, the first Discord in Musick. **1704** HARRIS *Ditone*, a double Tone, or the greater Third, is an Interval of Musick, which comprehends two Tones. The Proportion of the Tones that make the *Ditones*, is as 4 to 5, and that of the *Semi-ditones* as 5 to 6. **1706** KERSEY-PHILLIPS (6th edn) *Ditone* (in *Musick*) a double Tone, or the greater Third, an Interval which comprehends two Tones. The proportion of the Parts that make the *Ditones* is as 4 to 5, and that of the *Semi-Ditones*, as 5 to 6. **1728** CHAMBERS *Ditone, Ditonum*, in Music, an Interval comprehending two Tones. See *Interval*, and *Tone*. ¶ The Proportion of the Sounds that form the *Ditone* is 4 to 5; and that of the *Semi-ditone*, as 5 to 6. *Fa. Parran* makes the *Ditone* the 4th Kind of simple Concords, as comprehending two Tones, a greater, and a lesser: Others make it the first Discord; dividing the *Ditone* into 18 equal Parts, or Comma's, the Nine on the acute Side make the greater Tone, as asserted by *Salomon de Caux*. ¶ The Word is form'd of δὶς, *twice*, and τόνος, *Tone*. **1737** DYCHE-PARDON (2nd edn) *Ditone* (S.) in *Musick*, an Interval comprehending two Tones, in Proportion, as 4 to 5.

1609 DOWLAND-ORNITHOPARCUS *Micrologvs* (p. 18) *A Ditone.* ¶ Is a perfect third: so called, because it containes in it two *Tones*, as *Placentine* and *Pontifex* witnesse. It hath likewise two kindes, the first is from *vt* to *mi*; the second from *fa* to *la*. **1617-24** FLUDD *Utriusque Cosmi Maioris: De Templo Musicæ* (p. 182) *Ditonus* est proportio inter tres notas immediatè se habentes, ut, *Fa*, & *La*, *Ut*, & *Mi*. **1636** BUTLER *Principles of Musik* (pp. 46-7) *Ditonus* is a perfect Third, consisting of a Tone and a Tone: as from *Ut* to *Mi*, from *Fa* to *La*, and from *Pha* to *Re*. **1664** BIRCHENSHA-ALSTED *Templvm Mvsicvm* (pp. 92-3) The *Ditonus* is a sharp and perfect third: and doth consist of two *Tones*, as is between *vt mi. fa la.* otherwise called the *Third*. **1665** SIMPSON *Division-Viol* (2nd edn, p. 13) Next follows a Third comprehending the perfect or greater Third by the name of *Ditonus*, and the Imperfect or lesser Third by the name of *Semeditonus*. **1698** WALLIS *Question in Musick* (*Philos. Trans.*, 1698, p. 83) ... And that of 5 to 4, is the Proportion of the Greater Third (commonly called a *Ditone*, or Two Tones,) as *fa la* (in *fa sol la*) ...

ditonus diapente *see* diapason ditone, semidiapason

1609 DOWLAND-ORNITHOPARCUS *Micrologvs* (p. 21) *Ditonus Diapente.* ¶ Is the distance of one Voyce from another by a perfect seuenth: consisting of fiue *Tones*, and one *semitone*, according to *Georg. Valla lib.* 3. *cap.* 26. **1636** BUTLER *Principles of Musik* (p. 47) *Ditonus-diapente* or *Semidiapason*, is a Sevnth perfect, or Eight imperfect, consisting of five Tones and a Hemitone: as from *Pha* to *La*, from *Fa* to *Mi*, and from ♮ sharp to b flat in the Eight.

ditty *see* dismal ditty, testo

1604 CAWDREY (1st edn) *dittie*, the matter of a song. **1656** BLOUNT (1st edn) *Ditty* (from the Ital. *detto, i. dictum*) a rime expressed in words, and sung to a musical tune *Min.* **1658** PHILLIPS (1st edn) *Ditty*, a Song which hath the words composed to a tune. **1676** COLES *Ditty*, Song. **1702** KERSEY *New Engl. Dict.* (1st edn) A *Ditty*, a sort of song. **1704** *Cocker's Engl. Dict.* (1st edn) *Ditty*, a Song. **1706** KERSEY-PHILLIPS (6th edn) *Ditty*, a Song that has the Words set in Musick. **1707** *Gloss. Angl. Nova* (1st edn) *Ditty*, a Song which is set to a Tune. **1708** KERSEY *Dict. Anglo-Brit.* (1st edn) *Ditty*, a Song that has the Words set in Musick. **1735** DEFOE *Ditty*, a Song, or Ballad. **1737** DYCHE-PARDON (2nd edn) *Ditty* (S.) a Song or Ballad.

divisi

1724 [PEPUSCH] *Short Explic. of Foreign Words in Mus. Bks.* (p. 28) *Divisi*, Divided. Thus, *Divisi in due Parte*, is Divided in two Parts. **1726** BAILEY *An Univ. Etymolog. Engl. Dict.* (3rd edn) *Divisi* (in *Musick Boaks* [sic]) signifies divided into two Parts. *Ital.*

division *see* correnti, descant, diminution, fioretti, flourish, fredon, ground, lesson, overture, quaver, supposition, variation

1706 KERSEY-PHILLIPS (6th edn) In *Musick Division*, is the dividing of a Tune into many small Notes; as *Quavers, Semiquavers*, &c. And *To run Divisions*, is to play on an Instrument, or to sing after such a manner. **1728** CHAMBERS *Division*, in Music, the dividing of the Interval of an Octave into a Number of lesser Intervals. See *Octave*, and *System*. ¶ The 4th, and 5th, each of 'em, divide, or measure the Octave perfectly, tho' differently. When the 5th is below, and serves as a Base to the 4th, the *Division* is call'd *Harmonical*; When the 4th is below, the *Division* is call'd *Authentic*. See *Scale*. See also *Concinnous*. **1737** DYCHE-PARDON (2nd edn) *Division* (S.) ... in *Musick*, it is the distinguishing a Tune into several Parts, or breaking of a long Note into several short ones, &c.

1659 SIMPSON *Division-Violist* (p. 29) *Mixt Division*, I call That, which mixeth *Descant*, and *Breaking* the *Ground*, One with the Other; under which Terme I comprehend all *Division*, which presents unto our *Eares*, the Sounds of *two*, or *more* Parts moving together; ... **1665** SIMPSON *Division-Viol* (2nd edn, p. 35) *Descant Division* is that which makes a Different-concording-part unto the *Ground*.

divoto

1724 [PEPUSCH] *Short Explic. of Foreign Words in Mus. Bks.* (p. 28) *Divoto*, signifies a Grave, Serious Manner, or Way of Playing, or Singing, proper to inspire Devotion. **1726** BAILEY *An Univ. Etymolog. Engl. Dict.* (3rd edn) *Divoto* (in *Musick Books*) signifies a grave, serious manner or way of Playing or Singing, proper to inspire Devotion. *Ital.* **1737** DYCHE-PARDON (2nd edn) *Divoto* (S.) a grave, solemn Kind of Musick, such as is proper for Devotion.

1731 PRELLEUR *Modern Musick-Master* (Dictionary, p. 2) *Divoto*, in a Grave and serious manner. **1736** TANS'UR *Compleat Melody* (3rd edn, p. 68) *Divoto*, (Ital.) signifies a grave and serious Way of Singing; proper to inspire Devotion.

d la sol re *see* penultima divisarum

1671 PHILLIPS (3rd edn) *D. La sol re.* the name of the fifth Note in each of the 3 Septenaries in the *Gam ut*, or ordinary Scale of Musick, only in the lowermost Septenarie, *La* is wanting, and in the uppermost *Re.* **1676** COLES *D. La sol re*, the fifth note in the common Gamut or Scale of Musick **1678** PHILLIPS (4th edn) *D. La sol re*, the name of the Fifth Note in each of the three Septenaries in the *Gam ut*, or ordinary Scale of Musick, only in the lowermost Septenary, *La* is wanting, and in the uppermost *Re.* It answers in the lowest to the Greek, Λιχανός ὑπατη, in the next to παρανητη συνημμενον; in the last to παρανητη Διεζευγμενον. **1706** KERSEY-PHILLIPS (6th edn) *De-la-sol-re*, the Name of the Fifth Note, in each of [the] three Septenaries or Combinations of Seven in the *Gam-ut*, or ordinary scale of Musick; only in the lowermost Septenary *La* is wanting, and *Re* in the uppermost. **1708** KERSEY *Dict. Anglo-Brit.* (1st edn) *D-la-sol-re*, the Name of the Fifth Note, in each of the three Septenaries in the *Gam-ut*.

doced *see* dulcimer

1658 PHILLIPS (1st edn) *Doced*, or *Douced*, a Musical instrument, otherwise called a Dulcimer. **1676** COLES *Doced, Douced*, a Dulcimer. **1678** PHILLIPS (4th edn) *Doced* or *Douced, (old word)* a Musical instrument, otherwise called a *Dulcimer*. **1706** KERSEY-PHILLIPS (6th edn) *Doced* or *Douced* (old Word) a Musical Instrument commonly call'd a

Dulcimer. **1707** *Gloss. Angl. Nova* (1st edn) *Doced* or *Douced,* (old Word) a Dulcimer. **1708** KERSEY *Dict. Anglo-Brit.* (1st edn) *Doced* or *Douced,* (*O.*) a Musical Instrument commonly call'd a *Dulcimer.* **1737** BAILEY *The Univ. Etymolog. Engl. Dict.* (3rd edn, vol. 2) *Doced, Doucet,* a musical instrument commonly called a dulcimer. **1737** DYCHE-PARDON (2nd edn) *Doced* or *Douced* (S.) a Musical Instrument called a Dulcimer.

doctor

1676 COLES *Doctor, Latin.* teacher, he that hath taken the highest degree in Divinity, Physick, Civil-law or Musick. **1706** KERSEY-PHILLIPS (6th edn) *Doctor* (*Lat. i.e.* Teacher) one that has taken the highest Degree at an University, in any Art or Science, as *A Doctor of Divinity, Law, Physick, Musick,* &c.

doi

1724 [PEPUSCH] *Short Explic. of Foreign Words in Mus. Bks.* (p. 28) *Doi,* Two. § (p. 28) *A Doi Canti,* for two Voices. **1726** BAILEY *An Univ. Etymolog. Engl. Dict.* (3rd edn) *Doi* (in *Musick Books*) signifies Two, as *Doi Canto,* two Songs. *Ital.*

dolce *see* doux, gratieusement

1724 [PEPUSCH] *Short Explic. of Foreign Words in Mus. Bks.* (p. 28) *Dolce,* or *Dolcemento,* is Soft and Sweet. Thus, ¶ *Con Dolce Maniera,* is to play or sing in a soft, sweet, pleasing and agreeable Manner. **1726** BAILEY *An Univ. Etymolog. Engl. Dict.* (3rd edn) *Dolce* (in *Musick Books*) signifies soft and sweet[.] *Ital.* § *Con Dolce Maniera,* signifies to Play or Sing in a soft, sweet, pleasant, and agreeable manner. **1737** DYCHE-PARDON (2nd edn) *Dolce* (S.) in *Musick,* soft, gentle, low.

c.1710 ANON. *Preceptor for Improved Octave Flageolet* ('Explanation of Words', p. 82) *Dolce*—Sweet and Soft **1736** TANS'UR *Compleat Melody* (3rd edn, p. 67) *Con Dolce Maniere, Dolce, Doux, Gratioso, Gratiusement* [sic]. (Ital.) Either of those *Terms,* denotes that you must *sing* or *play* in a very soft, sweet and agreeable Manner.

dolcemelle *see* dulcimer

dolcemento

1726 BAILEY *An Univ. Etymolog. Engl. Dict.* (3rd edn) *Dolcemento,* the same as *Dolce. Ital.*

dolzaina *see* dulcian

domatum

1500 *Ortus Vocabulorum* L→E Domatum ti. fistula cannalis vel fistule yemales quibus stillicidia defluebant. vel sunt fistule aquarum siue cantorum. cor ma. n.s.

dominant *see* final

early 18th C. ANON. Essay on Musick BODLEIAN Rawl. D. 751, ff. 3v-4 It was first remark'd that between the two extremities of the octave, for example between C below, & C above, there was in ascending, a degree which was G and the 5th from C below, which with this C had the greatest affinity that might be after that of the octave. This degree in relation to the first is call'd the Fifth: it is also call'd the *Dominant* for a reason not unworthy of observation, & which will more plainly manifest the affinity of this Fifth with C below. This is, that in the series or progression of a tune of which C below makes the basis or foundation, (that is to say the principal Chord in which the tune terminates,) in this series I say, it will always be found that the chord of the Fifth, viz. G, will be more frequently struck & repeated than any other, which has given it the name of *Dominant.* **1721** MALCOLM *Treatise of Musick* (p. 277) *Observe* next, that of the natural Notes of every *Mode* or *Octave,* ... The 5*th* is called the *Dominante,* because it is the next principal Note to the *final,* and most frequently repeated in the Song; and if 'tis brought in as a new *Key,* it has the most perfect Connection with the *principal Key:* ...

donadello

1598 FLORIO It→E *Donadello,* ... Also a fiddle or a croude. **1611** FLORIO It→E *Donadello,* a croud or kit or little fidle. **1659** TORRIANO-FLORIO It→E **Donadello,* ... a kind of little croud, kit, or Country-fiddle

doppio *see* sonare

1611 FLORIO It→E *Doppio,* ... Also a tolling for the dead. **1659** TORRIANO-FLORIO It→E *Doppio,* ... also a ringing, a jangling, or a tolling of two or more bells together, and in tune, also a double peal, or toling for the dead

1731 PRELLEUR *Modern Musick-Master* (Dictionary, p. 2) *Doppio,* Double.

dorick *see* collateral, mode, mood, tone

1500 *Ortus Vocabulorum* L→E Dorica ce. a maner of speche f.p. Ipodorus. i. gr[a]uis sonus in musica et iocundus. m.s. **1552** HULOET L→E *Doricæ* Musycke vsed in comodyes and playes. **1587** THOMAS L→E *Dorica*, *A certaine kind of musicke representing a grauitie, and therefore was assigned to noble men and greate personages. *Dorion, rij, n.g.* *A certaine kinde of musicke representing gravitie. *Hypodorius, Isid. est accentus vel tenor in voce omnium gravissimus.* **1589** RIDER L→E *Dorica, f. dorion, n.* A certaine kind of musicke, representing gravitye, and therefore was assigned to noblemen and great personages. **1598** FLORIO It→E *Dorica*, ... Also a kinde of graue solemne musicke. *Dorico*, a graue solemn musition, representing grauitie. *Hipodorio*, a kind of graue accent in musicke. **1599** MINSHEU-PERCYVALL Sp→E **Dorico*, a graue solemne musition representing grauitie. **Dorio*, a musition playing graue musicke. **1611** FLORIO It→E *Dorica*, ... Also a kind of graue solemne musicke. *Dorico*, a solemne or graue Musitian. *Hipodorio*, a kinde of graue accent in Musicke. *Hippodonio* [sic], a kind of musicke or sound in musicke. **1656** BLOUNT (1st edn) § *Dorick Musick (Dorica musica)* a kind of grave and solemn Musick, and therefore assigned to great Personages. **1658** PHILLIPS (1st edn) § *Dorick*, Musick, a kinde of grave and solemne Musick **1659** TORRIANO-FLORIO It→E *Dorica, Dorico*, ... also a kind of grave and solemn Musick *Hipodorio, Hipofrigio*, a kinde of grave accent in musick. *Hippodomio* [sic], a kinde of note, tone, or accent in Musick. **1661** BLOUNT (2nd edn) § *Dorick* or *Dorian Musick (Dorica musica)* a kind of grave and solemn Musick, and therefore assigned to great Personages; and so called because the *Dorians* first devised it. **1671** PHILLIPS (3rd edn) § *Dorick*-mood, in Musick among the ancients was that which consisted of a slow solemn Spondaic time, it commonly began that Key which we call *C. sol fa ut*, and reacht to *A la mi re* above: **1676** COLES § *Dorick-mood, Dorian-musick*, of a slow solemn time, from *C sol fa ut* to *A la mi re*. **1704** *Cocker's Engl. Dict.* (1st edn) § *Dorick Musick*, grave solemn Musick. **1706** KERSEY-PHILLIPS (6th edn) § *Dorick Mood* (in *Musick*) one of the Five *Moods* or *Tones* in use among the Ancients, which consisted of slow-tun'd Notes, and was proper for stirring up Persons to Sobriety and Piety; so call'd from one of the Provinces of *Greece*, where it was first invented. **1707** *Gloss. Angl. Nova* (1st edn) § *Dorick Musick*, so call'd from the *Dorians*, is a kind of grave and solemn Musick, consisting of a slow spondaick Time. **1728** CHAMBERS *Doric*, in Music. The *Doric Mode* is the first of the authentic Modes of the Ancients. ¶ Its Character is to be severe, temper'd with Gravity, and Joy; And it is proper for Occasions of Religion, and War. It begins with *D, Sol, Re*. See *Mode*. ¶ *Plato* admires the Music of the *Doric* Mode; and judges it proper, to preserve good Manners, as being Masculine. And on this Account allows of it in his Common-wealth. ¶ The Ancients had likewise their *Subdoric Mode*, which was one of their Plagal Modes. Its Character was to be very grave, and solemn. It began with *G Ut*, a *Diatessaron* lower than the *Doric* Mode. **1730** BAILEY *Dict. Britannicum* (1st edn) § *Dorick Mood* (in *Musick*) a kind of grave and solid musick, consisting of slow, spondaick time. *Musick* (of the *Dorick Mood*) was grave and modest, and therefore called religious musick. **1736** BAILEY *Dict. Britannicum* (2nd edn) § *Doric Mode* (in *Musick*) was a mixture of gravity and mirth invented by *Thamyras* of *Thrace*. **1737** DYCHE-PARDON (2nd edn) § *Dorick Mood*, a grave, slow, solemn Kind of Musick, very proper either for the Church or the Camp.

1636 BUTLER *Principles of Musik* (p. 1) The *Dorik* Moode consisteth of sober slow-timed Notes, generally in Counter-point, set to a Psalm or other pious Canticle, in Meeter or Rhythmical vers: the notes answering the number of the Syllables. This mooveth to sobrieti, prudence, modesti, and godlines. § (p. 4) [marginalia: '*Dorik*.'] The first [of the five moods] hath his name of *Doria* a civil parte of Greece, neere Athens: the other 4 had their beginnings and names from certain Regions of Asia minor, which bordering upon Greece were peopled by Graecian Colonies. **early 18th C.** PEPUSCH various papers BL Add. 29429, f. 5v ... Of which ye C Plagal, being ye lowest Mode of all, is also calld the *Dorius*, because it begins with ye very lowest soand [sic] of all, viz Γ, Gamma ut, calld by ye Greecians Hypodorius. **1721** MALCOLM *Treatise of Musick* (p. 530) The Seven Species of *Octaves*, as they proceed in Order from *A. B. C. D. E. F. G*, are the Seven *Tones*, which differ in their Modulations, *i.e.* in the Distances of the successive Sounds, according to the fixt *Ratios* in the *System*. These Seven *Ptolomy* calls, The 1*st*, *Dorick*, the same with the *System*, or beginning in *A* or *Proslamb*. 2*d*, *Hypo-lydian*, beginning in and following the Order from *B* or *Hyp-hyp*. 3*d*, *Hypophrygian*, beginning at C or *Parh-hy*. 4*th*, *Hypodorian* at D. 5*th*, *Mixolydian* in E. 6*th*, *Lydian* in *F*. 7*th*, *Phrygian* in G.

dorito

1598 FLORIO It→E *Dorio*, a musition that plaies graue musicke. **1611** FLORIO It→E *Dorito*, one that plaies graue musicke.

dot

1683 GREETING *Pleasant Companion* (n.p.) All Tunes or Lessons for the *Flagelet* are prick'd upon six Lines, answering to the six Holes on that Instrument, by certain Characters called *Dots*: These *dots* direct what *Holes* are to be stopt, there being so many ...

double *see* alt

1696 [PURCELL] *Choice Collection of Lessons* (n.p.) All lessons on ye Harpsicord or Spinnet, are prickt on six lines, & two staves, in score ... to some Harpsicords they add to that number [being 'thirty black Keyes'] both above & below[;] notes standing below ye six lines, which have leger lines added to them are calld double, as double CC-fa-ut, or double DD-sol-re, soe they are above on ye treble hand, but then they are call'd in alt as being ye highest ... **1696** [after PURCELL] *Harpsicord Master* (f 3) All lessons on the Harpsicord or Spinnet are prickt on six lines and two staves, in score ... Notes standing below the six lines, which have leger lines added to them are called double, as double fa-ut, or double DD sol-re, Soe they are above on ye treble hand, but then they are call'd in alt, as being ye highest.

double backfall *see* backfall, elevation

double bar *see* bar, repeat, strain

c.1710 NORTH Short, Easy, & plaine rules BL Add. 32531, f. 23 [quoting Prendcourt:] A Mark like this. :||:. is called a Repetition, wch shews you that you must play over againe what is from the beginning of ye peice, to such a signe, or what is between 2 of such signes... [annotation by North:] NB. This with us is called a double barr wch with 2 pricks or pricks on either [?side] means as he says that such strain is to be played or sung over again.

double bass *in pitch notation*

c.1710 NORTH (draft for) Musicall Grammarian BL Add. 32537, f. 15 ... I will mention some of the remarkable methods used by ye organ makers. first they note all ye Naturalls by ye comon Letters thro all the Octaves; The lowest by ye seven capitalls. as. G. A. B. &c. If Any Notes fall lower, then by doubling. as GG. AA. BB. &c for wch reason they are called Double Bases ...

double bass *as instrument, see* violin, violone

double cadence

1731 PRELLEUR *Modern Musick-Master* (III *re* flute, p. 9) The double Cadence is an ordinary Shake follow'd by two Semiquavers Slur'd or tip't...

double counterpoint *see* double descant, harmonia gemina

double descant *see* descant, harmonia gemina

1704 HARRIS *Double-descent* [sic], See *Descant*.

1597 MORLEY *Plaine and Easie Introdvction* (p. 105) [marginalia: 'Double descant'] There is also a manner of composition vsed amongst the *Italians*, which they call *Contrapunto doppio*, or double descant, and though it be no Canon, yet is it verie neere the nature of a Canon: ... and it is no other thing, but a certaine kind of composition, which beeing sung after diuers sortes, by changing the partes, maketh diuers manners of harmonie: and is founde to be of two sortes. The first is, when the principall (that is the thing as it is firste made) and the replie (that is it which the principall hauing the partes changed dooth make) are sung, changing the partes in such maner, as the highest part may be made the lowest, and the lowest parte the highest, without anie change of motion: that is, if they went vpward at the first, they goe also vpward when they are changed: and if they went downeward at the first, they goe likewise downward being changed. And this is likewise of two sortes: for if they haue the same motions being changed, they either keepe the same names of the notes which were before, or alter them: if they keepe the same names, the replie singeth the high part of the principall a fift lower, and the lower part an eight higher: and if it alter the names of the notes, the higher part of the principal is sung in the replie a tenth lower, and the lower part an eight higher. ¶ The second kinde of double descant, is when the partes changed, the higher in the lower, go by contrarie motions: that is, if they both ascende before, beeing chaunged they descend: or if they descend before, they ascend being changed. **1667** SIMPSON *Compendium of Practical Musick* (p. 169) It is called Double Descant when the Parts are so contrived, that the *Treble* may be made the *Bass*, and the *Bass* the *Treble*. **1694** PURCELL-PLAYFORD *Intro. to Skill of Musick* (12th edn, 'A Brief Introduction to the Art of Descant', n.p.) There is a seventh sort of Fugeing called *Double Descant*, which is contrived so, that the Upper Part may be made the Under in the *Reply*; ...

double fugue *see* fugue

double gamut

1676 Mace *Musick's Monument* (p. 218) [*re* strings of the theorboe] Besides, to amplifie *Gam-ut* at any time; if It be a Long Note, you may put to It the *Greatest Long Diapason;* which we call *Double-Gam-ut:* ...

double shake

1700 Anon. *Compleat Instructor to the Flute* (p. 6) [*re* 'the proper Graces'] ... this mark (⌣̇⌣̇) is only over *G sol re ut.* in alt and is call'd the double Shake and to Strike it first Sound *A la mi re* in alt and then take of your thumb and first Finger with the third Finger of the left hand and Shake that very Strong, but lett the proper Note be he[a]rd at last.

double stop

1722 B., T. *Compleat Musick-Master* (p. 32) [*re* the viol] ... you will find 2[,] 3 or 4 Notes standing over one another, which we call Double stops, where there is but 2 of them standing you must hit both the Strings equal, stopping at the place or places so requiring, but if more let the bottom Note sound first, touching the middle Notes in the passing the Bow to the highest. **1725** De La Fond *New System of Music* (preface, lxiii) As for what is called *Double Stops* for Bow-Instruments; that method of playing, as far as I can find, has not been known long...

double time *see* gavotte

double transposition

1731 [Pepusch] *Treatise on Harmony* (2nd edn, p. 96) We proceed now to explain what we call *Double Transposition.* This is chiefly of Use for *Instruments,* for most of them, especially *Wind Instruments,* are confin'd as to *Pitch,* or as to *Compass,* and cannot therefore go so *high,* or so *low,* as some Compositions require; and, besides this Defect, by their being *fram'd* or *adapted* for some particular *Pitch* or *Key;* ...

doussaine *see* dulcian

doux *see* dolce, gratieusement

1724 [Pepusch] *Short Explic. of Foreign Words in Mus. Bks.* (p. 28) *Doux,* Soft and Sweet, much the same in Musick as *Piano.* **1726** Bailey *An Univ. Etymolog. Engl. Dict.* (3rd edn) *Doux* (in *Musick Books*) soft and sweet, much the same as *Piana* [sic]. *Ital.*

down *see* burden, refret

doxology

1656 Blount (1st edn) *Doxology* (Gr.) a song of praise, a speaking or giving glory; As when we say, *Glory be to the Father, &c.* that is properly *Doxology,* and is said to be composed by the first Council of *Nice,* and St. *Jerome,* to be the Author of adding the other Versicle, *As it was in the beginning, &c. View of Directory, fo.* 32. 33. **1658** Phillips (1st edn) *Doxology,* (Greek) a Verse or Song of praise, anciently instituted in the Church which was to be recited in Divine-service after the Prayers and Psalmes. **1706** Kersey-Phillips (6th edn) *Doxology (Gr.)* a Verse or short Hymn of Praise, anciently appointed in the Church, to be said in Divine Service, after the Prayers and Psalms; as the *Gloria Patri, i.e.* Glory be to the Father, *&c.* The Conclusion of the Lord's Prayer, *viz. for thine is the Kingdom, the Power and the Glory,* &c. which is sometimes left out, is also termed the *Doxology.* **1707** *Gloss. Angl. Nova* (1st edn) *Doxology,* (Gr.) a Song of Praise, a giving of Praise. **1708** Kersey *Dict. Anglo-Brit.* (1st edn) *Doxology,* (G.) a Verse or short Hymn of Praise, said in Divine Service; as the *Gloria Patri, i.e.* Glory be to the Father, *&c.* **1726** Bailey *An Univ. Etymolog. Engl. Dict.* (3rd edn) *Doxology* (Δοξολογία, of δόξος Glory and λόγος a Word, *Gr.*) a Song or short Hymn of Praise said in Divine Service; as the *Gloria Patri,* i.e. Glory be to the Father, *&c.* **1730** Bailey *Dict. Britannicum* (1st edn) To *Doxologize* ... to say the hymn called *Gloria Patri,* &c. *Doxology* ... a verse or short hymn of praise appointed anciently in the church to be said after the prayers and psalms in divine service, as the *Gloria Patri,* &c.

dragina

1500 *Ortus Vocabulorum* L→E Dragina atis. est questio siue interrogacio vel genus cantici n.t.

draw

1676 Mace *Musick's Monument* (p. 72) But *This* you must *remember,* viz. when ever you *strike* a *Bass,* be sure, you let your *Thumb rest it self,* upon the *next String,* and *There* let it *remain,* till you have *Vse of It* elsewhere. ¶ And this is the only way, to *draw from a Lute* (as we term it) the *sweetest Sound, that a Lute is able to yield;* which being perfected, you may conclude, *half the work of your Right Hand accomplished.*

drawing pen *see* music-line, patte
1706 KERSEY-PHILLIPS (6th edn) *Drawing-pen*, an Instrument made with a pair of Steel-chaps, and govern'd by a Screw, to draw Lines finer or thicker; as also to draw Five or Six Lines together, for Musick books, &c.

drenso
1587 THOMAS L→E *Drenso, as, Philom.* To sing as a Swanne. **1589** RIDER L→E *Drenso.* To sing as a swan doth.

driving note *see* syncopation, syncope
1724 TURNER *Sound Anatomiz'd* (p. 63) The most difficult Thing to a Beginner, in beating the *Measures*, is in such *Notes* as we call driving *Notes*, where we beat with the *Hand*, or *Foot*, in the Middle of a *Sound*, or *Note*, that shews the Length of it, and at the next *Note*, lift it up again. This was formerly practised, by drawing the *Bars* thro' the Heads of such *Notes*, before *Crotchets* and *Quavers* were in Use; for which Reason, they were then called *Notes* of Syncopation, which signifies cutting.

drone *see* bagpipe, burden, busone, faux-bourdon, ronfo, succino, sveglia
1730 BAILEY *Dict. Britannicum* (1st edn) *Drone*, a musical instrument, called also a bassoon. **1737** DYCHE-PARDON (2nd edn) *Drone* (S.) ... also the deep holding Key Note of a Bagpipe.

drub
1721 BAILEY *An Univ. Etymolog. Engl. Dict.* (1st edn) *Drug* [sic], (*Tromme, Dan. Trommel, Du.*) a Musical Warlike Instrument: **1730** BAILEY *Dict. Britannicum* (1st edn) To *Drub* (*q.d.* to *Dub*, *i.e.* to beat upon a drum, or *druben, Teut.*) to cudgel or bang soundly.

drum *see* atabal, caisse, caxa, kettle drum, pandera, taballi, tabour, tambour, tambourine, terga taurea, timbon, timbrel, tympany
1702 KERSEY *New Engl. Dict.* (1st edn) A *Drum.* To *drum, or* beat the drum. **1706** KERSEY-PHILLIPS (6th edn) *Drum*, a well known Warlike Musical Instrument, or the Man that beats it: **1707** *Gloss. Angl. Nova* (1st edn) *Drum*, a well known Instrument of Martial Musick: **1721** BAILEY *An Univ. Etymolog. Engl. Dict.* (1st edn) To *Drum*, (*Trommelen, Du.*) to beat upon a Drum. **1728** CHAMBERS *Drum, Tympanum*, a Military, Musical Instrument, of Use principally among the Foot, serving to call the Soldiers together, to direct their March, Attack, Retreat, *&c.* ¶ The Body of the *Drum* is made of a very thin Oak beat into a Cylinder, and cover'd at each End with Parchment, which is strain'd, or braced more or less, according to the Height, or Depth of the Sound required, by Strings; and struck with Sticks. The Height of the *Drum* is equal to its Breadth, which does not exceed two Foot and a half, by reason, no Skins can be had to cover bigger. There are also *Drums*, whose Body is of Brass. ¶ *Drum*, or *Drummer*, is also a Soldier destined to beat the *Drum*. ¶ In each Company of Infantry there is at least one *Drum*, and a *Drum-Major* in every Regiment. ¶ There are divers Beats of the *Drum*: As the *March, Double March, Assembly, Charge, Retreat, Alarm, Chamade*, &c. **1735** DEFOE *Drum*, a musical warlike Instrument; **1736** BAILEY *Dict. Britannicum* (2nd edn) A *Drum* (*tromme, Dan. trommel, Du.* and G.) a warlike musical instrument. **1737** DYCHE-PARDON (2nd edn) *Drum* (S.) a Musical Instrument, that is generally made use of in the Army, to call the Soldiers together, and direct them how to act; the Body of it is made of a thin Piece of Oak, bent in a Cylindrical Form, and each End or Bottom is covered with Parchment, to make it sound, one of the Ends is struck with a Stick, and there are Braces on the Side, whereby the Sound may be rendered louder or slacker. *Drum* (V.) to play or beat upon the Instrument called a Drum;

drum major *see* retreat
1702 KERSEY *New Engl. Dict.* (1st edn) A *Drum-major, or* chief of the Drummers. **1708** KERSEY *Dict. Anglo-Brit.* (1st edn) *Drum-major*, the chief of the Drummers. **1730** BAILEY *Dict. Britannicum* (1st edn) *Drum-Major*, the chief drummer of a regiment. **1737** DYCHE-PARDON (2nd edn) *Drum-Major* (S.) the chief, principal, or head Drummer in an Army, Regiment, &c.

drummer *see* atambor, tympanist, valigiaro
1702 KERSEY *New Engl. Dict.* (1st edn) A *Drummer.* **1737** DYCHE-PARDON (2nd edn) *Drummer* (S.) one who beats or plays upon a Drum skilfully, particularly for Warlike Exercises.

drumslade *see* classicum, Corybant, naccara, symphoniacus, taballi, tambour, tambourine, tympanist, tympany

drumstick *see* bacchetta

drum strings *see* timbre

d sol re *see* diatonos
1676 MACE *Musick's Monument* (p. 197) ... *D-sol-re*, which is likewise [with *C-fa-ut-Key*] a very *Stately, Noble*, and *Majestick useful Key*; ...

dub *see* drub, rombo, tamburagione, tambussare

due
1724 [PEPUSCH] *Short Explic. of Foreign Words in Mus. Bks.* (p. 28) *Due, Dui*, and *Duo*, is the same as *Doi* above. **1726** BAILEY *An Univ. Etymolog. Engl. Dict.* (3rd edn) *Due*, two. *Ital.*

duet *see* duo
1724 [PEPUSCH] *Short Explic. of Foreign Words in Mus. Bks.* (p. 28) *Duetti*, or *Duetto*, are little Songs or Airs in two Parts. **1726** BAILEY *An Univ. Etymolog. Engl. Dict.* (3rd edn) *Duetti, Duetto*, (in *Musick Books*) signifies little Songs, or Airs in two Parts. *Ital.* **1737** BAILEY *The Univ. Etymolog. Engl. Dict.* (3rd edn, vol. 2) *Duet* (in *Musick*) a song or air compos'd for 2 voices. **1737** DYCHE-PARDON (2nd edn) *Duet* (S.) a musical Term for a Song or Air composed for two Voices.

c.1710 ANON. *Preceptor for Improved Octave Flageolet* ('Explanation of Words', p. 82) *Duetto* or *Duo*—Musick in two parts **1736** TANS'UR *Compleat Melody* (3rd edn, p. 72) *Duett*, or *Duetto*. (Ital.) signifies two Part.

dulcian
1598 FLORIO It→E *Dolzaina*, as *Dolcemelle.* **1599** MINSHEU-PERCYVALL Sp→E **Dulçayna*, f. a kinde of trumpet. **Dulzayna*, vide *Dulçayna.* **1611** COTGRAVE Fr→E *Doussaine: f.* A certein musicall instrument. **1611** FLORIO It→E *Dolzaina*, as *Dolcemelle.*

dulcimer *see* barbiton, citrial, doced, entata, harpsichord, pettine, sambuke
1598 FLORIO It→E *Dolcemelle*, a kinde of musicall instrument called a dulcimer. **1604** CAWDREY (1st edn) *dulcimur, dulcimar*, (Greeke) instrument. **1611** FLORIO It→E *Dolcemelle*, a musicall instrument called a Dulcimell or Dulcimer. **1656** BLOUNT (1st edn) *Dulcimer* or *Dulcimel (sambuca)* so called *quasi, dulce melos* i. sweet melody) [sic] a musical instrument. **1658** PHILLIPS (1st edn) *Dulcimer*, a kind of Musical Instrument, otherwise called a Sambuc. **1659** TORRIANO-FLORIO It→E *Dolce melle*, hony-sweet, also a kind of musicall instrument called a *Dulcimer*, or *Dulcimell* **1661** BLOUNT *Dulcimer* or *Dulcimel (sambuca)* so called, *quasi, dulce melos, i* sweet melody) [sic] a musical Instrument; A Sambuke. **1671** PHILLIPS (3rd edn) *Dulcimer*, a kind of Musical Instrument, otherwise called a Sambuc, in Greek ψαλτήριον. **1676** COLES *Dulcimer*, a wire-string'd instrument. **1702** KERSEY *New Engl. Dict.* (1st edn) A *Dulcimer*, a kind of musical instrument. **1704** *Cocker's Engl. Dict.* (1st edn) *Dulcimer*, a wire stringed Instrument. **1706** KERSEY-PHILLIPS (6th edn) *Dulcimer*, a kind of Musical Instrument. **1708** KERSEY *Dict. Anglo-Brit.* (1st edn) *Dulcimer*, a Musical Instrument. **1721** BAILEY *An Univ. Etymolog. Engl. Dict.* (1st edn) *Dulcimer, (Dolcemelle, Ital.)* a musical Instrument. **1737** BAILEY *The Univ. Etymolog. Engl. Dict.* (3rd edn, vol. 2) *Dulcimer* a musical instrument something like a harpsicord; but that whereas in making the strings of the latter sound by pushing down the keys, *&c.* the strings of the former are struck with small iron or brass pins. **1737** DYCHE-PARDON (2nd edn) *Dulcimer (S.)* a musical Instrument, somewhat resembling a Harpsicord, but instead of making the Strings speak by the pushing down of Keys, &c. they are struck with small Iron or Brass Pins, to bring out the Tones.

dulcino
1724 [PEPUSCH] *Short Explic. of Foreign Words in Mus. Bks.* (p. 28) *Dulcino*, a little or small Bassoon. **1726** BAILEY *An Univ. Etymolog. Engl. Dict.* (3rd edn) *Dulcino*, a small Bassoon. *Ital.* **1730** BAILEY *Dict. Britannicum* (1st edn) *Dulcino*, a small bassoon, *Ital.*

dulcisonant
1500 *Ortus Vocabulorum* L→E Dulcisonus a um. idest dulcis sonans. swete soundynge o.s. **1656** BLOUNT (1st edn) *Dulcisonant (dulcisonus)* that sounds sweetly. **1658** PHILLIPS (1st edn) *Dulcisonant*, (lat.)

sweetly sounding. **1676** COLES *Dulcisonant, Latin.* sweet-sounding.

dump *see* cantus

duo *see* duet, opera

1728 CHAMBERS *Duo,* in Music, a Song, or Composition to be perform'd in two Parts only; the one sung, and the other play'd on an Instrument; or by the two Voices alone. ¶ It is also call'd a *Duo,* when two Voices sing different Parts, accompanied with a Third, which is a thorough Bass. Unisons and Octaves must rarely be used in *Duo's,* except at the Beginning and End. **1730** BAILEY *Dict. Britannicum* (1st edn) *Duo* (in *Musick Books*) a song or composition to be performed in 2 parts only; the one sung, and the other plaid on an instrument; or by 2 voices alone.

dupla, duple *see* character, common time, imperfect of the less, ionick, pavan time, pointing, proportion, time

1596 ANON. *Pathway to Musicke* [E iii] *VVhat is the proportion called Dupla.* ¶ It is that vvhich taketh from all noates and rests the halfe vs[ual value] of the same sort, are vvorth but one; and it is knovvne vvhen the higher number doth conteine the lovver tvvice as thus. $\frac{2}{4}$ ... **1597** MORLEY *Plaine and Easie Introdvction* (pp. 27-8) *Phi.* What is *Dupla* proportion in Musicke? ¶ *Ma.* It is that which taketh halfe the value of euery note and rest from it, so that two notes of one kinde doe but answere to the value of one: and it is knowen when the vpper number contayneth the lower twise thus. $\frac{2}{1}\ \frac{4}{2}\ \frac{6}{3}\ \frac{8}{4}\ \frac{12}{6}$ &c. But by the way you must note that time out of minde we haue tearmed that dupla where we set two Minymes to the Semibriefe, which if it were trew, there should be few songs but you should haue dupla quadrupla and octupla in it, and then by consequent must cease to be dupla. But if they thinke that not inconuenient, I pray them how will they answere that which from time to time hath been set downe for a general rule amongst all musitions, that *proportions of the greater inequalitie, do alwaies signifie dimunution* [sic], and if their *minyms* be diminished, I pray you how shall two of them make vp the time of a full stroke, for *in all proportions the vpper number signifieth the semibriefe, and the lower number the stroke* ... § (p. 78) [marginalia: 'Descant commonly called Dupla.'] The making of twoe or more notes for one of the plainsong, which (as I tolde you before) is falslie termed *dupla,* and is, when for a semibriefe or note of the plainsong, wee make two minimes. **1609** DOWLAND-ORNITHOPARCUS *Micrologvs* (p. 62) *Of the Duple Proportion.* ¶ *Dvpla Proportio,* the first kind of the *Multiplex,* is when the greater number being in relation with the lesse, doth comprehend it in it selfe twise: as 4. to 2: 8 to 4. But Musically, when two Notes are vttered against one, which is like them both in nature and kinde. The signe of this some say is the number of 2: others (because *Proportion* is a Relation not of one thing, but of 2) affirme that one number is to be set vnder another, thus; $\frac{2}{1}\ \frac{4}{2}\ \frac{6}{3}$. And make no doubt but in all the rest this order is to be kept. **1636** BUTLER *Principles of Musik* (p. 24) *Duple* Proportion is, when to a *Stroke,* or *Sembrief-time,* is sung 2 *Minims,* (or one Sembrief which countervaileth them,) (and consequently 4 Crochets, 8 *Qavers,* and 16 *Semiqavers,*) one to the *Thesis* or Fall, and the other to *Arsis* or Rise of the Hand: the Signe whereof is this: ₵.

duplo

1731 PRELLEUR *Modern Musick-Master* (Dictionary, p. 2) *Duplo,* Double.

duration *see* echometer

1721 MALCOLM *Treatise of Musick* (pp. 265-6) The other chief Ingredient in *Musick* is the *Duration,* or Difference of Notes with respects to their uninterrupted Continuance in one *Tune,* and the Quickness or Slowness of their Succession; ...

durezza

c.1668-71 *Mary Burwell's Instruction Bk. for Lute* (*TDa* p. 45) ... If by his disapparition he brings night upon our hemisphere it is a chromatic in his music; the Italians call it a *durezza,* the English a thing hard in appearance to the ear ...

dwelling

c.1715-20 NORTH Theory of Sounds BL Add. 32534, f. 62v ... but If the string is but touched & let goe, then the Cooperating springs of y[e] air & y[e]. other of the spring susteine each other, Not Intirely but wasting, tho Not so fast as either would wast if not so susteined, and this is what they call y[e] dwelling of y[e] Sound that Recomends an Instrument; ...

E

e *see* ela
1737 Dyche-Pardon (2nd edn) *E* ... it also denotes the Tones *E la mi* on the Keys of Organs and Harpsichords, &c.

ebasis
1500 *Ortus Vocabulorum* L→E Ebasis. songe without maner f.t.

ecclesiastic style *see* church music, countertenor, modi melopœiæ, style

ecclesiastic tone *see* tuono di chiesa
1721 Malcolm *Treatise of Musick* (pp. 567-8) You may also *observe,* that what they [in former times] called the *Ecclesiastick Tones,* are no other than certain Notes in the *Organ* which are made the *Final* or *Fundamental* of the Hymns; and as Modes they differ, some by their Place in the Scale, others by the *sharp* and *flat 3d;* but even here every Author speaks not the same Way: 'Tis enough we know they can differ no other Way, or at least all their Differences can be reduced to these. At first they were Four in Number, whose *Finals* were *d, e, f, g.* constituted *authentically*: This Choice, we are told, was first made by St. *Ambrose* Bishop of *Milan;* and for being thus chosen and approven, they pretend the Name *Authentick* was added: Afterwards *Gregory* the *Great* added Four *Plagals a, b, c, d,* whose Finals are the very same with the first Four, and in effect are only a Continuation of these to the *4th* below; and for this Connection with them were called *plagal,* tho' the Derivation of the Word is not so plain.

echo *see* counterfugue, organ, p, pianissimo, piano, resonance
1724 [Pepusch] *Short Explic. of Foreign Words in Mus. Bks.* (p. 29) *Ecco,* or *Echus,* is an Eccho, which in Musick is the Repetition of some Part of a Song or Tune in a very low and soft Manner, in Imitation of a real or natural Eccho; the same is signified by the Words *Doux,* or *Piano.* **1726** Bailey *An Univ. Etymolog. Engl. Dict.* (3rd edn) *Ecco* (in *Musick Books*) signifies the Repetition of some Part of a Song or Tune in a very low or soft manner, in Imitation of a real or natural Eccho. *Ital. Echus* (in *Musick Books*) the same as *Ecco,* which see. **1728** Chambers *Echo,* or *Eccho,* a Sound reflected, or reverberated .... Lastly, *Echoing* Bodies may be so order'd, that from any one Sound given, they shall produce many *Echo's,* different both as to Tone and Intension. By which Means a Musical Room may be so contrived, that not only one Instrument playing therein, shall seem many of the same Sort and Size, but even a Consort of different Ones; only by placing certain *Echoing* Bodies so, as that any Note play'd, shall be return'd by them in 3ds, 5ths, and 8ths. **1737** Dyche-Pardon (2nd edn) *Eccho* or *Echo* (S.) ... and in *Musick,* it is the repeating some Part of the Strain over again in a very low or soft Tone;

1731 Prelleur *Modern Musick-Master* (Dictionary, p. 2) *Ecco* or *Echus* in imitation of a Natural Eccho, this Word is sometimes used instead of *Piano.* **1736** Tans'ur *Compleat Melody* (3rd edn, p. 68) *Echo, Echus,* (Ital.) Either of those Terms denote that such a *Part,* or *Strain* must be repeated over again in a very soft and low Manner; immitating a *Natural Eccho*: being respective to the *Organ, Harpsichord,* &c.

echometer
1728 Chambers *Echometre,* in Music, a Kind of Scale, or Rule, with several Lines divided thereon, serving to measure the Duration, or Length, of Sounds, and to find their Intervals and Ratio's. ¶ The Word is form'd of the *Greek,* ἦχος, *Sound,* and μετρον, *Measure.* **1730** Bailey *Dict. Britannicum* (1st edn) *Echometre* (of 'Ηχος sound, and μετρον, measure) a scale or rule divided on it, which serves to measure the duration or length of sounds, and to find their intervals and ratio's. **1737** Dyche-Pardon (2nd edn) *Echometere* (S.) in *Musick,* a Scale serving to measure the Length or Duration and Ratio of Sounds.

eclisse, esclisse
1650 Howell-Cotgrave Fr→E *Eclisse.* Look *Esclisse. Esclisses.* ... also, the sides of a Violl, or Fiddle. **1688** Miege-Cotgrave Fr→E *Eclisse,* (f.) ... the wooden part of a Childs Drum; the side of a Lute.

eclogue *see* bucolick
1500 *Ortus Vocabulorum* L→E Egloga est pars bucolici carminis. alij volunt ecloga scribi per c f.p. **1598** FLORIO It→E *Egloga,* an eglogue, a choice discourse. *Eglogare,* to write or sing eglogues. **1599** MINSHEU-PERCYVALL Sp→E *Egloga,* f. an eglog, a pastorall dittie. **Hegloga,* vide *Egloga,* f. a pastorall speech or heardmans song. **1706** KERSEY-PHILLIPS (6th edn) *Ægloga,* a Pastoral Song. See *Eclogue. Eclogue* (*i.e.* a choice Piece) the title of *Virgil*'s Pastoral Poems; a Shepherd's Song, or Rural Ditty. **1708** KERSEY *Dict. Anglo-Brit.* (1st edn) *Ægloga,* a Pastoral Song.

1589 [PUTTENHAM] *Arte of English Poesie* (p. 30) *Of the Shepheards or pastorall Poesie called Eglogue, and to vvhat purpose it vvas first inuented and vsed.* Some be of opinion, and the chiefe of those who haue written in this Art among the Latines, that the pastorall Poesie which we commonly call by the name of *Eglogue* and *Bucolick,* a tearme brought in by the Sicilian Poets, should be the first of any other, and before the *Satyre* comedie or tragedie, because, say they, the shepheards and haywards assemblies & meetings when they kept their cattell and heards in the common fields and forests, was the first familiar conuersation, and their babble and talk vnder bushes and shadie trees, the first disputation and contentious reasoning, and their fleshly heates growing of ease, the first idle wooings, and their songs made to their mates or paramours either vpon sorrow or iolity of courage, the first amorous musicks, sometime also they sang and played on their pipes for wagers, striuing who should get the best game, and be counted cunningest.

eighth *see* diapason, octave
1596 ANON. *Pathway to Musicke* [B iv] An eight is the distance of the voice by an eight, consisting of fiue tunes and tvvo halfe tunes: Of vvhich there be seauen kindes, from euerie key to his like, vvith like names of notes. **1597** MORLEY *Plaine and Easie Introdvction* (p. 70) ... *an Vnison, a Fift,* and their eights. ¶ *Phi.* What do you meane by *their eights.* ¶ *Ma. Those notes which are distant from them eight notes,* as from an *vnison,* an *eight,* from a *fift,* a *twelfe.* **1721** MALCOLM *Treatise of Musick* (p. 246) And now at last we understand from whence the Names of *8ve, 6th, 5th,* &c. come; the Relations to which these Names are annexed are so called, because in the *natural Scale* of *Musick* the Terms [intervallic members] that are in these Relations to the *Fundamental* are the *Third, Fourth, &c.* in order from that *Fundamental* inclusively. Or thus, because the *harmonical Intervals* being *concinnously* divided, contain betwixt their Extremes (including both) so many Terms or Notes as the Names *8ve, 6th, &c.* bear.

eighth tone
1609 DOWLAND-ORNITHOPARCUS *Micrologvs* (p. 35) The Eight *Tone* is a Rule determining the *plagall* of the fourth sort. Or it is the *plagall* Progression of the fourth, possessing the same end that his *Authenticke* doth. The beginnings of it are *D. F. G. a.* and *c.*

ela *see* e, elio
1656 BLOUNT (1st edn) *Ela,* the highest note in the *Gamut.* **1658** PHILLIPS (1st edn) *Ela,* the highest note in the scale of Musick, or *Gam ut.* **1659** TORRIANO-FLORIO It→E **Ela,* the highest note of the Gamuth. **1671** PHILLIPS (3rd edn) *Elami,* the name of the sixth note of each septenary of the ordinary scale of Musick, onely in the uppermost S[e]ptenary *Mi* is wanting, and the note is called *Ela,* only. **1676** COLES *Ela,* the highest note in the Common scale of Musick. *Elami,* the sixt note in Musick. **1704** *Cocker's Engl. Dict.* (1st edn) *Ela,* the highest Note in the common Scale of Musick; as *gamut* is the lowest. **1706** KERSEY-PHILLIPS (6th edn) *E-la-mi,* the Name of the sixth ascending Note of each Septenary or Order of Seven Notes in the Scale of *Musick,* only in the uppermost Septenary *mi* is wanting, and the Note is call'd *E-la.* **1708** KERSEY *Dict. Anglo-Brit.* (1st edn) *E-la-mi,* the sixth ascending Note of each Septenary or Order of Seven Notes in the Scale of *Musick.* **1721** BAILEY *An Univ. Etymolog. Engl. Dict.* (1st edn) *Ela,* (perhaps of *Eleva,* L.) the highest Note in the Scale of Musick. **1737** DYCHE-PARDON (2nd edn) *Ela* (S.) the highest Note in the common Scale of Musick.

elegiographer
1538 ELYOT L→E *Elegiographus,* a writer of lamentable versis, or balades. **1552** HULOET L→E *Elegiographus* Wryter of lamentable verses, or balades. **1565** COOPER L→E *Elegiógraphus, phi, mas. g.* A writer of lamentable verses or balades. **1587** THOMAS L→E *Elegiographus,* *A writer of lamentable verses. **1589** RIDER L→E *Elegiographus, m.* A writer of lamentable verses. **1611** FLORIO It→E *Elego,* a writer of elegies. **1623** COCKERAM *Elegiographer.* Which writes mournefull songs.

1656 BLOUNT (1st edn) *Elegiographer (elegiographus)* a writer of Elegies, or lamentable verses. **1676** COLES *Elegiographer*, a writer of Elegies. **1706** KERSEY-PHILLIPS (6th edn) *Eliographus*, a Writer of Elegies. **1721** BAILEY *An Univ. Etymolog. Engl. Dict.* (1st edn) *Elegiographer*, (*Elegiographus*, L. ἐλεγειογράφος, *Gr.*) a Writer of Elegies.

elegy *see* dirge, epicedy, epitaph, monody, nænia, obit, threnody

1538 ELYOT L→E *Elegia*, a lamentable songe or verse. *Elegus*, the same. *Elegiacus, ca, cum*, pertaynynge therto. **1552** HULOET L→E *Elegeia, Elegia, Epiodium, Epicedium, Epiædium canticum, monodia, nænia, æ, & orum*, Lamentable songe or verse. **1565** COOPER L→E *Elegia, æ, f.g.* Lamentablenes: a lamentable songe. **1587** THOMAS L→E *Elegia, æ, f.g p b. Ovid.* Lamentablenes, a lamentable song. *Elegia, orum, n.g. p.l Plaut* Lamentable verses. **1589** RIDER L→E *Elegia, threnodia, f. threnum, n. threnos.* A lamentable, or mourning song. *Elegidium, elegia, n. elegus, m. elegia, monodia, f. epiodium, threnos, threnum, n, canticum.* A lamentable song, verse, or verses. **1598** FLORIO It→E *Elegia*, an elegie or mournfull verse. *Elegiaco*, an elegiacal or mournful verse. *Elegiare*, to sing or make elegies in wailfull verse. *Elegidio*, a kind of lamentable verse. **1599** MINSHEU-PERCYVALL Sp→E *Elegia*, f. a mournefull song. **Elegiaco*, of or pertaining to a mournfull song. **1611** COTGRAVE Fr→E *Elegiaque*. Elegiacall, belonging to an Elegie; lamenting, mournefull. *Elegie: f.* An Elegie; a mournefull verse, Poeme, Song, or Dittie. **1611** FLORIO It→E *Elegia*, an elegie or mournefull verse. *Elegiaco*, an elegiacall or mournefull verse. *Elegiare*, to singe or make elegies in wailefull verse. *Elegidio*, a kind of wailefull verse. **1616** BULLOKAR *Elegie.* A mournefull song vsed in funerals, or other passions of sorrow. **1623** COCKERAM *Elegie.* A mournefull song vsed at funeralls. *Elegies, Monodies.* mournfull Songs **1656** BLOUNT (1st edn) *Elegy (elegia)* a mourneful song or verse, commonly used at Funerals, or upon the death of any person. *Elegiacal (elegiacus)* belonging to an Elegy or lamentation. **1658** PHILLIPS (1st edn) *Elegie*, (Greek) a kinde of mournefull verse, or Funeral song. **1661** BLOUNT (2nd edn) *Elegy (elegia)* a mournful song or verse, commonly used at Funerals, or upon the death of any person, and composed of unequal verses. **1676** COLES *Elegie, Greek.* a kind of mournfull verse, or funeral song. **1704** *Cocker's Engl. Dict.* (1st edn) *Elegy*, a Mournful song, commonly used at Funerals. **1706** KERSEY-PHILLIPS (6th edn) *Elegy*, a Mournful Poem, a Funeral Song, a lamentable Ditty. **1707** *Gloss. Angl. Nova* (1st edn) *Elegy*, a mourneful Song or Verse, commonly used at Funerals, or upon the death of any Person. **1708** KERSEY *Dict. Anglo-Brit.* (1st edn) *Elegey*, a Mournful Poem, a Funeral Song.

1589 [PUTTENHAM] *Arte of English Poesie* (p. 39) [*re* the history of poetry] ... The third sorrowing was of loues, by long lamentation in *Elegie*: so was their song called, and it was in a pitious maner of meetre, placing a limping *Pentameter*, after a lusty *Exameter*, which made it go dolourously more then any other meeter.

elevation *see* beat, grace

1659 SIMPSON *Division-Violist* (p. 9) Sometimes a *Note* is graced by sliding to it from the *Third below*, called an *Elevation*, now something obsolete. Sometimes from the *Third above*; which we call a Double *Backfall*. This sliding a *Third, up*, or *down*, is alwayes done upon one String. Again; a *Note* is sometimes graced by joyning part of its sound to the *Note* following; like a *Prickt-Crochet*: whose following *Quaver* is Placed with the ensuing *Note*, but Played with the same *Bow* of his *Prickt-Crochet*: This we will call a *Cadent*.

elio *see* ela

1598 FLORIO It→E *Elio*, a kind of musicke or concord. **1611** FLORIO It→E *Elio*, a kind of musike or concord.

elysian fields

1736 BAILEY *Dict. Britannicum* (2nd edn) *Elysian Fields* ... a certain paradise of delightful groves and smiling meadows, into which, the heathens held that the souls of good men passed after death; ... all agree that in these *Elysian* fields, there was a perpetual spring, gentle breezes, a pure and temperate air, ... that the ear was delighted with a perpetual harmony either of birds or musicians; that the souls there celebrated a perpetual festival, with merriment and dancing;

embouchure *see* tampon

embroidery *see* variation

emiolio *see* hemiola

1659 TORRIANO-FLORIO It→E *Emiolio*, a kind of musical harmony.

emmeli

1609 DOWLAND-ORNITHOPARCUS *Micrologvs* (pp. 78-9) ... Voyces are called some *Vnisons*; some not *Vnisons*... Of not *Vnisons*, some are *æquisons*; some *Consones*; some *Emmeles*; ... *Emmeles* are they, which being not *Consones*, yet are next to *Consones*: as those which sound thirds, sixts, or other imperfect *Concords*. **1721** MALCOLM *Treatise of Musick* (p. 508) [*re* Ptolomy]... the other *Intervals* belonging to *Musick* [after the omophoni and synphoni] he calls *Emmeli* or *concinnous*...

emmelia *see* dance

1565 COOPER L→E *Emelia, æ, fœ. ge.* A certayne quiet kynde of daunsing, as it were a pauion. **1587** THOMAS L→E *Emmelia, æ, f.g.* *A certaine quiet kinde of daunse, as it were a pavion. **1589** RIDER L→E *Eumelia.* A certaine quiet kind of dance, as it were a pavin. **1598** FLORIO It→E *Emmeli, Ecmeli*, a worde of arte about musicke. Some take it to be a lowe silent musicke. **1611** COTGRAVE Fr→E *Emmelie.* A quiet kind of daunce, as the Pauin, Measure, &c: *Rab.* **1611** FLORIO It→E *Emmeli, Ecmeli*, a word of arte about musicke, some take it for low silent musicke.

1712 WEAVER *Essay towards History of Dancing* (p. 95) Among the Ancients (*viz.* the *Greeks* and *Romans*,) there were three sorts of *Dancing*; one Grave call'd **Emmelia*; [marginalia: '*which belong'd to Tragedies, and wherein the Majesty of Princes was shewn...'] one Gay or Brisk call'd *Cordax*, and another nam'd *Sicinis*, a *Satyrical Dance*, wherein the Grave and Brisk were intermix'd.

emodulor *see* modulor

1565 COOPER L→E *Emodulor, pen. cor. emodulâris, emodulâtus sum, emodulari, Ouid.* To singe in measure or proportion. **1587** THOMAS L→E *Emodulor, aris, depon. p.l Ovid.* To sing in measure or proportion.

emolia

1598 FLORIO It→E *Emolia*, a proportion or vnion in musicke. **1611** FLORIO It→E *Emolia*, a proportion or vnion in Musicke. **1659** TORRIANO-FLORIO It→E *Emolia*, a just proportion, or harmonious union in musick.

empneusta *see* entata

enchafouiné

1611 COTGRAVE Fr→E *Enchafouiné: m. ée: f.* Out of tune, out of temper ... **1650** HOWELL-COTGRAVE Fr→E † *Enchafouine: m. ée: f.* Out of tune, out of temper ...

enclavijado *see* claveta

1599 MINSHEU-PERCYVALL Sp→E **enClavijado*, m. ... wound vp or wrested as pegs or pins of an instrument

encomium

1565 COOPER L→E *Encomion, mij, neut. gene.* Prayse: a songe made in ones prayse. **1587** THOMAS L→E *Encomiastes*, *He that praiseth another, or singeth that song. *Encomnum* [sic], *mij, n.g.* *A praise, a song in the commendation of a mans vertues. **1598** FLORIO It→E *Encomio*, a song of praise or commendations. **1611** FLORIO It→E *Encomio*, a song of praise or commendation. **1656** BLOUNT (1st edn) *Encomium* (Lat.) a praise or song in commendation of any person. *Encomiastick (encomiasticus)* belonging to (or one that writes) an Encomium; **1659** TORRIANO-FLORIO It→E *Encomiasto*, a singer of an encomium, or of another mans praises. **1702** KERSEY *New Engl. Dict.* (1st edn) An *Encomium*, a speech, *or* song in commendation of one. **1706** KERSEY-PHILLIPS (6th edn) *Encomiast*, a Maker of Encomiums. *Encomium*, a Speech, or Song, in Commendation of a Person; Praise.

1589 [PUTTENHAM] *Arte of English Poesie* (p. 35) [*re* the history of poetry] ... So haue you how the immortall gods were praised by hymnes, the great Princes and heroicke personages by ballades of praise called *Encomia*, both of them by historicall reports of great grauitie and maiestie, the inferiour persons by other slight poemes. § (p. 37) [*re* the history of poetry] ... Those that were to honour the persons of great Princes or to solemnise the pompes of any installment were called *Encomia*, we may call them carols of honour.

encore *see* repeat, repetatur

enharmonic *see* genus, scale, species

1598 FLORIO It→E *Enarmonico*, a certaine harmonie and concord in musicke of nine voices or nine strings. **1611** FLORIO It→E *Enarmonico*, an harmonie or concord in Musicke of nine voices or nine strings. **1661** BLOUNT (2nd edn) *Enharmoniack (enharmonion)* one of the three general sorts of Musick; song of many parts, or a curious concent of sundry Tunes. **1671** PHILLIPS (3rd edn) *Enharmonic,* one of those Genus's of Musick which makes a different mode of harmony and air from the other two; viz. the *Chromatic,* and *Diatonic.* **1676** COLES *Enharmonick, -iack,* [(] Musick) of many parts, differing from the other 2 kinds, *Chromatick,* and *Diatonick.* **1696** PHILLIPS (5th edn) *Enharmonick,* one of those Genus's of Musick which makes a different Mode of Harmony and Air, from the other two, *viz.* the *Chromatick* and *Diatonick;* and which abounds in *Dieses's* or Sharps. **1704** HARRIS *Enharmonical, Enharmonick,* a Term in Musick, usually applied to the last of the three Kinds of Musick, abounding in *Diesis,* which are the least sensible Division of a Tone. See *Diesis.* **1706** KERSEY-PHILLIPS (6th edn) *Enharmonical* or *Enharmonick Musick, (Gr.)* the last of the three kinds of Musick in use among the Ancients abounding with Diesis; a particular manner of turning the Voice, and disposing the Intervals with such Art, that the Melody becomes more moving. See *Chromatick* and *Diatonick.* § *Enharmonical Diesis.* See *Diesis.* **1707** *Gloss. Angl. Nova* (1st edn) *Enharmonical,* a Musical Term, usually apply'd to the last of the three sorts of Musick, and abounds in Diesis's or Sharps. **1720** KERSEY-PHILLIPS (7th edn) *Enharmonical Diesis,* is the Difference between the greater and the lesser Semi-tone. These *Dieses* are the least sensible Divisions of a Tone, and are mark'd on the Score, in form of St. *Andrew*'s Cross. **1728** CHAMBERS *Enharmonic,* the last of the three *Genera,* or Kinds of Music. See *Genera.* ¶ The *Enharmonic* Genus, is said to have been thus called by Reason of its superior Excellence; Tho' wherein that consists, says Mr. *Malcolm,* we don't see. It was by all acknowledged so difficult, that few could practise it. ¶ The several *Genera* are divided into Diastems, upon which the Differences depend: Those of the *Enharmonic* are the *Diesis* and *Ditonum*: Those of the *Chromatic,* the *Hemitonium* and *Triemitonium;* and in the *Diatonic,* the *Hemitonium,* or *Limma,* and the *Tonus.* ¶ But under these general Names, which distinguish the *Genera,* there are several different Intervals, or Ratio's, which constitute the *Chroai,* or *Colores Generum,* or Species of *Enharmonic, Chromatic,* and *Diatonic.* See *Diatonic,* and *Chromatic.* **1730** BAILEY *Dict. Britannicum* (1st edn) *Enharmonical, Enharmonick,* of or pertaining to enharmonick musick. *Enharmonic Music,* a particular manner of tuning the voice, and disposing the intervals with such art, that the melody becomes more moving. The last of the three kinds of musick used by the ancients, and abounding in *Dieses* or *Sharps.* See *Cromatick* and *Diatonick.*

1597 MORLEY *Plaine and Easie Introdvction* (annotations to Part I) *Enharmonicum,* is that [kind of music] which riseth by *diesis, diesis,* (*diesis* is the halfe of the lesse halfe note) and *ditonus.* But in our musicke, I can giue no example of it, because we haue no halfe of a lesse *semitonium,* but those who would shew it, set downe this example of *enharmonicum,* and marke the diesis thus X as is were the halfe of the *apotome* or greater halfe note, which is marked thus ✕. This signe of the more halfe note, we now adaies confound with our *b* square [sic], or signe of *mi* in *b fa* ♮ *mi,* and with good reason: for when *mi* is sung in *b fa* ♮ *mi,* it is in that habitude to *alamire,* as the double *diesis* maketh *Ffaut* sharpe to *Elami,* for in both places the distance is a whole note. **1688** SALMON *Proposal to Perform Musick* (p. 16) *Enharmonick* Musick is that which ascends and descends gradually by quarter Notes, which the Ancients called Dieses: I don't mean that the whole Octave, either in this or the *Chromatick* Music, did consist only of these; but after having used some of them, they took wider Steps and larger Intervals afterwards to compleat the Fourth and Fifth. **1721** MALCOLM *Treatise of Musick* (p. 516) As to the Names of the *Genera* themselves, the *Enharm.* was so called as by a general Name; or some say for its Excellence (tho' where that lies we don't well know.) ... **1728** NORTH Musicall Grammarian (*C-K MG* f. 110) ... The other scale is called enharmonick; which by its name one would expect had most of harmony, but in truth there is litle or none belongs to it. For the steps are by 2 dieses or (as wee terme them) quarter notes, and then into the fourth by a ditone, or 3d sharp.

entata

1636 BUTLER *Principles of Musik* (p. 93) Instruments ar of 2 sorts: (*Entata,* and *Empneusta*: String- and Winde-Instruments. ¶ Of bothe these sorts, the pregnant wits of industrious Artists have devised many different kindes: as (of *Entata*) *Harp, Lute, Bandora, Orpharion, Cittern, Gittern, Cymbal, Psalteri, Dulcimer, Viol, Virginal, &c.* and (of *Empneusta*) *Pipe, Organ, Shalm, Sagbut, Cornet, Recorder, Fluit, Waits or Hobois, Trumpet,* &c.

entertain
1737 Dyche-Pardon (2nd edn) *Entertain* (V.) ... also to please or amuse them by Singing, playing upon Musical Instruments

entertainment *see* ridotta
1737 Dyche-Pardon (2nd edn) *Entertainment* (S.) ... also any Diversion, as a Play, Consort of Musick, &c.

enthusiasm *see* Corybant
1728 Chambers *Enthusiasm*, a prophetic, or poetic Rage, or Fury, which transports the Mind, enflames and raises the Imagination, and makes it think and express Things extraordinary and surprizing.... This is the *Enthusiasm* felt in Poetry, Oratory, Music, Painting, Sculpture, *&c.*

entonacion, entonnement *see* intonation

entrée *see* branle, intrada, overture, prelude
1724 [Pepusch] *Short Explic. of Foreign Words in Mus. Bks.* (p. 29) *Entree*, or *Entre*, is a particular Kind of Air so called. **1726** Bailey *An Univ. Etymolog. Engl. Dict.* (3rd edn) *Entre, Entree*, (in Musick Books) signifies a particular sort of Air. *Ital.*

entry *see* grave

entunes
1676 Coles *Entunes, Old word.* tunes. **1726** Bailey *An Univ. Etymolog. Engl. Dict.* (3rd edn) *Entunes*, to tune, to sing. *Chaucer.*

envoy
1593 Hollyband Fr→E *Envoy*, the rifreine of a Ballade, that is, the foote of a song: *m.* **1611** Cotgrave Fr→E *Envoy*... also, th'Enuoy, or conclusion of a Ballet, or Sonnet; **1706** Kersey-Phillips (6th edn) *Envoy, (Fr.)* ... Also the Conclusion of a Ballad or Song. **1708** Kersey *Dict. Anglo-Brit.* (1st edn) *Envoy*, (F.) ... Also the Conclusion of a Ballad, or Song

c.1726 North Musicall Gramarian BL Add. 32533, ff. 160v-161 The method of the old fancy's was to begin with a solemne fuge, and ... A tripla perhaps, or some yet freer aire, but ye tripla for the most part is of ye Graver sort. And Concluded often with a Lenvoy'e as they called it, & not with a jigg as now ye mode is, but rather an adagio with this stately semiclose... [gives example: see *JWi* p. 290]

eolic *see* æolian

Epaminondas *see* Olympiodorus
1565 Cooper L→E *Epaminondas*, A Theban borne, (sonne of an honest gentyll manne called Polymnus) in sundrie qualities excellent, as wel of the bodie as of the mynde, in all kyndes of musyke perfectly instructed, and danced exceadingly well.

epicedy *see* dirge, elegy, epiod, epitaph, monody, nænia, obit, præfica, threnody
1500 *Ortus Vocabulorum* L→E Epicedium. est carmen de aliquo mortuo factum n.s. **1552** Huloet L→E *Epicedium, Epi[c]ædium, Canticum, Epiodium, monodia, Nænia. æ. Naeua. orum, Threnodia æ*, Mournynge songe for the deade. **1565** Cooper L→E *Epicedium.* Verses made in prayse of a dead man. **1587** Thomas L→E *Epicedium, dij, n.g. p.b. in exequiis fiebat, dum iusta funeri persolvebantur, Iun.* A funerall song sung before the course [sic] be buried. **1598** Florio It→E *Epicedio*, a funerall song, sung before the corps be buried. **1611** Florio It→E *Epicedio*, a funerall song, sung before the corpes be buried. **1613** Cawdrey (3rd edn) *epiced*, funerall song. **1656** Blount (1st edn) *Epicedium* (Lat.) a Funeral Song, or verses in praise of the dead, which were wont to be sung before the Corps were buryed. **1658** Phillips (1st edn) *Epicedie*, (Greek) a certain mournful Song, which used to be sung before the corps at a Funeral. **1676** Coles *Epicedie, Greek. -ium*, a funeral song. **1704** *Cocker's Engl. Dict.* (1st edn) *Epicedium*, a Funeral Song before the Interring a Corps, also verses in praise of the dead. **1706** Kersey-Phillips (6th edn) *Epicedium*, a Funeral Song, or Copy of Verses in praise of the Dead. **1708** Kersey *Dict. Anglo-Brit.* (1st edn) *Epicedium*, a Funeral Song, or Copy of Verses in praises of the Dead.

1589 [Puttenham] *Arte of English Poesie* (p. 39) [*re* the history of poetry] ... And the lamenting of deathes was chiefly at the very burialls of the dead, also at monethes mindes and longer times, by custome continued yearly, when as they vsed many offices of seruice and loue towardes the dead, and thereupon are called *Obsequies* in our vulgare, which was done not onely by cladding the mourners their friendes and seruauntes in blacke vestures, of shape dolefull and sad, but also by wofull countenaunces and voyces, and besides by Poeticall mournings in verse. Such funerall songs were called *Epicedia* if they were song by many, and *Monodia* if they were vttered by one alone, and this was vsed at the enterment of Princes and others of great accompt, and it was reckoned a great ciuilitie to vse such ceremonies, as at this day is also in some countreys vsed.

epicitharisma

1587 THOMAS L→E *Epicitharisma, p.b. Tertull.* The last parte of an enterlude, wherein, after the auditours had bin wearied, a harper stepped forth and played. **1589** RIDER L→E *Epicitharisma, n.* The last part of an enterlud, wher [sic] in after the auditors haue beene wearied, a harper steppeth forth & plaied. **1598** FLORIO It→E *Epicitharisma,* the last part of the enterlude, wherein after the auditors had bin wearied musitians stept foorth and plaide. **1611** FLORIO It→E *Epicitharisma,* the last part of the interlude, wherein after the auditors had beene wearied musicians stept foorth and plaid. **1659** TORRIANO-FLORIO It→E *Epicitharisma,* the last part of a Comedy, wherein after the auditors had been wearied, Musitians stept forth and plaid. **1706** KERSEY-PHILLIPS (6th edn) *Epicitharisma,* (in the ancient Theaters) the last part of the Interlude, or a Flourish of Musick after the Play was done.

epigonium *see* bridal, epithalamy, hymen, thalassion

1598 FLORIO It→E *Epigonea,* a kinde of musicall instrument or musicke plaide at mariages. **1611** FLORIO It→E *Epigonea,* a kinde of musicall instrument or musike plaide at marriages.

1721 MALCOLM *Treatise of Musick* (p. 468) *Epigonius* was the Author of an Instrument called *Epigonium,* of 40 Strings; ...

epilemie

1611 COTGRAVE Fr→E *Epilemie.* A song of the superscription of a thing. *Rab.*

epinette *see* spinet

epinicion

1587 THOMAS L→E *Epinicia, orum, n.g. p.b. Suet.* A feast made in reioycing for a victorie, as a feast at a bonfire: verses or songes of triumph. **1598** FLORIO It→E *Epinicie,* verses or songs of triumph after some victorie. **1611** COTGRAVE Fr→E *Epinices.* Feasts, verses, or songs of triumph after a victorie. *Rab.* **1611** FLORIO It→E *Epinicie,* verses or songes of triumph after some victory. **1706** KERSEY-PHILLIPS (6th edn) *Epinicion,* a Song of Triumph after a Victory. **1707** *Gloss. Angl. Nova* (1st edn) *Epinicion,* a Triumphal Song. **1730** BAILEY *Dict. Britannicum* (1st edn) *Epinicion* (ἐπιμύθιον, Gr.) a triumphal song, or song for victory, also a feast or rejoycing on that account. **1737** DYCHE-PARDON (2nd edn) *Epinicion* (S.) among the *Greeks,* was a Feast or publick Rejoicing for a Victory obtained, or a triumphal Song or Poem.

epiod *see* elegy, epicedy

1565 COOPER L→E *Epicœdium, dij, n.g.* A songe songe [sic] before the corse be buried. **1623** COCKERAM *Epiædean* [sic] *Song.* A Song sung, ere the corps bee buried. *Epiodian-Songe,* a Song sung ere the corse bee buried **1661** BLOUNT (2nd edn) *Epiod (epiodium)* a song sung before the Corps were buried. **1676** COLES *Epiod, Greek.* a song before the burying of the corps.

episode *see* act, chorus, pavan, tragedy

1611 FLORIO It→E *Episodio,* ... Also a pleasing or delightfull digression, as in Homers Iliade the description of the number of the ships. Also a Panegyrike verse sung in praise of any Emperour or Prince at his first entry into a towne or principality. **1728** CHAMBERS *Episode, Episodium,* in dramatic Poetry, was the second part of the ancient Tragedy. See *Tragedy.* ¶ The Origin and Use of *Episodes,* is admirably described by M. *Hedelin,* and Fa. *Bossu.* Tragedy, in its Original, being only a Hymn sung in Honour of *Bacchus,* by several Persons, who made a Kind of Chorus, or Consort of Music, with Dancing, and the like; to diversify the Representation a little, and divert the Audience, they bethought themselves at length to divide the Singing of the Chorus into several parts; and to have something rehears'd in the Intervals. ¶ At first, a single Person, or Actor, was introduced, then two, then more; and what the Actors thus rehearsed, or entertain'd the Audience withal, being something foreign, or additional to, or beside, the Song of the Chorus, and no necessary part thereof, was call'd Επεισοδιον, *Episode.* ¶ And hence Tragedy came to consist of four parts, the *Prologue, Episode, Exode,* and *Chorus.* ¶ The *Prologue* was all that preceded the first Entrance of the Chorus. See *Prologue.* ¶ The *Episode,* all that was interposed between the Singings of the Chorus. ¶ The *Exode,* all that was rehearsed after the Chorus had done singing. See *Exordium.* ¶ And the *Chorus,* was the Grex [sic], or Company that sung the Hymn. See *Chorus.... Episode* in *Epic* Poetry.... But further, as all that was sung in the Tragedy, was call'd the *Chorus,* in the singular Number; yet this Singularity did by no means prevent every Part or Division of the same from being call'd a *Chorus,* without making several *Chorus's*: So 'twas with the *Episode*: Each Incident, and part of the Fable and Action, is not only a part of the *Episode,* but an *Episode* it self.

epistomium

1587 THOMAS L→E *Epistomium, ij, n.g. p.b. Sen. ... also,* the stop in a paire of organes, whereby the sound is made high or low. **1598** FLORIO It→E *Epistomio,* a stop in a paire of organes whereby the sound is made high or low. **1611** FLORIO It→E *Epistomio,* a stop in a paire of organes whereby the sound is made high or low. **1706** KERSEY-PHILLIPS (6th edn) *Epistomium,* ... Also the stop in a pair of Organs, whereby the Sound is made high or low. **1720** KERSEY-PHILLIPS (7th edn) *Episcomium* [sic], ... Also the stop in a pair of Organs, whereby the Sound is made high or low.

epitaph *see* dirge, elegy, epicedy, monody, nænia, obit, threnody

1587 THOMAS L→E *Epitaphium, ij, n.g. p.b.* ... a funeral song vsed at the tomb. **1598** FLORIO It→E *Epitaphio, Epitafio,* ... Also a funerall song vsed or sung at a tombe. **1611** FLORIO It→E *Epitaphio, Epitafio,* ... Also a funerall song vsed or sung at a tombe or buriall. **1656** BLOUNT (1st edn) *Epitaph (epitaphium)* an inscription or writing, set upon a Tomb, most commonly in lamentation or praise of the party there buried: The invention whereof is referred to the Scholars of *Linus,* who first bewailed their Master when hee was slain, in doleful verses, then called of him *Ælina,* afterwards *Epitaphia,* for that they were first sung at burials, after engraved upon the Sepulchers...

epithalamy *see* bridal, epigonium, hillulim, hymen, marriage music, nuptial, pitalamio, thalassion

1500 *Ortus Vocabulorum* L→E Epitalamium mij. i. cantus qui fit super thalamum. i. super sponsum et sponsam n.s. **1538** ELYOT L→E *Epithalamium,* a songe beinge songe atte a weddynge, or verses made in the praise of them that are maried. **1565** COOPER L→E *Epithalamium, mij, n.g.* A songe or prayse, songe at a weddyng. **1587** THOMAS L→E *Epithalamium, n.g. p.b. Isid.* A song sung at a wedding. **1598** FLORIO It→E *Epitalamio,* a song sung at a wedding. **1611** COTGRAVE Fr→E *Epithalme.* A wedding Song, or Poeme; verses made, or a song sung, at a wedding, in commendation of the parties married. **1611** FLORIO It→E *Epitalamio,* a song sung at mariages. **1656** BLOUNT (1st edn) *Epithalamy (epithalamium)* a Bridal, Song, or Poem, or a Song at a Wedding, in commendation of the parties married; Such was that of *Solomon, Psal.* 45 wherein the praise of the Church and her spiritual Marriage and Union with Christ is set down. Such also is that of *Stella* in *Statius,* and of *Julia* in *Catullus, &c.* It is so called from the Greek word *epi. i. apud,* and *Thalamus,* which signifies a Bed-Chamber, but more properly a Bride-Chamber, because this Song was used to be sung at the door of the Bride-Chamber, when the Bride bedded. There are two kinds of *Epithalamies,* the one used to be sung at night, when the married couple entred [sic] Bed; the other in the morning, to raise them up. *Min.* **1658** PHILLIPS (1st edn) *Epithalamy,* (Greek) a Nuptial Song, or Poem which useth to be recited at Weddings in praise of the Bride, and Bridegroom. **1659** TORRIANO-FLORIO It→E *Epitalamio,* a marriage song, a song sung at marriages. **1661** BLOUNT (2nd edn) *Epithalamize,* to make or sing an Epithalamy or Bridal song. **1671** PHILLIPS (3rd edn) *Epithalamy, (Greek)* a Nuptial Song, or Poem (which used anciently to be recited at Weddings) in praise of the Bride and Bridegroom, wishing a fruitfull Issue, and all things conducing to a future happy life, and now and then wantonly glancing upon the pleasures of the marriage bed. **1676** COLES *Epithalamie, -mium, Greek.* a nuptial or wedding song. **1702** KERSEY *New Engl. Dict.* (1st edn) An *Epithalamium,* a nuptial, *or* wedding song. **1704** *Cocker's Engl. Dict.* (1st edn) *Epithalamium,* a Nuptial or Marriage Song, in praise of Matrimony. **1706** KERSEY-PHILLIPS (6th edn) *Epithalamium,* a Nuptial Song or Poem, which anciently us'd to be rehearsed at Weddings, in Praise of the Bride and Bridegroom; wishing them a fruitful Issue, and all things conducing to a future happy Life; also now and then wantonly glancing upon the Pleasures of the Marriage-bed. **1707** *Gloss. Angl. Nova* (1st edn) *Epithalamium,* a Nuptial Song or Poem in praise of the parties married. **1721** BAILEY *An Univ. Etymolog. Engl. Dict.* (1st edn) *Epithalamium, (Epithalame, F.* of Ἐπιθαλάμιον, *Gr.)* a Nuptial Song or Poem in the Praise of the Bride and Bridegroom, and wishing them

Happiness and a Fruitful time, formerly sung at Weddings. *L.* **1728** CHAMBERS *Epithalium,* in Poetry, a *Nuptial Song;* or a Composition, usually in Verse, on Occasion of a Marriage between two Persons of Eminence. ¶ The Topicks it chiefly insists on, are the Praises of Matrimony, and of the Married Couple; with the Pomp and Order of the Marriage Solemnity. It concludes, with praying to the Gods for their Prosperity, their happy Offspring, *&c. Catullus* exceeded all Antiquity, in his *Epithalamiums;* and the Cavalier *Marino,* all the Moderns. **1737** DYCHE-PARDON (2nd edn) *Epithalamium* (S.) a Nuptial Song, or a poetical Composition, or Poem made fit for, or upon the Marriage between two Persons of Distinction.

1589 [PUTTENHAM] *Arte of English Poesie* (p. 37) [*re* the history of poetry] ... Those to celebrate marriages were called songs nuptiall or *Epithalamies,* but in a certaine misticall sense ... § (pp. 41-3) [*re* poetry at marriages and weddings] ... This was done in ballade wise as the natall song, and was song very sweetely by Musitians at the chamber dore of the Bridegroome and Bride at such times as shalbe hereafter declared and they were called *Epithalamies* as much to say as ballades at the bedding of the bride: for such as were song at the borde at dinner or supper were other Musickes and not properly *Epithalamies* ... Thus much touching the vsage of *Epithalamie* or bedding ballad of the ancient times ...

epitonium

1589 RIDER L→E § *Epitoniorum manubria.* The keyes of the organes. **1706** KERSEY-PHILLIPS (6th edn) *Epitonium,* an Instrument to wrest or stretch Cords, a Pin or Peg in a stringed Musical Instrument:

epode *see* hymn, strophe

1538 ELYOT L→E *Epos, epodos,* a kinde of verse, or songe, which contayneth thynges concernyng as well god as manne. **1587** THOMAS L→E *Epos, odos, n.g. Horat.* A kinde of verse or song containing things touching both God and man. **1611** COTGRAVE Fr→E *Epodes.* A kind of Lyricke verses; the first whereof is longer then the second. **1728** CHAMBERS *Epode,* in Poetry. In the *Lyric* Poetry of the *Greeks,* the *Epode* is the third Part, or End of the Ode: Their Ode, or Song, being divided into Strophe, Antistrophe, and *Epode.* See *Ode.* ¶ The *Epode* was sung by the Priests, standing still before the Altar, after all the Turns and Returns of the Strophe and Antistrophe. See *Strophe.* ¶ But when the Ode contain'd several *Epodes,* Strophes, *&c.* they were all alike. ¶ As the Word *Epode,* then, properly signifies the End of the Song; and as in Odes, what they call'd the *Epode,* finish'd the Singing: It became customary, as M. *Dacier* shews, for a little Verse, which being put after another, closed the Period, and finish'd the Sense which had been suspended in the first Verse, to be call'd *Epode,* ἐποδος. **1730** BAILEY *Dict. Britannicum* (1st edn) *Epode* (Ἐποδός, of ἐπὶ after and ᾠδαὶ, *Gr.* songs) one of the numbers of that sort of Lyrick poetry, of which the odes of *Pindar* consist. The other two being *Strophe* and *Antistrophe,* which answer each other in every ode, whereas one epode answers to another in several odes. ¶ The epode was sung by the priests standing still before the altar, after all the turns and returns of the *Strophe* and *Antistrophe.*

epopeia

1598 FLORIO It→E *Epopeia,* a verse or song containing things both of god and man. **1611** FLORIO It→E *Epopeia,* a verse or songe containing things both of God and man.

equal *see* sostenuto, uguale

equal time *see* tempo giusto

equison

1598 FLORIO It→E *Equisono,* an equall or tunable sounding. **1611** FLORIO It→E *Equisono,* an equall or tunable sounding. **1659** TORRIANO-FLORIO It→E *Equisono,* an equal or tuneable sound.

1609 DOWLAND-ORNITHOPARCUS *Micrologvs* (pp. 78-9) ... Voyces are called some *Vnisons;* some not *Vnisons*... Of not *Vnisons,* some are *æquisons;* ... *Aequisons* are those, which being stroke together, make one sound of 2. as *Diapason* and *Disdiapason.*

Erato *see* Muse

1737 BAILEY *The Univ. Etymolog. Engl. Dict.* (3rd edn, vol. 2) *Erato* (is represented in *Painting, &c.*) as a young virgin, of gay humour, crowned with myrtle and roses, holding a harp in her right hand, and a bow in the other, with a little winged cupid by her side, armed with a bow and arrows.

esacordo *see* hexachord

1598 FLORIO It→E *Esacordo,* an instrument of sixe strings. **1611** FLORIO It→E *Esacordo,* an instrument of sixe strings.

eschrakites

1728 CHAMBERS *Eschrakites*, or *Esrakites*, a Sect of Philosophers among the *Mahometans*, who adhere to the Doctrines and Opinions of *Plato*.... They are very careful in avoiding Vice, preserve an equal and easy Temper, love Music, and divert themselves with composing little Poems, or spiritual Songs. **1736** BAILEY *Dict. Britannicum* (2nd edn) *Eschrakites* ... a sort of *Mahometan Platonists*, who place their *summum bonum* or chiefest good and happiness in the contemplation of the Divine Majesty; despising the gross imaginations of the *Alcoran* concerning *Paradise*. They are very careful in shunning vice, preserve an equal and easy temper, love musick, and divert themselves with composing hymns or spiritual songs. **1737** DYCHE-PARDON (2nd edn) *Eschrakites* (S.) a Sect of Philosophers among the *Mahometans*... They studiously avoid Vice, love Musick, and always appear good-humoured.

esclisse *see* eclisse

esclop, esclot

1611 COTGRAVE Fr→E *Esclot: m.* ... also, a Rest in Musicke; **1650** HOWELL-COTGRAVE Fr→E *Esclop: m.* ... also, a Rest in Musick;

espineta, espinetta, espinette *see* spinet

essential notes *see* final, mode, natural

1721 MALCOLM *Treatise of Musick* (p. 277) *Observe* next, that of the natural Notes of every *Mode* or *Octave*, Three go under the Name of the *essential Notes*, in a peculiar Manner, *viz.* the *Fundamental*, the 3*d*, and 5*th*, their *Octaves* being reckoned the same, and marked with the same Letters in the *Scale*; the rest are particularly called *Dependents*... But the 3*d* and 5*th* of any *Mode* or *Key* deserve the Name of essential *Notes*, more particularly with respect to their Use in *Harmony*, because the *Harmony* of a 3*d*, 5*th* and 8*ve*, is the most perfect of all others; so that a 3*d* and a 5*th*, applied in *Consonance* to any *Fundamental*, gives it the Denomination of the *Key*; for chiefly by Means of these the Cadence in the *Key* is performed.

estampie *see* stampita

estrindore

1611 COTGRAVE Fr→E *Estrindore*. A kind of Brittish daunce. *Rab.*

eunuch *see* castration

1728 CHAMBERS *Eunuch* .... Great Numbers of Children, from one to three Years of Age, are yearly castrated in *Italy*, to supply the Opera's and Theaters, not only of *Italy*, but other Parts of *Europe*, with Singers: Tho' 'tis not one in three, that after having lost their Virility, they have a good Voice for a Recompence.

euphony *see* accent

1538 ELYOT L→E *Euphonia*, a good sounde. **1598** FLORIO It→E *Eufonia*, a good sound, a pleasant noise or vtterance of words. **1611** FLORIO It→E *Eufonia*, a good sound, a pleasing noise, a smooth vtterance of words. **1656** BLOUNT (1st edn) *Euphony (euphonia)* a good sound or voice, as they use to say in Schooles, *Euphoniæ gratia*, for good sound sake. **1658** PHILLIPS (1st edn) *Euphonie*, (Greek) a gracefull sound, a smooth running of words. **1676** COLES *Euphanie, Greek.* a graceful sound. **1737** DYCHE-PARDON (2nd edn) *Euphony* (S.) ... also Harmony or Musick.

1582 *Batman vppon Bartholome* (p. 422) ... And such according of voice is called *Euphonie*, that is sweetnesse of voyce, and is called also *Melodia*, & hath that name of sweetenesse and of *Mel*, that is honie: and the contrary is *Diophonia*, foule voyce and discording. **1736** TANS'UR *Compleat Melody* (3rd edn, p. 67) *Euphony*. (Lat.) Denotes a very graceful Sound; or a smooth running of Words.

eurhythmia

1706 KERSEY-PHILLIPS (6th edn) *Eurthythmia*, the true Measure observ'd in Dancing after Musick:

eurythmoi

1721 MALCOLM *Treatise of Musick* (p. 456) Again, explaining the Difference of *Rythmus* and *Metrum*, he [Quintilian] tells us, That *Rythmus* is applied Th[r]ee Ways; either to immoveable Bodies, which are called *Eurythmoi*, when their Parts are right proportioned to one another, as a well made Statue; or to every Thing that moves...

Euterpe *see* Muse

1706 KERSEY-PHILLIPS (6th edn) *Euterpe*, one of the Nine Muses, the Inventress of the Flute and other Musical Instruments. **1730** BAILEY *Dict. Britannicum* (1st edn) *Euterpe* ... the inventress of the mathematicks and playing on the pipe. The ancients painted or carved *Euterpe* crowned with a garland of flowers, holding in each hand sundry wind-instruments. **1737** Dyche-Pardon (2nd edn) *Euterpe* (S.) one of the nine Muses, to whom the Invention of the Mathematicks, and playing upon the Pipe is attributed; the Antients represented her crowned with a Garland of Flowers, holding in each Hand sundry Wind Musical Instruments.

evensong *see* primer

exclamation *see* trill
1680 B., A. *Synopsis of Vocal Musick* (p. 44) An Exclamation is a slacking of the Voice to reinforce it afterwards, and is especially used in Minims and Crotchets with a prick, whom shorter Notes do follow.

exharmonia
1661 Blount (2nd edn) *Exharmonians*, discords, or dissonances in musick. **1676** Coles *Exharmonia*, discords in Musick. **1704** *Cocker's Engl. Dict.* (1st edn) *Exharmonia*, discords in Musick.

exodium *see* episode
1500 *Ortus Vocabulorum* L→E Exodium dij. idest primus cantus inicium cantilene n.s. **1538** Elyot L→E *Exodium*, a songe at the ende of a comedy or interlude. also at the ende of a matter. **1728** Chambers *Exode*, or *Exodium*, in the antient *Greek* Drama, was one of the four Parts or Divisions of Tragedy. See *Tragedy*. ¶ The *Exodium*, according to *Aristotle*, was so much as was rehearsed after the Chorus had ceas'd to sing for the last Time; so that *Exodium* with them, was far from being what the Epilogue is with us, as several People have imagined it was. See *Epilogue*. ¶ The *Exode* was so much of the Piece as included the Catastrophe and unravelling of the Plot; which Catastrophe, *&c.* in Pieces regularly composed, always begun after the last singing of the Chorus; answering nearly to our 4th and 5th Acts.... *Vigenere* on *T. Livy*, says ... that the *Exodes* were a Kind of Interludes, in the Intervals, between the Acts, partly Fable and Pleasantry, partly Music, *&c.* to give Time both for the Spectators and Actors to recover Breath.... *Exodium*, was also the Name of a Song, sung at the Conclusion of a Meal. **1730** Bailey *Dict. Britannicum* (1st edn) *Exodium* (εξοδιον, Gr.) an interlude or farce at the end of a tragedy; also a song sung at the conclusion of a meal.

extempore *see* descant, improvisation, interlude, prelude, provisanti, ricercar, toccata, voluntary

F

f *as abbreviation of forte, see* forte
1724 [Pepusch] *Short Explic. of Foreign Words in Mus. Bks.* (p. 30) *F*. This Letter is often used as an Abbreviation of the Word *Forte*. **1726** Bailey *An Univ. Etymolog. Engl. Dict.* (3rd edn) *F* (in *Musick Books*) is an Abbreviation of the word *Forte*. Ital. **1737** Bailey *The Univ. Etymolog. Engl. Dict.* (3rd edn, vol. 2) *FF* (in *Musick Books*) stands for *forte forte*, and denotes very loud.

1731 Prelleur *Modern Musick-Master* (Dictionary, p. 2) *F*. or *Forte* signifies Loud or Strong ¶ *F.F.* or *Piu Forte*, Louder then [sic] Forte. ¶ *F.F.F.* or *Fortissimo* very Loud

f *as clef*
1730 Bailey *Dict. Britannicum* (1st edn) *F* (in *Musick*) is one of the signed clefs or keys placed at the beginning of one of the lines of a piece of musick.

fa
1598 Florio It→E *Fa*, a note in musicke. *Fama vt*, a note in musicke **1611** Florio It→E *Fa*, ... Also a note in musike. *Famaut*, a note in musike **1659** Torriano-Florio It→E *Famaut*, a note in Musick, as *Gamaut* **1671** Phillips (3rd edn) *F Fa ut*, the seventh or last note of the two first Septenaries of the *Gam Ut* (the last reaching no farther than *E*) being also the *Cliff* note of the Bassus or lowest part. **1676** Coles *F fa ut*, the seventh musick note, the Cliff-note of the basse-part. **1678** Phillips (4th edn) *F. Fa ut*, the seventh or last Note of the two first Septenaries of the *Gam Ut* (the last reaching no farther than E) being also the *Cliff* Note of the Bassus or the lowest part. In the first it answers to the Greek Ὑπάτη μέσων, in the other to τρίτη υπερβολαίων. **1688** Miege-Cotgrave Fr→E *Fa*, (m.) fa, a Musical Note. **1696** Phillips (5th edn) *Fa*, a Note in Musick. **1704** *Cocker's Engl. Dict.* (1st edn) *F, fa, ut*, seventh note in Musick, the Cliff note of the Bass part. **1706** Kersey-Phillips (6th edn) *Fa*, one of the Notes in *Musick*. *Fa-fa-ut*,

the seventh or last Note of the three Septenaries of the Scale of *Musick*, call'd the *Gam-ut*; being also the Cliff Note of the Bass, or lowest Part. **1728** CHAMBERS *F*, in Musick, is one of the signed Clefs or Keys, plac'd at the Beginning of one of the Lines of a piece of Musick. See *Clef*. ¶ F is the Bass-clef, and is plac'd on the fourth Line upwards. See *Bass*. ¶ Indeed, the Character or Sign by which the *f* and *c* Clefs are mark'd, bear no Resemble to those Letters. Mr. *Malcolm*, thinks it were as well if we used the Letters themselves, but Custom has carried it otherwise. The ordinary Character of the F or Bass-clef is [bass clef sign] which *Kepler* takes a deal of pains to deduce, by Corruption, from the Letter F it self. See *Character*. § *F-Ut-Fa*, in Musick, one of the Clefs. See *Clef*. § *Fa* is one of the Notes of Music, being the fourth in rising in this order of the Gamma, Ut, re, mi, fa. See *Note*. **1737** BAILEY *The Univ. Etymolog. Engl. Dict.* (3rd edn, vol. 2) *F Faut* (in the scale of *Musick*) the seventh or last note of the 3 septenaries of the *Gamut*. **1737** DYCHE-PARDON (2nd edn) *Fa* (S.) the Name of one of the Notes in the common Scale of Musick, which is naturally but half a Note or Tone, and is what is called a flat Note, unless made a whole or sharp Note, by prefixing this Mark [#] before it. *F. Faut* (S.) the Name of the seventh or last Note of the three Septenaries of the Gamut, or common Scale of musical Tones or Notes.

faburden *see* falso bordone, faux-bourdon
after 1517 ANON. Art of Mvsic BL Add. 4911, f. 94 *Quaht is faburdoun* ¶ Faburdoun is ane melodius kynd of harmony quhilk dois transnwt and brek sympill noitte in figure colorat be Numerarum trimar and bynar conform to ye Way of Music mensurall

fading *see* Jubal

fagottino
1724 [PEPUSCH] *Short Explic. of Foreign Words in Mus. Bks.* (p. 30) *Fagottino*, a single Curtail, a musical Instrument, somewhat like unto a small Bassoon. **1726** BAILEY *An Univ. Etymolog. Engl. Dict.* (3rd edn) *Fagottino* (in *Musick Books*) a single Curtail, a Musical Instrument, somewhat like a small Bassoon. *Ital.*

fagotto *see* bassoon, obligata
1598 FLORIO It→E *Fagotto*, ... Also a kinde of musicall instrument. **1611** FLORIO It→E *Fagotto*, ... Also a fardell, a bundle, a trusse, a packe. Also a kind of round musicall instrument. **1659** TORRIANO-FLORIO It→E *Fagotto*, any bundle, fardle ... also a kind of round country musicall instrument. **1724** [PEPUSCH] *Short Explic. of Foreign Words in Mus. Bks.* (p. 30) *Fagotto*, is a double or large Bass Curtail. § (p. 60) *Quart Fagotta*, a small Bassoon. **1726** BAILEY *An Univ. Etymolog. Engl. Dict.* (3rd edn) *Fagotto*, a double or large Bass, [sic] Curtail. *Ital.* *Quartfagotta*, a small Bassoon. *It.* **1730** BAILEY *Dict. Britannicum* (1st edn) *Fagotto*, a double or large bassoon, *Ital.* *Quartfagotta*, a small Bassoon, *Ital.*

1731 PRELLEUR *Modern Musick-Master* (Dictionary, p. 2) *Fagotto*, a Wind Instrument answering to a Bassoon.

fa la *see* æolian, balletto
1597 MORLEY *Plaine and Easie Introdvction* (p. 180) There be also an other kind of *Ballets*, commonlie called *fa las*, the first set of that kind which I haue seene was made by *Gastaldi*, if others haue laboured in the same field, I know not but a slight kind of musick it is, & as I take it deuised to be daunced to voices.

falcinine *see* by by, lallatio, lullaby
1500 *Ortus Vocabulorum* L→E Falcinine arum. cradell sanges f.p.

false *see* semidiapente, tritone
1721 MALCOLM *Treatise of Musick* (p. 260) ... of the *4ths* [32:45, 20:27, 3:4] and *5ths* [2:3, 27:40, 45:64] Two are *Discords*, and called *false 4ths* and *5ths*; and therefore when we speak of a *4th* or *5th*, without calling it *false*, 'tis understood to be of the true *harmonical* Kind; ...

false close
1597 MORLEY *Plaine and Easie Introdvction* (p. 127) ... and as for those waies which here you see marked with a starre thus * [in the various examples] they be passing closes, which we commonly cal false closes, being deuised to shun a final and and [sic] go on with some other purpose, & these passing closes be of two kinds in the base part, that is, either ascending or descending, if the passing close descend in the base it commeth to the sixth, if it ascend it commeth to the tenth or third ...

false fifth *see* fifth lesser, semidiapente, tritone
c.1710 NORTH (Prendcourt's) Treatise of Continued or thro-base BL Add. 32531, f. 35v [annotation by North:]

... and In its place, it is exceeding good. and this is the tritone or fals fifth as it is called, that is a flatt 5th. or sharp fourth. **1726-8** NORTH Theory of Sounds BL Add. 32535, ff. 110-110v ... Nay the 4#. or triton, called a fals fifth, wch is a very harsh sound ...

false relation *see* true relation

1730 [PEPUSCH] *Short Treatise on Harmony* (p. 2) *False* Relations, are Those wherein the Agreement is so distant and so small, that it is not sensible, at least not obvious or agreeable to the Ear.

false string

c.1698-c.1703 NORTH Cursory Notes (*C-K CN* p. 41) ... hence it is concluded, that the lighter and looser parts of the string vibrate in quicker transits, then the heavyer and stiffer. This is what musitians call fals in a string ... **c.1710** NORTH (draft for) Musicall Grammarian BL Add. 32537, f. 84 It is likewise reasonable here to observe the nature of confused tones wch are such as flow from such as they call fals strings, or crack't pipes. a fals string is when one part is larger then another, so as to make divers vibrations slower on one part & faster on another ... **1721** MALCOLM *Treatise of Musick* (p. 25) ... We have a notable Example of a *rough* and *harsh* Sound in Strings that are unevenly and not of the same Constitution and Dimension throughout; and for this Reason that their Sounds are very grating, they are called false Strings.

false third

1721 MALCOLM *Treatise of Musick* (p. 259) The Three *2ds* or *Degrees* or *Degrees* [8:9, 9:10, 15:16] are all *concinnous Intervals;* of the *3ds* [4:5, 5:6, 27:32] one is *Discord*, viz. 27:32, and therefore called a *false 3d;* the other Two are particularly known by the Names of *3d g.* and *3d l.* ...

falsetto *see* chroma, incino, minurize

1598 FLORIO It→E *Falsetto*, a false treble or countertenor in musicke. **1611** COTGRAVE Fr→E *Faulset: m.* A fayning, in song; also, a discord. § *Chanter en faulset.* To faine; also, to sing louder and louder, or to rise from note to note, in singing. *Chanter en faulset.* To faine; also, to sing louder and louder, or higher and higher; to rise from note to note, in singing. **1611** FLORIO It→E *Falseggiare*, ... Also to faine a voice. *Falsetto*, a false treble or countertenor in musicke. **1659** TORRIANO-FLORIO It→E *Falseggiare*, ... also to faign a voice in singing. *Falsetto*, a false treble, or faigning in Musick. **1688** MIEGE-COTGRAVE Fr→E *Fausset*, (m.) ... a feigned Treble, in Musick.

falso bordone *see* burden, faburden, faux-bourdon

1597 MORLEY *Plaine and Easie Introdvction* (annotations to Part II) As for singing vppon a plainsong, it hath byn in times past in England (as euery man knoweth) and is at this day in other places, the greatest part of the vsuall musicke which in any church is sung... It is also to be vnderstood, that when they did sing vpon their plainsongs, he who sung the ground would sing it a sixt vnder the true pitche, and sometimes would breake some notes in diuision, which they did for the more formall comming to their closes: but euery close (by the close in this place, you must vnderstand the note which serued for the last syllable of euery verse in their hymnes,) he must sing in that tune as it standeth, or then in the eight below: & this kind of singing was called in Italy *Falso bordone*, and in England a Fa burden ...

fancy *see* envoy, fantasia, lesson, pavan

c.1710 NORTH (draft for) Musicall Grammarian BL Add. 32537, ff. 101-101v [*re* plainsong music to which was added descant] ... If wee observe ye carracter of this sort of musick, among wch I account the Elabourate compositions of the masters in those times, when they began to come forward & Improve a litle, and called their works Fancy's. **c.1726** NORTH Musicall Gramarian BL Add. 32533, ff. 159v-160 In some old musick books, I have found divers formed consorts, with a latin or Itallian Epigrafe; being either the Initiall words of songs, or Names of family's, as La Martinenga, piccolhomini, & ye like, These I guess were songs for many voices composed and printed in Italy, and here transcribed for ye use of Instruments (for composers then were raritys) and without doubdt, however devested of their significant words (If they ever had any) were very good Musick. And it was from ye Italian model that wee framed those setts of musick, wch were called fancy's, and In Imitation of them Inscribed Fantazia. These were much of the same nature with our Modern Sonnata's, but had ye stamp of Elder times, wch are Enough to distinguish them. **1728** NORTH Musicall Grammarian (*C-K MG* f. 70v) The old masters seldome affected fuges but in those peices, which are not unlike our sonnatas, and by them were called fancys.

fanfare
1593 HOLLYBAND Fr→E *Fanfare*, it is the sound of the trumpets when they runne at the Tilt, a bragge. **1611** COTGRAVE Fr→E *Fanfare: f.* A sounding of Trumpets, or a comming into the Lists with sound of Trumpets, at a publicke Iusts; *Fanfarer.* To sound, or resound, as Trumpets; to challenge, or braue one another with sound of Trumpets; *Fanfaronnades: f.* Resoundings of Trumpets; **1659** TORRIANO-FLORIO It→E **Fanfara, Fanfarata*, a trumpeting, or sounding of many trumpets together, as at publick triumphs or tiltings **1688** DAVIS-TORRIANO-FLORIO It→E **Fanfara, Fanfatara*, a trumpeting, or sounding of many trumpets together, as at publick triumphs or tiltings **1688** MIEGE-COTGRAVE Fr→E *Fanfare*, (f.) *air de Trompette*, a Trumpet-Tune, or Note.

fantasia, fantasie *see* fancy, imperfect of the less, lesson, phantastic, prelude, research, style (stylo phantastico), time
1611 COTGRAVE Fr→E *Fantasie: f.* ... also, the Musicall lesson, tearmed a Fancie. **1659** TORRIANO-FLORIO It→E § *Passa fantasia, Passa tempo*, a pastime, sport, sollace, recreation, also a jews-harp or trump. **1696** PHILLIPS (5th edn) In Musick, a Fantasie is a Piece of Composition full of Harmony, but which cannot be reduc'd under any of the regular kinds. **1724** [PEPUSCH] *Short Explic. of Foreign Words in Mus. Bks.* (pp. 30-1) *Fantasia*, is a Kind of Air, wherein the Composer is not tied up to such strict Rules, as in most other Airs, but has all the Freedom and Liberty allowed him for his Fancy or Invention, that can reasonably be desir'd. ¶ *N.B.* Some Sonatas are so called. **1726** BAILEY *An Univ. Etymolog. Engl. Dict.* (3rd edn) *Fantasia* (in *Musick Books*) a kind of Air, in which the Composer is not tied up to such strict Rule, as in most other Airs; but is allow'd all the Freedom of Fancy or Invention that can reasonably be desir'd. This Title is given to some *Sonata*'s. *Ital.*

1597 MORLEY *Plaine and Easie Introdvction* (pp. 180-1) [marginalia: 'Fantasies.'] The most principall and chiefest kind of musicke which is made without a dittie is the fantasie, that is, when a musician taketh a point at his pleasure, and wresteth and turneth it as he list, making either much or little of it according as shall seeme best in his own conceit. In this may more art be showne then in any other musicke, because the composer is tide to nothing but that he may adde, deminish, and alter at his pleasure. And this kind will beare any allowances whatsoeuer tolerable in other musick, except changing the ayre & leauing the key, which in fantasie may neuer bee suffered. Other thinges you may vse at your pleasure, as bindings with discordes, quicke motions, slow motions, proportions, and what you list. Likewise, this kind of musick is with them who practise instruments of parts in greatest vse, but for voices it is but sildome vsed. **1676** MACE *Musick's Monument* (pp. 128-9) [marginalia: 'The Fancy, or Voluntary.'] ... after they have *Compleated Their Tuning* [on the lute by way of a prelude], They will (if They be *Masters*) fall into some kind of *Voluntary*, or *Fansical Play*, more *Intelligible;* which (if He be a Master, Able) is a way, whereby He may more *Fully*, and *Plainly* shew *His Excellency*, and *Ability*, than by any other kind of undertaking; and has an *unlimited*, and *unbounded Liberty;* In which, he may make use of the *Forms*, and *Shapes of all the rest.* **c.1715-20** NORTH Essay of Musical Ayre BL Add. 32536, ff. 68v-69 [*re* the history of English music] ... they had from abroad peices of Consort musick Express called fantasias, And also lighter Ayres .... the English Masters laboured Most upon that sort they Called fantazias, w[ch] at first were not much Removed from the plain song way, and yet better accepted, as being accounted more substantial then the lighter Ayers. **1728** NORTH Musicall Grammarian (*C-K MG* ff. 127v-128) [*re* viol music in England] ... the earlyer consorts were composed for 3, 4, and more parts, for songs in Itallian or Latine out of the psalmes; of which I have seen divers and mostly in print, with the names of the patroni inscribed. And in England when composers were scarce, these songs were copyed off, without the words, and for variety used as instrumentall consorts, with the first words of the song for a title. And of this printed musick vocally performed, many will shine against the best moderne compositions, and I suppose instrumentally would not loos much of their excellence. And as alterations with endeavour to advance are continually profered, so the Itallian masters, who allwais did, or ought to lead the van in musick, printed peices they called fantazias wherein was air, and variety enough, and afterwards these were imitated by the English, who working more elabourately, improved upon their patterne ...

farce *see* exodium, opera, revels
1593 HOLLYBAND Fr→E *Vne Farce*, a niggard: *m.* a playe, an Enterlude: *f.* **1611** COTGRAVE Fr→E *Farce: f.* A (fond and dissolute) Play, Comedie, or

Enterlude; also, the Iyg at the end of an Enterlude, wherein some pretie knauerie is acted; **1676** COLES *Farce, French...* a knavish jig at the end of an interlude, a fond and dissolute play. **1704** *Cocker's Engl. Dict.* (1st edn) *Farce,* ... also a short mock-play; as the *Mock Empress* of *Morocco, &c.*

fare ala

1598 FLORIO It→E *Fara ala,* the name of a certaine march sounded vpon drum and trumpet in time of warre. **1611** FLORIO It→E *Fare ala,* ... Also a certaine march vpon drum and trumpet in time of war. **1659** TORRIANO-FLORIO It→E **Fare ala,* ... also the name or sound of a march or point of war upon the drum or trumpet in time of battle or war.

Farinel's ground *see* follia

c.1715-20 NORTH Essay of Musical Ayre BL Add. 32536, f. 76v [*re* the arrival of foreign musicians in England] There was one Farrinell a frenchman, who had a Notable devision upon ye follia Lespagne, wch made it in those days be Called Farrinells Ground.

faucet

1706 KERSEY-PHILLIPS (6th edn) *Faucet,* ... also a kind of Pipe or Flute, us'd in former Times. **1708** KERSEY *Dict. Anglo-Brit.* (1st edn) *Faucet,* ... also a kind of Flute, us'd in former Times.

fausetum

1706 KERSEY-PHILLIPS (6th edn) *Fausetum,* (in old *Latin* Records) a Musical Pipe, or Flute

fausset *see* falsetto

faux-bourdon *see* burden, faburden, falso bordone

1611 COTGRAVE Fr→E *Faux-bourdon.* The drone of a Bagpipe. **1650** HOWELL-COTGRAVE Fr→E § *Chanter en faux bourdon.*

favorito

1731 PRELLEUR *Modern Musick-Master* (Dictionary, p. 2) *Favorito,* a Favourite.

feeling

c.1668-71 *Mary Burwell's Instruction Bk. for Lute* (*TDa* p. 45) ... When you have prepared the attention of the company with a preludium, or some strokes which we call the 'feeling' of the lute (to know whether it be perfectly in tune) you shall begin with the gravest lessons and the most airy...

feigning *see* falsetto, minurize, musica ficta

feint

1611 COTGRAVE Fr→E *Feinte: f.* ... also, a Sharp, in Musicke. **1728** CHAMBERS *Feint,* in Musick, a Semitone; the same with what we also call *Diesis.* See *Diesis.* **1730** BAILEY *Dict. Britannicum* (1st edn) A *Feint* (in *Musick*) a semi-tone, the same that is call'd *Diesis.*

fellio

1598 FLORIO It→E *Fellio,* a kind of musicall instrument. **1611** FLORIO It→E *Fellio,* a kind of musicall instrument. **1659** TORRIANO-FLORIO It→E *Fellio,* a kind of musical instrument.

fenico

1598 FLORIO It→E *Fenico,* a kinde of musicall instrument with strings. **1611** FLORIO It→E *Fenico,* a kind of musicall instrument. **1659** TORRIANO-FLORIO It→E *Fenico,* as *Fellio.*

Ferrabosco, Alfonso [the younger] *see* Alphonso, leero

f fa ut clef *see* c sol fa ut clef

f-fa-ut-key

1676 MACE *Musick's Monument* (p. 197) ... *F-fa-ut-Key,* which is an exceeding *Brisk, Lofty,* and *Sparkling Key;* ...

fiabbare

1611 FLORIO It→E *Fiabbare,* to chant or sing idle songs merily, as nurses doe in dandling of children. **1659** TORRIANO-FLORIO It→E **Fiabbamenti, Fiabbe, Fiabberie,* all manner of idle chantings to beguile time with, or to keep one from sleep, as nurses sing in dandling their children **Fiabbare, Fiabbeggiare,* to sing or chaunt merry tunes, and idle songs, as nurses do in dandling and rocking their children **Fiabbatore,* a foolish chanter, an idle singer

fiauto *see* flute

fictitious note *see* accidental, musica ficta

early 17th C. ANON. Praise of musicke BL 18. B. xix, f. 13v ... And the Third propertye of singinge called B *molles* (or as some other call *Fictye* rather) is when (besides the placinge of one of ye foresaid three principall Cliffes at the beginninge of the songe (or part) there is added also, and sett vpon the lines or spaces two b. flatt claves in different places ... **1721** MALCOLM *Treatise of Musick* (p. 317) The *diatonick* Series, beginning at the lowest Note, being first settled upon any Instrument, and distinguished by their Names *a. b. c. d. e. f. g.* the other Notes are called *fictitious* Notes, taking the Name or Letter of the Note below with a ✖ as *c*✖, signifying that 'tis a *Semitone* higher than the Sound of *c* in the *natural* Series, or this Mark ♭ with the Name of the Note above signifying a *Semitone* lower, as *d*♭;

fiddle *see* baldosa, biffara, biumbe, cacapensiere, crowd, cucutremma, donadello, fidicula, giga, kit, rebeck, ribibble, tempella, violin, vitula, zaramella, zimbello
1702 KERSEY *New Engl. Dict.* (1st edn) A *Fiddle*, a musical instrument. To *fiddle*, to play upon a *fiddle* **1721** BAILEY *An Univ. Etymolog. Engl. Dict.* (1st edn) *Fiddle*, (Fiꝺele, *Sax. Vedel, Du. Fidel, Teut.* of *Fidicula, L.*) a Musical Instrument. To *Fiddle, (Fidlen, Teut.)* to play upon a Fidle. *Teut.* **1730** BAILEY *Dict. Britannicum* (1st edn) *Fiddle* (*fidicula*, L. *fidel, Teut.* ſiεele, *Sax.*) a musical instrument well known. **1736** BAILEY *Dict. Britannicum* (2nd edn) *Fiddle* (*fidicula*, L. *veel, Du fiddel*, G. *fedel, Su. fidel, Teut.* ſiꝛhele, *Sax.*) a musical instrument well known. **1737** DYCHE-PARDON (2nd edn) *Fiddle* (S.) the most common Musical Instrument now in Use; called also a Violin. *Fiddle* (V.) to play ordinarily or indifferently upon the Musical Instrument called a Fiddle;

fiddler *see* crowder, minstrel, violinist
1702 KERSEY *New Engl. Dict.* (1st edn) A *Fidler*. **1721** BAILEY *An Univ. Etymolog. Engl. Dict.* (1st edn) Fiddler, (*Vedeler, Du.*) One who plays on a Fiddle. **1730** BAILEY *Dict. Britannicum* (1st edn) *Fidling* (of *fidlen, Teut.*) playing upon a fiddle; **1736** BAILEY *Dict. Britannicum* (2nd edn) *Fiddler* (of ſiꝛhele, *Sax.*) one who plays upon a fiddle. **1737** DYCHE-PARDON (2nd edn) *Fidler* (S.) a contemptuous Name for Musicians, but particularly for an indifferent or bad Player upon the Fiddle; *Fidling* (S.) playing upon a Fiddle;

1728 NORTH Musicall Grammarian (*C-K MG* f. 106v) [*re* ancient Greek music] ... And instruments are scarce ever mentioned, but with respect to poeme. So that so farr as I can see, a poet and a fidler were termes convertible, and meant almost the same thing.

fiddle stick *see* arco, bow, plectrum
1702 KERSEY *New Engl. Dict.* (1st edn) A *Fiddle-stick*.

fides *see* chord, nervo
1500 *Ortus Vocabulorum* L→E Fidis dis. a harpe strynge. f.t. vus. § Virgo fides fidis est: resonat fidis in citharaudo. **1538** ELYOT L→E *Fides, fidis*, the strynge of any instrument. sometyme a harpe or lute. **1565** COOPER L→E *Fides, fidis, f.g. Cic.* A stringe of an instrument: a harpe or lute. § *Adhibere fides epulis. Quintil.* To vse playinge of instrumentes at feastes. *Assumpta fide pulsus luctus. Valer. Flac.* Takyng his instrument. *Conspicuus fide. Ouid.* Notable for his playinge on instrumentes. *Contentae fides. Cic.* Stringes stretched or sette vp. *Mouere fides. Ouid.* To play on the lute, &c. **1587** THOMAS L→E *Fides, is, f.g.* A string of an instrument, a harpe or lute.

fidibus *see* canere, citharist, sambuke
1538 ELYOT L→E § *Scire fidibus*, to be perfytte in playenge on instrumentes. **1565** COOPER L→E § *Canere fidibus. Quintil.* To play on the harpe or lute. *Discebant fidibus antiqui. Cic.* Men of ancient tyme learned to plaie on the harpe or lute. *Discere fidibus. Cic.* To learne to play on the instrumentes. *Docere aliquem fidibus. Cic.* To teach one to play on the lute or harpe. To teache one to playe on the instrumentes. *Iungere vocem fidibus. Quintil.* To singe to. To singe to an instrument. *Modulanda verba fidibus. Horat.* Verses or meter to be songe to the lute. *Mouere fides. Ouid.* To play on the lute, &c. *Scire fidibus. Terent.* To be perfitte in playinge on instrumentes.

fidicen *see* cantor, chelys, citharist, lyre, lyrick
1500 *Ortus Vocabulorum* L→E Fidicen inis. qui canit cum fide vel cum chorda. m.t. **1538** ELYOT L→E *Fidicen, cinis*, a harpe: it maye be called a fyddell. it is also he that playeth on the instrument. *Fidicina*, a woman harper or luter. **1552** HULOET L→E *Fidicen. cinis.* Lute. *Fidicen, inis.* Luter. *fidicina, æ*, a woman luter, *Quasi fidibus canens.* **1565** COOPER L→E *Fídicen, pen. corr. fidícinis, pen. etiam corr. m.g. Cic.* An harper or minstrell that playeth on any stringed instrument. *Fidícina, fidícinæ, fœ. g. pen. corr. Terent.* A woman harper: a singynge wenche. *Fidícinius, Adiect. vt, Ludus fidicinius. Plaut.* A schoole where men are taught

to play on stringed instrumentes. **1587** THOMAS L→E *Fidicen, inis, m.g.* An harper or minstrell that playeth on any stringed instrument: he that playeth and singeth to that instrument. *Fidicina, æ, f.g. Terent.* A woman harper or luter: a singing wench. *Fidicinius, a, um, Plaut.* Belonging to the play of the harpe. **1589** RIDER L→E *Fidicen, Amphion, m.* A fidler. *Fidicen, tibicen, aulædus, choraules, choraulis, choraula, auletes, cantator fidibus, ginzeriator, m.* A Minstrell. *Fidicina, f.* She that plaieth on a lute, or any other instrument. *Fidicina, tibicina, f.* A woman minstrell.

fidicinales

1726 BAILEY *An Univ. Etymolog. Engl. Dict.* (3rd edn) *Fidicinales* (with *Anatomists*) the Muscles of the Fingers called *Lumbricales,* from the Use they are put to by Musicians, in playing upon some Instruments. *L.*

fidicula *see* rebeck

1500 *Ortus Vocabulorum* L→E Fidicula le. i. pua fidis. f.p. **1538** ELYOT L→E *Fidicula,* a rebecke, or gytterne. **1552** HULOET L→E *Fidicula. æ.* Gitterne or rebecke. *Fidicula. æ* Rebecke or gytterne. **1565** COOPER L→E *Fidícula, fidículæ, f.g. pen. corr. Parua cithara. Cic.* A little lute: a rebecke: a gitterne. **1587** THOMAS L→E *Fidicula, æ, f.g. dim. à Fides, is.* A little lute, a rebeck, a gitterne. Columella calleth it the harpe of heauen, which is a certaine companie of starres resembling an harpe. **1589** RIDER L→E *Fidicula, f.* A gitterne. *Fidicula, pandura, f.* A Rebecke. *Fidicula, pandura, vitulia, f* A Fiddle. *Fidiculizo.* To play on the Gitterne. **1706** KERSEY-PHILLIPS (6th edn) *Fidicula,* a little Lute, a Gittern, a Fiddle: **1708** KERSEY *Dict. Anglo-Brit.* (1st edn) *Fidicula,* a little Lute, a Fiddle:

1582 *Batman vppon Bartholome* (p. 424) Men in olde time called ye harpe *Fidicula,* and also *Fidicen,* for ye strings thereof accord, as well as some men accordeth in faith...

fife *see* buccina, flute, zuffolo

1593 HOLLYBAND Fr→E *Vn Fifre,* a fife, a flute playing with a drumme: *m.* **1598** FLORIO It→E *Fifaro,* as *Pifaro. Pifara, Piffara,* a flute, a pipe, a fife, a recorder, a bagpipe. *Pifaro, Piffaro,* a musition that plaies vpon any wind instrument. *Pifero, Piffero,* as *Pifaro. Piferoni, Pifferoni,* all manner of great winde instruments. Also musitions. **1599** MINSHEU-PERCYVALL Sp→E **Pifano,* or *Pifaro,* a fife or flute to play on. † *Pifaro,* vide *Pifano.* **1611** COTGRAVE Fr→E *Fifre: m.* A Fife; a Flute, or little pipe accorded with a Drumme, or Taber. *Phiphre: f.* A Fife, or small Pipe. **1611** FLORIO It→E *Fifaro,* a piper, a fluter. *Pifara,* any kind of pipe, fife or flute. *Pifarata,* a piping or fit of mirth. *Pifaro,* a Piper, a Fifer, a Fluter. † *Pifaro,* vide *Pifano. Pifero,* as *Pifaro. Piferoni,* Pipers, Fifers, Fluters. *Piffara,* as *Pifara.* **1659** TORRIANO-FLORIO It→E *Fifaro,* a piper, a fifer, a fluter. *Pifaro, Pifero, Piffaro, Piffero,* any pipe, fife, or flute. *Pifarata, Pifferata,* a piping, a fit of mirth, hunts up upon a pipe or flute. *Piferone, Pifferone,* a piper, a fifer, a fluter. **1688** MIEGE-COTGRAVE Fr→E *Fifre,* (f.) Fife, a kind of Musical Instrument; a player upon a fife. **1702** KERSEY *New Engl. Dict.* (1st edn) A *Fife,* a sort of pipe. **1706** KERSEY-PHILLIPS (6th edn) *Fife,* a sort of Wind-Musick, sometimes us'd in a Company of Foot-Soldiers. **1707** *Gloss. Angl. Nova* (1st edn) *Fife,* an Instrument for Wind Musick. **1721** BAILEY *An Univ. Etymolog. Engl. Dict.* (1st edn) A *Fife, (Fifre, F.)* a sort of Pipe, or Wind Musick. **1724** [PEPUSCH] *Short Explic. of Foreign Words in Mus. Bks.* (p. 31) *Fiffaro,* is a Fife, or small Pipe, Flute, or Flagelet, made Use of by the *Germans* in their Armies, to play with a Drum. (p. 55) *Piffaro,* is an Instrument somewhat like a Hautboy. *Piffero,* is a small Flute or Flagelet. **1726** BAILEY *An Univ. Etymolog. Engl. Dict.* (3rd edn) *Fiffaro,* a Fife, or small Pipe, Flute, or Flagelet, used by the *Germans,* with a Drum in the Army. *Ital. Piffaro,* an Instrument somewhat like a Hautboy. *Ital. Piffero,* a small Flute or Flagelet. *Ita.* **1730** BAILEY *Dict. Britannicum* (1st edn) *Fife (fifre, F.)* a sort of wind-musick, a small pipe. **1736** BAILEY *Dict. Britannicum* (2nd edn) *Fife (fifre,* F. *piffero,* Sp. *pfeiffe,* H.G.) a sort of wind musick, a small pipe. **1737** DYCHE-PARDON (2nd edn) *Fife* (S.) a small wind-musical Instrument, by some called a Flagellet, very shrill in its Tone, much used by the *Swissers, &c.*

fifth *see* diapente, false fifth, fifth lesser, perfect fifth, quinte

1704 HARRIS *Fifth,* a term in Musick, the same with *Diapente;* which see. **1706** KERSEY-PHILLIPS (6th edn) *Fifth,* a Term in *Musick.* See *Diapente.* **1721** BAILEY *An Univ. Etymolog. Engl. Dict.* (1st edn) *Fifth, (in Musick)* the same as Diapente. **1728** CHAMBERS *Fifth,* in Musick, one of the harmonical Intervals, or Concords. See *Interval.* ¶ The *Fifth* is the Third in order, of the Concords. The Ratio of the Chords that afford it, is 3:2. See *Concord.* ¶ It is called *Fifth,* because containing *five Terms,* or

Sounds between its Extremes; and four Degrees: So that in the natural Scale of Musick it comes in the *fifth* Place, or Order, from the Fundamental. See *Degree*, and *Scale*. ¶ The Antients called this Interval, *Diapente*. See *Diapente*. ¶ The *imperfect*, or *defective Fifth*, by the Antients called *Semi-Diapente*, is less than the *Fifth* by a mean Semi-tone. See *Tone*, and *Semi-Tone*. **1737** DYCHE-PARDON (2nd edn) *Fifth* (S.) ... and in *Musick*, it is called Diapente.

1584 BATHE Briefe Intro. to True Art of Music (MS copy, 1st half 16th c., *CHi* p. 8) The concord called a fyft, doth consist of fyue notes in distance, for so it appeareth by the denomination, that their foir it is called a fyft ... **1596** ANON. *Pathway to Musicke* [B iii *verso*] A Fift is the distance of voices by a Fift, and commeth of three tunes & a halfe tune, of vvhich there be foure kindes, *re la mi*, in *fa fa*, *vt sol*. **1726-8** NORTH Theory of Sounds BL Add. 32535, f. 36v ... And the consonance of 3. to 2. is that w[ch.] the Musitians call a fifth ... **1728** NORTH Musicall Grammarian (*C-K MG* ff. 55v-56) ... The other falling on a fifth was not allowed by our former English masters; they called it dashing a 5th in the face. But the fullness of harmony which it brings justifies it, but more the authority of Corelli who perpetually in his full consorts makes use of it.

fifth, lesser *see* false fifth, semidiapente, tritone

1721 MALCOLM *Treatise of Musick* (p. 262) [*re* the tritone] ... its Complement to an *Octave*, viz. 45:64, which is the least of the 5*ths*, is particularly called a lesser 5*th* or *Semidiapente* .... And because in common Practice the Difference of *t g.* and *t l.* is neglected, tho' it has its Influence, ... therefore these *Intervals* are only called *false*, which exceed or come short by a *Semitone*; ...

fifth tone

1609 DOWLAND-ORNITHOPARCUS *Micrologvs* (p. 33) The fift *Tone* is a Rule, determining the *Authenticke* of the third manner, or it is an *Authenticall* Progression of the third. Whose regular end is in *Ffaut*; and irregular end in *Csolfaut*. The beginnings of it (as *Franchinus* witnesseth) are Foure, *F. G. a*, and *c*. ...

figura

1617-24 FLUDD *Utriusque Cosmi Maioris: De Templo Musicæ* (p. 190) *Figura voce exprimenda*, quâ tempus describitur, est repræsentatio soni in aliquo modorum ordinati; per quod patet, quod figuræ significari debent modis & non aliter; vel notula seu figura est, quâ sonorum singulorum quantitas congruens ad motum tactu mensuratum notatur.

figurate counterpoint *see* counterpoint

figuration *see* canto figurato

1597 MORLEY *Plaine and Easie Introdvction* (p. 90) *Phi*. What is Figuration? ¶ *Ma*. When you sing one note of the plainsong long, & another short, and yet both prickt in one forme. Or making your plainesong as your descant notes, and so making vpon it, or then driuing some note or rest through your plainsong, making it two long, three long, &c. Or three minimes, fiue minimes, or so forth, two minimes and a crotchet, three minimes and a crotchet, fiue minimes and a crotchet, &c. with infinite more, as mens inuentions shall best like: for, as so manie men so manie mindes, so their inuentions will be diuers, and diuerslie inclined. The fift waie is called *Tripla*, when for one note of the plainsong, they make three blacke minimes ... though (as I tolde you before) this is not the true tripla, yet haue I set it down vnto you in this place, that you might know not onlie that which is right, but also that which others esteemed right.

figurative descant *see* canto figurato, counterpoint, descant, fugue

1704 HARRIS *Figurative Descant*. See *Descant*. **1706** KERSEY-PHILLIPS (6th edn) *Figurate Descant*, See *Descant*.

figure *as notational symbol, see* character, infigura, sign

1609 DOWLAND-ORNITHOPARCUS *Micrologvs* (p. 39) Wherefore a *Figure* [such as a large, long, breve etc.] is a certaine signe which represents a voyce, and silence. A Voyce, (I say) because of the kindes of Notes which are vsed: Silence, because of the Rests which are of equall value with the Notes, and are measured with Artificiall Silence.

figure *in thorough bass notation, see* thorough bass

1737 DYCHE-PARDON (2nd edn) *Figure* (V.) ... also to set over or put the Figures of the Concords over the Thorough Bass of a Piece of Musick, for the Use of the Harpsichord or Organ;

fileur

1688 Miege-Cotgrave Fr→E *Fileur,* (m.) a String-maker for musical Instruments;

filibustacchina *see* lerelot

1598 Florio It→E *Filibustacchina,* the burden of a countrie song, as we say hay doune a doune douna. **1611** Florio It→E *Filibustacchina,* the burden of a countrie song, as wee say, hay downe a downe a.

filum

1565 Cooper L→E § *Fila sonantia. Ouidius.* The ringinge or shrill stringes of an harpe. *Sonantia fila mouere. Ouid.* To strike the stringes of an instrument. **1587** Thomas L→E *Filum, li, n.g.* ... the string in an instrument:

fin *see* da capo

1611 Florio It→E *Finimondi,* ... Also a conclusion or cloze in Musicke. **1659** Torriano-Florio It→E *Fini mondi,* ... by Met. the end of any matter, also a close in Musick. **1724** [Pepusch] *Short Explic. of Foreign Words in Mus. Bks.* (p. 31) *Fin, Finis,* or *Finale,* is the End or last Note of a Piece of Musick. **1726** Bailey *An Univ. Etymolog. Engl. Dict.* (3rd edn) *Fin, Finale,* (in *Musick Books*) signifies the End or last Note of a Piece of Musick. *Ital. Finis* (in *Musick Books*) signifies the same as *Fin* or *Finale;* which see.

final *see* affinal key, ecclesiastic tone, repercussion

1609 Dowland-Ornithoparcus *Micrologvs* (p. 11) *Of the Finals belonging to the Tones.* ¶ *Finals,* (as Saint *Bernard* in his Musicke saith, both truely and briefely) are the Letters which end the Songs. For in these must be ended euery Song which is regular, and not transposed, and are in number Foure, as *Guido* writeth in the Dialogue of his *Doctrinall:* ... **1721** Malcolm *Treatise of Musick* (p. 277) ... the *Fundamental* is also called the *final,* because the Song commonly begins and always ends there: ... **1731** Prelleur *Modern Musick-Master* ('A Brief History of Musick', p. 15) ... there are three *Essential Sounds* or *Notes,* to be observed, the first is that by which the Tune ought to end, which is called the *Final,* The Second is that which is most heard, or oftenest repeated, this they call'd y[e] *Predominant* or *Ruling Note.* The third is called the *Mean* or *middle Note* and is generally a third above the Final.

fioretti

1598 Florio It→E *Fioretti,* ... Also flourishings or quaverings vpon any musicall instruments or running vpon them. **1611** Florio It→E *Fioretti,* ... Also quauerings or flowrishings or running diuisions vpon any musicall instruments or in singing. **1659** Torriano-Florio It→E **Fioretto, Fioretti,* ... also quaverings, flourishings, or running-divisions in singing, or upon any musical instruments.

first tone

1609 Dowland-Ornithoparcus *Micrologvs* (p. 29) The first *Tone* (as S. *Bernard* saith) is a Rule determining the *authentick* of the first kinde. Or it is the *authenticall* progression of the first. Now an *authenticall* progression, is the ascending beyond the *Finall Key* to an eight, & a tenth. And the progression of the first is formed by that kind of *Diapente,* which is from *d* to *a*: and of that kind of *Diatessaron,* which is from *a* to *d,* saith *Franchinus lib.* 1. *pract. cap.* 8. It hath his *Finall* regular place in *Dsolre,* or his vnregular in *alamire.* The beginnings of it according to *Guido* are *C. D. E. F. G.* and *a* ...

fissaye

1611 Cotgrave Fr→E *Fissaye: f.* A quicke, and violent daunce much vsed by the French.

fistula *see* afistolar, aula, aulos, calamus, cantes, domatum, tibia, trifistulary

1500 *Ortus Vocabulorum* L→E Fistula le. est quoddam instrumentum ad canendum ex canulis compactum. f.p. § Arbor aque ductus: est fistula musica morbus. **1538** Elyot L→E *Fistula,* a pype, as well to conuey water, as an instrument of musyke. **1552** Huloet L→E *Fistula* is the generall latyne for any thinge that is hollowe, and of the shape of a pype, or wherof a pipe may be made, as an oate strawe, or other strawe, reede. &c *Fistulator, sibilator, sifilator* Whistler. **1565** Cooper L→E *Fistula, fistulæ, f.g. pen. corr. Cic.* ... an instrument of musike. **1587** Thomas L→E *Fistula, æ, f.g.* ... also a pipe, or flute, whether it be of reed or other stuff: *Fistulator, oris, m.g. verb.* A piper: one that playeth on a flute or pipe. **1589** Rider L→E *Fistula, f. Calamus, m.* A Whistle. *Fistulatio, f.* A piping. *Fistulo.* To Pipe. **1611** Cotgrave Fr→E *Fistule: f.* A pipe, or flute; **1676** Coles *Fistula, Latin.* a pipe **1706** Kersey-Phillips (6th edn) *Fistula,* ... a Pipe or Flute, a Musical Instrument: **1707** *Gloss. Angl. Nova* (1st edn) *Fistula,* a Pipe, or Flute; **1721** Bailey *An Univ. Etymolog. Engl. Dict.* (1st edn)

Fistula, ... Also a Flute. *L.* **1728** CHAMBERS *Fistula*, in the antient Musick, An Instrument, of the Wind kind, resembling our Flute, or Flageolot [sic]. See *Flute.* ¶ The principal Wind Instruments of the Antients, are the *Tibia*, and *Fistula*: Tho' how these were constituted; or wherein they differ'd; or how they were play'd on, does not appear. All we know, is that the *Fistula* was at first made of Reeds, and afterwards of other Matters. Some had Holes; some none: Some again were single Pipes; others a Combination of several; Witness the Syringa of *Pan*. See *Tibia.* **1730** BAILEY *Dict. Britannicum* (1st edn) *Fistula*, a pipe, a musical instrument; **1737** DYCHE-PARDON (2nd edn) *Fistula* (S.) among the Antients, was an Instrument of Musick of the Wind Kind

fiutino *see* flautino, flute

1598 FLORIO It→E *Fiutino*, a little flute. **1611** FLORIO It→E *Fiutino*, a little flute.

fiuto *see* flute

flageolet *see* fistula, flute, zuffolo

1593 HOLLYBAND Fr→E *Flageolet*, a whistle, a pipe: *m.* **1611** COTGRAVE Fr→E *Flageoler*. To pipe, or play on a whistle. *Flageoleur: m.* A piper, a whistler; *Flageollet: m.* A pipe, whistle, flute; also, as *Flageollet.* **1658** PHILLIPS (1st edn) *Flajulet*, (French) a certain Musical instrument, being a kinde of Pipe, or Fluite, but somewhat lesse. **1670** BLOUNT (3rd edn) *Flageolet* (Fr) a small pipe or whistle, of late much used. **1671** PHILLIPS (3rd edn) *Flageolet, (French)* a certain Musical Instrument, being a kind of Pipe, or Fluit, but somewhat lesse. **1676** COLES *Flageolet, French.* a small pipe. **1688** MIEGE-COTGRAVE Fr→E *Flageolet*, (m.) *Instrument de Musique à Vent*, a flagellet. **1702** KERSEY *New Engl. Dict.* (1st edn) A *Flagelet*, a kind of pipe. **1706** KERSEY-PHILLIPS (6th edn) *Flagelet* or *Flageolet, (Fr.)* a Musical Instrument; a kind of Pipe. **1707** *Gloss. Angl. Nova* (1st edn) *Flagellet*, a Musical Instrument. **1721** BAILEY *An Univ. Etymolog. Engl. Dict.* (1st edn) *Flagelet, (Flageolet, F.)* a musical Instrument. **1726** BAILEY *An Univ. Etymolog. Engl. Dict.* (3rd edn) *Flagelet (Flageolet, F.)* a musical wind Instrument. A Pipe. **1728** CHAMBERS *Flageolet*, or *Flajolet*, a kind of little Flute, or musical Instrument of the Flute kind; used chiefly by the Shepherds and Country-People. See *Flute.* ¶ 'Tis usually made of Box, or other hard Wood; sometimes of Ivory. It has six Holes, or Stops, beside that at [the] Bottom, the Mouth-piece, and that behind the Neck. **1730** BAILEY *Dict. Britannicum* (1st edn) *Flagelet (flageolet*, F.) a musical pipe. **1737** DYCHE-PARDON (2nd edn) *Flagellet* (S.) a small, musical Pipe, or diminutive Flute.

1721 MALCOLM *Treatise of Musick* (p. 12) ... I have never indeed seen Flutes of any Matter but Wood, except of the small Kind we call Flageolets, of which I have seen Ivory ones, whose Sound has no remarkable Difference from a wooden one; ...

flamen

1538 ELYOT L→E *Flamen, hoc*, the blaste in an instrument. **1565** COOPER L→E *Flamen, flaminis, pen. corr. neut. gen. Horat.* ... a blaste in an instrument. **1587** THOMAS L→E *Flamen, inis, n.g.* ... a blast or sound in an instrument. **1589** RIDER L→E *Flamen, n.* A blast, or sounde of an instrument.

flat *see* character, key, molle

1728 CHAMBERS *Flats*, in Musick, a kind of additional Notes, contriv'd, together with *Sharps*, to remedy the Defects of Musical Instruments. See *Sharp.* ¶ The Natural Scale of Musick being limited to fix'd Sounds, and adjusted to an Instrument; the Instrument will be found defective in several Points: As particularly, in that we can only proceed from any Notes, by one particular Order of Degrees; that for this Reason we cannot find any Interval required from any Note or Letter upwards and downwards; and that a Song may be so contrived, as that if it be begun by any particular Note, or Letter, all the Intervals, or other Notes, shall be justly found on the Instrument, or in the fix'd Series; yet were the Song begun with any other Note, we could not proceed. See *Scale.* ¶ To remove, or supply this Defect, the Musicians have Recourse to a Scale proceeding by twelve Degrees, that is, thirteen Notes, including the Extremes, to an Octave; which makes the Instruments so perfect, that there is but little to complain of. This, however, is the present System or Scale for Instruments, *viz.* betwixt the Extremes of every Tone of the Natural Scale is put a Note, which divides it into two unequal Parts, called *Semi-tones*; and the Whole may be called the *Semitonic Scale*, containing twelve Semi-tones betwixt thirteen Notes, in the Compass of the Octave. See *Semi-tone*, and Scale of *Semi-tones.* ¶ Now, to preserve the Diatonic Series distinct, these inserted Notes either take the Name of the natural Note next below, with a Character # called a *Sharp*; or they take the Name of the natural Note next above, with the Mark ♭ called a *Flat*: Thus D ♭ or D *Flat* signifies a Semi-tone below the D natural. And it is indifferent in the main, whether the inserted Note be accounted as a *Flat*, or *Sharp*. ¶ This Semitonic Series or Scale is very exactly represented by the Keys of a Spinet: The foremost Range of Keys being the natural Notes; and the Keys behind, the artificial Notes, or the *Flats* and *Sharps*. See *Spinet*. **1730** BAILEY *Dict. Britannicum* (1st edn) *Flats* (in *Musick*) a kind of additional notes, as (♭) contrived together with sharps (♯) to remedy the defects of musical instrumen[t]s. **1731** KERSEY *New Engl. Dict.* (3rd edn) A *Flat*, or *Flat Sound* in *Musick*. **1737** DYCHE-PARDON (2nd edn) *Flat* (S.) ... in *Musick*, it is marked thus ♭, and imports that the particular Note against which it stands, is to be played or sung half a Note or Tune lower than it naturally would be, and when put at the Beginning of a Line or Space, affects all the Notes upon that Line or Space, &c. by causing them to be sung or played half a Note or Tone lower than they would be if they were not so affected.

1694 HOLDER *Treatise of Natural Grounds* (pp. 79-80) Of these [the concords], the *Third's* being Two, and *Sixth's* being also Two, want better distinguishing Names. To call them Flat and Sharp Thirds, and Flat and Sharp Sixths is not enough, and lies under a mistake; I mean, it is not a sufficient Distinction, to call the greater Third and Sixth, Sharp Third, and Sharp Sixth; and the lesser, Flat. They are so, indeed, in ascending from the Unison; but in descending they are contrary; so to the Octave, that greater Sixth is a lesser Third, and the greater Third is a lesser Sixth; which lesser Third and Sixth cannot well be called Flat, being in a Sharp Key; Flat and Sharp therefore do not well distinguish them in General. The lesser Third from the Octave being sharp, and the greater Sixth flat. So, from the Fifth descending by Thirds, if the First be a *Minor* Third, it is Sharp, and the other being a *Major* Third, cannot be said to be Flat. § (p. 198) [*re* variety of air in music] Which is also improved by the Differences of those we call Flat, or Sharp Keys; The Sharp, which take the Greater Intervals within *Diapason*, as 3ds, 6ths, and 7ths. *Major*; are more Brisk and Airy; and being assisted with Choice of Measures last spoken of, do Dilate the Spirits, and Rouze them up to Gallantry, and Magnanimity. The Flat, consisting of all the less Intervals, contract and damp the Spirits, and produce Sadness and Melancholy. **1724** TURNER *Sound Anatomiz'd* (p. 47) The *Mark* for *Contraction* is called a *Flat*; the con[t]racting of a *Sound* being called the flattening of it. This *Mark* is thus; ♭ which like the *Sharp*, is also placed on the left Side of the *Note*. **1731** PRELLEUR *Modern Musick-Master* (I, p. 5) There are two other Characters of great Use, called a Flat ♭ and a Sharp ✕. If a Flat be placed before any Note, you must sing such a Note half a Note lower than its natural Pitch: If a Sharp be set before any Note, you must sing it half a Note higher than it's natural heighth [sic].

flat cord

1737 LAMPE *Plain and Compendious Method* (p. 14) ... (E *nat*.-C *nat*.-A *nat*.) make a *Common Cord* with a flat Third, and is therefore called a flat Cord ...

flatness

1698 WALLIS *Letter to Samuel Pepys* (*Philos. Trans.*, 1698, p. 249) ... each *Pipe* in the Organ is intended to express a distinct *Sound* at such a *Pitch*; That is, in such a determinate Degree of *Gravity* or *Acuteness*; or (as it is now called) *Flatness* or *Sharpness*.

flator *see* aulœdus

1565 COOPER L→E § *Flatu spissa implere sedilia Horat.* with the sowne or noyse of fluites & pipes, to fill the Theater replenished with company of men. **1587** THOMAS L→E *Flator, oris, m.g. Fest.* One that doth blow, a piper.

flauta, flauto, fleute *see* flute

flautino *see* fiutino

1724 [PEPUSCH] *Short Explic. of Foreign Words in Mus. Bks.* (p. 31) *Flautino*, a little or small Flute, of the common Sort; like what we call a Sixth Flute, or an Octave Flute. **1726** BAILEY *An Univ. Etymolog. Engl. Dict.* (3rd edn) *Flautino*, a small Flute like a sixth Flute, or an Octave Flute. *Ital.*

flexibilis *see* concord

1565 COOPER L→E § *Flexibilis vocis genus. Cic.* A tunehable voyce. **1587** THOMAS L→E *Flexibilis, le.* ... tender, tractable, tuneable:

flexus

1565 COOPER L→E § *Flexus Vocis. Quintil.* The altering of the tune of the voyce in rising or fallyng when he singeth or speaketh. **1587** THOMAS L→E § *Flexus sonus.* A sound reverberated or beaten backe by reflection: *also* altered in tune.

flond [sic, for 'florid']
1704 HARRIS *Flond*, or *Figurate Descant*, a Term in Musick. Pee [sic] *Descant*. **1706** KERSEY-PHILLIPS (6th edn) *Flond*, or *Figurate Descant*, a Term in *Musick*. See *Descant*. **1708** KERSEY *Dict. Anglo-Brit.* (1st edn) *Flond* the same as *Figurate Descant*.

floralia *see* play
1728 CHAMBERS *Floral Games*. There are a kind of *Floral Games* observ'd at this day in *France*. They were first instituted in 1324. ¶ The Design and Establishment is owing to seven Persons of Condition, Lovers of Poetry, who about *All-Saints Day*, in 1323. sent a Circular Letter to all the Provincial Poets, called *Troubadours*, to meet at *Tholouse* on *May-day* following, there to rehearse their Poems; promising a Violet of Gold to the Person whose Piece shou'd be judg'd the best.... The Ceremony begins on *May-day*, with a solemn Mass, Musick, *&c*. The Corporation attend; and Poems are rehearsed every day: **1736** BAILEY *Dict. Britannicum* (2nd edn) *Floralia*, a feast and sports in honour of *Flora*, who having left a certain sum of money for the celebration of her birth, day [sic], these games were celebrated with obscenities and debaucheries, not only with the most licentious discourses; but the courtesans being call'd together by sound of trumpet made their appearance naked and entertain'd the people with abominable shews and postures. **1737** DYCHE-PARDON (2nd edn) *Floralia* (S.) among the *Romans*, Sports instituted in Honour of *Flora*, and observed the four last Days in *April*, and the first of *May*, at which Time shameless Strumpets went up and down the Streets naked, using lascivious Gestures and obscene Speeches, who were usually called together by the Sound of a Trumpet;

floting
1676 COLES *Floting, Old word.* whistling, piping. **1721** BAILEY *An Univ. Etymolog. Engl. Dict.* (1st edn) *Floting*, Whistling, Piping. *O*.

flourish *see* assay, epicitharisma, fioretti, half cadence, key, overture, pavan, precention, prelude, prelusion, proludium, prolusion
1706 KERSEY-PHILLIPS (6th edn) *Flourish, (Lat.)* an Ornament in Writing, Rhetorick, Musick, &c. **1737** DYCHE-PARDON (2nd edn) *Flourish* (S.) ... in *Musick*, a wild Sort of Overture, to try whether the Instrument is, or to bring the Voice in Tune, and to bring the Hand into a proper Position for the Key of the Composition, then going to be be [sic] play'd or sung. *Flourish* (V.) ... also to run over the several Keys, Strings, &c. of a musical Instrument, before the Beginning of a grand Performance, to see whether the Instruments are in Tune, and to put the Hand in a proper Position for the Key of the Composition.

c.1710 NORTH (draft for) Musicall Grammarian BL Add. 32537, f. 94v ... Nay it is y[e] use of Masters at the overture of a musicall Enterteinm[t], to possess y[e] ear of y[e] audience, with y[e] Key of y[e] following Musick, to flourish as they call it, upon y[e] Key; ... **c.1715-20** NORTH Essay of Musical Ayre BL Add. 32536, ff. 20-20v ... there is a sort of Musick, w[ch] carrys variety Enough, and yet departs not from y[e] Aire of the Key w[ch] with its full accord may Sound along with it. And this is Called flourish, devision, or breaking, whereof the manner is, when the Sound passeth from the Key Note to the severall notes of the accord, either per saltum, or by such degrees as the scale of the Key hath prefixt; and thro all the varietys of this Kind, the air of the Key is preserved; ...

flusteau
1611 COTGRAVE Fr→E *Flusteau*. A little Flute, or Pipe;

flute *see* aula, auleta, aulœdus, aulos, calamus, canna, cannella, colonna, faucet, fausetum, fife, fistula, fiutino, flageolet, flautino, hemiope, larigot, magade, record, recorder, sampogna, siringa, stifello, stufallo, succhiello, syrinx, tibia, tibicen, zuffolo
1570/71 *Dict. Fr. and Engl.* Fr→E *Fleute, ou Flute, ou Flageolet*, a flute, a whistle, a pype, a fife. *Fleuteur, ou Fluteur*, a pyper, a fluter, a fife [sic]. § *Iouer de fleute*, a player on the Flute. *Orgues à flutes, qui sonnent à soufflets*, recorders. **1593** HOLLYBAND Fr→E *Fleute, ou flute, flageol*, or *flageolet*, a flute, a whistle, a pipe: *f*. *Fleuter, ou fluteur*, a piper, a fluter: *m*. § *Animer & inciter à son de fleutes les gents à frapper*, to encourage, or harten men to fight, by the sound of a flute. *Iouëur de fleute*, a player on a Flute: *m*. **1598** FLORIO It→E *Fiuto*, ... Also a flute. *Flautare*, to play vpon a flute. *Flauto*, a flute, a player vpon a flute. **1599** MINSHEU-PERCYVALL Sp→E *Flauta*, f. a pipe of a reed, a flute, a fife. *Flautador*, m. a player on a fife or flute. **1611** COTGRAVE Fr→E *Fleute: f.* A flute; a pipe. *Fleuter*. To play on the flute. *Fleuteur: m.* A Fluter, a Piper. *Fleuteuse: f.* A Fluteresse; a woman that playes on a flute. § *Micocoulier d'Afrique*. Th'African Lote, or Nettle, tree; of

whose blacke wood excellent Flutes are made. **1611** FLORIO It→E *Fiuto,* a flute. *Flautare,* to play vpon a Flute. *Flauto,* a Flute. Also a Flutist. **1659** TORRIANO-FLORIO It→E **Fiuto, Fiutino,* a scent, a smell, also a flute. *Flautatore,* a flutist, a fluter. *Flauto,* a flute. *Frauto,* as *Flauto,* a flute. **1688** MIEGE-COTGRAVE Fr→E *Flute,* (f.) a flute, or pipe; .... Ps. 149. 2. you will find for the word *flute* that of Dance in the English Translation. † *Fluter,* to pipe, to play upon the pipe, or flute. § *Flute doulce,* the sweet flute, a flute that hath nine holes. *Jouër de la flute,* to play upon the flute. *Nous vous avons fluté, & vous n'avez point dansé,* (Matt. 11. 17.) we have piped unto you, and you have not danced. *Un Jouëur de flute,* a Player upon the flute. **1696** PHILLIPS (5th edn) *Flute,* a Musical Wind-Instrument; **1702** KERSEY *New Engl. Dict.* (1st edn) A *Flute, or* recorder, a kind of pipe. **1707** *Gloss. Angl. Nova* (1st edn) *Flute,* an Instrument of Wind Musick. **1721** BAILEY *An Univ. Etymolog. Engl. Dict.* (1st edn) A *Flute, (Fleute, F.* and *Teut.)* an Instrument of wind Musick: **1724** [PEPUSCH] *Short Explic. of Foreign Words in Mus. Bks.* (pp. 31-2) *Fiauto* is a Flute in general, of any Kind or Sort. *Flauto,* is a Flute; to be understood chiefly of the common Sort. § *Fiauto Traverso,* is a *German* Flute. *Flute a bec,* is a Common Flute. *Flute d'Allemanda,* is a *German* Flute. **1726** BAILEY *An Univ. Etymolog. Engl. Dict.* (3rd edn) *Fiauto,* a Flute, *Ital. Flauto,* a Flute. *Ital.* § *Fiauto Transverso,* a *German* Flute, *It. Flute a Bec,* a common Flute. *Ital. Flute d'Allemanda,* a *German* Flute. *Ital.* **1728** CHAMBERS *Flute,* an Instrument of Musick, the simplest of all those of the Wind kind. See *Musick.* ¶ It is play['']d, by blowing in it with the Mouth; and the Tones or Notes form'd and changed by stopping or opening Holes disposed for that purpose all along it. ¶ The *Latins* call it *Fistula,* and sometimes *Tibia,* Pipe; from the former of which, some derive the Word *Flute*: Tho' Borel will have it derived from *Flutta,* a Lamprey, thus called *a fluitando in Fluviis*; in regard the *Flute* is long, like the Lamprey, and has Holes all along it, like that Fish. ¶ The antient *Fistulæ* or *Flutes* were made of Reeds; afterwards they were of Wood; and at length, of Metal. But how they were blown, whether as our *Flutes,* or Hantboys, does not appear. ¶ 'Tis plain, some had Holes, which at first, were but few; but afterwards increased to a greater Number: And some had none. Some were single Pipes; and some a Combination of several, particularly *Pan's Syringa,* which consisted of seven Reeds, join'd together sideways. ¶ The *German Flute* is different from the common one: 'Tis not put into the Mouth, by the End, as the ordinary ones are: The End is stop'd up with a Plug, or Tampion; but the lower Lip is applied to a Hole about half an Inch distant from it. ¶ 'Tis usually a Foot long; equally big every where, and perforated with six Holes, beside that of the Mouth. It is us'd as a Treble in a Concert of several Parts. ¶ Its Bass is double, or quadruple that Length. **1737** BAILEY *The Univ. Etymolog. Engl. Dict.* (3rd edn, vol. 2, cant section) *Flute,* the Recorder of *London,* or of any other Town. **1737** DYCHE-PARDON (2nd edn) *Flute* (S.) a Wind-Musical Instrument very much in Use, of which there are various Sorts, as Consort Flute, Octave Flute, German Flute, &c.

1726-8 NORTH Theory of Sounds BL Add. 32535, f. 141v Now I proceed to that manner of voicing wch I distinguished by a terme wch may be comon to all, and that is, Flute. This is knowne by the ordinary Organ pipes, mouth flutes, flageoletts, Germane flutes, and other whistling devises. **1731** PRELLEUR *Modern Musick-Master* (Dictionary, p. 2) *Flauto,* any Kind of Flute.

flying a cadence

1731 [PEPUSCH] *Treatise on Harmony* (2nd edn, p. 57) ... We will conclude this Subject by mentioning what is call'd the *Flying* or *Avoiding* a Cadence. What is meant hereby is, that after the having Prepar'd and Resolv'd the *Discord* that precedes the Cadence, instead of proceeding afterwards to the Note on which it ought to conclude, we go to some *Other Note,* and thereby break off the Cadence, instead of compleating it.

follia *see* Farinel's ground, variation

1599 MINSHEU-PERCYVALL Sp→E **Fulia,* f. a daunce or song. **Fuliador,* m. a dauncer or singer of such daunce or song. **1724** [PEPUSCH] *Short Explic. of Foreign Words in Mus. Bks.* (p. 32) *Follia,* the Name of a particular Air, known by the Name of *Fardinal*'s Ground. ¶ *N.B.* The last of *Corelli*'s Solos is so called. **1726** BAILEY *An Univ. Etymolog. Engl. Dict.* (3rd edn) *Follia* (in *Musick Books*) signifies a particular Air, known by the Name of *Fardinal*'s Ground. *Ital.* **1730** BAILEY *Dict. Britannicum* (1st edn) *Follia* (in *Mus. Books*) a particular air commonly called *Fardinal's ground.*

fonticus

1500 *Ortus Vocabulorum* L→E Fonticus a. um. i. consonans vel musicus. o.s.

forefall *see* backfall, half-fall, whole-fall
c.1710 NORTH Short, Easy, & plaine rules BL Add. 32531, f. 24 [quoting Prendcourt:] A litle short stroke [⟋]set thus before a note is called a fore-fall ...

forlana
1724 [PEPUSCH] *Short Explic. of Foreign Words in Mus. Bks.* (p. 32) *Forlana*, a slow Kind of Jig. See *Saltarella.* **1726** BAILEY *An Univ. Etymolog. Engl. Dict.* (3rd edn) *Forlana*, a slow kind of Jig, the same as *Starella* [sic]. *Ital.* **1730** BAILEY *Dict. Britannicum* (1st edn) *Foriana* [sic], a slow kind of jig, the same as *Starella* [sic], Ital.

formality
1636 BUTLER *Principles of Musik* (p. 81) *Of Ornaments. Of Formaliti.* ¶ The last and chiefest Ornament is Formaliti: which is the mainteining of the Air, or Tone of the Song, in his Partes. ¶ This is *Ornamentum Ornamentorum*: the Ornament of Ornaments: with which the Partes ar sweetely conformed one to an other, and each of them to it self: and without which, not onely the other Ornaments lose their vertue and ceas to bee Ornaments; but also bothe Melodi and Harmoni themselvs, lose their Grace, and wil bee neither good Melodi nor good Harmoni: the whole Song beeing nothing els, but a Form-les *Chaos* of confused sounds.

forsongen
1676 COLES *Forsongen, Old word.* weary with singing. **1721** BAILEY *An Univ. Etymolog. Engl. Dict.* (1st edn) *Forsongen*, weary with Singing. *O.* **1726** BAILEY *An Univ. Etymolog. Engl. Dict.* (3rd edn) *Forsongin*, tired with Singing. *Ch.* **1740** BAILEY *An Univ. Etymolog. Engl. Dict.* (9th edn) *Forsongen*, weary with Singing. *O. Forsongin*, tired with Singing. *Ch.*

forte *see* f, piano
1721 BAILEY *An Univ. Etymolog. Engl. Dict.* (1st edn) *Forte*, (of *Fortis, L.*) a Term in Musick when the Movement is Strong and Bold. **1724** [PEPUSCH] *Short Explic. of Foreign Words in Mus. Bks.* (p. 32) *Forte*, or *Fortement*, is to play or sing loud and strong; and *Forte Forte*, or *FF*, is very loud. (p. 96) *Forte*, or *F*, Loud. § (p. 32) *Piu Forte*, or *P F*, is a Degree louder than *Forte* only. (p. 96) *Forte Forte*, or *FF*, Very Loud. **1726** BAILEY *An Univ. Etymolog. Engl. Dict.* (3rd edn) *Forte* (in *Musick-Books*) signifies, to play or sing loud and strong. *Ital. Forte Forte*, or *F.F.* signifies, to play or sing very loud and strong. *Ital. FF*, (in *Musick-Books*) stands for *Forte, forte*, and denotes very loud. *Ital. Fortement*, signifies the same as *Forte. Ital.* § *Piu Forte*, or *P.E* [sic]. (in *Musick-Books*) denotes a Degree louder than only *Forte. Ital.*

1680 B., A. *Synopsis of Vocal Musick* (p. 42) ... *Italians* only, and some that them do follow, do use these two words, *Forte* and *Piano*, signifying that such part of a song must be sung clearer and fuller, under which is written *Forte*, but softer and smaller, under which is written *Piano.* **c.1710** ANON. *Preceptor for Improved Octave Flageolet* ('Explanation of Words', p. 82) *For.* or *Forte*—Loud **1736** TANS'UR *Compleat Melody* (3rd edn, p. 68) *Forte, Fortement, Fortismo*, or *F.* or *Fe*, (Ital.) Either of those Terms denote that you must sing, or play very loud. ¶ *Piu Forte*, or *P.F.* denote one Degree louder than *Forte.* ¶ *Forte Forte*, or *F.F.* denotes as loud as possible.

fortissimo
1724 [PEPUSCH] *Short Explic. of Foreign Words in Mus. Bks.* (p. 96) *Fortissimo*, or *FFF*, Extream Loud. **1726** BAILEY *An Univ. Etymolog. Engl. Dict.* (3rd edn) *Fortissimo* (in *Musick-Books*) signifies extreme loud. *Ital.*

c.1710 ANON. *Preceptor for Improved Octave Flageolet* ('Explanation of Words', p. 82) *Fortissimo*—Very loud

fourth *see* diatessaron, imperfect fourth, quarte
1706 KERSEY-PHILLIPS (6th edn) *Fourth*, a Term in *Musick.* See *Diatessaron.* **1728** CHAMBERS *Fourth*, in Musick, one of the Harmonic Intervals, or Concords. See *Concord.* ¶ The *Fourth*, is the Fourth, in order, of the Concords. It consists in the Mixture of two Sounds, which are in the Ratio of 4 to 3; *i.e.* of Sounds produ'd by Chords, whose Lengths are to each other as 4:3. See *Chord*, and *Interval.* ¶ 'Tis call'd *Fourth*, because containing *four* Terms, or Sounds between its Extremes; and three *Degrees*: Or, as being the *fourth* in the Order of the Natural Scale from the Fundamental. See *Degree*, and *Fundamental.* ¶ The Antients call the *Fourth, Diatessaron*, and speak of it as the first and principal of all Concords; and yet the Moderns find it one of the most imperfect. 'Tis so very barren, and jejune, that it affords nothing good, either by Multiplication, or Division. See *Diatessaron.* ¶ The *Redundant Fourth* is a Discord compos'd of the Ratio's of 27 to 20; and of 4 to 5. See *Discord.* **1737** DYCHE-PARDON (2nd edn) *Fourth* (S.) in *Musick*, is

one of the harmonick Intervals or Concords, it is sometimes called Diatessaron, which the Ancients deemed one of the greatest or most perfect Concords, but by the Moderns is esteemed a very imperfect one.

1596 ANON. *Pathway to Musicke* [B iii] A fourth is the distance of the voice by a fourth standing of tvvo tunes and a halfe, of vvhich are three kinds, *re sol. mi la. vt fa.* **1698** WALLIS *Letter to Samuel Pepys* (*Philos. Trans.*, 1698, p. 250) [*re* the Aristoxenians and Pythagorians] They both agreed thus far; That *Dia-tessaron* and *Dia-pente*, do together make-up *Diapason*; that is (as we now speak) a *Fourth* and *Fifth* do together make an *Eighth* or *Octave*:

fourth, greater *see* tritone

fourth tone

1609 DOWLAND-ORNITHOPARCUS *Micrologvs* (p. 32) The Fourth *Tone* (as witnesseth *Bernard*) is a Rule determining the *plagall* of the second manner. Or it is a Progression of the second *plagall*, holding the same end that his *Authenticke* doth. It hath sixe beginnings, *C. D. E. F. G.* and *a* ...

fredon *see* descant

1593 HOLLYBAND Fr→E *Fredonner*, to warble or quauer. *Fredons*, warbling of voyce in musicke: *m.* **1611** COTGRAVE Fr→E *Fredon: m.* A Semie-quauer, or Semie-semie-quauer, in Musicke; and hence, Diuision; and a warbling, shaking, or quauering. *Fredonner.* To shake, diuide, warble, quauer in singing, or playing on an instrument. *Fredonneux: m. euse. f.* Full of Semie-semie-quauers; or of quauering, shaking, warbling; diuiding much. *Fredonnisé.* Shaked, quauered, warbled, diuided. **1688** MIEGE-COTGRAVE Fr→E *Fredon,* (m.) a division, in Musick;

free fugue *see* fuga ligata

freeman's song *see* virelay

french horn *see* sound

1726-8 NORTH Theory of Sounds BL Add. 32535, f. 138v ... That wch is called the french horn, used by Hunters, is a trumpet tube, turned in 2. or 3. rounds about.

frequentamentum *see* descant

1565 COOPER L→E *Frequentamentum, frequentamenti, n.g. vt, Frequentamenta vocis. Gell.* In musike, warblyng of the voyce. **1587** THOMAS L→E *Frequentamentum, ti, n.g. Gell.* ... In musicke warbling of the voice.

fret *see* laying, tastame, tastare, tastatura, tasto, touch, traste

1706 KERSEY-PHILLIPS (6th edn) *Fret,* ... also a particular Stop in a Musical Instrument, such as are usually distinguish'd by Strings or Wires ty'd round it at Certain Distances. *Fretted,* ... Viols, Lutes, and other Instruments are said to be *fretted*, when they have their several Frets or Stops marked on them. **1737** BAILEY *The Univ. Etymolog. Engl. Dict.* (3rd edn, vol. 2) *Fret* (in *Musick*) a string tied round the finger-board of an instrument to shew the proper distance upon the string that each note should be struck. **1737** DYCHE-PARDON (2nd edn) *Fret* (S.) ... in *Musick*, it is a String tied round the Finger-Board of some Instruments, to shew the proper Distance upon the String that each Note should be struck at; *Fretted* (A.) ... also Musical Instruments divided into Portions or Distances upon the Finger-Board, to shew the regular Places where to stop or put the Finger, in order to produce the Tone required by the Composition.

1568 LE ROY *Briefe and Easye Instrution* (p. 4) We call the frettes, the stringes that be tyed about the necke of the Lute, which be ordinarily eight in number represented and figured by the letters. b. c. d. e. f. g. h. i. and be called stoppes, because that whereas those sayte letters be sound, followyng the order of our tablytorie, the spaces betwixt the frettes must be stopped with the left hand. In the French tablytory is vsed the letters of the Alphabete, and the Italions and other Nacions in steade thereof, vse Siphers and other Carecters. **1596** BARLEY *New Booke of Tabliture* (n.p.) The freets are those strings that are tied about the necke of the Lute, and are ordinarilie eight in number represented and marked with these letters, b. c. d. e. f. g. h. i. and they are called stops, in regard that where these letters are found, following the order of the tabliture, and the spaces betwixt the freets must bee stopped with the fingers of the left hand.

frifolare

1611 FLORIO It→E *Frifolare,* to bestir ones fingers nimbly vpon a pipe, flute or virginalls. *Frisolista* [sic], a nimble piper or virginalls plaier, a light fingered fellow. **1659** TORRIANO-FLORIO It→E *Frifolare,* to bestir ones fingers nimbly upon any musical instrument *Frifolista,* a nimble fingred Musician

frigdores

1676 COLES *Frigdores, Old word.* Musick-measures (*q. Frigian* and *Lorrick* [sic].)

frigio *see* phrygian

fringoter

1593 HOLLYBAND Fr→E *Fringoter,* to quauer in singing. **1611** COTGRAVE Fr→E *Fringoter.* To quauer, to diuide in singing;

fritino

1500 *Ortus Vocabulorum* L→E Fritino as. to synge as a swalo/ [sic] or as other smalle burdys. n.p.

frizzare

1598 FLORIO It→E *Frizzante,* shrill, quauering *Frizzare,* to frie, to quauer vpon any instrument **1611** FLORIO It→E *Frizzare,* to bite, to burne or be tarte vpon the tongue. Also to spurt as good wine doth being poured into a flat glasse, to friske and skip nimbly. Also to quauer or run nimbly vpon any instrument. Also to fry or scorch or parch. Also to crush, to squash, to bruise or squatter. **1659** TORRIANO-FLORIO It→E **Frizzamento, Frizzata,* a spirting, a frisking, a startling, also a quavering with voice, or a nimble running and trebling upon any instrument **Frizzante,* spirting, frisking, or startling as good wine doth being poured into a flat glasse, also nimbly quavering with the voice when one singeth, also swift running upon an instrument **Frizzare,* to spirt, to frisk ... also to quaver with the voice, or run nimbly upon any instrument

frottola

1598 FLORIO It→E *Frottola,* a countrie gigge, or round, or countrie song, or wanton verse. *Frottolare,* to sing gigges, rounds, countrie songs, or wanton verses. **1611** FLORIO It→E *Frottola,* a countrie song or roundelay, a wanton tale, or skeltonicall riming. *Frottolare,* to sing countrie songs or gigges, to tell wanton tales, to rime dogrell. **1659** TORRIANO-FLORIO It→E *Frottola,* a country jigg, ditty or song, a roundelay, a skeltonical rithming. *Frottolante,* a composer or singer of Frottole. *Frottolare,* to compose, to sing, or tell wanton country jiggs, ditties or dogrel rhimes.

fuga in nomine

1731 [PEPUSCH] *Treatise on Harmony* (2nd edn, p. 88) The *Fuga in Nomine* is also an *Imitation,* but of another Kind than the *last mention'd* [simple imitation]; for, as the former are *Imitations* of *Fugues* only in respect to the *Lines* and *Spaces* in the *Staff,* so *these,* as their Name implies, are only so *as to the Solmisation,* and not at all *as to the Intervals.* In these *Imitations* the Composition is so contriv'd, as that the *Guide* and its *Answer* do *Solfa alike,* but proceed by very *dissimilar Intervals.*

fuga ligata

1636 BUTLER *Principles of Musik* (p. 75) *Fuga ligata.* ¶ Iterating of the whole modulation of a Song (namely when two or more Partes ar made in one) is a kinde of Fuga: which *Calvisius* calleth *Fuga ligata.* ¶ These Partes (Principal and Replie) soomtime they prik doun severally by themselvs: as in Mr *Morleys* examples of two Partes in one, in Epidiatessaron and Epidiapente, bothe in Counterpoint and Discant. ¶ Sometime they write onely the Principal: and prefix a Title, declaring bothe the Distance of the Replie, and the time when it coometh in: (adding afterward, in his due place, the marke of his Cloze) which Title the Musicians call Canon. **1731** [PEPUSCH] *Treatise on Harmony* (2nd edn, p. 86) Regular *Fugues* are of *two* sorts; the one is call'd by the Italians *Fuga Legata,* and the other *Fuga Sciolta.* The *first* sort is in English generally call'd *Canon;* and we may express the *other* sort by the Name of *Free Fugue.*

fuga sciolta *see* fuga ligata

fugue *see* arsis & thesis, augmentation, canon, counterfugue, descant, double descant, fancy, guide, harmonia gemina, imitation, in nomine, overture, pathetic music, point, recte & retro, revert, simple, two parts in one

1611 COTGRAVE Fr→E *Fugue: f.* A chace, or report of Musicke, like two, or more parts in one. **1656** BLOUNT (1st edn) *Fugue* (Fr.) a chase or report of Musick; as when two or more parts chase one another in the same point. **1658** PHILLIPS (1st edn) *Fugne* [sic], (French) a Term in Musick, when two parts answer one the other in the same point. **1671** PHILLIPS (3rd edn) *Fugue, (French)* a Term in Musick, when two parts answer one the other in the same point, or several points follow one another in the same part in several keys. **1676** COLES *Fugue, French.* when two or more parts (in musick) chase one another in the same point. **1688** MIEGE-COTGRAVE Fr→E *Fugue,* (f.) *Terme de Musique,* a fugue, or chace, in Musick. § *Faire une fugue,* to maintain a fugue. **1702** KERSEY *New Engl. Dict.* (1st edn) A *Fugue, or* chace in musick. **1704** HARRIS *Fugue,* in Musick, is some Point consisting of 4, 5, 6, or any other Number of Notes begun by some one single Part, and then seconded by a Third, Fourth, Fifth and Sixth Part (if the Composition consists of so many) repeating the same or such like Notes, so that the several Parts follow, or come in one after another in the same manner, the leading Part still flying before those that follow. § *Fugue-double,* is when two or more different Points move together in a *Fugue,* and are alternately interchang'd by the several Parts. **1706** KERSEY-PHILLIPS (6th edn) *Fugue,* or *Chace,* (in *Musick*) a Point consisting of several Notes, begun by some one single Part, and then seconded by a third, fourth, fifth and sixth Parts, according to the Nature of the Composition, repeating the same or such like Notes: So that the several Parts answer or come in one after another in the same manner; the leading Parts flying as it were before those that follow. § *Double Fugue,* is when two or more different Points move together in a Fugue, and are chang'd by turns one with another, by the several Parts. **1707** *Gloss. Angl. Nova* (1st edn) *Fugue,* (Fr.) a Chase of Musick, as when two or more parts chase one another in the same Point. **1724** [PEPUSCH] *Short Explic. of Foreign Words in Mus. Bks.* (p. 32) *Fugha,* a Fuge; which is a particular Way or Manner, according to which some Musick is compos'd, and of which there are several Sorts. **1726** BAILEY *An Univ. Etymolog. Engl. Dict.* (3rd edn) *Fugha* (in *Musick-Books*) denotes a particular Way or Manner, according to which some Musick is compos'd, and of which there are several Sorts. *Ital.* **1728** CHAMBERS *Fugue,* in Music, is when the different Parts of a musical Composition follow each other; and repeating what the first had perform'd. ¶ There are three kinds of *Fugues*: The Single *Fugue*; Double *Fugue,* and *Counterfugue.* ¶ The *Single,* or *Simple Fugue,* is some Point consisting of 4, 5, 6, or any other Number of Notes, begun by one single Part, and then seconded by a third, fourth, fifth, and sixth Part, if the Composition consists of so many, repeating the same, or such like Notes; so that the several Parts follow, or come in, one after another in the same manner, the leading Parts still flying before those which follow. ¶ *Fugue-Double,* is when two or more different Points move together in a *Fugue,* and are alternately interchanged by several Parts. ¶ *For the* Counter *Fuge,* see *Counter Fugue.* **1737** DYCHE-PARDON (2nd edn) *Fuge* (S.) in *Musick,* is when the different Parts of a Composition follow each other, each repeating what the first had performed; and according to what and how it is performed, is called a single Fuge, which consists of 5, 6, or any other Number of Notes begun by a single Part, and followed by a second, third, &c. Part; a double Fuge, is when two or more different Points move together in a Fuge, and are alternately interchanged by several Parts.

1597 MORLEY *Plaine and Easie Introdvction* (p. 76) We call that a Fuge, when one part beginneth and the other singeth the same, for some number of notes (which the first did sing) ... **1636** BUTLER *Principles of Musik* (p. 71) Fuga is the Repeating of soom Modulation or Point, in Melodi and Harmoni: an Ornament exceediug [sic] delightfull, and without satieti: and therefore Musicians the more they ar exercised in Setting, the more studdi and pains they bestow in this Ornament.... The Partes of *Fuga* ar two, the Principal, which leadeth; the Replie, which followeth. And the Sorts like wise two, Reporte and Revert. § (p. 80) *Fvga est certa alicusus modulationis Repetitio.* Calvisius C. 15. **late 17th C.** ANON. Tractatus de Musicâ BL Add. 4923, f. 12 Figuratum est vel *Fuga,* vel Canon. Fuga est, quando idem punctum à diversis partibus successive repetitur vel in eâdem, vel in diversâ clavi: ... § f. 12 Fuga inversa est, quotios punctum unium partis, in alterâ fertur notibus plaxe contraijs: v: g: in unâ assurgit ad quintam, in alterâ tantumdem descendit &c. **1667** SIMPSON *Compendium of Practical Musick* (pp. 128-9) *Of Fuga or Fuge.* ¶ This is some Point ... begun by some one single Part, and then seconded by a following Part ... The Fifth, and Sixth Parts (if the Composition consists of so many) do follow or come in after the same manner, one after the other; the leading Parts still flying before those that follow; and from thence it hath its name *Fuga* or Fuge. **1676** MACE *Musick's Monument* (p. 116) This *Term Fuge,* is a *Term* used among *Composers; by which They understand a certain intended Order, Shape, or Form of Notes; signifying, such a Matter, or such an Extension; and is used in Musick, as a Theam, or as a subject Matter in Oratory, on which the Orator intends to Discourse.* **1694** PURCELL-PLAYFORD *Intro. to Skill of Musick* (12th edn, 'A Brief Introduction to the Art of Descant', n.p.) *Of Fuge, or Pointing.* ¶ A *Fuge,* is when one part leads one, two, three, four, or more Notes, and the other repeats the same in the *Unison,* or such like in the *Octave,* a *Fourth* or *Fifth* above or below the Leading Part. § The third sort of Fugeing is called a *Double Fuge*; which is, when one Part leads a *Point*, and the following Part comes in with another, and so the Parts change ... **after 1698** ANON. Musical Observations and Experiments BL Harley 4160, f. 41 Ther is 2 sorts of points or fugues in descanting, the one is cald a direct fugue the other is a revers fugue, the direct is when the one part answers directly the other cald the revers answers contrary **1711** BEDFORD *Great Abuse of Musick* (p. 225) Another *Improvement* of *Musick* is by *Fuges*, or carrying on of Points, when one *Part* leads, and another follows in Imitation of it. **1728** NORTH Musicall Grammarian (*C-K MG* f. 69v) It seems proper in this place to produce all I have to say concerning fuges; and first that they mean no other then a short parcell of notes distinguishable by their melody, and native of the key in which they are profered and variously repeated. And these the masters have called points, and the elder musicians professed wonderfull art in the management of them, which so far as was reasonable, consisted in pure repetition... **1731** [PEPUSCH] *Treatise on Harmony* (2nd edn, p. 79) A *Fugue* is a Piece of Musick in *Two* or more *Parts*, wherein the Parts which *lead* and *answer* in *Fugue* must proceed by the *same Species* of *Intervals*; that is, that the *Tones* and *Semitones* must stand in the same Order in *One Part* as they do in the *Other*. **1731** PRELLEUR *Modern Musick-Master* (Dictionary, p. 2) *Fugha* or *Fuge* is when some of the parts begin a certain Aire and the other parts begin some time after that imitating the first and repeating the same Aire, Throughout all the parts. ¶ *Fuga per Arsin* and *Thesin* is what the Italians call by contrary motion, and is when the leading part descends the other instead of Imitating of it, ascends. ¶ *Fuga Doppia*, signifies Double Fuge that is when the leading part proposes a Subject; and the Second part instead of repeating the first Subject proposes a different. **1736** TANS'UR *Compleat Melody* (3rd edn, p. 63) A *Fuge*, or *Fuga*, is a Quantity of *Notes* of any Number; which is begun by any *single Part* and carried on; and afterward is Sounded again, by some other *Part*; which Repeats the same (or such like *Notes*) either in the *Unison*, or 8th; but more commonly in the latter; in a 4th, or 5th, above, or below, the *leading Part*: which is properly Termed, *The Prime Flower of Florid*, or *Figurate-Descant*. § (pp. 63-4) Note, *Well*, That *Fuges* have several *Terms*, or *Denominations (Ex. Gr.)* The First ... is called *Single Fuge*, or, *Imitation*; By reason the *Parts* do imitate one another.—*Double Fuge*, is when two several *Points*, or *Fuges* fall one after another.—*Arsis* and *Thesis*, is when your *Point* rises in one *Part*, and falls in another.—*Per Augmentation*, is when the *Notes* of the following *Parts* are Augmented, or made as long again as the *Leading-Part*.—*Diminution*, is when the Notes of the following *Parts* are made as quick again as the *Leading-Part*. *Double-Descant*, is contrived so, that in *Replication*, or *Answer*, the *Upper-part* may be made *Bass*; or the *Bass* be made the *Upper-part*. § (p. 71) *Fuge*, or *Fuga*, (Lat.) signifies *flying*, or *running*: And used when *Parts*, or *Points* fly one before another; which is properly called *Fugeing*.

full accord *see* accord, daccordo, triad

1726-8 NORTH Theory of Sounds BL Add. 32535, f. 111v ... Wherein may be observed, first the tone or key, and next to that the 3#. and above that the fifth. Where at every fourth puls of the tone, there is a coincidence of all these sounds, In w[ch] are comprized first a 3#. then between that and the 5[th.] a 3b. so the whole consists of a 5[th.] and the two thirds sharp and flatt, all sounding together; this is called the full accord, and belongs to every key note, and declares that these meeting in sound together, the lowest is a proper key that rules the scale, & y[e] rest its accords.

full stop

1652 PLAYFORD *Musicks Recreation on Lyra Viol* (n.p.) ... In this Example you see the places of the Letters as they are stopt on the neck of your Violl, and though heere they be of one sort together, in your Lessons you will meet with them mixt with other Letters one under another, which are called a full stop, or the striking three or foure strings together with once drawing the Bow, according to your numbers of Letters so placed. **1682** PLAYFORD *Musick's Recreation on Viol* (2nd edn, preface) ... In this Example you see the places of the Letter, as they are assigned to the Stops or Frets on the neck of the *Viol*, and though here they be all of one sort together, in the Lessons you will meet with them mixt with other Letters one under another according to Art, which are called full, which is the striking two, three, or four strings together with one stroke of the Bow, according to the number of Letters so placed.

fundamental *see* ecclesiastic tone, essential notes, final, key, supposed bass, triad

1728 CHAMBERS *Fundamental,* in Music, the principal Note of a Song, or Composition, to which all the rest are in some measure adapted, and by which they are sway'd; call'd also the *Key* of the Song. See *Key.*

1721 MALCOLM *Treatise of Musick* (p. 201) ... Let us suppose Four Sounds *A. B. C. D.* whereof *A* is the *gravest, B* next *acuter,* then *C,* and *D* the *acutest; A* is called the *Fundamental,* and the Relations of *B, C,* and *D,* to *A,* are *primary Relations:* ...

furia

1724 [PEPUSCH] *Short Explic. of Foreign Words in Mus. Bks.* (p. 33) *Furia,* or *Con Furia,* is with Fury and Violence; and this is to be understood not so much with Respect to the Loudness of the Sound, as to the Quickness of the Time or Movement. **1726** BAILEY *An Univ. Etymolog. Engl. Dict.* (3rd edn) *Furia,* or *Con Furia,* (in *Musick Books*) signifies, with Fury and Violence; and is to be understood not so much in respect to the Loudness of the Sound, as the Quickness of the Time and Movement. *Ital.*

fusa *see* demisemiquaver (chroma)

1617-24 FLUDD *Utriusque Cosmi Maioris: De Templo Musicæ* (p. 191) *Fusa* est dimidia pars semiminimæ.

fusano

1659 TORRIANO-FLORIO It→E **Fusano, Fusaggine,* spindle-tree, prick-wood, prick-timber, whereof they make the best spindles, archets, or bowes to play on Lira's or violins.

G

g

1728 CHAMBERS *G* is also us'd in Music, to signify one of the Clefs. See *Clef.* ¶ *G* is the Clef of the highest Part, call'd the *Treble,* or *Alt.* See *Treble.* **1737** DYCHE-PARDON (2nd edn) *G* ... in *Musick,* it is the Mark for the Treble Cliff, and is now made Use of for almost all the upper Parts above the Base, except in Church Musick, where the tenor Cliff is still retained;

galletto *see* wrest

1598 FLORIO It→E *Galletto,* ... Also a stop of any instrument, wherewith the strings are wreathed higher or lower. **1611** FLORIO It→E *Galletto,* ... a spiggot or tap of a barrell. Also a musitions wrest.

galliard *see* baladin, ball, chipassa, dance, lesson, saltarella, tresca, vergaye

1552 HULOET L→E [no Latin headword given] Galiard songe. **1598** FLORIO It→E *Gagliarda,* a dance called a galliard. **1611** COTGRAVE Fr→E *Gaillard: m. arde: f.* Lustie, liuelie ... well disposed, in good tune; **1611** FLORIO It→E *Gagliarda,* a dance called a galliard. **1650** HOWELL-COTGRAVE Fr→E *Gaillard: m. arde: f.* Lusty, lively ... well disposed, in good time; **1658** PHILLIPS (1st edn) *Galliard,* (French) lusty, also substantively taken for a kind of dance. **1659** TORRIANO-FLORIO It→E *Gagliarda,* a galliard-dance. **1671** PHILLIPS (3rd edn) *Galliard, (French)* lusty: also substantively taken for a kind of dance, or lusty jovial air. **1688** MIEGE-COTGRAVE Fr→E *Gaillarde, sorte de Danse gaie,* Galliard, the Galliard Dance. **1702** KERSEY *New Engl. Dict.* (1st edn) A *Galliard,* a kind of merry-dance. **1706** KERSEY-PHILLIPS (6th edn) *Galliard, (Fr.)* a kind of merry Dance. **1708** KERSEY *Dict. Anglo-Brit.* (1st edn) *Galliard,* (*F.*) a kind of merry Dance. **1724** [PEPUSCH] *Short Explic. of Foreign Words in Mus. Bks.* (p. 34) *Galliarda,* the Name of an ancient Dance, or Tune belonging thereunto, commonly in Triple Time, of a brisk, lively Humour, somewhat like a Jig. **1726** BAILEY *An Univ. Etymolog. Engl. Dict.* (3rd edn) *Galliarda* (in *Musick-Books*) is the Name of the Tune that belongs to a *Galliard,* and is commonly in tripple Time, of a brisk lively Humour, somewhat like a Jig. *Ital.* **1728** CHAMBERS *Galliard,* or *Gaillarde,* in Music, and Dancing, a sort of Dance, antiently in great Request; consisting of very different Motions, and Actions, sometimes proceeding *terra a terra,* or smoothly along; sometimes capering; sometimes along the Room, and sometimes a-cross. ¶ It was also called *Romanesque,* because brought from *Rome.* ¶ *Thoinot Arbeau,* in his Orchesography, describes it as consisting of five Steps, and five Positions of the Feet, which the Dancers perform'd before each other, and whereof he gives us the

Score, or Tablature, which is of six Minims, and two triple Times.— ¶ The Word is *French*, and literally signifies gay, merry, sprightly. **1730** BAILEY *Dict. Britannicum* (1st edn) *Galliard*, a sort of Dance, consisting of very different Motions and Actions, sometimes gliding smoothly, sometimes capering, and sometimes across. **1737** DYCHE-PARDON (2nd edn) *Galliard* (S.) a brisk, lively Dance much like to a Jigg, the Musick whereof is composed in Triple Time.

1597 MORLEY *Plaine and Easie Introdvction* (p. 181) [marginalia: 'Galliards.'] After euery pauan we vsually set a galliard (that is, a kind of musicke made out of the other) causing it go by a measure, which the learned cal *trochaieam rationem*, consisting of a long and short stroke successiuelie, for as the foote *trochæus* consisteth of one sillable of two times, and another of one time, so is the first of these two strokes double to the latter: the first beeing in time of a semibrefe, and the latter of a minime. This is a lighter and more stirring kinde of dauncing then the pauane consisting of the same number of straines, and looke howe manie foures of semibreues, you put in the straine of your pauan, so many times sixe minimes must you put in the straine of your galliard. The Italians make their galliardes (which they tearme *saltarelli*) plaine, and frame ditties to them, which in their *mascaradoes* they sing and daunce, and many times without any instruments at all, but in steed of instrumentes they haue Curtisans disguised in mens apparell, who sing and daunce to their owne songes. **1676** MACE *Musick's Monument* (p. 129) *Galliards*, are *Lessons* of 2, or 3 *Strains*, but are perform'd in a *Slow, and Large Triple-Time*; and (commonly) *Grave, and Sober*. **1728** NORTH Musicall Grammarian (*C-K MG* f. 74) ... I have observed in other sorts of musick of the Spanish cutt, that fullness of harmony was very much affected by that nation; and there was a time when the English masters imitated them, as in those peices they called galliardos. It may be described by a small 3 part song printed in old Playford's catch book viz. Dellos ochos di me morena, etc. **1731** PRELLEUR *Modern Musick-Master* (Dictionary, p. 2) *Gagliarda*, Gay, Brisk, Lively, &c.

galliard time *see* imperfect of the more, tripla

1636 BUTLER *Principles of Musik* (p. 8) ... and therefore the triple is oft called Galliard-time, and the duple, Pavan-time.

gamba

1724 [PEPUSCH] *Short Explic. of Foreign Words in Mus. Bks.* (p. 34) *Gamba*. See *Viola di Gamba*.

gamma

1598 FLORIO It→E *Gamma*, ... Also a note in musicke. **1611** FLORIO It→E *Gamma*, a note in Musike. Also a pipe or reede. **1659** TORRIANO-FLORIO It→E *Gaume*, a shrill sounding note of a huntsman. **1724** [PEPUSCH] *Short Explic. of Foreign Words in Mus. Bks.* (p. 34) *Gama*, or *Gamma*, is what we call the Gamut, or Gam-ut; by which is meant the first Note in the Scale of Musick; also the Scale it self. **1726** BAILEY *An Univ. Etymolog. Engl. Dict.* (3rd edn) *Gama*, the Gamut in Musick. *Ital.* *Gamma*, the Gamut in Musick. *Ital.* **1730** BAILEY *Dict. Britannicum* (1st edn) *Gam, Gama, Gammot*, the first or gravest Note in the modern Scale of Musick.

gamut *see* diagram, double gamut, scale, scale of music

1598 FLORIO It→E *Gamaut*, a note in musicke **1611** COTGRAVE Fr→E *Game: f.* Gamvt (in Musicke.) **1611** FLORIO It→E *Gamaut*, a note in Musike. **1656** BLOUNT (1st edn) *Gammut* or *Gamut*, the first note in Musick, from whence the whole number of notes take denomination. As the Greek Cross-row is called *Alphabet* from the two first letters, *Alpha* and *Beta*. **1658** PHILLIPS (1st edn) *Gamut*, the first note in the scale of Musick. **1670** BLOUNT (3rd edn) *Gamut* or *Gam-ut*, the first note in Musick, from whence the whole number of notes take denomination. As the Greek Cros-row is called *Alphabet* from the two first letters, *Alpha* and *Beta*. This Gam-ut was composed by *Guido Aretinus* about the year 900, as the ground and foundation of Musick. **1671** PHILLIPS (3rd edn) *Gamut*, the first note in the ordinary scale of Musick: also the Scale it self is usually called the *Gam Ut*. **1676** COLES *Gam 'Vt*, the scale of Musick, also the first or lowest note thereof. **1688** MIEGE-COTGRAVE Fr→E *Gâme*, (f.) Gamut, a certain Number of Notes containing all the principles of Musick. § *Apprendre sa Gâme*, to learn his Gamut. *Savoir sa Gâme*, to know his Gamut. **1702** KERSEY *New Engl. Dict.* (1st edn) The *Gam-ut, or* scale of musick; also the first, or lowest note of it. **1704** *Cocker's Engl. Dict.* (1st edn) *Gammut*, the lowest note in Musick, as *Ela* is the highest. **1706** KERSEY-PHILLIPS (6th edn) *Gam-ut*, the first Note in the Scale of Musick; also the Scale it self commonly so call'd. *See Scale of Musick*. **1707** *Gloss. Angl. Nova* (1st edn) *Gammut*, the first Note in the ordinary Scale of

Musick; also the Scale it self is usually called by this name. **1728** CHAMBERS *Gamm, Gammut* ... [*see* Appendix] **1737** DYCHE-PARDON (2nd edn) *Gamut* (S.) the Scale or Alphabet of Musick, whereby a Person in vocal or instrumental Musick knows how to distinguish and regulate the Tones in a Composition.

1584 BATHE Briefe Intro. to True Art of Music (MS copy, 1st half 16th c., *CHi* pp. 2-3) ... the schall of: *gam ut*: vhich is so named becaus: *gam ut*: is ye lowest place, and as it var ye foundation in that scalle ... **c.1596** BATHE *Briefe Intro. to skill of Song* [A iv *verso*] The Scale of Musick, which is called Gam-vt, conteineth 10 rules, and as many spaces; and is set downe in letters and sillables, in which you must beegin at the lowest word, Gam-vt, and so go vpwards to the end still ascending, and learne it perfectly without booke, to say it forwards and backewards: to know, wherein euery key standeth ... **1596** ANON. *Pathway to Musicke* [A ii] ... first of all it is needfull for him that vvill learn to sing truely, to vnderstand his *Scale*, or (as they commonly call it) the *Gamma-vt*: ... **1597** MORLEY *Plaine and Easie Introdvction* (p. 2) ... the Scale of Musicke, which wee terme the *Gam*. **early 17th C.** RAVENSCROFT Treatise of Musick BL Add. 19758, f. 2 Musicke must bee directed and gouerned by an Index (or a scale) or ladder. the w[ch] musick is built by: This same scale in o[r] Mother tongue is called Gamut the w[ch] procedeth from a greek letter called *Gam. ma* ... **1665** SIMPSON *Principles of Practical Mvsick* (pp. 4-5) On the bottom-Line is commonly placed this Greek Letter Γ *Octave* to the *G* above (whence it appears, that the Author of the Scale derived his knowledg in Musick from the Greeks) and from that Letter our Scale of Musick had the name of *Gamma* or *Gamvt*. **1677** NEWTON *English Academy* (p. 91) And thus they ['cliffs'] were wont to be placed in the Scale, in which the first Name *ut* being placed upon the same line with the Greek *Gamma*, hath caused the whole Scale to be called the *Gamut*; ... **early 18th C.** ANON. Essay on Musick BODLEIAN Rawl. D. 751, f. 2v The *Gamut* is a table of several words, syllables, figures, letters, numbers, &c. which serve to denote the grave and the acute sounds, their differences, proportions, intervals, &c. § f. 3v However Aretine still retain'd the letters of the Alphabet, with the Greek letter Gamma, from whence comes the word *gamut*. **1721** MALCOLM *Treatise of Musick* (pp. 554-5) [*re* Guido d'Arezzo] ... he added a Chord, a *Tonus* below *Proslam.* and called it *Hypo-proslambanomenos*, and after the Latins *g.* but commonly marked with the Greek Gamma Γ; to shew by this, say some, that the Greeks were the Inventors of *Musick*; but others say he meant to record himself (that Letter being the first in his Name) as the Improver of *Musick*; hence the *Scale* came to be called the *Gamm*. **1723** CHURCH *Intro. to Psalmody* (p. 2) ... *Gamut* which is a Scale of Musick so call'd from the first Note in it ... **1724** TURNER *Sound Anatomiz'd* (p. 36) The *Scale* it self is called the *Gamut*, from the *Greek* Letter, *Gamma*, which *Guido Aretinus* placed at the Bottom ...

gansar

1610 R. DOWLAND *Varietie of Lute-Lessons* [Dv] ... Likewise there is a kinde of strings of a more fuller and larger sort then ordinary (which we call *Gansars*.)

garrire

1598 FLORIO It→E *Garrire, Garrisco, Garrito*, ... Also to chirpe, to chante, to sing as birdes do, to chat, or to chaunt. **1611** FLORIO It→E *Garrire, risco, rito*, to chirp, to chant, to chat or sing as birdes.

Gastoldi, Giovanni *see* fa la

gavotte *see* dance, motion, repeat, rondeau, sonata, style (stylo choraico), tempo

1598 FLORIO It→E *Gauotta*, a French dance or round so called. **1611** COTGRAVE Fr→E *Gavote: f.* A (kind of) Brawle, daunced, commonly, by one alone. **1611** FLORIO It→E *Gauotta*, the name of a french dance. **1688** MIEGE-COTGRAVE Fr→E *Gavote*, (f.) *sorte de Dance gaie*, Gavot, a kind of Dance. § *Danser une Gavote*, to dance a Gavot. **1702** KERSEY *New Engl. Dict.* (1st edn) A *Gavot*, a sort of dance. **1706** KERSEY-PHILLIPS (6th edn) *Gavot, (Fr.)* a kind of Dance. **1708** KERSEY *Dict. Anglo-Brit.* (1st edn) *Gavot*, (*F.*) a kind of Dance. **1724** [PEPUSCH] *Short Explic. of Foreign Words in Mus. Bks.* (pp. 34-5) *Gavotta*, a Gavot, an Air of a brisk, lively Nature, always in Common Time, divided in Two Parts, each to be play'd twice over, the first Part commonly in Four or Eight Bars, and the second Part in Four, Eight, Twelve, Sixteen Bars, or more. **1726** BAILEY *An Univ. Etymolog. Engl. Dict.* (3rd edn) *Gavotta* (in *Musick Books*) a Gavot, an Air of a brisk lively Nature, and always in common Time; divided into two Parts, each to be play'd twice over; the first Part commonly in 4 or 8 Bars, and the second part in 4, 8, 12 or 16 Bars or more. *Ital.* **1731** KERSEY *New Engl. Dict.* (3rd edn) A *Gavot*, a kind of *French*-Dance. **1737** DYCHE-PARDON (2nd edn) *Gavot* (S.) a short, brisk, lively, musical Air, always composed in common Time, consisting of two Parts or Strains, each Strain or Part being played twice over, the first commonly consisting of four or eight Bars, and the last of eight, twelve, &c. Bars.

c.1715-20 NORTH Essay of Musical Ayre BL Add. 32536, f. 55 ... as A Gavott, w[ch] is an old french dance; ... **c.1726** NORTH Musicall Gramarian BL Add. 32533, f. 66 ... But Nothing can be so plaine, but capriccio will have to doe with it, as with Comon time, w[ch] in some Instances is struck by 2. Crotchets, w[ch] they call tempo di Gavotta, and In others, Each Note is counted by half ... I never yet could find the vertue of these accounts, unless the first, by a Quick snapp at Every 2[d] Note humours the dance called the Gavot (Not now used)... **1731** PRELLEUR *Modern Musick-Master* (Dictionary, p. 2) *Gavotta*, a Gavott name of a Tune

gay

1724 [PEPUSCH] *Short Explic. of Foreign Words in Mus. Bks.* (p. 35) *Gay*, or *Gayement*, is gay, brisk, or lively. **1726** BAILEY *An Univ. Etymolog. Engl. Dict.* (3rd edn) *Gay*, or *Gayment* (in *Musick Books*) signifies gay, brisk, lively. *Ital.*

gayta

1599 MINSHEU-PERCYVALL Sp→E † *Gaita*, vide *Gayta*, a bagpipe. † *Gaitero*, vide *Gaytero*, a plaier on bagpipes. † *Gayta*, f. a bagpipe. **Gaytero*, m. a plaier on bagpipes.

gazouiller

1570/71 *Dict. Fr. and Engl.* Fr→E *Gazouiller*, To whistle, sing, chirp, or warble, as birdes do. **1593** HOLLYBAND Fr→E *Gazouiller*, to whistle, sing, chirpe, or warble as birds do. **1611** COTGRAVE Fr→E *Gazouiller*. To sing, whistle, chirpe, as many birds together; **1688** MIEGE-COTGRAVE Fr→E *Gazouillement*, (m.) *certain Chant agreable que sont les Oiseaux*, a chirping, or singing.

gazzarra

1611 FLORIO It→E *Gazzarra*, ... Also a confused reioycing noise mixed with shouting and clapping of hands. **1659** TORRIANO-FLORIO It→E *Gazzarra*, a confused rejoycing noise mixed with shoutings and clappings of hands, and warlike musical instruments, but tending to joy and mirth

general *see* beat

1688 MIEGE-COTGRAVE Fr→E § *batre la Generale*, to beat the Drum for all the Infantry to march, to beat a general March. **1706** KERSEY-PHILLIPS (6th edn) A *General*, ... also a Beat of Drum so call'd, being the first that gives notice early in the Morning for the Foot to be in readiness to march. **1721** BAILEY *An Univ. Etymolog. Engl. Dict.* (1st edn) *General* (in the *Militay Art)* a particular Beat of Drum early in the Morning, to give Notice for the Foot to be in Readiness to march. **1728** CHAMBERS *General* is also used in the *Military* Art for a particular March, or Beat of Drum. ¶ To beat the *General*, is to give Notice to the Infantry to march. See *Drum.* **1730** BAILEY *Dict. Britannicum* (1st edn) A *General* (in *Military Affairs*) a particular Beat of Drum early in the Morning, to give notice for the Foot to be in readiness to March.

genethliaci

1589 [PUTTENHAM] *Arte of English Poesie* (p. 37) [*re* the history of poetry] ... Others for magnificence at the natiuities of Princes children, or by custome vsed yearely vpon the same dayes, are called songs natall or *Genethliaci*.

Geneva jig

1619 WITHER *Preparation to the Psalter* (p. 8) ... yet I vnderstand, that some sectaries and fauourers of the Church of *Rome*, haue of late yeares disapproued the translation of these *Psalmes* into the vulgar tongues, & scoffed at the singing of them in the reformed Churches; in so much, that they haue in scorne tearmed them *Geneua Iiggs*, and *Beza's Ballets*: ...

genus *see* colores generum, diatonum, species

1728 CHAMBERS *Genus*, in Musick, by the Antients called *Genus Melodiæ*, is a certain manner of subdividing the Principles of Melody, *i.e.* the consonant Intervals, into their concinnous Parts. See *Interval, Concord*, and *Concinnous*. ¶ The Moderns, considering the Octave, as the most perfect Interval, and that whereon all the other Concords depend in the present Theory of Musick; the Division of that Interval is consider'd as containing the true Division of the whole Scale. See *Octave*, and *Scale*. ¶ But the Antients went to work somewhat differently: The Diatessaron, or Fourth, was the least Interval which they admitted as Concord; and therefore they sought first how that might be most concinnously divided; from which they constituted the Diapente, or

Fifth, and Diapason, or Octave. ¶ The Diatessaron being thus, as it were, the Root or Foundation of the Scale; what they call the *Genera*, Kinds, arose from its various Divisions; and hence they defined the *Genus modulandi*, the manner of dividing the Tetrachord, and disposing its four Sounds as to Succession. See *Tetrachord*. ¶ The *Genera* of Musick were three, *viz.* the *Enharmonick, Chromatick,* and *Diatonick*: The two last whereof were variously subdivided; and even the first, though 'tis commonly reckon'd to be without any Species, yet different Authors have propos'd different Divisions under that Name, tho' without giving particular Names to the Species as was done to the other two. See *Species*. ¶ *For the Character*, &c. *of the several* Genera, *see Enharmonick, Chromatick,* and *Diatonick*. ¶ The Parts, or Divisions of the Diatessaron they call'd the *Diastems* of the several *Genera*, upon which their Differences depend; and which in the Enharmonick are particularly call'd the *Diesis*, and *Ditonum*; in the Chromatick, the *Hemitonium*, and *Triemitonium*; and in the Diatonic, the *Hemitonium*, or *Limma*, and the *Tonus*. ¶ But under these general Names, which distinguish the *Genera*, there are other different Intervals, or Ratio's which constitute the *Colores Generum*, or Species of Enharmonic, Chromatic, and Diatonic. Add, that what is a Diastem in one *Genus*, is a System in another. See *Diastem, System, Chroai* [no entry 'chroai']; see also *Diagramma*. **1730** BAILEY *Dict. Britannicum* (1st edn) *Genus* (in *Musick*) a certain manner of subdividing the Principles of Melody, *i.e.* the consonant Intervals into their concinnous Parts. **1737** DYCHE-PARDON (2nd edn) *Genus* (S.) ... in *Musick*, it is a particular Manner of subdividing the Principles of Melody.

1721 MALCOLM *Treatise of Musick* (pp. 512-13) *Of the Genera*. By this Title is meant the various Ways of subdividing the consonant *Intervals* (which are the chief Principles of *Melody*) into their *concinnous* Parts. As the *Octave* is the most perfect Interval, and all other *Concords* depend upon it, so according to the modern *Theory* we consider the Division of this *Interval*, as containing the true Division of the whole Scale: ... Now the *Diatessaron* being as it were the Root or Foundation of their Scale, what they call'd the *Genera* arose from its various Divisions: Hence they defined the *Genus (modulandi) the manner of dividing the Tetrachord, and disposing its four Sounds* (as to their Succession:) And this Definition shews us in general, That the 4*th* was divided into 3 *Intervals* by the middle Terms [intervallic members], so as to contain 4 Sounds betwixt the Extremes: Hence we have the Reason of the Name *Diatessaron*, (i.e. *per quator;*) and because from the 4*th* to the 5*th* was always the *Tone*, the 5*th* contained 5 Notes, and hence called *Diapente* (i.e. *per quinque*:) And with respect to the *Lyra* and its Strings, these Intervals were called *Tetrachordum* and *Pentechordum*. But the 8*ve* was called *Diapason*, (as it were *per omnes*) because it contains in a manner all the different Notes of Musick; for after one *Octave* all the rest of the Notes of the Scale were reckoned but as it were Repetitions of it: Yet with respect to the Lyre, it was also called *Octochordum*. The *Disdiapason* and all other Names of this Kind being now plain enough ...

geresol

1728 CHAMBERS *Geresol*, in Music, one of the Clefs. See *Clef*. **1730** BAILEY *Dict. Britannicum* (1st edn) *Geresol* (in *Musick*) one of the Cliffs.

gesticula

1589 RIDER L→E *Gesticula, f.* A Morrice daunce.

gesticulation *see* morris dance

1587 THOMAS L→E *Gesticulator, oris, m.g. verb. Col.* One that vseth much gesture: a dauncer or player with puppets: a morise dauncer. *Gesticulor, aris, depon. Colum.* ... to daunce by measures, *Suet.* **1589** RIDER L→E *Gesticulator, m.* A morrice dauncer. **1616** BULLOKAR *Gesticulation*. A moouing of the fingers, hands or other parts, eyther in idle wantonnesse, or to expresse some matter by signes, in dauncing, singing, or other such like exercise. **1623** COCKERAM *Gesticulation*. A mooving of the fingers, hands, or othet [sic] parts, either in idle wantonnesse, or to expresse some matter by signes, in dancing, singing, or the like. **1658** PHILLIPS (1st edn) *Gesticulation*, (lat.) ... also a kinde of Morrice dancing.

giga

1550 THOMAS It→E *Giga*, a certein instrument, as I thinke a bagpype. **1598** FLORIO It→E *Ghiga*, a croud, a fidle, a violin. *Ghigaro*, a crouder or fidler, a minstrell. *Giga*, a fiddle, a croud, a kit, a violin. *Gigaro*, a fidler, a crowder. **1611** FLORIO It→E *Ghiga*, a fidle or a croud. *Ghigare*, to fidle or croud. *Ghigaro*, as *Ghigatore*. *Ghigatore*, a fidler, a crouder. *Giga*, a Violin, a fiddle, a croud, a kit. *Gigare*, to play vpon a fidle. *Gigaro*, a fidler, a minstrell, a crouder. **1659** TORRIANO-

FLORIO It→E *Ghiga*, a country croud or fiddle. *Ghigaro, Ghigatore*, a fidler, a crouder, a minstrel. *Giga*, a certain musical instrument with strings.

gigue *see* barzelletta, dance, jig, sonata

1688 MIEGE-COTGRAVE Fr→E *Gigue*, (f.) *sorte de Dance Angloise*, a Jig, an English Jig. † *Giguer, cd. dancer, sauter*, to dance, to caper. § *Dancer une Gigue*, to dance a Jig. **1724** [PEPUSCH] *Short Explic. of Foreign Words in Mus. Bks.* (p. 35) *Giga, Gicque*, or *Gigue*, is a Jig, which is a Dance or Air very well known, of which some are to be play'd slow, and others brisk and lively, and always in Triple Time, of one Kind or other. **1726** BAILEY *An Univ. Etymolog. Engl. Dict.* (3rd edn) *Giga, Gigque, Gigue*, (in *Musick Books*) is a Jig, some of which are to be play'd slow, and others brisk and lively, but always in triple Time of one Kind or other. *Ital.* **1728** CHAMBERS *Gigg, Gigue*, or *Jig*, in Music and Dancing, a gay, brisk, sprightly Composition, and yet in full Measure, as well as the *Allemand*, which is more serious. See *Dance*. ¶ *Menage* takes the Word to arise from the Italian *Giga*, a musical Instrument mentioned by *Dante*. **1735** DEFOE *Gigue*, a Jigg, a brisk or lively Movement of Time in Musick.

1731 PRELLEUR *Modern Musick-Master* (Dictionary, p. 2) *Gigha, Giga* or *Gigue*, a Jig

gingeriator

1565 COOPER L→E *Ginzeriator, toris, m.g.* A minstrell. *Fest.* **1587** THOMAS L→E *Gingeriator, girenator, vel gingrinator, oris, m.g. Fest.* A minstrell or piper.

gingrina

1565 COOPER L→E *Gingrîna, næ, f.g.* A kinde of small pipes makynge a noyse like the chirkyng [sic] of birdes. **1587** THOMAS L→E *Gingrina, æ, f.g. Iun.* A short pipe with a small and dolefull sound, and tooke it name of *Adonis*, who was called *Gingris*, or for that it counterfaiteth the noise that geese doe make, or because this pipe was made of the bones of geese. **1589** RIDER L→E *gingrina*. A short pipe with a small and dolefull sound, counterfaiting the noise of gese [sic], because it was made of the bones of geese.

girometta

1611 FLORIO It→E *Girometta*, a merry wanton country-lasse. Also the name of a country song. **1659** TORRIANO-FLORIO It→E *Girometta*, a Country jig or dance.

gittern *see* cetara, chitariglia, chitarra, cithara, entata, fidicula, guitar, quiterne

1593 HOLLYBAND Fr→E *Guiterne, jouër sur la guiterne*, or *de la guiterne*, a Gitterne: *f.* **1611** COTGRAVE Fr→E *Guiterne*; or *guiterre*: f. A Gitterne. **1671** PHILLIPS (3rd edn) *Ghittern*, a sort of Musical Instrument for the manner of playing not much unlike a *Cittern*. **1676** COLES *Ghittern*, a small sort of Cittern. **1702** KERSEY *New Engl. Dict.* (1st edn) A *Gittern*, or *Cittern*, a musical instrument. **1706** KERSEY-PHILLIPS (6th edn) *Gittern*, a kind of Cittern, a Musical Instrument. **1721** BAILEY *An Univ. Etymolog. Engl. Dict.* (1st edn) *Gittren* [sic]. See *Ghittar*.

giusto *see* tempo giusto

Glareanus, Heinrich *see* concord, mode, tripla, tune

gloria in excelsis *see* hymn

1728 CHAMBERS *Gloria in Excelsis*, a kind of Hymn also rehearsed in the Divine Office; beginning with the Words *Gloria in Excelsis Deo, & in terra pax hominibus*, &c. Glory be to God on High, on Earth Peace, *&c.* **1730** BAILEY *Dict. Britannicum* (1st edn) *Gloria in Excelsis*, (*i.e.* Glory in the Highest) a kind of Hymn also rehearsed in the Divine Office. *L.*

gloria patri *see* doxology

1728 CHAMBERS *Gloria Patri*, in the Liturgy, a Formula, or Verse, repeated at the End of each Psalm, and on other Occasions, to give Glory to the Holy Trinity; call'd also Doxology. **1737** BAILEY *The Univ. Etymolog. Engl. Dict.* (3rd edn, vol. 2) *Gloria Patri, i.e.* glory be to the father. A set form of praise to the holy Trinity, appointed by the church to be repeated after many parts of the liturgy, and particularly the psalms; so called because when the offices are performed in *Latin*, those are the two first words of that *Hymn, Conclusion* or *Doxology*, as it is frequently called. There have been great contests about the antiquity, manner of wording and other particulars of this hymn; some contending that it was used in the apostles time; but tis generally allowed to have remained as a token of *Orthodoxy*, ever since it was appointed by pope *Damasus*. **1737** DYCHE-PARDON (2nd edn) *Gloria Patri* (S.) a set Form of Praise to the Holy Trinity, appointed by the Church, to be repeated after many Parts of the Liturgy, and particularly the Psalms; so called, because when the Offices are performed in *Latin*, those are the two first Words of that Hymn, Conclusion, or Doxology, as it is frequently called; ...

glory

1706 Kersey-Phillips (6th edn) A *Glory,* (in *Painting*) ... In an *Opera,* or Stage-Play, it is a Representation of Heaven.

gnaccara *see* naccara

1598 Florio It→E *Gnaccara,* a musicall instrument, a cymball or a rattle or a bagpipe. **1611** Florio It→E *Gnaccara,* a Cimball. Also a Rattle. Also a Bag-pipe. **1659** Torriano-Florio It→E *Gnacchera,* any ratling instrument, a kettle-drum, also a bag pipe, also a cymbal.

goat tuning

c.1668-71 *Mary Burwell's Instruction Bk. for Lute* (*TDa* p. 21) Old Gaultier's new tuning, called 'the goat tuning', because the first lesson he made upon that tuning is called The Goat (and indeed represents the leaps and skippings of a goat): ...

gobbo

1659 Torriano-Florio It→E **Gobbo,* a hulch, a bunch, or crook-backt man ... also the usual name of a Fool in Opera's or playes sung in musick.

gorgheggiare

1611 Florio It→E *Gorgheggiare,* to gargarize, to gurgle or ratle in the throate. Also to warble or quauer singing. **1659** Torriano-Florio It→E **Gorgare, Gorgheggiare,* ... to gurgle, to rattle in the throat, also to warble or quaver in singing, also to wharle or speak in the throat as the Florentines do.

grace *see* acute, backfall, beat, beat up, double shake, elevation, legare, pearled playing, plain beat, shake, slide, slur, spinger, sting, stoccata, transition, tremola, trill, tut, variation, whole-fall

1676 Mace *Musick's Monument* (p. 102) I will now ... lay down, all the other *Curiosities,* and *Nicities,* in reference to the *Adorning of your Play*: (for your *Foundations being surely Laid,* and your *Building well Rear'd,* you may proceed to the *Beautifying,* and *Painting* of your *Fabrick.*) And those, we call the *Graces* in our *Play.* ¶ The Names of such, which we must commonly use upon the *Lute,* be *These.* ¶ The 1*st.* and *Chiefest,* is the *Shake,* Marked *Thus,* with a *Prick* before it, as here you may see, (·*a*) The 2*d.* the *Beate, Thus,* ('*a*) The 3*d.* the *Back-fall, Thus,* ('*a*) The 4*th.* the *Half-fall, Thus,* (⁄*a*) The 5*th.* the *Whole-fall, Thus,* (+*a*) The *Sixth,* the *Elevation, Thus,* (⁎*a*) The 7*th.* the *Single Relish, Thus,* (∴*a*) The 8*th.* the *Double Relish, Thus,* (⁘*a*) The 9*th.* the *Slur, Thus,* (*a*) the 10*th.* the *Slide,* (the same) *Thus,* (*a*) the 11*th.* the *Spinger, Thus,* (*a*⁄) The 12*th.* the *Sting, Thus,* (~*a*) The 13*th.* the *Futt, Thus,* (:*a*) The 14*th.* the *Pause, Thus,* (*a*) or Thus, (â) The 15*th.* and last, *Soft and Loud Play, Thus,* (so: lo:) which is as *Great, and Good a Grace, as any other, whatever.* These are the 15 *Graces,* which may be used upon the *Lute*; yet *Few,* or *None* use them All. **1736** Tans'ur *Compleat Melody* (3rd edn, p. 20) *Scholar. What* is a Grace? ¶ *Master.* A *Grace* is a *Shake, Turn,* or *Humour* of the *Voice* or *Instrument*; which when used in a proper place, and performed to perfection; is so ornamental to *Musick,* that it fills the *Heart* with the Spirit of *Harmony*; so that nothing is required after it; if it ends right, and in a regular *Key.*

gradual

1616 Bullokar *Gradual.* That which was said or sung, betweene the Epistle and the Gospell. **1656** Blount (1st edn) *Gradual (graduale)* that part of the Mass which was said or sung between the Epistle and the Gospel, as a *grade* or step from the first to the later, signifying that the profession of a Christian is to be ascending from the *Epistle* to the *Gospel,* from the doctrin of the Prophets and Apostl[e]s to Christs, from one degree of vertue to another. **1658** Phillips (1st edn) *Gradual,* that part of the Mass, which uses [sic] to be sung between the Epistle and Gospel. **1704** *Cocker's Engl. Dict.* (1st edn) *Gradual,* ... also part of the Mass sung between the Epistle and Gospel, signifying, that Christians ought to ascend from the Apostles Doctrine, to Christs, from one degree of grace, and vertue to another. **1706** Kersey-Phillips (6th edn) The *Gradual,* a part of the Mass, which is said or sung, between the Epistle and Gospel. **1708** Kersey *Dict. Anglo-Brit.* (1st edn) The *Gradual,* a part of the Mass. **1728** Chambers *Gradual, Graduale,* was antiently a Church-book, containing divers Prayers, rehearsed, or sung after the Epistle. ¶ After reading the Epistle, the Chantor ascended the Ambo with his *Gradual,* and rehears'd the Prayers, *&c.* therein; being answer'd by the Choir: .... In the *Romish* Church, the Name *Gradual* is still retain'd to a Verse which they sing after the Epistle, and which antiently rehears'd on the Steps of the Altar: Tho' *Ugotio* gives another Account, and says it took its Denomination *Gradual*, because sung in a gradual Ascent from Note to Note. *Magri* speaks differently still, and will have it to have took this Name, because while the Deacon went up the *Steps* to the Pulpit, to sing the Gospel. ¶ *Graduals, Graduales*, is also applied to the fifteen Psalms sung, among the *Hebrews*, on the fifteen Steps of the Temple.— Others are of Opinion they were thus denominated, because the Singers rais'd their Voices by degrees, from the first to the last. **1730** BAILEY *Dict. Britannicum* (1st edn) The *Gradual* (*le graduel*, F.) that Part of the Mass, which is Sung between the Epistle and the Gospel. **1737** DYCHE-PARDON (2nd edn) *Gradual* (S.) a Part of the Mass sung between the Epistle and Gospel; there are 15 Psalms called Graduals or Psalm of Degrees, which are supposed to have been sung by the *Jewish* Priests standing upon the 15 Steps of the Temple.

gradual psalm *see* psalm

1656 BLOUNT (1st edn) *Gradual Psalms*, are fifteen Psalms so called, that is, those fifteen together from the 118. to 133. or from the 120. to 135. they are so called from a custom the Jews observed of singing them, as they ascended up fifteen steps or *degrees* (in Latine *gradus*) towards *Solomons* Temple, where the *Levites* did praise God with a great voyce, 2 *Chron*. 20. 19. **1706** KERSEY-PHILLIPS (6th edn) *Gradual Psalms*, fifteen Psalms together from 118th to the 133d. or from the 119th to the 134th, which the Levites us'd to sing, as they went up the fifteen Steps of *Solomon*'s Temple, on every step a Psalm. **1708** KERSEY *Dict. Anglo-Brit.* (1st edn) *Gradual Psalms*, fifteen Psalms together from 118th to the 133d. or from the 119th to the 134th, which the Levites us'd to sing, as they went up the fifteen Steps of *Solomon*'s Temple, on every step a Psalm.

grailler *see* blur, bombus, clang

1593 HOLLYBAND Fr→E *Grailler*, to blow a horne, to trumpet hoarsely, with a hoarse noyse § *Grailleren chantant*, to sing vntunably. **1611** COTGRAVE Fr→E *Grailler*. To winde a Horne hollowly; to blurre a Trumpet; to speake hoarsely, or with a broken voice; to sing harshly, vntuneably; **1650** HOWELL-COTGRAVE Fr→E † *Grailler*. To winde a Horne hollowly; to blurre a Trumpet; to speake hoarsely, or with a broken voice; to sing harshly, untunably;

grande

1724 [PEPUSCH] *Short Explic. of Foreign Words in Mus. Bks.* (p. 35) *Grande*, is Great, or Grand, and is used to distinguish the Great or Grand Chorus from the rest of the Musick. **1726** BAILEY *An Univ. Etymolog. Engl. Dict.* (3rd edn) *Grande* (in *Musick-Books*) signifies grand or great, and is used to distinguish the grand or great *Chorus* from the rest of the Musick. *Ital.*

gratieusement *see* dolce

1724 [PEPUSCH] *Short Explic. of Foreign Words in Mus. Bks.* (p. 36) *Gratieusement*, the same as *Gratioso*. **1726** BAILEY *An Univ. Etymolog. Engl. Dict.* (3rd edn) *Gratieusement* (in *Musick-Books*) signifies the same as *Gratioso, Ital.* which see.

gratioso *see* dolce

1724 [PEPUSCH] *Short Explic. of Foreign Words in Mus. Bks.* (p. 35) *Gratioso*, is a graceful and agreeable Manner of playing. **1726** BAILEY *An Univ. Etymolog. Engl. Dict.* (3rd edn) *Gratioso*, signifies an agreeable Manner of Playing. *Ital.*

grave *see* accent, allemande, divoto

1724 [PEPUSCH] *Short Explic. of Foreign Words in Mus. Bks.* (p. 36) *Grave*, signifies a very Grave and Slow Movement, somewhat faster than *Adagio*, and slower than *Largo*. (p. 95) *Grave*, Grave, or Gravely. § (p. 95) *Grave Assai*, not too Grave. **1726** BAILEY *An Univ. Etymolog. Engl. Dict.* (3rd edn) *Grave* (in *Musick Books*) denotes a very grave and slow Motion, somewhat faster than *Adagio*, and slower than *Largo. Ital.* **1728** CHAMBERS *Grave*, in Music, is applied to a Sound, which is in a low, or deep Tune. See *Sound*, and *Tune*. ¶ The thicker the Chord, or String, the more *grave* the Tone, or Note: And the smaller, the acuter. See *Chord*. ¶ Notes are supposed to be the more *grave*, in proportion as the Vibrations of a Chord, are less quick. See *Gravity*. **1737** DYCHE-PARDON (2nd edn) *Grave* (A.) ... in *Musick*, it is those Parts of the Composition whose Notes are long and slow, and in which the Harmony of the Concords is perfectly distinguished, and melodiously [contrived to] entertain, compose, and prepare the Hero for what follows;

1683 PURCELL *Sonnata's of III Parts* (*To the Reader*) ... It remains only that the English Practitioner be enform'd, that he will find a few terms of Art perhaps unusual to him, the chief of which are these following: *Adagio* and *Grave*, which import nothing but a very slow movement: ... **c.1715-20** NORTH Essay of Musical Ayre BL Add. 32536 (*JWi* p. 117) ... And now in our comon Sonnatas for Instruments, the entrance is usually with all the fullness of harmony figurated and adorned that the master at that time could contrive, and this is termed *Grave*, and sometimes, but as I take it, not so properly, *Adagio*, for that supposeth some antecedent nimble imployment, and a share of ease and repose to come after. But to returne, this *Grave* most aptly represents seriousness and thought... **c.1726** NORTH Musicall Gramarian BL Add. 32533, f. 65v Grave, is somewhat faster [than adagio] ... **1731** PRELLEUR *Modern Musick-Master* (Dictionary, p. 2) *Grave*, a Slow Movement.

gravement

1724 [PEPUSCH] *Short Explic. of Foreign Words in Mus. Bks.* (p. 36) *Gravement*, is the same as *Grave*. **1726** BAILEY *An Univ. Etymolog. Engl. Dict.* (3rd edn) *Gravement* (in *Musick Books*) signifies a very slow Movement, the same as *Grave*, which see. *Ital*.

gravicembalo *see* cembalo

1598 FLORIO It→E *Grauicembalo*, a musicall instrument like our claricoes. **1611** FLORIO It→E *Grauicembalo*, an instrument of Musicke like our Claricoes. **1659** TORRIANO-FLORIO It→E *Gravecembalo*, an instrument so called. *Gravicembalo*, a musical instrument like our Clarico's.

graviter sonare *see* imus sonus

1565 COOPER L→E *Grauissimus sonus. Cic.* A very low and base tune. *Grauiter sonare. Cic.* To haue a base or loe tune. *Grauiusculus sonus. Gell.* Somewhat a base low low tune. **1587** THOMAS L→E *Graviter sonare.* To haue a base or loe tune.

gravity

1728 CHAMBERS *Gravity*, in *Music*, an Affection of Sound, whereby it becomes denominated *grave, low*, or *flat*. See *Sound*. ¶ *Gravity* stands in Opposition to *Acuteness*, which is that Affection of Sound, whereby it is denominated *Acute*, Sharp, or high. See *Acuteness*. ¶ The Relation of *Gravity*, and Acuteness, is the principal thing concerned in Music; the Distinctness, and Determinateness of which Relation, gives Sound the Denomination of *Harmonical*, or *Musical*. See *Music* and *Harmony*. ¶ The Degrees of *Gravity, &c.* depend on the Nature of the Sonorous Body itself, and the particular Figure and Quantity thereof: Tho, in some Cases, they likewise depend on the Part of the Body where it is struck. Thus, *e. gr.* the Sounds of two Bells of different Metals, and the same Shape and Dimensions, being struck in the same Place, will differ as to Acuteness and *Gravity*; and two Bells of the same Metal will differ in Acuteness, if they differ in Shape or Magnitude, or be struck in different Parts. See *Bell*. ¶ So in Chords, all other things being equal, if they differ either in Matter, or Dimension, or Tension; they will also differ in *Gravity*. See *Chord*. ¶ Thus again, the Sound of a Piece of Gold is much graver than that of a Piece of Silver of the same Shape and Dimensions; and in this Case, the Tones are, *cæteris paribus*, proportional to the Specific Gravities; so a solid Sphere of Brass, two Foot diameter, will sound graver than another of one Foot diameter; and here the Tones are proportional to the Quantities of Matter, or the Absolute Weights. ¶ But it must be observed, that Acuteness and *Gravity*, as also Loudness and Lowness, are but relative Things. We commonly call a Sound *acute* and loud, in respect to another which is *grave*, or low with respect to the former: So that the same Sound may be both *grave* and acute, and also loud and low, in different Comparisons. ¶ The Degrees of Acuteness, and *Gravity*, make the different *Tones*, or *Tunes* of a Voice, or Sound: So we say one Sound is in Tune with another, when they are in the same Degree of *Gravity*. See *Tune*. ¶ The immediate Cause, or Means of this Diversity of Tone lies deep. The modern Musicians fix it on the different Velocity of the Vibrations of the Sonorous Body: In which Sense *Gravity* may be defined, a relative Property of Sound, which, in respect to some other, is the Effect of a lesser Number of Vibrations accomplish'd in the same Time, or of Vibrations of a longer Duration: In which Sense also, Acuteness is the Effect of a greater Number of Vibrations, or Vibrations of a shorter Duration. ¶ If two, or more Sounds be compared in the Relation of *Gravity*, &c. they are either *Equal*, or *Unequal*, in the Degree of Tune. ¶ Such as are equal, are call'd *Unisons*. See *Unison*. ¶ The Unequal including, as it were, at a Distance between each other, constitute which we call an *Interval* in Music, which is properly the Different in Point of *Gravity*, between the two Sounds. See *Interval*. ¶ Upon this Unequality, or Difference, does the whole Effect depend; and in respect hereof, these Intervals are divided into *Concords* and *Discords*. See *Concord* and *Discord*. See also *Scale*. **1730** BAILEY *Dict. Britannicum* (1st edn) *Gravity* (in *Musick*) an Affection of Sound, whereby it becomes denominated grave, low or flat.

greater fourth *see* tritone

Greeks

1737 Bailey *The Univ. Etymolog. Engl. Dict.* (3rd edn, vol. 2) *Greeks*, ... a people once famous for courage and learning, so that they were resorted to from most parts of *Europe, &c.* for instruction in arts and sciences, they being either the inventors or improvers of most arts, *&c.* .... [*re* the present] they do not use musick in their churches.

Gregorian *see* affinal key, chant, key

Gresham College

1658 Phillips (1st edn) *Gresham Colledge*, a fair house in the Citie of *London*, once the habitation of Sir *Thomas Gresham*, who constituted it a Colledge, and endowed it with Revenues for the maintaining of Professours of Divinity, Law, Physick, Astronomy, Geometry, and Musick; **1676** Coles *Gresham Colledge*, the house of Sir *Thomas Gresham*, who endowed it with Revenues for the maintenance of Professours of Divinity, Law, Physick, Astronomy, Geometry and Musick. **1728** Chambers *Gresham College*, or *College of Philosophy*; a *College* founded by Sir *Tho. Gresham*, and endow'd with the Revenue of the *Royal-Exchange*: One Moiety of this Endowment the Founder bequeath'd to the Mayor, and Aldermen of *London*, and their Successors, in trust, that they should find four able Persons to read within the *College*, Divinity, Geometry, Astronomy, and Musick; and to allow each, besides Lodging, 50 Pounds *per Ann.* ¶ The other Moiety he left to the Company of Mercers, to find three more able Persons, to read Civil Law, Physick, and Rhetorick, on the same Terms; with this Limitation, that the several Lecturers should read in Term-time, every Day in the Week, except Sundays; in the Morning in *Latin*, in the Afternoon the same in *English*: that in Musick to be only read in *English*. **1736** Bailey *Dict. Britannicum* (2nd edn) *Gresham College* (in *Bishopsgate street, London*) was the dwelling-house of Sir *Thomas Gresham* ... who by his last will and testament did in the year 1575 give the *Royal Exchange*, and all the buildings thereunto pertaining, the one moiety to the mayor and commonality of *London*, and their successors in trust, to find four persons to read lectures of *Divinity, Astronomy, Musick* and *Geometry* within his said dwelling-house, allowing them 50 pounds *per annum* a-piece salary... these lectures are read daily in *Term time*, by every one upon his day, in the morning between 9 and 10 in *Latin*, and in the afternoon between 2 and 3 in *English*, except that the *Musick* lecture is read in *English* only on *Thursday* and *Saturday* in the afternoon. **1737** Dyche-Pardon (2nd edn) *Gresham-College* (S.) a College founded by Sir *Thomas Gresham* a Merchant of *London* in the Year 1579. By the Statutes of the Foundation, there are seven Lectures settled in the several Faculties of Learning, *viz.* Divinity, Civil Law, Physick, Rhetorick, Astronomy, Geometry, Musick, for which there is a Salary of seven Times fifty Pounds *per Annum* to seven Professors, with the Conveniency of Lodgings, in the College; ...

gringoter

1570/71 *Dict. Fr. and Engl.* Fr→E *Gringoter, ou Gringuenoter*, to chaunt, to sing as birds do. *Gringuenotant*, quauering, warbling. *Gringuenotis*, quanering [sic] or deliuering of the voyce. **1593** Hollyband Fr→E *Gringoter, ou Gringuenoter*, to chaunt, to sing as birds doe, to quauer. *Gringuenotant*, quauering, warbling. *Gringuenotis*, or *gringotis*, quauering or deliuering of the voyce: *m.* **1611** Cotgrave Fr→E *Gringotement: m.* A quauering, or shaking with the voice. *Gringoter.* To warble, quauer, shake with the voice. *Gringotis: m.* A quauering, warbling, diuision. *Gringuenotant.* Warbling, quauering, shaking of the voice. *Gringuenoteur: m.* A warbler, shaker, quauerer; one that in singing vseth to diuide much. *Regringoté.* Chaunted, quauered, often. *Regringoter.* To chaunt, warble, or quauer often.

ground *see* breaking, canto fermo, chaconne, contrapeso, counterpoint, descant, Farinel's ground, lesson, subchanter, theorbo

1659 Simpson *Division-Violist* (p. 47) A *Continued Ground*, used in Playing, or Making *Division* upon, is (for the most part) the *Through-Basse*, of some *Motett*, or *Madrigall*, proposed, or selected, for That purpose. **1676** Mace *Musick's Monument* (p. 129) The *Ground*, is a set Number of *Slow Notes*, very *Grave*, and *Stately*; which, (after It is express'd Once, or Twice, very *Plainly*) then He that hath *Good Brains*, and a *Good Hand*, undertakes to Play several *Divisions* upon It, *Time* after *Time*, till he has shew'd his *Bravery*, both of *Invention*, and *Hand*. **c.1698-c.1703** North Cursory Notes (*C-K CN* p. 201) There is a sort of musick called a ground, which is onely a plain base, and the upper part varying the movement in true consonancy with it, as copiously as may be done, or is designed. This shews what liberty there is for the upper part to expatiate according to the subject, whatever the base is. Therefore to doe right to the upper parts that they may not wander, great care is to be had of the base on which they lean. **1736** TANS'UR *Compleat Melody* (3rd edn, p. 71) A *Ground*, is a *Bass*, composed of long *Notes, &c. the Division* being run in the other *Parts*.

group

1728 CHAMBERS In Music, a *Group* is one of the Kinds of Diminutions of long Notes, which in the Working, forms a sort of *Group*, Knot, Bush, or the like. ¶ The *Group* usually consists of four Crotchets, Quavers, or Semiquavers tied together, at the Discretion of the Composer. **1730** BAILEY *Dict. Britannicum* (1st edn) *Group* (in *Musick*) is one of the kinds of Diminutions of long Notes, which in the working forms a sort of Group, Knot, Bush, *&c.* a Group commonly consists of four Crotchets, Quavers, *&c.* tied together.

gruppo *see* trill

g sol re ut clef *see* c sol fa ut clef, treble clef

guide, guidon *as notational aid, see* direct, index, mostra

guide *as subject of fugue, see* point

1731 [PEPUSCH] *Treatise on Harmony* (2nd edn, p. 79) The *Part* which introduces the *Subject* of the *Fugue* is call'd the *Guide* or *Leader*; and *that* which follows and repeats what the *first* has said, is call'd the *Answer*.

Guido Aretinus *see* gamut, scale

guidonian system *see* harmonical hand

1721 MALCOLM *Treatise of Musick* (p. 558) ... Thus far go the Improvements of *Guido Aretinus*, and what is called the *Guidonian System*; to explain which he wrote a Book he calls his *Micrologum*. ...

guitar *see* baterie, castanet, cithara, citrial, gittern, saraband, spagnuola

1599 MINSHEU-PERCYVALL Sp→E *Guitarra*, f. a rebecke, a gitterne, a small instrument to play on. **1671** PHILLIPS (3rd edn) *Guittar*, a sort of Musical Instrument heretofore very much in use among the *Italians* and *French*, and now of late among the *English*. **1676** COLES *Ghittar*, an instrument somewhat like a Cittern, only the strings are guts. **1678** PHILLIPS (4th edn) *Ghittar*, a sort of Musical Instrument heretofore very much in use among the *Italians* and *French*, and now of late among the *English*. Some derive it from the Latin *Cithara*. **1688** MIEGE-COTGRAVE Fr→E *Guitarre*, (f.) a Guitar. ¶ Some pronounce and write it *Guiterre*, but Guitarre is the right Word. § *Apprendre de quêcun à jouër de la Guittarre*, to learne of one to play upon the Guitar. *jouër de la Guitarre*, to play upon the Guitar. **1702** KERSEY *New Engl. Dict.* (1st edn) A *Guitar*, a musical instrument. **1704** *Cocker's Engl. Dict.* (1st edn) *Ghittar*, an Instrument like a *Cittern*, only the strings are guts. **1706** KERSEY-PHILLIPS (6th edn) *Guitar*, a kind of Musical Instrument. **1707** *Gloss. Angl. Nova* (1st edn) *Ghittar*, a sort of musical Instrument, heretofore very much in use among the *Italians* and *French*, and now of late among the *English*; some say 'tis derived from *Cithara* a Harp. **1721** BAILEY *An Univ. Etymolog. Engl. Dict.* (1st edn) *Ghittar, Ghittern*, (*Guitern, F.* probably of *Cithara, L.*) a musical Instrument formerly much in Use among the *Italians* and *French*, and now among the *English*. **1724** [PEPUSCH] *Short Explic. of Foreign Words in Mus. Bks.* (p. 36) *Guitare*, a Guittar, a musical Instrument, now out of Use with us. **1726** BAILEY *An Univ. Etymolog. Engl. Dict.* (3rd edn) *Guitare*, a Guittar, a Musical Instrument now out of Use. *Ital.* **1735** DEFOE *Ghittar*, a musical Instrument formerly much used by the *Italians* and *French*. *Guitarre*, a musical Instrument, now out of use. **1737** DYCHE-PARDON (2nd edn) *Ghittar* or *Guittar* (S.) a musical Instrument, formerly much used by the Ladies, especially of *France* and *Italy*, but now almost out of Use, made in the Shape of a Lute, and resembling it in Tone.

guiterne *see* gittern

gymnopædia

1728 CHAMBERS *Gymnopædia*, a kind of Dance, in Use among the antient *Lacedæmonians*. It was performed during their Sacrifices, by young Persons who danced naked, singing at the same Time a Song in Honour of *Apollo*. See *Dance*. ¶ One *Terpander* is recorded as the Inventor of the *Gymnopædia*. **1730** BAILEY *Dict. Britannicum* (1st edn) *Gymnopædia* (γυμνοπαιδία, *Gr.*) a kind of Dance in use among the *Lacedæmonians*, performed by young Persons dancing naked, during the Time of the Sacrifices, and singing a Song in honour of *Apollo.* **1737** DYCHE-PARDON (2nd edn) *Gymnopædia* (S.) a Dance used by the antient *Lacedemonians*, that was performed during their Sacrifices by young Persons naked, who sang at the same Time a Song in Honour of *Apollo.*

gymnopædice

1728 CHAMBERS *Gymnopædice*, a kind of Dance, in Use among the Antients. ¶ *Athenæus* describes it as a *Bacchic* Dance, perform'd by Youths strip'd quite naked, with certain interrupted, tho' agreeable Motions, and Gestures of the Body, the Arms and Legs being flourished and directed after a peculiar Manner, representing a sort of real Wrestling. ¶ The Word is compounded of γυμνός, naked, and παῖς, Child.

H

h

1728 NORTH Musicall Grammarian (*C-K MG* f. 24) ... The occasion of all which is from the organ builders, for they tune all from C which they account naturall, and the order of that key requires B to be flat, and the B♮ in the gamut, they call H or K which in the G key is the naturall. And becaus the organs make B to be flat, that letter, viz. B is taken for the flat mark thro out, and is so used on all occasions; and then the mark H restoring B♮ to the gamut or G key, that letter corrupted, viz. ♮ is made the mark of naturall thro out, that is a restorer of every note de[s]turbed back to the scale of the gamut, as was touched before.

Halesina regio

1565 COOPER L→E *Halesino regio*, A countrey, wherein as a well, the water whereof beynge alwaies quiete & plaine, if one standynge by it dooe playe on a shaulme, or other lyke pype, the water in the well wyll ryse as it daunced, in so muche, that at the last it wyll mounte and renne ouer the brymme of the well: and the pype ceassynge, the water wil foorth with fall and become quiete.

half cadence *see* imperfect cadence

1728 NORTH Musicall Grammarian (*C-K MG* f. 53) There is another sort of close, which is usually called the half cadence. One manner is very solemne and often concludes grave musick; and it is onely by returning from a close [note] to the cadence note back again, and ending with a short flourish ...

half-fall *see* backfall, forefall, whole-fall

1676 MACE *Musick's Monument* (p. 105) The *Half-fall*, is ever from a *Half Note beneath*, (as is the *Beate*) and is performed, by striking that *Half-Note* first; but so soon, as that is so *struck*, you must readily *Clap down the True Note*, (with the *proper Finger*, standing ready) without any further *striking*.

half note *see* hemitone

halleluia *see* alleluia

hammering

c.1668-71 *Mary Burwell's Instruction Bk. for Lute* (*TDa* p. 36) *Of the hammering of the strings of the lute* ¶ Hammering comes from the word 'hammer'. It is done [by] beating the strings several times without taking off the finger very much from it.

Handel, G.F. *see* opera

hardiment *see* vigoroso

1724 [PEPUSCH] *Short Explic. of Foreign Words in Mus. Bks.* (p. 37) *Hardiment*, much the same as *Vivace.* **1726** BAILEY *An Univ. Etymolog. Engl. Dict.* (3rd edn) *Hardiment* (in *Musick Books*) signifies with Life and Spirit. *Ital.*

harigot *see* arigot, larigot

1611 COTGRAVE Fr→E *Harigot.* A kind of Jigge.

Harmonia

1658 PHILLIPS (1st edn) *Harmonia*, the daughter of *Mars* and *Venus*, and the wife of *Cadmus*, to her is attributed by some, the first invention of Musical Harmony.

harmonia *see* exharmonia, harmony

1728 CHAMBERS *Harmonia*, in Music, *&c.* See *Harmony.*

harmonia gemina *see* counterpoint, double descant

1636 BUTLER *Principles of Musik* (p. 78) *Harmonia Gemina.* ¶ There remaineth yet a kinde of *Fuga,* which the Italians call *Contrapunto doppio* (Dubble Counterpoint:) (belike becaus it was at first practised onely in eqal-timed Notes) & the English (because it is nou made in qicker Figures also) dooe call it Dubble Discant: but *Calvisius* more fitly termeth it *Harmonia Gemina*: (a general name, that comprehendeth bothe:) and becaus they have gon so far in this strange Invention, as to invert a third Part also; hee addeth *Tergemina.* ¶ This qeint Harmoni hee dooest thus define: *Harmonia Gemina aut Tergemina est, qua, vocibus inversis, secundâ aut tertiâ vice cani potest: ubi semper alius atq; alius concentus exauditur.* ¶ That which Inverteth onely two Partes, hee describeth thus: *Gemina harmonia fit ex duabis vocibus, si Gravis exaltetur, Acuta verò deprimatur*: that is, when 2 Partes (which ar called the Principal) ar so Composed, that beeing bothe mooved out of their Keys, the Superior dounward, and the Inferior upward, they dooe yet agree together in an other Harmoni: which 2 Partes thus inverted ar called the Replie.

harmonic *see* harmonious

1500 *Ortus Vocabulorum* L→E Armoniacus. vel armonicus a. um. idest dulcis suauis. sweet. o.s. **1565** COOPER L→E *Harmónicus, penult. corr. Adiectiuum.* Melodious. **1589** RIDER L→E *Harmonicus, canorus, ad.* Melodious. **1611** FLORIO It→E *Armonico,* harmonicall melodious. **1656** BLOUNT (1st edn) *Harmonical (harmonicus)* melodious, harmonious, musical, proportionate. **1658** PHILLIPS (1st edn) *Harmonical,* or *Harmonious,* full of Harmony, *i.* musical consent or agreement. **1659** TORRIANO-FLORIO It→E **Harmonicamente,* harmoniously. **1661** BLOUNT (2nd edn) *Harmonick (harmoniacus)* melodious, or that pertains to harmony, which is the accord of divers sounds or notes, or an apt proportion. **1704** HARRIS *Harmonical Proportion,* or *Musical,* is when of four Numbers, as the first is to the fourth, so is the difference of the first and second, to the difference of the third and fourth. ¶ As 5:8:12:30, are *Musical Proportionals,* because 5:30::8-5:30-12::3:18. **1706** KERSEY-PHILLIPS *Harmonical,* or *Harmonick,* belonging to Harmony. **1707** *Gloss. Angl. Nova* (1st edn) *Harmonical,* Musical; **1728** CHAMBERS *Harmonica, Harmonicks,* a Branch, or Division of the antient Music. See *Music.* ¶ The *Harmonica* is that Part which considers the Differences, and Proportion of Sounds, with Respect to acute and grave: In Contradistinction from *Rythmica* and *Metrica.* See *Rythmica* and *Metrica.* ¶ The only Part of their Music the Antients have left us any tolerable Account of, is the *Harmonica;* which it self is but very general and theoretical. ¶ Mr. *Malcolm* has made a very industrious, and learned Inquiry into the *Harmonica,* or Harmonic Principles of the Antients.—They reduced their Doctrines into seven Parts, *viz.* of *Sounds;* of *Intervals;* of *Systems;* of the *Genera;* of the *Tones,* or *Modes;* of *Mutations;* and of the *Melopœia.* See each consider'd under its proper Article *Sound, Interval, System, Genera, Mode, Mutation* and *Melopoeia.* § *Harmonical* ... [*see* Appendix] **1730** BAILEY *Dict. Britannicum* (1st edn) *Harmonical Composition,* in a general Sense, includes the Composition both of harmony and melody. *Harmonical Intervals,* is an interval or difference of two Sounds, which are agreeable to the Ear, whether in Consonance or Succession. *Harmonical Proportion* (in *Musick*) three or four Quantities are said to be in an *harmonical Proportion;* when in the former Case, the difference of the first and second shall be to the difference of the second and third, as the first is to the third; and in the latter, the difference of the first and second to the difference of the third and fourth, as the first is to the fourth. ¶ If there are three Quantities in an *harmonical Proportion,* the difference between the second and twice the first, is to the first as the second is to the third; also the first and last is to twice the first, as the last is to the middle one. ¶ If there are four Quantities in an *harmonical Proportion,* the difference between the second and twice the first, is to the first as the third to the fourth. **1737** BAILEY *The Univ. Etymolog. Engl. Dict.* (3rd edn, vol. 2) *Harmonical Sounds,* such sounds as always make a certain determinate number of vibrations in the time that same other fundamental sound, to which they are referred, make one vibration. **1737** DYCHE-PARDON (2nd edn) *Harmonical* (A.) something that is agreeing, or pertaining to Sound, or Proportion Musical.... In *Musick, Harmonical Proportion,* is when the String or Line is so divided, that the Difference of the first and second, shall be to the Difference of the second and third, as the first is to the third. ¶ *Harmonical Composition,* is the composing or making Musick, so as to be agreeable to the Laws of Harmony and Melody. ¶ *Harmonical Sounds,* are such as make a determinate Number of Vibrations, in the Time that some other fundamental Sound, to which they are referred, makes one.

harmonica *see* harmonic

1730 BAILEY *Dict. Britannicum* (1st edn) *Harmonica* (in *Musick*) a term given by the Antients to that part which considers the difference and proportion of Sounds, with respect to acute and grave.

1688 SALMON *Proposal to Perform Musick* (p. 30) [from remarks by John Wallis:] ... the proportion of Sounds, as to their Graveness and Acuteness, which by the Ancients was called *Harmonica.* **1721** MALCOLM *Treatise of Musick* (pp. 32-3) The First general Branch of this Subject [the divisions of music], which is the *contemplative* Part, divides naturally into these. *First,* the Knowledge of the Relations and Measures of *Tune.* And *Secondly,* of *Time.* The First is properly what the Ancients called *Harmonica,* or the Doctrine of *Harmony* in Sounds; because it contains an Explication of the Grounds, with the various Measures and Degrees of the Agreement (*Harmony*) of Sounds in respect of their *Tune.*

harmonical hand *see* guidonian system

1728 CHAMBERS *Harmonical Hand,* in Music, is used by some Writers for the ancient Diagramma, or Scale of Music, upon which they learn'd to sing. See *Gammut, Scale, Diagram, &c.* ¶ The Reason of the Appellation was, that *Guido Aretin,* upon inventing the Notes, *ut, re, mi, fa, sol, la,* disposed them on the Fingers of the Figure of a *Hand* stretch'd out. See *Note.* ¶ He changed the Letters of the Alphabet, used till that Time to express the Notes, for these six Syllables, which he took out of the first Strophe of the Hymn of St. *John Baptist,* composed by *Paulus Diaconus.* ¶ Ut *queant Laxis* re-*sonare fibris* ¶ Mi-*ra Gestorum* fa-*muli tuorum* ¶ Sol-*ve polluti* la-*bii reatum.* ¶ *Sancte* Joannes.

harmonici *see* canonici

harmonic music

1609 DOWLAND-ORNITHOPARCUS *Micrologvs* (p. 2) *Harmonicall Musicke,* is a faculty weighing the differences of high and low sounds by sence and reason, *Boetius*: Or, it is a cunning, bringing forth the sounds with Humane voyce, by the helpe of naturall Instruments, and iudging all the Sounds which are so brought forth. This as *Placentinus* writeth in the third Chapter of the second booke of his Musicke: is twofold, *Inspectiue* and *Actiue.*

harmonic proportion *see* contra harmonical proportion

1721 MALCOLM *Treatise of Musick* (pp. 165-6) And here I shall observe, That the *harmonical* Proportion received that Denomination from its being found among the Numbers, applied to the Length of Chords, that express the chief *Concords* in *Musick, viz.* the *Octave, 5th,* and *4th,* as here, 3, 4, 6. But this Proportion does not always constitute *Concords,* nor can possibly do, because betwixt the Extremes of any *Interval* we can put an *harmonical Mean,* yet every *Interval* is not resolvable into Parts that are *Concords;* therefore this Definition has been rejected, particularly by *Kepler;* and for this he institutes another Definition of *harmonical Proportion, viz.* When betwixt the Extremes of any *Ratio* or *Interval,* one or more middle Terms are taken, which are all *Concord* among themselves, and each with the Extremes, then that is an *harmonical* Division of such an *Interval;* so that *Octave, 6th* and *5th* are capable of being *harmonically* divided in this Sense; ...

harmonic series *see* natural series

1721 MALCOLM *Treatise of Musick* (p. 173) ... All which Numbers make up this Series, *viz.* 1, 2, 3, 4, 5, 6, 8, 10, 12, 16, 20, 24, 32, 40, 48, 64, 80, *&c.* which is continued after the Number 5, by multiplying the last Three by 2, and their Products *in infinitum* by 2; whereby 'tis plain, we shall have all the Multiples of these original Numbers 1, 3, 5, arising from the continual Multiplication of them by 2. And this I call the *Harmonical Series,* because it contains all the possible *Ratios* that make *Concord,* either *simple* or *compound*: And not only so, but every Number of it is *Concord* with every other ...

harmonic sound

1721 MALCOLM *Treatise of Musick* (p. 28) ... there are also Sounds which have a certain *Tone,* yet being excessive either in Acuteness or Gravity, bear not that just Proportion to the Capacity of the Organs of Hearing, as to afford agreeable Sensations. Upon the Whole then we shall call that *harmonick* or *musical Sound,* which being *clear* and *evenly* [sic] is agreeable to the *Ear,* and gives a certain and discernible *Tune* (hence also called *tunable Sound*) which is the Subject of the whole Theory of Harmony.

harmonicum
1587 THOMAS L→E *Harmonicum, Iun.* Pleasant concent in sundrie tunes: a kinde of musick verie hard to be applyed vnto song, and requiring much exercise and vse ere it can be obtained. *Harmonicus, a, um, Plin.* Melodious. **1589** RIDER L→E *Harmonicum, n.* A kinde of musicke very harde to be applied to a song.

harmonious *see* harmonic, trumpet harmonious
1598 FLORIO It→E *Armonioso, Armonico,* harmonious, melodious, well tuned, musicall. *Harmonioso,* harmonious, musicall, sweetelie sounding, melodious. **1611** COTGRAVE Fr→E *Harmonieux: m. euse: f.* Harmonious, musicall, melodious, tunably sounding, sweetly resounding. **1611** FLORIO It→E *Armonioso,* harmonious, melodious. *Harmonioso,* harmonious, melodious, sweetley sounding. **1616** BULLOKAR *Harmonious.* Sweete, pleasant, delightful to the eare. **1623** COCKERAM *Harmonious.* Sweet, pleasant. **1671** PHILLIPS (3rd edn) *Harmonious,* full of Harmony, i.e. musical consent, or agreement. **1676** COLES *Harmonious, -ick, -ical,* full of ¶ *Harmony, Greek.* Musical consent or agreement. **1678** PHILLIPS (4th edn) *Harmonious,* or *Harmonical,* full of Harmony, *i.e.* Musical consent, or agreement. **1688** MIEGE-COTGRAVE Fr→E † *Harmonieusement,* cd. *avec harmonie,* harmoniously. *Harmonieux,* harmonious. § *La Harpe est harmonieuse,* the Harp is harmonious. **1702** KERSEY *New Engl. Dict.* (1st edn) *Harmonious,* full of ¶ *Harmony,* melody, musical consent, *or* agreement. *Unharmonious,* without harmony, *or* jarring. **1704** *Cocker's Engl. Dict.* (1st edn) *Harmonious,* delightful to the Ear. **1706** KERSEY-PHILLIPS (6th edn) *Harmonious,* full of Harmony or Melody, Musical **1730** BAILEY *Dict. Britannicum* (1st edn) *Harmoniousness* (of ἁρμονία, Gr. *harmonia,* L.) agreeableness in Sound, or musical Proportion. **1735** DEFOE *Harmonious,* full of Harmony, agreeable, melodious. **1736** BAILEY *Dict. Britannicum* (2nd edn) *Unharmonious* (of *un* and *harmonieux,* F. of *harmonia,* L.) discordant, jarring disagreeing. **1737** BAILEY *The Univ. Etymolog. Engl. Dict.* (3rd edn, vol. 2) *Unharmonious* (of *in* and *harmonieux,* F.) not musical, not agreeing one with the other. **1737** DYCHE-PARDON (2nd edn) *Harmonious* (A.) melodious, agreeable, pleasing, charming.

harmony *see* composition, concent, concinnous, concord, consonance, disharmony, euphony, melody, modulation, music, symphony
1500 *Ortus Vocabulorum* L→E Armonia e. i. dulcoratio vel consonantia plurimorum cantuum. vel communis cantus celi vel cantus angelorum. f.p. **1538** ELYOT L→E *Harmonia,* harmonie or melody. **1552** HULOET L→E *Harmonia. æ, Melodia. æ. Melos dis, Numerus. ri, Symphonia. æ.* Armonye or melodye. **1565** COOPER L→E *Harmonia, harmóniæ, pen. corr. Cicer.* Harmonie: melodie: pleasant conceyt in musike. § *Ad harmoniam canere. Cic.* To make a melodious tune. *Harmonica ratio. Plin.* Melodie: pleasant concent in sundrie tunes. **1587** THOMAS L→E *Harmonia, æ, f.g.* Harmonie, melodie, the accord of diuerse sounds or notes: a consort of musick either vocall or instrumentall: *also* the apt proportion of, *Lucret.* **1589** RIDER L→E *Harmonia, f. melos, n. melodia, f. concentus, concentio, incentio, f.* Harmony, or melody *Harmonia, symphonia, f.* Concord in musick, or any tune. *Harmonia, f. vide* concent. A Consorte. **1593** HOLLYBAND Fr→E *Harmonie,* Harmonie, melodie: *f.* **1598** FLORIO It→E *Armonia,* harmonie, melodie, accord in musike. *Armonizzante,* harmonious, melodious, full of melodie. *Armonizzare,* to make harmonie, to make melodie. *Harmonia,* harmonie, musike, melodie. *Harmonizzante,* as *Harmonioso.* Also melodiouslie. *Harmonizzare,* to harmonize, to make musike. **1599** MINSHEU-PERCYVALL Sp→E **Armonia,* or *Harmonia,* harmonie, a sweete agreement in musicall voices, or instruments. **Harmonia,* vide *Armonia,* musicke, melodie, harmonie. **1604** CAWDREY (1st edn) *harmonie* (Greeke) agreement of diuers sounds in musicke. **1611** COTGRAVE Fr→E *Harmonie: f.* Harmonie, melodie, tunablenesse, a sweet consent of sounds; **1611** FLORIO It→E *Armonia,* harmonie, acoord [sic] in musicke. *Armonizzante,* harmonious. *Armonizzare,* to make harmonie. *Harmonia,* harmonie, melodie. *Harmonizzare,* to make harmonie. **1616** BULLOKAR *Harmonie.* Delightfull musicke of many notes. **1623** COCKERAM *Harmonie.* Delightfull musicke of many notes. *Harmonie, Melodie.* Musicke. **1659** TORRIANO-FLORIO It→E *Armonia,* harmonie, accord in musick, tunablenesse, concent of sounds. *Armonico, Armonioso, Armonizzante,* harmonious, melodious. *Armonizzare, Armoneggiare,* to harmonize, to make harmonie. **1688** MIEGE-COTGRAVE Fr→E *Harmonie,* (f) *accord de Sons differens,* harmony. § *Une belle & charmante harmonie,* a fine and charming harmony. **1696** PHILLIPS (5th edn)

Harmony, a Word proper to Sounds that are made in Harmonical Proportion, which is different from Arithmetical and Geometrical Proportion. Music, or a Mixture of Sounds pleasing to the Ear. **1704** *Cocker's Engl. Dict.* (1st edn) *Harmony*, Musical consent, or agreement. **1704** HARRIS *Harmony*, in an agreeable or pleasing Union between two or more Sounds, continuing together at the same time. ¶ Harmony is naturally produced by *Consonances*, but Art has discover'd the way to make it yet more agreeable by the mixture of *Dissonances.* **1706** KERSEY-PHILLIPS (6th edn) *Harmony*, a Consort, an Agreement, or pleasing Union between several Sounds continuing at the same time, either of Voices or Musical Instruments; *Harmonia, (Lat.)* Harmony, Melody, a Consort of Musick. **1707** *Gloss. Angl. Nova* (1st edn) *Harmony*, is an agreeable or pleasing Union between two or more Sounds, continuing together at the same time. **1721** BAILEY *An Univ. Etymolog. Engl. Dict.* (1st edn) *Harmony, (Harmonie, F. harmonia, L.* of ἁρμονία*, Gr.)* Melody, a musical Consort, a due Proportion or agreement Union in Sounds; **1724** [PEPUSCH] *Short Explic. of Foreign Words in Mus. Bks.* (p. 37) *Harmonia*, Harmony, the Result or Agreement of several different Notes or Sounds joyned together in Accord. **1726** BAILEY *An Univ. Etymolog. Engl. Dict.* (3rd edn) *Harmonia*, Harmony: The Result or Agreement of several different Notes or Sounds, join'd together in Accords. *Ital.* **1728** CHAMBERS *Harmony* ... [*see* Appendix] **1730** BAILEY *Dict. Britannicum* (1st edn) *Compound Harmony*, is that, which to the simple harmony of one Octave, adds that of another Octave. *Simple Harmony*, is that, where there is no concord to the Fundamental, above an Octave. **1737** DYCHE-PARDON (2nd edn) *Harmony* (S.) ... also *Musick* justly performed, according to the strict Laws thereof.

1635 ANON. Papers rel. to Writings of Birchensha BL Add. 4388, f. 46v *Harmonia* est ordinata successio *sonorum* gravitate. & acumine *differentium* **1636** BUTLER *Principles of Musik* (p. 46) Harmoni is a delightful congruiti of all the Partes of a Song among themselvs, throogh the Concordance of certain Intervalls, which *God* in Nature (not without a wonder) hath made to agree together; whereas others dooe sound so harshly one to another, that no Musical ear can endure them. § (p. 52) *Harmonia est diversorum sonorum unio. redacta ad concentum. Non enim tantùm simplicem, in acutioribus aut remissioribus sonis, Modulationem* (hoc est singularis vocis Melodiam) *admittit, & ab intervallo ad intervallum, vel velociore vel tardiore motu, secundùm Tempus in Figuris Musicis præscriptum, procedit; sed etiam alias voces, quæ concentum faciunt, accinentes habet: ex quibus, tanquam ex Partibus, Harmonia componitur.* Sethus Cap. 2. **1677** [F. NORTH] *Philosophical Essay of Musick* (p. 28) *Harmony* is the gratefull sound produced by the joyning of several *Tones* in Chord one to another. **1721** MALCOLM *Treatise of Musick* (pp. 200-1) ... I shewed you the Distinction that is made betwixt the Word *Concord*, which is the Agreement of Two Sounds considered either in *Consonance* or *Succession*, and *Harmony*, which is the Agreement of more, considered always in Consonance, and requires at least Three Sounds. In order to produce a perfect *Harmony*, there must be no *Discord* found between any Two of the simple Sounds; but each must be in some Degree of *Concord* to all the rest. Hence *Harmony* is very well defined, *The Sum of Concords* arising from the Combination of *Two* or more *Concords, i.e.* of Three or more simple Sounds striking the Ear all together; and different Compositions of *Concords* make different *Harmony.* § (p. 205) *Harmony* is a *compound* Sound consisting (as we take it here) of Three or more *simple* Sounds; the proper Ingredients of it are *Concords;* and therefore all *Discords* in the *primary Relations* especially, and also in the *mutual Relations* of the several *acute* Terms [intervallic members] are absolutely forbidden. § (p. 415) *Harmony* is the agreeable Result of the Union of Two or more *musical* Sounds heard at one and the same Time; so that *Harmony* is the Effect of Two Parts at least: As therefore a continued Succession of *musical* Sounds produces *Melody*, so does a continued Combination of these produce *Harmony.* § (p. 419) And here *observe*, that the Word *Harmony* is taken somewhat larger than above in *Chap.* 7. [pp. 385-413] for *Discords* are used with *Concords* in the *Composition* of *Parts*, which is here exprest in general by the Word *Harmony;* which therefore is distinguished into the *Harmony* of *Concords* in which no *Discords* are used, and that of Discords which are always mixt with *Concords.* § (pp. 499-500) ... My Business here is with the Part they [the ancient writers] called *Harmonica*, which treats of Sounds and their Differences, with respect to *acute* and *grave. Ptolomy* calls it *a Power or Faculty perceptive of the Difference of Sounds, with respect to* Acuteness *and* Gravity; and *Bryennius* calls it a speculative and practical Science, of the Nature of the *harmonick* Agreement in Sounds. § (p. 579) The

Word *Harmonia* signifies more generally the Agreement of several Things that make up one Whole; but so do several Sounds in Succession make up one *Song*, which is in a very proper Sense a Composition. And in this Sense we have in *Plato* and others several Comparisons to the *Harmony* of Sounds in *Musick*. But 'tis also used in the strict Sense for *Consonance*, and so is equivalent to the Word *Symphonia*. **1721 or after** ANON. Institutions of Musick (rear of LC copy of Bayne, p. 2) Harmony is the agreeable Result of the union of two or more Musical sounds heard at one and the same Time, so that Harmony is the Effect of two parts at least as therefore a continued succession of Musical sounds produce Melodie, so does a continued Combination of these produce Harmony. **1721 or after** ANON. Treatise of Thoro' Bass BEINECKE OSB. MS 3, p. 11 ... Whereas by the word Harmony is meant the agreeable result of two or more parts together, when the sounds that enter into the Composition of any piece are Juditiously Combined, so as not only to be agreeable when the parts are heard singly, but also when they are joyned and heard at one and the same time; ... **1730** [PEPUSCH] *Short Treatise on Harmony* (p. 4) *Harmony*, is the Agreeable Union of Sounds in several Parts, when Sung or Play'd together.

harmony of the spheres *see* music
1728 CHAMBERS *Harmony of the Spheres*, or *Celestial Harmony*, is a Sort of Music, much spoke of by many of the Philosophers and Fathers; supposed to be produced by the regular, sweetly tuned Motions of the Stars and Planets. See *System*. ¶ *Plato, Philo Judæus*, St. *Augustine*, St. *Ambrose*, St. *Isidore, Boetius*, and many others, are strongly possess'd with the Opinion of this *Harmony*, which they attribute to the various and proportionate Impressions of the heavenly Globes upon one another; which acting under proper Intervals, form a *Harmony*. ¶ It is impossible, according to them, that such spacious Bodies, moving with so much Rapidity, should be silent; on the contrary, the Atmosphere, continually impell'd by them, must yield a Set of Sounds, proportionate to the Impulsions it receives: Consequently, as they do not all run the same Circuit, nor with one and the same Velocity, the different Tones arising from the Diversity of Motions, directed by the Hand of the Almighty, form an admirable Symphony, or Concert. See *Music*. ¶ St. *Irenæus*, St. *Basil*, and St. *Epiphanius*, have appeared against the Notion. **1730** BAILEY *Dict. Britannicum* (1st edn) *Harmony of the Spheres, Harmony Celestial*, (with the *Philosophers*) a kind of Musick, supposed to be produced by the sweetly tuned Motions of the Stars and Planets. They attribute this harmony to the various and proportionate Impressions of the heavenly Globes upon one another, which, by acting under proper Intervals, form a harmony. For, as they thought it not possible that such large Bodies, moving with great rapidity, should be silent, and that the Atmosphere continually impelled by them must yield a set of Sounds proportionate to the impulsions it receives, and they not running all in the same Circuit, nor with the same Velocity, different Tones must arise from this diversity of Motions, which being all directed by the Hand of the Almighty, do form an admirable Symphony or Concert.

harp *see* alpa, barbiton, cetara, chelys, chevalet, cithara, entata, fides, fidicula, jessean harp, jews harp, lirone, lyre, sambuke, wega
1550 THOMAS It→E *Harpa*, an harpe. **1565** COOPER L→E § *Docto pollice sollicitat stamina. Ouid.* He playeth cunningly on the harpe. *Stamina sollicitat docto pollice. Ouidius.* He playeth on the harpe cunningly. **1570/71** *Dict. Fr. and Engl.* Fr→E *Vne harpe*, a harpe. **1593** HOLLYBAND Fr→E *Vne harpe*, a Harpe: *f.* **1598** FLORIO It→E *Harpa*, a harpe. **1599** MINSHEU-PERCYVALL Sp→E *Harpa*, f. an instrument of musicke called a harpe. **1611** COTGRAVE Fr→E *Harpe: f.* A Harpe; **1611** FLORIO It→E *Arpa*, any kind of harp. *Harpa*, a Harpe. **1650** HOWELL-COTGRAVE Fr→E § *Il mania tresbien ses harpes*. He stirred his fingers very nimbly. **1659** TORRIANO-FLORIO It→E **Harpa*, as *Arpa*, a harp. **1688** MIEGE-COTGRAVE Fr→E **Harpe*, (f.) an Harpe. § *Toucher (jouër de) la harpe*, to play upon the harp. **1696** PHILLIPS (5th edn) *Harp*, a Musical Instrument of a triangular Form, consisting of 78 Strings. **1702** KERSEY *New Engl. Dict.* (1st edn) A *Harp*, a musical instrument. To *Harp, or* play on the *harp*. **1708** KERSEY *Dict. Anglo-Brit.* (1st edn) *Harp*, a Musical Instrument. **1721** BAILEY *An Univ. Etymolog. Engl. Dict.* (1st edn) A *Harp*, (ꞅeaꞃpe, *Sax.* Harp[e], *Du. Harpe, F.*) a Musical Instrument. **1728** CHAMBERS *Harp*, a Musical Instrument, of the String Kind; being of a triangular Figure, and placed an End between the Legs to be play'd on. See *Instrument*. ¶ There is some Diversity in the Structure of *Harps*.—That call'd the *Triple Harp*, has 78 Strings, or Chords, in three Rows, 49 in each, which make four Octaves; The first Row is for the Semitones; and the third is in Unison with the

first. There are two Rows of Pins, or Screws, on the right Side, serving to keep the Strings tight in their Holes, which are fasten'd at the other End to three Rows of Pins on the upper Side. ¶ This Instrument is struck with the Finger and Thumb of both Hands. Its Music is much like that of the Spinett; all its Strings going from Semitone to Semitone: Whence some call it an *inverted Spinett.* See *Spinett.* ¶ It is capable of a much greater Degree of Perfection than the Lute. See *Lute.* ¶ King *David* is usually painted with a *Harp* in his Hands; but we have no Testimony in all Antiquity, that the *Hebrew Harp,* which they call *Chinnor,* was any Thing like ours.—On a *Hebrew* Medal of Simon *Machabæus* we see two Sorts of Musical Instruments; but they are both of them very different from our *Harp,* and only consist of three or four Strings. ¶ *Papias,* and *du Cange* after him, will have the *Harp* to have took its Name from the *Arpi,* a People of *Italy,* who were the first that invented it; and from whom it was borrowed by other Nations. ¶ All Authors agree, that it is very different from the *Lyra, Cythara,* or *Barbiton,* used among the *Romans.* See *Lyra.* ¶ *Fortunatus, L.* VII. *Carm.* 8. witnesses, that it was an Instrument of the *Barbarians.* ¶ *Romanusq; Lyra, plaudet tibi Barbarus* Harpâ ¶ *Græcus Achilliaca, Crotta Britannia canat.* ¶ *Menage,* &c. derive the Word from the *Latin, Harpa;* and that from the *German, herp,* or *harpff.* Others bring it from the *Latin Carpo,* because touch'd, or thrum'd with the Fingers. Dr. *Hicks* derives it from *Harpa,* or *Hearpa,* which signify the same Thing; the first in the Language of the *Cimbri,* the second in that of the *Anglo Saxons.* ¶ The *English* Priest who wrote the Life of St. *Dunstan,* and who lived with him in the X*th* Century, says; C.2. N.12. *Sumpsit secum ex More Citharam suam, quam paterni lingua* Hearpam *vocanius;* which intimates the Word to be *Anglo-Saxon.* **1730** BAILEY *Dict. Britannicum* (1st edn) *Harp* (heaꞃpe, *Sax.*) a musical Instrument of a triangular Form, having 72 Strings, *F.* and *Du.* **1735** DEFOE *Harp,* a musical stringed Instrument. **1736** BAILEY *Dict. Britannicum* (2nd edn) *Harp* (heaꞃpe, *Sax. harpa,* Su. *harpe,* Du. and L.G. *harsse,* H.G. *harpe,* F. *arpa,* It. *harpa,* Sp. and Port) a musical Instrument of a triangular Form, having twenty-seven Strings. **1737** DYCHE-PARDON (2nd edn) *Harp* (S.) an ancient Musical Instrument which the Moderns have very much improved, and now make of a triangular Form, which is held upright between the Person's Legs, that plays on it: It has three Parts; the main Body of it, which consists of the right Side, is made of eight flat Fronts of Wood, upon which is placed the Table, which hath two Holes made like Trefoil. It has three Rows of Strings, which in all make seventy eight; the first Row contains nine and twenty, which make four Octaves; the second Row makes the half Turn; the third is the Unison of the first Row; there are two Rows of Pins, which are called Buttons, on the right Side, which serve to keep the Strings tight in their Holes, and are fastened at the other End to the three Rows of Pins placed on the upper Side, which are called Keys; it is play'd on with both Hands, by pinching them in the same Manner together; its Musick is like that of a Spinnet, all the Strings going by Semi-tones; that in Use among the antient *Jews,* is supposed to have but very few Strings, and more like a Lute or Guitar than the Instrument above described, which is supposed to be derived both Name and Thing, from *Cimbri* or *English Saxons;* there are among us two Sorts *Viz.* the *Irish* Harp strung with Wire, and the *Welch* [sic] Harp strung with Gut, but in other Respects much alike. *Harp* (V.) to play upon the Musical Instrument so called;

harpeggio *see* arpeggio

harper *see* Argon, Arion, Aspendius, blind harper, brother of the string, citharist, Demodocus, fidicen, lyrist, Orpheus, Terpnus
1593 HOLLYBAND Fr→E *Harper,* or *jouër sur la harpe,* to play vpon the harpe. *Harpeur, m:* an harper or player vpon the harpe. **1599** MINSHEU-PERCYVALL Sp→E **Harpador,* m. ... Also a harper. **1611** COTGRAVE Fr→E *Harper.* To harpe, or play on a Harpe. *Harpeur: m.* A Harper; one that playes on the Harpe. **1611** FLORIO It→E *Harpatore,* a Harper. **1688** MIEGE-COTGRAVE Fr→E † **Harper, pour dire jouër de la Harpe,* to play upon the Harp. **1702** KERSEY *New Engl. Dict.* (1st edn) An *Harper.* **1708** KERSEY *Dict. Anglo-Brit.* (1st edn) *Harper,* one that plays on the Harp: **1737** DYCHE-PARDON (2nd edn) *Harper* (S.) one who plays upon the Instrument called a Harp;

harpsichord *see* basso continuo, clavecymbal, clavicembalo, polyplectra, spinet
1598 FLORIO It→E *Arpicordo,* an instrument like clarigols. **1611** COTGRAVE Fr→E *Harpechorde: f.* An Arpsicord, or Harpsicord; a Dulcimer. **1611** FLORIO It→E *Arpicordo,* an instrument like Clarigols called a harpers cord. **1659** TORRIANO-FLORIO It→E *Arpicordo,* a musicall instrument, like a Clarigoll, called a Harpers chorde. **1688** DAVIS-TORRIANO-

FLORIO It→E *Arpicordo,* a musical instrument, like a Claricord, called a Harper's Chord, or Harpsical. **1702** KERSEY *New Engl. Dict.* (1st edn) An *Harpsecord,* or *harpsecol,* a musical instrument. **1706** KERSEY-PHILLIPS (6th edn) *Harpsecord,* or *Harpsecol,* a kind of Musical Instrument. **1707** *Gloss. Angl. Nova* (1st edn) *Harpsicord,* a Musical Instrument like Virginals. **1721** BAILEY *An Univ. Etymolog. Engl. Dict.* (1st edn) *Harpsicord, Harpsicol, (Harpsicorde, F.)* a musical Instrument **1728** CHAMBERS *Harpsichord,* or *Harpsichol,* a Musical Instrument of the Wind-Kind; play'd after the Manner of an Organ. See *Organ.* ¶ The *Italians* call it *Clave Cimbala,* and the *French Clavecin.* In *Latin* it is usually call'd *Grave Cymbalum,* q.d. a large or deep Cymbal. See *Cymbal.* ¶ The *Harpsichord* is furnish'd with a Set of Keys; sometimes two Sets:—The touching, or striking of these Keys, moves a Kind of little Jacks, which move a double Row of Chords, or Strings of Brass and Iron, stretch'd on the Table of the Instrument over four Bridges. See *Music.* **1730** BAILEY *Dict. Britannicum* (1st edn) *Harpsicord, Harpsicol, (harpsicorde,* F.) a kind of musical string Instrument well known. **1737** DYCHE-PARDON (2nd edn) *Harpsicord* (S.) a string'd musical Instrument, much used and played on, especially by Organists in particular.

haut *see* acute, high
1724 [PEPUSCH] *Short Explic. of Foreign Words in Mus. Bks.* (p. 37) *Haut,* High or Shrill.

hautboy *see* hobois, oboe, piva, sveglia
1611 COTGRAVE Fr→E *Haultebois: m.* A Hobois, or Hoboy. § *Languette de hault-bois.* The little pipe, tongue, or tenon, which is in the mouth of a Hoeboy, &c. **1650** HOWELL-COTGRAVE Fr→E *Haultbois: m.* A Hobois, or Hoboy. **1688** MIEGE-COTGRAVE Fr→E **Haut-bois,* (m.) an hoboy. § *Jouër du haut-bois,* to play upon the hoboy. **1696** PHILLIPS (5th edn) *Hautboy,* a sort of Loud Wind-Instrument. **1702** KERSEY *New Engl. Dict.* (1st edn) A *Haut-boy,* or *hoboy* a musical instrument. A *Hoboy, or hautboy,* a Musical Instrument. **1706** KERSEY-PHILLIPS (6th edn) *Hautboy,* or *Hoboy,* a Musical Wind-Instrument. **1721** BAILEY *An Univ. Etymolog. Engl. Dict.* (1st edn) *Hautboy,* a Musical Instrument call'd a Hoboy. **1724** [PEPUSCH] *Short Explic. of Foreign Words in Mus. Bks.* (pp. 37-8) *Hautbois,* a Hoboy, or Hautboy, an Instrument of Musick very common, and therefore well known. **1726** BAILEY *An Univ. Etymolog. Engl. Dict.* (3rd edn) *Hautbois,* a Hoboy, or Hautboy. *Ital.* **1728** CHAMBERS *Hautboy,* or *Hoboy,* a Sort of Musical Instrument, of the Wind-kind, with a Reed to blow or play it withal. See *Instrument.* ¶ The *Hautboy* is shaped much like the Flute, only that it spreads, or widens, more toward the Bottom. The Treble is two Foot long: The Tenor goes a fifth lower, when blown, or sounded open. It has only seven Holes: The Bass is five Foot long, and has eleven Holes. ¶ The Word is *French, Haut-bois,* q.d. *High-Wood;* and is given to this Instrument, by Reason its Tone is higher than that of the Violin. **1737** DYCHE-PARDON (2nd edn) *Hautboy* or *hoboy* (S.) a Musical Instrument of the Wind-kind, blown with the Mouth thro' a Reed, and play'd upon with the Fingers;

c.1710 NORTH (draft for) Musicall Grammarian BL Add. 32537, f. 182v The next order of sounding tubes, are the Reedalls wch are of Excellent use, and Exercise the statelyest of pipes now knowne by ye name of Hautboys; and anciently as they say were called clavions, and are ye best companions for trumpetts. **c.1715-20** NORTH Theory of Sounds BL Add. 32534, f. 75v [*re* the hautboy] ... litle Inferior to the trumpet. hath made it to be Imployed on, ye most solemne occasions, as for triumphs In Warr and in church servi[ces] as well as Civill Rejoycings, In ye former of wch the sp[a]niards, & after them the Rest of Europe ha[ve] called the Curgh [?church] Hautboys clavion, and In ye latter, menestreles, becaus anciently there was litle or No ordinary [mu]sick but such as sounded by wind, and tha[t] perfor[med] onely by Exclesiasticks or Monastery Men.

haut-dessus *see* dessus, treble
1724 [PEPUSCH] *Short Explic. of Foreign Words in Mus. Bks.* (p. 38) *Haut Dessus,* First Treble. **1726** BAILEY *An Univ. Etymolog. Engl. Dict.* (3rd edn) *Haut Dessus,* first Treble. *Ital.*

1731 PRELLEUR *Modern Musick-Master* (Dictionary, p. 2) *Haut-Dessus,* First Treble.

haute-contre *see* cantus
1593 HOLLYBAND Fr→E *Haulte-contre,* the contrary is, *Basse-contre*: the base in musicke. **1611** COTGRAVE Fr→E *Haulte-contre: com.* The Countertenor part in singing; also, (a Countertenor) he that beares it. *Haute-contre: com.* The Countertenor part, in singing, &c; also (a Countertenor, or) he which bears that part. **1688** MIEGE-COTGRAVE Fr→E **Haute-contre,* (f.) *Terme de Musique,* the Counter-Tenor, in Musick. *Haute-contre,* (m.) he that sings the Counter-Tenor. **1724** [PEPUSCH] *Short Explic. of

Foreign Words in Mus. Bks. (p. 38) *Haut Contre,* Counter Tenor. **1726** BAILEY *An Univ. Etymolog. Engl. Dict.* (3rd edn) *Haut Contre* (in *Musick Books*) signifies Counter-Tenor. *Ital.*

1731 PRELLEUR *Modern Musick-Master* (Dictionary, p. 2) *Haut-Contre,* Counter Tenor.

hay *see* ridda, rosina
1702 KERSEY *New Engl. Dict.* (1st edn) To dance the *Hay.* **1706** KERSEY-PHILLIPS (6th edn) *Hay,* ... also a sort of Country-dance; **1708** KERSEY *Dict. Anglo-Brit.* (1st edn) *Hay,* ... also a sort of Country-dance; **1721** BAILEY *An Univ. Etymolog. Engl. Dict.* (1st edn) ... to dance the *Hay,* is to dance in a Ring. **1730** BAILEY *Dict. Britannicum* (1st edn) § *To dance the Hay,* to dance in a Ring.

haydegines *see* heidegiver
1662 PHILLIPS (2nd edn) *Haydegines,* (old word) a Countrey-dance, or round. **1676** COLES *Haydegines, Old word.* a Country dance. **1678** PHILLIPS (4th edn) *Haydegines, (old word)* a Countrey dance, or round.

hay down *see* carol, filibustacchina

head *see* joug
1728 CHAMBERS In Music, the *Head* of a Lute, Theorbo, or the like, is the Place where the Pins or Pegs are screw'd, to stretch or slacken the Strings. See *Lute, &c.*

hederal
1656 BLOUNT (1st edn) *Hederal (hederalis)* of or pertaining to Ivy; the Hederal Crown or Garland was given to Poets, and excellent Musitians, *Fern.* 27. 33.

heidegiver *see* haydegines
1707 *Gloss. Angl. Nova* (1st edn) *Heidegiver,* a Country Dance. *Spencer.*

hemiola *see* emiolio, tripla
1728 CHAMBERS *Hemiolus,* an antient Mathemetical Term, occurring chiefly in Musical Writers.—It signifies the Ratio of two Things, whereof the one contains the other once and an half; as 3:2, or 15:10. See *Ratio.* ¶ *Macrobius,* on the *Somnium Scipionis,* L. II. C. 1. observes, that the Concord, call'd in the antient Music *Diapente,* and in the Modern a *Fifth,* arises from this Proportion. See *Fifth.* ¶ The Word is compounded of ἥμι, *half,* and ὅλος, whole. **1736** BAILEY *Dict. Britannicum* (2nd edn) *Hemiolus* (of ἥμι Half, and ὅλος, Gr. the Whole) an ancient Mathematical Term, occurring chiefly in Musical Writers, signifying the Ratio of a Thing, whereof one contains the other once and a half.

1609 DOWLAND-ORNITHOPARCUS *Micrologvs* (p. 66) ... For *Hemiola* is that, which *Sesquialtera* is, saith *Aulus Gellius lib.* 19. *cap.* 14. ...

hemiope
1728 CHAMBERS *Hemiope,* or *Hemiopus,* a Musical Instrument in Use among the Antients. See *Music.* ¶ The *Hemiopus* was a Flute with only three small Holes. See *Flute.* ¶ The Word is compounded of ἥμι, and πλήσσω, *I strike,* or *seize.*

hemisphero
1587 THOMAS L→E *Hemisphærium, rij. n.g...* and it is taken for *Magas* [*see* magade]. **1598** FLORIO It→E *Hemispero* [sic], *Emisfero,* ... Also a kinde of musicall instrument. **1611** FLORIO It→E *Hemisphero,* ... Also a halfe round musicall instrument.

hemitone *see* semitone, tri-hemitone
1721 BAILEY *An Univ. Etymolog. Engl. Dict.* (1st edn) *Hemiton,* (in *Musick*) a half Tone. **1728** CHAMBERS *Hemitone,* in the antient Music, was, what we now call an half Note or Tone. See *Note* and *Tone.* **1730** BAILEY *Dict. Britannicum* (1st edn) *Hemitone* (in *Musick*) half a Tone. **1737** DYCHE-PARDON (2nd edn) ... in *Musick,* Hemitone is half a Note or Tone.

1698 WALLIS *Letter to Samuel Pepys* (*Philos. Trans.,* 1698, p. 253) ... the whole *Octave* is divided into Twelve Parts or Intervals (contained between Thirteen Pipes) which are commonly called *Hemitones* or *Half-notes.* Not, that each is precisely *Half a Note,* but somewhat near it, and so called.

heptachord *see* seventh
1728 CHAMBERS *Heptachord,* in the antient Poetry.—*Heptachord Verses,* were those sung or play'd on seven Chords; that is, in seven different Notes, or Tones; and probably on an Instrument with seven Strings. ¶ The Word is compounded of ἑπτά, *septem,* and χορδή, *Chord, String.* **1730** BAILEY *Dict. Britannicum* (1st edn) *Heptachord Verses* (of ἑπτά, seven, and χορδή, String) Verses

sung or play'd on seven Chords, *i.e.* in seven different Tones or Notes, and probably on an Instrument of seven Strings.

herenuela

1599 MINSHEU-PERCYVALL Sp→E **Hereñuela,* a kinde of musicall instrument, vsed in inchantments.

heroic *see* Calliope

1500 *Ortus Vocabulorum* L→E Heroicus ca. cuz dicit ab heros hoc est heroicum carmen. Heroica gesta que sunt de magnis viris & heroicis. o.s.

1711 BEDFORD *Great Abuse of Musick* (p. 28) ... And as the *Hexameter Verses* of *Orpheus, Homer, Hesiod, Tyrtæus, &c.* were compos'd for an *antient, grave,* and *equal* (such as we call *common*) *Time;* so I suppose, that these were the *Measures sung* on those Occasions [before battle], and that they might for this Reason be call'd *Heroick.*

hesychiastic *see* diastaltic

hexachord *see* esacordo

1696 PHILLIPS (5th edn) *Hexachord,* an Interval in Musick, called a Sixth. **1704** HARRIS *Hexachord,* a certain Interval of Musick, or Concord, commonly called a *Sixth;* and is two-fold, *viz.* The *Greater* and *Lesser.* ¶ The *Greater Hexachord,* is composed of two Greater Tones, two Lesser Tones, and one Greater Semi-Tone, which are five Intervals: But the *Lesser Hexachord,* consists only of two Greater Tones, on[e] Lesser Tone, and two Greater Semi-Tones. ¶ The Proportion of the former, in Numbers, is as 3 to 5; and that of the other as 5 to 8. **1706** KERSEY-PHILLIPS (6th edn) *Hexachord, (Gr.)* an Interval or Concord in *Musick,* commonly call'd a Sixth. **1707** *Gloss. Angl. Nova* (1st edn) *Hexacord,* a certain interval of Musick commonly called a *Sixth.* **1728** CHAMBERS *Hexachord,* in the antient Music, a Concord commonly called by the Moderns, a *Sixth.* See *Concord* and *Sixth.* ¶ The *Hexachord* is two-fold, *Greater* and *Lesser.*—The *Greater Hexachord,* is composed of two greater Tones, two lesser Tones, and one greater Semitone; which make five Intervals. The *Lesser Hexachord* consists only of two greater Tones, one lesser Tone, and two greater Semitones. See *Tone.* ¶ The Proportion of the former, in Numbers, is as 3 to 5; and that of the other, as 5 to 8. ¶ The Word is *Greek,* compounded of ἕξ, *Sex,* Six; and χορδη, *Corda,* Chord, or String. **1730** BAILEY *Dict. Britannicum* (1st edn) *Hexachord* (ἑξαχόρδον, Gr.) a Chord in Musick, commonly call'd by the Moderns a sixth. **1737** DYCHE-PARDON (2nd edn) *Hexachord* (S.) a Term in *Musick,* for the imperfect Chord, which we now call a Sixth.

hey down *see* carol, filibustacchina

hiastio

1598 FLORIO It→E *Hiastio,* a kind of musicke among the Grecians. **1611** FLORIO It→E *Hiastio,* a kind of musike among the Grecians. **1659** TORRIANO-FLORIO It→E *Hiastio,* a kinde of musick among the Grecians.

high *see* acute, haut

1728 CHAMBERS *High,* in Music, is sometimes used in the same Sense with *loud,* in Opposition to *low:* And sometimes in the same Sense with *Acute,* in Opposition to *Grave.* See *Sound, Acuteness, Gravity, &c.*

hilarodus

1538 ELYOT L→E *Hilarodus,* a synger of a wanton and delycate songe. **1552** HULOET L→E *Hilarodus* Singer of a delicate or wanton song. **1565** COOPER L→E *Hilarodus, di, m.g.* A singar of wanton songes. **1587** THOMAS L→E *Hilarœdus, di, Fest.* A singer of mery wanton songes. **1589** RIDER L→E *Hilarædus* [sic], *m.* A singer of delicate, or merrie songs. **1623** COCKERAM *Hilarode.* A singer of wanton songs. *Hilarode.* a Singer of wanton songs **1728** CHAMBERS *Hilarode,* or *Hilarodus,* in the antient Music and Poetry, a sort of Poet among the *Greeks,* who went about singing little gay Poems, or Songs; tho' somewhat graver than the *Ionic* Pieces. See *Rhapsodus.* ¶ The *Hilarodes* appear'd dress'd in white, and were crown'd with Gold. At first they wore Shoes; but afterwards assumed the *Crepída,* which was only a Soal, tied over the Foot with Straps. ¶ They did not sing alone; but had always a little Boy, or Girl, to attend them, playing on some Instrument. ¶ From the Streets, they were at length introduced into the Tragedy; as the Magodes were into Comedy. See *Magodes, Tragedy. &c.* ¶ The *Hilarodes* were afterwards call'd *Simodes,* from a Poet named *Simus,* who excell'd in this Kind of Poetry. ¶ The Word is compounded of ἱλαρὸς, *joyful,* and ᾠδὴ, *Singing, Song.* See *Hilarodia.* § *Hilarodia,* a Poem, or Composition in Verse, made, or sung by a Sort of Rhapsodists call'd *Hilarodes.* See *Hilarode.* **1730** BAILEY *Dict. Britannicum* (1st edn) *Hilarodia* (of ἡλαρός, cheerful, and ᾠδὴ, Gr. a Song) a Poem or Composition in Verse, sung by a sort of Rhapsodists called *Hilarodes.*

hillulim *see* marriage music
1661 BLOUNT (2nd edn) *Hillulim* (Hebr.) praises; a Song sung at the Jews marriages, by the Bridegrooms intimate friends. **1676** COLES *Hillulim, Hebrew.* praises, a Jewish wedding-song.

Hippomachus
1565 COOPER L→E *Hippómachus*, The name of a famous minstrell. **1678** PHILLIPS (4th edn) *Hippomachus*, an excellent Flutinist among the ancient *Greeks*. He held it the greatest argument of defect in Art, to be praised by the ignorant vulgar. Ælian.

hobois, hoboy *see* empneusta (under entata), hautboy, oboe
1706 KERSEY-PHILLIPS (6th edn) *Hoboy*. See *Hautboy*. **1731** KERSEY *New Engl. Dict.* (3rd edn) A *Hoboy*, a Musical Instrument.

1636 BUTLER *Principles of Musik* (p. 93) ... *Fluit, Waits* or †*Hobois, Trumpet*, &c. ... [marginalia: '†So also dooeth the French sound it, thowgh they write it Haultbois (high or loud sounding wooden Instruments.)']

hold *as fingering technique*
1665 SIMPSON *Division-Viol* (2nd edn, p. 5) When you set any Finger down, hold it on there; and play the following Notes with other Fingers, until some occasion require the taking it off... Instances of these Holds (for so they are called) you have, where you see such a Stroke as this √ drawn from One to some other distant Note unto which you must hold it.

hold *as pause, see* pause, sostenuto, soustenir, stay
1721 MALCOLM *Treatise of Musick* (p. 413) You'll find over some single Notes a Mark like an Arch, with a Point in the Middle of it which has been used to signifie that that Note is to be made longer than ordinary, and hence called a *Hold*; but more commonly now it signifies that the *Song* ends there, which is only used when the *Song* ends with a Repetition of the first Strain or a Part of it; and this Repetition is also directed by the Words, *Da capo, i.e.* from the Beginning.

holding note
1740 LAMPE *Art of Musick* (p. 31) Parts vary with only changing the Quality of a continued Sound, called a holding Note, and others by their moving, produce new Species of Harmony.

holocaust *see* sacrifice
1737 BAILEY *The Univ. Etymolog. Engl. Dict.* (3rd edn, vol. 2) *Holocaust* ... a sacrifice among the *Jews* which was all burnt upon the altar, ... while the victim was burning, the musick play'd, and the priest offered up a prayer that God would accept the sacrifice. **1737** DYCHE-PARDON (2nd edn) *Holocaust* (S.) the same with Burnt-Offering; in the *Jewish Church*, was a Sacrifice, which was all burnt upon the Altar, ... there was a Libation of Wine added to the Burnt-Offering, and while the Victim [a bullock] was burning, the Musick played, and the Priests made a Prayer to God to accept the Sacrifice; ...

hop merchant
1737 BAILEY *The Univ. Etymolog. Engl. Dict.* (3rd edn, vol. 2, cant section) *Hop Merchant*, a Dancing-Master.

horn *see* buccina, bugle, call, clarion, classicum, cor, cornet, cornicen, corno, cornu, french horn, kern, lituus, trantrana, trompe, ward-corn
1728 CHAMBERS *Horn* is also a Sort of musical Instrument, of the Wind Kind; chiefly used in Hunting, to animate and bring together the Dogs, and the Hunters. See *Hunting*. ¶ The *Horn* may have all the Extent of the Trumpet. See *Trumpet*. ¶ The Term anciently was, *Wind a Horn*; all *Horns* being in those Times compass'd: But since straight *Horns* are come in fashion, they say, *Blow a Horn*, and sometimes, *Sound a Horn*. ¶ There are various Lessons on the *Horn*; as the *Recheat, Double Recheat, Royal Recheat, Running* or *Farewel Recheat*, &c. See *Recheat*. ¶ The *Hebrews* made use of *Horns* form'd of Rams *Horns*, to proclaim the Jubilee; whence the Name *Jubilee*. See *Jubilee*.

c.1710 NORTH (draft for) Musicall Grammarian BL Add. 32537, f. 182 The comon horn y[e] hunters use is of this Genus [flatile], and more especially that semicircular one, called y[e] sow gelders Horne, w[ch] sounds very loud, and break's well into a 3[d] & fifth, and those Notes backwards and forwards is the tune of that Instrument.

horner *see* cornaro, corneur

hornet *see* cornemuse, cornu

hornpipe *as dance, see* jig, rigoletto
1597 MORLEY *Plaine and Easie Introdvction* (p. 181) ... There bee also many other kindes of dances [after the volte, courante and country dances] (as *hornepypes[,] Iygges* and infinite more) which I cannot nominate vnto you, but knowing these the rest can not but be vnderstood, as being one with some of these which I haue alreadie told you.

hornpipe *as instrument, see* buccina, cornemuse, corno, piva, stifello, villanella, zaino

horse-ballet
1670 BLOUNT (3rd edn) *Horse-ballet*, a Dance or Ball performed by Horses; such was that at the Emperors wedding, 1666. **1676** COLES *Horse-ballet*, a horse-danse.

hosanna
1598 FLORIO It→E *Osannare*, to sing or crie praises vnto God. **1611** FLORIO It→E *Osannare*, to sing and call on God with great ioy and praise-giuing for sauing vs. **1659** TORRIANO-FLORIO It→E *Osannare*, to sing and call on God with great joy and praise-singing for quickning and saving us.

hum
1737 DYCHE-PARDON (2nd edn) *Hum* (V.) ... to sing a Tune to a Person's self without opening his Lips;

human music *see* musica humana

humour *see* air, suit

hunting horn *see* bugle, cor, trompe

[hurdy-gurdy] *see* symphony, vielle

hutchet *see* cor, cornette, cornetto, corno
1593 HOLLYBAND Fr→E *Huchet, m*: the little horne which guides of the post doe vse. **1611** COTGRAVE Fr→E *Huchet: m.* A Hutchet, Bugle, or small Horne; such a one as Post boyes vse.

hydraulicks *see* æolipile, clepsiambo, organ, organum hydraulicum
1538 ELYOT L→E *Hydraulis*, an organ player. **1552** HULOET L→E *Hydraulis* Organ player. **1565** COOPER L→E *Hydáulicus, pen. cor. Adiect.* Perteinynge to organs ... *Hydraulos, m.g. Plin.* ... Also a payre of organs. *Vitr. Vall.* **1587** THOMAS L→E *Hydraula, æ, f.g. Suet.* An organe player *Hydraulicus, a, um, Plin.* Pertaining to organes: *Hydraulus, li, & hydraulis, m.g. Plin.* ... a paire of organes. **1589** RIDER L→E *Hydraula, organista, Psaltes, m.* An organe plaier. *Hydraulicus, ad.* Pertaining to organes. *Hydraulus, m. Hydraulis, f. Organum pneumaticum, n.* A paire of organes. **1611** COTGRAVE Fr→E *Hydraulique. voix hy.* The sound of (running) waters; or Musicke made thereby. **1658** PHILLIPS (1st edn) *Hydraulicks*, (Greek) certain water-works, whereby musick is made by the running of waters. **1676** COLES *Hydraulicks, Greek.* musical water-works. **1704** *Cocker's Engl. Dict.* (1st edn) *Hydraulicks*, Musical water works. **1706** KERSEY-PHILLIPS (6th edn) *Hydraulicks*, ... The Word in *Greek* signifies Sounding-Water, because the Ancients made use of falling Waters to get Wind into Organ-pipes, instead of Bellows. *Hydraulus*, a Musical Instrument, an Organ that plays by the motion of Water. **1730** BAILEY *Dict. Britannicum* (1st edn) *Hydraulick Organ*, an Organ which plays by the means of Water. *Hydraulicks* (ὑδραυλικός of ὑδραυλος, sounding Water, of ὕδωρ, Water, and αὐλός, Gr. a Pipe) pertaining to a Water Organ.

hylariani
1586 ANON. *Praise of Mvsicke* (p. 111) For in the time of Saint *Hylary* Bishoppe of *Poyters* in *Fraunce*, it is testified by *Isidorus* that this custome [of singing hymns from the book of Psalms] was confirmed in the church. In somuch that *Hylary* himselfe a man of wonderful eloquence, made *Hymnes* which were song in his church & called after his name *Hylariani*.

hymen *see* bridal, epigonium, epithalamy, hillulim, marriage music, nuptial, thalassion
1538 ELYOT L→E § *Concelebrare plateam hymeneo*, to make ioye abrode with synginge and daunsyng in the honour of mariage. **1565** COOPER L→E *Hymen, minis, n.g.* ... Also a songe songen at weddynges. *Hymenæus*. Mariage: a songe or verses songe at mariage. **1587** THOMAS L→E *Hymen, nis, n.g. p.b.* *... also a song sung at weddinges. *Hymeneus, nei, m.g. p.b. Iun.* Mariage, also a song sung at a mariage. **1589** RIDER L→E *Hymeneus, m. talassio, thalassio, f. thalassus, m. epithalmium, n. Hymen.* A song at a bridal, or mariage. **1611** COTGRAVE Fr→E *Hymenée: f.* ... also, a wedding song, or song of ioy at a wedding; **1613** CAWDREY (3rd edn) *hymen*, songs sung at marriages. **1616** BULLOKAR *Hymen.* A poeticall word, it is taken for the God of marriage, sonne vnto *Bacchus* and *Venus*; and sometime for a

song at a mariage feast. **1656** BLOUNT (1st edn) *Hymen* (Gr.) the God of marriages, or a song sung at marriages. The Greeks at their marriages were wont to sing *Hymen, Hymenæe*, as the Romans did *Talassio, Talassio.* **1676** COLES *Hymen, -næus*, Son of *Bacchus* and *Venus*, the God (or first instituter) of Marriage, also a nuptial or wedding Song. **1704** *Cocker's Engl. Dict.* (1st edn) *Hymen*, the God of Marriage; sometimes a Marriage Song.

hymn *see* alleluia, anthem, canticle, canto, carol, dithyramb, doxology, gloria in excelsis, hylariani, lauds, missura, ode, pæan, primer, procession, psalm, salve regina, song, Te Deum, trisagium, venitarium

1500 *Ortus Vocabulorum* L→E Himnus ni. i. laus dei cum cantico. angl. an hympue [sic]. m.s. § Himnus cum cantu: laus facta deo phibet Aspires primam p. non intercipiet. **1538** ELYOT L→E *Hymnus*, a praise in a songe. **1550** THOMAS It→E *Himno*, an hympne, or a praisyng songe. **1552** HULOET L→E *Hymnus, pæan.* Hympne, psalme, or prayse in a songe **1565** COOPER L→E *Hymnus, huius hymni, m.g. Martial.* A prayse in a songe: an hymne. **1587** THOMAS L→E *Hymnifer, a, um, Ovid.* Bringing forth himmes or songes. *Hymnus, ni, m g. Mart.* A song in the praise of one: an hymme. **1589** RIDER L→E *Hymnizo, psallo.* To sing Hymnes. *Hymnus, m. enchomium, n.* A song in the commendation of a mans vertue. *Hymnus, pean.* A Hymne. **1598** FLORIO It→E *Hinno*, a hymne, a praising song. **1599** MINSHEU-PERCYVALL Sp→E **Himno*, m. a song, a dittie, a hymne, a psalme, singing to the praise of God. **Hymnos*, m. songs to the praise of God. **1604** CAWDREY (1st edn) *hymne*, (Greeke) kinde of song to the prayse of GOD. **1611** COTGRAVE Fr→E *Hymne: m.* A hymne; a song of praise. **1611** FLORIO It→E *Hinno*, a Himne, a praising song. **1616** BULLOKAR *Hymne.* A song to praise God. **1623** COCKERAM *Hymne.* A song. **1658** PHILLIPS (1st edn) *Hymne*, (Greek) a spiritual Song, or Psalm sung to the praise of God. **1659** TORRIANO-FLORIO It→E *Hinno*, a hymn, a song of praises. **1676** COLES *Hymn, Greek.* a Psalm or sacred Song. *Hymniferous*, bringing or making hymns. **1688** MIEGE-COTGRAVE Fr→E *Hymne*, (fem, and sometimes masc.) an Hymn, or spiritual Song; a praising piece of Poetry. **1702** KERSEY *New Engl. Dict.* (1st edn) A *Hymn*, or spiritual song. **1704** *Cocker's Engl. Dict.* (1st edn) *Hymn*, a Psalm, or sacred song. **1706** KERSEY-PHILLIPS (6th edn) *Hymn*, a Spiritual Song, or Psalm sung to the Praise of God. **1708** KERSEY *Dict. Anglo-Brit.* (1st edn) *Hymn*, a Spiritual Song, or Psalm. **1721** BAILEY *An Univ. Etymolog. Engl. Dict.* (1st edn) *Hymniferous, (Hymnifer, L.)* bringing or producing Hymns. **1724** [PEPUSCH] *Short Explic. of Foreign Words in Mus. Bks.* (p. 39) *Inno*, a Hymn or Spiritual Song. **1726** BAILEY *An Univ. Etymolog. Engl. Dict.* (3rd edn) *Inno* (in *Musick-Books,*) signifies a Hymn, or Spiritual Son[g]. *Ital.* **1728** CHAMBERS *Hymn*, a Song or Ode in Honour of God; or, a Poem proper to be sung, compos'd in Honour of some Deity. See *Song* and *Ode.* ¶ The *Hymns* or Odes of the Ancients generally consisted of three Stanzas or Couplets; the first call'd *Strophe*; the second, *Antistrophe;* and the last *Epode*. See *Strophe, Antistrophe,* and *Epode.* ¶ The Word is form'd of the *Greek*, ὕμνος, *Hymn*, of the Verb ὕδω, *celebro*, I celebrate.—*Isidore*, on this Word, remarks, that *Hymn* is properly a Song of Joy, full of the Praises of God; by which, according to him, it is distinguish'd from *Threna*, which is a mourning Song, full of Lamentation. See *Threna.* ¶ St. *Hilary*, Bishop of *Poictiers*, is said to have been the first that compos'd *Hymns* to be sung in Churches: He was follow'd by St. *Ambrose.* Most of those in the *Roman* Breviary were compos'd by *Prudentius.* They have been translated into *French* Verse by the Messieurs *de Port Royal.* See *Psalm.* ¶ The *Te Deum* is also commonly call'd a *Hymn*, tho' it be not in Verse; so is the *Gloria in excelsis.* See *Te Deum* and *Gloria in excelsis.* ¶ In the *Greek* Liturgy, there are four Kinds of *Hymns*; but then the Word is not taken in the Sense of a Praise offer'd in Verse, but simply of Laud or Praise.—The Angelic *Hymn*, or *Gloria in excelsis*, makes the first Kind; the Trisagion the second; the Cherubic *Hymn* the third; and the *Hymn* of Victory and Triumph, call'd ἐπινίκιον, the last. See *Trisagion.* **1730** BAILEY *Dict. Britannicum* (1st edn) A *Hymn* (ὕμνος of ὑμνωδέω Gr. to celebrate) a Song or Ode in honour of God; or a Poem proper to be sung in honour of some Deity. § *Inno* (in *Mus. Books*) a Hymn or spiritual Song. **1737** DYCHE-PARDON (2nd edn) *Hymn* (S.) a religious Song or Ode, at first used by the Heathens in Praise of their false Deities, and afterwards introduced both into the *Jewish* and *Christian* Church; it frequently is used as synonymous to the Words Canticle, Song or Psalm; 'tis supposed when it is said that Christ having supped, sung an Hymn, &c. that it was one of the Psalms the *Jews* used to sing, after they had eaten the Passover.

1737 BANNER *Use and Antiquity of Musick* (pp. 1-2) My Business being at present to speak ... to explain ... and to shew, how those several Terms of Psalms,

Hymns and Spiritual Songs, tho' each of them are included under the general Term of Thanksgiving, are yet notwithstanding, distinguished and differenced one from another. An Hymn then is properly a Song of Praise only. An Ode, or Spiritual Song, contains not only the Praises of God, but likewise Arguments of Exhortation, Excitements to Vertue and the like. These two may be the Subject both of our private as well as publick Devotions, but Psalms seem to be appropriated to the publick Service of God in the Temple, being always accompanied with the Psaltery, Harp, or other Instruments of Musick, exciting and assisting Us to praise God with all our might.

hymnicanus

1500 *Ortus Vocabulorum* L→E Hymnicanus: & hymnidicus. a synger or a seyer of ympnes. m.s. **1589** RIDER L→E *Hymnicanus, hymnicinus.* A singer of hymnes.

hymniferous

1656 BLOUNT (1st edn) *Hymniferous (hymnifer)* that bringeth hymns.

hymnigrapher

1500 *Ortus Vocabulorum* L→E Hymnigraphus phi. i. scriptor hymnorum a wryter of ympnes. m.s. **1589** RIDER L→E *Hymnigraphus, m.* A writer of hymnes. **1656** BLOUNT (1st edn) *Hymnigrapher (hymnigraphus)* a writer of hymns. **1676** COLES *Hymnigrapher,* a writer of hymns.

hymnist

1500 *Ortus Vocabulorum* L→E Himnista te. q facit vel cantat himnos. c.p. **1656** BLOUNT (1st edn) *Hymnist (hymnista)* a singer of hymns. **1676** COLES *Hymnist,* a singer of hymns.

hymnology

1730 BAILEY *Dict. Britannicum* (1st edn) *Hymnology* (ὑμνολογία, Gr.) a singing of hymns or psalms.

hymnopolist

1730 BAILEY *Dict. Britannicum* (1st edn) *Hymnopolist* (ὑμνοπώλους, Gr.) a seller of hymns.

hypate *see* diagram, hyper-hypate, parhypate

1587 THOMAS L→E *Hypate, Iun.* A base or base string: that string that maketh the base sound. *Hypate hypaton, Iun.* B. mi. *Hypate meson, Iun.* F. la. mi. **1589** RIDER L→E *Hypate.* The base string. **1611** COTGRAVE Fr→E *Hipate: f.* A sixt; or the proportion of six, in Musicke. **1611** FLORIO It→E *Ipate,* a string of any musicall instrument that is euer graue. **1659** TORRIANO-FLORIO It→E **Hipate,* the proportion of six in Musick.

early 18th C. PEPUSCH various papers BL Add. 29429, f. 6 Hypate hypaton, i.e. y[e] first, or Principal, String, Sound or Note of y[e] first Tetrachord, in both y[e] Ac: and Gr: Parhypate Hypat, y[e] nexfollowing [sic] to Hyp: hypat. Lychanos hypaton, y[e] Index to y[e] foregoing Hypate Meson, y[e] first Sound of y[e] Meson Tetrachd. **1721** MALCOLM *Treatise of Musick* (p. 519) While the *Lyre* was *Tetra.* (or had but Four Strings) these were called in order from the *gravest* Sound *Hypate, Parhypate, Paranete, Nete;* which Names are taken from their Place in the *Diagram,* in which anciently they set the *gravest* uppermost, or their Situation in the *Lyre,* hence called *Hypate, i.e. suprema, (Chorda, scil.)* the next is *parhypate, i.e. subsuprema* or *juxta [s]upremam;* then *Paranete, i.e. penultima* or *juxta ultimam,* and then *Nete, i.e. ultima* ... **1731** PRELLEUR *Modern Musick-Master* ('A Brief History of Musick', p. 6) *Explanation of the Names by which the* Greeks *used to Distinguish their Notes....* The lowest *Tetrachord* they called *Tetrachordon Hypaton* that is to say *Tetrachord of the Prin[ci]pals.* The lowest String of this *Tetrachord* was called *Hypate Hypaton,* which signifies the *Principal of the Principals;* this answers to our *B mi* in the Bass. ¶ The next was called *Parhypate Hypaton,* which signifies near y[e] *Principal of Principals;* this note is a *Semitone* sharper than y[e] former and answers to *C-fa-ut.* ¶ The next was called *Lycanos Hypaton* or *Hypaton Diatonos,* that is to say the *Index of the Principals,* or a *Principal extended;* this answers to *D-sol-re*[.] This *Tetrachord* had but three Strings the uppermost being the same as the lowest in the next *Tetrachord* by reason of their joyning them ...

hyperbolæon *see* diagram

1721 MALCOLM *Treatise of Musick* (p. 523) [*re* development of the ancient lyre] At length another Tetrachord was added, called *Hyperbolæon* (*i.e. excellentium* or *excedentium*) the acutest of all; which being conjunct with the *Diezeugmenon,* the *Nete Diezeugmenon* was its gravest Chord, the other Three being called *Trite, Paranete,* and *Nete Hyperbolæon;* ... **1731** PRELLEUR *Modern Musick-Master* ('A Brief History of Musick', pp. 6-7) *Explanation of the Names by which the* Greeks *used to Distinguish their Notes....* The next *Tetrachord* was Called *Tetracordon Hyperboleon,* or *Tetrachord of the Acutest* or *the most Excellent.*

There are but three Strings in this *Tetrachord* because the lowest is the same as y[e] highest in the last they being joyned in the same manner as the two lowest *Tetrachords* are: I shall therefore proceed to the next String w[ch.] they called *Trite Hyperboleon*, that is to say the *Third Excellent;* this answers to our *F-fa-ut.* ¶ The next was called *Paranete Hyperboleon*, or *Hyperboleon Diatonos*, i.e[.] *the last but one of the Acutest*, this answers to our *G-sol-re[-]ut* the Treble Clif. *Nete-Hyperboleon* is the name they gave to the highest String on this *Tetrachord*, which signifies the *Acutest* or the *highest excellent;* this note answers to *A-la-mi-re*, the note above the Treble Clif.

hyper-hypate

1721 Malcolm *Treatise of Musick* (p. 521) ... there was another *octichord Lyre* attributed to *Terpander;* where instead of disjoining the Two Tetrachords of the *septichord Lyre*, he added another Chord a *Tone* lower than *Hypate*, called *Hyper-hypate, i.e. super supremam*, because it stood above in the *Diagram;* or *Proslambanomenos, i.e. assumptus*, because it belonged to none of the Two Tetrachords: The rest of the Names were unchanged.

hyper-hyperbolæon

1721 Malcolm *Treatise of Musick* (p. 555) [*re* the reforms of Guido d'Arezzo] Above *Nete Hyperbolæon* he added [an]other 4 Chords, which he made a new disjunct *Tetrachord*, he called *Hyper-hyperbolæon;* so that his whole *Scale* contained 20 *diatonick Notes*, (for this was the only *Genus* now used) besides the *b* flat, which corresponded to the *Trite Synemmenon* of the Ancients, and made what was afterwards called the Series of *b molle* ...

hypermixolydian *see* mixolydian

1586 Anon. *Praise of Mvsicke* (pp. 54-5) ... for *Plutarck* in his treatise of musick recordeth that *Modi Musici* were also distinguished by the names of nations: such were principally these foure, *Modos Dorius, Modus Phrygius, Modus Lydius*, and *Modus Myxolydius.* Hereunto were added as collaterall other three, *Hypodorius, Hypolydius*, and *Hypophrygius*: making seuen in number, aunswerable to the 7. planets: whereunto *Ptolomæus* added an 8. which is called *Hypermyxolydius*, sharpest of them al and attributed to the firmament.

hypodiapente *see* diapente

1597 Morley *Plaine and Easie Introdvction* (p. 100) ... if your Canon be in the fourth, and the lower part lead, if you sing the leading part an eight higher, your Canon will be in *Hypodiapente*, which is the fift below, and by the contrarie, if your Canon be in the fift, the lower part leading, if you sing the leading part an eight higher, your Canon wil bee in *hypodiatessaron*, or in the fourth below.

hypodorian *see* dorick

hypolydian *see* lydian

hypophrygian *see* phrygian

hyporchemata *see* style (stylo hyperchematico)

1712 Weaver *Essay towards History of Dancing* (p. 12) [*re* dance traditions in ancient times] ... And their Songs deriv'd the Name of *Hyporchemata*, from being used with *Dancing*.

I

idoraula

1500 *Ortus Vocabulorum* L→E Idoraula le. i. sonus organi vel genus organorum. f.p.

imitation *see* fugue, simple

1724 [Pepusch] *Short Explic. of Foreign Words in Mus. Bks.* (p. 39) *Imitatione*, or *Imitazione*, Imitation, by which is meant a particular Way of Composition, wherein each Part is made to Imitate each other. **1726** Bailey *An Univ. Etymolog. Engl. Dict.* (3rd edn) *Imitatione, Imitazzione*, (in *Musick-Books*) denotes a particular Way of Composition, wherein each Part is made to imitate each other. *Ital.* **1728** Chambers *Imitation*, in Music, is where one Party imitates the singing of another either throughout the whole Piece, which is one of the Kinds of Canon, or only during some Measures, which is a simple *Imitation.* Sometimes the Motion or the Figure of the Notes, alone, is imitated; and that, sometimes even by a contrary Motion, which makes what they call a Retrograde *Imitation*. The *Imitation* differs from the Fugue, in regard, in the former the Repetition must be a 2d, a 3d, a 6th, 7th, or 9th, either above or below the first Voice: Whereas were the Repetition to an Unison a 4th, 5th, or 8th, it would be a Fugue.

1694 PURCELL-PLAYFORD *Intro. to Skill of Musick* (12th edn, 'A Brief Introduction to the Art of Descant', n.p.) There is another diminutive sort of Fugeing called *Imitation* or *Reports*; which is, when you begin *Counterpoint*, and answer the *Treble* in some few Notes as you find occasion when you set a *Bass* to it. **1731** [PEPUSCH] *Treatise on Harmony* (2nd edn, pp. 87-8) A Simple *Imitation* appears to the Eye like a *Fugue*, its *Parts* seeming to proceed in the *same manner*, if we only consider the *Lines* and *Spaces* on which they are written. In *these* the *Answer* may be made to follow the *Guide* in any *Interval*; as, of a 2^d^, 3^d^, 4th, 5th, 6th, 7th. *&c.* But, as in *all* these Cases, the *several Parts* do not strictly proceed by the *same Intervals*, (the *Semitones* being plac'd differently in *one Part* from what they are in *another*) they are not properly to be call'd *Fugues*, but *Imitations* only. That the *Intervals* in these *Imitations* are not *Similar* in the *Guide* and *Answers*, is easily discover'd by their not *solfaing alike*; ... **1736** TANS'UR *Compleat Melody* (3rd edn, p. 71) *Imitation, Imitatione, Imitazzione,* (Ital.) signifies a way of Composing, where *Parts* are made to immitate one another.

immodulatus *see* modulation
1565 COOPER L→E *Immodulatus, Adiectiuum: vt Poemata immodulata. Horat...* without proportion or melodie. **1587** THOMAS L→E *Immodulatus, a, um, adiect.* Without proportion: without melodie. **1589** RIDER L→E *Immodulatus, ad.* Without melodie.

immusical
1656 BLOUNT (1st edn) *Immusical*, that hath no musick or harmony. **1676** COLES *Immusical*, having no musick or harmony. **1704** *Cocker's Engl. Dict.* (1st edn) *Immusical*, without harmony. **1726** BAILEY *An Univ. Etymolog. Engl. Dict.* (3rd edn) *Immusical*, not Harmonious, not Musical.

imperfect *see* imperfection
1736 TANS'UR *Compleat Melody* (3rd edn, p. 30) The meaning of the Word *Imperfect*, signifies that it wants a *Semitone* of its Perfection to what it does when it is *Perfect*; for as the *Lesser*, or *Imperfect*, or *Minor Third* includes three *Half-Tones*; the *Greater*, or *Perfect*, or *Major Third*, includes four *Half-Tones*, &c.

imperfect cadence *see* half cadence
1636 BUTLER *Principles of Musik* (p. 67) The Imperfect Cadence dooeth signifie very little rest, either of Harmoni or of Ditti: but that they ar bothe to proceede further: and it differeth from the perfect in the third or least Note: which either it silenceth ... or mooveth from the proper key of an Eight or Unison, to soom other: ... **early 18th C.** NORTH (Prendcourt's) Treatis of Continued or Through Basse BL Add. 32549, f. 27v Imperfect close is that when a final note falls downe a fourth instead of a fifth, this is frequently used in church musick and then ye penultiue note is figured with a 5b. and this is called an Imperfect cadence... **c.1710** NORTH (Prendcourt's) Treatise of Continued or thro-base BL Add. 32531, f. 39 [quoting Prendcourt:] An Imperfect close is that when a finall Note falls down a fourth Instead of a fifth, this is frequently used in church musick and then the penultime note is figured with a 5b. and this is called an Imperfect Cadence.

imperfect concord *see* concord
1597 MORLEY *Plaine and Easie Introdvction* (p. 71) *Phi.* What is an *vnperfect concord?* ¶ *Ma. It is that which maketh not a full sound, and needeth the following of a perfect concord to make it stand in the harmonie....* [They are] A third, a sixt, and their eightes: a tenth, a thirteenth, &c.

imperfect fifth *see* semidiapente

imperfect fourth *see* tritone
1724 TURNER *Sound Anatomiz'd* (p. 11) The *Fourth* may become a *Discord* to the *Base* two Ways; *First*, by extending the *Base* ... which is the Quantity of a *major Third*, but yet is a *Discord*, and may be called an *imperfect Fourth*; but is seldom used.

imperfection *see* discolouration, imperfect
1596 ANON. *Pathway to Musicke* [D iii] *Of Imperfection and vvhat it is.* ¶ Imperfection is the taking avvay of the third part of the value of the perfect note, vvhich containe three of the lesse, and is only in perfect degrees. **1597** MORLEY *Plaine and Easie Introdvction* (p. 24) *Phi.* What is *imperfection?* ¶ *Ma. It is the taking away of the third part of a perfect notes value,* and is done three maner of wayes, *By note, rest, or cullor.* Imperfection by note, is when before or after anie

note there commeth a note of the next lesse value ... By rest, when after any note there commeth a rest of the next lesse value ... Imperfection by coullor, is when notes perfect are prickt blacke, which taketh awaie the third part of their value ... **1609** DOWLAND-ORNITHOPARCUS *Micrologvs* (p. 54) Wherefore *Imperfection* is the degrading of perfect Notes. For to imperfect is to make a perfect Note imperfect. Or it is this, to bring it from his value...

imperfect of the less *see* dupla, mood, semibreve time, whole time
1654 PLAYFORD *Breefe Intro. to Skill of Musick* (p. 17) The fourth and last Mood, which is the *Imperfect of the Lesse*, is when all goes by two, as two Longs to a Large, two Briefs to a Long, two Sembriefs to a Briefe, two Minims to a Sembriefe, two Crochets to a Minim, &c. and this is called the Duple or Sembrief Time, and this *Mood* is thus marked ₵, and is usuall in Songs, Fantasies, Pavins and Almans, and the like. **1665** SIMPSON *Principles of Practical Mvsick* (pp. 18-19) *Of the Old Moods....* The *fourth Mood* they named *Imperfect of the Less*, which we call the *Common Mood;* the other three being (in a manner) worn out of use.... In this last or *Common Mood, two Longs* make a *Large; two Breves*, a *Long; two Semibreves*, a *Breve*, &c. **1667** PLAYFORD *Brief Intro. to Skill of Musick* (4th edn, p. 34) The *fourth* or last *Mood* which is called the *Imperfect of the Less* ... is called the Duple or *Semibrief Time*, (many call it the *Common Time*, because most used) ...

imperfect of the more *see* galliard time, mood, tripla
1654 PLAYFORD *Breefe Intro. to Skill of Musick* (p. 16) *The Imperfect of the More*, is when all goes by two, except the Minims, which goes by three, as two Longs to a Large, two Briefs to a Long, two Sembriefs to a Briefe, three Minims to a Sembriefe, with a prick of Augmentation (else it would not beare the proportion of three Minims, which is called a Time) and two Crochets to a Minim, &c. his Mood is thus signed Ͼ and this is called the Triple Time.... This Mood is much used in *Ayery songs* and *Galliards*, and is usually called *Galliard* or *Triple time*, and this *Triple time* is in some Lessons, as *Coranto's, Sarabands*, and *Jigs* brought into a Measure, as swift againe, for as before three Minims or Sembriefs with a prick made a Time, in this three Crochets makes a Time, or one Minim with a prick, and this measure is knowne by this signe or mark 3j, which is usually called *Three to one.* **1665** SIMPSON *Principles of Practical Mvsick* (p. 18) *Of the Old Moods....* The *third Mood* was *Imperfect of the more.* In which a *Large* contained two *Longs*, a *Long*, two *Breves;* a *Breve*, two *Semibreves;* and a *Semibreve*, three *Minims...*

improvisation *see* provisanti
1598 FLORIO It→E *Improuisare*, to sing or speake extempore. *Improuisatore*, a speaker or singer extempore. **1611** FLORIO It→E *Improuisare*, to sing, or say extempore. **1659** TORRIANO-FLORIO It→E *Improvisatore, Improvisore*, one that sings or speaks ex tempore.

imus sonus *see* graviter sonare, medius, sonus summus
1552 HULOET L→E *Imus sonus, uel Tonus.* Base in musyke. **1565** COOPER L→E *Imus sonus. Plin.* The base in songe and musike.

incension *see* harmony, incino
1538 ELYOT L→E *Incentio, onis*, the sowning of instrumentes. **1552** HULOET L→E *Incentio. onis* Soundynge of instrumentes. **1565** COOPER L→E *Incentio, huius incentiônis, f.g. Gell.* Harmonie or melodie of instrumentes, or of men singyng together. **1587** THOMAS L→E *Incentio, onis, f.g. verb. ab. Incino, Gel.* Harmony or melody of instruments, or of men singing togither: *Incentivum, vi, n.g. Pli. Iun.* ... the assay, triall, or proofe that musicians vse to make before their instruments or voices fall in tune. **1589** RIDER L→E *Incentio, f.* Melodie of instrumentes, or men singing together. *Incentivum, n.* The proofe that minstrels make before their instrumenes [sic] bee in tune. **1656** BLOUNT (1st edn) *Incension (ab incino)* melody of Instruments, or of men singing together. **1676** COLES *Incension, Latin.* Musick in Consort. **1704** *Cocker's Engl. Dict.* (1st edn) *Incension*, ... also a Consort of Musick.

incentor *see* intercentor, intercentus, intercino
1587 THOMAS L→E *Incentor, oris, m.g.* *He that stingeth [sic] the descant. **1589** RIDER L→E *Incentor, m.* A singer of descant. *Intercentus, m.* The meane in a song. **1656** BLOUNT (1st edn) *Incentor* (Lat.) he that singeth the descant. In singing there are three degrees, the first *Succentor*, the second *Incentor*, and the third *Accentor. Rider.* **1658** PHILLIPS (1st edn) *Incentor*, (lat.) ... also Incentor, Accentor, and Succentor, are three sorts of Singers in parts. **1676** COLES *Incentor* ... also a singer of descant, between Succentor and Accentor. **1696** PHILLIPS (5th edn)

Incentor, (Lat.) ... also Incentor, Accentor, and Succentor, are three sorts of Singers in parts. *Accentor*, he that sings the highest. *Incentor*, he that sings the middle part. And *Succentor*, he that sings the lower part. **1704** *Cocker's Engl. Dict.* (1st edn) *Incentor*, a singer of Descant in Musick. **1706** KERSEY-PHILLIPS (6th edn) *Incentor, (Lat.)* ... also one of the three sorts of Singers in Parts; thus *Accentor* is he that sings the highest, or Treble, *Incentor* he that sings the middle part, or Tenour, and *Succentor* he that sings the Bass, or lowest part. **1708** KERSEY *Dict. Anglo-Brit.* (1st edn) *Incentor, (L.)* ... also one of the three sorts of Singers in Parts; he that sings the middle part, or the Tenour.

incino *see* incension

1538 ELYOT L→E *Incino, ni, nere*, to synge, proprely to fayne a small breste. **1552** HULOET L→E *Incino. is* Syng a tryple properly to feyne a smal breast **1565** COOPER L→E *Incino, íncinis, pen. corr. incínui, incentum, incínere. Propert.* To singe: to feine a small voice: to sowne pleasantly and with melodie. **1587** THOMAS L→E *Incino, is, nui, entum, ere, ex In & Cano, Prop.* To sing: properly to faine a smal boeast: to sound pleasantly and with melodie. **1589** RIDER L→E *Incino.* To faine in singing.

inconcinnous *see* concinnous, system

increspare la voce

1659 TORRIANO-FLORIO It→E *Increspare la voce*, to quaver with ones voice in singing.

index *see* direct, mostra

1724 [PEPUSCH] *Short Explic. of Foreign Words in Mus. Bks.* (p. 39) *Index*, is a little Mark at the End of each Line in Musick, shewing what Note the next Line begins with, this being a *Latin* Word, is called by the *Italians Mostra*, and by the *French Guidon*. **1726** BAILEY *An Univ. Etymolog. Engl. Dict.* (3rd edn) *Index* (in *Musick Books*) is a little Mark at the End of each Line of a Tune, shewing what Note the next Line begins with. The same that the *French* call *Guidon*, and the *Italians Mostra*.

1736 TANS'UR *Compleat Melody* (3rd edn, p. 67) *Index.* (E.) *Guidon.* (Fr.) *Monstra* (Ital.) Either of those Terms is a *Name* given to this *Character* [music symbol] which we call a *Direct*.

indico

1598 FLORIO It→E *Indico*, ... Also a kinde of musicall instrument with strings. **1611** FLORIO It→E *Indico*, a precious stone in India that is euer sweating. Also blew Inde. Also a kinde of musicall instrument with strings.

induction

1597 MORLEY *Plaine and Easie Introdvction* (p. 92) [marginalia: 'Inductions & what they be.'] Here they set downe certaine obseruations, which they termed *Inductions*, as here you see in the first two barres *Sesqui altra* perfect [gives example]: that they called the induction to nine, to two, which is *Quadrupla Sesquialtra*. In the third barre you haue broken *sesquialtra*, & the rest to the end is *Quadrupla sesquialtra*, or as they termed it, nine to two, and euerie proportion whole, is called the Induction to that which it maketh being broken. As tripla being broken in the more prolation, wil make *Nonupla*, & so is tripla the Induction to *nonupla*: Or in the lesse prolation wil make *sextupla*, and so is the induction to *sextupla*: ...

infigura *see* tablature

1611 FLORIO It→E *Infigura*, ... Also set as a song. **1659** TORRIANO-FLORIO It→E *Infigura*, ... also set as a song in tablature

inflatus *see* classicum, cornicen, tibia

1565 COOPER L→E *Inflo, inflas, inflâre.* ... to blow in an instrument. § *Audierant inflari classica. Virg.* They hearde the trumpets blowen. *Buccinam inflare. Varro.* To blowe a trumpette. *Inflare sonum. Cic.* To make a sowne with a pipe: to blowe in an instrument. **1587** THOMAS L→E *Inflatus, us, m.g.* ... a blowing in an instrument: *Inflo, as.* ... to blow in an instrument **1589** RIDER L→E *Inflo.* To blow in an instrument.

ingenuity

1737 DYCHE-PARDON (2nd edn) *Ingenuity* or *Ingeniousness* (S.) the natural and improved Disposition, Skill, or Parts of a Person that produces fine Works, Writings, Paintings, or Performances of any Sort.

in nomine *see* fuga in nomine, plainsong

c.1698-c.1703 NORTH Cursory Notes (*C-K CN* pp. 211-12) When the church musick was in request; it was much in use to descant as they called it upon plain song, which plain song was some himne used in devine service; and particularly one called; In Nomine; whither it was used in the same notes, as the plain song was allwais, I thinck not worth inquiry nor easy finding out. But the In Nomines I have met with were onely the 8 notes, which might be sung, with the sillables In, No, mi, ne, Do, mi, ni, or ut, re, mi, fa, sol, la. And these 8 notes were to be sounded by some midle voice, very loud and strong; and both base and upper parts, descant upon them, working about with fuges, sincops, and such ornaments as they had then in use, allwaies holding fair with the plainesong, whose motions were religiously complyed with. And this useth to be done with voices, and pretended to be extempore, mostly, as I suppose, the practise of monks and church men. **c.1710** NORTH (draft for) Musicall Grammarian BL Add. 32537, f. 101 [*re* compositions on plainsong melodies] ... and made descants upon them. as that they call In Nomine; as also ye 6. notes of ye Scale they used to ye same porpose. In ye managem^t^ of wch They Introduced all the modulation of harmony that could be Imagined, with wonderfull subtilety making 4. or 5. parts move with a plain song In ye midst driving points, & comixing discords plentifully, notwithstanding the great confinem^t^ of ye plain sing [sic]. **c.1726** NORTH Musicall Gramarian BL Add. 32533, ff. 157-8 [marginalia: 'Old musick sung or playd on a plainsong & called In Nomine'] ... The first of these, of wch I have seen coppy's of 4. 5. & 6. parts were descants upon plaine song. The plain song was an order of plaine notes of considerable length perhap's a large or .2. breifs; ⊨. very often the Gamut Notes ascending or descending, wch were sung to ye syllables of—In nomine domini,—The Descant was the working of the parts attending, with Intire Regard to the Harmony. Not onely of the plainsong, But also of each other, with perpetuall and Intermiscuous syncopation's and halvings of notes amongst them, there scarce passing a note without a discord (as they accounted them) halved upon it, and striktly tyed to ye authentick rules; And this sort of Consort was called an In Nomine, and Divers past about under the Great Master's names that composed them, who were admired and valued accordingly. and I presume these were first designed for voices, and as Instruments came in use devolved upon them; and when the humour began to Refine, they left ye dull series of Graduall plainesong, and took other Notes, that looked towards Ayre; and any part back the plain song, Except the base, wch I never saw in that office, and seldome ye treble, but for ye Most part the tenor held ye plow. The last of these In Nomines (for they were all so called) was a 6p^t^ consort of W^m^ [sic] Jenkins who afterwards turned Reformer, and with very great success ... **1728** NORTH Musicall Grammarian (*C-K MG* f. 126v) [*re* descanting upon plainsong in England] ... And I guess that in some times, litle of other consort musick was coveted or in use, but that which was styled In Nomine was yet more remarkable, for it was onely descanting upon the 8 notes with which the sillables (In Nomine Domine) agreed. And of this kind I have seen whole volumes, of many parts, with the several authors' names (for honour) inscribed.

insono

1565 COOPER L→E *Insono, ínsonas, pen. corr. insónui, insonâre. Lucan.* To sowne: to play on a pipe or like instrument. **1587** THOMAS L→E *Insono, as, Luc.* To sound, to plaie on a pipe or like instrument, to make a noyse. **1598** FLORIO It→E *Insonare,* to sound or play vpon an instrument.

insonoro

1599 MINSHEU-PERCYVALL Sp→E *Insonoro,* vntunable, that cannot be set in tune.

inspective music *see* harmonic music

1609 DOWLAND-ORNITHOPARCUS *Micrologvs* (p. 2) *Inspectiue Musicke,* is a knowledge censuring and pondering the Sounds formed with naturall instruments, not by the eares, whose iudgement is dull, but by wit and reason.

instrument

1598 FLORIO It→E *Instrumento,* ... a musicall instrument *Stormento,* any kind of musicall instrument *Stromento,* ... an instrument of musike. § *Sonare d'instrumento,* to play vpon any instrument. **1599** MINSHEU-PERCYVALL Sp→E *Instrumento,* m. ... an instrument of musicke. **1611** FLORIO It→E *Stormento,* any kind of instrument either musicall or mechanicall. *Stromento,* any kind of toole or instrument mechanicall or musicall. § *Sonare d'instrumento,* to play on instruments. *Stromento di fiato,* a winde instrument. **1659** TORRIANO-FLORIO It→E **Stromentista,* a player on instruments. § *Sonare d'istrumento,* to sound or play upon an instrument. **1688** MIEGE-COTGRAVE Fr→E *Instrument,* (m.) ... a musical instrument; § *Je n'aime pas ce Instrumens dont l'harmonie est bruyante & tumultueuse,* I don't like those musical Instruments that make a loud and obstreperous noise. *Jouër de quêque Instrument*, to play upon an Instrument. *Jouër de quêque Instrument de Musique*, to play upon an Instrument of Musick. *Un Jouëur d'Instrumens*, a Player upon Instruments. **1702** KERSEY *New Engl. Dict.* (1st edn) A Mathematical, *or* Musical ¶ *Instrument-maker*. **1724** [PEPUSCH] *Short Explic. of Foreign Words in Mus. Bks.* (p. 73) *Stromento*, Instrument. **1737** DYCHE-PARDON (2nd edn) *Instrument* (S.) ... in a particular Manner, all Sorts of Musical Instruments;

instrumental music *see* style (stylo symphoniaco)

1609 DOWLAND-ORNITHOPARCUS *Micrologvs* (pp. 1-2) *Instrumentall Musicke*, is an Harmony which is made by helpe of *Instruments*. And because Instruments are either artificiall, or naturall, there is one sort of Musicke which is made with artificiall Instruments; another, which is made with naturall instruments. The Philosophers call the one *Harmonicall*; the other *Organicall*.

intavolatura *see* tablature

integer tonus *see* diatonic

1704 GORTON *Catechetical Questions in Musick* (pp. 26-7) *Q*. What is the difference between a Sound and Note? ¶ *A*. A Sound is the thing exprest, but a Note is the difference between any two sounds and is term'd *Integer Tonus*; and may be according to the distance, a whole Note or a half Note.

intercalarity

1538 ELYOT L→E § *Intercalaris uersus*, a syngular verse, often repeted amonge other verses. Some doo call it, in englyshe balades and songes, the foote or refrette of a ditie. **1589** RIDER L→E § *Versus intercalaris m. Intercalaraitas, f.* The burden of a song. **1656** BLOUNT (1st edn) *Intercalarity (intercalaritas)* the burden of a song; the putting between, as the *burden* is between the *verses*. **1676** COLES *Intercalarity*, the burden of a Song

intercentor *see* incentor

1589 RIDER L→E *Intercentor, m.* He that singeth the meane.

intercentus *see* incentor, medius

1500 *Ortus Vocabulorum* L→E Intercentus tus. a meane of a songe m.s. **1589** RIDER L→E *m.* The meane in a song.

intercino *see* incentor

1538 ELYOT L→E *Intercino, nere*, to synge betwene or in the myddell of a thynge. **1565** COOPER L→E *Intercino, intércinis, pen. corr. intercínui, intercentum, intercínere. Horat.* To singe between or in the middle of a thyng: as between the actes of comedies. **1587** THOMAS L→E *Intercino, is, ui, entum, ere, ex Jnter & Cano, Horat.* To sing betweene or in the middle of a thing, as betweene the acts of Comedies. **1589** RIDER L→E *Intercino, intercento.* To sing between, or to sing a mean.

interlude *see* epicitharisma, exodium, farce, intermedia, jig, joüarre, recitative, song, sorracus, symphony, thymelici, voluntary

1658 PHILLIPS (1st edn) *Interlude*, (lat.) a kind of Stage-play, that which is sung or represented between the several Acts. **1702** KERSEY *New Engl. Dict.* (1st edn) An *Interlude*, that which is done between the acts of a Stage-play. **1707** *Gloss. Angl. Nova* (1st edn) *Interlude*, (Lat.) a Play or Comedy; that which is sung or acted between the Acts. **1708** KERSEY *Dict. Anglo-Brit.* (1st edn) *Interlude*, part of a Stage-Play, that which is sung or represented between the several Acts. **1728** CHAMBERS *Interlude*, an Entertainment exhibited on the Theatre between the Acts of a Play; to amuse the Spectators while the Actors take breath, and shift their Dress; or to give time for changing the Scenes and Decorations. These *Interludes* usually consist of Songs, Dances, Feats of Activity, Consorts of Music, *&c.* In the antient Tragedy, the Chorus sung the *Interludes*, to shew the *Intervals* between the Acts. *Aristotle* and *Horace* give it for a Rule, that the *Interludes* should consist of Songs built on the principal Parts of the Drama: But since the Chorus has been laid down, Dancers, Buffoons, *&c.* ordinarily furnish the *Interludes*. **1735** DEFOE An *Interlude*, that which is sung or represented between two Acts in a Play. **1737** DYCHE-PARDON (2nd edn) *Interlude* (S.) in a *Play*, is any Sort of Amusement or Diversion between the Acts, while the Actors change their Dress to perform the remaining Parts, as Singing, Dancing, &c. in *Musick*, especially in *Church Musick*, and other vocal Performances, it is the voluntary Overture, or other Performance upon one or more Instruments, to give the Quiristers or Songsters Time to recover Breath, &c.

1736 TANS'UR *Compleat Melody* (3rd edn, p. 71) *Interlude, Rescerch* [sic], *Ricercate, Ritornello, Riternello*, (Ital.) Either of those *Terms* is a *Name*

given to short *Airs* or *Symphonies* play'd between many *Strains* of a Piece of *Musick* to grace and ornament it, sometimes by *Rule*, and sometimes *Extempore*.

intermedia *see* intercino
1598 FLORIO It→E *Intermedio, Intermezzo,* ... the musicke that is betweene the actes in a play. **1611** FLORIO It→E *Intermedio,* ... an Intermedium, the musike that is, or shewes that are betweene the acts of a play. **1659** TORRIANO-FLORIO It→E *Intermedio,* ... also the musick or dum-shews that are between the acts of a Play. **1737** DYCHE-PARDON (2nd edn) *Intermedia* (S.) in *Tragedies* and *Comedies*, is that which is played or sung between the Acts, to divert the Spectators; after the *Romans* took away the Chorus, instead thereof they introduced their *Mimi* and *Embolariæ*, the *Mimi* were a Sort of Persons that acted a dumb Comedy, and expressed their Meanings by their Gestures without Words, and the *Embolares* did the same by their Songs and Jests; we now call these Interludes, which see.

intersonant
1587 THOMAS L→E *Intersono, as, ui, are, Stat.* To sound betweene or in the meane season. **1656** BLOUNT (1st edn) *Intersonant (intersonans)* that soundeth between, or in the mean season. **1658** PHILLIPS (1st edn) *Intersonant,* (lat.) sounding between or in the midst.

interval *see* canon, chord, concinnous, concord, cord, diastem, diminished interval, spiss interval
1587 THOMAS L→E *Intervallum, li, n.g.* ... *also* a space or rest in musick, or the taking of the tune, *Vitru.* **1589** RIDER L→E *Intervallum, n.* The distance, or tune in musicke **1656** BLOUNT (1st edn) *Interval (intervallum)* ... also a Rest in Musick. **1696** PHILLIPS (5th edn) *Interval, (Lat.)* a Distance or Space, either of place or time. Said also of Numbers and Proportions, as well in Music as Arithmetick. **1704** HARRIS *Interval,* in Musick, is the Distance or Difference between any two Sounds, whereof one is more Grave, and the other more Acute. They make several Divisions of an *Interval,* as first into *Simple* and *Compound*; the *Simple Intervals*, are the *Octave*, and all that are within it, as the *Second, Third, Fourth, Fifth, Sixth* and *Seventh*, with their Varieties. The *Compound* ones are all those that are greater than an *Octave*, as the *Ninth, Tenth, Eleventh,* &c. with their Varieties. ¶ An *Interval* is also divided into *Just* or *True*, and into *False*: All the above mentioned *Intervals* with their Varieties, whether *Major* or *Minor* are *Just*; but the diminutive or superfluous ones are all *False*: See *Ozanum's Dict. Matth.* p. 653. An *Interval* is also divided into a *Consonance* and a *Dissonance*; which see. **1706** KERSEY-PHILLIPS (6th edn) *Interval,* ... In *Musick* it is the Distance or Difference between any two Sounds, of which one is more grave, and the other more acute. **1707** *Gloss. Angl. Nova* (1st edn) *Interval,* (Lat.) ... also the distance or difference between any two Sounds, whereof one is more grave, and the other more acute. **1728** CHAMBERS *Interval* ... [*see* Appendix] **1737** DYCHE-PARDON (2nd edn) *Interval* (S.) ... in *Musick*, it is the Difference between any two Tones or Notes, as they are Graver or Acuter the one than the other, and this, as it is greater or lesser, constitutes what is called Chords or Discords.

1609 DOWLAND-ORNITHOPARCUS *Micrologvs* (p. 17) An *Interuall* (as *Boêtius*, whose conceit for Musicke, no man euer attained *lib.* 1. *cap.* 8. writeth) is the distance of a base and high sound. Or (as *Placentinus lib.* 2. *cap.* 8. saith) it is the way from lownesse to height, and contrarily. Or it is the distance of one *Voyce* from another, considered by rising and falling. Whence it is manifest, that an *Vnison* is not a *Moode*, although it be the beginning of *Moodes*, as vnitie is of numbers... **1636** BUTLER *Principles of Musik* (p. 46) Intervalls ar the different distances of high and low sounds. ¶ And they ar either Simple, or Compound. ¶ Simple Intervalls ar the distances of all the Sounds within the compas of a Diapason, from their Ground: the which, increasing by half-tones, ar in number twelv: (1 Semitonium, 2 Tonus, 3 Sesquitonium or Semiditonus, 4 Ditonus, 5 Diatessaron, 6 Tritonus or Semidiapente, 7 Diapente, 8 Semitonium-diapente, 9 Tonus-diapente, 10 Semiditonus-diapente, 11 Ditonus-diapente or Semidiapason, 12 Diapason. § (p. 52) *Intervallum est soni acuti gravisq; distantia. Consonantia est acuti soni gravisq; mixtura suaviter auribus accidens. Dissonantia est duorum sonorum fibimet permixtorum ad aurem veniens aspera atq; injucunda percussio.* Boetius l. 1, c. 8. ... **1667** SIMPSON *Compendium of Practical Musick* (p. 37) An *Intervall* in Musick is that Distance or Difference which is betwixt any two Sounds, where the One is more Grave, the other more *Acute*. **c.1700** NORTH Capt. Prencourts rules BL Add. 32549, f. 12v An Intervall is a certein distance from one key to another, wch upon ye lines is from one line to one space, or from one line to other spaces, or from a space to other lines or spaces. **early 18th C.** ANON. Essay on Musick BODLEIAN Rawl. D. 751, f. 2 An Interval is the distance between a grave and an acute sound, & between an acute & a grave sound. **c.1710** NORTH Short, Easy, & plaine rules BL Add. 32531, f. 24v [quoting Prendcourt:] An Intervall is a certein distance from one key to another, w[ch] upon the lines is from one line to one space, or from one line to other spaces or from a space to other lines or spaces. **1721** MALCOLM *Treatise of Musick* (pp. 35-6) If Two or more Sounds are compared ... they are either *equal* or *unequal* in the Degree of *Tune*: ... the *unequal*, being at Distance one from another ... constitute what we call an *Interval* in *Musick*, which is properly the Difference of *Tune* betwixt Two Sounds. § (p. 39) *Intervals* are distinguished into *simple* and *compound*; a *simple Interval* is without Parts or Division; a *compound* consists of several lesser *Intervals*. Now 'tis plain this Distinction has a Regard to Practice only, because there is no such Thing as a least *Interval*: Besides, by a *simple Interval* is not meant here the least practised, but such as, tho' it were equal to Two or more lesser which are in Use, yet, when we would make a Sound move so far up or down, we always pass immediately from its one Term [intervallic member] to the other; what is meant then by a *compound Interval* will be very plain, it is such whose Terms are, in Practice, taken either in immediate Succession, or we make the Sound to rise and fall from the one to the other by touching some intermediate Degrees, so that the Whole is a Composition of all the *Intervals* from one Extreme to the other. What I call a *simple Interval* the Ancients called a *Diastem*; and they called the *compound* a *System*: Each of these has Differences; even of the *simple* there are some greater and lesser, and they are always *Discord*; but of the *compound* or *System*, some are *Concord*, some *Discord*. § (p. 259) We have already settled the Definition of a 3*d*, 4*th*, &c. as they are *harmonical Intervals*, they are either to be taken from the true *Ratios* of their Extremes; or, respecting the *Scale* of *Musick*, from the Number and particular Kinds of *Degrees*; yet we may make a general Definition that will serve any Part of the *Scale*, and call that *Interval*, which is from any Letter of the *Scale* to the 2*d*, 3*d*, 4*th*, &c. *inclusive*, a 2*d*, a 3*d*, a 4*th*, &c. § (p. 502) An *Interval* is the Difference of Two Sounds, in respect of *acute* and *grave*; or, that imaginary Space which is terminated by Two Sounds differing in *Acuteness* or *Gravity*. **1740** LAMPE *Art of Musick* (p. 39) [*re* Zarlino] ... And Chap 15 Part 2. describing an Interval thus: *l'acuto & il grave sono gli estremi dello Intervallo.*

intervalla concinna *see* concinnous

intonation

1598 FLORIO It→E *Intonare*, to make to sound, to tune, to raise the voice, to resound, to tune a voice or instrument. *Intuonare*, ... to tune, to raise the voice. **1599** MINSHEU-PERCYVALL Sp→E **Entonacion*, a tuning, a setting of tune. *Entonado*, m. tuned, brought into tune, set in tune. *Entonar*, to tune, to set in tune, to bring into tune, to set descant. **1611** COTGRAVE Fr→E *Entonné: m. ée: f.* Singing, sounding, resounding; also, sung, tuned, or sounded; *Entonnement.* A sounding, or singing; also, a tuning, or giuing of a tune. *Entonner.* ... Also, to tune, sing, chaunt it; sound, resound; and most properly, to begin, or giue a tune, in singing &c. *Intonation: f.* A lowd noise, tune, sound; § *Intonation de gare & serre.* The sounding of Drumme, or Trumpet, whereby souldiors are warned to stand close, and looke vnto themselues. **1611** FLORIO It→E *Intonare*, to entune, to make to sound, to tune voice or instrument, to raise the voice, to resound. **1659** TORRIANO-FLORIO It→E **Intonare*, to entune either voice or instrument **Intonatione, Intonatura*, an entuning. *Intonatore*, an entuner. **1688** MIEGE-COTGRAVE Fr→E *Entonné*, ... tuned, sung. *Entonner*, ... to tune, or sing. *Intonation*, (f.) *Terme de Musique*, the Diversity of Tones in Musick, or that Part of Musick which concerns the Diversity of Tones. § *Entonner des Louänges*, to sing Praises. *Entonner la Trompette*, to sound (or blow) the Trumpet. *Entonner les Notes, chanter du Ton qu'il faut chanter*, to sing the Notes. **1696** PHILLIPS (5th edn) *Intonation, (Lat.)* the giving the Tune or Key by the Chanter to the rest of the Quire. **1706** KERSEY-PHILLIPS (6th edn) *Intonation*, (in *Musick*) a giving the Tone or Key by the Chanter in a Cathedral to the rest of the Choir. **1737** DYCHE-PARDON (2nd edn) *Intonation* (S.) in *Musick*, is the giving the Pitch, Tone, or Key of the Song or Composition.

1736 TANS'UR *Compleat Melody* (3rd edn, p. 68) *Intonation*, (Ital.) is a *Term* commonly set at the beginning of a Piece of *Vocal-Musick*, which signifies the giving of a *Tone*, or the *Sound* of the *Key* to the rest of the *Quire*; which is commonly done by the head Cantor, or Singer.

intrada *see* entrée, overture, prelude

1724 [PEPUSCH] *Short Explic. of Foreign Words in Mus. Bks.* (p. 39) *Intrada*, Entry, much the same as

Prelude, or *Overture*. **1726** BAILEY *An Univ. Etymolog. Engl. Dict.* (3rd edn) *Intrada* (in *Musick Books*) signifies an Entry, much the same as *Prelude* or *Overture. Ital.*

intunable

1706 KERSEY-PHILLIPS (6th edn) *Intunable*, that cannot be tuned, or put in Tune. **1708** KERSEY *Dict. Anglo-Brit.* (1st edn) *Intunable*, that cannot be tuned, or put in Tune.

ionick *see* mode, mood, tune

1565 COOPER L→E § *Ionici motus. Horat.* The Jonike measures in daunsing. **1598** FLORIO It→E *Ionica*, ... Also a kinde of musicke among the Grecians. **1611** FLORIO It→E *Ionica*, ... Also a kind of ancient Architecture and Musike among the Grecians. **1656** BLOUNT (1st edn) *Ionick (Ionicus)* ... also wanton; as *Ionica Saltatio*, a wanton or effeminate dance. **1706** KERSEY-PHILLIPS (6th edn) § *Ionick Mood*, a kind of Musick that consisted of light, soft, and melting Strains, as amourous Songs, Sarabands, Courtants [sic], Jiggs, &c. **1707** *Gloss. Angl. Nova* (1st edn) *Ionick Mood*, a light and airy sort of Musick, of soft and melting Strains.

1636 BUTLER *Principles of Musik* (p. 2) The *Ionik* Moode is contrary to the Phrygian: an effeminate and delicate kinde of Musik, set unto pleasant songs and sonnets of loov, and such like fancies, for honest mirth and delight, chiefly in feasting and other merriments. § (p. 4) The *Ionian* [mood was so called] of *Ionia*, which lyest betweene *Æolia* and *Caria*; for the goodnes of aier and the commodious situation, inferiour to none of the Asian Regions: whose plenty and idlenes turned their honest mirth into lasciviousnes: .... This Moode is also called *Modus Chromaticus (i. coloratus, fucatus,)* of *chroma, color*: becaus as pictures ar beautifyed with trim lively coolors, to pleaz the wanton ey; so this kinde is as it were coollored with delicate lively sounds to pleaz the wanton ear.

iperlirica *see* lyrick

1500 *Ortus Vocabulorum* L→E Iperlirica. i. dulcedo cantus. f.p.

Ismenias

1538 ELYOT L→E *Ismenias*, the name of an excellent minstrel, whiche played on the shalmes. **1565** COOPER L→E *Ismenias*, The name of an excellent minstrel, which played on the shaulmes.

J

jack *see* bischero, key, saltarella, sautereau

1702 KERSEY *New Engl. Dict.* (1st edn) The *Jacks* in Virginals. **1706** KERSEY-PHILLIPS (6th edn) *Jacks*, small pieces of Wood fix'd to the Keys of a pair of Virginals, Harpsichord, or Spinet. **1737** DYCHE-PARDON (2nd edn) *Jack* (S.) ... among the *Musicians*, the small Pieces of Wood that are fixed to the Keys of Harpsicords, Spinnets, and Virginals, and which are cloathed with small Bits of List [sic] or Cloth, are called Jacks;

jangle

1730 BAILEY *Dict. Britannicum* (1st edn) To *Jangle* ... also to make a noise, as Bells when rung in no set Tune. **1737** DYCHE-PARDON (2nd edn) *Jangle* (V.) ... also any untuneable Noise, as a Confusion of Bells, or Sounds of Instruments of different Tunings, &c.

jar

1706 KERSEY-PHILLIPS (6th edn) To *Jarr* ... in *Musick* to disagree, or go out of Tune. **1735** DEFOE To Jarr, ... In *Musick*, to disagree in Sound. **1737** DYCHE-PARDON (2nd edn) *Jarr* (V.) ... and in *Musick*, it is being out of Tune or Time, so that the several Instruments do not perform their Parts harmoniously;

Jenkins, John *see* in nomine, rant

jessean harp

1623 COCKERAM *Iessean Harpe. Dauids* musicke. *Iessean harpe*. Dauids musick.

jeu

1611 COTGRAVE Fr→E *Ieu: m.* ... also, a lesson on the Lute, &c;

jews harp *see* resonance, sampogna, scacciapensiere, trompe, trumpet (trompa de Paris)

1702 Kersey *New Engl. Dict.* (1st edn) The *Jews-harp.* **1737** Dyche-Pardon (2nd edn) *Jews-Harp* or *Trump* (S.) a Mock Sort of Musical Instrument that Children play with.

jews trump

1702 Kersey *New Engl. Dict.* (1st edn) A *Jews-trump*, a kind of musical instrument. **1706** Kersey-Phillips (6th edn) *Jews-trump*, a sort of Musical Instrument.

c.1715-20 North Theory of Sounds BL Add. 32534, f. 59v ... So also that clownish Toy called a Jewstrump affords a like Remarque. For it is a pure spring, w[ch] In y[e] open air hath litle Sound, but augmented by y[e] air of y[e] mouth or breath is heard at a distance; ...

jig *see* baladin, ballata, barzelletta, cantilena, cobbola, contadinella, farce, forlana, frottola, Geneva jig, gigue, girometta, harigot, hornpipe, imperfect of the more, ionick, lesson, nonupla, rispetto, rondeau, saltarella, selve, siciliano, strambotto, toy, tripla, villanata, villanella

1702 Kersey *New Engl. Dict.* (1st edn) A *Jig*, a kind of dance. **1706** Kersey-Phillips (6th edn) *Jig*, a kind of Dance. **1721** Bailey *An Univ. Etymolog. Engl. Dict.* (1st edn) A *Jig*, (probably of *Geige, Teut. Gige, Dan.* a Fiddle.) a kind of Dance. **1730** Bailey *Dict. Britannicum* (1st edn) *Jig* (of *gige*, Dan. a Fiddle, according to *Skinner*, or of *gigue*, F.) an airy brisk kind of Dance. **1736** Bailey *Dict. Britannicum* (2nd edn) *Jig* (of *gige*, Dan. or *geig*, G. a Fiddle, according to *Skinner*; or of *gigue*, F. *giga*, It.) an airy, brisk Kind of Dance. **1737** Dyche-Pardon (2nd edn) *Jig* (S.) a brisk, merry Dance, or airy light Tune;

c.1715-20 North Essay of Musical Ayre BL Add. 32536, f. 61v [*re* plays and interludes] ... And after all Ends with what should be a dance called a jigg, but so swift, that no man living can run so fast as y[e] Measure is; It is Impossible for a dancer to keep such time, & his whole action, Must be running about like a Madman.

jig time *see* pointing

1731 Prelleur *Modern Musick-Master* (I, p. 4) There are three other sorts of Common Time as $\frac{12}{8}$, $\frac{6}{8}$, and $\frac{6}{4}$. the first contains twelve Quavers in a Bar, the second six Quavers in a Bar, and the last six Crotchets in a Bar[;] these are called Jigg Times.

jongleur

1688 Miege-Cotgrave Fr→E † *Jongleur*, (m.) a French Poet of old, such as went to great Men's Houses [to] sing their Exploits with a Viol.

Jopas

1658 Phillips (1st edn) *Jopas*, an *African* King, who was one of those that sought to have married *Dido*, he was a great Musician, and sung in verse, of the course of the Moon, and the motion of the Stars. **1676** Coles *Jopas*, a musical King of *Africa*, one of *Dido*'s Suiters.

joüarre

1611 Cotgrave Fr→E *Ioüarre: m.* An old rimer, ballade-maker; or maker of Enterludes for children, and countrey folke to act. **1650** Howell-Cotgrave Fr→E † *Ioüarre: m.* An old rimer, ballad-maker, or maker of Enterludes for children; and country folke to act.

joube *see* jubé, pulpit

1593 Hollyband Fr→E *Le Ioube*, or *poulpitre*, the singing place, the place of musicke: *m.*

joug *see* head, jugum

1611 Cotgrave Fr→E *Ioug: m.* ... also, the head of a Lute, Violl, &c;

Jubal *see* jubilee, music

1671 Phillips (3rd edn) *Jubal, (Hebr.)* fading, or a trumpet; the son of *Lamech*, and the Inventour of the harp and organ. **1676** Coles *Jubal, Hebrew.* fading, or a trumpet. **1706** Kersey-Phillips (6th edn) *Jubal*, (*Heb.* fading, or a Trumpet) the Son of *Lamech*, the Inventor of the Organ and Harp. **1708** Kersey *Dict. Anglo-Brit.* (1st edn) *Jubal* (*H* fading, or a Trumpet) the Son of *Lamech.*

jubé *see* joube, pulpit

1611 Cotgrave Fr→E *Iubé: m.* ... Also, a high place made for singers, or other Musitians, ouer stages, &c. **1688** Miege-Cotgrave Fr→E *Jubé*, (m.) *Terme d'Eglise*, a high Place for Singers in a Church, or Chappel, a singing Place. § *Un beau Jubé*, a fine singing Place.

jubilation

1500 *Ortus Vocabulorum* L→E Iubilatio onis. est cantus continuus. an[e]. a ioyng. **1730** Bailey *Dict.*

Britannicum (1st edn) *Jubilant* (*jubilans*, L.) Singing for Joy. *Milton*. **1737** DYCHE-PARDON (2nd edn) *Jubilant* (A.) joyful, merry, singing or exalting for Joy.

jubilee *see* horn, overture

1728 CHAMBERS *Jubilee*, a Church-Solemnity, or Ceremony observed at *Rome* .... *Masius* derives the Word from *Jubal*, the first Inventor of Musical Instruments, which for that reason were call'd by his Name; whence the words *Jobel* and *Jubilee* came to signify the Year of Deliverance and Remission, because proclaim'd with the Sound of one of those Instruments, which at first was no more than the Horn of a Ram.

jugum *see* joug, lyre, manche

1587 THOMAS L→E *Iugum, gi, n.g.* ... *also* the necke of a lute or such instrument, whereinto the pins be put, *Iun.*

julus

1538 ELYOT L→E *Iulus*, ... it is moreouer a songe dedicate to Diana. **1565** COOPER L→E *Iulus*, Otherwyse named Ascanius, the sonne of Aeneas. Also the name of a songe dedicated to Diana.

justiniana

1597 MORLEY *Plaine and Easie Introdvction* (p. 180) [marginalia: 'Iustinianes.'] There is likewise [with the vinate] a kind of songs) [sic] which I had almost forgotten) called *Iustinianas*, and are al written in the *Bergamesca* language a wanton and rude kinde of musicke it is, and like enough to carrie the name of some notable Curtisan of the Citie of *Bergama*, for no man will denie that *Iustiniana* is the name of a woman.

K

kern

1658 PHILLIPS (1st edn) *Kern*, an old Brittish word, signifying a horn. **1676** COLES *Kern, Brittish.* a horn. **1708** KERSEY *Dict. Anglo-Brit.* (1st edn) *Kern*, (B.) a Horn: Also an *Irish* Foot-Soldier **1706** KERSEY-PHILLIPS (6th edn) *Kern*, an old *British* Word, signifying a Horn: **1730** BAILEY *Dict. Britannicum* (1st edn) *Kern* (in Old *British* prob. of *Cornu*, L.) an Horn.

kettle drum *see* atabal, cymbal, gnaccara, naccara, timbrel, tympany

1702 KERSEY *New Engl. Dict.* (1st edn) A *Kettle-Drum*. A *Kettle-Drummer*. **1737** DYCHE-PARDON (2nd edn) *Kettle Drum*, is one, the Sides whereof are Brass.

key *as part of instrument, see* bischero, claveta, clavier, epitonium, jack, marche, musicis, musics, pedal, tastatura, tasto, touch

1702 KERSEY *New Engl. Dict.* (1st edn) The *Keys* of an Organ. **1728** CHAMBERS *Keys* also signify those little Pieces in the forepart of an Organ, Spinette, or Virginal, by means whereof the Jacks play, so as to strike the Strings of the Instrument; and Wind given to the Pipes, by raising and sinking the Sucker of the Sound-board. They are in number 28 or 29. In large Organs there are several Sets of these *Keys*, some to play the small secondary Organ, some for the main Organ, some for the Trumpet, and some for the Echoing-Trumpet. In some there are but a part that play, the rest being for Ornament. There are twenty Slits in the large *Keys*, which make the Half-Notes. M. *Baljouski* or *Douliez* pretends to have invented a new kind of *Keys* vastly preferable to the common ones. With these, he says, he can express Sounds, which follow each other in a continual Geometrical Proportion, and so can furnish all the Sounds in Music, and by consequence all the imaginary Intervals and Accords; whereas the common *Keys* do but furnish some of them. **1730** BAILEY *Dict. Britannicum* (1st edn) *Keys* (of *Spinnets, Organs*, &c.) little bits, by means of which the Jacks play, so as to strike the Strings of the Instrument; and Wind is given to the Pipes of an Organ, by raising and sinking the Sucker of the Sound board. **1731** KERSEY *New Engl. Dict.* (3rd edn) The *Keys*, or Stops of an Organ, Harpsichord, *&c*.

1725 DE LA FOND *New System of Music* (preface, xvi) ... as the word *Key*, which stands for no fewer than five very different things, *viz. 1.* An instrument to open a lock with. *2.* A piece of ground between a row of houses, and the side of a river, as the Custom-house *Key*. *3.* Those parts of a *Harpsicord* that move the Jacks. *4.* The last Note of a Tune. 5. Another thing in *Music*, which I shall explain in its proper place... § (p. 45) The word *Key* is used to signify, 1. The pieces of wood or ivory, by which the strings of a Harpsicord are struck ...

key *as tonal characteristic, see* affinal key, air, beemol, c-fa-ut-key, chiave, clef, d sol re, f-fa-ut-key, fundamental, mode, modulation, mood, song, tone

1671 PHILLIPS (3rd edn) § *Flatt Key* in Musick, see *Cliff*. **1676** COLES *Key* (in Musick) as *Cliff*. **1702** KERSEY *New Engl. Dict.* (1st edn) A *Key, or* cliff in musick. **1704** *Cocker's Engl. Dict.* (1st edn) *Key*, ... a Cliff in Musick **1704** HARRIS *Key*, in Musick, is a certain Tone, whereto every Composition, whether it be long or short, ought to be fitted or design'd: And this Key is said to be either *Flat* or *Sharp*, not in respect of its own Nature, but with Relation to the Flat or Sharp Third, which is joyned with it. **1706** KERSEY-PHILLIPS (6th edn) *Key*, ... In *Musick*, a certain Tone, to which every Composition ought to be fitted or apply'd; said to be either Flat or Sharp, upon Account of the flat or sharp Third which is joyn'd with it. **1707** *Gloss. Angl. Nova* (1st edn) *Key*, in Musick, is a certain Tone whereunto every Composition, whether it be long or short, ought to be referred, and this *Key*, is either *flat* or *sharp*, not in respect of its own Nature, but with relation to the flat or sharp third which is joined with it. **1723** PERKS *Musick* (*Lexicon Technicum*, 2nd edn, vol. 2) The *Key* is the Principal or Fundamental Note of a Tune, to which the rest have proper Relations, and with which the Bass always concludes. **1728** CHAMBERS *Key* ... [*see* Appendix] **1737** DYCHE-PARDON (2nd edn) *Key* (S.) ... in *Musick*, it is that Note in which the Airs of every Composition are supposed to close or end, and which is called flat or sharp, according as the third Note above it is two whole Tones, or one and a half; A and C are two natural Keys that use no artificial Sharps or Flats; A is naturally flat, and has one whole Tone and a half above it, and a whole Tone below it; C is naturally sharp, and has two whole Tones immediately above it, and a half Note or Tone below or under it, and whenever the other Letters are used they must be flatted or sharped [sic] to make them answer this Definition;

1597 MORLEY *Plaine and Easie Introdvction* (pp. 165-6) *Phi.* What do you mean by the high key? ¶ *Ma.* All songs made by the Musicians, who make songs by discretion, are either in the high key or in the lowe key... **1609** DOWLAND-ORNITHOPARCUS *Micrologvs* (pp. 7-8) *Of the Keyes.* ¶ The Wisedome of the Latine Musitians, imitating the diligence of the Græcians (whereas before the Singers did marke their Cords with most hard signes) did first note a musicall Introduction with Letters. To this *Guido Aretinus* ioyned those Voices he found out, and did first order the Musicall *Keyes* by lines and spaces, as appeareth in his Introductory. Therefore a *Key* is a thing compacted of a Letter and a Voyce. For the beginning of euery *Key* is a Letter, and the end a Syllable: Of a Voice (I say) not of Voyces, both because all the Keyes haue not many Voyces, and also because the names of *Generalities*, of *Specialties*, and of *Differences*, of which a definition doth consist, cannot be expressed in the plurall number. For *Animal* is the *genus*, not *Animalia*; a *Man* is the *species*, not men: *rationale* is the *difference*, not *rationabilia*: Or more formally, A *Key* is the opening of a Song, because like as a *Key* opens a dore, so doth it the Song. ¶ *Of the Number and Difference of Keyes.* ¶ *Keyes*, (as *Franchinus lib.* 1. *pract. cap.* 1. doth write) are 22. in number. Though Pope *Iohn*, and *Guido* (whom hee in his Fift Chapter saith to haue been the most excellent Musitians after *Boëtius*) onely make 20. These Two and Twentie *Keyes* are comprehended in a three-fold order. The first is of Capitall Letters; the Second of small; the Third of double Letters. And all these *Keyes* differ one from the other in *sight, writing*, and *naming*: because one is otherwise placed, written, or named than the other. Of the Capitall there be eight, *viz.* Γ. A. B. C. D. E. F. G. Of the small also Eight, *a.b.c.d.e.f.g.* for *b fa* ♮ *mi.* is not one *Key* onely, but two: which is prooued by *mutations, voyces*, and *instruments*. The same you must account of the vpper *bb fa* ♮♮ *mi* his Eight: of the double ones there be Six, *viz. aa.bb.* ♮♮ *cc.dd.* and *ee*... § (p. 9) Of *Keyes* some are to be marked, or (as others call them) *marked Keyes*, others are called *vnmarked Keyes*. Of the marked, there are fiue principall, *viz.* Γ *vt, F faut, C sol faut, G sol reut*, and *Dd la sol*: which the Ambrosians (as *Franch. lib.* 1. *pract. cap.* 3. reports) did mark with colours. *F faut*, with red, *C sol faut* with blew, double *bb* with skie-colour. But the Gregorians (whom the Church of Rome doth imitate) marking all the lines with one colour, to describe each of the marked *Keyes* by his first Letter, or some other signe, as in the Scale was mentioned. ¶ Those *Keyes* which are lesse principal, are two, *b* round, and ♮ square: The first shews that the Voyce is to be sung *fa*, the second that it is to be sung *mi* in the place wherein it is found. And vnlesse one doe heedily discerne *b* from ♮, he doth confound the Song (as *Berno* sayth) euen as wine and water mingleth together, one can discerne neither. **[1610]** CAMPION *New Way of Making Fowre Parts* [D4] Of all things that belong to the making vp of a Musition, the most necessary and vsefull for him is the true knowledge of the Key or Moode, or Tone, for all signifie the same thing, with the closes belonging to it, for there is no tune that can haue any grace or sweetnesse, vnlesse it be bounded within a proper key, without running into strange keyes which haue no affinity with the aire of the song. **1659** SIMPSON *Division-Violist* (p. 11) Next; you must know, that every Composition in *Musick*, be it long or short, is designed to some one *Key, Mood*, or *Tone*, in which the *Basse* doth alwayes conclude. This *Key*, or *Tone*, is said to be either *Flat*, or *Sharp*, in respect of the lesser or greater Third taking its place immediately above it. As for Example, suppose the *Key* to be in *G*, with a *b Flat* in *B*. Then I say, it is a *flat Key*; because from *G* to *b Flat* is the lesser Third. But if there be no such *b Flat* standing in *B*, it is then the greater Third, and called a *sharp Key*. **c.1668-71** *Mary Burwell's Instruction Bk. for Lute* (*TDa* p. 51) Of all things that belong to the making up a musician, the most necessary and useful for him is the true knowledge of the key (or mode or tone, for all signify the same thing) with the closes belonging unto it; for there is no tune that can have any grace or sweetness unless it be bounded within a proper key, without running into strange keys which have no affinity with the air of the song. **1676** MACE *Musick's Monument* (p. 225) *Secondly*, Observe whether It be a *Sharp*, or a *Flat Key*; which you shall know by the *Third* above your *Key*. As for Example, If *Gam-ut* be the *Key*; and if no *Flat* be set in *B-mi*: then It is call'd a *Sharp Key*, in respect that the *Third* to the *Key* is *Two Full Notes*; but if the *Third* be but a *Note* and a *Half*; then tis call'd a *Flat Key*; and for *That Cause* is the *General Custom* of calling a *Key Flat* or *Sharp*. **after 1695** NORTH untitled notebook BL Add. 32532, f. 13v The greatest difficulty beginner's ffind, In learning Composition is the understanding what is meant by a Key as when wee say a tune is in this or that key. and master's doe not take the right cours to Informe them. generally they say the last note of y[e] tune is the key. w[ch] is generally, but not allwais true, Nor doth y[e] learner know either why or wherefore, from that Item, Nor is y[t] neerer understanding the nature of the thing from a trick taught for finding In what bar it ly's. ¶ Now giving a good and clear notion of a key letts y[e] learner in to the full skill of composition, & that I thinck is no hard matter to doe. ¶ The Key, In Etimology, is nothing but one of those wee call Key's upon an organ, w[ch] y[e] finger toucheth in playing and mean's onely a Note, referred to some Instrument capable of musick, take y[e] note when you will, that is your key. **c.1698-c.1703** NORTH Cursory Notes (*C-K CN* p. 158) The first thing to be well apprehended in order to know the very secret of composition is that called the key, which however the word is derived means onely a note, or musicall tone. That is the plainest and most single thing to begin with. And lett any one but conceiv he hears a single sound that is a true tone, he is possest of a key; ... **c.1715-20** NORTH Essay of Musical Ayre BL Add. 32536, f. 32 ... that Note which is called the Key, or whereof the Scale is chosen ffor the gradation of the Consort. **1717** B[AYNE] *Intro. to Knowledge and Practice of Thoro' Bass* (p. 4) ... and in every Part and Portion of each Piece, there is one Sound or Tone predominant to which all the other Sounds that enter into the Composition do refer, which Tone is commonly called *the Key*. **1721** MALCOLM *Treatise of Musick* (p. 240) ... And this accounts for that *Maxim* in Practice, That all *Musick* is counted *upwards*; the Meaning is, that in the Conduct of a successive Series of Sounds, the lower or *graver* Notes influence and regulate the *acuter*, in such a Manner that all these are chosen with respect to some *fundamental* Note which is called the *Key*; ... § (p. 252) We shall still want something toward a complete and finished Notion of the Use and Office of the *Scale* of *Musick*, till we understand distinctly what a *Song* truly and naturally *concinnous* is, and particularly what that is which we call the *Key* of a *Song*; § (pp. 266-7) ... in every regular and truly *melodious Song*, there is one Note which regulates all the rest; the Song begins, and at least ends in this, which is as it were the principal Matter, or *musical Subject* that demands a special Regard to it in all the other Notes of the Song. And as in an Oration, there may be several distinct Parts, which refer to different Subjects, yet so as they must all have an evident Connection with the principal Subject which regulates and Influences the Whole; so in Melody, there may be several subprincipal Subjects, to which the different Parts of that Song may belong, but these are themselves under the Influence of the principal Subject, and must have a sensible Connection with it. This principal Note is called the *Key* of the Song, or the *principal Key* with respects to these others which are the *subprincipal Keys*. But a Song may be so short, and simply contrived, that all its Notes refer only to one *Key*. § (pp. 269-70) Let us suppose a Song begun in any Note, and carried on upwards or downwards by *Degrees* and *harmonical Distances*, so as never to touch any Notes but what are referable to that first Note as a *Fundamental, i.e.* are the true Notes of the *natural Scale* proceeding from that *Fundamental;* and let the *Melody* be conducted so through these natural Notes, as to close and terminate in that *Fundamental*, or any of its *8ves* above or below; that Note is called the *Key* of the *Melody*, because it governs and regulates all the rest ... and when any other Note is brought in, then 'tis said to go out of that *Key*: And by this Way of speaking of a Song's continuing in or going out of a *Key*, we may observe, that the whole *8ve*, with all its natural and *concinnous* Notes, belong to the *Idea* of a *Key*, tho' the *Fundamental*, being the principal Note which regulates the rest, is in a peculiar Sense called the Key, and gives Denomination to it in a System of fixt Sounds, and in the Method of marking Sounds by Letters ... And in this Application of the Word *Key* to one *fundamental* Note, another Note is said to be out of the *Key*, when it has not the Relation to that Fundamental of any of the natural Notes that belong to the *concinnous* Division of the *8ve*. § (p. 273) ... and this Distinction is marked with the Names of *A Sharp Key*, which is that with the *3d g*, &c. and *A Flat Key* with the *3d l*, &c. § (p. 274) And the Word *Key* may be applied to every Note of a Song, in which a *Cadence* is made; so that all these (comprehending the whole *Octave* from each) may be called different *Keys*, in respect of their different *Degrees* of *Tunes* ... § (pp. 275-7) 'Tis plain then, that a *Mode* (or *Key* in this Sense) is not any single Note or Sound, and cannot be denominated by it, for it signifies the particular Order or Manner of the *concinnous Degrees* of an *8ve*, the *fundamental* Note of which may in another Sense be called the *Key*, as it signifies that principal Note which regulates the rest, and to which they refer: And even when the Word *Key*, applied to different Notes, signifies no more than their different Degrees of *Tune*, these Notes are always considered as *Fundamentals* of an *8ve* *concinnously* divided, tho' the Mode of the Division is not considered when we call them different *Keys*; so that the whole *8ve* comes within the *Idea* of a Key in this Sense also: Therefore to distinguish properly betwixt *Mode* and *Key*, and to know the real Difference, take this Definition, *viz.* and *8ve* with all its natural and *concinnous* Degrees is called a *Mode*, with respect to the Constitution or the Manner and Way of dividing it; and with respect to the Place of it in the *Scale* of *Musick, i.e.* the *Degree* or Pitch of *Tune*, it is called a *Key*, tho' this Name is peculiarly applied to the *Fundamental*. Hence it is plain, that the same *Mode* may be with different *Keys*, that's to say, an *Octave* of Sounds may be raised in the same Order and Kind of *Degrees*, which makes the same *Mode*, and yet be begun higher or lower, *i.e.* taken at different *Degrees* of *Tune*, with respect to the Whole, which makes different *Keys*. It follows also from these Definitions, that the same *Key* may be with different *Modes*, that is, the Extremes of Two *Octaves* may be in the same *Degree* of *Tune*, and the Division of them different. The Manner of dividing the *Octave*, and the *Degree* of *Tune* at which it is begun, are so distinct, that I think there is Reason to give them different Names; yet I know, that common Practice applies the Word *Key* to both, so the same *Fundamental* constitutes Two different *Keys*, according to the Division of the *Octave;* and therefore a Note is said to be out of the *Key*, with respect to the same *Fundamental* in one Division, which is not so in another ... and the same Song is said to be in different *Keys*, when there is no other Difference, but that of being begun at different Notes. Now, if the Word *Key* must be used both Ways, to keep up a common Practice, we ought at least to prevent the Ambiguity, which may be done by applying the Words *sharp* and *flat*. For *Example*. Let the same *Song* be taken up at different Notes, which we call C and *A*, it may in that respect be said to be in different *Keys*, but the Denomination of the *Key* is from the Close; and Two Songs closing in the same Note, as C, may be said to be in different *Keys*, according as they have a greater or lesser *3d;* and to distinguish them, we say the one is in the *sharp Key* C, and the other in the *flat Key* C; and therefore, when *sharp* or *flat* is added to the Letter or Name by which any *fundamental* Note is marked, it expresses both the *Mode* and *Key*, as I have distinguished them above; but without these Words it expresses nothing but what I have called the *Key* in Distinction from *Mode*. § (p. 342) ... and whatever Difference you may make in the absolute Pitch of the whole Notes, or of the first Note which limites all the rest, the same individual Song must still be in the same *Mode;* and by the *Key* I understand only that Pitch or Degree of *Tune* at which the *fundamental* or close Note of the *Melody*, and consequently the whole *8ve* is taken; and because the *Fundamental* is the principal Note of the *8ve* which regulates the rest, it is peculiarly called the *Key*. § (pp. 343-4) ... But from what has been explained, you'll easily understand what Difference I put betwixt a *Mode* and a *Key*; of *Modes* there are only Two, and they respect what I would call the *Internal Constitution* of the *8ve*, but *Keys* are indefinite in the more general and abstract Sense, and with regard to their Denominations in Practice they are reduced to Twelve, and have respect to a Circumstance that's *external* and *accidental* to the *Mode*; and therefore a *Key* may be changed under the same *Mode*, as when the same Song, which is always in the same *Mode*, is taken up at different Notes or Degrees of *Tune*, and from the same *Fundamental* or *Key* a Series may proceed in a different *Mode*, as when different Songs begin in the same Note. But then because common Use applies the Word *Key* in both Senses, *i.e.* both to what I call a *Key* and a *Mode*, to prevent Ambiguity the Word *sharp* or *flat* ought to be added when we would express the *Mode*; so that a *sharp Key* is the same as a greater *Mode*, and a *flat Key* a lesser *Mode*; ... § (p. 416) The *Key* in every Piece and in every Part of each Piece of *musical* Composition is that *Tone* or Sound which is predominant and to which all the rest do refer .... Every Piece of *Musick*, as a *Concerto, Sonata* or *Cantata* is framed with due regard to one particular Sound called the *Key*, and in which the Piece is made to begin and end; but in the Course of the *Harmony* of any such Piece, the Variety which in *Musick* is so necessary to please and entertain, requires the introducing of several other *Keys*. § (pp. 417) As therefore the *3d* and *6th* may be either greater or lesser, from thence it is that the *Key* is denominated *sharp* or *flat*; the *sharp Key* being distinguished by the *3d g.* and the *Flat* by the *3d l.* **1721 or after** ANON. Institutions of Musick (rear of LC copy of Bayne, p. 3) The Key in every Piece and in every part of each piece of Musicall Composition is that Ton or Sound which is predominant and to which all the rest do referr. ¶ Every Piece of Musick as a Concerto, Sonata, or Cantata is fram'd with due Regard to one Particular sound called the Key and in which the Piece is made to begin and end, But in the course of the Harmony of any such Piece, The variety which in Musick is so necessary to please and entertain requires the Introduseing of several other Keyes. **1721 or after** ANON. Treatise of Thoro' Bass BEINECKE OSB. MS 3, p. 3 The Key in every piece, and in every part of each piece of Musicall Composition, is that Tone or Sound which is predominant, and to which all the rest referr. **1723** CHURCH *Intro. to Psalmody* (p. 29) *Phil.* Pray w^t^ do y^u^ mean by a Key? ¶ *Theo.* 'Tis a certain Sound or Note, wch ye Tendency of ye Air of any piece of Musick inclines it to end in, & takes it's name from one of ye 1st. 7 Notes in ye Gamut. for Instance, suppose ye last Note in a Psalm tune is in Gamut or G solreut, in ye Base or Treble y^n^ we say, That Tune is in Gamut; ... **1724** TURNER *Sound Anatomiz'd* (p. 6) The *Sound* given is called the *Key* to the rest, whose *Third* (which is the *Second* above it, the *Key* itself being always included as the *First*) must be either a *Major*, or a *Minor*; that is, a whole *Tone* or a *Semitone* to its *Second*; ... **1725** DE LA FOND *New System of Music* (p. 45) ... The word *Key* is used likewise to signify *the Note in which a piece of* Music *ends*. § (p. 48) The word *Key* in its third acceptation signifies *the general humor or mode of an air*. § (pp. 48-9) ... this notable difference in the *mode* or *humor* of a tune, which is the third signification of the term *Key*, is nam'd *Flatness or Sharpness, from the flatness or sharpness of the Third*, which occasions this great difference. When the Third is flat, the air is soft, serious, and bordering a little upon melancholy: and when the Third is sharp, the air is gay, lively and joyful. **c.1726** NORTH Musicall Gramarian BL Add. 32533, ff. 67-8 ... whereby the sence of the word Key, ambiguously used by ye artists, may be cleared up. The definition of it ... is but this. The word Key, Referred to musick, is the lower or leading tone of that scale, wch is Intended to direct the tones that follow Into proper & aggreable harmony. For wch Reason, at Enterteinm^ts^ of Musick by way of preludium it is usuall to flourish it forth, to prepare ye ear. If one asks some artists, what is a Key? they will answer, the Note that a Sonnata beginns or Ends with, wch is going from the Question, for that is generall and the answer is but a practise in particularibus; ... And ye fact is not allwais so, for a sonnata, may begin in one Key and End In another and change 40 times by ye way, and If artfuly done, No solascisme in ye Musick. but yet such use of the word, In comon practise, is not amiss, becaus it is a light to ye performers what Key to prepare for. tho in truth Nothing is more confused then the comon notion of a Key In Musick ... I must precaution, that for ye most part, speaking of a Key, it Refferrs not to the whole lesson but the particular notes there under consideration, (as certain phrases in language) are Interpreted according to some Key, Regarded together with them without heed to y^e^ Generall Key as will appear afterwards. § f. 73 ... As to 3^ds^ altho the septenary from G. leads thro A. to B. being the ♯3^d^. wch is 2. whole tones, yet if B, is flatened a semitone, and ♭B. put in y^e^ place of ♮B. the accord with. G. termed a $\flat 3^{d.}$ will be nearly as pleasing & aggreable as y[e] other. Therefore the Artists have full liberty to use either, as their subject Invites. The former is Called a sharp and the latter a flatt Key, and those termes in Musicall Language have no other signification then what is expressed here. **1726-8** NORTH Theory of Sounds BL Add. 32535, f. 35 The Scale I mentioned is derived from the Mononochord [sic], of w[ch] y[e] open sound is termed the Key and is y[e] first tone in y[e] scale ... **1728** NORTH Musicall Grammarian (*C-K MG* f. 37) The key defined ¶ It hath bin insisted that the septenary tones according to the scale, are fixed by a consonantiall relation to the first or leader (whatever that tone is) and by like relation of one to another. The primary tone being prefixt[,] laying aside vocall syllables, and using (as, from henceforward I shall) onely the letters, wee call it, (as hath bin hinted), the key. And whither it hath the name of A, B or C, it is all one, for the proper consonances, and no other are attendant upon it. Whereupon the key in musick may be thus defined: the lower or leading tone of that scale which is chosen to determine the accordant notes of the following harmony. The word is often used loosly sometimes for the claves of instruments, and often declaring the note of the scale, which is predominant in any peice of musick, which may often change, but wee confine it striktly to the leading tone, and doe not allow it to make any escapes for other porposes, of any kind, whatsoever. **1730** PLAYFORD *Intro. to Skill of Musick* (19th edn, p. 23) ... before I proceed any further, I think it requisite to let you know what a *Key* is. For Instance; Suppose you have a Lesson or Song prick'd down, you must observe in what Space or Line the last Note of it stands on, and that is the *Key*. Now it very often begins in the *Key*, but sometimes a *Third* or *Fifth* above it, and so you cannot so well tell, but it certainly ends in it. ¶ A *Key* is a Song or Tune depending on a Sound given, as a Sermon does on a Text, and when it ends right, it gives such Satisfaction to the Ear, that nothing more is expected after it; like a Period at the end of a Sentence, when the Sense is full, and no more depending upon it. **1731** [PEPUSCH] *Treatise on Harmony* (2nd edn, p. 3) By a *Key* is meant any particular Octave of Notes, taken from the General Diatonick Scale of Musick; whereof the Lowest Note is consider'd as the Principal, and therefore is call'd *The Key Note;* all the other Notes in that Key being consider'd as subordinate to it. **1736** TANS'UR *Compleat Melody* (3rd edn, p. 23) *Scholar*. What is a *Key*? or what is meant by the Word *Key*? ¶ *Master*. A *Key*, or *Key-Note*, as the last *Note* of the *Bass;* which contains the Air and Judgment of the whole Song; ... § *Scholar*. What difference is there in two *Keys*? and why is one called *Flat*, and the other *Sharp*? ¶ *Master*. The first is called A, the *Natural Flat Key*, by reason it hath the lesser *third, sixth*, and *seventh* above its *Key*. The second is called C, the *Natural Sharp Key*, it having the greater *third, sixth*, and *seventh* above its *Key*; ... **1740** LAMPE *Art of Musick* (p. 53) From hence what is practically called a *Key* in Musick took its Foundation having its proper Limits, and a certain Number of relative Harmonies, whose melodious Distances form a certain Species of an *Octave* gradually filled up, called the System, or *Scale* of a Key.

kit *see* cacapensiere, cetara, cithara, donadello, giga, hop merchant, mandora, pandora, poche, rebeck, ribecchino, tempella, vitula
1702 KERSEY *New Engl. Dict.* (1st edn) A *Kit, or* pocket-Violin. **1706** KERSEY-PHILLIPS (6th edn) *Kit*, a Pocket-Violin; a Musical Instrument: **1707** *Gloss. Angl. Nova* (1st edn) *Kit*, a Pocket-Violin; **1708** KERSEY *Dict. Anglo-Brit.* (1st edn) † *Kit*, a Pocket-Violin; a Musical Instrument: **1730** BAILEY *Dict. Britannicum* (1st edn) *Kit*, ... also a small Violin for the Pocket; **1737** BAILEY *The Univ. Etymolog. Engl. Dict.* (3rd edn, vol. 2, cant section) *Kit*, a Dancing Master. **1737** DYCHE-PARDON (2nd edn) *Kit* (S.) ... also a small Fiddle that Dancing-Masters carry in their Pockets;

knell *see* campana, carillon, scampanare
1702 KERSEY *New Engl. Dict.* (1st edn) A *Knell, or* passing-bell. **1706** KERSEY-PHILLIPS (6th edn) *Knell*, a Passing-bell, the ringing of a Bell at the Departure of a dying Person. **1707** *Gloss. Angl. Nova* (1st edn) *Knell*, the sound of a Bell, a Passing-Bell. **1708** KERSEY *Dict. Anglo-Brit.* (1st edn) *Knell*, a Passing-Bell, the ringing of a Bell at the Departure of a dying Person. **1730** BAILEY *Dict. Britannicum* (1st edn) *Knell* (of *cnyllan, Sax.* to knock or strike) a Passing-Bell, antiently rung at the Departure of a Person just ready to expire; but now when dead. **1731** KERSEY *New Engl. Dict.* (3rd edn) To *Knowl a Bell*, to toll it, to ring a Knell. **1737** DYCHE-PARDON (2nd edn) *Knell* (S.) the Sound of a passing Bell, formerly rung or tolled at a dying Person's Departure, and now at the Time of Burial, or quickly after their Death; also the Tone or Sound of a Bell rung upon any such like mournful Occasion.

L

la

1598 Florio It→E *La,* ... It is also a note in musicke, *La.* **1611** Florio It→E *La,* a note in musicke, La. **1659** Torriano-Florio It→E *La,* a note in Musick so called. **1688** Miege-Cotgrave Fr→E *Lâ,* (m.) *Terme de Musique,* la, one of the chief Notes of Musick.

ladetta *see* lauda, lauds

1598 Florio It→E *Ladetta,* a hymne, a psalme or song of praise. *Laldetta,* a song of praise, a thankesgiuing song. **1611** Florio It→E *Ladetta,* a Hymne, a Psalme or Song of praises. *Laldetta,* a song of praise or thankesgiuing. **1659** Torriano-Florio It→E *Ladetta,* a laudet, a hymn, a psalm of praises and thanksgiving. *Laldetta,* as *Ladetta.*

lai *see* lay

lallatio *see* falcinine, lullaby

1552 Huloet L→E *Lallatio. onis, Nenia* Song whych the nource singeth in dandlyng the chyld. **1589** Rider L→E *Lallatio, fascinina, f.* A song which the nurse singeth in dandling the childe. *Lallo.* To sing as the nurse doth to her childe.

Lambert, Michel *see* style

lamentatione *see* languissant

1724 [Pepusch] *Short Explic. of Foreign Words in Mus. Bks.* (p. 40) *Lamentatione,* is to play or sing in a Lamenting, Doleful, Mournful, Melancholy, Manner, and therefore, consequently, pretty Slow. **1726** Bailey *An Univ. Etymolog. Engl. Dict.* (3rd edn) *Lamentatione* (in *Musick Books*) signifies to play or sing in a lamenting, melancholly, mournful, doleful manner, and therefore of consequence pretty slow. *Ital.*

1736 Tans'ur *Compleat Melody* (3rd edn, p. 67) *Lamentatone, Languemente, Languissant,* (Ital.) Either of those *Terms,* denote that you must sing or play in a very grave, slow, lamenting, and mournful Manner.

lamnazzeath

1586 Anon. *Praise of Mvsicke* (p. 138) That he [the Holy Ghost] would haue them song most cunningly, hee directeth many Psalms especially and by name *Lamnazzeath.*

lampon *see* stramboccolo

1688 Miege-Cotgrave Fr→E *Lampon,* (m.) ... a drunken Song. § *Chanter des Lampons,* to sing drunken Songs.

languemente *see* lamentatione

languente

1724 [Pepusch] *Short Explic. of Foreign Words in Mus. Bks.* (p. 40) *Languente,* or *Languido,* the same as the foregoing Word [lamentatione]. **1726** Bailey *An Univ. Etymolog. Engl. Dict.* (3rd edn) *Languente* (in *Musick Books*) signifies the same as *lamentatione,* which see. *Ital. Languido* (in *Musick Books*) signifies the same as *lamentatione,* which see. *Ital.*

1731 Prelleur *Modern Musick-Master* (Dictionary, p. 2) *Languente,* in a languishing-manner.

languette *see* anche

1611 Cotgrave Fr→E § *Languette de hault-bois.* The little pipe, tongue, or tenon, which is in the mouth of a Hoe-boy, &c. **1688** Miege-Cotgrave Fr→E *Languette,* (f.) the little pipe (or tongue) of some musical Instruments.

languissant *see* lamentatione

1724 [Pepusch] *Short Explic. of Foreign Words in Mus. Bks.* (p. 40) *Languissant,* Languishing; this signifies much the same as *Lamentatione* above. **1726** Bailey *An Univ. Etymolog. Engl. Dict.* (3rd edn) *Languissant* (in *Musick Books*) signifies *languishing,* and much the same with *lamentatione,* which see. *Ital.*

large

1671 Phillips (3rd edn) *Large,* the greatest measure of Musicall quantity in use, one *Large* containing two Longs, one Long two Briefs, one Brief two Semi Briefs. See Brief [breve], and is thus Charactered, ПП **1676** Coles *Large,* (in Musick) eight Sem'briefs. **1702** Kersey *New Engl. Dict.* (1st edn) A *Large* in Musick, consisting of eight sembriefs. **1706** Kersey-Phillips (6th edn) A *Large,* the greatest Measure of Musical Quantity; one Large containing two Longs, one Long two Briefs, and one Brief two

Semi-briefs: But the *Large* and the *Long* are now of little Use, as being too long for any Voice or Instrument (the Organ only excepted[)], to hold ont [sic] to their full Length. **1737** DYCHE-PARDON (2nd edn) *Large* (S.) in *Musick*, is the Note, Mark, or Character that expresses the longest Time that is plaid, and is seldom used but for the close Note upon an Organ.

after 1517 ANON. Art of Mvsic BL Add. 4911, f. 1v *The larg* is one figur of quilk the leynth dois ye bodie triplicat halb and one virgill in the rytht part up or doun ... **1609** DOWLAND-ORNITHOPARCUS *Micrologvs* (p. 39) A *Large* is a figure, whose length is thrise as much as his breadth, hauing on the part toward your right hand a small tayle, bending vpward, or downeward. **1617-24** FLUDD *Utriusque Cosmi Maioris: De Templo Musicæ* (p. 191) *Larga* sive *maxima* est inter omnes figuras mensurabiles major. **1665** SIMPSON *Principles of Practical Mvsick* (p. 16) The first two Notes in use were *(Nota Longa, & Brevis)* a *Long* and a *Breve*, in order to a long and short syllable. Only they doubled or trebled the length of their *Longa*, and called it *Larga*, or *Maxima Nota*, our *Large*.

larghetto

1724 [PEPUSCH] *Short Explic. of Foreign Words in Mus. Bks.* (p. 40) *Largetto*, or *Larghetto*, denotes a Movement a little quicker than *Largo*. **1726** BAILEY *An Univ. Etymolog. Engl. Dict.* (3rd edn) *Largetto* (in *Musick Books*) signifies a Movement a little quicker than *Largo* which see. *Ital. Larghetto*, signifies the same as *Largetto. Ital.*

c.1710 ANON. *Preceptor for Improved Octave Flageolet* ('Explanation of Words', p. 82) *Larghetto*—Not so slow as Largo **1731** PRELLEUR *Modern Musick-Master* (Dictionary, p. 2) *Largetto* not Slow as Largo. **1736** TANS'UR *Compleat Melody* (3rd edn, p. 66) ... *Largetto*, (Ital.) signifies, one Degree quicker than *Largo*

largo *see* lent, tardo

1724 [PEPUSCH] *Short Explic. of Foreign Words in Mus. Bks.* (p. 41) *Largo*, Slow; by which Word is commonly to be understood a Slow Movement, yet quicker by one Degree than *Grave*, and by two than *Adagio*. (p. 95) *Largo*, Slow or Gently. § (p. 95) *Largo Assai*, or *Poco Largo*, not too Slow. **1726** BAILEY *An Univ. Etymolog. Engl. Dict.* (3rd edn) *Largo*, (in *Musick Books*) signifies *slow*, i.e. you are to understand by it, a slow Movement; yet quicker by one Degree than *Grave*, and by two than *Adagio*. **1737** DYCHE-PARDON (2nd edn) *Largo* (S.) a *Musical Term*, importing that the Movement tho' slow is one Degree quicker than Grave, and two than Adagio.

1683 PURCELL *Sonnata's of III Parts* (*To the Reader*) ... It remains only that the English Practitioner be enform'd, that he will find a few terms of Art perhaps unusual to him, the chief of which are these following: ... *Presto Largo, Poco Largo*, or *Largo* by it self, a middle movement: ... **c.1710** ANON. *Preceptor for Improved Octave Flageolet* ('Explanation of Words', p. 82) *Largo*—Not so slow as Adagio **c.1726** NORTH Musicall Gramarian BL Add. 32533, f. 65v ... Largo is strong, & bold. **1731** PRELLEUR *Modern Musick-Master* (Dictionary, p. 2) *Largo*, Very Slow. **1736** TANS'UR *Compleat Melody* (3rd edn, p. 66) *Largo, Lentment, Lento, Lent, Tardo*, (Ital.) Either of those *Terms*, or Words, denotes one Degree quicker than *Alemand*.

larigot *see* arigot, harigot

1611 COTGRAVE Fr→E *Larigau*. ... also, a Flute or Pipe is called so by the clownes in some parts of France. **1688** MIEGE-COTGRAVE Fr→E † *Larigot*, (m.) the head of the Wind-pipe; a kind of Flute, or Pipe.

Lasus

1565 COOPER L→E *Lasus*, A man in the tyme of Darius, that wrote fyrst of Musyke.

laud *see* lute

lauda *see* ladetta

1550 THOMAS It→E *Lauda*, preise, as of psalmes, himpnes or songes. *Laudesi*, schoolefelowes that vse to synge laudes or preises. **1565** COOPER L→E § *Laudes alicuius saltare. Plin. iun.* In daunsyng to synge ones prayses. **1598** FLORIO It→E *Lauda*, ... a hymn, a song or psalme *Laude*, praise ... as *Lauda*. *Laudesi*, schoole-masters or such as sing in churches songs of praises. **1611** FLORIO It→E *Lauda*, as *Laude*. *Laude*, laud, praise, commendation, thanksgiuing. *Laudesi*, such as sing songs of praises or thanksgiuing.

lauds *see* ladetta, primer

1658 PHILLIPS (1st edn) *Lauds*, (lat.) ... also certain Psalms of *David*, beginning with these words *Laudate dominum*, which use to be recited by the Roman Catholicks between the Nocturns and the Howres, which are certain other prayers or psalms so called. **1707** *Gloss. Angl. Nova* (1st edn) *Lauds*,

(Lat.) Praises read or sung last in either Morning or Evening Service. **1728** CHAMBERS *Lauds*, or *Laudes*, the second Part of the ordinary Office of the Breviary, said after Matins, though heretofore it ended the Office of the Night. The *Laudes* consist principally of Psalms, Hymns, *&c.* whence they took their Name. See *Matins* and *Breviary*. **1737** DYCHE-PARDON (2nd edn) *Lauds* (S.) the second Part of the *Roman* Breviary, said or sung now after Matins, but heretofore they ended the Office at Night; it consisted of Psalms, Hymns, &c.

lavolta *see* volta

1656 BLOUNT (1st edn) *Lavolta* (Ital.) a Dance so called; **1658** PHILLIPS (1st edn) *Lavolta*, (Ital.) ... also a kind of dance. **1676** COLES *Lavolta, Italian*. a kind of dance

lay *see* cançion, canzona, chanson, chant, motet, note, ode, raye, roundelay

1611 COTGRAVE Fr→E *Lay: m.* A Lay, Song, Roundelay; **1616** BULLOKAR **Laye*. A song. **1623** COCKERAM *Lay*. A song. **1658** PHILLIPS (1st edn) *Lay*, (French) a song. **1659** TORRIANO-FLORIO It→E *Lai*, layes, woes, moanings. **1676** COLES *Lay, French*. a song **1688** MIEGE-COTGRAVE Fr→E *Lai*, (a masc. Subst.) the Lyrick Poesy of the old French Poets. ¶ *C'est une sorte de Poëme qui contient quêque chose de triste, d'amoureux, ou de moral. Et il y en a de deux Sortes, le grand, & le petit. Le grand Lai est un Poëme composé de douze Couplets de Vers, de differente mesure sur deux Rimes. Le petit est un Poëme de 16. ou de 20. Vers, divisez en quatre Couplets, presque toujours sur deux Rimes.* **1721** BAILEY *An Univ. Etymolog. Engl. Dict.* (1st edn) *Lay*, (Ley, *Sax.*) a Song, or Poem. **1737** DYCHE-PARDON (2nd edn) *Lay* (S.) a Song or Poem, consisting of short and mournful Strains;

laying

1676 MACE *Musick's Monument* (p. 41) Again, There is found by *Experience* a *Better* manner of *Laying our Lutes*, (as we term it) which is done, by causing the *Fingerboard*, 1. to lye a little *Round*, or *Vp* in the *middle*; as also that the *Bridge* (answerably) *rise a little Round* to it. ¶ Then 2dly. to lay the *Strings so close* to the *Finger-board*, that the Strings may almost seem to *touch* the *first Fret*. This is call'd *Laying of a Lute Fine*, when all the *Strings* lye near the *Frets*.

leader *see* guide

ledger line *see* clef, double

1730 PLAYFORD *Intro. to Skill of Musick* (19th edn, p. 6) ... Now, altho' there is but Twenty two Notes set down in the *Scale, Musick* is not confin'd to that Number, but sometimes you'll meet with Notes both below and above what I have set down, (according to the Will of the Composer) and then you add a Line or two to the five Lines, as the Song requires, those Lines so added being called *Ledger-Lines*; ... **1731** PRELLEUR *Modern Musick-Master* (VI, from table facing p. 4) ... the four Notes above the Treble stave are called in alt; and those below the Bass stave are called double; these Notes are helped by additional lines which are also called Ledger lines.

leero *see* Alphonso, lyra viol, lyrick, lyrick verse, viol

1656 BLOUNT (1st edn) *Leero*, corruptly from *Lyra*, is a way of tuning, or playing on a Viol, different from that of *Alphonso*. **1658** PHILLIPS (1st edn) *Leero*, see *Lyrick*. **1676** COLES § *Leero-way, Lyra-way*, a tuning or playing on the Viol, differing from that of *Alphonso*. **1708** KERSEY *Dict. Anglo-Brit.* (1st edn) *Leero*, or *Leero-Viol*; a kind of Musical Instrument, corruptly for *Lyra*-Viol. **1721** BAILEY *An Univ. Etymolog. Engl. Dict.* (1st edn) *Leero-Viol*, (corruptly for *Lyra-Viol*) a kind of Musical Instrument.

1682 PLAYFORD *Musick's Recreation on Viol* (2nd edn, preface) The *Lero* or *Lyra-Viol*, is so called from the Latin word *Lyra*, which signifies a *Harp*, alluding to the various Tuning, under the name of *Harp-way, Sharp* and *Flat*. This way of playing on the *Viol*, is but a late Invention, in imitation of the Old *English Lute* or *Bandora*; whose Lessons were prickt down in like manner by certain Letters of the Alphabet, upon six Lines or Rules; which six Lines did allude to the six course of Strings upon those Instruments, as they do now unto the six single Strings upon the *Viol*.

legare *see* slur

1727 [RIVA] *Advice to Composers and Performers* (pp. 14-15) The Binding together or Stringing the Notes firm and distinct with the Voice, which the *Italians* express by the Terms (*Legare* and *Staccare la Voce*) are Graces equally agreable [presumably as other graces, not named], although contrary to each other; and nothing but good Judgment can direct the Singer how to use them properly, (that is to say) according to the Nature and Design of the Composition; ...

legerement

1724 [Pepusch] *Short Explic. of Foreign Words in Mus. Bks.* (p. 41) *Legerement* is to play Lightly, Gently, and with Ease. **1726** Bailey *An Univ. Etymolog. Engl. Dict.* (3rd edn) *Legerment* (in *Musick-Books*) signifies to play lightly, gently, and with ease. *Ital.*

1736 Tans'ur *Compleat Melody* (3rd edn, p. 68) *Legermente.* (Ital.) Denotes you must sing or play very gently, lightly, and with ease.

legno

1598 Florio It→E *Legno,* ... Also a kinde of musicall instrument. **1611** Florio It→E *Legno,* any kind of wood... Also a kind of musicall instrument. Also taken for the wood Guaiaco. **1659** Torriano-Florio It→E **Legno,* any kind of wood ... also the name of a kinde of musical instrument, also the Wood Guaicum

lent *see* largo

1724 [Pepusch] *Short Explic. of Foreign Words in Mus. Bks.* (p. 41) *Lent,* or *Lento,* or *Lentement,* do all denote a Slow Movement, and signify much the same as *Largo. Tres Lentement,* is very slow, and may signify a Movement between *Largo* and *Grave,* the same as when the Word *Largo* is repeated thus, *Largo, Largo.* **1726** Bailey *An Univ. Etymolog. Engl. Dict.* (3rd edn) *Lent* (in *Musick Books*) denotes a slow Movement, and signifies much the same as *Largo. Ital. Lentement,* signifies the same as *Lent. Tres Lentement,* signifies very slow, or a Movement between *Largo* and *Grave,* and the same as when *Largo* is repeated as *Largo, Largo. Lento* (in *Musick Books*) signifies a slow Movement, the same as *Lent* or *Lentement.* which see. *Ital.*

1731 Prelleur *Modern Musick-Master* (Dictionary, p. 2) *Lent, Lento* or *Lentement,* Slow

lenvoy *see* envoy

lerelot *see* burden, filibustacchina

1611 Cotgrave Fr→E *Lerelot: m.* The foot, or downe of a countrey-maidens song.

lero *see* leero

lesser fifth *see* fifth lesser

lesser second *see* second lesser

lesser semitone *see* semitone lesser

less half note *see* diatonic

lesson *see* jeu, suit, tablature

1737 Dyche-Pardon (2nd edn) *Lesson* (S.) something to be learnt, studied, spoke, played, sung, &c. by one that is Scholar to another.

1676 Mace *Musick's Monument* (p. 88) [*re* 'The 1st. Lesson, being a Præludium for the Hand in *C-fa-ut-Key*'] This I'l [sic] call a *Lesson;* All the other were only *Rudiments,* and of no further use, than to give you *Insight, Thus far:* Therefore, when you have made your intended use of Them, leave them, and adhere to your *Lessons* only. ¶ This may serve you, as a *Prælude,* at any time, upon *This Key;* being call'd *C-fa-ut-Key.* § (p. 128) And that you may hereafter know how to give *Right,* and *Proper Names* to all *Lessons* you meet with, take notice of *This General way,* how you may know Them, and how you may *Order Them.* ¶ There are first *Præludes,* then 2*dly. Fancies,* and *Voluntaries,* 3*dly. Pavines,* 4*thly. Allmaines,* 5*thly. Ayres,* 6*thly. Galliards,* 7*thly. Corantoes,* 8*thly. Serabands,* 9*thly. Tattle de Moys,* 10*thly. Chichona's,* 11*thly. Toyes,* or *Jiggs,* 12*thly. Common Tunes;* But lastly, *Grounds,* with *Divisions* upon them. **c.1715-20** North Essay of Musical Ayre BL Add. 32536, f. 71v [*re* the history of English music] And it was a declension, when they began to leav out y[e] fantasia, w[ch] was the most Elabourate, and best of their musick, and make setts of lessons, as they were called, consisting of Allemands Courants, &c.

levet

1598 Florio It→E *Leuata,* ... Also a kind of march sounded vpon drum and trumpet in time of war. **1611** Florio It→E *Leuata,* ... Also the name of a march vpon a Drumme and Trumpet in time of warre. Also a hunt is vp. **1659** Torriano-Florio It→E **Levata, Levatione, Levamento, Levatura,* ... also the name of a march or point of war sounded upon drum or trumpet, at the raising of a camp, or upon a retreat, also musick sounded under ones window in the morning, as we say, a Hunts up **1708** Kersey *Dict. Anglo-Brit.* (1st edn) *Levet,* a kind of Lesson on the Trumpet. **1726** Bailey *An Univ. Etymolog. Engl. Dict.* (3rd edn) *Levet,* a Lesson on the Trumpet. **1737** Dyche-Pardon (2nd edn) *Levet* (S.) a Lesson or Tune on the musical Instrument called a Trumpet.

libitum *see* ad libitum, bene placito
1724 [PEPUSCH] *Short Explic. of Foreign Words in Mus. Bks.* (p. 42) *Libitum*, or *Ad Libitum*, is as much to say, you may if you please, or if you will. **1726** BAILEY *An Univ. Etymolog. Engl. Dict.* (3rd edn) *Libitum, Ad Libitum*, at your Pleasure, *L.* (in *Musick-Books*) it signifies, you may if you please, or if you will.

libro *see* livre
1724 [PEPUSCH] *Short Explic. of Foreign Words in Mus. Bks.* (p. 42) *Libro*, a Book. This Word is often met with in the Title Page of Musick Books, in the following Manner: ¶ *Libro Primo*, First Book. ¶ *Libro Secondo*, Second Book. **1726** BAILEY *An Univ. Etymolog. Engl. Dict.* (3rd edn) *Libro* (in *Musick-Books*) signifies a Book. *Libro Primo*, the first Book. *Ital. Libro Secondo*, the second Book. *Ital.* and so of the rest. **1730** BAILEY *Dict. Britannicum* (1st edn) *Libro*, a Book, *Ital.*

lichanos *see* diagram, hypate, mese
1587 THOMAS L→E *Lichanos, Iun.* The forefinger string, or the third string. *Also*, D. sol. re. *Iun.* **1589** RIDER L→E *Lichanos*. The 3 string.

early 18th C. PEPUSCH various papers BL Add. 29429, f. 6 Lichanos, i.e. ye Index. viz Lichanos Meson, ye Index to Mese

lidio *see* lydian

ligature *see* note
after 1517 ANON. Art of Mvsic BL Add. 4911, f. 2 *Ligatur quhat is it.* Gaforus dois vrit in the fyrst chaptur of the secund buck. That a ligatur is of simpill figur ... **1596** ANON. *Pathway to Musicke* [C ii] *VVhat is a Ligature?* ¶ It is a coupling together of simple Notes by a little stroke on the right hand or left side, and of tvvo sorts on this manner as followeth, that is to say, square and ouerthvvart... **1597** MORLEY *Plaine and Easie Introdvction* (p. 9) *Phi.* What is a Ligature? ¶ *Ma. It is a combination or knitting to gether of two or more notes*, altering by their scituation [sic] and order the value of the same. **early 17th C.** RAVENSCROFT Treatise of Musick BL Add. 19758, f. 11v *A Compownd* note (or other wise called a ligature) is like a nowne Adiectiue wch cannot stand by himselfe but must needes require another to be joyned wth him both for to shew his nature and propertye. **1609** DOWLAND-ORNITHOPARCUS *Micrologvs* (p. 40) Wherefore a *Ligature* (as *Gaff.* writes in the fift chap. of his second Booke) is the conioyning of simple Figures by fit strokes. Or (according to the strokes vpward or downward) it is the dependence of the principall figures in straightnesse, or crookednesse. § (p. 41) ... Euery Note betwixt the first and the last, is called middle. **1617-24** FLUDD *Utriusque Cosmi Maioris: De Templo Musicæ* (p. 191) *Notulæ ligatura*, est conjunctio duarum vel plurium figurarum simul. **1636** BUTLER *Principles of Musik* (p. 38) *Ligature.* Of *Ligare*, to binde or tye: becaus it tyeth many Notes to one syllable of the Ditti. Which Adjunct *Franchinus* dooeth thus define: *Omnis Ligatura, quanquam multas complexa est notulas, unicam subtrahit syllabam pronunciandam.* **1662** [DAVIDSON] *Cantus, Songs and Fancies* (n.p.) Q. *What is a Legature?* ¶ A. It is a combination or knitting together of two or more Notes, altering by their situation and order the value of the same, holding out if your first Note lack a tayle, the second descending, it is a long.

limbuto
1611 FLORIO It→E *Limbuto*, a kinde of instrument so called. **1659** TORRIANO-FLORIO It→E *Limbuto*, a kind of musical instrument.

limma *see* colores generum, diastem
1694 HOLDER *Treatise of Natural Grounds* (p. 152) The *Pythagoreans*, not using *Tone Minor*, but two Equal *Tones Major*, in a Fourth, were forced to take a lesser Interval for the *Hemitone*; which is called their *Limma*, or *Pythagorean Hemitone*; and, which added to those two *Tones*, makes up the Fourth: it is a *Comma* less than *Hemitone Major*, (16 to 15;) and the Ration of it, is 256 to 243.

linguella
1598 FLORIO It→E *Linguella, Linguetta*, ... Also the tongues of a rauens quill in virginals, &c. **1611** FLORIO It→E *Linguella*, as *Linguetta*. *Linguetta*, ... the tongues of a Rauens quils vsed in Virginals. *Lingula*, as *Linguetta*. **1659** TORRIANO-FLORIO It→E *Linguella*. *Linguetta*, as *Lingula*. *Lingula*, ... also the little pieces of ravens quils used in the jacks of virgianalls [sic]

Linus *see* epitaph
1658 PHILLIPS (1st edn) *Linus*, the son of *Apollo*, and *Psammas* ... also the son of *Apollo* and *Terpsichore*, one of the nine Muses, he proved a very famous Musitian, taught *Thamyras, Orpheus*, and *Hercules*, by whom, as some say, he was knockt on the head, because he laught at him for playing

unhandsomely. **1676** Coles *Linus,* the Son of *Apollo* and *Psammas* ... also a famous Musician who taught *Orpheus* and *Hercules,* who knockt him (they say) on the head for laughing at his unhandsom playing. **1678** Phillips (4th edn) *Linus,* the Son of *Apollo* and *Psammas,* the Daughter of *Crotopus,* King of *Argos* ... also the Son of *Apollo* and *Terpsichore,* one of the Nine Muses. He proved a very famous Musician, taught *Thamiras, Orpheus,* and *Hercules,* by whom, as some say, he was knocked on the head, because he laught at him for playing unhandsomely.

linus *as song*
1706 Bedford *Temple Musick* (p. 13) [*re* the ancient Egyptians] ... That they were anciently addicted to *Musick* is also evident, since we are told by an *Historian* [marginalia: '*Herodot. Euterpe.* pag. 52.'] who travelled into those Parts, that *the* Egyptians *sang a Song like the* Greeks, *which they called* Linus, *or in the* Egyptian *Language* Maneros, *which was composed to lament the Death of the only Son of their first King,* who (as the same Author tells us) was called *Menes.* **1711** Bedford *Great Abuse of Musick* (p. 5) [*re* the musical skill of shepherds in ancient Egypt] ... This gave the first Rise to *Elegies,* and accordingly *Herodotus* informs us, That *the* Egyptians *sang a Song which they call'd* Linus, *or in their own language* Maneros, *which was compos'd to lament the Death of the only Son of their first King.*

lira, lire *see* lyre

lire-liron *see* burden
1611 Cotgrave Fr→E *Lire-liron.* The burthen of a song.

lirone
1611 Florio It→E *Lirone,* ... Also any kind of great Lira. **1659** Torriano-Florio It→E *Lirone,* ... also any great Harp or Lira. **1688** Davis-Torriano-Florio It→E *Lirone,* ... also any great Harp.

litany *see* prosodion
1598 Florio It→E *Letania,* a letanie sung or saide in churches. **1611** Florio It→E *Letania,* a Letanie sung in churches, a publicke praier *Letanizzare,* to say or sing Letanies. **1688** Miege-Cotgrave Fr→E § *Chanter la Litanie,* to sing the Litany. **1706** Kersey-Phillips (6th edn) *Litany, (Gr.)* a general Supplication, or Prayer; especially one in the Common-Prayer-Book of the Church of *England,* appointed to be Said or Sung on certain Days. **1728** Chambers *Litany,* an old Church-Term, signifying the Processions, Prayers, and Supplications, used to appease the Wrath of God, to avert his Judgments, or to procure his Mercies .... *Litany,* among us, is a Form of Prayer sung or said in Churches, consisting of several Periods, or Articles; at the End of each whereof, is an Invocation in the same Terms. The Word comes from the *Greek* λιτανεία, *Supplication. Pezron* would go further, and derive the λίττω, or λίσσω of the *Greeks,* from *Celtic Lit,* Feast, Solemnity.

liticen *see* buccinator
1538 Elyot L→E *Liticen,* a blower of a smalle trumpette. **1552** Huloet L→E *Liticen. nis, Tibicen.* Blower of small Trumpettes. **1587** Thomas L→E *Liticen, inis, m.g. Non.* A blower of a small trumpet.

lituus *see* aes, buccina, wind
1500 *Ortus Vocabulorum* L→E Lituus a. um. i. cornu gracile. angl. a smale horne **1538** Elyot L→E *Lituus,* ... Also a scepter, and a trumpette. **1565** Cooper L→E *Lituus. Virg.* An horne, or trumpette like Corneilis horne. § *Acuti litui. Stat.* Shrill hornes or trumpettes. *Lituos pati. Virgil.* To abide the sounde of trumpets. *Strepunt litui. Horat.* The trumpettes sowne. *Stridor lituûm, clangórque tubarum. Lucan.* The noyse of hornes and sounde of trumpettes. **1587** Thomas L→E *Lituus, tui, m.g.* ... a horne, a writhen or crooked trumpet like a Corneilis horne: **1589** Rider L→E *Lituus, m.* A crooked horne, or trumpet. *Lituus, m. concha, f.* A writhed, or crooked trumpet, like a Corneilis horne. **1598** Florio It→E *Lituo,* ... Also a kinde of crooked horne or trumpet. **1611** Florio It→E *Lituo,* a crooked staffe ... Also a kind of crooked horne or trumpet or horne-pipe. **1659** Torriano-Florio It→E **Lituo,* a crooked staff ... also a kind of crooked trumpet or horne-pipe. **1728** Chambers *Lituus,* among Medalists, is a Staff used by the Augurs, made in form of a Crozier. We frequently see it in Medals, along with other Pontifical Instruments. *Aulus Gellius* says, it was bigger in the place where it was crooked than elsewhere. Some derive the Word from the *Greek* λιτος, something that makes a shrill acute Sound, which was a Property of this Instrument.

liuto *see* lute

livre *see* libro
1724 [PEPUSCH] *Short Explic. of Foreign Words in Mus. Bks.* (p. 42) *Livre*, a Book. Thus, ¶ *Livre Premier*, First Book. ¶ *Livre Second*, Second Book.

long
1598 FLORIO It→E *Longa*, a long in musicke. **1611** FLORIO It→E *Lunga* [sic], a long in Musike. **1659** TORRIANO-FLORIO It→E **Longa*, a long in musick **1702** KERSEY *New Engl. Dict.* (1st edn) A *Long* in Musick. **1706** KERSEY-PHILLIPS (6th edn) A *Long*, a Musical Note, or Measure of Time, containing two *Briefs*. See *Large*. **1707** *Gloss. Angl. Nova* (1st edn) *Long*, is a Musical Note, equal to two Briefs. **1728** CHAMBERS *Long Measure*. See *Measure*.

after 1517 ANON. Art of Mvsic BL Add. 4911, f. 1v *The long is* a figur of quhilk ye Lynth dois dubill ye breid halv a virgle to ye similitud of the larg ... **1609** DOWLAND-ORNITHOPARCUS *Micrologvs* (p. 39) A *Long* is a Figure, whose length is twise as much as his breadth, hauing such a tayle as the *Large* hath. **1617-24** FLUDD *Utriusque Cosmi Maioris: De Templo Musicæ* (p. 191) *Longa* est dimidia pars largæ.

loure
1611 COTGRAVE Fr→E *Loure: f.* A bagpipe: *Poictevin*. *Lourette: f.* A small bagpipe. **1724** [PEPUSCH] *Short Explic. of Foreign Words in Mus. Bks.* (pp. 42-3) *Loure*, is the Name of a *French* Dance, or the Tune thereunto belonging, always in Triple Time, and the Movement, or Time, very Slow and Grave. **1726** BAILEY *An Univ. Etymolog. Engl. Dict.* (3rd edn) *Loure*, the Name of a *French* Dance, or the Tune that belongs to it, always in triple Time, and the Movement or Tune very low and grave.

ludo
1565 COOPER L→E *Ludo, ludis, lusi, lusum, lúdere. Plaut.* ... to play as one doth on instrumentes. § *Ludere in numerum. Virg.* To daunce measures. **1587** THOMAS L→E *Ludo, is, si, sum, ere.* ... to play as one doth on instruments: *also* to mooue, to daunce, or to write verses, epigrams, or like pleasant things, *Virg.* to sing, *Gell.*

lugubre *see* cantus, chanson, chant
1593 HOLLYBAND Fr→E § *vn chant lugubre*, a sorrowfull singing, *com.* **1611** COTGRAVE Fr→E *Lugubre: com.* Dolefull, mourning, mournefull, sorrowfull, wayling, funerall.

lullaby *see* by by, falcinine, lallatio, nænia, nanna, ninnare
1702 KERSEY *New Engl. Dict.* (1st edn) A *Lullaby-song*. **1731** KERSEY *New Engl. Dict.* (3rd edn) A *Lullaby*, or *Lullaby-Song*, a Tone to hush a Child to sleep. **1737** DYCHE-PARDON (2nd edn) *Lullaby* (S.) the singing to, or amusing of a Child by its Nurse to compose it to sleep.

Lully, Jean-Baptiste *see* branle, style, violin

lutanist *see* barbitist
1598 FLORIO It→E *Liutiere*, one that plaieth vpon a lute. **1611** FLORIO It→E *Liutiere*, as *Liutista*. *Liutista*, a professor or player on a Lute. **1702** KERSEY *New Engl. Dict.* (1st edn) A *Lutanist, or* lute-player. **1706** KERSEY-PHILLIPS (6th edn) *Lutanist*, one skilful in playing on the Lute; a Lute-Master. **1737** DYCHE-PARDON (2nd edn) *Lutanist* (S.) one skilled in playing upon the musical Instrument called the Lute.

lute *see* archlute, barbiton, chelys, close play, cut lute, draw, entata, feeling, fides, fidicula, hammering, laying, pearled playing, pinceter, strike, testudo, theorbo
1550 THOMAS It→E *Leuto*, a lute. *Liuto*, a Lute. **1570/71** *Dict. Fr. and Engl.* Fr→E *Vn Luc*, a lute. **1593** HOLLYBAND Fr→E *Luc*, a Lute: *m.* *Vn Lut*, or *luth*, a Lute: *m.* § *Le printens d'yver, et pincetant sur les chanterelles de son luth obeïssant, &c.* playing upon the singing cords of her obedient Lute, &c. *Maistre jouëur de Luc*, a Master that teacheth to play vpon the lute: *m.* **1598** FLORIO It→E *Liuto, Liutto*, an instrument called a lute. § *Sonare di lauto*, to play vpon a lute. **1599** MINSHEU-PERCYVALL Sp→E **Laud*, m. a lute. **1611** COTGRAVE Fr→E *Luc: m.* A Lute. *Lut: m.* A Lute; *Luth: m.* A Lute. § *Empointer les doigts sur le luth.* To finger a Lute; also, handsomely to set, couch, or place, the fingers ends thereon. *La table d'un Luc.* The bellie of a Lute. *Tablature d'un Luc.* The bellie of a Lute. *Vn luth à 16 rangs.* A sixteene-stringd Lute; or a Lute with sixteene strings. **1611** FLORIO It→E *Liutaro*, a Lute player or maker. *Liuto*, any kind of Lute. § *Sonare di lauto*, to play vpon a Lute. **1659** TORRIANO-FLORIO It→E *Dislutare*, to unlute. *Leuto, Leutto*, any kinde of Lute. *Liutaro[,] Liutiere, Liutista*, a professor, a teacher, or player on the lute, a lutanish [sic], also a maker or seller of lutes. **Liuto, Liutto*, any kinde of lute *Lotare*, as *Lutare*, to lute. § *Sonare di liuto*, to play upon a lute. **1688** MIEGE-COTGRAVE Fr→E *Lut*, (m.) Lute, a musical

Instrument; *Luth* See Lut. § *Bander les cordes d'un Lut,* to string a Lute. *desaccorder un Lut,* to put a Lute out of tune. *Il jouë fort bien du Lut,* he play's very well upon the Lute. *Il touche bien un Lut,* cd. *il jouë bien du Lut,* he touches a Lute finely. *Jouër du Lut, toucher le Lut,* to play upon the Lute. *Poser de bonne grace la main sur le Lut,* to lay his hand with a good grace on the Lute. **1696** PHILLIPS (5th edn) *Lute* also is a Musical Instrument consisting of a Belly, a Neck, and several rows of Gutstrings, to be touch'd with the Finger. **1702** KERSEY *New Engl. Dict.* (1st edn) A *Lute,* a Musical instrument. **1706** KERSEY-PHILLIPS (6th edn) *Lute,* a Musical Instrument **1721** BAILEY *An Univ. Etymolog. Engl. Dict.* (1st edn) *Lute, (Lut,* F. *liuto* Ital. *lulte, Dan.)* a musical Instrument. **1724** [PEPUSCH] *Short Explic. of Foreign Words in Mus. Bks.* (p. 41) *Leuto,* or *Lieuto,* a Lute, an Instrument of Musick. **1726** BAILEY *An Univ. Etymolog. Engl. Dict.* (3rd edn) *Leuto* (in *Musick-Books*) signifies a Lute or musical Instrument. *Ital.* **1728** CHAMBERS *Lute,* a Musical Instrument with Strings. It had antiently but five Rows of Strings; but in course of time four, five, or six more have been added. The *Lute* consists of four principal Parts, the Table, the Body or Belly, which has nine or ten Sides, the Neck, which has nine or ten Stops or Divisions mark'd with Strings, and the Head or Cross, wherein are Screws for raising or lowering the Strings to the proper Tone. In the middle of the Table is a Rose or Passage for the Sound. There is also a Bridge that the Strings are struck with the right Hand, and with the left the Stops are pressed. We call Temperament of the *Lute* the proper Alternation that is to be made in the Intervals, both with regard to Consonances and Dissonances, in order to render them more just on the Instrument. Some derive the word from the *German Laute,* which signifies the same thing, or from *lauten, sonare. Scaliger* and *Bochart* derive it from the *Arabic, Allaud.* The *Lutes* of *Boulogne* are esteem'd the best, on account of the Wood, which is said to have an uncommon Disposition for producing a sweet Sound. **1737** DYCHE-PARDON (2nd edn) *Lute* (S.) a musical Instrument of very antient Invention, and indeed almost all stringed Instruments bear a great Resemblance to it, and are properly so many Lutes differently modified; but at present the real Lute is in *England* almost wholly laid aside, as too troublesome.

luter

1500 *Ortus Vocabulorum* L→E *Luter* eris. i. concha vel cantarus aquarius: ...

lute string

1702 KERSEY *New Engl. Dict.* (1st edn) *Lute-string,* a sort of silk. **1706** KERSEY-PHILLIPS (6th edn) *Lustring* or *Lute-string, (Fr.)* a sort of Silk that has a Closs set on it. **1731** KERSEY *New Engl. Dict.* (3rd edn) *Lutestring* or *Lustring,* a kind of Silk for Hoods, Scarves, *&c.*

lutier

1688 MIEGE-COTGRAVE Fr→E *Luthier* See Lutier. *Lutier,* (from *Lut*) *faiseur d'Instrumens de Musique,* a Musick-Instrument Maker.

lutrin

1688 MIEGE-COTGRAVE Fr→E *Lutrin,* (m.) a Desk, a Querister's Desk in a Church-Quire. § *Chanter au Lutrin,* to sing at the Desk.

lydian *see* collateral, mixolydian, mode, mood, motet, tone

1598 FLORIO It→E *Hipolidio,* a kind of accent or note in musicke. *Lidio,* a kinde of mournefull solemne musicke. **1611** FLORIO It→E *Hipolidio,* a kinde of accent or note in graue Musicke. *Hippolidio,* a kind of musicke or sound in musicke. *Lidio,* ... Also a kinde of mournefull solemne musike. **1659** TORRIANO-FLORIO It→E *Hipolidio,* a grave accent or note in Musick. *Lidio,* a touch-stone, also a kind of mourning musick. **1661** BLOUNT (2nd edn) § *Lydian Musick* (*Lydius modus*) doleful and lamentable musick. **1676** COLES § *Lydian Musick,* dolefull. **1678** PHILLIPS (4th edn) § *Lydian Mood in Musicke,* that sort of Musick which is of the most soft, amorous, and melting strain. **1706** KERSEY-PHILLIPS (6th edn) § *Lydian Mood,* a sort of Harmony which was us'd in solemn grave Musick; the Descant or Composition being of slow Time, suited to Sacred Hymns or Anthems. **1730** BAILEY *Dict. Britannicum* (1st edn) § *Lydian Mood* (in *Musick*) a doleful and lamenting kind of it [music], the Descant being in slow time. *Musick* (of the *Lydian Mood*) was shrill. **1736** BAILEY *Dict. Britannicum* (2nd edn) § *Lydian Mode* (in *Musick*) was proper for funeral songs, and invented by *Amphion.* **1737** DYCHE-PARDON (2nd edn) § *Lydian-mood* (S.) a musical, doleful, and lamenting Manner of Expression, by Instruments or Voices, slow in Motion, and used at Funeral or Penitentiary Exercises.

1636 BUTLER *Principles of Musik* (p. 1) The *Lydian* Moode is a grave, ful, solemn Musik in Discant, for the moste parte, of slow time, set to a Hymn,

Anthem, or other spiritual song in prose, and soomtime in vers, the notes exceeding often the number of the syllables: which throogh his heavenly harmoni, ravisheth the minde with a kinde of ecstasi, lifting it up from the regarde of earthly things, unto the desire of celestiall joyz: ... which it dooeth lively resemble. § (p. 4) The *Lydian* Moode was so called of *Lydia*, famous for the golden River *Pactolus*, and the winding retrograde *Mæander*: the one resembling the treasure and glorious matter of the Ditti; the other the pleasing Reports and Reverts, with other admirable varieties of the Musik.

lyra *see* lyre

lyra viol *see* leero, viol
1702 KERSEY *New Engl. Dict.* (1st edn) A *Lyra-viol*, a musical instrument. **1706** KERSEY-PHILLIPS (6th edn) *Lyra Viol*, a sort of Viol. **1708** KERSEY *Dict. Anglo-Brit.* (1st edn) *Lyra-Viol* a sort of Viol: Whence the Expression of playing Leero-way, corruptly us'd for *Lyra*-way. **1730** BAILEY *Dict. Britannicum* (1st edn) *Lyra Viol*, a musical Instrument, whence comes the common Expression of playing *leero way*, corruptly for *lyra way*.

lyre *see* aime-lyre, chelys, cithara, harp, lirone, testudo
1500 *Ortus Vocabulorum* L→E Lira re. prima breuis est instrumentum musicum. i. cithara vel eius corda. anglice an harpe. f.p. Liro ras. i. liram facere vel arare liram. etiam est fistulare. a.p. **1538** ELYOT L→E *Lira*, ... sometyme it sygnifyeth an harpe. *Lyra*, an harpe. **1565** COOPER L→E *Lyra, lyræ, foe. gen. Plin.* An harpe. § *Bellus es arte lyra ... Martial.* Thou arte good at the harpe *Canor lyræ. Ouid.* The tune of the harpe. *Canoræ lyrae. Claud.* Lowde harpes. *Fidicen lyræ. Ouid.* An harper. *Inauratæ lyræ fila mouet pollice. Ouid.* He playeth on a gilted harpe. *Increpare lyram digitis. Ouid.* To play on the harpe. *Institui lyra. Quintil.* To be taught to play on the harpe. *Laudes alicuius canere lyra. Ouid.* To singe ones prayses to the harpe. *Lyra percussa. Ouid.* An harpe played on. *Lyræ parens, Mercurius. Horat.* Mercurie first inuentour of the harpe. *Lyram increpuisse digitis. Ouid.* To haue made the harpe go with his fyngers: to haue played on, &c. *Scitus lyræ. Ouid.* A cunnyng player on the harpe. **1587** THOMAS L→E *Lira, æ, f.g. Colum* ... an harp. *Lyra, ræ, f.g. Plin.* An harpe. **1593** HOLLYBAND Fr→E *Vn Lire*, a Citterne or instrument of musicke. *Lyre*, an harpe: *f.* **1598** FLORIO It→E *Lira*, an instrument of musicke called a lyre or a harp. **1599** MINSHEU-PERCYVALL Sp→E *Lira*, f. a harpe. **1611** COTGRAVE Fr→E *Lire: f.* The musicall Instrument Lyra. *Lyre: f.* A Lyra, or Harpe. **1611** FLORIO It→E *Lira*, an instrument of musike called a Lyra or Harp. *Lirare*, to play vpon a Lyra. **1658** PHILLIPS (1st edn) *Lyra*, one of the celestial Astorismes, which the Poets feigned to be *Arions* Harp. **1659** TORRIANO-FLORIO It→E *Lira*, an instrument of Musick, called a Lyra, some use it for a Harp *Lirare, Lireggiare*, to play upon a Lyra or Harpe **1676** COLES *Lyre, Latin.* a harp. *Lyra, (Arion's)* harp, a constellation. **1688** DAVIS-TORRIANO-FLORIO It→E *Lira*, an instrument of Musick, called a Harp; *Lirare, Lireggiare*, to play upon a Harp; **1696** PHILLIPS (5th edn) *Lyre*, a Musical Instrument, of which there are two sorts, the one strung with gutts, the other with wire strings. The Poets make use of this word for all manner of Harmony. **1702** KERSEY *New Engl. Dict.* (1st edn) A *Lyre, or* harp. **1704** *Cocker's Engl. Dict.* (1st edn) *Harp*, a Harp. **1706** KERSEY-PHILLIPS (6th edn) *Lyra*, the Lyre or Harp, a Musical Instrument, of which there are two sorts, one strung with Guts, and the other with Wire-strings: **1724** [PEPUSCH] *Short Explic. of Foreign Words in Mus. Bks.* (p. 42) *Lira*, or *Lyra*, or *Lyre*, a Viol so called from the Way of Tuning. **1726** BAILEY *An Univ. Etymolog. Engl. Dict.* (3rd edn) *Lira, Lyra, Lyre*, (so called from the way of Tuning) a Viol. **1728** CHAMBERS *Lyra*, or *Lyre*, the same with *Cithara*, a Harp; a stringed Instrument much used among the Antients; said to have been invented by *Mercury*, on occasion of his finding a dead Shell-Fish, call'd by the *Greeks Chelone*, and the *Latins Testudo*, lest, on an Inundation of the *Nile*; of the Shell whereof he form'd his *Lyre*, mounting it with seven Strings, according to *Lucian*, and adding a kind of *Jugum* to it, to stretch or loosen the Strings. *Boethius* relates the Opinion of some, who say that *Mercury*'s *Lyre* had but four Strings, in imitation of the Mundane Music of the four Elements. *Diodorus Siculus* says it had but three Strings, in imitation of the three Seasons of the Year; which were all the *Greeks* counted, *viz.* Spring, Summer and Winter. *Nicomachus, Horace, Lucian*, and others, make it have seven Strings, in imitation of the seven Planets. This three, four, or seven-stringed Instrument *Mercury* gave to *Orpheus*; who being torn to pieces by the *Bacchanals*, the *Lyre* was hung up by the *Lesbians* in *Apollo*'s Temple. Others say, *Pythagorus* found it in some Temple in *Egypt*, and added an eighth String. *Nicomachus* says, that when *Orpheus* was kill'd, his *Lyre* was cast

into the Sea, and thrown up at *Antissa* a City of *Lesbos*; where the Fishers finding it, gave it to *Terpander*; who carried it into *Egypt*, and call'd himself the Inventor. The seven Strings were diatonically disposed by Tones and Semi-Tones, and *Pythagoras*'s eighth String made up the Octave. ¶ From the *Lyra*, which all agree to be the first Instrument of the stringed kind in *Greece*, arose an infinite Number of others, differing in Shape and Number of Strings; as the *Psalterium, Trigon, Sambuca, Pectis, Magadis, Barbiton, Testudo*, (the two last used promiscuously by *Horace* with the *Lyra* and *Cithara*) *Epigonium, Simmicium* and *Pandura*; which were all struck with the Hand or a *Plectrum*. **1730** BAILEY *Dict. Britannicum* (1st edn) *Lyre* (*lyra*, L.) a Harp, some of which are strung with Wire, and others with Guts. **1737** DYCHE-PARDON (2nd edn) *Lyre* (S.) a Harp or other stringed Instrument with Wire Strings; the Painters, Statuaries, &c. represent *Apollo* always with a Lyre in his Hand;

1582 *Batman vppon Bartholome* (chap. 134) *Lira* hath that name for diuersitye of sounds: for *Lira* giueth diuers sounds, as *Isid.* saith. **1721** MALCOLM *Treatise of Musick* (p. 471) Of stringed Instruments [mentioned in ancient accounts] the first is the *Lyra* or *Cithara* (which some distinguish:) *Mercury* is said to be Inventor of it, in this Manner; after an Inundation of the *Nile* he found a dead Shell-fish, which the *Greeks* call *Chelone*, and the *Latins Testudo*; of this Shell he made his *Lyre*, mounting it with Seven Strings, as *Lucian* says; and added a Kind of *jugum* to it, to lengthen the Strings ...

lyricen *see* citharist

1500 *Ortus Vocabulorum* L→E Liricen inis. i. canens cum lira. Liricus ci. id est. an harper. m.t. Liricina ne. mulier q cum lira canit. a woman herper. f.p. **1538** ELYOT L→E *Lyricen, cinis*, an harper. **1565** COOPER L→E *Lyricen, pen. corr. lyrícinis, pen. corr. masc. gen.* An harper, or one that singeth to the harpe. **1587** THOMAS L→E *Lyricen, p.b. Horat. vid. Lyristes* [*see* lyrist].

lyrick *see* harp, iperlirica

1500 *Ortus Vocabulorum* L→E Lirica corum. sunt carmina dulcia & amena. n.s. Lirici sunt poete diuersa describentes carmina. m.s. Liricus ca. cum. perti. ad liram. Et componitur pliricus ca. cum. i. dulcis & delectabilis super alios vel super canum lire. o.s. **1565** COOPER L→E *Lyricus, pen. corr. Adiect.* Pertaynyng to an harpe. **1587** THOMAS L→E *Lyrica, orum, n.g. Plin.* A song to the Harpe. *Lyricus, a um, p.b.* Pertaining to an harpe, a player on a harpe. § *Carmen lyricum, Iun.* A song to the harpe: it consisted of *Strophe, Antistrophe, & Epodos.* **1589** RIDER L→E *Lyrica, orum, n. strophe, f. carmen lyricum.* A song to the harpe. *Lyricina, citharistria. fidicina, f.* A woman harper. *Lyricus, citharædicus, ad.* Belonging to the harpe. **1593** HOLLYBAND Fr→E *Lyrique*, as *le poete lyrique*, we meane Horace, because he hath written verses fit to be played vpon the harpe or other instrumentes of musicke. **1598** FLORIO It→E *Lirico*, a kinde of verse or song made to the harpe. **1611** COTGRAVE Fr→E *Lyrique: com.* Lyricke; of a Harpe; sung to the Harpe; playing on a Harpe. **1611** FLORIO It→E *Lirico*, a kind of verse or song made to the Harpe. **1616** BULLOKAR *Lyrike.* A Poet which maketh verses to be sung vnto the harp. The best of these Poets among the Grecians was *Pindarus*, and among the Latines, *Horace.* **1656** BLOUNT (1st edn) *Lyrick (lyricus)* a Poet that makes verses to be sung to the Harp. The best of these among the Grecians was *Pindarus*; and among the Latins, *Horace. Lyrick*, taken adjectively, is pertaining to a Harp, that playes on a Harp, or to *Lyrick* verses, which the antients applied to Songs and Hymms. **1658** PHILLIPS (1st edn) *Lyrick*, verses, or songs, songs composed to the Lyre, or Harp, whence we say vulgarly, playing Leero-way on the Viol, which is corruptly used for Lyra-way, *i.e.* Harp-way. **1659** TORRIANO-FLORIO It→E *Lirico*, a lirike Poem, or verses sung to the Lira or Harp. **1661** BLOUNT (2nd edn) *Lyrick (lyricus)* a Poet that makes verses to be sung to the Harp or Lute. The best of these among the Grecians was *Pindarus*; among the Latins *Horace.* Lyrick, taken adjectively, is pertaining to a Harp, that plays on a Harp, or to *Lyrick* verses, which the antients applied to Songs and Hymns. **1676** COLES *Lyrick*, belonging to an harp. § *Lyrick poets*, (as *Pindar* and *Horace*) who make ¶ *Lyrick-verses*, (not Heroick) composed to the Harp or Lute. **1688** DAVIS-TORRIANO-FLORIO It→E *Lirico*, a lyrick Poem, or verses sung to the Harp. **1702** KERSEY *New Engl. Dict.* (1st edn) *Lyrick*, belonging to a harp; as *lyrick* Verses, that were sung to that instrument. **1704** *Cocker's Engl. Dict.* (1st edn) *Lyrick*, a Poet, who frames verses to be sung to the Harp. The best of the *Greeks*, was *Pindarus*; and of the *Latins, Horace.* **1706** KERSEY-PHILLIPS (6th edn) *Lyrick*, belonging to the Harp; as *Lyrick Poesy.* **1728** CHAMBERS *Lyric*; something sung, or play'd on the Lyre or Harp. The Word is particularly applied to the antient Odes and Stanza's; which answer to our

Airs or Tunes, and may be play'd on Instruments. The Antients were great Admirers of *Lyric* Verses, which Name they gave to such Verses as do not come under either of the two ordinary Kinds of Verse, *viz.* Hexameters and Iambics. These were principally used in Odes, and in the Chorus's of Tragedies. The Characteristic of *Lyric* Poetry, and that which distinguishes it from all others, is Sweetness. As Gravity rules in Heroic Verse, Simplicity in Pastoral, Tenderness and Softness in Elegy, Sharpness and Poignancy in Satire, Mirth in Comedy, the Pathetic in Tragedy, and the Point in Epigram; so in the *Lyric,* the Poet applies himself wholly to sooth the Minds of Men by the Sweetness and Variety of the Verse, and the Delicacy of the Words and Thoughts, the Agreeableness of the Numbers, and the Description of Things most pleasing in their own Nature. See *Ode, Song,* &c. **1730** Bailey *Dict. Britannicum* (1st edn) *Lyrick (lyricus, L.)* of or pertaining to a Lyre or Harp. **1737** Dyche-Pardon (2nd edn) *Lyrick* (A.) something pertaining or be-belonging [sic] to the Lyre, Harp, &c. from whence the Odes or Stanzas of the Antients are called Lyrick Verses, answering to our Airs or single Tunes for Songs, &c. which were composed in the most soothing Strains, and varied by all the Art of the Poet, in Delicacy of Language and Turn of Thought to render them agreeable and entertaining.

1589 [Puttenham] *Arte of English Poesie* (p. 20) [*re* poets in ancient times] Others who more delighted to write songs or ballads of pleasure, to be song with the voice, and to the harpe, lute, or citheron & such other musical, instruments, they were called melodious Poets (*melici*) or by a more common name *Lirique* Poets, of which sort was *Pindarus, Anacreon* and *Callimachus* with others among the Greeks: *Horace* and *Catullus* among the Latines.

lyrick verse *see* æolian, epode, ode, sociandus

1706 Kersey-Phillips (6th edn) *Lyrick Verses* or *Songs,* such as are set to the Lyre or Harp; whence the Common Expression of *Playing Leero-way,* which is corruptly us'd for Lyra-way. **1707** *Gloss. Angl. Nova* (1st edn) *Lyrick Verses,* are Verses made to be sung to the Harp or Lute, such as are the Odes of *Horace, Pindar,* &c. **1730** Bailey *Dict. Britannicum* (1st edn) *Lyrick Verse, &c.* are such as are set to the Lyre or Harp, apply'd to the antient Odes and Stanza's, and answer to our Airs or Tunes, and may be play'd on Instruments.

lyrist

1587 Thomas L→E *Lyristes, stæ, m.g. Plin. Iun.* An harper, or one that singeth to the harpe. **1611** Florio It→E *Lirista,* a player on the Lira. **1656** Blount (1st edn) *Lyrist (lyristes)* a Harper, or one that sings to the Harp. **1676** Coles *Lyrist,* he that plaies on, or sings to the ¶ *Lyre* **1688** Davis-Torriano-Florio It→E *Lirista,* a harper. **1706** Kersey-Phillips (6th edn) *Lyrist,* an Harper, one that plays on, or sings to the Harp. **1731** Kersey *New Engl. Dict.* (3rd edn) A *Lyrist,* one skilled in playing on the Harp. **1737** Dyche-Pardon (2nd edn) *Lyrist* (S.) a Player upon or Singer to the Harp, Lyre, or other stringed Instrument.

M

madama d'Orliens

1611 Florio It→E *Madama d'Orliens,* the name of a kind of french dance.

madrigal *see* æolian, barzelletta, canzonet, contadinella, ground, song, style (stylo madrigalesco)

1550 Thomas It→E *Madriali,* songes or baletts. **1598** Florio It→E *Madrigaletti,* short madrigals. *Madrigali, Madriali,* madrigals, a kind of short songs or ditties in Italie. **1611** Florio It→E *Madrigaletti,* Songs called Madrigals. *Madrigali, madriali,* Madrigall songs. **1616** Bullokar *Madrigals.* A kind of Sonnets. **1623** Cockeram *Madrigall.* a kinde of Song *Madrigalls.* A kinde of Sonnets. **1656** Blount (1st edn) *Madrigal* (Ital. *madrigali*) a kind of song. **1658** Phillips (1st edn) *Madrigal,* (Ital.) a kind of Song. **1659** Torriano-Florio It→E **Madrigali, Madriali,* madrigals, which is properly a kinde of Lyricke Poesie, not subject to measure of feet, or strict rules of rhimes. **1671** Phillips (3rd edn) *Madrigal, (Ital.)* a kind of *Italian* air or song, to be set to musick, consisting but of one single rank of verses, and therein different from the *Canzon,* which *B* [sic] consists of several Strophs or ranks of verses returning in the same order and number. **1674** Blount (4th edn) *Madrigal,* (Ital. *Madrigali*) a kind of Song or Aire. **1676** Coles *Madrigal,* an *Italian* air, of one single rank of Verses. **1702** Kersey *New Engl. Dict.* (1st edn) A *Madrigal,* an *Italian* amorous sonnet. **1706** Kersey-Phillips (6th edn) *Madrigal, (Ital.)* a kind of *Italian* Air, or Song to be set to Musick, consisting only of a single Rank of Verses, and therein differing from the *Canzonet,* which is made up of several *Strophe*'s, or Ranks of Verses, returning in the same Order and Number. **1707** *Gloss. Angl. Nova* (1st edn) *Madrigal,* (Ital.) a kind of *Italian* Air or Song. **1724** [Pepusch] *Short Explic. of Foreign Words in Mus. Bks.* (p. 44) *Madrigale,* a particular Kind of Vocal Musick, formerly very much in Esteem, some for two, three, four, five, six, seven, and eight Voices; and was so called from the Kind of Poetry with which it was composed. **1726** Bailey *An Univ. Etymolog. Engl. Dict.* (3rd edn) *Madrigal* (so called from the kind of Poetry, with which it was compos'd) an *Italian* Air or Song; also a particular kind of Vocal Musick, formerly very much in request, some for two, three, four, five, six, seven and eight Voices. **1728** Chambers *Madrigal,* a Term in the modern *Italian, Spanish,* and *French* Poetry, signifying a little amorous Piece, containing a certain Number of loose unequal Verses, not tied either to the scrupulous Regularity of a Sonnet, or the Subtlety of an *Epigram;* but consisting of some tender, delicate, yet simple Thought, suitably expressed. The *Madrigal,* according to Mr. *le Brun,* is an Epigram without any thing very brisk and sprightly in its Fall or Close: something very tender and gallant is usually the Subject of it; and a certain beautiful, noble, yet chaste, Simplicity, makes its Character. ¶ The *Madrigal* is usually looked on as the shortest of all the little kinds of Poems, and may consist of fewer Verses than either the Sonnet or Roundelay. There is no other Rule regarded in mingling the Rhimes and Verses of different kinds, but the Choice and Convenience of the Author. This Poem, however, really allows of less Licence than any other; whether we regard the Rhyme, the Measures, or the Purity of Expression. ¶ *Menage* derives the Word from *Mandra,* which, in *Latin* and *Greek,* signifies a Company of Cattel; imagining it to have been originally a kind of Pastoral or Shepherd's Song; whence the *Italians* formed their *Madrigale,* and we *Madrigal.* Others rather chuse to derive the Word from *Madrugar,* which, in the *Spanish* signifies to rise in the Morning: the *Madrigals* being formerly sung early in the Morning, by those who had a mind to serenade their Mistresses. **1737** Dyche-Pardon (2nd edn) *Madrigal* (S.) a Love Song, or little amorous Poem, of uncertain or unequal Measures.

1597 Morley *Plaine and Easie Introdvction* (p. 180) [marginalia: 'A Madrigal'] ... the light musicke hath beene of late more deepely diued into, so that there is no vanitie which in it hath not beene followed to the full, but the best kind of it is termed *Madrigal,* a word for the *etymologie* of which I can giue no reason, yet vse sheweth that it is a kinde of musicke made vpon songs and sonnets, such as *Petrarcha* and many Poets of our time haue excelled in. This kind of musicke weare not so much disalowable if the Poets who compose the ditties would abstaine from some obscenities, which all honest eares abhor, and sometime from blasphemies to such as this, *ch'altro di te iddio non voglio* which no man (at least who hath any hope of saluation) can sing without trembling. As for the musick it is next vnto the Motet, the most artificiall and to men of vnderstanding most delightfull. If therefore you will compose in this kind you must possesse your selfe with an amorous humor (for in no composition shal you proue admirable except you put on, and possesse your selfe wholy with that vaine wherein you compose) so that you must in your musicke be wauering like the wind, sometime wanton, somtime drooping, sometime graue and staide, or herwhile effeminat, you may maintaine points and reuert them, vse triplaes and shew the verie vttermost of your varietie, and the more varietie you shew the better shal you please... **1636** Butler *Principles of Musik* (p. 8) The *Madrigal* is a Chromatik Moode in Discant, whose notes dooe often exceede the number of the syllables of the Ditti; soomtime in Duple, soomtime in Triple Proportion: with qik and sweete Reportes, and Repeats, and all pleasing varietiz of Art, in 4, 5, or 6 Partes having, in one or more of them, one or more Rests, (especially in the beginning) to bring in the Points begun in an other Parte.

maestoso

1724 [Pepusch] *Short Explic. of Foreign Words in Mus. Bks.* (p. 44) *Maestoso,* or *Maestuoso,* is to play with Majesty, Pomp, and Grandure, and consequently Slow, nevertheless with Strength and Firmness of Hand. **1726** Bailey *An Univ. Etymolog. Engl. Dict.* (3rd edn) *Maestoso, Maestuso,* (in *Musick Books*) signifies to play with Majesty, Pomp, and Grandeur, and so of consequence slow; nevertheless with Strength and Firmness of Hand. *Ital.*

1736 Tans'ur *Compleat Melody* (3rd edn, p. 68) *Maestoso, Maestuso,* (Ital.) Either of those Terms denote that you must sing, or play with Majesty and Grandure; but slow, strong, and steady.

maestro *see* capella, virtuosa

1659 Torriano-Florio It→E § **Maestro di canto, Maestro di capella,* a Singing-master, a Master of a Princes Chappel or Quire of Musick. **1724** [Pepusch] *Short Explic. of Foreign Words in Mus. Bks.* (pp. 44-5) *Maestro,* is Master. Thus, *Maestro de Capella,* is Master of the Chapel Musick, or Master of Musick only, meaning thereby one of the first Rank. **1726** Bailey *An Univ. Etymolog. Engl. Dict.* (3rd edn) *Maestro,* Master. *Ital. Maestro de Capella,* Master of the Chapel Musick, or Master of Musick only; meaning thereby one of the first Rank. *Ital.*

maestro bigo

1659 Torriano-Florio It→E **Maestro Bigo,* the name of an Old Song in *Italy,* as common as *Selengers-*Round is with us, by Met. a silly gull, onely good to sing an old song.

magade, magas *see* hemisphero, lyre

1565 Cooper L→E *Magas, magadis,* An instrument of musike: also a parte of an harpe. **1587** Thomas L→E *Magadium, dij, n.g. Iun.* The bridge of a lute or other instrument, that holdeth vp the strings. *Magas, adis, f.g. Iun,* An instrument of musick: *vid. Pectis* [*see* pecten], *Magadium, & Chelis* [chelys]. **1589** Rider L→E *Magadium, n.* The bridge of a lute, gitterne, or anie such like instrument. **1598** Florio It→E *Magace,* a kinde of musicall instrument. *Magade,* a musicall instrument of twenty strings. Also the bridge of a lute that holdeth vp the strings. **1611** Florio It→E *Magace,* a kind of musicall instrument of twentie strings. Also the bridge of a Lute that holdeth vp the strings. *Magade,* as *Magace.* **1659** Torriano-Florio It→E *Magace, Magade,* a kinde of musical instrument of twenty strings, also the bridge of a Lute or Viol, that holdeth up the strings. **1728** Chambers *Magas,* or *Magade,* the Name of a musical Instrument in Use among the Antients. There were two kinds of *Magades;* the one a string Instrument, the Invention whereof is ascribed by some to *Sappho,* and by others to the *Lydians,* and by others to *Timotheus* of *Miletum.* The other *Magade* was a kind of Flute, which at the same time yielded very high and very low Notes; the former kind was much improved by *Timotheus* of *Miletum,* who is said to have been impeached of a Crime; for that by increasing the Number of Chords, he spoiled and discredited the antient Music. **1736** Bailey *Dict. Britannicum* (2nd edn) *Magades* certain musical instruments us'd by the antients.

1721 Malcolm *Treatise of Musick* (pp. 580-2) ... this Word *magadised,* [is] taken from the Name of an Instrument μαγάδιος, in which Two Strings were always struck together for one Note. *Athenæus* makes the *Magadis* the same with the *Barbiton* and *Pectis;* and *Horace* makes the Muse *Polyhymnia* the Inventor of the *Barbiton.—Nec Polyhymnia* Lesboum *refugit tendre* Barbiton.—And from the Nature of this Instrument, that it had Two Strings to every Note, some think it probable the Name *Polyhymnia* was deduced... He [the comic poet Alexandrides] reports also the Opinion of the Poet *Jon,* that the *Magadis* consisted of Two Flutes, which were both sounded together. From all this 'tis plain, That by *magadised,* Aristotle [*Probl.* 18] means such a Consonance of Sounds as to be in every Note at the same Distance, and consequently to be without *Symphony* and Parts according to the modern Practice. *Athenæus* reports also of *Pindar,* that he called the Musick sung by a Boy and a Man *Magadis;* because they sung together the same Song in Two *Modes.* Mr. Perault concludes from this, that the Strings of the *Magadis* were sometimes 3*ds,* because *Aristotle* says, the 4*th* and 5*th* are never *magadised*: ...

Magnes

1658 Phillips (1st edn) *Magnes,* a youth of *Smyrna,* the most beautiful of his age, and excellent in musick and poetry, for which he was in high esteem with *Gyges* King of *Lydia*

magnificat

1598 Florio It→E *Magnificat,* the song of our Ladie, called Magnificat. **1599** Minsheu-Percyvall Sp→E **Magnifica cosa,* ... Also the song of our Ladie called Magnificat. **1611** Florio It→E *Magnificat,* the song of our Lady in Luke the first Chapter. **1656** Blount (1st edn) *Magnificat,* part of the Even-song among the Romanists, or the song of the Blessed Virgin *Mary, Luk* 1. 46. beginning thus *Magnificat anima mea, &c. My soul doth magnifie our Lord, &c.* At saying of which, they use to stand up, as being a Canticle or Song of joy, for the delivery whereof, the posture of standing is most proper. **1658** Phillips (1st edn) *Magnificat,* the

Song of the Virgin *Mary*, so called because it beginneth with these words, *Magnificat anima mea*, &c. **1659** TORRIANO-FLORIO It→E *Magnificat*, the Song of our Lady in the first Chapter of St. *Luke*. **1676** COLES *Magnificat*, (My Soul) doth magnifie, the Song of the Virgin *Mary*, (*Luke* 1. 46.) **1702** KERSEY *New Engl. Dict.* (1st edn) The *Magnificat, or* soug [sic] of the blessed Virgin *Mary*. **1706** KERSEY-PHILLIPS (6th edn) *Magnificat, (Lat.)* the Song of the Blessed Virgin *Mary;* so call'd, because it begins with these Words, *Magnificat anima mea Dominum, i.e.* My Soul doth magnify the Lord, &c. **1721** BAILEY *An Univ. Etymolog. Engl. Dict.* (1st edn) *Magnificat*, the Song of the blessed Virgin *Mary*, so call'd from *Magnificat* being its first Word in Latin.

maid marrion *see* morisco, morris dance

1658 PHILLIPS (1st edn) *Maid Marrian*, or *Morion*, a boy dressed in womans apparel to dance the *Morisco*, or *Morrisdance*. **1676** COLES *Maid-Marrian*, (or *Morion*) a boy drest in Maids Apparel, to dance the *Marisco*. **1696** PHILLIPS (5th edn) *Maid marrion*, or *Morion*, a Boy dressed in Womans apparel to dance the Morisco, or Morisdance. **1702** KERSEY *New Engl. Dict.* (1st edn) A *Maid-marrion*, a boy drest up in girl's cloths in a morrice dance. **1706** KERSEY-PHILLIPS (6th edn) *Maid Marrion* or *Maid Morion*, a Boy dress'd up in Girl's Cloaths, to dance the Morisco, or Morris-dance. **1708** KERSEY *Dict. Anglo-Brit.* (1st edn) *Maid Marrion* or *Maid Morion*, a Boy dress'd up in Girl's Cloaths, to dance the Morris-dance. **1730** BAILEY *Dict. Britannicum* (1st edn) *Maid Morion, Maid Marrion*, a Boy dressed in a Girl's Habit, having his Head gaily trimmed, who dances with the Morris-Dancers.

major

1688 MIEGE-COTGRAVE Fr→E §*Un Ton majeur (en Termes de Musique)* a greater Tone. *Tierce majeure*, a greater third. **1724** [PEPUSCH] *Short Explic. of Foreign Words in Mus. Bks.* (p. 45) *Maggiore*, Major or greater, a Term in Musick. **1726** BAILEY *An Univ. Etymolog. Engl. Dict.* (3rd edn) *Maggiore* (in *Musick-Books*) signifies major or greater. *Ital.* **1728** CHAMBERS *Major* and *Minor*, in Music, are spoken of the Concords which differ from each other by a Semi-tone. There are *Major* and *Minor* Thirds, *&c.* The *Major* Tone is the Difference between the 5th and 4th, and the *Major* Semitone is the Difference between the *Major* 4th and the 3d. The *Major* Tone surpasses the *Minor* by a Comma. See *Concord*. **1730** BAILEY *Dict. Britannicum* (1st edn) *Major and Minor* (in *Musick*) are spoken of the Concords which differ from each other by a Semi-tone. **1737** DYCHE-PARDON (2nd edn) *Major* (A.) .... *Major Concord*, in *Musick*, exceeds the lesser by half a Tone, as the greater or sharp Third is two whole Tones, or four Semitones, whereas the lesser or flat Third is but three Semitones &c.

manche *see* jugum

1611 COTGRAVE Fr→E *Manche: m.* ... also, the necke of a musicall Jnstrument; **1688** MIEGE-COTGRAVE Fr→E § *Manche de Violon, de Guitare, & autres Instrumens de Musique*, the Neck of a Violin, Guitar, and other Musical Instruments.

mandora *see* pandora

1611 COTGRAVE Fr→E *Mandore: f.* A Kitt, small Gitterne, or instrument resembling a small Gitterne. **1659** TORRIANO-FLORIO It→E *Mandora*, a musical instrument somewhat like a gittern. **1688** MIEGE-COTGRAVE Fr→E *Mandore*, (f.) better than *Mandole* [no such entry given], Mandore, a Musical Instrument something like a Lute.

mandron

1599 MINSHEU-PERCYVALL Sp→E *Mandron*, m. a kinde of instrument.

manequin

1611 COTGRAVE Fr→E *Manequin: m.* ... also, a rude instrument of Musicke; § *Iouër des cymbales, & manequins.* To leacher. *Iouër des manequins à basses marches.* The same.

manganello

1598 FLORIO It→E *Manganello*, ... Also a musicall rusticall instrument. **1611** FLORIO It→E *Manganello*, ... Also a kind of poore garment that shepheards weare. Also a kinde of bag-pipe. **1659** TORRIANO-FLORIO It→E *Manganello*, ... also a kind of great bag-pipe

manichord *see* claricords, monochord

1593 HOLLYBAND Fr→E *Manicordion*, or *Epinettes*, a paire of Virginals: *m.* **1598** FLORIO It→E *Manicordo*, an instrument like vnto a rigoll or paire of virginals, a claricorde, guise. *Manocordo*, as *Manicordo*. **1611** COTGRAVE Fr→E *Manicordion: m.* An (old-fashioned) Claricord. **1611** FLORIO It→E *Manicordo*, a rigoll or claricords. *Manocordo*, as *Manicordo*. **1659** TORRIANO-FLORIO It→E *Manacordo*, as *Monacordo*. *Manicordo*, a Rigols, a Claricord. **1688** MIEGE-COTGRAVE Fr→E *Manicordion*, (m.) Claricord, an old fashion Claricord. ¶ *Manicordion* *est un Instrument de Musique à cordes, qui a beaucoup de rapport avec le Clavecin. Et de fait il a, comme le Clavecin, un Clavier de cinquante touches, ou environ; qui a cinq chevalets sur sa table, & qui rend un son sourd & doux.* **1728** CHAMBERS *Manicordion*, a Musical Instrument, in form of a Spinett: See *Spinett*. Its Strings are cover'd with pieces of Scarlet Cloth, to deaden, as well as soften, the Sound; whence it is also call'd the *Dumb Spinett*, and is much used in Nunneries for the Religious to learn to play on; so as not to disturb the Silence of the Dormitory. *Scaliger* makes the *Manicord* more antient than the Spinett and Harpsichord. *Du Cange* derives the word from *Monochord*, from a supposition this Instrument has but one Cord; but he is mistaken, if has fifty, or more. **1730** BAILEY *Dict. Britannicum* (1st edn) *Manicordium*, a musical Instrument in form of a Spinet, its Strings are covered with scarlet Cloth to deaden and soften the Sound. It is used in Nunneries by the Nuns to learn to play, and not disturb the Silence of the Dormitory.

manner *see* style
1704 HARRIS *Manner*. A Word now much in use, which we have borrowed from the French *Maniere*. In Painting it signifies the Usage, Way, *Mode*, or *Manner* any Painter hath acquired, not only in the Management of his Hand or Pencil, but also as to his Observance of ... So 'tis also in Sculpture; and now adays in *Singing*, or *Playing* on any Instrument: When we would express our Approbation of any one's Way of *Singing* or *Playing*, we say *He hath a very Good manner*. **1706** KERSEY-PHILLIPS (6th edn) *Manner* ... Also when we would express our Approbation of any one's particular Way of Singing, or Playing on a Musical Instrument; we say, *He has a very good Manner*. **1707** *Gloss. Angl. Nova* (1st edn) *Manner*, (Fr.) is used to signifie a peculiar way of Managing one's skill in Painting, Sculpture, Singing, or Playing on an Instrument. **1730** BAILEY *Dict. Britannicum* (1st edn) *Manner* (with *Music*.) is a particular way of singing or playing; which is often express'd by saying, *he has a good Manner*.

manuductor *see* beating, stroke, tact, tactus
1728 CHAMBERS *Manuductor*, a Name given to an antient Officer in the Church, who, from the middle of the Choir where he was placed, gave the Signal to the Choristers to sing, mark'd the Measure, beat Time, and regulated the Music. The *Greeks* call'd him *Mesacoros*, because seated in the middle of the Choir. But in the *Latin* Church, he was call'd *Manuductor*, from *Manus*, and *duco, I lead*; because he led and guided the Choir by the Motions and Gesture of the Hand. **1737** DYCHE-PARDON (2nd edn) *Manuductor* (S.) an antient Church Officer, who from the Middle of the Choir gave the Signal to the Choristers to begin to sing, and marked the Measure, beat Time, and regulated the Musick;

march *see* a cavallo, alarm, allegrezza, alostendardo, assembly, baterie, beat, buccina, diana, drum, fare ala, general, levet, oghetto, ordinanza, palalalan, phrygian, procession, serra serra, tampon, trombeggiata, troop, vedere l'inimica, volta-faccia
1598 FLORIO It→E *Marcia*, a march or marching of souldiers or vpon the drum. **1611** FLORIO It→E *Marchiare*, to march in order by sound of drum. **1659** TORRIANO-FLORIO It→E *Marciare*, to march or go in order by sound of drum and fife.

marche
1611 COTGRAVE Fr→E *Marche: f.* ... also, a Virginall, or Organ, key; also, the finger-boord of a Violl. *Marchettes*. Small Organ keyes. § *Basses marches*. Pedalls; the low keyes of some Organs to be touched with the feet; whence; *Iouër des manequins à basses marches*. To leacher; **1688** MIEGE-COTGRAVE Fr→E *Marche*, (f.) march ... that which an Organist sets his foot upon, to make the pedals (or the low keys) play.

marriage music *see* bridal, epigonium, epithalamy, hillulim, hymen, nuptial, teda, thalassion, zigia
1702 KERSEY *New Engl. Dict.* (1st edn) § A *Marriage-song*. **1737** DYCHE-PARDON (2nd edn) *Marriage Musick* (S.) a sneering, bantering Appellation for the crying of young Children, by way of ridiculing that honourable State.

Marsyas *see* Apollo, Babys, Celænæ, phrygian
1565 COOPER L→E *Marsyas*, ... Also a ryuer of Phrygia, named of one *Marsyas* a minstrell. **1623** COCKERAM *Marsyas*, a Musitian that contended with *Phœbus*. **1658** PHILLIPS (1st edn) *Marsyas*, a certain Musitian of *Phrygia*, instructed by *Minerva*, he provoking *Apollo* to a contest in Musick, was overcome and flead for his presumption **1662** PHILLIPS (2nd edn) § *Celænæ*, a Hill in *Asia*, where *Marsyas* is said to have contended with *Apollo* for the mastery upon the

Flute. **1676** COLES *Marsyas*, a *Phrygian* Musician, who chalenged *Apollo*, and (being overcom'n) was flead for his presumption.

martello *see* campana
1611 FLORIO It→E *Martello*, a hammer. § *Sonare a martello*, to ring the bells backward in time of danger. *Sonare le campane a martello*, to ring the bels backward as in times of warre, of danger or of fire. *Toccare a martello*, to ring the bels with a hammer or as we say backe-ward. **1659** TORRIANO-FLORIO It→E § *Sonare a martello*, to ring the bells backward, as they do in times of danger. *Toccare a martello*, to ring the bells with a hammer, or as we say backward.

martengalle
1611 COTGRAVE Fr→E *Martengalle: f.* A kind of daunce, as common in *Provence*, as the Bransle in other parts of France.

maschil
[1733] BEDFORD *Excellency of Divine Musick* (pp. 27-8) ... The *Hebrew* is, *Sing Maschil*, a Word used in the *Title* of some of the *Psalms*, and seems to direct to some particular *Musick*, or *Tune* in principal Use among them [the original singers of psalms].

mask *see* balletto, canto, revels

masquerade *see* galliard, saltarella

mass *see* chantry, gradual, offertory, preface, requiem, sequence, tract, troper
1593 HOLLYBAND Fr→E *La Messe, f:* the masse. *Messiffier*, to say or sing a masse. **1611** COTGRAVE Fr→E *Messe: f.* The Masse, a Masse. *Messiffiant.* Massing, saying or singing Masse. *Messiffier.* To sing, or say Masse. § *Enfans de choëur de la messe de minuict.* Quirresters of midnights Masse; night-walking rakehells, or such as haunt those nightlie Rites, not for any deuotion, but onely to rob, abuse, or play the knaues with, others. **1611** FLORIO It→E *Messificare*, to sing or say Masse. **1659** TORRIANO-FLORIO It→E *Messificare*, to sing or say Masse. *Missificare*, to sing or say Masse. **1724** [PEPUSCH] *Short Explic. of Foreign Words in Mus. Bks.* (p. 46) *Messa*, are [sic] particular Pieces of Divine Musick, frequently made Use of in the *Roman* Church. **1726** BAILEY *An Univ. Etymolog. Engl. Dict.* (3rd edn) *Messa*, (in *Musick Books*) are particular Pieces of divine Musick, frequently made Use of in the *Roman* Church. *It.* **1728** CHAMBERS *Messe*, or *Masse*, or *Missa*, the Office, or public Prayers made in the Romish Church, at the Celebration of the Encharist .... *High Mass*, called also *Grand Mass*, is that sung by the Choristers, and celebrated with the Assistance of a Deacon and Subdeacon. ¶ *Low-Mass* is that wherein the Prayers are all barely rehearsed without any Singing, and performed without much Ceremony, or the Assistance of any Deacon or Subdeacon. **1730** BAILEY *Dict. Britannicum* (1st edn) *High Mass*, is that sung by the Choristers, and celebrated with the Assistance of a Deacon and Sub-deacon. **1737** DYCHE-PARDON (2nd edn) *Mass* (S.) ... in the Church of *Rome*, ... When the Prayers are sung by the Choristers, and all the Magnificence of Ceremonies are used it is called High Mass.

master note *see* measure, mi
1706 KERSEY-PHILLIPS (6th edn) *Master-Note*, in Musick. See *Measure-Note.* **1708** KERSEY *Dict. Anglo-Brit.* (1st edn) *Master-Notes*, in Musick, the same as *Measure-Note.*

1667 PLAYFORD *Brief Intro. to Skill of Musick* (4th edn, p. 24) The *Semibrief* being the last of *Augmentation*, is the Shortest, and in *Time* is called the *Master Note*, being of one *Measure* by himself; all the other *Notes* are reckoned by his value ... **1677** NEWTON *English Academy* (p. 99) ... The *Large* being the first [note] of Augmentation, and longest in Sound; the *Semi-breve* is the last of Augmentation, & the shortest in Sound, and in *Time* is called the Master Note, being of one Measure by himself, all the other Notes are reckoned by his value, both in Augmentation and Diminution. **1694** PURCELL-PLAYFORD *Intro. to Skill of Musick* (12th edn, n.p.) ... the *Semibreve* being the longest Note now in use; and called the *Master-Note*, or a *Whole Time*: ...

matachin *see* morris dance
1593 HOLLYBAND Fr→E *Matassiner*, to iest with his handes like a iester or tumbler. § *Iouër aux matassins*, to play a morris daunce, at matachine, or the antique: *m.* **1598** FLORIO It→E *Mattacini*, a kinde of antique daunce or morris vsed in Italy. *Mattinata*, ... mornings musike or hunts vppe plaid in a morning vnder ones window. **1611** COTGRAVE Fr→E *Matachin: m.* The Matachin daunce; also, those that daunce it. **1611** FLORIO It→E *Mattacinare*, to play or dance the Mattachino. *Mattacini*, ... a kinde of antique moresco or mattacino dance. **1658** PHILLIPS (1st edn)

Matachin, (French) a kinde of French dance. **1659** TORRIANO-FLORIO It→E *Mattaccinare,* to dance or play the Mattachino's or Morris-dancers. *Mattaccini,* an antick, a *Moresco,* or *Mattachino* dance. **1676** COLES *Matachin, French.* an antick or morrice dance. **1688** MIEGE-COTGRAVE Fr→E *Matassins,* (m.) *sorte de Danse folâtre,* Matachin Dance. § *Danser les Matassins,* to dance Matachin Dances. **1696** PHILLIPS (5th edn) *Matachin,* or *Mattasin, (French)* a kind of silly *French* dance. **1702** KERSEY *New Engl. Dict.* (1st edn) A *Marachin*-dance [sic], a kind of morris-dance. **1706** KERSEY-PHILLIPS (6th edn) *Matachin* or *Matassin,* a kind of antick *French* Dance. **1708** KERSEY *Dict. Anglo-Brit.* (1st edn) *Matachin* or *Matassin,* an antick *French* Dance.

mathematicks

1500 *Ortus Vocabulorum* L→E Mathematicus ca. cum. i. expers in scientia quadruuiali. s. musica: geometria astronomia et diasintastica. o.s. **1538** ELYOT L→E *Mathematicus,* he that is cunnynge in aulgryme, musyke, geometry, and astronomy. **1552** HULOET L→E *Ars Mathematica,* Science of Algryme, or Algorisme, Astronomy, Geometrie, or Musycke. ¶ *Mathematicus. a. um,* is he that is conning in any of these sciences[.] **1616** BULLOKAR *Mathematickes.* A terme applyed to such arts, as treate onely of quantities imaginarily abstracted from bodies. The arts commonly so called, are Arithmeticke, musicke, Geometry, Geography, Astronomie, Cosmography, and Astrology. **1623** COCKERAM *Mathematicks.* The Arts of Arithmaticke, Musicke, Geometrie, Geographie, Astronomie, Astrologie, and Cosmographie. **1650** HOWELL-COTGRAVE Fr→E *Mathematiques: f.* The Mathematickes; (comprehend soure [sic] of the liberall Sciences; *viz.*) Arithmetick, Geometry, Musicke, and Astronomy or Astrologie. **1656** BLOUNT (1st edn) *Mathematicks (mathematica)* Sciences or Arts, taught by demonstration, and comprehended four of the liberal Sciences (viz.) *Arithmetick* (wherein *Algæbra* is comprehended) *Geometry, Musick, Astronomy;* wherein the Ægyptians and Caldeans first excelled. **1658** PHILLIPS (1st edn) *Mathematician,* (lat.) one that is skilfull in the Mathematicks, that is, those Sciences which are understood by demonstration, of these there are four in all, Arithmetick, Geometry, Astronomy, and Musick. **1676** COLES *Mathematicks, Greek.* Sciences taught by Demonstration, *viz.* Arithmetick, Astronomy, Geometry and Musick. **1704** *Cocker's Engl. Dict.* (1st edn) *Mathematicks,* Sciences taught by demonstration, *viz.* Arithmetick, Musick. [sic] Geometry, Geography, Astronomy, Cosmography, and Astrology. **1736** BAILEY *Dict. Britannicum* (2nd edn) *Practical Mathematicks,* are such as shew how to demonstrate something that is useful, or to perform something proposed to be done, which may tend to the benefit of mankind. As *Astronomy, Architecture, Catoptricks, ... Mechanicks, Musick, Opticks, ...* &c.

matins

1598 FLORIO It→E *Mattinata,* ... mornings musike or hunts vppe plaid in a morning vnder ones window. Also a mattins. *Mattino,* as *Mattina.* Also mattins sung in churches. **1599** MINSHEU-PERCYVALL Sp→E *Maytinero,* m. one that saieth or singeth mattens. **1611** FLORIO It→E *Mattinare,* to sing or say Mattins. Also to sing or giue musike in a morning at some window. *Mattinata,* a Mattins ... Also a hunt is vp or musike plaid vnder ones window in a morning. *Mattino,* ... Also a Mattins sung in Churches. *Mattutinare,* to sing or say Mattins **1659** TORRIANO-FLORIO It→E *Mattinare, Mattineggiare, ...* to sing or say Mattins, to sing or give musick early in the morning under some gentlewomans window **Mattinata,* a Mattins ... also a hunts-up, or musick in a morning under ones window. **Mattino,* sub. a Mattins sung in Churches.

mean *as name of string*

c.1668-71 *Mary Burwell's Instruction Bk. for Lute* (*TDa* p. 17) ... For the placing [of] the second string (or the small mean, as we call it) ...

mean *as vocal part, see* cantus, incentor, intercentor, intercentus, intercino, medius, setting

1656 BLOUNT (1st edn) *Mean,* the Tenor in Song or Musick, it is an inner part between the *Treble* and *Base,* so called, because *medium locum obtineat.* **1658** PHILLIPS (1st edn) The *Mean,* in Musick the Tenor, or middle part **1676** COLES § *Mean part* (in Musick,) the Tenour, between treble and Basse. **1702** KERSEY *New Engl. Dict.* (1st edn) § The *mean-part, or* tenor in Musick, between bass and treble. **1706** KERSEY-PHILLIPS (6th edn) *Mean* or *Mean Part,* (in *Musick*) is the Tenor, or middle Part. **1708** KERSEY *Dict. Anglo-Brit.* (1st edn) *Mean* or *Mean Part,* (in *Musick*) is the Tenor, or middle Part. **1731** KERSEY *New Engl. Dict.* (3rd edn) The *Mean,* or *Mean Part,* (in *Musick*), the middle Part between Bass and Treble.

1636 BUTLER *Principles of Musik* (p. 42) The Mean is so called, becaus it is a midling or mean high part, betweene the Countertenor, (the highest part of a man) and the Treble, (the highest part of a boy or woman:) and therefore may bee sung by a mean voice. **1721** MALCOLM *Treatise of Musick* (pp. 332-3) ... All the other *Parts* [after the treble and bass], whose particular Names you'll learn from Practice, I shall call *Mean Parts*, whose *Clef* is *c*, sometimes on one, sometimes on another Line; and some that are really *mean Parts* are set with the *g Clef*. **1724** TURNER *Sound Anatomiz'd* (p. 36) ... in former Times the *Tenor Cliff* was as often placed upon the second *Line* as it was on any of the others, being called the *Mean Part*, but it is now wholly laid aside in Singing, except in *Cathedral Musick*, and very rarely in that, but for the *Organ Parts*; it is also pretty much used in *Instrumental-Musick*, as the *Tenor-Violin*, &c. but is never placed upon the fifth *Line*, neither for *Voices*, nor for *Instruments*.

mean note *see* final

mean proportional

1708 KERSEY *Dict. Anglo-Brit.* (1st edn) *Mean Proportional*, ... In *Arithmetick* and *Musick*, the Second of any three Proportionals is termed the Mean. **1730** BAILEY *Dict. Britannicum* (1st edn) *Mean proportional* (in *Musick*) the second of any three Proportionals.

measure *see* binary measure, mood, time

1593 HOLLYBAND Fr→E § *Mesure brusque*, a swift quicke measure in musicke. **1611** COTGRAVE Fr→E *Mesure: f.* ... also, modulation, or time, in Musicke; § *Mesure brusque*. A swift measure, or fast time in Musicke. **1688** MIEGE-COTGRAVE Fr→E *Mesure*, (f.) ... time, in Musick; ... measure, or time, in Dancing; § *Batre les tems de la mesure*, to beat the time. *Il y a diverses mesures dans la Musique*, there are several Times in Musick. **1704** HARRIS *Measure*, in Musick, is a Quantity of the Length and Shortness of Time, either with respect to Natural Sounds, pronounced by the Voice; or Artificial, drawn out of Musical Instruments: Which Measure is adjusted in Variety of Notes, by a constant Motion of the Hand or Foot, *down* or *up*, successively and equally divided; so that every *Down* and *Vp* is called a *Time* or *Measure*, whereby the Length of a *Semi-breve* is measured, which is therefore termed the *Measure-Note*, or *Time-Note*. **1706** KERSEY-PHILLIPS (6th edn) In *Musick*, *Measure* is a Space of Time, set out by a constant equal Motion of the Hand or Foot, down and up successively; which is sometimes swifter, sometimes slower, according to the Nature of the Musick. § *Measure-Note*, *Master-Note*, or *Time-Note*. the Semebreve, a Musical Note, so call'd because it is of a certain determinate Measure, or Length of Time by it self; and all the other Notes are measur'd by, or adjusted to its Value. **1707** *Gloss. Angl. Nova* (1st edn) *Measure in Musick*, is a Quantity of the length and shortness of Time, either with respect to natural sounds pronounced by the Voice; or Artificial drawn out Musicial [sic] Instruments, which Measure is adjusted in variety of Notes by a constant Motion of the Hand or Foot, *down* or *up*, is called a *Time* or *Measure* whereby the length of a *Semibreve* is measured, which is therefore the *Measure Note* or *Time Note*. **1728** CHAMBERS *Measure* is also used to signify the Cadence, and Time observed in Poetry, Dancing, and Music, to render them regular, and agreeable.... *Measure*, in Music, is the Interval, or Space of Time, which the Person, who regulates the Music, takes between the raising and letting fall of his Hand, in order to conduct the Movement sometimes quicker, and sometimes slower, according to the Kind of Music, or the Subject that is sung or play'd. See *Time*. The ordinary or common *Measure*, is one Second, or sixtieth part of a Minute, which is nearly the Space between the Beats of the Pulse or Heart; the Systole, or Contraction of the Heart, answering to the Elevation of the Hand, and its Diastole, or Dilation, to the letting it fall. The *Measure* usually takes up the Space that a Pendulum, of two Foot and a half long, employs in making a Swing or Vibration. See *Vibration*. ¶ The *Measure* is regulated according to the different Quality of Value of the Notes in the Piece; by which the Time that each Note is to take up, is express'd. The Semi-Breve, for instance, holds one Rise, and one Fall; and this is call'd the whole *Measure*: the Minim, one Rise, or one Fall; and the Crochet, half a Rise, or half a Fall, there being four Crochets in a full *Measure*. See *Note*. ¶ *Binary*, or *Double Measure*, is that wherein the Rise and Fall of the Hand are equal. ¶ *Ternary*, or *Triple Measure*, is that wherein the Fall is double to the Rise; or where two Minims are play'd during a Fall, and but one in a Rise: To this purpose, the Number 3 is placed at the beginning of the Lines, when the *Measure* is intended to be triple; and a *C*, when the *Measure* is to be common or double. ¶ This rising and falling of the Hands, was call'd by the *Greeks* ἄρσις and θέσις St. *Angustin* calls it *Plausus*, and the *Spaniards*, *Compass*. See *Beating of Time*.

after 1517 ANON. Art of Mvsic BL Add. 4911, f. 1 *Misur quhat is it*. It is of a certane moking with alternatie be one equall strock or anchoip [?] distinctlye proporcionat Throu ye quhilk. all nottis and pausis of sangis for the qualitie of euerie sing or figur or is mensurall proportion deducit **1614** RAVENSCROFT *Briefe Discovrse* (p. 1) *Measure* in this *Science* [of music] is a *Quantity* of the *length and shortnes* of *Time*, either by *Naturall sounds* pronounced by *Voice*, or by *Artificiall*, vpon *Instruments*.

mediant

1721 MALCOLM *Treatise of Musick* (p. 277) The 3*d* is called the *Mediante*, because it stands betwixt the *Final* and *Dominante* as to its Use.

mediation *see* tune

meditor

1500 *Ortus Vocabulorum* L→E Meditor aris. qua mellicari. i. modulari. i. dulciter melodiam decantare... **1538** ELYOT L→E *Meditor, aris, ari*, to thynke deepely ... to synge or playe swetely. **1552** HULOET L→E *Meditor. aris*. Rendre or recorde lessons, songes, or verses *Meditor. aris, Modulor aris Verno. nas*, Syng swetelye... properlye as byrdes do *Meditor. ris* Playe vpon an instrument swetely. **1587** THOMAS L→E *Meditor, aris, depon*. To thinke deeplie ... to sing & play sweetlie: **1589** RIDER L→E *Meditor*. To plaie, or sing sweetly.

medius *see* cantus, mean

1565 COOPER L→E § *Sonus medius, summus, imus. Plin*. The meane: the trebble: the base. **1589** RIDER L→E *Medius, intercentus, m*. The meane.

melicus *see* lyrick, musicus

1538 ELYOT L→E *Melicus*, a musycyan. **1552** HULOET L→E *melicus, musicus* Musician. **1565** COOPER L→E *Melicus*. A Musician. *Melicus, melici, m.g. Ausonius*. A musition. **1587** THOMAS L→E *Melicus, a, um*. A musitian. **1598** FLORIO It→E *Melico*, musicall, or musician-like. **1611** FLORIO It→E *Melico*, musicall or musician-like. § *Melico poema*, a lyrike poeme. **1659** TORRIANO-FLORIO It→E *Melico*, musically sweet. § *Melico poema*, a Lyrick Poem.

melismatic *see* style (stylo melismatico)

melodious

1593 HOLLYBAND Fr→E *Melodieux*, full of melodie. § *Melodieusement chanter*, to sing sweetely, with great melodie. **1598** FLORIO It→E *Melodioso*, melodius, harmonius, sweete singing. **1599** MINSHEU-PERCYVALL Sp→E **Melodioso*, melodious. **1611** COTGRAVE Fr→E *Melodieusement*. Melodiously, harmoniously, musically, tunably. *Melodieux: m. euse: f*. Melodious, musicall, harmonious, tunable, eare delighting, full of concords. **1611** FLORIO It→E *Melodioso*, melodious, harmonious. **1688** MIEGE-COTGRAVE Fr→E *Melodieusement, avec melodie*, melodiously, harmoniously. *Melodieux*, melodious, harmonious. § *Une Voix melodieuse*, a melodious Voice. **1702** KERSEY *New Engl. Dict.* (1st edn) *Melodious, or* harmonious. **1706** KERSEY-PHILLIPS (6th edn) *Melodious*, full of Melody, Musical, well-tuned, warbling. **1730** BAILEY *Dict. Britannicum* (1st edn) *Melodiousness*, fulness of melody, harmoniousness of Sound. **1737** DYCHE-PARDON (2nd edn) *Melodious* (A.) musical, harmonious, pleasant or charming in Sound. *Melodiousness* (S.) the Delicateness, Musicalness, or Harmoniousness of any Sounds.

melody *see* air, cantus, composition, genus, harmony, song, tune

1500 *Ortus Vocabulorum* L→E Melodia die. i. dulcis cantus. an[e]. melody Melodiana ne. idem est. f.p. **1538** ELYOT L→E *Melodia*, melodye. **1550** THOMAS It→E *Melode, melodia*, melodie or mirthe. **1552** HULOET L→E *melodes* Melodious synger. **1565** COOPER L→E *Melodia, melodiæ, f.g*. Melodie: sweete singynge. **1570/71** *Dict. Fr. and Engl.* Fr→E *Melodie*, melodie, sweet tune. **1587** THOMAS L→E *Melodes, dis, Sidon*. A sweet and cunning singer. *Melodia, æ, f.g* Melodie, sweet singing. **1589** RIDER L→E *Melodes, melicus, m*. A melodious singer. *Melodes, melosonus, m*. A sweete singer. *Melodia, harmonia, f*. Sweete singing. **1593** HOLLYBAND Fr→E *Mélodie*, melodie, sweete tunes: *f*. *Melodieux*, full of melodie. § *Melodieusement chanter*, to sing sweetely, with great melodie. **1598** FLORIO It→E *Melode*, melodious, harmonious, musicall, sweetlie singing. *Melodia*, melodie, harmonie, sweete singing, a tunable songing, whereof be three kinds, that is to say Harmonia, Chronia, and Diatonia. **1599** MINSHEU-PERCYVALL Sp→E *Melodia*, f. melodie, sweete musicke. § **Salteada melodia*, musicke broken off, vpon some sudden fright or accident. **1604** CAWDREY (1st edn) *melody*, (Greeke) sweete sounding, or sweete musick **1611** COTGRAVE Fr→E *Melodie: f*. Melodie, harmonie, a tunable sound, or singing; a musicall, or sweet Ayer. **1611** FLORIO It→E *Melode*, melodious, harmonious. *Melodia*, melodie, harmonia, sweete or tunable singing, whereof be three kinds, Harmonia, Chronia, Diatonia. *Melodiare*, to sing or make melody.

1623 COCKERAM *Melodied.* with Musicke satisfied. **1656** BLOUNT (1st edn) *Melody (melodia)* harmony, sweet singing, a musical or sweet aire. **1658** PHILLIPS (1st edn) *Melody*, a musical sound, or sweet aire, from the Greek words, *meli*, i. honey, and *ode*, i. a song, as it were a honey'd or sweet song. **1659** TORRIANO-FLORIO It→E *Melode, Melodico, Melodioso*, melodious, sweetly tuned. *Melodia*, melody, harmony, sweet and tunable singing, whereof be three kinds, *Harmonia, Chronia, Diatonia*. **1676** COLES *Melody, Greek.* harmony, a sweet-song. **1688** MIEGE-COTGRAVE Fr→E *Melodie*, (f.) *douceur de Chant, ou de Son*, melody, harmony. *Melodie*, Musick, Luke 15. 25. § *Faire une agreable melodie*, to make a pleasant harmony. *Une charmante melodie*, a charming melody. **1696** PHILLIPS (5th edn) *Melody*, Harmony, a Mixture of Sounds pleasing and delightful to the Ear; a Musical sound, or sweet Air, from the *Greek* words, *meli*, *i.e.* honey, and *ode*, *i.e.* a song; as it were, a honeyed, a sweet song. **1702** KERSEY *New Engl. Dict.* (1st edn) *Melody*, a sweet Consort in Musick. **1707** *Gloss. Angl. Nova* (1st edn) *Melody*, (Gr.) Harmony, sweet Singing. **1708** KERSEY *Dict. Anglo-Brit.* (1st edn) *Melody*, Harmony, a mixture of Musical Sounds delightful to the Ear. **1724** [PEPUSCH] *Short Explic. of Foreign Words in Mus. Bks.* (p. 45) *Melodia*, Melody, it is the Effect of several musical Notes, so placed, contrived, and disposed, that the singing or playing them one after another, give Delight and Pleasure to the Ear. **1728** CHAMBERS *Melody*, in Music, is the agreeable Effect of different Musical Sounds, ranged or disposed in Succession. So that Melody is the Effect only of one single Part, Voice, or Instrument; by which it is distinguish'd from *Harmony*; tho' in common Speech, these two are frequently confounded. Harmony is the agreeable Result of the Union of two or more concording musical Sounds heard in Consonance, *i.e.* at one and the same time; so that Harmony is the Effect of two Parts at least: As therefore a continued Succession of musical Sounds produces *Melody*, so does a continued Combination of these produce Harmony. See *Harmony* and *Concord*; see also *Music in Parts.* ¶ Tho' the Term *Melody* be chiefly distinguish'd by its Air; yet so far as the Bass may be made airy, and to sing well, it may also properly said to be *Melodious*. See *Treble* and *Bass*. ¶ Of the twelve harmonical Intervals of Musical Sounds, distinguish'd by the Names of *Second lesser, Second greater; Third lesser, Third greater; Fourth; false Fifth; Fifth; Sixth lesser, Sixth greater; Seventh lesser, Seventh greater*; and *Octave*; all *Melody*, as well as Harmony, are compos'd: For the Octaves of each of these are but Replications of the same Sounds; and whatever is said of any, or all of these Sounds, is to be understood also of their Octaves. See *Octave.* ¶ For the Rules of *Melody*, see *Composition*. The Word comes from the *Greek* μελι, *Honey*; and ωδή, *Singing*. **1730** BAILEY *Dict. Britannicum* (1st edn) *Melody* (μελωδία of μελος, a Verse, and ᾠδή, a Song, *Gr.*) a sweet Ayre, or pleasing musical Tune; Harmony, a mixture of musical Sounds, delightful to the Ear. **1731** KERSEY *New Engl. Dict.* (3rd edn) *Melody*, a delightful Mixture of Musical Sounds. **1737** DYCHE-PARDON (2nd edn) *Melody* (S.) Harmony, Musicalness, or Pleasantness of an Air or Song Tune.

1597 DOWLAND *First Booke of Songes* (dedicatory) ... So that *Plato* defines melody to consist of harmony, number, & wordes; harmony naked of it selfe, words the ornament of harmony, number the common friend & vniter of them both. **1617-24** FLUDD *Utriusque Cosmi Maioris: De Templo Musicæ* (p. 209) *Melodia* est sonorum continuata connexio, ita, ut alter post alterum fluxu continuo sonet, & propriè dicitur cantio unius vocis. **1636** BUTLER *Principles of Musik* (p. 44) *Melodi* is the sweete modulation or tune of each part in it self. **1721** MALCOLM *Treatise of Musick* (p. 38) ... The Effect of an agreeable *Succession* of several Sounds being particularly called *Melody*. § (p. 265) When several simple Sounds succeed other agreeably in the Ear, that Effect is called *Melody*; ... § (p. 414) *Melody* is the agreeable Effect of different *musical* Sounds, successively ranged and disposed; so that *Melody* is the Effect only of one single Part; and tho' it is a Term chiefly applicable to the *Treble*, as the *Treble* is mostly to be distinguished by its *Air*, yet in so far as the *Bass* may be made airy, and to sing well, it may be also properly said to be *melodious*. § (pp. 585-6) ... In order to [make] this Comparison [between melody of the ancients and moderns], I shall distinguish *Melody* into *vocal* and *instrumental*. By the first I mean *Musick* set to Words, especially Verses; and by the other *Musick* composed only for Instruments without Singing. For the *vocal* you see by the Definition that *Poetry* makes a necessary Part of it: This was not only of ancient Practice, but the chief, if not their only Practice, as appears from their Definitions of *Musick* already explain'd. **1721 or after** ANON. Institutions of Musick (rear of LC copy of Bayne, p. 2) Melodie is the agreeable Effect that different Musical Sounds successively rang'd and dispos'd have upon the sense of Hearing; so that Melodie is the Effect only of one single Part, and tho it is a Term chiefly applicable to the Treble as the Treble is mostly to be distinguished by it's aire yet in so far as the Bass may be made airy and to sing well it may be also properly said to be Melodious. **1721 or after** ANON. Treatise of Thoro' Bass BEINECKE OSB. MS 3, p. 11 By Melody is understood the agreeable Air of one single part of Musick, which is the result of Single Sounds succeeding one another after a manner that pleases, whether those single Sounds are diversified with the variety of Time and Tune, or varied only by the Diversifying of either; So that the Melody of a piece is said to be good, when the severall parts viz: the Trebles, Tenors & Bases, taken separately, sing well, as the phrase is, or are melodious; ... **1730** [PEPUSCH] *Short Treatise on Harmony* (p. 4) *Melody*, is the Proceeding of a single Part, from One Note or Sound to another. **1731** [PEPUSCH] *Treatise on Harmony* (2nd edn, p. 3) *Melody* is the Progression of Sound proceeding from one Note to another successively in a single Part. **1740** LAMPE *Art of Musick* (p. 45) *Melody*, says our Author [Vincentino] Pag. 3. is the Progressions of Sound proceeding from one Note to [a]nother successively in a single Part. § (p. 46) *Melody*, I think, is a Series of Sound, whose regular and agreeable *Succession* are expressed by a *single* performing Part, and arise from, are conformable to, or grounded upon Species of Harmonies, which are *mutually* related.

melopeus

1500 *Ortus Vocabulorum* L→E Melopeus dulcis cantus: vel cantus fictor et dicitur a melos: et peo q est fingo. m.s.

melopœia *see* harmonic, modi melopœiæ, musical faculty, mutation, pathetic music, petteia

1721 MALCOLM *Treatise of Musick* (p. 33) The Second general Branch [of music, after the contemplative part], which is the *Practical* part, as naturally divides into Two Parts answering to the Parts of the First: That which answers to the *Harmonica*, the Ancients called *Melopœia*; because it contains the Rules of making Songs with respect to *Tune* and *Harmony* of Sounds, tho' indeed we have no Ground to believe that the Ancients had any Thing like Composition in Parts. That which answers to the *Rythmica*, they called *Rythmopœia*, containing the Rules concerning the Application of the *Numbers* and *Time*. § (p. 500) [*re* the ancient 'Doctrine of *Harmonicks*'] ... the *Melopœia* or Art of making *Melody* or Songs. § (p. 541) [*re* the ancient Greek theory of melopœia] The substance of their Doctrine according to *Euclid* is this. After he has said that the *Melopœia* is the Use of the Parts (or Principles) already explained. He tells us, it consists of Four Parts, first αγογη, which the *Latins* called *ductus, that is*, when the Sounds or Notes proceed by continuous Degrees of the *Scale*, as *a. b. c.* 2*d* πλοκή, *nexus*, which is, when the Sounds either ascending or descending are taken alternately, or not immediately next in the *Scale*, as *a, c, b, d.* or *a, d, b, e, c, f,* or these reversely *d, b, c, a.* 3*d.* πεττεία, *Petteia*, (for the *Latins* made this *Greek* Name their own) when the same Note was frequently repeated together, as *a, a, a.* 4*th*, τονή, *Extensio*, when any one Note was held out or sounded remarkably longer than the rest. This is all *Euclid* teaches us about it. But *Aristides Quintilianus*, who writes more fully than any of them, explains the *Melopœia* otherwise. He calls it the *Faculty* or *Art* of making *Songs*, which has Three Parts, *viz.* λῆψις, μιξίς, χρῆσις, which the *Latins* call *Sumtio, mistio, usus.* § (pp. 543-4) [*re* the three parts of melopœia in ancient Greek music, being sumtio, mistio and usus] Not to trouble our selves with long *Greek* Passages, I shall give you the Definitions of these in *Meibomius*'s Words, 1. *Sumtio est per quam musico datur a quali vocis loco Systema sit faciendum, utrum ab* Hypatoide *an reliquorum aliquo.* 2. *Mistio, per quam aut sonos inter se aut vocis locos coagmentamus, aut modulationis genera, aut modorum Systema.* 3 *Usus, certa quædam modulationis confectio, cujus species tres,* viz. *Ductus, Petteia, Nexus.* As to the Definitions of the Three principal Parts, the Author of the *Dictionaire de Musique* puts this Sense upon them, *viz. Sumtio* teaches the Composer in what System he ought to place his Song, whether high or low, and consequently in what *Mode* or *Tone*, and at what Note to begin and end. *Mistio*, says he, is properly what we call the Art of *Modulating* well, *i.e.* after having begun in a convenient Place, to prosecute or conduct the Song, so as the Voice be always in a convenient *Tension*; and that the essential Chords of the *Mode* be right placed and used, and that the Song be carried out of it, and return again agreeably. *Usus* teaches the Composer how the Sounds ought to follow ane another, and in what Situations each may and ought to be in, to make an agreeable *Melody*, or a good *Modulation*. For the Species of the *Usus: Aristides* defines the *ductus* and *nexus* the same Way as *Euclid* does; and adds, that the *ductus* may be performed Three Ways, or is threefold, *viz.*

ductus rectus, when the Notes ascend, as *a, b, c*; *revertens*, when they descend *c, b, a*; or *circumcurrens*, when having ascended by the *systema disjunctum*, they immediately descend by the *systema conjunctum*, or move downwards betwixt the same Extremes, in a different Order of the intermediate Degrees, as having ascended thus, *a:b:c:d*, the Descent is *d:c:♭:a*, or *c:d:e:f*, and *f:e♭. d:c*. But the *Petteia* he defines, *Qua cognoscimus quinam sonorum omittendi, & qui sunt adsumendi, tum quoties illorum singuli: porro a quonam inciniendum, & in quem definiendum: atque hæc quoque morem exhibet*. In short, according to this Definition the *Petteia* is the whole Art.

melos *see* canor, canticum, cantion, harmony, phrygium melos
1500 *Ortus Vocabulorum* L→E Melos. i. dulcis cantus: dulcis modulatio. neutri genis indecli. Melos dis. quedam insula vel dulcis cantus. angl. a melody. f.t. Melus li. idest dulcis cantus. m.s. Melum li. idem est. Melus la. lum. i. dulcis vel pertinens ad melodias vel quod tractat de melodijs. ois genis scde decit. **1538** ELYOT L→E *Melos, odis*, melodye, armonye. **1565** COOPER L→E *Mele, Nominatiuus pluralis Græcus. Lucr.* Songes: balades. *Melos, neut. gen. indeclinabile. Pers.* Melodie: harmonie. **1587** THOMAS L→E *Mele, Lucret.* Songs, ballats. *Melos, n.g. defect. ablat. Melo, Lact.* Melodie, harmonie, a song, singing in measure, or tuneable singing: musick. Hereof there be three kindes: *Harmonia, Chronia* [sic], and *Diatonium*. **1589** RIDER L→E *Mele, n.* Songs. *Melos, n. harmonia, melodia, symphonia, f. cantus canor. Concentus numerus. modulus, m. modulatio, consonantia, f.* Melodie, or sweete consent in musicke.

Melpomene *see* Muse
1706 KERSEY-PHILLIPS (6th edn) *Melpomene*, one of the Nine Muses, said to have been the Inventress of Tragedies, Odes and Songs. **1707** *Gloss. Angl. Nova* (1st edn) *Melpomene*, one of the nine Muses, to whom is attributed the Invention of Tragedies, Odes, and Songs.

men *see* assai, poco
1724 [PEPUSCH] *Short Explic. of Foreign Words in Mus. Bks.* (p. 45) *Men*, less, or not so much. Thus *Men Allegro*, is a Movement not so gay and brisk, as the Word *Allegro* alone does signify and require. §*Men Forte*, not too loud, or less loud. *Men Presto*, not too quick, or less quick. **1726** BAILEY *An Univ. Etymolog. Engl. Dict.* (3rd edn) *Men* (in *Musick*) [sic] *Books*) signifies less, or not so much thus. § *Men Allegro* denotes a Movement not so gay and brisk as *Allegro*, signifies and requires when it stands alone. *Men Forte* (in *Musick Books*) signifies not too loud, or less loud. *Men Presto* (in *Musick Books*) signifies not too quick or less quick.

1731 PRELLEUR *Modern Musick-Master* (Dictionary, p. 3) *Men*, signifies Less as [sic] *Men Allegro* Not so quick as Allegro. ¶ *Men Forte*, not so Loud. ¶ *Men Presto*, not so Quick, &c.. **after 1731** ANON. *Directions for Playing on the Flute* (Dictionary, n.p.) *Men*: v. *Poco*. **1736** TANS'UR *Compleat Melody* (3rd edn, p. 66) *Men, Poco, Pico*, (Ital.) Either of those Words are often set before another Word, which signifies, *Less*, or not so much, as it was before; as, *Men Allegro*; is not quite so brisk as if *Allegro* was alone.

menacorda *see* claricords
1598 FLORIO It→E *Menacordo*, the instrument wee call Claricords. **1611** FLORIO It→E *Menacordo*, a Claricord instrument. **1659** TORRIANO-FLORIO It→E *Mena corda*, a Claricord or Rigoll.

menadi
1598 FLORIO It→E *Menadi*, certaine women that were wont to sacrifice to Bacchus, dancing at the sound of hornes, and crying as mad women, carying staues wreathed about with vine leaues. **1611** FLORIO It→E *Menadi*, certaine women that were wont to sacrifice to Bacchus, running and dancing at the sound of hornes, carying certaine iauelins or staues in their hands, wreathed about with vine-leaues, chanting and crying as mad women.

menes *see* linus

menestrail *see* minstrel

menestrandier *see* minstrel

menone *see* minstrel
1611 COTGRAVE Fr→E *Menone*. A Minstrell. *Poictevin*.

mensural music *see* active music
after 1517 ANON. Art of Mvsic BL Add. 4911, f. 1 Musi[c]o mensurall (as ornitoparchus one doctur of Music dois porit) is discretion of modulation and forme in discreit figuris In Mud, tyme and prolation

quantificat. Or it is ye artt of full harmony yat is perfytlie constitut throw deversitie of figuram and vocis. Or it is of augmentation and diminution Mud tyme prolation the perfyt securitie and evident distinction, of all senciall notte mesure and pausis. **1609** DOWLAND-ORNITHOPARCUS *Micrologvs* (pp. 2-3) *Mensurall Musicke,* is the diuers quantitie of Notes, and the inequalitie of figures. Because they are augmented or diminished according as the *moode, time,* and *prolation* doth require: ... § (pp. 38-9) *Boêtius* that Romane, (whose wit in Musicke no man euer mended; nay, neuer attained to, in the first Chapter of his Musicke) writes, That there is such efficacie in Harmonicall Consents, as a man though he would, cannot want them. For Musicke driueth away those cares which driue away sleepe, stilleth crying children, mitigateth the paine of those which labour, refresheth wearied bodies, reformeth appassionate minds. And euery liuing soule is so ouercome with Musicall sounds; that not onely they which are of the gallanter sort (as saith *Macrobius*) but euen all barbarous Nations doe vse Songs, either such as stirre them vp to an ardent embracing of vertue; or doe melt them in vnworthy pleasures: and so are they possessed with the sweetnesse of Harmony, that by Musicke the *Alarum* to warre is giuen, by Musicke the Retraite is sounded, as if the Note did both stirre vp, and after allay that vertue of fortitude. Now of the two [types of music, plainsong and mensural], that Musicke which we call Mensurall, doth specially performe these effects ... Therefore *Mensurall Musicke* is a knowledge of making Songs by figures, which are in forme differing, and hauing the quantity of *Moode, time,* and *Prolation*: Or it is an Art, whose Harmony is effected by the variety of figures and voyces. **1614** RAVENSCROFT *Briefe Discovrse* (p. 1) *Mensurabilis Musice* is defined to be a *Harmony* of diuers sortes of *Sounds,* exprest by certaine *Characters* or *Figures* called *Notes,* described on *Lines & Spaces,* different in *Name, Essence, Forme, Quantity,* and *Quality,* which are sung by a *Measure* of *Time*; or as *Io: Dunstable,* the man whome *loan. Nucius* in his Poeticall *Musicke* (and diuers others) affirme to be the first that inuented *Composition*) saith, it hath his beginning at an *Vnite,* and increaseth vpward by two and by three infinitely, and from the highest decreaseth in like manner downe againe to an Vnite. **1617-24** FLUDD *Utriusque Cosmi Maioris: De Templo Musicæ* (p. 190) *Mensura Musica* est habititudo quantitativa, longitudinem & brevitatem cujuslibet cantus mensurabilis manifestans.

menuet, minuet *see* minuetto, mood, passepied, rondeau, saraband, sonata, style (stylo choraico), tempo

1702 KERSEY *New Engl. Dict.* (1st edn) A *Menuet*, a sort of dance. **1706** KERSEY-PHILLIPS (6th edn) *Menuet* or *Minuet, (Fr.)* a sort of *French* Dance, or the Tune belonging to it. *Minuet*. See *Menuet*. **1721** BAILEY *An Univ. Etymolog. Engl. Dict.* (1st edn) *Menuet, Minuet*, a Sort of *French* Dance, or the Tune belonging to it, *F.* **1728** CHAMBERS *Menuet*, or *Minuet*, a kind of Dance, the Steps whereof are extremely quick, and short: It consists of a Coupee, a high Step, and a Balance; it begins with a Beat, and its Measure, or Motion, is Triple. **1731** KERSEY *New Engl. Dict.* (3rd edn) A *Minuet*, a *French* Dance, *or* the Tune belonging to it. **1737** DYCHE-PARDON (2nd edn) *Minuet* (S.) a particular Sort of Dance for one or two Persons, or the Musical Tune play'd or sung to the Dancers to regulate their Motions, which is always in Triple Time.

Mercury *see* caduceus, lyre, mese, music, Orpheus, Pandora, testudo

1565 COOPER L→E *Mercurius*, The sonne of Jupiter by Maia, whome poetes faigne to haue wynges on his head and feete ... He fyrste inuented the harpe ... **1656** BLOUNT (1st edn) *Mercury (mercurius)* the son of *Jupiter* and *Maia*; he was the messenger of the gods ... also author of the Harp, and guider of the way, he was said to have wings on his arms, and feet. **1658** PHILLIPS (1st edn) *Mercury*, ... he was counted the god of Eloquence, of Merchandry, of Handy-crafts-men, and the first inventour of the Harpe **1737** BAILEY *The Univ. Etymolog. Engl. Dict.* (3rd edn, vol. 2) *Mercury* ... To him is attributed the invention of the lute, and a kind of harp which he presented to *Apollo*.

mermaid *see* siren

1656 BLOUNT (1st edn) *Mermaid*, Seamaid, or Siren, whereof the Poets had three, *Parthenope, Leucosia* and *Ligea*; the first used her voyce, the second a Cittern, the third a Pipe; and so are said to entice Marriners and Seamen to them, by the sweetness of their musick, and then destroy them. The upper part of their bodies, was like a beautiful Virgin, the neather was fishy. By these *Syrens*, pleasures are emblematically understood, from which unless a man abstain, or at least use moderately, he shall be devoured in their waves. *Min.* **1676** COLES *Mermaides, Syrens, (Ligæa, Leucosia* and *Parthenope,)* Seamaids (with their neather parts fishy) who were said with their musick to entice Seamen & then destroy them.

Mersenne, Marin *see* antipathy, psaltery, waits

mese *see* diagram, mezzana, paramese
1587 THOMAS L→E *Mese, Iun.* The middle string: *also* A. la. mi. re. *Vitriv.* **1589** RIDER L→E *Mese.* The middle string of an instrument. **1598** FLORIO It→E *Mese,* ... the middle string. Also a-lam-ire in musicke. **1611** COTGRAVE Fr→E *Mese: f.* An eighth, or proportion of eight, in Musicke; **1611** FLORIO It→E *Mese,* ... Also the middle string of any instrument. Also a lamire in musike. **1661** BLOUNT (2nd edn) *Mese* (from the Gr. μεσόν, i. *medium*) ... Also the middle string, or mean of a musical instrument.

early 18th C. PEPUSCH various papers BL Add. 29429, f. 6 Mese, i.e, ye Middle sound between ye 2. Octaves. Paramese ye nex[t] following to Mese. **1721** MALCOLM *Treatise of Musick* (p. 520) Next to this [the ancient lyra] succeeded the *Septichord Lyre* of *Mercury,* which stands thus. *Mese* is *media. Lichanos,* so called from the *digitus index* with which the Chord was struck, as some say, or from its being the *Index* of the *Genus,* according to its Distance from *Hypate*; it was also called *Hypermese, i.e. supra mediam. Trite* so called as the Third from *Nete*; and it is also called *Paramese, i.e. juxta mediam.* This contains Two Tetrachords conjunct in *Mese,* which is common to both, and are particularly called the Tetrachords *Hypaton,* and *Neton*; so that these which were formerly Names of single Chords, are now Names of whole Tetrachords; but as yet there was no great Necessity for the Distinction ... **1731** PRELLEUR *Modern Musick-Master* ('A Brief History of Musick', p. 6) *Explanation of the Names by which the* Greeks *used to Distinguish their Notes....* The next *Tetrachord* was called *Tetracordon Meson,* that is, *Tetrachord* of the *means* or middle notes. The lowest String of this *Tetrachord* they called *Hypate-meson,* i.e. *the Principal of the Means,* this answers to our *E-la-mi.* ¶ The next was called *Parhypate Meson,* i.e. *near the Principal of the Means,* and answers to *F-fa-ut,* the Bass-Cliff. ¶ The next was called *Lychanos Meson* or *Meson Diatonos,* that is to say the *Index of the Means* or also *a mean extended*; this answers to *G-sol-re-ut.* The highest String of this *Tetrachord* they called *Mese,* i.e. *the Mean,* because this is the middle Note of y^e *Greek System* and answers to *A-la-mi-re.*

mesochorus *see* precentor
1538 ELYOT L→E *Mesochorus,* he that plaieth on a flute or other pype in the myddes of the daunsers. **1552** HULOET L→E *mesochorus* Player on a flute or like instrument. **1565** COOPER L→E *Mesochorus, ri, m.g.* He that playeth on a flute in the mids [sic] of the daunsers. **1587** THOMAS L→E *Mesochorus, ri, m.g. Sidon.* He that standing in the midst of the companie, giveth vnto others a signe to sing, or to doe some other thing. **1598** FLORIO It→E *Mesochoro,* one that standeth among singers giueth a signe when they should begin to sing. **1611** FLORIO It→E *Mesochoro,* one that standing amongst singers giueth a signe when they should begin to sing. **1659** TORRIANO-FLORIO It→E *Mesochoro,* one that standeth among singers, giveth a sign when they should begin to sing.

messe *see* mass

messe di voce
1709 [RAGUENET] *Comparison betw. Fr. and It. Musick and Opera's* (p. 44) ... the *Italians* themselves are unacquainted with it [the echo], for I am inform'd by some Masters of that Country, that their Distinctions are **loud,* and *soft* [marginalia: '**Forte, e piano.*'], or else a *Swelling* of the Voice, call'd by them *Messe di Voce*...

metter' in voce
1611 FLORIO It→E *Metter' in voce,* ... Also to set a dittie into musicall parts. **1659** TORRIANO-FLORIO It→E *Mettere in voce,* ... also to set a song.

mezzana *see* contramezzana, mese
1598 FLORIO It→E *Mezzana,* ... Also a meane string of an instrument. *Mezzano,* a meane or countertenour in musicke or singing. **1611** FLORIO It→E *Mezzana,* Also a meane string of an instrument. Also a middle bell of any ring. *Mezzano,* ... Also a meane, or countertenor in musike.

mi
1598 FLORIO It→E *Mi,* ... Also a note in musicke. **1611** FLORIO It→E *Mi,* ... Also a note in Musike.

1636 BUTLER *Principles of Musik* (p. 12) ... Of these sevn Notes thus Named, *Mi* is the principal, or Master-note: which beeing found, the six servil

Notes dooe follow, (both ascending and descending) in their order.

mi-clef

1636 BUTLER *Principles of Musik* (p. 14) Besides these Signed Cliefs, there ar also in the Scale to be noted 3 *Mi*-cliefs: (*B, E,* and *A*:) so called, becaus in one of these 3, is placed the Master-note *Mi*, by which the names of all other Notes (as before is shewed) ar known.

Midas

1565 COOPER L→E *Midas*, ... when the rusticall God Pan, chalenged to contende in musike with Apollo, and Tmolus the iudge appointed of that corntrouersie had geuen sentence on Apollos syde: All other that weare present dyd alowe his iudgement as good and true, onely kynge Midas reproued it, and in his estimation preferred Pan with his screakyng pypes. **1658** PHILLIPS (1st edn) *Midas* ... afterwards *Pan* having challenged *Apollo* to a musick duell; *Tmolus* being chosen Judge, *Midas* being the onely man that gave the victory to *Pan*, was adjudged for his ignorance to have Asses ears grow to his head ... **1736** BAILEY *Dict. Britannicum* (2nd edn) *Midas* ... a rich king in *Phrygia*, who reigned about *A.M.* 2648. in the time that *Deborah* judged *Israel* ... he being judge between *Pan* and *Apollo*, who sang best, he gave his verdict for *Pan*; at which *Apollo* being provoked gave him asses ears ...

mimo subservire

1565 COOPER L→E *Mimo subseruire. Bud.* To beare the bourden: to singe the playnesong: to healpe forwarde. **1587** THOMAS L→E *Mimo subservire, Bud.* To beare the burden, to sing the plaine song, to helpe forward. **1589** RIDER L→E *Mimo observire*. To sing the plaine song. *Mimo subservire*. To beare a Burden in a song.

minim *see* blanche, semi-minim, souspir

1593 HOLLYBAND Fr→E *Vne minime*, a minim in musicke: *f.* **1598** FLORIO It→E *Minima*, a minim in musicke. **1611** COTGRAVE Fr→E *Minime (blanche.)* A Minume, in Musicke. § *Minime noire*. A Crochet. **1611** FLORIO It→E *Minima*, a minime in musike. **1658** PHILLIPS (1st edn) *A Minime*, a certain quantity in musick, containing one time up, or down, from the Latin word *Minimus*, i. least **1659** TORRIANO-FLORIO It→E *Minimo*, the least of all, a minime. **1661** BLOUNT (2nd edn) *Minime* (Fr.) a slow time in Musick. **1670** BLOUNT (3rd edn) *Minim* (Fr.) a slow time in Musick. See *Sembrief*. **1676** COLES *Minim*, half a Sembrief. **1688** MIEGE-COTGRAVE Fr→E *Minime*, (f.) *Terme de Musique*, a Minum, in Musick. **1702** KERSEY *New Engl. Dict.* (1st edn) A *Minim*, a musical note; **1704** HARRIS *Minim*, a Term in *Musick*; see *Notes* and *Time*. **1706** KERSEY-PHILLIPS (6th edn) *Minim*, a Musical Note of a slow Time, two of which go to a Semibrief; as two Crotchets make a Minim, two Quavers a Crotchet, and two Semiquavers a Quaver: **1707** *Gloss. Angl. Nova* (1st edn) *Minim*, a Term in Musick, signifying half a *Semibreve*. **1724** [PEPUSCH] *Short Explic. of Foreign Words in Mus. Bks.* (p. 46) *Minima*, a Minim, a Note or Character in Musick so called. **1726** BAILEY *An Univ. Etymolog. Engl. Dict.* (3rd edn) *Minima* (in *Musick-Books*) a *Minium* [sic]. A Note or Character so called. **1728** CHAMBERS *Minim*, in Music, a Note, or Character of Time; equal to two Crotchets, or half a Semibreve. See *Time*, and *Characters of Music*. **1737** DYCHE-PARDON (2nd edn) *Minim* (S.) ... with the *Musicians*, is a Note that must be sounded by an Instrument or Voice so long as a Person may leisurely pronounce the Words one, two;

1609 DOWLAND-ORNITHOPARCUS *Micrologvs* (p. 39) A *Minime* is a Figure like a *Sembreefe*, hauing a tayle, ascending or descending. **1617-24** FLUDD *Utriusque Cosmi Maioris: De Templo Musicæ* (p. 191) *Minima* est dimidia quantitas Semibrevis, cujus medietas est Semiminima. **1724** TURNER *Sound Anatomiz'd* (p. 16) The first *Note* that shews these Divisions [of duration], is called a *Minim*; marked like the *Semibreve*, and is distinguished from it by the Addition of a Tail, thus; which being but half the Length of the *Semibreve*, divides it into two equal Parts.

minim time

1614 RAVENSCROFT *Briefe Discovrse* (p. 21) [*re* divisions of tact or time] The first is the *Perfect Diuision* of the *Semi-breue* which is by 3. the which we call *Minime Time*, & as some say, from the *Proportionate Rule*.

minnekin *see* cantarella, canto, pistoy bass, prima

1702 KERSEY *New Engl. Dict.* (1st edn) *Minnekins*, ... *also* a kind of gut-strings for musical instruments. **1706** KERSEY-PHILLIPS (6th edn) *Minnekins*, ... also a kind of small Catgut Strings for Violins, and other Musical Instruments. **1721** BAILEY *An Univ.*

Etymolog. Engl. Dict. (1st edn) *Minnikins,* ... Also a small Cat-gut strings for Violins, *&c.*

minor *see* flat

1696 Phillips (5th edn) *Minor,* ... In Musick it is attributed to Sixths and Thirds, as a sixth or third Minor, a lesser Third or Sixth. **1706** Kersey-Phillips (6th edn) *Minor* ... In *Musick,* it is apply'd to Sixths and Thirds; as *A Sixth* or *Third Minor, i.e.* one that is Lesser. **1724** [Pepusch] *Short Explic. of Foreign Words in Mus. Bks.* (p. 46) *Minore,* a Minor or lesser, a Term in Musick. **1728** Chambers *Minor,* in Music, is apply'd to certain Concords, which yet differ from others of the same Denomination by a half Tone. See *Semi-tone.* ¶ Thus we say, a third *Minor,* or lesser third: A sixth Major, and *Minor.* See *Third, Sixth, &c.* ¶ Concords that admit of Major and *Minor, i.e.* greater, and less, are said to be *Imperfect Concords.* See *Concord.*

minstrel *see* ambubaia, aubade, aulœdus, biffara, canto, choraula, cillone, citharist, fidicen, giga, gingeriator, menone, sonata, stampinata, tibicen

1570/71 *Dict. Fr. and Engl.* Fr→E *Menestrier,* a minstrell. **1589** Rider L→E [no headword given] A place ordained for minstrels, or singers, to play, or sing in. **1593** Hollyband Fr→E *Menestrier,* a minstrell: *m.* § *Danser au son du menestrier,* to daunce after the minstrels piping. **1599** Minsheu-Percyvall Sp→E *Menestrail,* m. a minstrel, a fidlar. **1611** Cotgrave Fr→E *Menestranderie: f.* A company of Minstrells. *Menestrandier: m.* A Minstrell, or Fidler. *Menestrel.* The same. *Menestrier: m.* The same; **1611** Florio It→E *Ministriere,* ... Also a Minstrell or a fidler. **1650** Howell-Cotgrave Fr→E † *Menestranderie: f.* A company of Minstrells. † *Menestrandier: m.* A Minstrell, or Fidler **1676** Coles *Minstrel, (French. Menestril)* a fidler or piper. **1688** Miege-Cotgrave Fr→E † *Menetrier,* (m.) a Fiddler. Say *Jouëur de Violon.* **1702** Kersey *New Engl. Dict.* (1st edn) A *Minstrel,* fiddler *or* Piper. **1706** Kersey-Phillips (6th edn) *Minstrel, (Fr.)* a Player on the Violin; a Fidler, or Piper. **1707** *Gloss. Angl. Nova* (1st edn) *Minstrel,* a Player on a Musical Instrument, a Fidler or Piper. **1708** Kersey *Dict. Anglo-Brit.* (1st edn) *Minstrel, (F.)* a Fidler, or Piper. **1728** Chambers *Minstrel,* an antient Term for a *Fidler,* or a Player on any other kind of Musical Instrument. ¶ The Word *Minstrel* in its Original, was used for People who sung and serenaded their Mistresses. Afterwards it became a Name for all kinds of Musicians: and at length pass'd to Buffoons and Country Scrapers. **1730** Bailey *Dict. Britannicum* (1st edn) *Minstrel (menestrier,* F.) a Musician. **1737** Dyche-Pardon (2nd edn) *Minstrel* (S.) any one whether Male or Female, that plays upon musical Instruments or sings methodically.

c.1726 North Musicall Gramarian BL Add. 32533, ff. 156-7v ... And one may Imagin that In the then earlyer times, the comon Country Musick was ordinarily of the flatile kind, such as wee call weights or wakes from waking ye people in Great townes, and those belonged to the Cathedrall, or Minster, (quasi Monastery church,) and thence musitioners were termed minstrells, and their profession the minstrelsye. **1728** North Musicall Grammarian (*C-K MG* ff. 128-128v) ... But now taking a stand [in the] reign [of] Henry 8 and looking backwards for some time and then forewards downe to [the] reign [of] James I there will be small show of skill in musick in England except what belonged to the cathedrall churches, and monasterys (when such were) and for that reason the consortiers wherever they went, (from ministers, as the word was) were called minstrells, and then the whole faculty of musick [was called] the minstrelsie. And the word is (nearly) so interpreted by Howell in his etimologys, and by Minshew in his Spanish dictionary.

minstrelsy

1726 Bailey *An Univ. Etymolog. Engl. Dict.* (3rd edn) *Minstralcie, Minstrelsy,* Musick. *Chaucer.* **1730** Bailey *Dict. Britannicum* (1st edn) *Minstrelsy* the Musician's Art. **1737** Dyche-Pardon (2nd edn) *Minstrelsy* (S.) the Art or Science of Musick practically performed, either by Voice or Instrument.

minuet *see* menuet

minuetto

1724 [Pepusch] *Short Explic. of Foreign Words in Mus. Bks.* (p. 46) *Minuetto,* a Minuet, a *French* Dance so called, or the Tune or Air belonging thereunto. This Dance or Air being so well known, that it needs no Explanation.

minugia

1659 Torriano-Florio It→E *Minugia,* ... the treble or smallest gut-strings of any musical instrument

minuire

1598 FLORIO It→E *Minuire, isco, ito,* ... Also to fauour the voice in singing, as it were to fall from the highest to the lowest. **1611** FLORIO It→E *Minuire, isco, ito,* to diminish ... Also to fauour the voice in singing, or fall with the voice. **1659** TORRIANO-FLORIO It→E *Minuire, Minuare,* ... to make less among musitians, to fall or decline with the voice, and favour it with singing. **1688** DAVIS-TORRIANO-FLORIO It→E *Minuire, Minuare,* ... among musicians, to fall or decline with the voice, and favour it with singing.

minurio

1500 *Ortus Vocabulorum* L→E Minurio ris. i. minutum cantare. to pype as smale byrdys.

minurize *see* descant

1538 ELYOT L→E *Minurizo, are,* to synge smalle, or to feyne in syngynge. **1552** HULOET L→E *Minurizo, as* Syng small. **1587** THOMAS L→E *Minurizo, vel minurio, as, Sidon.* To sing small or with a lowe voice, to feigne in singing. **1623** COCKERAM *Minurize.* to Sing small *Minurize.* To sing small, to faine in singing.

Misenus

1565 COOPER L→E *Misenus,* The sonne of Aeolus, Aeneas trumpettoure.

miskin

1671 PHILLIPS (3rd edn) *Miskin,* (old word) a little Bagpipe. **1676** COLES *Miskin, Old word.* a little bag-pipe. **1708** KERSEY *Dict. Anglo-Brit.* (1st edn) *Miskin,* (O.) a little Bag-pipe.

missura *see* Nunc Dimittis

1706 KERSEY-PHILLIPS (6th edn) *Missura,* (in old *Latin* Records) a singing the Hymn call'd *Nunc dimittis;* and performing other Superstitious Ceremonies, to recommend and dismiss a dying Person. **1708** KERSEY *Dict. Anglo-Brit.* (1st edn) *Missura,* (O. L.) a singing the Hymn call'd *Nunc dimittis;* and performing other Superstitious Ceremonies, to recommend and dismiss a dying Person. **1726** BAILEY *An Univ. Etymolog. Engl. Dict.* (3rd edn) *Missura* (*i.e.* about to send) a singing the Hymn called *nunc dimittis,* and performing other Superstitious Ceremonies to recommend and dismiss a dying Person, us'd by the *Roman* Catholicks. **1737** DYCHE-PARDON (2nd edn) *Missura* (S.) the singing the Hymn called *Nunc Dimittis,* and performing certain superstitious Ceremonies by the Papists, to recommend and dismiss a dying Person.

mixolydian *see* collateral, hypermixolidian, lydian

1598 FLORIO It→E *Misolidio,* a kinde of song or musicke. *Missolidio, Mixolidio,* mournefull, melancholike, or graue musike. **1611** FLORIO It→E *Misolidio,* mournefull or graue Musike. *Missolidio,* as *Misolidio.* **1659** TORRIANO-FLORIO It→E **Misolidio, Missolidio,* grave or mournful musicke. **1676** COLES *Mixolydian, (q. Mixt Lydian)* Musick, lamentable, fit for Tragedies.

mock song

1737 DYCHE-PARDON (2nd edn) *Mock-Song* (S.) one that banters another's Song in the same Words or Tune.

mode *as proportional phenomenon, see* mood

1565 COOPER L→E *Modus* Tyme or measure in musike. *Modus Cic.* Measure and time in singyng. **1587** THOMAS L→E *Modi, orum, m.g.* The measures, rests, times or pauses in singing or playing. *Modus, di, m.g.* ... time or measure in musicke. **1589** RIDER L→E *Modi, m.* The measure, time, rest, or pause in singing. *Modi, orum, m.* Measures, tunes, and pauses in singing. **1598** FLORIO It→E *Modi,* ... Also the measures, rest, times, or pauses in singing or playing. **1611** FLORIO It→E *Modi,* ... Also times, rests, or pauses in Musike. **1659** TORRIANO-FLORIO It→E *Modi, Modo,* ... also times, rests, or pauses in Musick. **1688** MIEGE-COTGRAVE Fr→E *Mode, en Termes de Musique,* modulation, or measure, in Musick. **1704** HARRIS *Modes in Musick.* See *Mood.* **1728** CHAMBERS *Mode* ... [*see* Appendix]

1721 MALCOLM *Treatise of Musick* (p. 560) ... *Again,* respecting the mutual Proportions of the Notes, they [in former times] had what they called *Modes, Prolations* and *Times*: The Two last were distinguished into *Perfect* and *Imperfect;* and first into *greater* and *lesser,* and each of these into *perfect* and *imperfect*: But afterwards they reduced all into 4 *Modes* including the *Prolations* and *Times.* I could not think it worth Pains to make a tedious Description of all these, with their Marks or Signs, which you may see in the already mentioned *Dictionaire de Musique*: ...

mode *as scalic phenomenon or key, see* collateral, mood, position, tune

1587 THOMAS L→E § *Modos concidere & frangere.* The voice falling to sing and as it were to gather strength, or to fal from the highest tune to the lowest. **1728** CHAMBERS *Mode* ... [*see* Appendix] **1730** BAILEY *Dict. Britannicum* (1st edn) *Mode* (in *Musick*) the particular manner of constituting the Octave, as it consists of seven essential or natural Notes, besides the Key.

1597 MORLEY *Plaine and Easie Introdvction* (p. 147) [*re* leaving the key] A great fault, for euery key hath a peculiar ayre proper vnto it selfe, so that if you goe into another then that wherein you begun, you change the aire of the song, which is as much as to wrest a thing out of his nature, making the asse leape vpon his maister and the Spaniell beare the loade. The perfect knowledge of these aires (which the antiquity termed *Modi*) was in such estimation amongst the learned, as therein they placed perfection of musicke, as you may perceiue at large in the fourth booke of *Seuerinus Boetius* his musick, and *Glareanus* hath written a learned booke which he tooke in hand onely for the explanation of those moodes; ... **1667** SIMPSON *Compendium of Practical Musick* (pp. 111-12) That which the *Grecians* called Mode or Mood, the *Latins* termed Tone or Tune. The design of either was, to shew in what Key a Song was set, and which Keys had affinity one with another. **1698** WALLIS *Letter to Samuel Pepys* (*Philos. Trans.*, 1698, p. 254) ... if all Musick were Composed to the same *Key*, or (as the Greeks call it) the same *Mode*... **1721** MALCOLM *Treatise of Musick* (pp. 274-5) ... I would propose the Word *Mode*, to express the *melodious Constitution* of the *Octave*, as it consists of Seven essential or natural Notes, besides the *Fundamental*; and because there are Two Species, let us call that with a *3d g.* the *greater Mode*, and that with a *3d l.* the *lesser Mode*: ... but with respect to the essential Difference in the Constitution of the *Octaves*, on which the *Melody* depends, there are only Two different *Modes*, the greater and the lesser. Thus the Latin Writers use the Word *Modus*, to signify the particular *Mode* or Way of constituting the *Octave*; and hence they also called it *Constitutio*; ... § (pp. 528-9) ... it must be owned there is an unaccountable Difference among the [ancient] Writers, in their Definition, Divisions and Names of the *Modes*. As to the Definition, I find an Agreement in this, that a *Mode*, or *Tone* in this Sense, is a certain *System* or *Constitution* of Sounds; and they agree too, that an *Octave* with all its intermediate Sounds is such a Constitution: But the specifick Differences of them some place in the Manner of Division or Order of its *concinnous* Parts; and others place merely in the *Tension* of the Whole, *i.e.* as the whole Notes are *acuter* or *graver*, or stand higher and lower in the *Scale* of *Musick*, as *Bryennius* says very expresly. *Boethius* has a very ambiguous Definition, he first tells us, that the *Modes* depend on the Seven different Species of the *Diapason*, which are also called *Tropi*; and these, says he, are *Constitutiones in totis vocum ordinibus, vel gravitate vel acumine differentes*. Again he says, *Constitutio est plenum veluti modulationius corpus, ex consonantiarum conjunctione consistens, quale est* Diapasaon, &c. *Has igitur constitutiones, si quis totas faciat acutiores, vel in gravius totas remittat secundum supradictas* Diapason *consonantiæ species, efficiet modos septem*. This is indeed a very ambiguous Determination, for if they depend on the Species of *8ves*, to what Purpose is the last Clause; and if they differ only by the Tenor or Place of the whole *8ve*, i.e. as 'tis taken at a higher or lower Pitch, what Need the Species of *8ves* to be all brought in: His Meaning perhaps is only to signify, that the different Orders or Species of *8ves* ly[e] in different Places, *i.e.* higher and lower in the *Scale*. § (pp. 562-4) The last Thing I shall consider here is, how the *Modes* were defined in these Days of Improvement [presumably the period from Guido to de Muris]; and I find they were generally characterized by the Species of *8ve* after *Ptolomy*'s Manner, and therefore reckoned in all 7. But afterwards they considered the *harmonical* and *arithmetical* Divisions of the *8ve*, whereby it resolves into a *4th* above a *5th*, or a *5th* above a *4th*. And from this they constituted 12 *Modes*, making of each 8ve two different Modes according to this different Division; but because there are Two of them that cannot be divided both Ways, therefore there are but 12 Modes. To be more particular, consider, in the natural System there are 7 different *Octaves* proceeding from these 7 Letters, *a, b, c, d, e, f, g*; each of which has Two middle Chords, which divide it *harmonically* and *arithmetically*, except *f*, which has not a true *4th*, (because *b* is Three Tones above it, and a *4th* is but Two *Tones* and a *Semitone*) and *b*, which consequently wants the true *5th* (because *f* is only Two *Tones* and Two *Semitones* above it, and a true *5th* contains 3 *Tones* and a *Semitone*) therefore we have only 5 *Octaves* that are divided both Ways, *viz. a, c, d, e, g*, which make 10 Modes according to these different Divisions, and the other Two *f* and *b* make up the 12. These that are divided harmonically, *i.e.* with the 5*ths* lowest were called *authentick*, and the other *plagal* Modes.... To these Modes they gave the Names of the ancient *Greek Tones*, as *Dorian*, *Phrygian*: But several Authors differ in the Application of these Names, as they do about the Order, as, which they shall call the first and second, *&c.* which being arbitrary Things, as far as I can understand, it were as idle to pretend to reconcile them, as it was in them to differ about it. The material Point is, if we can find it, to know what they meant by these Distinctions, and what was the real Use of them in *Musick*; but even here where they ought to have agreed, we find they differed. The best Account I am able to give you of it is this: They considered that an 8*ve* which wants a 4*th* or 5*th*, is imperfect; these being the *Concords* next to 8*ve*, the Song ought to these Chords most frequently and remarkably [sic]; and because their *Concord* is different, which makes the Melody different, they established by this Two Modes in every natural *Octave*, that had a true 4*th* and 5*th*: Then if the Song was carried as far as the *Octave* above, it was called a *perfect Mode*; if less, as to the 4*th* or 5*th*, it was *imperfect*; if not moved both above and below, it was called a *mixt Mode*: Thus some Authors speak about these *Modes*.

mode *as style, see* modi melopœiæ

moderato

1724 [PEPUSCH] *Short Explic. of Foreign Words in Mus. Bks.* (p. 46) *Moderato*, is with Moderation.

1731 PRELLEUR *Modern Musick-Master* (Dictionary, p. 3) *Moderato*, Moderately. **after 1731** ANON. *Directions for Playing on the Flute* (Dictionary, n.p.) *Moderato*: moderately

modi melopœiæ *see* melopœia

1721 MALCOLM *Treatise of Musick* (p. 544) There were also what they [the ancient Greeks] called, The *modi melopœiæ*, of which *Aristides* names these, *Dithyrambick*, *Nomick*, and *Tragick*; called *Modes* for their expressing the several Motions and Affections of the Mind. The best Notion we can form of this is, to suppose them something like what we call the different Stiles in *Musick*, as the *Ecclesiastick*, the *Choraick*, the *Recitative*, &c. But I think the *Rythmus* must have a considerable or the greatest Share in these Differences.

modulamen *see* acroamatick

1500 *Ortus Vocabulorum* L→E Modulamen inis. i. cantatio dulcis & mellica. a sweett song. n.t. Modulantia tie. idem est. f.p. **1552** HULOET L→E *Modulamen. inis, Modulus. li,* Syngynge tyme. **1587** THOMAS L→E *Modulamen, nis, Sen. & modulamentum, ti, n.g. Gell. vid. Modulatio* [*see* modulation].

1721 MALCOLM *Treatise of Musick* (p. 584) ... then [in ancient Greece] the Word *Modulamen* was never applied any other way than to successive Sounds.

modulans

1500 *Ortus Vocabulorum* L→E Modulans tis. i. dulciter cantans. syngyng sweetly. p. pen.

modulate *see* admodulate, recitative

1623 COCKERAM *Modulate*. To sing by measure. **1721** BAILEY *An Univ. Etymolog. Engl. Dict.* (1st edn) To *Modulate*, (*modulatum*, L.) to Sing, or make an Harmony. **1737** DYCHE-PARDON (2nd edn) *Modulate* (V.) to regulate the Sounds or Harmony of a Piece of Musick, and to make a regular Transition from one Key to another.

modulation *see* accent, chroma, counterpoint, descant, fugue, immodulatus, in nomine, measure, melody, melos, mode, repercussion

1500 *Ortus Vocabulorum* L→E Modulatio onis. dulcis cantus. anglice a songe. f.t. **1565** COOPER L→E *Modulátio, onis, f.g. Verbale. Quintil.* Musicall measure: modulation: pleasant tuninge. *Modulâtus, huius modulátus, pen. prod. m.g. Seneca.* A tunyng: a singinge in measure. *Modulâtus, pen. prod. Participium.* Done or songe by measure: tuned. § *Modulata cantica. Quintil.* Songes tuned in measure. **1587** THOMAS L→E *Modulatio, onis, f.g. verb. à Modulor, Quint.* Musicall measure, modulation, pleasant tuning. *Modulatus, a, um, Quint.* Done, or song by measure: tuned, well ordered and ruled, tempered. *Modulatus, us, m.g. Sen.* A tuning, a singing in measure. **1589** RIDER L→E *Modulatè. adu.* Aptely, with sweete accente and measure. *Modulatio, f. modulatus, m. modulamen.* A pleasant tuning, or tuning in measure. *Modulatus, m. modulatio, f modulamen, n.* A singing in measure. *Modulatus, p.* Tuned. **1598** FLORIO It→E *Modolantia*, singing, musicall measure, pleasant tuning, modulation. *Modolatione*, as *Modolantia*. **1611** COTGRAVE Fr→E *Modulation: f.* Modulation, harmonie, musicall proportion, pleasant tuning. **1611** FLORIO It→E

Modolantia modulation, musicall measure, tuneable singing. *Modolatione*, as *Modolantia*. **1616** Bullokar *Modulation*. A pleasant tuning or sweete singing. **1623** Cockeram *Modulation*. A singing by measure, sweet singing. *Modulation*. Measure in Musique. **1656** Blount (1st edn) *Modulation (modulatio)* a pleasant tuning, a singing or playing by number or measure. **1658** Phillips (1st edn) *Modulation*, (lat.) an exact singing, a keeping time and measure in singing. **1659** Torriano-Florio It→E *Modulanza, Modulatione, Modulame, Modolatione, Modolanza, Modolame*, musical-measure, modulation, tunable-singing, harmonious-proportion. **1676** Coles *Modulation, Latin*. an exact singing or warbling. **1696** Phillips (5th edn) *Modulation, (Lat.)* a carrying on a Song in the same Key, sometimes passing out of it, then getting into it again, without offending the Ears. **1702** Kersey *New Engl. Dict.* (1st edn) *Modulation*, tuning, *or* warbling in musick. **1706** Kersey-Phillips (6th edn) *Modulation*, (in *Musick*) Tuning or Warbling, the carrying of a Song in the same key, sometimes passing out of it, and then getting into it again; an agreeable Harmonie. **1707** *Gloss. Angl. Nova* (1st edn) *Modulation*, (Lat.) Tuneing, Composing in Musick, Setting of Notes. **1728** Chambers *Modulation*, in Music, is the Art of keeping in, or changing the *Mode* or Key. See *Mode*. ¶ Under this Term is comprehended the regular Progression of the several Parts thro the Sounds that are in the Harmony of any particular Key, as well as the preceeding naturally and regularly from one Key to another. ¶ The Rules of *Modulation* in the first sense belong to Harmony and Melody. See *Harmony* and *Melody*. ¶ We shall here only add a word with regard to the Rules of *Modulation* in the latter sense. ¶ As every Piece must have a principal Key; and since the Variety so necessary in Music to please and entertain, forbids the being confined to one Key; and that therefore it is not only allowable, but necessary, to *modulate* into, and make Cadences on several other Keys, having a Relation and Connection with the principal Key: It must be consider'd what it is that constitutes a Connection between the Harmony of one Key and that of another, that it may be hence determin'd into what Keys the Harmony may be conducted with Propriety. See *Key*. ¶ As to the Manner in which the *Modulation* from one Key to another is to be perform'd, so that the Transition may be easy and natural; 'tis not easy to fix any precise Rules: for tho it is chiefly perform'd by the help of the 7th *g* of the Key, into which the Harmony is to be changed, whether it be flat or sharp; yet the Manner of doing it is so various and extensive, as no Rules can easily circumscribe. A general Notion of it may be conceiv'd under the following Terms. ¶ The 7th *g* in either sharp or flat Key, is the 3d *g* to the 5th *f* of the Key, by which the Cadence in the Key is chiefly perform'd; and by being only a Semi-tone under the Key, is thereby the most proper Note to lead into it, which it does in the most natural manner imaginable. Insomuch that the 7th *g* is never heard in any of the Parts, but the Ear expects the Key should succeed it; for whether it be used as a 3d, or as a 6th, it always affects us with so imperfect a Sensation, that we naturally expect something more perfect to follow, which cannot be more easily and smoothly accomplish'd, than by the small Interval of a Semi-tone, to pass into the perfect Harmony of the Key. Hence it is, that the Transition into one Key is best effected, by introducing its 7th *g*, which so naturally leads to it. **1737** Dyche-Pardon (2nd edn) *Modulation* (S.) the Act of tuning, warbling, or regulating the Voice or Instrument to perform a Piece of Musick harmoniously.

1721 Malcolm *Treatise of Musick* (p. 441) Under the Term of *Modulation* may be comprehended the regular Progression of the several Parts thro' the Sounds that are in the *Harmony* of any particular *Key* as well as the proceeding naturally and regularly with the *Harmony* from one *Key* to another: ... § (p. 546) ... what we call Modulation or keeping in and changing the *Mode* or *Key*; ... **1721 or after** Anon. Institutions of Musick (rear of LC copy of Bayne, p. 17) Under the Term of Modulation may be Comprehended the Regular Progression of the several Parts through the Sounds that are in the Harmony of any Particular Key: as well as the proceeding naturally & regularly with the Harmony from one Key to another. **1725** De La Fond *New System of Music* (p. 78) ... what is called by some, the *modulation* in the works of our great Composers... This term signifies singing and playing in general, and is derived from *mode* or *modus*, which in the *Latin* signifies sometimes *Music* it self, or rather a piece of *Music*. § (p. 79) ... What here call'd modulation by some, is a particular beauty in *Composition*, which beauty consists in passing or sliding gracefully, tho' almost imperceptibly, out of one *Nota* [= key] into another, and back again to the first, or only out of one *Nota* into another, either ascending or descending, without going back to the first. **1730** [Pepusch] *Short Treatise on Harmony* (p. 4) *Modulation*, is the Transition of a melody or single Part; or of several Parts in Harmony, from one key to another. **1731** [PEPUSCH] *Treatise on Harmony* (2nd edn, p. 3) *Modulation* is the Art of rightly ordering the Melody of a single Part, or the Harmony of many Parts; either keeping in One Key, or in passing from One Key to Another. **1731** PRELLEUR *Modern Musick-Master* ('A Brief History of Musick', p. 15) Every one of these Notes [C, D, E, F, G, A, B] has another an [sic] Octave above it so y[t.] there are seven sorts of *Octaves*, in the extremities of which the Ancients limited the Extent of their Moods, so y[t] what they meant by *Modulation*, was only makeing a tune pass through all the Sounds comprehended between these two extremities, however in such a manner as the *Essential Sounds* might be heard oftener than any other, and this was always *Diatonically* ...

modulator

1565 COOPER L→E *Modulâtor, pen. prod. toris, m.g. Aliud verbale.* He that singeth or tuneth in measure. § *Vocis & cantus modulator. Colum.* A pleasant tuner and accenter of his woordes and voice. **1587** THOMAS L→E *Modulator, oris, m.g. verb. Colum.* He that singeth, or learneth to sing in measure: a pleasant tuner and accenter of, &c. **1589** RIDER L→E *Modulator, m.* He that tuneth in measure. **1598** FLORIO It→E *Modolatore,* he that singeth or learneth to sing in measure, in tune and accent. **1611** FLORIO It→E *Modulatore,* he that singeth in measure, tune, and accent. **1659** TORRIANO-FLORIO It→E *Modulatore, Modolatore,* one that singeth in tune and measure.

modulor *see* emodulor

1500 *Ortus Vocabulorum* L→E Modulo as. idem est. Modulor aris. i. dulciter cantare: melodias facere. to syng sweetly. d.p. Modulus li. i. peruus modus. Item hic modulus li: tropus: cantus qui precinitur in pricipio misse vel matutini vel vesperarum. m.s. **1538** ELYOT L→E *Modulor, aris, ari,* ... also to synge. *Modulus, et Modulamen,* a songe, a modulation, the tyme in syngynge. **1565** COOPER L→E *Módulor, penul. corr. modulâtis, modulâtus sum, modulári. Gell.* ... to singe: to speake with pleasant tune and accente. § *Modulari carmen. Virgil.* To singe a verse: to singe meter. *Orationem modulari. Cic.* To tune and accent. *Vocem modulari. Cic.* To measure and tune the voyce. **1587** THOMAS L→E *Modulare, adverb.* Aptlie, with sweete accent and measure. *Moduli, oram, vid. modi* [*see* mode]. *Modulor, aris. depo.* To make or do by number or measure, to sing, to sing tunably, to plaie or pipe: to measure, tune, and accent. *Modulus, li, m.g. dim. à Modus, Vitruv.* ... measure in musicke: a song: modulation, a, [sic] melodie **1589** RIDER L→E *Modulor.* To tune in measure. *Modulor,* To Tune, or measure: also to tune, or accent *Modulor, admodulator, emodulor, modulo, meditor.* To sing tuneably. *Modulus, modus, m.* A measure in musicke. **1598** FLORIO It→E *Modolare,* to sing or make harmonie, to measure, to tune and accent, to sing tunable, and according to due number. **1611** COTGRAVE Fr→E *Module: m.* ... also, modulation, melodie, or measure, in Musicke. **1611** FLORIO It→E *Modolare,* to sing tuneable, or according to due accent and number. *Modulo,* a measure in Musike. Also melodie. **1659** TORRIANO-FLORIO It→E *Modulare, Modolare,* to sing tuneably, or according to due number or accent. **Modulo, Modolo,* a due measure, tune, accent, or proportion in Musick

moduloscropus

1500 *Ortus Vocabulorum* L→E Modoloscropus est cantus factus in principio misse. m.s. **1589** RIDER L→E *Moduloscropus, m.* A Psalme sung before the sermon.

modus *see* mode

modus chromaticus *see* ionick

molle *see* beemol, b molle, chromatic, colores generum, properchant, toniæum

1598 FLORIO It→E *Molle,* ... in musicke it is taken for flat. **1611** FLORIO It→E *Molle,* ... Also a flat in Musike. **1659** TORRIANO-FLORIO It→E **Molle,* sub. a flat in Musick

1694 HOLDER *Treatise of Natural Grounds* (pp. 133-4) The *Chromatic* [genus in ancient Greek music] had three Colours; by which it was divided into *Molle, Sescuplum,* and *Toniæum.* ¶ 1[st.] *Molle,* in which the Tetrachord rose by a *Triental Diesis* ... or third part of a *Tone;* and another such *Diesis;* and an Incomposit Interval, containing a *Tone,* and half, and third part of a *Tone:* and it was called *Molle,* because it hath the least, and consequently most Enervated *Spiss* Intervals within the Chromatic *Genus*...

monaulos *see* aulos

1565 COOPER L→E *Monaulos.* A pipe: a recorder. **1587** THOMAS L→E *Monaulos, li. f.g. subauditur tibia,*

Plin. A pipe, a recorder. **1598** FLORIO It→E *Monaulo,* a pipe or a recordor [sic]. **1611** FLORIO It→E *Monaulo,* a Piper or a Recorder.

monochord *see* false, manichord, system, trumpet marine, tuba marine
1538 ELYOT L→E *Monochordium,* an Instrumente, hauynge manye strynges of oone sowne, sauynge that with smalle pieces of cloth, the sounes be distincte, as Clauycordes be. **1565** COOPER L→E *Monochordium, dij, n.g.* An instrument hauing many stringes of one sowne, sauynge that with small pieces of clothe the sowne is distincte, as in Clauicordes. **1587** THOMAS L→E *Monochordum, di, n.g.* *An instrument hauing manie strings of one sound, sauing that with small peeces of cloth the sound is distinct: some call it the Claricordes. **1589** RIDER L→E *Monocordium. n. espineta.* Claricordes, or instruments so called. **1598** FLORIO It→E *Monacordo,* an instrument with one string. Also as *Monocordo. Monocordo,* an instrument hauing manie strings of one sound, which with little peeces of cloth make distinct sounds, called claricords. **1599** MINSHEU-PERCYVALL Sp→E *Monacordio,* m. an instrument with one string. **Monicordio,* m. an instrument of one string. **1611** COTGRAVE Fr→E § *Monochordiser des doigts.* To quauer with the fingers, to wag or play with them, as if he touched a Manicordion. **1611** FLORIO It→E *Monocordo,* an instrument with many stringes of one sound, which with little pieces of cloth make distinct sounds. **1650** HOWELL-COTGRAVE Fr→E † *Monochordiser des doigts.* To quaver with the fingers, to wag or play with them, as if he touched a manicordion. **1661** BLOUNT (2nd edn) *Monochord* (Gr.) that hath but one string. **1676** COLES *Monochord, Greek.* having but one string **1688** MIEGE-COTGRAVE Fr→E *Monocorde,* (m.) a kind of Musical Instrument. ¶ *C'est un Instrument de Musique, monté sur du bois resonnant, où il y a des Cordes & des Chevalets. Il est tres propre, pour regler les Sons. Et il a eté appelé Monocorde, non pas qu'il n'ait qu'une Corde, mais parce que toutes ses cordes sont à l'Unisson.* **1696** PHILLIPS (5th edn) *Monochord,* an Instrument to prove the Variety and Proportion of Musical Sounds. **1702** KERSEY *New Engl. Dict.* (1st edn) A *Monocord,* a sort of musical instrument with one string. **1704** HARRIS *Monochord,* a kind of Instrument anciently of singular Use for the Regulating of Sounds; but some appropriate the Name of *Monochord* to an Instrument that hath only one single String, as the *Trumpet Marine.* ¶ The Ancients made use of the *Monochord* to determine the Proportion of Sounds to one another: When the *Chord* was divided into two equal Parts, so that the Terms were as 1 and 1, they called them *Vnisons;* but if they were as 2 to 1, they called them *Octaves* or *Diapasons;* when they were as 3 to 2, they called them *Fifths,* or *Diapentes;* if they were as 4 to 3, they called them *Fourths,* or *Diatessarons;* if the Terms were as 5 to 4, they called it *Diton,* or a *Tierce major;* but if the Terms were as 6 to 5, then they called it a *Demiditon,* or a *Tierce minor;* and lastly, if the Terms were as 24 to 25, they called it a *Demiton* or *Dieze.* ¶ The *Monochord* being thus divided, was properly that which they called a *System,* of which there were many kinds, according to the different Divisions of the *Monochord.* **1706** KERSEY-PHILLIPS (6th edn) *Monochord,* an Instrument, made use of by the Ancients, to determine the Proportion of Sounds; but some apply the Name to a Musical Instrument, that has only one single String; as the *Trumpet-marine.* **1707** *Gloss. Angl. Nova* (1st edn) *Monochord,* a kind of Instrument, anciently of singular use in the Regulation of Sounds; but some appropriate the Name of *Monochord* to an Instrument, that hath only one String, as the *Trumpet marine.* **1724** [PEPUSCH] *Short Explic. of Foreign Words in Mus. Bks.* (p. 46) *Monocordo,* or *Monochordo,* is a very long Instrument with only one String, made Use of to find out the true and exact Distance of each Note and Half Note the one from the other. **1726** BAILEY *An Univ. Etymolog. Engl. Dict.* (3rd edn) *Monochord* (*monochorde,* F. *monochordum,* L. μονόχορδον, of μόνος one, and χορδή the String of a musical Instrument, *Gr.*) a kind of Instrument anc[i]ently of singular Use in the Regulation of Sounds: But some appropriate the Name of *Monochord* to an Instrument which hath only one String. *Monocordo, Monochordo,* (in *Musick Books*) signifies a very long Instrument that has but one String, the Use of which is to find out the true and exact Distance of each Note and half Note, the one from the other. *Ital.* **1728** CHAMBERS *Monochord,* a musical Instrument wherewith to try the Variety and Proportion of musical Sounds. See *Tune.* ¶ It is compos'd of a Rule, divided and subdivided into divers Parts, whereon there is a String pretty well stretch'd upon two Bridges, at each Extreme thereof. In the middle between both is a moveable Bridge, by whose means, in applying it to the different Divisions of the Lnei [sic], you find that the Sounds are in the same Proportion to one another, as the Divisions of the Line cut by the Bridge were. ¶ The *Monochord* is also call'd the *Harmonical Canon,* or *Canonical Rule;* because

serving to measure the Degrees of Gravity, and Acuteness of Sounds. See *Gravity, &c.* ¶ There are also *Monochords* with 48 fix'd Bridges; the Use of all which may be supply'd by one single moveable Bridge; which are placed in the middle, by only shifting it under new Chords or Strings, always representing the entire Sound, or the open Note. ¶ *Pythagoras* is held to have been the Inventor of the *Monochord. Ptolemy* examined his Harmonical Intervals with the *Monochord.* See *Canon.* ¶ When the Chord was divided into equal parts, so that the Terms were as 1 and 1, they call'd them *Unisons;* if they were as 2 to 1, *Octaves,* or *Diapasons;* when they were as 8 to 2, *Fifths,* or *Diapentes;* if they were as 4 to 3, they called them *Fourths,* or *Diatessarons;* if the Terms were as 5 to 4, *Diton,* or a *Tierce Major;* if as 6 to 5, a *Demi-Diton,* or a *Tierce Minor;* lastly, if as 24 to 25, *Demi-diton* or *Dieze.* See *Unison, Octave, Diapason, Diapente, Diatessaron, &c.* ¶ The *Monochord* being thus divided, was properly what they call'd a System, of which there were many kinds, according to the different Divisions of the *Monochord.* See *System.* ¶ Dr. *Wallis* has taught the Division of the *Monochord* in the *Philosophical Transactions;* but thet [sic] Instrument is now disused, the modern Music not requiring such Division. ¶ *Monochord,* is also used for any musical Instrument, consisting of only one Chord, or String. See *Chord.* ¶ The Trumpet Marine is a *Monochord.* See *Trumpet.* ¶ The Word is *Greek,* form'd of μόνος *solus,* single, and χορδή Chord. **1737** DYCHE-PARDON (2nd edn) *Monochord* (S.) an Instrument that Organ and other Musical Instrument-makers try the Tones of their Instruments by or with; it is composed of a Rule divided or subdivided into divers Parts, upon which a String is stretched pretty tight over two Bridges placed at the two Extreams, which has likewise a moveable Bridge to set at the several Intervals, it will be found the Sounds or Tones bear the same Proportion to one another as the Distances upon the Line; it is sometimes called the Harmonical Canon; there are Monochords with 48 fixed Bridges to save the Trouble of moving; this Term is also applied to some practical Instruments with one String, as the Trumpet Marine, &c.

1609 DOWLAND-ORNITHOPARCUS *Micrologvs* (p. 22) A *Monochord,* that is, an Instrument of one string ... § (p. 23) A *Monochord* (as *Guido* proues in the beginning of his *Doctrinall*) is a long square peece of wood hollow within, with a string drawne ouer it; by the sound whereof, we apprehend the varieties of sounds ... Now it is called a *Monochord,* because it hath but one string, as a *Tetrachord* is called that which hath foure. And a *Decachord* which hath tenne, saith *Ioan. Pont.* 22. *cap.* 7. of his Musicke. **1731** PRELLEUR *Modern Musick-Master* ('A Brief History of Musick', p. 13) ... He [Pythagoras] also invented a *Monochord* an Instrument so called by reason of its haveing but one String which he divided in several equal parts by a Line under it; Then a small moveable Bridge being placed under the String divided it into two parts which yielded a *Grave* or *Acute Sound* according to the different Length of each portion; ...

monody *see* dirge, elegy, epicedy, epitaph, nænia, obit, threnody

1538 ELYOT L→E *Monodia,* a lamentable or mournyng song, suche as is songen in funeralles. **1565** COOPER L→E *Monodia.* A lamentable mournyng songe. **1587** THOMAS L→E *Monodia, æ, f.g. Iun.* A lamentable or funerall song: a song where one singeth alone, *Isid.* **1589** RIDER L→E *Monodia, f.* A song wherein one singeth alone. *Monodia, nænia, threnodia,* A mourning song for the dead. *vide* lamentable song [elegy] **1598** FLORIO It→E *Monodia,* a mourefull [sic] song where one singeth alone. **1611** FLORIO It→E *Monodia,* a mournefull song where one singeth alone. **1623** COCKERAM *Monodies.* Mournefull songs. **1656** BLOUNT (1st edn) *Monodie (monodia)* a lamentable or funeral song, where one sings alone. *Monodical,* pertaining to such a song. **1658** PHILLIPS (1st edn) *Monodical,* (Greek) belonging to Monody, *i.* a kind of Funeral-song, wherein one sings alone. **1676** COLES *Monody, Greek.* a funeral ditty sung by one alone. **1707** *Gloss. Angl. Nova* (1st edn) *Monody,* (Lat.) a Mournful or Funeral Song, where one Sings alone. *Monodical,* (Lat.) pertaining to a *Monody,* or Funeral Son[g]. **1728** CHAMBERS *Monody, Monodia,* in the antient Poetry, a kind of mournful Song, or Ditty, sung by a Person all alone; to utter his Grief. ¶ The Word is compounded of μονος *solus,* and ωδη, Song. **1730** BAILEY *Dict. Britannicum* (1st edn) *Monody* (*monodia,* L. μονωδία of μονος alone, and ωδε a Song, *Gr.*) a Song where one sings alone; also a lamentable or funeral Song. **1737** DYCHE-PARDON (2nd edn) *Monody* (S.) a Song of Sorrow or Lamentation sung by one Person.

monologie

1589 RIDER L→E *Monologia, f.* The Cuckoes tune, or the singing alwaies one tune *Monologus, m.* He that singeth like a cuckoe. **1656** Blount (1st edn) *Monologie (monologia)* singing always one tune, speaking still of one matter...

monstra *see* direct, index

monta in sella *see* butta in sella, serra serra
1598 Florio It→E *Monta in sella,* a charge that trumpetters vse to sound to prepare and call men to take horse and get vp. **1611** Florio It→E *Monta in sella,* a charge that Trumpeters vse to sound to prepare and call men to take horse and get vp. **1659** Torriano-Florio It→E *Monta in sella,* a charge, or point of war, a larum [sic] that Trumpeters use to sound, for a warning unto men to prepare themselves to take horse, and get up into the saddle.

mood *as proportional phenomenon, see* degree, mode, prolation, retorted time, time
1704 Harris *Mood* in *Musick,* signifies certain Proportions of the *Time,* or Measure of Notes. These *Moods* or *Modes* of measuring Notes, were formerly Four in Number, *viz.* ¶ 1. *The Perfect of the More,* in which a *Large* contain'd three *Longs,* a *Long* three *Breves,* a *Breve* three *Semi-breves,* and a *Semi-breve* three *Minims.* ¶ 2. *The Perfect of the Less,* wherein a *Large* comprehended two *Longs,* a *Long* two *Breves,* a *Breve* three *Semi-breves,* and a *Semi-breve* two *Minims.* ¶ 3. *The Imperfect of the More,* in which a *Large* contained two *Longs,* a *Long* two *Breves,* a *Breve* two *Semi-breves,* and a *Semi-breve* three *Minims.* ¶ 4. The *Imperfect of the Less,* is the same with that which we call the *Common Mood,* the other three being now altogether out of Use; altho' the Measure of our *Common Triple-time* is the same with the *Mood Imperfect of the More,* except that we reckon but two *Minims* to a *Semi-breve,* which in that *Mood* comprehend three. ¶ In our *Common Mood,* two *Longs* make a *Large,* two *Breves* a *Long,* two *Semi-breves* a *Breve,* &c. proceeding in the same Order to the last or shortest Note: So that a *Large* contains two *Longs,* four *Breves,* eight *Semi-breves,* sixteen *Minims,* thirty two *Crotchets,* fixty [sic] four *Quavers,* &c. **1706** Kersey-Phillips (6th edn) In *Musick, Moods,* signifie certain Proportions of the Time, or Measure of Notes, and were formerly four in Number, *viz. The Perfect of the More, The Perfect of the Less, The Imperfect of the More,* and *The Imperfect of the Less.* These Moods are now altogether out of Use, except the last, being the same with that which we call *The Common Mood;* in which a *Large* contains two *Longs,* four *Breves,* eight *Semi-breves,* sixteen *Minims,* thirty-two *Crotchets,* sixty-four *Quavers,* &c. **1728** Chambers *Mood,* in Music, See *Mode.*

after 1517 Anon. Art of Mvsic BL Add. 4911, f. 5 *Mŭd* (as *franchinus* in ye Secund builk dois attest) It is ye mesŭr of Longe in Largis or of brewis in Longe; Or it is the begining of quantatie and forme of largis and longe mesur ... **1596** Anon. *Pathway to Musicke* [C iii] *VVhat is a Moode?* ¶ It is a formall quantitie of longes in larges, measuring them by three or tvvo, and it is either perfect or imperfect. **1597** Morley *Plaine and Easie Introdvction* (pp. 12-13) Those who within these three hundred yeares haue written the Art of Musicke, haue set downe the Moodes otherwise then they eyther haue been or are taught now in England.... Those which we now call Moodes, they tearmid degrees of Musick: .... *Phi.* What did they tearme a *Moode?* ¶ *Ma. The dew measuring of Longes and Larges,* and was either *greater or lesser.* ¶ *Phi.* What did they tearme the *great moode?* ¶ *Ma. The dew measuring of Larges by Longes,* and was either perfect or vnperfect. ¶ *Phi.* What did they tearme the Great *moode perfect?* ¶ *Ma. That which gaue to the Large three Longes,* for in both Moode, time, and prolation, that they tearme perfect which goeth by three: as the great Moode is perfect when three *longes* go to the *large.* The lesse Moode is perfect when three *briefes* go to the *long*: and time is perfect when three *semibriefes* go to the *briefe.* And his signe is thus. O3 ... ¶ *Phi.* Which Moode did they terme, the great one imperfect? ¶ *Ma.* That *which gaue to the Large but two Longes.* His signe is thus, C3 ... ¶ *Phi.* What did they call the *lesser Moode?* ¶ *Ma. That moode which measured the Longes by Breeues,* and is either perfect or vnperfect. The lesse Moode perfect was *when the Long contained three Breeues,* and his signe is thus O2 § (pp. 18-19) *Phi.* You haue declared the *Moodes* vsed in old times so plainly, that I long to heare the other sort of *Moodes,* and therefore I pray you now explaine them. ¶ *Ma.* Although they differ in order of teaching & name, yet are they both one thing in effect and therefore I will be the more brief in the explaining of them. There be foure *Moodes* now in common vse: *Perfect of the more prolation. Perfect of the lesse prolation. Imperfect of the more prolation.* And *Imperfect of the lesse prolation. The moode perfect of the more is, when all go by three*: as three Longes to the Large: three Breeues to the Long: three Semibreeues to the

Breefe: three Minomes to the Semibreefe. His signe is a whole cirkle with a pricke or point in the center or middle thus: ⊙ ... *The Moode perfect of the lesse prolation is, when all go by two, except the Semibreefe*: as two Longes to the Large. [sic] two Breeues to the Long: three Semibreeues to the Breefe: two Minoms to the Semibreefe. And his signe is a whole cirkle without any poynt or pricke in the middle ... *The Moode Imperfect of the more prolation is, when all go by two, except the Minome which goeth by three*: as two Longes to the Large, two Breeues to the Longe, two Semibreeues to the Briefe, and three Minomes to the Semibriefe: so that though in this Moode the Briefe be but two Semibriefes, yet you must vnderstand that he is sixe Minomes, and euery Semibriefe three Minomes. His signe is a halfe cirkle set at the beginning of the song, with a prick in the middle ... *The Moode Imperfect of the lesse prolation is, when all go by two*: as two Longes to the Large, two Breeues to the Longe, two Semibriefes to the Briefe, and two Minomes to the Semibriefe, two Crotchets to the Minome, &c. His signe is a halfe cirkle without a pricke or poynt set by him .... This Moode is in such vse, as *when so euer there is no Moode set at the beginning of the song, it is alwaies imagined to be this*: and in respect of it, all the rest are esteemed as strangers. § (annotations to Part I) By the name of *Mood* were signified many thinges in Musicke. First those which the learned call *moodes*, which aftetward [sic] were tearmed by the name of *tunes*. Secondly a certaine forme of disposition of the Church plainsongs in *longes* and *Breues* example. If a plainsong consisted al of Longes, it was called the first mood: if of a Long & a Briefe successiuely, it was called the second mood, &c. Thirdly, for one of the degrees of musick, as when we saie mood, is the dimension of Larges and Longes. And lastly, for al the degrees of Musicke, in which sence it is commonlie (though falsly) taught to all the young Schollers in Musicke of our time: for those signes which we vse, do not signifie any moode at all, but stretche no further then time, so that more properly they might cal them time perfect of the more prolation, &c. then *mood* perfect of the more prolation. **early 17th C.** RAVENSCROFT Treatise of Musick BL Add. 19758, f. 12v A moode is a quantitye of longes & larges measurd by 2 or by 3 ... **1609** DOWLAND-ORNITHOPARCUS *Micrologvs* (p. 42) A *Moode* (as *Franchinus* saith in the second Booke, *cap.* 7. of his *Pract*:) is the measure of *Longs* in *Largs*, or of *Breefes* in *Longs*. Or it is the beginning of the quantitie of *Largs* and *Longs*, measuring them either by the number of two or the number of three... *Moode* (as it is here taken) is two-fold; to wit, The greater, which is in the *Largs* and *Longs*, and the lesser, which is in the *Longs* and *Breefes*. And each of these is diuided into the perfect and imperfect... The greater perfect *Moode* is, when a *Larg* containes in it three *Longs*: or it is the measuring of three *Longs* in one *Larg*. The signe hereof is a perfect circle accompanied with the number of three, thus; O3. The greater imperfect is a *Larg*, comprehending in it two *Longs*: which is knowne by an imperfect circle, ioyned to the number of three, thus; C3.... The lesser perfect *Mood* is a *Long* hauing in it three *Breefes*. Or it is the measuring of three *Breefes* in one *Long*, whose signe is a perfect Circle, accompanied with the number of 2, thus; O2. But the lesser imperfect, is a *Long* which is to be measured onely with two *Breefes*. The signe of this is the absence of the number of 2. Or a *Semicircle* ioyned to a number of 2. thus; C2. O. C... **1614** RAVENSCROFT *Briefe Discovrse* (p. 1) The *Scales or Tables* (by him [Franchinus de Coloniâ] instituted) of diuers are vulgarly termed *Moodes*, by some of better vnderstanding, *Measures*; and consist of *Notes, Pauses, Degrees, Signes, Perfection*, and *Imperfection*. **1636** BUTLER *Principles of Musik* (p. 28) These 4 Proportions of 2, 3, 6, and 9 to one, (beeing peculiar to the Mesure-note) as now they ar in respect to the *Sembrief-time*; so were they formerly to the Brief time, when that was the *Mesure-note*: beeing then called the 4 Moodes: (the Perfect and imperfect of the more, ⊙, Ͼ and the Perfect and Imperfect of the les, O, C.) **1662** [DAVIDSON] *Cantus, Songs and Fancies* (n.p.) Q. *What is Moode?* ¶ A. It is a measuring of Longs by Larges, and Briefs by Longs, and is either greater or lesser. **1724** TURNER *Sound Anatomiz'd* (p. 19) There are several other *Characters* called *Moods*, by which ... the different Divisions of *Parts* or *Measures*, in *Songs* and *Tunes* of a different *Stamp*, are distinguished. Of these, there are twelve Sorts in Use; but none of them confined to keep the same Pace in each different *Mood* in all *Tunes*, unless it be in what we call *Common-Time*, (from the equal Divisions of its *Measures*, as two *Minims*, four *Crotchets*, eight *Quavers*, &c.) for which there are four *Moods*.

mood *as scalic phenomenon or key, see* mode, song, tune

1670 BLOUNT (3rd edn) *Mood* or *Mode* (*modus*) ... In Grammar there are six *Moods*, well known in Musick, five; viz. the *Doric, Lydian, Æolic,*

Phrygian, and *Ionic*; so called from the Countries in which they were invented and practised. V. *Playfords Introduction* to Musick, pa. 37. **1676** COLES *Moods in Musick*, Dorick Lydian, Æolick, Phrygian and Ionick. **1678** PHILLIPS (4th edn) *Moods*, ... In Musick, the *Æolian*, the *Dorian*, the *Lydian*, and the *Phrygian*. **1696** PHILLIPS (5th edn) In Musick, the Mood is a certain Order in the composing of a Song, which obliges the Musician to make a more frequent use of some Notes rather than others, because they are Natural to the Mood, and to avoid others, as not being so; and to close in a certain Note that gives a Denomination to the Mood. Six of these Moods have the Fifth below, and the Fourth above, and six the Fourth below, and the Fifth above. **1704** HARRIS *Mood* in *Musick* .... Besides these *Moods* of *Time*, Five others relating to Tune, were in Use among the Ancient *Grecians*, which were termed *Tones* or *Tunes* by the *Latins*; the Design of either being to shew in what Key a Song was set, and how the different Keys had relation one to another. ¶ These sorts of *Moods* were distinguish'd by the Names of the several Provinces of *Greece*, where they were first invented; as the *Dorick, Lydian, Ionick, Phrygian*, and *Æolick*. ¶ *Dorick Mood*, consisted of slow-tun'd Notes, and was proper for the exciting Persons to Sobriety and Piety. ¶ *Lydian Mood*, was likewise used in Solemn Grave Musick; and the Descant or Composition was of slow Time, adapted to Sacred Hymns or Anthems. ¶ *Ionick Mood*, was for more light and soft Musick; such as pleasant amorous Songs, Sarabands, Corants, Jiggs, *&c*. ¶ *Phrygian Mood*, was a Warlike kind of Musick, fit for Trumpets, Hautboys, and other Instruments of the like Nature; whereby the Minds of Men were animated to undertake Military Atchievements, or Martial Exercises. ¶ *Æolick Mood*, being of a more airy, soft, and delightful Sound, such as our *Madrigals*, served to allay the Passions by the means of its grateful Variety and melodious Harmony. ¶ These *Moods* or *Tones* were distinguished into *Authentick* and *Playal* [sic], with respect to the dividing of the *Octave* into its Fifth and Fourth: The Former was when the Fifth possessed the Lower Place, according to the Harmonical Division of an *Octave*; and the other was when it stood in the Upper Place, according to the Arithmetical Division of the same *Octave*. **1706** KERSEY-PHILLIPS (6th edn) *Moods* .... Among the Ancient *Greeks*, there were also five other *Moods*, termed *Tones* or *Tunes* by the *Latins*; the Use of which was to shew in what Key a Song was set, and how the different Keys had relation one to another: These sorts of Moods were distinguish'd by the Names of the several Provinces of *Greece*, where they were first invented; as the *Dorick, Lydian, Ionick, Phrygian* and *Æolick*; some being proper for grave Musick, others for warlike Tunes, and others for more light and soft Airs: All which See under those respective Articles. **1728** CHAMBERS *Mood*, in Music, See *Mode*. **1730** BAILEY *Dict. Britannicum* (1st edn) *Moods* (among the antient *Greeks*) were five; the Use of which was to shew in what Key a Song was set, and how the different Keys had relation one to the other. These moods were called after five Provinces of *Greece*, viz. the *Dorick, Lydian, Ionian, Phrygian* and *Æolick*; some of which were suited for light and soft Airs, others to warlike Tunes, and others to grave Musick. *Moods of Musick*, are denominated, according to divers Countries, for whose particular Genius they seemed at first to have been contrived; and these are three; the *Lydian*, the *Phrygian*, and the *Dorick*.... To these three *Sappho*, the *Lesbian* added a fourth, called the *Mixolydian Mood*, which was only fit for Tragedies, and to move Compassion. ¶ There have also been three other moods added to them, equal to the Number of the Planets; the *Hypolygian* [sic], *Hypophrygian* and *Hypodorian*, and these were called Collateral ones. And there were also an eighth added by *Ptolemy*, called the *Hypermixolydian*, which is the sharpest and shrillest of all. **1737** DYCHE-PARDON (2nd edn) *Mood* (S.) ... the *Musicians* also use this Term, and call those Airs or Lessons that are of a slow and solemn Motion, fitted for Devotion or Mourning, the Dorick or Lydian Mood; light and soft Musick fitted to amorous Songs, Jigs, Courants, Sarabands, Minuets, &c. the Ionick Mood; that which was airy of an harmonious Sound, fit to allay and sooth the Passions, the Eolick Mood, and those that by their Sprightliness animated Men to courageous and daring Exploits of War, &c. the Phrygian Mood.

1597 MORLEY *Plaine and Easie Introdvction* (annotations to Part I) By the name of *Mood* were signified many thinges in Musicke. First those which the learned call *moodes*, which aftetward [sic] were tearmed by the name of *tunes*. Secondly a certaine forme of disposition of the Church plainsongs in *longes* and *Breues* example... **1731** PRELLEUR *Modern Musick-Master* ('A Brief History of Musick', p. 20) ... But if a Tune should go both 8 or 9 Notes higher, and 4 or 5 Notes lower than its *Final*, (as may be seen in several old Anthems used in the Church of Rome) then it is called a *Mixt*

Mood because it includes both the *Authentic* and the *Plagal*.

morisco *see* baioccare, maid marrion, morris dance, paganina, pyrricha

1570/71 *Dict. Fr. and Engl.* Fr→E § *Vn danseur de morisque*, a moresque daunser. **1593** Hollyband Fr→E § *Vn danseur de morisque*, a morrice daunser: *m*. **1611** Cotgrave Fr→E *Morisque: f.* A Morris (or Moorish) daunce; **1611** Florio It→E *Moresca*, a Morice, or Antique dance. **1656** Blount (1st edn) *Morisco* (Span.) a Moor; also a Dance so called, wherein there were usually five men, and a Boy dressed in a Girles habit, whom they call the *Maid Marrian* or perhaps *Morian*, from the Ital. *Morione* a Head-peece, because her head was wont to be gaily trimmed up. The common people call it a *Morris Dance*. **1658** Phillips (1st edn) *Morisco*, (Span.) ... also a kind of Dance which seemeth to be the same with that which the Greeks call *Pyrricha*, we vulgarly call it the Morris Dance, as it were the Moorish Dance. **1659** Torriano-Florio It→E *Moresca*, a Morisco, a Moris-dance, an antick dance. *Moreschiere*, a Moris dancer. **1676** Coles *Morisco, Spanish*. ... a Morrice (or moorish) dance **1702** Kersey *New Engl. Dict.* (1st edn) A *Morisco, or* morris-dance. **1707** *Gloss. Angl. Nova* (1st edn) *Morisco*, (Span.) a Moor, also a Morris (or Moorish) Dance. **1708** Kersey *Dict. Anglo-Brit.* (1st edn) *Morisco, (Sp.)* ... Also a Morris-Dance. **1721** Bailey *An Univ. Etymolog. Engl. Dict.* (1st edn) *Morisco*, a Moor, also a Morris (or Moorish) Dancer. *Span*. **1730** Bailey *Dict. Britannicum* (1st edn) *Morisco*, a *Morris Dance*, much the same with that which the *Greeks* call'd *Pyrrhica*. *Span*. **1737** Dyche-Pardon (2nd edn) *Moresk Dances* vulgarly called *Morrice Dances* (S.) are a Sort of sportive Dances in Imitation of the *Moors*, and which are performed either with Castanets, Tabours, Bells tied to the Legs, &c. and these are also called Chacones, Sarabands, &c.

Morley, Thomas *see* fuga ligata, syncope

morris dance *see* ballonchio, bouffons, chironomica saltatio, gesticulation, maid marrion, matachin, morisco, paganina, stampinata, thymelici, tresca, valets de la feste

1702 Kersey *New Engl. Dict.* (1st edn) A *Morrice-dance*, a kind of antick dance, usually perform'd by five Men and a Boy in Girls habit. A *Morris-dancer*. **1706** Kersey-Phillips (6th edn) *Morris-dance* (q.d. *Moorish* Dance) a kind of antick Dance, commonly perform'd by five Men and a Boy dress'd in a Girl's Habit, who is call'd the *Maid Marrion*, and has his Head gaily trimm'd up. **1730** Bailey *Dict. Britannicum* (1st edn) *Morris Dance* (or a Dance *a le Morisco*, or after the manner of the *Moors*; a Dance brought into *England* by the *Spaniards*) the Dancers are clad in white Wastcoats [sic] or Shirts and Caps, having their Legs adorn'd with Bells, which make a merry jingling, as they leap or dance.

mort *see* call

1726 Bailey *An Univ. Etymolog. Engl. Dict.* (3rd edn) A *Mort*, ... To blow a *Mort* (Hunting Term) is to sound a particular Air call'd a *Mort*, to give Notice that the Deer that was hunted is taken and is kill'd or killing. **1730** Bailey *Dict. Britannicum* (1st edn) § *To Blow a Mort (Hunt. Term)* is to sound a particular Air, called a *Mort*, to give notice to the Company that the Deer that was hunted is taken and killed, or a killing. **1736** Bailey *Dict. Britannicum* (2nd edn) *Mort (Hunting Term)* a certain note or tune blown with a horn.

mostra *see* direct, index

1724 [Pepusch] *Short Explic. of Foreign Words in Mus. Bks.* (p. 47) *Mostra*, is a little Mark or Character in Musick. For which see the Word *Index*. **1726** Bailey *An Univ. Etymolog. Engl. Dict.* (3rd edn) *Mostra (in Musick Books)* a little Mark at the End of each Line in Musick, shewing what Note the next Line begins with. The *French* call it *Guidon*. *Ital*.

mot

1593 Hollyband Fr→E *Vn mot*, a word, it is also the sound of the horne among hunters: *m*. **1611** Cotgrave Fr→E *Mot: m*. ... also, the note winded by a huntsman on his horne; **1656** Blount (1st edn) *Mot*, is also a Note, which a Huntsman winds on his horn. **1658** Phillips (1st edn) *Mot*, ... also a certain note which hunts-men wind on their horn. **1659** Torriano-Florio It→E *Motto*, ... among hunters it is used for any note that they wind on their horns. **1676** Coles *Mot*... also a lesson which Hunstmen wind on their horn. **1696** Phillips (5th edn) *Mot* or *Motto* (*French* and *Italian*) ... also a certain Note which Huntsmen wind on their Horn. **1708** Kersey *Dict. Anglo-Brit.* (1st edn) *Mot*, a certain Note, which Huntsmen wind on their Horn.

1730 BAILEY *Dict. Britannicum* (1st edn) *Mot (Hunting Term)* a certain Note or Tune blown with a Horn.

motet *see* ground, recitative, research, style (stylo motectico), symphony, tenor

1593 HOLLYBAND Fr→E *Vn motet*, a verse: *m*. 1598 FLORIO It→E *Mottetto, Mottino*, a dittie, a verse, a iigge, a short song. 1611 COTGRAVE Fr→E *Moté*. as *Motet*. *Motet: m*. A verse in Musicke, or of a Song; a Poesie; a short Lay. *Motté: m*. as *Motet*. 1611 FLORIO It→E *Mottetto*, ... Looke *Villancicco*. 1656 BLOUNT (1st edn) *Motet* (Fr.) a verse in Musick, or of a Song, a Poesie, a short-lay. 1658 PHILLIPS (1st edn) *Motet*, (French) a verse in Musick, a stanza of a song, also a short poesie. 1659 TORRIANO-FLORIO It→E *Mottino, Mottetto*, the dim of *Motto*, specially a spiritual himn sung on solemn daies by the Eunuchs or Nuns in *Rome* 1676 COLES *Motet, French*. a verse or stanza in Musick, in short poem. 1688 MIEGE-COTGRAVE Fr→E *Motet*, (m.) from *Mot, Terme de Musicien*, a kind of Musical Composition. 1706 KERSEY-PHILLIPS (6th edn) *Motet, (Fr.)* a sort of Musical Composure, a Stanza, or Staff of a Song; also a short Posy. 1707 *Gloss. Angl. Nova* (1st edn) *Motet*, (F.) a Verse in Musick, a Stanza of a Song; also a short Poesie. 1724 [PEPUSCH] *Short Explic. of Foreign Words in Mus. Bks*. (p. 47) *Motetto*, or *Motetti*, are what we call Motets; they are a kind of Church Musick, made Use of among the *Romans*, and composed with much Art and Ingenuity, some for one, two, three, four, or more Voices, and very often with several Instruments. They are of much the same Kind or Nature in Divine Musick, as Cantatas are in Common Musick. 1726 BAILEY *An Univ. Etymolog. Engl. Dict*. (3rd edn) *Motets*. See *Motetto*. *Motetto, Motetti*, (in *Musick Books*) denotes a kind of Church Musick made use of among the *Roman* Catholicks; and are composed with much Art and Ingenuity; some of them for one, two, three, four or more Voices, and very often with several Instruments. *Motetto*'s are much of the same Kind or Nature in divine Musick, as *Cantatas* are in common. 1737 DYCHE-PARDON (2nd edn) *Motets* (S.) in *Musick*, are divine Songs or Anthems, compos'd after the Manner of Cantata's in Civil Musick.

1597 MORLEY *Plaine and Easie Introdvction* (p. 179) [*Ma.*] ... I say that all musicke for voices (for onlie of that kinde haue we hetherto spoken) is made either for a dittie or without a dittie, if it bee with a dittie, it is either graue or light, the graue ditties they haue stil kept in one kind, so that whatsoeuer musicke bee made vpon it, is comprehended vnder the name of a Motet: a Motet is properlie a song made for the church, either vpon some hymne or Antheme, or such like, and that name I take to haue beene giuen to that kinde of musicke in opposition to the other which they called *Canto fermo*, and we do commonlie call plainsong, for as nothing is more opposit to standing and firmnes than motion, so did they giue the Motet that name of mouing, because it is in a manner quight to the other, which after some sort, and in respect of the other standeth still. This kind of al others which are made on a ditty, requireth most art, and moueth and causeth most strange effects in the hearer, being aptlie framed for the dittie and well expressed by the singer, for it will draw the auditor (and speciallie the skilfull auditor) into a deuout and reuerent kind of consideration of him for whose praise it was made... But to returne to our Motets, if you compose in this kind, you must cause your harmonie to carrie a maiestie taking discordes and bindings so often as you canne, but let it be in long notes, for the nature of it will not beare short notes and quicke motions, which denotate a kind of wantonnes. ¶ This musicke (a lementable case) being the chiefest both for art and vtilitie, is notwithstanding little esteemed, and in small request with the greatest number of those who most highly seeme to fauor art ... 1636 BUTLER *Principles of Musik* (p. 5) Of the *Lydian* Moode ar those solemn Hymns and other sacred Chyrch-songs, called *Moteta, à motu*: becaus they moove the harts of the hearers, striking into them a devout and reverent regard of him for whose praiz they were made. These *Motets* require most Art, of all Musik, in Setting: fitly to take Discords and Bindings, using plain, soft, sweete Discanting, with freqent, gracefull Reports and Reverts. Agreeable unto the art of the *Setters* shoolde bee the art of *Singers*: sweetely and plainly to expres the woords and syllables of the Ditti, that they may bee understood of the Congregation, and being like their *Motets* (grave, sober, holy) to sing with a grace to the Lord in their harts...

motion

1728 CHAMBERS *Motion*, in Music, is the manner of beating the Measure, to hasten or slacken the Time of the Pronunciation of the Words, or Notes. See *Measure* and *Time*. ¶ The *Motion*, in Songs compos'd in double Time, differs from those in triple Time. 'Tis the *Motion* that distinguishes Courants and

Sarabands, from Gavots, Borees, Chacones, *&c.* **1730** BAILEY *Dict. Britannicum* (1st edn) *Motion* (in *Musick*) is the manner of beating the measure, to hasten or slacken the Time of the Pronunciation of the Words or Notes. **1737** DYCHE-PARDON (2nd edn) *Motion* (S.) ... in *Musick*, it is the Manner of playing slow or quick, according to the Nature of the Composition;

moto contrario

1730 [PEPUSCH] *Short Treatise on Harmony* (p. 4) ... Contrary Motion, Moto contrario in Italian; which is, when the Parts move in a contrary direction, The One Ascending at the same time that The Other Descends. **1731** [PEPUSCH] *Treatise on Harmony* (2nd edn, p. 5) ... The Third *Motion* is in Italian styled *Moto Contrario,* and in English *Contrary Motion;* which is, when one Part moves downwards, while the other moves upwards.

moto obliquo

1730 [PEPUSCH] *Short Treatise on Harmony* (p. 4) ... Oblique Motion, called by the Italians Moto obliquo; which is, when Either Part keeps on in the same place, whilst the other moves Upwards or Downwards. **1731** [PEPUSCH] *Treatise on Harmony* (2nd edn, p. 5) ... The First of these Ways [of movement between parts] is call'd by the Italians *Moto Obliquo,* in English *Oblique Motion;* which is, when one Part repeats the same Note, or holds on, whilst the other goes, upwards or downwards, from one Note to another.

moto retto

1730 [PEPUSCH] *Short Treatise on Harmony* (p. 4) ... Similar Motion, call'd Moto Retto by the Italians; which is, when Both Parts move the same way Upwards or Downwards. **1731** [PEPUSCH] *Treatise on Harmony* (2nd edn, p. 5) ... The Second *Motion* is call'd in Italian *Moto Retto,* in English *Direct* or *Similar Motion;* which is, when both Parts move the same Way.

mouth

c.1710 NORTH (draft for) Musicall Grammarian BL Add. 32537, f. 201v [*re* a 'sonorous tube' such as an organ pipe] The breath enters by an oblong, but very narrow duct, w[ch] passing an apperture they call the mouth, falls upon a thin edg cut upon y[e] side of y[e] pipe and stands opposed to the Entrance of the thin filme of air, as if it were Intended to splitt it in too airs.

mouthpiece *see* bocciuolo, tampon

muance

1611 COTGRAVE Fr→E *Muance: f.* Change, alteration; and particularly, a variation, or change of notes in singing; *viz.* when in going either aboue, or below the six Notes (*Vt, re, mi, fa, sol, la*) one of them is changed in the middle to gaine ground, and to knit the gradation; as if in stead of *Vt, re, mi, fa, sol, la,* in ascending, one should sing *Vt, re, mi, fa, re, mi, fa sol, &c.* **1688** MIEGE-COTGRAVE Fr→E *Muance,* (f.) *Changement de Note,* a variation, or change of Notes, in Singing. § *Il faloit faire une muance en cet endroit,* you should have changed your Note in this place.

mundane music *see* music of the world

1664 BIRCHENSHA-ALSTED *Templvm Mvsicvm* (p. 11) *The Exemplary Cause of Harmonical Musick; is that Musick which is called mundane.* ¶ This is discerned in the Order, Disposition, and admirable proportion which doth occur in the Celestial, and subcelestial Region; ... **1721** MALCOLM *Treatise of Musick* (pp. 452-5) ... *Hermes Trismegistus* says, *That* Musick *is nothing but the Knowledge of the Order of all Things;* which was also the Doctrine of the *Pythagorean* School, and of the *Platonicks,* who teach that every Thing in the Universe is *Musick.* Agreeable to this wide Sense, some have distinguished Musick into *Divine* and *Mundane;* the first respects the Order and Harmony that obtains among the Celestial Minds; the other respects the Relations and Order of every other Thing else in the Universe. But *Plato* by the *divine Musick* understands, that which exists in the *divine* Mind, *viz.* these archetypal Ideas of Order and Symmetry, according to which *God* formed all Things; and as this Order exists in the Creatures, it is called *Mundane Musick*: Which is again subdivided, the remarkable Denominations of which are, *First, Elementary* or the Harmony of the first Elements of Things; ... 2*d. Celestial,* comprehending the Order and Proportions in the Magnitudes, Distances, and Motions of the heavenly Bodies, and the Harmony of the Sounds proceeding from these Motions: ... This Species is by some called particularly the *Mundane Musick.* 3*d. Human,* which consists chiefly in the Harmony of the Faculties of the human Soul, and its various Passions; and is also considered in the Proportion and Temperament, mutual Dependence and Connection, of all the Parts of this wonderful Machine of our Bodies. 4*th.* Is what in a more limited and peculiar Sense of the Word was called *Musick;* which has for its Object *Motion*, considered as under certain regular Measures and Proportions, by which it affects the Senses in an agreeable Manner. All Motion belongs to Bodies, and Sound is the Effect of Motion, and cannot be without it; but all Motion does not produce Sound, therefore this was again subdivided. Where the Motion is without Sound, or as it is only the Object of Seeing, it was called *Musica Orchestria* or *Saltatoria,* which contains the Rules for the regular Motions of *Dancing;* also *Hypocritica,* which respects the Motions and Gestures of the *Pantomimes.* When Motion is perceived only by the Ear, *i.e.* when Sound is the Object of *Musick,* there are Three Species; *Harmonica,* which considers the Differences and Proportion of Sounds, with respect to *acute* and *grave; Rythmica,* which respects the Proportion of Sounds as to Time, or the Swiftness and Slowness of their Successions; and *Metrica,* which belongs properly to the *Poets,* and repects the versifying Art: But in common Acceptation 'tis now more limited, and we call nothing *Musick* but what is heard; and even then we make a Variety of *Tones* necessary to the Being of *Musick.*

musa *see* acroamatick, cantion
1500 *Ortus Vocabulorum* L→E Musa se. a swete songe or wysdome. dicitur a moys quod est aqua. f.p. § Musa metrum cantus: instrumentumque sonorum. **1538** ELYOT L→E *Musa,* a swete songe. **1552** HULOET L→E *Musa.* æ Swete song. **1565** COOPER L→E *Musa, musæ, f g Virgil.* A sweete songe. § *Agrestem tenui meditabor arundine musam. Virg.* I will play an homely songe vpon a sclender pipe. I will write of base mattier in a low stile. *Musa syluestris. Virg.* An vplandish songe. *Musæ deditus. Horat.* Geuen to musike. **1587** THOMAS L→E *Musa, sæ, f.g.* A sweete song. **1589** RIDER L→E *Musa, f.* A sweete song. **1598** FLORIO It→E *Musa,* a Muse, or a sweet song. **1599** MINSHEU-PERCYVALL Sp→E **Musa,* f. a muse, a song, musicke. **1611** FLORIO It→E *Musa,* a Muse. Also a sweet song. **1659** TORRIANO-FLORIO It→E *Musa,* the sing. of *Muse,* a muse, a poetical vein, also a sweet song, or studious invention ... also a kind of horn or bag-pipe.

Muse *see* camena
1538 ELYOT L→E *Muse, Muses,* were maydens, whome poetes fayned to be the doughters of Jupiter and Memorie, and that they were ladyes and gouernours of poetrie & musyke, whiche were in numbre nyne. Some call them gyuers of eloquence, and doo name them goddesses. **1565** COOPER L→E *Musæ, arum,* The Muses: whiche were maydens, whome poetes feygned to bee the daughters of Jupiter and Memorie, and that they weare ladyes and gouernours of poetrie and Musyke. They were in numbre nyne, or after some but three. Some call them geuers of eloquence, and dooe name theim [sic] goddesses. **1587** THOMAS L→E *Musæ, arum, f.g.* The muses or godesses of learning, poesie, and musicke: *also* poetrie **1598** FLORIO It→E *Muse,* ... properlie the muses or goddesses of learning, poesie & musike. **1611** COTGRAVE Fr→E *Muse: f.* One of the nine Muses; also, a Muse, Poeticall conceit, Vaine, Poeme, or Song; **1611** FLORIO It→E *Muse,* Muses or Nimphes, properly the nine muses or Goddesses of learning, poesie and musike. **1616** BULLOKAR *Muses.* The feyned goddesses of poetry, and musicke, which were nine in number and daughters vnto *Iupiter* and *Mnemosyne*: Their names were *Cleio, Melpomene, Thaleia, Euterpe, Terpsichore, Erato, Calliope, Vrania* and *Polymneia.* **1650** HOWELL-COTGRAVE Fr→E *Muse: f.* One of the nine Muses; also, a Muse, Poeticall conceit, Vaine, Poem, or Song; **1656** BLOUNT (1st edn) *Muses (Musæ)* the feigned Goddesses of Poetrie and Musick, which were nine in number, and Daughters to *Jupiter* and *Mnemosyne.* **1658** PHILLIPS (1st edn) *Muses,* the 9 daughters of *Jupiter* and *Mnemosyne,* ... they were accounted the goddesses of Musick and Poetry, and the rest of the ingenuous [sic] Arts and Sciences, their names were *Calliope, Clio, Erato, Thalia, Melpomene, Terpsichore, Euterpe, Polyhymnia,* and *Vrania.* **1659** TORRIANO-FLORIO It→E *Muse,* Muses, Nimphs, or Goddesses of learning, of Poetry, and of Musick, which are said to be nine, that is to say, *Clio, Euterpe, Thalia, Melpomene, Polihinnia, Erato, Terpsicore, Urania, Caliope* **1676** COLES *Muses, (Calliope, Clio, Erato, Thalia, Melpomene, Terpsichore, Polyhymnia, Vrania)* Daughters of *Jupiter* and *Mnemosyne,* Goddesses of Poetry and Musick. **1702** KERSEY *New Engl. Dict.* (1st edn) The nine *Muses,* taken by the ancients for the Goddesses of *Musick,* and *Poetry* and the patronesses of Learning. Their names are *Calliope, Clio, Erato, Thalia, Melpomene, Terpsichore, Euterpe, Polyhymnia,* and *Urania.* **1706** KERSEY-PHILLIPS (6th edn) *Muses, (Gr.)* the nine Daughters of *Jupiter* and *Mnemosyne,* accounted the Godesses of Musick and Poetry, as also Patronesses of the other Liberal Arts and Sciences: Their Names are *Calliope, Clio, Erato, Euterpe, Melpomene, Polyhymnia, Terpsichore, Thalia* and *Urania;* which See in their proper Places. **1728** CHAMBERS

Muses, Fabulous Divinities of the antient Heathens, who were supposed to preside over the Arts, and Sciences. ¶ The Antients admitted nine *Muses*, and made them the Daughters of *Jupiter* and *Mnemosyne*, or Memory. ¶ At first, indeed, their Number was but three, viz. *Melete, Mneme*, and *Aœde*; *Greek* Words signifying Memory, Singing, and Meditation.... Each of these [nine Muses] were supposed to preside over their respective Art; *Calliope* over Heroic Poetry; *Clio* over History; *Melpomene* over Tragedy; *Thalia* over Comedy; *Euterpe* over Wind-Music; *Urania* over Astronomy; *Terpsichore* over the Harp; *Erato* the Lute; *Polyhymnia* Rhetoric. **1730** BAILEY *Dict. Britannicum* (1st edn) *Muses* ... These Muses, by the assistance of *Apollo*, invented Musick. Their chief Office was to be present at solemn Festivals, and sacred Banquets; and there to sing the Praises of famous Men, that they might encourage others to undertake glorious Actions... The *Muses* ... are fabulous Divinities of the antient Heathens, who were suppos'd to preside over the Arts and Sciences, and to be the Daughters of *Jupiter* and Μν[ε]μοσινη, *i.e.* Memory; which Fiction is introduc'd, bebause [sic] *Jupiter* was esteemed the first Inventor of Disciplines which are necessary in order to a regular Life. ¶ These indeed were at first but three, *viz.* Μελετή, *i.e.* Meditation; Μνήμη, *i.e.* Memory; and 'Αοιδή, Singing.... *Calliope* was suppos'd President of heroick Poetry; *Clio* of History; *Erato* of the Lute; *Thalia* of Comedy; *Melpomene* of Tragedy; *Terpsichore* of the Harp; *Euterpe* over Wind Musick; *Polyhymnia* of Musick; *Urania* of Astronomy. **1737** DYCHE-PARDON (2nd edn) *Muses* (S.) certain Goddesses among the Antients, reputed Daughters of *Jupiter* and *Mnemosyne*, nine in Number, to whom the Invention of Sciences is attributed, particularly the various Sorts of Poetry, called by the Names of *Clio, Urania, Calliope, Euterpe, Erato, Thalia, Melpomene, Terspychore* and *Polyhymnia*, some call them the Daughters of *Cœlus* and the Earth, that express the Qualities of the Body and Spirit for they were at first but three, *viz. Meditation, Memory*, and *Singing* ...

musella

1611 FLORIO It→E *Musella*, an Oaten-pipe, a pipe of Reedes. *Musellare*, to play on Oaten-pipes.

musette *see* bagpipe, porte-vent, sourdeline

1593 HOLLYBAND Fr→E *Musette*, or *cornemuse*, *f*: a little bag-pipe. **1611** COTGRAVE Fr→E *Musette: f.* A little Bag-pipe; or (more properly) as *Vielle*; **1688** MIEGE-COTGRAVE Fr→E *Musette*, (f.) *sorte d'Instrument de Musique à anches & à vent*, a Bag-pipe. *Musette*, (Ps. 71, 22, and Ps. 150. 3.) Psaltery. § *Jouër de la Musette*, to play upon the Bag-pipe.

music *see* active music, church music, diatonic music, harmonic music, inspective music, instrumental music, marriage music, mensural music, mundane music, organical music, pathetic music, plain music

1500 *Ortus Vocabulorum* L→E Musica ce. vna est de septes artibus liberalibus. & dicit a moys q est aqua qr aquaticis instrumentis inuenta est. angl. crafte of sange musike. f.p. **1538** ELYOT L→E *Musica, & musice*, musyke. **1551** HULOET L→E *musice* after good or true musycke **1565** COOPER L→E *Música, músice, vel Músice, músices, pen. cor. Cic.* Musike: it was vsed for studie of humanitie and especially poetrie. *Música, musicorum. Cic.* Musike. *Músice, pen. cor. Aduerbium. Plaut.* Delectably: in an harmonie: § *Conterere se in musicis. Cicero.* To spende his time in musike. *Musica ars. Plin.* The science of musike. **1570/71** *Dict. Fr. and Engl.* Fr→E *Musique*, musike, or harmonie of instruments. **1587** THOMAS L→E *Musica, cæ, vel Musice, es, f.g.* Musike: it was vsed for studie of humanitie, and especially poetrie. Hereof some make 3. kindes, 1. with the voice. 2. with the hand. 3. with blowing: or (as the masters of musike call it) Vocall, instrumentall, & proportionall. *Also* of musicall instruments there be 3. kindes. 1. in blowing, as the Organes, the Flute, &c. 2. in strings or wyers, as the Lute, the Virginalles, &c. 3. in striking or beating, as the Drum, &c. *Iun. Musica, orum. Idem. Musice, adverb. Plaut.* Delectably: in an harmony: § *Ars musica. Terent.* Comedies. **1589** RIDER L→E *Musica.* Musicke. *Musice, musica, f.* Musicke, or the arte of musicke. **1593** HOLLYBAND Fr→E *Musique*, musicke, or harmonie of instruments: *f.* **1598** FLORIO It→E *Musica*, the arte of Musike, it was vsed for studie of humanitie, and namely poetrie: hereof some make three kindes, first, with the voice, 2. with the hand, 3. with blowing, or as some call it vocall, instrumentall, and proportionall. Also of musicall instruments there be three kindes, one in blowing, as the organs, or the flute, &c. 2. in strings or wyers as the Lute, the Virginals, &c. the third, in striking or beating, as the drumme, &c. *Musicare*, to play the Musition. **1599** MINSHEU-PERCYVALL Sp→E *Musica*, f. musicke. § **Arrebatada musica*, sudden musicke quickely gone. **Musica de responso*, singing of friers or priestes at a dead mans buriall. **1611** COTGRAVE Fr→E *Musique: f.* Musicke, melodie, harmonie. § *Vn Asne n'entend rien en musique: Pro.* An Asse hath little skill in harmonie. *Vn asne n'entend rien en musique: Pro.* An asse is but a bad Musician; or, cannot judge of Musicke. **1611** FLORIO It→E *Musica,* the Arte of Musike. Also any kinde of musike whether vocall, that is with the voice, Instrumentall, that is with the touch of the hand vpon any instrument, or Proportionall, that is with blowing or any winde instrument, it hath beene vsed for study of humanity, namely Poetry. *Musicare,* to play musike. *Musicheuole,* musicall, proportionall. **1659** TORRIANO-FLORIO It→E *Musica,* the art of musick, also any kind of musick, harmony or melody, whether vocal, that is, with the voice, instrumental, that is, with the touch of the hand upon any Instrument, or Proportional, that is, with blowing, or with any wind-instrument, it hath also been used for study of humanity, namely of poetry, also in a jearing way for any business, action or story, *non gli piace questa musica,* he cannot endure to hear on that ear. § *La musica si puo dire effemiinatrice degli animi. Musicare,* to play or study musick. **1688** MIEGE-COTGRAVE Fr→E *Musique,* (f.) Musick, or the Art of Singing; Musick, or Harmony. § *Apprendre la musique,* to learn Musick. *Cette Musique m'endort,* this Musick charms me asleep. *Cette Musique me ravit,* this Musick ravishes me, I am ravished with this Musick. *Donner un plat de son Metier,* ... to give somthing of what one knows, or does. So a Master of Musick, that gives a Consort of Musick, is said to give *un Plat de son Metier. Enseigner la Musique,* to teach Musick. *Il a du panchant pour la Musique,* his Genius is for Musick. *La Musique charme les Oreilles, & ravit l'Esprit,* Musick charmes the Ears, and ravishes the Mind. *Maitre de Musique,* a Master of Musick. *Piece,* (f.) a piece, as of Musick, Poesy, Painting ... *Une bonne, une excellente Musique,* a good (rare, or excellent) Musick. *Une mechante Musique, une Musique enragée,* paultry (mad) Musick. *Une Musique ravissante,* a ravishing (or charming) Musick. *Un Livre de Musique,* a Musick-book. **1696** PHILLIPS (5th edn) *Musick,* one of the Seven Liberal Sciences, and a fourth Branch in the General Division of the Mathematicks, having for its Object discrete Quantity or Number, though it considers it not absolutely like Arithmetick, but with proportion of Time and Sound, and in order to making a delightful Harmony. So that Musick is nothing but the Agreement, apt Proportion, and Mixture of Acute, Grave, and Mixt Sounds. **1702** KERSEY *New Engl. Dict.* (1st edn) *Musick, or* the art of singing and playing upon musical instruments. § A *Musick-house.* A *Musick-master.* A *Musick-school.* **1704** HARRIS *Musick* is one of the Seven Sciences, commonly called *Liberal,* and comprehended also among the *Mathematical;* as having for its Object *Discreet Quantity* or *Number,* but not considering it in the Abstract, like *Arithmetick,* but with relation to *Time* and *Sound,* in order to make a delightful Harmony. ¶ This Science is also *Theorical,* which examineth the Nature and Properties of Concords and Discords, explaining the Proportions between them by Numbers: And *Practical,* which teacheth not only Composition, that is to say, the manner of Composing all sorts of Tunes or Airs; but also the Art of singing with the Voice, or playing upon Musical Instruments. **1706** KERSEY-PHILLIPS (6th edn) *Musick,* one of the seven Liberal Sciences, and a Branch of the *Mathematicks;* having for its Object discreet Quantity or Number, tho' not considering it in the Abstract like *Arithmetick,* but with Respect to Time and Sound, in order to make a delightful Harmony; also the Harmony it self that is so made. This Science is also *Theorieal* [sic] and *Practical.* § *Theorical Musick,* is that which searches into the Nature and Properties of Concords and Discords, and explains the Proportions between them by Numbers. *Practical Musick,* shews the manner of composing all sorts of Tunes or Airs, with the Art of Singing, and playing on all sorts of Musical Instruments. **1721** BAILEY *An Univ. Etymolog. Engl. Dict.* (1st edn) *Musick, (musique, F. musica,* L. of μουσικός, *Gr.)* one of the 7 Sciences term'd *Liberal,* belonging to the *Mathematicks* which considers the Number Time and Tune of Sounds, in Order to make delightful Harmony: Also the Art of singing and playing on all Sorts of Musical Instruments. **1724** [PEPUSCH] *Short Explic. of Foreign Words in Mus. Bks.* (pp. 47-8) *Musica,* Musick, by which Word is to be understood sometimes the Art or Science of Musick, sometimes the Books or Instruments of Musick; sometimes the Melody or Harmony of Musick; sometimes the Company of Musicians that do, or that are to perform Musick: Besides several other Significations, too many to be here inserted. **1726** BAILEY *An Univ. Etymolog. Engl. Dict.* (3rd edn) *Musica (in Musick Books)* sometimes signifies the Art or Science of Musick; sometimes the Books or Instruments of Musick; sometimes the Melody or Harmony of Musick; sometimes the Company of Musicians that perform the Musick. *Ital.* **1728** CHAMBERS *Music* ... [*see* Appendix] **1730** BAILEY

Dict. Britannicum (1st edn) *Musick* .... The Exercise of musick is salutory, in that it expels melancholy; vocal musick opens the Breast and Pipes, and is good to remedy stammering in Speech. Antient Historians, as *Ælian, Pliny* and *Plutarch* relate, that the antient musicians have moved the Passions of Mens Minds at their Pleasure, appeased the Disconsolate and Desperate, tempered the Amorous, and healed even the Sick, and wrought wonderful Effects. *Musick (Hieroglphically)* was represented by the ancient *Egyptians*, by a Swan and a Grashopper, the first of which is said to sing sweetly, immediately before her Death. § *Celestial Musick*, the Musick of the Spheres, comprehends the Order and Proportion in the Magnitudes, Distances and Motions of the heavenly Bodies, and the Harmony of the Sounds resulting from those Motions. *Elementary Musick*, the Harmony of the Elements of Things. *Human Musick*, is that which consists chiefly in the Faculties of the human Soul and its various Passions. **1737** DYCHE-PARDON (2nd edn) *Musick* (S.) is that Art which teaches how to form Concords, and bring agreeable Sounds to the Ear; and this is performed by certain Mathematical Rules or Proportions found out by various Experiments, and at last reduced to a demonstrative Science, so far as relates to the Tones and Intervals of Sounds only, so that indeed Musick is nothing else but the Agreement, apt Proportion, and Mixture of acute, grave and mixed Sounds, but is considered under many Distinctions; and sometimes it is applied to the Tone or Voice used by Orators, Players, Singers, &c. sometimes to the making or composing Pieces for Instrumental Performances; sometimes to the Harmony and Agreement between Friends, &c. it is sometimes Practical, and sometimes Speculative, &c. The Invention of the Science properly so called, or the Performance upon Musical Instruments is very antient, being earlier than the Flood; for *Jubal* is said to be the Father, or first Teacher of those that handled the Harp or Organ; some of the Heathens attribute the Invention to *Pythagoras*, and say he took the Hint of a *Diatessaron*, a *Diapente*, and a *Diapason*, from the beating of Hammers in a Smith's Shop. The Poets make *Mercury* and *Apollo* the first Musicians; the present Scale or Gamut now used was invented by one *Guido*, an Abbot, about 700 Years ago; the Use and Design of this Art is to recreate and compose the Mind, and to allay and excite the Passions; of the extraordinary Effects of Practical Musick, both profane and sacred History are loaded with Accounts and Examples, for which Reason the Solemnities of all Religions have been performed with the Sound of proper Instruments; the *Heathens*, the *Jews*, and the *Christians* have added the human Voice to the artificial Sounds, to make their Service the more affecting and grand.

1596 ANON. *Pathway to Musicke* [A ii] Mvsicke is a science, vvhich teacheth hovv to sing skilfullie: that is, to deliuer a song svveetly, tuneably, and cunningly, by voyces or notes, vnder a certaine rule & measure; ... **1597** MORLEY *Plaine and Easie Introdvction* (annotations to Part I) I haue omitted the definition and diuision of musicke because the greatest part of those, for whose sake the booke was taken in hand, and who chieflie are to vse it: be either altogither vnlearned, or then haue not so farre proceeded in learning, as to vnder stand the reason of a definition: and also because amongst so many who haue written of musicke, I knew not whom to follow in the definition. And therefore I haue left it to the discretion of y[e] Reader, to take which he list of all these which I shal set downe. The most auncient of which is by *Plato* set out in his *Theages* thus. Musicke (saith he) *is a knowledge* (for so I interpret the worde σοφια which in that place he vseth) *whereby we may rule a company of singers, or singers in companies* (or *quire*, for so the word χορος signifieth.) But in his *Banquet* he giueth this definition. *Musick*, saith he, *is a science of loue matters occupied in harmonie and rythmos. Boetius* distinguisheth and theoricall or speculatiue musicke he defineth, in the first chapter of the fift booke of his musicke, *Facultas differentias acutorum & grauium sonorum sensu ac ratione perpendens.* A facultie considering the difference of high and lowe soundes by sence and reason. *Augustine* defineth practicall musicke (which is that which we haue now in hand) *Recte modu landi* [sic] *scientia*, A science of well dooing by time, tune, or number, for in al these three is *modulan di* [sic] *peritia* occupied. *Fanchinus* [sic] *gaufurius* thus *Musica est proportionabilium sonorum concinnis interuallis disiunctorum dispositio sensu ac ratione consonantiam monstrans.* A disposition of proportionable soundes deuided by apt distances, shewing by sence and reason, the agreement in sound. Those who haue byn since his time, haue doon it thus, *Rite & bene canendi scientia*, A Science of duly and wel singing, a science of singing wel in tune and number *Ars bene canendi*, an Art of wel singing. Now I saie, let euery man follow what definition he list. As for the diuision, Musicke is either *speculatiue* or *practicall. Speculatiue is that kinde of musicke* which by Mathematical helpes, seeketh out the causes, properties, and natures of soundes by themselues, and compared with others proceeding no further, but content with the onlie contemplation of the Art. *Practical* is that which teacheth al that may be knowne in songs, eyther for the vnderstanding of other mens, or making of ones owne, and is of three kindes: *Diatonicum, chromaticum,* and *Enharmonicum.* **early 17th C.** RAVENSCROFT Treatise of Musick BL Add. 19758, f. 2 Musick is an Art in wch all Discords ar made to agree wth the concords in a sweet and well tund harmonye .... Practiue Musick is that wch doth teach one ... to singe skilfully: tunably: the wch dothe consist only in sownds and agreeable harmonye: ¶ Speculatiue Musick is that wch dothe way the the [sic] proportions of diuers sownds and dothe only require knowledge of thinges (not by sound) but by Judgment; not by care or Learning; but by witt and understanding; the wch is very harde for any practicall Musitian to attayne unto: **1609** DOWLAND-ORNITHOPARCUS *Micrologvs* (p. [0]) Mvsicke (as *Franchinus Gafforus* in the third Chapter of the first booke of *Theorie* writeth) is a knowledge of *Tuning,* which consists in *sound* and *Song.* In *sound* (I say) because of the musicke which the motion of the cœlestiall Orbes doth make. In *Song,* least that melody which our selues practise, should be secluded out of our definition.... *Boêtius* (to whom among the Latine writers of Musicke, the praise is to be giuen) doth shew in the second Chapter of his first booke of Musicke, that Musicke is three-fold. The *Worlds Musicke*: *Humane Musicke*: and *Instrumentall Musicke.* **1617-24** FLUDD *Utriusque Cosmi Maioris: De Templo Musicæ* (p. 164) *De Musicæ Definitione, Etymologia, & Inventoribus.* ¶ *Generaliter definitur,* scientia divina, qua omnia mundana inviolato vinculo connectuntur, & qua, in re unaquaque par æquali proportione pari refertur. Hæc Musices definitio mundanæ, humanæ & instrumentali convenit. ¶ *Specialiter definitur,* scientia bene canendi, fides pulsandi, cantúsque bene & congruè componendi, in gravibus & acutis; Atque de hujus Musicæ subjecto hoc in templo tractabimus. **1636** BUTLER *Principles of Musik* (p. 1) Musik is the Art of modulating Notes in voice or instrument. The which, having a great pouer over the affections of the minde, by its various Moodes produceth in the hearers various effects. § (p. 2) ... So dooest St *Augustine* define it [marginalia: *'De Musica,* l. 1, c. 2.']: *Musica est scientia bene modulandi.* **1677** NEWTON *English Academy* (p. 89) *Musick* is the Art of modulating Notes in Voice or Instrument. **1704** GORTON *Catechetical Questions in Musick* (p. 1) *Quest.* What is Musick? ¶ *Answ.* A composition of Proportionated sounds, put together by Art to delight the Ear. **1706** BEDFORD *Temple Musick* (p. 11) The word Μοῦσα, which signifies a *Muse,* and consequently Μουσικὴ *Musick* is of an *Egyptian* Derivation, and as from hence they took the *Name,* so it is evident that from hence they took the thing signified thereby. This the Learned *Kircher* positively affirms, and saith, That *after the Flood the* Egyptians *were the first Revivers of the lost* Musick. *For they being taught by Ham, and* Mizraim *his Son,* had made so great *an Improvement thereof, that the Word* Musick, *in other Languages, takes its Etymology or Derivation from the* Egyptian *Word* Moys, *which signifies* Water; *because Musick was found out, or at least improved near the standing Pools or Marshes of* Nilus, *and this Improvement was occasioned by the Reeds or Rushes which grew there in great abundance, and of which at first they made their Trumpets.* And therefore he concludes, that *without doubt* Musick *was brought out of* Egypt, *as appears from the* Egyptian *Word* Moys, *which signifies* Water. § (p. 33) ... The Word *Musick,* (as it was in Use among them [the ancient Greeks]) came from the *Greek* Word Μοῦσαι (*the Muses*) which they rather fansied to be the *Nine Goddesses* or *Patronesses of Poetry;* and accordingly they were invoked by the *Poets* upon all Occasions; and each of them had their particular Verses assigned to them. One of them was the Goddess of *Elegies,* another of *Dramaticks,* another of *mystical Poetry,* and another of *Epicks, &c*[;] and perhaps the Word Μυσικη might be thought by some of the *Greeks* to intend no more, and was therefore reckoned one of the *Liberal Arts* (as well as *Rhetorick*) instead of *Poetry*: and it seems probable that the several different *Moods* of *Musick,* so much talk'd of among the *Greeks,* might be more properly called *Modi loquendi* than *Modi cantandi.* **1721** MALCOLM *Treatise of Musick* (p. 1) *Musick* is a Science of *Sounds,* whose *End* is *Pleasure. Sound* is the *Object* in general; or, to speak with the *Philosophers,* it is the *material Object.* But it is not the Business of *Musick,* taken in a strict and proper Sense, to consider every Phenomenon and Property of Sound; that belongs to a more universal Philosophy: ... § (pp. 29-30) We may ... affirm, That *Musick* has for its Object, in general, *Sound;* and particularly, *Sounds* considered in their Relations of *Tune* and *Duration,* as under that *Formality* they are capable of affording agreeable Sensations. I shall therefore define *Musick, A Science that teaches how Sounds, under certain Measures of Tune and Time, may be produced; and so ordered or disposed, as in Consonance* (i.e. *joynt sounding*) or *Succession, or both, they may raise agreeable Sensations.* § (pp. 451-2) The Word *Musick* comes to us from the Latin Word *Musica,* if not immediately from a Greek Word of the same Sound, from whence the *Romans* probably took theirs; for they got much of their Learning from the *Greeks.* Our Criticks teach us, that it comes from the Word *Musa,* and this from a Greek Word which signifies to search or find out, because the *Muses* were feigned to be Inventresses of the *Sciences,* and particularly of *Poetry* and these *Modulations* of Sound that constitute *Musick.* But others go higher, and tell us, the Word *Musa* comes from a Hebrew Word, which signifies *Art* or *Discipline;* hence *Musa* and *Musica* anciently signified *Learning* in general, or any Kind of *Science;* in which Sense you'll find it frequently in the Works of the ancient Philosophers. But *Kircher* will have it from an *Egyptian* Word; because the Restoration of it after the Flood was probably there, by reason of the many Reeds to be found in their Fens, and upon the Banks of the *Nile. Hesychius* tells us, that the *Athenians* gave the Name of *Musick* to every *Art.* From this it was that the *Poets* and *Mythologists* feigned the nine *Muses* Daughters of *Jupiter,* who invented the Sciences, and preside over them, to assist and inspire these who apply to study them, each having her particular Province. In this gene[r]al Sense we have it defin'd to be, the orderly Ar[r]angement and right Disposition of Things; in short, the Agreement and *Harmony* of the Whole with its Parts, and of the Parts among themselves. § (pp. 455-6) *Aristides Quintialianus,* who writes a profest Treatise upon *Musick,* calls it the Knowledge of singing, and of the Things that are joyned with singing (ἐπιστήμη μέλους καὶ τῶν περὶ μελος συμβαινόντων, which *Meibomius* translates, *Scientia cantus, eorumq; quæ circa cantum contingunt*) and these he calls the Motions of the Voice and Body, as if the *Cantus* it self consisted only in the different Tones of the Voice. *Bacchius* who writes a short Introduction to Musick in Question and Answer, gives the same Definition. Afterwards, *Aristides* considers *Musick* in the largest Sense of the Word, and divides it into *Contemplative* and *Active.* The first, he says, is either *natural* or *artificial;* the *natural* is *arithmetical,* because it considers the Proportion of Numbers, or *physical* which disputes of every Thing in Nature; ... **1725** De La Fond *New System of Music* (pp. 1-3) The word *Music* is taken in two different senses. Sometimes it signifies *pleasing sounds;* and sometimes *the science of pleasing sounds.* This distinction at once gives us the definition of *Music,* in both the senses of the word. ¶ *Music* in the first signification or definition, *pleasing sounds,* is naturally distinguished in two parts, *passion* and *harmony.... Music* in the second signification or definition, *the science of pleasing sounds,* does not allow of any distinction; 'tis plainly understood: but, notwithstanding, it is to make the business of this whole Book. § (p. 10) *Pleasing sounds!* some will say, this is but a poor definition of *Music*: It cannot be a learned one. No matter for the learnedness of it; but only for the plainness, truth, nativeness or nature of it... That definition of *Music,* as short and as plain as it is, comprehends more than can be reduced to notes, consequently more than can be brought into practice; ... **1726** Jackson *Preliminary Discourse to a Scheme* (preface, vii) *Musick* is a harmonical Disposition of *Tones*: ... **1730** Playford *Intro. to Skill of Musick* (19th edn, p. 103) *Musick* is an Art of expressing perfect Harmony, either by *Voice* or *Instrument;* which Harmony ariseth from well taken *Concords* and *Discords.* **1736** Tans'ur *Compleat Melody* (3rd edn, p. 70) *Musica.* (Ital.) Signifies the *Art* of *Musick;* made either by a *Natural Voice;* or by an *Artificial Instrument.* § (p. 70) *Theoretical Musick,* is that which searches into the true *Grounds* of it; and into the true Nature of *Concords,* and *Discords;* explaining their true *Nature, Number,* and *Proportions,* &c. ¶ *Practical-Musick,* is that which Designs, Contrives, and Composes all *Sounds* into *Musical Parts.*

musica canonica

1721 Malcolm *Treatise of Musick* (p. 487) ... As they [in ancient Greece] had poetical Compositions upon various Subjects for their publick Solemnities, so they had certain determinate *Modes* both in the *Harmonia* and *Rythmus,* which it was unlawful to alter; and which were hence called *Nomi* or *Laws,* and *Musica Canonica.*

musica di camera *see* camera

musica ficta *see* accidental, fictitious note

1609 Dowland-Ornithoparcus *Micrologvs* (p. 24) *Of Musica Ficta.* ¶ Fained Musicke is that, which the Greekes call *Synemenon,* a Song made beyond the regular compasse of the Scales. Or it is a Song, which is full of Coniunctions.... The fained Scale exceedes the others both in height and depth. For it addeth a *Ditone* vnder *Vt* base, because it sings *fa* in *A*, and it riseth aboue *eela* by two degrees, for in it it sounds *fa*...

musica humana *see* music

1609 DOWLAND-ORNITHOPARCUS *Micrologvs* (p. 1) *Hvmane Musick*, is the Concordance of diuers elements in one compound, by which the spirituall nature is ioyned with the body, and the reasonable part is coupled in concord with the vnreasonable, which proceedes from the vniting of the body and the soule. For that amitie, by which the body is ioyned vnto the soule, is not tyed with bodily bands, but vertuall, caused by the proportion of humors. For what (saith *Cœlius*) makes the powers of the soule so sundry and disagreeing to conspire oftentimes each with other? who reconciles the Elements of the body? what other power doth soder and glue that spiritual strength, which is indued with an intellect to a mortall and earthly frame, than that Musicke which euery man that descends into himselfe finds in himselfe? For euery like is preserued by his like, and by his dislike is disturbed. Hence it is, that we loath and abhorre discords, and are delighted when we heare harmonicall concords, because we know there is in our selues the like concord.

musical *see* immusical

1598 FLORIO It→E *Musicale, Musicheuole*, musicall, according to musicke. **1609** CAWDREY (2nd edn) *musicall*, that loueth or hath skill [in] musicke. **1611** COTGRAVE Fr→E *Musicalement.* Musically, melodiously, harmoniously. **1611** FLORIO It→E *Musicale*, musicall, accroding [sic] to musike. **1659** TORRIANO-FLORIO It→E *Musicale, Musichevole, Musico*, musical, according to musick. **1688** MIEGE-COTGRAVE Fr→E *Musical*, musical, harmonious. **1702** KERSEY *New Engl. Dict.* (1st edn) *Musical*, of, *or* belonging to *Musick.* **1704** *Cocker's Engl. Dict.* (1st edn) *Musical*, Melodious. **1706** KERSEY-PHILLIPS (6th edn) *Musical*, belonging to Musick. **1707** *Gloss. Angl. Nova* (1st edn) *Musical*, belonging to Musick, Harmonious. **1730** BAILEY *Dict. Britannicum* (1st edn) *Musicalness*, harmoniousness of Sound. **1737** DYCHE-PARDON (2nd edn) *Musical* (A.) something belonging or appertaining to Musick, harmonious, pleasant Sounding, &c.

musical faculty

1721 MALCOLM *Treatise of Musick* (p. 456) The musical Faculties, as they [the ancient writers] call them, are, *Melopœia* which gives Rules for the *Tones* of the Voice or Instrument, *Rythmopœia* for Motions, and *Poesis* for making of Verse.

musici *see* canon

musician *see* melicus, musico, musicus

1570/71 *Dict. Fr. and Engl.* Fr→E *Musicien*, a musician or player on instruments. **1593** HOLLYBAND Fr→E *Musicien*, a Musition or player on instruments: *m.* **1611** COTGRAVE Fr→E *Musicien: m.* A Musician; a professor of Musicke. **1688** MIEGE-COTGRAVE Fr→E *Musicien*, (m.) Musician, that understands Musick. *Musicienne*, (f.) a Musician, a she Musician. § *C'est un excellent Musicien*, he is an excellent Musician. *Elle est bonne Musicienne*, she is a good Musician. **1702** KERSEY *New Engl. Dict.* (1st edn) A *Musician*, one well skill'd in ¶ *Musick* **1704** *Cocker's Engl. Dict.* (1st edn) *Musician*, a professor of Musick. **1706** KERSEY-PHILLIPS (6th edn) *Musician*, one well skill'd in, or that professes the Science of Musick. **1721** BAILEY *An Univ. Etymolog. Engl. Dict.* (1st edn) *Musician, (musicien*, F. *musicus*, L. of μουσικός, *Gr.*) a Professor or Practitioner of Musick.

1609 DOWLAND-ORNITHOPARCUS *Micrologvs* (p. 4) Therefore he is truely to be called a *Musitian*, who hath the faculty of speculation and reason, not he that hath onely practicke fashion of singing: for so saith *Boëtius lib.* 1. *cap.* 35. He is called a Musitian, which taketh vpon him the knowledge of Singing by weighing it with reason, not with the seruile exercise of practise, but the commanding power of speculation, and wanteth neither speculation nor practise. Wherefore that practise is fit for a learned man: *Plutarch* in his Musicke sets downe (being forced vnto it by *Homers* authoritie) and proues it thus: *Speculation breedeth onely knowledge, but practise bringeth the same to worke.* § (p. 5) ... there is great difference in calling one a Musitian, or a Cantor. For *Quintilian* saith, That Musitians were so honoured amongst men famous for wisdome, that the same men were accounted *Musitians* and *Prophets*, and *wise men*. But *Guido* compareth those *Cantors*, which haue made curtesie a farre off to Musicke) to brute Beasts.

musicians, company of

1737 Bailey *The Univ. Etymolog. Engl. Dict.* (3rd edn, vol. 2) *Musicians*, this company is composed of *Masters of musick, Dancing masters, &c.* they have no hall, but meet sometimet [sic] at *Embroiderers-Hall* in *Gutter-Lane*. They consist of a master, 2 wardens, about 20 assistants, they are also on the livery, the fine for which is 8*l*. Their armorial ensigns are *azure*, a swan with her wings expanded, chanting within a double tressure counter flory *argent*. On a chief *gules* 2 lions of *England*, and between them a pale *or* charged with a rose of *York*

musicis *see* musics

1736 Tans'ur *Compleat Melody* (3rd edn, p. 72) *Musicis's* (Lat.) is a Name given to Narrow *Keys* of the *Organ, Virginals, Harpsichord*, or *Spinnet*. They are commonly made of *Ivory*, and are tuned *Semitones*; and are placed between the *whole Tones* of the *proper Keys*; The *proper Keys* are commonly black; to give the Performer a Distinction one from the other...

music-line *see* drawing pen, staff

1636 Butler *Principles of Musik* (p. 90) A Musik-line is 5 parallel Rules, with their Spaces: devised for the distinguishing of Tones, drawn out to the length of a Ditti-line, whereof it is so called.

musico

1598 Florio It→E *Musico*, a musition, or singing man. **1599** Minsheu-Percyvall Sp→E *Musico*, m. a musicion, belonging to musicke. **1611** Florio It→E *Musico*, any kind of musition. **1659** Torriano-Florio It→E *Musico*, a Musitian, a Professor of musick. **1724** [Pepusch] *Short Explic. of Foreign Words in Mus. Bks.* (p. 48) *Musico*, is a Musician, or Musick-Master; or one who either Composes, Performs, or Teacheth Musick. **1726** Bailey *An Univ. Etymolog. Engl. Dict.* (3rd edn) *Musico*, a Musician or musick Master; or one who either composes, performs, or teaches Musick. *Ital.*

1736 Tans'ur *Compleat Melody* (3rd edn, p. 70) *Musico*. (Ital.) Signifies, either a *Musician*, or *Master* of *Musick*; or one that either teacheth, maketh, or performeth *Musick*.

music of the spheres *see* harmony of the spheres

music of the world *see* mundane music

1609 Dowland-Ornithoparcus *Micrologvs* (pp. [0]-1) *Of the Musicke of the World*. ¶ VVhen God (whom *Plutarch* prooues to haue made all things to a certaine harmonie) had deuised to make this world moueable, it was necessary, that he should gouerne it by some actiue and moouing power, for no bodies but those which haue a soule, can moue themselues, as *Franchinus* in the first Chapter of his first booke of *Theoric* saith. Now that motion (because it is the swiftest of all other, and most regular) is not without sound: for it must needs be that a sound be made of the very wheeling of the Orbes, as *Macrobius in Somnium Scip. lib.* 2. writeth. The like sayd *Boêtius*, how can this quick-mouing frame of the world whirle about with a dumb and silent motion? From this turning of the heauen, there cannot be remoued a certaine order of Harmonie. And nature will (saith that prince of Romane eloquence *Cicero*, in his sixt booke *de Reipub.*) that extremities must needs sound deepe on the one side, & sharp on the other. So then, the worlds Musicke is an Harmonie, caused by the motion of the starres, and violence of the Spheares. *Lodouicus Cœlius Rodiginus, lectionum antiquarum lib.* 5. *cap.* 25. writeth, That this Harmony hath been obserued out of the consent of the heauens, the knitting together of the elements, and the varietie of times. Wherefore well sayd *Dorilaus* the Philosopher, That the World is Gods Organe. Now the cause wee cannot heare this sound according to *Pliny* is, because the greatnesse of the sound doth exceede the sence of our eares. But whether wee admit this Harmonicall sound of the Heauens, or no, it skils not much; sith certaine it is, that the grand Work-maister of this *Mundane Fabricke*, made all things in number, weight, and measure, wherein principally, *Mundane Musicke* doth consist.

musics *see* musicis
1694 HOLDER *Treatise of Natural Grounds* (pp. 155-6) Take the First Scale of Ascent to *Diapason* ... as they are usually placed in the Keys of an Organ; ... The *Breves* representing the *Tones* of the broad Gradual Keys of an Organ; the *Semibreves* representing the Narrow Upper Keys, which are usually called *Musics*.

musicus *see* melicus
1500 *Ortus Vocabulorum* L→E Musicus ca. cum. Et musicalis & hoc lq. in eodem sensu. o.s. Musicus ci. qui tractat de musica vel qui docet eam. m.s. **1538** ELYOT L→E *Musicus*, a musycion. **1552** HULOET L→E *musicus. a. um* Musicall, or perteynyge to musycke. **1565** COOPER L→E *Músicus, ci, m.g. Substantiuum. Cic.* A musician: a singyng man. *Músicus, pen. corr. Adiectiuum.* Pertaynyng to musike. **1587** THOMAS L→E *Musicus, a, um.* Pertaining to musicke. *Musicus, ci, m.g.* A musition, a singing man. **1589** RIDER L→E *Musicus, ad.* Of musicke. *Musicus, melicus, m.* A Musition.

musurgus
1587 THOMAS L→E *Musurgus, gi, m.g. Iun.* A composer or maker of songes, a setter of notes, &c. **1589** RIDER L→E *Musurgus, m.* A composer, or setter of songs.

mutation *see* harmonic, pathetic music, rythmus, tone, vocal
1728 CHAMBERS *Mutation*, in the antient Music, signifies the Changes, or Alterations that happen in the Order of the Sounds which compose the Melody. ¶ *Aristoxenus* says it is, as it were, a kind of Passion in the Order of the Melody. See *Melody*. ¶ The Changes are, first, in the *Genera*; when the Song begins in one, as the *Chromatic*, and passes into another, as the *Diatonic*. Secondly, In the System; as when the Song passes out of one *Tetrachord*, as *Meson*, into another, as *Diazeugmenon*; or more generally, when it passes from a high place of the Scale to a lower, or contrarily, *i.e.* part of it is sung high, and part low. Thirdly, In the Mode or Tone, as when the Song begins in one, as the *Doric*; and passes into another, as the *Lydian*. Fourthly, In the *Melopœia*, that is, when the Song changes the very Air, so as from Gay and Sprightly, to become Soft and Languishing; or from a Manner that expresses one Passion or Subject, to the Expression of some other. **1730** BAILEY *Dict. Britannicum* (1st edn) *Mutation* (in the *antient Musick*) the Changes or Alterations that happen in the order of the Sounds, which compose the Melody.

1597 MORLEY *Plaine and Easie Introdvction* (annotations to Part I) Mutation is the leauing of one name of a note and taking another in the same sound, and is done (sayeth the Author of *quatuor principalia*) either by reason of propertie, or by reason of the voice. **1609** DOWLAND-ORNITHOPARCUS *Micrologvs* (p. 16) Whereupon *Mutation* (as *Georg. Valla lib.* 3. *cap.* 4. of his Musicke proueth) is the putting of one *Voyce* for another. But this definition, because it is generall, doth not properly agree to a Musitian: therfore *Mutation* is (to apply it to our purpose) the putting of one concord for another in the same *Key*. And because all *Voyces* are not concords, al do not receiue *Mutation*. Therfore it is necessary to consider, to which *Voyces Mutation* doth agree, and to which not; for ♮ *dures* are not changed into *b mols*, nor co[n]trarily: ... **1721** MALCOLM *Treatise of Musick* (p. 540) *Of Mutations*. This signifies the Changes or Alterations that happen in the Order of the Sounds that compose the *Melody*. *Aristox.* says, 'tis as it were a certain *Passion* in the Order of the *Melody*.

mute *see* piva, sordine
c.1710 NORTH (draft for) Musicall Grammarian BL Add. 32537, f. 84v ... A weight put upon y[e] bridge y[t] cloggs y[e] tremolo [and] hinders y[e] sound (w[ch] they call muting a violl) ... § f. 165v It is found that no materiall whatever, without a body of air Included, will give a sound by y[e] touch of a string; as those made for silent porposes, w[ch] have all the advantages that may be, except a body of air, & are called mutes.

mutilate
1737 DYCHE-PARDON (2nd edn) *Mutilate* (V.) ... to castrate Persons to make them Eunuchs, ... a Practice also in *Italy* to make the Males sing finely.

N

nablium *see* psaltery, viol, violin
1500 *Ortus Vocabulorum* L→E Nablum grece: latine psalterium vel organum. Nablum li. est instrumentum musicum admodum psalterij hns duodecim sonos. n.s. **1538** ELYOT L→E *Nablum, & nablium*, an instrument of musyke, called a psaltrie. **1565** COOPER L→E *Nablium, nablij, Instrumentum musicum, quod aliàs psalterium dicitur. Ouid.* **1587** THOMAS L→E *Nablium, blii, n.g. Ovid.* An instrument of musick called *Psalterion.* **1589** RIDER L→E *Nablium, n.* A instrument in musicke called Psalterion. **1611** FLORIO It→E *Nablio*, a musicall instrument called a Saltery or Viole, some say it is a wind-instrument. **1659** TORRIANO-FLORIO It→E *Nablio*, a musical instrument, called a Nablie, a Saltery, or a Violl, some say, that it is a wind-instrument. **1688** DAVIS-TORRIANO-FLORIO It→E *Nablio*, an instrument of musick, called a Psaltery, a wind-instrument.

naccara *see* gnaccara, naquaire
1550 THOMAS It→E *Nacchere*, the baggepipes, and as some say, the dromslades. **1598** FLORIO It→E *Nacca*, a cradle, a childs rattle to play with. *Naccare*, bagpipes, dromslades, a childes rattle. **1611** FLORIO It→E *Nacca*, a childes rattle to play with. *Naccare*, drom-slades. Also childrens rattles. Also a kinde of bag-pipe or Country-croud. Also a kind of Musike, made with two Drum-stickes beaten one against another. *Nacchere*, as *Naccare*. **1659** TORRIANO-FLORIO It→E *Naccare, Nacchere*: Drum sledes or kettle-drums, also a kind of long Bag-pipe or Country-croud, also a kind of antick made with two drum-sticks beating one against another, also childrens playing rattles, also snappers to play with ones fingers as boyes do in the streets, or *Castagnette*, that dancers use to rattle withall when they dance antick dances or the like

naccherino
1611 FLORIO It→E *Naccherino*, a kinde of winde-instrument or Cornet of Brasse. **1659** TORRIANO-FLORIO It→E *Naccarino, Naccherino*, a player upon *Nacare*, also a kind of wind-Instrument or Cornet of brasse

nænia *see* admetinænia, dirge, elegy, epicedy, epitaph, monody, nanna, obit, threnody
1500 *Ortus Vocabulorum* L→E Nenia e. carmina que fiunt super mortuos: vel est cantilena qua mulieres sopiunt pueros suos: vel est fabula vana vel est caro mortuorum: et est nomen onomatopeium vel ficticium quasi fictuz a sono. vt ne. ne. ne. [sic] et maxime super cantilenam que fit in cunis puerorum. f.p. Nenior aris. i. vana loqui vel cantilenam super mortuum facere vel lamentare vel nugari. d.p. **1538** ELYOT L→E *Nænia*, a mournynge songe, wont to be songen at burielles, somtyme it signifieth the songe that the mother or norice doth singe dandyllynge of her chylde. **1565** COOPER L→E *Nænia, næniæ. vel Næniæ, næniarum. Quintil.* A lamentable songe at the death or buriall of a man. § *Puerorum nænia. Horat.* A triflyng songe of yonge children. **1587** THOMAS L→E *Nænia, æ, f.g.* A lamentable song at the death or buriall of a man: a trifling song. **1589** RIDER L→E *Nænia, f.* A lamentable song at the death of one. *Nænia, f. threnos, threnum, n.* A lamentable song at burialles. **1611** FLORIO It→E *Nenia*, the name of a custumarie ceremonie vsed among the ancient Grecians in the funerals or burials, which was to hire a companie of men and women to accompanie them, and with wringing hands, piteous gestures, mournefull wailings and lored [sic] acclamations, to proclaime the noble deedes as well of the partie dead, as of his familie, and fore-fathers. Also as *Nanna.* **1658** PHILLIPS (1st edn) *Nænia*, (lat.) Funeral-songs, Funeral-prayers or praises. **1676** COLES *Næniæ*, Funeral songs. **1706** KERSEY-PHILLIPS (6th edn) *Nænia, (Lat.)* funeral Songs, Lamentations, or mournful Tunes, anciently sung at the burying of the Dead. **1707** *Gloss. Angl. Nova* (1st edn) *Nænia*, Funeral Songs, or Songs which were wont to be sung in old time at the Funerals of the Dead. **1728** CHAMBERS *Nenia*, or *Nænia*, in the antient Poetry, a kind of Verses sung at the Obsequies of the Dead. See *Obsequies.* ¶ Authors represent them as sorry Compositions, sung by hired Women-Mourners. The first Rise of these *Nenia* is ascribed to the *Phrygians.* ¶ The Word comes from the Greek νηνία, on which *Scaliger* observes that it should be wrote in *Latin Nenia*, not *Nænia.* ¶ *Guichart* notes *Nænia* to have antiently been the Name of a Song to lull Children a-sleep, and conjectures it to come from the *Hebrew* נין *Nin*, Child. ¶ In the Heathen Antiquity, the Goddess of

Tears and Funerals was call'd *Nænia,* whom some suppose to have given that Name to the *Funeral-Song;* and others to have taken her Name from it. Some will have the one, and some the other, form'd from the Sound or Voice of those that weep. **1737** Bailey *The Univ. Etymolog. Engl. Dict.* (3rd edn, vol. 2) *Nænia* (with the *Romans*) a goddess supposed to preside over mourning ditties sung at funerals, *&c.* to flutes and other instruments, *&c.* She had a temple built to her without the city, near the gate called *Viminalis.* **1737** Dyche-Pardon (2nd edn) *Naenia* (S.) Dirges, Funeral Songs, or Lamentations in mournful Tunes, antiently sung at Funeral Solemnities in Honour of the Dead, by Women hired on purpose called Preficæ, to Flutes and other Instruments, the Tones of which regulated both the Voice of the Singers, and directed the Mourners to knock or strike their Breasts, as if they, or those they represented were extreamly grieved for the Loss of the Friend;

nanna *see* ninnare

1598 Florio It→E *Nanna,* ... Some thinke it may be vsed for mournefull songs, or alluring verses. **1611** Florio It→E *Nanna,* ... Also a word that Nurces vse to still their children, as we say lullaby. Some thinke it may be vsed for a mourning songs, and others say for alluring verses. Also as *Nenia. Nannare,* to lullaby, to rocke or sing children a sleepe. **1659** Torriano-Florio It→E *Nannare, Nanneare, Nanneggiare,* to lullaby, to sing, to rock or dandle children asleep in the cradle, or in ones lap.

naquaire *see* naccara

1593 Hollyband Fr→E *Naquaires,* as *les trompes tabours & Naquaires commencerent à sonner,* the trumpets, drummes and haltbois began to sound out. **1611** Cotgrave Fr→E *Naquaire.* A lowd instrument of Musicke, somewhat resembling a Hoboy.

natural *see* character

1728 Chambers *Natural,* in Music, is used variously. Sometimes, it is taken for *Diatonic;* and sometimes for *Physical,* in which latter Sense, *Natural Music* is that performed by *Natural* Organs, *i.e.* Vocal Music, in contradistinction to Artificial, or Instrumental. ¶ *Natural Harmony* is that produced by the *Natural,* and Essential Chords of the Mode. See *Harmony.* ¶ *Natural Note* is used in opposition to *Flat* and *Sharp* Notes, which are call'd Artificial Notes. See *Note, Scale, &c.* **1730** Bailey *Dict. Britannicum* (1st edn) *Natural Harmony (Musi.)* is that produced by the natural and essential Chords of the Mode.

1721 Malcolm *Treatise of Musick* (p. 291) ... And to preserve the *diatonick* Series distinct, these inserted Notes [semitones] take the Name of the *natural* Note next below, with this Mark ✕ called a *Sharp,* as C ✕ or C *sharp,* to signify that it is a *Semitone* above C (*natural;*) or they take the Name of the *natural* Note next above, with this Mark ♭, called a *Flat* as D♭ or *D flat,* to signifie a *Semitone* below *D* (*natural;*) and tho' it be indifferent upon the main which Name is used in any Case, yet, for good Reasons, sometimes the one Way is used, and sometimes the other ... **1723** Church *Intro. to Psalmody* (p. 14) ... There is one other Character call'd a Natural made thus ♮ ye quality of it is to reduce any Note made flat or sharp by ye governing flats or sharps plac'd at the beginning of ye Lines, to its primitive Sound, as it stands in the Gamut. **1724** Turner *Sound Anatomiz'd* (p. 47) [*re* a note previously sharpened or flattened] ... if it be required to have its former *Tone;* it has always this Mark; ♮ placed before it, which is called a *Natural,* or the *Mark* of *Restoration* ... **1728** North Musicall Grammarian (*C-K MG* ff. 18v-19) ... Thus farr very well; for here is the letter, which is of universall regard, and is called the naturall, and when any tone used as a member of any other scale is reduced to the naturall it hath this mark ♮. **1731** Prelleur *Modern Musick-Master* (I, p. 6) There is a Character called a Natural made thus ♮ and is used to contradict such Flats and Sharps as are set at the Beginning, and to bring that Note to it's natural Sound; ... § (II, p. 2) There is an other Character called a Natural and made thus ♮, the Quality of which is to reduce any Note made flat or sharp by governing Flats or Sharps placed at the beginning of the Lines, to it's primitive Sound as it stands in the Gamut, as for Instance, a Flat being placed in *B* at the beginning of the Line makes all the Notes in that Line flat: then if the Composer should have a Mind to have some one or more of them sharp then this Natural is used instead of a Sharp.

natural bass

1737 Lampe *Plain and Compendious Method* (p. 18) That *Sound,* that gives the *Cord* the Name, is called the *Natural Bass,* which differs from the *Thorough Bass* in this, that the latter sounds *any* Part or Note of a *Cord as a Bass,* but the Former keeps its place as *Ground-Note* of the Cord ...

natural scale *see* diatonic music

1721 MALCOLM *Treatise of Musick* (p. 247) ... we call it [the diatonic scale] also the *Natural Scale,* because its *Degrees* and their Order are the most agreeable and *concinnous,* and preferable, by the Approbation both of Sense and Reason, to all other Divisions that have ever been instituted... I shall always call this, *The Scale of Musick,* without Distinction, as 'tis the only true *natural System.* § (p. 370) ... the seven plain Letters, *c, d, e, f, g, a, b,* which we call the *natural Scale* ...

natural series *see* harmonic series

1721 MALCOLM *Treatise of Musick* (pp. 318-19) ... beginning at any Note, if we take an 8*ve* *concinnously* divided by *Tones* and *Semitones* in the *diatonick* Order (which will be found more exact from some Notes than others because of the small Errors that still remain) that may be justly called a *natural Series,* and all these Notes *natural Notes* with respect to the First or *Fundamental* from which they proceed; and yet in the common Way of speaking about these Things, no 8*ve* is called a *natural Key* that takes in any of these Notes marked ✕ or ♭, in order to make it a concinnous Series. And ... there is no *Key* called *natural* in the whole Scale but *C* and *A*.

nazard

1611 COTGRAVE Fr→E *Nazard: m.* A kind of harsh, or iarring wind instrument.

neapolitan

1597 MORLEY *Plaine and Easie Introdvction* (p. 180) [marginalia: 'Napolitans'] ... Of the nature of these [canzonets] are the *Neapolitans* or *Canzone a la Napolitana,* different from them in nothing sauing in name, so that whosoeuer knoweth the nature of the one must needs know the other also ...

necessario *see* obligata

1724 [PEPUSCH] *Short Explic. of Foreign Words in Mus. Bks.* (p. 49) *Necessario,* Necessary, the same as *Concertante.* **1726** BAILEY *An Univ. Etymolog. Engl. Dict.* (3rd edn) *Necessario* (in *Musick Books*) signifies those Parts of a Piece of Musick, which play throughout the whole, to distinguish them from those which play only in some Parts.

neglectus

1587 THOMAS L→E *Neglectus, a, um, part.* ... vnorderly tuned.

nergal

1730 BAILEY *Dict. Britannicum* (1st edn) *Nergal* ... a continual Fire, which the *Persian Magi* preserved upon the Altar in honour of the Sun, and the Lights of the Firmament. This Fire was always kept burning, like the Vestal Fire of the *Romans;* whensoever they meddled with this Fire, they used to sing Hymns in honour of the Sun...

nervo *see* chord, cord, string

1538 ELYOT L→E *Neruiæ,* harpe strynges, or lute stringes. **1552** HULOET L→E *Neruuli. orum,* small strynges **1565** COOPER L→E *Nerui. Cic.* The strynge of an harpe, lute, or other instrument. § *Concordia neruorum. Quint.* The agreement of stringes of an instrument in tune. *Elicere sonum neruorum. Cic.* To play on some instrument of musike: to strike the stringes. *Neruorum elicere sonos. Cic.* To make stringes sounde. *Probare neruos. Quint.* To try or assay strynges, whether they be in tune. **1587** THOMAS L→E *Nervia, æ, f.g. & nervium, vii, n.g. Non.* The string of an Harpe or Lute. *Nervus, vi, m.g.* ... the string of an Harpe, Lute, or other instrument: **1589** RIDER L→E *Nervia, chorda, fides, f. nervium, Filum, n. nervus, m.* A string of an harpe, or other instrument. **1598** FLORIO It→E *Neruo, Nerbo,* ... Also the string of a harpe, of a lute or other instrument. **1611** FLORIO It→E *Neruo,* ... Also a string of any instrument. § *Nerui sonori,* gut-strings for instruments. **1659** TORRIANO-FLORIO It→E *Nervo, Nerbo,* ... also a gut-string for any Instrument **1706** KERSEY-PHILLIPS (6th edn) *Nervus, (Lat.)* ... the String of a Bow, or of a Musical Instrument: **1708** KERSEY *Dict. Anglo-Brit.* (1st edn) *Nervous, (L.)* ... the String of a Bow, or of a Musical Instrument:

1728 NORTH Musicall Grammarian (*C-K MG* f. 123) The invention of the viol Gothick ¶ Nothing made so great a denouement in musick as the invention of hors hair with rozin and the gutts of animalls twisted and dryed. I scarce think that the strings of the old lyra used in either the Jewish or Greek times[,] which in Latine are termed nerves, were such, becaus it was more or less piacular, to deal in that manner with the extra of dead animalls.

nespola

1598 FLORIO It→E *Nespola,* ... also a kind of musicall instrument without strings. **1611** FLORIO It→E *Nespola,* a Medlar, an open-arse-fruite. Also a kind of musicall instrument without strings. **1659** TORRIANO-FLORIO It→E *Nespola,* ... also a kind of round musical Instrument without strings, as *Nicchio*.

nete *see* diagram, diezeugmenon, paranete
1587 THOMAS L→E *Nete, Iun*. The seauenth string in the Harpe, making an high and small sound. *Nete diezeugmenon, Iun*. E. la. mi. *Nete hyperbolinon* [sic], *Iun*. A. la. mi. *Nete symemmenon* [sic], *Iun*. D. la. sol. **1589** RIDER L→E *Nete*. The sixt string, or next the seventh **1611** FLORIO It→E *Nete*, a string of any musicall instrument but euer sharpe. **1728** CHAMBERS *Nete Hyperboleon*, in the antient Music, the name of the highest and most acute of the Chords of the Lyre, or the ancient Scale, or Diagramma. See *Diagramma*. ¶ It answer'd to the *A, mi, la*, of the third Octave of the Organ, or the modern System. ¶ The Word is composed of the *Greek* νητη and ὑπερβολεων, i.e. *The last of the highest Chords*. ¶ *Nete Diazeugmenon*, in the Antient Music, was one of the Chords of the Lyre, or System of the Antients. See *Diagramma*. ¶ It answers to the *E, si, mi*, of the third Octave of the Organ, or modern System. ¶ The Word comes from the *Greek* νητη and διεξευγμένον, *last of the separate ones*; where is understood the word *Chord*. ¶ *Nete Synemmenon*, in the Antient Music, the Name of the highest Chord of a Tetrachord of the *Greek* System, added to make the *b soft* fall between the *Mese* and *Paramese, i.e.* between *la* and *si*. See *Diagramma*. ¶ This chord had the same Sound with the *Paranete Diazeugmenon*, or our *la* by *b mollis*. ¶ The Word comes from the *Greek* νητη and συνεμμένον, *the last of those added*; where is understood the word *Chord*. **1736** BAILEY *Dict. Britannicum* (2nd edn) *Nete Diazeugmenon* (νητη διεξευγμένον, last of the separate ones sc. *Chord*) one of the chords of the ancient lyre, answering to *E, si, mi*, of the third octave of the organ, *&c*. *Nete Hyperboleon*, (νητη ὑπερβολεων, *i.e.* the last of the highest chords) the name of the highest and most acute of the chords of the antient lyre, or the antient scale, or diagramma, and answered to the *A, mi, la*, of the third octave of the organ or modern system. *Nete Synemmenon* (νητη συνεμμένον, the last of those added, sc. *Chord*) the name of the highest chord of a tetrachord of the *Greek* system, added to make the *b* soft fall between the *Mese* and the *Paramese*, i.e. between *la* and *si*. **1737** BAILEY *The Univ. Etymolog. Engl. Dict*. (3rd edn, vol. 2) *Nete Diazeugmenon* (νητη διεξευγμένον, the last of the separate ones sc. *Chord*) one of the chords of the ancient lyre, answering to *E, si, mi*, of the third octave of the organ, *&c*. *Nete Hyperboleon* (νητη ὑπερβολεων, *i.e.* the last of the highest chords) the name of the highest and most acute of the chords of the ancient lyre, or the ancient scale, or diagramma; and answered to *A, mi, la*, of the third octave of the organ or modern system. *Nete Synemmenon* (νητη συνεμμένον, the last of those added, sc. *Chord*) the name of the highest chord of a tetrachord of the *Greek* system, added to make the *b* soft fall between the *Mese* and the *Paramese*, i.e. between *la* and *si*.

early 18th C. ANON. Essay on Musick BODLEIAN Rawl. D. 751, f. 3 ... the highest chord which [in ancient Greek music] was an A, and which made the most acute sound, was call'd *Nete hyperboleon*, that is to say, the last of the most excellent, or most acute, &c. **early 18th C.** PEPUSCH various papers BL Add. 29429, f. 6 Nete, i.e. ye last (: or Newest:) of each of the 2. Second Conjoins Tetr. Hyperbolæon, i.e, ye most Exceeding of all, in both ye Ac: & Gr:

neume *see* paraneuma
1500 *Ortus Vocabulorum* L→E Neuma atis. i. modulatio cantus. et spiritus sanctus. n.t. Neuma me. idem est. f.p. Neumaticus ca. cum. i. modulator dulcis et suauis consonans. o.s. § Spiritus est pneuma: sed cantus sit tibi neuma. Et cum p primum: sed sine p reliquum. **1611** COTGRAVE Fr→E *Neume: m*. A sound, song, or close of song after an Antham; or the long holding of the last note of an Antham, &c; used much in the Quires of Cathedrall Churches.

neutral
1609 DOWLAND-ORNITHOPARCUS *Micrologvs* (p. 13) ... there be certain Songs, which do ascend as an *Authentical*, & descend as a *Plagall*, and those are called *Neutrall*, or mixt Songs, though indeede Saint *Bernard* doeth not allow of them: for he saith, what execrable licentiousnesse is this, to ioyne together those things, which are contrary one to the other, transgressing the bonds of Nature?

nicchio *see* nespola, symphony, vielle
1611 FLORIO It→E *Nicchio*, any close nooke or corner... Also a kind of musicall instrument. **1659** TORRIANO-FLORIO It→E *Nicchio*, ... also a kind of round musical Instrument which is plaid upon with turning a little wheel that is in it, with a handle

nille
1611 COTGRAVE Fr→E *Nille: f*. The turning peg of a *Vielle*;

nimfale

1659 TORRIANO-FLORIO It→E *Nimfale, Nimphale,* a certain musical Instrument anciently used in Churches before Organes were devised, which he that plaid upon it did gird about him

ninnare *see* nanna

1659 TORRIANO-FLORIO It→E *Ninnare, Ninnellare,* to rock, to sing, to lull or dandle children asleep, to lullabie

ninth

1721 MALCOLM *Treatise of Musick* (p. 436) The *Ninth* which is in effect the *2d*, and is only called the *Ninth* to distinguish it from the *2d*, which under that Denomination is used in a different Manner, is in its own Nature a *Discord*.

nizzarda

1659 TORRIANO-FLORIO It→E *Nizzarda,* the name of a French dance.

nocturne *see* lauds

1737 DYCHE-PARDON (2nd edn) *Nocturns* or *Nocturnals* (S.) the *Roman* Catholicks bestow this Name upon that Part of the Church Office or Prayers, which they call also Mattins, which are commonly divided into three Parts, Portions, or Nocturns, because they used to be sung or performed only in the Night, which is still observed in some Cathedrals, where they sing their Mattins at Midnight, in Imitation of the Primitive Christians, who for Fear of Persecution, used to meet only in the Night, which gave their Adversaries an Opportunity to load and accuse them with heinous Crimes.

noel *see* carol

1593 HOLLYBAND Fr→E § *Chanter Noël,* to sing a Christmas Caroll. **1611** COTGRAVE Fr→E *Noel: m.* ... also, a Christmas Caroll; *Nouël: m.* ... also, a Christmas Caroll, or song made to the honour of Christ; § *Nouël nouvelet.* The burden of a Christmas Caroll: *Rab.* **1688** MIEGE-COTGRAVE Fr→E *Noël,* (m.) ... Carol, a Christmas Song, a Song upon our Saviour's Birth.

nola *see* sance bell, tintinabulum

1500 *Ortus Vocabulorum* L→E Nola le. quedam ciuitas campanie. Item nola Illud tintinabulum quod appendit collis canum vel pedibus auium vel aliud quod appenditur frenis & pectoribus equorum: ut cum quodam sonitu incedant equi. Et ampliato noie in uenitur nola pro qualibet parua campana vel pro qualibet campanella refectorij. **1587** THOMAS L→E *Nola, læ, Iun.* A little bell, a saunce or sacring bell. § *Nolæ curator, Iun.* The clocke keeper, the bell or chimekeeper.

non

1724 [PEPUSCH] *Short Explic. of Foreign Words in Mus. Bks.* (p. 49) *Non,* not. Thus, ¶ *Non Troppo Presto,* not too quick. ¶ *Non Troppo Largo,* not too slow. **1726** BAILEY *An Univ. Etymolog. Engl. Dict.* (3rd edn) *Non Troppo Presto* (in *Musick Books*) signifies not too quick, and *Non troppo largo,* not too slow.

1731 PRELLEUR *Modern Musick-Master* (Dictionary, p. 3) *Non,* not as ¶ *Non troppo Presto,* not too Quick ¶ *Non troppo Largo,* not too Slow

nona

1724 [PEPUSCH] *Short Explic. of Foreign Words in Mus. Bks.* (p. 49) *Nona,* Nine, or the Ninth in Number. Thus, ¶ *Opera Nona,* is the Ninth Opera.

nonupla *see* induction, sesqui

1656 BLOUNT (1st edn) *Nonupla,* a quick time in Musick peculiar to Gigs and such like; having nine Crotchets between Bar and Bar. **1658** PHILLIPS (1st edn) *Nonupla,* (a Term in Musick) being a very quick time, and peculiar to *Jiggs.* **1676** COLES *Nonupla,* a quick time (of 9 Crochets) peculiar to Jigs, &c. **1708** KERSEY *Dict. Anglo-Brit.* (1st edn) *Nonupla,* (in *Musick*) a very quick Time, peculiar to Jiggs.

1636 BUTLER *Principles of Musik* (p. 25) *Noncupla* is the *Triple* of the Minim in *Triple* Proportion: when to each Minim in *Triple* Time, is sung 3 blak Minims, 6 to the Fall, and 3 to the Rise of the Hand: which *Triple* is therefore called *Noncupla;* becaus nine of these blak Minims goe to one Sembrief-time. **1736** TANS'UR *Compleat Melody* (3rd edn, p. 66) *Nonupla,* denotes that a *Jigg* must be play'd in very quick Time.

nosegay dance *see* branle

note *see* clef note, degree, driving note, essential notes, holding note, master note, passing note, relative note, tone, trumpet note, whole note

1550 THOMAS It→E *Nota,* a note of songe, or voice. **1598** FLORIO It→E *Nota,* ... a note of musicke. **1611** COTGRAVE Fr→E *Note: f.* also, a note, or tune of Musicke; **1611** FLORIO It→E *Nota,* ... Also a note in

Musike. *Note*, all manner of notes, but often vsed of Poets for pliants, layes, or lamentations. **1688** MIEGE-COTGRAVE Fr→E § *Noter un Livre de Musique*, to prick down the Notes in a Musick-book. **1704** HARRIS *Notes* in Musick, are certain Terms invented to distinguish the Degrees of Sound in Tuning, and the Proportion of Time thereto belonging: For in regard that a Voice doth express a sound best, when it pronounceth some Syllable or Word with it, six select Syllables were formerly used to that purpose, ascending and descending in order, *viz, Vt, Re, Mi, Fa, Sol, La*; but four of them, *viz. Mi, Fa, Sol, La*, being found sufficient for the right Tuning of all the Degrees of Sound, and less burthensome to the Memory, the other two, *Vt* and *Re*, are generally now laid aside as superfluous. It is reported, That *Guido Aretinus*, having undertaken to reduce the *Greek* Scale of Musick to a more regular form about *A.D.* 960, assumed for the Names of those Notes as many Syllables taken out of the *Sapphick* Hymn of St. *John Baptist*, which began thus: ¶ Ut *queant Laxis* REs*onare fibris*, / MI*ra Gestorum* FA*muli tuorum*, / SOL*ve polluti* LA*bii reatum*. ¶ As for other sort of Notes relating to Time, they are Nine in Number, viz. *Large, Long, Breve, Semi-breve, Minim, Crotchet, Quaver, Semi-quaver*, and *Demi-Semiquaver*. The four first are usually termed *Notes of Augmentation*, or *Increase*, and the five last of *Diminution* or *Decrease*. The *Semi-breve* being the last of Augmentation, is commonly called the *Master-Note*, or *Measure-Note*, because it is of a certain determinate *Measure* or Length of *Time* by it self; and all the other Notes both of *Augmentation* and *Diminution*, are measured by, or adjusted to its value: But it ought to be observed, that the *Large* and *Long* are now of little use, as being too long for any Voice or Instrument (the *Organ* only accepted) to hold out to their full length; altho' their *Rests* are still very often used, more especially in Grave Musick, and Songs of many Parts. **1706** KERSEY-PHILLIPS (6th edn) In *Musick*, Notes are certain Terms invented to distinguish the Degrees of Sound, and the Proportion of Time belonging thereto: For this Purpose six choice Syllables were formerly made use of, *viz. Ut, Re, Mi, Fa, Sol, La*; but four of them, *viz. Mi, Fa, So, La*, being found sufficient for the right tuning of all Degrees of Sound; the other two are now generally lade aside as needless. ¶ There are also other sorts of *Notes*, relating to Time, being Nine in Number, *viz.* the *Large, Long, Breve, Semi-breve, Minim, Crotchet, Quaver, Semi-quaver*, and *Demi-Semiquaver*; all which See in their proper Places. The Marks of these Notes are usually set down on a Scale of five or six Lines, to serve as Directions for keeping Time in Singing, or Playing on any Musical Instrument. ¶ Notes of *Augmentation* and *Diminution*. See *Augmentation* [no such entry given] and *Diminution*. **1708** KERSEY *Dict. Anglo-Brit.* (1st edn) *Notes*, ... In *Musick*, certain Terms invented to distinguish, and tune the Degrees of Sound, which are now, generally express'd by four choice Syllables, viz. *Mi, Fa, Sol, La*. ¶ There are also other sorts of *Notes*, relating to Time, *viz.* the *Large, Long, Breve, Semi-breve, Minim*, &c. **1724** [PEPUSCH] *Short Explic. of Foreign Words in Mus. Bks.* (p. 49) *Nota*, a Note, or Character in Musick, of which there are upwards of Fifty different Sorts **1726** BAILEY *An Univ. Etymolog. Engl. Dict.* (3rd edn) *Nota*, a Note or Character. *L.* **1728** CHAMBERS *Notes* ... [*see* Appendix] **1730** BAILEY *Dict. Britannicum* (1st edn) *Notes Musical* (in relation to *Time*) are nine, *viz.* the *Large*, the *Long, Breve, Semi-breve, Minim, Crotchet, Quaver, Semi-quaver*, and *Demi-semi quaver*, all which are to be found in their proper Places. The Characters or Marks of these Notes are usually set down on a Scale of five or six Lines, to serve as Directions for keeping Time in singing, or playing on any sort of musical Instrument. *Notes of Augmentation* (in *Musick*) is the increasing or enlarging somewhat to the full Quantity or Value of any Note. *Notes of Diminution* (in *Musick*) is the diminishing or abating somewhat of the full Quantity or Value of any Note. **1737** DYCHE-PARDON (2nd edn) *Notes* (S.) in *Musick*, are certain Marks or Characters, by which both the Composer and Performer express the several Tones that are designed in the Composition; and those are commonly wrote upon five Lines with additional ones added as Occasion may require, or else with the Cliff changed;

1596 ANON. *Pathway to Musicke* [C] *VVhat is a Note?* ¶ It is a signe shevving the lovvdnes, or stilnes of the voice, and is of tvvo sorts, one simple, & the other ioyned, vvhich are called Ligatures. **early 17th C.** RAVENSCROFT Treatise of Musick BL Add. 19758, f. 9 A note is a sound well tuned shewing allso the Lowdnes or stilnes of the voice; ... **1609** DOWLAND-ORNITHOPARCUS *Micrologvs* (p. 6) ... Now Notes is that by which the highnes, or lownes of a Song is expressed. **1688** SALMON *Proposal to Perform Musick* (p. 31) [from remarks by John Wallis:] And here we are to take notice of the ambiguous or double sence of the word *Note*. Before, it signified one particular Sound or Note, as *la, mi, fa*, &c. but here, when we speak of *Notes* and *Half-*

notes, it signifies an Interval between Note and Note. The *Greeks* had two words for it, *Phthongus*, and *Tonus*; but we use *Note* promiscuously for both. **1725** De La Fond *New System of Music* (p. 12) A *note*, I define, *a musical sound considered with relation to its highness or lowness in the Scale.* § (p. 13) I must distinguish here between *Note* and *Tone*. Some will say, This distinction is so obvious, there's no occasion to spend any time about it. But notwithstanding, *Notes* and *Tones* are strangely confounded, and that, in no less an instance than this very article. They give us not only a self-inconsistent scale of notes, but they likewise call their *notes tones*; and those two names are used promiscuously. For example, their seven natural *notes* are call'd full or whole *tones*, two of them excepted and not excepted, as will soon appear; and their Semi-*tones* are call'd half *notes*. **1731** Prelleur *Modern Musick-Master* ('A Brief History of Musick', p. 12) The Ancients had not the use of five parallel Lines, but instead of them they used but one on which they writ the Names of their Notes which Method he [Guido Aretinus] might have followed with much more ease than they, by reason of the shortness of the Monosyllables before mentioned; but thinking that way not sufficient to express y^e *Grave* and *Acute Sounds*, he brought in the use of four parallel Lines, on and between which he placed certain points & characters which he called Notes.... [*re* the supposed lack of different time values in ancient music] ... Their want of *Notes* of an unequal Length was supplied by one *Iohn de Muris* who about the Year 1330, invented the following Characters [maxima, longa, breve, semibreve, minima, semiminima, croma, semicroma] which have since been called *Notes*, ascribing to every of them a certain length, & proportion in relation to each other.

nugicanoricrepe
1611 Cotgrave Fr→E *Nugicanoricrepe: m.* An idle singer of lyes, or trifling matters. **1650** Howell-Cotgrave Fr→E † *Nugicanoricrepe: m.* An idle singer of lies, or trifling matters.

numero
1724 [Pepusch] *Short Explic. of Foreign Words in Mus. Bks.* (p. 49) *Numero*, Number.

numerus
1552 Huloet L→E *Numerus* Rest in song whyche is a poynct of taciturnitie. § *remittere numeros in cantu* Rest in song. **1565** Cooper L→E § *Canere in cantu numeros. Cic.* To singe measures. *In numerum ludere. Virg.* To daunce or play in measures. **1589** Rider L→E *Numerus, m* A rest in a song.

Nunc Dimittis *see* missura
1619 Wither *Preparation to the Psalter* (p. 111) ... It is further recorded, that *Symeon*, who tooke *Christ* in his armes when hee was an Infant, and sang the Song called *Nunc Dimittis*, was the last in the Temple that euer pronounced יהלה with the proper vowels belonging therevnto; ...

nuptial *see* bridal, epigonium, epithalamy, hillulim, hymen, marriage music, thalassion
1706 Kersey-Phillips (6th edn) *Nuptial*, belonging to a Marriage, or Wedding; as *A Nuptial Song*, the *Nuptial Bed*, &c.

nut *see* sillet
1702 Kersey *New Engl. Dict.* (1st edn) The *Nut* of a cross-bow, musical instrument ...

o
1728 Chambers A Majuscule *O*, in Music, is a Note call'd by us *Semibreve*; by the *Italians*, *Circulo*; making what they call *Tempo perfetto*. See *Note*. ¶ The Antients used *O* as a Mark of triple Time; from a Notion that the Ternary, or Number 3, was the most perfect of Numbers, and therefore properly express'd by a Circle, the most perfect of Figures.

obit *see* dirge, elegy, epicedy, epitaph, monody, nænia, threnody
1656 Blount (1st edn) *Obit (obitus)* .... It is also sometimes taken for an Elegy or Funeral Song. **1676** Coles *Obit, Latin.* ... also a Funeral Song or Office for the dead. **1696** Phillips (5th edn) An *Obit, (Lat.)* an Anniversary-Office for the Dead, an Obsequie, Dirge, or Funeral-Song. **1702** Kersey *New Engl. Dict.* (1st edn) An *Obit*, dirge, *or* Office said for the dead. **1706** Kersey-Phillips (6th edn) *Obit*, a Funeral Solemnity, a Dirge, or Funeral

Song; an Office for the Dead, said every Year: **1708** Kersey *Dict. Anglo-Brit.* (1st edn) *Obit*, a Funeral Solemnity, a Funeral Song; an Office for the Dead, said every Year:

obligata *see* necessario
1724 [Pepusch] *Short Explic. of Foreign Words in Mus. Bks.* (pp. 50-1) *Obligata*, Necessary, Expressly, or on Purpose. Thus, ¶ *A doi Violini Obligati*, on Purpose for Two Violins. ¶ *Con Fagotto Obligate*, on Purpose for the Bassoon. ¶ *Con Viola Obligate*, on Purpose for the Viol. ¶ *Con il Violoncello Obligati*, hereby signifying that the Violoncello Part is very necessary to be performed, and therefore ought not to left out. ¶ It is often used to signify the same Thing as the Words *Necessario* and *Concertante*, for which see the last. **1726** Bailey *An Univ. Etymolog. Engl. Dict.* (3rd edn) *Obligata* (in *Musick Books*) signifies necessary, expresly, or on purpose, as *A doi violini obligati*, on purpose for two Violins; *con Fagotto obligate*, on purpose for the Bassoon; *con il violoncello obligati*, Means that the *Violoncello* Part is very necessary to be perform'd, and therefore ought not to be left out. It also sometimes signifies the same as the Words *Necessario* or *Concertante*, which see. *Ital.*

1736 Tans'ur *Compleat Melody* (3rd edn, p. 72) *Obligato*, (Ital.) signifies, *Necessary*, or on purpose, *i.e.* an *Instrumental Part* is necessary, and ought not to be left out. This is also a Name given to some *Sonata's*.

oboe *see* hautboy, hobois
1724 [Pepusch] *Short Explic. of Foreign Words in Mus. Bks.* (p. 51) *Oboe*, or *Oboy*, is a Hautboy, or Hoboy. **1726** Bailey *An Univ. Etymolog. Engl. Dict.* (3rd edn) *Oboe, Oboy*, (in *Musick Books*) a Hautboy or Hoboy.

occano
1500 *Ortus Vocabulorum* L→E Occano is. nui. occentum. i. contra vel vl undique canere cor. ca. **1538** Elyot L→E *Occano, & occino, occanui, & occini, occanere, & occinere*, to synge agaynst one, to laye in rebuke. **1552** Huloet L→E *Occano. nis. cinui, uel cecini*, Synge agaynste one. **1587** Thomas L→E *Occano, is, ere, entum, Liv.* To sing against one, to say in rebuke.

occentor
1587 Thomas L→E *Occentor, oris, m.g. Iun.* He that singeth the treble. **1589** Rider L→E *Occentor, m.* He that singeth the countertenor.

occentus *see* countertenor
1538 Elyot L→E *Occentus, tus*, where one syngeth against another. It maye be also taken for a countretenor. **1552** Huloet L→E *Occentus. us.* Contratenor in musycke. **1565** Cooper L→E *Occentus, huius occentus, m.g.* Syngyng. **1587** Thomas L→E *Occentus, us, m.g. verb. ab Occino, Valer. Max.* Singing, squeaking

occino
1500 *Ortus Vocabulorum* L→E Occino nis. iui. occentum. to synge agaynn **1538** Elyot L→E *Occino, nere*, to synge to another. **1565** Cooper L→E *Occino, óccinis, pen. corr. occínui, occentum, occínere. Liu.* To singe to an other: to singe agaynst. **1587** Thomas L→E *Occino, is, ui, entum, ere, ex Ob & Cano, Liv.* To sing to another, to sing against. **1589** Rider L→E *Occino, occento, occano, occanto.* To sing to, or against, or the contratenour.

Ockeghem, Johannes *see* counterpoint

octave *see* diapason, eighth, sesquioctava
1598 Florio It→E *Ottauo*, the eight in order, an eight in musicke. **1611** Florio It→E *Ottaua*, an octaue or eight in Musike. **1656** Blount (1st edn) *Octave (octavus)* an eighth in Musick, a proportion or the number of eight. **1658** Phillips (1st edn) *Octave*, (lat.) a musical proportion called an eighth **1676** Coles *Octave*, an Eighth. **1688** Miege-Cotgrave Fr→E *Octave*, (f.) *(en Termes de Musique) la Repetition du premier Son*, an Octave, in Musick. **1702** Kersey *New Engl. Dict.* (1st edn) An *Octave*, the eighth note in Musick; **1704** *Cocker's Engl. Dict.* (1st edn) *Octave*, a Note in Musick, called an Eight. **1704** Harris *Octave*, or *Eighth* in Musick, is an Interval of Eight Sounds; every Eighth Note in the Scale of the *Gam-ut*, being the same as far as the Compass of Musick requires. Tho' an Humane Voice can reach only to three of these *Octaves*, but the Tones of the Organ go as far as Eight. **1706** Kersey-Phillips (6th edn) *Octave*, ... In *Musick*, an Eighth, or an Interval of eight Sounds; every eighth Note in the Scale of the *Gam-ut*, being the same. See *Diapason* and *Tone*. **1707** *Gloss. Angl. Nova* (1st edn) *Octave*, or *Diapason*, an Interval in Musick, whose terms are as 2 to 1. **1724** [Pepusch] *Short Explic. of Foreign Words in Mus. Bks.* (pp. 51-2) *Octava*, or *Ottava*, is Octave; a Term in Musick, otherwise called an Eighth, or an Interval of Eight Sounds. *Ottava*, Octave. See *Octava* above. ¶ This Word also signifies the Number Eight or Eighth. Thus, ¶

Opera Ottava, the Eighth Opera. **1726** BAILEY *An Univ. Etymolog. Engl. Dict.* (3rd edn) *Ottava*, an Octave, an Eighth or Interval of 8 Sounds, *Ital.* **1728** CHAMBERS *Octave* ... [*see* Appendix] **1737** DYCHE-PARDON (2nd edn) *Octave* (S.) is a *Musical Term*, and signifies an Interval of eight inclusive Sounds, or different Degrees of Tone; some make no Difference between the Unison and Octave, but the Truth is, there is a great deal, for the Vibrations of the acuter Tone are twice repeated, for once of the graver; so that the Proportion of Sound forming the two Extreams of an Octave are in Numbers or Lines, as 2 to 1, so that two Chords or Strings of the same Matter, Thickness, and Tension, one whereof is double the Length of the other, produces the Octave, this is also called the Diapason; the Division of the Octave forms all the possible Chords that can be made.

1664 BIRCHENSHA-ALSTED *Templvm Mvsicvm* (p. 59) ... a *Diapason*, which vulgarly they call an *Octave* ... § (p. 93) ... the Distance of a Voice from a Voice by an Eighth; whence it is called an *Octave*. **1705** SALMON *Theory of Musick reduced to Arith. and Geom. Proportions* (*Philos. Trans.*, 1705, p. 2080) Three Tones Major, two Tones Minor, and two of the foresaid Hemitones, placed in the order found in the Scheme [not reproduced here], exactly constitute the practical Octave; which is so call'd because it consists of eight sounds, that contain the seven gradual intervals. **1731** PRELLEUR *Modern Musick-Master* (Dictionary, p. 3) *Octava* or, *Ottava*, an Octave, or an Interval of Eight Notes.

octochordon

1636 BUTLER *Principles of Musik* (p. 20) Octochordon. [marginalia: '*Boet. l.* 1. *c.* 20.'] *Musica quator nervis tota constabat: idq; usq; ad Orpheum duravit, ad imitationem Musicæ Mundanæ, quæ ex quatuor constat elementis. Cujus Quadrichordi Mercurius dicitur Inventor.*

ode *see* cantion, epode, hymn, lyrick, Melpomene, rhapsodi, song, strophe, tragedy, verse

1500 *Ortus Vocabulorum* L→E Odeporium dicit laus cantilene. n.s. **1538** ELYOT L→E *Ode*, a songe. **1565** COOPER L→E *Oda, odæ: siue Ode, odes, f.g.* A songe. **1587** THOMAS L→E *Oda, æ, vel Ode, es, f.g. p.l. Iun.* A song. *vid. Psalmus* [*see* psalm]. **1598** FLORIO It→E *Oda*, a kinde of verse or song, called an ode. *Ode*, songs called odes. **1611** COTGRAVE Fr→E *Ode: f.* ... also, a Poeticall Ode, or Song. **1611** FLORIO It→E *Oda*, a song called an Ode. *Ode*, Odes, songs. **1616** BULLOKAR *Ode.* A song. **1623** COCKERAM *Ode.* A song. *Ode, Hymne, Laye, Caroll.* a Song **1656** BLOUNT (1st edn) *Ode (oda)* a Song, or Poem pronounced with singing. **1658** PHILLIPS (1st edn) *Ode*, (Greek) a Song or Lyrick Poem. **1676** COLES *Ode, Greek.* a song or Lyrick poem. **1702** KERSEY *New Engl. Dict.* (1st edn) An *Ode*, a Poem that is sung to the harp, *or* a copy of *Lyrick* verses; *as* ¶ *Horace's Odes.* **1704** *Cocker's Engl. Dict.* (1st edn) *Ode*, a short Song or Poem, in lyrick verse. **1708** KERSEY *Dict. Anglo-Brit.* (1st edn) *Ode*, a Song, a Poem sung to the Harp, or a Copy of Lyrick Verses. **1728** CHAMBERS *Ode* ... [*see* Appendix] **1737** DYCHE-PARDON (2nd edn) *Ode* (S.) among the *Antients*, signified a Song or Poetical Composition fit for Singing, which was usually performed with the Instrument called the Lyre accompanying the Voice, in Honour of their Gods, Heroes, and Great Men, and sometimes upon other Subjects, from whence such Poems were in general called Lyrick Poems; in the *Modern Poetry*, it is what is called a Lyrick Poem

odelet

1611 COTGRAVE Fr→E *Odelette: f.* A small, or short Ode. *Odette.* as *Odelette.* **1656** BLOUNT (1st edn) *Odelet* (Diminutive of *Ode*) a small or short *Ode.* **1658** PHILLIPS (1st edn) *Odelet*, (dimin.) a short Ode. **1676** COLES *Odelet*, a short or little ¶ *Ode*

odeum

1538 ELYOT L→E *Odæa*, places, wherin syngynge is exercysed. **1552** HULOET L→E *Odæa* the place where musycke is exercised. *Odeum. dei* Place where musycke or songe is exercised. **1565** COOPER L→E *Odeum, odéi, pen. prod. Vitrunius* [sic]. A place wherin singyng is vsed: a place of musike. **1587** THOMAS L→E *Odeum, i, n.g. p.l.* A place in the house appointed for singers or musicke. *vid. Pulpit.* **1589** RIDER L→E *Odæum, n.* A place in the house appointed for singers. *Odeum, n.* A place ordained for minstrels, or singers, to play, or sing in. **1688** DAVIS-TORRIANO-FLORIO It→E *Odeo*, a musick-house, or a place appointed for musick. **1706** KERSEY-PHILLIPS (6th edn) *Odeum*, (among the Ancients) a kind of Musick-Theater; a Place for Rehearsal and Practice, before the Actors and Musicians appear'd, to perform their several Parts on the great Theater. **1728** CHAMBERS *Odeum*, among the Antients, was a Place destined for the Rehearsal of the Music to be sung on the Theatre. ¶ *Odeum* was also used for other Buildings that had no relation to the Theatre: *Pericles* built an *Odeum* at *Athens*, where musical Prizes were contended for. *Pausanias* says, that *Herod* the *Athenian* built a magnificent *Odeum* for the Sepulchre of his Wife. ¶ The *Latin* Writers also used the Word *Odeum* for the Choir of a Church. Grammarians are exceedingly in the dark about the signification of the Word among the Antients. **1737** DYCHE-PARDON (2nd edn) *Odeum* (S.) a Place among the Antients, where the Musicians practised, tried, or rehearsed their Musick before they play'd in the publick Theatres; also where Musical Prizes were strove for by the several Performers; sometimes it signifies the Choir of a Church where they sing the Service.

offertory

1728 CHAMBERS *Offertory*, an Anthem sung, or play'd on the Organ, at the time the People are making an Offering. See *Anthem* and *Offering*. ¶ Antiently the *Offertory* consisted of a Psalm sung with its Anthem; tho it is somewhat dubious whether the Psalm was sung entire; St. *Gregory* mentioning, that when it was time, the Pope looking at the Choir who sung it, gave the Sign when they should end. **1730** BAILEY *Dict. Britannicum* (1st edn) *Offertory* (*offertorium*, L.) ... also a Part of the Popish Mass, an Anthem sung or play'd on the Organ, at the Time the People are making an Offering. **1737** DYCHE-PARDON (2nd edn) *Offertory* (S.) ... in the Church of *Rome*, it is a Part of the Service or Anthem sung to or played upon an Organ, &c. while the People are making their Offering.

office *see* ufficina

oghetto

1598 FLORIO It→E *Oghetto*, a marche that drummers and trumpetters sound, called to the watch, to the round or sentinell. **1611** FLORIO It→E *Oghetto*, a march that Trumpeters and Drummers sound, called, to the watch, to the round or sentinell. **1659** TORRIANO-FLORIO It→E *Oghetto, quasi Au guet* in French, a march or point of war, that Trumpeters or Drummers sound, called, to the watch, to the round, or to the sentinel.

olympicum certamen

1565 COOPER L→E *Olympicum certamen*, Was a game or pryce kept on the hyll of *Olympus*, by all the princes and cities of Greece euery fyfte yere, in the honour of Hercules, who fyrst beganne it. ... There was also contention and victorie of poetes, rhetoricians, musitians, and subtile disputers.

Olympiodorus

1678 PHILLIPS (4th edn) *Olympiodorus*, a famous Musitian, who taught *Epaminondas* to play on the Flute.

omnes

1724 [PEPUSCH] *Short Explic. of Foreign Words in Mus. Bks.* (p. 51) *Omnes*, all; of much the same Use and Signification in Musick as the Word *Tutti*, for which see.

omnicantus

1587 THOMAS L→E *Omnicanus, a, um, Apull.* That can sing or frame it selfe to al tunes. **1589** RIDER L→E *Omnicantus, ad.* That can sing any thing. *Omnicanus* [sic], *ad.* That can sing, or frame himselfe to al tunes.

omophoni *see* symphony

1721 MALCOLM *Treatise of Musick* (pp. 507-8) The Extremes *Dia-pason* and *Disdia-pason*, *Ptolomy* calls *Omophoni* or *Unisons*, because they agree as one Sound... Others call those [intervals] of equal Degree *Omophoni* ...

opera *as stage work, see* academy, carnival, dialogue, eunuch, glory, gobbo, overture, recitative, ridotta, symphony, violone

1656 BLOUNT (1st edn) *Opera* (Lat.) ... In Italy it signifies a Tragedy, Tragi-comedy, Comedy or Pastoral, which (being the studied work of a Poet) is not acted after the vulgar manner, but performed by Voyces in that way, which the Italians term *Recitative*, being likewise adorned with Scenes by Perspective, and extraordinary advantages by Musick. The common Plays (which are not *Opera's*) are performed *ex tempore* by the Actors, and are but in the nature of *Farces* or Gigs, wanting the above mentioned adoruments [sic] **1658** PHILLIPS (1st edn) *Opera*, a kinde of Dramatick Poem, in use among the *Italians*, performed by voyces and instrumental Musick in a recitative stile, and adorned with Scenes by Perspective. **1659** TORRIANO-FLORIO It→E *Opera, Opra*, ... now adaies taken for a Comedy or Tragedy sung all in Musick, and represented with variety and change of scenes, as is annually to be seen at *Venice* in Carneval times, and in other Cities of *Italy* upon great occasions, as of Marriages or reception of great Personages **1676** COLES *Opera, Latin.* (labour) an Italian Recitative play performed by voices, adorned with Musick and Perspective Scenes. **1688** MIEGE-COTGRAVE Fr→E

Opera, (m.) *sorte de Comedie en Musique,* an Opera, a kind of Play with Songs and Musick. § *L'Opera a eté long,* it was a long Opera. *Un bel Opera,* a fine Opera. **1702** KERSEY *New Engl. Dict.* (1st edn) An *Opera,* a kind of play, with variety of songs and musick. **1704** *Cocker's Engl. Dict.* (1st edn) *Opera,* the *Italian* stage-plays, with Scenes, Musick, Singing, and Dancing. **1704** HARRIS *Opera,* is a sort of Solemn Entertainment of Musick upon the Theatre or Stage, and is very common in *France* and *Italy*: It usually begins with an *Ouverture,* which commonly ends with a *Fugue;* the rest is composed of *Symphonys, Recitativo's, Chacoons, Preludes,* &c. with all sorts of Vocal and Instrumental Musick. **1706** KERSEY-PHILLIPS (6th edn) *Opera,* a kind of Stage-Play, very common among the *Italians* and *French,* performed by Voices and Instrumental Musick, and adorn'd with variety of Scenes in Perspective. **1707** *Gloss. Angl. Nova* (1st edn) *Opera,* is a sort of Solemn Entertainment of Musick upon the Theatre or Stage, and is very common in *France* and *Italy.* **1728** CHAMBERS *Opera,* a Dramatic Composition set to Music, and sung on the Stage; accompanied with musical Instruments; and enrich'd with magnificent Dressings, Machines, and other Decorations. ¶ *Bruyere* says, that 'tis essential to the *Opera* to keep the Mind, the Eyes, and Ears in an Enchantment: *S. Evremond* calls the *Opera* a chimerical Assemblage of Poetry and Music; where the Poet and Musician each cramp the other. ¶ The *Opera* we derive from the *Venetians,* among whom 'tis held one of the principal Glories of their Carneval. See *Comedy.* ¶ While the *English* and *French* Comic and Tragic Theatres were forming, the *Venetians* invented the *Opera*: The Abbot *Perrin,* Introductor of Embassadors to *Gaston* Duke of *Orleans,* was the first who form'd the Design of introducing 'em into *Paris;* and he obtain'd the King's Privilege for the same in 1669. And it was not long e'er it pass'd thence into *England.* The Spectator observes, that the *French* Music agrees with their Accent and Pronunciation, much better than the *English;* and are at the same time better calculated for the gay Humour of that People. See *Recitative.* ¶ At *Rome* they have a kind of *Spiritual Opera's,* frequent in Lent; consisting of Dialogues, Duos, Trios, Ritornella's, Chorus's, *&c.* The Subject whereof is taken out of the Scripture, the Life of some Saint, or the like. The *Italians* call 'em *Oratorio*: The Words are frequently *Latin;* and sometimes *Italian.* **1730** BAILEY *Dict. Britannicum* (1st edn) *Opera,* a dramatick Composition, set to Musick, and sung on the Stage, attended with musical Instruments, and inrich'd with stately Dressings, Machines and other Decorations; the *Opera* was first used by the *Venetians,* with whom it is one of the principal Glories of their *Carnaval.* It was afterwards used by the *French,* and now by us. **1731** KERSEY *New Engl. Dict.* (3rd edn) An *Opera,* a Kind of Stage-play with variety of Scenes and Musick. **1735** DEFOE *Opera,* a sort of musical Entertainment upon the Stage or Theatre. **1737** DYCHE-PARDON (2nd edn) *Opera* (S.) a Play or Dramatick Performance set to Musick, and sung with the Accompaniment of Instruments, rich Machines, and extraordinary Habits; the *Venetians* were the first Inventors of this Manner of acting, it being the chief Glory of their Carnival; about the Year 1669, the Abbot *Perrin* obtained a Grant from *Lewis* XIV. to set up an Opera at *Paris,* who in 1672 acted *Pomona;* now they are in great Esteem in *England,* and generally set to Musick by Mr. *Handel.*

c.1698-c.1703 NORTH Cursory Notes (*C-K CN* p. 227) An entertainment composed is called an opera, an Itallian terme, opposed to the free buffoon performances of the ordinary actors of comedy, who by custome, play the fool upon the stage without premeditation, and to use the similitude act plays voluntary... **1709** [RAGUENET] *Comparison betw. Fr. and It. Musick and Opera's* (p. 65) [*re* the Italians and their invention of opera] Some Years ago, they gave the Name of Opera to all those Plays here in *London* as had any Musical Dialogues intermix'd with the Scenes; for no other reason, in my Opinion, but because there were several Chorus's and Dances added, after the manner of the *French.* **c.1726** NORTH Musicall Gramarian BL Add. 32533, f. 119 ... Here at present wee drop these, and Retire from the Church to the theater, where in our age Musick seem's to Mount her throne. There are the Enterteinem^{ts} called Operas, or Composures, to distinguish them from the ordinary Itallian comedy's, wch were sciolti, or loosly acted quasi Extempore. **1728** NORTH Musicall Grammarian (*C-K MG* ff. 138-138v) The semi-operas at the theaters ¶ It had bin strange if the gentlemen of the theaters had sate still all this while [i.e. during the existence of the 'musick meeting'], seeing as they say a pudding creep, that is a violent inclination in the towne to follow musick, and they not serve themselves of it. Therefore Mr. Betterton who was the cheif inginerr of the stage, contrived a sort of plays, which were called operas but had bin more properly styled semioperas, for they consisted of half musick, and half drama; the cheif of these were Circe, The Fayery Queen, Dioclesian and King Arthur; which latter was composed by Purcell and is unhappyly lost.

opera *as works*
1724 [PEPUSCH] *Short Explic. of Foreign Words in Mus. Bks.* (pp. 51-2) *Opera;* the Signification of this Word is so well known that it needs no Explanation: I shall only observe, That it properly signifies Work, and is thus often used. ¶ *Opera Prima,* First Work. ¶ *Opera Seconda,* Second Work.

1731 PRELLEUR *Modern Musick-Master* (Dictionary, p. 3) *Opera,* signifies properly a Work as Opera prima the first Work, Opera II[a.] Second Work, Opera III[a.] Third Work, &c. It signifies also a Tragedy or Pastoral &c set to Musick **after 1731** ANON. *Directions for Playing on the Flute* (Dictionary, n.p.) *Opera*: signifies properly a work, as *Opera prima,* first work. also a tragedy, or pastoral, set to musick.

opera tone *see* tone

opunculo
1538 ELYOT L→E *Opuncalo,* he that syngethe lyke to a sheparde. **1552** HULOET L→E *Opuncalo. onis* Singer lyke a shepard. **1587** THOMAS L→E *Opunculo, onis, m.g. Fest.* He that singeth like a sheapheard. **1589** RIDER L→E *Opunculo, m.* A singer like a sheepheard.

oratorio *see* opera
1659 TORRIANO-FLORIO It→E *Oratorio, Oratoio, ...* also an oratory, a closet or private chappel where prayers are said, anthems sung, also a Pulpit.

1709 [RAGUENET] *Comparison betw. Fr. and It. Musick and Opera's* (p. 29) [marginalia for '**Oratorio's*':] *A piece of Sacred History Compos'd in three or four Parts.

orchessa
1611 FLORIO It→E *Orchessa,* as *Orca* [being 'a kind of great vessell, or earthen pot']. Also a kinde of great base Violl, or such instrument. **1659** TORRIANO-FLORIO It→E *Orchessa,* as *Orca,* by Met. a great or base-viol.

orchestra
1587 THOMAS L→E *Orchestra, æ, f.g.* A place betweene the stage and the common seats, wherein Senatours and Noble personages satte to behold plaies and open games: sometime the sessions of the Senate: a theatre or scaffold whereon musitians, singers, and such like shew their cunning. **1598** FLORIO It→E *Orchestra,* a theatre or scaffolde where musitions and singers sit, a chiefe place in a theatre. **1611** FLORIO It→E *Orchestra,* a Theater wherein musitions and singers sit, a chiefe place betweene the Stage and the common seates of a Theater. Also a dancing place. **1658** PHILLIPS (1st edn) *Orchester,* (Greek) that part of the Scene in a Theater, where the *Chorus* useth to dance; it is also sometimes taken for the place where the Musicians sit. **1659** TORRIANO-FLORIO It→E *Orchestra,* a chief place between the common seats and the stage of a Theater whereon Players or Dancers act their parts, or where Musitians and Singers sit privately, used also for a dancing place or School § *Orchestrica prosessione,* the dancing procession. **1662** PHILLIPS (2nd edn) *Orchestre,* (Greek) that part of the Scene in a Theater, where the *Chorus* useth to dance; it is also sometimes taked [sic] for the place where the Musicians sit. **1676** COLES *Orchestre, Greek.* the place where the Chorus danceth, or where the Musicians sit. **1688** MIEGE-COTGRAVE Fr→E *Orchestre,* (f.) *Terme de Comedie,* the Musick-Room. ¶ This Word comes originally from the Greek Word ὀρχήστρα, and this from ὀρχέομαι to dance, because 'twas in the *Orchestra,* being the Stage (or middle) of the Theater, whereon the Chorus danced. Whereas, among the Romans, Orchestra was the Space between the Stage and the common Seats, wherein Senators and noble Personages sat to see Play's acted, such as are now our Boxes by the Stage. But *Orchestre* in French do's signify now adais the Musick-room. ¶ *Presentement* (say's *Mr. Richelet) on appelle Orchestre parmi nous le Lieu où l'on enferme la Symphonie & tous les Jouëurs d'Instrumens de Musique, qui jouënt entre les Actes des Pieces dramatiques, & les Entrées des Balets.* **1696** PHILLIPS (5th edn) *Orchestre, (Greek)* that part in a Theatre between the Scene where the Players acted, and the Seats where the Spectators sate. **1706** KERSEY-PHILLIPS (6th edn) *Orchestra (Gr.)* the Pit of the *Roman* Playhouse, where the Senators were seated; but among the *Greeks,* it was the Place where they danc'd or kept their Balls, which made part of their Plays: It is now taken for the Musick-Gallery, or Place where the Musicians sit. **1707** *Gloss. Angl. Nova* (1st edn) *Orchestre,* the place where the Chorus Danceth, or where Musitians sit. **1724** [PEPUSCH] *Short Explic. of Foreign Words in Mus. Bks.* (p. 52) *Orchestra,* is that Part of the Theater, where the Musicians sit with their Instruments to perform. **1730** BAILEY

Dict. Britannicum (1st edn) *Orchestra* (of ὀρχεῖσθαι, Gr. to dance) the lower part of the antient Theatre, where they kept their Balls; it was in Form of a Semicircle and surrounded with Seats. It is now taken for a Musick Gallery.

1712 WEAVER *Essay towards History of Dancing* (p. 9) [marginalia:] **Orchestra* was the place in which the Chorus us'd to Dance and Sing.

ordinanza

1598 FLORIO It→E *Ordinanza,* ... Also the name of a march, sounded in time of warre by trompetters, an array, or marshalling in order. **1611** FLORIO It→E *Ordinanza,* ... Also a march vpon Drum or Trumpets, calling to an armie, or filing of men. **1659** TORRIANO-FLORIO It→E *Ordinanza,* ... also the name of a March upon Drumm and Trumpet to call Souldiers to their colours, to their files, and to range and marshal themselves in due order.

ordines majores

1706 KERSEY-PHILLIPS (6th edn) *Ordines Majores* (*i.e.* Superior Orders) the Holy Orders of Priest, Deacon, and Sub-Deacon, anciently so call'd; as the Inferiour Orders of Chanter, Psalmist, Ostiary, Reader, Exorcist, and Acolyte, were termed *Ordines Minores.*

ordines minores

1708 KERSEY *Dict. Anglo-Brit.* (1st edn) *Ordines Minores,* the Inferiour Orders of Chanter, Psalmist, Reader, *&c.*

organ

see basso continuo, bearing, bellows, cabinet organ, canon, cantes, diapason, double bass, hydraulicks, marche, musics, organum hydraulicum, orgues, positive, stop

1500 *Ortus Vocabulorum* L→E Organum ni. est generale nomen omniuz instrumentorum: vel vasoruz musicorum. **1538** ELYOT L→E *Organa,* all instrumentes of musyke. **1552** HULOET L→E *Organa. orum* Instrumentes of musicke. *Organa. orum* Organes. **1565** COOPER L→E § *Afficiuntur animi in diuersum habitum organis. Quintil.* with musicall instrumentes mens mindes are moued to sundrie affections. *Organa per excellentiam dicuntur omnia musicorum instrumenta. Quint.* All musicall instrumentes. **1587** THOMAS L→E *Organum, ni, n.g.* ... an instrument of musicke § *Organum pueumaticum* [sic], *Vitruv.* The organes or organ pipes. **1599** MINSHEU-PERCYVALL Sp→E *Organo,* m. an instrument, the organes. **1611** FLORIO It→E *Organeggiare,* to play on Organes **1659** TORRIANO-FLORIO It→E *Organare,* ... also to give Organes motion or voice. **1676** COLES *Organ, Greek.* an instrument. **1696** PHILLIPS (5th edn) *Organ,* the noblest of Musical Instruments, serving for Church-Musick. **1702** KERSEY *New Engl. Dict.* (1st edn) An *Organ, or* instrument. A *pair of Organs,* a most melodious musical instrument. § The *Organ-keys.* The *Organ-pipes.* **1706** KERSEY-PHILLIPS (6th edn) *Organ* (Gr.) properly signifies an Instrument us'd in the carrying on of any Work, and it was often taken for a Musical one: Whence the word is now generally apply'd to the Noblest of Musical Instruments which serves for Church-Musick. **1721** BAILEY *An Univ. Etymolog. Engl. Dict.* (1st edn) *Organ,* (*Organe, F. Organum, L.* of ὄργανον, *Gr.*) the noblest of Musical Instruments, commonly used in Churches. **1724** [PEPUSCH] *Short Explic. of Foreign Words in Mus. Bks.* (p. 52) *Organo,* an Organ, an Instrument very well known. § (p. 52) *Organo Picciolo,* a Small or Chamber Organ is so called. **1726** BAILEY *An Univ. Etymolog. Engl. Dict.* (3rd edn) *Organo,* an Organ. *Ital.* as *organo Picciolo,* a small or Chamber Organ. **1728** CHAMBERS *Organ* ... [*see* Appendix] **1730** BAILEY *Dict. Britannicum* (1st edn) Organ ... also a musical Instrument used in Churches. ¶ *Organs* were first introduced into the Church about the Year 657. In the Cathedral of *Ulm* in *Germany* is an *Organ* 93 foot high, and 28 broad (the biggest Pipe 13 Inches diameter) and has 16 pair of Bellows to blow it. **1731** KERSEY *New Engl. Dict.* (3rd edn) An *Organ,* a Pair of *Organs,* a noble Sort of Musical Instrument. **1737** DYCHE-PARDON (2nd edn) *Organ* (S.) ... in *Musick,* it is the largest and most harmonious of all Instruments, being a Collection or Imitation of all others, and now generally used only in Churches, of which there are Differences, both according to the Art of the Builder, and the Charge bestowed on it; there are some of a smaller Size for the Use of the Chamber, and therefore called Chamber Organs.

1582 *Batman vppon Bartholome* (p. 423) *Organum* is a generall name of all instruments of musicke, and is neuerthelesse specially appropriate to the instrument that is made of many pipes, and blowen with bellowes, and vsed onelye in Churches, in Proses, Sequences, and Himnes. ¶ (*Or is for his [the organ's] loudnesse, neerest agreeing to the voyce of man.) **1619** WITHER *Preparation to the Psalter* (p. 88) The Church of the Christians hath made use of many [instruments]: as, the *Harpe, Psaltery, Violls, Sackbut, Trumpet, Cornet,*

Recorder, Orphurion, Bandore, Organs, and such like: but the Instrument, which hath beene accounted as the principall of all these, and most fit for Church assemblies, is that which we call the *Organnes;* An Instrument, as S. *Ierome* writes, vsed in *Ierusalem*, and yeelding such a sound, that might haue beene heard a myle; ... **1636** BUTLER *Principles of Musik* (p. 94) *Organ*. Of the Greeke ὄργανον, *Propriè Instrumentum*: and Synecdochicè *Instrumentum Musicum*: (as *Plut.* [sic] Sympos. 9. 'Οργάνων καίρουσι τοῖ επιτερπὲς ἤκουσι: and 1 Chron. 23 5. 4000 praised the Lord with the Instruments which *David* made: which, because they were used in the service of God, ar elswhere called the Instruments of God) and, by a Metalepsis of the same Synecdoche, this *Polyaulon organon*, this grand winde-Instrument is signifyed: (as Iob 21. 12. and Psal. 150. 4.) beeing so called κατεξοχήν (*per excellentiam*) becaus it is the most excellent Musical Instrument of all. **c.1714-20** TUDWAY history of music BL Harley 7342 (*CHo* f. 13) The word Organum, is of so extensive a signification, that tis almost imposible to guess what maner of instrument, a Musical Organ, so often mention'd in scripture, was; it is certain, that Organs, whatever they were, have not been us'd in ye Western X^tian^ Church, above 4 or 500 years, & tis as certain, that ye inventors therof, made but a small progress, in comeing to any perfection; ¶ A Church Organ consisted then, but of 5 or 6 stops, wch might perhapps take up, 200, or 250 pipes of wood; whereas, tis nothing now, to have Organs, of 15, or 20 stopps, all, or most of Metal, consisting of 1200, or 1500 pipes; Besides those stops, properly call'd Organical, our Modern Artists, have invented stops, wch imitate ye Cornet, Trumpet, flute, Vox humane, Ecchos, Bassones, violins & wth severall others, less frequent; ... **1731** PRELLEUR *Modern Musick-Master* (Dictionary, p. 3) *Organo*, signifies properly an Organ, but when it is written over any Piece of Musick, then it signifies ye Thorough Bass.

organarius

1538 ELYOT L→E *Organarij*, makers of instrumentes. **1552** HULOET L→E *Organarij, orum*. makers of such instrumentes [organa]. **1565** COOPER L→E *Organárius, huius organárij, m.g. Firmicus*. A maker of instrumentes. **1587** THOMAS L→E *Organarius, rij, m.g. Firm.* A maker of instrumentes ... **1589** RIDER L→E *Organarius, m.* A maker of instrumentes. **1599** MINSHEU-PERCYVALL Sp→E **Organero*, one that maketh or selleth organs. **1611** FLORIO It→E *Organaro*, an Organe-maker.

organetti

1598 FLORIO It→E *Organetti*, little slender organs or pipes. **1611** FLORIO It→E *Organetti*, claricords, little Organes.

organical

1728 CHAMBERS *Organical*, in the antient Music, was that Part performed with Instruments. See *Music*. ¶ The *Organical* comprehended three Kinds of Instruments; *viz. Wind Instruments*, as the Trumpet, Flute, *&c. Stringed Instruments*, as the Lute, Lyre, *&c.* And *Pulsatile Instruments*, or those play'd on by beating, as Drums, *&c.* See each in its place, *Trumpet, &c.*

organical music

1609 DOWLAND-ORNITHOPARCUS *Micrologvs* (p. 2) *Organicall Musicke* (as *Cœlius* writeth) is that which belongeth to artificiall Instruments: or it is a skill of making an *Harmony* with beating, with fingring, with blowing: with beating, as Drums, Tabors, and the like: with blowing, as Organs, Trumpets, Fluits, Cornets: with fingring, as those Instruments which are commanded, either with the touching of the fingers, or articulating of the Keyes. Yet such Instruments as are too voluptuous, are by *Cœlius Rodiginus* reiected.

organist *see* accompaniment, harpsichord, marche, pedal, positive

1500 *Ortus Vocabulorum* L→E Organista te. qui vel q in tali instrumento canit. an^e^. an organyster. c.p. **1565** COOPER L→E *Organici. Lucret.* They that play on instrumentes. **1587** THOMAS L→E *Organici, orum, m.g. Lucr.* They that play on instruments. *Organista, Iun.* An organe player. **1593** HOLLYBAND Fr→E *Organiste*, he that plaieth vpon the Organes: *m.* **1598** FLORIO It→E *Organista*, an organist, a plaier on organs. **1599** MINSHEU-PERCYVALL Sp→E **Horganista*, vide *Organista*, an organist, a plaier on the organes. *Organista*, m. a player on the organes. **1611** COTGRAVE Fr→E *Organiste: m.* An Organist; one that vsually playes on a paire of Organs. **1611** FLORIO It→E *Organista*, an Organist, a Player on Organes. **1616** BULLOKAR *Organist*. A player vpon Organs. **1623** COCKERAM *Organist*. That playeth on Organs. **1656** BLOUNT (1st edn) *Organist (organista)* an Organ player. **1676** COLES *Organist*, an Organ-player. **1688** MIEGE-COTGRAVE Fr→E *Organiste*, (m.) from *Orgue*, an Organist; a Player on the Organes. § *Un bon Organiste*, a good Organist. **1696** PHILLIPS (5th edn) *Organist*, one that plays upon the Organ

1702 KERSEY *New Engl. Dict.* (1st edn) An *Organist*, a player on ¶ A *pair of Organs* 1704 *Cocker's Engl. Dict.* (1st edn) *Organist*, one that plays on a Musical Instrument, called an *Organ.* 1706 KERSEY-PHILLIPS (6th edn) *Organist*, one Skill'd in Playing upon the Musical Organ. 1737 DYCHE-PARDON (2nd edn) *Organist* (S.) a Musician that is skilled in, or plays upon the Instrument called the Organ.

organizo
1500 *Ortus Vocabulorum* L→E Organizo as. i. organo cantare ... 1589 RIDER L→E *Organizo.* To plaie vpon the Organes.

organon
1728 NORTH Musicall Grammarian (*C-K MG* ff. 120v-121) [*re* music in the time of the later Roman emperors] Wee allow it to have flourished in the courts of the latter emperors, for in one of the august historians it is complained that the emperor spent his time in his pallaces with hearing of organs. This is the first notice taken of organs in history. The word organon is to be mett with in authors sooner, but crittiques say that organon was a word comonly applyed to most musicall instruments, and the organon hydraulicon distinguish't the multifistular engin; and it may be depended on that this was the mother of our musicall scale, and of all consort of harmony.

organum hydraulicum *see* hydraulicks, organ
1721 MALCOLM *Treatise of Musick* (p. 470) We hear [in ancient accounts] also of *Organs*, blown at first by a Kind of Air-pump, where also Water was some way used, and hence called *Organum Hydraulicum;* but afterwards they used Bellows.

orgues *see* pedal, souffler
1611 COTGRAVE Fr→E *Orgues: f.* Organs; wind-instruments; § *Suppied d'orgues.* The footstoole, or pedalls to a paire of Organs. 1688 MIEGE-COTGRAVE Fr→E *Orgue*, (masc. and fem. in the Sing. Number, and always fem. in the Plural) an Organ, a pair of Organs. § *De belles Orgues*, fine Organs. *Toucher (jouër) de l'Orgue*, to play on the Organs. *Toucher l'Orgue*, to play upon the Organ *Tuiau d'Orgue*, an Organ-pipe. *Tuyaux, Claviers, & Souflets d'Orgue*, the Pipes, the Keyes, and Bellows of an Organ. *Un Facteur d'Orgues*, an Organ-maker. 1706 KERSEY-PHILLIPS (6th edn) *Orgues (Fr.)* a pair of Organs, a Musical Instrument;

orgy
1538 ELYOT L→E *Orgia*, ceremonies or songes, pertaynyng to infernall goddes, or to Bacchus. 1565 COOPER L→E *Orgia, ôrum, n.g. plur.* Ceremonies or songes perteyninge to infernall goddes, or to Bacchus.

oricalco
1598 FLORIO It→E *Oricalco*, ... Also taken for a trumpet. 1611 FLORIO It→E *Oricalco*, shining-brasse. Also a Trumpet. 1659 TORRIANO-FLORIO It→E *Oricalco*, any kind of shining brasse or copper mixed with some Gold, and of its colour, used also for a shrill sounding Trumpet.

Orion
1500 *Ortus Vocabulorum* L→E Orion etiam inuenitur pro quodam citharedo et tune produ. pe. sed primam cor.

ornament *see* formality, grace

Ornithoparcus *see* mensural music, time

orpharion *see* entata, orphean harp (Orpheus)

Orpheus *see* heroic, Linus, lyre, octochordon, siren
1565 COOPER L→E *Orpheus*, A Thracian borne, sonne of Negrus, and Polymnia, or (as some write) of Apollo and Calliope, an auncient poete and harper moste excellent. He (as the poetes surmised) dyd with his musike delyte wylde beastes and infernall spirites, and moued stones with his sweete harmonie: wherby he recouered his wyfe *Eurydice* out of hel. At the last he was slayne with lightnyng, or (as some write) torne in peeces by women, because that for the sorow of his wyfe *Eurydice*, he did not onely himselfe refuse the loue of many women, and lyued a sole lyfe, but also disswaded other from the company of women. 1623 COCKERAM *Orpheus*, a cunning Harper, who by his excellent Musique, drew after him wilde beasts, Woods, and mountaines, and thereby recouered his wife from hell. 1656 BLOUNT (1st edn) *Orphean*, belonging to *Orpheus* the *Thracian* Poet, who is feigned to have plaid so excellently upon the Harp, that he drew Stones, Woods and Trees after him, *&c.* Hence we say, an *Orphtan* [sic] *Harp.* 1658 PHILLIPS (1st edn) *Orpheus*, a famous Poet, and Musician of *Thrace*, the son of *Calliope* and *Apollo*, he took so heavily the losse of his wife *Euridice* ... that he utterly abandoned the

company of women, for which he was torn in pieces by the *Mænades* at the Feast of *Bacchus*, and his several members being cast down the River *Hebrus* were gathered up by the Muses and buried, and his Harp translated up to Heaven. **1678** PHILLIPS (4th edn) *Orpheus*, a famous Poet and Musician of *Thrace*, the Son of *Calliope* and *Apollo*. He took so heavily the loss of his Wife *Euridice* ... that he utterly abandoned the company of Women; for which he was torn in pieces by the *Mænades*, at the Feast of *Bacchus*, and his several Members being cast down the River *Hebrus*, were gathered up by the Muses and buried, and his Harp translated up to Heaven. Others say, he was the Son of *Oeagrius*, and that receiving a Harp from *Mercury*, he became so excellent a player on it, that he charmed the most savage Creatures into civility, and gave Sence to the very Stones and Trees. **1736** BAILEY *Dict. Britannicum* (2nd edn) *Orpheus* ... according to the poets, was the son of *Apollo* and *Calliope*, a very great philosopher and an extraordinary musician, and as such bore away the palm from all that had been before him. *Mercury*, they say, made him a present of his harp, and he play'd so exquisitely well upon it, that he stopp'd the course of rivers, laid storm, drew the most savage animals after him, to divert themselves with his excellent harmony; and that rocks and trees were seen to move at the sound of his musick: But besides having lost by death his wife *Euridice*, he went after her to the gates of hell, where he play'd with that dexterity, that *Pluto*, *Prosperine*, *&c.* were ravish'd with the melody, and granted him to carry his wife back with him, to live on earth again, upon condition, that in his return he should not look back upon her till he was come to the light; but he breaking the condition by looking back upon her, her guard dragg'd her back to Hell, at which he grew so disconsolate, that he resolved never more to entertain any affection for a woman **1737** DYCHE-PARDON (2nd edn) *Orpheus* (S.) a Person famous for all Sorts of Learning among the Antients, but especially for Musick, for which Reason the Poets have made him the Son of *Apollo*, and say that his Harmony was so very efficacious, that it would stop the Course of Rivers, and that Rocks, Trees, and Beasts would dance after him; he is said to go down into Hell, and there so charmed *Cerberus*, that he brought away *Eurydice* his Wife; that some *Thracian* Woman killed him, for his endeavouring to persuade Men to live unmarried; but the *Muses* took Care of his Body, and his Harp was translated among the Stars, where it is now a Constellation.

oscillation *see* vibration
1736 TANS'UR *Compleat Melody* (3rd edn, p. 72) *Oscillancy*, *Oscillation*, or *Vibration*. (Lat.) signifies, either swinging, waving, shaking, or trembling, *&c.*

oscula *see* ventige
1706 KERSEY-PHILLIPS (6th edn) *Oscula (Lat.)* the holes in a Pipe:

ottava *see* octave

ovation *see* ovo
1538 ELYOT L→E *Ouatio*, a small triumph of a prince or captayne, whiche had victorie of his enmies [sic] without slaughter of men, or where battayle was not denounced: in the whyche tryumph the capitayne went on foote, or onely dyd ryde on a horse, with a garland of myrtelles on his heed, and his souldyours syngynge aboute hym. **1565** COOPER L→E *Ouátio, huius ouatiônis, f.g. Verbale. Gell.* A small triumph of a prince or capitaine for a victorie without slaughter of men. In which he did eyther goe on foote, or ride on horsebacke with his souldiours aboute him singynge or shoutynge for ioye, and wearyng on his heade a garlande of mirtell. **1587** THOMAS L→E *Ovatio, onis, f.g. p.b. ab Ovo, as.* A small triumph of a Prince or Captaine for a victorie without slaughter of men, in which he did either goe on foote, or ride on horsebacke with his souldiers about him singing, or shouting for ioy, and wearing on his head a garland of mirtle. **1589** RIDER L→E *Ovatio, f.* A triumph of a Prince, or captaine, for a victory without slaughter of men, in which hee, with his souldiers did sing, and shoute forth. **1611** FLORIO It→E *Ouare*, to shout for ioy, to reioyce with noise **1656** BLOUNT (1st edn) *Ovation* ... a smal triumph of a Prince or Captain for a Victory obtained without slaughter of men, in which he did either go on foot or ride on horseback with his Souldiers about him, singing or shouting for joy **1659** TORRIANO-FLORIO It→E *Ovare*, ... also to shout, to hollow, to sing, to joy or rejoyce with making a great noyse. *Ovatione*, an ovation, which was a kind of mean and ordinary triumph of a Captain or General for any victory obtained without slaughter of men, or effusion of blood which was done riding on horse-back before his Souldiers, singing and shouting for joy, and crowned with a Garland of Mirtle leaves **1706** KERSEY-

PHILLIPS (6th edn) *Ovation* (among the *Romans*) a kind of petty Triumph for a Victory, won without the spilling of much Blood, or for the defeating of Rebels, Slaves, Pirates, or other unworthy Enemies of the Common-wealth. It is so call'd from the Soldiers following their Commander, shouting and singing *O, O*; or from *Ovis, i.e.* a Sheep, which us'd to be sacrific'd to *Jupiter*, upon that occasion; **1737** DYCHE-PARDON (2nd edn) *Ovation* (S.) was an inferior Sort of Triumph, which the *Romans* allowed the Generals of their Army, when the Victory they had obtained was not very considerable, or when the War had not been declared according to Form of Law; ... The triumphing Party entered with Flutes, and not with Trumpets, nor were they admitted to wear an embroidered Garment, as at the great Triumphs

overture *see* entrée, flourish, interlude, intrada, opera, prelude, ricercar, toccata, voluntary
1702 KERSEY *New Engl. Dict.* (1st edn) An *Overture*, ... *also* a flourish of musick before the opening of the Scenes in a stage-play. **1704** HARRIS *Ouverture*, is a kind of Musick, usually played at the Opening or Beginning of an Opera; it commonly ends with a *Fugue*. **1706** KERSEY-PHILLIPS (6th edn) *Overture (Fr.)* ... also a Flourish of Musick, before the Scenes are open'd in a Play-house, especially before the beginning of an *Opera*. **1724** [PEPUSCH] *Short Explic. of Foreign Words in Mus. Bks.* (p. 52) *Overture*, is the Beginning, or First Part, or Strain of a Piece of Musick, and is much the same as *Prelude*. **1728** CHAMBERS *Ouverture*, or *Overture, Opening*, or *Preluding*; a Term used for the Solemnities at the beginning of a public Act, or Ceremony; as of an Opera, Tragedy, Concert of Music, *&c.* ¶ The *Overture* of the Theatre, or Scene, is a piece of Music, usually ending with a Fugue. ¶ The *Overture* of the Jubilee is a general Procession, *&c.* **1735** DEFOE *Overture*, ... also a piece of Musick before the Scenes are opened in a Play. **1737** DYCHE-PARDON (2nd edn) *Overture* (S.) ... in *Musick*, it is a fine Flourish, or running Division played by one or many Instruments, commonly before the Beginning of an Opera.

1731 PRELLEUR *Modern Musick-Master* (Dictionary, p. 3) *Ouverture* the Opening or Be[ginning] of an Opera or sometimes as a Prelude to any Piece of Musick.

ovo *see* ovation
1565 COOPER L→E § *Acies iuuenum ouans. Virgil.* Singyng or reioysinge triumphantly. **1587** THOMAS L→E *Ovo, as, p.b. Valer.* To reioyse with noyse, or shout with a multitude: to sing for ioy. **1589** RIDER L→E *Ovo.* To sing for ioy.

P

p *see* piano, piu
1724 [PEPUSCH] *Short Explic. of Foreign Words in Mus. Bks.* (p. 53) The Letter P is often used as an Abbreviation of the Word *Piano*: And *PP* as an Abbreviation of the Words *Piu Piano*: And *PPP* as an Abbreviation of the Word *Pianissimo*, for which see. **1726** BAILEY *An Univ. Etymolog. Engl. Dict.* (3rd edn) *P* (in *Musick Books*) stands for *Piando* [sic]. *Ital.* *P.P.* (in *Musick Books*) stands for *piu piano*. Ital. *P.P.P.* is an Abbreviation of the Word *Pianissimo*. Ital. **1728** CHAMBERS *P* in the *Italian* Music frequently represents *piano*; which is what in our Music we call *soft*, i.e. the Force of Voice, or Instrument, are to be diminish'd, so as to make a Kind of Eccho. ¶ *PP* signifies *piu piano*, i.e. *more soft*, or a second Eccho weaker or more remote than the former: and *PPP* signifies *pianissimo* softest of all, or a third Eccho, the Voice being, as it were, lost in the Air.

1731 PRELLEUR *Modern Musick-Master* (Dictionary, p. 3) *P. Pia* or *Piano*, Soft

paduana *see* pavan
c.1726 NORTH Musicall Gramarian BL Add. 32533, f. 167 During this flourishing time [the reign of Charles I], It became usuall to compose for Instruments In setts, that is After a fantazia, an aiery lesson of two straines, and a tripla by way of Galliard. w[ch] was stately; courant, or otherwise, Not unsuitable too, or rather Imitatory of the Dance: Instead of the fantazia, they often used, a very Grave kind of Ayre, w[ch] they called a padoanna, or pavan; this had had [sic] 3. straines, Each being twice played went of heavyly, Especially when a Rich veine failed the Master; ... **1728** NORTH Musicall Grammarian (*C-K MG* f. 70v) [*re* instrumental music of the 'old masters'] ... But for solemne musick they had a grave air which they called padoano or pavan, wherein they mad the most they could of pure harmony without much of melody becaus, the

parts were equally concerned to make good the consort ...

pæan *see* hymn, prosodion

1538 ELYOT L→E *Pæan,* an hymne in the prayse of *Apollo.* sommetyme the same *Apollo.* It is nowe taken for any hymne, made to the laude of God, or our Ladye. **1565** COOPER L→E *Pæan, pænis, m.g.* An hymne in the prayse of Apolly [sic]. Sometyme the same Apollo. *Pæan, pæânis, pen. prod. m. gen. Virg.* An hymne made to the prayse of God. § *Herculeum pæana canunt. Stat.* They singe an hymne to the honour of Hercules. **1587** THOMAS L→E *Pæan, anis, m.g.* An hymne or song of praise made to Apollo the God of the Painimes, at such time as any plague or pestilence raged, and also after the obtaining of some victorie and triumph. § *Pæanem citare.* By litle and litle to lift vp the voice, to arise from note to note, or to sing lowder and lowder. **1589** RIDER L→E *pæan.* A song made to Apollo. § *Pæanem citare.* To sing louder and louder. **1598** FLORIO It→E *Peani,* hymnes or songs of praises made & sung to Apollo at such time as anie plague or pestilence raged, and also after the obtaining of some victorie or triumphe. **1611** FLORIO It→E *Peani,* hymnes, or songs of praises made or sung, to Apollo when any plague raged, as also after the obtayning of some victory. **1656** BLOUNT (1st edn) *Pæan* (Gr.) a hymne or song of praise made to *Apollo,* at such time as any plague or pestilence raged; and also after the obtaining some victory or triumph **1658** PHILLIPS (1st edn) *Pæan,* (Greek) a certain Hymn which the ancient Greeks used to sing to *Apollo.* **1676** COLES *Pæan, Greek.* a Song to *Apollo.* § *Iö Pæan,* a voice or song of rejoicing (to *Apollo.*) **1707** *Gloss. Angl. Nova* (1st edn) *Paean,* a Hymn or Song of Praise made to *Apollo,* at such time as any Plague or Pestilence raged. **1728** CHAMBERS *Pæan,* in Antiquity, a Hymn in Honour of *Apollo,* or some of the other Gods; chiefly used on Occasions of Victory and Triumph. See *Hymn.* ¶ The *Pæan* took its Name from *Apollo* himself; who was denominated *Pæan,* because, in his Combat with the Serpent *Python,* his Mother *Latona* incouraged him to make use of his Arrows, by crying frequently ιω παίαν *Io Pæan,* i.e. *smite, shoot.* ¶ Thus *Festus,* but *Hesychius* rather takes *Apollo* to have been denominated *Pæan* from παίω, θεραπεύω, I *heal;* in Allusion to his being the Deity of Medicine. **1730** BAILEY *Dict. Britannicum* (1st edn) *Paean, Paeon,* (in *antient Poetry*) a Foot; so called, because supposed to be appropriated to the Hymn *Paean.* **1737** DYCHE-PARDON (2nd edn) *Paean* (S.) a Hymn or Song of Praise sung to *Apollo,* or some other of the more favourite Gods, upon a Victory, or at the Entrance of a Battle or Contest.

paganina

1598 FLORIO It→E *Paganina,* a kinde of dance vsed in Italy. **1611** FLORIO It→E *Paganina,* a kinde of Moris-dance in Italie. **1659** TORRIANO-FLORIO It→E *Paganina,* the *Morisco,* or *Canary* dance.

palalalan *see* pata-pata-pan

1611 COTGRAVE Fr→E *Palalalan.* The sound of the French march.

Palestrina, alla

1709 [RAGUENET] *Comparison betw. Fr. and It. Musick and Opera's* (p. 31) Among the ancient Composers of Church Musick, besides *Carissimi,* we may add, *Oratio Benevoli,* and *Francisco Foggia,* and one more ancient than either, *Palestrina* who was the Inventor of a Style in Musick, call'd from his own Name, *alla Palestrina,* or rather, *à Capella,* being the only Style suffer'd to be perform'd in the Pope's Chappel, a Style which none but *Palestrina* cou'd Invent, so none but Foggia has been ever able to Copy after him. These Compositions consist of four or five Parts...

palinodia

1500 *Ortus Vocabulorum* L→E Palinodia die. i. reiteratio. s. quando quis illum laudat quem prius vituperauerat. a[e]. a song or a praysyng rehersyde. f.p. Palinodicus ci. qui palinodia facit vel dicit vel iterator cantus. m.s. Palinodium dij. est cantus iteratus dicitur a palin quod est iterum et odo quod est cantus vel laus. n.s. Palinodius a. um. i. iterum cantatus. vel laudatus. o.s. **1538** ELYOT L→E *Palinodia,* a contrarye songe, or retractynge of that, whiche oone hathe spoken or wryten: Nowe of somme menne called a recantynge. **1565** COOPER L→E *Palinodia, huius palinódiæ, f.g.* A contrary songe: a retractation: a recantation: **1587** THOMAS L→E *Palinodia, æ, f.g.* A recantation, a contrarie song: **1598** FLORIO It→E *Palinodia,* ... a contrarie song. **1611** FLORIO It→E *Palinodia,* a recantation, or vnsaying of what one hath spoken, sung, or written. **1656** BLOUNT (1st edn) *Palinode, Palinodie (palinodia)* a contrary song, an unsaying that one hath spoken or written... **1676** COLES *Palinode, -dy, Greek.* recantation, another (kind of) Song. **1688** DAVIS-TORRIANO-FLORIO It→E *Palinodia,* a recantation or the sound of a retreat. **1728** CHAMBERS *Palinody,* a Discourse contrary to a preceding one. ¶ Hence the Phrase *Palinodiam Canere*, to sing *Palinody*; to make a Recantation. ¶ The Word, in the original *Greek*, signifies to sing *a-fresh*.

palmula

1721 MALCOLM *Treatise of Musick* (p. 558) ... he [Guido d'Arezzo] contrived what is called the *Abacus* and the *Palmulæ*, that is, the *Machinery* by which the String is struck with a Plectrum made of Quills.

Pan *see* Midas, pandora, Syrinx

1658 PHILLIPS (1st edn) *Pan*, the son of *Demogorgon*, he was worshipp'd in *Arcadia*; as the God of sheapherds, being smitten by Cupid, he fell in love with the Nymph *Syrinx*, who passing over the River *Ladon*, was turned into a Reed, which *Pan* beholding, made him a Pipe with the same Reed, whence he is said to have first found out the use of the Pipe and Oaten Reed. **1730** BAILEY *Dict. Britannicum* (1st edn) *Pan (Hieroglyphically)* is pictured with two Horns on his Head, and a Garment of a Leopard's Skin about his Shoulders, and a Rank of seven slender Pipes in his Hand, so joined together that their Musick could make an harmonious Consort, to signify the Harmony and rare Correspondency that is in the World between the several Parts that compose it.... They call him Σύρτον, either because he is blown through by all Winds ... or that he is not accommodated to Dancing genteelly; but skips like Country-clowns that have not the Knowledge of more polite Musick, ἀπὸ τοῦ σκίρταν, *i.e.* skipping. **1736** BAILEY *Dict. Britannicum* (2nd edn) *Pan* .... His goat's feet signifying the *solidity* of the earth, and his pipe of seven reeds, that celestial harmony supposed to be made by the seven planets.

pandera

1599 MINSHEU-PERCYVALL Sp→E **Pandera*, a taber, a rattle or such like toie for children to play with. *Panderetero*, m. a drumplaier, a taborer. Also one that selleth or maketh them. *Pandero, Adufe*, or *Atabal*, a drum, a tabor.

Pandora

1565 COOPER L→E *Pandôra*, A woman, vnto whom sundry goddes gaue sundrie giftes. Pallas gaue hir wisdome, Venus beautie, Apollo musike, Mercurius eloquence ... **1730** BAILEY *Dict. Britannicum* (1st edn) *Pandora* (πάντων δῶρα, *i.e.* receiving the Gifts of all the Gods) a Woman (according to the Poets) made by *Vulcan*, at the Command of *Jupiter*, to whom every God adorned with several Gifts. *Pallas* gave her Wisdom, *Venus* Beauty, *Apollo* Musick, *Mercury* Eloquence;

pandora *see* bandora, fidicula, lyre, pandurist

1500 *Ortus Vocabulorum* L→E Pandura ce. est genus organi. angl. a bagge pype. f.p. **1587** THOMAS L→E *Pandura, ræ, f.g. Iun.* A musical instrument hauing but 3. strings, a rebecke, a violen. **1589** RIDER L→E *Pandura, f.* A viole. *Pandura, f.* An instrument having but three stringes. **1598** FLORIO It→E *Pandora, Pandura*, a musical instrument with three strings, a kit, a croude, a rebecke. **1611** FLORIO It→E *Pandora*, a Croud, a Kit, or Rebecke with three strings. **1658** PHILLIPS (1st edn) *Pandure*, (lat.) a kinde of Musical instrument, called also a rebeck. **1659** TORRIANO-FLORIO It→E *Pandora*, a Greek word, signifying, All-gifts, among Poets it signifies a most beautiful woman, on whom all the Gods bestowed gifts, ... but now used for a croud, a kit, a rebeck with three strings, though we use it for a Bandora. **1676** COLES *Pandure*, a Rebeck, or rather a *Bandore*. **1678** PHILLIPS (4th edn) *Pandure, (Lat.)* a kind of Musical Instrument. See *Bandore* [bandora]. **1688** MIEGE-COTGRAVE Fr→E *Pandore*, (f.) *Instrument de Musique à cordes de leton*, Bandore, a Musical Instrument, with brass strings. § *La Pandore ressembloit au Lut en quêque façon*, the Bandore was something like a Lute. **1704** *Cocker's Engl. Dict.* (1st edn) *Pandure*, a Musical Instrument. *Pandurist*, he that has skill to play on it. **1706** KERSEY-PHILLIPS (6th edn) *Pandore* or *Pandure*, a kind of Musical Instrument. **1707** *Gloss. Angl. Nova* (1st edn) *Pandore*, a kind of Musical Instrument. **1708** KERSEY *Dict. Anglo-Brit.* (1st edn) *Pandore* or *Pandure*, a Musical Instrument. **1728** CHAMBERS *Pandoron*, a musical Instrument, used among the Antients; resembling the Lute. See *Lute*. ¶ It has the same Number of Strings; but they are of Brass, and of Consequence give a more agreeable Sound. ¶ Its Frets are of Copper, like those of the Cistron; its Back flat, like that of the Guitarre; and the Rims of its Table, as well as its Ribs, cut in Semi-circles. ¶ *Du Cange* observes, that *Varro, Isidore*, and others of the Antients, mention it as having only three Strings. ¶ The Word, according to some, is form'd from the *Greek* πᾶν and δόρον *i.e.* all Gift, or all Sorts of Gifts. *Isidore* derives the Name from its Inventor *Pandorus*; others from *Pan*, to whom they attribute its Invention, as well as that of the Flute. **1730** BAILEY *Dict. Britannicum* (1st edn) *Pandore* (*pandura*, L.) a musical Instrument resembling a Lute.

1721 MALCOLM *Treatise of Musick* (p. 583) ... [Perault] observes, that the Ancients probably had a Kind of simple Harmony, in which Two or Three Notes were tuned to the principal Chords of the *Key*, and accompanied the Song. This he thinks probable from the Name of an Instrument *Pandora* that *Athenæus* mentions; which is likely the same with the *Mandora*, an Instrument not very long ago used, says he, in which there were Four Strings, whereof one served for the Song, and was struck by a *Plectrum* or Quill tied to the Forefinger: The other Three were tuned so as Two of them were an *8ve*, and the other a Middle dividing the *8ve* into a *4th* and *5th*: They were struck by the Thumb, and this regulated by the *Rythmus* or Measure of the Song, *i.e.* Four Strokes for every Measure of common Time, and Three for Triple. He thinks *Horace* points out the Manner of this Instrument in *Ode* 6... This instrument is parallel to our common Bagpipe.

pandurarius

1589 RIDER L→E *Pandurarius*. A viole maker, or he that plaieth on a viole.

pandurist

1587 THOMAS L→E *Pandurizo, as, Lamprid*. To plaie on such an instrument. **1589** RIDER L→E *Pandurizo*. To play on a Viole, an instrument of musicke. **1656** BLOUNT (1st edn) *Pandurist (panduristes)* he that plays on a musical instrument called a *Rebech*, or on a Violin. **1676** COLES *Paudurist* [sic], he that playes on a ¶ *Pandure*

panegricus *see* episode, song

1500 *Ortus Vocabulorum* L→E Panegricus ca. cum. i. laudando decantatus. o.s.

pango *see* cano, cella

1500 *Ortus Vocabulorum* L→E Pangeto as. i. sepe vel frequenter canere vel cantare. Pango gis. panxi: caret supino. i. cantare. § Pango actiuum est in duobus significatis: sed pro cantare simpliciter est neutrum. Inuenitur etiam pango vndecimo pro palum figere vel plantare. **1538** ELYOT L→E *Pango, pepegi, & panxi, pangere*, ... to wryte, to singe, to tel. **1565** COOPER L→E *Pango, pangis, pépigi & panxi, pactum, pángere*. ... to singe: to tell. **1587** THOMAS L→E *Pango, is, xi. & pepegi, ctum, ere*... to write, to sing or tell, to make:

para

early 18th C. PEPUSCH various papers BL Add. 29429, f. 6 Para, i.e[.] ye next to ye foregoing or to ye following. viz Paranete Hyperb: Paranete Diezeugm:

paramese *see* diagram, mese

1587 THOMAS L→E *Paramese, Iun*. The fift string, being the verie next to the midlemost: *also* B. fa. b. mi. *Vitruv*. **1589** RIDER L→E *Paramese*. The fifth string. **1598** FLORIO It→E *Paramese*, the fift string or next to the middlemost. Also B. fa. b. mi. **1611** COTGRAVE Fr→E *Peramese: f.* A Ninth, or a proportion of nine, in Musicke. **1611** FLORIO It→E *Paramese*, the fifth string, or next to the middlemost. Also B. fa. b. mi. **1706** KERSEY-PHILLIPS (6th edn) *Paramese* (*Gr.* in *Musick*) the Sound of the fifth String, being next to the middlemost; also the Note call'd *B-fa-be-mi*. **1728** CHAMBERS *Paramese*, in the antient Music, the ninth Chord or Sound in the *Diagramma* or Scale of Music. See *Diagramma*. ¶ The Word is *Greek*, and signifies *juxta mediam*, next to the Middle; its Situation in the first State of the Scales, being next the Mese or Middle Chord. See *Chord*.

paranete *see* diagram, nete

1587 THOMAS L→E *Paranete, Iun*. The sixth string. *Paranete diezeugmene, Iun*. D. la. sol. re. *Paranete hyperbolænôn, Iun*. G. sol. re. ut. *Paranete synemmenôn, Iun*. C. sol. fa. **1659** TORRIANO-FLORIO It→E *Peramete, Corda d'instromento musicale*, a nineth, or a proportion of Nine in musick. **1706** KERSEY-PHILLIPS (6th edn) *Paranete* (*Gr.* in *Musick*) the Sound of the sixth String, so call'd as being next the last. *Paranete Synemmenon* the Note call'd C-sol-fa. *Paranete Diezeugmenon*, D-la-sol-re. *Paranete Hyperbolæon*, G-sol-re-ut.

paraneuma *see* neume

1500 *Ortus Vocabulorum* L→E Paraneuma me. an^e^. swette sange. dulce melos et melodia. f.p.

paraphoni

1721 MALCOLM *Treatise of Musick* (p. 508) ... Others [as distinct from Ptolomy] call ... the *4ths* and *5ths* *Paraphoni*; others call the *5ths* only *Paraphoni* ...

paraphonista *see* chorister

1500 *Ortus Vocabulorum* L→E Paraphonista. idest cantator. angl. or querester. c.p. § Cantores proprie: paraphonistas dabis esse. Parophonista te. i. cantator. dicit a paro as. et phonos quod est sonus. q. parans idest incipiens cantus

parhypate *see* diagram, hypate
1587 THOMAS L→E *Parhypate, Vitruv.* The string next to the base. *Parhypate hypatôn. Iun.* C. fa. vt. *Parhypate mesôn, Iun.* F. fa. vt. **1589** RIDER L→E *Parhypate.* The second, or next to the base. **1706** KERSEY-PHILLIPS (6th edn) *Parhypate (Gr.)* in *Musick* the Sound of the String next the Bass. *Parhypate Hapatôn,* the Note *C-fa-ut. Parhypate Meson,* the Note *F-fa-ut.*

parley *see* beat, chamade
1706 KERSEY-PHILLIPS (6th edn) § *To Beat or Sound a Parley,* to give the Signal for such a Conference, by beat of Drum, or sound of Trumpet; which is usually done by the Besiegers to have leave to bury their Dead, and by the Besieged, in order to surrender the Place upon certain Terms. **1708** KERSEY *Dict. Anglo-Brit.* (1st edn) § *To Beat or Sound a Parley,* to give the Signal for such a Conference, by beat of Drum, or sound of Trumpet. **1728** CHAMBERS *Parley,* a Conference with an Enemy, *&c.* of the *French Parler* to speak, talk. ¶ Hence to *beat* or *sound a Parley,* is to give a Signal for the holding of such a Conference by Beat by Drum, or Sound of Trumpet. **1737** DYCHE-PARDON (2nd edn) *Parley* (S.) a Conference, Dispute, or talking about any Thing, especially in *War,* when any Thing is desired by the Besiegers or the Besieged they beat a Drum, which they call beating a Parley

parola
1724 [PEPUSCH] *Short Explic. of Foreign Words in Mus. Bks.* (p. 53) *Parola,* Word or Words in general, but more particularly in Musick they are to be understood of those Words of which a Song or Cantata is composed. **1726** BAILEY *An Univ. Etymolog. Engl. Dict.* (3rd edn) *Parola,* a Word or Words. *Ital. Parola,* (in *Musick Books*) signifies those Words of which a Song or Cantata is compos'd. *Ital.*

part *see* counterpart
1728 CHAMBERS *Part,* in Music, a Piece of the Score or Partition, wrote by itself, for the Convenience of the Musician; or it is one or more of the Successions of Sounds which make the Harmony, wrote *a-part.* See *Partition.* ¶ Or, the *Parts* are the Sounds made by several Persons singing, or playing in Concert. See *Concert.* ¶ Music in *Parts* was unknown to the Antients; they had but one *Part;* all their Harmony consisted in the Succession of Notes; none in the Consonance. See *Music* and *Symphony.* ¶ There are four principal *Parts;* the *Treble, Bass, Tenor,* and *Counter-tenor.* See *Treble, Bass, Tenor,* and *Counter-tenor.* See *Treble, Bass, Tenor, &c.* ¶ Some compare the four *Parts* in Music, to the four Elements: The *Bass* represents the Earth; the *Tenor,* Water; *Counter-tenor,* Air; and the *Treble,* Fire. **1730** BAILEY *Dict. Britannicum* (1st edn) *Part* (in *Musick*) a Piece of the Score or Partition, written by itself for the Conveniency of the Musician. **1737** DYCHE-PARDON (2nd edn) *Part* (S.) ... in *Musick,* it signifies that which is plaid or sung by any one particular Person or Instrument.

1721 MALCOLM *Treatise of Musick* (pp. 331-2) A *Song* is either *simple* or *compound.* If it is a *simple Song,* where only one Voice performs; or, tho' there be more, if they are all *Unison* or *Octave,* or any other *Concord* in every Note, 'tis still but the same Piece of *Melody,* performed by different Voices in the same or different Pitches of *Tune,* for the *Intervals* of the Notes are the same in them all. A *compound Song* is where Two or more Voices go together, with a Variety of *Concords* and Harmony; so that the *Melody* each of them makes, is a distinct and different *simple Song,* and all together make the *compound.* The *Melody* that each of them produces is therefore called a *Part* of the *Composition;* and all such *Compositions* are very properly called *symphonetick Musick,* or *Musick* in *Parts;* taking the Word *Musick* here for the *Composition* or *Song* it self. **1731** PRELLEUR *Modern Musick-Master* (Dictionary, p. 3) *Parte,* a Part as *Parte Prima,* the First Part[,] *Parte Secunda,* the Second Part, &c.

parte
1724 [PEPUSCH] *Short Explic. of Foreign Words in Mus. Bks.* (pp. 53-4) *Parte,* is Part. Thus, ¶ *Parta Prima,* is First Part. ¶ *Parta Seconda,* the Second Part. **1726** BAILEY *An Univ. Etymolog. Engl. Dict.* (3rd edn) *Parte,* a part. *Ital.*

particular system *see* system
1721 MALCOLM *Treatise of Musick* (p. 332) ... therefore the Staff of Five Lines upon which each *Part* is written, is to be considered as a *Part* of the *universal System* or *Scale,* and is therefore called a *particular System;* ...

partition *see* score
1728 CHAMBERS *Partition,* in Music, the Disposition of the several Parts of a Song, set on the same Leaf; so as upon the uppermost Ranges of Lines are found the *Treble;* in another the *Bass;* in another the

Tenor, &c. that they may all be sung or play'd jointly or separately. See *Part, Music, &c.*

pascha floridum
1706 KERSEY-PHILLIPS (6th edn) *Pascha Floridum*, Palm-Sunday, or the Sunday before Easter, when the proper Hymn or Gospel sung was, *Occurrunt turbæ cum floribus & palmis*, &c. *i.e.* The Multitude come forth with Flowers and Palm-branches.

passacaglia *see* sonata, variation
1724 [PEPUSCH] *Short Explic. of Foreign Words in Mus. Bks.* (p. 54) *Passacaglio*, or *Passacaille*, or *Passagillio*, is a Kind of Air somewhat like a Chacoone, but of a more slow or graver Movement. **1726** BAILEY *An Univ. Etymolog. Engl. Dict.* (3rd edn) *Passacaclio, Passacaille, Passacillio, (in Musick Books)* signifies a kind of Air something like a *Chacoone*; but of a more slow or graver Movement. *Ital.*

passage *see* transition
1611 COTGRAVE Fr→E *Passage: m.* ... also, musicall diuision, or warbling; § *Passager, & varier la voix.* To warble, or diuide, in singing, &c. **1728** CHAMBERS *Passage*, in Music, a Portion of an Air, or Tune, consisting of several little Notes, as Quavers, Demi-quavers, *&c.* lasting one, two, or at most, three Measures. ¶ Thus what the *Italians* call *contra punto d'un sol passo*, in a Portion in the Beginning of the Song, consisting of one, two, or three Measures, which is to be imitated in other Notes; not with the same Strings or Tones, but only observing the same Motion, Number, and Figure as in the Notes of the first *Passage*; which is one of the Kinds of *contra punto perfidiato*.

passamezzo *see* pastorella
1598 FLORIO It→E *Passa mezzo*, a passameasure, or a cinquepace. *Passamezzo*, a passameasure in dancing a cinquepace. **1611** FLORIO It→E *Passamezzo*, a passemeasure, a cinqu-pace [sic].

passepied *see* saraband
1593 HOLLYBAND Fr→E § *Danseur de Passe-pieds*, he that danceth on tiptoe, or capers: *m.* **1611** COTGRAVE Fr→E *Passe-pied: m.* A caper, or loftie tricke in dauncing; also, a kind of daunce, peculiar to the youth of *La haute Bretaigne.* **1724** [PEPUSCH] *Short Explic. of Foreign Words in Mus. Bks.* (p. 54) *Passepied*, is an Air very much like a Minuet in all Respects, only to be play'd more brisk and lively. **1726** BAILEY *An Univ. Etymolog. Engl. Dict.* (3rd edn) *Passepied (in Musick Books)* signifies an Air very like a Minuet in all Respects, only to be play'd more brisk and lively. *Ital.*

passing note
c.1710 NORTH (draft for) Musicall Grammarian BL Add. 32537, f. 29 From hence wee have leav to double, and thro these discords procure excellent harmony ... It is comon to pass these notes quick and then they are called passing notes & by y[e] managem[t] of y[e] voice or Instrument give an Emphasis upon the Concords. **c.1726** NORTH Musicall Gramarian BL Add. 32533, f. 133v ... And it is obvious that all the lesser [notes], called passing Notes, may be left out, and then the accords are touched one after the other ... **1731** [PEPUSCH] *Treatise on Harmony* (2nd edn, p. 41) What has been said hitherto in relation to the *Discords*, has been as to the regularly Preparing and Resolving them: We will mention now how they may be used without that Regularity, but then they are no longer properly to be call'd *Discords*, but *Passing* or *Transient Notes*: ...

passion, passionate *see* accent, æolian, air, mood, mundane music, music, mutation, pathetic music, petteia, pythagoreans, research, rest, rythmica, saraband, style (stylo madrigalesco, stylo motectico, stylo recitativo)

pastoral *see* bucolick, eclogue, opera, troubadour
1656 BLOUNT (1st edn) A *Pastoral (pastorale carmen)* a song of Herdsmen or Shepherds. **1658** PHILLIPS (1st edn) *Pastoral*, (lat.) belonging to a shepherd or rural life, whence a pastoral Song. **1676** COLES *Pastoral* (Song) of Herdsmen. **1704** *Cocker's Engl. Dict.* (1st edn) *Pastoral*, ... also a Song or Poem about Herdsmen or Husbandry. **1706** KERSEY-PHILLIPS (6th edn) *Pastoral*, belonging [to] a Shepherd, or to a Church-Minister; as *A Pastoral Song, a Pastoral Letter.* **1707** *Gloss. Angl. Nova* (1st edn) *Pastoral*, (Lat) belonging to a Shepherd, or Rural Life, whence Pastoral Song; **1708** KERSEY *Dict. Anglo-Brit.* (1st edn) A *Pastoral*, a sort of Poem relating to Affairs between Shepherds and Shepherdesses. **1724** [PEPUSCH] *Short Explic. of Foreign Words in Mus. Bks.* (p. 54) *Pastorale*, is an Air composed after a very sweet, easy, gentle Manner, in Imitation of those Airs which Shepherds are supposed to play. **1726** BAILEY *An*

Univ. Etymolog. Engl. Dict. (3rd edn) *Pastorale (in Musick Books)* signifies an Air composed after a very sweet, easy, gentle Manner, in Imitation of those Airs which Shepherds are supposed to play. *Ital.* **1730** BAILEY *Dict. Britannicum* (1st edn) *Pastoral (pastorale)* a Shepherd's Song, or Poem by way of Dialogue, between Shepherds and Shepherdesses. **1737** DYCHE-PARDON (2nd edn) *Pastorale* (S.) a Poetical Performance or Composition by way of Dialogue between Shepherds and Shepherdesses about Country Affairs, such as the Complaints of Lovers, the Cruelty of Shepherds, Disputes who sung best, the Ambushes of Satyrs, ravishing of Nymphs, &c.

1731 PRELLEUR *Modern Musick-Master* (Dictionary, p. 3) *Pastorale* after a Sweet easy Gentle manner, as Shepherds are supposed to play.

pastorella

1597 MORLEY *Plaine and Easie Introdvction* (p. 180) [marginalia: '*Pastorelle* [and] *passamezzos* with ditties'] There be also many other kindes of songes [after the vinate and justinianas] which the Italians make as *Pasterellas* and *Passamesos* with a dittie and such like, which it would be both tedious and superfluons to delate [sic] vnto you in words ...

pata-pata-pan *see* palalalan

1688 MIEGE-COTGRAVE Fr→E † *Pata-pata-pan, Mots imaginez pour representer le Son du Tambour.* These are made Words to express the beat of a French Drum.

pathetic music

1728 CHAMBERS *Pathetic,* in Music, something very moving, expressive, passionate, capable of exciting Pity, Compassion, Anger, or the like Passion. ¶ In this Sense, we say a *Pathetic Fugue, Pathetic Song, &c.* ¶ The Chromatic Genus, with its major and minor Semi-tones, either ascending or descending is very proper for the *Pathetic;* as is also an artful Management of Discords; Variety of Motions, now brisk, now languishing, now swift, now slow. ¶ *Niewentiit,* tells us of a Musician at *Genoa,* who excell'd in the *Pathetic;* to that Degree, that he was able to play any of his Auditors into Distraction; he adds, that the great Means he made Use of, was the Variety of Motions, *&c.* **1730** BAILEY *Dict. Britannicum* (1st edn) *Pathetick Musick,* Musick that is very moving, expressive, passionate, capable of exciting Pity, Compassion, Anger, or the like Passion.

1721 MALCOLM *Treatise of Musick* (p. 541) [*re* mutations in the melopœia in ancient Greek music] ... In the *Melopœia,* that is, when the Song changes the very *Air,* so as from gay and sprightly to become soft and languishing, or from a *Manner* that expresses one Passion or Subject to the Expression of some other; and therefore some of them call this a Change in the *Manner* (*secundum morem*): But to express Passion, or to have what they called *Pathetick Musick,* the various *Rythmus* is abolutely necessary to be join'd; ...

patte *see* drawing pen

1688 MIEGE-COTGRAVE Fr→E *Patte,* (f.) .... *On appelle Patte un petit Instrument à plusieurs pointes, qui sert à regler les Livres de Musique, & à faire plusieurs raies tout d'un coup.*

pause *see* counterpoint, diapsalma, diastema, grace, hold, mode, rest, selah, tacet

1688 MIEGE-COTGRAVE Fr→E § *Pause de Musique, certaine marque dans les Livres de Musique qui vaut une mesure,* a pause, in Musick. **1704** HARRIS *Pause* or *Rest,* in Musick, is a Silence or Artificial Intermission of the Voice or Sound, proportion'd to a certain Measure of Time, by the Motion of the Hand or Foot. ¶ These *Pauses* or *Rests* are always equal to the Length or Quantity of the Notes whereto they are annex'd, and are therefore called by the same Names as a *Long-rest*[,] *Breve-rest, Semi-breve-rest,* &c. ¶ *Odd Rests* are those which take up only some part of a *Semi-breve*'s Time or Measure, and have always reference to some *Odd Note;* for by those two *Odds* the Measure is made even. **1706** KERSEY-PHILLIPS (6th edn) In Musick, *Pause* or *Rest,* is an artificial Discontinuance of the Voice or Sound. See *Rest.* **1728** CHAMBERS *Pause,* in Music, a Character of Silence and Repose; call'd also by some, a *Mute figure;* because it shews that some of the Parts are to be Silent, while the others continue the Song; either for the sake of some Fugure [sic] or Imitation, or to give a breathing Time, or to give room for another Voice, *&c.* to answer what this Part sung, as in Dialogues, Echoes, *&c.* ¶ The Antients had two kinds of Pauses; the one call'd by the *Italians, Initial Pauses;* because, first placed at the Beginning of the Piece, tho' sometimes after, and regularly before the Circle O, or the Semi-circle C. ¶ They had also Pauses after the Characters of the

Measure, and in the Course of the Piece. ¶ A *general Pause* is a general Cessation or Silence of all the Parts. ¶ *Demi-pause* is a Cessation for the Time of half a Measure. ¶ We also say *Pause of a Minim, Pause of a Semi-breve, long Pause, Pauses of Croma,* and *Semi-Croma;* which are Names given by the *Italians,* to express the different values of Pauses. For the Signs or Characters of Pauses. See *Character.* **1730** BAILEY *Dict. Britannicum* (1st edn) § *A Demy Pause* (in *Musick*) a Cessation for the Time of half a Measure. *A General Pause,* a general Cessation or Silence of all the Parts. **1737** DYCHE-PARDON (2nd edn) *Pause* (S.) a Stop, resting, thinking, or forbearing to speak, sing, or play upon an Instrument for a Time.

1636 BUTLER *Principles of Musik* (pp. 37-8) A Pauz is a mark of rest or silence in a song, for the time of soom Note: whereof it hath his name. ¶ A line depending from a superiour rule, and not touching the rule below, is a Sembrief-rest: the like line rising from an inferiour rule, and not touching the rule aboov, is a Minim-rest: the same with a crooke to the right hand, is a Crochet-rest, and to the left hand, a Qaver-rest. Also a line reaching from rule to rule, is a Brief-rest, or a Pauz of 2 Sembriefs: a line from a rule to a third rule, is a Long-pauz, or of 4 Sembriefs: and 2 of them together make a Large-pauz, or of 8 Sembriefs. **1665** SIMPSON *Principles of Practical Mvsick* (p. 17) ... The Strokes or Marks which you see set after them [the notes], are called *Pauses,* or *Rests;* that is a Cessation or Intermission of Sound, and are of the same length or quantity (as to Measure of time) with the Notes which stand before them; and are likewise called by the same Names, as *Long Rest, Breve Rest,* and *Semibreve Rest,* &c. **1667** PLAYFORD *Brief Intro. to Skill of Musick* (4th edn, p. 26) *Pauses* or *Rests* are silent *Characters,* or an *Artificial* omission of the *Voyce* or *Sound,* proportioned to a Certain *Measure* of *Time,* by *Motion* of the hand (whereby the Quantity of *Notes* and *Rests* are directed) by an Equal *Measure* ... **1677** NEWTON *English Academy* (p. 102) A *Pause* is a mark of rest or silence in a Song for the time of some Note, whereof it hath its name. **1726** BRUCE *Common Tunes* (p. 27) Q. *What call you Pauses or Rests?* ¶ *A.* They are silent Characters, or artful Omission of the Voice or Sound, agreeable to a certain Measure of them, by Motion of the Hand in an equal Measure, as such and such Pauses or Rests do require.

pavan *see* dance, emmelia, imperfect of the less, lesson, paduana, sonata, time

1598 FLORIO It→E *Pauana,* a dance called a pauine. **1611** COTGRAVE Fr→E *Pavane: f.* A Pauane. *Pavanier: m.* A pauine-maker; a dauncer of Pauines. **1611** FLORIO It→E *Pauana,* a dance called a Pauen. **1656** BLOUNT (1st edn) *Pavin* (Fr. *Pavâne*) a kind of Dance; perhaps so called *à pavienda terra,* of paving the ground. *Min.* **1658** PHILLIPS (1st edn) *Pavin,* (Span.) a kind of Dance so called. **1659** TORRIANO-FLORIO It→E *Pavana, Pavaniglia,* a pavan dance **1676** COLES *Pavin, Pavane, French.* a kind of Dance. **1678** PHILLIPS (4th edn) *Pavin, (Ital.)* a kind of Dance so called, as some conjecture from *Pavia,* once the chief of *Lombardy,* as it were a Dance invented, or first used by the people of those parts. **1688** DAVIS-TORRIANO-FLORIO It→E *Pavana, Pavaniglia,* a stately, majestick dance, so called from *Pavone,* the Peacock. **1688** MIEGE-COTGRAVE Fr→E *Pavanne,* (f.) *sorte de Branle ancien,* a Pavane, or Pavane-Dance. § *Danser la Pavane,* to dance a Pavane. **1696** PHILLIPS (5th edn) *Pavan,* A grave and majestick sort of Dance that came from *Spain,* wherein the Dancers turn round and wheel about one after another: Also the gravest and the slowest sort of Instrumental Musick, consisting generally of three Strains. **1702** KERSEY *New Engl. Dict.* (1st edn) A *Pavan,* a kind of dance. **1704** *Cocker's Engl. Dict.* (1st edn) *Pavin,* a kind of Musical Air or Dance, of slow time. **1706** KERSEY-PHILLIPS (6th edn) *Pavan* or *Pavane,* a grave and majestick sort of Dance, that came from *Spain,* wherein the Dancers turn round, and wheel about one after another: Also the gravest and slowest sort of Instrumental Musick, consisting generally of three Strains. **1707** *Gloss. Angl. Nova* (1st edn) *Pavan,* a grave sort of Dance; also the slowest sort of Instrumental Musick. **1708** KERSEY *Dict. Anglo-Brit.* (1st edn) *Pavan* or *Pavane,* a grave and majestic Spanish Dance: Also the gravest and slowest sort of Instrumental Musick. **1728** CHAMBERS *Pavan,* or *Pavane,* a Grave Dance, derived from the *Spaniards;* wherin the Dancers make a kind of Wheel, or Tail before each other, like that of a Peacock, whence the Name. See *Dance.* ¶ The *Pavane* was antiently in great repute; and was danced by Gentlemen with Cap and Sword; by those of the Long Robe, with their Gowns; by Princes with their Mantles, and by the Ladies with their Gown-tails trailing on the Ground. ¶ It was called the *Grand Ball;* from the Solemnity, wherewith it was perform'd. ¶ To moderate its Gravity, 'twas usual to introduce several Flourishes, Passades, Capers, *&c.* by way of *Episodes.* ¶ Its Tablature or Score is given at large by *Thoinot Arbeau* in his *Orchesographia.*

1730 Bailey *Dict. Britannicum* (1st edn) *Pavan, Pavane*, a grave and majestick *Spanish* Dance, wherein the Dancers turn round, and make a Wheel or Tail before them like that of a Peacock; also the gravest, and slowest Sort of Instrumental Musick, consisting generally of 3 Strains.

1597 Morley *Plaine and Easie Introdvction* (p. 181) [marginalia: 'Pauens.'] The next in grauity and goodnes vnto this [the fantasie] is called a pauane, a kind of staide musicke, ordained for graue dauncing, and most commonlie made of three straines, whereof euerie straine is plaid or sung twice, a straine they make to containe 8. 12. or 16. semibreues as they list, yet fewer then eight I haue not seene in any pauan. In this you may not so much insist in following the point as in a fantasie: but it shal be inough to touch it once and so away to some close. Also in this you must cast your musicke by foure, so that if you keepe that rule it is no matter howe many foures you put in your straine, for it will fall out well enough in the ende, the arte of dauncing being come to that perfection that euerie reasonable dauncer wil make measure of no measure, so that it is no great matter of what number you make your strayne. **1667** Simpson *Compendium of Practical Musick* (p. 142) The next in dignity after a Fancy, is a *Pavan*; which some derive from *Padua* in Italy; ... **1676** Mace *Musick's Monument* (p. 129) *Pavines*, are *Lessons* of 2, 3, or 4 *Strains*, very *Grave*, and *Sober; Full of Art, and Profundity*, but seldom us'd, in These our Light Days.

pavan time *see* dupla

1636 Butler *Principles of Musik* (p. 8) ... and therefore the triple is oft called Galliard-time, and the duple, Pavan-time.

pearled playing

c.1668-71 *Mary Burwell's Instruction Bk. for Lute* (*TDa* pp. 34-5) Many hold that for making a good shake and the other graces (which is called the 'pearled' playing) the strings upon the lute must not be too stiff; ...

pecten *see* plectrum

1500 *Ortus Vocabulorum* L→E Pecten inis... vel texendi plectrum cythare. **1538** Elyot L→E *Pecten, inis*, ... it is also the stickes, wherwith a man stryketh doulcemers whan he doeth playe on them **1552** Huloet L→E *Pecten. inis, Plectrum. tri.* Stycke wherwith a man stricketh dulcimers or like instrumentes. **1565** Cooper L→E *Pecten. Virg.* A sticke wherwith thei play on doulcimers. **1587** Thomas L→E *Pecten, inis, n.g. Ovid.* ... a sticke wherewith they play on dulcimers, *Virg.* **1589** Rider L→E *Pecten, instrumentum.* A quill, or bowe to play on the harpe, rebecke, or dulcimer.

pectide *see* pettido

1598 Florio It→E *Pectide*, a musical instrument like a psalterie. **1611** Florio It→E *Pectide*, a musicall instrument like a Psalterie. **1659** Torriano-Florio It→E *Pectide*, as *Pettide*.

pectis

1587 Thomas L→E *Pectis, Iun.* A kinde of musical instrument in some points all one with the psalter. **1589** Rider L→E *Pectis, f.* A kinde of instrument, in some pointes all one with the Psalter.

pecto

1538 Elyot L→E *Pecto, xui, tere*, ... to sette a harpe or other lyke instrument. **1552** Huloet L→E *Pecto. is* Tunable to make, or set in tune. **1565** Cooper L→E *Pecto, pectis, pexui vel pexi, pexum, péctere. Virg.* ... to strike the Doulcimers or Harpe. **1587** Thomas L→E *Pecto, is, xi, & ui, tum, ere* ... to strike the dulcimer or harpe. **1589** Rider L→E *Pecto.* To strike the Dulcimer, or harp.

pedal *see* marche

1688 Miege-Cotgrave Fr→E *Pedale*, (f.) *Terme de Facteur d'Orgue & d'Organiste*, a pedal, or low key of some Organs to be touched with the feet. § *Toucher une Pedale*, to touch a Pedal. **1702** Kersey *New Engl. Dict.* (1st edn) The *Pedals, or* low Keys of some Organs, to be touch'd with the Foot. **1728** Chambers *Pedals*, the large Pipes of an Organ, so call'd, because play'd and stop'd with the Foot. See *Organ.* ¶ The *Pedals* are the largest Pipes in the Machine, they are made Square, of Wood; usually thirteen in Number. ¶ They are of modern Invention, and serve to carry the Sounds an *Octave* deeper than the rest. **1730** Bailey *Dict. Britannicum* (1st edn) *Pedals* (*pedales*, L.) the large Pipes of an Organ, so called because play'd and stopp'd with the Foot.

1676 Mace *Musick's Monument* (p. 235) Concerning *This Instrument*, (call'd the *Pedal* (because It is contriv'd to give *Varieties* with the *Foot*) I shall bestow a few *Lines* .... *This Instrument* is in *Shape and Bulk* just like a *Harpsicon*; only It differs in the *Order* of *It*, Thus, *viz.* There is made right underneath the *Keys*, near the *Ground*, a kind of *Cubbord*, or *Box* ...

peg *see* bischero, cavicchia, claveta, enclavijado, epitonium, nille, perno, pirolo, ritornello, verticuli¡
1737 DYCHE-PARDON (2nd edn) *Peg* (S.) a small Piece of Wood used sometimes to screw up or tighten the Strings of a Musical Instrument

pendaglio *see* bandrol, cascata, scatta, soga
1598 FLORIO It→E *Pendaglio*, a tassell or pendant of a trumpet **1611** FLORIO It→E *Pendaglio*, any pendent or downe dangling thing as of a Trumpet.

pentachord
1728 CHAMBERS *Pentachord*, an ancient musical Instrument, with five Strings; whence the Name, of πέντε, five, and χοροδα Chord, String. ¶ The Invention of the *Pentachord* is referr'd to the *Scythians*: The Strings were of Bullocks Leather, and were struck with a *Plectrum* made of Goats Horn. **1730** BAILEY *Dict. Britannicum* (1st edn) *Pentachord* (of πέντε five, and χορδή, *Gr.* string) a musical Instrument having 5 Strings. **1737** DYCHE-PARDON (2nd edn) *Pentachord* (S.) any Musical Instrument that has five Strings.

pentatonon *see* sixth
1728 CHAMBERS *Pentatonon*, in the ancient Music, a Concord, by us call'd the greater Sixth. See *Sixth.* ¶ It consists of four Tones, and a major and minor Semitone; whence the Name *Pentatonon*, *q.d.* five Tones. **1730** BAILEY *Dict. Britannicum* (1st edn) *Pentatonon* (in antient *Musick*) a Concord, with us call'd the greater Sixth.

penultima divisarum *see* d la sol re
1587 THOMAS L→E *Penultima divisarum, Iun.* D. la. sol, re.

percantatrix
1565 COOPER L→E *Percantatrix, penult prod. percantatrîcis, f.g. Plaut.* A singyng wench: also an enchauntresse. **1587** THOMAS L→E *Percantatrix, icis, f.g. Plaut.* A singing wench: *also* a shee witch, or enchauntresse.

percino
1538 ELYOT L→E *Percino, nere*, to synge stylle, to contynewe syngynge. **1552** HULOET L→E *Percino. is* Syng continuallye or styll. **1587** THOMAS L→E *Percino, is, ere.* *To sing still continuing to the end. **1589** RIDER L→E *Percino.* To sing to the end.

percussio
1565 COOPER L→E *Percussio, pro Ictu, de dimensione temporum in pedibus aut musica.* The tune and measure of a foote in meter, conteinyng both the eleuatinge & depressyng of the voice.

percussion *see* repercussion
1696 PHILLIPS (5th edn) *Percussion, (Lat.)* ... Drums and Bells make a great noise, by reason of the violent percussion of the Air.

peregrine tone
1609 DOWLAND-ORNITHOPARCUS *Micrologvs* (p. 35) *Of the strange Tone.* ¶ There is another *Tone* [distinct from the eight regular ones], which many call the *Peregrine*, or strange *Tone*, not that it is of strange Notes, but that it is very seldome vsed in our Harmony. For his Tenor is not sung to any but to one *Antiphone, Nos qui viuimus, &c.* and to two Psalmes, *In exitu &c.* and *Benedicite.* His end is in the finall Note of the Seuenth *Tone*, as *Franchinus* demonstrates it...

perfect
1728 CHAMBERS *Perfect* in Music, something that fills and satisfies the Mind and the Ear. ¶ In this Sense we say, *Perfect Cadence, Perfect Concord,* &c. See *Concord, Cadence, &c.* ¶ The Ancients has two kindes of Modes, the Major and Minor; and each of these again was either *Perfect* or *Imperfect*. See *Mode.* ¶ The Word *Perfect* when join'd with the Words *Mode* and *Time*, usually express triple Time or Measure; in opposition to double Time, which they call'd imperfect. See *Time, Triple, &c.*

perfect cadence
1636 BUTLER *Principles of Musik* (p. 66) A perfect Cadence is that which to the disjoined Mesure-note and the Binding Concord, addeth a third Note in the key of the disjoined: which must bee either an Eight or an Unison to the Base: ...

perfect concord *see* concord
1704 HARRIS *Perfect Concords*, in Musick. See *Concords.* **1706** KERSEY-PHILLIPS (6th edn) *Perfect Concords*, in Musick. See *Concords.*

1597 MORLEY *Plaine and Easie Introdvction* (p. 71) ... a vnison, a fift, an eight, a twelfth, a fifteenth, a nineteenth, and so forth *in infinitum*, be perfect cordes. **1721** MALCOLM *Treatise of Musick* (p. 415) Of these [12] *Intervals* Two, *viz.* the *Octave* and *Fifth*, are called *perfect Concords*; Four, *viz.* the

Two *3ds* and Two *6ths*, are called *imperfect Concords;* Five *viz.* the false *Fifth*, the Two *Seconds* and Two *Sevenths*, are *Discords...* § (p. 422) The *Harmony* of *Concords* is composed of the *imperfect*, as well as of the *perfect Concords;* and therefore may be said to be *perfect* and *imperfect*, according as the *Concords* are of which it is composed; thus the *Harmony* that arises from a Conjunction of any Note with its *5th* and *Octave* is *perfect*, but with its *3d* and *6th* is *imperfect*.

perfect fifth

1704 HARRIS *Perfect Fifth*, the same with *Diapente;* which see. **1706** KERSEY-PHILLIPS (6th edn) *Perfect Fifth*, See *Diapente*.

perfect of the less *see* mood

1654 PLAYFORD *Breefe Intro. to Skill of Musick* (p. 15) The *Perfect of the Lesse* is when all goe by two, except the Sembriefs, as two Longs to a Large, two Briefs to a Long, three Sembriefs to a Briefe, two Minims to a Sembrief, &c. and his signe or marke is made thus (|)3. **1665** SIMPSON *Principles of Practical Mvsick* (p. 18) *Of the Old Moods....* The *Second Mood* was named *Perfect of the less;* In which a *Large* contained *two Longs;* a *Long*, two *Breves*, a *Breve*, *three Semibreves;* and a *Semibreve*, *Two Minims...*

perfect of the more *see* mood

1597 MORLEY *Plaine and Easie Introdvction* (annotations to Part I) *Perfect of the more*) This (as I said before) ought rather to be tearmed time perfect of the more prolation, then mood perfect, and yet hath it been receiued by consent of our Eng lish [sic] practicioners, to make the Long in it three briefes, and the Large thrice so much. **1654** PLAYFORD *Breefe Intro. to Skill of Musick* (p. 15) The *Perfect of the More* is when all go by three, as three Longs to a Large, three Briefs to a Long, three Sembriefs to a Brief, three Minums to a Sembrief, and his signe or mark is thus ⊙3. **1665** SIMPSON *Principles of Practical Mvsick* (p. 18) *Of the Old Moods.* ¶ The Antients had *four Moods, Modes* or *Measures* of Notes. The *first* they called *perfect of the more*, (*prolation* being implyed) in which a *Large* contained *three Longs*, a *Long*, *three Breves;* a Breve, *three Semibreves;* and a *Semibreve*, *three Minims:* ...

perfidia *see* passage

1728 CHAMBERS *Perfidia*, in Music, a Term borrowed from the *Italian;* signifying an Affection of doing always the same Thing, of following the same Design, continuing the same Motion, the same Song, the same Passage, and the same Figures of Notes. ¶ Such are the stiff Basses of Chacones, *&c.* because depending wholly on the Caprice of the Composer. **1730** BAILEY *Dict. Britannicum* (1st edn) *Perfidia* (in *Musick*) an Affectation of doing always the same Thing, of following the same Design, of continuing the same Motion, the same Song, the same Passage, the same Figures of Notes. *Ital.*

peripate

1659 TORRIANO-FLORIO It→E *Peripate*, the name of a certain string upon a musical instrument.

perno

1659 TORRIANO-FLORIO It→E **Perno*, ... also a peg or pin of any musical instrument

petteia *see* melopœia

1728 CHAMBERS *Petteia*, or *Pettia*, in the ancient Musick, a *Greek* Term, to which we have no corresponding one in our Language. ¶ The Melopoeia, *i.e.* the Art of arranging Sounds in Succession so as to make Melody, is divided into three Parts, which the *Greeks* call *Lepsis*, *Mixis*, and *Chresis*, the *Latins Sumptio*, *Mixtio*, and *Usus;* and the *Italians Presa*, *Mescolamento*, and *Uso*. ¶ The last is also call'd by the *Greeks* Πεττεία, *Petteia*, and by the *Italians Pettia*. ¶ *Petteia* or *Pettia*, then is the Art of making a just Discernment of all the Manners of ranging, or combining Sounds among themselves, so as they may produce their Effect, *i.e.* so as they may express the several Passions intended to be rais'd; thus, *E. gr.* it shews what Sounds are to be us'd, and what not, how often any of 'em are to be repeated, with which to begin, and with which to end, whether with a grave Sound to rise, or an Acute one to fall, *&c.* ¶ 'Tis the *Petteia* that makes the Manners of the Musick; it being this that chuses out this or that Passion, this that or [sic] Motion of the Soul to be awaken'd, and whether it be proper to excite it in this or that occasion. ¶ The *Petteia* therefore is in Musick what the Manners are in Poetry. See *Manners*. ¶ We don't see whence the Word shou'd have been taken by the *Greeks* unless from Πεττεία their Game of Chess; the musical *Petteia* being a Combination and Arrangement of Sounds, as Chess is of Pieces call'd πέττοι, *Calculi*, Chess-Men. **1730** BAILEY *Dict. Britannicum* (1st edn) *Petteia* (in *Musick*) the Art of making a just Discernment of all

Manners of ranging or combining Sounds among themselves, so as they may produce their Effect.

pettido *see* pectide, pittide
1598 FLORIO It→E *Pettido,* a kind of musicall instrument. **1611** FLORIO It→E *Pettido,* a kind of musi[c]all instrument. **1659** TORRIANO-FLORIO It→E *Pettido,* a musical instrument like a Psaltery.

pettine
1598 FLORIO It→E *Pettine,* ... Also a stick wherewith they play on dulcimers. **1611** FLORIO It→E *Pettine,* ... Also a kind of stick wherewith they play on Dulcimers. **1659** TORRIANO-FLORIO It→E *Pettine,* ... also a certain stick wherewith they play on Dulcimers

phantastic *see* style (stylo phantastico)
1728 CHAMBERS *Phantastic,* in Musick. *Phantastic Style,* is a Style proper for Instruments; or a free, easy manner of Composition. See *Style.*

phigthongo *see* phthongus
1611 FLORIO It→E *Phigthongo,* a kind of tune or harmony in musike. **1659** TORRIANO-FLORIO It→E *Phithongo,* a kind of note, tune, or harmony in Musick. *Phtongo,* a sound, a tune or note.

philosophy
1616 BULLOKAR *Philosophie.* The study of wisdome: a deepe knowledge in the nature of things. There are three different kindes hereof. 1. *Rationall* Philosophy, including, Grammar, Logick, and Rhetorick. 2. *Naturall* Philosophy teaching the nature of all things, and conteining besides Arithmetick, Musick, Geometry and Astronomy. 3. *Morall* Philosophy, which consisteth in the knowledge and practise of ciuilitie & good behauiour. **1656** BLOUNT (1st edn) § *Natural Philosophie,* searching into the obscurity of natures secrets, containing besides, Arithmetick, Musick, Geometry, and Astronomy.

phonascia
1587 THOMAS L→E *Phonaschus, i, m.g. Quint.* A master that learneth or teacheth to sing, and and [sic] to pronounce and moderat [sic] the voice. **1589** RIDER L→E *Phonascus, m.* A man which teacheth to sing. **1728** CHAMBERS *Phonascia,* the Art of forming the human Voice .... [in ancient Greece] the Masters of this Art, or those who taught the Art of managing the Voice, were call'd *Phonasci;* under whose Tutorage were put all those destin'd to be Orators, Singers, Comedians, *&c.*

phrygian *see* collateral, mode, mood, phrygium melos, tone
1500 *Ortus Vocabulorum* L→E Ipofrigicus a. um. i. consonans vel dulcit sonans. o.s. **1598** FLORIO It→E *Frigio,* ... Also a melodie or tune wherein seemed to be a deuine furie. *Hipofrigio,* as *Hipodorio* [sic]. *Hippofrigio, Hippolidio, Hippodonio* [sic], certaine kindes of musicke or accent in musicke. *Phrigio,* a melodie, a musicke or tune, wherein seemed to be a diuine furie. **1611** COTGRAVE Fr→E *Phrygie: f.* Phrygian melodie; a kind of tune, or musicke, wherein there seemed to be a diuine furie. **1611** FLORIO It→E *Frigio,* ... Also a kind of tune or melodie wherin seemed to be a diuine furie. *Hippofrigio,* a kind of musicke or accent and sound in musicke. *Phrigio,* a melody, tune or musicke wherin seemeth to be a deuine fury. **1659** TORRIANO-FLORIO It→E *Frigio,* a kind of melody or tune ancient[l]y used among the Grecians, wherein seemed to be some divine fury *Phrigio,* a tune or melodious musick wherein seemeth to be a divine fury. **1678** PHILLIPS (4th edn) § *Phrygian Mood in Musick.* See *Mood.* **1706** KERSEY-PHILLIPS (6th edn) § *Phrygian Mood,* (among the Ancients) a Warlike kind of Musick, fit for Trumpets, Hautboys, &c. which serv'd to raise the Minds of Men for undertaking Military Atchievements or Martial Exercises: Also a chearful, sprightly Measure in dancing. **1707** *Gloss. Angl. Nova* (1st edn) § *Phrygian Mood,* a Warlike kind of Musick fit for Trumpets, Hautboys, *&c.* Also a sprightly Measure in Dancing. **1728** CHAMBERS § *Phrygian Mode,* in Music. See *Mode.* **1730** BAILEY *Dict. Britannicum* (1st edn) § *Musick* (of the *Phrygian Mood*) was martial, and excited Men to Fury and Battel; by this mood *Timotheus* stirred up *Alexander* to Arms. **1736** BAILEY *Dict. Britannicum* (2nd edn) § *Phrygian Mode* (in *Musick*) was adapted to the hindring of rage invented by *Marsyas* the *Phrygian.* **1737** DYCHE-PARDON (2nd edn) § *Phrygian Mood* (S.) the *Musical Term* for such Sort of Compositions as are usually play'd upon Trumpets, Hautboys and other Warlike Instruments, intended to excite Chearfulness, Courageousness, &c.

1586 ANON. *Praise of Mvsicke* (p. 55) *Modus Phrygius* distracting the mind variably, also called *Bacchicus* for his great force & violence aunswereth to that which I called warlik ... **early 17th C.** ANON. Praise of musicke BL 18. B. xix, f. 11 [marginalia: 'Phrigian musick'] Another kynd or mood of musick of a more stirringe disposition comonly vsed in warre, Truimphes and such like, named *Phrigian* musick, the manner of wch: musick consisteth of skippinge and Jumpinge notes, of vneven and distracted measures and sounds, not so much respectinge the truthe of number, as the sudden cominge from longe notes to very short ones, the which musick was acted vpon instruments either single, as Trumpetts, Cornetts, Shalmes, Flutes, and such lyke violent instruments, or in that musick, where these together with voyces were conioyned. **1636** BUTLER *Principles of Musik* (p. 2) The *Phrygian* Moode is a manly and coorragious kinde of Musik, which, with his stately, or loud and violent tones, rouseth the spirit, and inciteth to arms and activiti: such ar Marches, Almains, and the warlike sounds of Trumpet, Fife, and Drum. § (p. 4) The *Phrygian* Moode [was so called] of *Phrygia*, a region bordering upon Lydia and Caria: in which is *Cios* that martiall Mart-toun, and the most high hil *Ida*, famous for the Trojan war.

phrygium melos

1565 COOPER L→E *Phrygium melos*, A melodie or tune in instrumentes, wherein seemed to bee (as Lucianus sayeth) a maner of diuine furie, all be it Porphyrius called it barbarous. Cassiodorus sayeth, that the melody, called *Dorium*, geueth wysedome, and chastitie: *Phrygium* styrreth to battayle, and inflameth the desyre of furie: *Aeolium* appeaseth the tempestes of the mynde, and bryngeth in sleape. *Lydium* quickeneth vnderstanding in them that be dull, and induceth appetite of celestiall thynges. **1587** THOMAS L→E *Phrygium melos*, *A melody or tune, wherein seemed to be a diuine furie. **1589** RIDER L→E *Phrygium melos*. A melodie in singing, wherein seemed to be a divine furie.

phthongus *see* note, phigthongo

1587 THOMAS L→E *Pthongus, i, m.g. Plin.* A sownd, tune, or note. **1598** FLORIO It→E *Phtongo*, a sound, a tune, or a note. **1611** FLORIO It→E *Phtongo*, a sound, a tune or a note. **1706** KERSEY-PHILLIPS (6th edn) *Phthongus*, a Sound, Tune or Note in Musick.

pianissimo

1724 [PEPUSCH] *Short Explic. of Foreign Words in Mus. Bks.* (p. 54) *Pianissimo*, or *PPP*, is extream Soft or Low. See the Word *Eccho*. (p. 96) *Pianissimo*, or *PPP*, Extream Soft. **1726** BAILEY *An Univ. Etymolog. Engl. Dict.* (3rd edn) *Pianissimo* (in *Musick Books*) signifies extreme soft or low. *Ital.* See *Eccho*.

c.1710 ANON. *Preceptor for Improved Octave Flageolet* ('Explanation of Words', p. 82) *P.P.* or *Pianissimo*—Very soft **1731** PRELLEUR *Modern Musick-Master* (Dictionary, p. 3) *Pianissimo* or *P.P.P.* very Soft

piano *see* doux, echo, forte, p

1598 FLORIO It→E *Piano*, ... Also low, as *Parlar piano, cantar piano*, to speake or sing low. **1611** FLORIO It→E *Piano*, ... Also low, as *Cantar Piano*, to sing low. **1724** [PEPUSCH] *Short Explic. of Foreign Words in Mus. Bks.* (p. 54) *Piano*, or the letter *P*, signifies Soft or Low. (p. 96) *Piano*, or *P*, Soft. § (p. 96) *Piano Piano*, or *Piu Piano*, or *PP*, Very Soft. (p. 54) *Piu Piano*, or *PP*, is very Soft or Low. **1726** BAILEY *An Univ. Etymolog. Engl. Dict.* (3rd edn) *Piano* (in *Musick Books*) signifies soft or low. *Ital.* **1730** BAILEY *Dict. Britannicum* (1st edn) *P.P.* (in *Musical Books*) is used for *piu, piano*, Ital. *i.e.* more soft. **1737** DYCHE-PARDON (2nd edn) *Piano* (A.) a Term in *Musick*, that signifies a Part of the Air or Strain repeated very softly, or like a gentle Echo.

1680 B., A. *Synopsis of Vocal Musick* (p. 42) ... *Italians* only, and some that them do follow, do use these two words, *Forte* and *Piano*, signifying that such part of a song must be sung clearer and fuller, under which is written *Forte*, but softer and smaller, under which is written *Piano*. **1683** PURCELL *Sonnata's of III Parts* (*To the Reader*) ... It remains only that the English Practitioner be enform'd, that he will find a few terms of Art perhaps unusual to him, the chief of which are these following: ... *Piano*, soft. **1706** BEDFORD *Temple Musick* (p. 194) ... *and the Intermissions of a certain silence, is signified by this Word* [selah], *which is also expressed in the* Italian Songs *by these Words* Piano, *and* Forte... **c.1710** ANON. *Preceptor for Improved Octave Flageolet* ('Explanation of Words', p. 82) *Pia*: or *Piano*—Soft **1736** TANS'UR *Compleat Melody* (3rd edn, p. 67) *Piano, P.*—*Pianissimo, P.P.P.* (Ital.) Either of those *Terms*, denote that you must *sing* or *play* very soft and low. *Piu Piano*, or *P.P.* signifies a little more soft and low.

pibole

1611 COTGRAVE Fr→E *Pibole: f.* A kind of Bagpipe. *Piboleur: m.* A Piper. *Poictevin.*

pico *see* men

picque *see* andante
1724 [PEPUSCH] *Short Explic. of Foreign Words in Mus. Bks.* (p. 55) *Picque*, the same as *Pointe*, which see. **1726** BAILEY *An Univ. Etymolog. Engl. Dict.* (3rd edn) *Picque* (in *Musick Books*) is to separate or divide each Note one from another, in a very plain and distinct manner. *Ital.*

piece
1688 MIEGE-COTGRAVE Fr→E *Piece*, (f.) ... a piece, as of Musick, Poesy, a Painting ... § *Piece de Musique*, ... a piece of Musick

pieno *see* ripieno
1724 [PEPUSCH] *Short Explic. of Foreign Words in Mus. Bks.* (p. 55) *Pieno*, signifies full; and is often used instead of the Words *Tutti*, *Grande*, or *Grose*. Thus, ¶ *Pieno Choro*, Full Chorus. **1726** BAILEY *An Univ. Etymolog. Engl. Dict.* (3rd edn) *Pieno* (in *Musick Books*) signifies full; and is frequently us'd instead of the Words *Tutti*, *Grande*, or *Grose*, as *Pieno Chero* [sic], a full Chorus. *Ital.*

pifara *see* fife

piladion
1661 BLOUNT *Pyladion*, a kind of Song; see *Bachyllion*. **1676** COLES *Piladion*, a song or dance of ¶ *Pilades*, a notable Comedian. *Pyladion*, as *Piladion*.

pinax
1587 THOMAS L→E *Pinax, Vitruv.* A boord in the vpper part of the organs, wheron the pipes stand.

pinceter
1593 HOLLYBAND Fr→E *Pinceter*, to pinch thicke, to play swift and fine vpon a lute. § *le printens d'yver, et pincetant sur les chanterelles de son luth obeïssant, &c.* playing vpon the singing cords of her obedient Lute, &c. **1611** COTGRAVE Fr→E *Pinceter*. To pinch thicke ... also, to touch a Lute, &c, nimbly;

pipe *see* appeau, aulos, avena, biumbe, busciarella, busine, buxum, calamus, canna, ceramella, chalemie, chalumeau, cicuticen, cifello, cingria, colonna, concionatorius, faucet, fistula, flageolet, flusteau, gingrina, monaulos, musella, piva, sampogna, sibbio, siringa, stifello, succhiello, syrinx, tibia, zigia, zuffolo
1688 MIEGE-COTGRAVE Fr→E *Pipeau, ou chalumeau*, (m.) a pipe, an oaten-pipe; **1696** PHILLIPS (5th edn) *Pipe*, ... Also the Shepherds Musick commonly called an Oaten Reed. **1702** KERSEY *New Engl. Dict.* (1st edn) A *Pipe*, ... a sort of musical instrument, *&c.* To *pipe, or* play upon the pipe. A *Piper, or* player on the pipe; **1706** KERSEY-PHILLIPS (6th edn) *Pipe*, ... a sort of Musical Instrument: **1721** BAILEY *An Univ. Etymolog. Engl. Dict.* (1st edn) *Pipe*, (Pipe, *Sax. piepe*, *Du. pipeau*, F. pfeiffe, *Teut. Fifaro*, Ital.) a musical Instrument, a Reed, ... **1728** CHAMBERS *Pipe* .... *For the Pipes of Organs*: See *Organ*. **1731** KERSEY *New Engl. Dict.* (3rd edn) To *pipe*, to play upon a Pipe *or* Flute. **1737** DYCHE-PARDON (2nd edn) *Pipe* (S.) an Instrument applied to various Uses, ... to produce Musical Sounds, &c. *Pipe* (V.) to play upon the Flute, Hautboy, &c. also to cry. *Piper* (S.) one who goes about the Country playing upon a small Pipe or musical Instrument, for the Country Folks to dance after, &c.

pirolo
1598 FLORIO It→E *Pirolo*, ... Also a pinne or a peg for an instrument of musick. **1611** FLORIO It→E *Pirolo*, ... Also any woodden peg or pinne for an instrument of musike. **1659** TORRIANO-FLORIO It→E *Pirolo*, any turned or round wooden peg or pin, namely of a musical Instrument

pirrica *see* pyrricha

Piseus
1565 COOPER L→E *Piseus*, He that first inuented the brasen trumpet.

pistoy bass
1676 MACE *Musick's Monument* (pp. 65-6) The first and *Chief Thing* [in stringing your lute] is, to be carefull to get *Good Strings*, which would be of *three sorts*, viz. *Minikins*, *Venice-Catlins*, and *Lyons*, (for *Basses*:) There is another sort of *Strings*, which they call *Pistoy Basses*, which I conceive are none other than *Thick Venice-Catlins*, which are commonly *Dyed*, with a *deep dark red colour*. ¶ They are indeed the *very Best*, for the *Basses*, being *smooth* and *well-twisted Strings*, but are hard to come by; However out of a *Good parcel of Lyon Strings*, you may (with care) pick those which will serve *very well*.

pitalamio *see* epithalamy
1598 FLORIO It→E *Pitalamio*, a kind of marriage song. **1611** FLORIO It→E *Pitalamio*, a kind of mariage song. **1659** TORRIANO-FLORIO It→E *Pitalamio*, as *Epitalamio*.

pitch *see* agreslir la voix, clef, consort pitch, falso bordone, flatness, intonation, part, tension, tone, transposition
1725 De La Fond *New System of Music* (p. 14) ... I call the *pitch, the most agreeable degree or place to fix the scale upon.*

pithaules
1587 Thomas L→E *Pithaules, Iun.* A player on a bagpipe.

pittide *see* pettido
1659 Torriano-Florio It→E *Pittide,* a doleful Instrument.

piu *see* p
1724 [Pepusch] *Short Explic. of Foreign Words in Mus. Bks.* (p. 55) *Piu,* signifies a little more, and increaseth the Strength of the Signification of the Word it is joyned with. Thus, ¶ *Piu Allegro* is to play a little more gay or brisk than the Word *Allegro* only does require, and *Piu Presto* is to play somewhat quicker than the Word *Presto* only does require. **1726** Bailey *An Univ. Etymolog. Engl. Dict.* (3rd edn) *Piu* (in *Musick Books*) signifies a little more, and increases the Strength of the Signification of the Word it is joined with § *Piu Allegro,* i.e. Play a little more gay and brisk than *Allegro* by it self requires. *Ital. Piu Piano* (in *Musick Books*) signifies soft and slow. *Ital. Piu Presto,* i.e. Play quicker than *Presto* it self requires. *Ital.*

1731 Prelleur *Modern Musick-Master* (Dictionary, p. 3) *Piu Piano* or *P.P.* Softer.... *Piu Allegro,* more Brisk then *Allegro.* ¶ *Piu Presto* Quicker then *Presto.* **after 1731** Anon. *Directions for Playing on the Flute* (Dictionary, n.p.) *Piu*: signifies more, as *Piu Allegro,* more brisk than *Allegro* **1736** Tans'ur *Compleat Melody* (3rd edn, p. 66) *N.B.* That *Piu,* (Ital.) signifies a little *more.*

piva *see* mute, sordine
1598 Florio It→E *Piua,* a pipe, a bag-pipe. *Piua sorda,* a sourdine put in a trumpet, to still the shrilnes of it. **1611** Florio It→E *Piua,* any kind of pipe or bag-pipe. *Piuasorda,* a still bag-pipe. Also a sordine to still the shrilnesse of a Trumpet. **1659** Torriano-Florio It→E *Piva,* any musical pipe, namely, a bag-pipe, or horn-pipe *Pivaro,* a piper § *Piva sordina, Piva sorda,* a surdin put in at the mouth end of a Trumpet or Cornet to still the shrillnesse of it, also a still horn-pipe **1724** [Pepusch] *Short Explic. of Foreign Words in Mus. Bks.* (p. 56) *Piva,* a Hautboy is sometimes so called. **1726** Bailey *An Univ. Etymolog. Engl. Dict.* (3rd edn) *Piva,* a Hautboy. *Ital.*

place
c.1596 Bathe *Briefe Intro. to skill of Song* [C] [*re* two and three parts in one] First it is to be vnderstanded by this word place, is ment the distance of the following part, to the former part, as the same place or vnison, is called the first place, the next or second place is called the second place, whether it be vp or downe, &c.

plagal *see* ecclesiastic tone, mode, mood, tone, tune
1664 Birchensha-Alsted *Templvm Mvsicvm* (p. 77) ... But the *Latines* more narrowly considering the ascension and descension of every *Tone,* have constituted to every *Mood* a subjugal *Mood;* and those four they call *Plagal;* also subjugal, servile, and the like. § (p. 80) *The nature of the Plagal Moods is this.* This Mood is called Plagal, as if we should say oblique or inversed; which hath its final Key in the lowest part of the fifth, but above the fourth: and is divided arithmetically. **1667** Simpson *Compendium of Practical Musick* (p. 113) These Moods or Tones had yet another distinction; and that was, *Authentick,* or *Plagal.* This depended upon the dividing of the *Octave* into its *5th.* and *4th... Plagal,* was when the *5th.* possest the upper place, according to the Arithmetical division thereof.

plain beat *see* beat
1659 Simpson *Division-Violist* (p. 9) *Graces* done with the *Fingers,* are of two sorts: *viz, smooth,* and *shaked. Smooth* is, when in rising, or falling, a *Tone,* or *Semitone,* we seem to draw as it were, the Sound from one *Note* to another, in imitation of the *Voice;* and is expressed by setting down, or taking off the Finger, a little after the touch of the *Bow.* In ascending, it makes that Grace which we call a *Plain-Beat* or *Rise;* in descending, that called a *Backfall.*

plainchant *see* recitative
1688 Miege-Cotgrave Fr→E *Plain-chant* See *Plein-chant. Plein-chant,* (m.) a singing by the Notes.

plain counterpoint *see* canto fermo

plain descant

1706 KERSEY-PHILLIPS (6th edn) *Plain Descant.* See *Descant.*

plain music

1609 DOWLAND-ORNITHOPARCUS *Micrologvs* (p. 3) *Plaine Musicke,* (as *Saint Bernard* an excellent searcher into regular and true Concinence) doth write in the beginning of his Musicke, saying: It is a rule determining the nature and forme of regular Songs. Their nature consists in the disposition, their forme in the progression and composition. Or plaine Musicke is a simple and vniforme prolation of Notes, which can neither be augmented nor diminished.

plainsong *see* accino, canto fermo, chant, contrapeso, contre, counterpoint, descant, diatonic, diatonic music, falso bordone, figuration, in nomine, mimo subservire, motet, tenor

1597 MORLEY *Plaine and Easie Introdvction* (p. 70) *Phi.* What is the mean to sing vpon a playne song. ¶ *Ma.* To know the distances both Concords and Discords.

after 1695 NORTH untitled notebook BL Add. 32532, f. 10v [*re* the history of English music] The oldest Musick was that used in churches called plaine song. for ye Salmes & himnes... **c.1715-20** NORTH Essay of Musical Ayre BL Add. 32536, f. 67 [*re* the history of English church music] ... It became ordinary to take some church Anthem or part of it, for that they Called a plain-song, and particularly the words In Nomine domini, wch fitt ye 8. notes of the scale ascending or descending ffor in all voicing some syllables must be used.

plango

1552 HULOET L→E *Plango. is. anxi, Plecto. is Pulso. as* Stryke an instrument.

Plato *see* apotome, choreuma, chorodidascalus, dorick, eschrakites, harmony, harmony of the¡ spheres, melody, mundane music, music¡

play *see* floralia, secular plays

1737 DYCHE-PARDON (2nd edn) *Plays* (S.) by this Term the Antients understood all Manner of Diversions whatever, ... the Plays of the Capitoline were also another Sort of solemn Horse-Races, Wrestlings, &c. here were also Concerts of Musick performed by the best Masters, Rehearsals of Poems, and other Trials of Wit, by the best Poets and Orators; ... the Plays of *Flora* were so offensive that they were forced to be put down, common Women appearing publickly naked, and in the Night-Time ran about with Links in their Hands, dancing in lascivious Postures to the Sound of musical Instruments, and singing immodest Songs; ... in the *Pyrrhick Plays,* the young Soldiers ... also exhibited by their Gestures all the full Duties of Soldiers in War, ... during which the Musick both animated the Soldiers, and diverted the Spectators with the Sound of many Flutes, &c.

Playford, John *see* galliard, mood, syncopation

plectrum *see* linguella, palmula, pecten, plango, polyplectra

1500 *Ortus Vocabulorum* L→E Plectrum tri. gubernaculum nauis vel lingua in corpore vel potus vltima pers lingue et percussorium cythare n.s. vus § Est nauis plectrum lingue cythare regimenque texendi plectrum cythare. **1538** ELYOT L→E *Plectrum,* an instrument, wherwith menne played on the harpe or doulcymers, for hurtynge of their fyngers. **1552** HULOET L→E *Plectrum. tri, pecten nis,* Quyll, with whiche a musician vseth to play to saue his fingers, or any lyke thinge ... but more artly a musicians sticke. &c. **1565** COOPER L→E *Plectrum, plectri, n.g. Martial.* An instrument wherewith men played on the harpe and dulcimers. **1587** THOMAS L→E *Plectropœus, Iun. qui plectra & cytharas parat. Plectrum, ri, n.g.* A quill, bowe, or such like thing to play withall vpon the strings of a harp, rebeck, or dulcimer. **1589** RIDER L→E *Plectrum, n. Dædala, f.* A bowe, wherewith they play on a fidle, or viole. *Plectrum, n. dædala, f. pecten, m.* A fidle sticke. **1598** FLORIO It→E *Pletro,* a fidling sticke, a bowe, a sticke or quill to play vpon any instrument of musicke. **1599** MINSHEU-PERCYVALL Sp→E **Plectro,* m. a quill or such like thing to strike the strings of a harpe, psalterie or such like instrument. **1611** COTGRAVE Fr→E *Plectre: m.* The quill, or bow, wherewith a Citterne, or Violl, is played on. **1611** FLORIO It→E *Pletro,* a fidling sticke or bow. Also a quill to play vpon any instrument. **1659** TORRIANO-FLORIO It→E *Pletro,* an arket, a bow, a fidling-stick to play upon the strings of any Instrument

1582 *Batman vppon Bartholome* (chap. 134) [*re* the harp] ... & the wrest is called *Plectrum.*

pneumatica *see* hydraulicks
1565 Cooper L→E § *Organ pneumatica. Plin.* ... also Organes, pipes, and such like goeyng with winde. **1611** Florio It→E *Pneumatica*, all manner of wind-musike.

poche *see* kit
1611 Cotgrave Fr→E *Poche: f.* A pocket ... also, the little narrow, and long Violin (hauing the backe of one peece) which French dauncers, or dauncing Maisters, carrie about with them in a case, when they goe to teach their Schollers. **1688** Miege-Cotgrave Fr→E *Poche*, (f.) a pocket ... a Kit, or pocket Violin;

poco *see* assai, largo, men, un poco
1724 [Pepusch] *Short Explic. of Foreign Words in Mus. Bks.* (p. 56) *Poco*, a little less, and is just the contrary to the foregoing Word *Piu*, and therefore lessens the Strength of the Signification of the Words joyned with it. Thus, ¶ *Poco Allegro* is to play not quite so brisk as the Word *Allegro* if alone would require. *Poco Presto* not quite so quick as *Presto* if alone would require; and *Poco Largo* is not quite so slow as the Word *Largo* alone does require. ¶ *Poco Piu Allegro*, is a little more brisk; but *Poco Meno Allegro*, is a little less brisk. **1726** Bailey *An Univ. Etymolog. Engl. Dict.* (3rd edn) *Poco* (in *Musick Books*) signifies a *little less*, and is just the contrary to *Piu*, and therefore lessens the Strength of the Signification of the Words joined with it. *Poco Allegro*, directs to play not quite so brisk as *Allegro* requires, if it stood alone. *Poco Piu Allegro*, signifies a little more brisk. *Poco Meno Allegro*, signifies a little less brisk. *Poco Largo*, signifies not quite so slow, as the Word *Largo* requires when it stands alone. *Poco Presto*, signifies not quite so quick, as *Presto* if it stands alone requires. **1737** Dyche-Pardon (2nd edn) *Poco* (A.) a *Musical Term*, signifying Diminution, or making the Word to which it is joined somewhat less, as *Poco Allegro* is somewhat slower than *Allegro*.

1728 North Musicall Grammarian (*C-K MG* ff. 74v-75) ... some masters write poco allegro, or assai to temper the impertinent hast[e] that some self conceipted performers are apt to make more for ostentation of hand then justice to the musick. When the master is for that sport, he writes presto, or prestissimo, but never when any fuge is thought of. **1731** Prelleur *Modern Musick-Master* (Dictionary, p. 3) *Poco Allegro*, not so Brisk as *Allegro* ¶ *Poco Presto*, not so Quick as *Presto* ¶ *Poco Largo* not so Slow as *Largo* **after 1731** Anon. *Directions for Playing on the Flute* (Dictionary, n.p.) *Poco*: signifies less, as *Poco largo*, not so slow as *Largo*.

point *see* arsis & thesis, fugue, guide, report, revert
1728 Chambers *Point*, in Musick, a Mark or Note anciently used to distinguish the Tones. See *Note.* ¶ Hence we still call it *Simple Counter-Point*, when a Note of the Bass, answers precisely to that of the Treble; and *Figurative Counter-Point*, when a Note is syncopeed [sic], and one of the Parts makes several Inflexions of the Voice or Tone, while the other only makes one. See *Counter-Point*, [sic] ¶ We still use a *Point* to raise the Value of a Note, and prolong its Time by one half, *e. gr*, a *Point* added to a Semibreve, instead of two Minims, makes it equal to three. See *Time*, and *Characters in Musick.* **1730** Bailey *Dict. Britannicum* (1st edn) *Point* (in *Musick*) a Mark or Note antiently used to distinguish the Tones.

1636 Butler *Principles of Musik* (p. 71) A Point is a certain number and order of observable Notes in any one Parte, iterated in the same or in divers Partes: within the time commonly of two Sembriefs in qik Sonnets, and of fowr or five in graver Musik. **1667** Simpson *Compendium of Practical Musick* (p. 128) [*re* the fugue] This is some Point, (as we term it in Musick) consisting of 4, 5, 6, or any other number of Notes; begun by some one single Part, and then seconded by a following Part ... **after 1695** North untitled notebook BL Add. 32532, f. 9v ... But having this foundation of a fuge, or a short tune, w[ch] they call a point, it is not unpleasing if y[e] same part Repeat's it.

pointe *see* andante
1724 [Pepusch] *Short Explic. of Foreign Words in Mus. Bks.* (p. 57) *Pointe*, the same as *Staccato*, or *Spiccato*, for which see those Words. (p. 59) *Punctus*, a Point, the same as the following Word. *Punto*, a Point, a Character in Musick very well known. **1726** Bailey *An Univ. Etymolog. Engl. Dict.* (3rd edn) *Pointe* (in *Musick Books*) signifies to separate or divide each Note one from another, in a very plain and distinct Manner. *Ital. Punto*, a Point. *Ital.*

pointing *as fugal writing, see* fugue

pointing *as rhythmic inequality*
[1729] HOTTETERRE *Rudiments or Principles of German Flute* (p. 17) ... You must observe that Quavers are not always to be play'd equally, but that you must in certain movements make one long, and one short, which is also regulated by their number when they are even. You make the first long, the second short, and so on. when [sic] they are odd, you do quite the reverse, that is called pointing; the movements in which 'tis most commonly used is Duple, or Common Time. **1731** PRELLEUR *Modern Musick-Master* (III *re* flute, p. 7) Quavers are not always to be play'd equally, but you must in certain movements make one long, and one short, which is also regulated by their number, for when they are even, You must make the first long[,] the second short and when they are odd, you do quite the reverse, that is call'd pointing; the movements in which 'tis most commonly used is common Time, Triple Time, and Jigg Time of $\frac{6}{4}$. You must pronounce *Ru* on the Note which follows y[e.] Quaver w[n.] it ascends, or descends by one step only.

poliphant *see* polyphon
1694 PURCELL-PLAYFORD *Intro. to Skill of Musick* (12th edn, preface) Queen *Elizabeth* ... she did often recreate herself on an excellent Instrument called the *Poliphant*, not much unlike a *Lute*, but strung with Wire: ...

Polyhymnia *see* Muse
1706 KERSEY-PHILLIPS (6th edn) *Polyhymnia* or *Polymnia*, one of the nine Muses, who presided over the Hymns and Songs that were play'd on the Lute and Harp. **1708** KERSEY *Dict. Anglo-Brit.* (1st edn) *Polyhymnia* or *Polymnia*, one of the nine Muses, who presided over Hymns and Songs play'd on the Lute, *&c.* **1730** BAILEY *Dict. Britannicum* (1st edn) *Polyhymnia* (πολυύμνεια of πολύς and ὕμνος, Gr. a Hymn) one of the 9 Muses, the President of Hymns, Songs, and Musick. **1737** DYCHE-PARDON (2nd edn) *Polyhymnia* (S.) one of the nine Muses; ... others said that she presided over Hymns, Songs, and Musick.

polyphon *see* poliphant
1656 BLOUNT (1st edn) *Polyphon* (Gr.) multiplicity of sound; also a musical instrument so called, having many strings, and by consequence several sounds. **1676** COLES *Polyphon, Greek.* (an instrument with) a multiplicity of sounds. **1702** KERSEY *New Engl. Dict.* (1st edn) A *Polyphon*, a musical Instrument, that has many things and a great variety of sounds. **1704** *Cocker's Engl. Dict.* (1st edn) *Polyphon*, a Musical Instrument which hath divers sounds. **1706** KERSEY-PHILLIPS (6th edn) *Polyphon*, a kind of Musical Instrument that has many Strings and Sounds. **1726** BAILEY *An Univ. Etymolog. Engl. Dict.* (3rd edn) *Polyphones* (of πολύς and φονή the Voice) Instruments to multiply Sounds.

polyplectra
1721 MALCOLM *Treatise of Musick* (p. 558) He [Guido d'Arezzo] is also said to be the Contriver of those Instruments they call *Polyplectra*, as *Spinets* and *Harpsichords*: However they may now differ in Shape, he contrived what is called the *Abacus* and the *Palmulæ*, that is, the *Machinery* by which the String is struck with a Plectrum made of Quills.

port de voix *see* slur
[1729] HOTTETERRE *Rudiments or Principles of German Flute* (p. 12) ... the *Port de voix*, which hereafter I shall call a Sigh ... **1731** PRELLEUR *Modern Musick-Master* (III *re* flute, p. 9) The Port-de-voix is a tipping with the Tongue, anticipated by one Note below the Note on which we design to make it.

porte-vent
1688 MIEGE-COTGRAVE FR→E *Porte-vent*, (m.) *la partie de la Musette par où l'on fait entrer le Vent*, the pipe of a Bag-pipe.

posaune *see* sackbut
1724 [PEPUSCH] *Short Explic. of Foreign Words in Mus. Bks.* (p. 57) *Posaune*, a Sackbut, an Instrument of Musick made Use of as a Bass to a Trumpet. **1726** BAILEY *An Univ. Etymolog. Engl. Dict.* (3rd edn) *Posaune*, a Sackbut, an Instrument of Musick, made use of as a Base to a Trumpet. *Ital.* **1730** BAILEY *Dict. Britannicum* (1st edn) *Posaume* [sic], a Sackbut, a musical Instrument, used as a Bass to a Trumpet.

position
1721 MALCOLM *Treatise of Musick* (pp. 530-1) Now, every *Mode* being considered by it self as a distinct *System*, may have the Names *Proslamb. hyp-hyp.* &c. applied to it; for these signify only in general the Positions of the Chords in any particular *System*; if they are so applied, he [Ptolomy] calls them the *Positions*; for *Example*, the first Chord, or gravest Note of any *Mode* is called its *Proslamb.*

positione, and so if the rest in Order. But again these are considered as coinciding, or being unison, with certain Chords of the *System*; and these Chords are called the *potestates*, with respect to that *Mode*; for *Example*, the *Hypodorian* begins in *D*, or *Lichanos hypaton* of the System, which therefore is the *potestas* of its *Proslamb.* as *Hyp[o]meson* is the *potestas* of its *hyp-hyp.* and so of others, *that is*, these Two Chords coincide and differ only in Name; and we also say, that such a numerical Chord as *Prosl. positione* of any Mode is such a Chord, as *hyp-hyp. potestate*, which is equivalent to saying, that *hyp-hyp.* of the System is the *Potestas* of the *Proslamb. positione* of that Mode.

positive

1728 CHAMBERS *Positive*, in Musick, the little Organ usually behind, or at the foot of the Organist, play'd with the same Wind, and the same Bellows, and consisting of the same Number of Pipes with the large one; tho, those much smaller, and in a certain Proportion. See *Organ*. ¶ In the Organs of the Jesuits, the *Positive* is in the grand Body. **1730** BAILEY *Dict. Britannicum* (1st edn) *A Positive* (in *Musick*) the little Organ usually behind or at the Foot of the Organist, play'd with the same Wind, and the same Bellows, and consisting of the same Number of Pipes with the large one.

postposition *see* anticipation, resolution

1730 [PEPUSCH] *Short Treatise on Harmony* (p. 37) *Postposition*, or Retardation of Harmony, is the putting a Discord upon the Accented Part of the Bar, follow'd by a Concord on the Unaccented Part, but not Prepared and Resolved, according to the Regular Rules for Discords.

practick music *see* active music

præcino *see* precention

1538 ELYOT L→E *Præcino, nui, nere*, to synge before or fyrst **1552** HULOET L→E *Præcinno. is* Syng before. *Præcinno. is*, Syng fyrst. **1565** COOPER L→E *Præcino, præcinis, penult. corr. præcínui, præcentum, præcínere. Plin.* To beginne to singe: to singe before or first: **1587** THOMAS L→E *Præcino, is, ui, entum, ere, ex Præ & Cano.* To begin to sing, to sing before or first: **1589** RIDER L→E *Præcino.* To sing before, or beginne the song.

præcoseralis

1589 RIDER L→E *Præcoseralis. Stratileus, parisius. m.* A bell-man.

præfica *see* nænia

1552 HULOET L→E *Praefica* (as *Neuius* sayeth) is the woman that syngeth such songe [an epicedium] to cause the company to mourne **1589** RIDER L→E *Præfica, f.* A vvoman hired to mourne at a buriall, to praise the life & deeds of the dead bodye *Præfica, f.* The woman which singeth such songes [monodiæ].

praesica

1552 HULOET L→E *praesica. æ* Priest whyche begynneth the office or songe in the churche.

preamble *see* prelude, proludium

precantation

1587 THOMAS L→E *Præcantatio, onis, f.g. Quint.* A singing before, a charming, an inchaunting. **1589** RIDER L→E *Præcantatio, f. antecantamentum, n.* A singing before. **1623** COCKERAM *Præcantation.* A singing before. *Precantation.* a Singing before

precention *see* prelude, proludium

1538 ELYOT L→E *Præcentio*, that whiche is songen or playde at the beginning of a songe or balade. **1552** HULOET L→E *Præcentio. onis.* Dittye (as some do call) of a songe, or that whych is played or songe, at the begynninge of a songe or balade. **1565** COOPER L→E *Præcentio, onis, f.g. Verbale. Cic.* That is played or songen at the beginnyng of a songe or balade: the floorish. **1587** THOMAS L→E *Præcentio, onis, f.g. verb. à Præcino.* The entrance or beginning of a ballade, the onset of a song, the floorish. **1589** RIDER L→E *Præcentio, f.* An entrance to a balad. **1658** PHILLIPS (1st edn) *Præcention*, (lat.) the flourish, or entrance of a song, or ballad. **1661** BLOUNT (2nd edn) *Precention (præcentio)* a singing before; the on-set or flourish of a Song. **1676** COLES *Precention*, the flourish or Entrance of a Song. **1704** *Cocker's Engl. Dict.* (1st edn) *Precention*, the flourish before the Musick, or song begins.

precentor *see* chanter, præcino, praesica

1500 *Ortus Vocabulorum* L→E Precentor oris. qui in ecclesia vocem permittit in cantu. anglice a chauntour. s. principalis cantor m.t. Precentus tus tui. est dignitas precentoris. or a trebell m.q. **1538** Elyot L→E *Præcentor, toris*, he that first singeth. it may be taken for the chaunter in a quyre. **1552** Huloet L→E *Præcentor. ris*. Chaunter in a quier, or he that syngeth ye base, or fyrste, or is the chiefe synger. *Præcentor. ris*, he that singeth fyrst **1565** Cooper L→E *Præcentor, præcentôris, m.g.* He that singeth firste. A chaunter in a quiere. **1587** Thomas L→E *Præcentor, oris, m.g. Iun.* The Chanter, he that beginneth the tune. **1589** Rider L→E *Præcentor, mesochorus, m* He which beginneth the song. **1676** Coles *Precentor*, the Chantor, that begins the tune. **1704** *Cocker's Engl. Dict.* (1st edn) *Precentor*, the principal singing man in a Cathedral, who sets the Tune for the rest. **1706** Kersey-Phillips (6th edn) *Precentor*, the Chanter that begins the Tune in a Cathedral. **1728** Chambers *Precentor*, or *Præcentor*, a Dignitary in Cathedral Churches, popularly call'd the *Chanter*, or *Master of the Choir*. See *Chanter*. ¶ The *Præcentor* is so call'd, from the *Latin præ*, and *cano*; because he is supposed to lead the Choir, and *sing before* the rest. **1737** Dyche-Pardon (2nd edn) *Precentor* (S.) he that begins or leads the Chant or Tune in a Cathedral Church.

precentura

1500 *Ortus Vocabulorum* L→E Precentura re. an[e]. a chauntrye f.p.

predominant note

see dominant, final, key, repercussion

preface

1688 Miege-Cotgrave Fr→E *Dans l'Eglise Romaine on appelle aussi Preface la partie de la Messe qu'on di immediatement devant le Canon, & qui se chante aux grandes Messes.* **1728** Chambers *Preface, Præfatio* .... The *Romanists* call that part of their Mass which precedes the Consecration, and which is to be rehearsed in a peculiar Tone, *Preface*.

prelude

see fantasia, feeling, flourish, intrada, key, lesson, opera, overture, precention, prelusion, prohemium, proludium, prolusion, research, ricercar, ritornello, sonata, suit, symphony, toccata, voluntary

1538 Elyot L→E *Præludium*, a proheme, or that which Musicians and Mynstrelles doo playe at the begynnynge, er they come to the songe, which they purpose to playe. *Præludo, si, dere*, to playe before. **1565** Cooper L→E *Prælúdium, præludij, neut. gen. Cic.* A proheme: in musike a voluntarie before the songe: a floorish: a preamble or entrance to a mattier, and, as ye would say, signes and profers. *Præludo, prælûdis, prælúsi, prælûsum, penult. prod. prælúdere. Virg.* To play before: in musike to play a voluntary before the songe. **1587** Thomas L→E *Præludium, ij, n.g.* A proheme: in musicke a voluntary before the song: a floorish, preamble or entrance to a matter, & (as ye would say) signes and proffers. *Præludo, is, si, sum, ere, Virg.* To play before: in musicke to play a voluntarie before the song: **1598** Florio It→E *Preludio*, a proheme in musicke, a voluntary before the song **1611** Cotgrave Fr→E *Prelude: m.* ... and in Musicke, voluntarie before a lesson, &c. **1611** Florio It→E *Preludio*, a proheme in Musike, a flourish or voluntarie before a song or any musike. **1656** Blount (1st edn) *Preludium* (Lat. *præludium*) ... In musick, a *voluntary* before the Song, a flourish or preamble, and (as you would say) signs and proffers. **1658** Phillips (1st edn) *Prælude*, (lat.) ... also in Musick it is taken for a voluntary or flourish upon any instrument. **1659** Torriano-Florio It→E *Preludio*, ... a proem, a flourish, or voluntary before a song or any musick. **1676** Coles *Prelude, -dium*, a proem or Entrance, and (in Musick) a Voluntary or flourish before a song or lesson. *Prelusion*, the same. **1688** Miege-Cotgrave Fr→E *Prelude*, (m.) *tout ce qu'on jouë d'abord sur quêque Instrument de Musique, pour se concilier les Gens devant qui on doit jouër*, a Prelude. † *Preluder, cd. commencer à jouër un peu sur quêque Instrument de Musique, pour se mettre en train*, to prelude, to play a Prelude. **1702** Kersey *New Engl. Dict.* (1st edn) A *Prelude*, a flourish of musick, before the playing of a tune; **1704** *Cocker's Engl. Dict.* (1st edn) *Preludium*, a *Prologue*, or Speech before any song, or play: A flourish before the Musick begins the Tune. **1704** Harris *Prelude*, in Musick, signifies any Flourish that is Introductory to Musick which is to follow after. **1706** Kersey-Phillips (6th edn) *Prelude*, properly the preparatory Notes of Musicians before they begin to play, a Voluntary, or Flourish; **1707** *Gloss. Angl. Nova* (1st edn) *Prelude*, (Lat.) a Flourish of Musick before the Playing of a Tune **1724** [Pepusch] *Short Explic. of Foreign Words in Mus. Bks.* (p. 57) *Preludio*, a Prelude; the first Part or Beginning of a Piece of Musick is often so called; and is much the same as *Overture*. **1726** Bailey *An Univ. Etymolog. Engl. Dict.* (3rd edn) *Preludio* in ([sic] *Musick Books*) signifies a Prelude; the first Part or Beginning of a Piece of Musick, and is much the same as *Overture*. Ital. **1728** Chambers *Prelude*, in Music, a *Flourish*, or an irregular Air which the Musician plays off-hand, to see if his Instrument be in Tune; and to lead him into the piece to be play'd. **1730** BAILEY *Dict. Britannicum* (1st edn) To *Prelude* (*præludere*, L. *preluder*, F.) to flourish before or make a Prelude, to play an irregular Air off Hand, to try if the Instrument be in Tune, and to lead into the Piece to be play'd. **1737** DYCHE-PARDON (2nd edn) *Prelude* (S.) in *Musick*, is an Overture or Sort of Flourish in the Key, to try whether the Instrument is in Tune, and to dispose the Hand to stop the following Lessons the better; *Prelude* (V.) ... also to run over the Strings or Stops of a musical Instrument, to prepare the Hand, and try whether the Instrument is in Tune.

1597 HOLBORNE *Cittharn Schoole* (preface) ... in the front of the booke (as the first step or key to open a way to thy beginnings) I haue prefixed some fewe tastes, which by another name I call *Præludia*: things short and not hard: deliuered vnto thee of purpose to guide thy hand to some proper vse of plaie, and withall to search and feele if thy *Cytharn* be well in tune: thinges verie well also becomming any man as a preface before he shall proceede to do any determinate matter. Next vnto them as in an orderly consequence I haue conioyned the most vsuall and familiar grounds of these our times, for consort or thine owne priuate selfe: together with some such other light fansies of vulgar tunes for variety as I could best call to memory: ... **1676** MACE *Musick's Monument* (p. 120) The First [lesson in a '*Sett*, or a *Suit of Lessons*'] always, should begin, in the Nature of a *Voluntary Play*, which we call a *Præludium*, or *Prælude*. § (p. 128) The *Prælude* is commonly a *Piece of Confused-wild-shapeless-kind of Intricate-Play*, (as most use It) in which no perfect *Form, Shape*, or *Uniformity* can be perceived; but a *Random-Business, Pottering*, and *Grooping*, up and down, from one *Stop*, or *Key*, to another; And generally, so performed, to make *Tryal*, whether the *Instrument* be *well in Tune*, or not; ... **1736** TANS'UR *Compleat Melody* (3rd edn, p. 71) *Prelude, Preludo, Preludium* (Ital.) Either of those *Terms*, are a Name given to a short *Air*, or *Symphony*, play'd before a Piece of *Musick* begins; sometimes by *Rule*, and oftentimes Extempore.

prelusion *see* prelude, prolusion

1656 BLOUNT (1st edn) *Prelusion* (*prælusio*) a playing before, a flourish, the same with *præludium*.

preparation

1728 NORTH Musicall Grammarian (*C-K MG* f. 43) ... And from thence I extract this generall and infallible rule: the air of any key may pass immediately into that of any other key which is a prime accord, (that is a 3d or 5th) of the former ascending or descending; and into no other without large circuitations, and interpositions, which the masters call preparation. Such preparation is sometimes necessary, and sometimes used for elegance, and often not needful at all, altho there are formes which usually taken them in.

presa *see* ripresa

1724 [PEPUSCH] *Short Explic. of Foreign Words in Mus. Bks.* (p. 57) *Presa*, is a Character in Musick called a Repeat. **1726** BAILEY *An Univ. Etymolog. Engl. Dict.* (3rd edn) *Presa* (in *Musick Books*) a Character in Musick call'd a Repeat. *Ital.*

prestissimo *see* velocissimo

1724 [PEPUSCH] *Short Explic. of Foreign Words in Mus. Bks.* (p. 57) *Prestissimo*, is Extream Fast or Quick. (p. 95) *Prestissimo*, Extream Quick. **1726** BAILEY *An Univ. Etymolog. Engl. Dict.* (3rd edn) *Prestissimo* (in *Musick Books*) signifies extreme fast or quick. *Ital.*

c.1710 ANON. *Preceptor for Improved Octave Flageolet* ('Explanation of Words', p. 82) *Prestissimo*—Very fast or quicker than Presto **1731** PRELLEUR *Modern Musick-Master* (Dictionary, p. 3) *Prestissimo*, very Quick.

presto *see* promptement, pronto, veloce, vistamente, vite

1724 [PEPUSCH] *Short Explic. of Foreign Words in Mus. Bks.* (p. 57) *Presto*, Fast or Quick. (p. 95) *Presto*, Quick. § (p. 57) *Men Presto*, not too Quick; or not quite So Quick. (p. 58) *Non Troppo Presto*, not Too Quick. *Poco Presto*, not very Quick. *Presto Presto*, or *Piu Presto*, very Fast or Quick. See *Piu*. (p. 95) *Presto Presto*, or *Piu Presto*, very Quick. **1726** BAILEY *An Univ. Etymolog. Engl. Dict.* (3rd edn) *Presto* (in *Musick Books*) signifies fast or quick. *Ital.* § *Presto Presto*, signifies very fast or quick. *Men Presto*, not too quick. *Ital.* *Non troppo Presto*, not too quick. *Ital.* **1737** DYCHE-PARDON (2nd edn) *Presto* (S.) in *Musick*, signifies quick or very fast;

1680 B., A. *Synopsis of Vocal Musick* (p. 19) The secondary signs of the Tact or Time are certain words used by the *Italians*, and afterwards also of others, to wit, *Adagio*, and *Presto*, signifying, that such a part of a Song where *Adagio* is written, is to be Sung slower, and where *Presto*, swifter. **c.1710** ANON. *Preceptor for Improved Octave Flageolet* ('Explanation of Words', p. 82) *Presto*—Quick, or faster than Allegro **c.1726** NORTH Musicall Gramarian BL Add. 32533, f. 65v ... then comes presto, away, and If faster, prestissimo, and I wonder they stopp there and doe Not goe on to prestititissimo **1731** PRELLEUR *Modern Musick-Master* (Dictionary, p. 3) *Presto*, Fast or Quick. **1736** TANS'UR *Compleat Melody* (3rd edn, p. 66) *Presto, Prestissimo, Pronto, Veloce, Velocement, Velocissamente, Vite, Visto, Vistamente*, (Ital.) Either of those *Terms*, denote that you must *sing*, or *play* as quick as possible: To lose no *Time*. § (p. 66) *Men Presto*, not too quick; *Non Troppo Presto*, signifies the same. *Non Troppo Largo*, not too slow.

prick *see* alteration

1706 KERSEY-PHILLIPS (6th edn) To *Prick*, ... to set down a Tune or Song **1708** KERSEY *Dict. Anglo-Brit.* (1st edn) To *Prick*, ... to set down a Tune or Song **1737** DYCHE-PARDON (2nd edn) *Prick* (V.) ... also to write down in proper Notes a Lesson of Musick upon ruled Paper;

1597 MORLEY *Plaine and Easie Introdvction* (p. 22) [marginalia: 'A pricke of alteratiou [sic]'] You must then knowe, that *if you finde a prick so following a Minyme in this Moode* [the moode imperfect of the less prolation], *it doubleth the value therof & maketh it two Minymes*, and then is the pricke called *a pricke of alteration*. § (annotations on Part I) A pricke is a kinde of Ligature, so that if you would tie a semibrief and a minime together, you may set a pricke after the semibriefe, and so you shal binde them. § (annotations on Part I) *A pricke of augmentation.*) Some tearme it a pricke of addition, some also a pricke of perfection, not much amisse: but that which now is called of our musicians a pricke of per fection [sic], is altogither superfluous and of no vse in musicke: for after a semibriefe in the more prolation, they set a pricke, though another semibriefe follow it: but though the pricke were away, the semibriefe of it selfe is perfect. § (annotations on Part I) So that by these his wordes [i.e. of the author of *De quatuor principalibus*] it euidentlie appeareth, that in those daies (that is about twoe hundred yeares agoe) musicke was not so farre degenerate from theoricall reasons as it is now. But those who came after, not only made foure kinds of pricks, but also added the fift, thus. There bee say they in all fiue kindes of pricks, a pricke of addition, a pricke of augmentation, a pricke of perfection, a pricke of deuision, and a pricke of alteration. A pricke of augmentation they define, that which being sette after a note, maketh it halfe as muche longer as it was before: the pricke of Addition they define, that which being set after a sembriefe in the more prolation, if a minime follow, it causeth the semibriefe to be three white minimes. A pricke of perfection they define, that which being set after a semibriefe in the more prolation, if an other semibriefe follow, it causeth the first to be perfect. The pricke of deuision and alteration they define, as they be in my booke... **1609** DOWLAND-ORNITHOPARCUS *Micrologvs* (p. 52) Wherefore a *Pricke* is a certaine indiuisible quantity, added to the Notes, either for *Diuision*, or for *Augmentation*, or for *Certainty* sake. Or it is a certaine Signe lesser than any other accidentally set either before, or after, or betweene Notes.... Ovt of this Definition, there are collected three kindes of *Prickes*, to wit: That of *Addition*, and that is the *Augmentation* of the figures. Or it is the perfection of imperfect Notes... **1614** RAVENSCROFT *Briefe Discovrse* (p. 21) A *Prick* is a *Signe* of an *indiuisible Quantity* placed either before, after, on the vpper, nether ends, or sides of a *Note*, and there seruing for the aforesaid distinctions [of perfection, addition, division, alteration and augmentation]. **1726** BRUCE *Common Tunes* (p. 27) Q. *What call you Pricks?* ¶ *A*. They are large Points or Puncts thus, . and consist of two essential Parts, *viz*. Pricks of Perfection or Addition. **1736** TANS'UR *Compleat Melody* (3rd edn, p. 9) *Scholar*. Sir, I have often seen a little *Dot* set on the right side of a Note; and should be very glad to know its *Name*, and also its *Use*. ¶ *Master*. That *Dot* is called the *Prick* of *Perfection*, or *Point* of *Addition*; which adds to the *Sound* of a *Note* half as much as it was before. When this *Point* is set to the *Semibreve*, it must be held as long as three *Minims, &c*.

pricksong *see* set of pricksong, solfa, tablature

prima *as number*

1724 [PEPUSCH] *Short Explic. of Foreign Words in Mus. Bks.* (p. 58) *Prima*, or *Primo*, the First, or Number One. This Word is commonly used on the Top of each Page of the First Treble, in the following Manner. ¶ *Violino Primo*, First Violin. ¶ *Canto Primo*, First Voice. ¶ *Viola Prima*, First Viol. ¶ And in the Title Page of Musick Books. Thus, ¶ *Opera Prima*, the First Opera, or First Work. **1726** BAILEY *An Univ. Etymolog. Engl. Dict.*

(3rd edn) *Prima* (in *Musick Books*) signifies the first or Number one. *Ital.*

1731 PRELLEUR *Modern Musick-Master* (Dictionary, p. 3) *Primo*, First as *Violini Primo*, First Violin. ¶ *Fagotto Primo*, First Bassoon &c

prima *as string*

1599 MINSHEU-PERCYVALL Sp→E *Prima*, f. ... the minikin or small string of an instrument.

primer

1656 BLOUNT (1st edn) *Primer*, a Prayer book of the Romanists so called; containing the Office of the *Virgin Mary*, which is divided into seven several houres (as a memorial of the seven principall parts and hours of our Saviors Passion), *viz.* the *Mattins* and *Laudes* ... The *Evensong* and *Compline* for the Eveniug [sic]; and these seven houres are composed of Psalms cheifly; Hymns, Canticles, Antiphones, Versicles, Responsories and Prayers.

primicerius *see* chanter

1728 CHAMBERS *Primicerius*, in Antiquity, the first, or chief Person in any Office, or Dignity.... The *Ecclesiastical Primicerius, Du Cange* observes, was the same with the *Chanter* among us. See *Chanter*.

principal *see* fugue, harmonia gemina

procession *see* litany, trisagium, villancico, waits, whiffler

1658 PHILLIPS (1st edn) *Procession*, (lat.) ... also a custom among Clergy-men of passing along the streets singing of Psalms, making supplications and visiting the bounds of the Parish. **1704** *Cocker's Engl. Dict.* (1st edn) *Procession*, in *Popish* Countreys is a solemn service, where the Host, Sacrament, or some Image is carried before, and followed by Priests singing: **1704** HARRIS *Procession*, in Cathedral and Conventual Churches, the members formerly had their stated Processions, wherein they walked two and two in their most Ornamental Habits, with Hymns, Musick, and other suitable expressions of Solemnity, and respect to the occasion... **1706** KERSEY-PHILLIPS (6th edn) *Procession*, ... a solemn walking of the Clergy and People of the Church of *Rome*, in their Ornamental Habits, with Hymns, Musick, &c. **1728** CHAMBERS *Procession*, is also a Ceremony in the *Romish* Church, consisting in a formal March of the Clergy in their Robes, and the People after them, putting up Prayers, singing Hymns, *&c.* and in this manner, making a Visit to some Church, or other holy Place. **1730** BAILEY *Dict. Britannicum* (1st edn) *Procession (*in *cathedral and conventual Churches)* in former Times the Members had their stated Processions, in which they walked, 2 and 2, in their most ornamental Habits, with Musick, singing Hymns, and other Expressions of Solemnity, agreeable to the Occasion. **1737** BAILEY *The Univ. Etymolog. Engl. Dict.* (3rd edn, vol. 2) *Procession* a ceremony in which both the clergy and laity walk together singing litanies and other prayers, as they march along.... The Christian clergy likewise have their processions on the same accounts. The first of these were begun by *Chrysostom*, at *Constantinople*, which was designed by way of opposition to the great appearances of the *Arians*. For they being discountenanced, were wont to meet without the town, singing anthems as they went along. ¶ These processions were set on foot to prevent their having any influence on the orthodox; they bearing crosses with flambeaux upon them, singing their prayers. ¶ From this original processions have grown into their present use in the *Roman* church, wherein the priests and people proceed from one church to another, singing prayers and litanies; *Procession* (in *Cathedral and Conventual Churches*) in former times the members had their stated processions, in which they walked two and two, in their most ornamental habits, with musick, singing hymns, and other expressions of solemnity, agreeable to the occasion... **1737** DYCHE-PARDON (2nd edn) *Procession* (S.) ... the first Processions among the Christians mentioned by the Ecclesiastical Writers with the Clergy at the Head of them, are those set on Foot at *Constantinople* by St. *Chrysostom*, to oppose the resembling Appearance of the *Arians*, who being forced to hold their Assemblies without the Town, went thither Night and Morning singing Anthems; ... the Custom of the Church of *Rome*, from the Time of *Gregory the Great*, has been for the Clergy and People to go in Procession from one Church to another, singing Prayers and Litanies; and when they came to the Church designed, they sang the Service of the Day, and Mass, which they called the Station;

procino *see* accino

1538 ELYOT L→E *Procino, cinui, nere*, to pronounce in singing, to synge out. **1552** HULOET L→E *Procino. is. nui* Syng aloft. **1589** RIDER L→E *Procino*. To sing aloude.

proclamation *see* ban, banoyement, cor, trompe, trumpeter
1696 PHILLIPS (5th edn) *Proclamation,* a Publication made by sound of Trumpet, and beat of Drum. **1706** KERSEY-PHILLIPS (6th edn) *Proclamation,* the Act of proclaiming, a solemn publishing, with sound of Trumpet, or beat of Drum: **1708** KERSEY *Dict. Anglo-Brit.* (1st edn) *Proclamation,* the Act of proclaiming a solemn publishing with sound of Trumpet, or beat of drum:

profetare *see* prophetize, propheto
1598 FLORIO It→E *Profetiggiare,* ... Also to sing praises to God, to preach, to interpret. **1611** FLORIO It→E *Profetare,* as *Profetizzare. Profetizzare,* ... Also to preach, to interpret, or sing praises to God. **1659** TORRIANO-FLORIO It→E *Profetare, Profeteggiare, Profetizzare,* ... used also to preach, to interpret, or sing praise unto God.

prohemium *see* prelude
1500 *Ortus Vocabulorum* L→E Prohemium mij. the fyrst sange. est sermo generalis preambulans in principijs librorum ostendens in generali q postea otineat in speciali n.s.

prolation *relating to mensuration, see* mensural music, mode, mood, sign, time
1596 ANON. *Pathway to Musicke* [C iii *verso*] *VVhat is Prolation?* ¶ It is a formall quantitie of Minoms and Sembriefes, measuring them by three, or by tvvo, and it is evther [sic] perfect or imperfect. **1597** MORLEY *Plaine and Easie Introdvction* (p. 14) *Phi.* What is *Prolation?* ¶ *Ma. It is the measuring of* Semibriefs *by* Minoms, and is either more or lesse. *The more prolation is, when the* Semibrief *contayneth three* Minoms, his signes be these: ʘ Ͼ ... *The lesse prolation is when the* Semibriefe *contayneth but two* Minomes: The signe wherof is the absence of the pricke thus. O C
early 17th C. RAVENSCROFT Treatise of Musick BL Add. 19758, f. 12v Prolation is a formall quantity of minimes and Semibrieves mesurd by 3 ... **1609** DOWLAND-ORNITHOPARCUS *Micrologvs* (p. 43) Wherefore *Prolation* is the essentiall quantitie of *Semibreefes*: or it is the setting of two or three *Minims* against one *Semibreefe.* And it is twofold, to wit the greater, (which is a *Semibreefe* measured by three *Minims,* or the comprehending of three *Minims* in one *Semibreefe,* whose signe is a point inclosed in a signe thus, ʘ.Ͼ) The lesser *Prolation* is a *Semibreefe* measured with two *Minims* onely, whose signe is the absence of a pricke. For *Franchinus* saith, They carry with them the imperfecting of the figure, when the signes are wanting ... **1614** RAVENSCROFT *Briefe Discovrse* (p. 5) *Prolation* signifieth an extending or putting foorth; and it is of the *Degrees* from the first measuring *Note* to the last measured, through the *Perfect* and *Imperfect* figures; vnto which terme *Prolation* is applyed, a Note of a *Circular* body, but with a *Stroke,* as a head ioyned to that Body, which is term'd the *Minime;* (which *Minime* measuring the *Semi-breue*) thereby comes it, that the Tearme *Prolation* is appropriated to the *Semi-breue,* as being the first *Note* measured by the *Prolationate,* or extending *Note.* **1662** [DAVIDSON] *Cantus, Songs and Fancies* (n.p.) Q. *What is Prolation?* ¶ A. It is a measuring of Minims by Semi-briefs, and is either perfect or imperfect.

prolation *relating to ornament*
1728 CHAMBERS *Prolation,* in Music, the Act of Shaking, or making several Inflections of the Voice, on the same Syllable. **1730** BAILEY *Dict. Britannicum* (1st edn) *Prolation* (in *Musick*) the Act of shaking or making several Inflections of the Voice on the same Syllable. **1737** DYCHE-PARDON (2nd edn) *Prolation* (S.) in *Musick,* is the Act of forming the Trill or Shake with the Voice, which occasions various Inflections upon the same Syllable.

proludium *see* precention, prelude
1538 ELYOT L→E *Proludo, dere,* to flourysshe, as musytians doo, before they come to the principalle mattier: **1565** COOPER L→E *Proludium, proludij. Gell.* A flourish: a voluntarie: a preamble: an entrance or beginninge: an assaye or proffe before the mattier. *Proludo, prôludis, pen. prod. prolúsi, prolûsum, pen. prod. prolúdere. Virgil.* To flourish as musitians, or men of sense doe before they play earnestly. **1587** THOMAS L→E *Proludium, ij, n.g.* A flourish, a voluntarie: a preamble, an assay or proofe before the matter. *Proludo, is, si, sum, ere.* To flourish as musicians or fensers doe before they play in earnest, to proue or assay what he can doe before he come to the thing, to begin, to make a preamble, to goe before.

prolusion *see* prelude, prelusion
1676 COLES *Prolusion, Latin.* as *Preludium.* **1704** *Cocker's Engl. Dict.* (1st edn) *Prolusion,* a flourish before a Song or Lesson in Musick.

promptement *see* presto
1724 [PEPUSCH] *Short Explic. of Foreign Words in Mus. Bks.* (p. 58) *Promptement,* the same as *Pronto.* **1726** BAILEY *An Univ. Etymolog. Engl. Dict.* (3rd edn) *Promptement* (in *Musick Books*) signifies quick or nimbly, without losing Time. *Ital.*

pronto *see* presto
1724 [PEPUSCH] *Short Explic. of Foreign Words in Mus. Bks.* (p. 58) *Pronto,* Quick or Nimbly, without losing Time. **1726** BAILEY *An Univ. Etymolog. Engl. Dict.* (3rd edn) *Pronto* (in *Musick Books*) signifies quick or nimbly, without losing Time. *Ital.*

properchant *see* b molle, b quarre
1597 MORLEY *Plaine and Easie Introdvction* (pp. 4-5) *Phi.* What is *Properchant?* ¶ *Ma.* It is a propertie of singing, wherin you may sing either *fa* or *mi* in *b fa* ♮ *mi* according as it shalbe [sic] marked *b* or thus ♮ and is when the *vt* is in *C fa vt.* **early 17th C.** ANON. Praise of musicke BL 18. B. xix, f. 13v ... And that propertie of singinge is called *Properchant* which (besides one of the Three principall Claves aforesaid beinge placed at y[e] beginninge of the songe) hath also either vpon one of the lynes or spaces, one b. flatt Clave ... **1667** SIMPSON *Compendium of Practical Musick* (pp. 112-13) From these six Notes, *Vt, Re, Mi, Fa, Sol, La,* did arise three properties of Singing; which they named *B Quarre, B Molle,* and *Properchant* or *Naturall... Properchant* was when their *Vt* was applyed to C; so, that their six Notes did not reach so high as to touch *B* either *flat* or *sharp.*

prophetize *see* profetare
1656 BLOUNT (1st edn) *Prophetize (propheto)* ... to sing praises to God;

propheto *see* profetare
1500 *Ortus Vocabulorum* L→E Propheto. as. idem est vel prophesiam recitare laudes deo canere vel docere vel preloqui vel prelocutores officium excercere vel prefigurare. **1538** ELYOT L→E *Propheto, are,* to prophesye, to syng prayses to god: **1587** THOMAS L→E *Propheto, as,* *To prophesie, or foretell things to come: to sing praises to God:

proportion *see* harmonic proportion, mean proportional, ratio
after 1517 ANON. Art of Mvsic BL Add. 4911, f. 113 *Quhat is proportion? Nicholae Barrodncensis.* dois determ. That proporcion is of tua quantateis of the samy kynd. **1596** ANON. *Pathway to Musicke* [E ii] *Of proportion in Musicke and what is a proportion.* ¶ It is the conferring of two numbers perpendicularly placed as $\frac{2}{1}$ is a double proportion: $\frac{3}{1}$ a triple proportion: $\frac{4}{1}$ is a proportion quadruple. **1597** MORLEY *Plaine and Easie Introdvction* (p. 27) *Phi.* What is *Proportion?* ¶ *Ma.* It is *the comparing of numbers placed perpendicularly one ouer another....* Proportion is either of equalitie or vnequalitie. *Proportion of æqualitie,* is the comparing of two æquall quantities togither ... *Proportion of inæqualitie* is, when two things of vnequall quantitie are compared togither, and is either of the more or lesse inæqualitie. Proportion of the more *inæqualitie* is, when a greater number is set ouer and compared to a lesser, and *in Musicke doeth alwaies signifie diminution. Proportion of the lesse inæqualitie* is, where a lesser number is set ouer, and compared to a greater, as $\frac{2}{3}$, *and in Musicke doeth alwaies signifye augmentation....* there be but fiue [proportions] in most common vse with vs: *Dupla, Tripla, Quadrupla, Sesquialtera, and Sesquitertia.* § (p. 183) And although it be true that the proportions haue not such vse in musicke in that forme as they be nowe vsed, but that the practise may be perfect without them, yet seeing they haue beene in common vse with the musicians of former time, it is necessarie for vs to know them, if we meane to make any profit of their works. **1609** DOWLAND-ORNITHOPARCUS *Micrologvs* (p. 59) *What Proportion is fit for Musitians.* ¶ Because the dissimilitude, and not the similitude of voyce doth breede Harmonie: therefore the Art of Musicke doth onely consider of the *Proportion* of inequalitie. This is two-fold; to wit, the *Proportion* of the greater or of the lesse inequalitie. The *Proportion* of the greater inequalitie, is the relation of the greater number to the lesse, as 4. to 2. 6. to 3. The *Proportion* of the lesser inequalitie is contrarily the comparison of a lesse number to greater, as of 2. to 4. of 3. to 6.

proslambanomenos *see* burden, diagram, gamut, scale, supernumerary, tone
1587 THOMAS L→E *Proslambanomenos, Vitruv.* A. re. **1598** FLORIO It→E *Proslanuanomeno* [sic], a kinde of musicall note, or tune. **1611** FLORIO It→E *Proslanaunomeno,* a kind of tune or note in Musike.

1728 NORTH Musicall Grammarian (*C-K MG* f. 111) Greek [music] continually disposed to change ¶ These scales were extended by setting one over another, and the 2d tetrachord came up within a tone of the diapason, but another like tetrachord following did not answer by diapasons to the first, therefore a stop was made there, and to fullfill the diapason, a note was added below, out of all tetrachord[s]; which was called proslamb[an]omenas, as if 2 tetrachords reached from G to F[,] then ff was the gained note, and thus the compass of a full diapason was gained ... **1731** PRELLEUR *Modern Musick-Master* ('A Brief History of Musick', p. 4) *Pythagoras* (who is reported to have laid down rules for finding the Proportions of Sounds) perceiving that the first string in the upper *Tetrachord* and the last String in the lower one, *ie, A* and *B* were disagreeable in themselves (they being what we call a Seventh) added another under y[e] lowest of the Second *Tetrachord,* viz an *A*, which he called *Proslambanomenos* that is to say *added* or *Super numery,* & so compleated the Octave. § ('A Brief History of Musick', p. 7) ... The lowest Note of this *System* [of tetrachords] was called *Proslambanomenos,* and signifies *added* or *Supernumery;* this answers to *A-re,* This note does not help to make up the lowest *Tetracord,* but has been added to compleat the lowest Octave.

prosodion

1712 WEAVER *Essay towards History of Dancing* (pp. 12-13) [*re* dance traditions in ancient times] ... The *Prosodion,* or Litany, or Supplication, was said with a Hymn, when they approach'd towards the Gods, and brought the Sacrifices to the Altar. Some are of Opinion, that this was only the Song that contain'd the Hymn of that God; for the *Athenians* sung *Pæans* and *Prosodia's* to *Demetrius* on his Approach: But when the Word *Prosodia* is of the Feminine Gender, and join'd with a Musical Instrument, it signifies a Song.

provisanti *see* improvisation

1598 FLORIO It→E *Prouisanti,* ... Also such as sing extempore and speake at randome. *Prouisare,* to speake or sing extempore. **1611** FLORIO It→E *Prouisanti,* such as speake at random or sing extempore.

psallens

1500 *Ortus Vocabulorum* L→E Psallens tis. i. cantans gaudens o.t.

psallo *see* cano, hymn, psalm

1500 *Ortus Vocabulorum* L→E Psallo is li. i. exultare iubilare congaudere vel cantar a.t. Sallio sallo sale salio pede cantica psallo. **1538** ELYOT L→E *Psallo, li, lere,* to synge. **1552** HULOET L→E *Psallo. as, Propheto. as* Synge lawdes and prayses to God. *Psallo. li. ere,* to synge psalmes **1565** COOPER L→E *Psallo, psallis, psalli, psallere. Horat.* To synge: to play on harpe or lute. **1587** THOMAS L→E *Psallo, is, li, ere.* To sing, to play on the harp or lute.

psallocitharist

1565 COOPER L→E *Psallocitharistæ. Sueton.* Syngers to the harpe. **1587** THOMAS L→E *Psallocitharista, æ, m.g. Suet.* A singer to the harp. **1589** RIDER L→E *Psallocitharista, lyricen, lyristes, m.* A singer to the harpe. **1656** BLOUNT (1st edn) *Psallocitharist (Psallocitharista)* a singer to the Harp. **1676** COLES *Psallocitharist, Greek.* a singer to the harp.

psalm *see* anthem, antiphon, book of psalms, canere, chanter, diapsalma, dismal ditty, doxology, gradual psalm, hymn, ladetta, lauda, lauds, maschil, moduloscropus, offertory, primer, procession, psallo, psalter, psaltery, respond, sacrum, selah, sinassi

1500 *Ortus Vocabulorum* L→E Psalma tis. et hec psalma me. i. psalmus et oponit diapsalma n.t. Psalmus mi. anglice a salme m.s. **1538** ELYOT L→E *Psalmus,* a songe proprely to god, or of God. **1552** HULOET L→E *Psalmo. as, psallo. as,* Hympne to singe *Psalmus me,* Psalme, prayse, or songe to God, or of God. **1565** COOPER L→E *Psalmus, mi, m.g.* A songe of or to god. **1587** THOMAS L→E *Psalmus, mi, m.g. Iun.* A song of or to God: a Psalme sung to the psaltery, or a song sung by the voyce. **1589** RIDER L→E *Psalmus, m.* A song to God. *v.* hymnes [*see* hymn]. *Psalmus, m. psalma, f.* A Psalme. **1593** HOLLYBAND Fr→E *Vn Psalme,* or *pseaulme,* a psalme: *m.* **1598** FLORIO It→E *Psalmo,* as *Salmo. Salmeggiare,* to sing, speake, write or compose Psalmes. *Salmo,* a psalme, a song of thanks-giuing and praise to God, a psalme sung to the psalterie, or a song sung by the voice. **1599** MINSHEU-PERCYVALL Sp→E *Salmo,* a psalme. **1611** COTGRAVE Fr→E *Psalme: m.* A Psalme; a song made of, or vnto, God. **1611** FLORIO It→E *Psalmo,* as *Salmo,* a Psalme. *Salmeggiare,* to sing, to speake, to write or compose Psalmes. *Salmo,* a Psalme, or song of thanksgiuing and praises to God. **1656** BLOUNT (1st edn) *Psalm (psalmus)* a song made of short verses, and sentences, where many superfluous words are cut off: It comes of an Hebrew word, which hath the signification of pruining or cutting of superfluous twigs. **1659** TORRIANO-FLORIO It→E *Salmeggiare, Salmodiare,* to sing, to write, to speak, or to compose Psalmes or praises unto. *Salmo,* a song of thanks-giving and praises to God, namely sung unto *Decacordo.* **1676** Coles *Psalm, Greek.* a Divine Song. **1688** Miege-Cotgrave Fr→E *Pseaume,* (m.) a Psalm. § *Chanter un Pseaume,* to sing a Psalm. *le chant des Pseaumes,* the singing of Psalms. **1696** Phillips (5th edn) *Psalm,* a Hymn upon sacred Subjects; a Word seldom attributed to any other than the Psalms of *David.* **1702** Kersey *New Engl. Dict.* (1st edn) A *Psalm,* hymn, *or* divine song, *as David's* Psalms. **1704** *Cocker's Engl. Dict.* (1st edn) *Psalm,* Sacred Poem or Song. **1706** Kersey-Phillips (6th edn) *Psalm, (Gr.)* a Hymn upon some Sacred Subject, a Divine Song. **1724** [Pepusch] *Short Explic. of Foreign Words in Mus. Bks.* (p. 59) *Psalmus,* Psalms. (p. 66) *Salmo,* or *Psalmo,* a Psalm or Spiritual Song. **1726** Bailey *An Univ. Etymolog. Engl. Dict.* (3rd edn) *Salmo,* a Psalm or Spiritual Song. *Ital.* **1728** Chambers *Psalm,* a Divine Song, or Hymn. See *Song,* and *Hymn.* ¶ The Word is now appropriated to the CL *Psalms* of *David;* and the Name *Canticle,* or Song, given to other pieces of the same kind, composed by other Prophets and Patriarchs. ¶ The Antients, as is observ'd by St. *Augustin,* made this difference between a *Canticle* or Song, and a *Psalm;* that the former was sung solitarily, or by the Voice alone; but the latter accompany'd with a Musical Instrument. ¶ The *Psalms,* in the antient Editions, are divided into five Books; nor is *David*'s Name found at the Head of more than seventy-three of them; tho' some, and among the rest, St. *Augustia,* and St. *Chrysostom,* attribute all the hundred and fifty to him without exception. ¶ The *Jews,* however, were always of another Sentiment; and 'tis certain there are some few, at least, that are not his—St. *Jerom* observes, among the Number, several that were composed [a] long time after *David. Du Pin* adds, that 'tis difficult to ascertain the Authors; all we know of the Book, is, that 'tis a Collection of Songs, made by *Esdras.* ¶ The *Gradual Psalms,* were those antiently sung on the Steps of the Temple. See *Gradual.* ¶ The *Penitentiary Psalms,* were not formerly the same with those now call'd by that Name. See *Penitentiary.* ¶ The Word is form'd of the *Latin Psalmus;* and that from the *Greek* ψάλλω, *I sing.* **1737** Dyche-Pardon (2nd edn) *Psalm* (S.) a divine Hymn or Song upon religious Matters, but now commonly restrained to those contained in that Book of the *Old Testament,* call'd the Book of Psalms, consisting of one hundred and fifty, generally called *David*'s, tho' it is supposed they were not all wrote by him, some having the Names of *Asaph, Eman, Ethan, &c.* at the Head of 'em, which some suppose were only either Musicians, that composed proper Tunes to sing them in, or chief Singers, to lead the Tune, &c. Much Debate has been among the Learned, whether and what Sort of Verse they were composed in, but that Part of *Hebrew* Knowledge is not exactly known, so that it probably was only a poetical Sort of Prose the Authors made use of, to make them more easily conform to the Musick of those Times, which together with their Instruments are wholly unknown to us.

1609 Dowland-Ornithoparcus *Micrologvs* (p. 30) *Of the Diuisions of the Psalmes.* ¶ I Find there are two sorts of Psalmes, which we vse in praising God, the greater and the lesser: all Psalmes are called lesser, except those two, *viz.* Of the blessed Virgin, and of *Zacharias.* Also the Song of *Symeon,* in some Diocesse is accounted for a greater Psalme, in some for a lesser; as I in going ouer the world haue found. **1619** Wither *Preparation to the Psalter* (pp. 53-4) The principall things mentioned in the *Tiles* are sixe: and in euery *Psalme,* some one or more of them is considerable: to wit, either the Name of the *Psalme,* or the name of some Person, or the Manner of singing, or the Instrument, or the Time in which it was appointed to be sung. The Names of the *Psalmes* are many: such as these, *A Psalme: A Song: A Hymne: A Prayer: Instructions: Remembrances: Of Degrees: Halleluiah,* or *Praises. A Psalme a Song; and a Song a Psalme.* By a *Psalme,* the Auncient Expositors vnderstood such verses as being composed in the honour or prayse of some Subiect, were indifferently intended, to be either read or sung; as are our ordinary English Sonnets, consisting of fourteene lines. A *Song* was made of *Measures,* composed purposely to be Sung. *Hymnes* were Songs, in which were the praises of God onely, and that with ioy and triumph; and therefore the Songs of *Ieremy* cannot be properly called *Hymnes,* but rather Tragedies, or Lamentations: those that are intituled *Halleluiah,* are *Hymns* also, mentioning particularly the praises of God for benefits receiued. Now of what nature they are which be called *Prayers, Psalms of Instruction,* or such like; the very names of some of them doe plainely enough declare: the rest shall bee opened in the Exposition of the Psalmes; ... Those that are Inscribed, *A Psalme a Song;* and those that haue the words transposed, *A Song a Psalme,* are such as were both sung and playd together; but with this difference: Where it is intituled, *A Psalme a Song,* there the Instruments beganne the *Psalme;* and the

Quire sang the next verse: where it is, *A Song a Psalme*, there the company of Singers beganne the *Psalme*, and the Instruments sounded the second verse.

psalmist *see* ordines majores, ordines minores
1500 *Ortus Vocabulorum* L→E Psalmista te. qui psalmum dicit. vel cantat vel componit com. p. **1552** HULOET L→E *Psalmista. æ* Psalme maker or synger. *Idem* Psalmist and psalme maker. **1589** RIDER L→E *Psalmista, psalmistes, m.* A Psalmist. **1598** FLORIO It→E *Salmista*, a psalmist, a composer or singer of psalmes. Also a psalter. **1599** MINSHEU-PERCYVALL Sp→E *Salmista*, a psalmist or maker of psalmes. **1611** COTGRAVE Fr→E *Psalmiste: m.* A Psalmist, a maker of Psalmes. **1611** FLORIO It→E *Salmista*, a Psalmist, a composer or singer of Psalmes. Also a Psalter. **1616** BULLOKAR *Psalmist.* A maker or singer of Psalmes. **1623** COCKERAM *Psalmist.* A maker of singing Psalmes. *Psalmist.* a maker of singing Psalmes **1656** BLOUNT (1st edn) *Psalmist (psalmista)* he that makes or sings Psalms; an attribute usually and most properly given to King *David.* **1676** COLES *Psalmist*, the composer of it [a psalm]. **1688** MIEGE-COTGRAVE Fr→E *Psalmiste*, (m.) Psalmist. § *le Psalmiste David*, the Psalmist Kind David. **1696** PHILLIPS (5th edn) *Psalmist*, a Title given to King *David*, as being a Writer of Psalms or sacred Hymns. **1702** KERSEY *New Engl. Dict.* (1st edn) A *Psalmist, or* writer of *psalms.* **1704** *Cocker's Engl. Dict.* (1st edn) *Psalmist*, the Authour or Composer of a Psalm. **1706** KERSEY-PHILLIPS (6th edn) *Psalmist*, a Title given to King *David* by way of Eminence, upon account of his admirable Skill in composing Psalms or Sacred Hymns. **1721** BAILEY *An Univ. Etymolog. Engl. Dict.* (1st edn) *Psalmist*, ... one who makes or sings Psalms. **1730** BAILEY *Dict. Britannicum* (1st edn) *Psalmist* (*psalmistes*, L. pſalm-ſcop, *Sax.*) a Composer or Singer of Psalms. **1737** DYCHE-PARDON (2nd edn) *Psalmist* or *Psalmographist* (S.) a Composer or Singer of Psalms, Hymns or divine Songs; and among the *Divines*, commonly means *David* King of *Israel.*

1737 BANNER *Use and Antiquity of Musick* (p. 16) How far the Christian, has followed the Example of the Jewish Church in this particular, may be gathered from the Canons and Constitutions of the first and purest Ages of it, for as her Service was, as it were, one continued Act of Praise and Thanksgiving, so there was a certain Order of Men, called *Psalmistæ* or Singers, set apart for the more decent, and regular Performance thereof.

psalmodi
1589 RIDER L→E *Psalmodi, Antipsalmodi.* Those that sing in the church on both sides [of] the quier.

psalmody
1500 *Ortus Vocabulorum* L→E Psalmodia die. i. cantus psalmorum f.p. **1538** ELYOT L→E *Psalmodia*, a dyuerse or mixt songe. **1552** HULOET L→E *Psalmodia* Singyng of psalmes. *Psalmodia* Song diuers or mixt. **1565** COOPER L→E *Psalmodia.* Syngynge and playinge together on an instrument. **1587** THOMAS L→E *Psalmodia, æ, f g.* *A singing or playing togither on an instrument: a singing togither of Psalmes. **1589** RIDER L→E *Psalmodia, f.* A singing to instruments, or a singing together of Psalmes. **1593** HOLLYBAND Fr→E *Psalmodie*, the singing of psalmes: *f. Psalmodier*, to sing songes to God, to sing psalmes. **1598** FLORIO It→E *Salmodia*, a singing or playing together on an instrument, a singing together of psalmes. **1611** COTGRAVE Fr→E *Psalmodie: f.* The singing of Psalmes. *Psalmodier.* To sing Psalmes. **1611** FLORIO It→E *Psalmodia*, as *Salmodia. Psalmodiare*, to sing Psalmes. *Salmodia*, a singing together of Psalmes or playing together on instruments. *Salmodiare*, to sing Psalmes together. **1616** BULLOKAR *Psalmodie.* A singing of Psalmes. **1623** COCKERAM *Psalmodie.* A singing of Psalmes. *Psalmodie.* Singing of Psalmes **1656** BLOUNT (1st edn) *Psalmody (psalmodia)* a singing or playing together on an instrument; a singing of Psalms together. **1658** PHILLIPS (1st edn) *Psalmodie*, (Greek) a singing of Psalms, or verses made of short songs, or sentences. **1659** TORRIANO-FLORIO It→E *Salmodia*, a singing together of Psalms. **1676** COLES *Psalmody, Greek.* a singing of Psalms. **1688** MIEGE-COTGRAVE Fr→E *Psalmodie*, (f.) *le Chant des Pseaumes*, a singing of Psalms. *Psalmodier, cd. chanter les Pseaumes*, to sing Psalms. **1704** *Cocker's Engl. Dict.* (1st edn) *Psalmody*, singing of Psalms. **1706** KERSEY-PHILLIPS (6th edn) *Psalmody*, a singing and playing together on a Musical Instrument; a singing of Psalms. **1724** [PEPUSCH] *Short Explic. of Foreign Words in Mus. Bks.* (p. 66) *Salmodia*, to sing Psalms, or Spiritual Songs. **1726** BAILEY *An Univ. Etymolog. Engl. Dict.* (3rd edn) *Salmodia* (in *Musical Books*) signifies to sing Psalms, or Spiritual Songs. *It.* **1728** CHAMBERS *Psalmody*, the Art of singing Psalms. See *Psalm* and *Singing.* **1730** BAILEY *Dict. Britannicum* (1st edn) *Psalmody* (*F.* and *L.* of ψαλμοδία, of ψαλμός and ἀειδω, to sing, *Gr.*) singing of Psalms, or singing and playing on an Instrument at the same Time. **1737** DYCHE-PARDON (2nd edn) *Psalmody* (S.) the

Art of singing or playing the Musical Tunes of the Psalms upon Instruments.

psalmography

1500 *Ortus Vocabulorum* L→E Psalmographia phie. i. descriptio psalmorum f.p. Psalmographo as. idest describere psalmos a.p. Psalmographus phi. i. scriptor psalmorum **1589** RIDER L→E *Psalmographia, f.* The writing of Psalmes. *Psalmographo.* To write Psalmes. *Psalmographus, m.* A writer of Psalmes. **1598** FLORIO It→E *Salmografo,* a writer or composer of psalmes. **1611** FLORIO It→E *Salmografo,* a writer of Psalmes. **1656** BLOUNT (1st edn) *Psalmography (psalmographia)* the writing of Psalms. **1658** PHILLIPS (1st edn) *Psalmographie,* (Greek) a writing of Psalms. **1676** COLES *Psalmography, Greek.* a writing of Psalms. **1704** *Cocker's Engl. Dict.* (1st edn) *Psalmography* one that writes Psalms, or Spiritual Songs. **1721** BAILEY *An Univ. Etymolog. Engl. Dict.* (1st edn) *Psalmographer,* ... a Writer of Psalms. **1730** BAILEY *Dict. Britannicum* (1st edn) *Psalmographist* (ψαλμογράφος of ψαλμός, and γραφειν, Gr. to write) a Writer of Psalms. **1737** DYCHE-PARDON (2nd edn) *Psalmography* (S.) the Art of Writing or Composing divine Songs, Hymns, or Psalms.

psalter *see* book of psalms, venitarium

1598 FLORIO It→E *Psalterio,* as *Salterio. Salterio,* ... Also a psalter or psalme booke. **1611** FLORIO It→E *Psalterio,* as *Salterio,* a Psalter. **1702** KERSEY *New Engl. Dict.* (1st edn) The *Psalter, or* book of *Psalms.* **1706** KERSEY-PHILLIPS (6th edn) *Psalter,* a Collection of *David's* Psalms, a Book of Psalms. **1708** KERSEY *Dict. Anglo-Brit.* (1st edn) *Psalter,* a Collection of *David's* Psalms; a Book of Psalms. **1728** CHAMBERS *Psalter,* the Book, or Collection of Psalms, ascrib'd to *David.* See *Psalm.* ¶ There are an Infinity of Editions of the *Psalter—Augustin Justinian,* a Dominican, and Bishop of *Nebo,* publish'd a *Polyglot Psalter* at *Genoa,* in 1516; *Contarinus* publish'd the *Psalter* in *Hebrew, Greek, Chaldee,* and *Arabic,* with *Latin* Notes and Glosses. See *Polyglot.* **1737** DYCHE-PARDON (2nd edn) *Psalter* (S.) the Book of Psalms

1619 WITHER *Preparation to the Psalter* (p. 44) [*re* the Psalter] This Booke is knowne by diuers names. The *Hebrewes* call it *Sepher Thehillim,* that is, the Booke of *Praises.* Some call it, the *Psalter*: as, S. *Augustine,* S. *Ierome,* and other of the Auncients haue tearmed it; and this name might be giuen for diuers respects: either a *Psallendo,* and for that it is written in verse, appertaining to *Musicke;* or else it was borrowed from that Instrument, whereunto it was vsually sung: For that which the *Iewes* called *Nebel,* was an Instrument, which the *Latines* call *Psalterium.* It consisted of ten strings, and differed from the *Viole* or *Harpe,* in that they gaue forth their sound belowe, and the Psaltery aboue. Moreouer; some thinke, that it might be called the *Psaltery,* in respect of the things signified by that Instrument: for the Psaltery, on which they vsually praysed God in the olde Law, had (as I said before) tenne strings, which signified the ten precepts of the Law; & by that, the mysticall *Psaltery* of the *Gospel* was also figured; whose ten strings, are the ten mysteries of Christ, & his Church...

psaltery *see* musette, nablium, psalter, sautry, shawm

1500 *Ortus Vocabulorum* L→E Psalterium greci: nos organa nabla iudei Psalterium rij. grece pablum hebraice organum latine an[e]. a sawter n.s. **1538** ELYOT L→E *Psalterium,* an instrument lyke to a harp, also the Psalmes called the Psalter. **1552** HULOET L→E *Psalterium,* Psalter, or boke of psalmes, or place wrytten wyth psalmes. *Psalterium* is also an instrument of musicke lyke a harpe **1565** COOPER L→E *Psalterium, psalterij, n.g. Quint.* An instrument like to an harpe but more pleasaunt. Also the psalter. **1587** THOMAS L→E *Psalterium, rij, n.g. Quint.* An instrument of musick like an harp, but more pleasant: some call it a Psaltry to play holie hymnes vpon, & to sing vnto in playing. **1589** RIDER L→E *Psalterium, n.* A Psalter, or booke of Psalmes: also an instrument of musicke like a harpe, called a Psalterie. *Psalterium, organum, n.* An instrument of musicke. **1598** FLORIO It→E *Salterio,* an instrument of musicke like a harpe of ten strings, but more pleasant, called a shalme or psaltery to play holie hymnes vpon, and to sing vnto. **1599** MINSHEU-PERCYVALL Sp→E *Salterio,* a psalter or psalme booke, or a musicall instrument called a psalterie. **1611** COTGRAVE Fr→E *Psalterion: m.* A Psalterie; a melodious Instrument which resembles a Harpe. **1611** FLORIO It→E *Salterio,* an instrument of musike like a harpe with ten strings, but more pleasant, called a Shalme or Psaltery, to play holy hymnes vpon and to sing vnto. Also a Psalter or Psalme book. **1616** BULLOKAR *Psalterie.* A sweet instrument like a Harpe. **1656** BLOUNT (1st edn) *Psaltery (psalterium)* an Instrument of Musick like an Harp, with ten strings, but more pleasant; Some call it a Shalme, to play holy Hymns upon, and to sing unto in playing; Others say, it was an Instrument three square, of seventy two strings, and of incomparable sweetness, As *Mersenius* describes it. **1658** PHILLIPS (1st edn) *Psaltery,* (Greek) a certain Musical instrument with ten strings, somewhat like a Harp, some call it a Shalm. **1659** TORRIANO-FLORIO It→E *Salterio, Saltero,* an instrument of musick like a harp of ten strings, called a Shalm or Psaltery, to play holy Hymnes upon, and to sing unto, also a Psalter or Psalm-book **1676** COLES *Psaltery, Greek.* a shalm, (like a harp) with 10 strings. **1688** MIEGE-COTGRAVE Fr→E *Psalterion,* (m.) *sorte d'Instrument de Musique fort harmonieux,* Psaltery, a melodious Instrument of Musick. § *Toucher le Psalterion,* to play upon the Psaltery. **1696** PHILLIPS *Psaltery, (Greek)* a certain musical Instrument with Ten Strings, somewhat like a Harp. **1702** KERSEY *New Engl. Dict.* (1st edn) A *Psaltery,* a kind of musical instrument like a harp, but more pleasant. **1704** *Cocker's Engl. Dict.* (1st edn) *Psaltery,* a Musical Instrument, with ten strings like an Harp. **1706** KERSEY-PHILLIPS (6th edn) *Psaltery,* a kind of Musical Instrument with ten Strings, somewhat like a Harp, but more pleasant. **1728** CHAMBERS *Psaltery, Psalterion,* a Musical Instrument, much in use among the antient *Hebrews;* who call'd it *Nebel.* ¶ We know but little of the precise Form of the antient *Psaltery*: That now in use, is a flat Instrument, in form of a *Trapezium;* or a Triangle truncated a-top. ¶ It is strung with thirteen Wire Chords, set to Unison or Octave; and mounted on two Bridges on the two sides—It is struck with a *Plectrum,* or little Iron Rod; or sometimes a crooked Stick; whence it is usually ranked among the Instruments of Percussion. ¶ Its Chest, or Body, is like that of a Spinet. It has its Name *à Psallendo;* some also call it *Nablum,* or *Nablium.* ¶ *Papias* gives the Name *Psaltery* to a kind of Flute used in Churches, to accompany the Singing; in *Latin, Sambucum.* **1737** DYCHE-PARDON (2nd edn) *Psaltery* (S.) sometimes signifies the Psalter or Book of Psalms; and sometimes a Musical Instrument used by the Antients to play the Psalm Tunes, and by us now is generally understood the latter, which was an Instrument of Wood, having Strings somewhat like our Harp; the modern Psaltery is a flat Instrument in a triangular Form, strung with three Rows of Strings of Iron, or Brass Wire, tuned to an Unison, or an Octave, raised upon two Bridges, which are upon the two Sides, and the Strings extended from Side to Side.

1582 *Batman vppon Bartholome* (chap. 134) The *Psalterie* is called *Psalterium,* & hath that name of *Psallendo,* singing: for the consonant answereth to the note therof in singing... The Hebrewes calleth the Psalterie *Decacordes,* an instrument hauing ten strings, by number of the ten Commaundements ... **1619** WITHER *Preparation to the Psalter* (p. 137) ... Yea, then we sing *Psalmes* vnto the *Psaltery,* when we both meditate the doctrines of Saluation through Christ mentioned in them, and striue also, as we are able, to make our actions answerable to the Commandements of God. For, the *Psaltery* was an Instrument to be played on with the hand: which consisting of ten strings was aunciently vsed by those who sung these *Psalms* in the Temple. And it was appoynted for that purpose, mystically to teach vs, that hee whose tongue shall truely prayse God, with the Songs of Faith in the Gospell, must also haue hands, making the *Musicke* of good workes vpon the ten strings of the Law.

psaltes

1500 *Ortus Vocabulorum* L→E Psaltes tis. dicitur pertus in cithara vel organo **1538** ELYOT L→E *Psaltes,* a synynge man. **1552** HULOET L→E *Psaltes* Singyng man. *Psaltes. tis* Player on an instrument. **1565** COOPER L→E *Psaltes, psaltis, masc. gen.* A syngyng man. **1587** THOMAS L→E *Psaltes, is, m g Iun.* A singing man, or Organ player. **1589** RIDER L→E *Psaltes, organicus, masc. psaltria, f.* One that plaieth on an instrument.

psaltria

1538 ELYOT L→E *Psaltrix, tricis, & Psaltria,* a synynge woman. **1552** HULOET L→E *Psaltria. æ, Ambubaia, Psaltrix* Syngynge woman. **1565** COOPER L→E *Psaltria, psaltriæ, foem. gen. Terent.* A syngyng wenche. **1587** THOMAS L→E *Psaltria, æ, f.g.* A singing wench.

pseaume

see psalm

Ptolomy

see canonici, colores generum, dorick, emmeli, harmony, mode, monochord, omophoni, position, synphoni, tone

pulpit

see joube, jubé, odeum, oratorio

1587 THOMAS L→E *Pulpitum, ti, n.g. Mart.* The higher parte of the stage where the musitians were and delighted the people with their musicall playing: **1611** COTGRAVE Fr→E *Poulpitre: m.* ... also, a Stage, or part of a Theater wherein Players act; also, a roome for Musicians in th'vpper part of a

Stage; **1707** *Gloss. Angl. Nova* (1st edn) *Pulpit,* (Lat.) the higher part of the Stage on which the Musicians were; **1726** BAILEY *An Univ. Etymolog. Engl. Dict.* (3rd edn) *Pulpit* (*pulpitum*, L.) anciently the higher Part of a Stage, on which the Musicians were; **1728** CHAMBERS *Pulpit* .... Among the *Romans*, the *Pulpit* was a part of the Theatre, call'd also *Proscenium*; or what we now call the *Stage*, whereon the Actors trod; tho' some say it was properly an Eminence thereon for the Music, or a *Suggestum* whence Declamations, *&c.* were spoke. **1730** BAILEY *Dict. Britannicum* (1st edn) *Pulpitum* (among the *Romans*) a Place raised on which the Actors acted their Plays, or what we now call the Stage; tho' some say it was an Eminence for the Musick; or a Place from whence Declamations were spoken.

pulsation

1538 ELYOT L→E *Pulsatus, ta, tum,* striken as a harpe or other instument is, whyche hath strynges. *Pulso, are,* to beate, to stryke, to hurte, to play on a harpe, or other lyke instrument. **1552** HULOET L→E *Pulsatus. a. um* Stryken as an instrument is in playing. **1565** COOPER L→E *Pulsans, Participium: vt Cymbala pulsans. Iuuenal.* Playing on Cymballes. *Pulsatio, onis, f.g. Verbale. Liu.* ... A strikyng of strynges or playing on instrumentes. *Pulso, pulsas, pulsàre, Frequentatiuum. Cic.* ... to playe on an harpe or lyke instrumente. § *Citharæ pulsator. Valer. Flac.* A player on an harpe. *Lyra pulsa manu. Ouid.* The harpe striken or played on. *Nerui in fidibus pulsi. Cic.* Stringes stroken. *Pulsare lyram, vel citharam pectine. Virgil.* To play on the harpe with, &c. **1587** THOMAS L→E *Pulsatio, onis, f.g. verb.* ... a striking of strings or playing on instruments. *Pulsator, oris, m.g. verb. Val. Max.* ... a player on instruments. *Pulsatus, a, um, part. Plin.* Beaten, knockt, striken, played on. *Pulso, as frequent. à Pello.* to play on an harp or like instrument. **1589** RIDER L→E *Pulsator, m.* A plaier vppon instruments. *pulso, præmoderor.* To plaie on the harpe. *Pulsus, pulsatus, p.* Plaied on an instrument. **1656** BLOUNT (1st edn) *Pulsation (pulsatio)* ... a striking of strings, or playing on Instruments. **1676** COLES *Pulsation, Latin.* a beating upon.

punctus *see* point

punto *see* point

Purcell, Henry *see* opera

purfle

1702 KERSEY *New Engl. Dict.* (1st edn) A *Purfle*, ... *also* a kind of ornament about the edges of some musical instruments, *as* Viols, Violins, *&c.* **1706** KERSEY-PHILLIPS (6th edn) *Purfle, (Fr.)* ... Also a kind of Ornament about the Edges of Musical Instruments, particularly of Viols, Violins, *&c.*

purl *see* arpeggio, warble

1737 DYCHE-PARDON (2nd edn) *Purl* (S.) ... also the fine, clear, resounding Tone of a Musical Instrument.

pyladion *see* piladion

pyrricha *see* morisco

1598 FLORIO It→E *Pirrica,* a kinde of dancing in armour vsed in Athens. Also a kinde of verses or song to dance by. **1611** COTGRAVE Fr→E *Pyrrique.* A souldierlie forme of dauncing in Armour; inuented by *Pyrrhus* King of Macedonia. **1611** FLORIO It→E *Pirrica,* a kind of verse or song to dance by. Also a kind of dancing in Armorie. **1659** TORRIANO-FLORIO It→E *Pirrica,* a kind of song to dance by, also a dancing in armour. **1706** KERSEY-PHILLIPS (6th edn) *Pyrrhicha,* a kind of Dance invented by *Pyrrhus* the Son of *Achilles,* which was perform'd by Soldiers in Arms, with which they struck certain Shields by the Cadence and Sound of Musical Instruments.

Pythagoras *see* apotome, canon, lyre, monochord, mundane music, music, proslambanomenos

1565 COOPER L→E *Pythágoras,* A man of excellent witte, borne in an yle called Samos ... He was in sharpenesse of wit passyng al other, and found the subtile conclusions and misteries of arithmetike, musike, and geometrie.

pythagoreans *see* limma

1728 CHAMBERS *Pythagoreans,* a Sect of antient Philosophers, who retain'd to the Doctrines of *Pythagoras*.... He [Pythagoras] endeavour'd to assuage the Passions of the Mind with Verses, and Numbers; and made a Practice of composing his Mind every Morning by his Harp; frequently singing the *Pœans* [sic] of *Thales.* See *Music.*

Q

quadrimode *see* diapente

quadrivium
1552 Huloet L→E *Grammatica, Logica, Rhetorica dicunter simplex triuium, Arithmetica, Astron, Geometri. Musica, censentur quadriuiæ.*

quadrupla
1596 Anon. *Pathway to Musicke* [E iii *verso*] *VVhat is the proportion called Quadrupla.* ¶ It is that which diminisheth the value by foure partes, and thus it is knowen, when the higher number doth containe the lower number by foure times as thus $\frac{4}{1}$ ... **1597** Morley *Plaine and Easie Introdvction* (p. 31) *Ma.* Quadrupla is a proportion deminishing the value of the notes to the quarter of that which they were before, & it is perceiued in singing, when a number is set before the song, comprehending another foure times, as $\frac{4}{1}$ $\frac{8}{2}$ $\frac{16}{4}$ &c. **1609** Dowland-Ornithoparcus *Micrologvs* (p. 64) The *Quadrupla* is the third kind of the *Multiplex*, and is, when a greater number doth comprehend a lesse in it selfe foure times, as 8. to 2:12 to 3. But Musically, when 4. Notes are sounded to one: the signes of it are these $\frac{4}{1}$ $\frac{8}{2}$...

quarta
1724 [Pepusch] *Short Explic. of Foreign Words in Mus. Bks.* (p. 60) *Quarta*, or *Quarto*, Four, or the Fourth in Number. Thus, ¶ *Opera Quarta*, the Fourth Opera. ¶ *Violino Quarto*, the Fourth Violin. **1726** Bailey *An Univ. Etymolog. Engl. Dict.* (3rd edn) *Quarta, Quarto,* (in *Musick Books*) signifies Four, or the Fourth in Number. *Ital.*

1736 Tans'ur *Compleat Melody* (3rd edn, p. 72) *Quarta* (Ital.) signifies four Parts.

quarte *see* diatessaron, fourth
1611 Cotgrave Fr→E *Quarte: f.* ... also, a fourth, in Musicke. **1688** Miege-Cotgrave Fr→E *Quarte*, (a fem. Subst.) ... a fourth, in Musick

quarter note *see* enharmonic

quart fagotta *see* fagotto

quartuor
1724 [Pepusch] *Short Explic. of Foreign Words in Mus. Bks.* (p. 60) *Quartuor*, Musick for Four Voices is so called. **1726** Bailey *An Univ. Etymolog. Engl. Dict.* (3rd edn) *Quatuor Four*, L. *(in Musick Books)* signifies Musick composed for 4 Voices. *Ital.*

quasi modo Sunday
1706 Kersey-Phillips (6th edn) *Quasi modo Sunday*, Low-Sunday, or the next after Easter, so call'd from the first Words of the *Latin* Hymn sung at Mass on that Day, beginning thus, *Quasi modo geniti, &c.* **1707** *Gloss. Angl. Nova* (1st edn) *Quasi-modo-Sunday*, Low-Sunday, being the next after Easter. 'Tis so nam'd from the Words of a *Latin* Hymn us'd that Day at Mass. **1708** Kersey *Dict. Anglo-Brit.* (1st edn) *Quasi modo Sunday*, Low-Sunday, or the next after Easter, so call'd from the first Words of the *Latin* Hymn sung at Mass on that Day, beginning thus, *Quasi modo geniti, &c.* **1730** Bailey *Dict. Britannicum* (1st edn) *Quasi Modo Sunday*, so called from the first Words of the *Latin* Hymn, sung at Mass on that Day, which begins thus, (*Quasi modo geniti*, &c.) Low-Sunday.

quaver *as note value, see* crotchet, semicrome
1656 Blount (1st edn) *Quaver* in singing (from *quatio*, to shake; *Quia vox cantando quatitur*) and *semiquaver* are the quickest times in Musick. **1658** Phillips (1st edn) *Quaver*, one of the quickest times or pauses in Musick. **1670** Blount (3rd edn) *Quaver* in singing (from *quatio*, to shake; *Quia vox cantando quatitur*) and *semi-quaver* are the quickest times in Musick. See *Sembreif* [sic]. **1671** Phillips (3rd edn) *Quaver*, a measure of time in Musick, being the half of a Crochet, as a Crochet the half of a Quaver, a Semiquaver, *&c.* **1676** Coles *Quaver* (in Musick,) half a Crochet. **1678** Phillips (4th edn) *Quaver*, a measure of time in Musick, being the half of a Crochet, as a Crochet the half a Minim, a Semiquaver the half of a Quaver, *&c.* **1702** Kersey *New Engl. Dict.* (1st edn) A *Quaver*, or half a crotchet in musick. **1704** *Cocker's Engl. Dict.* (1st edn) *Quaver*, a term in Musick, called half a Crotchet. **1704** Harris *Quaver*, a Note in Musick so called: See the Words *Notes* and *Time*. **1707** *Gloss. Angl. Nova* (1st edn) *Quaver*, a Measure of Time in Musick, being half a Crotchet. **1728** Chambers *Quaver*, in Music, a

Measure of Time, equal to one half of the Crochet, or one eighth of the Semibreve. See *Time.* ¶ The *Quaver* is mark'd by the Character ♪. See *Character.* ¶ The *English Quaver* makes what the *French* call their *Crochue,* Crochet; because of the Hook at bottom. See *Crochet.* ¶ The *Quaver* is divided into two Semiquavers noted ♬, and four Demisemiquavers mark'd ♬. **1737** DYCHE-PARDON (2nd edn) *Quaver* (S.) the Name of a musical Note used to prick Songs, &c. in, or the eighth Part of a Bar in common Time;

1609 DOWLAND-ORNITHOPARCUS *Micrologvs* (p. 40) A *Quauer* is a figure like a *Crochet,* hauing a dash to the right hand-ward. **1614** RAVENSCROFT *Briefe Discovrse* (pp. 3-4) And as for our *Crotchets, Quauers, & Semiquauers,* I yet finde not the Inuention of them; and therefore I suppose no great heede was taken of the Inuentor, yet they were accepted vpon sufferance; yet so, as that we now differ from the auntient in the naming of them, for that which wee terme our *Quauer* they term'd a *Crotchet,* & that which we terme a *Crotchet,* they term'd a *Semi-Minime,* the halfe of our *Minime,* as the *Semibreue* is the halfe of the *Breue.* And these *Simple* and *Compound Notes* are they, which wee commonly call the *Inward signes* of *Measurable Musicke.* **1724** TURNER *Sound Anatomiz'd* (p. 16) The Third [note of duration, after the minim and crotchet] is called a *Quaver*; marked like the Crotchet, and is distinguished from it, by the Tail's being turned up again, thus; ♪ which being but half the Length of the *Crotchet,* divides the *Semibreve* into *Eight* Parts.

quaver *as ornament, see* brillante, chroma, fioretti, fredon, fringoter, frizzare, gorgheggiare, gringoter, increspare la voce, quiver, ritornello, roulade, taratantara, tremante, tremblement, tremola, trill, vibrante, vibrissation, warble
1702 KERSEY *New Engl. Dict.* (1st edn) A *Quaver, or* shake in singing. To *quaver, or* run a division. **1706** KERSEY-PHILLIPS (6th edn) *Quaver,* ... Also a Shake or Trill in Singing. To *Quaver,* to run a Division with the Voice. **1728** CHAMBERS *Quavering,* in Music, the Act of trilling, or shaking; or running of a Division with the Voice. See *Division.* **1730** BAILEY *Dict. Britannicum* (1st edn) *Quaver* (prob. of *quatere,* L. to shake) to shake or trill a Note, or run a Division with the Voice. **1737** DYCHE-PARDON (2nd edn) *Quaver* (S.) ... also the Manner of shaking or ornamenting Notes in a Song, by what is called the Trill or Shake. *Quaver* (V.) to ornament a Song or Note by shaking or expressing the Trill, or descanting or dividing upon a Note with the Voice.

querulous

1538 ELYOT L→E *Quærulus, la, lum,* that which complaineth, or is full of complayntes. It is put some tyme of the Poetes for shrylle or lowde in syngynge. **1565** COOPER L→E *Querulus. Virg.* Lowde in singynge or chirpynge: shrylle. § *Chordæ querulæ. Ouid.* Lowde stringes. **1587** THOMAS L→E *Querulus, a, um, Mart.* That complaineth or is full of complaints: loud in singing or chirping, shrill. **1656** BLOUNT (1st edn) *Querulous (querulus)* that complains, or is full of complaints; sounding, singing, chirping, shrill. **1658** PHILLIPS (1st edn) *Querulous,* (lat.) singing or cherping sorrowfully, declaring ones complaints.

queuë

1688 MIEGE-COTGRAVE Fr→E *Dans les Instrumens de Musique, on appelle Queuë le morceau de bois au bout de la Table, où les Cordes sont attachées.*

quilio

1611 FLORIO It→E *Quilio,* the burdon of a song.

quill *see* linguella, palmula, pandora, pecten, plectrum

quinible

1676 COLES *Quinible,* (*q.* whinable) a treble. **1704** *Cocker's Engl. Dict.* (1st edn) *Quinible,* in Musick signifies a Treble. **1726** BAILEY *An Univ. Etymolog. Engl. Dict.* (3rd edn) *Quinible,* a Treble. *Chauc.*

quinque

1724 [PEPUSCH] *Short Explic. of Foreign Words in Mus. Bks.* (p. 60) *Quinque,* is Musick composed for Five Voices. **1726** BAILEY *An Univ. Etymolog. Engl. Dict.* (3rd edn) *Quinque Five (in Musick Books)* signifies Musick composed for five Voices. *Ital.*

1736 TANS'UR *Compleat Melody* (3rd edn, p. 72) *Quinque,* (Ital) signifies five Parts.

quinta *see* diapente
1659 TORRIANO-FLORIO It→E *Quinta,* a fifth part, a fifth in musick **1724** [PEPUSCH] *Short Explic. of Foreign Words in Mus. Bks.* (pp. 60-1) *Quinta,* or

Quinto, is Five, or the Fifth in Number. Thus, ¶ *Opera Quinta*, is the Fifth Opera. Or, ¶ *Libro Quinto*, the Fifth Book. **1726** BAILEY *An Univ. Etymolog. Engl. Dict.* (3rd edn) *Quinta, Quinto*, signifies five or the fifth. *Ital.*

quinte *see* fifth

1611 COTGRAVE Fr→E *Quinte: f.* ... also, a fift (or the proportion of fiue) in Musicke, &c; **1688** MIEGE-COTGRAVE Fr→E *Quinte*, (f.) ... a fifth, or the proportion of five, in Musick; .... *Quinte est d'ailleurs un Instrument de Musique à cordes, & à archet. C'est aussi la partie de la Viole ou du Violon, qui est entre la basse & la taille.*

Quintilian *see* æolian, melopœia, music

quinto

1597 MORLEY *Plaine and Easie Introdvction* (p. 166) ... But if you would make your song of two trebles you may make the two highest parts both with one cliffe, in which case one of them is called *Quinto*. If the song bee not of two trebles, then is the *Quinto* alwaies of the same pitch with the tenor, your *Alto* or meane you may make high or lowe as you list, setting the cliffe on the lowest or second rule.

quire *see* choir

1702 KERSEY *New Engl. Dict.* (1st edn) A *Quire*, or *choir*, the company, and the place in a Church where the divine service is sung. **1706** KERSEY-PHILLIPS (6th edn) *Quire*, that part of a Church, where the Divine Service is said or sung. See *Choir*; **1707** *Gloss. Angl. Nova* (1st edn) *Quire*, that part of a Church where divine Service is performed; **1730** BAILEY *Dict. Britannicum* (1st edn) *Quire* (of *le chœur*, F.) the Choir of a Church; also a Set of Singers; **1736** BAILEY *Dict. Britannicum* (2nd edn) *To Quire* it, to sing in Consort, as the Choir does. **1737** DYCHE-PARDON (2nd edn) *Quire* (S.) sometimes means that Part of a Church where the Service is performed, called also the *Choir*; and sometimes it means the Singers who perform the Service; **1740** BAILEY *An Univ. Etymolog. Engl. Dict.* (9th edn) To *Quireit*, to sing in Consort as the Choir does. *Shakesp.*

quirister *see* chorister, clerizon

1656 BLOUNT (1st edn) *Quirister*, a Singer in a Quire, a Quire-man, a Chorister. **1658** PHILLIPS (1st edn) *Quirister*, see *Chorister*. **1676** COLES *Quirister*, as *Chorister*. **1702** KERSEY *New Engl. Dict.* (1st edn) A *Querister, or* quirister. A *Quirister, or* singer in a quire. **1704** *Cocker's Engl. Dict.* (1st edn) *Quiresters, Choresters*, or singing Men perform their service. **1706** KERSEY-PHILLIPS (6th edn) *Querista*, (in old *Records*) a Querister or Boy that sings in the Quire of a Church. *Quirister*, one that sings in the Quire of a Cathedral, or Collegiate Church. **1726** BAILEY *An Univ. Etymolog. Engl. Dict.* (3rd edn) *Querista, Querister*, a Boy who sings in the Quire of a Church. *O.L.* **1728** CHAMBERS *Quirister*, or *Chorister, Chorista*, a Person appointed to sing in the Quire or Choir of a Cathedral. See *Chorister*. **1730** BAILEY *Dict. Britannicum* (1st edn) *Querista (old Rec.)* a Querister or Chorister, a Boy who sings in the Choir of a Church, *L. Quirester* (of Choir) a Singing-Man or Chorister. **1737** DYCHE-PARDON (2nd edn) *Quirister* or *Chorister* (S.) a Singer, especially of Anthems and other Church Musick;

quiterne

1611 COTGRAVE Fr→E *Quiterne: f.* A Gitterne.

quiver *see* quaver

1737 DYCHE-PARDON (2nd edn) *Quiver* (V.) ... also to warble or sing melodiously and ornamentally.

R

rabel *see* rebeck

1599 MINSHEU-PERCYVALL Sp→E † *Rabel*, m. an instrument called a rebecke.

raccolta

1611 FLORIO It→E *Raccolta*, ... Also the call of souldiers together vnto any place of retreate of stand or rendezuous by sound of drum or trumpet. § *Sonare a raccolta*, to sound a retreat. *Sonare raccolta*, to sound a retreat. **1659** TORRIANO-FLORIO It→E *Raccolta, Raccoltata*, ... also the call of souldiers together unto their colours, unto a stand, or unto a Rendevouze by sound of drum or trumpet

ramager *see* chant, rossignoler

1593 HOLLYBAND Fr→E *Ramage, les petits oiseaux oublient leur ramage*, the braunch song of birds: *m.* § *Vn chant Ramage*, a wild song, a tune vsed among the boughes and Forest: rusticall. **1611** COTGRAVE Fr→E *Ramage* ... hagard, wild, homelie, rude. § *Chant ramage.* Naturall chaunting, rurall singing. **1688** MIEGE-COTGRAVE Fr→E *Ramage,* (m.) *le Chant naturel d'un Oiseau,* the natural Note of a Bird. *Ramager,* cd. *chanter,* to sing. § *Ramage doux, charmant, ravissant, agreable,* a sweet, charming, or pleasant Note.

rant

1728 NORTH Musicall Grammarian (*C-K MG* f. 132) [*re* Jenkins] ... He would be often in a merry humour; and make catches, and some strains he called rants, which were like our stoccatas.

ratio *see* proportion

1736 TANS'UR *Compleat Melody* (3rd edn, p. 71) *Ratio.* (Ital.) signifies, the *Ration,* or *Rate,* or *Proportion,* &c.

rattle *see* cascabel, chapas, crecerelle, crepitaculum, crotalum, gnaccara, naccara, pandera, sistrum, sonagliera, sonaglio

1728 CHAMBERS *Rattle,* among the Antients, was accounted a Musical Instrument, of the pulsatile Kind; call'd by the *Romans, Crepitaculum.* See *Musick.* ¶ Mr. *Malcolm* takes the *Tintirnabulum* [sic], *Crotalum,* and *Sistrum,* to have been only so many different Kinds of Rattles. See *Crotalum, Sistrum, &c.* ¶ The Invention of the *Rattle* is ascribed to *Archytas;* whence *Aristotle* calls it, ἀρχύτου πλαταγη, *Archytas's Rattle.* ¶ *Diogenianus* adds the Occasion of the Invention; *viz.* that having Children, he contriv'd this Instrument to prevent their tumbling other things about the House. So that how much soever some Instruments have chang'd their uses, the Rattle we are sure has preserv'd it.

rauca

1500 *Ortus Vocabulorum* L→E Rauca & ramilla. for sange hosse. f.p. **1565** COOPER L→E § *Concentus rauci. Stat.* Tunes disagreyng.

raye *see* lay

1676 COLES *Rayes, Reies, Old word.* Roundelaies, Songs.

re

1598 FLORIO It→E *Re,* ... Also a note in musike. **1611** COTGRAVE Fr→E *Re.* ... a Musicall, or singing Note **1611** FLORIO It→E *Re,* ... Also a note in musike. **1656** BLOUNT (1st edn) *Re,* ... a Musical or singing Note **1688** MIEGE-COTGRAVE Fr→E *Ré,* (m.) *une des sept principales Voix de la Musique,* Re, one of the seven chief Musical Notes. **1728** CHAMBERS *Re,* in Musick. See *Note.*

rebeck *see* fidicula, guitar, pandora, rabel, ribebba, ribecchino, ribibble

1550 THOMAS It→E *Ribeca,* or *ribeba,* a rebecke or a kitte. **1593** HOLLYBAND Fr→E *Vn Rubec* [sic], an instrument of musicke a rebecke, a fiddle: *m.* § *Qui jouë du rebec,* a fidler. **1598** FLORIO It→E *Rebechista,* as *Ribechista. Ribecca,* a musicall instrument so called, a rebeck, or a croud, or a kit. *Ribecchista,* a fidler or player vpon a rebeck, or croud. *Ribichista,* as *Ribechista.* **1611** COTGRAVE Fr→E *Rebec: m.* The fiddle tearmed a Rebeck. **1611** FLORIO It→E *Rebechista,* as *Ribechista. Ribecca,* an instrument called a Rebecke, a Croud, or Fidlers kit. *Ribecchista,* a fidler vpon a rebecke or croud. *Ribichiste,* as *Ribecchista.* **1656** BLOUNT (1st edn) *Rebeck* (Fr. *Rebéc*) a Fiddle, or certain Musical Instrument of three strings. **1658** PHILLIPS (1st edn) *Rebeck,* ... also a certain Musical instrument of 3 strings, called in Latin *Sistrum,* or *Fidicula.* **1659** TORRIANO-FLORIO It→E *Ribecca, Ribecchino,* a rebeck, a croud, or a fidlers kit. *Ribeccare,* to play upon a rebeck *Ribecchista,* a player upon a rebecca. **1661** BLOUNT (2nd edn) *Rebeck* (Fr. *Rebéc*) a Fiddle, or musical Instrument of three strings. *Chaucer* uses it for an old Trot. **1676** COLES *Rebeck,* a 3 string'd fidle **1688** MIEGE-COTGRAVE Fr→E *Rebec,* (m.) *Instrument de Musique qui est hors d'Usage, & qui n'avoit que trois Cordes,* a Rebeck. **1702** KERSEY *New Engl. Dict.* (1st edn) A *Rebeck,* a kind of musical instrument. **1704** *Cocker's Engl. Dict.* (1st edn) *Rebeck,* a Musical Instrument with three strings. **1708** KERSEY *Dict. Anglo-Brit.* (1st edn) *Rebeck,* ... also a certain Musical Instrument of Three Strings. **1721** BAILEY *An Univ. Etymolog. Engl. Dict.* (1st edn) *Rebeck,* (*rebec,* F.) a Musical Instrument, having three Strings.

recant

1565 COOPER L→E *Recantare. Martial.* To singe agayne: to singe after. *Recantâtus, penult. prod. Participium: vt Opprobria recantata. Horat.* Songe or repeated agaìne. **1587** THOMAS L→E *Recano, is, ui, tum, ere, Plin.* To sing againe: to sing after another. *Recantatus, a, um, part. Horat.* Sung or repeated againe: *Recanto, as, Plin.* To sing againe, to sing after another: **1598** FLORIO It→E *Recantare,* ... also to sing againe. **1611** COTGRAVE Fr→E *Rechanté: m. ée: f.* Resounded, or sung againe;

Rechanter. To sing, ring, or sound, againe; **1611** FLORIO It→E *Ricantare*, to recant or sing againe. *Ricantatione*, a recantation or singing againe. **1656** BLOUNT (1st edn) *Recant (recanto)* to sing after another **1688** MIEGE-COTGRAVE Fr→E *Rechanté*, sung again. *Rechanter*, to sing again. § *Il rechante la fin quatre ou cinq fois de suite*, he sings the end four or five times over.

recheat *see* call, horn

1656 BLOUNT (1st edn) *Recheat*, the name of one of those Lessons which Hunters use in winding a Horn; perhaps from the Fr. *Rechercher*, *i.* to seek diligently; because most commonly, when they winde this *Lesson*, the Hounds have lost their game, or hunt a game unknown. **1658** PHILLIPS (1st edn) *Recheat*, a certain lesson, which Hunters wind on their Horn, when the Hounds have lost their Game. **1676** COLES *Recheat*, a Hunters lesson when they lose the game &c. **1696** PHILLIPS (5th edn) *Recheat*, a certain Lesson which Hunters wind upon their Horn, when the Hounds have lost their Game. **1702** KERSEY *New Engl. Dict.* (1st edn) A *Recheat*, a hunter's lesson when they lose the game. **1704** *Cocker's Engl. Dict.* (1st edn) *Recheat*, a Lesson or Tune of the Hunting horn, when the Dogs have lost their scent. **1706** KERSEY-PHILLIPS (6th edn) *Recheat*, a certain Lesson, which Huntsmen wind upon the Horn, when the Hounds have lost their Game, to call them back from pursuing a Counter-scent. **1707** *Gloss. Angl. Nova* (1st edn) *Recheat*, the name of those Lessons which Hunters wind upon their Horn, when they have lost their Game. **1728** CHAMBERS *Recheat*, in Hunting, a Lesson which the Huntsman winds on the Horn, when the Hounds have lost their Game; to call them back from pursuing a Counter-scent. **1740** BAILEY *An Univ. Etymolog. Engl. Dict.* (9th edn) *Recheat* (among *Hunters*) a Lesson which Huntsmen wind with the Horn, to call the Hounds back from a false Scent.

recherche *see* research

recino

1500 *Ortus Vocabulorum* L→E Recino cinis. i. retro canere. **1538** ELYOT L→E *Recino, ere*, to synge agayne. **1565** COOPER L→E *Recino, recinis, pen. corr. recínui, recentum, recínere. Cic.* To singe or sowne agayne: to ringe againe. **1587** THOMAS L→E *Recino, is, ui, entum, ere.* To sing, sound, or ring again: **1589** RIDER L→E *Recino, recano, recanto.* To sing againe.

recitative *see* adagio, basso recitante, cantata, chorus, continued bass, modi melopœiæ, opera, style (stylo recitativo), symphony, tragedy, trio

1598 FLORIO It→E *Recitante*, ... Also an enterlude plaier. **1611** FLORIO It→E *Recitante*, ... Also an enterlude plaier. *Recitare*, to recite, to rehearse, to relate, to tell by heart or without booke, as players doe their parts in commedies. § *Recitatare una comedia*, to recite a commedie. **1656** BLOUNT (1st edn) *Recitative (recitativus)* that is openly read, or rehearsed aloud. Among the *Italians* it is an artificial way of singing. See *Opera*. **1658** PHILLIPS (1st edn) *Recitation*, (lat.) a reciting, or rehearsing, whence Recitative stile in Musick is a kinde of singing, wherewith Heroick, or Dramatick Poems are rehearsed upon the stage. **1659** TORRIANO-FLORIO It→E *Recitabile, Recitativo, Recitevole*, recitable, rehearsable, also the stile and method now adays, used in singing of Comedies, commonly called by the name of *Opera's*. **1676** COLES *Recitative*, rehearsed (in *Operaes*.) **1704** *Cocker's Engl. Dict.* (1st edn) *Recitative*, rehearsing, or repeating in Musick, Poetry, or Plays. **1706** KERSEY-PHILLIPS (6th edn) § *Recitative Musick* or *A Recitative*, a kind of Singing that comes near plain Pronunciation, after such a manner as Dramatick Poems are rehearsed upon the Stage. *Recitative Style*, a Style or Way of Writing fitted for that purpose. **1724** [PEPUSCH] *Short Explic. of Foreign Words in Mus. Bks.* (p. 62) *Recetitavo*, or *Recitativo*, or *Recitatif*; or by Way of Abbreviation *Recit°*. or *Rec°*. or *Re°*. The Adagio, or Grave Parts, in Cantata's, Motetts, and Opera's, have generally this Word fixed thereto, by which is to be understood a particular Way or Manner of Singing, which those Grave Parts require. **1726** BAILEY *An Univ. Etymolog. Engl. Dict.* (3rd edn) *Recitatif, Recitativo*, (in *Musick Books*) signifies the Adagio or grave Parts, in Cantata's, Motets and Opera's; a particular Way or Manner of Singing, which those grave Parts require. *Ital. Recitative Style*, a Way of Writing fitted for that Purpose. *Recit°*, is an Abbreviation of Recitativo, which see. **1728** CHAMBERS § *Recitative Music*, a Kind of Singing, that differs but little from ordinary Pronunciation; such as that wherein several Parts of the Liturgy are rehears'd in Cathedrals; or that wherein the Actors ordinarily deliver themselves on the Theatre, at the Opera, *&c.* See *Singing* and *Opera*. ¶ The *Italians* value themselves on their Performance in the *Recitative* Way. The *Recitatives*, or *Recitativo's*, in our Opera's, usually tire the Audience, by reason they don't understand the Language; the Songs make them amends. See *Song.* ¶ *Recitative Style,* is the Way of Writing accommodated to this Sort of Music. See *Style.* **1730** BAILEY *Dict. Britannicum* (1st edn) § *Recitative Musick,* a Sort of Singing that differs but little from plain Pronunciation, such as some Parts of the Liturgy rehearsed in Cathedrals; or after the Manner that dramatick Poems are rehearsed on the Stage. **1737** DYCHE-PARDON (2nd edn) *Recitative* (A.) ... and in *Musick,* it is a Sort of speaking in a plain but musical singing Manner, much like the plain Chant used in Cathedrals at reading the Psalms, Confession, Creed, &c. and particularly used at the rehearsing or acting dramatick Performances in Operas, &c.

1721 MALCOLM *Treatise of Musick* (p. 596) ... the recitative Kind [of music, as exemplified by the ancient Greeks], *that is,* only a more *musical* Speaking, or *modulated* Elocution; the Character of which is to come near Nature, and be only an Improvement of the natural Accents of Words by more pathetick or emphatical *Tones;* the Subject whereof may be either Verse or Prose. **1731** PRELLEUR *Modern Musick-Master* (Dictionary, p. 3) *Recitativo* or *Rec$^{o.}$* to express a Sort of Speaking in Singing, This Word is very common in Cantatas

record *see* recorder

1706 KERSEY-PHILLIPS (6th edn) To *Record,* ... also to begin to sing or tune Notes, as a Bird does. **1721** BAILEY *An Univ. Etymolog. Engl. Dict.* (1st edn) *Record, (among Fowlers)* to begin to Sing or tune Notes as a Bird does. **1737** DYCHE-PARDON (2nd edn) *Record* (V.) ... also to sing like Birds, or to play upon an Instrument now commonly called the Flute.

recorder *see* arigot, canna, cannamella, cannella, empneusta (under entata), fife, flute, monaulos, record, siringa, stifello, stufallo, syrinx, tibia

1678 PHILLIPS (4th edn) *Recorder* ... also an instrument of Wind Musick which is common. **1731** KERSEY *New Engl. Dict.* (3rd edn) A *Recorder* or *Flute,* a a [sic] Musical Instrument. **1737** DYCHE-PARDON (2nd edn) *Recorder* (S.) ... also the antient Name of a Musical Instrument now called the Flute.

recte & retro

1667 SIMPSON *Compendium of Practical Musick* (p. 166) Some Canons are made to be Sung *Recte & Retro* (as they phrase it;) that is Forward and Backward; or one Part forward and another backward. **1694** PURCELL-PLAYFORD *Intro. to Skill of Musick* (12th edn, 'A Brief Introduction to the Art of Descant', n.p.) There is a sixth sort of Fugeing called *Recte & Retro,* which is repeating the Notes backward; therefore you must avoid Prick'd Notes, because in the Reverse it would be of the wrong side of the Note. **1736** TANS'UR *Compleat Melody* (3rd edn, p. 72) *Recte,* (Lat.) signifies, *Forewards*: *Retro,* signifies *Backwards;* both pertaining to *Canon.* (Lat.)

reditta *see* repeat, repetatur, riditta

1724 [PEPUSCH] *Short Explic. of Foreign Words in Mus. Bks.* (p. 62) *Reditta,* the same as *Replica,* to repeat. **1726** BAILEY *An Univ. Etymolog. Engl. Dict.* (3rd edn) *Redita* (in *Musick Books*) signifies to repeat. *Ital.*

redondilla

1599 MINSHEU-PERCYVALL Sp→E **Redondillas,* a kinde of verse, roundelayes.

refrain *see* balade, burden, reprise

1570/71 *Dict. Fr. and Engl.* Fr→E § *Refrains des balades,* the burthen of a song. **1593** HOLLYBAND Fr→E § *Refrain des balades,* the burthen of a song, the holding of a song or ballet, the refret, the foote of a song, ballet or dittie: the verse enterlaced or often repeated in a dittie, song or ballet. **1611** COTGRAVE Fr→E § *Refrain d'une balade.* The Refret, burthen, or downe of a Ballade. **1688** MIEGE-COTGRAVE Fr→E *Refrein,* (m.) burden. § † *C'est là le Refrein de la Balade, Expression Proverbiale le refrein d'une Chanson,* the burden of a Song. *Le Refrein doit être natural, plaisant, & ingenieux,* the Burden ought to be natural, pleasant, and ingenious. *On appelle Refrein un même Vers, qu'on repete à la fin des Couplets de la Balade, du Chant Royal, & de quêques autres Poëmes à peu prês de cette nature.*

refret *see* burden, intercalarity, reprise

1656 BLOUNT (1st edn) *Refret* (Fr. *refrain*) the the [sic] Burthen or Down of a Song or Ballad. **1658** PHILLIPS (1st edn) *Refret,* (French *Refrain*) the burthen of a Ballade or Song. **1676** COLES *Refret, (French. refrain)* the burden of a song. **1704** *Cocker's Engl. Dict.* (1st edn) *Refret,* a *French* word for the burden of a Song. **1707** *Gloss. Angl. Nova* (1st edn) *Refret,* the Burden of a Song or Ballad. **1708** KERSEY *Dict. Anglo-Brit.* (1st edn) *Refret,* the Burden of a Ballad, or Song. **1728** CHAMBERS

Refret, in Musick. See *Ritornello*. **1730** BAILEY *Dict. Britannicum* (1st edn) *Refret (refrein*, F.) the Burden of a Ballad or Song.

regal *see* rigols

1598 FLORIO It→E *Regali*, a musicall instrument called rigoles. **1611** COTGRAVE Fr→E *Regales, des reg*. The musicall Instrument, called Rigolls. **1611** FLORIO It→E *Regali*, ... Also instruments called Rigoles. **1656** BLOUNT (1st edn) *Regal (regalis)* ... also a certain Musical Instrument, so called: **1659** TORRIANO-FLORIO It→E *Regale*, a pair of Rigols **1688** MIEGE-COTGRAVE Fr→E *Regale*, (f.) ... Rigol, a kind of Musical Instrument, that comes from Flanders.

c.1698-c.1703 NORTH Cursory Notes (*C-K CN* p. 97) That other sort of voicing pipes in organs is called the regoll; perhaps from regula, the barr that is managed to tune them, or from golla, a throat, from the resemblance to the sound of humane voice at the larinx; no matter which... **c.1715-20** NORTH Theory of Sounds BL Add. 32534, f. 69 ... I come next to consider the state of the comon sonorous tubes, wch are voiced by a proper Energye within themselves. and these are of many kinds, and Inventions, but I think all may be Reduced to. 3. Manners. 1. Such a sound by an eruption of air from the lipps of the performer. 2. by ye action of a spring or reed, wch ye German's in their organs call a Reedall, & wee by corruption a Regall. and 3. by ye working of ye air it self, of wch are those of all sorts called flutes. § f. 74 The next manner of voicing tubes made to sound by Inflation, is by a Redall, or as our organ makers (corrupting the german word[)] terme it a Regall. there are. 2. sorts, one of can or Reed (whence ye name), the other of Mettall. **1726-8** NORTH Theory of Sounds BL Add. 32535, f. 64 The comon reed pipe, wch the waits (as they are called) Insert into their Haut-boy's or shawmes, works In the same manner, by stop & let goe, but being formed of Reed (literally whence the terme, Reedall vulgo' Regall) and not of Mettall, and made with express designe, is altogether plyant ...

regola

1724 [PEPUSCH] *Short Explic. of Foreign Words in Mus. Bks.* (p. 62) *Regola*, or *Regula*, a Rule or Canon. **1726** BAILEY *An Univ. Etymolog. Engl. Dict.* (3rd edn) *Regola* (in *Musick Books*) signifies a Rule or Canon. *Ital.*

rehearsal

1728 CHAMBERS *Rehearsal*, in Musick and the Drama, an Essay or Experiment of some Composition, made in private, previous to the Representation or Performance thereof in publick; to habituate the Actors or Performers, and make them more ready and perfect in their Parts. ¶ There is a new Tragedy in *Rehearsal*.—The *Rehearsal* of the Anthem, *&c.* **1737** DYCHE-PARDON (2nd edn) *Rehearsal* (S.) ... also the trying or private practising of Players or Musicians of a Play or Concerto before they venture to play or act it openly upon the Stage.

relation *see* false relation, true relation

relation inharmonical

1704 HARRIS *Relation Inharmonical*, a Term in Musical Composition, signifying a harsh Reflection of Flat against Sharp, in a cross form, *viz.* When some harsh and displeasing Discord is produced, in comparing the Present Note of another Part. **1706** KERSEY-PHILLIPS (6th edn) *Relation Inharmonical*, (in Musical Composition) a harsh Reflection of Flat against Sharp in a cross Form; *viz.* when some harsh and displeasing Discord is produc'd in comparing the present Note of another Part. **1708** KERSEY *Dict. Anglo-Brit.* (1st edn) *Relation Inharmonical*, (in Musical Composition) a harsh Reflection of Flat against Sharp in a cross Form. **1728** CHAMBERS *Relation Inharmonical*, is a Term in musical Composition, signifying a harsh Reflection of Flat against Sharp, in a cross Form; *viz.* When some harsh and displeasing Discord is produced, in comparing the present Note of another Part.—*Harris.*

1636 BUTLER *Principles of Musik* (p. 49) ... And therefore, as in the true *Diatessaron*, the respect or relation of *Ut* to *Fa* or of *Re* to *Sol*, and, in a true *Diapente*, the relation of *Vt* to *Sol*, or of *Re* to *La* (becaus they ar Concords) is Harmonical; so, in the excessive Diatessaron, the relation of *Pha* to *Mi*, and, in the defective *Diapente*, the relation of *Mi* to *Pha*, (becaus they ar Discords) is called *Relatio non Harmonica.* **1659** SIMPSON *Division-Violist* (p. 11) ... so you avoid *Relation* not *Harmonical;* that is, a harsh and unpleasing Reflection of *Flat* against *Sharp.* § (p. 44) ... *in foure* Notes Asccending [sic], *or* Descending *by* Degrees, *we seldome exceed the distance of a* Full, *or* Perfect 4th. lest we produce unto the *Eare* that harshness, which is called *Relation not Harmonicall.* **1667** SIMPSON *Compendium of Practical Musick* (p. 56) ... the harsh reflection of *E sharp* against *B flat* the foregoing Note of the *Bass*: which is that we call *Relation Inharmonical* ... § (p. 91) Relation, or

Respect, or Reference Inharmonical, is a harsh reflection of *Flat* against *Sharp*, in a cross form: that is, when the present Note of one Part, compared with the foregoing Note of an other Part, doth produce some harsh and displeasing Discord. **1721** Malcolm *Treatise of Musick* (p. 227) ... But let me make this last Remark, which we have also confirmed from Experience, *viz*. That of Two Sounds in *Consonance*, 'tis required not only that every Note they make together be *Concord* (I have said already that there are some Exceptions to this Rule) but that, as much as possible, the present Note of the one Voice be *Concord* to the immediately preceeding Note of the other; which can be done by no Means so well as by such *Degrees* as are the Differences of *Concords* (where these happen to be *Discord, Musicians* call it particularly *Relation inharmonical.*)

relatio non harmonica *see* relation inharmonical

relative note

1717 B[ayne] *Intro. to Knowledge and Practice of Thoro' Bass* (pp. 5-6) Now, of these twelve Intervals of Sound, which are within the Compass of the *Octave* of any one Key, whether it be a sharp or a flat one; seven do in some respect or other naturally refer to the *Key*, which seven shall therefore be call'd *the relative Notes* of the Key; and the five of the twelve which never can enter into the Harmony of the Key, shall therefore be denominated *extraneous*. ¶ The seven relative Notes in a *sharp Key*, are the *great Second, great Third, Fourth, Fifth, great Sixth, great Seventh, and Octave*: And the five extraneous are the *less Second, less Third, false Fifth, less Sixth and less Seventh*. ¶ The seven relative Notes in a *flat Key*, are the *great Second, less Third, Fourth, Fifth, less Sixth, great Seventh*, and *Octave*: The five extraneous are the *less Second, great Third, false Fifth, great Sixth* and *less Seventh*.

relish *see* beat, grace, trill

remonter

1688 Miege-Cotgrave Fr→E *Remonte*, to get (or go) up again ... to new-string. § *Remonter un Lut de Cordes*, to new-string a Lute.

reorgarza

1598 Florio It→E *Reorgarza*, the name of a french dance vsed in Italie. **1611** Florio It→E *Reorgarza*, a French dance vsed in Italie. **1659** Torriano-Florio It→E *Reorgarza*, a French dance.

repeat *see* presa, reditta, repetatur, repetition, replica, replicato, reprise, riditta, ripresa, strain

1728 Chambers *Repeat*, in Musick, a Character shewing that what was last play'd or sung, must be *repeated*, or gone over again. See *Repetition*. ¶ The *Repeat* serves instead of writing the same thing twice over.—There are two Kinds of *Repeats*; the *great* and the *small*. ¶ The first is only a *double Bar*, dotted on each Side; or two parallel Lines drawn perpendicular a-cross the Staff; with Dotts on either Hand: See its Form under *Characters of Musick*. ¶ This Mark shews that the preceding Strain is to be *repeated*; that is, if it be near the Beginning of the Piece, all hitherto sung, or play'd, is to be *repeated*; or if towards the End of a Piece, all from such another Mark. ¶ In Gavots, we usually find the *Repeat*, at about the third Part of the Piece.—In Minuets, Borees, Courants, *&c*. towards the end. ¶ Some make this Rule, that if there be Dotts on each Side [of] the Bar, they direct to a *Repetition* both of the preceding and the following Strain; if there be only Dotts on one Side then, only the Strain on that Side [is] to be *repeated*. ¶ The *small Repeat* is where only some of the last Measures of a Strain are to be repeated.—This is denoted by a Character set over the Place where the *Repetition* begins, (see *Characters in Musick*) and continues to the End of the Strain. ¶ When the Song ends with a *Repetition* of the first Strain, or Part of it, instead of a *Repeat*, they use the Words *da Capo*, i.e. from the beginning. **1730** Bailey *Dict. Britannicum* (1st edn) *A Repeat* (in *Musick*) a Character shewing that what was last play'd or sung must be gone over again. **1737** Dyche-Pardon (2nd edn) *Repeat* (S.) in *Musick*, is a Mark or Character made thus, :S:, signifying that so much of the Strain as has this Mark set to it, must be repeated or played over again.

1665 Simpson *Principles of Practical Mvsick* (p. 29) This mark S: signifies a *Repetition* from that place only where it is Set; and is called a *Repeat*. **1700** Anon. *Compleat Instructor to the Flute* (p. 7) ... where you meet with this mark :S: sett over the Note thus :S: it is call'd a repeat and when you have play'd to the End of a Straine begin again that repeat and play to the next Double bar. **1706** Bedford *Temple Musick* (p. 194) ... *and the Intermissions of a certain silence* ... is also expressed in our *English* Anthems by a Mark which we call a *Repeat,* and which shews that the following *Part* to the end of a *Strain,* is to be *Repeated* with a *Lower Voice.* **1721** Malcolm *Treatise of Musick* (p. 411) A *Repeat* is a Mark which signifies the Repetition of a Part of the Piece; which is either of a whole Strain, and then the double *Bar,* at the End of that Strain, which is repeated, is marked with Points on each Side of it; and some make this the Rule, that if there are Points on both Sides, they direct to a Repetition both of the preceeding and following Strain, *i.e.* that each of them are to be play'd or sung twice on End; ... **1723** Church *Intro. to Psalmody* (p. 57) There is a character in Musick omitted, call'd a Repeat, which is mark'd Thus :S: it is commonly plac'd over some Note near the end of a piece of Musick, & directs you to repeat that part over again. **1731** Prelleur *Modern Musick-Master* (I, p. 5) There is a Character called a Repeat made thus :S: and is used to signifie that such a part of a Song must be sung over again from the Note over which it is placed[.] **1736** Tans'ur *Compleat Melody* (3rd edn, p. 9) A *Repeat,* is used to direct the Performer, that such a *Part,* or *Strain* must be repeated over again from the *Note* it is set over, or after; Either of these Words signifies the same; *viz. Repetatur, Represa, Replica, Replicato, Reditta, Riditta, Encore.*

repercussion *see* percussion, repetatur

1728 Chambers *Repercussion,* in Musick, a frequent Repetition of the same Sounds. See *Repetition.* ¶ This frequently happens in the Modulation; where the essential Chords of each Mode, or of the harmonical Triad, are to beat oftener than the rest; and of these three Chords the two Extremes, *i.e.* the final and the predominant one, (which are properly the *Repercussion* of each Mode) oftener than the middle one. **1730** Bailey *Dict. Britannicum* (1st edn) *Repercussion* (in *Musick*) a frequent Repetition of the same Sounds. **1737** Dyche-Pardon (2nd edn) *Re-percussion* (S.) ... and in *Musick* it is the frequent or often playing or repeating the same Notes or Sounds.

1609 Dowland-Ornithoparcus *Micrologus* (p. 12) *Of the Repercussions of Tones.* ¶ Whereupon the *Repercussion,* which by *Guido* is also called a *Trope,* and the proper and fit melodie of each *Tone.* Or it is the proper interuall of each *Tone* ...

repetatur *see* repeat

1724 [Pepusch] *Short Explic. of Foreign Words in Mus. Bks.* (p. 63) *Repetatur,* to Repeat. **1726** Bailey *An Univ. Etymolog. Engl. Dict.* (3rd edn) *Repetatur* (in *Musick Books*) signifies, let it be repeated or repeat. *Ital.*

1731 Prelleur *Modern Musick-Master* (Dictionary, p. 3) *Repetatur* to be Repeated. **1736** Tans'ur *Compleat Melody* (3rd edn, p. 67) *Repetatur, Replica, Re-percussion, Replicato, Represa, Reditta, Riditta, Come sopra,* (Ital.) *Encore.* (Fr.) Either of those *Terms* signify that such a *Part,* or *Strain* must be repeated over again: from the *Note* or Place it is set over. It is often set over this Character, :S: which is called a *Repeat;* and signifies the same.

repetition *see* double bar, repeat, strain

1728 Chambers *Repetition* .... Musicians and Comedians make several *Repetitions* of their Consorts and Comedies, e'er they perform for good. See *Rehearsal*.... *Repetition,* in Musick, a re-iterating or playing over again of the same Part of a Composition; whether it be a whole Strain, a Part of a Strain, or a double Strain. ¶ The *Repetition* is denoted by a Character, called a *Repeat,* which is varied so as to express the various Circumstances of the *Repetition.* See *Repeat.* ¶ When the Song *ends* with a *Repetition* of the last Strain, or a part of it; the *Repetition* is denoted by *da Capo;* that is, from the Beginning. ¶ *Repetition, Reply,* is also used in Musick, when after a little Silence, one Part *repeats* or runs over the same Notes, the same Intervals, the same Motions, in a word, the same Song, which a first Part had already gone over during the Silence of this. ¶ *Repetition, Reply* is also a doubling, or trebling, *&c.* of an Interval; or a Reiteration of some Consonance or Dissonance: Thus a fifteenth is a *Repetition* of the Octave, *i.e.* a double Octave or second Octave. See *Octave.* **1730** Bailey *Dict. Britannicum* (1st edn) *Repetition* (in *Musick*) a reiterating or playing over again of the same Part of a Composition, whether it be a whole Strain, a Part of a Strain, or a double Strain.

repicare

1598 Florio It→E *Repicare,* to sound or iangle as bells, to clatter or clash as armour doth. **1611** Florio It→E *Repicare,* to sound or iangle as Bells

repicco
1611 FLORIO It→E *Repiceo*, a chime of Bells. **1659** TORRIANO-FLORIO It→E *Repicco*, a jangling noise, a clattering sound, also a chime of bells.

repieno *see* ripieno

replica *see* repeat, repetatur
1724 [PEPUSCH] *Short Explic. of Foreign Words in Mus. Bks.* (p. 63) *Replica*, the same as *Repetatur*. § *Se Replica se Piace*, to Repeat if you please. **1726** BAILEY *An Univ. Etymolog. Engl. Dict.* (3rd edn) *Replica (in Musick Books)* signifies to repeat. *Ital.* as *Se replica se place* [sic], i.e. repeat if you please. *Ital.*

replicato *see* repeat, repetatur
1724 [PEPUSCH] *Short Explic. of Foreign Words in Mus. Bks.* (p. 63) *Replicato*, to Repeat, or Play over again. **1726** BAILEY *An Univ. Etymolog. Engl. Dict.* (3rd edn) *Replicato* (in *Musick Books*) signifies, repeat or play over again. *Ital.*

reply *see* fugue, harmonia gemina

report *see* descant, fugue, imitation, lydian, madrigal, motet, revert
1636 BUTLER *Principles of Musik* (p. 72) Reporte is the Iterating or mainteining of a Point in the like motion, *(per Arsin aut Thesin;)* the Principal and Replie both Ascending, or bothe Descending. ¶ Reporte is either Direct, which iterateth the Point in the same Cliefs and Notes (Unisons or Eights;) or Indirect, which iterateth the Point in other Cliefs: for it may bee taken at any distance from the first Note of the Point: but specially at a Fowrth or Fift. ¶ Direct Reporte, or in the same Cliefs, is commonly in divers Partes: Indirect, or in divers Cliefes, in the same Parte. **after 1695** NORTH untitled notebook BL Add. 32532, f. 10 [*re* consorts of 'ye old English musitians'] ... but to this purpose I cannot comend them. for they were not content to repeat their point, & In some, but Not much variety of Key's, wch they called Reporting, but they much take it backwards also, wch they called Reverting; ...

repose
1611 COTGRAVE Fr→E *Repose: f.* A Semibreefe Rest, in Musicke. **1688** MIEGE-COTGRAVE Fr→E *Repos*, (m.) ... a rest, in Musick;

represa *see* repetatur

reprise *see* refrain, refret, repeat
1706 KERSEY-PHILLIPS (6th edn) *Reprise*, ... also the Repetition, upholding, or Burden of a Ballad, or Song.

requiem
1656 BLOUNT (1st edn) *Requiem* ... is often used in English, especially in Poetry; As to sing a *Requiem* for the dead; whereby is understood a Mass for the dead, which begins with these words. *Requiem æternam dona eis, Domine, & lux perpetua luceat eis.* **1658** PHILLIPS (1st edn) To sing a *Requiem*, signifieth to sing a Masse for the eternal rest of the soules of those that are deceased, the word *Requies* signifying in Latin rest. **1704** *Cocker's Engl. Dict.* (1st edn) *Requiem*, ... A Popish Service or Mass sung for the rest of Souls departed. **1706** KERSEY-PHILLIPS (6th edn) *Requiem*, as To *sing a requiem, i.e.* to sing a Mass for the Souls of deceased Persons **1728** CHAMBERS *Requiem*, a Mass sung in the *Romish* Church for the rest of the Soul of a Person deceas'd. See *Mass.* ¶ It is thus called, because the *Introit* begins with, *Requiem æternam dona eis Domine*, &c. **1737** DYCHE-PARDON (2nd edn) *Requiem* (S.) .... *To sing a Requiem*, in the Church of *Rome*, is to say or sing Mass for the Soul of some departed Person.

research *see* fantasia, interlude, prelude, ricercar, voluntary
1728 CHAMBERS *Research*, in Musick, is a Kind of Prelude or Voluntary, play'd on the Organ, Harpsichord, Theorbo, *&c.* Wherein the Composer seems to *Search*, or look out for the Strains, and Touches of Harmony, which he is to use in the regular Piece to be play'd afterwards. See *Prelude.* ¶ This is usually done off-hand, and consequently requires a Master's Skill.—When in a Motet the Composer takes the Liberty to use any thing that comes in his Head, without applying any Words to it, or subjecting himself to express the Sense or Passion thereof; the *Italians* call it *Fantasia Ricercata*; the *French, Recherche*; and our Musicians, *Research.* **1730** BAILEY *Dict. Britannicum* (1st edn) *Re-Search* (in *Musick*) a Kind of Prelude or Voluntary played on an Organ, Harpsichord, *&c.* **1740** BAILEY *An Univ. Etymolog. Engl. Dict.* (9th edn) *Research* (in *Musick*) a sort of Prelude.

resine *see* colophony, nervo
1611 COTGRAVE Fr→E f. § *Resine Colophonienne.* Clarified, or hard Rozen; such as wee rub Violl stickes withall. *Resine Colophonienne.* Dry clarified Rosin; such as we rub Violl-sticks with.

resolution *see* anticipation, postposition
1728 CHAMBERS *Resolution,* in Musick, is when a Canon, or perpetual Fugue is not wrote all on the same Line, or in one Part; but all the Voices that are to follow the *Guida,* or first Voice, are wrote separately, either in *Score, i.e.* in separate Lines, or in separate Parts, with the Pauses each is to observe, in the Beginning, and in the Tone proper to each. **1730** BAILEY *Dict. Britannicum* (1st edn) *Resolution* (in *Musick*) is when a Canto or perpetual Fugue is not written all on the same Line, or in one Part; but all the Voices that are to follow the *Guido* are written separately, *&c.*

after 1517 ANON. Art of Mvsic BL Add. 4911, f. 30 *Quhat is resolutione* ¶ It is ane opnynge and furtli schawm of observir cantionis be Canonis Institat. Quhilk be way of resolution ar planlye resoluit. Or it is ane tangtription of notte in ane moir vvlgar forme in the quhilk vycht vyslye It is to be constatut. **early 18th C.** PEPUSCH various papers BL Add. 29429, ff. 3-3v The Resolution, is the Converting a Discord in a Concord, viz: a 3, 4, 5, or 6th. by Ascending or Descending a full Tone or More Tones in ye Bass. **1721** MALCOLM *Treatise of Musick* (p. 437) The *Discords* here treated of are introduced into the *Harmony* with due Preparation; and they must be succeeded by *Concords,* commonly called the *Resolution* of the *Discord.* **1721 or after** ANON. Institutions of Musick (rear of LC copy of Bayne, p. 14) The Discords here treated of, are to be introduced into the Harmony with due Preparation, and they must be succeeded by Concords commonly called the Resolutions of the Discord.

resonance
1611 COTGRAVE Fr→E *Resonnace: f.* A resounding; ringing; melodious Eccho, rebounding sound; a recording, as of birds; also, an accord, agreement, consent of harmonie. *Resonnamment.* Resoundingly, lowdly, shrilly, melodiously, with good correspondence of voices; Eccho-like. **1728** CHAMBERS *Resonance, Resounding,* in Musick, *&c.* a sound return'd by the Air inclosed in the Bodies of String-Musical-Instruments; as Lutes, *&c.* or even in the Bodies of Wind-Instruments, or Flutes, *&c.* See *Sound, Musick, Instrument, &c.* ¶ We also say, Elliptic, and parabolic Vaults, *resound* strongly, *i.e.* reflect or return the Sound. See *Eccho.* ¶ The Mouth, and the Parts thereof, as the Palate, Tongue, Teeth, Nose, and Lips, Mons. *Dodart* observes, contribute nothing to the Tone of the Voice; but their effect is very great as to the *Resonance.* See *Voice.* ¶ Of this we have a very sensible Instance in that vulgar Instrument called the *Jews-Harp,* or *Trompe de Bearn*: For, if you hold it in your Hand, and strike the Tongue or Spring thereof, which makes all the Sound of the Instrument, it scarce yields any Noise at all. But, holding the Body of the Instrument between the Teeth, and striking the Spring as before, it makes a musical Buzz, which is heard to a good Distance, and especially the lower Notes. ¶ So also in the Haut-bois, the Tone of the Reed is always the same; being a sort of a Drone: The Chief variety is in the Tone of the *Resonance,* produced in the Mouth by the greater or less Aperture, and the divers Motions of the Lips. See *Hautboy.*

respond
1704 *Cocker's Engl. Dict.* (1st edn) *Respond,* to answer to every other verse in the Psalms of the Common-Prayer; and from thence the Hymns or Psalms sung alternately in Cathedrals, are called. ¶ *Responsories,* because they answer one another.

responsory *see* anthem, antiphon, primer
1587 THOMAS L→E § *Responsorius cantus, Isid. quòd alio desinente, id alter respondet.* **1599** MINSHEU-PERCYVALL Sp→E § **musica de Responso,* singing of priests at burials, when they answere on the other. **1656** BLOUNT (1st edn) *Responsory* (as *Cantus responsorius,* where one verse or line answers another;) answerable... **1658** PHILLIPS (1st edn) *Responsory* song, an Anthem, wherein they sing by turns as it were, one answering the other. **1706** KERSEY-PHILLIPS (6th edn) *Responsory Song,* an Anthem, in which the Quiristers sing by turns, as it were one answering another. **1708** KERSEY *Dict. Anglo-Brit.* (1st edn) *Responsory Song,* an Anthem, in which the Quiristers sing by turns. **1728** CHAMBERS *Responsary* [sic] *Song,* an Anthem in which the Quiristers sing by turns. See *Anthem.* **1737** DYCHE-PARDON (2nd edn) *Responsory* (S.) a Song, Prayer or Anthem, wherein one Part of the Choir answers by Turns to the other.

1586 ANON. *Praise of Mvsicke* (p. 108) *Isidorus,* Archbishop of *Hispalis* in *Spaine* of whome I spake before, maketh a difference & distinction betweene *Anthems* and *Responsories*: for *Anthems* he said as I affirmed before, *that Ambrose was the first that translated them from the Greeke into the Latine Church: but for Responsories hee sheweth that they were long before that time vsed in the Churches of Italy, and were so called because when one sang, the quire answered him singing also, & then it was the vse either that euery man shuld sing by himself, or sometime one alone,* or at some other times two or three together, the quier for the most part making answere.

rest *see* course, hold, numerus, pause, repose, souspir, tacet

1706 KERSEY-PHILLIPS (6th edn) *Rest*, ... also a Term in Musick. See *Pause*. **1708** KERSEY *Dict. Anglo-Brit.* (1st edn) *Rest*, ... in *Musick*, the same as *Pause*. **1728** CHAMBERS *Rest*, in Musick, is a Pause or Interval of Time, during which there is an Intermission of the Voice or Sound. See *Pause* and *Time*. ¶ *Rests* are sometimes used in *Melody*, that is in Musick of a single Part, to express some simple Passion, or even for Variety sake; but more usually in *Harmony*, or in Compositions of several Parts, for the sake of the Pleasure of hearing one Part move on while another *rests*; and this interchangeably. See *Melody* and *Harmony*. ¶ *Rests* are either for a whole Bar, or more than a Bar, or but for the Part of a Bar.—When the *Rest* is for a part, it is express'd by certain Signs corresponding to the Quantity of certain Notes of Time; as Minim, Crotchet, *&c.* and is accordingly call'd *Minim-rest*, *Crotchet-rest*, &c. ¶ The Characters or Figures whereof, see under *Characters of Musick*; where the Note and corresponding *Rest* are found together. ¶ When any of those Characters occur either on Line or Space; that Part is always silent for the Time of a Minim, or Crotchet, *&c.*—Sometimes a *Rest* is for a Crotchet and Quaver together; or for other Quantities of Time, for which there is no particular Note: In which Case the Signs of Silence are not multiplied; but such Silence is express'd by placing together as many *Rests* of different Time, as make up the designed *Rest*. ¶ When the *Rest* is for a whole Bar, the Semibreve *Rest* is always used.—If the *Rest* be for two Measures, 'tis mark'd by a Line drawn a-cross a whole Space.—For three Measures 'tis drawn a-cross a Space and a half; and for four Measures a-cross two Spaces. But to prevent Ambiguity, the Number of Bars is usually writ over the Sign. ¶ Some of the more antient Writers in Musick, make these *Rests* of different Value in different Species of Time.—*E. gr.* The Character of a Minim-*Rest*, in common Time, say they, expresses the *Rest* of three Crotchets in triple Time; is that the Triples $\frac{6}{8}$, $\frac{6}{16}$, $\frac{12}{8}$, $\frac{12}{16}$, it always marks an half Measure, how different soever these may be among themselves. ¶ They add that the *Rest* of a Crotchet in common Time is a *Rest* of three Quavers in the Triple $\frac{9}{8}$; and that the *Quaver Rest* of common Time is to [sic] equal to three Semi-quavers in the Triple $\frac{9}{16}$. But this variety in the Use of the same Characters, is now laid aside. **1730** BAILEY *Dict. Britannicum* (1st edn) *Rest* (in *Musick*) a Pause or Interval of Time, during which there is an Intermission of the Voice or Sound. **1731** KERSEY *New Engl. Dict.* (3rd edn) A *Rest* (in *Musick*) a Pause, a Stop. **1737** DYCHE-PARDON (2nd edn) *Rest* (S.) ... and in *Musick*, is a Pause or Stop of the Voice or Instrument, or both for some Interval of Time.

1609 DOWLAND-ORNITHOPARCUS *Micrologvs* (p. 51) A *Rest* (as *Tinctoris* writeth) is the Signe of Silence. Or (as *Gafforus* saith) it is a figure which sheweth the Artificial leauing off from singing: Or it is a stroke drawne in line and space, which betokens silence. Now *Rests* are placed in songs after three manners, to wit; Essentially, Iudicially, and both wayes. Essentially, when they betoken silence. Iudicially, when they betoken not silence but the perfect *Moode*: and then their place is before the signe of Time. Both wayes, when they represent both. **1667** SIMPSON *Compendium of Practical Musick* (p. 27) *Odd Rests* we call those which take up only some part or parcel of a *Semibreves* Time or Measure, and have alwayes reference to some odd Note; for, by these two *Odds* the Measure is made even. **1722** B., T. *Compleat Musick-Master* (p. 5) A *Rest* or *Pause*, for so it may properly be called, denoteth a ceasing or intermission of sound for the Time or length of any of the foregoing Notes.

resveil *see* reveille

retornello *see* ritornello

retorted time

1597 MORLEY *Plaine and Easie Introdvction* (p. 27) [marginalia: 'A Retort.'] ¶ *Phi.* What do you terme a *retorted Moode*? ¶ *Ma*. It is *a Moode of imperfect time set backward*, signifying that the Notes before which it is set must be sung as fast againe as they were before ... **1715** ROBINSON *Essay upon Vocal Musick* (p 16) [*re* the moods of proportion] The last of all these is called Retorted Time, for it requires to be sung about as quick again as that of Common Time, it has the same Measure with both the other, and is known by this Mood ⊕, which you see stands by a great Figure of 2. **1731** PRELLEUR *Modern Musick-Master* (I, p. 4) ... sometimes you'll see this Mark $\frac{2}{4}$ at the beginning of a Song, then there is but 2 Crotchets or a Minim in a Bar. this is called retortive Time. § (III, p. 11) Common Time is known by some one of these Characters C, or ¢, Ↄ or $\frac{2}{4}$... The last of these marks never contains more than a Minim, or 2 Crotchets or four Quavers &c in a Bar. this [sic] is called retortive Time.

retreat *see* beat, cornet, drum, levet, mensural music, palinodia, raccolta, tattoo, volta-faccia
1593 HOLLYBAND Fr→E § *Sonner à la retraicte,* to sounde the retyre. **1706** KERSEY-PHILLIPS (6th edn) *Retreat,* ... Also a beat of Drum so call'd. See *Tattoo.* **1730** BAILEY *Dict. Britannicum* (1st edn) *Retreat,* a Beat of Drum in the Evening, at the Firing of a Piece, call'd the *Warning-Piece;* at which the Drum-Major, with all the Drums of the Battalion, beats round the Regiment. **1737** BAILEY *The Univ. Etymolog. Engl. Dict.* (3rd edn, vol. 2) *Retreat,* a beat of drum in the evening, at the firing of a piece, called the *Warning Piece;* at which the drum-major with all the drums of the battalion, beats round the regiment.

retro *see* recte & retro

reveille *see* beat
1611 COTGRAVE Fr→E *Resveil: m.* A Hunts-vp, or Morning song for a new-married wife, the day after the mariage. **1706** KERSEY-PHILLIPS (6th edn) *Reveiller,* (*Fr. i.e.* to awake) the Beat of Drum in a Morning, that summons the Soldiers from their Beds, and is commonly call'd the *Travelly.* **1708** KERSEY *Dict. Anglo-Brit.* (1st edn) *Reveiller,* (*F.*) the Beat of Drum in a Morning, that summons the Soldiers from their Beds. **1721** BAILEY *An Univ. Etymolog. Engl. Dict.* (1st edn) *Reveille,* (*reveil,* F.) the beat of a Drum in a Morning, which summoneth the Soldiers from their Beds. **1728** CHAMBERS *Reveille,* a Beat of the Drum, intended to give Notice that it is Day-break; and that the Soldiers are to rise, and the Centries forbear challenging. See *Drum.* ¶ The Word in *French,* form'd of the Verb *reveiller,* to awake. **1730** BAILEY *Dict. Britannicum* (1st edn) *Reveille, i.e.* to awake *F.* (in the *Milit. Art.*) a beat of Drum in the Morning, that summoneth the Soldiers from their Beds, and is usually called the *Travelly.*

revels *see* agonothet, ball, choragus
1616 BULLOKAR *Reuels.* Players and dancings, with other pleasant deuices, vsed sometimes in the Kings Court, and elsewhere in great houses. **1623** COCKERAM *Reuells.* Dancings, mummings [sic], &c. **1656** BLOUNT (1st edn) *Revels* (from the Fr. *Reveiller, i.* to awake from sleep) are with us, sports of Dancing, Masking, Comedies, and such like, used formerly in the Kings House, the Inns of Court, or in the Houses of other great personages; And are so called, because they are most used by night, when otherwise men commonly sleep: There is also an Officer, called, *The Master of the Revels,* who has the ordering and command of these pastimes. **1658** PHILLIPS (1st edn) *Revels,* sports of dancing, masking, comedies, *&c.* formerly used in the Kings house and Inns of Court, from the French *Reveiller,* to awake, because they were performed in the night time. **1676** COLES *Revels, French.* Night-sports of dancing &c. in the Innes of Court, &c. § *Master of the Reuels,* who hath the Ordering of the ¶ *Revels* **1702** KERSEY *New Engl. Dict.* (1st edn) *Revels,* sports of dancing, masking, dice-playing, *&c.* in the Inns of Court. § The *Master of the revels,* an officer that has the ordering of those pastimes. **1706** KERSEY-PHILLIPS (6th edn) *Revels,* Sports of Dancing, Masking, Dice-playing, acting Comedies, or Farces, &c. us'd in Prince's Courts, Noble-mens Houses, or Inns of Court, and commonly perform'd by Night; their Name in *French,* being derived from *Reveiller* to awake.

reversi
1611 COTGRAVE Fr→E *Reversi: m.* A kind of Trumpe (played backward, and full of sport) which the Duke of Savoy brought some ten yeares agoe into France.

revert *see* descant, fugue, lydian, motet, report
1597 MORLEY *Plaine and Easie Introdvction* (p. 85) [marginalia: 'What a reuert is.'] ¶ *Phi.* What doe you call the reuerting of a point? ¶ *Ma.* The reuerting of a point (which also we terme a reuert) is, when a point is made rising or falling, and then turned to go the contrarie waie, as manie notes as it did y[e] first. **1636** BUTLER *Principles of Musik* (p. 72) Revert is the Iterating of a Point in contrari Motion, *(per Arsin & Thesin;)* the Replie mooving *per Thesin,* if the Principal Ascend, and *per Arsin,* if the Principal descend. Which kinde of Fuga is much more difficult than Report. **1736** TANS'UR *Compleat Melody* (3rd edn, p. 72) *Reverted,* (Lat.)

signifies, turned back again, or *backwards;* pertaining to *Canon.*

rhapsodi *see* hilarodus

1728 CHAMBERS *Rhapsodi, Rhapsodists,* in Antiquity, Persons who made a Business of singing Pieces of *Homer*'s Poems. ¶ *Cuper* informs us, that the *Rhapsodi* were cloath'd in red when they sung the *Iliad;* and in blue when they sung the *Odyssee.* ¶ They perform'd on the Theatres; and sometimes for Prizes, in Contests of Poetry, Singing, *&c.* ¶ After the two Antagonists had finished their Parts, the two Pieces, or Papers they were wrote in, were joined together again; whence the Name, *viz.* from ῥάπτω, *suo,* I join together; and ᾠδή, Ode, Song. ¶ But there must have been other *Rhapsodi* of more Antiquity than these; People who composed Heroic Poems, or Pieces in Praise of Heroes and Great Men, and sung their own Compositions from Town to Town for a Livelihood: Of which Profession was *Homer* himself. ¶ *Philochorus,* again, derives the Word from ῥάπτειν εἴδην, *to procure Pieces of Poetry to be composed,* as if they were not the Authors of the Poems to be sung. This Opinion, to which *Scaliger* inclines, reduces these *Rhapsodi* to the first Kind.—In effect, 'tis probable that they were all of the same Class, whatever Distinction some Authors may Imagine; and that their Business was to sing or rehearse Poems, either of their own, or other People's Composition, as might best serve their Purpose, the getting of a Penny. So that we don't apprehend it any Injury to them, to set them on the Foot of our Ballad-singers; many of whom, no doubt, Pen their own Ditties. After *Homer*'s, 'tis no wonder they confined themselves altogether to his Pieces, for which the People had the utmost Veneration: Nor is it surprizing they should erect Stages, *&c.* and Dispute the Point of Recitation in Fairs and Markets.

rhapsody

1728 CHAMBERS *Rhapsody,* in Antiquity, a Discourse in Verse, sung or rehearsed by a *Rhapsodist.* See *Rhapsodi.* ¶ Others will have *Rhapsody* properly to signify a Collection of Verses, especially those of *Homer;* which having been a long time dispersed in Pieces and Fragments, were at length by *Pisitratus*'s Order, digested into Books, call'd *Rhapsodies:* From the *Greek* ῥάπτω, *suo,* I sew; and ᾠδή, Verse, Song. ¶ Hence, among the Moderns, *Rhapsody* is used for an Assemblage of Passages, Thoughts, and Authorities, raked together from divers Authors, to compose some new Piece.— *Lipsius*'s Politicks make such a *Rhapsody,* wherein there is nothing of the Author's own, but Conjunctions and Particles.

[rhetoric] *see* descant, flourish

rhythm *see* rythmus

1658 PHILLIPS (1st edn) *Rhythmical,* (Greek) belonging to Rhythme, or Meeter in verse; as also to proportion, or harmony in Musick. **1728** CHAMBERS *Rhythm* ... [*see* Appendix]

1635 ANON. Papers rel. to Writings of Birchensha BL Add. 4388, f. 46v *Rhythmus* est ordo motûs secundum celeritatem & tarditatem.

rhythmica *see* rythmica

ribebba *see* rabel, rebeck

1598 FLORIO It→E *Ribebba,* as *Ribecca.* **1611** FLORIO It→E *Ribebba,* ... Also as *Ribecca. Ribes,* as *Ribebba.*

ribecca *see* rebeck

ribecchino *see* rebeck

1598 FLORIO It→E *Ribecchino,* a little croud, kit, or fidle. **1611** FLORIO It→E *Ribecchino,* a little fidle, rebecke or croud.

ribibble

1658 PHILLIPS (1st edn) *Ribibble,* (old word) a Fiddle, or Cittern. **1676** COLES *Ribible, Old word.* a rebeck or fidle. **1706** KERSEY-PHILLIPS (6th edn) *Ribibble,* (old Word) a Cittern, or Fiddle. **1708** KERSEY *Dict. Anglo-Brit.* (1st edn) *Ribibble,* (*O.*) a Cittern, or Fiddle.

ricercar *see* fantasia, interlude, prelude, research, voluntary

1659 TORRIANO-FLORIO It→E *Ricerca, Ricercamento, Ricercata, Ricercatura,* a search, a searching, a seeking out, an enquiring out ... also a Musitians seeking out of new strains and touches before he will play any set lesson. **1724** [PEPUSCH] *Short Explic. of Foreign Words in Mus. Bks.* (p. 64) *Ricercate,* is a Kind of Extempory Prelude or Overture, the same as we call a *Voluntary.* **1726** BAILEY *An Univ. Etymolog. Engl. Dict.* (3rd edn) *Ricercate* (in *Musick Books*) signifies a kind of extempore Prelude or Overture; the same the *English* call a *voluntary. Ital.*

ridda

1550 THOMAS It→E *Ridda,* a round daunce. **1598** FLORIO It→E *Rida,* a kinde of countrie, rounde, hopping dance. *Ridda,* as *Rida. Riddare,* to dance in a round. **1611** FLORIO It→E *Ridda,* any kind of round Country dance as our Hay dance. *Riddare,* to dance round. **1659** TORRIANO-FLORIO It→E *Ridda,* a Country daunce like our Haye-dance. *Riddare,* to dance in a round as about a a [sic] May-pole, or else hand in hand, to dance the haye.

riditta *see* reditta, repeat, repetatur

1724 [PEPUSCH] *Short Explic. of Foreign Words in Mus. Bks.* (p. 64) *Riditta.* See the Words *Reditta, Replica, &c.* **1726** BAILEY *An Univ. Etymolog. Engl. Dict.* (3rd edn) *Riditta,* signifies the same as *Reditta,* and *Replica,* which see. *Ital.*

ridotta

1726 BAILEY *An Univ. Etymolog. Engl. Dict.* (3rd edn) A *Ridotto,* an Eutertainment [sic] of Singing, Musick, *&c.* an Opera. **1730** BAILEY *Dict. Britannicum* (1st edn) *Ridotta,* an Entertainment of Singing, Musick, *&c.* an Opera, or part of it, *Ital.* **1737** DYCHE-PARDON (2nd edn) *Ridotta* (S.) a Ball or Entertainment of Singing, Dancing, instrumental Musick, &c.

rigadoon *see* style (stylo choraico)

1728 CHAMBERS *Rigadoon,* a kind of Dance, borrowed originally from *Provence;* perform'd in Figure, by a Man and a Woman.—The *Rigadoon* is gay, pleasant, *&c.* The Word is form'd from the *French Rigodon,* which signifies the same thing. **1730** BAILEY *Dict. Britannicum* (1st edn) *Rigadoon,* a *French Dance,* performed in Figures by a Man and a Woman. **1735** DEFOE *Rigadoon,* a sort of Dance. **1737** DYCHE-PARDON (2nd edn) *Rigadoon* (S.) a *French* Dance performed by a Man and Woman in Figures. **1740** BAILEY *An Univ. Etymolog. Engl. Dict.* (9th edn) *Rigadoon,* a sort of Dance.

rigaletto

1659 TORRIANO-FLORIO It→E *Rigaletto,* certain musical instruments used antiently in churches before Organs were divised [sic], which some take to be the Rigols.

rigo

1611 FLORIO It→E *Rigo,* ... the name of an old common song. **1659** TORRIANO-FLORIO It→E *Rigo,* ... also the name of a common old song.

rigoletto

1598 FLORIO It→E *Rigoletto,* a countrie skipping dance, a merrie round or hornepipe, or gigge. **1611** FLORIO It→E *Rigoletto,* a country skipping dance, horne-pipe, merrie-round. Also a gigge. § *Mastro rigo,* the name of an old common song in Italy. **1659** TORRIANO-FLORIO It→E *Rigolare,* to sing or chant common songs *Rigoletto,* a country gig, a country dance, horn-pipe or merry round

rigols *see* clavicembalo, manichord, menacorda, regal, rigaletto

1658 PHILLIPS (1st edn) *Rigols,* a certain Musical instrument, called a *Clericord,* it comes from the French *Regalliadir,* i. to rejoyce. **1673** BLOUNT *World of Errors* (n.p.) *Rigols,* A certain Musical Instrument, called a *Clericord;* comes from the French *Regalliadir,* i.e. to rejoyce *(for* Regaillardir.) *Engl. Dict. Rigols,* Vox quæ mihi in solo *Dict. Angl.* occurrit, exponitur instrumentum musicum, quod alio nomine *Clavichordium, A Clavicord* dicitur. Author somniando, ut solet, suaviter deducit a Fr. Gal. Regalliadir, exhilarari. Sanè si talis vox sit, quod nullus credo, mallem deducere a Fr. Gal. *Se Rigoler,* derider, lascivire—Vel, quod magis placet, a Lat. *Lyricola.* Dr. *Skinner.* **1676** COLES *Rigols, Old word.* a claricord (instrument.) **1678** PHILLIPS (4th edn) *Rigols,* a certain Musical Instrument, by some supposed to be the same with a *Clavichord* or *Clerichord;* the derivation of it from the *French Regalliardir* to rejoyce, is not more strain'd, than Skinners from *Lyricula;* ... **1702** KERSEY *New Engl. Dict.* (1st edn) *Rigols,* a sort of musical instrument, us'd in *Flanders.* **1704** *Cocker's Engl. Dict.* (1st edn) *Rigols,* an old word for a Musical Instrument, now called a *Claricord.* **1706** KERSEY-PHILLIPS (6th edn) *Rigols,* a sort of Musical Instrument, by some suppos'd to be the same with *Clarichord* or *Clavichord.* **1708** KERSEY *Dict. Anglo-Brit.* (1st edn) *Rigols,* a Musical Instrument. **1726** BAILEY *An Univ. Etymolog. Engl. Dict.* (3rd edn) *Rigol,* a Musical Instrument, a *Clavicord,* or what makes merry or diverts. *Sh.* **1728** CHAMBERS *Rigol,* a kind of musical Instrument, consisting of several Sticks bound together, only separated by Beads.—It makes a tolerable Harmony, being well struck with a Ball at the End of a Stick. **1730** BAILEY *Dict.*

Britannicum (1st edn) *Rigols*, a Musical Instrument, consisting of several Sticks bound together, only separated by Beads.

rimesso *see* destendu
1598 FLORIO It→E *Rimesso*, ... Also sent or giuen againe, let downe or slacked the strings of an instrument. *Rimettere, metto, misi, messo*, ... to let downe as the strings of an instrument. **1611** FLORIO It→E *Rimesso*, ... Also slacked or let downe the strings of an instrument. **1659** TORRIANO-FLORIO It→E *Rimesso*, ... slacked or let down the strings of any instrument

ripieno *see* bass, pieno, tenor, violin
1724 [PEPUSCH] *Short Explic. of Foreign Words in Mus. Bks.* (p. 63) *Repieno*, or *Repiano*, signifies Full; and is used to distinguish those Violins in Concerto's, which play only now and then to fill up, from those which play throughout the whole Concerto. (p. 64) *Ripiano*. See the Word *Repieno*. § (p. 10) *Alto Ripieno*, the Tenor of the Great Chorus, or the Tenor that sings or plays now and then in some particular Places. (p. 15) *Basso Ripieno*, is the Bass of the Grand Chorus, or the Bass that plays now and then in some particular Places. (p. 18) *Canto Ripieno*, is the Treble of the grand Chorus, or that which sings only now and then in some particular Places. (p. 79) *Tenore Ripieno*, the Tenor which plays in some Parts only. **1726** BAILEY *An Univ. Etymolog. Engl. Dict.* (3rd edn) *Repiano, Repieno*, (in *Musick Books*) signifies full, is used to distinguish those Violins in *Concerto*'s, which play only now and then to fill up, from those which play throughout the whole *Concerto*. Ital. *Ripiano*, the same as *Repiano*, Ital, which see. *Ital.* § *Alto Ripieno* (in *Musick Books*) signifies the Tenor of the great Chorus, that sings or plays now and then in some particular places. *Basso Repieno* (in *Musick Books*) signifies the Bass of the Grand Chorus, or the Bass that plays now and then, in some particular Places. *Ital.* *Canto Ripieno* (in *Musick Books*) signifies the Treble of the Grand Chorus, or that which sings now and then in some particular Places. *Ital.* **1737** DYCHE-PARDON (2nd edn) *Repiano* or *Repieno* (S.) in *Musick*, is much the same with Chorus, or the coming in of several Instruments at particular Times, that rest at other Parts of the Concerto.

1728 NORTH Musicall Grammarian (*C-K MG* ff. 70v-71) Harmony is never so compleat as in full 4 parts; all inter-woven and alike airey, which is never so well when a part is thrust in for repien as they terme it ... **1731** PRELLEUR *Modern Musick-Master* (Dictionary, p. 2) *Basso Ripieno*, Bass of y[e] Great Chorus. **1736** TANS'UR *Compleat Melody* (3rd edn, p. 70) *Repieno*, or *Repiano*. (Ital.) signifies *Full*, or the same as *Chorus*: And directs those *Parts* to move in *Consort* that move but in some certain Places. Sometimes it is a Name given to those *Parts*, that move but some certain Places, as *Basso Repieno, Alto Repieno, Canto Repieno*, &c. which Parts are called, *The Parts of the little Chorus*.

ripresa *see* presa, repeat
1598 FLORIO It→E *Ripresa*, ... an answere in musike to begin when another leaues off. **1611** FLORIO It→E *Ripresa*, ... Also an answer in musike to begin when another leaues off. **1659** TORRIANO-FLORIO It→E *Ripresa*, ... among Musicians it is an answering one another, when one leaves off and another begins. **1724** [PEPUSCH] *Short Explic. of Foreign Words in Mus. Bks.* (p. 63) *Represa*, to Repeat; or a Repeat; a Character used in Musick, to shew where the Repeat begins. (p. 64) *Ripresa*. See the Word *Represa*. **1726** BAILEY *An Univ. Etymolog. Engl. Dict.* (3rd edn) *Represa* (in *Musick Books*) signifies a Repeat, or to repeat; a Character us'd to shew where the Repeat begins. *Ital.* *Ripresa*, the same as *Represa*, Ital. which see.

rise *see* beat, plain beat

rispetto
1598 FLORIO It→E *Rispetto*, ... Also a kind of countrie song or Iigge. **1611** FLORIO It→E *Rispetto*, respect, regard, or esteeme ... Also a kinde of Country song or roundely. **1659** TORRIANO-FLORIO It→E *Rispetto*, ... also a stanza or stave of verses or songs that Countrey people may sing or say

risvegliatoio *see* chanticleer, sveglia
1659 TORRIANO-FLORIO It→E *Risvegliatoio, Risveglio*, as *Svegliatoio*, also a hunt's-up sounded with horn or musick in a morning, also a chanti-clear, or night crowing cock.

ritornello *as part of a composition, see* interlude, opera, refret, roundo, tornello
1659 TORRIANO-FLORIO It→E *Ritornello, Ritornelgli*, ... also a quavering of ones voice in singing or burthen of a song. **1696** PHILLIPS (5th edn)

Ritornello, the Repeating a Couplet of Verses at the end of a Stanza, or of half a dozen Notes at the end of a Song. **1706** KERSEY-PHILLIPS (6th edn) *Ritornello (Ital.)* the repeating of a Couplet of Verses at the end of a *Stanza*, or Staff; or of six Notes at the end of a Song. **1707** *Gloss. Angl. Nova* (1st edn) *Ritornello*, (Ital.) the repeating of six Notes at the end of a Song, or of a Couplet of Verses at the end of a Stanza. **1708** KERSEY *Dict. Anglo-Brit.* (1st edn) *Ritornello*, (*I.*) the repeating of a Couplet of Verses at the end of a Stanza, or Staff. **1721** BAILEY *An Univ. Etymolog. Engl. Dict.* (1st edn) *Riternello* [sic], the Repeating 6 Notes at the End of a Song or of a Couplet of Verses at the End of a Stanza. *Ital.* **1724** [PEPUSCH] *Short Explic. of Foreign Words in Mus. Bks.* (pp. 63-4) *Retornello*, a Ritornel. Those short Symphonies for Violins, Flutes, or other Instruments, are so called, which either begins a few Bars before a Song, and sometimes plays a few Bars here and there in the Midst of a Song, and which also very often plays a few Bars after the Song is ended. *Ritornello.* See the Word *Retornello.* **1726** BAILEY *An Univ. Etymolog. Engl. Dict.* (3rd edn) *Retornello*, is a *Retornel* in Musick, so they call those short Symphonies for Violins, Flutes, or other Instruments, which either begin a few Bars before a Song, and sometimes play a few Bars here and there, in the midst of a Song; and which also often plays a few Bars after a Song is ended. *Ital. Ritornello*, the same as *Retornello*, Ital. which see. **1728** CHAMBERS *Ritornello*, or *Refrect* [sic], in Musick, the Burthen of a Song, or a Repetition of the first Verses of the Song, at the end of each Stanza or Couplet. See *Repetition.* ¶ The Word is *Italian*, and signifies properly a *little Return*, or a short Repetition, such as that of an Eccho; or of the last Words of a Song; especially when the Repetition is made after a Voice by one or more Instruments. ¶ But Custom has extended the use of the Word to all Symphonies, play'd before the Voices begin, and which serve by way of Prelude or Introduction to what follows. ¶ In the Partitions or Score of the *Italian* Musick, we frequently find the *Ritornello*'s signified by the Words *si suona*; to shew that the Organ, Spinet, or the like, are to repeat what the Voice has been singing. See *Repeat.* **1730** BAILEY *Dict. Britannicum* (1st edn) *Riternello* (in *Mu. Books*) the Burthen of a Song, repeating the six Notes at the End of a Song, or a Couplet of Verses at the End of a Stanza, *Ital.* **1737** DYCHE-PARDON (2nd edn) *Retornel* (S.) in *Musick*, is a short Symphony for many Instruments that begin a few Bars before a Song, and sometimes play a few in the Middle now and then, and generally after it.

1706 BEDFORD *Temple Musick* (p. 73) ... in our *Anthems* there are frequent *Intermissions* of all Voices, when the *Organ* Plays alone, that which we call a *Retornella*; ... **1731** PRELLEUR *Modern Musick-Master* (Dictionary, p. 3) *Ritornello* a short Symphony so call'd which either begins before the Song or sometimes in ye Middle or also after the Song is ended

ritornello *as part of an instrument, see* peg

1611 FLORIO It→E *Ritornello*, a twirle or turning about as of a pin or peg of a Lute. **1659** TORRIANO-FLORIO It→E *Ritornello, Ritornelgli*, any twirl or turning and winding about, as of the pegs of a lute

rodaja

1599 MINSHEU-PERCYVALL Sp→E † *Rodaja*, f. ... a dance called the round.

romance

1599 MINSHEU-PERCYVALL Sp→E *Romance*, the Castilian toong, a song in Spanish. **1611** FLORIO It→E *Romanzare*, to write or sing fabulous tales or faigned histories in rime. *Romanzatore*, a romant, a writer, a singer or speaker of fabulous tales or faigned stories in rime *Romanziere*, a pratling Mountibanke, a singer of fabulous poemes or ballads. **1659** TORRIANO-FLORIO It→E *Romanzare*, to write or sing *Romanzi. Romanzi*, Romances, fabulous tales, fained stories, either in rime or prose, of errant Knights and Paladines, used also for lying Mountebanks.

romanzina *see* rosina

1598 FLORIO It→E *Romanzina*, a kinde of dance, or trick in dancing. **1611** FLORIO It→E *Romanzina*, a kind of dance. Also a kind of tricke in dancing. **1659** TORRIANO-FLORIO It→E *Romanzina*, a lying, pratling ... also a kind of Country dance.

rombo *see* bombus, clang

1550 THOMAS It→E *Rombo*, for *bombo*, the sounde of a trompette. **1598** FLORIO It→E *Rombo*, ... the clang, sound or braying of a trumpet, the dubbing of a drum **1611** FLORIO It→E *Rombo*, ... the clang, sound or braying of a Trumpet, the dubbing of a Drum

ronde

1611 COTGRAVE Fr→E *Rond: m.* ... also, the daunce called a Round;

rondeau *see* balade, da capo
1724 [PEPUSCH] *Short Explic. of Foreign Words in Mus. Bks.* (pp. 64-5) *Rondeau,* all Songs or Tunes which end with the First Part or Strain, are called by this Name, let them be Minuets, Sarabands, Gavots, Jigs, or any other Kind of Air, and therefore they commonly have the Words *Da Capo,* or the Letters *DC* at the End of them, to signify that the first Part must be begun again; and commonly at the End of the said first Part there is the Word *Fin, Fine,* or *Finis,* to signify that it must be concluded there: Or if these Words are not there, there commonly is, or ought to be, a certain Mark over the last Note of the said First Part, which has the same Signification as the Word *Fin,* or *Finis.* **1726** BAILEY *An Univ. Etymolog. Engl. Dict.* (3rd edn) *Rondeau* (in *Musick Books*) is a Name that is apply'd to all Songs or Tunes that end with the first Part or Strain, whether they be *Minuets, Sarabands, Gavots, Jigs,* or any other kind of Air, and for that Reason, they have either the Letters *DC,* or the Words *Da Capo* at the End of them; which signify, that the first part must be begun again; and there is also commonly the Word *Fin, Fine* or *Finis,* at the End of the first Part, which signify that it must be concluded there. And if these Words are not there, either there is or ought to be a Character or Mark over the last Note of the said first Part, that signifies the Words *Fin,* &c. *Ital.* **1737** DYCHE-PARDON (2nd edn) *Rondeau* or *Round-o* (S.) in *Musick,* is a common Name to all those Airs or Tunes that end with the first Part or Strain, for which Purpose they are marked with the Words *Da Capo,* or Letters *D.C.* signifying that the first Part must be begun or played over again.

rondo
c.1710 ANON. *Preceptor for Improved Octave Flageolet* ('Explanation of Words', p. 82) *Rondo*—An Air ending with the first movement

ronfo
1611 FLORIO It→E *Ronfo,* the drone of a bagpipe.

rose *see* soundhole
1688 MIEGE-COTGRAVE Fr→E *Rose de Guitarre, de Luth, de Tuorbe, &c.* the Rose (or Rose-like Sound-hole) of a Guitarr, of a Lute, of a Theorbo, &c.

rosin *see* resine

rosina *see* romanzina
1611 FLORIO It→E *Rosina,* a little rose. Also a kinde of round dance as our hay.

rossignoler
1598 FLORIO It→E *Rossignolare,* to sing or chirpe as a nightingall. **1611** COTGRAVE Fr→E *Rossignoler.* To record, or sing, like a Nightingale. *Rossignolesque: com.* Nightingale-like, harmonious, melodious; dolefull, mournefull. **1611** FLORIO It→E *Rossignolare,* to sing as a Nightingall. **1659** TORRIANO-FLORIO It→E *Rossignolare,* to record or sing as a nightingale. **1688** MIEGE-COTGRAVE Fr→E § *Le Rossignol a un ramage tout à fait charmant,* the Nightingale has a most pleasant Note. *Le Rossignol aime extremement la Musique,* the Nightingale is a great lover of Musick.

rote *see* barbiton

roulade
1706 KERSEY-PHILLIPS (6th edn) *Roulade, (Fr.)* a Trill, Trilling, or Quavering: **1707** *Gloss. Angl. Nova* (1st edn) *Roulade,* (Fr.) a Trill, Quavering or Trilling. **1708** KERSEY *Dict. Anglo-Brit.* (1st edn) *Roulade, (F.)* a Trilling, or Quavering: **1728** CHAMBERS *Roulade,* in Musick, a trilling or quavering. See *Quavering.*

roulement
1688 MIEGE-COTGRAVE Fr→E *Roulement (en fait de Musique) l'action de chanter sur une même Syllabe plusieurs Notes avec harmonie,* a Trill, in Singing.

round *as composition, see* catch, ronde

round *as notational symbol*
1728 CHAMBERS *Round,* in Musick.—The *Italians* call b *round,* what we call b *flat,* and the *French* b *Mol;* and b *Square,* what we call b *sharp.* See *Flat* and *Sharp, &c.*

roundel
1726 BAILEY *An Univ. Etymolog. Engl. Dict.* (3rd edn) *Roundel,* a Song beginning and ending with the same Sentence. *Chauc.* **1730** BAILEY *Dict. Britannicum* (1st edn) *Roundel, Roundelay, Roundo,* a Song beginning and ending with the same Sentence, or one that turns back again to the first

Verse, and then goes round. **1737** DYCHE-PARDON (2nd edn) *Roundel, Rounelay,* or *Roundo* (S.) a Song that begins and ends with the same Words, or a Tune that begins and ends with the same Strain.

roundelay *see* balade, ballata, cançion, canzona, cascavelle, chanson, chant, cobbola, frottola, lay, raye, redondilla, tornello, vaudeville, villanata, villanella, virelay
1656 BLOUNT (1st edn) *Roundelay,* a Shepheards dance; Sometimes used for a Song. **1658** PHILLIPS (1st edn) *Roundelay,* a Sheapherds song, or dance. **1674** BLOUNT (4th edn) *Roundelay* (Fr. *Rundeau*) a Shepherds Dance; sometimes used for a Song, which ends as it begins. **1676** COLES *Roundelay, French.* a shepherds song or dance. **1678** PHILLIPS (4th edn) *Roundelay,* a Shepherds Song, as it were a Song sung in a round, by a company where each takes his turn. **1702** KERSEY *New Engl. Dict.* (1st edn) A *Roundelay,* a kind of catch, *or* song. **1704** *Cocker's Engl. Dict.* (1st edn) *Roundelay,* a Dance or Song among Shepherds. **1707** *Gloss. Angl. Nova* (1st edn) *Roundelay,* or *Roundell,* a *Shepherd's* Song sung by several in their turns, or as in a round. **1708** KERSEY *Dict. Anglo-Brit.* (1st edn) *Roundelay,* a Shepherd's Song. **1721** BAILEY *An Univ. Etymolog. Engl. Dict.* (1st edn) *Roundelay,* (of *round* and *lay,* a Song. *Roundeau,* F.) a *Shepherds,* [sic] Song, sung by several in their Turns, or as in a Round. **1728** CHAMBERS *Roundelay,* or *Roundo,* a kind of antient Poem ... **1730** BAILEY *Dict. Britannicum* (1st edn) *Roundelay, Roundo,* a Shepherd's Song; or, as it were, a Song sung in a Round by a Company where each takes his Turn. **1731** KERSEY *New Engl. Dict.* (3rd edn) A *Roundelay,* a Shepherd's Song *or* Dance.

roundo
1728 CHAMBERS *Roundo,* or *Roundelay,* in Musick, a kind of Burthen or Ritornello; where the beginning of each Couplet is repeated at the end thereof. See *Ritornello.*

Royal Exchange
1706 KERSEY-PHILLIPS (6th edn) *Royal Exchange,* a stately Pile of Building in the City of *London,* which was at first founded by Sir *Thomas Gresham,* a worthy Merchant, A.D. 1566. just a hundred Years before it was burnt: But it is now built of excellent Stone, with such curious and admirable Architecture, especially for a Front, a high Tower or Steeple, in which is an harmonious Chime of twelve Bells;

ruotata *see* torlo, volta, zurlo
1598 FLORIO It→E *Ruotata,* a kinde of round trick in dancing. **1611** FLORIO It→E *Ruotata,* a round tricke in dancing.

rythmica *see* harmonic, melopœia, mundane music
1728 CHAMBERS *Rhythmica, Rythmice,* in the antient Musick, that Branch of Musick which regulated the *Rhythmus.* See *Rhythmus.* ¶ The *Rhythmica* consider'd the Motions; regulated their Measure, Order, Mixture, *&c.* so as to excite the Passions, keep them up, augment, diminish, or allay them. ¶ *Aristides* and other antient Musical Writers, divided artificial Musick into *Harmonica, Rhythmica,* and *Metrica.* See *Musick.* ¶ But the *Rhythmica* with them likewise comprehends dumb Motions, and, in effect, all *Rhythmical,* i.e. regular, Motion. ¶ *Porphyry* divides Musick into *Harmonica, Rythmica, Metrica, Organica, Poetica,* and *Hypocritica.* See each under its proper Article. ¶ The Antients seem to have had no *Rhythm* in their Musick beside the long and short Syllables of their Words and Verses, which were sung, and always made a Part of their Musick; so that the *Rhythmica* with them was only the Application of the Metrical-Feet, and the various kinds of Verses used by them.—The Modern goes much further. See *Rhythm.* **1737** BAILEY *The Univ. Etymolog. Engl. Dict.* (3rd edn, vol. 2) *Rhythmica* (in *ancient Musick*) the branch of musick that regulated the rhymes.

1721 MALCOLM *Treatise of Musick* (pp. 32-3) The First general Branch of this Subject [the divisions of music], which is the *contemplative* Part, divides naturally into these. *First,* the Knowledge of the Relations and Measures of *Tune.* And *Secondly,* of *Time...* [which] they called *Rythmica,* because it treats of the Numbers of Sounds or Notes with respect to *Time,* containing an Explication of the Measures of *long* and *short,* or *swift* and *slow* in the Succession of Sounds.

rythmopœia *see* melopœia, musical faculty
1728 CHAMBERS *Rythmopæia*[,] one of the Musicial [sic] Faculties, as they are call'd; which prescribes Rules for the Motions, or *Rhythm.* ¶ The antient *Rhythmopœia* is very defective.—We find nothing of it in the Books of the Antients but some general Hints; which can scarce be call'd Rules. In their Explications there appears nothing but what belongs to the Words and Verses of their Songs, which is a strong Presumption they had no other.

See *Rhythm*. **1730** BAILEY *Dict. Britannicum* (1st edn) *Rhythmopoia* (of ῾Ρυθμοποιεια and ποιεω, to make Gr.) one of the Musical Faculties, as they are called, that prescribes Rules for the Motions.

1721 MALCOLM *Treatise of Musick* (p. 33) The Second general Branch [of music, after the contemplative part], which is the *Practical* Part, as naturally divides into Two Parts answering to the Parts of the First: ... That which answers to the *Rythmica*, they called *Rythmopœia*, containing the Rules concerning the Application of the *Numbers* and *Time*.

rythmus *see* eurhythmia, eurythmoi
1721 MALCOLM *Treatise of Musick* (p. 586) ... That under the Head of *Mutations*, those who consider the *Rythmus* makes the Changes of it no other than from one Kind of *metrum* or *Verse* to another, as from *Jambick* to *Choraick*: And we may notice too, That in the more general Sense, the *Rythmus* includes also their [the ancient Greeks'] Dancings, and all the theatrical Action.

S

s.
1724 [PEPUSCH] *Short Explic. of Foreign Words in Mus. Bks.* (p. 66) The Letter *S* is used as an Abbreviation of the Word *Solo*, and is met with in Pieces of Musick of several Parts, to signify that in such Places the Voice or Instrument performs alone. **1726** BAILEY *An Univ. Etymolog. Engl. Dict.* (3rd edn) *S.* (in *Musick Books*) is an Abbreviation of the Word *Solo*, and is put in Pieces of Musick of several Parts, to signify that in such Places, the Voice or Instrument performs alone. *Ital.*

sackbut *see* empneusta (under entata), posaune, sambuke, sarbataine, storta, tromba squarciata, trombeggiata, tromboncino, trombone, trumpet, trumpet harmonious, tuba
1599 MINSHEU-PERCYVALL Sp→E *Sacabuche*, an instrument of musicke called a sackbut. **1658** PHILLIPS (1st edn) *Sagbut*, (Span.) a kinde of Musical instrument, somewhat resembling a Trumpet. **1676** COLES *Sackbut, Spanish.* a drawing trumpet. **1678** PHILLIPS (4th edn) *Sackbut* or *Sagbut, (Spanish Sacabuche)* an Instrument of Wind Musick, somewhat like a Trumpet. *Sagbut.* See *Sackbut.* **1688** MIEGE-COTGRAVE Fr→E *Saquebut*, (f.) a Sackbut. § *La Saquebute est plus en usage en Allemagne, qu'en tout autre Païs de L'Europe*, the Sackbut is more used in Germany, than in any other Country of Europe. *La Saquebut est un Instrument de Musique, qui ressemble à la Trompette, hormis qu'il a plus de branches, & qu'il est bien plus long*, the sackbut is a musical Instrument, not unlike a Trumpet, except that it has more branches, and is withall much longer. *La Saquebute imite le Son de la Trompette*, the Sackbut imitates the Sound of the Trumpet. **1702** KERSEY *New Engl. Dict.* (1st edn) A *Sack-but*, a kind of musical instrument. **1704** *Cocker's Engl. Dict.* (1st edn) *Sackbut*, a Musical Instrument. **1708** KERSEY *Dict. Anglo-Brit.* (1st edn) *Sackbut* or *Sagbut*, an Instrument of Wind-Musick. **1721** BAILEY *An Univ. Etymolog. Engl. Dict.* (1st edn) *Sackbut*, (*sacabuche* of *sacar de buche*, Span. to fetch the Breath from the Bottom of the Belly (as we say) because it requires a strong Breath) an Instrument of Wind-Musick. **1728** CHAMBERS *Sackbut*, a musical Instrument of the Wind Kind; being a kind of Trumpet, tho' different from the common Trumpet both in Form and Size. 'Tis very fit to play Bass, and is contrived so as to be drawn out or shorten'd according to the Gravity or Acuteness of these Tones. The *Italians* call it *Trombone*, the *Latins, Tuba Ductilis*. It takes asunder into Four Pieces, or Branches; and hath frequently a Wreath in the middle; which is the same Tube, only twisted twice, or making two Circles in the middle of the Instrument; by which Means, it is brought down one fourth lower than its natural Tone. It has also two Pieces or Branches on the Inside, which don't appear, except when drawn out by means of an Iron Bar, and which, lengthen it to the Degree requisite to hit the Tone required. The *Sackbut* is usually Eight Foot long, without being drawn out, or without reckoning the Circles. When extended to its full Length, 'tis usually Fifteen Foot. The Wreath is Two Foot Nine Inches in Circumference. It serves as Bass in all Consorts of Wind Music. ¶ There are *Sackbuts* of different Sizes, serving to execute different Parts; particularly a small one, called by the *Italians*, Trombone *picciolo*, and the *Germans*, *Cleine alt-posaune*, proper for a Counter-Tenor. The Part assigned it, is usually called *Trombone primo*, of I°. There is another larger, called *Trombone maggiore*,

which may serve as a Tenor: Its Part is usually called *Trombone secondo*, or II°. or 2°. There is a third still bigger, called *Trombone grosso;* its Part is called *Trombone terzo*, or III°. or 3°. Lastly, there is another which exceeds all the rest, and which is much heard in the Music, especially in the Bass; its Part is called *Trombone quarto*, of IV°. or 4to. or simply *Trombone*. It has usually the Key of *Fa, ut fa* on the fourth Line; tho' frequently also on the fifth Line from the Top, by Reason of the Gravity or Depth of the Sounds. **1730** BAILEY *Dict. Britannicum* (1st edn) *Sackbut* (*Sacabuche* of *Sacar de buche*, Span. to fetch the Breath from the Bottom of the Belly) a Musical Instrument of the Wind-kind; being a Sort of Trumpet, tho' different from the common Trumpet, both in Form and Size. **1731** KERSEY *New Engl. Dict.* (3rd edn) A *Sackbut*, a musical Instrument like a Trumpet. **1737** DYCHE-PARDON (2nd edn) *Sackbut* (S.) an antient, shrill, musical stringed Instrument, tho' some think it was a Sort of Flute or Pipe of the Wind Kind.

c.1715-20 NORTH Essay of Musical Ayre BL Add. 32536, f. 65v [*re* the history of music in England] ... Wind Instruments had ye first possession here [in northern England], And were used in cathedrall churches And in the north at this day. When for a Base the trumpett was made ductile, & called a sackbutt.

sacrifice *see* holocaust
1730 BAILEY *Dict. Britannicum* (1st edn) *Sacrifice* .... The *Egyptians* and Inhabitants of *Palestine* offered their own Children to their Gods, and the *Israelites* themselves so far imitated their Bararites, as to cause their Children to pass between two Fires, till they were miserably scorched; and they also shut them up in a hollow Idol of Brass, call'd *Moloch*, made red-hot, and while these innocent Victims were in this Manner tormented, they sounded Trumpets, beat Drums, *&c.* to drown their Outcries.... [after animal sacrifices to Mars, Neptune, Bacchus, etc. in ancient times] Then they danced round the Altar, singing Hymns and Songs in Honour of the Deity to whom it was offered. These Hymns consisting of three Parts, or Stanza's; the first was sung in turning from East to West; the other in turning from West to East; and the third Part they sung standing before the Altar.... the Priest ... afterwards retired with the Assistants to feast upon the remaining Part of the Beast, singing the Praises of the Deity.... The Gods of the Air were adored with Musical Instruments, and melodious Songs ...

sacring bell *see* nola, sance bell, sonnette, tintinabulum

sacrum
1587 THOMAS L→E *Sacrum, cri, n.g* Any thing dedicated to God: ... hymnes and psalmes, holy mysteries: ... **1589** RIDER L→E *Sacrum*. Hymnes, or Psalmes.

salarian verse
1656 BLOUNT (1st edn) *Salarian Verse*, a kind of Song, which *Mars* his Priests, among the old *Romans*, were wont to sing. *Tac.* **1676** COLES *Salarian verse*, sung by the Priests of *Mars*.

sally
1702 KERSEY *New Engl. Dict.* (1st edn) *Sally*, and to *sally a bell*; a particular way of ringing it. **1706** KERSEY-PHILLIPS (6th edn) *Sally* ... Also a particular Way of Ringing a Bell. **1708** KERSEY *Dict. Anglo-Brit.* (1st edn) *Sally*, ... Also a particular Way of Ringing a Bell. **1721** BAILEY *An Univ. Etymolog. Engl. Dict.* (1st edn) A *Sally*, (among *Ringers*) a particular Way of Ringing a Bell. **1730** BAILEY *Dict. Britannicum* (1st edn) *Sally* (with *Ringers*) a particular Way of ringing a Bell.

salmo *see* psalm

saltabello
1550 THOMAS It→E *Saltabellare*, a certein daunce that leapeth forwards and back wardes. **1598** FLORIO It→E *Saltabello*, a kinde of hopping, or skipping dance. **1611** FLORIO It→E *Saltabello*, a kind of hopping or skipping dance.

saltarella *as dance, see* forlana, galliard
1724 [PEPUSCH] *Short Explic. of Foreign Words in Mus. Bks.* (p. 66) *Saltarella*, a particular Kind of Jig so called.

1597 MORLEY *Plaine and Easie Introdvction* (p. 181) ... The Italians make their galliardes (which they tearme *saltarelli*) plaine, and frame ditties to them, which in their *mascaradoes* they sing and daunce, and many times without any instruments at all, but in steed of instrumentes they haue Curtisans disguised in mens apparell, who sing and daunce to their owne songes.

saltarella *as part of instrument, see* sautereau
1598 FLORIO It→E *Saltarelli*, the iacks of a paire of virginals. **1611** FLORIO It→E *Saltarelli*, the iackes

of Virginals. **1659** TORRIANO-FLORIO It→E *Saltarelli, Salterelli,* the jacks of a pair of of [sic] virginals

salterio *see* psaltery

saltuaris
1587 THOMAS L→E *Saltuaris, re, Plin* That daunceth to the stroke of an instrument, or of and belonging to daunsing

salve regina
1688 DAVIS-TORRIANO-FLORIO It→E *Salve Regina,* a Hymn to our Blessed Lady, used in the Church-office.

sambuke *see* barbiton, dulcimer, psaltery, sarbataine
1500 *Ortus Vocabulorum* L→E Sambuca ce. est quoddam genus simphonie § Arbor sambucus: sambucaque musica res est. Pastor cambucam [sic]: sambucam fert falteratus. **1538** ELYOT L→E *Sambuca,* an instrument of musyke, now called doulcymers *Sambucina,* a woman whyche playeth on doulcymers. **1552** HULOET L→E *Sambucina, uel Sambucistria, ang.* a woman that playeth on the dulcimers. **1565** COOPER L→E *Sambuca, sambúcæ, f.g. pen. prod. Vitruu. lib. 6. cap. I.* An instrument of musike called a doulcimer. *Sambúcina, sambúcinæ, fœ. gen. pen. corr. Plaut.* A woman that playeth on doulcimers. **1587** THOMAS L→E *Sambuca, cæ, f.g. Pers.* An instrument of musicke, which we commonly take for a dulcimer. *Est triquetrum instrumentum, imparibus longitudine fidibus, Iun. Acuti soni & arguti, tetrachordum, Athen. Sambucina, næ, Plaut.* A woman that playeth on dulcimers. **1589** RIDER L→E *Sambucina, sambucistria, f* A woman that plaieth on a dulcimer. **1598** FLORIO It→E *Sambuca,* a kinde of horne pipe or dulcimer. **1611** FLORIO It→E *Sambuca,* a kind of Horne-pipe or Dulcimer. *Sambucina,* a Plaier on a Sambuca. **1656** BLOUNT (1st edn) *Sambuke (sambuca)* an instrument of Musick, which we commonly take for a *Dulcimer;* **1658** PHILLIPS (1st edn) *Sambuke,* a Musical instrument, called also a Dulcimer; **1659** TORRIANO-FLORIO It→E *Sambuca,* a kind of Dulcimer or Bagpipe, also a sack-butt **1676** COLES *Sambuke, Latin.* a dulcimer **1688** DAVIS-TORRIANO-FLORIO It→E *Sambuca,* a Dulcimer; **1704** *Cocker's Engl. Dict.* (1st edn) *Sambuke,* a Musical Instrument, now called a Dulcimer; **1706** KERSEY-PHILLIPS (6th edn) *Sambuca, (Gr.)* a Triangular Instrument of Musick, taken for a Dulcimer, an Harp, or a Sackbut: **1728** CHAMBERS *Sambucus,* an ancient musical Instrument of the Wind Kind, and resembling a Kind of Flute; probably thus called because made of Elder, which the *Latins* call *Sambucus.* **1730** BAILEY *Dict. Britannicum* (1st edn) *Sambucus,* an antient musical Instrument of the Wind-Kind, and resembling a Flute; so called because probably made of the *Sambucus,* or Elder-Tree.

sampogna, zampogna
1550 THOMAS It→E *Sampogna,* a baggepipe. **1598** FLORIO It→E *Sampogna,* a bagge-pipe, an oten-pipe. Also a bell hanged about sheepe or goates, a lowe-bell. *Sampognatta,* as *Sampogna. Zampogna,* an oaten pipe, a shepheards pipe, a bagge-pipe. Also a bell that is hung about a goate or bell-weathers necke. *Zampognare,* to sound or plaie vpon any kind of reede, pipe or bagge-pipe. *Zampognaro,* a plaier vpon anie pipe or bagge-pipe. Also a bell-weather. **1599** MINSHEU-PERCYVALL Sp→E **çampoña,* f. a bagpipe, an oten-pipe. **çampoñar,* to sound or play vpon any kind of reed or pipe. **† Sampoña,* vide *çampoña,* a fluite. **1611** COTGRAVE Fr→E *Sampogne: f.* A bagpipe, or oaten pipe; also, the bell hanged about the necke of a sheepe, or goat; some call it a Low-bell. **1611** FLORIO It→E *Sampogna,* a Low-bell or bell hanged about sheepes or Goates neckes. Also any kind of Oaten-pipe. Vsed also for a bag-pipe. *Zampogna,* an Oaten-pipe, Reede-pipe, a Sheapheards-pipe. Also a bell that is hung about a Goate or Bellweathers necke that leadeth the rest. *Zampognare,* to sound or play vpon any Sheapheards pipe or Reede. *Zampognaro,* a plaier vpon any Reede or Shepheards-pipe. **1659** TORRIANO-FLORIO It→E *Sampogna, Sampognare,* as *Zampogna. Zampogna,* an Oaten pipe, a Reed pipe, a Shepheards pipe, also a Bell hung about a Chief goats or Bell-weathers neck, that leadeth the rest, also a jews-harp. *Zampognare,* to sound or play upon any oaten or reed pipe *Zampognaro,* a player upon a *Zampogna,* by Met. an idle pratler. **1724** [PEPUSCH] *Short Explic. of Foreign Words in Mus. Bks.* (p. 66) *Sampogna.* See the Word *Zampogna.* (p. 94) *Zampogna,* a Common Flute or Whistle. **1726** BAILEY *An Univ. Etymolog. Engl. Dict.* (3rd edn) *Sampogna,* See *Zampogna. Zampogni,* a common Flute or Whistle. *Ital.*

sance bell *see* nola, sonnette
1656 BLOUNT (1st edn) A *Sance* or *Sacring Bell (campana sacra vel sancta)* so called because, *nos ad sacra seu sancta vocet.* **1706** KERSEY-PHILLIPS

(6th edn) *Sance-Bell,* or *The Sanctus Bell,* a little Bell, formerly us'd in every Church, and rung when the Priest said, *Sanctus, Sanctus Dominus Deus Sabaoth, i.e.* Holy, Holy Lord God of Sabaoth. **1708** KERSEY *Dict. Anglo-Brit.* (1st edn) *Sance-Bell,* or *The Sanctus Bell,* a little Bell, formerly us'd in Churches. **1721** BAILEY *An Univ. Etymolog. Engl. Dict.* (1st edn) *Sance-Bell,* (q.d. Saints Bell, or the *Sanctus* Bell, usually rung when the Priest said, *Sanctus, Sanctus Dominus Deus Sabaoth;*[)] a little Bell us'd in Churches. **1730** BAILEY *Dict. Britannicum* (1st edn) *Sance-Bell* (q. *Saint's-Bell,* or the *Sanctus-Bell,* formerly rung, when the Priest said, *Sanctus, Sanctus, Domine, Deus Saboath*) a little Bell in Church-Steeples.

saraband *see* castanet, chaconne, courante, imperfect of the more, ionick, lesson, morisco, rondeau, sextupla, sonata, suit, tattle de moy, tempo, tripla

1611 FLORIO It→E *Zarabanda,* a kind of tune or dance much vsed in Spaine. **1656** BLOUNT (1st edn) *Saraband* (Ital. *Zarabanda*) a kinde of lesson in Musick, and a Dance so called. **1658** PHILLIPS (1st edn) *Saraband,* (Ital.) a kind of Lesson or Air in Musick going with a quick time. **1659** TORRIANO-FLORIO It→E *Zarabanda,* a kind of Spanish tune or dance. **1676** COLES *Saraband, Italian.* a kind of quick air in Musick. **1688** MIEGE-COTGRAVE Fr→E *Sarabande,* (f.) a Saraband. § *La Sarabande a eté defendue par l'Inquisition d'Espagne, tant elle la jugea capable d'emouvoir les Passions tendres, de derober le Cœur par les Yeux, & de troubler la Tranquillité de l'Esprit,* the Saraband has been forbidden by the Inquisition of Spain, as being judged too apt to move tender Passions, to steal the Heart through the Eyes, and to disturb the Tranquility of the Mind. *La Sarabande est une sorte de Dance passionnée, qui vient d'Espagne, & dont les Maures de Grenade ont eté les Inventeurs,* the Saraband is a kind of passionate Dance, come out of Spain, and first invented by the Moors of Granada. **1696** PHILLIPS (5th edn) *Sarabrand, (Ital.)* a Musical Composition in Triple time, ending with the Hand up. Also a dance to the same measure. **1702** KERSEY *New Engl. Dict.* (1st edn) A *Saraband,* a kind of dance. **1704** *Cocker's Engl. Dict.* (1st edn) *Saraband,* a quick dance or air in Musick. **1706** KERSEY-PHILLIPS (6th edn) *Saraband,* a kind of Musical Composition in Triple Time; also a Dance to the same Measure. **1707** *Gloss. Angl. Nova* (1st edn) *Saraband,* a sort of Musical Composition in Triple-time; also a Dance in the same measure. **1721** BAILEY *An Univ. Etymolog. Engl. Dict.* (1st edn) *Saraband,* (*sarabande,* F.) a musical Composition in triple Time, also a Dance to the same Measure. **1724** [PEPUSCH] *Short Explic. of Foreign Words in Mus. Bks.* (p. 67) *Sarabande,* a Saraband, a Kind of Air always in Triple Time, and commonly play'd very Grave and Serious. ¶ *N.B.* A Saraband and a Minuet are very much alike in several Respects, excepting the different Time or Movement they are play'd in. ¶ A Minuet and a Passepied, differ also in the same Manner. (p. 68) *Serebanda.* See *Sarabande.* **1726** BAILEY *An Univ. Etymolog. Engl. Dict.* (3rd edn) *Saraband* (*sarabande,* F.) a Musical Composition always in triple Time; and commonly played very grave and serious; also a Dance to the same Measure. ¶ A Saraband and a Minuet are very much alike in several Respects, excepting the different Time or Movement they are played in; and a Minuet and a Passepied differ in the same Manner. **1728** CHAMBERS *Saraband,* a Musical Composition in Triple Time; being, in reality, no more than a Minuet, whose Motions are slow, and serious. *Saraband* is also a Dance to the same Measure, usually terminating when the Hand rises, whereby 'tis distinguish'd from the Courant, which Ends when the Hand that beats Time, falls. The *Saraband* is said to be derived originally from the *Sarazens,* as well as the *Chacone*: It had its Name, according to some Authors, from a Comedian called *Sarabande,* who first danc'd it in *France.* Others derive it from the *Spanish Sarao* Ball: 'Tis usually danced to the Sound of the Guitarre, or Castanettes. **1730** BAILEY *Dict. Britannicum* (1st edn) *Saraband* (*sarabande,* F.) a musical Composition always in triple time, and is in reality no more than a Minuet, the Motions of which are slow and serious. *Saraband,* a Dance to the same Measure which usually terminates when the Hand rises, whereby it is distinguished from a Courant, which usually ends when the Hand that beats Time falls; and is otherwise much the same as a Minuet. **1731** KERSEY *New Engl. Dict.* (3rd edn) A *Sataband* [sic], a quick Air in *Musick,* a kind of Dance. **1735** DEFOE *Saraband,* a sort of Dance, much like a Minuet. **1737** DYCHE-PARDON (2nd edn) *Saraband* (S.) a Term in *Musick* for a Composition or Air in Triple Time, of a slow Movement, and is properly when danced a Minuet.

1676 MACE *Musick's Monument* (p. 129) *Serabands,* are of the *Shortest Triple-Time*; but are more *Toyish,* and *Light,* than *Corantoes*; and commonly of Two *Strains.* **1728** NORTH Musicall

Grammarian (*C-K MG* f. 74) The sarabanda deserves to be mentioned. It is an air purely spagnuola, and corresponds [to] the rodomontade humour of that nation. It is an ayre that bears a basso andante exceeding well; ... **1731** PRELLEUR *Modern Musick-Master* (Dictionary, p. 3) *Sarabanda,* is a Tune always in Triple Time

sarbataine

1593 HOLLYBAND Fr→E *Vne sarbataine,* a long trunke, also an instrument of musicke, some doe call them Waites: *f.* **1611** COTGRAVE Fr→E *Sarbacane,* or (which is better) *Sarbataine: f.* A long trunke to shoot in; also, the musicall Instrument called a Sagbut.

sautereau *see* saltarella

1611 COTGRAVE Fr→E *Saultereau: m.* ... also, the Jack of a Virginall, &c; *Sautereau: m.* ... also, the Jacke of a Virginall, &c. **1688** MIEGE-COTGRAVE Fr→E *Sautereau,* (m.) Jack. § *les Sautereaux d'une Epinette,* the Jacks of a Virginal.

sautry *see* psaltery

1676 COLES *Sautry, Old word.* for *Psaltery.*

scacciapensiere *see* cacapensiere

1598 FLORIO It→E *Scacciapensiere,* a kind of musicall instrument. **1611** FLORIO It→E *Scacciapensiere,* a kind of Bag-pipe or such Country musicall instrument. **1659** TORRIANO-FLORIO It→E *Scaccia pensiere,* a kind of country croud or bag-pipe, a jews-harp or trump.

scagnello

1598 FLORIO It→E *Scagnello,* the bridge of a lute. **1611** FLORIO It→E *Scagnello,* ... Also the bridge of a Lute or any such corded instrument.

scale *see* diagram, diatonic scale, natural scale

1676 COLES § *Scale of musick,* the Gammut. **1702** KERSEY *New Engl. Dict.* (1st edn) § The *Scale of Musick,* in which the figure, order and names of the musical notes are set down. **1704** HARRIS § *Scale of the Gamut,* or *Musical Scale* is a kind of *Diagram,* consisting of certain Lines and Spaces drawn to shew the several Degrees, whereby a Natural or Artificial Voice or Sound may either ascend or descend. ¶ The Name thereof is taken from the *Greek* Letter *Gamma,* which *Guido Aretinus,* who reduced the *Greek* Scale into this Form, plac'd at the bottom, to signifie from whence it was derived; so that ever since, this Scale or *Gammut,* hath been taken for the Ground-work or first Foundation of all Musick, both Vocal and Instrumental. ¶ But there were three different Scales in use among the Ancients, which had their Denominations from the three several sorts of Musick, *viz.* The *Diatonical, Chromatical,* and *Enharmonical.* Which see. **1706** KERSEY-PHILLIPS (6th edn) § *Scale of Musick,* commonly call'd the *Gam-ut* or *Scale* of the *Gum-ut* [sic], is a kind of Scheme or Rule, consisting of certain Lines and Spaces on which the Figures of the Musical Notes are set down in their natural Order, so as to shew the several Degrees, whereby a Voice or Sound may either ascend or descend. The Name of it is taken from the *Greek* Letter *Gamma,* which *Guido Aretinus,* (who reduc'd the Musical Scale of the ancient *Greeks* into this Form) set at the bottom, to signifie from whence it was deriv'd; and this Scale or *Gam-ut* has been taken ever since for the First Foundation or Ground-work of all Musick both Vocal and Instrumental. **1707** *Gloss. Angl. Nova* (1st edn) § *Scale of the Gamut* or *Musical Scale,* is a kind of Diagram consisting of certain Lines and Spaces whereby an artificial Voice or Sound may either ascend or descend. **1728** CHAMBERS *Scale* ... [*see* Appendix] **1730** BAILEY *Dict. Britannicum* (1st edn) § *Scale of Musick, Scale of the Gamut,* a Series of Sounds rising or falling towards Acuteness or Gravity from any given Pitch of Tune to the greatest Distance.

1596 ANON. *Pathway to Musicke* [A iii] *Scala* in Lattine signifieth a Ladder, vvhich name is giuen as vvell for the likenes as the vse: For the likenes because it hath lines like steps in a Ladder, and spaces, in vvhich the *Cleues* or Keyes doe stand, for the vse because it serueth the learner to climbe vp to the knovvledge of Musicke: or that he must ascend and descend therevvith, as men doe in building... **1597** MORLEY *Plaine and Easie Introdvction* (annotations to Part I) That which we cal the scale of musicke, or the *Gam,* others cal the Scale of *Guido*: for *Guido Aretinus* ... changed the Greeke scale .... All the scale was diuided into foure *Tetrachordes* or fourths, the lowest of which foure was called *Tetrachordon hypate,* the fourth of principals. The second *tetrachordon meson,* the fourth of middle or meanes. The third *tetrachordon diezeugmenon,* the fourth of strings disioyned or disiunct. The fourth and last *tetrachordon hyperbolæon,* the fourth of stringes exceeding: the lowest string *Proslambanomene* is called assumed, because it is not accounted for one of any *tetrachorde,* but was taken in to be a *Diapason* to the *mese* or middle string. The *tetrachorde* of principals or *hypaton*, beginneth in the distance of one note aboue the assumed string, containing foure strings or notes, the last of which is *Hypatemeson*: the *tetrachorde* of *meson* or meanes, beginneth where the other ended (so that one string is both the end of the former, and the beginning of the next) and containeth likewise foure, the last whereof is *mese*. But the third *tetrachorde*, was of two maner of dispositions, for either it was in the natural kind of singing, and then was it called *tetrachordon diezeugmenon*, because the middle string or *mese*, was separated from the lowest stringe of that *tetrachorde*, by a whole note, and was not accounted for any of the foure belonging to it, as you may see in the scale, or then in the flat kind of singing: in which case, it was called *tetrachordon synezeugmenon*, or *synenmenon*, because the *mese* was the lowest note of that *tetrachorde*, all being named thus *mese*. *Trite synenmenon*, or *synezeugmenon*, *paranete synezeugmenon*, and *nete synezeugmenon*. **1725** De La Fond *New System of Music* (p. 12) ... I define *the Scale, a gradual division of those musical sounds.* But if these two definitions should not be thought pertinent enough, here are two others; *a Note is each of those sounds, with relation to highness or lowness only, that come into the constitution of an air or tune.* And *the Scale, a gradual distinction of Notes.*

scale of music *see* gamut

1704 *Cocker's Engl. Dict.* (1st edn) *Scale of Musick*, the Note called Gammut.

1664 Birchensha-Alsted *Templvm Mvsicvm* (p. 21) *The Series of Intension and Remission*: or of Ascension from a grave Sound into an Acute, and of the Descension from an acute into a grave, is called the *Scale of Musick*. **1680** B., A. *Synopsis of Vocal Musick* (p. 27) The Scale of Musick is an order of seven degrees, distant one from another by just intervals, according to which every sound in ascending and descending is to be directed. **1721** Malcolm *Treatise of Musick* (p. 40) A *System* is either *particular*, or *universal*, containing within it every particular System that belongs to *Musick*, and is called, *The Scale of Musick*, which may be defined, *A Series of Sounds rising or falling towards Acuteness* or *Gravity from any given Sound, to the greatest Distance that is fit and practicable, thro' such intermediate Degrees, as make the Succession most agreeable and perfect, and in which we have all the concording Intervals most concinnously divided.* § (p. 239) Now the System of *Octave* containing all the *original Concords*, and the *compound Concords* being the Sum of *Octave* and some lesser *Concord*, therefore 'tis plain, that if we would have a Series of *Degrees* to reach beyond an *Octave*, we ought to continue them in the same Order thro' a second *Octave* as in the first, and so on thro a third and fourth *Octave*, &c. and such a Series is called *The Scale of Musick*, which as I have already defin'd, expresses a Series of Sounds, rising or falling towards *Acuteness* or *Gravity*, from any given Pitch of *Tune*, to the greatest Distance that is fit or practicable, thro' such intermediate *Degrees* as makes the Succession most agreeable and perfect; and in which we have all the *harmonical Intervals* most *concinnously* divided. § (pp. 511-12) ... And therefore when we know how *8ve* was divided [by the ancient Greeks, according to the intervals of the system], we know the Nature of their *Diagramma*, which we now call the *Scale of Musick*; the Variety of which constitutes what they called the *Genera melodiæ*, which were also subdivided into Species; ...

scambietti

1611 Florio It→E *Scambietti*, ... Also friskes, leapings or nimble skippings, tumbling trickes or changings in dancing and tumblings.

scampanare

1598 Florio It→E *Scampanare*, to ring, toll, or iangle bels disorderly. **1611** Florio It→E *Scampanamento*, a ringing or iangling of bells. *Scampanare*, to ring, to tolle or iangle bels disorderly and out of tune. *Scampanate*, ringings, knells, tollings, peales or ianglings of bells. **1659** Torriano-Florio It→E *Scampanamento, Scampaneggio, Scampanata, Scampanio*, any ringing, jangling or tolling of bells, a knell or peal of bells. *Scampanare*, to ring, to toll, or jangle bells disorderly and out of tune.

scarabillare

1598 Florio It→E *Scarabillare*, to squeake as a bagge-pipe, to make an vnpleasant squeaking. **1611** Florio It→E *Scarabillare*, to squeake as a Bag-pipe **1659** Torriano-Florio It→E *Scarabillare*, to squeak as a door or a bag-pipe.

scatta *see* bandrol, cascata, pendaglio, soga

1611 Florio It→E *Scatta*, a string or scarfe tied to a hunters horne. **1659** Torriano-Florio It→E *Scatta*, a scarf or string whereat a hunter hangs his horn.

schism *see* diaschisma

1617-24 FLUDD *Utriusque Cosmi Maioris: De Templo Musicæ* (p. 182) *Schisma* est medietas differentiæ inter semitonium majus & minus, hoc est, dimidia pars Comatis. **1636** BUTLER *Principles of Musik* (p. 23) [quoting Boethius:] *Schisma est dimidium Commatis.* **1653** ?BROUNCKER *Renatvs Des-Cartes Exc. Comp. of Musick* (p. 30) ... the difference betwixt a Tone *major* and a Tone *minor*, which we nominate a *Schism*; [annotation by Brouncker, p. 74: 'Others do call it a *Comma majus*...'] ... **1680** B., A. *Synopsis of Vocal Musick* (p. 36) ... there must be a fraction, which is the difference of a *greater and lesser Tone*, and is commonly called a *Schisma* or *Comma* ... **c.1710** NORTH (draft for) Musicall Grammarian BL Add. 32537, f. 154v ... and If wee take monochords upon other places, as the tone, the 7th flat & sharp tritone or sixt flat and sharp, the sextupla devision's of them, will not Jump with the corresponding accords of the principall string but widely differ In many places, wch differences are called scismes...

science

1656 BLOUNT (1st edn) *Science (scientia)* ... The seven liberal Sciences are these, *Grammer, Logick, Rhetorick, Astrology, Geometry, Arithmetick* and *Musick* **1676** COLES § *Liberal Sciences*, Grammar, Logick, Rhetorick, Musick, Arithmetick, Geometry, Astronomy. **1696** PHILLIPS (5th edn) The seven Liberal *Sciences* are Grammar, Logic, Rhetoric, Astronomy, Geometry, Arithmetic and Musick. **1702** KERSEY *New Engl. Dict.* (1st edn) The seven liberal *Sciences*, viz. *Grammar, Logick, Rhetorick, Arithmetick, Geometry, Astronomy*, and *Musick.* **1704** *Cocker's Engl. Dict.* (1st edn) *Science*, ... The seaven Liberal Arts or ¶ *Sciences*, are *Astronomy, Geometry, Musick, Arithmetick, Logick, Rhetorick*, and *Grammer.* **1708** KERSEY *Dict. Anglo-Brit.* (1st edn) The Seven *Liberal Sciences*, are Grammar, Logick, Rhetorick, Arithmetick, Geometry, Astronomy, and Musick. **1737** DYCHE-PARDON (2nd edn) *Science* (S.) any Sort of Knowledge, ... there are seven Particulars, that by Way of Excellence are called Liberal Sciences upon account of opening Mind or Understanding, and enlarging its Faculties, *viz. Grammar, Logick, Rhetorick, Arithmetick, Geometry, Astronomy*, and *Musick*

scitala

1598 FLORIO It→E *Scitala*, ... Also a kinde of song among the Grecians. **1611** FLORIO It→E *Scitala*, a kind of secret cifer vsed among the Spartans. Also a kind of song among the Grecians. **1659** TORRIANO-FLORIO It→E **Scitala, Scitalca*, a kind of secret cypher used among the Spartans ... also a kind of song among the Grecians

sconcerto

1598 FLORIO It→E *Sconcertato*, disordered, out of tune, confused. **1611** FLORIO It→E *Sconcertato*, vntuned, out of tune. **1659** TORRIANO-FLORIO It→E **Sconcertatamente*, untunably. *Sconcertato*, out of tune or order. **Sconcerto*, a discordance, an untuned consort.

score *see* partition

1704 HARRIS *Score*, in Musick, is the Original Draught of the whole Composition, wherein the several Parts, *viz.* Treble, Second Treble, Base, *&c.* are distinctly scored or marked **1706** KERSEY-PHILLIPS (6th edn) *Score* ... In *Musick* it is taken for the Original Draught of the whole Composition, in which the several Parts, *viz.* Bass, Treble, Second Treble, &c. are distinctly scored or marked. **1728** CHAMBERS *Score*, in Musick, *Partition*, or the Original Draught of the whole Composition, wherein the several Parts, *viz.* Treble, Second Treble, Base, *&c.* are distinctly *scored* and marked. See *Partition.* **1737** DYCHE-PARDON (2nd edn) *Score* (S.) in *Musick*, is writing down the several Parts of the Composition immediately one under another;

1736 TANS'UR *Compleat Melody* (3rd edn, p. 72) *Score*, signifies the Original Draught of the whole *Composition*; wherein all *Parts* are distinctly marked, or set down, and distinguished and set one under another, in their proper *Places.*

Scylax

1565 COOPER L→E *Scylax*, A musician of Caria.

second *see* tone

1728 CHAMBERS *Second* in *Musick*, one of the musical Intervals; being only the Distance between any Sound, and the next nearest Sound; whether higher or lower. See *Interval.* As in the Compass of a Tone, there are reckoned Nine sensible, different Sounds, which form those little Intervals, call'd *Commas*; one might, in strictness, say, there are Eight kinds of Seconds. But as these minute Intervals, though sensible, are not yet so far so, as to contribute much to the Harmony, they usually only distinguish four Sorts. The First called, the *diminish'd Second*, containing Four Commas, and is the Difference, for

Instance of a natural *ut*, and an *ut* raised four Commas higher. The Second, call'd *Second Minor*, contains Five Commas, and is made either naturally, as from *mi* to *fa*, or from *si* to *ut*; or accidentally, by means of *b*, as from *ta* to *si*, *b flat*; or from *fa diesis* to *sol*; otherwise called a *Major Semitone*, or *imperfect Second*, or *Italian Semitone*. The Third is the *Major Second*, containing the Nine Commas, which compose the Tone. This the *Italians* call *Tono* or *perfect Second*. The Fourth is the *Second Redundant*, composed of a whole Tone and a minor Semitone. **1730** BAILEY *Dict. Britannicum* (1st edn) *Second* (in *Musick*) one of the musical Intervals, being only the Distance between any Sound and the next nearest Sound, whether higher or lower.

1636 BUTLER *Principles of Musik* (p. 49) A Second, a Third, a Fowrth, a Fift, a Sixt, a Sevnth, and an Eight, ar so called, becaus they contein so many severall Sounds. **1688** SALMON *Proposal to Perform Musick* (p. 13) ... Seconds, which is the name whereby the gradual Notes are commonly called: for reck[o]ning inclusively in Musick, one Interval, which must needs be contain'd between two Sounds, is term'd a Second. **1721** MALCOLM *Treatise of Musick* (p. 246) ... For the same Reason also, the *Tone* or *s*. (whichever of them stands next the *Fundamental*) is called a *2d*, particularly the *Tone* (whose Difference of greater and lesser is not strictly regarded in common Practice) is called the *2d g*. and *s*. the *2d l*. Also that Term [intervallic member] which is betwixt the *6th* and *8ve*, is called the *7th*, which is also the greater 8:15, or the lesser 5:9. **1724** [PEPUSCH] *Short Explic. of Foreign Words in Mus. Bks.* (p. 67) *Seconda*, or *Seconde*, the Second, or Number Two. Thus, ¶ *Violino Secondo*, the Second Violin. ¶ *Opera Seconda*, the Second Opera. ¶ *Parta Seconda*, the Second Part. ¶ *Libro Secondo*, the Second Book. **1726** BAILEY *An Univ. Etymolog. Engl. Dict.* (3rd edn) *Seconda, Seconde*, the second or two in Number. *Ital. Seconda, Seconde*, the second or two in Number. *Ital.* **1737** DYCHE-PARDON (2nd edn) *Second* (S.) ... and in *Musick*, it is the Distance between any two Tones or Sounds that lie orderly or next to one another in the Scale.

secondina

1598 FLORIO It→E *Secondina*, ... Also the second string of any instrument of musicke. **1611** FLORIO It→E *Secondina*, ... Also the second string of any musicall instrument.

second, lesser

1721 MALCOLM *Treatise of Musick* (p. 298) ... Thus an *Interval* of 1 *Semitone* is called a lesser Second or *2d l*. of 2 *Semitones* is a *2d g*. of 3 *Semitones* a *3d l*. of 4, a *3d g*. and so on ...

second tone

1609 DOWLAND-ORNITHOPARCUS *Micrologvs* (p. 31) The second *Tone*, (as Saint *Bernard* saith) is a Rule determining the *Plagall* of the first fashion. Or it is a plagall Progression of the first. Now a *plagall* Progression is a descending beyond the *Finall* to a Fift, or at least a fourth. His beginnings (according to *Guido*) are *A. C. D. F.* & *G.* & doth rightly posesse the extreames of the eight *Authenticke*, because the souldier by law of Armes, doth dwell in the Tents of his captaine...

secular plays

1737 DYCHE-PARDON (2nd edn) *Secular Plays* (S.) this was one of the greatest Solemnities of *Old Rome*, ... the third and last Day there were two Choirs of Musick one of Boys the other of Girls of the best Families, whose Fathers and Mothers were living, who sung Hymns composed for the Occasion.

selah

1658 PHILLIPS (1st edn) *Sela*, or *Selah*, an Hebrew word, used in several of *Davids* Psalms; being as some think a pause, or resting time in Musick. **1676** COLES *Selah, Hebrew*. a note of resting or of observation. **1704** *Cocker's Engl. Dict.* (1st edn) *Selah*, an *Hebrew* note of observation, pawsing, or resting. **1706** KERSEY-PHILLIPS (6th edn) *Selah*, or *Sela, (Heb.)* a Note of Musick, more especially us'd in *David*'s Psalms; some take it for a Note of Observation, some for a kind of Pause, or Rest, and others for the lifting up of the Voice. **1737** BAILEY *The Univ. Etymolog. Engl. Dict.* (3rd edn, vol. 2) *Selah* (סלה, *Heb.*) an *Hebrew* word which occurs frequently in the psalms, the meaning of which is variously conjectured; some supposing it was a pause or stop to the singers to raise their voices; and others that it directs the change of tune or person; but others think it was a direction to change the whole chorus; for sometimes the chorus broke off in the middle of a psalm, and another set of vocal musick went on with it; others say that it signified *Amen* and others *for ever*. **1737** DYCHE-PARDON (2nd edn) *Selah* (Part.) an *Hebrew* Word that occurs seventy three Times in the Psalms, and once in the Prophet *Habakkuk*; the Meaning whereof some affirm to be *for ever*; others *Amen*; and others only a Sign of a Pause or Stop of the Singers to raise their Voices; and others that it directs a Change in the Tune or Person; and others that it was a Direction to change the whole Chorus; for sometimes the Chorus broke off in the Middle of the Psalm, and another Set of vocal Musick went on with it.

1586 ANON. *Praise of Mvsicke* (p. 138) ... That he [the Holy Ghost] would haue them song with sundry seuerall and most excellent notes and varietie of tunes, in diuerse parts and places of sundry Psalmes, it is to bee seene by the word *Sela* set downe in sundry places, as Psalme 77. &c. which Hebrewe word properly signifieth, now change your voice and that cunningly, now lift vp your voice, and that with an other excellent tune, that the people may be more attentiue; and the word *Sela* is neuer written, but where the matter of the Psalme is most notable. **1619** WITHER *Preparation to the Psalter* (pp. 55-6) There is in the Booke of Psalmes the word *Selah* oftentimes vsed: and I find it no where else in all the holy Scripture, but among these *Hymns* [presumably meaning the psalms]; except in some places of the prayer of the Prophet *Habakuk*. ¶ The *Rabbines*, as S. *Ierome* testifies, will haue it to signifie a change, or distinction of the *verse* or *Ryme*: or else, an eleuation of the voyce. The *Septuagint*, *Theodotion*, and *Symmachus*, Interpret it Διαψαλμα; a word almost as obscure. Yet S. *Augustine*, in his Commentary vpon the fourth *Psalme*, takes it to meane some Moode, pause, or custome, to be obserued in the singing. And as *Sympsalma* among the *Greekes*, signifies a continuation of the *Psalme*, or singing of two as one; So *Diapsalma* (as the same Father saith) may bee the diuiding of one into two or more parts. And as our Church hath a custome at this day, to sing or say these words; *Glory bee to the Father, to the Sonne, and to the Holy Ghost, &c.* after the Gospels, and at the end of euery *Psalme*: So peraduenture (as some imagine) there might be some short or deuout sentence, which was to bee repeated where that word stood. Or it may bee, the *Psalme* was ordered to bee sung in parts, one part of the Quire answering the other: and *Selah* might bee placed as a note of Diuision. S. *Ierome*, in his Translation of the Bible, interprets it *Semper*, that is, *Always*, or *For euer*. And in one place he sayeth, that there be three Words, which the *Hebrewes* vsually set at the end of their Bookes, as we doe the word *Finis*. Among which *Selah* was one: the other two were *Amen*, and *Salom*. Some vnderstand it to be a note, warning the Reader, that there is somewhat extraordinarily to be heeded in the verse going before. Yea, many other Interpretations there be; and those so different, or irresolutely affirmed, that I know not to which I might peremptorily incline.... If (as some affirme) it signifie an Eleuation, or *lifting vp*, it may haue respect to the matter: and for ought I know to the contrary, it may as well signifie somewhat appertaining to the melodie or tune of the Psalme. But though it were but a note to direct the singer; yet I perswade my selfe, that it should not haue been placed there, vnlesse it had comprehended also some mysterie of the Euangelicall Law... there is nothing extant of the Auncient *Hebrew* Musicke, to informe vs what note it should be (if it be a note) nor other meanes whereby to gather what thing is satisfied; ... **1706** BEDFORD *Temple Musick* (pp. 98-9) [*re* ancient Jewish texts] ... And the word *Selah*, which is usually found in the End of a *Verse*, is also found at the End of the first Part, all which do make the Division of a Verse into two Parts to be very apparent, but especially in the Original; which seems for these Reasons to be more curiously Composed for such a way of sing[i]ng, which we call *The Canting of the Psalms*, than can be imitated in any exact Translation. § (pp. 193-4) ... The *First* is סלה *Selah*, a Word of frequent Use in the End, and once found in the middle of a Verse, and generally thought to have Reference to the *Jewish Musick*. The Word is derived from the *Verb* סלה to *prostrate* or *tread down*, and therefore may probably mean a *Repetition* of the aforegoing *Strain* with a *Softer Voice*, to introduce a *greater variety*, and make the *Musick* more Graceful. To this Opinion *Kircher* seems to incline, who relating the different Sentiments of others concerning the Word *Selah*, at last tells us his own Judgment in these Words: *From all which I collect, That the Lifting up of the Voice, and the Intermission of a certain silence, is signified by this Word* ...

selve

1659 TORRIANO-FLORIO It→E *Selve*, the name of a country jig.

semi

1736 TANS'UR *Compleat Melody* (3rd edn, p. 69) *N.B.* That the *Particle Semi*, in *Semidiapasion*, *Semidiapente*, *Semiditone*, &c. doth not mean the half of such an *Interval;* but that it wants a *Semitone* of its Perfection.

semibreve *see* master note, o

1598 FLORIO It→E *Semi breue,* a semibriefe in musike. **1611** FLORIO It→E *Semibreue,* a semy briefe in Musike. **1659** TORRIANO-FLORIO It→E *Semi-breve,* a semibrief in musick. **1661** BLOUNT (2nd edn) *Sembrief* (q. *Semibrief*) a slow time in Musick. **1670** BLOUNT (3rd edn) *Sembrief* (q. *Semibrief*) a slow time in Musick. We account two *Minims* to the *Sembrief,* two *Crotchets* to the *Minim,* two *Quavers* to the *Crotchet,* two *Semiquavers* to the *Quaver.* **1671** PHILLIPS (3rd edn) *Sembrief,* in Musick, is a note containing half the quantity of the *Brief,* see *Brief* [breve]. **1676** COLES *Sembrief,* a full time (in Musick.) **1702** KERSEY *New Engl. Dict.* (1st edn) A *Sem-brief,* a musical note, containing two minims, four crotchets, *&c.* **1704** *Cocker's Engl. Dict.* (1st edn) *Sembrief,* in Musick is the full time. **1704** HARRIS *Semi-breve,* a Term in Musick. See *Notes* and *Time.* **1706** KERSEY-PHILLIPS (6th edn) *Semi-breve,* or *Sem-brief,* a Musical Note of half the Quantity of the *Breve,* or *Brief,* containing two Minims, four Crotchets, &c. See *Brief.* **1724** [PEPUSCH] *Short Explic. of Foreign Words in Mus. Bks.* (p. 68) *Semi,* Half. Thus, ¶ *Semi Breve,* Half a Breve. One of the Notes or Characters in Musick is so called. **1728** CHAMBERS *Semi-breve,* in Music, a Note, or Measure of Time, comprehending the Space of Two Minims, or Four Crotchets, or Half a *Breve.* The *Semi-breve* is accounted one Measure of Time; or the Integer, in Fractions and Multiples whereof the Time of the other Notes is expressed. Thus the Minim is express'd by $\frac{1}{2}$; a Crotchet by $\frac{1}{4}$, *&c. i.e.* by $\frac{1}{4}$ of a Measure or *Semi-breve.* A *Breve* by 2; a *Long* by 4, that is, by 4 Measures or *Semi[-]breves.* The Character of the *Semi-breve* is 0. **1737** DYCHE-PARDON (2nd edn) *Sembrief* (S.) a *Musical* Note, containing two Minims, four Crotchets, &c. and in *common Time* is a whole Measure or Bar in the Division of the Musick both in playing and pricking, marked O.

after 1517 ANON. Art of Mvsic BL Add. 4911, f. 1v *The semibrewe* is a round figur formit to the one eg or as plesit franchinus, one triangli ... **1609** DOWLAND-ORNITHOPARCUS *Micrologvs* (p. 39) A *Sembreefe* is a Figure, which is round in forme of an egge, or (as *Franchinus* sayeth) Triangular. **1617-24** FLUDD *Utriusque Cosmi Maioris: De Templo Musicæ* (p. 191) *Semibrevis* est medietas quantitatis Brevis. **1636** BUTLER *Principles of Musik* (p. 24) [marginalia:] *The Semibrief is the Mesure-note.* **1665** SIMPSON *Principles of Practical Mvsick* (p. 16) When Musick grew to more perfection, they added two Notes more, under the Terms of *Semibrevis* and *Minima Nota;* (our *Semibreve* and *Minim*) which later was then their shortest Note. **1676** MACE *Musick's Monument* (pp. 78-9) I will begin first with the *Semibreve,* and give you *Its Definition* according to *Its General Use* .... 'Just as your saying *One,* your *Foot must knock,* and remain *down,* till you have counted the *Word Two;* then, just as you say the *Word Three,* your *Foot must rise,* and *continue up,* till you have said the *Word Four,* and then down again at the *Word One.* And thus must yonr [sic] *Foot constantly be in Motion, during your Play, and Equally dividing your Down from your Up,* so *Exactly,* that not the least *Difference* may be perceiv'd .... And here you must take notice, That *Those* 4 *Counts,* perform'd with your *Foot, down, and up,* is the *Time,* which we call a *Semibreve* ... **1724** TURNER *Sound Anatomiz'd* (pp. 15-16) Of these *Notes* [of duration], there are but six commonly used; the longest of which is called a *Semibreve,* or half the Measure of a *Breve,* .... Its Mark is this, ◇ **1731** PRELLEUR *Modern Musick-Master* (Dictionary, p. 3) *Semi breve,* is the name of a Note which is in value as much as two Minims or 4 Crotchets, &c. Or one Barr of Common Time.

semibreve time *see* common time, o, whole time

1666 PLAYFORD *Musick's Delight on the Cithren* (n.p.) The *Semibreve* or *Common-Time* is, when all Notes double their proportions by two to the *Semibreve;* that is, two *Minims* to the *Semibreve,* two *Crotchets* to the *Minim,* &c.

semicadence

c.1726 NORTH Musicall Gramarian BL Add. 32533, f. 94v But these Schemes properly belong to the cadence, there are others that appertaine to closes they call Semicadences; wch are such as fall Gradually from the Key note down to the fourth below ...

semichoro

1611 FLORIO It→E *Semichoro,* a demie-chorus. **1659** TORRIANO-FLORIO It→E *Semi-choro,* a demy-chorus.

semicrome

1598 FLORIO It→E *Semicrome,* a semie crochet in musike. **1611** FLORIO It→E *Semicrome,* a semiecrotchet in Musike. **1659** TORRIANO-FLORIO It→E *Semi-crome*, a semy-crotchet in Mnsick [sic].

semidiapason *see* ditonus diapente, interval
1704 HARRIS *Semi-diapason*, a Term in Musick, signifying a Defective or Imperfect *Octave*. **1706** KERSEY-PHILLIPS (6th edn) *Semi-Diapason*, a Term in *Musick*, signifying a defective, or imperfect *Octave*. **1728** CHAMBERS *Semi-diapason*, in Music, a defective Octave; or an Octave diminished, of a minor *Semi-tone*, or four Commas. See *Diapason*. **1730** BAILEY *Dict. Britannicum* (1st edn) *Semidiapason* (in *Musick*) a defective Octave, or an Octave diminished of a minor Semitone, or 4 Comma's.

1609 DOWLAND-ORNITHOPARCUS *Micrologvs* (p. 21) *Semidiapason*. ¶ Is an imperfect eight, consisting of foure *Tones*, and three *Semitones*, not to be vsed in any plaine Song, yet worthy to be knowne by componists. **1694** HOLDER *Treatise of Natural Grounds* (p. 172) The other [seventh, after the lesser seventh] is the greatest, called *Semidiapason*, whose Ration is 48 to 25; ...

semidiapente *see* false fifth, fifth lesser, interval, tritone
1704 HARRIS *Semi-diapente*, a Term in Musick, signifying an *Imperfect Fifth*. **1706** KERSEY-PHILLIPS (6th edn) *Semi-Diapente*, an imperfect Fifth. **1721** BAILEY *An Univ. Etymolog. Engl. Dict.* (1st edn) *Semi-diapente*, (in *Musick*) is half a Fifth, or an imperfect Fifth. **1728** CHAMBERS *Semi-diapente*, in Music, a defective Fifth, call'd usually by the *Italians*, *Falsa quinta*, and by us a *false Fifth*. See *Fifth*. **1730** BAILEY *Dict. Britannicum* (1st edn) *Semidiapente* (in *Musick*) a defective Fifth, called a false Fifth.

1609 DOWLAND-ORNITHOPARCUS *Micrologvs* (p. 20) *Semidiapente*. ¶ Is an *Interuall* by an imperfect fift, comprehending two *Tones*, with two *semitones*, which though it be not found in plaine-song, yet doth the knowledge thereof much profit composers, who are held to auoide it. **1636** BUTLER *Principles of Musik* (p. 49) ... from *Mi* to *Pha* aboov ar 5 distinct sounds, as in a *Diapente*: but they ar from the Ground, but 2 Tones and 2 Hemitones, whereof that Interval is called **Semidiapente*. [marginalia: '**Semidiapente. Semi* in this woord (as in *Semiditonus* and *Semidiapason*) dooeth not signifie half of the whole, but the whole save half a Note.'] **1694** HOLDER *Treatise of Natural Grounds* (p. 168) The *Semidiapente*, (or False Fifth) 64 to 45; is compounded of a Fourth, and *Hemitone Major*.

semidiatessaron
1728 CHAMBERS *Semi-diatessaron*, in Music, a defective Fourth, call'd, properly, a *false Fourth*. See *Fourth*. **1736** BAILEY *Dict. Britannicum* (2nd edn) *Semidiatessaron* (in *Mu.*) a defective fourth.

semiditie *see* diminution

semiditone *see* demiditone, interval
1598 FLORIO It→E *Semiditono*, a kinde of tune in musicke. **1611** FLORIO It→E *Semiditono*, a halfe tune in Musike. **1659** TORRIANO-FLORIO It→E *Semi-ditono*, a half tune in Musick. **1704** HARRIS *Semi-ditone*, in Musick, is the Lesser Third having its Terms as six to five. **1706** KERSEY-PHILLIPS (6th edn) *Semi-Ditone*, the lesser Third, having its Terms, as Six to Five. **1730** BAILEY *Dict. Britannicum* (1st edn) *Semiditone* (in *Mu.*) the After-third, having its Terms as 6 to 5.

1609 DOWLAND-ORNITHOPARCUS *Micrologvs* (p. 18) *A Semiditone*. ¶ Which *Faber Stapulensis* calleth *Sesquitonium*, is an *Interuall* of one *Voyce* from another by an imperfect third: consisting of a *Tone*, and a *semitone* according to *Placentinus*. It hath two kindes, as *Pontifex* in the eight Chapter saith; the first is from *re* to *fa*; the second from *mi* to *sol* ... **1636** BUTLER *Principles of Musik* (p. 46) *Semiditonus* is an imperfect Third, consisting of a Tone and a Half-tone: as from *Re* to *Fa*, from *Sol* to *Pha*, from *Mi* to *Sol*, and from *La* to *Ut*. **1692** Letters addressed to William Holder BL Sloane 1388, f. 63 [letter from John Baynard, 1692] ... Since I find in Kircher that he useth Semiditonus on all occasions for the 3rd Minor, as the most proper & most useful word; you may consider whether you were not better use it also instead of Sesquitone; though this last be used altogether by as great a man as any I know, viz. Pietro Mengoli, in his Speculationi di Musica.

semiditone diapason
1728 CHAMBERS *Diapasonsemiditone*, a Concord, whose Terms are in the Proportion of 12 to 5. **1730** BAILEY *Dict. Britannicum* (1st edn) *Diapasonsemiditone*, a concord, the terms of which are in proportion of 12 to 5. **1737** DYCHE-PARDON (2nd edn) *Diapasonsemiditone* (S.) in *Musick*, a Concord, in Proportion, as 12 to 5.

1609 DOWLAND-ORNITHOPARCUS *Micrologvs* (p. 21) *Semiditonus Diapason.* ¶ Is an *Interuall* by an imperfect Tenth, as witnesseth *Valla* the 31. Chapter, consisting of sixe *Tones*, and three *semitones*. A *Ditone* with a true *Diapason* is a perfect Tenth, consisting of seuen *Tones*, and two *semitones*.

semiditone diapente

1609 DOWLAND-ORNITHOPARCUS *Micrologvs* (p. 21) *Semiditonus Diapente.* ¶ Is an *Interuall* by an imperfect seuenth. This according to *Placentinus lib.* 3. *cap.* 24. comprehends foure *Tones*, and two *semitones*. **1636** BUTLER *Principles of Musik* (p. 47) *Semiditonus-diapente* is a Sevnth imperfect, of 4 Tones and 2 Hemitones: as from *Ut* to *Pha*, from *Mi* to *Re*, from *Sol* to *Fa*, and from *Re* to *Ut*.

semi-minim

1598 FLORIO It→E *Semiminima*, a semiminime in musicke. **1611** FLORIO It→E *Semiminima*, a semiminime in Musike, that is, halfe a crotchet. **1659** TORRIANO-FLORIO It→E *Semi-minima*, a half crotchet or semiminime in Musick.

seminiro, seminito

1611 FLORIO It→E *Seminiro*, a kind of tune in Musike. **1659** TORRIANO-FLORIO It→E *Seminito*, a tune in Musick.

semi-opera *see* opera

semiquaver *see* demi-crochue, demiquaver

1671 PHILLIPS (3rd edn) *Semiquaver*, a note in Musick containing half the Quaver. **1676** COLES *Semiquaver*, half a quaver. **1696** PHILLIPS (5th edn) *Semiquaver*, a Note in Musick, containing half the quantity of the Quaver, sixteen of which make a whole Time. **1702** KERSEY *New Engl. Dict.* (1st edn) A *Semi-quaver*, a note in Musick. **1704** *Cocker's Engl. Dict.* (1st edn) *Semiquaver*, in Musick is half a quaver. **1704** HARRIS *Semi-quaver*, a Term in Musick. See *Notes* and *Time*. **1728** CHAMBERS *Semi-quaver*, in Music. See *Quaver*. **1737** DYCHE-PARDON (2nd edn) *Semiquaver* (S.) a *Musical* Note, which in common Time is the sixteenth Part of a Bar.

1609 DOWLAND-ORNITHOPARCUS *Micrologvs* (p. 40) A *Semiquauer* is a figure like a *Quauer* which hath two dashes, and therby is distinguished from it [i.e. the quaver] ... **1724** TURNER *Sound Anatomiz'd* (p. 17) The Fourth [note of duration, after the minim, crotchet and quaver] is called a *Semiquaver*; which being but half the Length of the *Quaver*, has its Tail turned up with a double Stroke, thus; and divides the *Semibreve* into *Sixteen* Parts.

semi-sono

1659 TORRIANO-FLORIO It→E **Semi-sono*, a half or demy tune.

semitact *see* tactus

semitone *see* accidental, apotome, artificial sound, chromatic, comma, degree, fictitious note, hemitone, imperfect, interval

1500 *Ortus Vocabulorum* L→E Semitono as. to halfe tone a.p. **1587** THOMAS L→E § *Semitonium minus, Boet. vid. Diesis.* **1598** FLORIO It→E *Semitono*, a demitune, or halfe note in musicke. *Semituono*, a semitune, halfe a note in musicke. **1611** FLORIO It→E *Semitono*, a demie tune or halfe note in Musike. *Semituono*, as *Semitono*. **1659** TORRIANO-FLORIO It→E *Semi-tonare*, to play but half a tune. *Semi-tono*, a half note in musick. **1702** KERSEY *New Engl. Dict.* (1st edn) A *Semi-tone, or* half tone. **1704** HARRIS *Semi-tone*, a Term in Musick, of which there are two sorts, *viz*, a Greater and a Lesser; the *Enharmonical Deisis*, being the Difference between them. **1706** KERSEY-PHILLIPS (6th edn) *Semi-Tone*, (in *Musick*) a half Tone, of which there are two sorts, *viz*. a Greater and a Lesser; the *Enharmonical Diesis*, being the Difference between them. **1728** CHAMBERS *Semi-tone* ... [*see* Appendix] **1730** BAILEY *Dict. Britannicum* (1st edn) Semi-Tone (in *Mu.*) one of the Degrees of concinnous Intervals of Concords.

1609 DOWLAND-ORNITHOPARCUS *Micrologvs* (pp. 17-18) ... a *Semitone* ... is a rising from one *Voyce* to another, (by an imperfect second) sounding flatly: and it is onely betwixt the *Voyces Mi, fa*. It is called a *Semitone*, not because it is halfe a *Tone*, (for a *Tone* cannot be diuided into two equall parts) but because it is an imperfect *Tone*, for *Semum* is called that which is imperfect, as saith *Boêtius lib.* 1. *cap.* 16. **1617-24** FLUDD *Utriusque Cosmi Maioris: De Templo Musicæ* (p. 182) *Semitonus* est una proportio inter tres notas immediatè se habentes, ut *Mi* & *Sol, Re* & *Fa*. **1636** BUTLER *Principles of Musik* (p. 46) *Semitonium* is a Second imperfect: *i.* from *Mi* to *Fa* or from *La* to *Pha*. **1664** BIRCHENSHA-ALSTED *Templvm Mvsicvm* (p. 92) ... which Connexion is called a Semitone, which is the skipping of the Voice into a Voice by an imperfect Second, sounding flatly: as is the Leaping from *mi* into *fa*, and again from *fa* into *mi*... **1721** MALCOLM *Treatise of Musick* (p. 223) As to the *Semitone*, 'tis so called, not that it is geometrically the Half of either of these which we call *Tones* [being specifically the lesser and greater tones] (for 'tis greater) but because it comes near to it; and 'tis called the *greater Semitone*, being greater than what it wants of a *Tone*. § (p. 229) ... For the *Degrees* sought we have already assigned these, *viz*. ... 15:16 called a *greater Semitone*: § (p. 291) ... This therefore is the present *System* for Instruments, *viz*. betwixt the Extremes of every *Tone* of the natural *Scale* is put a Note, which divides it into Two unequal Parts called *Semitones*; and the whole may be called the *semitonick Scale*, containing 12 *Semitones* betwixt 13 Notes within the Compass of an *Octave*: ...

semitone diapason

1609 DOWLAND-ORNITHOPARCUS *Micrologvs* (p. 21) *Semitonium Diapason*. ¶ Is a leaping by an imperfect Ninth, consisting of fiue *Tones*, and three *semitones*. Now a *Tone* with a *Diapason* is a perfect Ninth, consisting of sixe *Tones*, and two *semitones*.

semitone diapente

1609 DOWLAND-ORNITHOPARCUS *Micrologvs* (p. 19) *Semitone Diapente*. ¶ Is an *Interuall* of one *Voyce* from another by an imperfect sixt, according to *Georgius Valla lib*. 3. *cap*. 21. consisting of three *Tones*, and two *Semitones*. **1636** BUTLER *Principles of Musik* (p. 47) *Semitonium-Diapente* is an imperfect Sixt, of 3 Tones and two Hemitones: as from *Re* to *Pha*, from *Mi* to *Vt*.

semitone, lesser

1721 MALCOLM *Treatise of Musick* (p. 261) [*re 'false Intervals'*] ... 24:25, the Difference of a *t l*. and *s*. which is sometimes called a lesser *Semitone*, because it is less than 15:16; then 128:135, the Difference of a *t g*. and *s*. which is a greater Difference than the last, and is also called a lesser *Semitone*, and is a Middle betwixt 15:16, and 24:25.

senza *see* con

1724 [PEPUSCH] *Short Explic. of Foreign Words in Mus. Bks*. (p. 68) *Senza*, without. This Word is used in the following Manner: ¶ *Senza l'Aria*, without the Air. ¶ *Senza Ritornello*, without the Retornel. ¶ *Senza Violino*, without the Violins. ¶ *Senza Stromenti*, without the Instruments. **1726** BAILEY *An Univ. Etymolog. Engl. Dict*. (3rd edn) *Senza* (in *Musick Books*) signifies without, as *Senza Stromenti*, without Instruments. *Ital*.

1731 PRELLEUR *Modern Musick-Master* (Dictionary, p. 3) *Senza*, Without, as *Senza Violini* without Violins, &c **1736** TANS'UR *Compleat Melody* (3rd edn, p. 72) *Senza*. (Ital.) signifies, without; as *Senza Stroment*, without Instruments.

se piace

1724 [PEPUSCH] *Short Explic. of Foreign Words in Mus. Bks*. (p. 69) *Se Piace*, if you please: The same as *Ad Libitum*. **1726** BAILEY *An Univ. Etymolog. Engl. Dict*. (3rd edn) *Sepiace*, if you please. *Ital*.

septenary *see* alamire, clef, d la sol re, ela, fa

sequence

1611 COTGRAVE Fr→E *Sequences: f*. Answering verses, or verses whereto answer is made, in the Masse.

serenade *see* aubade, minstrel

1598 FLORIO It→E *Serenata*, musike giuen vnder gentlewomens windowes in a morning or euening. **1611** COTGRAVE Fr→E *Serenade: f*. Euening Musicke played at the dore, or vnder the window, of a louelie, or beloued creature. **1611** FLORIO It→E *Serenata*, a fit of mirth or hunt is vp plaide in a morning or euening in the street. **1656** BLOUNT (1st edn) *Serenade* (Fr.) evening musick at the door or under the window of a lovely or beloved creature. Mr. *Cowley* in his Poems. **1658** PHILLIPS (1st edn) *Serenade*, (French) an evening-song sung by a Lover under his Mistresses window. **1659** TORRIANO-FLORIO It→E *Serenata*, a fit of mirth, a hunt is up, or musick plaid in a fair morning, or clear evening under some fair Mistresses window **1676** COLES *Serenade, French*. evening musick under his Mistresses window. **1696** PHILLIPS (5th edn) *Serenade, (French)* an Evening Song, sung by a Lover under his Mistresses Window. **1702** KERSEY *New Engl. Dict*. (1st edn) A *Serenade, or* night-musick, play'd by a lover to charm his mistress. To *serenade one, or* play love-musick at her door, *or* under her window. **1704** *Cocker's Engl. Dict*. (1st edn) *Serenade*, a Consort of Musick or Singing in the Night or Morning, under the Window of the beloved Mistress. **1706** KERSEY-PHILLIPS (6th edn) *Serenade*, Night-Musick, especially that which is performed by a Lover to Charm his Mistress, at her Door, or under her Window. **1707** *Gloss. Angl. Nova* (1st edn) *Serenade*, (Fr.) Night Musick, play'd by a Lover at his Mistresses Door, or under her Window. **1724** [PEPUSCH] *Short Explic. of Foreign Words in Mus. Bks.* (p. 68) *Serenata,* Serenade[,] a Consort of Musick is so called when performed in the Midst of the Night, or Morning early, in the open Air or Street. **1726** BAILEY *An Univ. Etymolog. Engl. Dict.* (3rd edn) *Serenata,* a Consort of Musick performed in the midst of the Night or Morning early, in the open Air or Street. *Ital.* **1728** CHAMBERS *Serenade,* a kind of Concert given in the Night-Time by a Gallant, at his Mistress's Door, or under her Window. Sometimes it consists wholly of Instrumental Music; sometimes Voices are added; and the Pieces compos'd or play'd on these Occasions, are also call'd *Serenades.* We don't know whence the Word should derive, unless from the *French, Serein,* the Dew falling in the Night-Time. **1730** BAILEY *Dict. Britannicum* (1st edn) A *Serenade* (prob. of *serein,* F.) a Kind of Concert given in the Night-time by a Gallant, at the Door, or under the Window of his Mistress. *To Serenade* (*donner de serenades,* F.) to play or sing to a Lady or Mistress, under her Door or Window, in the Night, or early in the Morning, *Ital. Serenata,* the same as Serenade, *Ital.* **1731** KERSEY *New Engl. Dict.* (3rd edn) To *serenade one,* to play Love-Musick at her Door *or* under her Window. **1737** DYCHE-PARDON (2nd edn) *Serenade* (S.) a vocal or instrumental Concert in the Night-time under the Window of a Mistress or Sweetheart. *Serenade* (V.) to play or sing under the Window of a Mistress or Sweetheart in the Night-time.

serpent

1688 MIEGE-COTGRAVE Fr→E *Serpent,* (m.) ... a sort of Wind-Instrument of Musick. § *Il ya aussi un Instrument de Musique à vent, de metal ou de bois de Noyer, couvert de Cuir, que l'on appelle Serpent. Il a six trous, & environ cinq ou six piez de long. On l'appelle Serpent, parce que sa figure approche en quêque sorre de celle d'un Serpent.* **1728** CHAMBERS *Serpent,* a Musical Instrument, serving as a Basse to the Cornet, or small Shawm, to sustain a Chorus of Singers in a large Vessel. It has its Name *Serpent,* from its Figure; as consisting of several Folds or Wreaths, serving to take off its Length, which would otherwise be Six or Seven Feet. 'Tis usually covered with Leather; and consists of Three Parts; a Mouth-piece, a Neck, and a Tail. It has Six Holes, by means whereof, they give it the Compass of Two Octaves. **1730** BAILEY *Dict. Britannicum* (1st edn) *Serpent,* a Kind of musical Instrument, serving as a Bass to the *Cornet* or small *Shawm,* to sustain a Chorus of Singers in a large Vessel. **1740** BAILEY *An Univ. Etymolog. Engl. Dict.* (9th edn) *Serpent,* a Musical Instrument serving a Base to the Cornet.

serra serra

see butta in sella, monta in sella
1598 FLORIO It→E *Serra Serra,* a kind of march sounded in warre. **1611** FLORIO It→E *Serra serra,* a kind of march sounded in times of battles or skirmishes or suddaine assaults, as you would say, stick close. **1659** TORRIANO-FLORIO It→E **Serra, Serra,* a kind of march or point of war sounded in times of battles, skirmishes or suddain assaults, as you would say, stick close, march close, or fight close.

sesqui

1728 CHAMBERS *Sesqui,* a *Latin* Particle, signifying a Whole and a Half; which, joined with *Altera, Terza, Quarta, &c.* is much used in the *Italian* Music, to express a Kind of *Ratio*'s; particularly, several Species of Triples. The *Ratio* express'd by *Sesqui,* is the Second *Ratio* of Inequality, called also *Super-particular Ratio*; and is, when the greater Term contains the Less, once, and some certain Part, over: As 3:2; where the First Term contains the Second once, and Unity over; which is a Quota Part of Two. Now, if this Part remaining, be just Half the less Term, the *Ratio* is called *Sesquialtera*: If the remaining Part be a Third Part of the lesser Term, as 4:3, the *Ratio* is called *Sesqui-tertia,* or *Sesqui-terza.* If a Fourth Part, as 5:4, the *Ratio* is called *Sesqui-quarta;* and thus to Infinity, still adding to *Sesqui* the ordinal Number of the smaller Term. In *English,* we may say *Sesqui-alteral, Sesqui-Third, Sesqui-fourth, &c.* ¶ As to the Kinds of Triples expressed by the Particle *Sesqui,* they are these: The *Greater Perfect Sesqui-alteral,* which is a Triple, where the Breve is three Measures, or Minims, and that without having any Point. The *Greater Imperfect Sesqui-alteral,* which is where the Breve, when pointed, contains three Measures, and without any Point, two. The *Less Perfect Sesqui-alteral,* which is where the Semi-breve contains three Measures, and that without any Point. The *Less Imperfect Sesqui-alteral,* a Triple, mark'd C $\frac{3}{2}$, where the Semi-breve, with a Point, contains three Measures, and two without. According to *Bontempi,* one may likewise call the Triples $\frac{6}{4}$ and $\frac{12}{8}$, *Sesqui-alteral.* ¶ The *Sesqui-octave,* is a Kind of Triple, mark'd C $\frac{8}{9}$, called by the *Italians Nonupla di Crome,* where there are 9 Quavers in every Measure or Bar, in Lieu of 8. The *Double Sesqui-quarta* is a Kind of

Triple mark'd C $\frac{9}{4}$, called by the *Italians Nonupladi Semi-minime,* where there are 9 Crotchets in each Measure, instead of 4.

sesquialtera *see* hemiola, proportion, tact, tripla

1538 ELYOT L→E *Sesquialtera,* so moche and halfe so moche, a proportion in musyke. **1565** COOPER L→E § *Sesquialtera pars. Cic.* So muche and halfe so much: a proportion in musike. **1704** HARRIS *Sesquialter,* in Musick. See *Time.* **1706** KERSEY-PHILLIPS (6th edn) *Sesquialter,* ... Also a Term in *Musick.* See *Time.* **1708** KERSEY *Dict. Anglo-Brit.* (1st edn) § *Sesquialteral Proportion,* ... In *Musick,* a triple Measure of three Notes to two such like Notes of Common Time.

1596 ANON. *Pathway to Musicke* [E iv] *VVhat is the proportion called Sesque altera.* ¶ It is when three noates is pronounced against two of the same likenesse, and it is when the higher number containeth the lower once and one second part ouer ... **1597** MORLEY *Plaine and Easie Introdvction* (pp. 32-3) *Phi.* Come then to *Se[s]quialtera,* what is it? ¶ *Ma.* It is when three notes are sung to two of the same kinde, and is knowne by a number contayning another once, and his halfe $\frac{3}{2}$ $\frac{6}{4}$ $\frac{9}{6}$ the example of this you shal haue amongst the others. § (annotations on Part I) *Sesquialtera,* is a musical proportion, wherin three notes are sung in the time of two of the same kinde, or rather thus. *Sesquialtera,* is a kinde of musicall diminution, wherein 3. semibriefes or their value in other notes are sung for two strokes. **1609** DOWLAND-ORNITHOPARCUS *Micrologvs* (p. 40) There is a certaine Figure, in shape like a *Minime,* but ioyned with the number of Three, which is called *Sesquialterata,* because three are sung for two. § (p. 64) The *Sesquialtera* is the first sort of the *Super particular,* and is, when a great number doth comprehend a lesse once, and some other part of it: as 6. to 4:9. to 6. But Musically, when three Notes are sounded against two of the same kinde: the signes of it are these; $\frac{3}{2}$ $\frac{6}{4}$ $\frac{9}{6}$ ... **1667** SIMPSON *Compendium of Practical Musick* (p. 34) Beside these several sorts of *Tripla's* before mentioned, you may sometimes meet with Figures set thus $\frac{3}{2}$ called *Sesquialtera* proportion, which signifies a *Triple* Measure of three Notes to two such like Notes of the Common Time. **1680** B., A. *Synopsis of Vocal Musick* (p. 14) Sesquialtre time is whose parts, the depression and elevation of the hand are equal, or even long, as in Common Time, yet by whom Notes and Pauses are measured, not according to their proper value, as in Common Time, but according to a certain proportion as in Triple: And is either Slower, Swifter, or Swiftest. **1736** TANS'UR *Compleat Melody* (3rd edn, p. 13) The first, and generally the slowest *Mood,* is called *Sesquialtern* [sic] *Proportion,* being a *Triple Measure* of three *Notes* to two, such like *Notes* in *Common-Time;* and sung, or play'd in the same *Tune;* which is one fourth Part quicker in every *Bar.*

sesquiditonus

1728 CHAMBERS *Sesquiditonus,* in Music, a Concord resulting from the Sounds of two Strings, whose Vibrations, in equal Times, are to each other in the *Ratio* of 5 to 6. See *Ditonus.* **1730** BAILEY *Dict. Britannicum* (1st edn) *Sesquiditonus* (in *Musick*) a Concord resulting from the Sound of two Strings, whose Vibrations, in equal Times, are to each other in the *Ratio* of 5 to 6.

sesquioctava

1609 DOWLAND-ORNITHOPARCUS *Micrologvs* (p. 65) The *sesquioctaua* Proportion is, when a greater number being compared with a lesse, doth comprehend it once, and with it his 8 part, as 9. to 8:18 to 16. But Musically, when 9. Notes are sung to 8, which are like themselues. The signe of it is the number of 9. set ouer 8, thus; $\frac{9}{8}$ *Or* $\frac{◌}{8}$

sesquitertia *see* proportion

1597 MORLEY *Plaine and Easie Introdvction* (p. 33) *Sesquitercia* is When foure notes are sung to three of the same kinde, and is knowen by a number set before him, contayning another once, and his third part thus. $\frac{4}{3}$ $\frac{8}{6}$ $\frac{12}{9}$ **1609** DOWLAND-ORNITHOPARCUS *Micrologvs* (p. 65) The *Sesquitertia* Proportion, which they cal *Epitrite,* because it is made by an *Epitrite, Macr.* saith, it is when the greater number of Notes, doth containe the lesser in it selfe, & besides his third part: as 4. to 3:8 to 6:12. to 9. But Musically, is when 4. Notes are sounded against 3. which are like themselues. The signes of it are these, $\frac{4}{3}$ $\frac{8}{6}$ $\frac{12}{9}$. There be that ascribe an inuerted *semicircle* to this *Proportion,* but *Tinctor* seemes to be against that.

sesta *see* sixth

1659 TORRIANO-FLORIO It→E **Sesta,* a sixth part, a sixth, or proportion of six in musick, the sixth string of any Instrument **1724** [PEPUSCH] *Short Explic. of Foreign Words in Mus. Bks.* (p. 69) *Sesta,* Six, or the Sixth in Number. Thus, ¶ *Opera Sesta,* the Sixth Opera. *Sexta,* Six: The same as *Sesta,* which see. (p. 70) *Sixte,* Six. See the Word *Sesta.*

sestina

1598 FLORIO It→E *Sestina,* a kind of song or verse riming sixe times to one word. **1611** FLORIO It→E *Sestina,* a stance of verses or of a song containing six lines. Also a kind of song of six stances riming together six times to one word. **1659** TORRIANO-FLORIO It→E **Sestina,* ... also a stanza or stave of a song, containing six verses, also a kind of posie of six stanza's riming together six times to every one word.

sestuple *see* sextupla

set of pricksong *see* staff

c.1596 BATHE *Briefe Intro. to skill of Song* [A v] ... I will begin from the first sight of the booke, that all things that doe belong to their knowledge, may be the better vnderstoode. First when a man seeth the booke before him he may see certaine rules which goe along lineally by 5 and 5 which number of 5 is called a set of pricksong (for a set of plainesong hath commonly but 4. rules,) ...

sett *see* branle, suit

settima

1724 [PEPUSCH] *Short Explic. of Foreign Words in Mus. Bks.* (p. 68) *Septima,* or *Septieme.* See the Word *Settima.* (p. 69) *Settima,* Seven, or the Seventh: The same as *Septima.* Thus, ¶ *Opera Settima,* or *Septima,* is the Seventh Opera.

setting *see* modulation, tablature

1636 BUTLER *Principles of Musik* (p. 40) Setting is the framing of a Song in Partes: which, for the most part, (specially in Counterpoint) ar fowr (Base, Tenor, Countertenor, Mean:) of which, in soom Songs, is wanting one or two: and in soom, for a voice of an high pitch, is added a Treble.

seventh *see* diminished flat seventh, heptachord, settima

1728 CHAMBERS *Seventh,* in Music, an Interval, called by the *Greeks Heptachordon;* whereof there are four Kinds: The First, The defective *Seventh,* consisting of three Tones, and 3 greater Semi-tones. The Second, called by *Zarlin,* and the *Italians, Semi-ditano condiapente,* or *Settimo Minore;* is composed Diatonically of seven Degrees, and six Intervals, four whereof are Tones, and the rest greater Semi-tones, as from *de* to *ut;* and Cromatically of ten Semi-tones, six whereof are greater, and four less: It takes its Form from the *Ratio Quadripartiens Quintas,* as 9 to 5. The Third, called by the *Italians, Il Ditono con Diapentes,* or *Settimo Maggiore,* is composed Diatonically, like the former, of seven Degrees, and six Intervals, six whereof are full Tones, and a single one a greater Semi-tone; so that only one major Semi-tone is wanting of the Octave: As from *ut* to *si,* and Cromatically of twelve Semi-tones, six whereof are greater, and five lesser. It takes its Form, or Origin, from the *Ratio* of 15 to 8. The Fourth, is the redundant *Seventh,* composed of five Tones, a greater Semi-tone, and a lesser; as from *si b* to *la:* So that it only wants a Comma of an Octave; that is, so much as it wants to render its second Semi-tone greater. Hence many confound it with the Octave itself; maintaining, with good Reason, That only the three first *Sevenths* can be of any Use.

seventh lesser, seventh greater

1721 MALCOLM *Treatise of Musick* (p. 260) ... the *7ths* [8:15, 5:9, 9:16] are neither *harmonical* nor *concinnous Intervals,* yet of Use in *Musick,* as I have already mentioned; the Two greater are particularly known by the Name of greater or lesser *7th,* tho' some I know make the least 9:16 the *7th* lesser; ...

seventh tone

1609 DOWLAND-ORNITHOPARCUS *Micrologvs* (p. 34) *Of the Seuenth Tone.* ¶ The Seuenth *Tone* is a Rule determining the *Authenticke* of the fourth sort. Or it is the *authenticall* Progression of the Fourth. It hath his end in *Gsolreut* regular only. To this belongs fiue beginnings, *viz. G. a.* ♮. *c.* & *d.*

sexte *see* sixth

1611 COTGRAVE Fr→E *Sexte: f.* ... also, a sixt, or proportion of six, in Musicke, &c. *Sixte: m.* A sixt, a proportion of six, in Musicke. **1688** MIEGE-COTGRAVE Fr→E *Sexte,* (f.) from *Six, Ton de Musique,* a Sixth, or Proportion of Six, in Musick.

sextupla

1656 BLOUNT (1st edn) *Sextuple (sextuplus)* ... A time in Musick, containing six *Crothets* [sic] to a Bar, appropriated chiefly to *Sarabands.* **1728** CHAMBERS *Sestuple*[,] *Sextuple,* in Music, a Kind of mix'd Triple-time. M. *Brossart* thinks, 'tis improperly thus called, and ought rather to be called *Binary-Triple*. We only find three Kinds of it in Authors; but one may add two others; the First, the Sestuple of the Semi-breve, or Triple, of 6 for 1, or Six-one. The Second, the Sestuple of Minims, or Triple of 6 for 2, or Six-two. The Third, the Triple of Semi-minim, or Triple of 6 for 4, or Six-four. The Fourth, the Sextuple of the Croma, or Triple of 6 for 8, or Six-eight. The Fifth, the Sextuple of Semi-croma, or Triple of 6 for 16, or Six-sixteen. See *Triple*.

1636 BUTLER *Principles of Musik* (p. 25) *Sextupla* is the *Triple* of the Minim in *Duple* Proportion: when to each Minim in *Duple* Time, is sung 3 blak Minims (or a blak Sembrief and a Minim,) (and conseqently 6 Crochets, which must have, for difference, the form of Qavers) 3 to the Fall, and 3 to the Rise of the Hand: (or, if you will keepe Minim-time, 3 to one stroke, and 3 to an other:) which *Triple* is therefore called *Sextupla*; becaus 6 of these blak Minims goe to one Sembrief-time.

shake *see* beat, cadence, double shake, fredon, grace, gringoter, pearled playing, prolation, quaver, tremblement, trill, undershake, vibrante, warble, wrist shake

1737 DYCHE-PARDON (2nd edn) *Shake* (S.) ... and in *Musick*, is one of the principal Graces.

1659 SIMPSON *Division-Violist* (p. 9) The other sort of Graces is done by the *Shake*, or *Tremble* of a Finger; of which, there are two kinds: *viz.* Close, and Open. *Close*, is that when wee shake a Finger as close and near to that which stoppeth as may be; touching the String, therewith, so gently, and nicely, as to make no Variation of *Tone*: This may be used where no other Grace is concerned. *Open* is, when a Finger is shaked in that distance from whence it was removed, or is to be set down; supposing the distance exceed not the wideness of a whole *Tone*, or two *Fretts*; for wider then that we never shake. **1676** MACE *Musick's Monument* (p. 103) The *Shake*, is 2 ways to be performed, either *Hard*, or *Soft*, the *Hard*, (or *Tearing-Shake*) is thus done, *viz.* If you *Shake any String Open*, you must first strike it with some *Right Hand Finger*, and then be ready with the *Fore-finger*, of the *Left Hand* to pick it up, with the very Tip (near the *Nail*) of your Finger; and so, by often, and quick picking it up in that manner, or (more plainly) Scratching It, in a *Smooth*, *Nimble*, and *Strong Agitation*, you will have performed It. ¶ The *Soft-Shake*, is done, in all respects, like the former, except the *Tearing*, and *Scratching*; and only by *Beating the String Strongly*, and with a *Quick Motion*, in the *same place*, as you did the other; which always must be either in *B*, or r-*Frett*; and if it be done *Evenly*, and *Strongly*, it gives a very *Pleasant Grace* unto your Play.... The *Stopt-Shake*, is (only) differing from the *Open-Shake*, in that you are always to use some One of your *Under-fingers*, in your *Shaking*, and to *Stop*, one of your *Upper-fingers*, upon some *Letter*, and then *Shake* with an *Under-Finger*. **1681** B[ANISTER] *Most Pleasant Companion* (p. 6) ... when your Mark is alone on any other Line underneath the Dots, the Fingers belonging to the Line on which it is set you must shake, taking it off before you play any other Note, you doing thus, this is called a *Shake*. **c.1700** NORTH Capt. Prencourts rules BL Add. 32549, f. 11v This Mark ᴧᴧ is called a shake, w[ch] is a swift movem[t] with 2. fingers upon 2. Keys, and at last Remaining with one finger upon that note before w[ch] y[e] signe stands **1726** BRUCE *Common Tunes* (pp. 29-30) Q. *What call you a* Shake? ¶ *A*. It is a sweetning of any Note or Sound, by shaking of it in small or strong Breathings, within its proper Sound. And its Mark is like unto a small *A*, thus *a*. And all this for the Harmony of Musick, when it preceeds a flat or dull Sound or Note. **[1729]** HOTTETERRE *Rudiments or Principles of German Flute* (pp. 7-8) ... least some shou'd not know what a Shake is, I'll give them a definition of it, (Viz.) 'Tis an agitation or mixture of two Sounds together, distant from each other but the space of a Tone, or Semitone, and several times beat upon after you begin with the Superior Note, and end with the lower and you give it but the first articulation, 'tis the finger continues it. **1736** TANS'UR *Compleat Melody* (3rd edn, p. 9) A *Shake*, called the *Trilloe*, is commonly placed over any Note that is to be *shaked*, or *graced*.

shamade *see* chamade

sharp *see* character, diesis, feint, key

1702 KERSEY *New Engl. Dict.* (1st edn) A *Sharp* in musick. **1728** CHAMBERS *Sharp*, in Music, a kind of artificial Note or Character, (thus form'd #) which being prefix'd to a Note, shews that it is to be sung or play'd a Semi-tone, or half a Note higher than the natural Note would have been without. When the Semi-tone takes the Name of the natural Note next above it, 'tis mark'd with a Character call'd a *Flat*. See *Flat*. 'Tis indifferent, in the Main, which of the Two be used, tho' there are sometimes particular Reasons for the one rather than the other. See *Semitone.* The Use of *Flats* and *Sharps,* is by way of Remedy to the Deficiencies of the fixed *Scales* of Instruments. See *Scale.* **1730** BAILEY *Dict. Britannicum* (1st edn) *Sharp* (in *Musick*) a kind of artificial Note or Character so formed (#) **1731** KERSEY *New Engl. Dict.* (3rd edn) A *Sharp,* a sharp Sound in *Musick.* **1737** DYCHE-PARDON (2nd edn) *Sharp* (S.) in *Musick,* is a Mark or Character made thus, #, importing that the Note to which it is adjoined must be half a Tone shriller than it naturally would be without it.

1724 TURNER *Sound Anatomiz'd* (p. 47) The Mark of *Extension* is called a *Sharp;* extending of a *Sound* being called in another Name, the sharpening of it. The *Mark* is this; # and is always placed on the left Side of the *Note* which is to be extended.

sharp cord

1737 LAMPE *Plain and Compendious Method* (p. 14) ... (E *nat.*-C *sharp.*-A *nat.*) make a Common Cord with a greater Third, and therefore called a *Sharp Cord.*

sharpness *see* flatness

shawm *see* aula, auleta, cano, cornet, empneusta (under entata), Ismenias, psaltery, serpent, tibia, tibicen, tibini, tonarion

1702 KERSEY *New Engl. Dict.* (1st edn) A *Shalm,* or *shawm,* a musical instrument. **1706** KERSEY-PHILLIPS (6th edn) *Shalm,* or *Shawm,* a kind of Musical Instrument. **1721** BAILEY *An Univ. Etymolog. Engl. Dict.* (1st edn) *Shalm, Shawm* (*Schallmey,* Teut.) a Sort of Musical Instrument. **1726** BAILEY *An Univ. Etymolog. Engl. Dict.* (3rd edn) *Shalm, Shawm,* (*Schallmey,* Teut.) a sort of Musical Instrument, a Psaltery. *Shawm,* a Musical Instrument, a sort of Psaltery.

shir

1586 ANON. *Praise of Mvsicke* (pp. 137-8) ... Therefore in our English church, the psalmes may be song, and song most cunningly, and with diuerse artificiall instruments of Musick, and song with sundry seuerall and most excellent notes. For proofe that the holy Ghost would haue them song, hee calleth diuerse Psalmes by the name of the Hebrew word *Shir,* which is a song, and such a song, as ought of necessity to be song: as Psalme 7. and 120.

shrill *see* acute, agreslir la voix, argutus, canor, haut, querulous, succortrilla

1737 DYCHE-PARDON (2nd edn) *Shrill* (A.) a loud, sharp, or acute Tone, Sound, or Noise in Musick, called the Treble.

si

1688 MIEGE-COTGRAVE Fr→E *Si, une des sept principales Voix de Musique*

sibbio

1598 FLORIO It→E *Sibbiolo,* ... also a kind of oten pipe or horne pipe. **1611** FLORIO It→E *Sibbio,* a whistle or a pipe. *Sibbiolo,* any kind of whistle or pipe. **1659** TORRIANO-FLORIO It→E **Sibbio, Sibbiolo, Sibilo,* any kind of whistle or whistling-pipe

siciliano *see* sonata

1724 [PEPUSCH] *Short Explic. of Foreign Words in Mus. Bks.* (p. 69) *Siciliane,* a Kind of Jig. See *Saltarella.* **1728** CHAMBERS *Sicilian,* in Music, *&c.* a Kind of gay sprightly Air, or Dance; somewhat of the Nature of an *English* Jig: usually marked with the Characters $\frac{6}{8}$ or $\frac{12}{8}$.

sicinnium *see* siticine, sticine

1538 ELYOT L→E *Sicinnium,* a kynde of daunsynge, wherein they that daunsed dyd synge, as they doo in Christmasse, whan they synge Carolles: and as maydens do nowe vse to doo in the streates. **1552** HULOET L→E *siciniuum.* Daunsynge wyth syngynge. *Sícinnium. ij. tamen usurp.* Christmas caroll. **1565** COOPER L→E *Sicinnium, nij.* A kynde of daunsing wherin they that daunsed did sing. **1587** THOMAS L→E *Sicinnis, f.g. vel Sicinnium, nij, n.g.* A kinde of daunsing, wherein they sung that daunsed. **1589** RIDER L→E *Sicinnium, vel sicinnis, f.* A kind of dancing, when they song [sic] that daunced. **1611** COTGRAVE Fr→E *Sicinnie: f.* A dauncing, and singing together. *Sicinnistes: m.* Such as daunce, and sing together; or, as *Siticines. Rab.* **1650** HOWELL-COTGRAVE Fr→E † *Sicinnie: f.* A dancing, and singing together.

sigh *see* port de voix, sospiro

sign *see* character, figure

1724 [PEPUSCH] *Short Explic. of Foreign Words in Mus. Bks.* (p. 69) *Signes,* or *Signo,* a Sign or Mark: All Notes, Marks, and Characters in Musick are called so, of which there is upwards of Fifty different Sorts. **1726** BAILEY *An Univ. Etymolog.*

Engl. Dict. (3rd edn) *Signes, Signo,* Signs, Notes, Marks or Characters, of which in Musick there are upwards of 50 different Sorts. *Ital.*

after 1517 ANON. Art of Mvsic BL Add. 4911, f. 10v *Sing* [?sign] *quhat is it?* It is ane evident takin quhilk giffis ye first knawleig of modulation fowart Mude tym and prolation quhan the ow ye cirkill saith and half ye quantatie of figure Insthe as determinit **1609** DOWLAND-ORNITHOPARCUS *Micrologvs* (p. 44) ... Therefore a signe is, a certain figure set before a Song, which sheweth the *Moode, Time,* and *Prolation.*

signature

1721 MALCOLM *Treatise of Musick* (p. 341) ... And in the Course of the Song, if the natural Note is sometimes required, it is signified by this Mark ♮. And the marking the *System* at the Beginning with Sharps or Flats, I call the *Signature* of the *Clef.*

signed clef

1597 MORLEY *Plaine and Easie Introdvction* (annotations to Part II) *Claues signata,* or signed Cliffes, ... they be signes for all songes, and vse hath receiued it for a generall rule, not to sette them in the space, because no Cliffe can be so formed as to stand in a space and touch no rule, except the B cliffe. And therefore least any should doubt of their true standing (as for example the G cliffe, if it stood in space and touched a rule, one might iustlie doubt, whether the Author meant G sol re vt in Base, which standeth in space, or G sol re ut in *alto* which standeth of the rule) it hath byn thought best by all the musytions, to set them in rule. Indeed I cannot denie, but that I haue seen some *Are* cliffes, and others in the space: but *Vna hirundo non facit ver.* **1721** MALCOLM *Treatise of Musick* (pp. 557-8) ... But to go one with *Guido;* the Letters he applied to his Lines and Spaces, were called *Keys,* and at first he marked every Line and Space at the Beginning of a Staff with its Letter; afterwards marked only the Lines, as some old Examples shew; and at last marked only one, which was therefore called the *signed Clef;* of which he distinguished Three different ones, *g, c, f;* (the three Letters he had placed his *ut* in) ... **1726** BRUCE *Common Tunes* (p. 6) ... True it is, that every Key in the Scale of Musick may be called a Cliff or Cleave; yet for the better, and more equal Harmony in Musick's Parts, the Learned and Judicious have rationally agreed to these three principal Cliffs, which they call ordinarily by the Name *signed Cliffs,* being assigned and destinate to such principal Parts of Musick as are most harmonious and agreeable. § (p. 10) Q. *Why are these three Cliffs called* signed Cliffs *or* Cleaves? ¶ *A.* As before was hinted, because they have and bear a certain Sign and Mark to distinguish the one Part of Musick from the other; and are called *Cleaves* or *Cliffs* because they open and yield Access one Sound to another, either higher or lower.

sillaba

1724 [PEPUSCH] *Short Explic. of Foreign Words in Mus. Bks.* (pp. 69-70) *Sillaba,* Syllable, an articulate or compleat Sound, made of One or several Letters.

sillet *see* nut

1611 COTGRAVE Fr→E *Scillet: m.* The Nut of a (musicall) Instrument. **1688** MIEGE-COTGRAVE Fr→E *Sillet,* (m.) *C'est le morceau de bois ou d'ivoire, sur lequel posent les Cordes d'un Instrument de Musique.*

simmicium *see* lyre

1721 MALCOLM *Treatise of Musick* (p. 468) ... *Simmicus* also invented an Instrument called *Simmicium* of 35 Strings.

simpla

1500 *Ortus Vocabulorum* L→E Simpla ple. an[e]. a crochette. f.p. **1589** RIDER L→E *Simpla, semiminnima* [sic], *f.* A Crotchet.

simple

1728 CHAMBERS *Simple,* in Music, is chiefly used in Opposition to *Double;* sometimes to a *Compound* of several Parts, or Figures of different Values, *&c.* *Simple Cadence,* is that where the Notes are all equal through all the Parts. *Simple Concords* are those, wherein we hear at least two Notes in Consonance; as a Third, and a Fifth; and, of consequence, at least three Parts: Which is either done immediately, and called the *Harmonical Triad;* or in a more remote Manner; that is, when the Sounds, that are not in the Base, are one or two Octaves higher. This Distance has no ill Effect in the Third; but in the Fifth it has; and, generally speaking, the nearer, or more immediate the Concords are, the better. We also say, *C Simple,* in Opposition to *c* Accented.—*Simple Counter-point,* is a Harmonical Composition, wherein Note is set against Note; in Opposition to a figurative Counter-point. *Simple Fugue,* or *Simple Imitation,* is, when one Part imitates the Singing of another for some Measures. *Simple Interval*: See *Interval. Simple Triple*: See *Triple.* **1730** Bailey *Dict. Britannicum* (1st edn) *Simple* (in *Musick*) is chiefly used in Opposition to Double; sometimes to a Compound of several Parts or Figures of different Values.

simpsalma *see* sympsalma

sinassi *see* synaxis
1611 Florio It→E *Sinassi*, a godly assembly in singing of Psalmes. **1659** Torriano-Florio It→E *Sinassi*, a godly or devout Assembly in singing of Psalms.

sincantor *see* succentor
1656 Blount (1st edn) *Sing-cantor*. See *Succentor.* **1676** Coles *Sing-cantor*, as *Succentor.*

sinfonia *see* symphony

sing *as in bell*
1593 Hollyband Fr→E *Sing*, sometime is a bell, or the ringing of belles: as *les sings sonnent*, the belles doe ring. **1611** Cotgrave Fr→E *Sing: m.* ... also, a bell, or the sound of a bell; whence, *Toc-sing*; an Allarum bell;

sing *as in vocal production, see* cano, chanter
1702 Kersey *New Engl. Dict.* (1st edn) To *sing, or* make melody with the voice. A *Singer*. *Sung* (from to *sing.*) § A *Singing-master.* **1728** Chambers *Singing*, the Action of making divers Inflexions of the Voice, agreeable to the Ear, and even answering to the Notes of a Song or Piece of Melody. See *Song*. ¶ The first thing done in learning to *sing*, is to raise a Scale of Notes by Tones and Semi-tones, to an Octave, and descend again by the same Notes; and then to rise and fall by greater Intervals, as a 3d, 4th, and 5th; and to do all this by Notes of different Pitch. Then these Notes are represented by Lines and Spaces, to which the Syllables *fa, sol, la, mi,* are applied, and the Pupil taught to name each Line and Space thereby; whence this Practice is usually call'd *Sol-fa-ing*. The Nature, Reason, Defects, *&c.* whereof, see under the Article *Sol-fa-ing.* **1736** Bailey *Dict. Britannicum* (2nd edn) *Sung, Sang, Irr. Imp.* (*sunge, sange*, G.) did sing. **1737** Dyche-Pardon (2nd edn) *Sing* (V.) to make Musick with the Voice, and is generally the Indication of Mirth and Pleasure. ¶ *Singing of Psalms*, this has been a very antient Custom both among the *Jews* and *Christians*. St. *Paul* mentions this Practice which was continued in all succeeding Ages with some Variations as to Mode and Circumstance; for so long as immediate Inspiration lasted the Preacher, &c. frequently gave out a Hymn; and when this ceased proper Portions of Scripture were selected, or Hymns agreeable thereto composed; but by the Council of *Laodicea* it was ordered, that no private Compositions should be used in the Church, who also ordered that the Psalms should no longer be one continued Service, but that proper Lessons should be interposed, to prevent the People's being tired. At first the whole Congregation bore a Part singing all together; afterwards the Manner was altered, and they sung alternately, some repeating one Verse and some another. After the Emperors became Christians, and Persecution was over, Singing grew much more in Use, so that not only in the Churches, but also in private Houses Psalms were frequently sung. The ancient Musick not being quite lost, they diversify'd into various Sorts of Harmony, and altered into soft and strong, gay or sad, grave or passionate, &c. Choice was always made of that which best agreed with the Majesty and Purity of Religion, and especial Care taken to avoid soft and effeminate Airs. In some Churches they ordered the Psalms to be pronounced with so small an Alteration of the Voice, that it was little more than plain speaking like the reading Psalms in our Cathedrals at this Day; but in Process of Time instrumental Musick was introduced first among the *Greeks*. Pope *Gregory the Great* refined upon the Church Musick, and made it more exact and harmonious; and that it might be general, he set up Singing Schools in *Rome*, wherein Persons were educated to be sent to foreign Churches, where it has remained ever since; only among the Reformed there are various Ways of performing, and even in the same national Church, particularly that of *England*, in which the Parish Churches differ in Mode very much from the Cathedrals. Most Dissenters comply with this Part of Worship in some Form or other.

1728 North Musicall Grammarian (*C-K MG* f. 105v) And that having such facultys they must necessarily stumble upon the exercise of what wee call singing, that is pronouncing with an open and extended voice; ...

singer
1609 Dowland-Ornithoparcus *Micrologvs* (p. 4) *Who be called Singers.* ¶ The *Practitioner* of this

facultie [of singing] is called a *Cantor*, who doth pronounce and sing those things, which the Musitian by a rule of reason doth set downe. So that the *Harmony* is nothing worth, if the *Cantor* seeke to vtter it without the Rules of reason, and vnlesse he comprehend that which he pronounceth in the puritie of his vnderstanding.

sinistra *see* tibia

siren *see* mermaid, Terpsichore
1500 *Ortus Vocabulorum* L→E Siren enis. i. tractus vel cantus eo q dulcedini sui cantus ad loca periculosa attrahunt nauigantes Pap. aunt puta sirenes esse demones vel dracones. f.t. **1565** COOPER L→E *Sirênes*, Were three daughters of Achelous & Calliope, which dwelled in an ile betweene Italie & Sicilie, who with their sweete synginge drewe suche vnto theim, as passed that sea, and than slewe theim. As it happened Ulysses to sayle that waye, he stopped the eares of all his company, to the entent they shoulde not heare the songes of the Sirenes, and caused himselfe to be bounde to the maste of the shyp, and so escaped. wherfore [sic] ye Sirenes sorowed so much, ye thei wer disapoinctted, that they threw themselues into the sea, whom poetes feigned to be mermaydens. **1616** BULLOKAR *Syren*. A Mermayde: Poets feine there were three Mer-mayds or *Syrens*, in the vpper part like maidens, and in the lower part fishes: which dwelling in the sea of Sicilie, would allure Saylers to them, and afterward destroy them; beeing first brought asleepe with harkening to their sweete singing. Their names were *Parthenope*, *Lygia*, and *Leucasia*; **1658** PHILLIPS (1st edn) *Sirens*, certain Sea-deities, three in number, *Parthenope*, *Ligea*, and *Leucosia*, the daughters of *Achelous* and *Calliope*, having their upper part like maids, and their lower parts like fishes; they used by the sweetnesse of their voices to allure Mariners to the rocks and cause them to be cast away: which *Vlisses* foreseeing, stopt the ears of his associates with soft wax, and caused himself to be bound to the mast of the ship; whereupon they seeing themselves contemned, cast themselves headlong into the Sea. **1688** MIEGE-COTGRAVE Fr→E *Sirene*, (f.) a Mermaid, or Meermaid. § Meermaids (as the Fables tells us, and as we paint them now adaies) are in their upper Parts like Women, and Fish below; or, according to Servius, part Virgins and part Birds; whence called *volueres Puellæ* by *Claud*. They were three of them, Daughters of Achelous and the Muse Calliope, and all of 'em rare Songsters. They ply'd upon the Coast of Sicily, and tempted Passengers on Shore, where they sung them asleep, and then killed and robbed them. The Truth is, they were tempting Harlots. However the Moral is, to shew the Peril of bodily Pleasures, which are likewise three, Meats, Drinks, and Venery. **1706** KERSEY-PHILLIPS (6th edn) *Sirens*, certain Sea-Monsters or Mermaids on the Coasts of *Sicily*, having the upper Parts of their Bodies like Women and the lower ones like Fishes, who (as the Story goes) us'd to allure Passengers on Shore, where they were robb'd and devour'd: But *Vlysses* being desirous to hear their Harmony, stopt the Ears of his Companions with soft Wax, and caus'd himself to be bound to the Main-mast of the Ship; whereupon being discontented at the loss of so great a Prize, they threw themselves into the Sea, and were chang'd into Rocks. Whence 'tis said of a Woman having a charming Voice, That she Sings like a Siren. **1707** *Gloss. Angl. Nova* (1st edn) *Sirens*, Sea-Monsters, that used to allure Men by singing sweetly. **1708** KERSEY *Dict. Anglo-Brit.* (1st edn) *Sirens*, certain fabulous Sea-Monsters or Mermaids on the Coasts of *Sicily*, who by singing us'd to allure Passengers on Shore, where they were robb'd and devour'd. Whence 'tis said of a Woman, having a charming Voice, *That she Sings like a Siren*. **1728** CHAMBERS *Syrens*, *Sirenes*, in Antiquity, *Mermaids*, or certain fabulous Beings .... Some Explainers of the ancient Fables, will have the Number and the Names of the Three *Syrens*, to have been form'd on the Triple Pleasure of the Senses, Wine, Love and Music; which are the three most powerful Means of seducing Men; and hence so many Exhortations to avoid the fatal *Syrens* Song.... Lastly, others allow them to have been certain Shores and Promontories, where the Winds, by the various Reverberations and Echo's, cause a kind of Harmony, that surprizes and stops Passengers. This, probably, might be the Origin of the *Syrens* Song, and of the giving the Name of *Syrens* to these Rocks. **1730** BAILEY *Dict. Britannicum* (1st edn) *Siren* ... a Sort of Monsters who are said to have their upper Parts like beautiful Virgins, and the lower like the Body and Tail of a Fish... These are said to have inhabited between the Coasts of *Italy* and *Sicily*, and to have play'd harmoniously on several Instruments of Musick, and to have sung so melodiously, that they allured Passengers to them to their Destruction. **1737** BAILEY *The Univ. Etymolog. Engl. Dict.* (3rd edn, vol. 2) *Sirens* ... sea monsters famous in the writings of poets .... Their dwelling was upon the coast of the *Sicilian* sea, where they are fabled to

have sung so harmoniously that the mariners who pass'd that way were in danger of being shipwreck'd, by approaching too near the shore, in stopping to hear them.... The poets tell us, that when the *Argonauts* passed that way, the *Sirens* did what they could to charm them; but *Orpheus* taking his harp, made their songs and other attempts useless: whereupon the *Sirens* in despair at being overcome, threw themselves into the sea, and became rocks. **1737** DYCHE-PARDON (2nd edn) *Sirens* (S.) certain Sea Monsters famous in the Writings of Poets, who make them the Daughters of the River *Achelous*, and of one of the nine Muses; they are said to be three in Number; they dwelt on the Coast of the *Sicilian* Sea, and sung so harmoniously that the Mariners were in great Danger of being shipwrecked by coming too near the Shore to hear their Melody; they were partly like beautiful Women, and partly like Birds, having the Wings and Feet of Birds, and other Parts like Women; it is further said, that attempting to charm the *Argonauts* in their Expedition, *Orpheus* so excelled them, that their Attempt proving fruitless, for Revenge they threw themselves into the Sea, and became Rocks; others say they became the Monsters commonly called Mermaids.

siringa *see* syrinx
1565 COOPER L→E *Siringa.* A pype, recorder or flute: **1587** THOMAS L→E *Siringa, vid. Syringa.* or *Syrinx.* **1598** FLORIO It→E *Siringa,* ... Also a reed, a pipe, a flute or a recorder. **1611** FLORIO It→E *Siringa,* ... Also a pipe made of a Cane. *Siringare,* ... Also to play vpon a pipe of a Cane.

sistrum *see* crotalum, rattle
1500 *Ortus Vocabulorum* L→E Sistrum tri. i lingua egipciaca dicit tuba vel instrumentum musicum usitatuz in bellis feiarum. **1538** ELYOT L→E *Sistrum,* an instrument lyke a horne, whiche was vsed in battayle, in the stede of a trumpet. **1565** COOPER L→E *Sistrum, sistri, n. gen. Ouid.* An instrument like an horne, vsed in battayle in steede of a trumpet. Also a brasen timbrell. § *Garrula sistra. Martialis.* Ringing timbrelles. *Tinnula sistra. Ouid.* Ryngyng timbrels. **1587** THOMAS L→E *Sistratus, a, um. Mart.* Holding the instrument *Sistrum.* *Sistrum, stri, n.g. Ouid.* An instrument like an horne, vsed in battell, in stead of a trumpet: *also* a brasen or iron timbrell, &c. *vid. Crotalum.* **1589** RIDER L→E *sistrum.* a brasen, or iron timbrel. *Sistrator, m.* he that playeth on such a timbrel. *Sistratus, m.* The playing on such a timbrel. **1593** HOLLYBAND Fr→E *Vn sistre,* a Citterne: *m.* **1598** FLORIO It→E *Sistro,* a kinde of musicall instrument of brasse, much like a horne. **1611** COTGRAVE Fr→E *Cistre: m.* A kind of brazen timbrell. *Sistre: m.* A kind of brasen Timbrell. **1611** FLORIO It→E *Sistro,* a kinde of musicall instrument of brasse like a horne or cornet, a brazen or iron Timbrell. **1659** TORRIANO-FLORIO It→E *Sistro,* a musical instrument of brasse or iron, called a Timbrel **1688** MIEGE-COTGRAVE Fr→E *Cistre* (m.) *Sistrum,* a kind of Musical Instrument having something of a Lute, and common in Italy. ¶ But, 2 Sam. 6. 5, for the word *Cistres* in French, you will find the word of Cornet, in the English Translation. **1706** KERSEY-PHILLIPS (6th edn) *Sistrum, (Gr.)* a sort of Musical Instrument of an Oval Shape like a Racket, in use among the Ancients. **1728** CHAMBERS *Sistrum* or *Cistrum,* an ancient musical Instrument, used by the Priests of *Isis* and *Osiris. Spon* describes it as of an oval Form, in manner of a Racket, with three Sticks traversing it breadth-wise, which playing freely, by the Agitation or Beating of the Instrument, made a kind of Sound, which to the Ancient seem'd melodious. Mr. *Malcolm* takes the *Sistrum* to have been no better than a kind of a Rattle. *Jer. Bosius* has an express Treatise on the *Sistrum,* intitled, *Isiacus de Sistro. Oiselius* observes, that the *Sistrum* is found represented on several Medals; and also on *Talismano. Osiris* on some Medals, is painted with a Dog's Head and a *Sistrum* in his Hand. **1730** BAILEY *Dict. Britannicum* (1st edn) *Sistrum,* an antient Musical Instrument used by the Priests of *Isis* and *Osiris,* L. **1737** DYCHE-PARDON (2nd edn) *Sistrum* (S.) an *Egyptian* Musical Instrument used by the Priests of *Isis,* who is said to be the Inventress thereof; 'twas of an Oval Figure, or a dilated Semi-circle, in the Shape of a Shoulder Belt, with Brass Wires across, which played in Holes, wherein they were stopped by their flat Heads, &c.

1582 *Batman vppon Bartholome* (chap. 134) *Sistrum* is an instrument of musicke, & hath the name of a Ladye that first brought it vp. For it is proued that *Isis* Queene of *Egypt,* was the first finder of *Systrum,* and *Iuuenal* speaketh thereof, and saith.

siticine *see* sicinnium, sticine
1538 ELYOT L→E *Siticen,* he that dyd blowe in a trumpet whan men were buryed. **1565** COOPER L→E *Siticen, ticinis.* He that did blow in a trumpette when men weare buried, or he that singeth at burials. **1587** THOMAS L→E *Siticen, inis, com. g.*

Cato. He that did blow in a trumpet, or sing to a pipe, when men were buried. **1589** RIDER L→E *Siticen, com. g.* A trumpeter at funeralles. **1611** COTGRAVE Fr→E *Siticines: m.* That sounded Trumpets, or sung vnto Pipes, at Funeralls: *Rab.* **1706** KERSEY-PHILLIPS (6th edn) *Siticines*, (*Lat.* among the *Romans*) were those who sounded upon a sort of Trumpet that had a very sorrowful and mournful Tone, at their Funeral Solemnities.

sixth *see* hexachord, minor, pentatonon, sesta, sexte

1728 CHAMBERS *Sixth*, in Music, one of the Simple Original Concords, or Harmonical Intervals. See *Concord*. The *Sixth* is of two Kinds; *greater* and *lesser*; and hence is esteem'd one of the Imperfect Concords; though each of them arise from a Division of the Octave. See *Octave*. The greater *Sixth* is the Concord resulting from a Mixture of the Sounds of two Strings, that are to each other as 3 to 5. The lesser *Sixth* results from two Strings, which are to each other as 5 to 8. See *Scale*. The lesser *Sixth* is composed Diatonically of Six Degrees, whence its Name; and of Five Intervals, Three whereof are Tones, and Two Semi-tones; Chromatically of Eight Semi-tones; Five whereof are greater, and Three less. It has its Form or Origin from the *Ratio, Super-tri-partiens quintas*, as of 8 to 5. The greater is composed Diatonically like the less, of Six Degrees and Five Intervals; among which are Four Tones, and a Semi-tone. And Chromatically of Nine Semi-tones; Five whereof are greater, and Four less; of Consequence it has a less Semi-tone more than the former. It has its Origin from the *Ratio Super-bi-partiens tertius*, as of 5 to 3. Anciently the *Sixth* had only one Reply, which was the 13th; but in the modern System, it has several, as the 20th, 27th, *&c.* all marked indifferently in the thorough Base, by the Figure 6. And even the *Sixth* itself, both greater and lesser, when used naturally, is not expressed any otherwise than by a Simple *Sixth*. But when 'tis greater or less accidentally, to the 6 is added some other Mark, as may be seen in M. *Brosset*. ¶ Besides the two kinds of *Sixth*'s have described, which are both good Concords; there are two others that are vitious and dissonant. The first is the *Defective Sixth*, composed of two Tones and three Semi-tones, or of Seven Semi-tones, five whereof are greater, and two less. The second is the *Redundant Sixth*, composed of Four Tones, a greater Semi-tone, and a less. Whence some call it *Pentatonon*, as comprehending Four Tones. These two being both dissonant, should never be used in Melody, and very rarely in Harmony. ¶ As to the two Consonant *Sixth*'s, they were anciently to be used very sparingly; but at present we make them as often as we please, as we do with Thirds; the *Sixths* being in reality, no other than inverted Thirds; but Care is usually taken, that the first *Sixth* that occurrs [sic] be less, and the last greater; and that from the greater, we rise to the Octave, and from the less, fall to the Fifth. **1730** BAILEY *Dict. Britannicum* (1st edn) *Sixth* (in *Musick*) one of the original 2 Concords or harmonical Intervals. **1737** DYCHE-PARDON (2nd edn) *Sixth* (A.) ... in *Musick*, it is deemed one of the original Concords, or harmonical Intervals.

sixth lesser, sixth greater

1721 MALCOLM *Treatise of Musick* (p. 260) ... of the *6ths* [16:27, 3:5, 5:8] one is *false*, and the other Two which are *harmonical*, are called *6th g.* and *6th l.*

sixth tone

1609 DOWLAND-ORNITHOPARCUS *Micrologvs* (p. 33) The Sixt *Tone* is a Rule, determining a *plagall* of the third sort. Or it is the *plagall* Progression of the third, participating iustly with his *Authenticall* in the finall Notes. To whom there befall foure beginnings, *viz. C. D. F.* and *a*, saith *Franchinus* in the 13. chapter of his *Practick*; and *Guido* in his doctrinall Dialogue.

slide *see* slur

1676 MACE *Musick's Monument* (p. 108) The *Slide*, is near of Kin to the *Slur*, and differs only *Thus*; your *Notes* are always *Descending*, and *Mark'd* with a *Hoop, or Slide*, as your *Slur*... **c.1695** NORTH Notes of Me BL Add. 32506 (*JWi* p. 19) Then next the grace of passing from one [note] to another, which in some sort connects them, though severall; as if they were links in a chaine, very distinct, yet connected all together. For if there be any pause between note and note, it is amiss; but with the same breath as one note ends, the next begins. And if you would take a distinct breath to each note, it must not begin with the entrance of [the] next, but with the expiring of the last, otherwise there will be a stopp more sensible upon the taking breath. This is that is called a slide, and in hand instruments is done with the finger, mixing the neighbour notes a litle in the transition. Even the organ and harpsicord will doe the same thing, as may be observed upon any one's playing, for nature itself almost leads to it. **1731** PRELLEUR *Modern Musick-Master* (III *re* flute, p. 9) ... the Slide is taken a Note above, and is never pratis'd by in descending to a third...

slow

1721 MALCOLM *Treatise of Musick* (p. 395) In the present Practice, tho' the same Notes of *Time* are of the same Measure in any one Piece, yet in different Pieces they differ very much, and the Differences are in general marked by the Words *slow, brisk, swift,* &c. written at the Beginning; but still these are uncertain Measures, since there are different Degrees of *slow* and *swift*; ...

slur *see* double cadence, grace, legare, slide, transition

1737 DYCHE-PARDON (2nd edn) *Slur* (S.) ... also a Mark in Musick made over the Heads of several Notes, to denote that so many as are contained under it are to be sounded with one drawing of the Bow, Breathing, &c. *Slur* (V.) ... also to play many Notes upon a Musical Instrument with one Drawing of the Bow, &c.

1676 MACE *Musick's Monument* (p. 108) The next therefore, is the *Slur*, and is no more than the *Falling* of so many *Letters, (Ascending)* as you can, upon *Any one String*; only by hitting the 1*st*. as you did the *Whole-fall*... **1681** B[ANISTER] *Most Pleasant Companion* (p. 6) The fourth Grace is called a slur, and *Beat*, and is played thus, hit your first Note with the tip of your Tongue, and continuing your Breath take up your second, and bring on the first Beating. **c.1700** NORTH Capt. Prencourts rules BL Add. 32549, f. 11v This mark .ε. signifyes a slurr, wch is a grace to be made to a note before wch it doth stand, you begin a 3rd below the Note, and goe quick thro ye second to it; It must be done very swift or ye Grace is lost. **c.1710** NORTH Short, Easy, & plaine rules BL Add. 32531, f. 24 [quoting Prendcourt:] This Mark. ε. signifies a Slurr, wch is a grace to be made to a Note before wch it doth stand. You begin a 3^{d} below ye Note, & goe quite thro ye second to it. It must be done very swift or ye Grace is lost. **1724** TURNER *Sound Anatomiz'd* (p. 63) When you see an *Arch* (which we call a Slur) over the Heads of two, or more *Notes*, thus; ⌒ or underneath thus; ‿ those *Notes* so arched in, are to be sung all in on[e] *Vowel* or *Syllable*. **c.1726** NORTH Musicall Gramarian BL Add. 32533, f. 109 That species wch I called the slur, hath some affinity with the beat up & back fall, onely Instead of one tone or semitone rising or falling this will will [sic] be of a 3^{d} or a fifth Asending [sic] or descending and, as I think hath the best effect of any Grace of the hand whatever, ffor (altho proceeding) consequentially it makes out the just accords of ye Notes, litle short of consonancys. **[1729]** HOTTETERRE *Rudiments or Principles of German Flute* (p. 12) ... First the little curve line over, or under y^{e} heads of two, or more Notes, commonly call'd a Slur, and markt as you see in this Example on y^{e} right hand;  Signifies, that you must only tip the first of them with your tongue, which here serves only as a preparation, (or what in French is call'd a *Port de voix*) to the Cadence, or Shake, and you are to continue ye same wind, without drawing your breath, to the end of the Cadence, or Shake, as I have already shew'd you. **1731** PRELLEUR *Modern Musick-Master* (III *re* flute, pp. 4-5) ... the little curve line over, or under the heads of two, or more Notes, commonly call'd a Slur, and ... Signifies, that you must only 'tip the first of them with your tongue w$^{ch.}$ here serves only as a preparation, (or what in French is call'd a *Port de voix*) to the Cadence, or Shake, and you are to continue y^{e} same wind. [sic] without drawing your breath, to the end of the Cadence or Shake ... § (III *re* flute, p. 9) Slur[r]ing is when two, or more Notes are pass'd over with only one tip with the tongue, which is markt by a Curve line, over or under ye Heads of the Notes... § (V *re* violin, p. 7) There is also another sort of Grace call'd a Slur and marked thus (⌒) which is sometimes set over two, three, or more Notes to shew that all the Notes comprehended within it must be drawn with one Bow ...

smuma

1500 *Ortus Vocabulorum* L→E Smuma me. i. canticum. f.p.

soave

1724 [PEPUSCH] *Short Explic. of Foreign Words in Mus. Bks.* (p. 70) *Soave*, Sweet or Agreeable. **1726** BAILEY *An Univ. Etymolog. Engl. Dict.* (3rd edn) *Soave*, sweet, agreeable. *Ital.*

1731 PRELLEUR *Modern Musick-Master* (Dictionary, p. 3) *Soave* or *Soavemente* Sweet or Agreable.

soavemente

1724 [PEPUSCH] *Short Explic. of Foreign Words in Mus. Bks.* (p. 70) *Soavemente*, Sweetly or Agreeably. **1726** BAILEY *An Univ. Etymolog. Engl. Dict.* (3rd edn) *Soavement*, sweetly, agreeably. *Ital.*

sociandus

1565 COOPER L→E *Sociandus. Aliud participium: vt Verba socianda chordis. Horat. Versus lyrici.* Balades to be songe to the harpe. **1587** THOMAS L→E *Sociandus, a, um, Horat.* To be ioyned, fitted, or sung to.

soga *see* bandrol, cascata, pendaglio, scatta

1611 FLORIO It→E *Soga,* ... Also a horne-string or scarfe fastned to a Hunters horne. **1659** TORRIANO-FLORIO It→E *Soga,* any horn-string or skarf fastned to a hunters horn

sol

1598 FLORIO It→E *Sol,* a note of musike. **1611** FLORIO It→E *Sol,* a note in Musike **1706** KERSEY-PHILLIPS (6th edn) *Sol, (Lat.)* ... Also the Name of one of the Musical Notes. See *Notes.* **1721** BAILEY *An Univ. Etymolog. Engl. Dict.* (1st edn) *Sol,* (in *Musick*) the Name of one of the Notes, in the Gamut. **1724** [PEPUSCH] *Short Explic. of Foreign Words in Mus. Bks.* (p. 70) *Sol,* one of the Notes in the Gamut is so called. **1728** CHAMBERS *Sol,* in Music, the Fifth Note of the Gamut: Ut, Re, Mi, Fa, Sol. See *Note* and *Gamut*; see also *Music.* **1737** DYCHE-PARDON (2nd edn) *Sol* (S.) ... in *Musick,* it is the contracted Name of several Notes in the Scale or Gamut, such as *G. sol re, &c. D. la. sol re, &c.*

solennité

1570/71 *Dict. Fr. and Engl.* Fr→E *Solennité,* sound, tune. **1593** HOLLYBAND Fr→E *Solennité,* sound, tune: *f.*

solfa

1598 FLORIO It→E *Insolfare,* to set pricke song. *Solfa,* prick-song. *Solfeggiare,* to sing prick-song, to solfa it. *Zolfa,* prick-song. **1611** COTGRAVE Fr→E *Solfe: f.* A solfa; a note in singing. **1611** FLORIO It→E *Insolfare,* ... Also to sol fa or set pricke-song. *Solfa,* a note in musike, pricke song. *Solfeggiare,* to sol-fa, or sing prike-song. *Zolfa,* solfa or prickesong. **1659** TORRIANO-FLORIO It→E **Insolfare, Insolferate,* ... also to Sol, Fa, or set prick-song. *Sol fa,* a note in Musick or prick-song. *Solfare, Solfeggiare,* to *Sol-fa,* or sing prick-song. *Zol-fa,* as *Sol-fa,* pricksong. **1704** *Cocker's Engl. Dict.* (1st edn) *Sol-fa,* two notes in Musick, the other three being *mi, re, ut.*

solfaing

1728 CHAMBERS *Sol-fa-ing* ... [*see* Appendix] **1730** BAILEY *Dict. Britannicum* (1st edn) *Sol-fa-ing* (in *Singing*) the naming and pronouncing the several Notes of a Song, by the Syllables *sol, fa, la, &c.* **1737** DYCHE-PARDON (2nd edn) *Sol-fa-ing* (S.) the Art and Act of singing a Tune by the contracted Names of the Notes in which it is composed, calling them sol, la, mi, fa, &c.

1609 DOWLAND-ORNITHOPARCUS *Micrologvs* (p. 14) *Solfaing* is the orderly singing of euery Song by Musicall *Voyces,* according as *Mi* and *Fa* shall require. For to *Sol fa* (as *Gafforus* witnesseth) is to expresse the Syllables, and the names of the *Voyces.*

sollecito

1724 [PEPUSCH] *Short Explic. of Foreign Words in Mus. Bks.* (p. 70) *Sollecito,* signifies Grief or Sorrow. **1726** BAILEY *An Univ. Etymolog. Engl. Dict.* (3rd edn) *Sollecito,* Grief, Sorrow. *Ital.*

solo *see* voce

1724 [PEPUSCH] *Short Explic. of Foreign Words in Mus. Bks.* (pp. 70-1) *Solo,* Singly, or Alone; or by Way of Abbreviation the Letter *S.* This Word or Letter is often met with in Pieces of Musick of several Parts, when one Part is to perform alone: Thus, ¶ *Violino Solo,* is the Violin alone. ¶ *Fiauto Solo,* the Flute alone. ¶ *Organo Solo,* the Organ alone. ¶ This Word is also used to distinguish those Sonatas for One Violin and a Bass, or One Flute and a Bass, from those with Two Violins and a Bass, or Two Flutes and a Bass. Thus the Fifth Opera of *Corelli's* Sonatas, which are composed for One Violin and a Bass, are commonly called Solo's, to distinguish them from the First, Second, Third, and Fourth Opera's, which are composed for Two Violins and a Bass. **1726** BAILEY *An Univ. Etymolog. Engl. Dict.* (3rd edn) *Solo* (in *Musick Books*) stands for singly or alone. It is frequently us'd in Pieces of Musick of several Parts, when one part is to perform alone, as *fiauto solo,* the Flute alone, *Organo solo,* the Organ alone, and *Violino solo,* the Violin alone. *Solo* (in *Musick*) is also used to distinguish those Sonatas, for one Violin and a Bass, or one Flute and a Bass, from those with 2 Violins and a Bass, or 2 Flutes and a Bass. And so the 5th Opera of *Corelli's* Sonatas, which are composed for one Violin and a Bass, are commonly call'd *Solo's,* to distinguish them from the 1st, 2d, 3d and 4th Operas, which are composed for 2 Violins and a Bass. *Ital.* **1737** DYCHE-PARDON (2nd edn) *Solo* (S.) something single or alone; but in *Musick,* it properly signifies those Compositions where there is but one single upper Instrument, whose Airs or Lessons would be very pleasant, even without the Accompaniment of a Bass, as are *Corelli's* Solo's, &c.

c.1715-20 NORTH Essay of Musical Ayre BL Add. 32536, f. 35 In the next place the superior parts are to be considered, and first that wch they Call a Solo with a Basso Continuo attending; ... **1731** PRELLEUR *Modern Musick-Master* (Dictionary, p. 3) *Solo,* Alone as *Violino Solo,* Violin Alone; *Flauto Solo;* Flute Alone; *Organo Solo,* the Organ Alone, &c. **1736** TANS'UR *Compleat Melody* (3rd edn, p. 71) *Solus,* or *Solâ,* signifies, *alone*; and often set over such *Parts* that are to be performed alone.—*Solâ,* is also a *Name* given to a Piece of *Musick* that is but for one *Violin,* one *Flute,* and a *Bass;* to distinguish it from those that are for two *Violins,* two *Flutes,* and a *Bass*: and are called *Solâ's,* (Ital.)

sommier *see* canon, soundboard

1593 HOLLYBAND Fr→E *Sommier musical, m*: see *Canon.* **1611** COTGRAVE Fr→E *Sommier: m.* ... also, the Sound-boord of an Organ;

son *see* sound

1570/71 *Dict. Fr. and Engl.* Fr→E *Son,* sound, tune. *Sonner,* to sound, to ring. § *Arains sonnans,* ringing plates. **1593** HOLLYBAND Fr→E *Son,* sound, tune: *m.* § *Arains sonnans,* ringing plates. **1611** COTGRAVE Fr→E *Son: m.* A sound; voyce, noyse, dinne; tune, musicke, melodie. **1688** MIEGE-COTGRAVE Fr→E *Son* (a masc. Subst.) sound; § *le Son d'une Cloche, d'un Verre, d'une Trompette, d'un Lut, d'une Guitare,* the sound of a Bell, of a Glass, of a Trumpet, of a Lute, or of a Guitar.

sonagliera *see* caxa

1550 THOMAS It→E *Sonagli,* hawkes belles. **1598** FLORIO It→E *Sonagliera,* ... Also a set of bels as morris dancers dance with. *Sonaglietti,* little haukes bels or childrens rattles. **1611** FLORIO It→E *Sonagliera,* a set of bells as Morice-dancers vse. *Sonalietti,* little bells for Hawkes, or about Dogs necks. Also childrens rattles. **1659** TORRIANO-FLORIO It→E *Sonaglietti, Sonaglini, Sonagliuoli,* any kind of hawks bells or such as Morice-dancers use

sonaglio

1598 FLORIO It→E *Sonaglio,* a little bell, a haukes bell, a rattle. **1611** FLORIO It→E *Sonaglio,* a Hawkes bell. Also a childes rattle.

sonante *see* absonant

1659 TORRIANO-FLORIO It→E *Sonante,* sounding, resounding, ringing, also playing upon any instrument.

sonare

1598 FLORIO It→E *Sonare,* to sound, to resound, to ring bels, to play on any instrument, to winde a horne, to sound a trumpet, to make a noise **1611** FLORIO It→E *Sonare,* ... to ring bells, to strike vp a drum, to winde a horne, to sound a trumpet, to play on instruments. **1659** TORRIANO-FLORIO It→E *Sonare,* to sound, to sound a trumpet, to wind a horn, to play on any instrument, to ring the bells § **Sonare a distesa,* to ring all out. **Sonare a doppio,* to ring a double peal *Sonare a festa,* to ring for an holyday. *Sonare in capitolo,* to ring out for all the the [sic] people to come together. **1688** DAVIS-TORRIANO-FLORIO It→E § **Sonare a distesa,* to sing all out. **Sonare in capitolo,* to ring out for the people to gather together.

sonata *see* camera, canzona, canzonetta, chiesa, concerto, descant, fancy, fantasia, grave, obligata, solo

1550 THOMAS It→E *Sonatore,* the sounner, as the minstrell or ringer of belles. **1598** FLORIO It→E *Sonata,* a sounding or fit of mirth. *Sonatore,* a sounder, a minstrell, a fidler, a musition, a plaier vpon instruments. **1611** FLORIO It→E *Sonatore,* a sounder, a plaier on instruments, a minstrell, a fidler, a musicion. *Suonata,* any sound of Musike. *Suonatore,* as *Sonatore.* **1659** TORRIANO-FLORIO It→E *Sonata,* a ringing, a sounding noise, a fit of mirth vpon instruments. *Sonato,* sounded, rung, played upon. *Sonatore,* a sounder, a ringer, a minstrel, a player on instruments. *Suonata,* a ring or peal, as *Sonata.* **1724** [PEPUSCH] *Short Explic. of Foreign Words in Mus. Bks.* (p. 72) *Sonata.* See the Word *Suonata.* (pp. 74-5) *Suonata,* or *Sonata,* is the Name of certain Pieces of Instrumental Musick, which being very common, and well known, needs no particular Description. Of these there are Two Sorts, One intended for the Churches or Chapels, and therefore called *Sonata di Chiesa,* or Church Sonatas; the others intended for Chambers or Private Consorts, and therefore called *Sonata da Camera,* or Chamber Sonatas. ¶ *N.B.* Of *Corelli's* Musick the First and Third Operas are Church Sonatas, and the Second and Fourth Operas are Chamber Sonatas; though the common Distinction among us is made by calling his First and Third Operas by the Name of Sonatas, and the Second and Fourth by the Name of Airs. **1726** BAILEY *An Univ. Etymolog. Engl. Dict.* (3rd edn) *Suonata, Sonata,* (in *Musick Books*) is the Name of certain Pieces of Instrumental Musick, well known. They are of two Sorts, one for Churches and Chapels called *sonata di Chiesa,* or Church *S[o]nata*'s; the other for Chambers or private Concerts, called *sonata de Camera,* or Chamber Sonata's. *Ital.* **1728** CHAMBERS *Sonata,* in Music, a Term called by the *Italians, Suonata,* or *Suono,* Sound, as signifying a Piece or Composition of Music, wholly executed by Instruments; and which is, with regard to the several Kinds of Instruments, what the *Cantata* is, with regard to Voices. See *Cantata.* ¶ The *Sonata,* then, is properly a grand, free, humorous Composition, diversified with a great Variety of Motions and Expressions, extraordinary and bold Strokes, Figures, *&c.* And all this purely accordingly to the Fancy of the Composer; who, without confining himself to any general Rules of Counter-Point, or to any fix'd Number or Measure, gives a Loose to his Genius, runs from one Mode, Measure, *&c.* to another, as he thinks fit. ¶ We have Cantata's of 1, 2, 3, 4, 5, 6, 7, and even 8 Parts; but usually they are performed by a single Violin, or with two Violins and a thorough Bass for the Harpsichord, and frequently a more figured Bass for the Bass-Viol, *&c.* ¶ There are a Thousand different Species of *Sonata*'s; but the *Italians* usually reduce them to three Kinds: *Suonata de Chiese;* that is, *Sonata*'s proper for Church-Music, which usually begin with a grave, solemn Motion, suitable to the Dignity and Sanctity of the Place and the Service; after which they strike into a brisker, gayer and richer Manner. These are what they properly call *Sonata*'s. ¶ The second Kind comprehends the *Suonate de Camera,* or *Sonata*'s proper for the Chamber, *&c.* These are properly Series's of several little Pieces, proper for Dancing; only composed to the same Tune. They usually begin with a Prelude or little *Sonata,* serving as an Introduction to all the rest: Afterwards come the *Alleman, Pavan, Courant,* and other serious Dances; then *Gigues, Gavots, Minuets, Chacons, Passecailles* and other gayer Airs: The whole composed in the same Tone or Mode. [no third category follows] **1730** BAILEY *Dict. Britannicum* (1st edn) *Sonata,* a Piece or Composition of Musick, wholly performed by Instruments. **1737** DYCHE-PARDON (2nd edn) *Sonata* (S.) among the *Musicians,* is a Piece or Composition of Musick in various Parts to be performed by Instruments only.

1721 MALCOLM *Treatise of Musick* (p. 406) We have also a Variety of such Pieces united in one principal *Key,* and such an Agreement of Air as is consistent with the different *Modes* of *Time;* and such Composition of different Airs is called, in a large Sense, one Piece of *Melody,* under the general Name of *Sonata* if 'tis designed only for Instruments, or *Cantata* if for the Voice; and these several lesser Pieces have also different Names, such as *Allemanda, Gavotta,* &c. (which are always *common Time) Minuet, Sarabanda, Giga, Corrante, Siciliana,* &c. which are *triple Time.* **1728** NORTH Musicall Grammarian (*C-K MG* f. 83v) The instrumentall musick of late hath bin listed mostly under the title of sonnatas which being consorts of 3 and rarely of 4 parts, and more hands requiring to be imployed, some parts have bin doubled; but that not succeeding well (plainely) the very doubling hath bin improved by art as in the conciertos, which have assigned the separations and conjunctions with better effect; ... **1731** PRELLEUR *Modern Musick-Master* (Dictionary, p. 3) *Suonata,* or *Sonata,* a Piece of Musick for Instruments. **after 1731** ANON. *Directions for Playing on the Flute* (Dictionary, n.p.) *Sonata*: a piece of musick for instruments. **1736** TANS'UR *Compleat Melody* (3rd edn, p. 71) *Sonata, Suonata, Scionata,* (Ital.) Either of those *Names* are applied to a Piece of *Musick* composed only for *Instruments,* &c.

sonatina

1724 [PEPUSCH] *Short Explic. of Foreign Words in Mus. Bks.* (p. 75) *Suonatina,* a Little, Short, Plain, or Easy Sonata. **1730** BAILEY *Dict. Britannicum* (1st edn) *Suonantina* [sic], a little, short, plain, and easy Sonata, *Ital.*

song *see* air, ballad, bargaret, berlingozzo, bucolick, canticle, cantion, canto, chanson, chant, dithyramb, ditty, hymn, mock song, ode, part, pastoral, plainsong, psalm, sonnet

1702 KERSEY *New Engl. Dict.* (1st edn) A *Song* (from to sing) **1721** BAILEY *An Univ. Etymolog. Engl. Dict.* (1st edn) A *Song,* (ſanȝ, *Sax. sang.* Du. *and* Dan.) a Verse or Composure sung **1728** CHAMBERS *Song,* in Poetry, a little Composition, consisting of simple, easy, natural Verses, set to a Tune, in order to be sung. See *Singing.* ¶ Each Stanza of a *Song,* is called a *Couplet.* See *Stanza* and *Couplet.* ¶ The *Song* bears a deal of Resemblance to the *Madrigal;* and move to the *Ode,* which is nothing but a Song according to the ancient Rules. See *Madrigal* and

Ode. ¶ Its Object is usually either Wine or Love; whence M. *le Brun* defines a modern *Song*, to be either a soft and amorous, or a brisk and bacchic Thought, express'd in a few Words. ¶ Indeed, this is to restrain it to too narrow Bounds; for we have devout *Songs*, satyrical *Songs*, and panegyrical *Songs*. ¶ But, be the *Song* what it will, the Verses are to be easy, natural, flowing, and to contain a certain Harmony, which neither shocks the Reason nor the Ear; and which unites Poetry and Music agreeably together. ¶ Anciently, the only Way of preserving the Memory of great and noble Actions, was, by recording them in *Songs;* and in *America* there are still People, who keep their whole History in *Songs*. See *Druid*. ¶ *Song*, in Music, is applied to the General, to any single Piece of Music, whether contrived for a Voice or Instrument. See *Music* and *Composition*. ¶ A *Song*, Mr. *Malcolm* observes, may be compared to an Oration: For, as in this latter, there is a Subject, *viz.* some Person or Thing the Discourse is referr'd to, and which is always to be kept in View throughout the whole; so, in every truly regular and melodious *Song*, there is one Note which regulates all the rest; wherein the *Song* begins, and at last ends, and which is, as it were, the principal Matter, or musical Subject, to be regarded in the whole Course of the *Song*. And, as in the Oration, there may be several distinct Parts, which refer to particular Subjects, yet must they have an evident Connection with the principal Subject, which regulates the whole; so in Melody, there may be several sub-principal Subjects, to which the different Parts of the *Song* may belong: But these are, themselves, under the Influence of the principal Subject, and must have a sensible Connection with it. This principal or fundamental Note, is called the *Key of the Song*. See *Key*. **1731** KERSEY *New Engl. Dict.* (3rd edn) A *Song*, any poetical Composition which is sung. **1737** DYCHE-PARDON (2nd edn) *Song* (S.) a particular Set of Words either in Prose or Verse set to Musick, in order to be sung or sounded with or by the Voice.

1589 [PUTTENHAM] *Arte of English Poesie* (p. 47) ... So haue we remembred and set forth to your Maiestie very briefly, all the commended fourmes of the auncient Poesie, which we in our vulgare makings do imitate and vse vnder these common names: enterlude, song, ballade, carroll and ditty: borrowing them also from the French al sauing this word (song) which is our naturall Saxon English word. **1609** DOWLAND-ORNITHOPARCUS *Micrologvs* (p. 26) Wherfore a Song is a melody formed of a *Sound, Mood,* & *Tone,* by a liuely Voice. I say by a *sound,* because of the writing of the Notes, which improperly we call a Song: By the *moode,* I vnderstand rising and falling, because of the prayers which are read in an Vnison. By the *Tone,* because of the chirping of birds, which is comprehended within no *Tone.* For [what] within a *Syllogisme* is *moode* and *figure*, that in a Song is the *Tone* and Scale. I say a liuely Voyce, because of Musicall Instruments. Or otherwise: A Song is the fitting of a liuely Voyce according to rising, and falling, Or (as *Gafforus* writeth in his *Theoricks lib.* 5. *cap.* 6.) it is the deduction of many Voyces from the same beginning. And this description doth properly agree to this progression of syllables, because it is not a Song. **1721** MALCOLM *Treatise of Musick* (pp. 266) ... a *melodious Song* may be brought under this general Definition, *viz. A Collection of Sounds or Notes (however produced) differing in* Tune *by the* Degrees *or* harmonious Intervals *of the* Scale *of* Musick, *which succeeding other in the Ear, after equal or unequal* Duration *in their respective* Tunes, *affect the Mind with Pleasure.*

songedest

1726 BAILEY *An Univ. Etymolog. Engl. Dict.* (3rd edn) *Songedest,* didst sing. *Chauc.*

songlietti *see* sonagliera

song of Solomon *see* canticle

songster

1702 KERSEY A *Songster, or* singer. **1730** BAILEY *Dict. Britannicum* (1st edn) *Songster* (ʃanᵹeꞃe, *Sax.*) a Singer of Songs. **1731** KERSEY *New Engl. Dict.* (3rd edn) A *Songster*, a Person that sings Songs. **1737** DYCHE-PARDON (2nd edn) *Songster* (S.) one that performs Musical Compositions with the Voice or sings Songs, to which particular Notes are adapted.

soniolo

1611 FLORIO It→E *Soniolo,* vsed for a low-bell.

sonnaille

1593 HOLLYBAND Fr→E *Sonnaille,* the bell which cattell haue about their necke: *f.* **1611** COTGRAVE Fr→E *Sonnaille: f.* A little bell; and particularly, the bell hung about the necke of a Weather, or heard-beast. *Sonnaillerie: f.* A tinkling, or the tingling of a little bell. *Sonnaillier: m. ere: f.* Carrying a bell;

sonnet
1550 THOMAS It→E *Sonetti,* baletts or short songes. **1598** FLORIO It→E *Sonettare,* to compose, write, or sing sonnets. *Sonetto,* a sonnet, a canzonet, a song. **1611** COTGRAVE Fr→E *Sonnet: m.* A sonnet, or canzonet, a song (most commonly) of 14 verses. **1611** FLORIO It→E *Sonettare,* to compose or sing Sonnets. *Sonettiere,* a composer or singer of Sonnets. *Sonetto,* a Sonnet, a Canzonet, a Song. **1702** KERSEY *New Engl. Dict.* (1st edn) A *Sonnet,* a sort of song *or* poem, consisting of 14 verses. **1730** BAILEY *Dict. Britannicum* (1st edn) *Sonnet* (*sonnet,* Ital.) a short Song, *&c.* a sort of *Italian* Poem ... **1737** DYCHE-PARDON (2nd edn) *Sonnet* (S.) a short Song or Poem sung to some pleasant Tune, especially Love Songs.

sonnette *see* sance bell
1570/71 *Dict. Fr. and Engl.* Fr→E *Sonnette,* a little bell. **1593** HOLLYBAND Fr→E *Sonnette,* a little bell: *f.* **1611** COTGRAVE Fr→E *Sonnette: f.* A little bell, Antham bell, Sans or sacring bell; any small tinging bell; as the bell about the necke of a Bell-weather, &c; **1688** MIEGE-COTGRAVE Fr→E *Sonnette,* (f.) *sorte de petit Cloche de cuivre, d'argent, ou de vermeil doré,* a little Bell, any small tinkling Bell.

sono *see* suona
1598 FLORIO It→E *Sono,* ... a worde, a tune, a note

sonorous
1737 DYCHE-PARDON (2nd edn) *Sonorous* (A.) sounding or that is capable and ready of yielding or producing Sounds, especially those proper for Musical Distinctions.

sono submisso
1565 COOPER L→E § *Sono submisso dicere aliquid. Tibull.* To vtter in a base tune.

sonus summus
1565 COOPER L→E *Sonus summus, medius, imus. Plin.* The treable, the meane, the base. **1587** THOMAS L→E *Sonus summus, medius, imus, Plin.* The treable, the meane, the base.

sopralto *see* soprano
1598 FLORIO It→E *Sopralto,* ... Also a chiefe treble in musicke. **1611** FLORIO It→E *Sopralto,* ... Also a chiefe treble in musike. **1659** TORRIANO-FLORIO It→E *Sopr'-alto,* high above others, also the trebble of any voice or instrument.

soprano *see* cantarella, contra-sovrano, sopralto
1598 FLORIO It→E *Soprana,* Also the treble string of any instrument. *Soprano,* ... Also the treble in musike. **1611** FLORIO It→E *Soprana,* ... Also the treble string of any instrument. *Soprano,* ... Also the treble voice or string. **1688** DAVIS-TORRIANO-FLORIO It→E *Soprano,* ... also the trebble string of any instrument.

sordine *see* buccina, mute, piva
1598 FLORIO It→E *Sordina,* a sordine to put in a trumpet to make it sound lowe. **1611** COTGRAVE Fr→E *Sourdine: f.* A Sourdet; the little pipe, or tenon put into the mouth of a Trumpet, to make it sound low; also, a Sordine, or a kind of hoarse, or low-sounding Trumpet. **1611** FLORIO It→E *Sordina,* a surdine to put in a trumpet to make it sound low. **1656** BLOUNT (1st edn) *Sordine* or *Sordet* (from the Fr. *Sourdine*) the little Pipe or Tenon, put into the mouth of a Trumpet, to make it sound low; also a kinde of hoarse or low sounding Trumpet. **1658** PHILLIPS (1st edn) *Sordet,* or *Sordine,* (French) a pipe put into the mouth of a Trumpet, to make it sound lower. **1676** COLES *Sordet, -ine, French.* the little pipe in the mouth of a trumpet. *Sourdine,* as *Sordet.* **1688** MIEGE-COTGRAVE Fr→E *Sourdine,* (f.) Sourdet, the little pipe put into the mouth of a Trumpet to make it sound low. § *La Sourdine est faite d'un morceau de bois qu'on pousse dans le pavillon de la Trompette, a fin que le bouchant en partie on affoiblisse le Son de la Trompette. On se sert de la Sourdine à la Guerre, lors qu'on veut deloyer sans que l'Enemi entende le Son de la Trompette. Sourdine (en Termes de Lutier) est un Instrument de Musique à Cordes, qui represente un Lut, ou un Violon. Mais il n'en a ni la Rose, ni les Ouïes; & ne sert que pour jouër d'une maniere sourde, & qui ne soit pas beaucoup entendue.* Sourdine *est le Terme Anglois, si je ne me trompe.* **1702** KERSEY *New Engl. Dict.* (1st edn) A *Sordine, or* little pipe put into the mouth of a Trumpet, to make it sound low. **1704** *Cocker's Engl. Dict.* (1st edn) *Sordiet,* or *Sordet,* a *French* word for the small pipe in the mouth of the trumpets. **1706** KERSEY-PHILLIPS (6th edn) *Sordet* or *Sordine, (Fr.)* a little Pipe put into the Mouth of a Trumpet, to make it sound lower. **1708** KERSEY *Dict. Anglo-Brit.* (1st edn) *Sordet* or *Sordine, (F.)* a little Pipe put into the Mouth of a Trumpet, to make it sound lower. **1730** BAILEY *Dict. Britannicum* (1st edn) *Sordet, Sordine,* (*sourdine,* F.) a small Pipe put into the Mouth of a Trumpet, to make it sound lower or shriller.

sorracus
1538 ELYOT L→E *Sorracus,* a cofer or baskette wherein are caried the instrumentes or apparayle seruynge for comedies or interludes.

sospiro *see* souspir, tacet
1724 [PEPUSCH] *Short Explic. of Foreign Words in Mus. Bks.* (p. 72) *Sospiro,* a little Character in Musick called a Rest. **1726** BAILEY *An Univ. Etymolog. Engl. Dict.* (3rd edn) *Sospiro* (in *Musick Books*) a little Character called a Rest. *Ital.*

sostenuto *see* continuato, dwelling, soustenir
1724 [PEPUSCH] *Short Explic. of Foreign Words in Mus. Bks.* (p. 72) *Sostenuto,* is to hold out the Sound of a Note Firmly, in an Equal and Steddy Manner. **1726** BAILEY *An Univ. Etymolog. Engl. Dict.* (3rd edn) *Sostenuto* (in *Musick Books*) signifies to hold out the Sound of a Note firmly, in an equal and steddy manner. *Ital.*

Soteridas
1678 PHILLIPS (4th edn) *Soteridas,* a Musician of *Epidaurus,* who wrote three Books of the Theory of Musick, mentioned by *Dionysius.*

sottana
1598 FLORIO It→E *Sottana,* ... Also the string next to the meane string of an instrument. **1611** FLORIO It→E *Sottana,* ... Also the string next to the meane string of an instrument. **1659** TORRIANO-FLORIO It→E *Sottana, Sottano,* ... also the string next to the mean of an instrument.

soubchanter *see* subchanter

souffler
1611 COTGRAVE Fr→E *Soufflé: m. ée: f.* ... also, sounded, or winded on a horne, &c. *Soufflement: m.* ... a winding of a horne, &c. *Souffler.* ... to sound, or wind, as a Cornet, horne, &c; **1688** MIEGE-COTGRAVE Fr→E § *les Souflets de l'Orgue,* the Bellows-Work of a pair of Organs.

sound *see* harmonic sound, son, sono, sonorous, sowned, standing sounds, suona
1702 KERSEY *New Engl. Dict.* (1st edn) *Sound,* the object of hearing, *as* the sound of a Bell, Glass, Musical Instrument, *&c.* **1704** HARRIS *Sound* .... Dr. *Holder* in his Book of the Natural Grounds and Principles of Harmony; says, That if the Tremulous Motion which causeth Sound, be Uniform, then it produces a Musical Note, or Sound: But if it be Difform, then it produces a Noise. **1706** KERSEY-PHILLIPS (6th edn) *Sound,* the Object of Hearing, which is caus'd by the tremulous Motion or Shaking of the Air; so that (according to Dr. *Holder*) if such Motion be *Vniform,* it produces a Musical Note or Sound; but if *Difform,* then it yields a Noise. **1721** BAILEY *An Univ. Etymolog. Engl. Dict.* (1st edn) A *Sound,* (*son,* F. of *sonus,* L.) the Object of Hearing, which is caused by the tremulous Motion or Shaking of the Air, so that if such Motion be *uniform,* it produces a Musical Note or Sound, but if *difform,* then it yields a Noise, according to Mr. *Holders* Definition. **1728** CHAMBERS *Sound* ... [*see* Appendix] **1730** BAILEY *Dict. Britannicum* (1st edn) *Sound* (in *Musick*) the Quality and Distinction of the several Agitations of the Air, considered as their Disposition, Measure, *&c.* may make Musick. **1737** DYCHE-PARDON (2nd edn) *Sound* (S.) that Reverberation or Modulation of Air that causes musical or disagreeable Tones; *Sound* (V.) to blow a Trumpet or *French* Horn, to beat a Drum, &c.

soundboard *see* belly, canon, sommier, table, trembloer
1702 KERSEY *New Engl. Dict.* (1st edn) The *Sound-board* of an Organ. **1728** CHAMBERS *Sound-Board,* the principal Part of an Organ, and that which makes the whole Machine play. See *Organ.* ¶ The *Sound-board* or *Summer,* is a Reservoir, into which the Wind drawn in by the Bellows, is conducted by a Port-vent, and hence distributed into the Pipes placed over the Holes of its upper Part. This Wind enters them by Valves, which open by pressing upon the Stops or Keys, after drawing the Registers, which prevent the Air from going into any of the other Pipes, but those 'tis required in. ¶ Organs, whose longest blind Pipes are four Foot, have their *Sound-Board* from five to six Feet. Organs of 16 Feet have two *Sound-Boards,* which communicate the Wind from one to the other, by a Pewter Port-vent.

soundhole *see* oscula, rose, ventige
1702 KERSEY *New Engl. Dict.* (1st edn) The *Sound-hole* ... of a musical instrument.

soundpost
1702 KERSEY *New Engl. Dict.* (1st edn) *sound-post* of a musical instrument.

c.1710 NORTH (draft for) Musicall Grammarian BL Add. 32537, ff. 165v-166 ... And viols & violin's will have very litle sound unless the back & belly are united by that they call a sound post. **1726-8** NORTH Theory of Sounds BL Add. 32535, f. 148v ... And If a small strutt be not put up stiff between ye bridg, and the back, wch in some manner unites both, ye Instrument will not sound. and for that reason it is called the sound post.

sourdeline

1688 MIEGE-COTGRAVE Fr→E *Sourdeline,* (f.) a kind of Bag-pipe. § *Le Sourdeline est une sorte de Musette assez agreable, qui est à plusieurs Chalumeaux, & qui n'est en usage qu'en Italie.*

sourdine *see* sordine

souspir

1611 COTGRAVE Fr→E *Souspir: m.* A sigh ... also, a Minime rest in Musice. § *Demy souspir.* A Crochet rest. **1688** MIEGE-COTGRAVE Fr→E *Soupir,* (m.) a Sigh ... a minime-rest, in Musick.

soustenir *see* sostenuto

1611 COTGRAVE Fr→E *Soustenir.* ... also, (in singing) to hold a note;

sowned

1704 *Cocker's Engl. Dict.* (1st edn) *Sowned,* proclaimed or published by sound of Trumpet.

spadico

1565 COOPER L→E *Spadix, Instrumentum musicum. Quintil.* An instrument of musike. **1587** THOMAS L→E *Spadix, icis,, adject. Virg. ... also* an instrument of musick. **1598** FLORIO It→E *Spadice,* ... Also a kinde of musicall instrument. **1611** FLORIO It→E *Spadico,* a scarlet or stammell colour. Also a bright bay-colour of a horse. Also a kind of musicall instrument. **1659** TORRIANO-FLORIO It→E *Spadico, Spadice,* ... also a kind of musical instrument

spagnuola

1724 [PEPUSCH] *Short Explic. of Foreign Words in Mus. Bks.* (p. 72) *Spagnuola,* a Guittar. See *Guitarra.*

species *see* genus

1728 CHAMBERS *Species,* in the ancient Music, a Subdivision of one of the Genera. ¶ The Genera of Music were Three, the *Enharmonic, Chromatic* and *Diatonic;* the two last of which were variously sub-divided into *Species;* nor was the First without *Species,* though those had not particular Names as the *Species* of the other Two had. ¶ These *Species* were also called the *Chroai,* Colours of the Genera: The Constitution whereof, see under the Article *Genera.* **1730** BAILEY *Dict. Britannicum* (1st edn) *Species* (in *antient Mu.*) a Subdivision of one of the General.

spiccato *see* andante, pointe, staccato

1724 [PEPUSCH] *Short Explic. of Foreign Words in Mus. Bks.* (p. 72) *Spiccato,* is to Separate or Divide each Note one from another, in a very Plain and Distinct Manner. **1726** BAILEY *An Univ. Etymolog. Engl. Dict.* (3rd edn) *Spiccato* (in *Musick Books*) signifies to separate or divide each Note one from another, in a very plain and distinct Manner. *Ital.*

spinet *see* basso continuo, claricords, manichord, polyplectra

1587 THOMAS L→E *Espineta, Iun.* A kinde of harp: the virginals, the clarichords. **1589** RIDER L→E *Espineta, f. clavecymbalum.* A pair of Verginals. **1593** HOLLYBAND Fr→E *Espinette,* a paire of Virginals: *f.* § *Espinette organisée,* a Bandora. **1598** FLORIO It→E *Espinetta,* virginals or claricords. *Spinetta,* a paire of virginals. **1611** COTGRAVE Fr→E *Epinette.* as *Espinette;* a paire of Virginals. *Espinette: f.* A paire of Virginalls. § *Espinette organisée.* A Virginall and wind Instrument ioyned together; a set of Pipes added to a Virginall. **1611** FLORIO It→E *Espinetta,* Virginals or Claricords. *Spinetta,* ... Also a paire of Virginalles. *Spinetteggiare,* to play vpon Virginalls. **1659** TORRIANO-FLORIO It→E *Espinette,* as *Spinette.* **1688** MIEGE-COTGRAVE Fr→E *Epinette,* (f.) *sorte d'Instrument de Musique,* Virginals, a pair of Virginals.... But Ps. 150. 4 you will find for the French Word *Epinette* that of stringed Instruments in the English Translation. § *Jouër de l'Epinette,* to play upon Virginals. **1706** KERSEY-PHILLIPS (6th edn) *Spinet,* a Musical Instrument, a sort of small Harpsichord. **1724** [PEPUSCH] *Short Explic. of Foreign Words in Mus. Bks.* (p. 72) *Spinetto,* a Spinet, an Instrument well known. **1726** BAILEY *An Univ. Etymolog. Engl. Dict.* (3rd edn) *Spinetto,* a *Spinet.* Ital *Spinet* (*spinetto,* Ital.) a Musical Instrument, a sort of small Harpsichord. **1728** CHAMBERS *Spinet,* a Musical Instrument, rank'd in the Second or Third Place among harmonious Instruments. See *Music.* ¶ In consists of a Chest or Belly, made of the most porous and resinous Wood to be found; and a Table of Firr fasten'd on Rods, call'd *Sound-boards,* which bear on the Sides. On the Table is raised a little Prominence, wherein are placed as many Pins as there are Chords to the Instrument. ¶ The Instrument is played by two Ranges of continued Keys, the foremost Range being in the Order of the Diatonick Scale; and the other Range set backwards in the Order of the Artificial Notes or Semi-tones. See *Scale.* ¶ The Keys are so many long, flat Pieces of Wood, which when touched and press'd down at one End, make the other raise a Jack, which sounds the Strings by means of the End of a Crow's Quill, wherewith 'tis armed. The 30 first Strings are of Brass, the other more delicate ones of Steel or Iron Wiar. They are all stretch'd over Two Bridges glued to the Table. ¶ The Figure of the *Spinet* is a long Square, and Parallelogram a Foot and Half broad; some call it a *Harp Couch'd,* and the Harp, an *Inverted Spinet.* ¶ The *Spinet* is generally tuned by the Ear; which Method of the practical Musicians, is founded on this Supposition, That the Ear is a perfect Judge of an Octave and Fifth. The general Rule, is to begin at a certain Note, as *c,* taken towards the middle of the Instrument, and tuning all the Octaves up and down, and also the Fifth's, reckoning Seven Semi-tones to each Fifth, by which means the whole is tuned. ¶ Sometimes to the common or fundamental Play of the *Spinet,* is added another similar one in Unison, and a Third is Octave to the first; to make the Harmony the fuller. They are play'd either separately or together, which is call'd the *double* or *triple Spinet.* Sometimes a Play of Violins is added, by means of a Bow, or a few Wheels parallel to the Keys, which press the Strings, and make the Sounds last as long as the Musician pleases; and heighten and soften them, as they are more or less press'd. The Harpsichord is a kind of *Spinet,* only with another Disposition of the Keys. See *Harpsichord.* ¶ The Instrument takes its Name from the little Quills Ends, wherewith the Strings are drawn, which are supposed to resemble *Spinæ,* Thorns. **1737** DYCHE-PARDON (2nd edn) *Spinet* or *Spinnet* (S.) a Musical key'd Instrument, or small Harpsicord, so contrived, that a Person may sit with Ease and play various Parts at once.

spinger *see* acute, grace

1659 SIMPSON *Division-Violist* (p. 9) There is yet another plain or smooth Grace, called a *Spinger,* which concludeth the sound of a *Note* more acute, by clapping down another Finger just at the expiring of it. **1676** MACE *Musick's Monument* (p. 109) The *Spinger,* is a *Grace,* very *Neat, and Curious,* for some sort of *Notes;* and is done *Thus,* viz. ¶ After you have *Hit your Note,* which you intend to make the *Grace upon,* you must (just as you intend to part with *your Note*) *Dab* one of your *next Fingers lightly upon the same String, a Fret, or 2 Fretts below,* (according to the *Ayre*) as if you did intend to *stop the String,* in that *Place; yet so Gently, that you do not cause the String to Sound, in That stop,* (so dab'd;) but only so, that it may *suddenly take away That Sound, which you last struck;* yet give some *small Tincture of a New Note;* but not *Distinctly to be heard,* as a *Note;* which *Grace* (if *Well done,* and *Properly*) is very *Taking, and Pleasant.*

spirito

1724 [PEPUSCH] *Short Explic. of Foreign Words in Mus. Bks.* (p. 72) *Spirito,* or *Spiritoso,* with Spirit and Life. **1730** BAILEY *Dict. Britannicum* (1st edn) *Spirito, Spiritoso,* (in *Mu. Books*) signifies with Life and Spirit, *Ital.*

spiss interval

1694 HOLDER *Treatise of Natural Grounds* (pp. 130-1) And to constitute these Degrees, some of them, *viz.* the Followers of *Aristoxenus,* divided a *Tone Major* into 12 Equal Parts; *i.e.* Supposed it so divided: Six of which being the *Hemitone,* (*viz.* half of it,) made a Degree of *Chromatic Toniæum.* And Three of them, or a Quarter called *Diesis;* a Degree *Enharmonic.* The *Chromatic* Fourth rose thus, *viz.* from the First Chord to the Second was a *Hemitone;* from the Second to the Third, a *Hemitone;* from the Third to the Fourth, a *Trihemitone;* or as much as would make up a just Fourth. And this last Space (in this case) was accounted as well as either of the other, but one Degree or undivided Interval. And they called them *Spiss* Intervals (πυκνά) when two of those other Degrees put together, made not so great an Interval as one of these; as, in the *Enharmonic* Tetrachord, two *Dieses* were less than the remaining *Ditone,* and in the common *Chromatic,* two Hemitone Degrees were less than the remaining *Trihemitone* Degree.

spissum

1721 MALCOLM *Treatise of Musick* (p. 545) ... Then as to the Two other *Genera* [i.e. the enharmonic and chromatic], to understand what he [Aristoxenus] says, *observe,* that the lower Part of the *Tetrachord* containing Two *Dieses* in the One, and Two *Hemitones* in the other *Genus* (whose Sums are always less than the remaining *Ditone* or *Triemitone* that makes up the *Diatessaron*) is called πυκνόν *spissum,* because the *Intervals* being small, the Sounds are as it were set thick and near other; opposite to which is απυκνόν *non spissum* or *rarum*: Notice too, that the Chords that belonged to the *spissum* were called πυκνοί, and particularly the lowest or *gravest* of the Three in every *Tetrachord* were called βαρύπυκνοι, (from βάρυς *gravis,*) the middle ὀξύπυκνοι (from μεσος *medius*) the acutest μεσόπυκνοι (from ὀξύς *acutus*) Those that belonged not to the πυκνόν were called ἀπυκνοί., *extra spissum.*

spondæus

1587 THOMAS L→E *Spondæus.* A foote consisting of 2. long syllables: it is so called, of drawing the voice in singing at diuine seruice.

spondalion

1656 BLOUNT (1st edn) *Spondalion* (Gr.) a himn consisting most of *Spondes;* sung to procure and settle the favor of the Gods, whilst the Incense was a burning **1676** COLES *Spondalion, Greek.* a heathen hymn sung at the burning of the incense. **1704** *Cocker's Engl. Dict.* (1st edn) *Spondalion,* a Song sung by the Gentiles or Heathens, when they burnt Incense to their Gods.

spondaules

1728 CHAMBERS *Spondaules,* in Antiquity, a Player of the Flute, or other Wind Instrument of that Kind, who, during the Offering of Sacrifice, performed some suitable Air in the Priest's Ear to prevent the hearing of any Thing that might distract him, or lessen his Attention. See *Sacrifice.* ¶ The Word is form'd from the *Greek* σπονδὴ *Libation,* and αὐλή, *Flute.* **1737** BAILEY *The Univ. Etymolog. Engl. Dict.* (3rd edn, vol. 2) *Spondaules* (of σπονδὴ, a libation, and αὐλή, Gr. a flute) a player on the flute, or such like wind instrument, who during the offering of the sacrifice, performed some suitable air in the priest's ear, to prevent the hearing of any thing that might distract him or lessen his attention.

spondeo piede

1598 FLORIO It→E *Spondeopiede,* a foote of a verse consisting of two long syllables in the last word, it is so called of drawing the voice in singing at deuine seruice. **1611** FLORIO It→E *Spondeo piede,* a foote of a verse consisting of two long sillables in the last word, so called of drawing the voice in singing at Deuine seruice.

spondiale *see* waits

1565 COOPER L→E *Spondylus, spondyli, pen. cor. m.g.* ... A brasen thynge, vsed at Athens in geuyng of voyces. **1587** THOMAS L→E *Spondiales, vel Spondiauli, Iun.* Such as plaied vpon long pipes at diuine seruice: they may be called the waites. **1589** RIDER L→E *Spondiales.* Waites, certain musicall instruments so called.

springer *see* spinger

squillare

1598 FLORIO It→E *Squillare,* to ring or iangle bels

stab *see* stoccata

staccare *see* legare

staccato *see* pointe, stoccata

1724 [PEPUSCH] *Short Explic. of Foreign Words in Mus. Bks.* (p. 73) *Staccato,* or *Stoccato.* See the Word *Spiccato.* **1726** BAILEY *An Univ. Etymolog. Engl. Dict.* (3rd edn) *Staccato, Stoccato,* (in *Musick Books*) signifies the same as *spiccato,* Ital. which see. **1737** DYCHE-PARDON (2nd edn) *Staccato* (A.) in *Musick,* is when the Players strike the Strings very smart and distinct.

1731 PRELLEUR *Modern Musick-Master* (Dictionary, p. 3) *Staccato* or *Stoccato,* in a plain and distinct Manner

staff *in notation, see* music-line, particular system, set of pricksong

1728 CHAMBERS *Staff,* in Music, five Lines, on which, with the intermediate Spaces, the Notes of any Song or Piece of Music are mark'd. See *Music.* ¶ *Guido Aretin,* the greater Author of the Modern Music, is said to be the first who introduced the *Staff;* marking his Notes, by setting Points (.) up and down them, to denote the Rise and Fall of the Voice; and each Line and Space he mark'd at the beginning of the *Staff* with *Gregory*'s Seven Letters, *a, b, c, d, e, f, g.* See *Note.* ¶ But others will have the Artifice of an older Date; and *Kircher* particularly affirms, That in the Jesuites Library at *Messina,* he found an old *Greek* MS. Book of Hymns, above 700 Years old; wherein some Hymns were written on a *Staff* of eight Lines, mark'd at the beginning with Eight *Greek* Letters. The Notes or Points were on the Lines, but no used made of the Spaces. See *Scale, Gamut, Solfaing, &c.*

staff *as poetic division*
1702 Kersey *New Engl. Dict.* (1st edn) A *Staff*, a division of a Psalm.

staffa
1598 Florio It→E *Staffetta*, ... Some haue vsed *Staffetta* for the instrument called *Crotalo*. Looke *Crotalo*. **1611** Florio It→E *Staffa*, a stirrop of a sadle... Also a musicall instrument as *Crotalo*. *Staffetta*, ... hath also beene vsed for the instrument called *Crotalo*. **1659** Torriano-Florio It→E *Staffa, Staffe*, ... any kind of stirrup ... also a certain musical instrument of iron made like a stirrup, round about, which is fastned, little jangling bells ...

stampinata
1598 Florio It→E *Stampinata*. [no definition given] **1611** Florio It→E *Stampinata*, a fit of mirth or fidling. Also a kind of country dancing, singing or fidling anciently vsed in Italie. **1659** Torriano-Florio It→E *Stampinata, Stampita*, any trampling noise, also a kind of moris-dancing, fidling or singing, anciently used in *Italy*, now used for a fit of mirth given by Minstrels.

stampita
1550 Thomas It→E *Stampita*, the plaiying of a daunce, or of a song. **1598** Florio It→E *Stampita*, a kinde of countrie dance, a fit of mirth or fidling. **1611** Florio It→E *Stampita*, as *Stampinata*.

standing sounds
1721 Malcolm *Treatise of Musick* (pp. 525-6) I have explained the *Diagram* in the *diatonick genus*; but the same Names are applied to all Three *Genera*; and according to the Differences of these, so are the Relations of the several Chords to one another. But since the Constitution of the *Scale* by *Tetrachords* is the same in all, and that the *Genera* differ only in the *Ratios* which the Two middle Chords of the *Tetrachord* bear to the Extremes; therefore these Extremes were called *standing* or *immoveable Sounds* (ἑστῶντες *soni stantes*) and all the middle ones were called *moveable* (κινητοι *soni mobiles*) for to raise a Series from a given *Fundamental* or *Proslambanomenos*, the first and last Chord of each *Tetrachord* is invariably the same, or common to every *Genus*; but the middle Chords vary according to the *Genus*.

stanza
1702 Kersey *New Engl. Dict.* (1st edn) A *Stanza, or* staff, a certain number of verses.

start *see* grave

stasimon
1611 Florio It→E *Stasimo*, the full subiect of the Chorus his speech. Lat. **1659** Torriano-Florio It→E *Stasimo*, the full subjest [sic] of the Chorus his speech.

1712 Weaver *Essay towards History of Dancing* (pp. 13-14) [*re* dance traditions in ancient times] ... The Song which succeeded the *Dance*, when all stood still, and were quiet, was call'd *Stasimon*.

stave *see* staff

stay *see* hold
1665 Simpson *Principles of Practical Mvsick* (p. 36) This Mark or *Arch* 𝄐 is commonly set at the End of a Song, or Lesson; to signifie the *Close* or Conclusion. It is also set, somtimes, over certain particular Notes in the middle of *Songs*, when (for humor) we are to insist or stay a little upon the said Notes: and therefore 'tis called a *Stay* or *Hold*.

stempellare *see* tempella
1598 Florio It→E *Stempellare*, to twangle or play foolishlie vpon any instrument, to fumble vpon a Lute. **1611** Florio It→E *Stempellare*, to fumble, to twangle, or play foolishly vpon any instrument. **1659** Torriano-Florio It→E *Stempellare, Stempellare*, as *Tempellare*.

Stesichorus
1538 Elyot L→E *Stesichorus*, a famouse poete, of whome it is writen, that whanne he was an infant in his cradelle, a Nyghtyngale satte on his mouthe, and dyd synge, sygnyfienge that he shulde be the sweetest poete, that euer was afore hym. Also he founde fyrste syngynge of songes in a daunse. **1565** Cooper L→E *Stesichorus*, A famous poete, of whom it is wrytten, that, when he was an infante in his cradell, a nyghtingale sat on his mouthe, and dyd synge, signifiyng that he shoulde

be the sweetest poete that euer was afore him: he found first singing of songes in a daunce.

sticine *see* sicinnium, siticine
1611 COTGRAVE Fr→E *Sticines: m.* Fluters, or Pipers. *Rab.*

stifello *see* stufallo, suffolo
1598 FLORIO It→E *Stifello,* a kinde of pipe, recorder, flute, or hornepipe. **1611** FLORIO It→E *Stifello,* a kind of pipe or recorder. **1659** TORRIANO-FLORIO It→E *Stifello,* any pipe or whistle.

stile *see* style

sting *see* grace
1676 MACE *Musick's Monument* (p. 109) The *Sting,* is another very *Neat, and Pritty Grace;* (But not *Modish* in *These Days*) yet, for some sorts of *Humours,* very *Excellent;* And is *Thus done,* (upon a *Long Note, and a Single String*) first strike your *Note,* and so soon as It is struck, *hold your Finger (but not too Hard) stopt upon the Place,* (letting your *Thumb loose*) and *wave your Hand (Exactly) downwards, and upwards, several Times, from the Nut, to the Bridge;* by which *Motion,* your *Finger will draw, or stretch the String a little upwards, and downwards, so,* as to make the Sound seem to *Swell* with pritty *unexpected Humour,* and gives much *Contentment, upon Cases.*

stoccata *see* rant, staccato, tremolo
c.1726 NORTH Musicall Gramarian BL Add. 32533, f. 114 Another Grace or rather manner Is the stoccata or stabb, wch is a peculiar art of the hand upon Instruments of the Bow; And as it is an occasion all Imitation so it hath a due acceptance; but to use it at all turnes, whensoever ye movement will allow it, creates a fastidium.

stop *in organ, see* epistomium, organ, theorbo stop, trayan, tremante, tremolo
c.1715-20 NORTH Theory of Sounds BL Add. 32534, f. 65v ... and what a felicity is it, when a stopp (as it is called) of an organ ...

stop *on string instrument, see* double stop, fret, full stop, grave

storia
1598 FLORIO It→E *Storia,* ... Also a kind of musicall instrument. **1611** FLORIO It→E *Storia,* a storie, a historie, a narration. Also a kind of musicall instrument. **1659** TORRIANO-FLORIO It→E *Storia,* ... also the name of a musical instrument.

stormento *see* instrument

storta
1598 FLORIO It→E *Storta,* ... also a sack-but or such other crooked instrument of musicke. **1611** FLORIO It→E *Storta,* any kind of withe or wreath... Also a sack-but or such other crooked musicall instrument. **1659** TORRIANO-FLORIO It→E *Storta, Stortola,* ... also a sack-but or such other winding or crooked musical instrument

stracantare
1550 THOMAS It→E *Stracantare,* to syng to muche. **1611** FLORIO It→E *Stracantare,* to sing and sing againe. **1659** TORRIANO-FLORIO It→E *Stra-cantare,* to sing and sing again.

strain
1706 KERSEY-PHILLIPS (6th edn) *Strain,* Tune, flight of Speech or Eloquence: **1707** *Gloss. Angl. Nova* (1st edn) *Strain,* Tune, flight of Speech or Eloquence; **1737** DYCHE-PARDON (2nd edn) *Strain* (S.) ... in *Musick,* it is the Part of a Tune or Air where the Composition makes a full Close.

1693 LENTON *Gentleman's Diversion* (p. 6) ... with a Repetition which is marked thus :S: which is to inform you when you have ended the *Strain or Lesson ... *Note that to any double Barr it is called a Strain.*

strambelli *see* strambotto

stramboccolo *see* lampon
1611 FLORIO It→E *Stramboccolo,* a kind of base, railing or filthy composition. **1659** TORRIANO-FLORIO It→E *Stramboccolo,* a base, scurril, or railing song or composition. **1688** DAVIS-TORRIANO-FLORIO It→E *Stramboccolo,* a lampoon, scurrillous song, or libel.

strambotto *see* catch
1598 FLORIO It→E *Strambelli,* as *Strambotti. Strambottare,* to sing rounds, gigs, catches or freemens songs. *Strambotti,* countrie gigs, rounds, catches or songs, virelaies. *Strambottiere,* a maker or singer of gigs, songs, catches or rounds. *Strambottino,* a short fine gig, round or catch. **1611** COTGRAVE Fr→E *Strambot: m.* A Jyg, Round,

Catch, countrey Song. **1611** FLORIO It→E *Strambelli,* as *Strambotti. Strambottare,* to sing rounds, catches, gigges, or three mens songs. *Strambotti,* Country gigges, rounds, catches, virelaies or three mens songs. *Strabottiere,* a maker or singer of *Strambotti. Strambottino,* any little *Strambotto.* **1650** HOWELL-COTGRAVE Fr→E † *Strambot: m.* A Jyg, Round, Catch, country Song. **1659** TORRIANO-FLORIO It→E *Strambottare,* ... also, to sing *Strambotti. Strambotti, Strambetti, Strambottini, Stramotti,* Country-gigs, rurelayes [sic], catches, three mens songs, clinches. *Strembottiere* [sic], a singer of *Stramboti,* a maker of clinches. **1688** DAVIS-TORRIANO-FLORIO It→E *Strambotti, Strambetti, Strambettini,* Country jiggs[,] catches of three parts, or clinches.

strange tone *see* peregrine tone

stravaganza

c.1715-20 NORTH Essay of Musical Ayre BL Add. 32536, f. 60 The other Error, wch hath divers branches, yet may fall aptly under the title of Stravaganze, And that is when to gaine a conceipt of somewhat new or admirable, the musick is steered out of the common cours, as If the buisness were not to manage by ye rules of an art of science already knowne but to Invent a new one. **c.1726** NORTH Musicall Gramarian BL Add. 32533, ff. 150-150v In a Word, as I said at first, musick is Impartial, and Enterteines both kinds with Equall favour; and The caracters of Each depends upon ye measure, the dupla may be ludicrous, fantasticall, and buffonesque, as well as the triple. for wch I may call to wittness certein consorts called 'stravaganze, and others that affect somewhat like them, especially In the high Arpeggio, wch really in value scarce exceed ye jingling of a Bunch of Keys...

strideo

1552 HULOET L→E *strideo. es, strido. is* Syng out of tune.

strike

1568 LE ROY *Briefe and Easye Instrution* (p. 6) And to the ende thou shalte not bæ abused by these termes, to strike dounwardes, to strike vpwardes, or to gripe, you shall vnderstande, to strike doune the strynges, is when the thombe plaieth alone, whiche striketh the stryng dounward, to lifte or strike vpwardes, those bee the fingers that striketh the strynges vpwardes, when the letters be marked with pointes or prickes, to gripe, is when the thombe and the fingers plaie together, the whiche notwithstandyng, doeth not lefe their office to strike vpwardes, or dounwardes, that is to saie, to strike dounwards with the thombe, and vpwardes with the fingers. **1596** BARLEY *New Booke of Tabliture* (n.p.) [*re* the lute] And to the end yee shall not be ignorant what these tearmes meane of striking downewardes, or vpwards, or to gripe, I meane by striking downewards the stringes, is when the thumb playeth alone, and to strike with the fingers is when the letters hath pricks vnder them, and the stringes are striken vpwardes, to gripe is when the fingers and the thumb playeth together, and yet not looseth their office in striking vpwardes and downewards, that is to say, to strike downeward with the thumb, and vpward with the fingers. **1603** ROBINSON *Schoole of Mvsicke* [Bv] ... now for your right hand, called the striking hand leane vpon the bellie of the Lute with your little finger onelie, & that, neither to far from the *Treble* strings, neither to neere ... § [C*v*] ... the right hand, called the striking hand. **1676** MACE *Musick's Monument* (pp. 73-4) And that you may learn to *strike a String Clear, and Clean,* take notice, that in *your stroke,* you strive to *draw your Finger a little Vpwards,* and not *Slanting,* for that will *endanger* the *hitting* of *another String, together* with *That String,* you intend to Strike *Single.* This is called *Clean Striking.*

string *see* boyautier, burden, cantarella, canto, catling, chanterelle, contramezzana, cord, diapason, false string, fides, fileur, filum, gansar, lichanos, mean, mese, mezzana, minnekin, minugia, nervo, nete, paramese, paranete, parhypate, peripate, pistoy bass, prima, secondina, soprano, sottana, trite;

1702 KERSEY *New Engl. Dict.* (1st edn) *Unstrung,* that has no *strings* (speaking of a Musical Instrument.) § *Wire-strings,* for Musical Instruments. **1721** BAILEY *An Univ. Etymolog. Engl. Dict.* (1st edn) *Strings, (streng, Dan.)* the Chords of a Musical Instrument. **1728** CHAMBERS *String* ... [*see* Appendix] **1731** KERSEY *New Engl. Dict.* (3rd edn) To *string,* ... to fix Strings to a Musical Instrument. **1736** BAILEY *Dict. Britannicum* (2nd edn) *To Unstring* (of *un* and ꞅꞇꞃænᵹ, *Sax,*) to take strings from a musical instrument **1737** DYCHE-PARDON (2nd edn) *Strings* (S.) in a peculiar Manner, are the Cords of Musical Instruments, which are either Gut or Wire. *String* (V.) ... also to fit up

Musical Instruments with Gut or Wire Strings, to make them fit for playing on. *Unstrung* (V.) ... also to take off the Strings from a Musical Instrument, &c.

stroke *see* beating, manuductor, tact, tactus
1597 MORLEY *Plaine and Easie Introdvction* (p. 9) *Phi.* What is *stroke?* ¶ *Ma. It is a successiue motion of the hand, directing the quantitie of euery note & rest in the song, with equall measure, according to the varietie of signes and proportions*: this they make three folde, *more, lesse, and proportionate. The More stroke they call, when the stroke comprehendeth the time of a Briefe. The lesse, when a time of a Semibriefe: and proportionat where it comprehendeth three Semibriefes,* as in a triple or three Minoms, as in the more prolation ...

strombettare *see* taratantara, trumpet
1611 FLORIO It→E *Strombettare,* to sound as in a Trumpet, but foolishly. *Strombettata,* a foolish trumpeting. **1659** TORRIANO-FLORIO It→E *Strombettata, Strombezzata,* a foolish trumpetting tara-tantara

stromento *see* instrument

strophe *see* antistrophe, couplet, epode, hymn
1587 THOMAS L→E *Strophæ, arum, f.g. Iun.* Songs sung to the harp. **1706** KERSEY-PHILLIPS (6th edn) *Strophe,* the first of the three Members of a *Greek* Lyrick Ode, or Poem; the second being the *Antistrophe,* which answers thereto; and the third the *Epode,* which answers to neither, but is answer'd in the next Return. *Strophe* is also the first turn of the *Chorus,* or Quire of Singers in a Tragedy on one side of the Stage, answering to the *Antistrophe* on the other. See *Antistrophe.* **1728** CHAMBERS *Strophe,* in the *Greek* and *Latin* Poetry, a Stanza, or certain Number of Verses including a perfect Sense; succeeded by another, consisting of the same Number and Measure of Verses, in the same Disposition and Rythmus, call'd the *Antistrophe.* ¶ What the *Couplet* is in Songs, and the *Stanza* in Epic Poetry; *Strophe* is in Odes. See *Couplet.* ¶ The Word is Greek, στροφή of στρέφω, I turn; because at the End of the *Strophe,* the same Measures returning again; or rather, as the Term related, principally, to the Music or Dancing, because at first coming in, the Chorus or the Dancers turn'd to the Left, and that Measure ended, they turn'd back again to the Right. **1730** BAILEY *Dict. Britannicum* (1st edn) *Strophe* ... the first of the three Members of a *Greek* Lyrick Ode or Poem; the second being the Antistrophe that answers to it; and the third is the *Epode* that answers to neither, but is answer'd in the next Return. *Strophe,* is also the first Turn of the *Chorus* or Choir of Singers in a Tragedy, on one side of the Stage, answering to the Antistrophe on the other.

1711 BEDFORD *Great Abuse of Musick* (pp. 24-5) ... when *Dramatick Poesy* was brought to some Perfection [in ancient Greece], there was also a *Chorus* between the *Acts,* consisting of several *Verses,* in the same Measure and Order like those in *Pindar,* and which was *sung* according to the *Musick* of those Times. It generally consisted of three Parts, and the *Verses* of each respective Part were usually the same both for *Number* and *Measure.* When the *first Part* was *sung,* the *Chorus* turn'd to the *Right Hand,* which they called *Strophe.* When the second Part was *sung,* the *Chorus* turn'd to the *Left Hand,* which they call'd *Antistrophe*: And when the *third Part* was *sung,* the *Chorus* turn'd to the *middle Part* of the *Audience,* which they call'd *Epodos.* This *Chorus* was a Company of *Actors,* representing the Assembly or Body of those vulgar Persons who either were present, or probably might be so upon that Place or *Scene* where the Business was suppos'd to be transacted...

strowler
1737 BAILEY *The Univ. Etymolog. Engl. Dict.* (3rd edn, vol. 2, cant section) *Strowlers,* Vagabonds, Itinerants, ... Mountebanks, Fidlers, Country-Players, Rope-dancers...

stufallo *see* stifello, suffolo
1611 FLORIO It→E *Stuffello,* a pipe, a fluite, a recorder. **1659** TORRIANO-FLORIO It→E *Stufallo,* a pipe, a flute, a recorder.

style *see* church music, manner, modi melopœiæ, Palestrina alla, phantastic, recitative
1728 CHAMBERS *Style,* in Music, the manner of Singing and Composing. ¶ The *Style* is, properly, the manner each Person has, either of Composing, or Performing or Teaching; which is very different, both in respect of the different Genius's of Countries and Nations, and of the different Matters, Places, Times, Subjects, Expressions, *&c.* ¶ Thus we say, the *Style* of the *Charissimi,* of *Lully,* or *Lambert*; the *Style* of the *Italians,* the *French,*

the *Spaniards, &c.* The *Style* of gay Pieces of Music, is very different from that of serious Pieces: The *Style* of Church Music, very different from Theatrical Music. The *Style* of the *Italian* Compositions, is poignant, florid, expressive; that of the *French* Compositions, natural, flowing, tender, *&c.* ¶ Hence, the various Epithets, given to distinguish these various Characters; as, the ancient and modern *Style,* the *Italian* and *German Style,* the Ecclesiastical and Dramatic *Style,* the gay, grave, majestic, natural, soft, familiar, gallant, low, sublime *Styles, &c.* ¶ The *Stylo Recitativo* or *Dramatico,* in the *Italian* Music, is a *Style* fit to express the Passions. The *Stylo Ecclesiastica* is full of Majesty, very grave, and fit to inspire Devotion. ¶ *Stylo Motectico,* is a various, rich, florid *Style,* capable of all Kinds of Ornaments, and, of consequence, fit to express various Passions, particularly Admiration, Grief, *&c.* ¶ *Stylo Madrigalesco,* is a *Style* proper for Love, and the other softer Passions. ¶ *Stylo Hyperchematico,* is a *Style* proper to excite Mirth, Joy, Dancing, *&c.* and, of consequence, full of brisk, gay Motions. ¶ *Stylo Symphoniaco,* is a *Style* fit for Instrumental Music: But as each Instrument has its particular Effect, there are as many different *symphonical Styles.* The *Style* of Violins, for Instance, is usually Gay; that of Flutes Melancholy and Languishing, and that of Trumpets, Sprightly and Animated. ¶ *Stylo Melismatico,* is a natural, artless *Style,* which any Body, almost, may sing. ¶ *Stylo Phantastico,* is a free, easy, humorous Manner of Composition, far from all Constraint, *&c.* ¶ *Stylo Choraico,* is the *Style* proper for Dancing; and is divided into as many different Kinds, as there are Dances; as the *Style* of Sarabands, of Minuets, of Gavots, of Rigadoons, *&c.* **1730** BAILEY *Dict. Britannicum* (1st edn) *Style* (in *Musick*) the Manner of Singing and Composing. § *Stylo Choraico,* the Style that is proper for Dancing, for either Sarabands, Minuets, Gavots, or Rigadoons. *Stylo Hyperchematico,* a Style proper to excite Mirth, Joy, Dancing, and of consequence full of brisk gay Motions. *Stylo Madrigalesco,* a Style proper for Love and other Passions. *Stylo Melismatico,* a natural, artless Style. *Stylo Motectico,* a various, rich, florid Style, capable of all kinds of Ornamentation, and fit to express the Passions, as Admiration, Grief, *&c.* *Stylo Phantastico,* a free, easy, humorous Manner of Composition. *Stylo Recitativo, Stylo Dramatico,* a Style fit to express the Passions. *Stylo Symphonico,* a Style fit for instrumental Musick.

subchanter *see* chanter, succentor, succino
1570/71 *Dict. Fr. and Engl.* FR→E *Soubchantre,* subchanter. **1593** HOLLYBAND FR→E *Soubchantre,* seeke *Subchanter* [no such entry given]. **1611** COTGRAVE FR→E *Soubchanter.* To sing vnder, or after, another; to hold the base or ground vnto; to follow, in a song of three, or foure parts in one. *Soubchantre: m.* An vnder-chaunter; an Officer in a Cathedrall Church inferiour to the head Chaunter. *Souschanter.* To sing vnder, to hold the base, or ground vnto; or as *Soubschanter.* **1650** HOWELL-COTGRAVE FR→E † *Soubchanter.* To sing under, or after, another; to hold the base or ground unto; to follow, in a song of three, or four parts in one. **1696** PHILLIPS (5th edn) *Subchanter,* An Officer in the Quire, that begins the Anthem in the absence of the Chanter. **1702** KERSEY *New Engl. Dict.* (1st edn) A *Sub-Chanter,* an inferiour *Chanter* in a Cathedral, *or* Collegiate Church. **1706** KERSEY-PHILLIPS (6th edn) *Sub-chanter,* an Officer in a Cathedral, or Collegiate Church, that begins the Anthem, in the Chanter's Absence. **1708** KERSEY *Dict. Anglo-Brit.* (1st edn) *Sub-chanter,* an Officer in a Cathedral, or Collegiate Church, that begins the Anthem in the Chanter's Absence. **1721** BAILEY *An Univ. Etymolog. Engl. Dict.* (1st edn) *Subchanter,* an under Chanter; an Officer in a Cathedral or Collegiate Church who begins the Anthem in the Absence of the Chanter. **1728** CHAMBERS *Sub-Chantor,* an Officer in the Choir, who officiates in the Absence of the Chanter, *&c.* See *Chantor.*

subito *see* verte, volti, vs
1724 [PEPUSCH] *Short Explic. of Foreign Words in Mus. Bks.* (p. 73) *Subito,* Quick or Nimbly. Thus, ¶ *Volti Subito,* is to turn over Quickly, without Loss of Time. ¶ These Words are met with at the Bottom of a Leaf on the right Hand Side, when the Leaf turns over in the Middle of a Part or Strain, to signify as above, that in turning over the Leaf you must be very Quick, that little or no Time may be lost thereby. **1726** BAILEY *An Univ. Etymolog. Engl. Dict.* (3rd edn) *Subito* (in *Musick Books*) signifies quick and nimbly, as *volti subito,* turn over quick, without loss of time. *Ital.*

1731 PRELLEUR *Modern Musick-Master* (Dictionary, p. 3) *Subito,* Quickly, v. *Volti.*

succentor *see* incentor, sincantor, subchanter, succino

1500 *Ortus Vocabulorum* L→E Succentus tus. tui. a tenore. m.q. **1538** ELYOT L→E *Succento, tare,* to synge a base. *Succentor, toris,* he that syngeth a base. **1552** HULOET L→E *succento. as, succino. is* Syng vnder. *Succento. as, succino. is,* to synge a tenor *Succentor. oris et succento. as,* Base synger. *Succentor. ris,* Tenor, or he that singeth a tenor. **1587** THOMAS L→E *Succento, as.* *To sing a base. *Succentor, oris, m.g.* He that singeth the base. **1589** RIDER L→E *Succentor, m.* He that singeth the base. **1623** COCKERAM *Succent.* to Sing a base **1656** BLOUNT (1st edn) *Succentor* (Lat.) he that singeth the Base. See *Incentor.* Our phrase, *an old Sincantor,* is either a corruption from this word, or if it be written with a C, then tis from the Fr. *Cinquante,* which signifies fifty, and so may be taken for one that is fifty years of age or above. **1658** PHILLIPS (1st edn) *Succentour,* (lat.) vulgarly *Sincantour,* see *Incentour.* **1676** COLES *Succentor, Latin.* a (bass or under) singing-man. **1704** *Cocker's Engl. Dict.* (1st edn) *Succentor,* corrupted to *Sincator,* he that in Musick sings the Base. **1706** KERSEY-PHILLIPS (6th edn) *Succentor.* See *Incentor.* **1708** KERSEY *Dict. Anglo-Brit.* (1st edn) *Succentor,* he that sings the Bass, or lowest Part, in a Consort of Musick. **1730** BAILEY *Dict. Britannicum* (1st edn) *Succentor,* he that sings the Bass or lowest Part, *L.*

succhiello

1598 FLORIO It→E *Succhiello,* ... Also a kind of little pipe or flute. **1611** FLORIO It→E *Succhiello,* an auger, a piercer, a wimblet, a gimblet, a boarer, a forcehead. Also a spigot. Also a little pipe or flut. **1659** TORRIANO-FLORIO It→E *Succhiello,* any little pipe or flute

succino *see* subchanter, succentor

1500 *Ortus Vocabulorum* L→E Succino is. cinni. centum. i. parum vel subtus vel submissa voce canere. **1538** ELYOT L→E *Succino, cinere,* to make a soft noise, to singe a base or tenour. **1552** HULOET L→E *succino. as. ang.* to synge the base. *succino. is* Syng softly wythoute noyse. **1565** COOPER L→E *Succino, succinis, pen. corr. succinere, Ex sub & cano compositum. Horat.* To make a softe noyse: to singe a base or tenor. **1587** THOMAS L→E *Succino, is, Horat.* To make a soft noise, to sing a base or tenour. **1589** RIDER L→E *Succino, succento.* To sing the base. **1598** FLORIO It→E *Succinare,* ... to sing a base or tenour. **1611** FLORIO It→E *Succinare,* ... Also to sing a base or drone tenor.

succortrilla

1538 ELYOT L→E *Succortrila,* a small voyce and a shryll. **1552** HULOET L→E *succortrila* Shyll [sic] voyce. **1587** THOMAS L→E *Succortrilla, succotilla, vel succotrilla, æ, f.g. Fest.* A small and shrill voice, the treble.

suffolo *see* cifello, stifello, stufallo, zuffolo

1550 THOMAS It→E *Suffolare,* to whistell. **1598** FLORIO It→E *Suffolino, Suffoletto,* a little whistle. *Suffolo,* a whistle. **1611** FLORIO It→E *Suffoletto,* a little whistle. *Suffolino,* a little whistle. *Suffolo,* any kind of whistle or hisse. **1659** TORRIANO-FLORIO It→E *Suffolo, Suffoletto, Suffolino, Sufolo,* any kind of whistle or whistling pipe. **1724** [PEPUSCH] *Short Explic. of Foreign Words in Mus. Bks.* (p. 73) *Suffolo,* a Bird Pipe, or Flagelet. See *Zufolo.*

suit *see* chichona, prelude, tattle de moy

1676 MACE *Musick's Monument* (p. 120) I will *now* set you a *Sett,* or a *Suit of Lessons,* (as we commonly call *Them*) which may be of any *Number,* as you please, yet commonly are about *Half a Dozen.* ¶ The First always, should begin, in the Nature of a *Voluntary Play,* which we call a *Præludium,* or *Prælude.* ¶ Then, *Allmaine, Ayre, Coranto, Seraband, Toy,* or what you please, provided They be all in the *same Key;* yet (in my opinion) in regard we call Them a *Suit of Lessons*) They ought to be something a Kin, (as we use to say) or to have some kind of *Resemblance in their Conceits, Natures, or Humours.*

suona *see* sono, sound

1611 FLORIO It→E *Disuono,* by sound or sounding. **1659** TORRIANO-FLORIO It→E § *Altri a suonare, altri a cantare,* some to play, others to sing. **1724** [PEPUSCH] *Short Explic. of Foreign Words in Mus. Bks.* (pp. 71-2) *Sona, Suona,* or *Suono,* Sound, or Sounds, which is the chief or proper Object of Musick, and which if performed in an agreeable Manner one after another is then called Melody; but if one with another in an agreeable Manner, is called Harmony. (p. 73) *Suona,* or *Suono,* or *Suonare.* See *Sona.* (p. 75) *Suono.* See the Word *Sono.* **1726** BAILEY *An Univ. Etymolog. Engl. Dict.* (3rd edn) *Sona,* a Sound or Sounds, which is the proper or chief Object of Musick, and which, if performed in an agreeable Manner one after another, is then called Melody, but if one with another in an agreeable manner, it is call'd Harmony. *Ital.* *Suona, Suono,* See Sona. *Ital.*

suonata *see* sonata

supernumerary
1728 CHAMBERS In Music, the *Supernumerary,* call'd by the *Greeks Proslambanomenos,* is the lowest of the Chords of their System; answering to *a, mi, la,* of the lowest Octave of the Moderns. See *Proslambanomenos* and *Diagram.*

supposed bass
1731 [PEPUSCH] *Treatise on Harmony* (2nd edn, p. 8) As those Melodies are most agreeable that go least by Leaps, and most by Degrees; and as the *Fundamental Bass* being only made use of, would occasion many Leaps in its Melody, we may therefore, to remedy that, use other Notes for Basses, which are then call'd *Suppos'd Basses.* These are necessary on many Occasions; for besides that they do not in reality change the Harmony, they make the Melodies capable of great Variety; for, by making use of the *Fundamental* and of the *Suppos'd Basses* as Occasion requires, we are enabled to make the Parts to move the more by Degrees, and consequently the Melodies will be the more agreeable, and Sing the better.

supposition *see* counterpoint
1728 CHAMBERS *Supposition,* in Music, the using of two successive Notes, of the same Value, as to Time; the one whereof being a Discord, *supposes* the other a Concord. See *Harmony.* ¶ The Harmony, Mr. *Malcolm* observes, is always to be full on the accented Parts of the Bar, or Measure, but not on the unaccented. Discords may transiently pass, without any Offence to the Ear. This transient Use of Discords, follow'd by Concords, makes what we from the *French* call *Supposition.* See *Concord* and *Discord.* ¶ There are several Kinds of *Supposition*: The first is, when the Parts proceed gradually from Concord to Discord; and Discord to Concord; the intervening Discord serving only as a Transition to the following Concord. ¶ Another Kind is, when the Parts do not proceed gradually from the Discord to the Concord, but descend to it by the Distance of a Third. ¶ A third Kind, like the second, is, when the rising to the Discord is gradual, but the descending from it to the following Concord, is by the Distance of a fourth. ¶ A fourth Kind, very different from all the rest, is, when the Discord falls on the unaccented Parts of the Measure, and the Rising to it is by the Distance of a fourth. In which Case 'tis absolutely necessary to follow it immediately, by a gradual Descent into a Concord, that has just been heard before the Harmony; to make the preceding Discord pass without Offence, and only seem a Transition into the Concord. **1730** BAILEY *Dict. Britannicum* (1st edn) *Supposition* (in *Musick*) is the Using 2 successive Notes of the same Value, as to Time, the one of which, being a Discord, supposes the other a Concord.

1721 MALCOLM *Treatise of Musick* (pp. 433-4) The *Harmony* must always be full upon the accented Parts of the *Measure,* but upon the unaccented Parts that is not so requisite: Wherefore *Discords* may transiently pass there without any Offence to the Ear: This the *French* call *Supposition,* because the transient *Discord* supposes a *Concord* immediately to follow it, which is of infinite Service in *Musick,* as contributing mightily to that infinite Variety of *Air* of which *Musick* is capable. **1721 or after** ANON. Institutions of Musick (rear of LC copy of Bayne, p. 12) The Harmony must alwayes be full upon the accented Parts of the measure, but upon the unaccented Parts that is not so requisite, wherefore Discords may transiently pass there without any offence to the Ear. This the French call Supposition, because the transient Discord supposes a Concord immediately to follow it, which is of infinite service in Musick as contributing mightily to that infinite variety of aire of which Musick is capable. **1731** [PEPUSCH] *Treatise on Harmony* (2nd edn, p. 42) There is a Way in *Division* of making use of Discords upon the second accented part of the Barr; this is call'd *Supposition,* because the Discord so brought in is *suppos'd* to be a Note higher, or a Note lower than it is; that is to say, 'tis suppos'd to be the Concord it goes to.

[suspension] *see* anticipation, postposition, resolution, supposition

sveglia *see* risvegliatoio
1598 FLORIO It→E *Sueglione,* a loude instrument called a hautboy. **1611** FLORIO It→E *Sueglia,* a kind of racke or torture in Florence. Also a hautboy or such winde instrument. *Sueglione,* a hautboy or loud instrument. Also the drone of a bagpipe. **1659** TORRIANO-FLORIO It→E *Sveglia,* a loud wind instrument called a Hautboy **Sveglione,* ... also a

Hautboy, or such loud wind instrument, also a Drone in a bag-pipe

sympathy *see* antipathy
1603 ROBINSON *Schoole of Mvsicke* [Cv] [*re* the lute] ... Note, that you strike cleane, plump together in a full stroke of many parts or strings, sometimes loude, sometimes soft, letting your right hand, answere the left hand at the instant, striuing with no stroke: and to conclude, the touch of the one hand, to answere the stop of the other hand, in the full harmony of consent, (called a *Simpathie*,) and then to know what strings to strike, with what fingers, mark all these rules following ... **c.1715-20** NORTH Theory of Sounds BL Add. 32534, f. 56v ... the manner how sounding strings tuned in just symphony affect each other so visibly as is comonly observed, w[ch] the admirers of such phenomena call sympathy ... **1726-8** NORTH Theory of Sounds BL Add. 32535, f. 33v ... there will be found of all sorts and degrees, w[ch] are comonly distinguisht by the termes of Concord, and discord. In the distinction of w[ch], wee must be very carefull, els wee shall be carryed Into great perplexity & confusion, therefore as before let us take another string of the same materiall, and of size length & tension exactly equall with the former, and place it at any distance in y[e] same room; and there will appear what fond people call sympathy, that is If one of these strings is made to sound, the other will of it self manifestly vibrate, and emitt a sound of the same condition, and tone with its fellow; ...

symphoniacus *see* chorister, style (stylo symphoniaco)
1538 ELYOT L→E *Symphoniacus*, a syngynge boye. **1552** HULOET L→E § *simphoniaci pueri* Syngyng boyes. *Symphoniacus seruus, Typanista, Tympanotriba*. Drumslade player. **1565** COOPER L→E *Symphoníacus. pen. corr. Adiectiuum*. Belongynge to concent and harmonie. § *Ducere pueros symphoniacos. Cic.* Singyng boyes. *Symphoniaci serui. Cic.* Seruaunts that in shippes, with playinge & singynge encourage souldiours to fighte more fiersely. **1587** THOMAS L→E *Symphoniacus, a, um*. Of or belonging to consent & harmonie: *also* a trumpeter in ships of war. § *Symphoniaci serui*. Seruants that in ships with playing & singing encourage souldiers to fight more fiercely: singing men, musicians. **1598** FLORIO It→E *Simphoniaco*, of or belonging to consent or harmonie. **1611** FLORIO It→E *Simphoniaco*, of or belonging to accord and consent in time, tune and harmony. **1659** TORRIANO-FLORIO It→E **Simphoniaco, Simphonico*, according to time, tune or harmonie.

symphonical
1656 BLOUNT (1st edn) *Symphoniacal (symphoniacus)* of or belonging to consent and harmony. **1658** PHILLIPS (1st edn) *Symphoniacal*, (Greek) belonging to Symphony, *i.* consent in Harmony, agreement in tune or time. **1676** COLES *Symphoniacal*, belonging to ¶ *Symphony* **1704** *Cocker's Engl. Dict.* (1st edn) *Symphonical*, Musically, Harmonically, Agreeably.

symphonio
1538 ELYOT L→E *Symphonio, are*, to agree or accord in one. **1552** HULOET L→E *Symphonio, as*. Accorden or agree in one tune. *symphonio. as*. Concorden or agree in musycke or tune *Symphonio. as*. Consenten or agre in musicke or tune. **1589** RIDER L→E *Symphonio* To concorde, or agree togeather in musicke. **1611** FLORIO It→E *Simphonio*, a Quire of singers. **1659** TORRIANO-FLORIO It→E *Simphonio*, a Quire of singing men.

symphonious
1730 BAILEY *Dict. Britannicum* (1st edn) *Symphonious*, pertaining to Symphony. *Milton*.

symphonist
1611 FLORIO It→E *Simphonista*, a Querister. Also a tuner of songs. **1656** BLOUNT (1st edn) *Symphonist (symphonista)* a Chorister, one that sings with true tune and time. **1659** TORRIANO-FLORIO It→E *Simphonista*, a tuner of songs or musick, also a Querister. **1676** COLES *Symphonista, Greek*. a Songster. **1704** *Cocker's Engl. Dict.* (1st edn) *Symphonists*, Musicians, Singing, Masters

symphony *as harmony or consort, see* asymphony, band, interlude, opera, prelude, ritornello, style (stylo symphonico), tone, voluntary
1500 *Ortus Vocabulorum* L→E Simphonia e. dicit a sin q est cum & phonos. sonus quasi consonancia vocum & et est proprie modulationis temperamentum ex graui & acuto consonantibus sonis siue in voce siue in flatu siue in pulsu. f.p. Simphonides nomen proprium Simphonizo as. i. cantare cum simphonia **1538** ELYOT L→E *Symphonia*, a consent in tune, also harmony. **1552** HULOET L→E *symphonia, sympsalma*. Concorde in

musycke or tune. *Symphonia, Sympsalma.* Consente in musyke or tune. *Symphonia, Sympsalmo* Tunable singyng. **1565** COOPER L→E *Symphonia, pen. corr. Cic.* Concent in tune: harmonie. § *Symphonia discors. Horat.* Vntunable musike. *Symphoniæ cantus. Cic.* The concent and harmonie of diuers playinge or singynge together. **1587** THOMAS L→E *Symphonia, æ, f.g.* Consent in tune, or harmonie, a tuneable singing without iarring, &c. **1589** RIDER L→E § *Symphonia concentio, f. concentus, m.* Tunable singing. *Symphonia discors, discordes modi.* Musicke disagreeing. **1593** HOLLYBAND Fr→E *Symphonie,* an agreement of voyces or instruments: *f.* **1598** FLORIO It→E *Simphonia,* an accord or consent in tune time or harmonie, a tunable singing without iarring. *Sinfonia, Sinphonia,* a concordance or consent in musicke. **1609** CAWDREY (2nd edn) *symphonie,* harmonie and consent in tune. **1611** COTGRAVE Fr→E *Symphonie: f.* Harmonie, tunable singing, &c, a consent in tune. **1611** FLORIO It→E *Simphonia,* an accord or consent in time, tune and harmony. Also a tunable singing without iarring. *Sinfonia,* as *Simphonia. Sinphonia,* as *Simphonia.* **1616** BULLOKAR *Symphonie.* Harmony or consent in Musick. **1623** COCKERAM *Symphony.* Harmony, consent in Musick. **1656** BLOUNT (1st edn) *Symphony (symphonia)* consent in tune or time, a tuneable singing without jarring, harmony. **1659** TORRIANO-FLORIO It→E *Simphonia,* an accord or consent in time, tune and harmonie, a tunable singing without any discordance or jarring *Sinfonia,* as *Simphonia. Zinfonia, Zimphonia,* as *Simphonia.* **1676** COLES *Symphony, Greek.* harmony, consent. **1688** MIEGE-COTGRAVE Fr→E *Symphonie,* (f.) cd. *harmonie,* symphony, harmony. § *Une belle, agreable, douce, merveilleuse, charmante, ou ravissante Symphonie,* a fine, agreeable, sweet, admirable, charming, or ravishing Symphony. **1696** PHILLIPS (5th edn) *Symphony,* Musick, Sounds and Concords pleasing to the Ear, whether Vocal or Instrumental. Sometimes a Consort of Instrumental Musick, is called a Symphony. **1702** KERSEY *New Engl. Dict.* (1st edn) A *Symphony,* a melodious harmony, *or* musical consort. **1704** *Cocker's Engl. Dict.* (1st edn) *Symphony,* agreement, consent, or harmony. **1706** KERSEY-PHILLIPS (6th edn) *Symphony,* Musical Sounds and Concords pleasing to the Ear, either Vocal or Instrumental; also a Consort of Instrumental Musick. **1707** *Gloss. Angl. Nova* (1st edn) *Symphony,* (Gr.) a melodious Harmony, or musical Consort. **1721** BAILEY *An Univ. Etymolog. Engl. Dict.* (1st edn) *Symphony,* (*symphony,* F. *symphonia,* L. of συμφωνία, *Gr.*) a Melodious Harmony or Musical Consort. **1724** [PEPUSCH] *Short Explic. of Foreign Words in Mus. Bks.* (p. 70) *Simphonia,* see the Word *Symphonia.* (p. 75) *Symphonia,* or *Simphonia,* a Symphony; by which is to be understood Airs in Two, Three, or Four Parts, for Instruments of any Kind; or the Instrumental Parts of Songs, Motets, Operas, or Concertos are so called. **1726** BAILEY *An Univ. Etymolog. Engl. Dict.* (3rd edn) *Symphony* (*Symphonie,* F. *Symphonia,* L. of συμφωνία of συμφωνέω to agree in one Sound, *Gr.*) a Melodious Harmony or Musical Consort, by which it is to be understood, Airs in 2, 3 or 4 Parts, for Instruments of any Kind; or the Instrument Parts of *Songs, Motets, Operas* or *Concerto*'s. **1728** CHAMBERS *Symphony,* in Music, a Consonance, or Consort of several Sounds agreeable to the Ear; whether they be Vocal or Instrumental, or both; call'd also *Harmony.* See *Harmony* and *Consonance.* ¶ Some Authors restrain *Symphony* to the sole Music of Instruments: In this Sense, say they, the Recitativo's in such an Opera were intolerable, but the *Symphonies* excellent. See *Song.* ¶ The *Symphony* of the Ancients went no further than to two or more Voices or Instruments set to Unison; for they had no such Thing as Music in Parts; as is very well prov'd by M. *Perrault*; at least, if ever they knew such a Thing, it must be allow'd to have been lost. See *Synaulia.* ¶ 'Tis to *Guido Aretine* we owe the Invention of Composition: 'Twas he [who] first join'd in one Harmony several distinct Melodies; and brought it even the Length of four Parts, *viz.* Bass, Tenor, Counter, and Treble. See *Harmony* and *Melody.* ¶ The Word is form'd from the Greek συν, with, and φώνη, Sound. **1730** BAILEY *Dict. Britannicum* (1st edn) *Symphony* (*symphonia,* L. συμφωνία, of συμφωνέω, Gr. to agree in one Sound) a Consonance or Concert of several Sounds agreeable to the Ear, whether they be vocal, or instrumental, or both, also called Harmony. **1737** DYCHE-PARDON (2nd edn) *Symphony* (S.) sometimes means the Agreement of several Voices, or a Concert of several Instruments; and sometimes a musical Instrument; and sometimes Harmony abstractly considered.

1582 *Batman vppon Bartholome* (p. 422) And so *Isid.* saith, that *Simphonia* is a temperate modulation and according in sounds high and low, and by this harmony, high voyce accordeth: so that if one discordeth the hearing. [marginalia: '*Simphonia, is a consent in tune, called harmony.*'] **1617-24** FLUDD *Utriusque Cosmi Maioris: De Templo*

Musicæ (p. 209) *Symphonia* est distinctorum sonorum & melodiarum concros harmonia seu congruens consensus. **1636** BUTLER *Principles of Musik* (p. 94) [*re* types of instrumental music] ... *Symphona*, that have a *Symphoni* or *Harmoni* of Partes in themselvs, (as *Organ, Harp, Lute*:) ... **1694** HOLDER *Treatise of Natural Grounds* (*Introduction*) ... This is properly in Symphony, *i.e.* Consent of more Voices in different Tones; ... **1721** MALCOLM *Treatise of Musick* (pp. 574-5) [*re* whether ancient music was superior to modern music] ... But that there be no Difference about mere Words, observe, that the Question is not, Whether the Ancients ever joyned more Voices or Instruments together in one *Symphony*; but, whether several Voices were joyned, so as each had a distinct and proper *Melody*, which made among them a Succession of various *Concords*; and were not in every Note *Unisons*, or at the same Distance from each other, as *8ves*? which last will agree to the general Signification of the Word *Symphonia*; yet 'tis plain, that in such Cases there is but one Song, and all the Voices perform the same individual *Melody*; ... § (p. 578) *Cassiodorus* says, *Symphonia est temperamentum sonitus gravis ad acutum, vel acuti ad gravem, modulamen efficiens, sive in voce sive in percussione, sive in flatu. i.e. Symphony* is an Adjustment of a grave Sound to an acute, or an acute to a grave, making *Melody*. § (pp. 579-80) [having established that Aristotle generally equated harmonia with symphonia:] ... Now we shall make Aristotle clear his own Meaning in the Passages adduced: He uses *Symphonia* to express Two Kinds of *Consonance*; the one, which he calls by the general Name *Symphonia*, is the Consonance of Two Voices that are in every Note *unison*, and the other, which he calls *Antiphonia*, of Two Voices that are in every Note *8ve*: In his *Problems*, § 19. *Prob*. 16. He asks why *Symphonia* is not as agreeable as *Antiphonia*; and answers because in *Symphonia* the one Voice being altogether like or as *One* with the other, they eclipse one another. The *Symphoni* here plainly must signify *Unisons*, and he explains it elsewhere by calling them *Omophoni*: And that the *8ve* is the *Antiphoni* is plain, for it was a common Name to *8ve*; and *Aristotle* himself explains the *Antiphoni* by the Voice of a Boy and a Man that are as *Nete* and *Hypate*, which were *8ve* in *Pythagoras*'s Lyre... his Meaning is plainly this, *viz.* that when Two Voices sing together one Song, 'tis more agreeable that they be *8ve* than *unison* with one another, in every Note: ... **1736** TANS'UR *Compleat Melody* (3rd edn, p. 70) *Symphony*, signifies an *Agreement*; or Consent in *Harmony*; also an *Interlude*, or *Prelude*, being agreeable, or in Symphony with a Piece of *Musick*.

symphony *as instrument, see* nicchio, vielle
1611 FLORIO It→E *Simphonia*, ... Also a kinde of musicall instrument. **1659** TORRIANO-FLORIO It→E *Simphonia*, ... also a kind of musical Instrument.

1582 *Batman vppon Bartholome* (p. 424) The Simphonye is an instrument of Musicke, and is made of an hollowe tree closed in leather on either side, and minstralls beateth it with stickes, and by accord of high and low, thereof commeth full sweete notes, as *Isi.* saith: neuertheles y[e] accord of all soundes be called Symphonia in like wise, as y[e] accord of diuers voyces is called *Chorus* ...

sympsalma *see* selah, symphony
1538 ELYOT L→E *Sympsalma*, a concorde in syngynge. **1587** THOMAS L→E *Sympsalma, Isid.* A concord in singing. **1589** RIDER L→E *Synpsalma* [sic]. Concord in singing. **1611** FLORIO It→E *Simpsalma*, concord in singing.

synaphe *see* tetrachord
1731 PRELLEUR *Modern Musick-Master* ('A Brief History of Musick', p. 7) [*re* the ancient diatonic system] ... By *Synaphe* they understood that *Conjunction* which is when two Tetrachords are joyned in one and the same Note both makeing no more than an *Eptachord*, or seven Strings; as it happens in the two highest and in the two lowest *Tetrachords* ...

synaulia *see* aula, aulos
1728 CHAMBERS *Synaulia*, in the ancient Music, a Contest of Pipes, performing alternately, without Singing. ¶ Mr. *Malcolm*, who doubts whether the Ancients had properly any such Thing as Instrumental Music, that is, Music composed wholly for Instruments, without any Singing; yet quotes the Practice of the *Synaulia* from *Athenæus*. See *Symphony, Harmony, Music, &c.* **1730** BAILEY *Dict. Britannicum* (1st edn) *Synaulia* (in *antient Musick*) a Contest of Pipes, performing alternately without Singing.

1721 MALCOLM *Treatise of Musick* (p. 587) ... *Athenæus* says, *The* Synaulia *was a Contest of Pipes performing alternately without singing.*

synaxis *see* sinassi
1589 RIDER L→E *Synaxis, f.* A godly assembly in singing of psalmes.

syncopation *see* cadence, diminution, driving note
1670 BLOUNT (3rd edn) *Syncopation (syncopatio)* ... It is a term in Musick, when the striking of time falls to be in the midst of a *Semibrief* or *Minim*, &c. or (as Musicians usually term it) Notes driven till the time falls even again. *Playford's Introd. to Musick. pa.* 28. **1676** COLES *Syncopation*, when the striking of time falls in the midst of a note, notes driven till the time falls even again. **1704** HARRIS *Syncopation*, a Term in Musick, which is when a Note of one Part ends and breaks off upon the middle of a Note of another part. **1706** KERSEY-PHILLIPS (6th edn) *Syncopation*, a Term in *Musick*, which is us'd when a Note of one Part ends and breaks off upon the middle of a Note of another Part. **1707** *Gloss. Angl. Nova* (1st edn) *Syncopation*, (Gr.) a Term in Musick, when a Note of one part ends and breaks off upon the middle of a Note of another part. **1737** DYCHE-PARDON (2nd edn) *Syncopation* (S.) in *Musick*, is when one Note both ends one Part of the Tune, or a Bar, and begins another.

1596 ANON. *Pathway to Musicke* [E ii] *Of Sincopation, and what it is.* ¶ It is when the smaller noates are pronounced by diuision of the greater, as an odde minome, by the diuiding of a sembrieffe, or of a crotchet by the diuiding of a minom ... **1597** MORLEY *Plaine and Easie Introdvction* (p. 152) *Phi.* ... is not the close of the counter a Cadence. ¶ *Ma.* No, for a Cadence must alwaies bee bound or then odde, driuing a small note through a greater which the Latins (and those who haue of late daies written the art of musicke[)], call *Syncopation*, for all binding and hanging vpon notes is called *Syncopation* ... **1659** SIMPSON *Division-Violist* (p. 15) ... *Syncopation*, or *Binding*: that is; when a *Note* of *One Part*, ends, and breaks off, upon the *middle* of some *Note* of a different *Part*; ... **1667** PLAYFORD *Brief Intro. to Skill of Musick* (4th edn, p. 26) ... *Sincopation*, or breaking of the *Time* by the Driving a *Minim* through *Semibriefs*, or Crotchets through *Minums*, which is is [sic] the beating the Time in the middle of a Note or Sound. § (p. 28) *Sincopation* is when the beating of *Time* falls to be in the midst of a *Semibrief* or *Minum*, &c. or, as we usually term it, *Notes driven* till the *Time* falls even again: ... **1694** PURCELL-PLAYFORD *Intro. to Skill of Musick* (12th edn, n.p.) Notes of *Syncopation*, or *Driving-Notes*, are, when your Hand or Foot is taken up, or put down, while the *Note* is sounding, which is very awkward ... **after 1698** ANON. Musical Observations and Experiments BL Harley 4160, f. 40v Sinchopation is that part of descant wherin a concord is bound to a discord & the one half or part of the note is a concord & the other is a discord ... **c.1715-20** NORTH Theory of Sounds BL Add. 32534, f. 46v ... For when wee hear a tone & semitone beat or wallow, or any other Notes not concords fall foul upon one & other, wch is called sincopation, or even plain out of tune sounds so long as the pulses of Each are Isochronicall, that very regularity in the particulars, sanctifies the mixt sounds, and the Ear bears a continuance of them; ... **1721** MALCOLM *Treatise of Musick* (pp. 412-13) *You'll* find a Mark, like the Arch of a Circle drawn from one Note to another, comprehending Two or more Notes in the same or different Degrees; ... If the Notes are in the same Degree, it signifies that 'tis all one Note, to be made as long as the whole Notes so connected; and this happens most frequently betwixt the last Note of one *Bar* and the first of the next, which is particularly called *Syncopation*, a Word also applied in other Cases: Generally, when any *Time* of a *Measure* ends in the Middle of a Note, *that is*, in *common Time*, if the Half or any of the 4*th* Parts of the *Bar*, counting from Beginning, ends in the Middle of a Note, in the *simplest Treble* if any 3*d* Part of the *Measure* ends within a Note, in the *compound Treble* if any 9*th* Part, and in the Two mixt *Triples*, if any 6*th* or 12*th* Part ends in the Middle of any Note, 'tis called *Syncopation*, which properly signifies a striking or breaking of the *Time*, because the Distinctness of the several *Times* or Parts of the *Measure* is as it were hurt or interrupted hereby, which yet is of good Use in *Musick* as Experience will teach. **c.1726** NORTH Musicall Gramarian BL Add. 32533, f. 92 ... it is usuall to tye ye hard & smooth accords, wch is called sincopation ... **1731** PRELLEUR *Modern Musick-Master* (I, p. 11) *Of Syncopation or driving Notes.* ¶ Syncopation is when the Hand or Foot is taking up or put down while a Note is sounding which is pretty hard to a Beginner; but this being once conquer'd he may think himself a pretty good Timist.

syncope *see* descant, driving note
1704 HARRIS *Syncope*, in Musick, is the driving a Note, when some shorter Note prefix'd at the beginning of the Measure, or Half-measure, is immediately follow'd by two, three, or more Notes

of a greater Quantity, before you meet with another short Note equivalent to that which began the driving, to make the Number even. As when an odd *Crotchet* comes before two, three, or more *Minims*, or an odd *Quaver* before two, three, or more *Crotchets*. **1706** KERSEY-PHILLIPS (6th edn) In *Musick, Syncope* is the driving of a Note, when some shorter Note, set at the beginning of the Measure, or Half-Measure, is immediately follow'd by two, three, or more Notes of greater Quantity, before you meet with another short Note, equivalent to that which began the Driving; so as to make the Number or Time fall even again: As when an odd *Crotchet* comes before two, three, or more *Minims*; or an odd Quaver before two, three, or more Crotchets. **1708** KERSEY *Dict. Anglo-Brit.* (1st edn) *Syncope*, ... In *Musick*, the driving of a Note. **1721** BAILEY *An Univ. Etymolog. Engl. Dict.* (1st edn) *Syncope*, (in *Musick*) is the driving of a Note, as when an odd *Crochet* comes before 2 or 3 *Minims*, or an odd *Quaver* between 2 or 3 or more *Crotchets*. **1724** [PEPUSCH] *Short Explic. of Foreign Words in Mus. Bks.* (p. 75) *Syncope* in Musick is the driving of a Note, as when an odd Crotchet comes before Two or Three Minims, or an odd Quaver between Two, Three, or more Crotchets. **1728** CHAMBERS *Syncope*, in Music, signifies the Division of a Note; used when two or more Notes of one Part answer to a single Note of the other Part: as when a Semibreve of the one answers to two or three Crotchets of the other. ¶ A Note is said to be *Syncope'd* when it has a Point added on the Side of it; which increases its Value by one half.

after 1517 ANON. Art of Mvsic BL Add. 4911, f. 23v ... as *franchinus gaforus* say, is. Sincopa is ane mensurall canticle. It is ane reductione of ane noitt beand mair nor and noit, or mair noittis, fill and vther or vthoris noittis. To ye quhilke in commeration it dois properlye conttein. Or cincopa is ane mensurall sang is ane passarg of ane semebrewe or ane Mynnym be the middis of tua. Ayrae four fyve or sax man noittis or of may noittis. eftir ye arbitry of Musicorams or of compositions of canticlis. **1636** BUTLER *Principles of Musik* (p. 64) Syncope is the Disjoining and Conjoining of a Mesure-note: when (in respect of Time) it is disjoined into 2 Partes; whereof the former is conjoined with the precedent half-note in one Time, and the later with his subsequent half-note in an other Time: The Conjoining of which latter with his half-note following, is called by *Sethus Alligatio*, and by *Morley*, Binding. In which, for distinction, the first of these two conjoined half-notes is called the Bound-note, and the second the Binding-note: unto which two, there answereth (either in the Base or in soom other Parte) one entire Mesure-note, which is as it were the Band, that holdeth them bothe together: ... § (p. 70) *Disjoining and Conjoining*. Agreeable heereunto is the Definition of †*Sethus* [marginalia: '†*Cap.* 12.']: *Syncope est irregularis applicatio Notulæ ad Tactum, facta propter minorem Figuram praecedentem*. which hee dooeth thus explane: *Semibrevis enim, cum Tactu suo absolvatur, Regulariter in Depressione Tactus inchoatur, & in Elevatione finitur. Quando autem ante Semibrevem Minima in Notulis vel Pausis collocatur, quae Tactum inchoat in Depressione; necesse est ut Semibrevis in altera parte Tactus, hoc est in Elevatione, incipiatur, & in Depressione sequentis Tactus desinat: atq; ita partibus suis ad diversos Tactus distrabatur*. **1653** ?BROUNCKER *Renatvs Des-Cartes Exc. Comp. of Musick* (p. 54) A *Syncopa* is, when the end of one Note in one voice is heard at the same time with the beginning of one other Note of an adverse part; ... **1665** SIMPSON *Principles of Practical Mvsick* (p. 30) *Syncope*, or *Driving* a Note, is, when, after some shorter Note which begins the Measure, there immediately follow two, three, or more Notes of a greater quantity, before you meet with another short Note (like that which began the *Driving*) to make the Number even, As, when an *odd Crochet* comes before two, three, or more *Minims*; or an odd *Quaver* before two, three, or more *Crochets*. **c.1698-c.1703** NORTH Cursory Notes (*C-K CN* p. 190) Hitherto of bare fac[ed] discords, as one may call them in counterpoint; the more ordinary and better mixture of them is in breaking notes upon one and another, which they call a sincope, and (improperly) binding.

synemmenon *see* diagram, musica ficta, nete, paranete, scale, systema conjunctum, trite
early 18th C. PEPUSCH various papers BL Add. 29429, f. 6 Synemmenon, i.e. accidental. **1721** MALCOLM *Treatise of Musick* (p. 522) ... Afterwards [in the development of the ancient septichord lyre] a third Tetrachord was added to the *septichord Lyre*; which was either conjunct with it, making Ten Chords, or disjunct, making Eleven. The Conjunct was particularly distinguished by the Name *Synemmenon, i.e. Tetrachordum conjunctarum*; and the other by the Name of *Diezeugmenon, i.e. disjunctarum*. And now the middle Tetrachord was called *Meson* (*mediarum*;) and to the Words *Hypate, Parhypate, Lichanos,*

Trite, Paranete, Nete, are now added the Name of the Tetrachord, which is necessary for Distinction; ... **1731** PRELLEUR *Modern Musick-Master* ('A Brief History of Musick', p. 7) [*re* the history of the ancient diatonic system] ... But finding between the *Mese* and the *Paramese*, i.e. between *A* and *B*, a Full Tone, that made the *fourth* from *F* to *B* and the *fifth* from *B* to *F*, very disagreeable (the one being a *Sharp Fourth* and the other a *flat fifth*) made another *Tetrachord* which they called *Tetrachordon Synemenon*, that is to say *Tetrachord of the Conjoyned* by which means they Caused a String to fall between the *Mese* and the *Paramese* (that is between *A* and *B*) which they called *Trite Synemenon*. i.e. the *Third of the Conjoyned*; this they marked with a *Flat*, in the Space between *A* and *B*.

synphoni

1721 MALCOLM *Treatise of Musick* (pp. 507-8) The *4th* and *5th* and their Compounds he [Ptolomy] calls *Synphoni* or *consonant* ... others call [only] ... the *4ths Synphoni* ...

sypharium

1538 ELYOT L→E *Sypharium*, a curtayne hanged before minstrels whan they synge. **1565** COOPER L→E *Sypharium*. A courtaine hangynge before minstrelles when they singe. **1587** THOMAS L→E *Sypharium, rij. n.g.* *A curten hanging before ministrels [sic] when they sing.

syren *see* siren

Syrinx *see* Pan

1658 PHILLIPS (1st edn) *Syrinx*, an *Arcadian* Nimph, one of the *Naiades*, who flying from the violence of *Pan*, was turned into a reed, of which *Pan* made his pastoral pipe, which for her sake he much delighted to play upon. **1676** COLES *Syrinx*, a Nymph (flying from *Pan*) turn'd into a reed, which he made his pipes of.

syrinx *see* aulos, siringa, tibia

1538 ELYOT L→E *Syrinx*, a pype or recorder. **1552** HULOET L→E *Syrinx* Pype called a recorder. *syrinx* Recorder or pype so called. **1565** COOPER L→E *Syrinx, syringis, fœm. g*... A pipe: **1587** THOMAS L→E *Syrinx. is, & Syringa, æ, f.g.* *A pipe, flute, or recorder: a reede **1589** RIDER L→E *Syrinx, Syringa, f. monaulos, vide* pipe [aula, tibia]. A Recorder, or fluite **1706** KERSEY-PHILLIPS (6th edn) *Syrinx*, a Reed, a Pipe, a Flute;

systaltic *see* diastaltic

system *see* concinnous, diastem, diatonic system, guidonian system, monochord, particular system, position, scale of music¡

1587 THOMAS L→E *Systema, Iun.* The compasse of a song. **1589** RIDER L→E *systema* The compass of a song. **1656** BLOUNT (1st edn) *Systeme (systema)* the compasse of a song **1658** PHILLIPS (1st edn) *System*, (Greek) ... also the compasse of a Song. **1676** COLES *System, Greek.* the compass of a song **1704** HARRIS *System*, in Musick, is the Extent of a certain Number of *Chords*, having its bounds toward the *Grave* and *Acute*, which hath been differently determin'd by the different Progress made in Musick, and according to the different Divisions of the *Monochord*. ¶ The *System* of the Ancients, was composed of four *Tetrachords*, and one *Supernumerary Chord*, the whole making Fifteen Chords. **1706** KERSEY-PHILLIPS (6th edn) In *Musick*, *System* is an extent of a certain number of *Chords*, having its Bounds toward the *Grave* and *Acute*; which has been differently determined by the different Progress made in that Science, and according to the different Divisions of the *Monochord*. **1708** KERSEY *Dict. Anglo-Brit.* (1st edn) *Systema, (G.)* a System, the Body of a Science, the compass of a Song: **1724** [PEPUSCH] *Short Explic. of Foreign Words in Mus. Bks.* (p. 76) *System* of Musick is a Treatise of Musick, or Book treating of Musick in all its several Parts, both Mathematical and Practical. **1726** BAILEY *An Univ. Etymolog. Engl. Dict.* (3rd edn) *System* (of *Musick*) is a Treatise of Musick, or a Book treating of Musick in all its several Parts, both Mathematical and Practical. **1728** CHAMBERS *System* ... [*see* Appendix] **1730** BAILEY *Dict. Britannicum* (1st edn) *System* (in *Musick*) a compound Interval, or an Interval composed of several lesser, such as is the *Octave*, &c. or it is an Extent of a certain Number of Chords, having its Bounds towards the Grave and Acute; which has been differently determined by the different Progress made in Musick, and according to the different Divisions of the Monochord. § *Concinnous Systems* (in *Musick*) are those which consist of such Parts as are fit for Musick, and those Parts placed in such an Order between the Extremes, as that the Succession of Sounds from one Extreme to the other may have a good Effect.

Inconcinnous Systems (in *Musick*) are those where the simple Intervals are inconcinnous or badly disposed betwixt the Extremes.

1617-24 FLUDD *Utriusque Cosmi Maioris: De Templo Musicæ* (p. 172) *Systema* est subjectum illud seu templi quadratum; quod ex clavis & sýllabis in lineis & spaciis dispositis constituitur, in quo sonorum ratio & cantus melodia consistit. **1664** BIRCHENSHA-ALSTED *Templvm Mvsicvm* (p. 25) *The greater System for the most part doth consist of ten Lines: and serveth for the Composing of a Song, called otherwise a conjoyned System.* ¶ *The lesser System doth consist of five Lines, and serveth chiefly to a Song pricked out. This is otherwise called a simple System.* **1721** MALCOLM *Treatise of Musick* (pp. 510-11) A *System* is an *Interval* composed, or conceived as composed, of several lesser. As there is no least *Interval* in the Nature of the Thing, so we can conceive any given *Interval* as composed of, or equal to the Sum of others; but here a *System* is an *Interval* which is actually divided in Practice; and where along with the Extremes we conceive always some intermediate Terms [intervallic members]. As *Systems* are only a Species of *Intervals*, so they have all the same Distinctions, except that of *Composite* and *Incomposite*. They were [in ancient Greece] also distinguished several other Ways not worth Pains to repeat. But there are Two we cannot pass over, which are these, *viz.* into *concinnous* and *inconcinnous*; the first composed of such Parts, and in such Order as is fit for *Melody*; the other is of an opposite Nature. Then into *perfect* and *imperfect*: Any *System* less than *Disdiapason* was reckoned *imperfect*; and that only called *Perfect*, because within its Extremes are contained Examples of the simple and original *Concords*, and in all the Variety of Order, in which their *concinnous* Part ought to be taken; which Differences constitute what they call'd the *Species* or *Figuræ consonantiarum*; which were also different according to the *Genera*: It was also called the *Systema maximum*, or *immutatum*, because they thought it was the greatest Extent or Difference of *Tune*, that we can go in making good *Melody*; tho' some added a 5*th* to the *Disdiapason* for the greatest System; and some suppose Three 8*ves*; but they all owned the *Diapason* to be the most *perfect*, with respect to the Agreement of its Extremes; and that however many 8*ves* we put in the *Systema maximum*, they must all be constituted or subdivided the same Way as the first: ... § (p. 518) We have already seen the essential Principles, of which the ancient *Scale* or *Diagramma*, which they called their *Systema perfectum*, was composed, in all its different Kinds.

systema conjunctum

1721 MALCOLM *Treatise of Musick* (p. 540) The *Tetrachord Synemmenon*, which makes what they called the *Systema conjunctum*, was added for joyning the upper and lower *Diapason* of the *Systema immutatum*; ...

systema temperato *see* temperament

1731 PRELLEUR *Modern Musick-Master* ('A Brief History of Musick', p. 13) ... There are yet several other Systems [of dividing the scale] besides these already mentioned but especially one worth more observation than the rest, which is what the Italians call *Systema Temperato* or *Participato* by reason of its being grounded upon *Temperament.* [sic]that is to say, the *increasing* of certain Intervals, and consequently the *decreasing* of others, which make it partake both of the *Diatonic* & *Chromatic* Systems. § ('A Brief History of Musick', p. 14) ... a learned Man (whose Name and the Age he lived in have been both lost as *Bontempi* reports) perceiving that the Ear was not offended at the decreasing of the *Fifth* of a Small matter; found by this means that admirable *Temperament* which allows the fourth, a little more extent, than its mathematical proportion does, and so makes the first & Second Tone of each *Tetrachord* equall; and consequently both capable of being divided into Semitones. This occasioned another System, which the Italians call *Systema-Temperato* or *Participato* because the addition of this *Chromatic String* causes the Octave to be divided into 12 Semitones, without leaving any Space [or] void either between, or in the two *Tetrachords* it consists of, and so joyns both the *Diatonic* and *Chromatic Systems* in one...

syzeugmenon

1587 THOMAS L→E *Syzeugmenon, Iun.* B. fa. b. mi. **1706** KERSEY-PHILLIPS (6th edn) *Syzeugmenon*, a Musical Note call'd *B-fa-be-mi.*

T

t

1724 [PEPUSCH] *Short Explic. of Foreign Words in Mus. Bks.* (p. 77) The Letter *T* is often used as an Abbreviation of the Word *Tutti*, for which see below. **1726** BAILEY *An Univ. Etymolog. Engl. Dict.* (3rd edn) *T.* (in *Musick Books*) is an Abbreviation of the *Italian* Word *Tutti, i.e.* all or altogther, which see. *T* (in *Mu. Books*) is used to denote the Tenor.

taballi *see* atabal

1598 FLORIO It→E *Taballi*, drums, drumslades, timbrels, or tabours. **1611** FLORIO It→E *Taballaro*, a Drummer, a Tabourer. *Taballi*, Drums, Drumslades, Tabours or Timbrels. **1659** TORRIANO-FLORIO It→E *Taballo, Taballi*, a drum, a drum-slade, a tabour, a timbrel.

taber *see* tabour

tablature *see* infigura, viol

1598 FLORIO It→E *Intauolare*, ... Also, to set any song to musicall notes. *Intauolato*, ... Also set in song or notes. *Intauolatura*, any song or musicke set in notes, pricke song. *Tauolare*, ... Also to set prick-song. *Tauolato*, ... set in prick-song. *Tauolatura*, a prick-song, a song set in prick-song. **1611** FLORIO It→E *Intauolatura*, ... Also set to prick-song. *Intauolare*, ... Also to set any dittie or song in prick-song or with notes. *Tauolare*, ... Also to set in Musike, or Prick-song. *Tauolato*, ... Also set to Musike or Prick-song. *Tauolatura*, any kind of Prick-song. **1659** TORRIANO-FLORIO It→E **Intavolare*, ... also to set a song or ditty in tablature, in pricksong, or notes. *Intavolatura*, ... a setting in Musick. **Tavolare*, ... also to set in musick, prick-song, plain song, or tablature *Tavolato*, ... also set to musick in tablature *Tavolatura*, any tablature or prick-song. **1688** MIEGE-COTGRAVE Fr→E *Tablature*, (f.) *Piece de Musique ecrite sur un Papier*, a Tablature, or Musick-book, directing one that plays upon the Lute or Guitarr, what Strings he is to strike by the letters of the Alphabet. § *donner une Leçon de Guitarre par Tablature*, to set down a Lesson upon the Guitar in Tablature. *Savoir (ou entendre) la Tablature*, to understand the Tablature. **1706** KERSEY-PHILLIPS (6th edn) *Tablature*, a sort of Musick-Book, directing one that plays upon the Lute or Guitar, what strings he is to strike, by the Letters of the Alphabet. **1707** *Gloss. Angl. Nova* (1st edn) *Tablature*, a kind of Musick Book directing to play on the Lute, Viol, *&c.* by the Letters of the Alphabet; **1724** [PEPUSCH] *Short Explic. of Foreign Words in Mus. Bks.* (p. 77) *Tabulatura*, or *Tablature*, is the old Way of writing Musick with Letters instead of Notes. **1726** BAILEY *An Univ. Etymolog. Engl. Dict.* (3rd edn) *Tablatura, Tablature*, is the old Way of Writing Musick with Letters instead of Notes. *Tablature*, a Musick Book, directing to play on the *Lute, Viol,* &c. *L.* **1728** CHAMBERS *Tablature*, in Music, in the general, is, when, to express the Sounds, or Notes of a Composition, we use Letters of the Alphabet, or Cyphers, or any other Characters, not usual in the modern Music. See *Score.* ¶ But in its stricter Sense, *Tablature* is the Manner of Writing a Piece for a Lute, Theorba, Guitarre, Bass-Viol, or the like; which is done by Writing on several parallel Lines (each whereof represents a String of the Instrument) certain Letters of the Alphabet; whereof, A marks that the String is to be struck open, *i.e.* without putting the Finger of the left Hand on the Head; B shews, that one of the Fingers is to be put on the first Stop; C on the second; D on the third, *&c.* See *Writing* of Music. ¶ The *Tablature* of the Lute is wrote in Letters of the Alphabet; that of the Harpsichord in the common Notes. See *Lute, Harpsichord, &c.* **1730** BAILEY *Dict. Britannicum* (1st edn) *Tablature* (of *tabula*, L.) a Musick-Book giving Directions for playing upon the Lute, Viol, *&c.* by Letters, Cyphers, *&c.* **1737** DYCHE-PARDON (2nd edn) *Tablature* (S.) the Manner of pricking or writing down Musical Lessons with Letters, &c. to direct the Player how to perform them.

1603 ROBINSON *Schoole of Mvsicke* [B ii] [*re* the lute] ... now hauing the names & knowledge of the strings and stops perfectly by roate, you shall also learne to know them by booke (called *Tablature.*)

table *see* belly, soundboard

1688 MIEGE-COTGRAVE Fr→E *Table d'Instrument de Musique*, cd, *le Dessus d'un Instrument*, the Belly of a musical Instrument.

tabour *see* accettabolo, adufe, atabal, atambor, bedon, pandera, tambour, tambourine, terga taurea, timbrel, tympany

1589 RIDER L→E A Tabret, *v.* taber [*see* tympanum]. **1611** COTGRAVE Fr→E *Tabour: m.* A Drumme; also, a Tabor. *Tabourasse: f.* A Drumme, or Tabor. *Tabourder.* To play on a Drumme, or Tabor; *Tabourdeur: m.* A Taborer, or Drummer. *Tabourement: m.* A Drumming; *Tabourer.* To drumme; *Taboureur: m.* A Drummer, or Taborer; **1650** HOWELL-COTGRAVE Fr→E † *Tabourasse: f.* A Drum, or Tabor. † *Tabourder.* To play on a Drum, or Tabor; † *Tabourdeur: m.* A Taborer, or Drummer. † *Tabourement: m.* A Drumming; † *Tabourer,* To drum; † *Taboureur: m.* A Drummer, or Taborer; **1702** KERSEY *New Engl. Dict.* (1st edn) A *Taber, tabor,* or *tabret,* a kind of drum. A *Taberer,* one that plays on the *taber.* A *Tabret, or* taber. § The *Taber and pipe.* **1706** KERSEY-PHILLIPS (6th edn) *Tabor* or *Tabret,* a kind of Drum. **1707** *Gloss. Angl. Nova* (1st edn) *Taber, Tabor,* or *Tabret,* a kind of Drum. **1708** KERSEY *Dict. Anglo-Brit.* (1st edn) *Tabor* or *Tabret,* a kind of Drum. **1721** BAILEY *An Univ. Etymolog. Engl. Dict.* (1st edn) *Taber, (Tabour, F.)* a small Drum. *Tabor, (Tabourin, F.)* a small Drum. **1728** CHAMBERS *Tabor, Tabourin,* a small Drum. See *Drum.* **1730** BAILEY *Dict. Britannicum* (1st edn) *Taber, Tabour, (tabour,* F.) a small Drum. *Taberer (un tambourineur,* F.) one that plays upon a small Drum, call'd a Tabour. *Tabret,* the same as *Tabor.* **1736** BAILEY *Dict. Britannicum* (2nd edn) *Taber, Tabour, (tambour de Basque,* or *Tambourin,* F. *Tamboril,* Sp.) a small Drum. *To Tabor,* to play upon the *Tabor.* **1737** BAILEY *The Univ. Etymolog. Engl. Dict.* (3rd edn, vol. 2) *Tabret,* a small drum. **1737** DYCHE-PARDON (2nd edn) *Taber* or *Tabour* (S.) a small Drum, which is beat or played upon with one Hand, and used as a Drone or Base to the Musick of a small Pipe played upon with the other, much in Vogue with the Country Folks at Wakes, Fairs, Weddings, and other Times of Festivity.

tabouren

1726 BAILEY *An Univ. Etymolog. Engl. Dict.* (3rd edn) To *Tabouren,* to make a drumming Noise. *Chauc.*

tabourin *see* tambourine

tabret *see* tabour, timbrel

tacet *see* rest

1688 MIEGE-COTGRAVE Fr→E *Tacet,* (m.) *la partie de Musique qui ne dit mot, & qui est marquée de pauses,* a Pause (or Rest) in Musick. § *Faire le Tacet,* to make a Pause (in Musick.) **1724** [PEPUSCH] *Short Explic. of Foreign Words in Mus. Bks.* (p. 77) *Tace,* or *Tacet,* to hold still, or keep Silence. **1726** BAILEY *An Univ. Etymolog. Engl. Dict.* (3rd edn) *Tace, Lat., Tacet, Ital.,* (in *Musick Books*) signifies to hold still or keep silence.

1736 TANS'UR *Compleat Melody* (3rd edn, p. 67) *Tace, Tacet, Sospiro,* (Ital.) Either of those Words signify, *Silence,* or to *Rest;* which Words are often set over those *Characters* called *Rests.*

tacitista

1611 FLORIO It→E *Tacitista,* ... Also a professor of silence.

tact *see* beating, manuductor, stroke, time, touch

1596 ANON. *Pathway to Musicke* [Ev] *Of tacture or striking, and what is tacture.* ¶ It is a successiue mouing of the hand, directing the quantity of all the noats and rests in the song. **1609** DOWLAND-ORNITHOPARCUS *Micrologvs* (p. 46) Wherefore *Tact* is a successiue motion in singing, directing the equalitie of the measure: Or it is a certaine motion, made by the hand of the chiefe singer, according to the nature of the marks, which directs a Song according to Measure.... *Tact* is three-fold, the greater, the lesser, and the proportionate. The greater is a Measure made by a slow, and as it were reciprocall motion. The writers call this *Tact* the whole, or totall *Tact.* And, because it is the true *Tact* of all Songs, it comprehends in his motion a *Semibreefe* not diminished: or a *Breefe* diminished in a duple. ¶ The lesser *Tact,* is the halfe of the greater, which they call a *Semitact.* Because it measures by it[s] motion a *Semibreefe,* diminished in a duple: this is allowed of onely by the vnlearned. ¶ The Proportionate is that, whereby three *Semibreefes* are vttered against one, (as in a Triple) or against two, as in a *Sesquialtera...* **1614** RAVENSCROFT *Briefe Discovrse* (p. 20) *Tact, Touch* or *Time,* is, a certaine *Motion* of the hand (whereby the quantity of *Notes* and *Rests* are directed) by an equall *Measure,* according to the properties of the *Signes* of the *Degrees...* **1636** BUTLER *Principles of Musik* (p. 24) ... the time of all Notes is ... mesured by *Tactus* or the Stroke of the Hand ...

tactus *see* arsis & thesis, beating, manuductor, stroke, time, touch
after 1517 ANON. Art of Mvsic BL Add. 4911, f. 24v *Tactus quhat is it?* It is ane continuall motion, or ane chop witht ye hand of the preceptour, dressand [sic] ye sang mensuraly that ye modulatoure evverrie ane till ane vther fail ye notht in ye perfyt mensuring of the quantaties of all noittis and pausis in equall voces devvydit. **1617-24** FLUDD *Utriusque Cosmi Maioris: De Templo Musicæ* (p. 190) *Tactus Musicus* est motus certus & æqualis, sonorum tempora metiens.

taille *see* tenor
1611 COTGRAVE Fr→E *Taille: f.* ... also, the Tenor part in singing, &c; **1688** MIEGE-COTGRAVE Fr→E *Taille,* (f.) ... the Tenor, or Treble in Musick; § *La basse Taille, en Termes de Musique,* the Tenor part in Musick. *La haute Taille,* the Treble. *Taille, ou Instrument de Musique sur lequel on jouë la Taille,* the Musical Instrument upon which the Tenor or the Treble is plaid. **1724** [PEPUSCH] *Short Explic. of Foreign Words in Mus. Bks.* (p. 77) *Taille,* the same as *Tenor,* for which see. **1726** BAILEY *An Univ. Etymolog. Engl. Dict.* (3rd edn) *Taille,* the same as *Tenor,* which see. *Ital.*

tail-piece *see* queuë, tyrouër

talassion *see* thalassion

Tallis, Thomas *see* countertenor

tambour *see* atambor, tabour
1550 THOMAS It→E *Tamburo,* a tabbour, a dromslade, or a tymbrell. **1598** FLORIO It→E *Tamburiere,* a drummer. *Tamburro,* a drum, a timbrell, a tabour, a drumslade. Also a drummer. § *Sonare di tamburo,* to dub or sound vpon a drum. **1611** COTGRAVE Fr→E *Tambour: m.* A Drumme; also, a Tabor. **1611** FLORIO It→E *Tamburiere,* a Drummer, a Tabourer. *Tamburro,* a Drum, a Timbrell, a Drumslade, a Tabour. Also a Drummer or a Tabourer. § *Sonare di tamburo,* to sound or dub a Drum. **1659** TORRIANO-FLORIO It→E **Tamburriere, Tamburiere,* a Drummer, a Tabourer **Tamburro, Tamburo,* a drum, a drumslade, a tabour, a timbrel, also a Drummer, or a Tabourer, ... also as *Bargello,* because he was wont to go about with a drum before him. § *Sonare di tamburro,* to sound or beat a drum. **1676** COLES *Tambour, French.* a Drum. **1688** MIEGE-COTGRAVE Fr→E *Tambour,* (m.) a Drum; a Drummer. *Tambour,* Ps. 149: 3, and 150. 4, Timbrel. § *Batre le Tambour,* to beat the Drum. *Ce Tambour est une sorte d'Instrument recreatif, composé d'un Bois large de trois bons doits, delié, plié en forme de Cerceau, & garni de Sonnettes, le Vuide du Bois etant environné d'une Peau de Mouton fortement bandée. Ainsi on jouë de ce Tambour, en le tenant d'une main, & le frapant de l'autre. baterie de Tambour à la pointe du Jour,* a beat of drum at break of day. *Fûte de Tambour,* the barrel of a Drum. *Jouër du Tambour de Basque,* to play upon the Tabor. *Le Son du Tambour,* the Noise of the Drum. *Sortir d'une Ville Tambour blatant, & la meche allumée,* to come out of a Town Drums beating, and match lighted. *sortir Tambour batant,* to come out Drum beating. *Tambour de Basque,* a Tabor. **1704** *Cocker's Engl. Dict.* (1st edn) *Tainbour* [sic], a *French* word for a Drum. **1706** KERSEY-PHILLIPS (6th edn) *Tambour, (Fr.)* a Drum, an Instrument of Martial Musick; **1721** BAILEY *An Univ. Etymolog. Engl. Dict.* (1st edn) *Tambour,* a Drum:

tambourine *see* timburins
1570/71 *Dict. Fr. and Engl.* Fr→E *Tabourin,* a drum, a tymbrell, a tabber. *Tabourineresse,* a woman that playes on a tymbrell. *Tabourineur,* a drumsleyer. **1593** HOLLYBAND Fr→E *Tabourin,* a drumme, a timbrell, a taber: *m. Tabouriner,* to play vpon the drum. *Tabourineresse,* or *tabourineuse,* a woman that plaieth on a timbrell: *f. Tabourineur,* a drumplayer: *m.* **1598** FLORIO It→E *Tamburrino,* a little drum, a tabour, a timbrell, a drum-slade. Also a drummer. ... Also a tabour and pipe. **1599** MINSHEU-PERCYVALL Sp→E **Tamborilero,* m. one that playeth on a taber. *Tamborin,* m. a taber. **1611** COTGRAVE Fr→E *Tabourin: m.* A Tabor; also, a Drumme; and a little Drumme; *Tabouriner.* To play on a Tabor; also, to drumme or strike vp a Drumme. *Tabourinesse: f.* A woman that playes on a Tabor, or strikes vp a Drumme. *Tabourinet: m.* A Drumme, or Tabor for a child; a little Drumme, or Tabor; *Tabourineur: m.* A Taborer; one that playes on a Tabor. § *Tabourin de Basque.* A kind of small, and shallow Drumme, or Tabor, open at the one end, and hauing the barrell stucke full of small bells, and other gingling knacks of lattin, &c, which, together with the Taborers fingers on the other end thats couered, make (in the ears of children and sillie people) a prettie noyse. *Tabourin de guerre.* Is properly, the Drumme. **1611** FLORIO It→E *Tamburrino,* a little Drum a Tabour, a Timbrell, a Drumslade. Also a Drummer, a

Timbrell or a Taboure and Pipe. **1650** HOWELL-COTGRAVE Fr→E † *Tabourin: m.* A Tabor; also, a Drum; and a little Drum; also, the Drum, or Drummer belonging to a compamy [sic] of footmen; † *Tabouriner.* To play on a Tabor; also, to drum, or strike up a drum. † *Tabourinesse: f.* A woman that plaies on a Tabor, or strikes up a Drum. † *Tabourinet: m.* A Drum, or Tabor for a child; a little Drum, or Tabor; † *Tabourineur: m.* A Taborer; one that plaies on a Tabor. **1659** TORRIANO-FLORIO It→E *Tamburrino, Tamburello, Tamburetto,* the dim. of *Tamburro,* as *Crotalo.* § *Fare il tamburino,* to do as the drum **1661** BLOUNT (2nd edn) *Tamburine,* an old kind of instrument, which by some is supposed to be the *Clarion. Spencer.* **1662** PHILLIPS (2nd edn) *Tambarine,* an old Instrument, supposed the *Clarion.* **1676** COLES *Tamburine,* an old kind of instrument disused. **1688** DAVIS-TORRIANO-FLORIO It→E § *Fare come il tamburino,* to do as the drum **1688** MIEGE-COTGRAVE Fr→E † *Tabourin,* (m.) *Tambour d'Enfant,* a little Drum, a Child's Drum. *Tabourin,* Ps. 68. 25, a Timbrel. † *Tambourin,* † *Tambouriner,* † *Tambourineur,* See *Tabourin. Tabouriner. Tabourineur.* † *Tabouriner,* to beat (or strike up) a Drum. † *Tabourineur,* (m.) a Drum-beater. **1704** *Cocker's Engl. Dict.* (1st edn) *Tamburine,* a Musical Instrument used in former Ages, now obsolete and out of use. **1706** KERSEY-PHILLIPS (6th edn) *Tambarine,* a Musical Instrument, us'd in old time, and suppos'd to be the same with the *Clarion.* **1730** BAILEY *Dict. Britannicum* (1st edn) *Tambarine,* a certain Kind of musical Instrument.

tamburagione

1598 FLORIO It→E *Tamburagione,* a drumming, a sounding of a drum. *Tambureggiare,* to drum, to tabour. **1611** FLORIO It→E *Tamburagione,* a dubadub vpon a Drum. *Tambureggiare,* to dubadub vpon a Drum. **1659** TORRIANO-FLORIO It→E *Tamburraggione, Tamburranza,* any dubba-dubbing upon a Drum. *Tamburreggiare, Tamburiere,* to dubba-dub, or strike up a Drum or Tabour.

tambussare

1598 FLORIO It→E *Tambussare,* ... a dub a dub, to drum **1611** FLORIO It→E *Tambussare,* to dubadub, to drum. **1659** TORRIANO-FLORIO It→E *Tambussare, Tambustare,* to rumble ... to drum, to dubba-dub

tampano

1598 FLORIO It→E *Tampano,* a kind of musicall instrument without strings. **1611** FLORIO It→E *Tampano,* as *Timpano.*

tampon

1611 COTGRAVE Fr→E § *Colin tampon.* The Drumme-sound of the Suissers march. **1688** MIEGE-COTGRAVE Fr→E *Tampon signifie aussi, en Termes d'Art, la partie du Hautbois, de la Flute, ou du Flageolet, qui en fait l'embouchure, & qui sert à donner le Vent.*

tañer

1599 MINSHEU-PERCYVALL Sp→E *Tañedor,* a plaier on instruments, a sounder on instruments. *Tañer,* to sound, winde, or play vpon any instrument.

tarantula

1598 FLORIO It→E *Tarantola,* ... some take it to be a flye whose sting is perillous and deadly, and nothing but diuers sounds of musicke can cure the patient. **1611** FLORIO It→E *Tarantola,* ... Some take it to be a flie whose sting is deadly, yet curable by diuers sounds of musike. **1656** BLOUNT (1st edn) *Tarantula* (Lat.) a most venemous spider, so called of *tarentum,* a neapolitan City, where they most abound; Some take it to be a flie, whose sting is deadly; yet curable by divers sounds of musick. See more of this in *Sands Travels.* fol. 249. **1658** PHILLIPS (1st edn) *Tarantula,* a kinde of venemous Creature, abounding in *Tarantum,* a Citie in the Kingdom of *Naples,* which casteth forth a sting, onely curable by the sound of Musick. **1659** TORRIANO-FLORIO It→E *Tarantola,* a Tarantula, which (as some say) is a kind of fly, or (as others write) a kind of Eft or Eute, which stingeth or biteth most deadly; yet is it curable by divers sorts of musick hastily played unto the patient **1676** COLES *Tarantula,* a most venomous spider, or a fly whose sting (they say) is only cured by Musick, from ¶ *Tarantum,* a City of *Naples* where they abound. **1702** KERSEY *New Engl. Dict.* (1st edn) A *Tarantula,* a venomous spider, ash-colour'd, speckled with little white and black, *or* red and green spots. 'Tis so call'd from *Taranto,* a City of *Naples,* where they abound, and its sting is said to be cur'd only by musick. **1707** *Gloss. Angl. Nova* (1st edn) *Tarantula,* a venemous Spider, ... they say its bite is of such a Nature, that it is to be cured only with Musick. **1721** BAILEY *An Univ. Etymolog. Engl. Dict.* (1st edn) *Tarantula,* (so called of *Taranto,* a City of *Naples* where they abound) a kind of Venemous, Ash-coloured Spider, speckled with little white and black, or red and green Spots, whose bite is of such a Nature, that it is to be cured only by Musick. **1737** DYCHE-PARDON

(2nd edn) *Tarantula* (S.) a Sort of venemous Spider, the Bite whereof affects the Patient with a Sort of Madness, said to be curable only by Musick.

taratantara *see* strombettare, trantrana
1565 COOPER L→E *Taratantara, pen. corr. Ennius*. The sowne of a trumpet. **1587** THOMAS L→E *Taratantara, Enn.* A sound of the trumpet. **1598** FLORIO It→E *Tara tantara,* the clang or sound of a trumpet. **1611** FLORIO It→E *Tarare,* ... Also to sound a Trumpet. *Taratantara,* the clang or sound of a Trumpet. *Taratantarare,* to sound a Trumpet. **1656** BLOUNT (1st edn) *Tara-tantara,* or tarantara (from the British *Taran. i.* thunder, or from *taro* and *taraw, i.* to strike, and so may signifie as much as *percutiens, percute*) it is a word of encouragement to battel which the trumpets do (as neere as they can) imitate. *Tarantarize (tarantarizo)* to sound a trumpet, to sing or sound *tarantara.* **1658** PHILLIPS (1st edn) *Taratantarize,* (Greek) to imitate the sound of a Trumpet, which seemeth to expresse the word *Taratantara.* **1659** TORRIANO-FLORIO It→E *Taratantara,* the clang or sounding of a trumpet, a Taratantara. *Taratantarare,* to taratantare, or sound a trumpet. § **Fare tantara,* to be lively and merry together, with musick and loud talking. **1676** COLES *Tarantara, Taratan-,* the sound of Trumpets (to battel.) **1696** PHILLIPS (5th edn) *Taratantara,* a word of encouragement to Battel, which Trumpets imitate as near as they can. **1704** *Cocker's Engl. Dict.* (1st edn) *Taratantara,* the blowing a Trumpet to Battel. **1706** KERSEY-PHILLIPS (6th edn) *Taratantara,* a Word of Encouragement to Battel, sounded by Trumpets. **1708** KERSEY *Dict. Anglo-Brit.* (1st edn) *Taratantara,* a Word of Encouragement to Battel, sounded by Trumpets. **1730** BAILEY *Dict. Britannicum* (1st edn) *Tarantara,* the Sound of a Trumpet, in calling to Battle.

1706 BEDFORD *Temple Musick* (p. 72) [*re* Jewish psalm singing in ancient times, quoting from Dr. Lightfoot] ... The *Singers* (saith he) *in singing* these *Psalms, divided each of them into three Parts, making three large Pauses, or Rests in them, and at these Intermissions the trumpets sounded, and the People worshipped.* This sounding he describes to be *a Plain-Blast,* then *another* with *Quaverings and Shakings,* and after that a *Plain-Blast* again, which he called a *Taratantara,* tho' he confesseth that this Word seems to put the *Quavering sound* before, and after, and the Plain in the midst, contrary to the *Jewish* description of it...

tardo *see* largo
1724 [PEPUSCH] *Short Explic. of Foreign Words in Mus. Bks.* (p. 77) *Tardo,* Slow, much the same as *Largo,* which see. **1726** BAILEY *An Univ. Etymolog. Engl. Dict.* (3rd edn) *Tardo* (in *Musick Books*) signifies slow, much the same as *Largo,* Ital. Which see.

1731 PRELLEUR *Modern Musick-Master* (Dictionary, p. 3) *Tardo,* Slow[,] much the same as *Largo.*

tarot
1688 MIEGE-COTGRAVE Fr→E *Tarot,* (m.) a kind of Musical Instrument. § *Le Tarot s'appelle ordinairement Basson. C'est un Instrument à anche & à vent, qui a onze trous, & qui sert de Basse aux Concerts de Musique.*

tastame *see* fret, tastatura, tasto, traste
1611 FLORIO It→E *Tastame,* ... Also the frets of Instruments. **1659** TORRIANO-FLORIO It→E *Tastame, Tastamento,* ... also the fret of any instrument.

tastare
1598 FLORIO It→E *Tastare,* ... Also to fret an instrument of musicke. **1611** FLORIO It→E *Tastare,* ... Also to fret an instrument of Musike. **1659** TORRIANO-FLORIO It→E *Tastare, Tasteggiare,* ... to touch or play upon the frets of an instrument

tastatura *see* fret, tastame, tasto, touch, traste
1611 FLORIO It→E *Tastatura,* that which is called the touch vpon an instrument of musike. Also the frame of the keyes or frets in any Instrument. **1659** TORRIANO-FLORIO It→E *Tastatura,* ... the touch upon an instrument, or the frame of the keys and frets of any musical instrument. **1724** [PEPUSCH] *Short Explic. of Foreign Words in Mus. Bks.* (p. 78) *Tastatura,* the Keys of Organs and Harpsicords. **1726** BAILEY *An Univ. Etymolog. Engl. Dict.* (3rd edn) *Tastatura,* the Keys of Organs and Harpsichords. *Ital.*

tasto *see* fret, tastame, tastatura, traste
1598 FLORIO It→E *Attasti,* the frets of any instruments. *Tasti,* the frets or keyes of any musicall instrument. § *Toccare li tasti,* to touch the keyes or frets of any instrument. **1611** FLORIO It→E *Attasti,* the frets of any instrument. *Tasti,* the frets or keyes of any musicall instruments. *Tasto,* a taste, a touch, an assaie, a feeling, a triall. Also a fret of an instrument. § *Toccare li tasti,* to touch

the keyes or frets of an instrument **1659** TORRIANO-FLORIO It→E *Tasti*, the frets or keyes of any musical instrument. **1724** [PEPUSCH] *Short Explic. of Foreign Words in Mus. Bks.* (p. 78) *Tasto*, is to Touch, which signifies that the Notes must not be held out their full Length, but only just touch'd. This has Respect chiefly to the Organ or Harpsicord in playing a Thorough Bass. **1726** BAILEY *An Univ. Etymolog. Engl. Dict.* (3rd edn) *Tasto* (in *Musick Books*) to touch, signifies that the Notes must not be held out their full Length, but only just touch'd. This chiefly respects the Organ or Harpsichord in playing a thorough Bass. *Ital.*

1736 TANS'UR *Compleat Melody* (3rd edn, p. 68) *Tasto*. (Ital.) Denotes that the *Notes* must be but just touched, yet hold their full Time. This *Term* is most respective to the *Organ*, *Harpsichord*, &c. in playing the *Thorow-Bass*, which is often marked with *Figures* over the *Notes*; which shews what Distance such *Notes* are struck from the *Ground*, or lowest *Notes*.

tatæ

1587 THOMAS L→E *Tatæ*, *Plaut*. A wanton word in singing wherewith one answereth another.

tattamelle

1598 FLORIO It→E *Tattamelle*, ... Also a kinde of instrument of musicke. **1611** FLORIO It→E *Tattamelle*, foolish, idle, or childish pratlings, toyes or vanities. Also a kind of musicall instrument.

tattle de moy *see* lesson

1676 MACE *Musick's Monument* (p. 129) A *Tattle de Moy*, is a *New Fashion'd Thing*, much like a *Seraband*; only It has more of *Conceit in It*, as (in a manner) *speaking the word*, (*Tattle de Moy*) and of *Humour*; (as you will find, quite through *This Book*, where they are set;) *That Conceit* being never before Published, but *Broached together with This Work*. ¶ It may supply the *Place* of a *Seraband*, at the *End of a Suit of Lessons*, at any Time.

tattoo *see* beat, retreat

1702 KERSEY *New Engl. Dict.* (1st edn) *Taptoo*, a particular way of drumming; *as* to beat the *taptoo* in a garrison. **1706** KERSEY-PHILLIPS (6th edn) *Tat-too* or *Tap-too*, the beat of Drum at Night for all Soldiers to repair to their Tents in the Field, or to their Quarters in a Garrison: It is sometimes call'd *The Retreat*. **1708** KERSEY *Dict. Anglo-Brit.* (1st edn) *Tat-too* or *Tap-too*, the beat of Drum at Night for all Soldiers to repair to their Tents in the Field, or to their Quarters in a Garrison. **1728** CHAMBERS *Tat-too, q.d. tap-to*, a Beat of a Drum, at Night, to advertise the Soldiers to repair to their Quarters in a Garrison, or to their Tents in a Camp. See *Drum*. **1730** BAILEY *Dict. Britannicum* (1st edn) *Tatto* (*tap-too*, q. of *taper*, F. to strike or beat, and *to*) a certain Beat or Tune play'd on a Drum in a Garrison or a Camp at Night, as a Notice for the Soldiers to repair to their Quarters or Tents. **1737** DYCHE-PARDON (2nd edn) *Tattoo* (S.) sometimes called the Retreat, a Beat of Drum at Night for all Soldiers in Garrison to repair to their Quarters, and in the Fields to their Tents; after which in frontier Towns where there is any Suspicion of the Inhabitants, they are not permitted to stir abroad, or at least without a Light.

tavolatura *see* tablature

tecla

1599 MINSHEU-PERCYVALL Sp→E **Tecla*, as *Musica de Tecla*, musicke of organes, virginalles, clauicordes or such like.

teda *see* marriage music

1565 COOPER L→E *Teda, tedæ, f.g. Plin.* ... A weddinge. A songe at a weddinge. **1598** FLORIO It→E *Teda*, ... Also a song at a wedding. **1611** FLORIO It→E *Teda*, ... Also a song sung at weddings. **1659** TORRIANO-FLORIO It→E *Teda, Tede*, ... some take *Teda* for a marriage or wedding-feast, and some others for a Song or merry Carol sung at weddings.

Te Deum *see* hymn

1688 MIEGE-COTGRAVE Fr→E § *Chanter le Te Deum*, to sing Te Deum. **1706** KERSEY-PHILLIPS (6th edn) *Te Deum*, a Hymn of Thanksgiving us'd in Churches upon Solemn Occasions, especially for the obtaining of a Victory, and so call'd from the first Words of it in *Latin, Te Deum Laudamus, i.e.* We praise thee O God, *&c.* **1708** KERSEY *Dict. Anglo-Brit.* (1st edn) *Te Deum*, a Hymn of Thanksgiving us'd in Churches upon Solemn Occasions. **1721** BAILEY *An Univ. Etymolog. Engl. Dict.* (1st edn) *Te Deum*, a Hymn of Thansgiving [sic] used in Churches upon solemn Occasions, so called from its first Words in *Latin*. **1728** CHAMBERS *Te Deum*, a kind of Hymn, or Song of Thanksgiving, used in the Church, beginning with the Words *Te Deum laudamus, We praise thee, O God*. ¶ 'Tis used to be sung in the *Romish* Church with extraordinary

Pomp and Solemnity, upon the gaining a Battle, or other happy Event. The *Te Deum* is usually ascrib'd to St. *Ambrose*, and St. *Augustin*. **1730** BAILEY *Dict. Britannicum* (1st edn) *Te Deum*, a Hymn frequently sung in Church on Thanksgiving Days for Victories gained, Deliverances from Dangers, *&c*, so called from the *Latin* Beginning of it, *Te Deum laudamus*, &c. *i.e.* we praise thee the Lord. **1737** DYCHE-PARDON (2nd edn) *Te-Deum* (S.) a famous Hymn that has been long used in the Church, and especially upon extraordinary Occasions, such as national Thanksgiving for a publick Victory, &c.

Tellen

1565 COOPER L→E *Tellen, tellinis*, A foolishe poete and minstrell.

tempella *see* stempellare

1598 FLORIO It→E *Tempella*, a fiddle, a croud, or kit. **1611** FLORIO It→E *Tempella*, any plaine fiddle, kit or croud. Also a huge twanger, a swagring toole, a filthy dildoe. **1659** TORRIANO-FLORIO It→E **Tempella*, any plain countrey fiddle, kit, or croud **Tempellare*, ... to shake fair and gently ... also to fumble or twangle upon a croud.

temperament *see* bearing, lute, systema temperato, tuning

1728 CHAMBERS *Temperament*, or *tempering*, in Musick, a rectifying or mending the false or imperfect Concords, by transferring to them part of the Beauty of the perfect ones. See *Concord*. ¶ The Degrees of the Octave, which may be call'd its *Elements*, as being the smallest Intervals it is resolvable into; are two greater Semitones, two lesser Tones, and three greater Tones. See *Tone* and *Octave*. ¶ Now the different Situation of these Elements, with respect to each other, occasions that Intervals or Concords of the same Name, as *Thirds, Fourths, &c.* don't consist of the same Degrees or Elements, tho' there be always the same Number of them; but one Fourth, for Instance, is agreeable and perfect, and another not. ¶ To mend these imperfect Concords, the Musicians have bethought themselves to *temper, i.e.* give them part of the Agreeableness of perfect ones. In order to [do] this, they take a Medium between the two, and this they call a *Temperament*, which necessarily produces a new Division of the Octave, or which amounts to the same new Elements. ¶ For Instance, whereas naturally its Elements are the greater Semitone, and the greater and lesser Tone; they take a middle Tone form'd of the greater and the less: And the only Elements now, are the greater Semitone, and this mean Tone, which renders the five Intervals that are Tones equal, and those that are Semitones less unequal to these. ¶ One might also divide each of the five Tones of the Octave into Semitones, which, join'd to the two it naturally has, make twelve: In which Case, the whole Octave would be divided into twelve equal Parts, which would be mean Semitones. ¶ 'Tis easy to form various other Kinds of *Temperaments*: All the Difficulty is to find such as are free from the two great Inconveniences, *i.e.* which don't alter either all the Concords too much, or, at least, some of them. ¶ All such Divisions of the Octave are call'd *temper'd*, or *temperative Systems*. See *System* and *Scale of Musick*. **1730** BAILEY *Dict. Britannicum* (1st edn) *Temperament, Tempering*, (in *Musick*) a Rectifying or Amending the false or imperfect Concords, by transferring to them Part of the Beauty of the perfect ones.

tempo *see* contratempo

1724 [PEPUSCH] *Short Explic. of Foreign Words in Mus. Bks.* (p. 78) *Tempo*, Time. Thus, ¶ *Tempo di Gavotta*, is Gavot Time, or the Time or Movement observed in playing a Gavot. ¶ *Tempo di Minuetto*, is Minuet Time. ¶ *Tempo di Sarabanda*, Saraband Time.

tempo di gavotta *see* gavotte

tempo giusto

1731 PRELLEUR *Modern Musick-Master* (Dictionary, p. 1) *A Tempo giusto* w$^{th.}$ an equal Time.

tempo perfetto *see* o, semibreve time

tempus *see* time

tendrement *see* affetto

1724 [PEPUSCH] *Short Explic. of Foreign Words in Mus. Bks.* (p. 78) *Tendrement*, is Tenderly or Gently; that is, to Play or Sing after a Sweet, Gentle, or Affecting Manner. **1726** BAILEY *An Univ. Etymolog. Engl. Dict.* (3rd edn) *Tenderement* (in *Musick Books*) signifies tenderly or gently; that is to sing or play after a sweet, gentle, or affecting Manner. *Ital.*

1736 TANS'UR *Compleat Melody* (3rd edn, p. 67) *Tenderment, Con Affetto, Affetto, Affettuoso.* (Ital.) Either of those *Terms* denote that you must *sing* or *play* in a very sweet, tender, and affecting Manner.

tenebres

1656 Blount (1st edn) *Tenebres* ... Also the service or mattins used in the Roman Church on *Wednesday, Thursday* and *Fryday* before *Easter*, and are cal'd *tenebræ*, (and thence *tenebræ, wednesday, thursday, &c.*) as being begun with many lights, and ending in darknesse, representing the nightly time of our blessed Saviours apprehension in the garden *Gethsemani*; in which office are lighted at the first on a triangular candlestick fifteen candles, *vid.* as many as there are *Psalmes* and *Canticles* in the office, and at the end of every *Psalme* one of the fifteen lights is extinguished till they be all put out; **1658** Phillips (1st edn) *Tenebres*, certain divine Services performed among the Catholicks some dayes of the week before Easter Sunday, in representation of our Saviours Agony in the Garden, there being put out, of the 15 lamps which they light, one at the end of every Psalm they repeat, untill all the lights are extinguished. **1676** Coles *Tenebres, French.* (darkness) the Roman service (on Wednesday, Thursday and Fryday before Easter) representing Christs apprehension in the Garden, when at the end of every Psalm they put out a Candle, till all the 15 are out, and he left friendless and under the power of darkness. **1706** Kersey-Phillips (6th edn) *Tenebræ* or *Tenebres, (Lat. i.e.* Darkness) a Service us'd in the *Roman* Church, on *Wednesday, Thursday* and *Friday* before *Easter*, in representation of our Blessed Saviour's Agony in the Garden: So that fifteen Lamps, or Candles (which is the number of Psalms, or Canticles in the Office) being at first lighted on a Triangular Sconce, one of them is extinguished at the end of every Psalm repeated by the Priest, till all the Lights be put out, and the Congregation left in utter Darkness.

tenor

see countertenor, decant, decantator, mean, part, succentor, t, taille

1552 Huloet L→E [no headword given] Syng a tenor. **1589** Rider L→E *Tenor, cantus* The tenour. **1598** Florio It→E *Tenore*, a tenor or degree in musicke **1599** Minsheu-Percyvall Sp→E *Tenor*, the tenor, sound, tune. **1611** Cotgrave Fr→E *Teneur: m.* The Tenor part in Musicke. **1611** Florio It→E *Tenore*, ... a tenor or degree in musik. **1656** Blount (1st edn) *Tenor* (Lat.) .... The *tenor* part in musick is that which is next above the base. ¶ The order in consort-vocal musick is thus; 1. *Base*; 2. *Tenor*; 3. *Counter-tenor*; 4. *Mean* or Contra-alto. 5. *Trebble* or Alto. **1658** Phillips (1st edn) *Tenor*, (lat.) ... also one of the five parts in Musick. **1659** Torriano-Florio It→E *Tenore*, ... a tenor in musick **1676** Coles *Tenor, Latin.* that part (in Musick) next the Bass. **1688** Miege-Cotgrave Fr→E † *Tenor, Partie de Musique, ce qui s'appelle presentement Taille*, Tenor, the Tenor in Musick. **1702** Kersey *New Engl. Dict.* (1st edn) The *Tenor* in musick. **1704** *Cocker's Engl. Dict.* (1st edn) *Tenor*, in Musick is that part next the Base; **1704** Harris *Tenor*, is the Name of the first Mean or middle Part in *Musick*. **1706** Kersey-Phillips (6th edn) *Tenor, (Lat.)* ... In *Musick*, it is the Name of the first Mean or middle Part, next the Bass. **1707** *Gloss. Angl. Nova* (1st edn) *Tenor*, in Musick, is that part which is next above the Base; **1724** [Pepusch] *Short Explic. of Foreign Words in Mus. Bks.* (p. 79) *Tenore*, a Part in Musick, called by us Tenor. **1726** Bailey *An Univ. Etymolog. Engl. Dict.* (3rd edn) *Tenore*, a Part of Musick called *tenor*, Ital. thus *tenore viola* is a tenor Viol, *tenore violino*, a tenor *Violin; tenore ripieno*, the tenor that plays in some Part only; *tenore concertante*, the tenor that plays throughout. *Ital.* **1728** Chambers *Tenor* in *Musick*, the first mean or middle Part; or that which is the ordinary Pitch or *Tenor* of the Voice, when not either rais'd to the Treble, or lower'd to the Base. See *Part* and *Music.* ¶ The *Tenor* is frequently mark'd on thorough Basses with the Letter T. ¶ The *Tenor* is a Part which almost all grown Persons can sing. But as some have a greater Compass of Voice upwards, others downwards, others are confin'd to a kind of Medium, and others can go equally either higher or lower; hence many Musicians make a Variety of *Tenors*, as a *low Tenor*, a *mean Tenor*, a *high Tenor*, a *natural Tenor*; to which is also added, a *reacting Tenor, Violin Tenor*, &c. ¶ The *Italians* usually distinguish no more than two Kinds of *Tenors, viz. Tenor primo*, or P° or I°, which answers to our upper *Tenor*; and *Tenore secundo*, or 2° or II°, which is our natural *Tenor*; confounding the others under the Word *Baritono.* ¶ *Tenor* is also us'd for a Person who says that Part in Concert; or for an Instrument proper to play it. **1730** Bailey *Dict. Britannicum* (1st edn) *Tenor* (in *Musick*) the first, mean or middle Part, or that which is the ordinary Pitch of the Voice, when neither raised to the Treble, nor lowered to the Bass. **1737** Dyche-Pardon (2nd edn) *Tenor* (S.) in *Musick*, is the natural or common Pitch of the Voice;

1609 DOWLAND-ORNITHOPARCUS *Micrologvs* (p. 84) A *Tenor* is the middle voyce of each Song, or (as *Gafforus* writes *lib.* 3. *cap.* 5.) it is the foundation to the Relation of euery Song: so called a *Tenendo*, of holding, because it doth hold the Consonance of all the parts in it selfe, in some respect.... *Of the higher Tenor.* ¶ The high *Tenor*, is the vppermost part, saue one of a Song: or it is the grace of the *Base*: for most commonly it graceth the *Base*, making a double *Concord* with it. **1617-24** FLUDD *Utriusque Cosmi Maioris: De Templo Musicæ* (p. 209) *Tenor* est vox media, per medios sonus præcipuam ferè melodiam informans. **1636** BUTLER *Principles of Musik* (p. 41) The Tenor is so called, becaus it was commonly in Motets the ditti-part, or Plain-song: which* [marginalia: '*Tenor, of *teneo*, signifyeth one continued order or fashion of a thing, held on without change.'] continued in the same kinde of Notes (usually briefs) much after one plain fashion: uppon which, the other Partes did discant in sundry sorts of Figures, and after many different ways: or (if you will) becaus neither ascending to any high or strained note, nor descending very low, it continueth in one ordinari tenor of the voice: and therefore may bee sung by an indifferent voice. **1653** ?BROUNCKER *Renatvs Des-Cartes Exc. Comp. of Musick* (p. 51) [*re* composition in four voices] The Second, being the next to the *Basse*, they call *Tenor*; this being also, in its kind, the chiefest, because it containes the Subject of the whole Modulation ... **1667** SIMPSON *Compendium of Practical Musick* (p. 112) ... The *Latins* reduced theirs [their modes or tones], to eight Plain-song Tunes; and those were set in the *Tenor*; so called, because it was the Holding Part to which they did apply their Descant. **1724** TURNER *Sound Anatomiz'd* (p. 38) ... the *Tenor* likewise, one wou'd from its Name be naturally apt to conclude, that it always carried the Subject of the *Air*, when it is engaged with other Voices; and that was indeed, the Reason formerly, for calling it the *Tenor*: For, always laying next to the *Base*, they used to make it the prime *Part*; but People, in aftertimes, thought it more agreeable to let the highest *Part* bear the Subject ... Yet notwithstanding this, the *Part* which lies next the *Base*, retains the Name of *Tenor* to this Day. **1736** TANS'UR *Compleat Melody* (3rd edn, p. 70) *Tenor*. Is the Name of the *Leading Part*, (tho' some-times 'tis called *Treble*.) Being the first, or next *Octave*, or *System* above the *Bass*.

tenor clef *see* c sol fa ut clef

1724 TURNER *Sound Anatomiz'd* (p. 35) Upon the second *Line* above that [the note *Gsolreut*], you see this *Mark*; [C clef sign] which is occasionally, placed upon either the third or fourth *Line*. If it be on the fourth; it is placed there to signify that such a *Part* is for a *Tenor Voice*; if on the third, it then signifies a *Contra-Tenor*, being variously placed, no otherwise than to keep the *Notes* within due *Sounds*, by hindering them from interfering with one another, according to the Compass of either, *Voices*, or *Instruments*. This *Cliff* is called in General, the *Tenor*, or *Csolfaut Cliff*.

tenorista *see* decantator

1659 TORRIANO-FLORIO It→E *Tenorista*, one that sings a tenor. **Tenorizzare*, to keep or sing a tenor **1724** [PEPUSCH] *Short Explic. of Foreign Words in Mus. Bks.* (p. 79) *Tenorista*, one that has a Voice proper for a Tenor. **1726** BAILEY *An Univ. Etymolog. Engl. Dict.* (3rd edn) *Tenorista*, one that has a Tenor Voice, *i.e.* a Voice proper for a Tenor. *Ital.*

tension

1736 TANS'UR *Compleat Melody* (3rd edn, p. 72) *Tension*, (Lat.) signifies the screwing of *Strings* to a certain *Pitch*, &c.

tercet *see* tierce

1706 KERSEY-PHILLIPS (6th edn) *Tercet*, a Third in *Musick*.

terga taurea

1587 THOMAS L→E *Terga taurea*. Drums made of bul-hides. *Terga taurea, Ovid.* Drums or tabrets made of a bulls hydes. **1589** RIDER L→E *Terga taurea* Drums made of bul-hides.

Terpandrus *see* gymnopædia, hyper-hypate, lyre

1538 ELYOT L→E *Terpander, dri*, an olde musytian, whyche added .vii. strynges to the harpe. **1565** COOPER L→E *Terpandrus, dri*, An olde musician, who added .vii. stringes to the harpe.

Terpnus

1565 COOPER L→E *Terpnus*, An harper in the tyme of Nero.

Terpsichore *see* Muse

1730 BAILEY *Dict. Britannicum* (1st edn) *Terpsichore* ... one of the Nine Muses, to whom is attributed the Invention of Dancing and Balls. The Antients used to represent her in Painting, *&c.* with a chearful

Countenance, and playing upon some Instrument, having her Head adorned with a Coronet of Feathers of divers Colours, but chiefly green, in Token of the Victory the Muses obtain'd over the Syrens, *&c.* by singing.

terza
1724 [PEPUSCH] *Short Explic. of Foreign Words in Mus. Bks.* (p. 79) *Terza,* a Third, a Term in Musick, also the Number Three, or the Third. Thus, ¶ *Opera Terza,* is the Third Opera. ¶ *Violino Terza,* Third Violin. **1726** BAILEY *An Univ. Etymolog. Engl. Dict.* (3rd edn) *Terza* (in *Musick Books*) signifies a third; also the Number 3, as *Terza Opera* the 3d Opera; *Terza Violina,* the 3d Violin. *Ital.*

terza, in *see* trio
1724 [PEPUSCH] *Short Explic. of Foreign Words in Mus. Bks.* (p. 80) *In Terza,* or *Un Terzo,* are Songs or Tunes in Three Parts, the same as *Trio* below. **1726** BAILEY *An Univ. Etymolog. Engl. Dict.* (3rd edn) *In Terza, In Terzo,* (in *Musick Books*) signifies Songs or Tunes in 3 Parts, the same as *Trio,* which see. *Ital.*

terzetto *see* tiercet
1659 TORRIANO-FLORIO It→E **Terzario, Terzaruolo, Terzeruolo,* ... also a writer or singer of Terzet-rimes as Petrarke was in his Triumphs **1724** [PEPUSCH] *Short Explic. of Foreign Words in Mus. Bks.* (p. 80) *Terzetto,* little Airs in Three Parts. **1726** BAILEY *An Univ. Etymolog. Engl. Dict.* (3rd edn) *Terzetto* (in *Musick Books*) signifies little Airs in 3 Parts.

testo *see* ditty
1724 [PEPUSCH] *Short Explic. of Foreign Words in Mus. Bks.* (p. 80) *Testo,* the Text or Words of a Song. *Textus.* See the Word *Testo.* **1726** BAILEY *An Univ. Etymolog. Engl. Dict.* (3rd edn) *Testo,* signifies the Text or Words of a Song. *Ital.*

testudo *see* chelys, lyre, viol
1565 COOPER L→E *Testudo. Cic.* The bealy of a lute: A lute whiche somewhat resembleth a Torteise his shelle. § *Caua testudo. Horat.* An holow lute. *Dulcis strepitus aureæ testudinis. Horat.* The sweete tune or sowne of the gilded lute. **1587** THOMAS L→E *Testudo, inis, f.g. Plin.* ... the belly of a lute, a lute which somwhat resembleth a Torteise his shell, *Cic.* **1589** RIDER L→E *Testudinarius, m.* A Lute maker. *Testudo, f.* The bellie of a Lute. **1598** FLORIO It→E *Testudine,* ... Also the belly of a lute, or a lute bicause it resembleth a tortoise shel. **1611** FLORIO It→E *Testudine,* ... Also the bellie of a Lute, or Lute it selfe, because it somewhat resembleth a Tortoise shell. *Testudo,* as *Testudine.* **1659** TORRIANO-FLORIO It→E *Testudine, Testude, Testudo,* ... any Sea or Land Tortoise ... by Met. the belly of a lute, or lute it self, because it somewhat resembleth a Tortoise-shell **1728** CHAMBERS *Testudo, in Antiquity,* was particularly us'd among the Poets, *&c.* for the ancient Lyre; by Reason it was originally made, by its Inventor *Mercury,* of the Back or hollow Shell of a *Testudo Aquatica,* or Sea Tortoise, which he accidentally found on the Banks of the River *Nile.* See *Lyre.* ¶ Dr. *Molyneux* has an express Discourse, in the *Philosophical Transactions,* to shew that the Tortoise-shell was the Basis of the ancient Lyre, and that the whole Instrument had thence the Denomination *Testudo;* which Account lets some Light into an obscure Passage in *Horace,* Ode 3. lib. 4. mistaken by all the Commentators. ¶ *O* Testudinis *Aureæ / Dulcem quæ strepitum, Pieri, temperas; / O Mutis quoque piscibus, / Donatura Cygni, si libeat, sonum.* **1730** BAILEY *Dict. Britannicum* (1st edn) *Testudo* (with *Poets*) a Lyre, because it is said to have been made by *Mercury,* its Inventer, of the Back or hollow Shell of the Sea-Tortoise.

c.1668-71 *Mary Burwell's Instruction Bk. for Lute* (*TDa* p. 9) ... as do testify and represent the Latin words *testudo,* which signifies 'a lute', and *tortu,* which is an animal that creeps slowly; and if the lute resembles the tortoise shell, 'tis but a little now that he is in his perfection.

tetrachord *see* colores generum, diatonic scale, genus, monochord, scale, system
1565 COOPER L→E *Tetrachordium, dij, n.g.* An instrument of foure strynges. **1587** THOMAS L→E *Tetrachordum, di, n.g.* *An instrument of foure strings. **1589** RIDER L→E *Tetrachordon.* An instrument having but foure strings. **1598** FLORIO It→E *Tetracordo,* an instrument of fower strings. **1611** FLORIO It→E *Tetracordo,* an instrument of foure strings. **1656** BLOUNT (1st edn) *Tetracord (tetrachordum)* an instrument with foure strings. **1658** PHILLIPS (1st edn) *Tetrachord,* (Greek) an instrument of four strings. **1661** BLOUNT (2nd edn) *Tetracord (tetrachordium)* an antient instrument with four strings; but now it is taken for every fourth in the Scale of Musick, or *Gamut.* **1676** COLES *Tetrachord, Greek.* an instrument of 4 strings, a forth in the Gamut. **1704** *Cocker's Engl. Dict.* (1st edn) *Tetrachord,* an ancient Musical Instrument

of four Strings or Chords. **1704** HARRIS *Tetrachord,* in Musick, is a Concord or Interval of 3 *Tones.* ¶ The *Tetrachord* of the Ancients was a rank of four Strings, accounting the *Tetrachord* for one Tone as it is often taken in Musick. **1706** KERSEY-PHILLIPS (6th edn) *Tetrachord,* (*Gr.* in *Musick*) a Concord, or Interval of three Tones: Among the Ancients, it was an Instrument, or rank of four Strings, accounting the *Tetrachord* for one Tone. **1707** *Gloss. Angl. Nova* (1st edn) *Tetrachord,* in Musick, is a Concord or interval of three Tones; also a Musical Instrument consisting of four Chords. **1708** KERSEY *Dict. Anglo-Brit.* (1st edn) *Tetrachord,* (*G.* in *Musick*) a Concord, or Interval of Three Tones. **1724** [PEPUSCH] *Short Explic. of Foreign Words in Mus. Bks.* (p. 80) *Tetrachordo,* Tetrachord, a Concord or Interval of Three Tones. **1726** BAILEY *An Univ. Etymolog. Engl. Dict.* (3rd edn) *Tetrachord* (*tetrachordus,* L. of τετράχορδον, Gr.) a Concord, or Interval of three Tones. *Tetrachordo,* the same as *Tetrachord* above. *Ital.* **1728** CHAMBERS *Tetrachord,* in the ancient Music, a Concord consisting of three Degrees, Tones, or Intervals, or four Sounds or Terms; call'd also by the Ancients διατέσσαρον, and by the Moderns a *Fourth.* See *Fourth.* ¶ This Interval had the Name *Tetrachord* given it with respect to the Lyra, and its Chords or Strings. See *Chord.* See also *Diatessaron.* ¶ Ancient Authors make frequent Mention of the Synaphe, or Conjunction; and Dieseusis, or Disjunction of *Tetrachords.* To conceive their Meaning, it must be observ'd, that two *Tetrachords* were said to be join'd, when the same Chord was the highest of the first, or lowest Instrument, and the lowest of the second; as was the Case in the two *Tetrachords* that compose the ancient Heptachord or Seventh. But when two *Tetrachords* had no common Chord; but, on the contrary, had each their different ones to begin and end withal, so that between the two there were two Intervals of a Tone, then the *Tetrachords* were said to be disjoin'd; which was the Case in the two *Tetrachords* that compose the Octochord or Octave. See *Octave.* ¶ The Word is form'd of the Greek, τετρα, four times, and χορδη, a Chord or String. **1730** BAILEY *Dict. Britannicum* (1st edn) *Tetrachord* (*tetrachordo,* Ital. *tetrachordus,* L. of τετράχορδον, Gr.) an Instrument with four Strings; also an Interval of three Tones, accounting the Tetrachord for one Tone, as it is often taken in Musick. **1737** DYCHE-PARDON (2nd edn) *Tetrachord* (S.) a Musical Instrument of four Strings; also an Interval of three Tones.

tetradiapason

1704 HARRIS *Tetradiapason,* a Quadruple Diapason, is a Musical Cord, otherwise called a Quadruple Eighth, or Nine and Twentieth. **1706** KERSEY-PHILLIPS (6th edn) *Tetradiapason,* (in *Musick*) a quadruple Diapason; a Chord otherwise call'd a Quadruple Eighth, or Nine and Twentieth. **1707** *Gloss. Angl. Nova* (1st edn) *Tetradiapason,* (Gr.) a Quadruple Diapason, is a musical Chord, otherwise called a Musical Eighth, or nine and Twentieth. **1728** CHAMBERS *Tetradiapason,* a *Quadruple Diapason*; a Musical Chord, otherwise call'd a quadruple eight or nine and twentieth. See *Diapason.*

1736 TANS'UR *Compleat Melody* (3rd edn, p. 69) A *Tetradiapason,* is a *Quadruple Diapasion,* or a *Fourth Octave*; being a 29th (Gr.)

thalassion *see* bridal, epigonium, epithalamy, hillulim, hymen, marriage music, nuptial

1500 *Ortus Vocabulorum* L→E Thalassion sij. i. mare quod et thalatum dicitur. Inde n.s. **1538** ELYOT L→E *Talassio,* was a songe contayned in certayn verses, sungen at weddynges. It was also a certayne exclamation or crie vsed at mariages, the begynnynge whereof beganne, whan Romulus and the Romaynes rauished the maydens of the Sabines, amonge whom was one of excellent beautie, whom whan many of the Sabines wold haue reskued, they whyche caried her toward Romulus, to th[e] intent that she shulde not be taken from them, cryed *Talassio,* whiche was the name of a noble prynce of the Sabines, as if they wold haue brought hyr to hym, and by that meane they escaped, & broughte hir to Romulus. And afterwarde they vsed at mariages to crie *Talassio.* **1552** HULOET L→E *Thalassio. onis, Talassio onis* Song contaynyng a certayn kynd of metre, or verse songe at bridalles & mariages. &c. **1565** COOPER L→E *Talasio & talassio.* A songe contayned in certaine verses songe at mariages. Also an exclamation or crie vsed at mariages, hauyng the beginnyng when Romulus and the Romans rauished the maydens of the Sabines: among which was one of excellent beautie that hir countreymen woulde haue reskewed, and then the Romaines cried *Talassio* (which was the name of a prince of the Sabines[)], makynge as though they woulde conueigh the mayden to him, and by that shifte or policie escaped and brought hir to Romulus. After whiche time they vsed that crye at mariages. *Thalassio, thalassiônis, mascu. ge. Martial.* A songe at a mariage **1587** THOMAS L→E *Talasio, onis. Fest.* A song contayned in certaine verses sung at mariages: an exclamation vsed in mariage. *Thalassio, onis, m.g. Mart. & Thassius, m.g. Liv.* A nuptiall song, or a song at a bridall. **1598** FLORIO It→E *Talasione, Talassione,* a song contained in certaine verses vsed to be sung at mariages, an exclamation or cry vsed at mariages hauing the beginning when Romulus and the Romanes rauished the maidens of the Sabines. **1611** FLORIO It→E *Talasione,* a song contained in certaine verses vsed to be sung at marriages, an exclamation or cry vsed at mariages, first begun when Romulus and his Romans rauished the maidens of the Sabines. **1656** BLOUNT (1st edn) *Talassion (talassio)* a song used to be sung at marriages. See *Thalassio. Thalassion (thalassio)* a nuptial song, or a song, at a bridal. *Thalassio* was used at Bridals or weddings in *Rome,* as an auspicate or lucky word; like this among the Greeks, *Hymen O Hymenæe, Hymen, &c. Catul.* **1658** PHILLIPS (1st edn) *Thalassion,* (lat.) a Nuptial Song, from *Thalassius* the god of Marriage Rites among the Romans. **1659** TORRIANO-FLORIO It→E *Talassione, Talasione,* a song an exclamation or crye used at marriages, first begun when *Romulus* and his Romans ravished the maidens of the Sabines. **1676** COLES *Thalassion, Latin.* a Nuptial song among the old *Romans.* **1704** *Cocker's Engl. Dict.* (1st edn) *Thalassion,* a Marriage Song among the Ancient Romans.

thalia *see* Muse
1500 *Ortus Vocabulorum* L→E Talia i. vua [sic] musarum. f.p. Thalia lie. est vua [sic] musarum f.p.

Thamyras *see* dorick, Linus
1538 ELYOT L→E *Thamaras,* was he, whiche fyrste playd on a harpe, withoute syngynge therto. **1565** COOPER L→E *Thamyras,* Was he, which first plaied on an harpe, without syngynge thereto.

theatre *see* interlude, ode, odeum, opera, orchestra, pulpit, recitative, rhapsodi
1589 [PUTTENHAM] *Arte of English Poesie* (p. 29) [*re* the performance of interludes in ancient Greek theatre] ... Afterward when Tragidies came vp they deuised to present them vpon scaffoldes or stages of timber, shadowed with linen or lether as the other, and these stages were made in the forme of a *Semicircle* ... Also there was place appointed for the musiciens to sing or play vpon their instrumentes at the end of euery scene, to the intent the people might be refreshed; and kept occupied. This maner of stage in halfe circle, the Greekes called *theatrum,* as much as to say a beholding place ...

theorbo *see* archlute, bass, basso continuo, colachon, research
1598 FLORIO It→E *Tiorba,* a kinde of musicall instrument vsed among countrie people. **1611** FLORIO It→E *Tiorba,* a musical instrument that blind men play vpon called a Theorba. **1656** BLOUNT (1st edn) *Theorba* (from the Ital. *Tiorba*) a certaine musical instrument different from the Lute, in that the head, or part of the head of this bends back, and the head of that is commonly strait. **1658** PHILLIPS (1st edn) *Theorba,* (Ital. *Tiorba*) a Musical Instrument, being a kind of base Lute. **1659** TORRIANO-FLORIO It→E *Tiorba,* a musical Instrument that men play upon, called a Theorba. **1671** PHILLIPS (3rd edn) *Theorba* (Ital. *Tiorba*) a musical Instrument, being a kind of Lute, used for the most part in playing of grounds and through bases. **1676** COLES *Theorba, Italian.* a large Lute. **1688** MIEGE-COTGRAVE Fr→E *Tuorbe,* (m.) *Instrument de Musique à cordes,* Theorbo, a Musical Instrument with Strings. § *Jouër du Tuorbe,* to play upon the Theorbo. *Un beau Tuorbe,* a fine Theorbo. **1702** KERSEY *New Engl. Dict.* (1st edn) A *Theorboe-lute,* a musical iustrument [sic]. **1704** *Cocker's Engl. Dict.* (1st edn) *Theorbo,* a large Musical Instrument called a Lute, for playing the lowest part or ground. **1706** KERSEY-PHILLIPS (6th edn) *Theorbo,* a Musical Instrument, being a large Lute, us'd for the most part in the playing of Grounds and Thorough-Basses. **1707** *Gloss. Angl. Nova* (1st edn) *Thoerbo,* a Musical Instrument. **1721** BAILEY *An Univ. Etymolog. Engl. Dict.* (1st edn) *Theorbo, (Teorbe, F. Tiorba, Ital.)* a kind of musical Instrument. **1724** [PEPUSCH] *Short Explic. of Foreign Words in Mus. Bks.* (p. 80) *Theorba,* or *Thiorba,* a large Lute made Use of by the *Italians* for playing a Thorough Bass, much the same as *Arcileuto,* or Arch-Lute. **1726** BAILEY *An Univ. Etymolog. Engl. Dict.* (3rd edn) *Theorbo* (*teorbe,* F. *thiorba,* Ital.) a musical Instrument; a large Lute made use of by the *Italians,* for playing a thorough Bass, much the same as *Arcileuto,* or Arch-lute. *Ital.* **1728** CHAMBERS *Theorbo, Theorba,* a Musical Instrument, made in Form of a Lute; except that it has two Necks, or Juga, the second and longer whereof sustains the four last Rows of Chords, which are to give the deepest Sounds. See *Lute.* ¶ The *Theorbo* is an Instrument, which for these last sixty or seventy Years, has succeeded to the Lute, in the playing of

thorough Basses: 'Tis said to have been invented in *France* by the Sieur *Hotteman*, and thence introduc'd into *Italy, &c.* ¶ The only Difference between the *Theorbo* and the Lute, is, that the former has eight Bass or thick Strings, twice as long as those of the Lute; which Excess of Length renders their Sound so exceedingly soft, and keeps it up for so long a Time, that 'tis no Wonder many prefer it to the Harpsichord itself. At least it has this Advantage, that it is easily remov'd from Place to Place, *&c.* ¶ All its Strings are usually single; tho' there are some who double the Bass Strings with a little Octave, and the small Strings with an Unison; in which Case, bearing more Resemblance to the Lute than the common *Theorbo*, the *Italians* call it the *Archiluto* or *Arch-Lute.* ¶ The Word *Theorbo* is form'd from the *French Theorbe*, of the *Italian Tiorba*, which signifies the same Thing, and which some will have the Name of the Inventor. **1730** BAILEY *Dict. Britannicum* (1st edn) *Theorbo* (*thiorba*, Ital.) a musical Instrument, a large Lute for playing a thorough Bass, used by the *Italians.* **1737** DYCHE-PARDON (2nd edn) *Theorbo* (S.) a large Lute, or Musical Instrument used to play thorough Basses on in Concerts.

1676 MACE *Musick's Monument* (p. 207) *The Theorboe*, is no other, than *That* which we call'd *the Old English Lute*; and is an *Instrument* of so much *Excellency*, and *Worth, and of so Great Good Use*, That in dispite of all *Fickleness*, and *Novelty*, It is still made use of, in the *Best Performances in Musick*, (*Namely, Vocal Musick.*) ¶ But because, I said It was the Old English Lute, It may be ask'd, Why is It not then still so Call'd; but by the Name of the *Theorboe*? ¶ I Answer, That although *It be the Old English Lute*, yet as to the *Use of It Generally, there is This Difference*, viz. *The Old Lute was Chiefly us'd, as we now use our French Lutes, (so call'd;) that is, only to Play Lone-Lessons upon*, &c. *But the Theorboe-Lute is Principally us'd in Playing to the Voice, or in Consort; It being a Lute of the Largest Scize;. and we make It much more Large in Sound*, by contriving unto *It a Long Head, to Augment and Increase that Sound, and Fulness of the Basses, or Diapasons, which are a great Ornament to the Voice, or Consort.* § (p. 208) Truly I cannot tell, why It was so called *Theorboe*; but for *These Reasons*; the *Distinction of Names*, between *It*, and the *Smaller Lute*, may well enough be maintained, seeing It has Now got the *Name.* (θε in *Greek*, begins a *very High Name.*) ...

theorbo stop

1676 MACE *Musick's Monument* (p. 236) I caus'd one of *Them* [an organ] to be made in my *House*, that has 9 several other *Varieties*, (24 in all) by reason of a *Stop* (to be *Slip'd* in with the *Hand*) which my *Work-man* calls the *Theorboe-Stop*; and indeed It is not much unlike It; But what It wants of a *Lute*, It has in Its own *Singular Prittiness.*

thesis & arsis *see* arsis & thesis

third *see* ditone, false third, mediant, minor, tercet, terza, tierce

1728 CHAMBERS *Third*, in Music, a Concord resulting from a Mixture of two Sounds, containing an Interval of two Degrees. See *Concord.* ¶ 'Tis call'd a *Third*, as containing *three* Terms, or Sounds between the Extremes. See *Interval.* ¶ The *Third*, in *Italian, Terza*, in *French Tierce*, in *Latin Tertia*, has no general Name in the *Greek*: 'Tis the first of the imperfect Concords, *i.e.* of such as admit of Majority and Minority, without ceasing to be Concords. ¶ And hence it is, that it is distinguish'd into two Kinds. ¶ The first, which the *Italians* call *Ditono*, (from the *Greek Ditonon*) or *Terza Maggiore*, and we *greater Third*, is compos'd diatonically of three Terms or Sounds, containing two Degrees or Intervals; one whereof, in the ancient System, is a greater Tone, and the other a lesser Tone; but in the modern temperate System they are both equal, as *ut, re, mi*, or *ut, mi.* See *Degree, Tone, Semitone, &c.* ¶ Chromatically it is compos'd of four Semitones; two whereof are greater, and the *third* less: It takes its Form from the Ratio sesqui-quarta 4:5. ¶ The second *Third*, which the *Italians*, like the *Greeks*, call *Trihemituono*, or *Semi-ditano*, or *Terza minore*, and we *lesser Third*, is compos'd, like the former, of three Sounds or Terms, and two Degrees or Intervals: But these Degrees, diatonically, are only a greater Tone, and a Semitone; and chromatically of three Tones, two greater, and one less, as *re, mi, fa*, or *re, fa*: It takes its Form from the Ratio Sesqui-quinta 5:6. ¶ Both these *Thirds* are of admirable Use in Melody, and make, as it were, the Foundation and Life of Harmony. See *Melody* and *Harmony.* ¶ They are us'd agreeably both ascending and descending; and that either in running over all the Degrees, as *ut, re, mi*, or *re, mi, fa*, or in skipping the middle Degree, as *ut, mi*, or *re, fa.* ¶ But it is to be observ'd, the *greater Third* has somewhat gay and sprightly in rising, and somewhat heavy and melancholic in falling: The *lesser Third*, on the contrary, has somewhat soft and tender in rising, and somewhat brisk in falling. ¶ *For the Use of the greater or lesser* Third *in the Series of the Scale.* See *Scale.* ¶ There are two other Kinds of *Thirds* that are dissonant and vicious; the first only compos'd of two greater Semitones, and, by Consequence, of a Semitone less than the *lesser Third*: This they call the *defective Third.* ¶ The second, on the contrary, has a Semitone more than the *greater Third;* and this they call *redundant Third.* ¶ The defective *Third* is very frequent in *Italian* Songs, especially those compos'd for Instruments; but is not to be us'd without Necessity, and a deal of Discretion. The redundant *Third* is absolutely forbidden. **1730** BAILEY *Dict. Britannicum* (1st edn) *Third* (in *Musick*) a Concord resulting from a Mixture of two Sounds, containing an Interval of two Degrees. **1737** DYCHE-PARDON (2nd edn) *Third* (S.) ... and in *Musick,* is an Interval of two Sounds or Degrees of Tone, and of this there is the greater and the lesser, the Third greater is called the sharp, and the lesser the flat Third.

third greater, third lesser

1721 MALCOLM *Treatise of Musick* (p. 260) The Three 2*ds* or *Degrees* [8:9, 9:10, 15:16] are all *concinnous Intervals;* ... Two [4:5, 5:6] are particularly known by the Names of 3*d g.* and 3*d l.*

third tone

1609 DOWLAND-ORNITHOPARCUS *Micrologvs* (pp. 31-2) The third *tone,* is a Rule determining the *Authenticall* of the second manner. Or it is the *authentical* progression of the second, hauing the final place regular in *Elami*: His beginnings (according to *Guido*) are *E. F. G.* &c.

thorough bass *see* andante, archlute, bass, basso continuo, B. C., c, cantata, continuato, continued bass, continuo, dialogue, duo, figure, ground, natural bass, organ, sonata, tasto, tenor, theorbo, through bass

1702 KERSEY *New Engl. Dict.* (1st edn) The *Thorough-bass.* **1708** KERSEY *Dict. Anglo-Brit.* (1st edn) *Thorough Bass,* (in *Musick*) is that which goes quite thro' the Composition. **1728** CHAMBERS *Thorough-Bass,* in Music, is that which goes quite through the Composition. See *Bass.* ¶ It is also call'd *Continu'd Bass.* See *Continu'd Bass.* **1737** DYCHE-PARDON (2nd edn) *Thorough-bass* (S.) in *Musick,* is the full Bass played with all the Chords, and which accompanies or goes thro' the whole Concert, tho' the particular Instruments change, or stand still often.

1717 B[AYNE] *Intro. to Knowledge and Practice of Thoro' Bass* (pp. 3-4) As by an agreeable and various Disposition and Distribution of the Sounds that rise out of the *Bass,* the upper Parts are composed, so these Sounds which so naturally grow out of the *Bass,* may naturally accompany it: But to preserve the Character of the *Bass,* wherein there ought always to appear the greatest Plainness, these Sounds must accompany it, undivided and uncompounded, in a plain and simple manner. ¶ The *Bass* then so accompany'd, is call'd the *Thoro' Bass;* in which are virtually comprehended all the upper Parts; for these Sounds, which by a various Division and Distribution, compose the upper Parts, are here in Substance collected into the *Bass.* **1721 or after** ANON. Treatise of Thoro' Bass BEINECKE OSB. MS 3, pp. 1-2 Of the Nature of the Thoro' Bass in generall, and the Reason of the Name.... This Bass is called by the Italians Basso-Continuo, by the French Basse continué, or Basse generale; That is, the generall Bass which is continued through the whole piece, and does not rest, as perhaps the other Basses do when the Musick consists of many Parts. From thence it is that we call it the Thoro' Bass, instead of continued, as being that part which Goes through the whole peice from beginning to end, without any long or sensible interruption: So that the appellation of Thoro' Bass is owing to the Nature of the Bass itself, and is not given it because of its being accompanyed.

three mens' song *see* berlingozzo, cantarini, strambotto

thremot *see* clang

1676 COLES *Thremot, (q. terræ mot) Old word.* the blast of a horn. **1704** *Cocker's Engl. Dict.* (1st edn) *Thremot* or *Teremot,* the blowing of an horn. **1726** BAILEY *An Univ. Etymolog. Engl. Dict.* (3rd edn) *Thremote,* the Blast of a Horn. *Chaucer.*

threne *see* threnody

1538 ELYOT L→E *Threnos,* a lamentacyon, whyche was vsyd at buryenge. **1587** THOMAS L→E *Threnos, vel threnum, ni, n.g. Isid.* Lamentation. *Also* a lamentable verse and song, a funerall song. *Iun.* **1589** RIDER L→E *Threnos. threnum, n. nænia epicedium, n.* A funeral song. **1623** COCKERAM *Threnes.* Mournings, lamentations. **1656** BLOUNT

(1st edn) *Threne (threnum)* lamentation; also a lamentable verse or song; a funeral song. **1659** TORRIANO-FLORIO It→E *Treni* any wailefull poems or Songs, chiefly the lamentations of *Jeremy*. **1676** COLES *Threne, Greek.* a lamentation (song[)]. **1704** *Cocker's Engl. Dict.* (1st edn) *Threne,* a Funeral Hymn or Song.

threnody *see* dirge, elegy, epicedy, epitaph, monody, nænia, obit, threne

1538 ELYOT L→E *Threnodia,* a mournyng songe. **1565** COOPER L→E *Threnodia.* A mournyng songe. **1587** THOMAS L→E *Threnodia, æ, f.g.* *A mourning song. **1656** BLOUNT (1st edn) *Threnody (threnodia)* a mourning song. **1658** PHILLIPS (1st edn) *Threnody,* (Greek) the singing of a Threne, *i.* a mourning or funeral-Song. **1661** BLOUNT (2nd edn) *Threnody (threnodia)* the singing of a funeral song. **1676** COLES *Threnody. Greek.* the singing of a funeral song. **1704** *Cocker's Engl. Dict.* (1st edn) *Threnody,* Singing a Song or Elegy on the Dead. **1706** KERSEY-PHILLIPS (6th edn) *Threnodia, (Gr.)* a mournful, or funeral Song; the *Greek* Title of the Book of Lamentations of the Prophet *Jeremiah.* **1707** *Gloss. Angl. Nova* (1st edn) *Threnody,* (Gr.) a mournful or funeral Song. **1728** CHAMBERS *Threnody, Threnodia,* a mournful, or Funeral Song. See *Funeral.* **1737** DYCHE-PARDON (2nd edn) *Threnodia* (S.) a Dirge, or mournful Song or Poem to sing at Funerals, &c.

through bass *see* ground, thorough bass

early 18th C. NORTH (Prendcourt's) Treatis of Continued or Through Basse BL Add. 32549, f. 17 The through bass is called that becaus It is y[e] basis or foundation of all the other parts; and it doth continue from one end to th[e] other without Intermission. **c.1710** NORTH (Prendcourt's) Treatise of Continued or thro-base BL Add. 32531, f. 29 [quoting Prendcourt:] The thro-bass is called thus, becaus It is the base or foundation of all the other parts, and It doth continue from one End to th'other without Intermission. 'Tis a true Composition at sight.

thrubal

1611 COTGRAVE Fr→E *Thrubal. Rab.* A Trumpettor.

thump

1652 PLAYFORD *Musicks Recreation on Lyra Viol* (n.p.) ... Also sometimes you will meet with a letter which hath this mark under it ⁛ which is called a Thump, or the striking the string onely with the Finger of your left hand.

thyasus

1538 ELYOT L→E *Thyasus,* a daunce dedycate to Bacchus. **1565** COOPER L→E *Thyasus, si,* A daunce dedicate to Bacchus. **1587** THOMAS L→E *Thyasus, si, m.g. p.b. Virg.* A daunce dedicated to Bacchus.

thymelici

1538 ELYOT L→E *Thymelici,* maye be callydde daunsers of Morysdaunces. **1552** HULOET L→E *Tlymelici* [sic]. Dauncers called morrys dauncers, or commune dauncers. **1565** COOPER L→E *Thymelici.* Players in interludes: common or open daunsers. **1587** THOMAS L→E *Thymele, es, f.g. *Pulpitum in orchestra altum pedes 5. in quo chorus tragædiarum, & comædiarum, cæteriq;* **1656** BLOUNT (1st edn) *Thymelical (thymelicus)* belonging to players in interludes and open dance.

tibia *see* aes, aula, calamus, fistula, flute, wind

1500 *Ortus Vocabulorum* L→E Tibia bie. in vno sensu est instrumentum musicum longum sicut tuba sectum diuersis foraminibus sic dicta q primo solet fieri de tibijs ceruorum ... f.p. **1538** ELYOT L→E *Tibia,* ... it is also an instrument callid a shalme. *Tibialis, le,* pertaynyng to shaulmes. § *Miluina tibia,* a cornette, or smalle shaulme. **1565** COOPER L→E *Tibia.Cic.* A shalme, pype, flute, or recorder. § *Canere tibijs. Quintil.* To play on pipes. *Cantus tibiarum. Quintil.* The playing on pipes or recorders: the melodie of, &c. *Inflare tibias. Cic.* To blow a pipe or recorder. *Ludicræ tibiæ. Plin.* Mynstrels pypes. *Tibia flatur. Ouid.* A pipe is blowen. *Tibia indixit choros. Virgil.* The pipe or flute called them to daunsinge. *Tibiarum tratatio. Cic. Nec verò ab aruspicibus accipiunt tibiarum tratationem, sed à musicis.* The plaiynge of flutes or recorders, the handlyng or vsinge. **1587** THOMAS L→E *Tibia, æ, f.g. ... also* a fluite, a pipe, &c. *vid. Classicum.* § *Dextræ, Iun.* Pipes that being plaied vpon, were held in the right side of the mouth and in the right hand. *Gingrina, vid. Gingrina. Milvina* [*see* tibia], *Iun.* A pipe that maketh a squeaking & sharp noise like a kite. *Ligula tibiæ, Iun.* The tongue, cane, or quill of a pipe. *Longæ tibiæ, Iun.* Pipes vsed in praying in temples making a long sound. *Milvina tibia, Fest.* A cornet or small shawme. *Phrygiæ, Iun.* Pipes that were not equall, or that had not euen holes but od. *Præcentoria. Iun.* A pipe whereon they plaid in temples before the shrines of their gods.

Puellaria, vel puellatoria, Iun. A pipe that made a shrill noise like a womans voice. *Sarranæ.* Pipes that had euen holes. *Sinistræ, Iun.* Pipes that beeing plaid vpon were held contrariwise [to tibiæ dextræ]. *Tibia Vtricularis, Iun.* A baggepipe. *Vasca, vel potiùs vasta, Iun.* A great pipe which was full of holes and sounded lowder then the first. **1589** RIDER L→E *Tibia, f.* A crowd or fidle. *tibia, fistula, syrinx, syringa, arundo, f. calamus.* A pipe. § *Tibia vtriculatis, ascaula, f.* A bagge pipe. **1598** FLORIO It→E *Tibia,* a flute, a recorder, a pipe. *Tibiare,* to sound vpon a flute, a pipe, or a recorder. *Tibiatore,* a piper vpon flutes, recorders or pipes. **1611** FLORIO It→E *Tibia,* any kind of flute, pipe, or recorder. Also a trumpet. *Tibiare,* to sound vpon any flute, a pipe or recorder. *Tibiatore,* a piper vpon pipes, flutes or recorders, a trumpeter. **1658** PHILLIPS (1st edn) *Tibial,* (lat.) belonging to a Pipe or Flute. **1659** TORRIANO-FLORIO It→E *Tibia,* any trumpet, pipe, flute, recorder, haut-boy, or other long wind-instrument *Tibiare,* to sound or play upon a *Tibia* *Tibiatore,* a plaier upon a *Tibia* **1676** COLES *Tibial, Latin.* belonging to pipes. **1706** KERSEY-PHILLIPS (6th edn) *Tibia, (Lat.)* a Pipe, Flute, or Flagelet; a Musical Instrument:

1582 *Batman vppon Bartholome* (p. 424) *Tibia* is a pipe, & hath that name, for it was first made of legs of Hartes, young & old, as men suppose, & the noice of pipes was called *Tibicen.* Or els as *Hugution* saith, this name *Tibia* commeth of *Tibin,* y[e] is a rush or a reede, for of certaine reedes, such an instrument was made in old time: & thereof is said *hic Tibicen, nis,* he y[e] plaieth on such pipes... **1586** ANON. *Praise of Mvsicke* (pp. 16-17) Nowe among the winde instrumentes the Pshalme was deuised either by *Euterpe* one of the nine Muses, or else by *Ardalus Vulcans* sonne, made at the first of the shanke bones of cranes, and therefore called *Tibia* by the Latines. Although afterwardes it was framed of the baytree in *Lybia,* of box in *Phrygia,* of the boanes of hinds in *Thebes* in *Scythia* of rauens & eagles, in *Aegypt* of barly stalks & so accordingly at other times & in other places of other matters. **1709** [RAGUENET] *Comparison betw. Fr. and It. Musick and Opera's* (p. 63) ... They [the ancients] had indeed another sort of Instrument, which they call'd *Tibiæ,* something like our Haut-bois; ... **1721** MALCOLM *Treatise of Musick* (p. 469) Of *Wind*-instruments we hear [in ancient accounts] of the *Tibia,* so called from the Shank-bone of some Animals, as Cranes, of which they were first made. **1728** NORTH Musicall Grammarian (*C-K MG* f. 115v) The tibiæ, were pipes that sounded by a reedall device like those affixed to bag-pipes, and foraminated for changing the tone when there was occasion. They were also termed dexteræ and sinistræ, becaus two pipes met in an angle at the mouth, so that to manage them, there was work for right hand and left; ...

tibicen *see* tubicen

1500 *Ortus Vocabulorum* L→E Tibicen inis. qui canit cum tibia vus § A cano si veniat nomen quod veni desinit in cen Tibicen longo liricen tubicen breuiando Tibicina e... vel mulier q canit cum tibia f.p. Tibicines penult cor. an[e]. trompers **1538** ELYOT L→E *Tibicen, & tibicina,* he or she that blowethe a trumpette or shalme. **1552** HULOET L→E § *Ad modos tibicinis saltare.* Daunce after the stroke or tune. **1565** COOPER L→E *Tibicen, pen. prod. tibícinis, pen. corr. masc. gen. Cic.* He that bloweth a trumpet, or playeth on a shalme, or flute. Any minstrell. *Tibícina, tibícinæ, pen. cor. fœm. gen. Martial.* A woman playing on a flute or shalme. § *Ad tibicinem immolare. Cic.* To have a minstrell playing while he doth sacrifice. **1587** THOMAS L→E *Tibicen, inis, m.g.* A plaier on the flute, a trumpeter, a minstrell. *Versus in quo aliquid infarcitur, quod metri legem hiulcam sustentet, Serv.* *Tibicina, æ, f.g. Mart.* A woman playing on a flute, or shalme. **1589** RIDER L→E *Tibicen, aulædus, fistulator, masc.* A plaier on the flute, or small trumpet. *Tibicen, Cheleus, m.* A Lute plaier, or luter.

tibicinate *see* tubicinate

1656 BLOUNT (1st edn) *Tibicinate* (*tibicino*) to sing or pipe. **1658** PHILLIPS (1st edn) *Tibicination,* (lat.) a playing on a Pipe. **1676** COLES *Tibicinate, Latin.* to pipe. **1704** *Cocker's Engl. Dict.* (1st edn) *Tibicinate,* to play upon the Hoboy, Recorder, or any other Pipe.

tibilustrium *see* tubilustrium

1538 ELYOT L→E *Tibilustria,* were dayes whan menne wente with trumpettes, as it were in processyon aboute their lambes [sic]. **1565** COOPER L→E *Tibilustria.* Dayes on which men wente with trumpets, as it weare in procession, aboute their landes. **1587** THOMAS L→E *Tibilustria,* *Daies in which men went with trumpets about their lands. **1598** FLORIO It→E *Tibilustri,* daies in which men went with trumpets as it were in procession about their lands. **1611** FLORIO It→E *Tibilustri,* daies in which men were wont to go with pipes and trumpets, as it were in procession about their lands

tibini

1538 ELYOT L→E *Tibini,* tunes made with shalmes. **1552** HULOET L→E *tibini* the tune of trompet or shalme. **1565** COOPER L→E *Tibini.* Tunes made with shalmes. **1587** THOMAS L→E *Tibini, Non.* Tunes made with shalmes. **1589** RIDER L→E *Tibini, m.* Tunes made with shalmes.

tie *see* ligature, syncopation

1677 NEWTON *English Academy* (p. 101) A *Tye* is a Semi-circle, whose two ends point to the two Notes conjoyned, as when two *Minums,* or one *Minum* and a *Crotchet* are Tyed together; as also, when two or more Notes are to be Sung to one Syllable, or two Notes or more to be plaid with one drawing of the Bow on the *Viol* or *Violin.* **1680** B., A. *Synopsis of Vocal Musick* (p. 43) A Tye is a crooked line, binding two or more Notes together, which to one Syllable are to be Sung. **c.1700** NORTH Capt. Prencourts rules BL Add. 32549, f. 12 This signe is called a tye .⌒. w[ch] is commonly set aboue two Notes upon the same space or the same line. and signifyes that you touch the first Note, and lye upon it till its value and that of the following note is past, for you must not touch the second note againe.

tierce *see* demiditone, tercet, third

1696 PHILLIPS (5th edn) *Tierce, (French)* ... In Musick, a Concord, or mixture of Two Sounds, which contain an interval of Two Tones and a half. **1704** HARRIS *Tierce,* or a *Third,* is a Term in *Musick,* signifying a certain Division of the *Monochord,* in which if the Terms be as 5 to 4, 'tis called, a *Tierce Major,* or a *Diton;* but if the Terms are as 6 to 5, then 'tis called, a *Tierce Minor,* or *Demi-Diton.* **1706** KERSEY-PHILLIPS (6th edn) *Tierce* or *A Third,* (in *Musick*) is a certain division of the Monochord, in which if the Terms be as 5 to 4, 'tis call'd a *Tierce Major,* or a *Diton;* but if they be as 6 to 5, then 'tis styl'd a *Tierce Minor,* or *Demi-Diton.* **1707** *Gloss. Angl. Nova* (1st edn) *Tierce,* or a *Third,* the difference of three Notes in Musick, which is either *Major* or *Minor;* the first in the division of a *Monochord,* being as 5 to 4, the last as 6 to 5. **1728** CHAMBERS *Tierce,* in Music. See *Third.* **1730** BAILEY *Dict. Britannicum* (1st edn) *Tierce* (in *Musick.*) See *Third.*

tiercet *see* terzetto

1611 COTGRAVE Fr→E *Tiercet: m.* A Song of triple Stanzoes, or Stanzo of three verses. **1656** BLOUNT (1st edn) *Tiercet* (Fr.) a song of triple *Stanzoes,* or *Stanzo* of three verses. **1704** *Cocker's Engl. Dict.* (1st edn) *Teircet* [sic], a Song or Poem, whereof every staff has only three Verses or Lines. **1706** KERSEY-PHILLIPS (6th edn) *Tiercet,* a Song consisting of triple Stanza's, or a Staff of three Verses. **1708** KERSEY *Dict. Anglo-Brit.* (1st edn) *Tiercet,* a Song consisting of triple Stanza's; or a Staff of three Verses.

tiger

1730 BAILEY *Dict. Britannicum* (1st edn) *A Tiger* (in *Hieroglyph.*) represented a Savege Nature, ... and is reported to fall into a violent Rage when it hears the Sound of a musical Instrument.

timbestoets

1704 *Cocker's Engl. Dict.* (1st edn) *Timbestoets,* an old word for small Bells.

timbestores

1676 COLES *Timbesteres, Old word.* timbrel-players. **1708** KERSEY *Dict. Anglo-Brit.* (1st edn) *Timbestores,* (*O.*) Timbrel-players. **1721** BAILEY *An Univ. Etymolog. Engl. Dict.* (1st edn) *Timbestores,* Players on Timbrels. *O.* **1726** BAILEY *An Univ. Etymolog. Engl. Dict.* (3rd edn) *Timbesters,* Players on Timbrels. *O.*

timbon

1611 COTGRAVE Fr→E *Timbon.* A kind of brasen Drumme. *Tymbon.* A kind of brasen drumme.

timbre

1593 HOLLYBAND Fr→E *Timbre de cloistre,* the Bell which is rung to come to dinner or supper, or assemble together *Tymbre,* ... the little bell in religious houses, Colleges, or Innes, to call the company togither: *m.* **1611** COTGRAVE Fr→E *Timbre: m.* A Colledge-bell; or the Hall-bell of a Colledge, or Cloister; also, the bell of a little Clocke; **1676** COLES *Timbres, French.* little bells. **1688** MIEGE-COTGRAVE Fr→E *Timbre,* (m.) bell ... strings, or Drum-strings; § *On a coupé le Timbre cette Caisse,* some body has cut the Strings of this Drum. **1704** *Cocker's Engl. Dict.* (1st edn) *Timbres,* a *French* word for small Bells.

timbrel *see* adufe, bacile, bacino, cembalo, crepitaculum, crusma, cymbal, sistrum, taballi, tambour, tambourine, timbestores, tympany

1611 COTGRAVE Fr→E *Tymbale.* A Timbrell; or, a little brasen drumme to daunce by. *Langued.* **1656** BLOUNT (1st edn) *Timbrel* (from the Belg. *Trommel*) a Taber. **1658** PHILLIPS (1st edn) *Timbrel,* (Dutch

Trommel) a kind of musical Instrument, by some called a Taber. **1676** COLES *Timbrel, (Dutch. Trommel)* a Taber. **1688** MIEGE-COTGRAVE Fr→E *Tymbale,* (f.) a Kettle- Drum. *Tymbalier,* (m.) *celui qui bat la Tymbale,* a Kettle-Drummer. § *Batre les Tymbales,* to beat the Kettle-Drums. **1702** KERSEY *New Engl. Dict.* (1st edn) A *Timbrel, or* taber. § A *Timbrel-player.* **1704** *Cocker's Engl. Dict.* (1st edn) *Timbrel,* a Musical Instrument, called also a Tabret. **1706** KERSEY-PHILLIPS (6th edn) *Timbrel,* a kind of Musical Instrument, which some call a *Taber.* **1737** DYCHE-PARDON (2nd edn) *Timbrel* (S.) a Musical Instrument formerly in Use, especially among the Women to dance and sing to, but now quite laid aside.

timburins *see* tambourine
1707 *Gloss. Angl. Nova* (1st edn) *Timburins,* an old kind of Instrument, some think a Clarion. *Spencer.*

time *see* common time, dupla, galliard time, jig time, measure, minim time, mood, pavan time, prolation, retorted time, semibreve time, tact, tripla, whole time
1688 MIEGE-COTGRAVE Fr→E *Tems,* (m.) Time ... in ... Musick **1704** HARRIS *Time,* in *Musick,* is that quantity, or length whereby is assign'd to every particular *Note,* its due Measure, without making it either longer or shorter than it ought to be; and it is twofold, *viz. Duple* or *Common,* and *Triple.* ¶ *Duple,* or *Semi-breve Time,* generally called *Common,* because most used, is when all the *Notes* are encreased by two: As 2 *Longs* make a *Large,* 2 *Breves* a *Long,* 2 *Semi-breves* a *Breve,* 2 *Minims* a *Semi-breve,* 2 *Crotchats* [sic] a *Minim,* 2 *Quavers* a *Crotchat,* 2 *Semi-quavers* a *Quaver,* and 2 *Demi-Semi-quavers* a *Semi-quaver.* ¶ This sort of *Time* is usual in *Anthems, Almains, Pavans, Fantasies,* &c. ¶ *Triple Time,* is that wherein the Measure is counted by *Three's*: As one *Semi-breve* is equivalent to 3 *Minims,* one *Minim* to 3 *Crotchats,* &c. So that this swifter *Time* or *Measure* is proper for Airy Songs, and Light Lessons: As *Corants, Sarabands, Jiggs,* &c. ¶ To these sorts of *Time* may be added, *Sesquialter Proportion,* which signifies a *Triple* Measure of three *Notes,* to two such like *Notes* of the *Common Time.* **1706** KERSEY-PHILLIPS (6th edn) In *Musick, Time* is that quantity or length, by which every particular Note has its due Measure appointed, without making it either longer or shorter than it ought to be; and it is twofold, *viz.* Duple or Common, and Triple. ¶ *Duple* or *Semi-breve Time,* generally call'd *Common,* because most us'd; is when all the Notes are encreased by two; as 2 *Longs* make a *Large,* 2 *Breves* a *Long,* 2 *Semi-breves* a *Breve,* 2 *Minims a Semi-breve,* 2 *Crotchets* a *Minim,* 2 *Quavers* a *Crotchet,* 2 *Semi-quavers* a *Quaver,* and 2 *Demi-Semi-quavers* a *Semi-quaver*: This kind of Time is usual in Anthems, Almains, Pavans, Fantasies, &c. ¶ *Triple Time,* is that in which the Measure is counted by Threes; as one *Semi-breve* is equivalent to three *Minims,* one *Minim* to three *Crotchets,* &c. So that this swifter Time, or Measure is proper for Airy Songs and light Lessons; as *Courants, Jiggs, Sarabands,* &c. ¶ To these sorts of Time may be added *Sesquialter Proportion,* which signifies a Triple Measure of three Notes to two such like Notes of the Common Time. **1728** CHAMBERS *Time* ... [*see* Appendix] **1731** KERSEY *New Engl. Dict.* (3rd edn) *Time,* ... In *Musick,* that Length by which a due Measure is fixt for every thing. **1736** BAILEY *Dict. Britannicum* (2nd edn) *Time* (in *Musick*) is the measures which are separated in writing by strokes or bars. § *To beat Time* (in *Musick*) to give or distinguish such time by a blow or motion of the hand or foot. **1737** DYCHE-PARDON (2nd edn) *Time* (S.) ... in *Musick,* it is the giving each Note according to the Composition its proper Length or continued Sound; and this is again called common, duple, or triple Time.

after 1517 ANON. Art of Mvsic BL Add. 4911, f. 6 Tym. (as *ornitoparchus* dois approve) is ane breif tua or thrie semebrewis in the solf Includit. Or it is of twa or thrie semebrewis in ane brieff a dimention mensurall or ellis in [other] wayis. *Tym* is ane mesur of ane preferrit or ane omittit voce continu allie proportionat under ane moving. The quhilk onderstand ye quantatie of brevis or of certane semebrewis in the respect of ane breffias It war ane positione of thrie or tua semebriwis **1596** ANON. *Pathway to Musicke* [C iii *verso*] *VVhat is time?* ¶ It is a formall quantitie of Sembriues, measuring them by three or by two, and eyther it is perfect or imperfect. **1597** MORLEY *Plaine and Easie Introdvction* (p. 9) [marginalia: 'Definition of time.'] ¶ *Phi.* What is *the timing of a note?* ¶ *Ma.* It *is a certayne space or length, wherein a note may be holden in singing.* § (pp. 12-13) *Phi.* What called they *time?* ¶ *Ma. The dimension of the Breefe by Semibreeues*: and is likewise perfect or vnperfect. *Perfect time is, when the Brief containeth three semibreeues.* His signes are these, O3 C3 O ... The time vnperfect is, *when the Briefe containeth but two Semibre[u]es,* whose signes are these: O2 C2 C **early 17th C.** RAVENSCROFT Treatise of Musick BL Add. 19758, f. 12v Tyme is a quantity of Semibrieues and minimes mesurid by 2 or by 3 ... **1609** DOWLAND-ORNITHOPARCUS *Micrologvs* (p. 42) *Of Time.* ¶ *Time* is a *Breefe* which containes in it two or three *Semibreefes*. Or it is the measuring of two or three *Semibreefes* in one *Breefe*. And it is two-fold, to wit, perfect: and this is a *Breefe* measured with three *Semibreefes*. Whose signe is the number of three ioyned with a Circle or a Semicircle, or a perfect Circle set without a number, thus; O3. C3. O. The imperfect is, wherein a *Breefe* is measured onely by two *Semibreefes*. Which is knowne by the number of two ioyned with a perfect Circle, or a Semicircle, or a Semicircle without a number, thus; O2. C2. **1614** RAVENSCROFT *Briefe Discovrse* (p. 5) *Tempus* signifieth a Time, which is ordained by order, hauing a iust *Measure*, set *Limits* & *Bonds*; and here is a figure or *Note* of a *Rhombus* or *Circular* forme, which we terme the *Semi-breue*; but the reason why the *Time* is appropriated to the *Breue* is in regard of the *Perfect Measure* of the *Breue* by this *Circular Note*, though in the forme it is applyed to the *Semi-breue*. **1617-24** FLUDD *Utriusque Cosmi Maioris: De Templo Musicæ* (p. 190) *Tempus* est spatium continuande vocis seu soni tam prolati, quàm omissi, quod certis figuris descriptum tactu mensuratur. **1662** [DAVIDSON] *Cantus, Songs and Fancies* (n.p.) Q. *What is Tyme?* ¶ A. It is a measuring of Semi-briefs by Briefs, and is either perfect or imperfect. **1665** SIMPSON *Principles of Practical Mvsick* (p. 22) [*re* keeping time] This Motion of the Hand is *Down*, and *Vp*, successively and equally divided. Every *Down* and *Vp*, being call'd a *Time*, or *Measure*. And by this we measure the length of a *Semibreve*: which is therefore called the *Measure-Note*, or *Time-Note*. **1680** B., A. *Synopsis of Vocal Musick* (p. 8) Time is a successive motion, depression and elevation, fall and rise of the hand, by which the length of all Sounds, Notes, and Pauses is measured: and is either dupla usually called common, or tripla, or sesquia[l]tera. **1686** ANON. *New and Easie Method to Learn to Sing* (p. 48) ... the next thing is to know, how to give every Note its true Time in any Song or Lesson; for which purpose, every Tune is divided into Parcels, called *Times*, by Lines or Bars struck across the Staff.

timoroso
1724 [PEPUSCH] *Short Explic. of Foreign Words in Mus. Bks.* (p. 80) *Timoroso*, is to play with Fear, or Great Care and Caution. **1726** BAILEY *An Univ. Etymolog. Engl. Dict.* (3rd edn) *Timoroso* (in *Musick Books*) signifies to play with great Fear, or great Care and Caution. *Ital.*

Timotheus *see* chromatic, magade, phrygian
1538 ELYOT L→E *Timotheus*, ... Also a cunnynge musitian, whiche vsyd to take of his scholers, which had lerned before, double salarie, that he toke of other, whiche neuer lerned, sayeng, that he toke with them double labours, that is to saye, to make them to forgette that which they hadde lernyd afore, and thanne to teache them perfytely. **1565** COOPER L→E *Timótheus* ... Also a cunning musitian, whiche vsed to take of his scholers, which had learned before, double salarie, that he toke of other which neuer learned: saiyng, that he tooke with them double labours, that is to say, to make them to forget that, whiche they had learned before, and then to teache them perfectly.

timpane *see* tympany

tintamar
1704 *Cocker's Engl. Dict.* (1st edn) *Tintamar*, a jangling of Bells.

tintene *see* tintinabulum
1598 FLORIO It→E *Tintene*, a kinde of musicall instrument without strings. Also a little shrill sounding bell. **1611** FLORIO It→E *Tintene*, a little shrill-sounding bell, a musicall instrument without strings.

tintillare
1659 TORRIANO-FLORIO It→E *Tintillante, Tintinnante*, tingling, gingling, or shrill ringing of bells. *Tintillare, Tintinare, Tintinuare, Tintinuire, nisco, nito*, to dingle, to tingle, to jangle, to gingle, to ding-dang, or ring shrill and sharp, as some bells do.

tintin
1611 COTGRAVE Fr→E *Tintin: m.* The tinging, or tolling of a bell; also, the warble, or song of a Nightingale.

tintinabulum
1500 *Ortus Vocabulorum* L→E Tintinnabulum li. i. nola que solet pendi collis canum vel pedibus auium. or a sacrynge belle n.s. **1565** COOPER L→E *Tintinnabulum, tintinnabuli, n. gen. penult. cor. Iuuenalis.* A little bell. **1587** THOMAS L→E *Tintinnabulum, li, n.g. Iuv.* A litle bell, *vid. Nola.* **1589** RIDER L→E *Tintinnabulum, n. campanula,*

campanella, f. campanellum. Crepitaculum, n. A little bell. *Tintinnaculus, m.* A ringer, or he that maketh a ringing. **1598** FLORIO It→E *Tintinabulo,* as *Tintene.* **1611** FLORIO It→E *Tintinabulo,* as *Tintene.* **1659** TORRIANO-FLORIO It→E *Tintinabulo, Tintina,* any shrill sounding bell, any musical instrument without strings.

1582 *Batman vppon Bartholome* (chap. 134) *Tintinabulum* is a bell or a Tamparnole, and hath the name of *Tiniendo* tinckeling or ringing.

tintination

1623 COCKERAM *Tintinate.* To ring like a bell. *Tintinate.* to Ring like a bell. **1656** BLOUNT (1st edn) *Tintinate (tintino)* to ring like a bell, to ting. **1658** PHILLIPS (1st edn) *Tintinnation,* (lat.) a ringing like a bell. **1704** *Cocker's Engl. Dict.* (1st edn) *Tintination,* Ringing of Bells.

tintinno

1550 THOMAS It→E *Tintinno,* the sharpe sounde that a basen, a bell, or suche other maketh, whan it is striken. **1598** FLORIO It→E *Tintino,* a shrill, sounding, or iangling of a bason or bels **1611** FLORIO It→E *Tintino,* any kind of shrill tingling, gingling, or sharp sounding, as of basons or bels.

tinton

1611 COTGRAVE Fr→E *Tinton: m.* The burthen of a song; also, the ting of a bell; also, a kind of dance.

tiorba *see* theorbo

tiple *see* cantor

1599 MINSHEU-PERCYVALL Sp→E **Tiple,* as *Cantor tiple,* one that singeth small, the treble voice. § **Tiple de la yglesia,* he that singeth the treble voice in the church.

tirelirer

1598 FLORIO It→E *Tirelirare,* to sing or chirp as a larke. **1611** COTGRAVE Fr→E *Tirelirer.* To warble, or sing like a Larke. **1611** FLORIO It→E *Tirelirare,* to sing as a Larke. **1659** TORRIANO-FLORIO It→E **Tirilirare,* to tiriliry, to sing or warble as a lark.

titeller

1611 COTGRAVE Fr→E *Titeller.* To ting, or tingle, as a (little) Bell. **1650** HOWELL-COTGRAVE Fr→E † *Titeller.* To ting, or tingle, as a (little) Bell.

tocar

1599 MINSHEU-PERCYVALL Sp→E *Tocar,* Præs. *yo Toco,* 1. Præt. *yo Toque,* Præs. Sub. *Toque,* to touch, to sound a trumpet, horne, or any winde instrument, to play vpon a drum or any musicall instrument § **Tocar a retirar,* to sound a retrait on the drum. **Tocar cuerno,* to winde a horne. **Tocar trompeta,* to sound a trumpet. **Toque del atambor,* a sounding or striking vp of a drum.

toccata

1611 FLORIO It→E § *Toccata d'vn musico,* a preludium that cunning musitions vse to play as it were voluntary before any set lesson. **1724** [PEPUSCH] *Short Explic. of Foreign Words in Mus. Bks.* (p. 81) *Toccata,* or *Toccato,* is of much the same Signification as the Word *Ricercata,* which see. **1726** BAILEY *An Univ. Etymolog. Engl. Dict.* (3rd edn) *Toccata, Toccato,* (in *Musick Books*) signifies the same as *Ricercate,* which is a kind of extempore Prelude or Overture, called in *English* a Voluntary. *Ital.* **1737** DYCHE-PARDON (2nd edn) *Toccata* or *Toccato* (S.) in *Musick,* means a voluntary or extemporary Overture or Piece of Musick played by a single Person.

toc-sing *see* sing

toll *see* bell, campana, cloche, copter, doppio, knell, martello, scampanare, tintin

1702 KERSEY *New Engl. Dict.* (1st edn) To *toll, or* ring a bell, after a particular manner. **1706** KERSEY-PHILLIPS (6th edn) To *Toll,* to ring a Bell after a paricular manner: **1708** KERSEY *Dict. Anglo-Brit.* (1st edn) To *Toll,* to ring a Bell after a particular manner: **1721** BAILEY *An Univ. Etymolog. Engl. Dict.* (1st edn) To *Toll a Bell,* is to ring it after a particular Manner to give Notice of the Death or Funeral of some Person. **1730** BAILEY *Dict. Britannicum* (1st edn) *Toll,* the Sound of a Bell, giving Notice of a Death or Funeral. **1737** DYCHE-PARDON (2nd edn) *Toll* (V.) to sound a Bell in a melancholy Manner, as at a Funeral, &c.

tonabulum

1500 *Ortus Vocabulorum* L→E Tonabulum li. a lytell belle n.s.

tonarion *see* aula

1538 ELYOT L→E *Tonarion,* a certayne shaulme with a softe sounde, on the whiche in the old time some oratours vsed to haue, to playe by theym, whan they pleaded, that by the tunes of the shalme, the oratour mought [sic] moderate and order his pronunciation. **1565** COOPER L→E *Tonarion*. A shalme of a softe tune, that some oratours in pleadyng vsed to haue by them to moderate their voyce. **1587** THOMAS L→E *Tonarion*, *A certaine shalme with a sweete sound. **1598** FLORIO It→E *Tonarione*, a certaine shalme with a sweete sound. **1611** FLORIO It→E *Tonarione*, a kind of shalme that hath a very sweet and shrill sound. **1659** TORRIANO-FLORIO It→E *Tonarione*, a shalm that hath a very shril and sweet sound.

tone *see* diazeutick tone, ecclesiastic tone, eighth tone, fifth tone, final, first tone, fourth tone, integer tonus, mode, note, peregrine tone, second tone, seventh tone, sixth tone, third tone, tune, tuono di chiesa

1538 ELYOT L→E *Tonus*, a tune or accent. **1552** HULOET L→E tonus, uocalitas, *Consonantia, quam græci etiam Euphoniam uocant* Tune. **1565** COOPER L→E *Tonus, toni, masc. gen.* Tune or accente. **1587** THOMAS L→E *Tonus, ni, m.g. Plin.* Tune, note, or accent: **1589** RIDER L→E *Tonus, phthongus, Cantus, sonus, sonitus, m. vox. et Vocalitas, f.* A tune. **1593** HOLLYBAND Fr→E *Ton*, a tune, as *garder le ton*, to keepe tune: **1598** FLORIO It→E *Tonare*, ... Also to tune an instrument or voice, to accent, to sounde. *Tono*, ... a tune, a note, an accent. *Tuonare*, ... to tune, to sound or giue a true accent. *Tuonante*, ... tuning, sounding, accenting. *Tuono*, ... a tune, a note, a sound, an accent. **1604** CAWDREY (1st edn) *tone*, (Greeke) a tune, note, or accent **1611** COTGRAVE Fr→E *Ton: m.* A tune, or sound; **1611** FLORIO It→E *Distuonare*, to vntune. *Tonare*, ... Also to tune any instrument or voice. Also to accent or set to any tune. *Tono*, ... Also any tune, note, ayre, accent or sound. *Tuonante*, ... Also tuning, sounding, accenting. *Tuonare*, ... Also to tune, to sound, or giue a true accent. *Tuono*, ... Also a tune, a sound, an accent. **1616** BULLOKAR *Tone*. A tune, note, or accent of the voice. **1623** COCKERAM *Tone*. Accent of voice, or note. *Tone, Symphonie*. Accent in tune. **1659** TORRIANO-FLORIO It→E *Tonare, Toneggiare, Tuonare*, ... also to tune an Instrument or voice, to accent. *Tono*, a tone, a tune, a sound, an accent, a note *Tuonare, Tuonante*, as *Tonare*. **1661** BLOUNT (2nd edn) *Tonical* (from *tonus*) pertaining to tone, note, tune or accent. Dr. *Br*. **1676** COLES *Tonical*, belonging to a ¶ *Tone, Latin*. tune, note, accent. **1688** MIEGE-COTGRAVE Fr→E *Ton* (a masc. Subst.) tone; sound; tune, or note. § *C'est sur ce Ton qu'il faut chanter*, this is the Tune we must sing upon. *Donner le Ton aux Musiciens*, to give the Musicians the Tune. *Hausser le Ton des Tuyaux de l'Orgue*, to raise the Sound of the Organ pipes. *Un Ton bas & cassé*, a low and faint Note. *Un Ton de Voix charmant, agreable, qui plait*, a charming, or ravishing Voice. *Un Ton haut & clair*, a high and clear Note. *Un Ton musical*, a musical Tone. **1696** PHILLIPS (5th edn) *Tone, (Lat.)* belonging to a Tone, or the elevation of the Voice, by certain equal or measured Degrees or Intervals that serve to form Concords, and are regulated by the Gammut. Tone is also the sound of the Voice, high or low, or mean, deep or shrill **1704** *Cocker's Engl. Dict.* (1st edn) *Tone*, the accent, tune, note of the voice **1704** HARRIS *Tone*, a Term in Musick, signifying a certain Degree of elevation, or depression of the Voice, or some other Sound. *Musicians* commonly determine it to be the sixth Part of an *Octave*, in which Sence, the *Octave* is said to be composed of Five *Tones*, and two *Semi-tones*; and the *Tone*, to be the Difference between the fourth and fifth. A *Tone*, or whole Note is divided into nine Particles called *Comma's*, five of which, are assigned to the greater *Semi-tone*, and four to the lesser. **1706** KERSEY-PHILLIPS (6th edn) *Tone, (Gr.)* ... In *Musick*, a certain Degree of raising or sinking the Voice: It is commonly defin'd to be the sixth part of an *Octave*; in which Sense the *Octave* is said, To be composed of five Tones, and two Semi-tones: A *Tone*, or whole Note is also divided into nine small Parts call'd *Comma's*, five of which are appropriated to the greater Semi-tone, and four to the lesser. **1707** *Gloss. Angl. Nova* (1st edn) *Tone*, a Term in Musick, signifying a certain degree of elevation or depression of the Voice or some other sound. **1724** [PEPUSCH] *Short Explic. of Foreign Words in Mus. Bks.* (p. 81) *Ton, Tono*, or *Tonus*, a Tone or Sound. (p. 83) *Tuono*. See the Word *Ton*. **1726** BAILEY *An Univ. Etymolog. Engl. Dict.* (3rd edn) *Ton*, a Tone or Sound. *Ital.* **1728** CHAMBERS *Tone*, or *Tune*, in Music, a Property of Sound, whereby it comes under the Relation of *Grave* and *Acute*; or, the Degree of Elevation any Sound has, from the Degree of Swiftness of the Vibrations of the Parts of the sonorous Body. See *Sound*. ¶ For the Cause, Measure, Degree, Difference, *&c.* of *Tones*. See *Tune*. ¶ The Variety of *Tones* in human Voices, arises partly from the Dimensions of the Wind-pipe, which, like a Flute, the longer and narrower it is, the sharper is the *Tone* it gives; but principally from the Head of the Larynx, or Knot of the Throat, call'd *Pomum Adami*; the *Tone* of the Voice being more or less grave, as the *Rima*, or Cleft thereof is more or less open. See *Voice*. ¶ *Tone*, is particularly us'd in Music for a certain

Degree or Interval of Tune, whereby a Sound may be either rais'd or lower'd from the Extreme of a Concord to the other; so as still to produce true Melody. See *Interval* and *Concord*. ¶ Musician, beside the Concords, or harmonical Intervals, admit three lesser Kinds of Intervals, which are the Measures and component Parts of the greater; and are call'd *Degrees*: The Nature, Origin, Use, *&c.* whereof, see under the Article *Degree*. ¶ Of these Degrees, two are call'd *Tones*, and a third a *Semitone*; their Ratio's in Number are 8:9, call'd a *greater Tone*; 9:10, call'd a *lesser Tone*; and 15:16, a *Semitone*. ¶ The *Tones* arise out of the simple Concords, and are equal to their Differences: Thus the *greater Tone* 8:9 is the Difference of a Fifth and a Fourth: The *lesser Tone* 9:10 the Difference of a lesser Third and Fourth, or of a Fifth and sixth greater: And the *Semitone* 15:16, the Difference of a greater Third and Fourth. See *Semitone*. ¶ Of these *Tones* and *Semitones* every Concord is compounded, and consequently is resolvable into a certain Number thereof: Thus, the lesser Third consists of one *greater Tone* and one *Semitone*; the greater Third of one *greater Tone* and one *lesser Tone*. See *Third*. ¶ The Fourth of one *greater Tone*, one *lesser Tone*, and one *Semitone*. See *Fourth*. ¶ The Fifth of two *greater Tones*, one *lesser Tone*, and one *Semitone*. See *Fifth, &c.* ¶ *For the Use of these* Tones, &c. *in the Construction of the Scale of Music*; See *Scale*. **1737** DYCHE-PARDON (2nd edn) *Tone* (S.) ... also the peculiar Sound of a Person's Voice, or a Musical Instrument, whether it be harsh, soft, melodious, &c.

1582 *Batman vppon Bartholome* (p. 422) *Tonus* is the sharpnesse of voyce, and is difference and quantitie of harmonie, and standeth in accent and Tenor of voyce: and Musitions make thereof fifteene parts. **1609** DOWLAND-ORNITHOPARCUS *Micrologvs* (pp. 10-11) A *Tone* (as *Guido* saith) is a rule iudging the Song in the end, or it is a knowledge of the beginning, middle, and end of euery Song, shewing the rising and falling of it.... By the authoritie of the Græcians, we should only obserue 4. *Tones*, (saith *Guido Microl.* 11. 1. *Proton*. 2. *Deuteron*, 3. *Triton*, 4. *Tetarton*. But the Latines considering the rising & falling, and diuiding each of the Greeke *Tones* into authenticke & plagall: to conclude euery thing that is sung within Eight *Tones*, agreeable to the eight parts of Speech. For it is not amisse, (saith *Ioan Pont. cap.* 10) that euery thing which is sung, may be comprehended within Eight *Tones*, as euery thing which is spoken, is confined within Eight parts of Speech. ¶ Now these Eight *Tones* (as *Franch. lib.* 5. *Theor.* and last Chapter, and *lib.* 1. *pract.* 7. *cap.* saith) are by the Authors thus named, The first *Dorian*; the second, *Hypodorian*; the third, *Phrygian*; (which *Porphyrio* cals barbarous; the fourth, *Hypophrygian*; the fift, *Lydian*; the sixt, *Hypolydian*; the seuenth, *Myxolydian*; the eight, some call *Hypermyxolydian*; others say it hath no proper name. § (p. 13) ... All the odde *Tones* are *Authenticall*, all the euen *Plagall*: these are so called because they descend more vnder the final *Key*: these, because they doe more ascend aboue the finall *Key*.... Euery Song in the beginning, rising straight beyond the finall Note to a Fift, is *Authenticall*: but that which fals straight way to a Third, or a Fourth, vnder the finall *Key*, is *Plagall*.... A Song not rising in the middle beyond the finall Note to an Eight, although it haue a Fift in the beginning, is *Plagall*: vnlesse the *Repercussion* of an *Authenticall* being there found, preserue it: as an *Antiphone* is newly found, which is iudged to be of the Eight *Tone*, because it hath not the rising of an *Authent* in the middle. But the *Repercussion* of a seuenth, appearing straight in the beginning, doth preserue it, and make it remaine *Authenticall*. See *Pontifex cap.* 12. § (p. 18) A *Tone* (as *Faber Stapulensis* writeth) is the beginning of *Consonances*: or it is a *Consonance* caused by the number of eight. For *Macrobius* saith, that the eight, is an number, by which *Symphonie* is bred; which *Symphonie* the Græcians call a *Tone*. Or it is the distance of one *Voyce* from another by a perfect second, sounding strongly, so called a *Tonando*, that is, *Thundring*. For *Tonare*, (as *Ioannes Pontifex* 12. *cap.* 8. saith) signifieth *to thunder powerfully*. Now a *Tone* is made betwixt all *Voyces* excepting *mi* and *fa*, consisting of two smaller *Semitones*, and one *Comma*. **1617-24** FLUDD *Utriusque Cosmi Maioris: De Templo Musicæ* (p. 182) *Thonus* est intervallum perfectum inter duas voces, duo semitonia non æqua continens, vel Tonus est quædam aëris percussio indissoluta usque ad auditum. **1636** BUTLER *Principles of Musik* (p. 46) *Tonus* is a Second perfect: as from *Ut* to *Re*, from *Re* to *Mi*, from *Fa* to *Sol*, from *Sol* to *La*, and from *Pha* to *Vt*. **1664** BIRCHENSHA-ALSTED *Templvm Mvsicvm* (p. 36) A Tone is a Space circumscribed by two Sounds; or, the distance of a grave and acute Sound: So that Tones are those Intervals, which are placed between the first and second Sound, the second and third, the third and fourth ... § (p. 92) A *Tone* is the skipping of a Voice from a Voice by a perfect Second sounding strongly. Hence it is called a Second. **1677** [F. NORTH] *Philosophical Essay of*

Musick (p. 7) A Tone is the repetition of Cracks or Pulses in equal spaces of time so quick that the interstices or intervals are not perceptible to sense. **1694** HOLDER *Treatise of Natural Grounds* (pp. 137-8) ... And the *Lichanos, Parypate, Paranete,* and *Trite,* are changeable; as upon our Instruments are the Seconds, and Thirds, and Sixths, and Sevenths: The *Proslambanomenos, Hypate, Mese, Paramese,* and *Nete,* are Immutable; as are the Unison, Fourths, Fifths, and Octaves. ¶ Now from the several changes of these Mutable Chords, chiefly arise the several Moods (some call'd them *Tones*) of Music, to which were joyned two more, *viz. Hyperæolian* and *Hyperlydian*; and afterwards Six more were added. **1698** WALLIS *Question in Musick* (*Philos. Trans.*, 1698, p. 83) ... that of 10 to 9, for (what they call) the *Lesser Tone*: And that of 9 to 8, for (what they call) the *Greater Tone*. **early 18th C.** ANON. Essay on Musick BODLEIAN Rawl. D. 751, f. 2 The Sounds which make the extremities of these Intervals, as well as the Intervals themselves are call'd Tones: but they are likewise distinguish'd by the particular name of the chord or degree. There are two other significations of this term; the first, that a Tone denotes a certain determinate degree of sound which serves to regulate all the others: thus we say the Church-Tone, the Opera-Tone, of Flute or Harpsichord is of such a Tone. This is otherwise call'd Pitch. The other signification of the word Tone is when it is taken for a certain manner of disposing the sounds in the series or progression of a Tune, which is likewise called Mood or Key. Thus we say one Tone is more lively, or more soft than another. But let us return to the first signification of the word Tone Viz. the intervals of sound, & the extremities of those intervals, which are design'd in Musick by these letters C. D. E. F. G. A. B[.] C. **c.1702** ANON. Practicall Theory of Musick BL Add. 4919, f. 3v The Progress from ye Key given to its Octave is thro' the foregoing gradual Notes placed in a certain order: They are by ye learned call'd Tones, from whence this sort of Musick has ye name of Diatonick; & if you place them one after another, as they stand in the Scheme, you will find that they exactly constitute those principall Concords wch. we stand most in need of. **1721** MALCOLM *Treatise of Musick* (p. 223) ... Hitherto we have used the Words, *Tone* and *Tune* indifferently, to signify a certain Quality of a single Sound; but here *Tone* is a certain *Interval*, and shall hereafter be constantly so used, and the Word *Tune* always applied to the other. § (p. 229) ... For the *Degrees* sought we have already assigned these, *viz.* 8:9 called a *greater Tone*, 9:10 called a *lesser Tone* ... § (p. 528) *Of Tones* or *Modes*. They [the ancient Greeks] took the Word *Tone* in four different Senses. 1. For a single Sound, as when they said the *Lyra* has seven *Tones*, i.e. Notes. 2. For a certain *Interval*, as the Difference of the *4th* and *5th*. 3. For the *Tension* of the Voice, as when we say, One sings with an *acute* or a *grave* Voice. 4. For a certain *System*, as when they said, The *Dorick* or *Lydian Mode*, or *Tone*; which is the Sense to be particularly considered in this Place. § (p. 535) Anciently there were but Three *Modes*, the *Dorick, Lydian* and *Phrygian*, so called from the Countries that used them, and particularly called *Tones* because they were at a *Tone's* Distance from each other; ... § (pp. 538-9) [Ptolomy in] *Lib.* 2. *Chap.* 7 of the *Mutations with respect to what they call* Tones... says in the Beginning of that *Chap.* "The *Mutations* which are made by whole *Systems*, which we properly call *Tones*, because these Differences consist in *Tension*, are infinite with respect to Possibility ..." § (p. 540) ... But there are *Modes* I call the *Antiquo-modern Modes*, which shall be considered afterwards. **1725** DE LA FOND *New System of Music* (p. 14) The word *Tone* is used in two different senses: sometimes it signifies an *inflection of one or several notes discovering either pleasure or pain*; and this is found in the voice particularly. Other times, the same word signifies *the difference of sound between the same notes, at the same pitch, in different voices and instruments*. ¶ This distinction at once gives us the definition of a *Tone* in both significations of the word. The first part of the distinction, or the first definition of *Tone*, is, I think, unexceptionable: but the second I own is somewhat defective, which defect could not be help'd so far. The defect lies in bringing in the *pitch* before the word is explain'd. **c.1726** NORTH Musicall Gramarian BL Add. 32533, f. 19 When the Ear perceivs a sound continuing without any manner of Deflection, It is certain that the voice is direct, and in a Musicall sence it is called a tone, and (alluding to wrighting) a note; wch termes meaning the same thing, are used promiscuously; But sometimes certain degrees of flexure are termed tones ... **1726-8** NORTH Theory of Sounds BL Add. 32535, f. 29v ... The most Eminent of that kind is what is called, Tone, or from the Greek (Imitatively); Thongos; And that is found to consist of pulses Iterated; ... **1728** NORTH Musicall Grammarian (*C-K MG* f. 12v) When the ear perceives a sound continuing without any manner of deflection, it is certein that voice is direct, and in a musicall sence is called a tone, or (alluding to wrighting) a note, which termes, meaning the same thing, are often used promiscuously; but sometimes one degree of flexure is called a tone ...

toniæum

1694 HOLDER *Treatise of Natural Grounds* (pp. 133-4) The *Chromatic* [genus in ancient Greek music] had three Colours; by which it was divided into *Molle, Sescuplum,* and *Toniæum*.... 3d. *Toniæum;* by a *Hemitone,* and *Hemitone,* and *Trihemitone;* and is called *Toniæum,* because the two *Spiss* Intervals make a *Tone.* And this is the ordinary *Chromatic.*

tonus diapente

1609 DOWLAND-ORNITHOPARCUS *Micrologvs* (p. 19) *Tonus Diapente.* ¶ Is the distance of one Voyce from another by a perfect sixt. Which *Stapulensis* affirmes to consist of foure *Tones,* and a lesser *semitone.* **1636** BUTLER *Principles of Musik* (p. 47) *Tonus-diapente* is a perfect Sixt, consisting of 4 Tones and a Hemitone: as from *Ut* to *La,* from *Fa* to *Re,* and from *Pha* to *Sol.*

tonus diazeucticus *see* diazeutick tone

tordiglione *see* tourdion

1611 FLORIO It→E *Tordiglione,* a kind of dance in Spaine. **1659** TORRIANO-FLORIO It→E *Tordiglione, Tordilione,* ... also a certain Spanish dance.

torlo *see* ruotata, zurlo

1598 FLORIO It→E *Torlo,* a twirle, a round turning tricke in dancing. **1611** FLORIO It→E *Torlo,* a top, a gigge ... Also a twirle or round turning tricke in dancing.

tornello *see* ritornello

1611 FLORIO It→E *Tornello,* ... Also the burden of a song. **1659** TORRIANO-FLORIO It→E **Tornello, Tornio, Tornolo,* ... used also for the burden of a Song that is often repeated, also a Roundelay.

torsello

1659 TORRIANO-FLORIO It→E **Torsello,* ... also leaden bullet, also a certain musicall instrument used in churches

touch *see* tact, tactus, tastatura, tocar

1611 COTGRAVE Fr→E *Touche: f.* ... also, a stop or fret in a Musicall Instrument; **1650** HOWELL-COTGRAVE Fr→E *Touch: f.* ... also, a stop or fret in a Musicall Instrument; **1688** MIEGE-COTGRAVE Fr→E *Touche,* (f.) ... a stop, or fret, in a Musical Instrument; a string, of a Musical Instrument; a key of a pair of Virginals, Organs, and the like. **1696** PHILLIPS (5th edn) *Touch,* ... In Musick we say an Organ or Harpsichord has a good Touch, when the Keys lye down, and are neither too loose nor too stiff. **1728** CHAMBERS *Touch,* in Music. An Organ is said to have a good *Touch,* when the Keys [are] close, and lie down well; being neither too loose, nor too stiff. See *Organ.* **1737** DYCHE-PARDON (2nd edn) *Touch* (S.) ... also the well or ill-making of a Musical Instrument, especially Organs, Harpsichords, &c. *Touch* (V.) ... also to play upon a Musical Instrument.

1664 BIRCHENSHA-ALSTED *Templvm Mvsicvm* (p. 67) [annotation by Birchensha:] **Touch* is that which *Musicians* call *Tactus,* or the *stroke* of the hand by which Time is measured. Or it is the successive Motion of the hand, directing by equal measure the Quantity of all *Notes* and *Pauses* in a Song, according to the variety of *Signes* and *Proportions.* The parts thereof are Elevation and Depression; or the Fall and Rise of the hand.

tourdion *see* tordiglione

1611 COTGRAVE Fr→E *Tourdion: m.* A turning ... also, the daunce tearmed a Round.

tourne-bout

1688 MIEGE-COTGRAVE Fr→E *Tourne-bout,* (m.) a kind of Musical Instrument.

tourniquet

1611 COTGRAVE Fr→E *Tourniquet: m.* The pinne of a *Vielle;* that which the *Vielleur* turnes with his hand as he playes.

toy *see* lesson, suit

1676 MACE *Musick's Monument* (p. 129) *Toys,* or *Jiggs,* are *Light-Squibbish Things,* only fit for *Fantastical,* and *Easie-Light-Headed People;* and are of any sort of *Time.*

tract

1656 BLOUNT (1st edn) *Tract (tracta)* ... In the *Masse* it is two or three versicles betwixt the Epistle and Gospel; and so called, because it is sung with a slow, long, *protracted* tone.

tragedy *see* choir, chorus, exodium, interlude, intermedia, opera, strophe

1656 BLOUNT (1st edn) *Tragedie (tragœdia)* is a lofty kinde of poetry, so called from τράγος, a goat, and ᾠδή, an ode or song; because the actors thereof had a goat given them as a reward. **1702** KERSEY *New Engl. Dict.* (1st edn) A *Tragedy*, a sort of lofty play in which great Persons are brought on the Stage, the subject being full of trouble, and the end always doleful; so called from two *Greek* words *tragos*, a goat, and *ode* a song; because the Actors usually had a goat given 'em for a reward. **1706** KERSEY-PHILLIPS (6th edn) *Tragedy*, a sort of Dramatick Poem ... It is so call'd from the *Greek* Words *Tragos*, a Goat, and *Ode*, a Song, because the Actors anciently receiv'd a Goat for their Reward, or else a Vessel made of Goat's-Skin filled with Wine. **1728** CHAMBERS *Tragedy*, a Dramatic Poem, representing some signal Action, perform'd by illustrious Persons, and which has frequently a fatal Issue or End. See *Drama*.... *Tragedy*, in its Original, M. *Hedelin*, observes, was only a Hymn sung in Honour of *Bacchus*, by several Persons, who, together, made a Chorus of Music, with Dances and Instruments. See *Chorus*. ¶ As this was long, and might fatigue the Singers, as well as tire the Audience; they bethought themselves to divide the singing of the Chorus into several Parts, and to have certain Recitations in the Intervals.... The Persons who made these Recitations on the Scene, were call'd *Actors*; so that *Tragedy* at first was without Actors. And what they thus rehearsed, being things added to the singing of the Chorus, whereof they were no necessary Part, were call'd *Episodes*. See *Episode*.... The *English* received the first Plan of their Drama from the *French*; among whom it had its first Rise towards the End of the Reign of *Charles* V. under the Title of *Chant-Royal*, which were Pieces in Verse, composed in Honour of the Virgin, or some of the Saints, and sung on the Stage; call'd by the Title of *Chant-Royal*, because the Subject was given by the King of the Year; or the Person who had bore away the Prize the Year preceding. See *Chant*. ¶ The Humour of these Pieces run wonderfully among the People, insomuch that in a little time there were form'd several Societies, who began to vie with each other: One of these, to engage the Town from the rest, began to intermix various Incidents, or Episodes, which they distributed into *Acts, Scenes*, and as many different *Persons* as were necessary for the Representation.

tranotare
1659 TORRIANO-FLORIO It→E **Tranotare*, to note between.

transient note *see* passing note

transition *see* breaking, counterpoint, descant, modulate, modulation
1704 HARRIS *Transition*, in Musick, is when a greater Note is broken into a lesser, to make smooth, or sweeten the roughness of a Leap, by a gradual *Transition*, or passing to the Note next following; whence it is commonly called, *the breaking of a Note*, being sometimes very necessary in musical Compositions. **1706** KERSEY-PHILLIPS (6th edn) In *Musick, Transition* is when a greater Note is broken into a lesser, to make smooth or sweeten the roughness of a Leap; so as to pass by Degrees to a Note next following: It is commonly call'd the breaking of a Note, and is sometimes very necessary in Musical Compositions. **1728** CHAMBERS *Transition*, in Music, is when a greater Note is broken into lesser, to make smooth the Roughness of a Leap, by a gradual Passage to the Note next following; whence it is commonly call'd the *breaking of a Note*; being sometimes very necessary in Musical Compositions. See *Note* and *Passage*. **1737** DYCHE-PARDON (2nd edn) *Transition* (S.) ... in *Musick*, it is the subdividing a Note to render the Passage of a Leap, which would otherwise sound rough to the Ear, smooth and pleasant.

1673 LOCKE *Melothesia* (p. 8) I have here annexed ... an Example or two by way of Transition, or passing from one *Key* to another; ... **1736** TANS'UR *Compleat Melody* (3rd edn, p. 21) There is another *Grace* used in *Musick* that requires much Judgment, called the *Grace* of *Transition*; that is to slur, or break a Note to sweeten the Roughness of a *Leap*; and in Instrumental-Musick, *Transition* is often used on the *Note* before a *Close*...

transposition *see* double transposition
1724 [PEPUSCH] *Short Explic. of Foreign Words in Mus. Bks.* (p. 81) *Transpositio*, Transposition, which in Musick is the writing a Song or Tune in any Key or Cliff different from the Key or Cliff it was first composed in; and this is often done for the greater Conveniency of the Voice, or some particular Instrument, as the Flute, which cannot reach so low as the Violin and other Instruments. **1726** BAILEY *An Univ. Etymolog. Engl. Dict.* (3rd edn) *Transposito* [sic] (in *Musick*) is Transposition, which is the Writing a Song or Tune in any Key or Cliff different from the Key or Cliff it was first composed in; this is frequently done for the greater

Conveniency of the Voice, or some particular instrument, as the Flute, which cannot reach so low, as the Violin and other Instruments. *L.* **1728** CHAMBERS *Transposition* ... [*see* Appendix] **1737** DYCHE-PARDON (2nd edn) *Transposition* (S.) ... in *Musick,* 'tis the changing a Tune or Lesson, and putting it into a higher or lower Key or Cliff, in order to sing or play it upon or with another Voice or Instrument than it was originally composed for.

1609 DOWLAND-ORNITHOPARCUS *Micrologvs* (p. 26) Whereupon *Transposition* is the remouing of a Song, or a *Key* from his proper place. For to transpose is to remoue a song, or a *Key* from the proper place. **1724** TURNER *Sound Anatomiz'd* (p. 70) In the Case of *Transposition,* which is to remove any *Song* or *Tune,* so many *Notes* or *Sounds* higher or lower, than what they were supposed to be before; ... **1731** [PEPUSCH] *Treatise on Harmony* (2nd edn, p. 5) *Transposition,* is the removing a Piece of Musick from one Pitch of Sound to another, without altering the Nature of it in any other respect.

trantrana *see* taratantara

1611 COTGRAVE Fr→E *Trantrac: m.* The lowd resounding, or sound, of a Hunters horne. *Trantran.* The same. *Trantraner.* To wind a horne verie lowd, to make it rattle. **1659** TORRIANO-FLORIO It→E *Trantrana,* a loud winding of a horn. *Trantranare,* to wind a horn and make it rattle.

traquear

1599 MINSHEU-PERCYVALL Sp→E *Traquear,* to crie ... Also to make a noise as the drum when it is strooken vp. *Traquido,* the noise of the blow of a peece, the noise the drum maketh when it is plaied on.

traste *see* fret, tastame, tastatura, tasto

1599 MINSHEU-PERCYVALL Sp→E *Traste,* m. ... or the fret of an instrument. § *Trastes de laud,* the frets of a lute.

travelly *see* reveille

trayan

1611 COTGRAVE Fr→E *Trayans: m.* The wires which are placed in the forepart of an arched, or old fashioned Organ; and serue to stop, or open the Pallets thereof.

tre

1724 [PEPUSCH] *Short Explic. of Foreign Words in Mus. Bks.* (p. 81) *Tre,* the Number Three. See *Terza* above.

treble *see* canto, dessus, haut-dessus, quinible, shrill, sonus summus, succortrilla, tiple

1616 BULLOKAR *Treble...* sometime it signifieth the highest note in musicke. **1623** COCKERAM *Treble...* sometime the highest note in musicke. **1671** PHILLIPS (3rd edn) *Treble,* the highest part in Musick called in Latin *Altus.* **1676** COLES *Treble,* ... also the highest part in Musick. **1702** KERSEY *New Engl. Dict.* (1st edn) § The *Treble-part,* in Musick. **1704** *Cocker's Engl. Dict.* (1st edn) *Treble,* the highest note in Musick; **1704** HARRIS *Treble,* is the last or highest of the four Parts in *Musical Proportion.* **1706** KERSEY-PHILLIPS (6th edn) *Treble,* ... Also the last or highest of the four Parts in Musick. **1707** *Gloss. Angl. Nova* (1st edn) *Treble,* the highest part in Musick, or the highest of the four Parts in Musical Proportion. **1708** KERSEY *Dict. Anglo-Brit.* (1st edn) *Treble,* ... Also the last or highest of the four Parts in Musick. **1728** CHAMBERS *Treble,* in Music, the highest or acutest of the four Parts in Symphony, or that which is heard the clearest in a Concert. See *Music, Gravity,* and *Symphony.* ¶ In the like Sense we say, a *Treble* Violin, *Treble* Hautboy, *&c.* See *Violin,* &c. ¶ In Vocal Music, the *Treble* is usually committed to Boys and Girls.—Their Part is the *Treble.* See *Part.* ¶ The *Treble* is divided into *first* or *highest Treble,* and *second* or *Base Treble.*—The half *Treble* is the same with Counter-Tenor. See *Harmony.* **1737** DYCHE-PARDON (2nd edn) *Treble* (S.) the upper or highest Part in a Musical Composition, where the Notes are the shrillest or weakest toned, and sung by Women or Children, or played by Flutes, &c.

1596 BARLEY *New Booke of Tabliture* (n.p.) Againe note that those six stringes [of the lute] be figured by sixe straight lines, whereof the first and highest is called the Trebble, and the next is the second string, and so forth to the next, three, foure, fiue, sixe ... **1636** BUTLER *Principles of Musik* (p. 42) The Treble is so ealled [sic], becaus his notes ar placed (for the most part) in the third Septenari, or the Treble cliefs: and is to bee sung with a high cleere sweete voice. **1721** MALCOLM *Treatise of Musick* (p. 332) The highest *Part* is called the *Treble,* or *Alt* whose *Clef* is *g,* set on the 2*d* Line of the *particular System,* counting upward: ... **1736** TANS'UR *Compleat Melody* (3rd edn, p. 70) *Treble,*

Tripla, Canto, Haut Dessius. (Ital.) Either of those signifies *Threefold;* which are the Name of the *Third,* or highest *System,* or *Octave* in Musick, or the *Highest Part* of Musical Composition.

treble clef

1724 TURNER *Sound Anatomiz'd* (pp. 35-6) This *Cliff* is (as you see) marked thus; [clef sign] and is called the *Treble Cliff,* or *G solreut Cliff.*

tremante

1598 FLORIO It→E *Tremante,* ... Also wauering or warbling. *Tremare,* ... to wauer, to warble. *Tremolante,* as *Tremante.* Also a stop in musicke called the quauering, wauering or warbling stop. *Tremolare,* as *Tremare,* but properly to quauer, to wauer, or warble. **1611** FLORIO It→E *Tremante,* trembling ... Also quauering or warbling with the voice. *Tremare,* to tremble ... Also to quauer or warble with the voice. *Tremolante,* ... Also a stop in some instruments called the quauering or warbling stop. *Tremolare,* as *Tremare.* **1659** TORRIANO-FLORIO It→E **Tremante, Tremolante, Tremoloso, Tremoroso,* ... also a quavering or warbling with the voice in singing *Tremare, Tremacciare, Tremolare, Tremiscere, misco, miscei, misciuto,* ... also to quaver or warble with the voice in singing. *Tremolante,* as *Tremante,* also a quavering-stop in an instrument

tremblement

1688 MIEGE-COTGRAVE Fr→E *Tremblement,* (m.) ... a quavering, in vocal Musick; a shake, in Instrumental Musick; *Trembler,* ... to make a shake in Musick. § *Faire de beaux Tremblemens, (en Termes de Musique,)* to make fine shakes in Musick.

trembloer *see* soundboard

1611 COTGRAVE Fr→E *Trembloer: m.* The Sound-boord of a Musicall Instrument. **1650** HOWELL-COTGRAVE Fr→E † *Trembloer: m.* The Sound-boord of a Musicall Instrument.

tremola *see* cantus, tremante

1565 COOPER L→E § *Cantus tremulus. Horat.* warblyng. **1589** RIDER L→E *Tremulus, ad.* VVarbling, or quauering. **1724** [PEPUSCH] *Short Explic. of Foreign Words in Mus. Bks.* (p. 82) *Tremola,* to Tremble, a particular Grace in Musick. **1726** BAILEY *An Univ. Etymolog. Engl. Dict.* (3rd edn) *Tremola* (in *Musick Books*) signifies to tremble; a particular Grace in Musick. *Ital.*

tremolo *see* grave

1728 NORTH Musicall Grammarian (*C-K MG* f. 73) ... There is another mode of the grave that frequently occurrs in our Italianezed sonnatas, which I have knowne intituled, tremolo, and is now comonly performed with a tempered stoccata. And that I take to be an abuse, and contrary to the genius of that mode, which is to hold out long notes inriched with the flowers of harmony and with a trembling hand, which of all parts together resembles the shaking stop of an organ; ...

tremulo *see* tremola

tresca

1550 THOMAS It→E *Tresca,* a galyard, or other suche leapyng daunce. **1598** FLORIO It→E *Tresca,* a kind of antike, or morice dance **1611** FLORIO It→E *Tresca,* a kinde of Antike or merrie dance. **1659** TORRIANO-FLORIO It→E *Tresca,* ... an Antick merrie dance

triad, trias *see* common cord, essential notes, flat cord, full accord, repercussion, sharp cord, simple

1728 CHAMBERS *Trias Harmonica,* or the *Harmonical Triad,* in Music, a Compound of three radical Sounds, heard all together; two whereof are a Fifth, and a Third above the other, which is the Fundamental. See *Concord, &c.* ¶ The *Triad* is properly a Consonance form'd of a Third and a Fifth; which, with the Bass, or fundamental Sound, makes three different Terms, whence the Name *Trias.*—That of *harmonical* is doubtless given it from that wonderful Property of the Fifth, which divides itself naturally into two Thirds, both excellent, and perfectly harmonical; so that this one Sound dispos'd between two others, makes two Thirds at once, and of Consequence a double Harmony. See *Fifth.* ¶ Hence it is, that in *Trio's,* particularly, this Concord is preferr'd to that which divides the Octave into a Fifth and a Fourth: In regard that, if there be a Concord on one Side, there is a Discord on the other; whereas here the Harmony is compleat on both Sides. ¶ Of the three Sounds which compose the harmonical *Triad,* the gravest is call'd the *Fundamental,* or *Bass;* the acutest, *i.e.* that which makes the Fifth, and which terminates the Concord upwards, is call'd the *excluded* or *highest* Sound; and that which divides the Fifth so agreeably into two Thirds, is call'd the *harmonical Mean.* ¶ The Division of the Fifth into two Thirds, may be perform'd two Ways, *viz.* 1°. Harmonically, when the great Third is lowest, and the less a-top; in which Case the *Triad* is perfect and natural. ¶ 2°. Arithmetically, when the less Third is lowest, and the greater a top; in which Case the *Triad* is imperfect and flat. Both are good; but the latter not to be often us'd. **1730** BAILEY *Dict. Britannicum* (1st edn) *Trias Harmonica* (in *Musick*) a Compound of three radical Sounds heard altogether, of which two are a Fifth, and a Third above the other, which is a Fundamental.

1664 BIRCHENSHA-ALSTED *Templvm Mvsicvm* (p. 55) *The Musical* Trias *is that which doth arise from three sounds and as many* Dyads: *otherwise called the* unitrisonous Radix. § (p. 56) *The Harmonical* Tryas *is the Root of all the Harmony that can be invented,* [sic] ¶ And may be called the *unitrisonous Radix*: because it doth consist of three *Monads* or *Sounds*, and as many *Dyads*: all of them in that whole *Tryas*, and every one most sweetly concenting one with another, because they are joyned together in a certain Order by just Proportions.

triccatina

1598 FLORIO It→E *Triccatina*, a kind of tripping dance vsed in Italy. Also a nimble dancing wench, a trifling, iesting wench. **1611** FLORIO It→E *Triccatina*, a kind of tripping dance. Also a nimble tripping or dancing wench.

trifistulary

1656 BLOUNT (1st edn) *Trifistulary (trifistularis)* pertaining to three pipes. *Br.* **1676** COLES *Trifistulary, Latin.* of three pipes. **1704** *Cocker's Engl. Dict.* (1st edn) *Trifistulary*, a Musica[l] Instrument of three pipes.

tri-hemitone

1698 WALLIS *Question in Musick* (*Philos. Trans.*, 1698, p. 83) ... that of 6 to 5, is the Proportion of a lesser Third (called a *Tri-hemitone*, or Tone and half,) as *la fa* (in *la mi fa*.) ...

trill *see* prolation, quaver, roulade, roulement, shake, warble

1611 FLORIO It→E *Trigliare*, to quauer or warble in singing. *Triglio*, a quauer or warble in singing. *Trillare*, as *Trigliare*. *Trillo*, as *Triglio*. **1656** BLOUNT (1st edn) *Trillo* (Ital.) an excellent grace in singing; being an uniform trembling or shaking of the same Note, either soft and smoothly in the throat, as naturally the *French* do, or more strongly or artificially from the stomack, as the *Italians*. **1658** PHILLIPS (1st edn) *Trillo*, (Ital.) a gracefull shake, or trembling of the voyce in singing. **1659** TORRIANO-FLORIO It→E *Trigliare, Trillare,* to quaver or to warbl[e] with the voice in singing. **1676** COLES *Trill, -o, Italian.* a quavering grace in singing. **1702** KERSEY *New Engl. Dict.* (1st edn) A *Trill*, and ¶ To *trill, or* quaver in singing. **1704** *Cocker's Engl. Dict.* (1st edn) *Trill* or *Trillo*, the art or grace of quavering in singing. **1706** KERSEY-PHILLIPS (6th edn) *Trill, (Ital.)* a quavering in *Musick*, a graceful shaking of the same Note in Singing. **1707** *Gloss. Angl. Nova* (1st edn) *Trill*, (Ital.) a quivering or shaking with Voice or Instrument. **1708** KERSEY *Dict. Anglo-Brit.* (1st edn) *Trill*, (*I.*) a quavering in *Musick*, a graceful shaking of the same Note in Singing. **1724** [PEPUSCH] *Short Explic. of Foreign Words in Mus. Bks.* (p. 82) *Trillo*, a Trill or Shake, a common Grace in Musick. **1726** BAILEY *An Univ. Etymolog. Engl. Dict.* (3rd edn) *Trill* (*trillo*, Ital.) a quivering or shaking with Voice or Instrument, a common Grace in Musick. **1731** KERSEY *New Engl. Dict.* (3rd edn) To *trill*, to quaver or shake with the Voice. **1736** BAILEY *Dict. Britannicum* (2nd edn) *To Trill*, to quaver or shake with the voice, or an instrument. **1737** DYCHE-PARDON (2nd edn) *Trill* (S.) in *Musick*, the fine Grace or Ornament to Singing, called a Shake.

1667 PLAYFORD *Brief Intro. to Skill of Musick* (4th edn, 'A Brief Discourse of, and Directions for Singing after the Italian manner' [after Caccini], p. 40) ... there is made now adayes an indifferent and confused use of those Excellent *Graces* and Ornaments to the good manner of Singing, which we call *Trills, Grapps* [sic], *Exclamations* of *Increasing* and *Abating* of the Voyce ... § (as above, p. 50) The *Trill* described by me is upon one Note only, that is to say, to begin with the first *Crotchet*, and to beat every Note with the throat upon the vowel unto the last Brief. As likewise the *Gruppo* or *double Relish*. § (as above, p. 54) [annotation:] ... *this chief or most usual Grace in Singing called the* Trill ... *some observe that is rather the shaking of the Uvula or Pallate on the Throat in one Sound upon a Note;* ... **1680** B., A. *Synopsis of Vocal Musick* (p. 44) A Trillo is a shaking of the Uvula on the Throat in one Sound or Note, as Gruppo is in two Sounds or Notes, the one being by one degree higher than the other, and are commonly used in cadences and closes. **c.1695** NORTH Notes of Me BL Add. 32506 (*JWi* p. 27) The trill is the sound of 2 notes seconds together; the beat, the same, onely that mixes the lower, as the trill the upper note, as the accessary; for the principall note that bears the weight must have its cheif emphasis, the other is but accessionall. **c.1710** NORTH Short, Easy, & plaine rules BL Add. 32531, f. 23v [quoting Prendcourt:] This mark. ~~~ . is called a shake, wch is a small movement with 2. fingers upon 2. Keys and at last Remaining with one finger upon ye Note before [on] wch ye Signe stands. [annotation by North:] NB. This [is] called the trill and upon an harpsichord is not cleverly performed ... **1731** PRELLEUR *Modern Musick-Master* (I, p. 11) The chief Grace in singing is the *Trillo* or Shake, and is much used of late ...

trilletto

1724 [PEPUSCH] *Short Explic. of Foreign Words in Mus. Bks.* (p. 82) *Trilletto*, a short or little Trill. **1726** BAILEY *An Univ. Etymolog. Engl. Dict.* (3rd edn) *Trilletto* (in *Musick*) a short or little Trill. *Ital.*

trio *see* opera, terza in

1724 [PEPUSCH] *Short Explic. of Foreign Words in Mus. Bks.* (p. 82) *Tria*, or *Trio*, Musick in Three Parts is so called, either for Voices or Instruments, or both together. *Trio.* See *Tria* above. **1726** BAILEY *An Univ. Etymolog. Engl. Dict.* (3rd edn) *Tria* (in *Musick Books*) is a Name given to the 3 Parts of Musick, either for Voices or Instruments, or both together. *Ital.* **1728** CHAMBERS *Trio*, in Music, a Part of a Concert, wherein there are only three Persons sing[ing]; or a musical Composition consisting of three Parts. ¶ *Trio's* are the finest Kind of Composition; and these and Recitativo's are what please most in Concerts. **1730** BAILEY *Dict. Britannicum* (1st edn) *Trio* (in *Musick*) a Part of a Concert, where only three Persons sing, or a musical Composition of three Parts.

1736 TANS'UR *Compleat Melody* (3rd edn, p. 72) *Trio*, or *Trezetto* [sic], or in *Trez.* (Ital.) signifies three Parts.

tripla, triple *see* character, galliard time, imperfect of the more, ionick, pointing, proportion, time, treble

1611 COTGRAVE Fr→E *Triple: m.* A Triple; also, Galliard-time, in Musicke. **1724** [PEPUSCH] *Short Explic. of Foreign Words in Mus. Bks.* (p. 82) *Tripola*, Triple, is one of the Sorts of Time or Movement made Use of in Musick, and of which there are several Sorts. **1726** BAILEY *An Univ. Etymolog. Engl. Dict.* (3rd edn) *Tripola* (in *Musick*) a triple; one of the Sorts of Time or Movement, of which there are several. *Ital.* **1728** CHAMBERS *Triple* ... [*see* Appendix]

1596 ANON. *Pathway to Musicke* [E iii *verso*] *VVhat is the proportion called Tripla.* ¶ It is that which diminisheth the value by three parts, for three Briues are set for one, and three sembriues for one, &c. and is knowen when the higher number containeth the lower thrise as thus, $\frac{3}{1}$ ... **1597** MORLEY *Plaine and Easie Introdvction* (pp. 29-30) *Phi.* What is *tripla proportion in musicke*? ¶ *Ma. It is that which diminisheth the value of the notes to one third part*: for three *briefes* are set for one, and three *semibriefes* for one, and is knowen when two numbers are set before the song, whereof the one contayneth the other thrise thus $\frac{3}{1}$ $\frac{6}{2}$ $\frac{9}{3}$ ... Heere is likewise another ensample wherein *Tripla* is in all the parts together, which if you pricke al in blacke notes, will make that proportion which the musitions falslie termed *Hemiolia*, when in deed it is nothing else but a round *Tripla*. For *Hemiola* doth signifie that which the *Latines* tearme Sesquipla or sesquialtra: but the good *Munks* finding it to go somwhat rounder then common tripla, gaue it that name of *Hemiolia* [for] lacke of another. But for their labour they were roundly taken vp by *Glareanus, Lossius* and others. § (annotations on Part I) *Tripla*) This is the common hackney horse of al the Composers, which is of so manie kindes as there be maners of pricking, sometimes al in blacke notes, sometimes all in white notes, sometimes mingled, sometimes in briefes, sometimes al in semibriefes, and yet all one measure. **1609** DOWLAND-ORNITHOPARCUS *Micrologvs* (p. 63) *Of the Triple.* ¶ The *Triple Proportion*, the second kinde of the *Multiplex* is, when the greater number, being in Relation with the lesse, doth comprehend it in it selfe 3. times, as 6. to 2:9. to 3. But Musically, when three Notes are vttered against one such, which is equall to it in kind. The signe of this is the number of three set ouer an Vnitie ... **1636** BUTLER *Principles of Musik* (p. 25) *Triple* Proportion is, when 3 Minims (or a Sembrief and a Minim,) (and conseqently 6 Crochets and 12 Qavers) goe to the Sembrief-stroke: 2 to the Fall, and the third to the Rise of the Hand: the proper Signe whereof is this Ͼ Unto which 3 Minims, 2 in *Dupla* are eqivalent: and therefore may bee sung to them by an other Parte: for in bothe Proportions, the Hand falleth in the same instant; thowgh it rise a little sooner in the *Dupla*, than in the *Tripla*: in that, when $\frac{1}{2}$, in this, when $\frac{2}{3}$ of the time is past. **1666** PLAYFORD *Musick's Delight on the Cithren* (n.p.) The *Tripla-Time* is, when the Time is measured by *three Minims* to a *Semibreve* with a *Prick of Addition*. Or, in more quicker Measure, the Time is measured by three *Crochets* to a *Minim* with a *Prick of Addition*, which *Prick* added to the *Semibreve* or to a *Minim*, make his measure half so much longer than he was before: the *Semibreve* which was but two ... **1667** PLAYFORD *Brief Intro. to Skill of Musick* (4th edn, p. 31) ... the *Imperfect of the More*, the *Imperfect of the Less*, one being called the *Triple Time*, the other the *Duple* or *Common Time* ... **1682** PLAYFORD *Musick's Recreation on Viol* (2nd edn, preface) The *Tripla* Time which is usual to *Corants, Sarabands*, and *Jiggs*, is a more light and quicker Measure of Time [than common or semibreve time], and his Time Note is measured by a *Minim* with a *Prick*, which amounts to three *Crochets*, or six *Quavers*, or twelve *Semiquavers*. **c.1700** NORTH Capt. Prencourts rules BL Add. 32549, f. 7v Of the Tripla time. ¶ This time is called thus, becaus a measure is devided into three parts. wth. two downe and one up. **c.1710** NORTH Short, Easy, & plaine rules BL Add. 32531, f. 18v Of the Tripla time. ¶ This time is called thus becaus a Measure is devided Into 3. parts. vizt 2. downe & one up. **1721** MALCOLM *Treatise of Musick* (pp. 400-1) *Triple Time* consists of many different Species, whereof there are in general 4, each of which have their Varieties under it; and the common Name of *Triple* is taken from this, that the Whole or Half *Measure* is divisible into 3 equal Parts, and so beat. ¶ The 1*st Species* is called the *simple Triple*, whose *Measure* is equal either to 3 *Semibreves*, to 3 *Minims*, or to 3 *Crotchets*, or to 3 *Quavers*, or lastly to 3 *Semiquavers*; which are marked thus; *viz.* $\frac{3}{1}$ or $\frac{3}{2}$ or $\frac{3}{4}$ $\frac{3}{8}$ $\frac{3}{16}$, but the last is not much used, nor the first, except in Church-musick. The *Measure* in all these, is divided into 3 equal Parts or *Times*, called from that properly *Triple-time*, or the *Measure* of 3 *Times*, whereof 2 are beat down, and the 3*d* up. ¶ The 2*d Species* is the *mixt Triple*: its *Measure* is equal to 6 *Crotchets* or 6 *Quavers* or 6 *Semiquavers*, and accordingly marked $\frac{6}{4}$ or $\frac{6}{8}$ or $\frac{6}{16}$, but the last is seldom used. Some Authors add other Two, *viz.* 6 *Semibreves* and 6 *Minims*, marked $\frac{6}{1}$ or $\frac{6}{2}$ but these are not in use. The *Measure* here is ordinarily divided into Two equal Parts or *Times*, whereof one is beat down, and one up; but it may also be divided into 6 *Times*, whereof the first Two are beat down, and the 3*d* up, then the next Two down and the last up, *that is*, beat each Half of the Measure like the *simple Triple* (upon which Account it may also be called a *compound Triple*,) and because it may be thus divided either into Two or 6 *Times* (*i.e.* Two *Triples*) 'tis called *mixt*, and by some called the Measure of 6 *Times*. ¶ The 3*d Species* is the *compound Triple*, consisting of 9 *Crotchets*, or *Quavers* or *Semiquavers* marked thus $\frac{9}{4}$, $\frac{9}{8}$, $\frac{9}{16}$; the first and the last are little used, and some add $\frac{9}{1}$ $\frac{9}{2}$ which are never used. This *Measure* is divided either into 3 equal Parts or *Times*, whereof Two are beat down and one up; or each Third Part of it may be divided into 3 *Times*, and beat like the *simple Triple*, and for this 'tis called the Measure of 9 *Times*. ¶ The 4*th Species* is a *Compound* of the 2*d Species*, containing 12 *Crotchets* or *Quavers* or *Semiquavers* marked $\frac{12}{4}$ $\frac{12}{8}$ $\frac{12}{16}$, to which some add $\frac{12}{1}$ and $\frac{12}{2}$ that are not used; nor are the 1*st* and 3*d* much in Use, especially the 3*d*. The *Measure* here may be divided into Two *Times*, and beat one down and one up; or each Half may be divided and beat at the 2*d* Species, either by Two or Three, in which Case it will make in all 12 *Times*, hence called the Measure of 12 *Times*. **1724** TURNER *Sound Anatomiz'd* (p. 21) The other *Moods* [besides those in common time], which are eight in Number, are proper to what we call *Tripple-Time*, and divide the *Measures* into three equal Parts; or sometimes but two; and at others into four; *i.e.* three Times *One*; (by *Minims, Crotchets* or *Quavers*) three Times *Three*; (by *Crotchets* or *Quavers*) two times *Three*; (by *Crotchets* or *Quavers*) and four Times *Three*; (by *Quavers*) ... **1728** NORTH Musicall Grammarian (*C-K MG* f. 35) ... And in a word a tripla is an emphatick breaking the ground tones into 3 as the comon time is into two ...

triplex, triplus *see* treble

tripode

1550 THOMAS It→E *Tripudio*, a base daunce. **1598** FLORIO It→E *Tripode*, a kinde of musicall instrument. *Tripudiare*, to dance, to trip on the toes. *Tripudij*, dancing of birds or trippings, trippings on the toes. *Tripudio*, a kind of foolish countrie dance or tripping on the toe. **1611** FLORIO It→E *Tripode*, a table of gold threefoote long ... Also a kind of musicall instrument. *Tripudiare*, to dance or trip on the tooes. *Tripudij*, dancings or trippings on the tooes. *Tripudio*, a kind of tripping dance. **1659** TORRIANO-FLORIO It→E *Tripode*, ... also a certain musical instrument *Tripudio*, a kind of nimble tripping or leaping dance, as the French-Branles.

trisagium *see* hymn
1656 BLOUNT (1st edn) *Trisagion* (Gr.) thrice holy, the *Sanctus, Sanctus, Sanctus,* mentioned in the Church-service. **1676** COLES *Trisagion, Greek.* Holy, Holy, Holy. **1706** KERSEY-PHILLIPS (6th edn) *Trisagium, (Gr.)* a kind of Hymn in the *Greek* Church; much of the same Nature with that in the Service of the Church of *England; Holy, Holy, Holy, Lord God of Sabaoth,* &c. **1708** KERSEY *Dict. Anglo-Brit.* (1st edn) *Trisagium,* (*G.*) a kind of Hymn in the *Greek* Church. **1728** CHAMBERS *Trisagion,* or *Trisagium,* in Church History, a Hymn, wherein the Word *holy* is repeated three Times. See *Hymn.* ¶ The proper *Trisagion* is those Words *holy, holy, holy, Lord God of Hosts,* which we read in *Isaiah* vi. 3. and in the Apocalypse. ¶ From these Words, the Church form'd another *Trisagion,* which is rehears'd in *Latin* and *Greek,* in the respective Churches, to this Effect: *Holy God, hold Fort, hold Immortal! have Mercy upon us.* ¶ *Petrus Fullensis* to this *Trisagion* added, *Thou who wast crucify'd for us, have Mercy upon us*: Thus attributing the Passion not to the Son alone, but to all the three Persons of the *Trinity,* and pronouncing Anathema to all such as would not say the same. ¶ The Use of this latter *Trisagion,* (exclusive of the Addition of *Fullensis*) begun in the Church of *Constantinople,* from whence it pass'd into the other Churches of the East, and afterwards into those of the West.—*Damascenus, Codin, Balsamon,* and others, say it was in the Time of the Patriarch *Proclus* that it was first introduc'd, and on the following Occasion: There being a violent Earthquake in the 35th Year of the younger *Theodosius,* the Patriarch made a grand Procession, wherein, for several Hours together, was sung the Kyrie Eleison, Lord have Mercy upon us. While this was in Hand, a Child was taken up into the Air, where, it seems, he heard the Angels a singing the *Trisagion* just mention'd. He return'd soon after, and told what he had heard: Upon which they began to sing that Hymn, and the more willingly too, as they attributed the Troubles they were then under to the Blasphemies which the Hereticks of *Constantinople* utter'd against the Son.—*Alclepiades, Cedrenus,* Pope *Felix, Nicephorus,* &c. relate the same Story. ¶ *Petrus Fullensis,* Patriarch of *Antioch,* and a zealous Partizan of *Nestorius,* endeavour'd to corrupt the Hymn, by adding, *who suffer'd for us*; but in vain: It still subsists in its primitive Purity, both in the *Latin, Greek, Ethiopic,* and *Mosarabic* Offices. See *Patripassions.* ¶ The Word is compounded of the *Greek,* τρεῖς, three, and ἅγιος, *sanctus,* holy. **1730** BAILEY *Dict. Britannicum* (1st edn) *Trisagium* (τρισαγιον, of τρις thrice, and ἅγος, Gr. holy) the Name of a particular Hymn used in the *Greek* Church, where the Word ἅγος is repeated three times.

trisdiapason
1704 HARRIS *Tris-diapason,* or *Triple-diapason,* a Chord in Musick, otherwise called a Triple, Eighth, or Fifteenth [sic]. **1706** KERSEY-PHILLIPS (6th edn) *Tris-diapason,* or *Triple-Diapason,* (in *Musick*) a Chord, otherwise call'd a Triple Eighth, or Fifteenth [sic]. **1730** BAILEY *Dict. Britannicum* (1st edn) *Trisdiapason* (in *Musick*) a Chord, otherwise called a triple 8th or 5th [sic].

1636 BUTLER *Principles of Musik* (p. 41) All these Partes [bass, tenor, countertenor and mean] set together (thowgh for the deepest Base-voice, and the loftieth Treble-voice) ar conteined within the compas of 22 Notes: which is a *Trisdiapason,* or the ful extent of the *Gam-ut*: but ordinarily they doe not exceede the number of 19 or 20. **1736** TANS'UR *Compleat Melody* (3rd edn, p. 69) A *Trisdiapasion* is a *Triple Octave;* being a 22d. (Gr.)

trite *see* diagram
1706 KERSEY-PHILLIPS (6th edn) *Trite, (Gr.)* the third Musical Chord: *Trite Diezeugmenon* the Note call'd *C-sol-fa-ut. Trite Hyperbolæon,* F-fa-ut. *Trite Synemmenon,* B-fa-be-mi. **1728** CHAMBERS *Trite,* in Music, the third musical Chord. See *Chord* and *Diagram.*

early 18th C. PEPUSCH various papers BL Add. 29429, f. 6 Trite, i.e[.] ye Third before. viz: Trite Hyperbolæon, Trite Diezeugmenon **1731** PRELLEUR *Modern Musick-Master* ('A Brief History of Musick', p. 9) This Note *Trite Synemenon* has since been used for *B* flat. This makes the *Fourth* and *Fifth* perfect. It has been called *Trite Synemenon* by reason of its being the third String of that Tetrachord.

Triton
1623 COCKERAM *Trytons.* Neptunes Trumpetors. **1658** PHILLIPS (1st edn) *Triton,* a Sea Deity, the son of *Neptune* and *Salacia,* faigned by the Poets to have been the Trumpeter of *Neptune.* **1676** COLES *Triton,* a Sea-god (*Neptunes* Trumpeter) **1696** PHILLIPS (5th edn) *Triton,* a Sea Deity, *Neptune*'s Trumpeter.

tritone *see* false, false fifth, fifth lesser, semidiapente
1598 FLORIO It→E *Tritono,* consisting of three tuns. **1611** FLORIO It→E *Tritono,* consisting of three tunes. **1704** HARRIS *Tritone,* a term in Musick, which signifies a greater Fourth. **1706** KERSEY-PHILLIPS (6th edn) *Tritone,* a Term in Musick which signifies a greater Fourth. **1728** CHAMBERS *Tritone, Triton,* in Music, a false Concord, consisting of three Tones, or a greater Third, and a greater Tone. See *Concord.* ¶ Its Ratio, or Proportion in Numbers, is of 45 to 32. In dividing the Octave, we find, on one Side, the false Fifth, and the *Tritone* on the other. See *Octave.* ¶ The *Tritone* is a kind of redundant Third, consisting of three Tones, whence its Name; or, more properly, of two Tones, with a greater Semitone, and a lesser, as of *ut* to *fa,* of *fa* to *si, &c.*—But it is not, as many imagine, a greater Fourth; for the Fourth is a perfect Interval, which does not admit of any majority or Minority: Nor must the *Tritone* be confounded with the false Fifth; for the *Tritone* only comprehends four Degrees, *viz. ut, re, mi, fa,* whereas the false Fifth comprehends Five, *viz. fa, sol, la, si, ut;* besides, that among the Six Semitones, which compose the *Tritone* chromatically, there are three greater and three lesser; whereas among the Six Semitones, which compose the false Fifth, there are only two lesser, and four greater. See *Third, Fourth, Fifth, &c.* **1730** BAILEY *Dict. Britannicum* (1st edn) *Tritone* (in *Musick*) a false Concord consisting of three Tones, or a greater Third and a greater Tone.

1609 DOWLAND-ORNITHOPARCUS *Micrologvs* (p. 20) *Tritonus.* ¶ And it is a leaping from one Voyce to another by a sharp Fourth, comprehending three whole *Tones* without the *semitone.* Wherefore it is greater than *Diatessaron; Stapulensis* saith thus, A *Tritone* doth exceed the Consonance of a *Diatessaron...* **1617-24** FLUDD *Utriusque Cosmi Maioris: De Templo Musicæ* (p. 183) *Tritonus* est intervallum duarum vocum secundùm ascensum & descensum, continens in se tres tonos ... **1636** BUTLER *Principles of Musik* (p. 47) *Tritonus,* or *Semidiapente,* is a Fift imperfect, consisting of 3 whole Tones, as from *Pha* to *Mi;* or of 2 *Tones* and 2 Hemitones, as from *Mi* to *Pha.* But *Calvisius* (for doctrines sake) dooest distinguish them: calling the Interval of *Pha* to *Mi, Tritonus;* and of *Mi* to *Pha, Semidiapente.* § (p. 49) ... 3 whole Tones from the Ground, whereof that Interval is called *Tritonus:* ... **1665** SIMPSON *Division-Viol* (2nd edn, p. 14) A Fourth is divided into the greater by the name of *Tritone,* which is a prohibited Intervall, and the lesser by the name of *Diatessaron.* **1694** HOLDER *Treatise of Natural Grounds* (p. 168) The *Tritone,* (or False Fourth) whose Ration is 45 to 32, consists of 3 whole Notes; *viz.* 2 *Tones Major,* and 1 *Minor.* **c.1698-c.1703** NORTH Cursory Notes (*C-K CN* p. 187) ... the sound of the 4th# or 5th flatt, which they call tritone or fals fifth. **early 18th C.** ANON. Essay on Musick BODLEIAN Rawl. D. 751, f. 3v ... Besides we see that the voice which naturally inclines to what flatters the ear, seems to reach with pain from the extremity of the octave to this half of it, which is call'd Triton, because the whole octave containing in its extent six full-tones, its half is very near three tones. **1721** MALCOLM *Treatise of Musick* (p. 262) *Observe* also, that the greatest of the *4ths* [32:45, 20:27, 3:4], viz. 32:45 is particularly called a *Tritone,* for 'tis equal to 2 *t g.* and 1 *t l.* ... § (p. 299) ... yet if we call every *Tritone* a *5th,* we shall still have an Exception, for then *f-b* contains only 4 Letters; and therefore 'tis best to call all *Intervals* of 6 *Semitones, Tritones* ... § (p. 415) ... *false Fifth,* (which is called *Tritone* or *Semidiapente* ... **1724** TURNER *Sound Anatomiz'd* (pp. 11-12) [the fourth] ... becomes a *Discord,* when it extends itself, while the *Base* keeps its proper Place, and is called the *Tritone,* or *greater Fourth,* being three whole *Tones* from the *Base,* which is just half the Distance between the *Base* and the *Octave.*

trochaieam rationem *see* galliard

tromba, trompe *see* trumpet

tromba squarciata
1611 FLORIO It→E *Trombetta squarciata,* a kind of trumpet. **1659** TORRIANO-FLORIO It→E *Tromba squarciata,* a sack-but.

trombeggiata
1598 FLORIO It→E *Trombeggiare,* to sound a trumpet, or play vpon a sackbut. *Trombeggiata,* any marche or point of warre sounded vpon a trumpet. *Trombeggiatore,* a trumpeter. **1611** FLORIO It→E *Trombeggiata,* any march or point of warre sounded vpon a Trumpet. *Trombeggiatore,* a Trumpeter.

trombetta
1598 FLORIO It→E *Trombetta,* a trumpet, a trump. Also a trumpeter. § *Sonare la trombetta,* to sound, to clange a trumpet. **1611** FLORIO It→E *Trombetta,* a trumpet. Also a trumpeter. **1659** TORRIANO-FLORIO It→E § *Sonare la trombetta,* to sound a trumpet.

1724 [Pepusch] *Short Explic. of Foreign Words in Mus. Bks.* (p. 82) *Trombetta*, a Small or Little Trumpet.

tromboncino

1598 Florio It→E *Tromboncino*, a treble or meane sackbut. **1611** Florio It→E *Tromboncino*, a treble Sackbut.

trombone *see* sackbut

1598 Florio It→E *Trombone*, a bace [sic] or great sackbut, a great trump. **1611** Florio It→E *Trombone*, a Base or great Trumpet, or Sackbut. **1659** Torriano-Florio It→E *Trombone*, any base trumpet or sack-but **1724** [Pepusch] *Short Explic. of Foreign Words in Mus. Bks.* (p. 82) *Trombone*, a very Large or Bass Trumpet, though more properly a Sackbut.

trompe *see* trump, trumpet

1570/71 *Dict. Fr. and Engl.* Fr→E *Trompe ou Trompette*, a trompet. **1593** Hollyband Fr→E *Trompe ou trompette*, a trumpet, *fem.* § *Publier à son de trompe & cri public*, to make a proclamation. **1611** Cotgrave Fr→E *Trompe: f.* A Trump, or Trumpet, or Trumpet; also, a writhen, and brazen Hunters horne; **1650** Howell-Cotgrave Fr→E § *Sasse bonne farine sans trompe ne buccine; Prov.* Boult thy fine meale, and eat good past, without report, or Trumpets blast. **1676** Coles *Trompe, French.* a trumpet. **1688** Miege-Cotgrave Fr→E *Trompe*, (f.) Horn, a Hunter's Horn, a Trumpet ... a Jews Harp, for Boys to play upon. § *Jouët de la Trompe*, to play upon the Jews harp. *Publier quêque Chose à son de Trompe*, to proclaim a Thing at the Sound of Trumpet. *Sonner de la Trompe*, to blow the Horn. **1704** *Cocker's Engl. Dict.* (1st edn) *Trompe*, in *French* a Trumpet.

tronfare

1659 Torriano-Florio It→E *Tronfare, Tronfiare*, ... also to trump.

troop *see* beat

1706 Kersey-Phillips (6th edn) *Troop*, as To *beat the Troop*, which is the second Beat of Drum, when the Foot are to march: So that *the General* is the first, to give notice of the March, and the Troop the next, for the Men to repair to their Colours. **1708** Kersey *Dict. Anglo-Brit.* (1st edn) *Troop*, as To *beat the Troop*, which is the second Beat of Drum, when the Foot are to march. **1728** Chambers *Troop .... To beat the Troop*, is the second Beat of a Drum, whereby the Foot are advertis'd to march. See *Drum.*

trope *see* mode, repercussion

1500 *Ortus Vocabulorum* L→E Trophus. i. cantus m.s.

troper

1706 Kersey-Phillips (6th edn) *Troper*, (in old Records) a Book of alternate Turns or Responses in singing Mass. **1708** Kersey *Dict. Anglo-Brit.* (1st edn) *Troper*, (in old Records) a Book of alternate Turns or Responses in singing Mass.

trophy

1696 Phillips (5th edn) *Trophy*, ... In Painting, Graving, *&c.* the Representation of Pikes, Drums, Corslets, and other Instruments of War, are called *Trophies.*

trophy money

1702 Kersey *New Engl. Dict.* (1st edn) *Trophy-money*, 4 *d.* paid yearly by House-keepers on the Train-bands, for the charge of Drums, Colours, Scarves, *&c.* **1706** Kersey-Phillips (6th edn) *Trophy-Money*, a Duty of four Pence paid yearly by House-keepers on the Trained Bands, but charged on the Land-lord, for the Drums, Colours, Scarves, *&c.* of their respective Companies. **1708** Kersey *Dict. Anglo-Brit.* (1st edn) *Trophy-Money*, a Duty of 4*d.* paid yearly by House-keepers on the Trained Bands; for the Drums, Colours, *&c.* of their respective Companies. **1728** Chambers *Trophy Money*, a Duty of 4 *d.* paid Annually by the House-keepers or the Trained Bands, for the Drums, Colours, *&c.* of their respective Companies. See *Militia.* **1737** Dyche-Pardon (2nd edn) *Trophy Money* (S.) a small Acknowledgment paid by House-keepers, or their Landlords annually for the finding Drums, Colours, &c. for the Militia.

troubadour *see* floralia

1728 Chambers *Troubadours*, or *Trouveours*, or *Trouvers*, a Name anciently, and to this Day, given [to] the ancient Poets of *Provence.* See *Poetry.* ¶ Some will have the Name borrow'd from *trouver*, to find, by reason of their *Inventions;* tho' others take them to have been call'd *Trombadous*, by reason they sung their Poems on an Instrument call'd a *Trompe* or *Trump.* ¶ The Poesy of the *Troubadours* consisted in Sonnets, Pastorals, Songs, Syrventes or Satyrs, which were much to their Taste; and in Tensions, which were Love Disputes. ¶ *Jean de Notre Dame*, commonly call'd

Nostradamus, a Procureur in the Parliament of *Provence*, wrote an ample Discourse of these Poets.—He makes their Number seventy-six. *Pasquier* tells us, he had an Extract of an ancient Book belonging to Cardinal *Bembo*, entitled, *Los Noms daquels qui firent Tensons & Syrventes*, which made their Number ninety-six, among which was an Emperor, *viz. Frederick* I. and two Kings, *viz. Richard* I. of *England*, and a King of *Arragon*, with a Dauphin, several Counts, *&c.* Not that all these had compos'd entire Works in Provincial; some of them had not brought forth any thing beyond Epigrams. ¶ *Petrarch* speaks with Applause of several *Troubadours* in the IVth Chapter of the Triumph of Love.—The *Italian* Poets are said to have borrow'd their best Pieces from the *Troubadours*. *Pasquier* declares expresly, that *Dante* and *Petrarch* are, indeed, the Fountains of the *Italian* Poetry; but Fountains which have their Sources in the Provincial Poetry. ¶ *Bouche*, in his History of *Provence*, relates, that about the Middle of the XIIth Century, the *Troubadours* began to be esteem'd throughout *Europe*, and that their Credit and Poesy was at the highest about the Middle of the XIVth. He adds, that it was in *Provence* that *Petrarch* learnt the Art of Rhiming, which he afterwards practis'd, and taught in *Italy*. **1730** BAILEY *Dict. Britannicum* (1st edn) *Troubadours*, ancient Poets of *Provence* in *France*.

true relation *see* false relation
1730 [PEPUSCH] *Short Treatise on Harmony* (p. 2) True Relations, are Those wherein the Two Notes which make the Terms of the Relation, have a certain Proportion of Agreement which is agreeably sensible to the Ear.

trump *see* jews trump, reversi, trompe, tronfare
1702 KERSEY *New Engl. Dict.* (1st edn) A *Trump, or* trumpet. **1721** BAILEY *An Univ. Etymolog. Engl. Dict.* (1st edn) *Trump, (Trompe, Du.)* a small Trumpet for Children. **1730** BAILEY *Dict. Britannicum* (1st edn) *Trump (trompe, Du.)* a Trumpet. **1737** DYCHE-PARDON (2nd edn) *Trump* or *Trumpet* (S.) a Musical Instrument used in Armies to excite Chearfulness and Courage in the Men, made of Brass or Silver, in the Form of a Conick Tube, &c.

trumpet *see* aes, agnafile, alarm, auricalco, bellicum, bemes, bozina, buccina, busine, buxum, cauum, clang, classicum, levet, oricalco, strombettare, taratantara, trompe, tuba
1550 THOMAS It→E *Tromba*, a trompette. **1565** COOPER L→E § *Dare signum militibus. Terent.* To cause the trumpet to be blowen to warne the souldiours. *Pronuntiare. Curtius.* To proclaime by trumpette. *Pronuntiare prælium in posterum diem. Liu.* By trumpette to proclaime battaile, &c. **1589** RIDER L→E To blow a trumpet, v: to sound § There are diverse soundes of a trumpet, 1 *Exorneticon.* when it soundeth the alarum. 2 *Paraceleusticon.* When it emboldeneth the skirmish. 3 *Anacleticon.* When it soundeth the retraite. 4 *Anapausterion.* When it soundeth of ceasing from labour, & to pitche their tentes. 5 *Pompicon, pollux.* When it is vsed in great solemnitie. **1598** FLORIO It→E *Tromba*, a trump, or a trumpet. Also a sackbut. *Trombare*, to sound a trumpet. **1599** MINSHEU-PERCYVALL Sp→E **Tromba*, f. a trumpet, a round instrument of brasse. *Trompa*, a trumpet *Trompeta*, a trumpet, a trumpeter. § **Trompa de Paris*, a Iewes harpe. **Trompeta de bueltas*, a sagbut. Also a trumpet with manie windings and turnings. **1611** COTGRAVE Fr→E *Trompette: f.* A Trumpet; *Trompetté: m. ée: f.* Trumpetted, or noised abroad; published, or proclaymed with sound of Trumpets. **1611** FLORIO It→E *Tromba*, any Trump or Trumpet. Also a Sackbut. *Trombare*, to sound a Trumpet... Also to play vpon a Sackbut. § *A suon di tromba*, by the sound of trumpet. *Ferro trombe tamburisonante professione*, a Rodomontall word, as one would say Sword-trumpet-drum-sounding profession [sic]. *Sonare la trombetta*, to sound a Trumpet. *Trombetta squarciata*, a kind of Trumpet. **1650** HOWELL-COTGRAVE Fr→E § *A pain, & oignon trompette, ne clairon; Prov.* Hard fare, poore dyet, course Acales [sic], require neither state in the serving, nor musicke in the eating; or, the sound of forraigne Trumpets is but seldome heard in a poore, and barren State. **1659** TORRIANO-FLORIO It→E *Trombare, Trombeggiare, Trombettare*, to sound a trumpet or a sack-but **1688** MIEGE-COTGRAVE Fr→E *Trompette*, (f.) a Trumpet. § *Addoucir le son de la Trompette*, to make the Trumpet sound sweeter. *La Trompette sonne*, the Trumpet sounds. *Le Son de la Trompette*, the Sound of the Trumpet. *Sonner (jouër) de la Trompette*, to sound the Trumpet. *Trompette harmonieuse, ou Saquebute*, a Sackbut. **1696** PHILLIPS (5th edn) *Trumpet*, a Warlike Musical Instrument, in use among the Cavalry, and serving for the same Purposes, as the Drum among the Infantry. **1702** KERSEY *New Engl. Dict.* (1st edn) A *Trumpet*, a musical Instrument. **1706** KERSEY-PHILLIPS (6th edn) *Trumpet, (Fr.)* a known warlike Musical Instrument, which is in use among the Horse, and serves for the same purposes as the

Drum among the Foot-Soldiers; also the Man that sounds it. **1721** BAILEY *An Univ. Etymolog. Engl. Dict.* (1st edn) A *Trumpet*, (*Une Trompette, F. Trompeta, Span. Trommet, Dan.)* a warlike musical Instrument. To *Trumpet, (Trompetter, F.)* to sound a Trumpet, to publish, to set or spread abroad **1724** [PEPUSCH] *Short Explic. of Foreign Words in Mus. Bks.* (p. 82) *Tromba*, a Trumpet. **1728** CHAMBERS *Trumpet* ... [*see* Appendix] **1730** BAILEY *Dict. Britannicum* (1st edn) *To Trumpet* (*trompetter*, F.) to blow a Trumpet. **1737** DYCHE-PARDON (2nd edn) *Trumpet* (V.) to sound or play upon the musical Instrument called a Trumpet.

trumpet air

c.1710 NORTH (draft for) Musicall Grammarian BL Add. 32537, ff. 181-181v ... but for the trumpett It ordinarily rising Gaines a Scale of successive notes In a sharp key, as farr as the sixt, and no higher, but those with y[e] fourth below, and a 3[d] under that make a chirping movement or peculiar tune, w[ch] is well knowne, and called the trumpet air, ffor the Instrument will not be made to sound any other Notes but these.

trumpeter *see* a cavallo, aeneator, bozina, buccinator, butta in sella, diana, liticen, monta in sella, oghetto, siticine, symphoniacus, thrubal, tibicen, trombetta, tubicen

1570/71 *Dict. Fr. and Engl.* Fr→E *Vn Trompetteur*, a trompeter. **1593** HOLLYBAND Fr→E *Vn Trompetteur*, a Trumpeter: *m*. **1598** FLORIO It→E *Trombattore*, a trumpetter. *Trombettaro*, a trumpeter. *Trombettero*, a trumpeter. *Trombettiero*, a trumpeter. **1599** MINSHEU-PERCYVALL Sp→E *Trompetear*, to sound a trumpet. *Trompetero*, m. a trumpeter. **1611** COTGRAVE Fr→E *Trompeter.* To trumpet, or sound a Trumpet. *Trompeteur: m.* A Trumpetter. *Trompetteur: m.* A Trumpetter. **1611** FLORIO It→E *Trombatore*, a *Trumpeter*. Vsed also for a cryer of a Proclamation. *Trombettaro*, a Trumpeter. *Trombettiere*, a Trumpeter **1659** TORRIANO-FLORIO It→E *Trombatore, Trombeggiatore*, a Trumpeter, also a proclaimer or crier of a Proclamation or any thing else by the sound of a trumpet. *Trombeggiata, Trombettata*, a trumpetting, any march or point of war sounded upon a trumpeting *Ttombetta* [sic], a trumpet, a Trumpeter *Trombettiere, Trombettaro, Trombatore, Trombeggiatore, Trombettino*, a Trumpeter **1688** MIEGE-COTGRAVE Fr→E *Trompette*, (m.) a Trumpeter. § *Trompetter, crier à son de trompe*, to proclaim (or publish) with sound of Trumpet. *un bon Trompette*, a good Trumpeter. **1702** KERSEY *New Engl. Dict.* (1st edn) A *Trumpeter*. **1706** KERSEY-PHILLIPS (6th edn) *Trumpeter*, he that blows or sounds a Trumpet:

trumpet harmonious

1728 CHAMBERS *Trumpet Harmonious*, is an Instrument which imitates the Sound of a *Trumpet*, and which resembles it in every thing, except that it is longer, and consists of more Branches. ¶ 'Tis ordinarily call'd *Sackbut*. See *Sackbut*.

trumpet maker *see* tubarius

trumpet marine *see* monochord, tuba marine

1688 MIEGE-COTGRAVE Fr→E *Trompette marine*, a Trump marine. *Trompette marine, sorte d'Instrument de Musique*, a Trump-marine. **1696** PHILLIPS (5th edn) *Trumpet Marine*, an Instrument with a Belly resembling a Lute, and a very long Neck, with one String, which being struck with a Hair Bow, makes a noise like a Trumpet. **1702** KERSEY *New Engl. Dict.* (1st edn) A *Trumpet-marine*, a kind of musical instrument. **1708** KERSEY *Dict. Anglo-Brit.* (1st edn) *Trumpet-Marine*, an Instrument with one String, which being struck with a Hair-bow, sounds like a Trumpet. **1728** CHAMBERS *Trumpet Marine*, is a musical Instrument consisting of three Tables, which form its triangular Body. ¶ It has a very long Neck, with one single String, very thick, mounted on a Bridge, which is firm on one Side, but tremulous on the other.—'Tis struck by a Box with the one Hand, and with the other the String is press'd or stopp'd on the Neck by the Thumb. ¶ 'Tis the Trembling of the Bridge, when struck, that makes it imitate the Sound of a *Trumpet;* which it does to that Perfection, that 'tis scarce possible to distinguish the one from the other. ¶ And this is what has given the Denomination of *Trumpet Marine*, tho', in Propriety, it be a kind of Monochord. ¶ The *Trumpet Marine* has the same Defects with the *Trumpet, viz.* that it performs none but *Trumpet Notes*, and some of those either too flat or too sharp.—The Reason, Mr. *Fr. Roberts* accounts for, only premising that common Observation of two unison Strings, that if one be struck, the other will move; the Impulses made on the Air by one String, setting another in Motion, which lies in a Disposition to have its Vibrations synchronous to them: To which it may be added, that a String will move, not only at the striking of an Unison, but also at that of an 8th or 12th, there being no

Contrariety in the Motions to hinder each other. See *Unison* and *Chord*. ¶ Now in the *Trumpet Marine* you do not stop close, as in other Instruments, but touch the String gently with your Thumb, whereby there is a mutual Concurrence of the upper and lower Part of the String to produce the Sound.—Hence 'tis concluded, that the *Trumpet Marine* yields no musical Sound, but when the Stop makes the upper Part of the String an Aliquot of the Remainder, and consequently of the whole; otherwise the Vibrations of the Parts will stop one another, and make a Sound suitable to their Motion, altogether confus'd. Now these aliquot Parts, he [Roberts] shews, are the very Stops which produce the *Trumpet Notes*. **1737** DYCHE-PARDON (2nd edn) *Trumpet Marine* (S.) a Musical Instrument of only one large String, which being sounded with a Hair Bow imitates the Tone or Sound of a Trumpet.

1677 [F. NORTH] *Philosophical Essay of Musick* (p. 18) The *Trumpet marine* ... is a large and long monochord play'd on by a Bow near the end, which causes the string to break into shrill Notes. The removing the thumb that stops upon the string gives measure to these breaks, and consequently directs the *Tone* to be produced. The jarr at the Bridge takes the same measure and makes the *Sound* loud, in imitation of a *Trumpet*, which otherwise would be like a *Whistle* or *Pipe*. **c.1715-20** NORTH Theory of Sounds BL Add. 32534, f. 51v ... But I find It needfull In the first place by way of preparation to Inspect that wonderfull Instrument called a Trumpett Marine. It is onely a direct Monachord Strained upon a sounding flat, as the string of a violl is strained, but longer & rounder then any there. It is touched by a bow, Not at ye bridg, as a viol, but above all near the Nutt. It yeilds all the tones as a wind trumpet doth, and within that Compas, No other; but it goes higher then ye trumpet, and thereby hath more latitude as will appear; ...

trumpet note

1692 ROBERTS *Discourse concerning Musical Notes of Trumpet* (*Philos. Trans.*, 1692, p. 559) Whence it comes to pass that the Trumpet will perform no other Notes (in that compass) but only those in the Table, which are usually called by Musicians Trumpet-Notes[.]

trumpet tuning

c.1668-71 *Mary Burwell's Instruction Bk. for Lute* (*TDa* p. 20) The trumpet tuning: this tuning is called so because of his loud effect. It was invented by the famous old Gaultier...

trutilare

1598 FLORIO It→E *Trutillare*, to sing as a thrush or a blacke birde. **1611** FLORIO It→E *Trutilare*, to chirpe or sing as a blackebird. **1659** TORRIANO-FLORIO It→E *Trutilare, Trutillare*, to sing as a blackbird.

tuba *see* aes, buccina, cauum, classicum, sackbut, trumpet

1500 *Ortus Vocabulorum* L→E Tuba be. dicitur fistula cantoris de argento que quator proprietates habebat in lege. scet conuocandum multitudinem ad mouendum castra bella et dies festos. dictum a tono as. anglice a trumpe f.p. vus § Legalem populum tuba cum clangore vocabat In bellis castris festisque sonora sonabat **1538** ELYOT L→E *Tuba*, a trumpette. § *Tuba ductilis*, a brason trumpette. **1550** THOMAS It→E *Tuba*, a trumpette. **1552** HULOET L→E *Ænea tuba, Tuba ductilis*. Brasen trompet. *Tuba ductilis* Trumpet of brasse. **1565** COOPER L→E *Tuba, tubæ, fœm. gen. Cic.* A trumpette. § *Addiscere tubas. Stat.* To learne to blow the trumpette. *Ante tubam. Virg.* Before the trumpette sowned. *Increpuit sonitum tuba. Virgil.* The trumpette sowned. *Signum tuba. Cæs.* To sowne the trumpette. *Tuba ductilis.* A brasen trumpet. **1587** THOMAS L→E *Tuba, æ, f.g.* A trumpet: § *Ductilis, vel ahenea, Iun.* A trumpet of copper or brasse. *Tuba classis, vel prœliaris, Iun.* A trumpet for war. *Tubæ varij soni*, 1. *Exorneticon*, when it soundeth the alarme. 2. *Paraceleusticon*. when it emboldneth & incourageth in the skirmish. 3. *Anacleticon*. when it soundeth the retrait. 4. *Anapausterion*. when it maketh sound of ceasing from labour, and to pitch their tents. 5. *Pompicon*. when it is vsed in great solemnitie, &c. *Pollux*. **1589** RIDER L→E *Tuba, buccina, f buccinum, classicum, & buxum, n salpinx.* A trumpet. § *Tuba classis. Tuba pralialis.* A trumpet for warre. **1598** FLORIO It→E *Tuba*, a trump or a trumpet. **1611** FLORIO It→E *Tuba*, a trumpe, or a trumpet. *Tubatore*, a Trumpeter. **1659** TORRIANO-FLORIO It→E *Tuba*, as *Tromba*. **1670** BLOUNT (3rd edn) *Tube (tuba)* ... also a Trumpet or any long Pipe.

1582 *Batman vppon Bartholome* (p. 423) And *Tuba* hath that name as it were *Tona*, that is holow within, and ful smooth for to take the more breath: & is round without and straight at the trumpeters mouth, and broad and large at the other end ... **c.1710** NORTH (draft for) Musicall Grammarian BL Add. 32537, f. 182 ... Therefore it hath bin contrived to lengthen out the tube as occasion requires to forme a scale of base notes; and this is called tuba ductilis, or Sackbutt. and is used in consorts of wind musick.

tuba marine *see* trumpet marine
1694 Holder *Treatise of Natural Grounds* (p. 200) ... the *Tube-Marine*, or Sea-Trumpet (a *Monochord*) ...

tubarius
1587 Thomas L→E *Tubarius, rij, m.g. Callistra.* A trumpet maker.

tubicen *see* tibicen
1500 *Ortus Vocabulorum* L→E Tubicen inis. q canit in tuba. anglice a trumper Tubicina ne. q canit in tuba **1538** Elyot L→E *Tubicen, cinis*, a trumpettour. **1565** Cooper L→E *Túbicen, pen. cor. tubícinis, m.g. Vegetius.* A trumpettour. **1587** Thomas L→E *Tubicen, inis, m.g. Veget.* A trumpetour. **1589** Rider L→E *Tubicina, f.* A woman trumpeter. **1611** Florio It→E *Tubicina*, a trumpeter. **1659** Torriano-Florio It→E *Tubicina*, a little trumpet, also a Trumpeter.

tubicinate *see* tibicinate
1611 Florio It→E *Tubicinare*, to sound a trumpet. **1656** Blount (1st edn) *Tubicinate (tubicino)* to sound the Trumpet. **1658** Phillips (1st edn) *Tubicination*, (lat.) a sounding of a Trumpet, Pipe, or Cornet. **1676** Coles *Tubicinate, Latin.* to trumpet. **1704** *Cocker's Engl. Dict.* (1st edn) *Tubicinate*, to blow with a Trumpet.

tubilustrium *see* tibilustrium
1587 Thomas L→E *Tubilustrium, n.g. Fest.* The daie wherein the trumpets are purged with water. **1589** Rider L→E *Tubilustrium, n.* The daie wherein the trumpets are purged with water. **1611** Cotgrave Fr→E *Tubilustre: m.* A day whereon the Trumpets dedicated vnto sacrifices were hallowed, and the Trumpetters with water purged. *Rab.* **1659** Torriano-Florio It→E *Tubilustti* [sic], games and sacrifices used among the Grecians in honour of Trumpetors. **1688** Davis-Torriano-Florio It→E *Tubilustri*, a day wherein the Trumpets were purged with a Lamb [sic]. **1728** Chambers *Tubilustrium*, in Antiquity, a Feast or Ceremony in use among the *Romans*. See *Feast*. ¶ This Name was given to the Day whereon they purified their sacred Trumpets; as also to the Ceremony of purifying them. It was held on the fifth and last Day of the Feast of *Minerva*, call'd *Quinquatrus* or *Quinquatria*, which was perform'd twice a Year. ¶ The Word is compounded of *Tubus*, and *Lustro*, I purify. **1730** Bailey *Dict. Britannicum* (1st edn) *Tubilustrium* (among the *Romans*) a Ceremony or Festival at the Purification of their sacred Trumpets.

tunable *see* intunable
1702 Kersey *New Engl. Dict.* (1st edn) *Tunable*, harmonious, *or* conformable to the rules of Musick. *Untuneable*, out of tune, jarring, *or* harsh. **1706** Kersey-Phillips (6th edn) *Tunable*, that may be tuned, or put in Tune; agreeable to the Rules of *Musick*. **1707** *Gloss. Angl. Nova* (1st edn) *Tunable*, harmonious or conformable to the Rules of Musick. **1726** Bailey *An Univ. Etymolog. Engl. Dict.* (3rd edn) *Tunable* (of *tonus*, L.) that may be tuned or put in Tune; harmonious, *i.e.* agreeable to the Rules of Musick. **1730** Bailey *Dict. Britannicum* (1st edn) *Tunableness* (of *tonus*, L. *ton*, F. *able* and *ness*) Melodiousness, Harmoniousness; also Capableness of being put into Tune. *Tunably*, harmoniously. **1736** Bailey *Dict. Britannicum* (2nd edn) *Untunable* (of *un tonus*, L. of *Gr.* and *able*) not melodious. **1737** Dyche-Pardon (2nd edn) *Tunable* (A.) musical, harmonious; *Untuneable* (A.) that has not a regular Proportion of Sound, that is not capable of being made melodious, or harmonious. **1740** Bailey *An Univ. Etymolog. Engl. Dict.* (9th edn) *Tunableness*, Harmoniousness.

tune *see* attone, cantus, common tune, entunes, mood, tone
1702 Kersey *New Engl. Dict.* (1st edn) A *Tune, or* musical air. To *tune, or* set an instrument in *tune*. A *Tuner*. **1706** Kersey-Phillips (6th edn) *Tune*, an Agreement in Sound, an Air, or Song; a particular Way of singing, or playing on Musical Instruments. **1728** Chambers *Tune* ... [*see* Appendix] **1730** Bailey *Dict. Britannicum* (1st edn) *Tune* (*tonus*, L. *ton*. F. of τόνος, Gr.) Agreeableness in Sound, a harmonious, musical Composition, Air, or Song. To *Tune*, to put into Tune, as an Instrument; also to sing or play a Tune. **1731** Kersey *New Engl. Dict.* (3rd edn) *To tune a Musical Instrument*, to set it in *Tune*. **1737** Bailey *The Univ. Etymolog. Engl. Dict.* (3rd edn, vol. 2) *Tune* (*tonus*, L. of τόνος, Gr.) agreeableness in sound, a harmonious composition. *Tuneless*, without any tune. **1737** Dyche-Pardon (2nd edn) *Tune* (S.) an Air judiciously composed according to the Rules of Musick, and variously denominated according to the Use it is designed for, or may be applied to, as a Minuet, Jigg, Hornpipe, &c. also a

Lesson for some particular Instrument only. *Tune* (V.) to screw up the Strings, or regulate the Pipes of musical Instruments in such a Manner that every Note shall have its true and exact harmonical Proportion of Tone to one another;

1597 Morley *Plaine and Easie Introdvction* (p. 147) ... the church men for keeping their keyes haue deuised certaine notes commonlie called the eight tunes, so that according to the tune which is to be obserued, at that time if it beginne in such a key, it may end in such and such others, as you shall immediatly know. And these be (although not the true substance yet) some shadowe of the ancient *modi* whereof *Botius* and *Glareanus* haue written so much. § (annotations on Part III) *The eight tunes*) The tunes (which are also called *modi musici*) the practitioners do define, to be *a rule whereby the melodie of euery song is directed.* Now these tunes arise out of the tunes of the eight, according to the diuersity of setting the fift and fourth together, for the fourth may be set in the eight, either aboue the fift, which is the harmonicall diuision or mediation (as they tearme it) of the eight, or vnder the fift, which is the Arithmeticall mediation: and seeing there be seauen kindes of eights, it followeth that there be 14. seuerall tunes, euery eight making two. But of these fourteene (saith *Glareanus*) the musicians of our age acknowledge but eight though they vse thirteen, some of which are in more vse, and some lesse vsual then others. And these eight which they acknowledge, they neither distinguish trulie, nor set downe perfectly, but prescribe vnto them certaine rules which are neither generall, nor to the purpose, but such as they be, the effect of them is this. Some tunes (say they) are of the odde number, as the first, third, fift and seuenth: others of the euen number: as the second, fourth, sixt and eight: the odde they call *Autentas*, the euen *Plagales*. To the *autentas* they giue more liberty of ascending then to the *Plagale*, which haue more liberty of descending then they, according to this verse, *Vult descendere par, sed scandere vult modus impar* ... Now these tunes consisting of the kinds of *diapason* or eights, it followeth to know which tunes ech kind of diapason doth make. It is therefore to be vnderstood, that one eight hauing but one diapente of fift, it followeth, that one diapente must be common to two tunes, the lowest key of which diapente ought to be the finall key of them both. It is also to be noted, that euery *autenta* may go a whole eight aboue the final key, and that the *Plagale* may go but a fift aboue it, but it may goe a fourth vnder it, as in the verses nowe set downe is manifest. So then the first tune is from *dsolre* to *dlasolre*, his fift being from *dsolre* to *Alamire*. The second tune is from Alamire to Are, the fift being the same which was before, the lowest key of which is common finall to both. In like maner, the third tune is from *elami* to *elami*, and the fourth from *b fa b mi* to ♮ *mi*, the diapente from elami to *b fa b* mi, being common to both. Now for the discerning of these tunes one from another, they make three waies, the beginning, middle, and ende: and for the beginning say they, euery song which about the beginning riseth a fift aboue the finall key, is of an autenticall tune: if it rise not vnto the fifth it is a plagall. And for the middle, euery song (say they) which in the middle hath an eight aboue the final keye, is of an autenticall tune: if not it is a plagal. And as for the ende, they giue this rule, that euery song (which is not transposed) ending in *G sol re ut*, with the sharpe in *b fa b mi*, is of the seuenth or eighth tune in f fa vt of the fifth or sixth tune, in *elami* of the thirde or fourth tune, in *dsolre* is of the firste or second tune. And thus muche for the eight tunes, as they be commonly taught. But *Glareanus* broke the yce for others to follow him into a further speculation & perfect knowledge of these tunes or *modi*, and for the means to discern one from another of them, he saith thus. The tunes or *modi musici* (which the Greeke writers cal ἁρμονίας, sometimes also νομος καὶ Τροπος) are distinguished no otherwise then the kinds of the diapason or eight from which they arise, are distinguished, and other kindes of eightes are distinguished no otherwise then according to the place of the halfe notes or *semitonia* conteined in them, as all the kindes of other consonants are distinguished. For in the diatessaron there be foure sounds, and three distances (that is two whole notes & one lesse halfe note) therefore there be three places where the halfe note may stand. For either it is in the middle place, hauing a whole note vnder it, and another aboue it, and so produceth the first kind of diatessaron, as from Are to dsolre, or then it standeth in the lowest place, hauing both the whole notes aboue it, producing the second kind of diatessaron, as from ♮ mi to elami, or then is in the highest place, hauing both the whole notes vnder it, in which case it pro duceth [sic] the third and last kind of diatessaron, as from c faut to effaut, so that how many distances any consonant hath, so many kindes of that consonant there must be, bicause the halfe note may stand in any of the places: and therefore diapente hauing fiue soundes and foure distances (that is three whole notes and a halfe note) there must be foure kindes of diapente: the first from dsolre to Alamire, the second from *elami* to *bfabmi*, the third from *F faut* to *c solfaut*, the fourth and laste, from *g solreut* to *dlasolre*. If you proceed to make any more, the fift wil be the same with the first, hauing the halfe note in the second place from below. Now the diapason conteining both the diapente & diatessaron, as consisting of the coniunction of them together, it must follow that there be as many kinds of diapason as of both the other, which is seuen. Therefore it is manifeste that our practicioners haue erred in making eight tunes, separating the nature of the eight from that of the firste, seeing they haue both one kinde of diapason, though diuided after another maner in the last then in the first. But if they wil separate the eight from the first, because in the eight the fourth is lowest, which in the first was highest: then of force must they diuide all the other sortes of the diapason, likewise after two maners, by which meanes, there will arose fourteene kindes of formes, tunes, or *modi*. And to begin at the first kind of diapason (that is from *are* to *alamire*) if you diuide it Arithmeticaly, that is, if you set the fourth lowest, & the fift highest, then shall you haue the compasse of our second mood or tune, thogh [sic] it be the first with *Boethius*, & those who wrote before him, and is called by them *Hypodorius*: also if you diuide the same kind of *diapason* harmonically, that is, set the fift lowest, and the fourth highest, you shal haue the compasse of that tune which the ancients had for their ninth, and was called *æolius*, though the latter age woulde not acknowledge it for one of the number of theirs. Thus you see that the first kind of the *diapason* produceth twoe tunes, according to two forms, of mediation or diuision. But if you diuide the second kind of *diap*. Arithmetically, you shal haue that tune which the latter age tearmed the fourth, and in the old time was the second called *hypophrygius*: but if you diuide the same harmonically, setting the fift lowest, you shall haue a tune or mood which of the ancients was iustly reiected: for if you ioine ♮ *mi* to *F faut*, you shal not make a ful fift[.] Also if you ioine F *fa ut* to *b fa b mi*, you shall haue a *tritonus*, which is more by a great halfe note then a fourth. And because this diuision is false in the diatonicall kind of musicke (in which you may not make a sharpe in *F fa ut*) this tune which was called *hyperæolius* arising of it was reiected. If you diuide the third kind of *diap*. from *Cfaut* to *csolfaut* Arithmetically, you shal haue the compasse and essential bounds of the sixt tune, which the ancients named *hypolydius*: if you diuide it harmonically, you shal haue the ancient *Ionicus* or *Iastius*, for both those names signifie one thing. If you diuide the fourth kind of *diap*. from D. to d Arithmetically, it wil produce our eight tune, which is the ancient *hyperiastius* or *hypomixolydius*: if harmonically, it is our first tune and the ancient *dorius*, so famous and recommended in the writinges of the Philosophers. If the fift kind of *diap*. from *Elami* to *elami*, bee diuided arithmeticallie, it maketh a tune which our age wil acknowledge for none of theirs, though it be our tenth indeed, and the ancient *hypoæolius*, but if it be harmonically diuided, it maketh our third tune, and the olde *phrygius*. But if the sixt kind of the *diap*. be diuided arithmetically, it will produce a reiected mood, because from F faut to b fa b mi, is a *tritonus*, which distance is not receiued in the diatonical kind, and as for the flat in b fa ♮ b mi, it was not admitted in diatonicall musicke, no more then the sharpe in F faut, which is a moste certaine argument that this musicke which we now vse, is not the true *diatonicum*, nor any *species* of it. But againe to our deuision of the eights. If the sixt kind be diuided harmonicallye, it is our fift tune and the auncient *lydius*. Lastly, if you diuide the seuenth kind of diap. (which is from G to *g*) arithmetically, it wil make the ancient *hypoionicus or hypoiastius* (for both those are one) but if you diuide it harmonically, it wil make our sea uenth [sic] tune, and the ancient *mixolydius*. Thus you see that euery kind of diap. produceth two seueral tunes or moods, except the second & sixt kinds, which make but one a peece, so that now there must be twelue and not only eight... It is also to be vnderstood that those examples which I haue in my booke set downe for the eight tunes, bee not the true and essentiall formes of the eight tunes or vsuall moodes, but the formes of giuing the tunes to their psalmes in the Churches, which the churchmen (falsly) beleeue to be the *modi* or tunes, but if we con sider [sic] them rightly, they be all of some vnperfect mood, none of them filling the true compas of any mood[.] And thus much for the twelue tunes, which if any man desire to know more at large, let him read the 2 & third bookes of *Glareanus* his *dodecachordon*, the fourth booke of *Zaccone* his practise of musicke, and the fourth part of *Zarlino* his harmonicall institutions ... **1721** MALCOLM *Treatise of Musick* (p. 17) How these Degrees [of highness or lowness] are measured, we shall learn again, only *mind* that these Degrees of *Acuteness* and *Gravity* are also called different and distinguishable *Tones* or *Tunes* of a Voice or Sound; so we say one Sound is in *Tune* with another when they are in the same Degree: *Acute* and *Grave* being but Relations, we apply the Name of *Tune* to them both, to express something that's constant and absolute which is the Ground of the Relation; ...

tuning *see* bearing, beating, consort pitch, goat tuning, temperament, trumpet tuning
1596 ANON. *Pathway to Musicke* [B ii *verso*] Tuning or tune keepeing is a lifting vp or letting dovvne of the voice, from one voice to another; eyther by Rules or Spaces in certaine distances: from vvhich definition, are excepted the vnisones, vvhich keepe in the selfe same place one certaine tune, eyther in strayning or remitting the voice. **c.1715-20** NORTH Theory of Sounds BL Add. 32534, f. 49v [*re* 'clavicall instruments'] ... By their separate strings, are. w[ch] latter sort cannot be adapted stricktly to accord upon any more then the scale of some one Key, and without a shift made by adjusting the accords in some Measure Indifferent to most Keys of y[e] scale and thereby, to suplant the scismes; that is an art called tuning, better understood by Instrument makers then by musitians; ... § f. 65 [*re* pipe instruments] Instrument makers sence themselves of demension for adjusting y[e] termes of pipes and come very near y[e] designe, but y[e] Ear is not satisfyed without consummate Exactness w[ch] no mechanisme will obtaine therefore moveable expedients are found out to adjust y[e] Measure of y[e] air Included, the application of w[ch] is called tuning

tuono di chiesa *see* ecclesiastic tone
1730 [PEPUSCH] *Short Treatise on Harmony* (p. 54) It is because of this Difference and Peculiarity, that the key of E is as it were dedicated and appropriated to Church Musick; this difference in its Modulation, making what is composed in it the most Solemn, and therefore the Italians call it *Tuono* di *Chiesa*. **1731** [PEPUSCH] *Treatise on Harmony* (2nd edn, p. 65) ... *this* Key [E] differs from all the others; for *they* are introduc'd by the Semitone major *below* them, but *this* is by the Semitone major *above* it; *they* by their *Seventh* major, but *this* by his *Second* which happens to be *minor; that is*, from *F* downwards to *E*. 'Tis because of this Difference and Peculiarity in its Modulation, which makes what is compos'd in it to be very *solemn*, that this Key is as 'twere appropriated to *Church-Musick*, and call'd by the Italians *Tuono di Chiesa*.

tuorbe *see* theorbo

turturi
1500 *Ortus Vocabulorum* L→E Turturi. dicuntur pastores qui fistulis canunt

tut
1676 MACE *Musick's Monument* (p. 109) [*re* the lute] The *Tut*, is a *Grace*, always performed with the *Right Hand*, and is a *sudden taking away the Sound of any Note*, and in such a manner, as it will seem to cry *Tut*; and is very *Pritty*, and *Easily done, Thus*. ¶ When you would perform *This Grace*, it is but to strike your *Letter*, (which you intend shall be so *Grac'd*) with one of your *Fingers*, and immediately *clap on your next striking Finger, upon the String which you struck*; in which doing, you suddenly *take away the Sound of the Letter*, which is that, we call the *Tut*; and if you do it clearly, it will seem to speak the word *Tut*, so plainly, as if it were a *Living Creature, Speakable*.

tutti *see* concerto, concerto grosso, omnes, pieno, t
1724 [PEPUSCH] *Short Explic. of Foreign Words in Mus. Bks.* (p. 83) *Tutti*, or *Tutto*, or by Way of Abbreviation the Letter *T* only. This Word or Letter signifies All, or All together, and is often met with in Musick of several Parts, especially after the Word *Solo*, or *Trio*; thereby signifying that in such Places all the several Parts are to perform together. **1726** BAILEY *An Univ. Etymolog. Engl. Dict.* (3rd edn) *Tutti, Tutto*, (in *Musick Books*) signifies *all* or *All-together*, and is often found in Musick of several Parts, and especially after the Word *solo* or *trio*, and signifies that in such Places all the several Parts are to perform together. *Ital.*

c.1715-20 NORTH Essay of Musical Ayre BL Add. 32536 (*JWi* p. 127) Where parts are multiplyed, the same thing ['loud and soft' play] is done by the resting of some, and then falling in alltogether, as when in the moderne *Concertos* they write *tutti*. **1731** PRELLEUR *Modern Musick-Master* (Dictionary, p. 3) *Tutti*, all, or all together.

twang
1702 KERSEY *New Engl. Dict.* (1st edn) To *Twang* like the string of an instrument. **1706** KERSEY-PHILLIPS (6th edn) To *Twang*, to sound like the String

of a Musical Instrument, or Whip, &c. **1735** DEFOE A *Twang*, ... a sharp Sound as of a Bow-String. **1737** DYCHE-PARDON (2nd edn) *Twang* (S.) sometimes means the Sound of a String of a Musical Instrument pulled rudely;

tweedle

1726 BAILEY *An Univ. Etymolog. Engl. Dict.* (3rd edn) To *Tweedle*, to play on a Fiddle or Bag-pipe. **1737** DYCHE-PARDON (2nd edn) *Tweedle* (V.) a mock Word, signifying to play upon a Musical Instrument.

two parts in one *see* canon, fugue

1597 MORLEY *Plaine and Easie Introdvction* (pp. 96-8) *Phi.* What doe you terme two partes in one? ¶ *Ma.* It is when two parts are so made, as one singeth euerie note and rest in the same length and order which the leading part did sing before.... Then it followeth to declare the kindes thereof, which wee distinguish no other waies, then by the distance of the first note of the following part, from the first of the leading which if it be a fourth, the song or *Canon* is called two partes in one in ye fourth[,] if a Fift, in the fift, and so foorth in other distances. [gives example entitled 'Two parts in one in the fourth' with accompanying marginalia: *'This waye, some terme a Fuge in epidiatessaron, that is in the fourth aboue. But if the leading part were highest, then would they call it in hypodiatessaron, which is in the fourth beneath: And so likewise in the other distances, diapente which is the fifth: & diapason which is the eighth.*]

twyer

1658 PHILLIPS (1st edn) To *Twyer*, (Sax.) to sing.

tymbale *see* timbrel

tymbon *see* timbon

tympanist

1500 *Ortus Vocabulorum* L→E Timpanaria. dictur planctus f.p. Timpanistria e. qui vel que canit cum timpano com. p. Timpanizo as. est canere cum timpano a.p. **1538** ELYOT L→E *Tympanista*, he that playeth on a drumslade or tymbrell. *Tympanistria*, a woman that playeth on a tymbrell. *Tympanizo*, to play on a tymbrell, tabour, or drumslade. *Tympanotriba, idem quod tympanista* **1552** HULOET L→E *tympanista* Tabourer. *tympanista, tympanotriba, tympanistria*, Tymbrell player. *tympanizo. as, ang.* to play on a tymbrell *tympanizo. as,* to playe on a tabour *Tympanizo. as ang.* to playe on the drunslade [sic]. *Tympanizo. as,* to playe on the timphan **1565** COOPER L→E *Tympanista, tympanistæ, masc. ge.* A player on a drunslade [sic] or tabber. *Tympanístria, tympanístriæ, fœ. gen. Sidonius.* A woman playinge on a tymbrell, or drumme. *Tympanízo, tympanízas, tympanizâre. Sueton.* To playe on a drumme, tabber, or tymbrell. *Tympanótriba, tympanótribæ, m.g. pen. corr. Plaut.* A player on a drumme. **1587** THOMAS L→E *Tympanista, vel tympanistes, æ, m.g. Iun.* The drumplaier or drumster. *Tympanistria, æ, f.g. Sidon.* A woman playing on a tymbrell or drumme. *Tympanizo, as, Suet.* To play on a drumme, taber, or tymbrell. *Tympanotriba, bæ, com. g. Plaut.* A drumster. **1589** RIDER L→E *Tympanista, tympanistes, tympanotriba, m.* A plaier on a drumme, a drumslade, or drumster. *Tympanista, tympanotriba, m.* A taberer, hee that plaieth on a taber. *Tympanista, & tympanotriba.* A timbrell plaier. *Tympanistria, f.* A woman taberer. *Tympanistria, f.* A woman that plaieth on a drumme. *Tympanizo* To plaie on the Taber. *Tympanizo.* To play on a Timbrell. *Tympanizo* To play on the drum. **1598** FLORIO It→E *Timpanista,* a drummer, a tabourer, a drum-player or drumster. **1611** COTGRAVE Fr→E *Tympaner.* To play on a Timpan, Timbrell, or Taber. *Tympaniste: m.* A Timpanist; a player on a Timpan, &c; also, one that hath a Timpanie. *Rab.* **1611** FLORIO It→E *Timpanista,* a Drumster, a Tabourer. **1623** COCKERAM *Tympanist.* To sound a drum. *Tympanize.* to beate a Drum. **1656** BLOUNT (1st edn) *Tympanist (tympanista)* a Drumster or Taberer *Tympanize (tympanizo)* to play on a Drum, Taber or Tymbrel. **1658** PHILLIPS (1st edn) *Tympanist,* he that playeth upon a Tymbrel, Taber, or Drum, called *Tympanum.* **1659** TORRIANO-FLORIO It→E **Timpanizzare,* co [sic] timpanize, to drum, to tabour **1676** COLES *Tympanist,* a drummer *Tympanize,* to play the [tympany.] **1704** *Cocker's Engl. Dict.* (1st edn) *Tympanist,* one that can ¶ *Tympanize,* or beat the Drum well; A Drummer.

tympany *see* bunda, drum, tampano

1500 *Ortus Vocabulorum* L→E Timpanum ni. est quoddam instrumentum musicum sicut pellis in ligno extenta in similitudinem cribri et virga breui concutitur cui si iuncta fuerit fistula dulciorem reddit melodiam dictum a tinuio is. an^{e}. a tymphan n.s. **1538** ELYOT L→E *Tympanum,* a tymbrel, a tabour, or drumslade. **1552** HULOET L→E *Tympanum. ni.* Drumslade. *Tympanum. ni,* Tabour. *Tympanum ni,* Tymphan instrument of musyke. **1565** COOPER L→E *Tympanum, tympani, n.g. pen. corr.* A tymbrell, tabber, or drunslade [sic]. § *Adhibeo ... tympanum. Plaut.* To call for a tabber. *Caua tympana ferire. Ouid.* To play on tabbers. *Reboant tympana. Catull.* The drummes sowne alowde. *Sæua tympana. Horat.* Cruell drunslades [sic]. *Taurina tympana. Claudian.* Made of oxe hydes. *Tympana concita pulsu. Horat.* Tabers or timbrels plaied vpon. *Tympana reddunt planctum. Claud.* The tabers make a sorowfull noyse. **1570/71** *Dict. Fr. and Engl.* Fr→E *Tympan,* a tympan. **1587** THOMAS L→E *Tympanum, ni, n.g. Ovid.* A timbrell, taber, drum or drumslade: **1589** RIDER L→E *Tympanum, crepitaculum, n.* A timbrell. *Tympanum, n.* A drum. *Tympanum, n.* A taber, or tabret. **1593** HOLLYBAND Fr→E *Tympan,* a timpan: *m* **1598** FLORIO It→E *Timpano,* a timbrell, a tabour, a drum, a drumslade. **1611** COTGRAVE Fr→E *Tympan: m.* A timpan, or Timbrell; also, a Taber; **1611** FLORIO It→E *Timpano,* a Timbrell, a Tabour, a drum, a Drum-slade. **1656** BLOUNT (1st edn) *Tympane (tympanum)* a Tymbrel, Taber, Drum or Drumstale [sic]; **1659** TORRIANO-FLORIO It→E *Timpano,* a Timbrel, a Drum, a Drumslade, a Tabour **1676** COLES *Timpane, Greek.* a drum **1688** MIEGE-COTGRAVE Fr→E *Tympanon,* (m.) a kind of German Instrument of Musick. § *Le Tympanon est un Instrument de Musique fort harmonieux, qui vient d'Allemagne, & qui est sur du bois monté de Cordes de laiton, qu'on touche avec une Plume.* **1704** *Cocker's Engl. Dict.* (1st edn) *Tympane,* a Drum; **1706** KERSEY-PHILLIPS (6th edn) *Tympane,* a kind of Musical Instrument us'd in *Germany. Tympanum,* a Drum, which among the Ancients was a thin piece of Skin or Leather stretch'd upon a Wooden or Iron-Circle, and beat with the Hand. **1721** BAILEY *An Univ. Etymolog. Engl. Dict.* (1st edn) *Tympan, (Tympanum, L.* of Τυμπανον, *Gr.)* a Timbrel or Drum. **1724** [PEPUSCH] *Short Explic. of Foreign Words in Mus. Bks.* (p. 81) *Timpano.* See the Word *Tympano.* (p. 83) *Tympano,* or *Tympanum,* a Drum in general, but in Musick it has respect more particularly to a Pair of Kettle Drums, which are often used in Consort as Bass to a Trumpet. **1726** BAILEY *An Univ. Etymolog. Engl. Dict.* (3rd edn) *Tympano* (in *Musick Books*) a pair of Kettle Drums, which are often used in Consort as a Bass to a Trumpet. *Ital.* **1728** CHAMBERS *Tympanum,* τυμπανον, *Drum;* a musical Instrument, which among the Ancients, consisted of a thin Piece of Leather or Skin, stretch'd upon a Circle of Wood or Iron, and beat with the Hand. See *Drum.* **1731** KERSEY *New Engl. Dict.* (3rd edn) The *Tympan,* ... The Word in *Greek* signifies a Drum.

tyrouër

1611 COTGRAVE Fr→E *Tyrouër: m.* Js, in a Violin, or small Fiddle, the flat peece behind the bridge whereto the strings be fastened;

U

ufficina

1688 DAVIS-TORRIANO-FLORIO It→E *Ufficina,* ... also morning and evening prayer or service customarily read, or sung, or publickly said in Churches.

uguale *see* continuato

1724 [PEPUSCH] *Short Explic. of Foreign Words in Mus. Bks.* (p. 85) *Uguale,* or *Ugualemente,* Equal or Equally. **1726** BAILEY *An Univ. Etymolog. Engl. Dict.* (3rd edn) *Uguale, Ugualement,* (in *Musick Books*) signifies equal or equally, *Ital.*

ule

1661 BLOUNT (2nd edn) *Ule, Yeule, Yool* or *Ule-Games,* in our Northern parts, are taken for Christmass games or sports ... In *Yorkshire* & our other Northern parts, they have an old custom, after Sermon or Service on Christmas day, the people will, even in the Churches cry *Vle, Vle,* as a token of rejoycing, and the common people run about the streets singing ¶ *Ule, Ule, Ule, / Three puddings in a Pule, / Crack nuts and cry Ule.*

undecima

1724 [PEPUSCH] *Short Explic. of Foreign Words in Mus. Bks.* (p. 91) *Undecima,* is the Number Eleven.

undershake *see* beat, shake

c.1700 NORTH Capt. Prencourts rules BL Add. 32549, f. 11v This mark. ⌇ I call an undershake for the Movem[t] is to be made, from y[e] key next under the note, by w[ch] this mark doth stand whereas y[e] upper shake, is to be made with the Key that's above y[e] Note, before w[ch] the proper signe doth stand.

unison *see* equison
1598 FLORIO It→E *Vnisone,* a vnison in musicke. **1611** COTGRAVE Fr→E *Vnisson: f.* An vnison; *Vnisonnant: m. ant: f.* Sounding alike, according, or agreeing in sound, of one and the same sound. *Vnissonnement.* All with one sound, voice, accord; in good harmonie. **1611** FLORIO It→E *Vnisone,* an vnison in musike. **1656** BLOUNT (1st edn) *Unison* (Fr. *unisson*) ... A term in Musick, when two Strings or Notes have one and the same tone. **1658** PHILLIPS (1st edn) *Unison,* (French) an agreement of two notes in one tone. **1659** TORRIANO-FLORIO It→E *Unisonante,* of one and the same sound, sounding alike. *Unisuono,* of one onely sound. **1676** COLES *Unison, French.* the agreement of 2 notes in one. **1688** MIEGE-COTGRAVE Fr→E *Unisson,* (f.) *l'union ou le mêlange de deux Sons, fait par un Nombre egal de batemens d'Air,* Unison. **1696** PHILLIPS (5th edn) *Unison, (French)* an Agreement of Two Notes in one Tone. The same with an Octave. **1702** KERSEY *New Engl. Dict.* (1st edn) *Unison* (a Musical Term) when two notes, or strings agree in the same tone. **1704** *Cocker's Engl. Dict.* (1st edn) *Unison,* a term in Musick of one and the same sound, two notes agreeing in one. **1704** HARRIS *Unison,* in Musick, is one or the same Sound, whether produced by one single Voice, or divers Voices sounding in the same Tone; so that an *Vnison* in this Science, may be considered as an Unite in Arithmetick. [sic] or as a Point in Geometry, not divisible into any Parts, in regard that it is the first Term to any Interval. When the Ancients divided their *Monochord,* so that the Parts were as 1 to 1, they called them *Vnisons.* **1706** KERSEY-PHILLIPS (6th edn) *Unison,* (in *Musick*) is one and the same Sound, whether produced by one single Voice, or divers Voices sounding the same Tone; the agreement of two Notes or Strings of an Instrument in one and the same Tone: **1707** *Gloss. Angl. Nova* (1st edn) *Unison,* (Fr.) a Term in Musick, an agreement of two Notes in one tone. **1724** [PEPUSCH] *Short Explic. of Foreign Words in Mus. Bks.* (pp. 91-2) *Unissono,* a Unison, by which in Musick is to be understood when Two or more Strings of an Instrument or Instruments, or any other Sounds are so well in Tune one with another, that in sounding them together, they appear to be but one String or Sound. This Word is also used when in Symphonies of Songs Two Violins both play the same Thing, or the Violin and Song, or the Bass and Song, *&c.* **1728** CHAMBERS *Unison* ... [*see* Appendix] **1737** DYCHE-PARDON (2nd edn) *Unison* (S.) a Musical Term for two Persons or Instruments that sound the same Note in such a perfect Manner, that there is no Difference in the Tone.

1596 ANON. *Pathway to Musicke* [B ii *verso*] The vnisone is so called because it is *vnius soni,* of one & the selfe same sound repeated in one place. **1665** SIMPSON *Division-Viol* (2nd edn, p. 13) ... an Unison; that is, One and the same Sound; whether produced by one single voyce, or divers voyces sounding together in the same Tone; ... **1667** SIMPSON *Compendium of Practical Musick* (p. 37) ... an Unison; that is, one, or the same sound; whether produced by one single Voyce, or divers Voyces sounding in the same Tone. **early 17th C.** ANON. Praise of musicke BL 18. B. xix, f. 3 ... But properly and more rightly two or more stringes being tuned in one self tune are called *Vnussonus,* and so are also two or more voyces singing in one and the same tune called *Vnussonus* (for yf either in the voyces or the stringes ([sic] the same beinge sunge or stricken together) there appeare any more different sounds then one ... **early 17th C.** RAVENSCROFT Treatise of Musick BL Add. 19758, f. 5v A unison is so termid because hee cometh of unius sonus of one sownd keeping all waies in one line or in one space. **1609** DOWLAND-ORNITHOPARCUS *Micrologvs* (p. 78) ... Voyces are called some *Vnisons;* some not *Vnisons. Vnisons* are those, whose Sound is one. **1636** BUTLER *Principles of Musik* (p. 48) ... the Unison: so called, becaus standing in the same Clief that the Ground dooeth, it yeeldeth, in an other Parte, such a sound, as seemeth one and the same with it. The which althowgh it bee noe Intervall; (as all other Concords ar) yet, the Ground and it beeing 2 individual concording sounds, it may wel bee called a Concord: and becaus, like an Eight, it dooeth sweetely resound in Harmoni; and with its sweetenes, is ofttimes necessari in contexing [sic] of Points, and other melodious passages; it is justly reckoned among the Chief of them. § (p. 56) Vnison. *Vnisonus dicitur quasi unus sonus: & definitur, quòd sit unio duorum aut plurium sonorum in eadem Clave consistentium. Intervallum autem Vnisonus non est, nec propriè Consonantia: idq; vel indè patet, quòd Intervallum distantia fit acuti soni gravisq; : Vnisonus autem distantiam sonorum, quoad acumen & gravitatem, non admittat. Adjungitui autem Consonantiis, & quidem perfectis; propterea quòd nihil magis consonum aut perfectum esse possit; quàm quod respectu sui unum est.* Sethus Calvis. c. 4. **1664** BIRCHENSHA-ALSTED *Templvm Mvsicvm* (p. 92) An equal *Mood* is that which is in the same Degree, and is called the *unison* or *Basis.* **1682** PLAYFORD *Musick's Recreation on Viol* (2nd edn, preface) An *Unison*, is the making of two strings to agree in one sound, the one open, the other stopt: ... **1694** HOLDER *Treatise of Natural Grounds* (p. 54) By Unison is meant, sometimes the Habitude or Ration of Equality of two Notes compared together, being of the very same Tune. Sometimes (as here) for the given single Note to which the Distance, or the Rations of other Intervals are compared. As, if we consider the Relations to *Gamut*, to which *A re* is a Tone or Second, *B mi* a Third, C a Fourth, D a Fifth, &c. We call *Gamut* the Unison, for want of a more proper Word. Thus *C fa ut*, or any other Note to which other Intervals are taken, may be called the Unison. **early 18th C.** ANON. Essay on Musick BODLEIAN Rawl. D. 751, f. 4v That if these vibrations are made in two different places of the air, but always equally frequent, & beginning at the same time; these two sounds will have such relation to each other, that to the ear they will make but one sound, though doubl'd; which is call'd *unison*. **1721** MALCOLM *Treatise of Musick* (pp. 35-6) If Two or more Sounds are compared ... they are either *equal* or *unequal* in the Degree of *Tune*: Such as are *equal* are called *Unisons* with regard to each other, as having one *Tune*; ... **1731** PRELLEUR *Modern Musick-Master* (Dictionary, p. 4) *Unisoni*, is set over a Piece of Musick, when all the parts play in the Unison, or Octave. **1740** LAMPE *Art of Musick* (p. 39) [*re* Zarlino] ... And he gives the further following Definition of a Unison in the third Part Chap. ii. of his Institutions: *Unisono è una Adunanza di due, over piu Suoni, o voci equali, che non fanno alcuno Intervallo—Questo non si pone tra le Consonanze & tra gli Intervalli—l'unisono è solamente principio della Consonanza o dell' Intervallo, ma non é Consonanza, ne Intervallo—& perche ogni Consonanza si ritrova tra due Suoni distanti per il grave & per l'acuto; i quali fanno uno Intervallo & è Mistura o compositione di suono grave & di acuto: però non havendo l'unisono alcuna di queste Qualità, non lo potiamo chiamare per alcun modo ne Consonanza, ne Intervallo...*

un poco *see* poco

1724 [PEPUSCH] *Short Explic. of Foreign Words in Mus. Bks.* (p. 92) *Un Poco*. See the Word *Poco*. **1726** BAILEY *An Univ. Etymolog. Engl. Dict.* (3rd edn) *Un Poco*. See *Poco*, Ital.

ut

1598 FLORIO It→E *Vt*, a note in musike vt. **1611** FLORIO It→E *Vt*, a note in Musicke, Vt. **1659** TORRIANO-FLORIO It→E *Ut*, a note in Musick. **1688** MIEGE-COTGRAVE Fr→E *Ut*, (m.) *une des principales Voix de la Musique*, Ut, one of the chief Musical Notes. **1728** CHAMBERS *Ut*, in Music, the first of the musical Votes [sic]. See *Note*. ¶ *Ut, re, mi, fa*; the Clef of *G, re, sol, ut*; of *C, sol, ut*, &c. ¶ This Note, with the rest, were taken out of the Hymn of St. *John Baptist*. *Vt queant laxis*, &c. See *Music*.

utricularius *see* tibia

1538 ELYOT L→E *Vtricularius*, he that pypeth in a botell. **1565** COOPER L→E *Vtriculárius, vtriculárij, m.g. Sueton*. A baggepiper. **1587** THOMAS L→E *Vtricularius, rij, m.g. p.b. Suet*. A player on a baggepipe. **1589** RIDER L→E *Vtricularius, pithaules, ascaules, m.* A baggepiper.

V

v

1724 [PEPUSCH] *Short Explic. of Foreign Words in Mus. Bks.* (p. 84) The Letter *V* is often used as an Abbreviation of the Word *Violino*. Thus, ¶ *V Primo*, stands for *Violino Primo*, or First Violin. And ¶ *V Secondo*, for *Violino Secondo*, or Second Violin.

valets de la feste

1611 COTGRAVE Fr→E *Valets de la feste*. A kind of Morrisdauncers, attired like fooles, and hauing, as ours, their legs gartered with bells.

valigiaro

1598 FLORIO It→E *Valigiaro*, ... Also a drummer. **1611** FLORIO It→E *Valigiaro*, a cloakebag ... it hath been vsed for a Drummer. **1659** TORRIANO-FLORIO It→E *Valigiaro*, a maile or budget-maker, by Met. a Drummer.

variation *see* descant, muance

1724 [PEPUSCH] *Short Explic. of Foreign Words in Mus. Bks.* (p. 85) *Variatio, Variato, Variation*, or *Variazione*, is a Variation, Variety, or Changing. **1726** BAILEY *An Univ. Etymolog. Engl. Dict.* (3rd edn) *Variatio* (in *Musick*) See *Variazione*. *Variation* (in *Musick*) See *Variazione*. *Variazione* (in *Musick Books*) signifies variation, variety or changing. *Ital.* **1728** CHAMBERS *Variation*, in the *Italian* Musick, is understood of the different Manners of playing or singing a Tune, or Song; whether by subdividing the Notes into several others, of lesser Value, or by adding Graces, *&c.*— In such manner, however, as that one may still discern the Ground of the Tune thro' all the Enrichments; which some call *Embroideries.* ¶ Thus, *e.g.* the divers Couples of Chacons, *Spanish* Folies, Gavots, *French* Passacailles, &c. are so many *Variations*: So also many Diminutions of Courants, Gavots, and other Pieces for the Lute, Harpsichord, *&c.* are real *Variations.* **1730** BAILEY *Dict. Britannicum* (1st edn) *Variazione* (in the *Italian Musick*) is the different Manner of playing or singing a Tune or Song, either by dividing the Notes into several others, or by adding of Graces, *&c.* Ital.

1731 [PEPUSCH] *Treatise on Harmony* (2nd edn, p. 46) There is another sort of *Division*, call'd *Variation*, by which we may subdivide also a Division. Variation is made by dividing a Note or Sound into two, three, or more Notes, in such a manner as that we must always retain the Note upon which we make the Variation, and make *that* the first Note of this Division, and afterwards proceed to make two, three, or more Notes upon it, without changeing the Air; that is, the Melody or the Harmony of the Note upon which we make the Variation.

vaudeville *see* virelay

1611 COTGRAVE Fr→E *Vaudeville: f.* A countrey ballade, or song; a Roundelay, or Virelay; so tearmed of *Vaudevire*, a Norman towne, wherin *Olivier Bassel*, the first inuentor of them, liued; **1656** BLOUNT (1st edn) *Vaudevil* (Fr.) a Countrey ballad or song, a Roundelay or *Virelay*, so tearmed of *Vandevire*, a Norman Towne wherein *Oliver Bassel*, the first inventer of them, lived; also a vulgar Proverb, a Country or common saying. **1658** PHILLIPS (1st edn) *Vaudevil*, (French) a Countrey ballade, roundelay, or song, it is also called a Virelay. **1676** COLES *Vaudeville, Virelay*, a Countrey ballad, or common proverb. **1688** MIEGE-COTGRAVE Fr→E *Vaudeville*, (m.) *sorte de Chanson populaire*, a kind of Ballad, or Song. **1706** KERSEY-PHILLIPS (6th edn) † *Vaudevil, (Fr.)* a Country-Ballad, or Song. **1708** KERSEY *Dict. Anglo-Brit.* (1st edn) *Vaudevil*, (*F.*) a Country-Ballad, or Song.

vaylar *see* baioccare, baylar, chioppare, chrich

1599 MINSHEU-PERCYVALL Sp→E **Vayladera*, ... Also a woman dauncer. **Vaylar*, to daunce with snapping the fingers.

vedere l'inimica

1598 FLORIO It→E *Veder l'inimico*, a kind of march sounded in time or war vpon the trumpet and drum. **1611** FLORIO It→E *Vedere l'inimico*, ... Also a kind of march sounded in time of warre vpon the Trumpet and Drum when they discover the enemie. **1659** TORRIANO-FLORIO It→E *Vedere l'inimico*, ... also a certain marche sounded in times of war upon the trumpet or drum when they discover the enemy.

veloce *see* presto

1724 [PEPUSCH] *Short Explic. of Foreign Words in Mus. Bks.* (p. 85) *Veloce*, or *Velocement*, is a Quick Movement, and is of much the same Signification as the Word *Presto*. **1726** BAILEY *An Univ. Etymolog. Engl. Dict.* (3rd edn) *Veloce, Velocement*, (in *Musick Books*) signifies a quick Movement, and is much of the same signification with *Presto*. Ital.

velocissimo

1724 [PEPUSCH] *Short Explic. of Foreign Words in Mus. Bks.* (p. 85) *Velocissimo*, or *Velocissimamente*, is Extream Quick, much the same as the Word *Prestissimo*. **1726** BAILEY *An Univ. Etymolog. Engl. Dict.* (3rd edn) *Velocissimo, Velocissimamente*, (in *Musick Books*) signifies extreme fast or quick, and much the same as *Prestissimo. Ital.*

venitarium *see* psalter

1706 KERSEY-PHILLIPS (6th edn) *Venitarium (Lat.)* the Hymn-book or Psalter, in which the Psalm *Venite exultemus Domino, i.e.* O come let us sing unto the Lord, *&c.* was wrote with Musical Notes, as it was to be sung in Cathedral Churches at the beginning of Matins. **1721** BAILEY *An Univ. Etymolog. Engl. Dict.* (1st edn) *Venitarium*, (so called of *Venite Exultemus Domine, L.* O come and let us sing unto the Lord, *&c.* which was written with Musical Notes, as it was to be sung in Cathedral Churches at the Beginning of Matins) a Hymn-Book or Psalter.

ventesimo

1724 [PEPUSCH] *Short Explic. of Foreign Words in Mus. Bks.* (p. 85) *Ventesimo*, the same as *Vigesimo*, Twenty. **1726** BAILEY *An Univ. Etymolog. Engl.*

Dict. (3rd edn) *Ventesimo* (in *Musick Books*) signifies Twenty. *Ital.*

ventige *see* oscula

1736 BAILEY *Dict. Britannicum* (2nd edn) *Ventiges,* the Holes of a Flute, Pipe, *&c.*

vergaye

1593 HOLLYBAND Fr→E *Vne vergaye,* a kinde of galliard or daunce: *f.* **1611** COTGRAVE Fr→E *Vergaye: f.* A kind of daunce.

verno

1587 THOMAS L→E *Verno, as, Colum. ... also* to sing cheerefully as birds doe, *Plaut.* **1589** RIDER L→E *Verno.* To sing cheerefully as birdes do.

verse *see* amebean verse, canta-versi, lyrick verse, salarian verse

1565 COOPER L→E § *Componere amores. Id est, versus de amore. Ouidius.* To make loue balades. *Contendere alternis versibus. Virgil.* To singe verses by course, whiche may doo best. *Versibus incomptis ludunt. Virg.* They singe songes in vnhandsome meter. **1587** THOMAS L→E *Versus, us, m.g.* A verse: *also* ... a song, *Plin.* **1724** [PEPUSCH] *Short Explic. of Foreign Words in Mus. Bks.* (p. 85) *Verso,* Verse, a Term in Poetry, though often made Use of in Musick. **1728** CHAMBERS *Verse,* in Poetry, a Line, or Part of a Discourse .... *Vossius* adds, that the antient Odes were sung, as to the *Rythmus,* in the same manner as we scan 'em: every *Pes* being a distant Bar or Measure, separated by a distinct Pause: Tho, in reading, that Distinction was not accurately observ'd.

versicle *see* primer

1656 BLOUNT (1st edn) *Versicle (versiculus)* a little verse or line; a short song or sentence.

verte *see* subito, volti

1724 [PEPUSCH] *Short Explic. of Foreign Words in Mus. Bks.* (p. 85) *Verte,* or *Verte Subito.* See the Words *Volti* and *Subito.* **1726** BAILEY *An Univ. Etymolog. Engl. Dict.* (3rd edn) *Verte* (in *Musick Books*) signifies turn over Leaf, as *verte subito,* turn over quickly. *L.*

1731 PRELLEUR *Modern Musick-Master* (Dictionary, p. 3) *Verte Subito,* Turn over Quickly **1736** TANS'UR *Compleat Melody* (3rd edn, p. 71) *Verte,* (Ital.) signifies to turn over the *Leaf;* as, *Verte Subito,* turn over quick.

verticuli

1587 THOMAS L→E *Verticuli, orum, m.g. Pli. ... also* the pinnes or pegs whereby the strings of an instrument are set high or low, *Var.*

vespers

1500 *Ortus Vocabulorum* L→E Vespere arum. significat tempus quod cantatur officium. euensonge tyme **1550** THOMAS It→E *Vespro,* the euenyng, or euensong. **1598** FLORIO It→E *Vespro,* ... Also euensong or euening praier. **1611** FLORIO It→E *Vespro,* ... Also euensong or euening praier. **1656** BLOUNT (1st edn) *Vesperas,* the Evening-song, or evening prayers; so called among Roman Catholicks. **1658** PHILLIPS (1st edn) *Vespers,* evening-song, prayers said about evening time. **1659** TORRIANO-FLORIO It→E *Vespro, Vespero,* ... also even-song, or evening-prayer. **1661** BLOUNT (2nd edn) *Vespers,* or *Vespera's,* Evening song, or Evening prayers; so called among Roman Catholicks. **1706** KERSEY-PHILLIPS (6th edn) *Vespers,* Even-song, or Evening-Prayers in the *Roman* Church. **1708** KERSEY *Dict. Anglo-Brit.* (1st edn) *Vespers,* Even-song, or Evening-Prayers in the *Roman* Church. **1728** CHAMBERS *Vespers,* in the *Romish* Church, *Evening Songs;* that Part of the Office which is rehearsed after Noon: answering to our Evening Prayers; except that it differs more from the Office of the Morning, call'd *Mattins.* See *Mattins.* **1737** DYCHE-PARDON (2nd edn) *Vespers* (S.) in the *Church of Rome,* is the Evening Service, Prayers, or Songs.

vettina

1598 FLORIO It→E *Vettina,* ... I finde it also vsed for a chime of bels **1611** FLORIO It→E *Vettina,* ... I finde it also vsed for a chime of belles ... **1659** TORRIANO-FLORIO It→E **Vette, Vettine, Vetticiuole,* ... some have used the word for a Chime or Carillion of Bells

veze

1611 COTGRAVE Fr→E *Veze: f.* A Bag-pipe. *Poictevin. Vezeur: m.* A Bagpiper. *Poictevin.* § *Iouër de la veze.* To play on the Bagpipe; also, to fizle.

vibrante

1550 THOMAS It→E *Vibrare,* to shake or warble, as to shake a sword ... **1598** FLORIO It→E *Vibrante,* ... Also warbling, or quauering. *Vibrare,* ... to quauer, or warble in musike. *Vibrire, risco, rito,* to warble or quauer in singing. *Vibro,* ... Also a quauering, a warbling, or running in musike. **1611** FLORIO It→E

Vibrante, ... Also warbling or quauering. *Vibrare*, ... Also to warble or quauer in musicke or singing. *Vibrire, risco, rito*, as *Vibrare*. *Vibro*, ... Also a warble, a quauer, or running in musicke or singing. **1659** TORRIANO-FLORIO It→E *Vibrante*, ... also quavering or warbling with the voice. *Vibrare, Vibrire*, ... also to warble or quaver with the voice as a cunning singer. *Vibro, Vibratione*, ... also a quavering, a warbling or running in musick or singing.

vibration *see* oscillation, sympathy

vibrissation
1538 ELYOT L→E *Vibrisso, are*, to quauer in syngynge. **1552** HULOET L→E *Vibrisso. as* Quauer in syngynge. **1565** COOPER L→E *Vibrisso, aui, are*. To quauer or warble in singeyng. **1587** THOMAS L→E *Vibrisso, as, Fest*. To quauer or warble in singing **1589** RIDER L→E *Vibrisso*. To Warble, or quaver in singing. *Vibro, vibrisso*. To Quaver as in singing **1656** BLOUNT (1st edn) *Vibrissation (vibrissatio)* a quavering or warbling in singing **1658** PHILLIPS (1st edn) *Vibrissation*, (lat.) a quavering, or shaking of the voice in singing. **1676** COLES *Vibrissation, Latin*. a quavering (in singing[)]. **1704** *Cocker's Engl. Dict*. (1st edn) *Vibrissation*, in Musick or Singing, signifies shaking or quavering.

vielle *see* musette, nicchio, nille, symphony, tourniquet
1593 HOLLYBAND Fr→E *Vielle, f*: a kinde of violl which beggers doe vse from house to house: *Vn vielleur*, a player vpon such instruments. *Vielles, viesles, violles*, or *violes*, Instruments of musicke. § *Raccorder ses Vieles*, to tune his violes. **1611** COTGRAVE Fr→E *Vielle: f*. A rude, or harsh-sounding Instrument of Musicke, vsually played on by base Fidlers, and blind men; *Vielleur: m*. One that vsually playes on, or gets a rascallie liuing by playing on, a *Vielle*; and thence, any base, or beggarlie Fidler. § *Ils accorderent tresbien leurs vielles ensemble*. They iumbled their fidles passing well together; (but this phrase hath a further (filthie) sence.) **1688** MIEGE-COTGRAVE Fr→E *Viele*, or *Vielle*, (f.) a Cymbal. *Vieler*, or *Vieller*, cd. *jouër de la Vielle*, to play upon the Cymbal. *Vieleur*, or *Vielleur*, (m.) a Player on the Cymbal. § *C'est un pauvre Aveugle, qui viele de Rue en Rue*, 'tis a poor Blindman, that plays about the Streets on the Cymbal. *Jouër de la Vielle*, to play upon the Cymbal. *La Viele est aujourd'hui peu estimée*, the Cymbal is slighted now adaies. *La Vielle est une sort d'Instrument de Musique, dont quêques pauvres Aveugles jouënt, & gagnent leur Vie*, the Cymbal is a sort of Musical Instrument, used by poor Blindmen, to pick a livelyhood.

vigesimo
1724 [PEPUSCH] *Short Explic. of Foreign Words in Mus. Bks*. (p. 86) *Vigesimo*, the Number Twenty, or Twentieth. Thus, ¶ *Opera Vigesimo*, the Twentieth Opera.

vigoroso *see* hardiment
1724 [PEPUSCH] *Short Explic. of Foreign Words in Mus. Bks*. (p. 86) *Vigoroso*, or *Vigorosamente*, is to Play or Sing with Strength or Vigor. **1726** BAILEY *An Univ. Etymolog. Engl. Dict*. (3rd edn) *Vigoroso, Vigorosamente*, (in *Musick Books*) signifies to play or sing with Strength and Vigour. *Ital*.

1736 TANS'UR *Compleat Melody* (3rd edn, p. 67) *Vigoroso, Vigorosemente, Hardimente*. (Ital.) Either of those *Terms*, denote that you must *sing*, or *play* with Life, and Spirit; But strong, and steady.

vihuela *see* violin
1599 MINSHEU-PERCYVALL Sp→E *Vihuela*, an instrument called a viall, sometime a bandore. § **Vihuela de arco*, a viall de Gamba, or a great viall that men set betweane their legs to play on.

villanata
1598 FLORIO It→E *Villanata*, a kinde of countrie song, iigge, or dance. **1611** FLORIO It→E *Villanata*, any kinde of Country song, gigge, or dance. **1659** TORRIANO-FLORIO It→E *Villanata*, ... also any Country-song, jigg, roundelay, or dance

villancico
1599 MINSHEU-PERCYVALL Sp→E **Villancico*, m. a song. **1611** FLORIO It→E *Villancicco, abbellirono la processione i mottetti et villancicchi chè cantò la capella*.

villanella, villanelle
1598 FLORIO It→E *Villanella*, a prettie little country wench lasse, or girle. Also a countrey daunce, a iigge, a round, a song, a horne-pipe, or a ballat, such as countrie milk-maids sing. **1611** COTGRAVE Fr→E *Villanelle: f*. A countrey daunce, round, or song. **1611** FLORIO It→E *Villanella*, a pretty Country-lasse ... Also any Country dance, gig, roundelay, song, ballad, dance or hornpipe, such as Country wenches sing. **1659** TORRIANO-FLORIO It→E *Villanella*,

Villanetta, ... also any Countrey-song, jig, roundelay, horne-pipe, ballade, or dance. **1688** DAVIS-TORRIANO-FLORIO It→E *Villanella, Villanetta,* ... also a Country jigg, roundelay, horn-pipe, ballad, or dance. **1688** MIEGE-COTGRAVE Fr→E *Villanelle,* (f.) *Chanson de Berger,* a Shepherd's Song.

1597 MORLEY *Plaine and Easie Introdvction* (p. 180) [marginalia: 'Villanelle.'] The last degree of grauetie [after the motet, madrigal and neapolitan] (if they haue any at all[)] is giuen to the *villanelle* or countrie songs which are made only for the ditties sake, for so they be aptly set to expresse the nature of the ditty, the composer (though he were neuer so excellent) will not sticke to take many perfect cordes of one kind together, for in this kind they thinke it no fault (as being a kind of keeping *decorum*) to make a clownish musicke to a clownish matter, & though many times the dittie be fine enough yet because it carrieth that name *villanella* they take those disallowances as being good enough for plow and cart[.]

vinate *see* justiniana

1597 MORLEY *Plaine and Easie Introdvction* (p. 180) [marginalia: 'Vinate'] The slightest kind of musick (if they deserue the name of musicke) are the *vinate* or drincking songes, for as I said before, there is no kinde of vanitie whereunto they haue not applied some musicke or other, as they haue framde [sic] this to be sung in their drinking, but that vice being so rare among the Italians, & Spaniards: I rather thinke that musicke to haue bin deuised by or for the Germains (who in swarmes do flocke to the Vniuersitie of Italie) rather then for the Italians themselues.

Vingt-quatre Violons du Roi *see* violin

vinolenta

1582 *Batman vppon Bartholome* (p. 423) [*re* qualities of the singing voice] The voyce *Vinolenta* is soft and plyant: that name *Vinolenta,* commeth of *Vino,* that is a lytle bell softly bent...

viol *see* Alphonso, bassetto, entata, leero, lyra viol, lyre, lyrick, nablium, orchessa, pandora, vihuela, viola da gamba

1593 HOLLYBAND Fr→E *Violles: f:* or *Violons: m:* viols, instruments of musicke. **1611** COTGRAVE Fr→E *Violle: f.* A (Musicall) Violl, or Violin. § *Les ouyes d'vne Violle.* The sound-holes of a Violl. *Vn ieu de violles.* A set, or chest of Violls. **1671** PHILLIPS (3rd edn) *Viol,* an Instrument of musick, played on with a bow, and used for the most part for the playing of a base in a Consort. **1676** COLES *Viol,* an instrument of six strings. **1678** PHILLIPS (4th edn) *Viol,* ... also (*Ital. Viola,* or *Viola di Gamba, Lat. Nablium*) a Musical Instrument of six strings, and play'd on with a Bow, and used for the most part for the playing of a Bass in Consort: when it is used for the playing of Tunes singly, it is call'd, *Leero,* or *Lyra-Viol,* and is somewhat of a less size. **1688** MIEGE-COTGRAVE Fr→E *Viole,* (f.) a Viol. § *Jouër de la Viole,* to play upon the Viol. *La Viole est un Instrument de Musique, qui se touche avec un Archet, & qui resemble au Violon. La Difference qu'il y a, c'est que la Viole est bien plus grosse & plus grande, qu'elle a six Cordes, & que ces Cordes vont toujours en augmentant de grosseur depuis la Chanterelle jusques à la siziéme.* **1702** KERSEY *New Engl. Dict.* (1st edn) A *Viol,* a Musical Instrument. § *A Bass-viol.* A *Viol-maker.* **1704** *Cocker's Engl. Dict.* (1st edn) *Viol,* a Musical Instrument with fix [sic] strings. § *Base Viol,* like the Treble with four strings. **1706** KERSEY-PHILLIPS (6th edn) *Viol,* a Musical Instrument of six Strings: **1721** BAILEY *An Univ. Etymolog. Engl. Dict.* (1st edn) *Viol, (Violle, F. Viola, Ital.)* a Musical Instrument. § *Bass-Viol,* a Musical Instrument. **1728** CHAMBERS *Viol,* a Musical Instrument, of the same Form with the *Violin;* and struck, like that, with a Bow. See *Violin.* ¶ There are *Viols* of divers Kinds: The first, and the principal, among us, is the *Bass-Viol,* call'd by the *Italians* Viola di *Gamba,* or the *Leg-Viol;* because held between the Legs. ¶ 'Tis the largest of all; and is mounted with six Strings, having eight Stops, or Frets, divided by Semi-tones. ¶ Its Sound is very deep, soft, and agreeable.—The Tablature, or Musick for the Bass-Viol, is laid down on six Lines, or Rules. ¶ What the *Italians* call *Alto Viola,* is the Counter-Tenor of this; and their *Tenore Viola* the Tenor. They sometimes call it simply the *Viol*: Some Authors will have it the *Lyra,* others the *Cithara,* others the *Chelis,* and others the *Testudo* of the Antients. See *Lyra, &c.* ¶ 2°, The *Love-Viol,* which is a kind of Triple *Viol,* or Violin; having six brass or steel Strings, like those of the Harpsichord.—It yields a kind of silver Sound, which has something in it very agreeable. ¶ 3°, A *Large Viol,* with 44 Strings, call'd by the *Italians Viola di Bardone;* but little known among us. ¶ 4°, The *Viola Bastarda,* or *Bastard Viol,* of the *Italians;* not used among us: *Brossard* takes it to be a kind of *Bass-Viol,* mounted with six or seven String, and as the common one. ¶ 5°, What the *Italians* call *Viola di Braccio*, Arm-*Viol;* or simply *Braccio, Arm;* is an Instrument answering to our Counter-Tenor, Treble, and Fifth Violin. ¶ 6°, Their *Viola Prima*, or *First Viol*, is really our Counter-Tenor Violin; at least, they commonly use the Cliff of *C sol ut* on the first Line, to denote the Piece intended for this Instrument. ¶ 7°, Their *Viola Secunda*, is much the same with our *Tenor* Violin; having the Key of *C sol ut* on the second Line. ¶ 8°, Their *Viola Terza*, is nearly our Fifth Violin; the Key *C sol ut* on the third Line. ¶ 9°, Their *Viola Quarta*, or Fourth *Viol*, is not known in *England* or *France*: Tho we frequently find it in the *Italian* Compositions; the Key on the fourth Line. ¶ Lastly, their *Violetta*, or little *Viol*; is, in reality, our Triple *Viol*: Tho Strangers frequently confound the Term with what we have said of the *Viola Prima, Secunda, Terza*, &c. § *Bass-Viol*, a Musical Instrument, of the same Form with that of the *Violin*, except that 'tis much larger. 'Tis struck like that, with a Bow; but has [six] Strings and eight Stops, divided into Half-Stops, or Semi-Tones. The Sound it yields is much more grave, sweet, and agreeable, than that of the *Violin*, and of much better effect in a Consort. See *Violin*. **1737** DYCHE-PARDON (2nd edn) *Viol* (S.) a Musical Instrument of various Sizes strung with six Strings, formerly very much in use for Chamber Airs, Songs, &c. but now almost out of Use, the Neck is strung or fretted with nine Strings, Frets, or Divisions, for the several Tones or half Notes to be expressed by; the common Tuning is by Fourths upon all the Strings except the third and fourth, which is a sharp Third.

1654 PLAYFORD *Breefe Intro. to Skill of Musick* (p. 29) The *Basse Violl* is that which usually playes the ground or lowest part, which is called the *Basse*, and hath six strings ... **1667** PLAYFORD *Brief Intro. to Skill of Musick* (4th edn, p. 75) The *Viol* (usually called the) *de Gambo* or *Consort Viol*, because the *Musick* thereon is play'd from the Rules of the *Gam-vt*, and not as the *Lyra Viol*, which is by Letters or *Tableture*.

viola *see* vivola

1598 FLORIO It→E *Viola*, ... Also an instrument called a Violl or a Violine. **1611** FLORIO It→E *Viola*, ... Also an instrument called a violl or violine. **1659** TORRIANO-FLORIO It→E *Viola, Viole*, ... also a viole-instrument. **1724** [PEPUSCH] *Short Explic. of Foreign Words in Mus. Bks.* (p. 86) *Viola*, a Viol, an Instrument of Musick well known, the Neck of which is divided in Half Notes by Seven Frets fixed thereon, and which is commonly strung with Six Strings, though sometimes with Seven. Of this Instrument there are several Sorts and Sizes, as first, ¶ *Viola Tenora*, a Tenor Viol. ¶ *Viola Basso*, a Bass Viol. (p. 10) *Alto Viola*, a small Tenor Viol. (p. 14) *Basso Viola*, is the Bass for the Bass Viol. (p. 79) *Tenore Viola*, a Tenor Viol. **1726** BAILEY *An Univ. Etymolog. Engl. Dict.* (3rd edn) *Viola*, a Viol, a musical Instrument, the Neck of which is divided into half Notes by 7 Frets fixed thereon, and is commonly strung with 6 Strings, and sometimes with 7. And they are of several Sorts and Sizes. *Ital.* § *Alto Viola* (in *Musick Books*) signifies a small Tenor Viol. *Basso Viola* (in *Musick Books*) signifies the Bass Viol. *Ital. Viola Tenera* [sic], a Tenor Viol. *Ital. Viola Basso*, a Bass Viol. *Ital.* **1735** DEFOE *Bass-Viol*, a large musical Instrument.

1731 PRELLEUR *Modern Musick-Master* (Dictionary, pp. 3-4) *Viola*, is properly a Viol, But it is commonly taken for a Tenor.

viola bastarda *see* viol

1724 [PEPUSCH] *Short Explic. of Foreign Words in Mus. Bks.* (p. 16) *Bastarda Viola*, a Bastard Viol: For which see *Viola*. (p. 87) *Viola Bastardo*, a Bastard Viol, which is a Bass Violin, strung and fretted like a Bass Viol. **1726** BAILEY *An Univ. Etymolog. Engl. Dict.* (3rd edn) *Bastardo Viola* (in *Musick Books*) signifies a Bastard Viol. *Ital. Viola Bastardo*, a Bastard Viol, *i.e.* a Bass Violin, strung and fretted like a Bass Viol. *Ital.*

viola da arco

1611 FLORIO It→E *Viola da arco*, a Bow-violin or Violl. **1659** TORRIANO-FLORIO It→E *Viola-da arco*, a bow-viol or violin.

viola da braccio *see* viol, violin

1611 FLORIO It→E *Viola da braccio*, a violin. **1659** TORRIANO-FLORIO It→E *Viola-da braccio*, an arm viol or violin.

1728 NORTH Musicall Grammarian (*C-K MG* f. 123v) [*re* the 'viol Gothick' and its spread to Italy and elsewhere] I doe suppose that at first it was, like its native country, rude and gross. And that at the early importation it was of the lesser kind, which they called viola da bracchio, and since the violin, and no better then as a rustique zampogna used to stirr up the vulgar to dancing, or perhaps to solemnize their idolotrous sacrifizes.

viola da gamba *see* gamba, viol, vivola

1598 FLORIO It→E *Viola di gamba,* a violl *de gamba.* **1611** FLORIO It→E *Viola di gamba,* a Violl de Gamba, because men hold it betweene or vpon their legges. *Viuola de gamba,* a violl de gamba. **1659** TORRIANO-FLORIO It→E *Viola-da gamba,* a violl *de gamba,* so called, because it is held between the legs. **1724** [PEPUSCH] *Short Explic. of Foreign Words in Mus. Bks.* (p. 87) *Viola da Gamba,* is the same as *Viola Basso,* or Bass Viol, and is so called by the *Italians* from the Word *Gamba,* which signifies Leg or Legs, because the common Way of playing upon that Instrument is to hold it with or between the Legs. **1726** BAILEY *An Univ. Etymolog. Engl. Dict.* (3rd edn) *Viola Di Gamba,* a Bass Viol, which is so called from *Gamba* the Leg; because the common Way of playing upon it is by holding it between the Legs. *Ital.*

1655 PLAYFORD *Intro. to Skill of Musick* (2nd edn, p. 41) The *Violl De Gambo* is so called because his *Musick* is play'd from the Rules of the *Gam-ut,* and not by Letters or *Tableture* as the *Lyra Violl* ...

viola d'amour *see* viol

1724 [PEPUSCH] *Short Explic. of Foreign Words in Mus. Bks.* (p. 87) *Viola d'Amour,* a Kind of Treble Viol, strung with Wire, and so called because of its soft and sweet Tone. **1726** BAILEY *An Univ. Etymolog. Engl. Dict.* (3rd edn) *Viola d'Amour,* a Kind of Treble Viol strung with Wire, and so called, because of its sweet Tone.

violetta *see* viol, violoncello

1724 [PEPUSCH] *Short Explic. of Foreign Words in Mus. Bks.* (p. 86) *Violetta,* a Small or Treble Viol. **1726** BAILEY *An Univ. Etymolog. Engl. Dict.* (3rd edn) *Violetta,* a small or Treble Violin. *Ital.*

violier

1570/71 *Dict. Fr. and Engl.* Fr→E *Violier,* a violer or player on the violl. **1593** HOLLYBAND Fr→E *Violier,* a violer or player on the violl: *m.* **1611** COTGRAVE Fr→E *Violier: m.* A Fidler, or common Musition, that playes on a Violin;

violin *see* bassetto, Cremona, entata, fiddle, giga, kit, pandurist, poche, v, viola da arco, viola da braccio

1598 FLORIO It→E *Violino,* ... Also an instrument of musicke called a violine. **1611** COTGRAVE Fr→E *Violon: m.* A Violin, or little Violl. **1611** FLORIO It→E *Violino,* a violin. **1659** TORRIANO-FLORIO It→E *Violino,* a violl, or a violin. **1671** PHILLIPS (3rd edn) *Violin,* a Musicall Instrument much after the same sort as the viol, but a great deal smaller, and used for the playing of the Treble part. **1676** COLES *Violin, French.* (a small Viol) with four [strings]. § *Base Violin,* with four, as the treble. **1678** PHILLIPS (4th edn) *Violin,* (qu. a little *Viol, Ital. Violino,* or *Viola da Braccio, Lat. parvum Nablium*) a small Musical Instrument of four Strings, and play'd on with a Bow, and for the most part used for the playing of the upper or treble part in Consort. **1688** MIEGE-COTGRAVE Fr→E *Violon,* (m.) a Violin, or Fiddle; a Player upon the Violin, or Fiddler; a Fop.... (But in the English Translation of the Bible you will find the Word Harp, for the French *Violon;* as 1 Sam. 16. 16. Ps. 137. 2 Ps. 150. 3.) § *C'est un des meilleurs Violons qu'il y ait,* he is one of the best Players upon the Violin. *Il jouë fort bien du Violon,* he plays very well upon the Violin. *Jouër du Violon,* to play upon the Violin. *Roi des Violons, le Chef des 24 Violons du Roi & de tous les Violons de France,* the Head-man of the King's Musick. **1702** KERSEY *New Engl. Dict.* (1st edn) A *Violin, or* little Viol. § A *Bass-violin.* **1704** *Cocker's Engl. Dict.* (1st edn) *Violin,* a lesser Instrument [than the viol] with four strings. **1706** KERSEY-PHILLIPS (6th edn) *Violin,* (*q.d.* a little Viol) a Musical Instrument with four Strings, which yields a very sprightly and delightful Sound. There is also a Bass-*Violin,* a large Instrument which has likewise four Strings, and in Shape resembles a Viol. **1708** KERSEY *Dict. Anglo-Brit.* (1st edn) § *Bass Violin,* a Musical Instrument. **1721** BAILEY *An Univ. Etymolog. Engl. Dict.* (1st edn) *Violin, (Violino, Ital. Violon, F.)* a musical Instrument well known. **1724** [PEPUSCH] *Short Explic. of Foreign Words in Mus. Bks.* (pp. 87-9) *Violino,* a Violin or Fiddle, an Instrument of Musick too well known to need any Description. This Word is often signified by the Letter *V,* which see. § *Violino Primo,* is the First Violin, or Upper Violin. *Violino Secondo,* the Second Violin. *Violino Terzo,* Third Violin. *Violino Quarta,* Fourth Violin. *Violino Tenora,* Tenor Violin. *Violino Concertante,* or *Concertini,* and *Violino di Concerto,* are the Violins either First or Second which play throughout, to distinguish them from those called *Ripieno,* which play only here and there, and in the full Parts or Chorus. *Violino Ripieno,* Violins of the Full Parts. (p. 10) *Alto Violino,* a small Tenor Violin. (p. 14) *Basso Violino,* is the Bass for the Bass Violin. (p. 79) *Tenore Violino,* a Tenor Violin. (p. 89) *Violino Basso,* a Bass Violin. **1726** BAILEY *An Univ.*

Etymolog. Engl. Dict. (3rd edn) *Violino*, A Violin or Fiddle. § *Alto Violino* (in *Musick Books*) signifies a small Tenor Violin. *Basso Violino* (in *Musick Books*) signifies the Bass for the Bass Violin. *Ital. Violino Concertant*, or *Concertini* or *di Concerto*, are Violins, either first or second, which play throughout, to distinguish them from those called *Ripieno*, which play only here and there, and in the full Parts or Chorus. *Ital. Violino Ripieno*, Violins of the full Parts. *Ital.* **1728** CHAMBERS *Violin*, or *Fiddle*, a Musical Instrument, mounted with four Strings, or Guts; and struck, or play'd with a Bow. ¶ The *Violin* consists, like most other Instruments, of three Parts; the *Neck*, the *Table*, and the *Soundboard*. ¶ At the Sides are two Apertures, and sometimes a third towards the Top, shaped like a Heart. ¶ Its Bridge, which is below the Aperture, bears up the Strings, which are fasten'd to the two Extremes of the Instrument; at one of them, by a Screw, which stretches, or loosens 'em at pleasure. ¶ The Style and Sound of the *Violin*, is the gayest and most sprightly of all other Instruments; and hence it is of all other the fittest for dancing. Yet there are ways of touching it, which render it grave, soft, languishing, and fit for Church or Chamber Musick, ¶ It generally makes the Treble, or highest Part in Consorts.—Its Harmony is from Fifth to Fifth. Its play is composed of Bass, Counter-Tenor, Tenor, and Treble; to which may be added, a Fifth Part: Each Part has four Fifths, which rise to a greater Seventeenth. ¶ In Compositions of Musick, *Violin* is express'd by V: two V V denote two *Violins*. ¶ The Word *Violin*, alone, stands for *Treble Violin*: When the *Italians* prefix *Alto*, *Tenore*, or *Basso*, it then expresses the Counter-Tenor, Tenor, or Bass *Violin*. ¶ In Compositions where there are two, three, or more different *Violins*, they make use of *primo*, *secundo*, *terzo*, or of the Characters I° II° III°, or 1° 2° 3°, *&c.* to denote the difference. ¶ The *Violin* has only Four Strings, each of a different thickness, the smallest whereof makes the *E si mi* of the highest Octave of the Organ; the second, a Fifth below the first, makes the *A mi la*; the third, a Fifth below the second, is *D la re*; lastly, the fourth, a Fifth below the third, is *G re sol*. ¶ Most Nations, ordinarily, use the Key *G re sol* on the second Line, to denote the Musick for the *Violin*; only in *France*, they use the same Key as the first Line at bottom: The first Method is best where the Song goes very low, the second where it goes very high. ¶ The *Violoncella* [sic] of the *Italians*, is properly our Fifth *Violin*; which is a little Bass *Violin* with five or six Strings. ¶ And their *Violone* is a Double Bass, almost twice as big as the common Bass *Violin*, and the Strings bigger and longer, in proportion; and consequently, its Sound an Octave lower than that of our Bass *Violin*, which has a noble Effect in great Concerto's. **1730** BAILEY *Dict. Britannicum* (1st edn) *Violin* (*violon*, F.) a Fiddle. § *Bass Violin*, a musical Wind [sic] Instrument, of the same Form with the Violin, but much larger. **1736** BAILEY *Dict. Britannicum* (2nd edn) *Violin* (*violino*, F. *violino*, It. *vihuela*, Sp.) a fiddle. **1737** DYCHE-PARDON (2nd edn) *Violin* (S.) a small Viol, or rather what is now called a Fiddle strung with four Strings, all commonly tuned by Fifths.

1731 PRELLEUR *Modern Musick-Master* (Dictionary, p. 4) *Violino*, a Violin.

violinist *see* fiddler

1724 [PEPUSCH] *Short Explic. of Foreign Words in Mus. Bks.* (p. 87) *Violinista*, is a Violinist, or one that plays on the Viol, or Violin. **1726** BAILEY *An Univ. Etymolog. Engl. Dict.* (3rd edn) *Violinista*, one who plays on a Viol or Violin. *Ital.*

violist *see* pandurarius, pandurist

1702 KERSEY *New Engl. Dict.* (1st edn) A *Violist*, one well skilled in playing on the *Viol*. **1706** KERSEY-PHILLIPS (6th edn) *Violist*, one that is skilled in, or Teaches the Art of Playing on the Viol. **1707** *Gloss. Angl. Nova* (1st edn) *Violist*, one well skilled in playing upon the Violin. **1721** BAILEY *An Univ. Etymolog. Engl. Dict.* (1st edn) *Violist*, one skill'd in playing upon the Violin, or that teaches the Art of playing on it. **1730** BAILEY *Dict. Britannicum* (1st edn) *Violist*, a Player on a Violin. **1731** KERSEY *New Engl. Dict.* (3rd edn) A *Violist*, one that is skilled in, or teaches the Art of playing on the Viol. **1737** DYCHE-PARDON (2nd edn) *Violist* (S.) one who plays upon a Viol or Violin.

violoncello *see* obligata

1724 [PEPUSCH] *Short Explic. of Foreign Words in Mus. Bks.* (p. 89) *Violoncello*, is a Small Bass Violin, just half as big as a common Bass Violin, in Length, in Breadth, and Thickness, the Strings of which being but half the Length of the Bass, makes them just an Octave higher than the Bass. This is made Use of to play a Bass Violin or Viol, and is very agreeable to the Ear. This Instrument is sometimes used to play a Tenor. ¶ *N.B.* A *Violetta*, or Treble Viol, if rightly strung and tuned, may answer the same End. **1726** BAILEY *An Univ. Etymolog. Engl. Dict.* (3rd edn) *Violoncello*, signifies a small Bass Violin, just half as big as a common Bass Violin, in Length, Breadth and Thickness, whose Strings being but half the Length of the Bass, makes them just an Octave higher than the Bass. Used to play a Bass upon with a common Bass Violin or Viol. *Ital.* **1737** DYCHE-PARDON (2nd edn) *Violoncello* (S.) a small Bass Violin, or Fiddle with a deep Belly.

1731 PRELLEUR *Modern Musick-Master* (Dictionary, p. 4) *Violoncello*, a Bass Violin.

violone *see* violin
1598 FLORIO It→E *Violone*, a great violl, or *Viole de gamba*. **1611** FLORIO It→E *Violone*, a great or base violl. **1659** TORRIANO-FLORIO It→E *Violone*, a great or base violl. § *Muta di violini*, a set or consort of viols. **1688** DAVIS-TORRIANO-FLORIO It→E § *Muto di violoni*, a set or consort of viols. **1724** [PEPUSCH] *Short Explic. of Foreign Words in Mus. Bks.* (p. 90) *Violone* is a very large Bass Violin, or Double Bass, it being as large again in every Way as a common Bass Violin, and the Strings twice as thick and twice as long, renders the Sound just an Octave lower than the common Bass Violin. This Instrument is used only in Great Consorts, as Operas, and other publick Musick. **1726** BAILEY *An Univ. Etymolog. Engl. Dict.* (3rd edn) *Violone*, is a very large Bass Violin, or double Bass, being every way as large again as a common Bass Violin, and the Strings twice as thick, and twice as long, which renders the sound just as Octave lower than the common Bass Violin. This Instrument is only used at great Concerts, as *Opera*'s, and other publick Musick. *It.*

1731 PRELLEUR *Modern Musick-Master* (Dictionary, p. 4) *Violone*, a Double Bass, that is an Octave lower then [sic] a Common Bass Violin.

virelay *see* cançion, canzona, chanson, chant, vaudeville
1611 COTGRAVE Fr→E *Virelay*: m. A Virelay, Round, freemans Song. **1656** BLOUNT (1st edn) *Virelay* (Fr.) a roundelay, Country-ballad, or Freemans Song. **1658** PHILLIPS (1st edn) *Virelay*, see *Vaudevill*. **1676** COLES *Virelay, French*. a Roundelay. **1704** *Cocker's Engl. Dict.* (1st edn) *Virelay*, a Shepherds Song or Dance, a Roundelay. **1706** KERSEY-PHILLIPS (6th edn) *Virelay, (Fr.)* a sort of comical Song; a Roundelay. **1707** *Gloss. Angl. Nova* (1st edn) *Virelay*, a light Song. *Spen.* **1721** BAILEY *An Univ. Etymolog. Engl. Dict.* (1st edn) *Virelay*, a sort of Comical Song, a Roundelay. *F. Spencer.* **1726** BAILEY *An Univ. Etymolog. Engl. Dict.* (3rd edn) *Verilayes*, a Roundelay, a rustick Song or Dance. *Chaucer.*

virginals *see* clavecymbal, clavicembalo, clavier, entata, manichord, spinet
1656 BLOUNT (1st edn) *Virginal (Virginalis)* Maidenly, Virgin-like; hence the name of that Musical Instrument, called *Virginals*, because Maids and *Virgins* do most commonly play on them. **1658** PHILLIPS (1st edn) *Virginalls*, a certain musical Instrument commonly known. **1671** PHILLIPS (3rd edn) *Virginals*, a certain Musicall Instrument commonly known, and played on after the manner of the Organ, and the Harpsicon. **1676** COLES *Virginals*, a Maidenly Instrument, with keys as the Organ and Harpsicon. **1678** PHILLIPS (4th edn) *Virginals, (Lat. Clavicymbalum)* a common, but noble sort of Musical Instrument, toucht in like manner as the Organ or Harpsichord, and probably so call'd, as having been thought a proper Instrument for Virgins to play on. **1702** KERSEY *New Engl. Dict.* (1st edn) A pair of *Virginals* a sort of Musical Instrument. **1704** *Cocker's Engl. Dict.* (1st edn) *Virginals*, a Musical Instrument for Women to play upon, with key[s] like an Harpsicon or Organ. **1706** KERSEY-PHILLIPS (6th edn) *Virginals*, a noble sort of Musical Instrument, touch'd after the same manner as the Organ and Harpsichord, and probably so call'd as having been counted a proper Instrument for Virgins to play on. **1708** KERSEY *Dict. Anglo-Brit.* (1st edn) *Virginals*, a noble sort of Musical Instrument touch'd after the same manner as the Instrument for Virgins to play on **1721** BAILEY *An Univ. Etymolog. Engl. Dict.* (1st edn) *Virginals*, (*Virginale, L.* probably so call'd, because a fit Instrument for Virgins to play upon) a Musical Instrument, touch'd after the same manner as the *Harpsichord* and *Organ*. **1735** DEFOE *Virginal*, a Musical Instrument touched like a *Harpsichord*. **1737** DYCHE-PARDON (2nd edn) *Virginals* (S.) a Musical Instrument with Keys like a Harpsichord, now quite out of Use.

virtuosa
c.1668-71 *Mary Burwell's Instruction Bk. for Lute* (*TDa* p. 45) The most part of your excellent masters are tetchy and humoursome; that makes them to be the more courted, as cruelty in a handsome woman inflames the hearts of lovers. But you must be an excellent man to take that privilege. Any ordinary master must have other ways to make himself

esteemed. He ought not to play in a debauched company, and himself must be moderate. Therefore the Italians call a person that have some good quality *virtuosus* or *virtuosa*, grounded upon the sentence of scripture that knowledge doth not enter into a wicked soul; ...

vistamente *see* presto
1724 [PEPUSCH] *Short Explic. of Foreign Words in Mus. Bks.* (p. 90) *Vistamente*, or *Visto*, much the same as *Presto.* **1726** BAILEY *An Univ. Etymolog. Engl. Dict.* (3rd edn) *Vistament* (in *Musick Books*) signifies very fast or quick, much the same as *Presto. Ital. Visto* (in *Musick Books*) the same as *Vistamente. Ital.*

vite *see* presto
1724 [PEPUSCH] *Short Explic. of Foreign Words in Mus. Bks.* (p. 90) *Vite*, Quick or Lively, much the same as *Presto.* **1726** BAILEY *An Univ. Etymolog. Engl. Dict.* (3rd edn) *Vite* (in *Musick Books*) signifies quick and lively, much the same as *Presto. Ital.*

1731 PRELLEUR *Modern Musick-Master* (Dictionary, p. 4) *Vite Vistamente*, or *Visto*, Fast or Quick.

vitula
1500 *Ortus Vocabulorum* L→E Vitula le. est instrumentum musicum vel dea leticie vel victorie. a fedyll f.p. **1552** HULOET L→E *Vitula* Kytte or fiddle. *Vitula. æ.* Ffidle.

vivace *see* allegro
1724 [PEPUSCH] *Short Explic. of Foreign Words in Mus. Bks.* (p. 90) *Vivace*, is as much as to say with Life and Spirit. By this Word is commonly understood a Degree of Movement between *Largo* and *Allegro*, but more inclining to the latter than the former. (p. 95) *Vivace*, with some Life or Spirit. § (p. 95) *Piu Vivace*, Lively. **1726** BAILEY *An Univ. Etymolog. Engl. Dict.* (3rd edn) *Vivace* (in *Musick Books*) signifies with Life and Spirit, and by it is commonly understood a Degree of Movement between *Largo* and *Allegro*; but more inclining to the latter than the former. *Ital.* **1737** DYCHE-PARDON (2nd edn) *Vivace* (A.) a Term in Musick, that directs the Strain or Air to be played with a moderate Swiftness and great Sprightliness of Stroke or Tone, by striking the Bow smartly cross the Strings, &c.

1683 PURCELL *Sonnata's of III Parts* (*To the Reader*) ... It remains only that the English Practitioner be enform'd, that he will find a few terms of Art perhaps unusual to him, the chief of which are these following: ... *Allegro*, and *Vivace*, a very brisk, swift, or fast movement: ... **1731** PRELLEUR *Modern Musick-Master* (Dictionary, p. 4) *Vivace*, with Life, and Spirit.

vivacemente *see* allegro
1724 [PEPUSCH] *Short Explic. of Foreign Words in Mus. Bks.* (p. 91) *Vivacemente*, or *Vivamente*, the same as *Vivace.* **1726** BAILEY *An Univ. Etymolog. Engl. Dict.* (3rd edn) *Vivacemente, Vivamente*, the same as *Vivace. Ital.*

1731 PRELLEUR *Modern Musick-Master* (Dictionary, p. 4) *Vivacemente* or *Vivamente*. much the same as *Vivace*.

vivacissimo
1724 [PEPUSCH] *Short Explic. of Foreign Words in Mus. Bks.* (p. 91) *Vivacissimo*, is a Degree or Two Quicker than *Vivace*, and may be look'd upon to signify a Movement near as Quick as *Allegro*. **1726** BAILEY *An Univ. Etymolog. Engl. Dict.* (3rd edn) *Vivacissimo* (in *Musick Books*) denotes a Degree or 2 quicker than *Vivace*, and may be taken as signifying a Movement near as quick as *Allegro. Ital.*

1736 TANS'UR *Compleat Melody* (3rd edn, p. 66) *Vivacissimo*, (Ital.) signifies one Degree quicker than *Allegro*; and more sprightly.

vivola *see* viola, viola da gamba
1550 THOMAS It→E *Viuola*, a viall. **1598** FLORIO It→E *Viuola*, ... Also a violine. **1611** FLORIO It→E *Viuola*, an instrument of musicke called a violl, or violin. *Viuuola*, a violin or violl. **1659** TORRIANO-FLORIO It→E *Vivola*, a viol or violin instrument

vocal
1538 ELYOT L→E *Vocalitas*, a tune or sounde of a voyce. **1565** COOPER L→E *Vocálitas, pen. corr. vocalitâtis, fœ. g. quam Græci euphoniam vocant. Quintil.* A tune or sounde of a voyce. § *Sonum vocis.* To apply the tune of his voyce. *Vox mutandis ingeniosa sonis. Ouid.* A very tunable voyce. **1587** THOMAS L→E *Vocalitas, atis, f.g. Quin.* A tune or sound of a voice. **1589** RIDER L→E *Vocalis, ad.* Wel tuned. **1593** HOLLYBAND Fr→E § *Allier la voix avec la corde*, to ioyne the voice with the string of the instrument, that is, to sing and play together.

1598 FLORIO It→E *Vocalita,* a tune, a sound, a voice, a calling. **1611** COTGRAVE Fr→E *Vocal: m. ale: f.* Vocall ... also, well-tuned, that maketh a distinct sound; *Voix: f.* A voyce; a sound, noise, tune, word, crie; **1611** FLORIO It→E *Vocalita,* ... a tune, a sound of a voice. **1623** COCKERAM *Vocalitie.* the Sound of a voyce or tune *Vocalitie.* The tune or sound of the voice. **1656** BLOUNT *Vocality (vocalitas)* a tune or sound of a voyce. **1659** TORRIANO-FLORIO It→E *Vocalita,* ... a tuning, a sounding the voice. **1696** PHILLIPS (5th edn) *Vocal Music,* perform'd by Voices.**1704** *Cocker's Engl. Dict.* (1st edn) *Vocal,* pertaining to singing. **1724** [PEPUSCH] *Short Explic. of Foreign Words in Mus. Bks.* (p. 92) *Vocale,* Vocale, Vocal, Musick for Voices is so called. **1726** BAILEY *An Univ. Etymolog. Engl. Dict.* (3rd edn) *Vocale, i.e.* Vocal, Musick for Voices. *Ital.* **1728** CHAMBERS *Vocal Music,* is Music set to Words, especially Verses; and to be perform'd with the Voice. In contra-distinction to *Instrumental Music,* composed only for Instruments, without Singing. See *Music.* ¶ Poetry then makes a necessary Part of *Vocal Musick;* and this appears to have been the chief, if not the only Practice of the Antients, from the Definitions which they gave us of Music. See *Harmony, &c.* ¶ Their *Vocal Music* seems to have had some Advantage over ours, in that the *Greek* and *Latin* Languages were better contrived to please the Ear than the modern ones.—In effect, *Vossius* taxes all the later Languages as unfit for Music, and says, 'We shall never have any good *Vocal Music* till our Poets learn to make Verses on the Model of the Antients,' *i.e.* till the antient metrical Feet and Quantities are restored. See *Verse,* and *Quantity.* ¶ But it is to be observ'd, that the *Rythmus* of their *Vocal Music,* was only that of their Poetry; and had no other Forms and Mutations than what the metrical Art afforded. See *Mutation.* ¶ Their Changes were no other than from one kind of *Metrum* or Verse, to another; as from *Iambic,* to *Choraic.* See *Measure,* and *Rythmus.* ¶ Their *Vocal Musick,* then, consisted of Verses set to musical Tunes, and sung by one or more Voices, in Chorus, or alternately; sometimes with, and sometimes without the Accompanyments of Instruments. See *Symphony.* ¶ For Instrumental Musick, in the manner we have defin'd it, 'tis not very clear they ever had any. See *Synaulia, &c.* **1730** BAILEY *Dict. Britannicum* (1st edn) § *Vocal Musick,* that Musick which is performed by the Voice only, Singing.

voce *see* increspare la voce, messe di voce, metter' in voce

1598 FLORIO It→E *Voce,* ... a crying, a tune, a saying **1611** FLORIO It→E *Voce,* ... a report, a tune, a saying. § *Porre in uoce,* to publish or set a song. **1659** TORRIANO-FLORIO It→E *Voce,* ... also a word, a tune, a report § *Scorgere la voce,* to distinguish or govern ones voice in singing. **1724** [PEPUSCH] *Short Explic. of Foreign Words in Mus. Bks.* (p. 92) *Voce* in general is a Noise or Sound, but more particularly in Musick it signifies a Humane Voice. Thus, ¶ *Voce Solo,* is for a Single Voice. **1726** BAILEY *An Univ. Etymolog. Engl. Dict.* (3rd edn) *Voce* in General, signifies a Noise or Sound; but in Musick it more particularly signifies a human Voice; as, *voce solo,* a single Voice. *Ital.*

1736 TANS'UR *Compleat Melody* (3rd edn, p. 72) *Voce Solo,* (Ital.) signifies a single Voice.

vocis mollitudo

1565 COOPER L→E *Vocis mollitudo. Author ad Heren.* The tunehablenesse [sic] of the voyce. **1587** THOMAS L→E *Vocis Mollitudo, ad Heren.* The tuneablenes of the voice.

voice

1688 MIEGE-COTGRAVE Fr→E *Voix,* (f.) Voice ... Note, a Musical Note. § *Les Sept Voix de Musique,* the Seven Musical Notes. *Musique de Voix & d'Instrumens,* Vocal, and Instrumental Musick. **1696** PHILLIPS (5th edn) A *Voice,* ... Also of those that sing, we say, such a one has a Charming Voice. **1728** CHAMBERS *Voice* ... [*see* Appendix]

1609 DOWLAND-ORNITHOPARCUS *Micrologvs* (pp. 5-6) *Of Voyces.* ¶ *Concord,* (which rules all the Harmony of Musicke) cannot be without a *Voyce,* nor a *Voyce* without a *Sound,* saith *Boêtius, lib.* 1. *cap.* 3. Wherefore in seeking out the description of a *Voyce,* we thought fit to search out this point, what *Sounds* are properly called *Voyces.* Note therefore, that the sound of a sensible creature is properly called a *Voyce,* for things without sence haue no *Voyce,* as *Cœlius* writes, *antiquar. lect. lib.* 10. *cap.* 53. When we cals pipes *Vocal,* it is a translated word, and a *Catachresis.* Neither haue al sensible cretures a *Voice*: for those which want blood, vtter no *Voice.* Neither do fishes vtter any *Voyce,* because a *Voyce* is the motion of the ayre, but they receiue no ayre. Wherefore onely a sensible creature doth vtter a *Voyce,* yet not all sensible creatures, nor with euery part of their bodies (for the hands being stroken together make a clapping, not a *Voyce.*) A *Voyce* therefore is a sound vttered from the mouth of a perfect creature, either by aduise, or signification. By aduise, (I say) because of the coffe, which is no *Voyce*: By signification, because of the grinding of the teeth. But because this description of a *Voyce*, doth agree onely to a liuely *Voyce*, and not to a deafe musicall *Voyce*, which especially, being a sole syllable is deafe, vnlesse it be actually expressed, we must find out another description more agreeable to it. Therefore a musicall *Voyce*, is a certaine syllable expressing a tenor of the Notes.

voix *see* port de voix

volta *see* dance, lavolta, ruotata, torlo, zurlo
1598 FLORIO It→E *Volta*, ... Also a dance called a *Volta*. **1611** FLORIO It→E *Volta*, a turne ... Also a kind of turning french dance called a *Volta*. **1656** BLOUNT (1st edn) *Volta* or *Lavolta* (Ital.) ... Also a turning dance so called. *Florio*. **1658** PHILLIPS (1st edn) *Volta*, (Ital.) a course, or turn in riding or in dancing. **1659** TORRIANO-FLORIO It→E **Volta*, ... also a French dance so called, as standing much on turnings **1676** COLES *Volta, Lav., Italian*. a course or turn (in riding, dancing, &c.[)] **1704** *Cocker's Engl. Dict.* (1st edn) *Volta*, a dance or turn in Musick in Italy;

1597 MORLEY *Plaine and Easie Introdvction* (p. 181) [marginalia: '*Voltes courantes*.'] Like vnto this [the bransle] (but more light) be the *voltes* and *courantes* which being both of a measure, ar notwithstanding daunced after sundrie fashions, the *volte* rising and leaping, the *courante* trauising and running, in which measure also our countrey daunce is made, though it be daunced after another forme then any of the former. All these be made in straines, either two or three as shall seeme best to the maker, but the *courant* hath twice so much in a straine, as the English country daunce.

volta-faccia
1598 FLORIO It→E *Volta faccia*, a kind of march sounded in time of war when they should retreat. **1611** FLORIO It→E *Voltafaccia*, a kind of march sounded in time of war as a warning to retreate. **1659** TORRIANO-FLORIO It→E *Volta-faccia*, a march sounded in time of warre, as a warning to retreat.

volti *see* subito, verte, vs
1724 [PEPUSCH] *Short Explic. of Foreign Words in Mus. Bks.* (pp. 92-3) *Volti*, or *Volta*, or *Voltare*, is to Turn, or Turn over. This Word is often met with at the Bottom of the Leaf on the right Hand Side in Musick Books, when the Sonata or Piece of Musick is not ended, to signify that there still remains more on the other Side [of] the Leaf, and therefore it must be turned over. When it happens that the Leaf must turn over in the Middle of a Strain there is the Word *Subito*, or the Letter *S* joyned with it; for which see the Word *Subito*. § (p. 93) *Volti Presto*, is the same as *Volti Subito*. *Volti se Piace*, Turn over if you please. **1726** BAILEY *An Univ. Etymolog. Engl. Dict.* (3rd edn) *Volta, Volti, Voltare*, (in *Musick Books*) signifies to *turn or turn over*, and is frequently met with at the bottom of a Leaf, on the right Hand Side, when the Sonata or Piece of Musick is not ended, to signify, that there still remains more on the other Side of the Leaf, and therefore it must be turned over. § *Volti Presto*, signifies the same, as *volti subito*. *Ital.* *Volti si place* [sic], is turn over if you please. *Ital.* *Volti Subito*, is turn over quick, and is used when it happens that the Leaf must be turn'd over in the middle of a Strain. *It.* **1730** BAILEY *Dict. Britannicum* (1st edn) *Volti si place* [sic], *i.e.* turn over if you please, *Ital.*

c.1710 ANON. *Preceptor for Improved Octave Flageolet* ('Explanation of Words', p. 82) *Volti Subito*—Turn quickly **1731** PRELLEUR *Modern Musick-Master* (Dictionary, p. 4) *Volta* or *Volti*, Turnover. ¶ *Volti Subito*, Turnover, Quickly. [sic] or without Loss of Time.

voluntary *see* fantasia, interlude, lesson, prelude, research, ricercar, suit, toccata
1702 KERSEY *New Engl. Dict.* (1st edn) A *Voluntary*, that which a Musician plays extempore. **1706** KERSEY-PHILLIPS (6th edn) A *Voluntary*, a Musician's Play *extempore*, such as comes next to his Fancy. **1707** *Gloss. Angl. Nova* (1st edn) *Voluntary*, ... that which a Musician plays *Extempore*. **1730** BAILEY *Dict. Britannicum* (1st edn) A *Voluntary* (in *Musick*) that which a Musician plays *Extempore*, according to his Fancy, at his beginning to play. **1737** DYCHE-PARDON (2nd edn) *Voluntary* (S.) in *Musick*, is an Overture or Descant made extempore, or Airs plaid without having been wrote down or precomposed.

c.1698-c.1703 NORTH Cursory Notes (*C-K CN* p. 203) ... profest masters have a faculty of expressing a world of variety, with out preparation, which they call voluntary, and is often done with admirable neatness and variety... **c.1710** NORTH (Prendcourt's) Treatise of Continued or thro-base BL Add. 32531, f. 29 [annotation by North:] ... to fill forbear, or adorne, with a just favour, that a thro-base master, & not an ayerist, is but an abcadarian, besides that wch is called voluntary, wch is a ready touching an air, with Ellegance & fullness, nay compleat art, & perfection of Musick (as is Expected) upon Every key, will not be done with out a mastery of Composition. **c.1715-20** NORTH Essay of Musical Ayre BL Add. 32536 (*JWi* p. 136) In short, Voluntary upon an Organ is the consumate office of a musitian. It is air, melody, harmony, humour imitation, and what not; ... **1736** TANS'UR *Compleat Melody* (3rd edn, preface) I cannot omit speaking in the *praise* of that most Heavenly and Laudable Custom perform'd on the *Organ*, just before the *first Lesson*, (which Piece of *Harmony* is commonly called a *Voluntary;*) by which we are supposed to be prepared for the Admission of those *Divine Truths* we are going to receive; ... § (p. 71) A *Voluntary*, is an Extempore Air, *Prelude*, *Interlude*, or *Symphony*; play'd either before, or in the middle, or at the End of a Piece of *Musick*, to ornament, or grace it; most respective to the *Organ*, *Harpsicord*, &c.

VS

1724 [PEPUSCH] *Short Explic. of Foreign Words in Mus. Bks.* (p. 84) The Letters *VS* at the Bottom of a Leaf are often used as an Abbreviation of the Words *Volti Subito*; for which see those Words.

waits *see* aula, auleta, empneusta (under entata), hobois, minstrel, regal, sarbataine, spondiale

1702 KERSEY *New Engl. Dict.* (1st edn) The *Waits*, a sort of musical instrument. **1706** KERSEY-PHILLIPS (6th edn) *Waits*, a sort of Wind-Musick. **1721** BAILEY *An Univ. Etymolog. Engl. Dict.* (1st edn) *Waits*, (either of *Waiting*, because they attend on Magistrates, Officers, *&c.* in Pomps and Processions; or of *Guet*, a Watch, of *Guetter*, to Watch, *F.* because they keep a sort of Watch a[t] Nights) a sort of Wind Musick. **1730** BAILEY *Dict. Britannicum* (1st edn) *Waites* (prob. q. *guettas* of *guetter*, F. to watch, or of *waiting* on Magistrates at Pomps and Processions) a sort of Musick or Musicians. **1735** DEFOE *Waits*, a sort of Musick, or Musicians who play in the Night. **1737** DYCHE-PARDON (2nd edn) *Waites* (S.) in *corporate Towns*, are a Set of Musicians that attend upon the Mayor, &c. at publick Processions, Feasts, &c. **1740** BAILEY *An Univ. Etymolog. Engl. Dict.* (9th edn) *Waits*, ... a sort of Musick, or Musicians.

c.1715-20 NORTH Essay of Musical Ayre BL Add. 32536, f. 6v History of Musick dark, the wind Instrument^s^ oldest or first in use, especially in cathedralls & monasterys, from going abroad, called Minstrells, & weights quasi wakes; Instruments taken up by Comon Musitians; ... § f. 65v [*re* the history of music in England] ... out of the minstrelsie our Night Musick In ye streets, called the weights, or rather wakes, are derived of viols, violins and all other Instruments of touch, as well as wind, enough is found in Mersennus; ... **1728** NORTH Musicall Grammarian (*C-K MG* f. 128v) [*re* English music from Henry VIII to James I] ... And as for corporation and mercenary musick, it was cheifly flatile; and the professors, from going about the streets in a morning, to wake folks, were, and are yet, called waits, quasi wakes.

warble *see* accent, chant, chanter, fredon, frequentamentum, gazouiller, gorgheggiare, gringoter, modulation, passage, quiver, tirelirer, tremante, tremola, trill, vibrante, vibrissation¡

1676 COLES *Warble*, to quaver (in singing[)]. **1702** KERSEY *New Engl. Dict.* (1st edn) To *Warble*, trill, *or* quaver in singing. **1704** *Cocker's Engl. Dict.* (1st edn) *Warble*, to quaver or shake in singing. **1706** KERSEY-PHILLIPS (6th edn) To *Warble*, to Chirp, Sing or Chatter, as a Bird does; to Sing in a trilling or quavering Way; to gargle or purl **1707** *Gloss. Angl. Nova* (1st edn) *Warble*, to sing as a Bird; to sing in a quavering way; **1708** KERSEY *Dict. Anglo-Brit.* (1st edn) To *Warble*, ... to Sing in a trilling or quavering Way; **1737** DYCHE-PARDON (2nd edn) *Warble* (V.) to sing in a melodious, ornamental, trilling Manner, like a Canary-Bird, &c.

ward-corn

1706 KERSEY-PHILLIPS (6th edn) *Ward-Corn*, a Duty heretofore enjoyned of keeping Watch and Ward with a Horn, to blow upon any occasion of Surprize. **1708** KERSEY *Dict. Anglo-Brit.* (1st edn) *Ward-Corn*, a Duty heretofore enjoyned of keeping Watch and Ward with a Horn, to blow upon any occasion of Surprize. **1721** BAILEY *An Univ. Etymolog. Engl. Dict.* (1st edn) *Ward Corn*, (of Ward and *Cornu*, *L.* a Horn) was a Duty anciently enjoyned on Tenants to

Guard a Castle by keeping Watch and Ward, with an Horn to blow on a sudden surprize. **1728** CHAMBERS *Wardecorne*, among our antient Writers, a Duty incumbent on the Tenants, to guard the Castle, by sounding a Horn upon the approach of an Enemy; call'd also *Cornage*. See *Cornage*. **1730** BAILEY *Dict. Britannicum* (1st edn) *Wardecord* [sic] (of þeaꞃδ, *Sax.* and *cornu*, L. an Horn) an antient Duty of watching and warding at a Castle, and blowing an Horn upon a Surprize; called *Cornage*.

wassaile
1704 *Cocker's Engl. Dict.* (1st edn) *Wassail bowl*, of spiced Ale, carried about at *Christmas*, with singing, to get money **1728** CHAMBERS *Wassaile*, or *Wassel*, a Festival Song, sung heretofore from door to door, about the Time of *Epiphany*.

watch-work *see* chime
1704 HARRIS *Watch-work* ... [*see* Appendix]

wavee *see* arcata, wrist shake
c.1726 NORTH Musicall Gramarian BL Add. 32533, f. 111v That w[ch] I have called the wavee, hath bin Intimated before, when I observed the philomelian tone, beginning as it were from nothing and swelling, and coming to y[e] ackme beginns to wave, & so more strong, as If a bow of a tree waved in ye Wind, not stopping the tone at all, and so dying with the sound into, (quasi,) Nothing again ...

wega
1696 PHILLIPS (5th edn) *Wega*, the shining harp.

whiffle
1730 BAILEY *Dict. Britannicum* (1st edn) To *Whiffle* (prob. of þæꞅan, *Sax.* to babble, or *weyfelen*, *Du.* to ramble or fluctuate) to play on a Pipe; **1737** DYCHE-PARDON (2nd edn) *Whiffle* (V.) to pipe or play upon a musical Wind Instrument;

whiffler
1706 KERSEY-PHILLIPS (6th edn) *Whiffler* is also taken for a Piper that plays on a Fife in a Company of Foot-Soldiers: **1708** KERSEY *Dict. Anglo-Brit.* (1st edn) *Whiffler*, a Piper that plays on a Fife in a Company of Foot-Soldiers: Also a young Freeman, that goes before and waits upon the Company to which he belongs, on some Publick Solemnity. **1730** BAILEY *Dict. Britannicum* (1st edn) *Whiffler* (þæꞅleꞃ, *Sax.*) one that plays on a Whiffle or Fife; a young Freeman that goes before the Companies of *London* on publick Processions. **1737** DYCHE-PARDON (2nd edn) *Whiffler* (S.) ... sometimes a Piper;

whistle *see* calamus, cifello, cimbello, fistula, gazouiller, sampogna, sibbio, stifello, suffolo
1721 BAILEY *An Univ. Etymolog. Engl. Dict.* (1st edn) To *Whistle*, ... to make Musical Sounds with the Lips and Breath without any Vocal Sounds. **1730** BAILEY *Dict. Britannicum* (1st edn) A Whistle (hþiꞅꞇle, Sax.) a sort of musical Pipe. To *Whistle* (of hþiꞅꞇan, *Sax.*) to play Tunes with the Lips and Breath, a sort of singing without speaking. **1737** DYCHE-PARDON (2nd edn) *Whistle* (S.) a small musical Pipe; also a Tune played by the Breath and Lips of any Person. *Whistle* (V.) to play Tunes with the Lips, and natural Breath, as tho' it were upon a musical Instrument.

whole-fall *see* backfall, forefall, half-fall
1676 MACE *Musick's Monument* (pp. 105-6) The *Whole-fall*, is a *Grace*, much out of use, in *These our Days*; yet because, in some Cases it is very *Good*, and *Handsome*, and may give *Delight*, and *Content* to many, who think fit to use it; know, it is *Thus Performed; viz.* It gives *Two False Letters*, before the *True intended Letter* comes in.... This is sufficient to Explain the *Whole-fall; Only Note*, That you always fall it, *through the proper Ayre-Notes of the Key*, (which to a *Musical Ear*, is *Naturally known*.)

whole note
1698 WALLIS *Letter to Samuel Pepys* (*Philos. Trans.*, 1698, p. 250) [*re* the Aristoxenians and Pythagoreans] ... the *Difference* of those two (of a Fourth and Fifth) they agreed to call a *Tone*; which we now call a *Whole note*.

whole time *see* common time, master note, semibreve time
1728 NORTH Musicall Grammarian (*C-K MG* f. 32) ... And there is a gage whereby the performers may know whither accounts of their devisions fall right or not, and these signalls allwais conclude an equall duration as prescribed; which is called an whole time, and in the notation is marked out by a line struck cross the scale, and that is called barr, and in comon time is noted by a 𝅝.

wind
1702 KERSEY *New Engl. Dict.* (1st edn) To *wind, or* blow a horn. **1728** CHAMBERS *Wind-Instruments,* in Music, are Instruments play'd by the *Wind,* chiefly the Breath; in contradistinction to String-Instruments, and Instruments of the pulsatile Sound. See *Music.* ¶ The *Wind-Instruments* known to the Antients, were the *Tibia, Fistula, Syringa* of *Pan,* consisting of seven Reeds join'd side-wise; *Organs, Tubæ, Cornua,* and *Lituus*: See *Tibia, Fistula, &c.* each under the proper Article. ¶ Those of the Moderns, are the *Flute, Bagpipe, Hautboy, Trumpet, &c.* See *Flute, Bagpipe, &c.*

wrest *see* galletto
1706 KERSEY-PHILLIPS (6th edn) *Wrest,* a sort of Bow to tune Musical Instruments with. **1730** BAILEY *Dict. Britannicum* (1st edn) A *Wrest,* a sort of Bow to Tune Musical Instruments with.

wrist shake *see* shake, wavee
c.1710 NORTH (draft for) Musicall Grammarian BL Add. 32537 (*JWi* p. 165) I must take notice of a wrist shake, as they call it, upon the violin, which without doubdt is a great art, but as I think injured by overdoing; for those who use it well never let a note rest without it, whereas it ought to be used as the swelling wavee, coming and going, which would have a much better effect. **c.1715-20** NORTH Essay of Musical Ayre BL Add. 32536, f. 38v ... And the late Invention, they Call a wrist-shake, Is Intended to that End, us$^{t.}$ that y^{e} sound may waive, but not stopp, or vary its tone, for all Interruption of y^{e} Sound where it ought to be heard is a fault; ...

Xenophilus
1565 COOPER L→E *Xenophilus,* A musician of Chalcis, whiche lyued 107. yeres in great felicitie and quietnesse. **1678** PHILLIPS (4th edn) *Xenophilus,* a Musician of *Chalcidia,* whom *Aristoxenus* affirms to have liv'd 105 years in very great honour and worldly felicity; he is also mentioned by *Pliny,* and *Valerius Maximus.*

Z

Zacconi, Lodovico *see* tune

zaino
1598 FLORIO It→E *Zaino,* ... Also a certaine musicall instrument that shepheards vse, as a horne pipe. **1611** FLORIO It→E *Zaino,* a little leather budget or Palmers scrip. Also a certaine musicall instrument that sheapheards vse as an horne pipe or bagpipe. **1659** TORRIANO-FLORIO It→E *Zaino,* any little leather budget, a shepheards or Palmers Scrip, also a certain musical instrument, that shepheards use, as an Horn-pipe, or Bag-pipe

zamara *see* çamarro
1598 FLORIO It→E *Zamara, zamarra,* ... Also a kind of musical instrument with strings. **1611** FLORIO It→E *Zamara,* ... a sheapheards frock, an Irish mantle. Also a kind of musical instrument with strings. **1659** TORRIANO-FLORIO It→E *Zamarra, Zamara, Zamarotto,* ... a Seamans or shepheards frock, also a kind of musical instrument with strings.

zampogna *see* sampogna

zarabanda *see* saraband

zaramella *see* ceramella, ciaramella
1598 FLORIO It→E *Zaramella,* a kinde of countrey fiddle, croud or bag-pipe, that boyes make of reedes. **1611** FLORIO It→E *Zaramella,* as *Ciaramella. Zaramellare,* as *Ciaramellare.*

Zarlino, Gioseffo *see* chromatic, composition, concord, interval, seventh, tune, unison

zigia
1538 ELYOT L→E *Zygia,* a pype, wherin menne dyd playe at weddynges. **1565** COOPER L→E *Zygia.* A pipe whereon men played at weddinges. **1587** THOMAS L→E *Zygia, æ, f.g. p.b. Plin.* A kinde of maple as some thinke: *also* a pipe whereon men

plaied at weddings. **1589** RIDER L→E *Zygia, f.* A pipe whereon men plaied at weddings. **1611** FLORIO It→E *Zigia,* a kinde of Maple-tree. Also a kind of pipe in ancient times vsed to play on at weddings. **1659** TORRIANO-FLORIO It→E *Ziglia,* ... also a kind of pipe in auncient times used to play on at weddings. **1688** DAVIS-TORRIANO-FLORIO It→E *Zigia,* ... also a kind of pipe in ancient times to play on at weddings.

zimbello *see* cimbello
1598 FLORIO It→E *Zimbello,* a kinde of crowde or fiddle. **1611** FLORIO It→E *Zimbello,* ... Also a bagge full of bran, sawdust or grauell, bound to a cord, with which children in Italy at Shrouetide goe about and strike at poore Country people. Also a kinde of musicall instrument, Croud or fiddle. **1659** TORRIANO-FLORIO It→E *Zimbello,* ... also a long little bag full bran, saw-dust, or gravell, bound to a cord, with which Children in *Italy* at Shrove-tide go about, and strike at poor Country people, also a kind of musicall countrey instrument, Croud or Fiddle

zimri
1676 COLES *Zimri, Hebrew.* a Song. **1696** PHILLIPS (5th edn) *Zimri, (Heb. a Song or Singing,)* an Usurper of the Kingdom of *Israel,* having first slain his Master *Elah* the Son of *Baashah.*

zuffoletto, zuffolino
1598 FLORIO It→E *Zuffolini,* little whistles or pipes. **1611** FLORIO It→E *Zuffoletto,* any little whistle. *Zuffolino,* any little whistle. **1659** TORRIANO-FLORIO It→E *Zuffoletto, Zuffolino,* a little whistle.

zuffolo *see* cifello, suffolo
1598 FLORIO It→E *Zuffo,* a whistle, a pipe, a flute, or fife. *Zuffolare,* to whistle, to pipe, to fife. *Zuffolatore,* a whistler, a piper, a fifer. *Zuffolo,* as *Zuffo.* **1611** FLORIO It→E *Zuffo,* any kind of whistle or pipe. *Zuffolare,* to whistle or pipe. *Zuffolata,* any kind of whistling. *Zuffolatore,* a whistler, a piper. *Zuffolo,* any whistle or pipe. **1659** TORRIANO-FLORIO It→E *Zuffolare,* to whistle, to pipe. *Zuffolata,* any whistling or piping. *Zuffolatore,* a whistler, a piper. *Zuffolo,* any whistle or pipe. **Zuffolone, Zuffolotto,* a great whistle. *Zuffurare,* ... also to whistle. **1688** DAVIS-TORRIANO-FLORIO It→E **Zuffolata,* any whistling or piping. **1724** [PEPUSCH] *Short Explic. of Foreign Words in Mus. Bks.* (p. 94) *Zufolo,* a Bird Pipe, or Small Flagelet. **1726** BAILEY *An Univ. Etymolog. Engl. Dict.* (3rd edn) *Zutolo* [sic], a Bird-pipe or small Flagelet. *Ital.*
1731 PRELLEUR *Modern Musick-Master* (Dictionary, p. 4) *Zufolo* or *Zuffolo* or *Suffolo* a little Flute, or Flageolet.

zurlo *see* ruotata, torlo, volta
1598 FLORIO It→E *Zurlo,* a round turning tricke in dancing. **1611** FLORIO It→E *Zurlo,* any kind of top ... Also a round or turning trick in dansing. **1659** TORRIANO-FLORIO It→E *Zurlo,* a twirl ... also a round trick, or turning on the toes in dancing

zygia *see* zigia

Appendix

Reproduced in this Appendix are longer encyclopedic articles from Chambers (1728) and Harris (1704). Each is cross-referenced in its relevant place in the Dictionary.

Contents

Articles from Chambers' *Cyclopedia*, 1728:

Article from Harris' *Lexicon Technicum*, 1704:

bell

1728 Chambers *Bell,* a popular Machine, rank'd by Musicians among the number of Musical Instruments *of Percussion.* Its Form needs no Description; its Parts are the *Body,* or *Barrel,* and *Clapper* with-in-side, and the *Ear* or *Cannon,* whereby it is hung to a large Beam of Wood; its Matter is a Metal compounded of twenty Pounds of Pewter to an hundred of Copper, call'd *Bell-Metal.* The thickness of its Edges is usually $\frac{1}{15}$ of the Diameter, and its Height twelve times its Thickness. The *Bell-Founders* have a *Diapason,* or *Bell-Scale,* wherewith they measure the Size, Thickness, Weight, and Tone of their *Bells.* The Uses of *Bells* are summ'd up in the *Latin* Distich:

Laudo Deum verum, Plebem voco, congrego Clerum,
Defunctos ploro, Pestem fugo, Festa decoro.

For the *Method of Casting Bells, &c.* see *Foundery* [entry not reproduced]. Mr *Hauksbee* and others, find by Experiment, the Sound of a *Bell* struck under Water, to be a fourth deeper than in the Air: But *Mersenne* says, 'tis of the same Pitch in either Element. *Bells* are observ'd to be heard further, placed on Plains, than on Hills; and still further in Vallies, than on Plains: the Reason of which is not difficult to assign, if it be considered, that the higher the sonorous Body is, the rarer is its Medium; consequently, the less Impulse it receives, and the less proper Vehicle it is to convey it to a Distance.

The first *Bells* are said to have been made at *Nola,* in *Campania,* whereof St. *Paulinus* was Bishop; at least, 'tis said, he was the first who brought 'em into the Church. And hence, 'tis added, they had their *Latin* Names, *Nolæ* and *Campanæ*: But others say, they take these Names, not from their being invented in *Campania,* but because 'twas here the manner of hanging and balancing of 'em, now in Use, was first practis'd; at least, that they were ballanced and hung on the Model of a Ballance invented or used in *Campania.* For, in *Latin* Writers we find *Campana Statera,* for a *Counter-poise,* and in *Greek* καμπανίξειν, for *ponderare,* to load or weigh. *Polydore Virgil* ascribes the Invention of *Bells* to Pope *Sabinian,* St. *Gregory*'s Successor; but by Mistake; for St. *Jerome,* Cotemporary [sic] with *Paulinus,* makes mention of a *Bell.* In effect, Pope *Sabinian* did not invent *Bells;* but he was the first who appointed the Canonical Hours to be distinguish'd by 'em. We even find mention made of *Bells* in *Ovid, Tibullus, Martial, Statius,* and *Manilius,* and the *Greek* Authors, under the Titles of *Tintinnabula,* and *Sounding Brass. Suetonius, Dion, Strabo, Polybius, Josephus,* and others, mention 'em under the Names of *Petasus, Tintinnabulum, Æramentum, Crotalum, Signum,* &c. But these appear to have been little else but Baubles, and little like the huge Bells in use among us.

Hieronymus Magius, who has a Treatise express on *Bells,* (wrote, when in Chains, in *Turkey,* and which is accounted very remarkable, purely from his Memory, without the Assistance of any Books) makes large *Bells* a modern Invention. Indeed, we don't hear of any before the sixth Century: In 610, we are told, *Loup,* Bishop of *Orleans,* being at *Sens,* then besieg'd by the Army of *Clotharius,* frighted away the Besiegers by ringing the *Bells* of St. *Stephen*'s. The first large *Bells* in *England* are mention'd by *Bede* towards the latter End of that Century. The *Greeks* are commonly said to have been acquainted with 'em till the ninth Century, when their Construction was first taught them by a *Venetian.* Indeed, 'tis not true that the Use of Bells was entirely unknown in the antient *Eastern* Churches, and that they call'd the People to Church, as at present, with wooden Mallets. *Leo Allatius,* in his *Dissertation of the Greek Temples,* proves the contrary from several antient Writers. 'Tis his Opinion, that *Bells* first began to be disused among 'em, after the taking of *Constantinople* by the *Turks*; who, it seems, prohibited 'em, lest their Sounds should disturb the Repose of Souls, which, according to them, wander in the Air. He adds, that they still retain the Use of *Bells* in Places remote from the Commerce of the *Turks*; particularly, very antient ones in Mount *Athos. F. Simon* thinks the *Turks* rather prohibited the *Christians* the Use of *Bells,* out of political, than religious Reasons; inasmuch as the Ringing of *Bells* might serve as a Signal for the Execution of Revolts, *&c*... The City *Bourdeaux* was deprived of its *Bells* for Rebellion; and when 'twas offer'd to have 'em restored, the People refus'd it, after having tasted the Ease and Conveniency of being freed from the constant Din and Jangling of *Bells.*

Matthew Paris observes, that antiently the Use of *Bells* was prohibited in Time of Mourning; tho at present they make one of the principal Ceremonies of Mourning. *Mabillon* adds, that 'twas an antient Custom to ring the *Bells* for Persons about to expire, to advertise the People to pray for 'em; whence our *Passing-Bells. Lobineau* observes, that the Custom of *ringing Bells,* at the Approach of Thunder, is of some Antiquity; but that the Design was not so much to shake the Air, and so dissipate the Thunder, as to call the People to Church, to pray the Parish may be preserved from that terrible Meteor.

The Custom of *baptizing,* or *blessing Bells,* is very antient. Some say 'tis evidently of an older standing; there being an express Prohibition of the Practice in a Capitulary of *John* XIII. *Alcuin* says 'twas establish'd long before Pope *John* XIII. Yet this is only to be understood of an Order of that Pope, for restoring the Practice which had been disused.... *Nankin*, a City of *China*, was antiently famous for the Largeness of its *Bells*; but their enormous Weight having brought down the Steeple, the whole Building fell to Ruin, and the *Bells* have ever since lain on the Ground. One of these *Bells* is near 12 *English* Foot high, the Diameter $7\frac{1}{12}$, and the Circumference 23; its Figure almost Cylindric, except for a Swelling in the middle; and the Thickness of the Metal about the Edges, seven Inches. From the Dimensions of this *Bell*, its Weight is computed at 50000 Pounds, which is more than double the Weight of that of *Erfort*, said by Father *Kircher* to be the greatest *Bell* in the World. These *Bells* were cast by the first Emperor of the preceding Dynasty, about 300 Years ago. They have each their Name, the Hanger *Schoui*, the Eater *Che*, the Sleeper *Choui*, the Will *Fi*. Father *le Compte* adds, that there are seven other *Bells* in *Pekin*, cast in the Reign of *Youlo*, each of which weighs 120000 Pounds. But the Sounds even of their biggest *Bells*, are very poor; being struck with a Wooden in lieu of an Iron Clapper. The *Ægyptians* have none but wooden Clocks, except one brought by the *Franks* into the Monastery of St. *Anthony*.

Bell: The Sound of a Bell consists in a vibratory Motion of the Parts thereof, much like that of a Musical Chord. The Stroke of the Clapper, 'tis evident, must change the Figure of the *Bell*, and of round, make it oval: But the Metal having a great degree of Elasticity, that Part which the Stroke drove furthest from the Centre will fly back again, and that even somewhat nearer to the Centre than before: So that the two Points which before were the Extremes of the longer Diameter, now become those of the shorter. Thus the Circumference of the *Bell* undergoes alternate Changes of Figure, and by means thereof gives that tremulous Motion to the Air wherein Sound consists. See *Sound*.

M. *Perrault* maintains, that the Sound of the same *Bell*, or *Chord*, is a Compound of the Sounds of the several Parts thereof; so that where the Parts are homogenous, and the Dimensions of the Figure uniform, there is such a perfect Mixture of all these Sounds, as constitutes one uniform, smooth, even Sound; and the contrary Circumstances produce Harshness. This he proves from the *Bell*'s differing in Tune according to the Part you strike; and yet strike it any where, there is a Motion of all the Parts. He therefore considers *Bells* as composed of an infinite Number of Rings, which, according to their different Dimensions, have different Tones, as Chords of different Lengths have: And when struck, the Vibrations of the Parts immediately struck, determine the Tone; being supported by a sufficient Number of consonant Tones in other Parts. See *Tune*.

chimes

1728 Chambers *Chimes of a Clock*, a kind of periodical Musick, produc'd at certain Seasons of the Day, by a particular Apparatus added to a *Clock*.... For the placing of these Pins [on the chime-barrel], you may proceed by the way of Changes on Bells, *viz*. 1, 2, 3, 4, *&c*. or rather, make use of the Musical Notes: where it must be observ'd, what is the Compass of the Tune, or how many Notes, or Bells, there are from the highest to the lowest; and accordingly, the Barrel must be divided from end to end.

Thus, in the following Examples, each of those Tunes are eight Notes in compass; and accordingly, the Barrel is divided into eight Parts. These Divisions are struck round the Barrel; opposite to which are the Hammer-Tails.

We speak here as if there was only one Hammer to each Bell, that it may be more clearly apprehended: but when two Notes of the same Sound come together in a Tune, there must be two Hammers to the Bell to strike it: So that if in all the Tunes you intend to *chime* of eight Notes compass, there should happen to be such double Notes on every Bell; instead of eight you must have sixteen Hammers; and accordingly you must divide the Barrel, and strike sixteen Strokes round it, opposite to each Hammer-Tail: Then you are to divide it round about, into as many Divisions as there are Musical Bars, Semibreves, Minims, *&c*. in the Tune.

Thus, the hundredth Psalm-Tune has twenty Semibreves, and each Division of it is a Semibreve: the first Note of it also is a Semibreve; and therefore on the *Chime*-Barrel must be a whole Division, from 5 to 5; as you may understand plainly, if you conceive the Surface of a *Chime*-Barrel to be represented by the following Tables; as if the cylindrical Superficies of the Barrel were stretch'd out at length, or extended on a Plane: and then such a Table, so divided, if it were to be wrapp'd round the Barrel, would shew the Places where all the Pins are to stand in the Barrel: For the Dots running about the Table, are the Places of the Pins that play the Tune.

Indeed, if the *Chimes* are to be compleat, you ought to have a set of Bells to the Gamut Notes; so as that each Bell having the true Sound of *sol, la, mi, fa*, you may play any Tune with its Flats and Sharps; nay, you may by this means play both a Bass and Treble with one Barrel: and by setting the Names of your Bells at the head of any Tune, that Tune may easily be transferr'd to the *Chime*-Barrel, without any Skill in Musick: But it must be observ'd, that each Line in the Musick is three Notes distant; that is, there is a Note between each Line, as well as upon it.

The Notes of the 100 *Psalm.*

A Table for dividing the Chime - *Barrel of the* 100 *Psalm.*

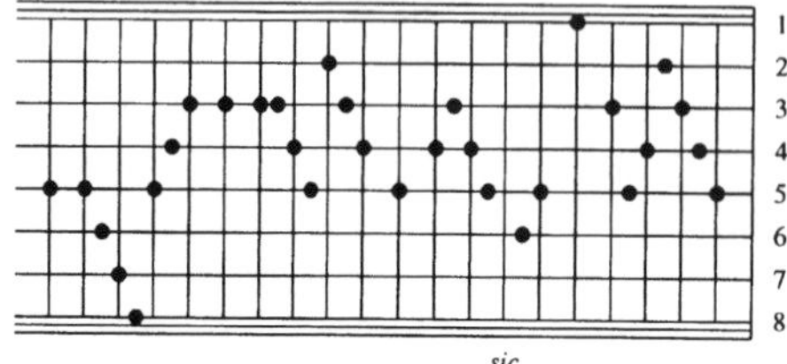

clef

1728 CHAMBERS *Clef, Cliff,* or *Key,* in Musick, a Mark at the Beginning of the Lines of a Song, which shews the Tone, or Key in which the Piece is to begin. Or, it is a Letter mark'd on any Line, which explains and gives the Name to all the rest. See *Key.*

Antiently, every Line had a Letter mark'd for a *Clef*; now a Letter on one Line suffices: since by this all the rest are known; reckoning up or down in the Order of the Letters.

'Tis call'd the *Clef,* or Key, because hereby we know the Names of all the other Lines and Spaces; and consequently the Quantity of every Degree, or Interval.

But because every Note in the Octave is call'd a *Key,* tho in another Sense, this Letter mark'd, is call'd in a particular manner the Sign'd Clef; because being written on any Line, it not only signs and marks that one, but explains all the rest.

By *Clef,* therefore, for distinction-sake, we mean that Letter sign'd on a Line, which explains the rest; and by *Key* the principal Note of a Song, in which the Melody closes.

There are three of these *Sign'd Clefs, c, f, g.* The *Clef* of the highest Part in a Song, call'd *Treble,* or *Alt,* is *g* set on the second Line counting upwards. The *Clef* of the Bass, or the lowest Part, is *f* on the fourth Line upwards: For all the other mean Parts, the *Clef* is *c,* sometimes on one, sometimes on another Line. Indeed, some that are really mean Parts, are sometimes set with the *g Clef.* See *Bass, &c.*

It must, however, be observ'd, that the ordinary Signatures of *Clefs* bear little resemblance to those Letters. Mr. *Malcolm* thinks it would be well if we us'd the Letters themselves. *Kepler* takes a world of Pains, to shew that the common Signatures are only Corruptions of the Letters they represent. See their Figure among the other *Characters of Musick.*

The *Clefs* are always taken Fifths to one another: That is, the *Clef f* is lowest, *c* a Fifth above it, and *g* a Fifth above *c.*

When the Place of the *Clef* is chang'd, which is not frequent in the *mean Clef,* 'tis with Design to make the System comprehend as many Notes of the Song as possible, and so to have the fewer Notes above or below it. If then there be many Lines above the *Clef,* and few below it, this Purpose is answer'd by placing the *Clef* in the first or second Line: If there by many Notes below the *Clef,* 'tis plac'd higher in the System. In effect, according to the Relation of the other Notes to the *Clef* Note, the particular System is taken differently in the Scale; the *Clef* Line making one in all the Variety. See *Scale.*

But still, in whatever Line of the particular System any *Clef* is found, it must be understood to belong to the same of the general System, and to be the same individual Note or Sound in the Scale.

By this constant Relation of *Clefs,* we learn how to compare the several particular Systems of the several Parts; and know how they communicate in the Scale, *i.e.* which Lines are Unison, and which not: for 'tis not to be suppos'd that each Part has certain Bounds, within which another must never come. Some Notes of the Treble, *v.g.* may be lower than some of the mean Parts, or even of the Bass. To put together therefore in one

System all the Parts of a Composition written separately, the Notes of each Part must be plac'd at the same Distances above and below the proper *Clef*, as they stand in the separate System; and because all the Notes that are consonant, (or heard together) must stand perpendicularly over each other, that the Notes belonging to each Part may be distinctly known, they may be made with such Differences as shall not confound or alter their Significations with respect to Time, but only shew that they belong to this or that Part. Thus shall we see how the Parts change and pass thro' one another; and which, in every Note is highest, lowest, or unison.

The Use of particular *Sign'd Clefs* then, is an Improvement with respect to the Parts of any Composition; for unless some one Key in the particular Systems were distinguish'd from the rest, and refer'd invariably to one Place in the Scale, the Relations could not be distinctly mark'd.

It must here be observ'd, that for the Performance of any single Piece, the *Clef* only serves for explaining the Intervals in the Lines and Spaces: so that we need not regard what Part of any greater System it is; but the first Note may be taken as high or as low as we please. For the proper Use of the Scale is not to limit the absolute Degree of Tone; so the proper Use of the *Sign'd Clef*, is not to limit the Pitch at which the first Note of any Part is to be taken; but to determine the Tune of the rest with relation to the first: And considering all the Parts together, to determine the relations of their several Notes by the Relations of their *Clefs* in the Scale: Thus, the pitch of Tune being determin'd in a certain Note of one Part; the other Notes of that Part are determin'd by the constant Relations of the Letters of the Scale, and the Notes of the other Parts by the Relations of their *Clefs*.

In effect, for performing any single Part, the *Clef* Note may be taken in any Octave, *i.e.* at any Note of the same Name, provided we do not go too high or too low for finding the rest of the Notes or a Song. But in a Concert of several Parts, all the *Clefs* must be taken, not only in the Relations, but also in the Places of the System abovemention'd; that every Part may be comprehended in it.

The difference of *Clefs* in particular Systems, makes the Practice of Musick much more difficult and perplex'd than it would otherwise be; both with respect to Instruments, and to the Voice. This occasion'd Mr. *Salmon* to propose a Method of reducing all Musick to one *Clef*; whereby the same Writing of any Piece of Musick, should equally serve to direct the Voice, and all Instruments; which he calls an *Universal Character*.

The Natural and Artificial Note express'd by the same Letter, as *c* and *c*✕; are both set on the same Line or Space. When there is no Character of Flat or Sharp at the beginning with the *Clef*, all the Notes are Natural: and if in any particular Place the Artificial Note be requir'd, 'tis signify'd by the Sign of a Flat or Sharp set on the Line a Space before that Note.

If a Sharp or Flat be set at the beginning in any Line or Space with the *Clef*, all the Notes on that Line or Space are Artificial ones; *i.e.* are to be taken a Semitone higher or lower than they would be without such Sign. The same affects all their Octaves above and below, tho they ben't mark'd so, [sic] In the course of the Song, if the Natural Note be sometimes requir'd, 'tis signify'd by ♮.

The marking of the System thus by Flats and Sharps, Mr. *Malcolm* calls the *Signature of the Clefs*. See *Note, Tune, Transposition, Flat, Sharp, &c.*

concord

1728 Chambers *Concord*, in Musick, is the Relation of two Sounds that are always agreeable to the Ear, whether applied in Succession or Consonance. See *Sound*.

If two single Sounds be in such a Relation, or have such a difference of Tune, as that being sounded together, they make a Mixture, or compound Sound, which affects the Ear with pleasure; that Relation is called *Concord*: and whatever two Sounds make an agreeable Compound in consonance, those same will always be pleasing, in Succession, or will follow each other agreeably. See *Tune*.

The Reverse of a *Concord*, is what we call a *Discord*; which is a Denomination of all the Relations or Differences of Tune that have a displeasing Effect. See *Discord*.

Concord and Harmony are, in effect, the same thing; tho Custom has applied them differently. As *Concord* expresses the agreeable Effect of two Sounds in Consonance; so Harmony expresses that Agreement in a greater Number of Sounds in Consonance: Add, that Harmony always implies Consonance; but *Concord* is sometimes applied to Succession: tho never but when the Terms will make an agreeable Consonance: whence it is that Dr. *Holder*, and some other Writers, use the Word *Consonance* for what we call *Concord*. See *Consonance*.

Unisonance, then, being the Relation of Equality between the Tunes of two Sounds, all Unisons are *Concords*, and in the first Degree: but an Interval being a Difference of Tune, or a Relation of Inequality between two Sounds, becomes a *Concord* or *Discord*, according to the Circumstances of that particular Relation. Indeed, some restrain *Concord* to Intervals, and make a difference of Tune essential thereto; but that is precarious: and Mr. *Malcolm* thinks, that as the Word implies Agreement, 'tis applicable to Unison in the first degree. See *Unison*.

'Tis not easy to assign the Reason or Foundation of *Concordance*: The differences of Tune, we have already observ'd, take their rise from the different Proportions of the Vibrations of the sonorous Body, *i.e.* of the Velocity of those Vibrations in their recourses; the frequenter those recourses are, the more acute being the Tune, and *vice versa*. See *Gravity, &c.* But the essential differences between *Concord* and Discord lies deeper: there does not appear any natural Aptitude in the two Sounds of a *Concord*, to determine it to give us a pleasing Sensation, more than in the two Sounds of a Discord. These different Effects are merely arbitrary, and must be resolv'd into the divine good pleasure. See *Sensation* [entry not reproduced].

We know by experience what Proportions and Relations of Tune afford Pleasure, [and] what [do] not; and we know also how to express the Differences of Tune by the Proportion of Numbers; we know what it is pleases us, tho we don't know why: We know, *v.g.* that the Ratio of 1:2 constitutes *Concord*, and 6:7 Discord; but on what original Grounds agreeable or disagreeable Ideas are connected with those Relations, and the proper Influence of the one on the other, is above our reach.

By Experience, we know that the following Ratios of the Lengths of Chords are all *Concord*, *viz.* 2:1, 3:2, 4:3, 5:4, 6:5, 5:3, 8:5; that is, take any Chord for a Fundamental, which shall be represented by the Number 1, and the following Divisions thereof will be all *Concord* with the whole, *viz.* $\frac{1}{2} \cdot \frac{2}{3} \cdot \frac{3}{4} \cdot \frac{4}{5} \cdot \frac{5}{6} \cdot \frac{3}{5} \cdot \frac{5}{8} \cdot$ So that the distinguishing Character between *Concords* and Discords, must be look'd for in these Numbers, expressing the Intervals of Sound; not abstractedly, and in themselves, but as expressing the Number of Vibrations.

Now, Unisons are in the first Degree of *Concord*, or have the most perfect Likeness or Agreement in Tune; and therefore have something in 'em accessory to that Agreement, which is found, less or more, in every *Concord*: but 'tis not true, that the nearer two Sounds come to an Equality of Tune, the more Agreement they have; therefore, 'tis not in the Equality or Inequality of the Numbers that this Agreement lies.

Further, if we consider the Number of Vibrations made in any given time by two Chords of equal Tune; on the Principle laid down, they are equal: And therefore, the Vibrations of the two Chords coincide, or commence together as frequently as possible, *i.e.* they coincide at every Vibration; in this frequency of which Coincidence, or united Mixture of the Motions of the two Chords, and of the Undulations of the Air occasion'd thereby, it is, that the Difference of *Concord* and Discord must be sought.

Now, the nearer the Vibrations of two Strings approach to a Coincidence as frequent as possible, the nearer they should approach the Condition and, consequently, the Agreement of Unisons; which agrees with Experience.

For if we take the natural Series 1, 2, 3, 4, 5, 6, and compare each Number to the next, as expressing the Number of Vibrations in the same time of two Chords, whose Lengths are reciprocally as those Numbers; the Rule will be found exact, for 1:2 is best, then 2:3; after 6 the Consonance is unsufferable; the Coincidences being too rare: tho there are other Ratios that are agreeable, besides those found in that continued Order, *viz.* 3:5, and 5:8, which, with the preceding five are all the *concording* Intervals within, or less than an Octave, or 1:2; that is, whose acutest Term is greater than half the Fundamental.

On this Principle, 3:5 will be preferable to 4:5; because being equal in the number of Vibrations of the acuter Term, there is an advantage on the Side of the Fundamental in the Ratio 3:5, where the Coincidence is made at every third Vibration of the Fundamental, and every fifth of the acute Term: So also the Ratio 5:8 is less perfect than 5:6; because, tho the Vibrations of each Fundamental are equal; yet in the Ratio 5:6, the Coincidence is at every sixth of the acute Term, and only at every eighth in the other Case.

Thus, we have a Rule for judging of the Preference of *Concords*, from the Coincidence of their Vibrations: agreeable to which Rule, they are dispos'd into the Order of the following Table; to which the *Names of the Concords* in Practice, the *Ratio of their Vibrations*, the *Lengths of the Chords*, and the *Number of Coincidences* in the same, are express'd. [see *Table of* CONCORDS below]

Tho this Order be settled by Reason, yet it is confirm'd by the Ear. On this bottom, *Concords* must still be the more perfect, as they have the greatest Number of Coincidences, with regard to the Number of Vibrations in both Chords; and where the Coincidences are equal, the Preference will fall on that Interval, whose acutest Term has fewest Vibrations to each Coincidence; which Rule, however, is in some Cases contrary to Experience; and yet it is the only Rule yet discover'd.

F. *Mersenne*, indeed, after *Kircher*, gives us another Standard for settling the comparative Perfection of Intervals with regard to the Agreement of their Extremes in Tune: And 'tis this.

Table of CONCORDS.

Ratio's, or Vibrations.				Coincid.
	Grave Term.		*Acute Term.*	
Unison	1	:	1	
Octave, 8ve	2	:	1	60
Fifth, 5th	3	:	2	30
Fourth, 4th	4	:	3	20
Sixth, gr.	5	:	3	20
Third, gr.	5	:	4	15
Third, lesser	6	:	5	12
Sixth, lesser	8	:	5	12
	Grave	*Lengths.*	*Acute*	

The Perception of *Concordance,* say they, is nothing but the comparing of two or more different Motions which in the same time affect the auditory Nerve: Now we can't make a certain Judgment of any Consonance, till the Air be as oft struck in the same time by two Chords, as there are Unites [sic] in each Member expressing the Ratio of that *Concord, v.g.* we can't perceive a Fifth, till two Vibrations of the one Chord, and three of the other are accomplish'd together; which Chords are in length as 3 to 2: The Rule then is, that those *Concords* are the most simple and agreeable, which are generated in the least time; and those, on the contrary, the most compound and harsh, which are generated in the longest time.

For instance, let 1, 2, 3, be the Lengths of 3 Chords 1:2 is an Octave; 2:3 a Fifth; and 1:3 an Octave and Fifth compounded, or a Twelfth. The Vibrations of Chords being reciprocally as their Lengths, the Chord 2 will vibrate once, while the Chord 1 vibrates twice, and then exists an Octave; but the Twelfth does not yet exist, because the Chord 3 has not vibrated once, nor the Chord 1 thrice, which is necessary to form a Twelfth.

Again, for generating a Fifth, the Chord 2 must vibrate thrice, and the Chord 3 twice; in which time, the Chord 1 will have vibrated 6 times; and thus the Octave will be thrice produc'd, while the Twelfth is only produced twice; the Chord 2 uniting its Vibration sooner with the Chord 1, than with the Chord 3; and they being sooner consonant than the Chord 1 or 2 with that 3.

Whence, that Author [Mersenne] observes, many of the Mysteries of Harmony, relating to the Performance of Harmonious Intervals and their Succession, are easily deduced.

But this Rule, upon examining it by other Instances, Mr. *Malcolm* has shewn defective, as it does not answer in all Positions of the Intervals with respect to each other; but a certain Order, wherein they are to be taken, being requir'd: and there being no Rule, with respect to the Order, that will make this Standard answer to Experience in every Case: So that at last we are left to determine the Degrees of *Concord* by Experience and the Ear.

Not but that the Degrees of *Concord* depend much on the more or less frequent uniting the Vibrations, and the Ear's being more or less uniformly mov'd, as above; for that this Mixture or Union of Motion, is the true Principle, or, at least, the chief Ingredient in *Concord,* is evident: But because there seems to be something further in the Proportion of the two Motions, necessary to be known, in order to fix a catholick Rule for determining all the Degrees of *Concord,* agreeable to Sense and Experience.

The Result of the whole Doctrine is summ'd up in this Definition.

Concord is the Result of frequent Union, or Coincidence of the Vibrations of two sonorous Bodies, and, by consequence, of the undulating Motions of the Air, which, being caus'd by these Vibrations, are like and proportionable to 'em; which Coincidence, the more frequent it is, with regard to the number of Vibrations of both Bodies, perform'd in the same time, *cæteris paribus,* the more perfect is that *Concord*: till the Rarity of the Coincidence, in respect of one or both the Motions, commence *Discord. See some of the remarkable Phænomena of Sounds accounted for from this Theory, under the Word Unison*; see also *Interval, &c.*

Concords are divided into *simple,* or original, and *compound.*

A *simple,* or original *Concord,* is that whose Extremes are at a Distance less than the Sum of any two other *Concords.*

On the contrary, a compound *Concord* is equal to two or more [simple] *Concords.*

Other Musical Writers state the Division thus: An Octave 1:2 and all the inferior *Concords* above express'd are all simple and original *Concords*: and all greater than an Octave, are called *compound Concords;* as being compos'd of, and equal to the Sum of one or more Octaves, and some single *Concord* less than an Octave, and are usually, in practice, denominated from that *simple Concord.*

As to the Composition and Relations of the original Concords, by applying to them the Rules of the Addition and Subtraction of Intervals, they will be divided into *simple* and *compound,* according to the first and more general Notion; as in the following Table.

Simple *Concords.*	Compound *Concords.*				
					5th 4 or
5 : 6 a 3d less.	5th	3d g.	and 3d l.	8ve. com-	6th g. 3dl.
4 : 5 a 3d gr.	6th l.	4th	3d l.	pos'd of	or 3d g.
3 : 4 a 4th	6th g.	4th	3d g.		3d l. 4th.

The Octave is not only the first *Concord* in point of Perfection, the Agreement of whose Extremes is greatest, and the nearest to Unison; insomuch that when sounded together, 'tis impossible to perceive two different Sounds; but 'tis also the greatest Interval of the seven original *Concords;* and as such, contains all the lesser, which derive their sweetness from it, as they arise more or less directly out of it; and which decrease gradually, from the Octave to the lesser Sixth, which has but a small degree of *Concord.* See *Octave.*

What is very remarkable, is the manner wherein these lesser *Concords* are found in the Octave, which shews their mutual Dependencies.

For, by taking both an Harmonical and Arithmetical Mean between the Extremes of the Octave, and then both an Harmonical and Arithmetical Mean betwixt each Extreme, and the most distant of the two Means last found, *viz.* betwixt the lesser Extreme and the first Arithmetical Mean, and betwixt the greater Extreme and the first Harmonical Mean, we have all the lesser *Concords.*

Thus, if betwixt 360 and 180 the Extremes of Octave, we take an Arithmetical Mean, it is 270; and an Harmonical Mean in 240: then, betwixt 360 the greatest Extreme, and 240 the Harmonical Mean, take an Arithmetical Mean, it is 300; and an Harmonical Mean, to 288. Again, betwixt 180 the lesser Extreme of the Octave, and 270 the first Arithmetical Mean, it is 225, and an Harmonical one 216.

Thus have we a Series of all the *Concords,* both ascending towards Acuteness from a common Fundamental, 360; and descending towards Gravity from a common acute Term, 180: which Series has this Property, that taking the two Extremes, and any other two at equal Distances, the four will be in Geometrical Proportion.

The Octave, by immediate Division, resolves it self into a Fourth and Fifth; the Fifth, again, by immediate Division, produces the two Thirds; the two Thirds are therefore found by Division, tho not by immediate Division; and the same is true of the two Sixths. Thus do all the original *Concords* arise out of the Division of the Octave; the Fifths and Fourths immediately and directly, the Thirds and Sixths mediately.

From the Perfection of the Octave arises this remarkable Property, that it may be doubled, tripled, *&c.* and yet still persevere [as] a *Concord, i.e.* the Sum of two or more Octaves are *concord;* tho the more compound will be gradually less agreeable: But it is not so with any other *Concord* less than [an] Octave; the Doubles, *&c.* whereof, are all Discords.

Again, whatever Sound is *concord* to one Extreme of the Octave is *concord* to the other also: and if we add any other simple *Concord* to an Octave, it agrees to both its Extremes; to the nearest Extreme it is a simple *Concord,* and to the farthest a compound one.

Another thing observable in this System of *Concords,* is, that the greatest Number of Vibrations of the Fundamental cannot exceed five; or that there is no *Concord* where the Fundamental makes more than five Vibrations, to one Coincidence with the acute Term. It may be added, that this Progress of the *Concords* may be carried on to greater degrees of Composition, even *in infinitum;* but the more compound, the less agreeable.

So a single Octave is better than a double one, and that than a triple one; and so of Fifths, and other *Concords.* Three or four Octaves is the greatest length we go in ordinary Practice: The old Scales went but to two; no Voice or Instrument will well go above four. See *Third, Fourth, Fifth, &c.*

counterpoint

1728 CHAMBERS *Counter-point*, in Musick, the Art of composing Harmony; or of disposing and concerting several Parts so together, as that they make an agreeable Whole. See *Composition*, and *Harmony*.

Counter-point is divided into *simple*, and *figurative*; agreeably to the Division of Harmony, into the Harmony of Concords, and that of Discords. See *Concord*.

Counter-point took its Name hence, when Musick in Parts was first introduc'd, their Harmony being so simple they us'd no Notes of different Time, and mark'd their Consonances by *Points* set *against* each other. Hence, in regard to the Equality of the Notes of Time, the Parts were made Concord in every Note.

This afterwards became denominated *simple* and *plain Counter-point*; to distinguish it from another Kind, wherein Notes of different Values were us'd, and Discords brought in betwixt the Parts, which they call *figurative Counter-point*.

Simple Counter-point, or the Harmony of Concords, consists of the imperfect, as well as the perfect Concords; and may therefore be denominated *perfect*, or *imperfect*, according as the Concords are, whereof it is compos'd: Thus, the Harmony arising from a Conjunction of any Note with its Fifth and Octave, is perfect; but with its Third and Sixth imperfect.

Now, to dispose the Concords or the Natural Notes and their Octaves in any Key in a simple *Counterpoint*, observe, with regard to the Distinction into perfect and imperfect Harmony, this general Rule, *viz.* to the Key *f*, to the 4th *f*, and to the 5th *f*, a perfect Harmony must be join'd; to the 2d *f*, the 3d *f*, and 7th, an imperfect Harmony is indispensible; to the 6th *f*, either an imperfect or perfect Harmony.

In the Composition of two Parts, observe, that tho a third appears only in the Treble on the Key *f*, the 4th *f*, and the 5th *f*; yet the perfect Harmony of the Fifth, is always suppos'd, and must be supplied in the Accompanyments of the thorow Bass to those fundamental Notes.

More particularly, in the Composition of two Parts, the Rules are, That the Key *f* may either have its Octave, its Third, or its Fifth; the fourth *f* and fifth *f* may have either their respective Thirds or Fifths, and the first may have its Sixth; as, to favour a contrary Motion, the last may have its Octave.

The sixth *f* may have either its 3d, its 5th, or its 6th.

The second *f*, third *f*, and seventh *f*, may have either their respective 3ds or 6ths; and the last, on many occasions, its false 5th. Which Rules hold the same both in flat and sharp Keys.

For the Rules of *Counter-point*, with regard to the Succession of Concords; it must be observ'd, That as much as can be in Parts, may proceed by a contrary Motion, *i.e.* the Bass may ascend when the Treble descends, and *vice versa*. The Parts moving either upwards or downwards the same way; two Octaves or two Fifths never to follow one another immediately. To Sixths never to succeed each other immediately. Whenever the Octave or Fifth is to be made use of, the Parts must proceed by a contrary Motion, except the Treble [must] move into such Octave or Fifth gradually. If in a Sharp Key, the Bass descend gradually from the 5th *f* to the 4th *f*, the last, in that Case, must never have its proper Harmony applied to it; but the Notes that were Harmony in the preceding 5th *f*, must be continu'd on the 4th *f*. Thirds and Fifths may follow one another as often as one has a mind.

Figurative Counter-point is of two Kinds: In the one, Discords are introduc'd occasionally; serving only as Transitions from Concord to Concord: In the other, the Discord bears a chief part in the Harmony. See *Discord*.

For the *first*; nothing but Concords are ever to be us'd on the accented Parts of the Measure: In the unaccented Parts, Discords may pass transiently, without any Offence to the Ear. This the French call *Supposition*; because the transient Discord always supposes a Concord immediately following it: Which is of infinite Service in Musick. See *Supposition*.

For the *second*, wherein the Discords are used as a solid and substantial Part of the Harmony; the Discords that have Place are the Fifth when join'd with the Sixth, to which it stands in the Relation of a Discord: the Fourth when join'd with the Fifth; the Ninth, which is in effect the Second; the Seventh, and the Second and Fourth.

These Discords are introduc'd into the Harmony with due Preparation; and are to be succeeded by Concords: which is commonly call'd the *Resolution of Discord*.

The Discord is prepar'd by first subsisting in the Harmony in quality of a Concord; *i.e.* the same Note which becomes the Discord is first a Concord to the Bass Note immediately preceding that to which it is a Discord. The Discord is resolv'd by being immediately succeeded by a Concord descending from it by the Distance only of Second *g*, or Second *l*.

As the Discord makes a substantial Part of the Harmony, so it must always possess an accented Part of the Measure. Now to introduce the Discords into Harmony; it must be consider'd what Concords may serve for their Preparation and Resolution: The Fifth, then, may be prepar'd, either by being an Octave, Sixth, or Third. It may be resolv'd either into the Sixth, or Third. The Fourth may be prepar'd in all the Concords, and may be resolv'd into the Sixth, Third, or Octave. The Ninth may be prepar'd in all the Concords except the Octave; and may be resolv'd into the Sixth, Third, or Octave. The Seventh may be prepar'd in all the Concords; and resolv'd into the Third, Sixth, and Fifth. The Second and Fourth are used very differently from the rest; being prepar'd and resolv'd into the Bass. See *Harmony, Concord, Discord, Key, Clef, Modulation, &c.*

discord

1728 CHAMBERS *Discord,* in Music, the Relation of two Sounds which are always, and of themselves, disagreeable, whether applied in Succession, or Consonance. See *Sound.*

If two simple Sounds are in such a Relation of Tune, that is, have such a Difference of Tune, as that being sounded together, they make a Mixture, or compound Sound, which the Ear receives with Displeasure, it is call'd a *Discord;* As, on the contrary, if it receive it with Pleasure, it is call'd a *Concord*: And whatever two Sounds make an agreeable, or disagreeable Compound, they will have the same Effects respectively, if they be applied in Succession. See *Tune, Concord.*

As Concords are denominated *Unharmonical Intervals;* so may *Discords* be denominated *Unharmonical Intervals.* See *Interval.*

Discords are distinguish'd into *Concinnous,* and *Inconcinnous Intervals.*

The *Concinnous,* by the Ancients call'd *Emmeli,* are such as are apt, or fit for Music, next to, and in Combination with Concords. These are Relations, which in themselves are neither very agreeable, no disagreeable; and have only a good Effect in Music by their Opposition, as they heighten, and illustrate the more natural and essential Principles of the Pleasure we seek for; or, as by their Mixture, and Combination with them, they produce a Variety necessary to our being better pleas'd.

Notwithstanding this they are still call'd *Discords;* as the Bitterness of some Things may help to set off the Sweetness of others, and yet still be better.

The *Inconcinnous Discords,* by the Ancients call'd *Ecmeli,* are such as are never chosen in Music; as having too great a Harshness in them: Tho' even the greatest *Discord* is not without its Use. See *Concinnous, &c.*

The Essential Principles of Harmony, Harmonical Intervals, or Concords, are but few, in Number only eight; the indefinite Number of other *Ratio's* are all *Discords.* Hence Mr. *Malcolm* shews the Necessity of taking some of the less untoward of these *Discords* into the System of Music: In order to this, he considers the Effect of having none but harmonical Intervals in the System of Music.

1. With respect to a single Voice; If that should move always from one Degree of Tune to another, so as every Note, or Sound to the next were in the *Ratio* of some Concord; the Variety, which is Life of Music, would soon be exhausted. For to move by no other, than Harmonical Intervals, would not only want Variety, and so weary us with a tedious Repetition of the same Things, but the very Perfection of such Relations of Sounds would cloy the Ear in the same Manner as sweet and luscious Things do the Taste, which for that reason are artfully season'd with the Mixture of Sower and Bitter. See *Degrees* [no such entry given].

2. With respect to Music in Parts, *i.e.* when two, or more Voices joyn in Consonance, the general Rule is, that the successive Sounds of each be so order'd, that the several Voices shall be all Concords. Now there ought to be a Variety in the Choice of those successive Concords, and also in the Method of their Successions; all which depends on the Movement of the single Parts. So that, if these could only move in an agreeable Manner by harmonical Distances, there are but a few different Ways wherein they could move from Concord to Concord; and hereby we should lose much of the Ravishment of Sounds in Consonance. As to this Part then; the Thing demanded is a Variety of Ways whereby each single Voice, or more in Consonance, may move agreeably in the successive Sounds, so as to pass from Concord to Concord, and meet at every Note in the same, or a different Concord, from what they stood in at the last Note.

In what Cases, and for what Reasons *Discords* are allow'd, the Rules of Composition must teach; But only joyning these two Considerations, *&c.* we see how imperfect Music would be without any other Intervals than Concords. See *Composition.*

Beside the *Concinnous Discords* used designedly in Music; there are several other *Discord* Relations, which happen unavoidably, in a Kind of accidental, and indirect Manner. Thus in the Succession of several Notes there are to be consider'd not only the Relations of those which succeed others immediately, but also of those betwixt which other Notes intervene. Now the inmediate [sic] Succession may be conducted so as to produce good Melody; yet among the distant Notes there may be very gross *Discords*, that would not be tolerable in immediate Succession, and far less in Consonance. And such *Discords* are actually contain'd in the Scale of Music. Thus, taking any one Species, *e.gr.* that with the greater Third, and marking the Degrees betwixt each Term and the next; and tho' the Progression be melodious, as the Terms refer to one common Fundamental, yet there are several *Discords* among the mutual Relations of the Terms, *e.gr.* from 4th to 7th *g* is 32:45; and from 2d *g* to 6th *g*, is 27:40; and from 2d *g* to 4th is 27:32 all *Discords*.

The Species of Counterpoint, wherein there is a Mixture of *Discords*, is call'd *Figurative Counterpoint*; Of which there are two Kinds: That wherein the *Discords* are introduced occasionally, to serve as Transitions from Concord to Concord; and that wherein the *Discord* bears a chief Part in the Harmony. See *Figurative Counterpoint*.

Upon the unaccented Parts of the Measure, *Discords* may transiently pass without any Offence to the Ear: This is call'd *Supposition*, by reason the transient *Discord* supposes a Concord immediately following. See *Supposition*.

The *Harmony of Discords* is that wherein the *Discords* are made Use of as the solid and substantial Part of the Harmony. For by a proper Interposition of a *Discord*, the succeeding Concords receive an additional Lustre. Thus the *Discords* are in Music what the strong Shades are in Painting. See *Harmony*.

The *Discords* are the 5th when joyn'd with the 6th; the 4th joyn'd with the 5th, the 9th is of its own Nature a *Discord*; so is the 7th.

The *Discords* are introduced into the Harmony of due Preparation, and must be succeeded by Concords; which is commonly call'd the *Resolution of the Discord*. The *Discord* is prepar'd by subsisting first in the Harmony in the Quality of a Concord; that is, the same Note which becomes the *Discord* is first a Concord to the Bass-Note immediately preceding that to which it is a *Discord*.

The *Discord* is *resolved* by being immediately succeeded by a Concord descending from it by the Distance only of greater 2d, or lesser 2d.

gamut

1728 CHAMBERS *Gamm, Gammut, Gamut*, or *Gam-ut*, in Music, a Scale, whereon we learn to sound the Musical Notes, *Ut, re, mi, fa, sol, la*, in their several Orders, and Dispositions. See *Note*, and *Scale*.

The Invention of this Scale is owing to *Guido Aretin*, a Monk of *Aretium*, in *Tuscany*; tho' it is not properly an Invention, as an Improvement on the Diagramma or Scale of the Antients. See *Diagram*.

The *Gammut* is also call'd the *Harmonical Hand*; by reason *Guido* first made use of the Figure of the Hand, to arrange his Notes on.

Finding the *Greek* Diagramma of too small Extent, *Guido* added five more Chords, or Notes to it: One, below the Proslambanomenos, or gravest Note of the Antients; and four, above the Nete, or Acutest. The first, he call'd Hypo-proslambanomenos; and denoted it by the Letter G, or rather the *Greek* Γ, *Gamma*: Which Note being at the head of the Scale, occasion'd the whole Scale to be call'd by the barbarous Name *Gamm*, or *Gammut*.

Some say, *Guido*'s Intention in calling his first Note Γ, *Gamm*, was to shew, that the *Greeks* were the Inventors of Musick: Others, that he meant hereby to record himself; this being the first Letter of his own Name.—

Guido's Scale is divided into three Series, or Columns; the first call'd *Molle*, or flat; the second *Natural*; and the third *Durum*, or Sharp, as represented in the Scheme, *Tab. Musick, Fig.* 3 [reproduced below]. But since his Time, some Alterations have been made there.

The Use of this Scale, is to make the Passages, and Transitions from B Molle, to B Durum, by means of the Tones and Semitones. The Series of B Natural standing betwixt the other two, communicates with both; so that to name the Chords of the Scale by these Syllables, if we would have the Semitones in their natural Places, *viz. b c* and *e f*, then we apply *ut* to *g*; and after *la* we go into the Series of *b* natural at *fa*; and after *la* of this, we return to the former at *mi*, and so on: Or, we may begin at *ut* in *c*, and pass into the first Series at *mi*, and then back to the other at *fa*: By which means the one Transition is a Semitone, *viz. la, fa*; and the other a Tone, *la, mi*. To follow the Order of *b* Molle, we may begin with *ut* in *c*, or *f*, and make Transitions after the same manner. See *Tone*, and *Semitone*.

Hence came the barbarous Names of *Gammut, Are, Bmi,* &c. But what a perplex'd Work is here, with so many different Syllables applied to every Chord; and all to mark the Places of the Semitones, which the simple Letters *a b c* &c. do as well, and with more Ease?

Several Alterations have since been made in the *Gamut.* M. *le Maire,* particularly, has added a seventh Note, *viz. si;* and the *English* usually throw out both *ut* and *si,* and make the other five serve for all: As will be shewn under the Article *Sol-fa-ing.*

Gamm, Gamma, or *Gammut,* is also the first, or gravest Note in the modern Scale of Music; the Reason whereof is shewn under the preceding Article [above].

TAB. MUSIC

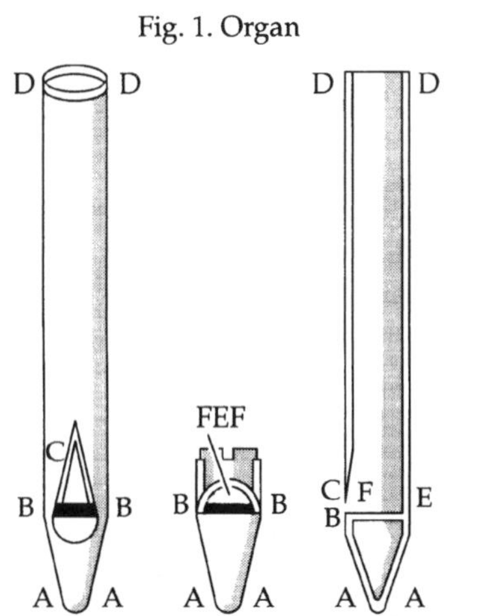

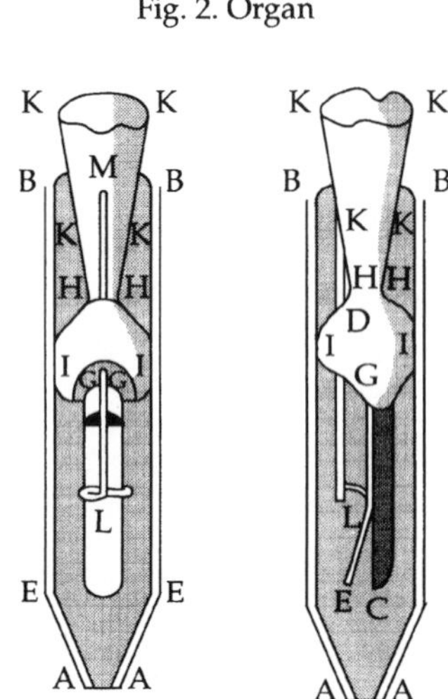

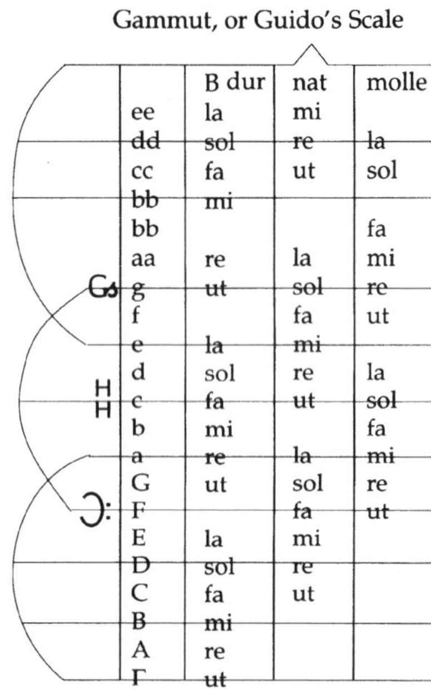

Gammut, or Guido's Scale
B dur
nat
molle
ee la mi
dd sol re la
cc fa ut sol
bb mi
bb fa
aa re la mi
g ut sol re
f fa ut
e la mi
d sol re la
c fa ut sol
b mi fa
a re la mi
G ut sol re
F fa ut
E la mi
D sol re
C fa ut
B mi
A re
Γ ut

[*Schematized after original illustration*]

harmonical

1728 Chambers *Harmonical* ... of Musical Intervals, which are expressed by Numbers, in order to our finding their mutual Relations, Compositions and Resolutions. See *Interval, &c.*

Harmonical Composition, in its general Sense, includes the Composition both of *Harmony* and *Melody,* i.e. of Music, or Songs, both in a single Part, and in several Parts. See *Composition.*

In its more proper and limited Sense, *Harmonical Composition* is restrain'd to that of Harmony. In which Sense it may be defined [as] the Art of disposing and concerting several single Parts together, in such Manner, as to make one agreeable whole. See *Song, &c.*

The Art of Harmony has been long known under the Name of *Counterpoint.* See *Counterpoint.*

As the Time when Parts were first introduced, Music being then very simple, there were no different Notes of Time; and the Parts were in every Note made Concord.

This they afterwards call'd *simple,* or plain *Counterpoint,* to distinguish it from another Kind, then introduced, wherein Notes of different Value were introduced, and Discords brought in between the Parts. See *Discord.*

This they call'd *Figurative Counterpoint.* See *Figurative Counterpoint.*

Harmonical Interval, in an Interval, or Difference of two Sounds which are agreeable to the Ear, whether in Consonance or Succession. See *Interval.*

Harmonical Intervals, therefore, are the same with *Concords.* See *Concord.*

They are thus call'd, as being the only essential Ingredients of Harmony. See *Harmony.... Harmonical Sounds,* in an Appellation given by M. *Sauveur* to such Sounds as always make a certain determinate Number of

Vibrations in the Time that some other fundamental Sound, to which they are referr'd, makes one Vibration. See *Sound* and *Vibration* [latter entry not reproduced].

Harmonical Sounds, are produced by the Parts of Chords, *&c.* which vibrate a certain Number of Times while the whole Chord vibrates once. See *Chord*.

By this they are distinguished from the third, fifth, *&c.* where the Relations of the Vibrations is 4 to 5, or 5 to 6, or 2 to 3. See *Third, &c.*

The Relations of Sounds, had only been consider'd in the Series of Numbers 1:2, 2:3, 3:4, 4:5, *&c.* which produced the Intervals call'd *Octave, Fifth, Fourth, Third,* &c. Mr. *Sauveur* first consider'd them in the natural Series, 1, 2, 3, 4, &c. and examined the Relations of the Sounds arising therefrom.—The Result is, that the first Interval 1:2, is an Octave; the second 1:3, a twelfth; the third 1:4, a fifteenth, or double Octave; the fourth 1:5, a seventeenth; the fifth 1:6, a nineteenth, *&c.*

This new Consideration of the Relations of *Sounds*, is more natural than the old one; and does express and represent the whole of Music, and is in Effect all the Music that Nature gives without the Assistance of Art.—The String of a Harpsichord, or a Bell, beside their general Sound, which is proportionate to their Length, Tension, *&c.* do also at the same Time yield other subordinate and acuter Sounds, which a nice Ear, with a good Attention, clearly distinguishes.

These subordinate *Sounds* arise from the particular Vibrations of some of the Parts of the String, or Bell, which are, as it were, detach'd from the rest, and make separate Vibrations: In Effect, every half, every third, every fourth, *&c.* of the Chord performs its Vibrations apart, while a general Vibration is made of the whole Chord.—Now all these subordinate Sounds are *Harmonical* with Regard to the whole Sound: The least acute, which we hear, is [an] Octave with the whole Sound; the least acute that follows, makes a twelfth with the whole Sound; the next a seventeenth, *&c.* till they grow too acute for the Ear to perceive them. Now throughout the whole, we hear no such Thing as a Sound that makes a fifth, or a third, *&c.* with the whole Sound; none in short, but what are comprized in the Series of *Harmonical* Sounds.

Add, that if the Breadth, or Bellows that blow a Wind Instrument, be play'd stronger and stronger, the Tone will be continually rais'd, but this only in the *Ratio* of the *Harmonical Sounds*.—So that it appears that Nature, when she makes as it were a System of Music her self, uses no other but this Kind of Sounds; and yet they had hitherto remained unknown to the Musicians: Not but that they frequently fell into 'em, but it was inadvertently, and without knowing what they did.—M. *Sauveur* shews that the Structure of the Organ depends entirely on this unknown Principle. See *Organ*.

harmony

1728 Chambers *Harmony*, in Music, the agreeable Result of an Union of several Musical Sounds, heard at one and the same Time; or, the Mixture of divers Sounds, which together have an Effect agreeable to the Ear. See *Sound*.

As a continued Succession of Musical Sounds produces *Melody*; so does a continued Combination of these produce *Harmony*. See *Melody*.

Among the Antients, however, as sometimes also among the Moderns, *Harmony* is used in the strict Sense of *Consonance*; and so is equivalent to the *Symphony*. See *Consonance* and *Symphony*.

The Words *Concord*, and *Harmony*, do really signify the same Thing; tho' Custom has made a little Difference between them. Concord is the agreeable Effect of two Sounds in Consonance: And *Harmony*, the Effect of any greater Number of agreeable Sounds in Consonance. See *Concord*.

Again, *Harmony* always implies *Consonance*: But *Concord* is also applied to Sounds in *Succession*; tho' never but where the Terms can stand agreeably in Consonance: The Effect of an agreeable Succession of several Sounds, is call'd *Melody*; as that of an agreeable Consonance, *Harmony*.

The Antients seem to have been entirely unacquainted with *Harmony*; the Soul of the modern Music.—In all their Explications of the *Melopœia*, they say not one Word of the Concept of the Concert, or *Harmony* of Parts. We have Instances, indeed, of their joyning several Voices, or Instruments, in Consonance: But then those Voices, *&c.* were not so joyn'd, as that each had a distinct and proper Melody, so making a Succession of various Concords; but were either Unisons, or Octaves, in every Note; and so all perform'd the same individual Melody, and constituted one Song. See *Song, Synaulia, &c.*

When the Parts differ, not in the Tension of the whole, but in the different Relations of the successive Notes; 'tis thus that constitutes the modern Art of *Harmony*. See *Music* and *Melopoeia*.

Harmony is well defined the Sum of Concords, arising from the Combination of two or more Concords, *i.e.* of three or more simple Sounds, striking the Ear all together: And different Compositions of Concords make different *Harmony*.

To understand the Nature, and determine the Number, and Preference of *Harmonies;* it is to be consider'd, that in every compound Sound, where there are no more than three simple ones, there are three Kinds of Relations, *viz.* the primary Relation of every simple Sound to the fundamental, or gravest, whereby they make different Degrees of Concord with it: The mutual Relations of the Acute sounds each with other, whereby they mix either Concord or Discord into the Compound: And the secondary Relation of the whole, whereby all the Terms unite their Vibrations, or coincide more or less frequently.

Suppose, *e. gr.* four Sounds, A, B, C and D, whereof A is the gravest; B next; then C; and D the acutest.—Here, A is the fundamental; and the Relations of B, C, and D, to A are primary Relations: So, if B be a 3d *g* above A, that primary Relation is 4 to 5; and if C be a 5th to A, that primary Relation is 2 to 3; and if D be 8ve to A, that is 1 to 2. For the mutual Relations of the acute Terms, B, C, D, they are had by taking their primary Relations to the fundamental, and subtracting each lesser from each greater: Thus, B to C is 5 to 6, a 3d *l*; B to D is 5 to 8, a 6th *l*, &c.—Lastly, to find the secondary Relation of the whole, seek the least common Dividend to all the lesser Terms or Numbers of the primary Relations, *i.e.* the least Number that will be divided by each of them exactly: This is the Thing sought; and shews that all the simple Sounds coincide after so many Vibrations of the Fundamental as the Number expresses.

So in the preceding Example, the lesser Terms of the three primary Relations are 4, 2, 1, whose least common Dividend is 4. Consequently, at every 4th Vibration of the Fundamental, the whole will coincide.

Now *Harmony*, we have observed, is a compound Sound, consisting of three, or more, simple Sounds.—Its proper Ingredients are Concords; and all Discords, at least in the primary and mutual Relations, are absolutely forbidden. 'Tis true Discords are used in Music; but not for themselves simply, but to set off the Concords by their Contrast and Opposition. See *Discord*.

Hence, any Number of Concords being proposed to stand in primary Relation with a common Fundamental; we discover whether or no[t] they constitute a perfect *Harmony* by finding their mutual Relations.—Thus, suppose the following Concords, or primary Relations, *viz.* the greater 3d, 5th, and Octave given; their mutual Relations are all Concord, and therefore may stand in *Harmony*. For the greater 3d and 5th are to one another, as 5:6, a lesser third. The greater 3d and Octave, are as 5:8 a lesser 6th. And the 5th and Octave are as 3:4 a lesser fourth. But if 4th, 5th, and 8ve, be proposed, 'tis evident they cannot stand in *Harmony;* by Reason betwixt the 4th and 5th there is a Discord, *viz.* the Ratio 8:9. Again, supposing any Number of Sounds which are Concord, each to the next, from the lowest to the highest; to know if they can stand in *Harmony*, we must find the primary, and all the mutual Relations, which must be all Concord. So let any Number of Sounds be as 4:5:6:8, they may stand in *Harmony* by Reason each to each is Concord: But the following ones cannot, *viz.* 4, 6, 9, because 4:9 is Discord.

The necessary Conditions of all *Harmony*, then, are Concords in the primary and mutual Relations; on which Footing, a Table is easily form'd of all the possible Varieties: But to determine the Preference of *Harmonies*, the secondary Relations are likewise to be consider'd.—The Perfection of *Harmonies* depends on all the three Relations: It is not the best primary Relations that make best *Harmony*: For then a 4th and 5th must be better than a 4th and 6th. Whereas the first two cannot stand together, because of the Discord in the mutual Relation: Nor does the best secondary Relation carry it; for then would a 4th and 5th, whose secondary Relation with a common Fundamental is 6, be better than a lesser 3d and 5th, whose secondary Relation is 10: [sic] But here also the Preference is due to the better mutual Relation.—Indeed, the mutual Relations depend on the primary; tho' not so, as that the best primary shall always produce the best mutual Relation: However, the primary Relations are of the most Importance; and together with the secondary, afford us the following Rule for determining the Preference of *Harmonies*.

Viz. Comparing two *Harmonies*, which have an equal Number of Terms, that which has the best primary and secondary Relations, is most perfect.—But in Cases, where the Advantage is in the primary Relation of the one, and the secondary of the other, we have no certain Rule: The primary are certainly the most considerable; but how the Advantage in these ought to be proportion'd to the Disadvantage in the other, or *vice versa*, we know not. So that a well turned [sic] Ear must be the last Resort in these Cases.

Harmony is divided into Simple and Compound.

Simple Harmony, is that where there is no Concord to the fundamental above an Octave.

The Ingredients of simple *Harmony*, are the seven simple original Concords, of which there can be but 18 different Combinations, that are *Harmony*; which we give in the following Table from Mr. *Malcolm*.

Table of simple HARMONIES.

5th	8ve	2	3d *g* 5th	4	3d *g*, 5th	8ve
4th	8ve	3	3d *l* 5th	10	3d *l*, 5th	8ve
6th *g*	8ve	3	4th, 6th *g*	3	4th, 6th, *g*	8ve
3d *g*	8ve	4	3d *g*. 6th *g*	12	3d *g*, 6th *g*	8ve
3d *l*	8ve	5	3d *l*, 6th *l*	5	3d *l*, 6th *l*,	8ve
6th *l*	8ve	5	4th, 6th *l*	15	4th, 6th *l*,	8ve

These are all the possible Combinations of the Concords that make *Harmony*: For the 8ve is compounded of a 5th and 4th, or a 6th and 3d; which have a Variety of greater and lesser; out of these are the first six *Harmonies* composed: Then, the 5th being composed of the greater 3d, and lesser 3d, and the 6th of 4th and 3d; from these proceed the next six of the Table: Then an 8ve joyn'd to each of these 6, make the last six.

The Perfection of the first twelve is according to the Order of the Table: Of the first six each has an Octave, and their Preference is according to the Perfection of the other lesser Concord joyn'd to the Octave.—For the next six, the Preference is given to the two Combinations with the 5th, whereof that which has the 3d *g* is best; then to these two Combinations with the 6th *g*, of which that which has the 4th is best.—For the last six, they are not placed last, as being the least perfect, but because they are the most complex, and are the Mixtures of the other 12 with each other. In Point of Perfection they are plainly preferable to the preceding six, as having the very same Ingredients, and an Octave more.

Compound Harmony, is that which to the simple *Harmony* of one Octave, adds that of another Octave.

For the Compound *Harmonies*, their Variety is easily found out of the Combinations of the simple *Harmonies* of several Octaves.

Harmony, again, may be divided into that *of Concords*, and that *of Discords*.

The *first* is that we have hitherto consider'd, and wherein nothing but Concords are admitted.

The *second* is that wherein Discords are used, intermix'd with the Concords. See *Harmonical Composition*.

Composition of Harmony. See *Harmonic Composition*.

Harmony, is sometimes also used in a laxer Sense, to denote an Agreement, Suitableness, Union, Conformity, *&c*.

The Word is form'd of the *Greek* ἁρμονία, of the Verb ἁρμόνειν, *convenire, congruere*, to agree, match, *&c*.

In Music, we sometimes apply it to a single Voice, when sonorous, clear, and soft; or to a single Instrument, when it yields a very agreeable Sound.—Thus, we say, the *Harmony* of her Voice: of his Lute, *&c*.

interval

1728 CHAMBERS *Interval*, in Music, is the Difference between two Sounds in respect of Acute and Grave, or that imaginary Space terminated by two Sounds differing in Acuteness or Gravity. When two or more Sounds are compared in this Relation, they are either equal or unequal in the Degree of Tune. Such as are equal are call'd *Unisons*, with regard to each other, as having one Tune; the other being at a distance from each other, constitute what we call an *Interval* in Music, which is properly the Distance in Tune between two Sounds. *Intervals* are distinguish'd into Simple and Compound. A simple *Interval* is without Parts or Division, a Compound consists of several lesser *Intervals*. But this Distinction regards Practice only, because there is really no such thing as a least *Interval*. Besides, by a simple *Interval* is not meant here the least practised, but such as tho it were equal to two or more lesser which are in use, yet when we would make a Sound move so far up or down, we always pass immediately from one of its Terms to the other. What is meant then by a compound *Interval*, will be very plain: It is such, whose Terms are in Practice taken either in immediate Succession, or such where the Sound is made to rise and fall from the one to the other, by touching some intermediate Degrees; so that the whole becomes a Composition of all the *Intervals* from one Extreme to the other. What we here call a simple *Interval*, the Antients call'd a *Diastem*, and the Compound they call'd a *System*. Each of these has Differences; even of the Simple there are some greater, and others less: but they are always Discord; but of the Compound or System, some are Concord, others Discord. *Unisons*, 'tis plain, cannot possibly have any Variety; for where there is no difference, as in Unisonance, which flows from a Relation of Equality, 'tis plain there can be no Distinction: Unisons therefore must all be Concords. But an *Interval* depending on a Difference of Tune, or a Relation of Inequality, admits of Variety; and so the Terms of every *Interval*, according to their particular Relation or Difference, make either Concord or Discord. Some indeed have restrained the word *Concord* to *Intervals*, making it include a Difference in Tune, but this is precarious; for as the word *Concord* signifies an Agreement of Sounds, 'tis certainly applicable to Unisons in the first Degree: *Intervals*, 'tis plain, may differ in Magnitude, and there may be an infinite Variety according to the possible Degrees of Tune; for there is no Difference so great or little, but a greater or a less may possibly be conceived. 'Tis true, with regard to Practice, there are Limits which are the greatest and least *Intervals* our Ears are Judges of, and which may be actually produced by Voice or Instrument.

The Degrees of Tune are proportional to the Numbers of Vibrations of the sonorous Body in a given Time, or the Velocity of their Courses and Recourses. Now these Differences in Tune constitute, as has been already said, the *Intervals* of Music; these therefore must be greater or less, as the Differences are; and 'tis the Quantity of these, which is the Subject of the Mathematical Part of Music. Those *Intervals* are measured not in the simple Differences or Arithmetical Ratio's of the Numbers expressing the Lengths or Vibrations, but in their Geometric Ratio's; so that the same *Interval* depends on the same Geometrical Ratio, and *vice versâ*. It is however to be observed, that in comparing the Equality of *Intervals*, the Ratio's expressing them must be all of one Species; otherwise this Absurdity will follow, that the same two Sounds may make different *Intervals*. To describe the particular Methods of measuring the Inequality of *Intervals*, would be too tedious: this one Rule may be observed, that, to determine in general, which of two or more *Intervals* are the greatest, take all the Ratio's as proper Fractions, and the least Fraction will be the greatest *Interval*.

The Antients were extremely divided about the measuring of *Intervals*. *Pythagoras* and his Followers measur'd them by the Ratio's of Numbers. They supposed the Differences of Gravity and Acuteness to depend on the different Velocities of the Motion that causes Sound; and thought, therefore, that they could only be accurately measured by the Ratio's of those Velocities. Which Ratio's were first investigated by *Pythagoras*, on occasion of his passing by a Smith's Ship, and observing a Concord betwixt the Sounds of Hammers striking on the Anvil. *Aristoxenus* opposed this. He thought Reason and Mathematics had nothing to do in the case, and that Sense was the only Judge in the Dispute; the other being too subtile to be of any use. He therefore determined the 8ve, 5th, and 4th, which are the most simple Concords, by the Ear; and by the Difference of the 4th and 5th, he found out the Tone: which once settled as an *Interval* the Ear could judge of, he pretended to measure every *Interval* by various Additions and Subtractions made of these mentioned one with another: But this Method is very inaccurate. *Ptolemy* keeps a middle Course betwixt the two. He finds fault with the one for despising Reason, and with the other for excluding Sense; and shews how these two may mutually assist each other in this Matter. See *Tone, &c.*

key

1728 CHAMBERS *Key*, in Music, is a certain fundamental Note or Tone, to which the whole Piece, be it Concerta, Sonata, Cantata, *&c.* is accommodated, and with which it usually begins, but always ends. To get an Idea of the Use of the *Key*, it may be observed, that as in an Oration there is a Subject, *viz.* some principle Person or Thing to which the Discourse is referred, and which is always to be kept in view, that nothing unnatural and foreign to the Subject may be brought in; so in every regular Piece of Music there is one Note, *viz.* the *Key*, which regulates all the rest. The Piece begins, and ends in this; and this is, as it were, the musical Subject, to which a regard must be had in all the other Notes of the Piece. Again, as in an Oration there are several distinct Articles, which refer to different Subjects, yet so as that they have all a visible Connection with the principal Subject, which regulates and influences the whole; so in Music there may be various subaltern Subjects, that is, various *Keys*, to which the different Parts of the Piece may belong: but then they must be all under the Influence of the first and principal *Key*, and have a sensible Connection with it. Now to give a more distinct Notion of the *Key*, we must observe, that the Octave contains in it the whole Principles of Music, both with respect to Consonance or Harmony, and Succession or Melody; and that if either Scale be continued to a double Octave, there will, in that Case, be seven different Orders of the Degrees of an Octave, proceeding from the seven different Letters with which the Terms of the Scale are marked. Any given Sound therefore, *i.e.* a Sound of any determinate Pitch or Tune, may he [sic] made the *Key* of the Piece, by applying to it the seven natural Notes arising from the Division of an Octave, and repeating the Octave above or below at pleasure. The given Note is applied as the principal Note or *Key* of the Piece, by making frequent Closes or Cadences upon it; and in the Progress of the Melody no other but those seven natural Notes can be admitted, while the

Piece continues in that *Key*, every other Note being foreign to the Fundamental, or *Key*: For Instance, suppose a Song begun in any Note, and carried on upwards or downwards by Degrees and Harmonical Distances, so as never to touch any Notes but what are referable to that first Note as a Fundamental, *i.e.* are the true Notes of the natural Scale proceeding from the Fundamental; and let the Melody be so conducted thro' those natural Notes, as to close and terminate in the Fundamental, or any of its Octaves above or below, that Note is called the *Key* of the Melody, because it governs all the rest, limiting them so far, as that they must be, to it, in relation of the seven essential Notes of an Octave; and when any other Note is brought in, 'tis called, going out of the *Key*. From which way of speaking, *viz.* a Song's continuing in, or going out of the *Key*, it may be observed, that the whole Octave, with its natural Notes, come under the Idea of a *Key*, tho the Fundamental, or principal Note is, in a peculiar Sense, called the *Key*. In which last Sense of the word *Key* (*viz.* where it is applied to one fundamental Note) another Note is said to be out of the *Key*, when it has not the Relation to that Fundamental of any of the natural Notes belonging to the concinnous Division of the Octave. Here too it must be added, with respect to the two different Divisions of the Octave, that a Note may belong to the same *Key*, *i.e.* have a just musical Relation to the same Fundamental in one kind of Division, and be out of the *Key* with respect to the other.

Now a Piece of Music may be carried through several *Keys*; i.e. it may begin in one *Key*, and be led out of that into another, by introducing some Note foreign to the first, and so on to another: but a regular Piece must not only return to the first *Key*, but those other *Keys*, too, must have a particular Connection with the first. It may be added, that those other *Keys* must be some of the natural Notes of the principal *Key*, tho' not any of them at pleasure.

As to the Distinctions of *Keys*, we have already observed, that to constitute any given Note or Sound, a *Key*, or fundamental Note, it must have the seven essential or natural Notes added to it, out of which, or their Octaves, all the Notes of the Piece must be taken, while it keeps within the *Key*, i.e. within the Government of that Fundamental. 'Tis evident therefore there are but two different Species of *Keys*, which arise according as we join the greater or less Third, these being always accompanied with the sixth and seventh of the same Species; the third *g*, for instance, with the sixth and seventh *g*; and the third *l* with the sixth and seventh *l*. And this Distinction is expressed under the Names of a *Sharp-Key*, which is that with the third *g*, *&c.* and the *Flat-Key*, which is that with the third *l*, *&c.* whence 'tis plain, that how many different Closes soever there be in a Piece, there can be but two *Keys*, if we consider the essential Difference of *Keys*; every *Key* being either flat or sharp, and every *Sharp-Key* being the same, as to Melody, as well as every flat one. It must be observed, however, that in common Practice the *Keys* are said to be different, when nothing is considered but the different Tune, or Pitch of the Note, in which the different Closes are made: In which Sense the same Piece is said to be in different *Keys*, according as it begun in different Notes, or Degrees of Tune. To prevent any Confusion which might arise from using the same Word in different Senses, M. *Malcolm* proposes the word *Mode* to be substituted instead of the word *Key*, in the former Sense; that is, where it expresses the melodious Constitution of the Octave, as it consists of seven essential, or natural Notes, besides the Fundamental; and in regard there are two Species of it, he proposes, that with a third *g* be called the greater Mode, and that with a third *l* the lesser Mode; appropriating the word *Key* to those Notes of the Piece in which the Cadence is made; all of which may be called different *Keys*, in respect of their different Degrees of Tune. To distinguish then accurately between a Mode and a *Key*, he gives us this Definition, *viz.* an Octave, with all its natural and essential Degrees, is a Mode, with respect to the Constitution or Manner of dividing it; but with respect to its Place in the Scale of Music, *i.e.* the Degree or Pitch of Tune, it is a *Key*; tho' that Name is peculiarly applied to the Fundamental: whence it follows, that the same Mode may be with different *Keys*, i.e. an Octave of Sounds may be rais'd in the same Order and Kind of Degrees which makes the same Mode, and yet be begun higher or lower, *i.e.* be taken at different Degrees of Tune with respect to the whole, which makes different *Keys*; and, *vice versa*, that the same *Key* may be with different Modes, *i.e.* the Extremes of two Octaves may be in the same Degree of Tune, yet the Division of them be different. See *Modulation, Harmony, Melody, Clef.*

mode

1728 CHAMBERS *Mode* in Music, is defined by some Authors, the particular Manner of constituting the Octave; or the melodious Constitution of the Octave, as it consists of seven Essential, or Natural Notes besides the Key, or Fundamental. See *Octave*.

A *Mode*, then, is not any single Note, or Sound; but the particular Order of the concinnous Degrees of an Octave: The fundamental Note whereof may, in another sense, be call'd the *Key*, as it signifies that principal Note which regulates the rest.

The proper difference between a *Mode* and a Key, consists in this, that an Octave with all its natural and concinnous Degrees, is call'd a *Mode*, with respect to the Constitution, or the manner and way of dividing it; and with respect to the place of it in the Scale of Music, that is, the Degree or Pitch of Tune, it is call'd a *Key*: that is, an Octave of Sounds may be rais'd in the same Order, and Kind of Degrees which makes the same *Mode*, and yet be begun higher or lower; that is, be taken at different Degrees with respect to the whole, which makes different Keys: and from the same Definition it follows, that the same Key may be found with different *Modes*; that is, the Extremes of two Octaves may be in the same Degree of Tune, and the Division of 'em different. See *Key*.

Now if it be further observed, that of the natural Notes of every *Mode*, or Octave, three go under the Name of the essential Notes in a peculiar manner, *viz.* the Fundamental, the Third, and Fifth; their Octaves being reckon'd the same, and mark'd with the same Letters in the Scale: the rest are particularly call'd Dependents. Again, the Fundamental is also call'd the final; the Fifth the Dominante; and the Third, as being between the other two, the Mediante. See *Key*.

The Doctrine of the Antients with regard to *Modes*, which they sometimes also call Tones, is sometimes obscure; there being an unaccountable Difference among their Authors as to the Definition, Divisions, and Names of their *Modes*. They agree indeed, that a *Mode* is a certain System or Constitution of Sounds; and that an Octave, with all its intermediate Sounds, is such a Constitution: but the specific difference of Tones, some place in the manner of Division, or Order of its concinnous parts; and others merely in the different Tension of the Whole, *i,e.* as the whole Notes are acuter or graver, or stand higher or lower in the Scale of Music.

Boethius is very dark on this head; and defines a *Mode* to be, as it were, an intire Body of Modulation, consisting of a Conjunction of Consonances, as the Diapason.

Ptolemy makes the *Modes* the same with the Species of the Diapasons; but at the same time speaks of their being at some distance from each other. Some contended for thirteen, some for fifteen *Modes*, which they placed at a Semitone's distance from each other; but it is plain, those understood the differences to be only in their place or distances from each other; and that there is one certain harmonious Species of Octave apply'd to all, *viz.* that Order which proceeds from the *Proslambanomenos* of the *Systema Imutatum*, or the A of the modern System. *Ptolemy* argues, that if this be all, they may be infinite, tho' they must be limited for Use and Practice. But, indeed, much the greater part define them by the Species *Diapason*; and therefore only make seven *Modes*; but as to their Use, we are left intirely in the dark.

If the *Modes* be nothing but the seven Species of Octaves, the Use of 'em can only be, that the *Proslambanomenos* of any *Mode* being made the principal Note of any Song, there may be different Species of Melody answering to those different Constitutions. But then we are not to conceive that the *Proslambanomenos*, or Fundamental of any *Mode* is fixed to any particular Chord of the System, *v.g.* the *Phrygian* to g; so that we must always begin there, when we would have a piece of Melody of that Species. When we say in general, that such a *Mode* begins in *g*, it is no more than to signify the Species of Octave as they appear in a certain fix'd System; but we may begin in any Chord of the System, and make it the *Proslam.* of any *Mode*, by adding new Chords, or altering the tuning of the old. If this were the true nature, and use of the Tones, most of these *Modes* must be imperfect, and incapable of good Melody, as wanting some of those which we reckon the essential and natural Notes of a true *Mode*. Again, if the essential difference of the *Modes* consist only in the Gravity of Acuteness of the whole Octave, then we may suppose one Species or concinnous Division of the Octave, which being apply'd to all the Chords of the System, makes them true Fundamentals for a certain Series of successive Notes, by changing, as above, the Tone of certain Chords in some cases, or by adding new Chords to the System. But that must have been a simple kind of Melody, produced by admitting only one concinnous Series, and that too wanting some useful and necessary Chords.

Music was considerably improved in the XIth Century, by *Guido Aretinus*; who, among other Innovations, reformed the Doctrine of *Modes*. It is true, they were still defined by the Species of the Octave, in *Ptolemy*'s manner, and their number was fix'd to seven; but afterwards taking occasion to consider the Harmonical and Arithmetical Divisions of the Octave, whereby it resolves into a 4th above a 5th, or a 5th above a 4th, they hence constituted 12 *Modes*, making of each Octave two different *Modes*, according to this different Division; but because there are two of them that cannot be divided both ways, there are but 12 *Modes*. Of these, such as were divided harmonically, that is, with the 5ths lowest (which were six) were call'd *Authentic;* and the other six which had the 5ths highest, were call'd *Plagal Modes.* See the Scheme annex'd.

Plagal. 8ve.		Authentic. 8ve.	
4th	5th	4th	
g	*c*	*g*	*c*
a	*d*	*a*	*d*
b	*e*	*b*	*e*
c	*f*	*c*	*f*
d	*g*	*d*	*g*
e	*a*	*e*	*a*

To these *Modes,* they gave the Names of the antient *Greek* Tones, as *Dorian, Phrygian, Lydian*: But the several Authors differ in the Application and Order of these Names. So that we are still in great measure at a loss what they meant by those distinctions, and what their real use was. The best Account we can give is this; They consider'd that an Octave which wants a 4th or 5th, is imperfect; these being the Concords next to Octave, the Song ought to touch those Chords most frequently and remarkably; and because their Concord is different, which makes the Melody different, they established by this two *Modes* in every natural Octave that had a true 4th and 5th: Then, if the Song was carried as far as this Octave above, it was call'd a *perfect Mode;* if less, as to the 4th or 5th, it was *imperfect,* it if moved both above and below, it was call'd a *mix'd Mode.* Thus it is some Authors speak about these *Modes.* Others, considering how indispensible a Chord the 5th is in every *Mode,* they took for the Final, or Key-Note in the Arithmetically divided Octaves, not the lowest Chord of that Octave, but that very 4th. The only difference then in the Method between the Authentic and Plagal *Modes* is, that the Authentic goes above its Final to the Octave; the other ascends a 5th, and descends a 4th; which will indeed be attended with different Effects, but the *Mode* is essentially the same, having the same Final to which all the Notes refer. We are now to consider wherein the *Modes* of one Species, as Authentic, or Plagal, differ among themselves. This must either be by standing higher or lower in the Scale, *i.e.* by the different Tension of the whole Octave, or rather by the different Subdivision of the Octave into its concinnous Degrees; there can be no other. We are to consider then, whether these Differences are sufficient to produce such very different Effects as are ascribed to the several *Modes;* for instance, that the one produces Mirth, another Sadness, a third is proper for Religion, a fourth for Love, *&c.* That these Effects are owing merely to the Constitution of the Octave, scarce any body will affirm. The differences in the Constitution will, indeed, have some influence, but it will be so little, as that by the various Combinations of other Causes, one of these *Modes* may be used to different purposes. The greatest difference is that of those Octaves which have the 3d *l*, or 3d *g*, making what on other occasions we call the *Sharp* and *Flat* Key.

However, if the *Modes* depend upon the Species of Octaves, how can they be more than seven? And as to the distinction between Authentic and Plagal, we have already observed, that it is imaginary with respect to any essential Difference constituted thereby in the Kind of the Melody; for tho' the carrying the Song above or below the Final, may have different Effects, yet this is to be ascribed to other Causes besides the Constitution of the Octaves. It is particularly observable, that those Authors who give us Examples in actual Composition of their twelve *Modes,* frequently take in the Artificial Notes # and ♭, to perfect the Melody of their Key; and by this means depart from the Constitution of the Octave, as it stands fix'd in the natural System. There is nothing certain or consisting therefore in their way of speaking; but the *Modes* are all really reducible to two, *viz.* the Sharp and Flat; the other differences respecting only the Place of the Scale where the Fundamental is taken.

The antient *Modes,* besides their general Division into Authentic and Plagal, had also their respective Names from the several *Greek* Provinces where they are supposed to have been invented. Originally, indeed, there were but three, *viz. Doric, Lydian,* and *Phrygian;* which were particularly call'd Tones, because at a Tone's distance from one another. The rest were added afterwards, and were some of them named from the relations they bore to the former, particularly the *Hypo-Doric,* as being below the *Doric.*

The *Doric Mode* was a mixture of Gravity and Mirth, invented by *Thamiras* of *Thrace.* See *Doric.*

The *Phrygian Mode* was adapted to the kindling of Rage; invented by *Marsyas* the *Phrygian*. See *Phrygian*.
The *Lydian Mode* was proper for Funeral Songs; invented, according to *Pliny*, by *Amphion*. See *Lydian*.
The *Myxolodian* [sic] was invented by *Sappho*.
The *Æolic*, *Ionic*, and *Hypo-Doric* were invented by *Philoxenus*.
The *Hypo-Lydian* by *Polymnestes*.
Besides these *Modes* of *Tune*, old Authors have also introduced *Modes of Time*, or Measures of Notes.

These at first were distinguished into Greater and Less, and each of these again into *Perfect* and *Imperfect*. But afterwards they reduced all into four *Modes*, which included the whole Business of Times. As those *Modes* are now disused, they are hardly worth the reciting.

The common *Mode* now in use, is much more Simple and Natural than any of those; the Proportion, which in theirs varied, being in ours fix'd, *viz.* 2:1. A Large equal to two Long; a Long to two Breves; a Breve to two Semibreves, *&c.* proceeding in the same Proportion to the last or lowest Notes. And if on some Occasions the Proportion of 3:1 betwixt two successive Notes is required, it is easily express'd by annexing a Point (.). See *Time, Note, &c.*

The Antients had likewise their *Modi Melopoeiæ*, of which Aristides names these, *Dithyrambic, Nomic*, and *Tragic*, call'd *Modes* from their expressing the several Motions and Affections of the Mind. See *Melopoeia* [no such entry given].

music

1728 Chambers *Music*, the Science of Sound, consider'd as capable of producing Melody, or Harmony: or, the Art of disposing and conducting Sounds, considered as grave and acute; and of proportioning them among themselves, and separating them by just Intervals, pleasing to the Sense. See *Sound*.

Mr. *Malcolm* better defines *Music*, a Science that teaches how Sounds under certain Measures of Tune, and Time, may be produc'd, and so order'd or dispos'd, as either in Consonance (*i.e.* joint Sounding) or Succession, or both, as they may raise agreeable Sensations.

From this Definition, the Science naturally divides itself into two general Parts, *Speculative* and *Practical*.

The *first*, the knowledge of the *Materia Musica*, or how to produce Sounds in such Relations of Tune, and Time, as shall be agreeable in Consonance, or Succession, or both: By which, we don't mean the actual Production of these Sounds by an Instrument or Voice, which is meerly the mechanical or effective Part; but the Knowledge of the various Relations of Tune or Time, which are the Principles, out of which the Pleasure sought derives. See *Tune*.

The 2*d*, How these Principles are to be apply'd; or how Sounds, in the Relations they bear to *Music* (as those are determin'd in the first part) may be order'd, and variously put together in Succession and Consonance, so as to answer the End: And this we call the Art of *Composition*, which is properly the practical Part of *Music*. See *Composition*.

Some add a third Branch, *viz.* the Knowledge of *Instruments*; but as this depends altogether on the first, and is only an Application or Expression of it, it cannot come regularly under the Definition, and consequently is no part of the Division of the Science.

The first Branch, which is the contemplative Part, divides itself into these two, *viz.* the Knowledge of the Relations and Measures of Time, and the Doctrine of Time itself.

The former is properly what the Antients call'd *Harmonica*, or the Doctrine of Harmony in Sounds, as containing an Explication of the Grounds, with the various Measures and Degrees of the Agreement of Sounds, in respect of their Tune. See *Harmonica*.

The latter is what they call'd *Rythmica*, because it treats of the Numbers of Sounds or Notes with respect to Time; containing an Explication of the Measures of long and short, or swift and slow, in the Succession of Sounds. See *Rythmica*.

The second Branch, which is the practical part, as naturally divides into two parts, answering to the parts of the first.

That which answers to the *Harmonica*, the Antients called *Melopœia*, because it contains the Rules of making Songs, with respect to Tune, and Harmony of Sounds; tho we have no reason to think the Antients had any thing like Composition in Parts. See *Melopoeia* [no such entry given].

That which answers to the *Rythmica*, they call'd *Rythmopœia*, containing Rules for the Application of the Numbers and Time. See *Rythmopoeia*.

We find a strange Diversity in the antient Writers, as to the Nature, Office, Extent, Division, *&c.* of *Music*.

The Name is suppos'd originally form'd from *Musa,* Muse; the Muses being suppos'd to be the Inventors thereof. *Kircher,* however, will have it take its Name from an *Egyptian* Word, as supposing its Restoration after the Flood to have begun there, by reason of the Reeds, *&c.* on the Banks of the *Nyle. Hesychius* tells us, the *Athenians* gave the Name Music to every Art.

Hermes Trismegistus defines *Music* to be the Knowledge of the Order of all things; which is also the Doctrine of the *Pythagorean* School, and of the *Platonists,* who teach, that every thing in the Universe is *Music.*

Agreeable to which wide Sense, some divide *Music* into *Divine* and *Mundane.*

The first respecting the Order and Harmony that obtains among the Celestial Minds; the other, the Relations and Order of every thing else in the Universe. *Plato,* however, by the *Divine Music,* understands that which exists in the Divine Mind, *viz.* those Archetypal Ideas of Order and Symmetry, according to which God formed all things: And as this Order exists in the Mundane Creatures, he calls it *Mundane Music.*

Which last Species they again subdivided into four, *viz.* 1. *Elementary Music,* or the Harmony of the Elements of Things.

2. *Celestial Music,* or the *Music* of the Spheres; comprehending the Order and Proportions in the Magnitudes, Distances and Motions of the heavenly Bodies, and the Harmony of the Sounds resulting from those Motions.

3. *Human Music,* which consists chiefly in the Harmony of the Faculties of the human Soul, and its various Passions; and is also consider'd in the Proportion, Temperament and mutual Dependance of the Parts of the Body.

4. What, in the proper and limited sense of the Word, is call'd *Music;* which has for its Object, Motion, consider'd as under certain regular Measures and Proportions, by which it affects the Senses in an agreeable manner.

Now as Motion belongs to Bodies, and as Sound is the Effect of Motion, and cannot be without it, but all Motions does not produce Sound; hence this last Branch of *Music* became subdivided.

Where the Motion is without Sound, or as 'tis only the Object of Sight, it was either call'd *Musica Orchestria* or *Saltatoria,* which contains the Rules for the regular Motions of Dancing; or *Musica Hypocritica,* which respects the Motion and Gestures of the Pantomimes.

When the Motion is perceiv'd only by the Ear, *i.e.* when Sound is the Object of *Music,* there were three Species; *viz. Harmonica,* which considers the Differences and Proportions with respect to Grave and Acute; *Rythmica,* which respects the Proportion of the Sounds as to Time, or the Swiftness and Slowness of their Successions; and *Metrica,* which belongs properly to the Poets, and respects the Art of making Verses.

Aristides Quintilianus, Bacchius, and other antient Writers, define *Music* the Knowledge of Singing, and of the Things belonging thereto; which he calls the Motions of the Voice and Body: as if the Singing itself consisted only in the different Tones of the Voice.

The same Author [presumably Quintilian], considering *Music* in the largest sense of the Word, divides it into *Contemplative* and *Active.* The first, he says, is either *Natural* or *Artificial.* The *Natural* is either *Arithmetical,* because it considers the Proportion of Numbers; or *Physical,* which examines the Order of the Things of Nature.

The artificial he divides, as above, into *Harmonica, Rythmica, Metrica.*

The active, which is the Application of the artificial, is either *Enuntiative* (as in Oratory;) *Organical* (or Instrumental Performance;) *Odical* (for Voice and singing of Psalms;) *Hypocritical,* in the Motions of the Pantomimes. To which some add *Hydraulical,* tho' in reality no more than a Species of the Organical; to which, Water is used, for the producing or modifying of Sound.

Porphyry makes another Division of *Music,* taking it in the limited Sense, as having Motion both dumb and sonorous for its Object; and without distinguishing the Speculative and Practical, he makes its Parts these six, *viz. Rythmica,* for the Motions of Dancing; *Metrica,* for the Cadence and Recitation; *Organica,* for the Practice of Instruments; *Poetica,* for the Numbers and Feet of Verses; *Hypocritica,* for the Gestures of the *Pantomimes;* and *Harmonica,* for Singing.

The *Musical Faculties,* as they call them, are *Melopœia,* which gives Rules for the Tones of the Voice or Instrument; *Rythmopœia,* for Motions, and *Poesis,* for making Verses.

Music appears to have been one of the most antient of Arts. And of all others, *Vocal Music* must undoubtedly have been the first Kind. For Man had not only the various Tones of his own Voice to make his Observations on, before any other Art or Instrument was found out, but had the various natural Strains of Birds, to give him occasion to improve his own Voice, and the Modulations of Sounds it was capable of.

Of many antient Authors who agree in this Conjecture, we shall only mention *Lucretius*, who says,

At Liquidas Avium Voces imitarier Ore,
Ante fuit multo quam levia Carmina Cantu,
Concelebrare Homines possent, Aureisque juvare.

The first Invention of string'd Instruments he ascribes to the Observation of the Winds whistling in the hollow Reeds.

As for other kind[s] of Instruments, there were so many Occasions for *Chords* or Strings, that Men could not be long in observing their various Sounds, which might give Rise to string'd *Instruments*. See *Chord*.

And for the pulsatile Instruments, as *Drums* and *Cymbals*, they might arise from the Observation of the hollow Noise of concave Bodies.

Plutarch, in one place, ascribes the first Invention of *Music* to the God *Apollo*, and in another to *Amphion*, the Son of *Jupiter* and *Antiope*. This last, however, is pretty generally allow'd to have been the first who brought *Music* into *Greece*, and to have been the Inventor of the *Lyre*. The Time he lived in, is not agreed upon. See *Lyra*.

To him succeeded *Chiron*, the Demi-God; *Demodocus; Hermes Trismegistus; Olympus; Orpheus*, whom some make the first Introducer of *Music* into *Greece*, and the Inventor of the *Lyra; Phemius; Terpander*, who was Contemporary with *Lycurgus*, and set his Laws to *Music*. To him some attribute the first Institution of *Musical* Modes, and the Invention of the *Lyre; Thales;* and *Thamyris*, who is said to have been the first Inventor of Instrumental *Music* without Singing.

These were the eminent Musicians before *Homer*'s Time. Others of a later Date, were *Lasus Hermionensis, Melnippides, Philoxenus, Timotheus, Phrynnis, Epigonius, Lysander, Simmicus*, and *Diodorus*; who were all considerable Improvers of *Music*. *Lasus* is said to have been the first Author who wrote on *Music* in the Time of *Darius Hystaspes; Epigonius* invented an Instrument of forty Strings, call'd the *Epigonium*. *Simmicus* also invented an Instrument, call'd *Simmicium*, of thirty-five Strings. *Diodorus* improv'd the *Tibia*, by adding new Holes; and *Timotheus* the *Lyre*, by adding a new String; for which he was fined by the *Lacedemonians*.

As the Accounts we have of the Inventors of *Musical* Instruments among the Antients, are very obscure; so are also the Accounts what those Instruments were; we scare knowing any thing of them besides the bare Name.

The general Division of Instruments, is into *Stringed Instruments, Wind Instruments*, and the *Pulsatile Kind*. Of *Stringed Instruments*, we hear of the *Lyra* or *Cythara*, the *Psalterium, Trigon, Sambuca, Pectis, Magadis, Barbiton, Testudo, Epigonium, Simmicium*, and *Pandura*, which were all struck with the Hand, or a *Plectrum;* and which see in their Places.

Of *Wind Instruments*, we hear of the *Tibia, Fistula, Hydraulic Organs, Tubæ, Cornua*, and *Lituus*.

The *Pulsatile Instruments*, were the *Tympanum, Cymbalum, Crepitaculum, Tintinnabalum, Crotalum*, and *Sistrum*; which see.

Music has even been in the highest Esteem in all Ages, and among all People. Nor could Authors express their Opinion of it strongly enough, but by inculcating, that it was used in Heaven, and was one of the principal Entertainments of the Gods, and the Souls of the Blessed.

The Effects ascribed to it by the Antients, are almost miraculous; by means hereof, Diseases are said to have been cured, Unchastity corrected, Seditions quell'd, Passions rais'd and calm'd, and even Madness occasion'd. *Athenæus* assures us, that antiently all Laws Divine and Human Things, Lives and Actions of illustrious Men, were written in Verse, and publickly sung by a Chorus to the Sound of Instruments; which was found the most effectual means to impress Morality, and a right Sense of Duty on the Mind.

Music made a great part of the Discipline of the antient *Pythagoreans*, and was used by them to draw over the Mind to laudable Actions, and settle in it a passionate Love of Virtue. It being their Doctrine, that the Soul itself consists of Harmony; and therefore by *Music*, they pretended to revive the primitive Harmony of its Faculties. By this primitive Harmony, they meant that which, according to their *Dogma*, was in the Soul, in its pre-existent State in Heaven. See *Pythagorean*.

Dr. *Wallis* has endeavour'd to account for the surprising Effects ascribed to the antient *Music;* and charges them principally on the Novelty of the Art, and the Hyperbola's of the antient Writers: Nor does he doubt but the modern *Music, cæteris paribus*, would produce Effects at least as considerable as the antient. The truth is, we can match most of the antient Stories of this kind in the modern Histories. If *Timotheus* could excite *Alexander*'s Fury with the *Phrygian* Sound, and sooth him into Indolence with the *Lydian;* a more modern

Musician is said to have driven *Eric* King of *Denmark* into such a Rage, as to kill his best Servants. Dr. *Niewentiit* tells us of an *Italian*, who by varying his *Music* from brisk to solemn, and so *vice versa*, could move the Soul, so as to cause Distraction and Madness. And Dr. *South* has founded his Poem, call'd *Musica Incantans*, on an Instance he knew of the same thing.

Music, however, is not only found to exert its Force on the Affections, but on the Parts of the Body also; witness the *Gascon* Knight, mention'd by Mr. *Boyle*, who could not contain his Water at the playing of a Bag-pipe; the Woman, mention'd by the same Author, who could burst out in Tears at the hearing of a certain Tune, with which other People were but little affected: To say nothing of the trite Story of the *Tarantula*. We have an Instance of the *French* Academy, of a Musician's being cured of a violent Fever, by a little Concert occasionally play'd in his Room.

Nor are our Minds and Bodies alone affected with Sounds, but even inanimate Bodies. *Kircher* tells us of a large Stone, that would tremble at the Sound of one particular Organ-pipe; and *Morhoff* mentions one *Petter*, a *Dutch man*, who could break *Rummer-Glasses* with the Tone of his Voice. *Mersenne* also tells us of a particular Part of a Pavement, that would shake and tremble, as if the Earth would open, when the Organs play'd. Mr. *Boyle* adds, that Seats will tremble at the Sound of Organs; that he has felt his Hat do so under his Hand, at certain Notes both of Organs and Discourse; and that he was well inform'd, every well-built Vault would answer some determinate Note.

There is a great Dispute among the Learned, whether the Antients or Moderns best understood and practised *Music*: Some maintaining that the antient Art of *Music*, by which such wonderful Effects were perform'd, is quite lost; and others, that the true Science of Harmony is now arrived to much greater Perfection, than was known or practised among the Antients.

This Point is no other way to be determined, but by comparing the Principles and Practice of the one with those of the other.

As to the Theory or Principles of Harmonics, 'tis certain we understand it better than they; because we know all that they knew, and have improved considerably on their Foundations. The great Dispute then lies on the Practice.

With regard to this, it may be observ'd, that among the Antients, *Music*, in the most limited Sense of the Word, included *Harmony, Rythmus*, and *Verse*; and consisted of Verses sung by one or more Voices alternately; or in Choirs, sometimes with the Sound of Instruments, and sometimes by Voices only.

Their Musical Faculties, we have already observed, were *Melopœia, Rythmopœia*, and *Poesis*. The first whereof may be consider'd under two Heads, *viz. Melody* and *Symphony*. As to the latter, it contains nothing but what relates to the Conduct of a single Voice, or making what we call *Melody*. Nor do they appear to have ever thought of the Concert, or Harmony of Parts. This then was no part of the antient Practice, but entirely a modern Invention, to which we are beholden to *Guido Aretinus*, a *Benedictine* Friar. We would not, however, be understood to mean, that the Antients never join'd more Voices or Instruments than one together in the same Symphony; but that they never join'd several Voices, so as that each had a distinct and proper Melody, which made among them a Succession of various Concords, and were not in every Note Unisons, or at the same Distance from each other as Octaves. This last indeed agrees to the general Definition of the Word *Symphonia*; yet 'tis plain that in such Cases, there is but one Song, and all the Voices perform the same individual Melody. But when the Parts differ, not by the Tension of the whole, but by the different Relations of the successive Notes, this is the modern Art, which requires so peculiar a Genius, and on which account the modern *Music* has much the advantage of the antient. For further satisfaction on the Subject, see *Kircher, Perrault*, Dr. *Wallis*, Mr. *Malcolm*, and others; who unanimously agree, that after all the pains they have taken to know the true State of the antient Music, they could not find the least reason to think there was any such thing in their Days as *Music* in Parts. See *Symphony, Synaulia, &c.*

The antient *Musical* Notes are very mysterious and perplexed: *Boetius* and *Gregory the Great* first put 'em into a more easy and obvious Method. It was in the Year 1204, that *Guido Aretine*, a Benedictine of *Aretium* in *Tuscany*, first introduced the Use of a Staff with five Lines, on which, with the Spaces, he marked his Notes by setting a Point up and down upon 'em, to denote the Rise and Fall of the Voice; tho *Kircher* mentions this Artifice to have been in use before *Guido*'s Time. See *Note, Staff, &c.*

Another Contrivance of *Guido*'s was to apply the six Musical Syllables *ut, re, mi, fa, sol, la*, which he took out of the *Latin* Hymn,

UT *queant Laxis* REsonare *fibris*
MI*ra Gestorum* FA*muli tuorum*

SOLve polluti LA*bii reatum.*

O Pater Alme.

Besides his Notes of *Music,* by which, according to *Kircher,* he distinguished the Tones, or Modes, and the Seats of the Semi-tones, he also invented the Scale, and several Musical Instruments, call'd *Polyplectra,* as Spinets and Harpsichords. See *Note, Gamut, &c.*

The next considerable Improvement was in 1330, when *Joannes de Muris,* Doctor at *Paris,* invented the different Figures of Notes, which express the Times, or Length of every Note, at least their true relative Proportions to one another, now call'd *Longs, Breves, Semi-breves, Crochets, Quavers,* &c.

The most antient Writer of *Music,* we have already observed, was *Lasus Hermionensis;* but his Work, as well as those of many others both *Greek* and *Roman,* are lost. *Aristoxenus,* Disciple of *Aristotle,* is the eldest Author extant on the Subject; after him came *Euclid,* Author of the Elements: *Aristides Quintilianus* wrote after *Cicero*'s time. *Alypius* stands next; after him *Gaudentius* the Philosopher, and *Nicomacus* the *Pythagorean,* and *Bacchius.* Of which seven *Greek* Authors, we have a fair Copy, with a Translation and Notes, by *Meibomius. Ptolemy,* the celebrated Mathematician, wrote in *Greek* of the Principles of Harmonics, about the time of the Emperor *Antoninus Pius.* This Author keeps a Medium between the *Pythagoreans* and *Aristoxenians.* He was succeeded at a good distance by *Manuel Bryennius.*

Of the *Latins* we have *Boethius,* who wrote in the time of *Theodoric* the *Goth,* and one *Cassiodorus;* about the same time *Martianus,* and St. *Augustin* not far remote. Of the Moderns are *Zarlin, Vincenzo Galileo, Doni, Kircher, Mersenne, Paran, de Caux, Perrault, Wallis, Des Cartes, Holdisworth, Malcolm,* &c.

Musical Sound, See *Sound. Musical String,* See *Chord. Musical Faculties,* See *Music. Musical Notes,* See *Note.*

note

1728 CHAMBERS *Notes* in Music, are Characters which mark the Tones, *i.e.* the Elevations, and Fallings of the Voice; and the swiftness, or slowness of its Motions. See *Sound.*

In the general, under *Notes* are comprehended all the Signs, or Characters used in Music, for the making Harmony of Sounds. See *Character.*

But, in Propriety, the Word only implies the Marks which *denote* the degree of Gravity, or Acuteness, to be given each Sound. See *Gravity.*

The *Greeks* used the common Letters of their Alphabet for musical *Notes;* and in regard more Notes were needed than they had Letters, the defect was supply'd by the different Situation of the Letters, *viz.* by placing of them upright, inverted, *&c.* and by cutting off, or doubling some Strokes.

Thus the same Letter *Pi,* express'd different *Notes* in all the following forms, ⊓ ⊔ ⊏ ⊐ ⌈ ⌉. For every several *Mode* they had 18 Signs.

Now, *Alipius* gives us Signs for 15 different *Modes,* which with the differences of the *Genera,* and the distinction between Voice and Instrument, Mr. *Malcolm* observes, makes in all 1620 *Notes.* Not that they had so many distinct Characters; but the same Character has different Significations, on different Occasions. Thus ϕ in the *Diatonic* Genus is *Lycanos Hypaton* of the *Lydian* Mode; and *Hypate meson* of the *Phrygian.*

The *Latins,* in the time of *Boethius,* had eased themselves of so needless a Burthen; and only used the first 15 Letters of their Alphabet for *Notes.* These, Pope *Gregory* considering that the Octave was the same in effect with the first, and that the order was the same in the upper and lower Octave of the Gamut, reduced to seven; which were to be repeated in a different Character.

At length, in the 11th Century, a *Benedictine,* one *Guido Aretin,* in lieu of the Letters, substituted the six Syllables *ut, re, mi, fa, sol, la;* placing them on different Lines, and marking them with Points. Lastly, it was thought proper to add *Notes* likewise in the Spaces. See *Gamut.*

Of the seven musical *Notes, ut, re, mi, fa, sol, la, si,* the first six are ascribed to *Aretine,* who is said to have invented them at *Pomposa* in the Dutchy of *Ferrara.* The seventh, *viz. si,* was added, according to some, by *Vander Putten;* according to others, by *Le Maire.* It serves very good purposes, in avoiding the difficulty of the Divisions remaining in *Guido*'s Scale.

Indeed *Vossius* won't allow *Guido* the Honour of inventing any of them; but shews that the *Egyptians* had used them long before him; in which he is confirmed by the Testimony of *Halicarnasseus*: However, common Fame ascribes to him not only the Notes, but also the Lines, Letters, or Clefs, Flats, and *Sharps.*

The *Notes ut, re, mi,* &c. he is said to have taken from a Hymn in the Vespers of S. *J. Baptist, Ut queant laxis resonare fibris, &c.* See *Music.*

Hitherto the *Notes* only served to express the Degrees of Tune; they were all of equal value as to time; till about the Year 1330, *John de Meurs,* a Doctor of *Paris,* gave different Figures to the different Points, to express the Quantity of Time each was to be dwelt upon.

There are three things to be consider'd in these *Notes.* 1. The *Quantity, i.e.* the size and figure of the head. 2. The *Quality, i.e.* the Colour of the head, whether it be white or black, full or open. 3. The *Properties,* as the *Italians* express themselves, *viz.* whether the Note is accompanied with a Virgula, or Comma, or not. It must likewise be consider'd whether the *Notes* be separate and distinct, or bound together.

The several musical *Notes,* are, the *Large,* which contains 8 Measures, tho *Mersennus* makes it 12. (see its Figure under *Character;*) the *Long,* containing 4 Measures; the *Breve,* containing 2; the *Semibreve,* containing 1; the *Minim* $\frac{1}{2}$; the *Crochet* $\frac{1}{4}$; the *Quaver* [$\frac{1}{8}$]; the *Semiquaver* $\frac{1}{16}$; and the Demisemiquaver $\frac{1}{32}$.

Usually we only distinguish six principal *Notes,* represented by as many different Characters, *viz.* the *Semibreve,* equal to two Minims; the *Minim,* equal to two Crochets; the *Crochet,* equal to two Quavers; the *Quaver,* equal to two Demiquavers; and the *Semiquaver,* equal to two Demi-semiquavers. See each under its proper Article, *Semibreve, Minim, Crochet, &c.*

octave

1728 Chambers *Octave,* in Music, an harmonical Interval consisting of 8 Tones, or Degrees of Sound. See *Interval* and *Degree.*

The most simple Perception the Soul can have of true Sounds, is that of *Unison;* in regard the Vibrations there begin and end together. The next to this is the *Octave;* wherein the more acute Sound makes precisely two Vibrations, while the graver or deeper makes one; and wherein, by consequence, the Vibrations of the two meet at every Vibration of the more grave. See *Tune, Gravity, &c.*

Hence Unison and *Octave* pass almost for the same Concord. See *Unison.*

Hence also the Proportion of the Sounds that form the *Octave* are in Numbers, or in Lines, as 2 to 1: so that two Chords or Strings of the same Matter, Thickness, and Tension, one whereof is double the length of the other, produce the *Octave.* See *Chord.*

The *Octave* is call'd by the Antients *Diapasan* [sic], because containing all the simple Tones and Concords; all of which derive their Sweetness from it, as they arise more or less directly out of it. See *Concord.*

To be just, it must contain diatonically 7 Degrees, or Intervals; and consequently 8 Terms, or Sounds, whence its Name, *Octave.*

The *Octave* containing in it all the other simple Concords, and the Degrees being the Differences of these Concords; it is evident the Division of the *Octave* comprehends the Division of all the rest. See *System.*

By joining, therefore, all the simple Concords to a common Fundamental, we have the following Series:

1 :	$\frac{5}{6}$:	$\frac{4}{5}$:	$\frac{3}{4}$:	$\frac{2}{3}$:	$\frac{5}{8}$:	$\frac{3}{5}$:	$\frac{1}{2}$.
Fund.	*3d* l,	*3d* 9,	*4th,*	*5th,*	*6th* l,	6th *g,*	*8ve.*

Again, the System of *Octave* containing all the original Concords; and the compound Concords being the Sum of *Octave,* and some lesser Concord; in order to have a Series to reach beyond an *Octave,* we must continue them in the same Order thro a second *Octave,* as in the first; and so on thro a third and fourth *Octave.* Such a Series is call'd the Scale of *Music.* See *Scale.*

Tho the Composition of *Octaves* may be carried on infinitely, yet three or four *Octaves* is the greatest length we go in ordinary Practice. The old Scales went no further than two, or at most three *Octaves,* which is the full compass of an ordinary Voice. And, notwithstanding the Perfection of the *Octave,* yet after the third, the Agreement diminishes very fast; nor do they ever go so far at one Movement, as from one extreme to the other of a double or triple *Octave;* seldom beyond a single *Octave*: Nor is either Voice or Instrument well able to go beyond. To form a fourth *Octave,* if the acuter String be half a Foot, which is but a small Length to give a clear Sound; the longer must be eight Feet. If then we go beyond the fourth *Octave,* either the acute Term will be too short, or the grave one too long.

The *Octave* is not only the greatest Interval of the seven original Concords, but the first in degree of Perfection. As it is the greatest Interval, all the less are contain'd in it: Indeed, the manner wherein the less Concords are found in the *Octave,* is somewhat extraordinary; *viz.* by taking both an harmonical and arithmetical Mean between the Extremes of the *Octave,* and then both an arithmetical and harmonical Mean between each Extreme, and the most distant of the two Means last found; *i.e.* between the less Extreme and the first arithmetical, and between the greater Extreme and the first harmonical Mean, we have all the lesser Concords. See *Concord.*

Mr. *Malcolm* observes, that any Wind-Instrument being over-blown, the Sound will rise to an *Octave,* and no other Concord; which he ascribes to the Perfection of the *Octave,* and its being next to Unison.

From this simple and perfect Form of the *Octave,* arises this peculiar Property, that it may be doubled, tripled, *&c.* and still be Concord; *i.e.* the Sum of two or more *Octaves* are Concord; tho the more Compound, gradually, the less agreeable. He adds, there is that Agreement between its Extremes, that whatever Sound is Concord to one Extreme of the *Octave,* is so to the other.

Des Cartes, from an Observation of the like kind, *viz.* that the Sound of a Whistle or Organ-Pipe, will rise to an *Octave,* if forcibly blown; concludes, that no Sound is heard, but its acute *Octave* seems someway to echo or resound in the Ear.

ode

1728 CHAMBERS *Ode,* in the antient Poetry, a *Song;* or a Composition proper to be sung, and composed for that purpose; the singing usually accompanied with some musical Instrument, chiefly the Lyre; whence the *Ode* became denominated *Lyric.* See *Song* and *Lyric.*

Ode, in the modern Poetry, is a Lyric Poem, consisting of long and short Verses, distinguish'd into *Stanza's,* or *Strophes,* wherein the same measure is preserved throughout.

The Word comes from the *Greek* ᾠδή, *Singing.*

The *Odes* of the Antients, *Vossius* observes, had a regular Return of the same kind of Verse, and the same Quantity of Syllables in the same Place of every similar Verse: "But there is nothing (says he) but confusion of Quantities in the modern *Odes;* so that to follow the natural Quantity of our Syllables, every Stanza will be a different Song."

He should have observ'd, however, that all the antient *Odes* were not of such kind. But he proceeds: "The Moderns have no regard to the natural Quantity of the Syllables, and have introduced an unnatural and barbarous Variety of long and short Notes, which they apply without any regard to the natural Quantity of the Syllables: so that it is no wonder our vocal Music has no effect." in *Poem. Cantu.* See *Verse, Vocal Music, Quantity, &c.*

Among the Antients, *Ode* signified no more than a *Song;* with us, they are different things. Their *Odes* were generally in honour of their Gods; as many of those of *Pindar* and *Horace*: sometimes on other Subjects; as those of *Anacreon, Sapho,* &c.

The *English Odes* are generally composed in praise of Hero's and great Exploits; as those of *Prior,* or *Welsted,* &c.

The distinguishing Character of the *Ode* is *Sweetness*: The Poet is to sooth the Minds of his Readers by the variety of the Verse, and the delicacy of Words, the beauty of Numbers, and the description of things most delightful in themselves. Variety of Numbers is essential to the *Ode.*

At first, indeed, the Verse of the *Ode* was but of one kind; but for the sake of Pleasure, and the Music to which they were sung, they by degrees so varied the Numbers and Feet, that their Kinds are now almost innumerable. One of the most considerable is the *Pindaric,* distinguish'd by the Boldness and Rapidity of its Flights. See *Pindaric* [entry not reproduced].

The antient *Ode* had originally but one *Stanza,* or *Strophe;* but was at last divided into three Parts: The *Strophe, Antistrophe,* and *Epode;* the Priests going round the Altar, singing the Praise of the Gods, call'd their first Entrance *Strophe, i.e.* turning to the left; the second, turning to the right, they call'd *Antistrophe; i.e.* returning. And accordingly, the Song, in those different Places, was call'd *Ode* and *Epode.* See *Strophe* and *Antistrophe.*

Lastly, standing still before the Altar, they sung the remainder; which they also call'd *Epode.* See *Epode.*

organ

1728 CHAMBERS *Organ,* in Music, the largest and most harmonious of all Wind-Instruments. See *Music.*

The Invention of the *Organ* is very antient, tho' tis is agreed it was very little used till the VIIIth Century. It seems to have been borrow'd from the *Greeks. Vitruvius* describes one in his tenth Book. The Emperor *Julian* has an Epigram in its praise. St. *Jerom* mentions one with twelve Pair of Bellows, which might be heard a thousand Paces, or a Mile; and another at *Jerusalem,* which might be heard to the Mount of Olives. The Structure of the modern *Organ* may be conceiv'd as follows.

The *Organ* is a Buffet containing several Rows of Pipes. The Size of the *Organ* is usually express'd by the length of its largest Pipe: Thus we say an *Organ* of 32 Feet, of 16 Feet, of 8 Feet, and of 2 Feet. Church *Organs* consist of two Parts, *viz.* the main Body of the *Organ*, call'd the *great Organ*; and the *Positive*, or *little Organ*, which is a small Buffet usually placed before the great *Organ*.

The *Organ* has at least one Set of Keys, when it has only one Body; and two or three, when it has a Positive. The large *Organs* have four, sometimes five Sets. Besides, the Pedals or largest Pipes have their Key, the Stops or Touches whereof are play'd by the Feet. The Keys of an *Organ* are usually divided into four Octaves; *viz.* the second *Sub-Octave*, first Sub-Octave, middle Octave, and first Octave. Each Octave is divided into twelve Stops or Frets; whereof the seven black mark the natural Sounds, and the five white the artificial Sounds; *i.e.* the Flats and Sharps. So that the Keys usually contain 48 Stops, or Touches. Some Organists add to this Number one or more Stops in the third Sub-Octave, as well as in the second. Note, in Harpsichords and Spinets, the natural Stops or Keys are usually mark'd white, the artificial ones black. The Pedals have about two or three Octaves at the pleasure of the Organist: So that the number of Stops is undeterminate.

Each Key or Stop press'd down, opens a Valve or Plug, which corresponds, lengthwise, to as many Holes as there are Rows of Pipes on the Sound-Board. The Holes of each Row are open'd and shut by a Register or Ruler pierced with 48 Holes. By drawing the Register, the Holes of one Row are open'd, because the Holes of the Register correspond to those of the Sound-board. So that by opening a Valve, the Wind brought into the Sound-board by a large Pair of Bellows, finds a Passage into the Pipe which corresponds to the open Hole of the Sound-board. But by pushing the Register, the 48 Holes of the Register, not answering to any of those of the Sound-board, that Row of Pipes answering to the push'd Register are shut. Whence it follows, that by drawing several Registers, several Rows of Pipes are open'd; and the same thing happens, if the same Register correspond[s] to several Rows. Hence the Rows of Pipes become either Simple, or Compound; *Simple*, when only one Row answers to one Register; *Compound*, where several. The Organists say, a Row is *Compound*, when several Pipes play upon pressing one Stop.

The Pipes of the *Organ* are of two kinds; the one with Mouths, like our Flutes; the other with Reeds. The first call'd *Pipes of Mutation*, consist,

1. Of a Foot AABB, (Tab. *Music, Fig.* 1.) [follows article on gamut] which is a hollow Cone, and which receives the Wind that is to sound the Pipe. 2. To this Foot is fasten'd the Body of the Pipe BBDD. Between the Foot and the Body of the Pipe is a Diaphragm, or Partition EEF, which has a little, long, narrow Aperture to let our the Wind. Over this Aperture is the Mouth BBCC; whose upper Lip CC, being level, cuts the Wind as it comes out at the Aperture.

The Pipes are of Pewter, Lead mix'd with a twelfth Part of Tin, and of Wood. Those of Tin are always open at their Extremities; their Diameter is very small, their Sound very clear and shrill. Those of Lead mix'd, are larger; the shortest open, the largest are quite stop'd; the mean ones partly stop'd, and having besides a little Ear on each side the Mouth, to be drawn closer, or set further asunder, in order to raise or lower the Sound. The wooden Pipes are made square, and their Extremity stop'd with a Valve or Tampion of Leather. The Sound of the wooden and leaden Pipes is very soft; the large ones stop'd, are usually of Wood; the small ones of Lead. The longest Pipes give the greatest Sound; and the shortest the most acute: Their Lengths and Widths are made in the reciprocal Ratio's of their Sounds; and the Divisions regulated by their Rule, which they call *Diapasan* [sic]. But the Pipes that are shut only have the Length of those that are open, and which yield the same Sound. Usually, the longest Pipe is 16 Feet; tho' in extraordinary *Organs* 'tis 32. The pedal Tubes are always open, tho' made of Wood and of Lead.

A *Reed-Pipe* consists of a Foot AABB, (Tab. *Music*, Fig. 2) which carries the Wind into the Shalot, or Reed CD, which is a hollow Demi-cylinder, fitted at its Extremity D, into a kind of a Mould II, by a wooden Tampion FG. The Shalot is cover'd with a Plate of Copper EEFF, fitted at its Extremity FF into the Mould by the same wooden Tampion: Its other Extremity EE is at liberty; so that the Air entring the Shalot, makes it tremble or shake against the Reed; and the longer that part of the Tongue which is at liberty FL, is made, the deeper is the Sound. The Mould II, which serves to fix the Shalot or Reed, the Tongue, Tampion, *&c.* serves also to stop the Foot of the Pipe, and to oblige the Wind to go out wholly at the Reed. Lastly, in the Mould is solder'd the part HHKK, call'd the Tube, whose inward opening is a continuation of that of the Reed. The Form of this Tube is different in the different Ranks of Pipes.

The degree of Acuteness and Gravity in the Sound of a Reed-Pipe, depends on the Length of the Tongue, and that of the Pipe CK, taken from the Extremity C of the Shalot, to the Extremity K of the Tube.

The Quality of the Sound depends on the Width of the Reed, the Tongue, and the Tube; as also on the Thickness of the Tongue, the Figure of the Tube, and the Quantity of Wind.

To diversity the Sounds of the Pipes, they add a Valve to the Port-vent, which lets the Wind go in Fits or Shakes.

Hydraulic Organ, a Musical Machine that plays by means of Water.

Of these there are several in *Italy* in the Grotto's of Vineyards. *Ctesebes* [sic] of *Alexandria*, who lived in the Reign of *Ptolemy Evergetes*, is said to have first invented *Organs* that plaid by compressing the Air with Water, as is still practised. *Archimedes* and *Vitruvius* have left us Descriptions of the *Hydraulic Organ*. *Felibien, de la Vie des Archit.*

In the Cabinet of Q. *Christina*, is a beautiful and large Medallion of *Valentinian*, on the reverse whereof is seen one of these *Hydraulic Organs*; with two Men, one on the right, the other on the left, seeming to pump the Water which plays it, and to listen to its Sound. It has only eight Pipes, placed on a round Pedestal. The Inscription is *Placea Spetri*.

rhythm

1728 CHAMBERS *Rhythm, Rhythmus*, in Musick, the Variety in the Movements, as to the quickness or slowness, length and shortness of the Notes. See *Note*.

Or, the *Rhythmus* may be defined more generally, the Proportion which the Parts of a Motion have to each other. See *Rhythmica*.

Aristides among the antient Musicians, applies the Word *Rhythmus* three Ways; *viz.* either to immoveable Bodies, when their Parts are rightly proportioned to each other; as a well-made Statue, *&c.* or to things that move regularly, as in handsome Walking, in Dancing, in the dumb Shews of the Phantomimes [sic], *&c.* or thirdly, to the Motion of Sound, or the Voice; in which, the *Rhythmus* consists of long and short Syllables or Notes, join'd together in Succession in some kind of order, so as their Cadence on the Ear may be agreeable.

This, in Oratory constitutes what we call a *numerous Style*, and when the Tones of the Voice are well chosen, a harmonious Stile. See *Style* and *Numbers* [entry not reproduced].

In effect, *Rhythmus* in the general is perceiv'd either by the Eye or Ear; and may either be with or, without Metre: But the strict musical *Rythm* [sic] is only perceiv'd by the Ear, and cannot exist without it.—The first exists without Sound, as in Dancing; in which Case it may be either without any Difference of Acute and Grave, as in a *Drum*, or with a Variety of these as in a *Song*.

The *Rythmus* of the Antients, Mr. *Malcolm* observes, was very different from the Moderns.—The former was only that of the long and short Syllables of the Words and Verses: It depended altogether on the Poetry, and had no other Forms or Varieties than what the metrical Art afforded. The Changes therein are none but those made from one Kind of Metrum to another, as from Jambic to Choraic, *&c.*

In the modern Musick, the Constitution of the *Rythmus* differs from that of the Verse, so far, that in setting Musick to Words, the thing chiefly regarded is to accommodate the long and short Notes to the Syllables in such manner, as that the Words be well separated; and the accented Syllable of each Word so conspicuous, that what is sung may be distinctly understood. See *Melody*.

Vossius in his Book *de Pœmatum Cantu & viribus Rythmi*, extols the antient *Rythmus*.—Though he owns 'twas confined to the metrical Feet; yet, so well did they cultivate their Language, especially in what relates to the *Rythmus*; that the whole effect of the Musick was ascribed to it, as appears, says he, by that saying of theirs, το πᾶν ποίει μουσικοῖς ὁ ῥυθμός. See *Music, Pantomime, &c.* See also *Ode, &c.*

Vossius attributes the whole Force of the antient Musick to their happy *Rythmus*. But this is somewhat inconceivable: Mr. *Malcolm* rather takes it that the Words and Sense of what was sung had the chief effect: Hence it was that in all the antient Musick the greatest Care was taken that not a Syllable of the Words should be lost, lest the Musick should be spoil'd.

Pancirollus seems of this Opinion; and the Reason he gives why the modern Musick is less perfect than the Antient, is, that we hear Sounds without Words. See *Musick*.

Vossius says, that *Rhythm* which does not express the very Forms and Figures of things, can have no effect; and that the antient poetical Numbers alone are justly contrived for this End.—He adds, that the modern Languages and Verse is altogether unfit for Musick; and that we shall never have right Vocal Musick till our Poets learn to make Verses capable to be sung, *i.e.* till we new model our Languages, restore the antient Quantities and Metrical-feet, and banish our barbarous Rhimes.

Our Verses, says he, run all as it were on one Foot; so that we have not any real *Rythmus* at all in our Poetry: He adds, that we mind nothing further than to have such a Number of Syllables in a Verse, of whatever Nature, and in whatever Order. But this is an unjust Exaggeration. See *Verse.*

scale

1728 CHAMBERS *Scale,* in Musick, a Series of Sounds rising or falling towards Acuteness or Gravity, from any given Pitch of Tune to the greatest Distance that is fit or practicable, through such intermediate Degrees as makes the Succession most agreeable and perfect, and in which we have all the harmonical Intervals most commodiously divided. This *Scale* is otherwise called an *Universal System,* as including all the particular Systems belonging to Musick. See *System.*

Origin and Construction of the Scale of Musick.

Every Concord or harmonical Interval, is resolvable into a certain Number of Degrees or Parts; the Octave, for Instance, into three greater Tones, two less Tones, and two Semi-Tones; the greater Sixth, into two greater Tones, one less Tones [sic], and two Semi-Tones; the less Sixth, into two greater Tones, one less Tone, and two Semi[-]Tones; the Fifth, into two greater Tones, one less Tone, and one Semi-Tone; the Fourth, into one greater Tone, one less Tone, and one Semi-Tone; the greater Third, into one greater Tone, and one less Tone; and the less Third, into one greater Tone, and one less Tone. 'Tis true, there are Variety of other Intervals or Degrees, besides greater Tones, less Tones, and Semi-Tones, into which the Concords may be divided; but these three are preferred to all the rest, and these alone are in Use: For the Reason whereof, see *Tone.* Further, 'Tis not any Order, or Progression, of these Degrees, that will produce Melody: A Number, for Instance, of greater Tones will make no Musick, because no Number of them is equal to any Concord, and the same is true of the other Degrees: There is a Necessity, therefore, of mixing the Degrees to make Music, and the Mixture must be such, as that no Two of the same Kind be ever next each other[.] A natural and agreeable Order of these Degrees Mr. *Malcolm* gives us in the following Division of the Interval of an Octave; wherein, (as all the lesser Concords are contained in the greater) the Divisions of all the other simple Concords are contained. Under the Series are the Degrees between each Term, and the next. In the first Series, the Progression is by the less Third; in the latter, by the greater Third.

	great 2d	gr. 3d	4th	5th	6th	7th	8th	
1	$:\frac{8}{9}$	$:\frac{4}{5}$	$:\frac{3}{4}$	$:\frac{2}{3}$	$:\frac{3}{5}$	$:\frac{8}{15}$	$:\frac{5}{2}$	[*sic*]
Key or Fund.	great Tone.	less Tone.	Semi-Tone.	great Tone.	less Tone.	great Tone.	Semi-Tone.	

	great Second.							
1	$:\frac{8}{9}$	$:\frac{5}{6}$	$:\frac{3}{4}$	$:\frac{2}{3}$	$:\frac{5}{8}$	$:\frac{5}{9}$	[:]$\frac{2}{2}$	[*sic*]
Key or Fund.	great Tone.	Semi-Tone.	less Tone.	great Tone.	Semi-Tone.	great Tone.	less Tone.	

Now, the System of Octave, containing all the Original Chords; and the Compound Concords being only the Sum of Octave and some less Concord; 'tis evident, That if we would have the Series of Degrees continued beyond Octave, they are to be continued in the same Order through a Second as through the First Octave, and so on through a Third and Fourth Octave, *&c.* and such a Series is what we call the *Scale of Musick.* Whereof there are two different Species; according as the less or greater 3d. or the less or greater 6th. are taken in; for both can never stand together in relation to the same Key or Fundamental, so as to make a harmonical Scale. But if, either of these Ways, we descend from a Fundamental or given Sound, to an Octave, the Succession will be melodious; tho' the Two make two different Species of Melody. Indeed, every Note is Discord with regard to the next; but each of them is Concord to the Fundamental, except the 2d and 7th. In continuing the Series, there are two Ways of compounding the Names of the simple Interval with the Octave. Thus: A greater or lesser Tone or Semi-tone above an Octave, or two Octaves, *&c.* or to call them by the Number of Degrees from the Fundamental, as 9th, 10th, *&c.* In the two *Scales* above, the several Terms of the *Scale* are expressed by the proportionable Sections of a Line, represented by 1, the Key or Fundamental of the Series: If we would have the Series expressed in the whole Numbers; they will stand as follows; in each whereof, the greatest Number expresses the longest Chord, and the other Numbers the rest in Order: So that if any Number of Chords be in these Proportions of Length, they will express the true Degrees and Intervals of the *Scale* of Musick, as contained in an Octave concinnously divided in the Two different Species abovementioned.

540 :	480 :	432 :	405 :	360 :	324 :	288 :	270
great Tone	less Tone	semi Tone	great Tone	less Tone	great Tone	less Tone	

216 :	192 :	180 :	162 :	144 :	135 :	120 :	108
great Tone	semi Tone	less Tone	great Tone	semi Tone	great Tone	less Tone	

This *Scale* the Ancients called the *Diatonic* Scale, because proceeding by Tones and Semi-tones. See *Diatonic*. The Moderns call it, simply, *The Scale*, as being the only one now in Use, and sometimes *The natural Scale*, because its Degrees and their Order are the most agreeable and concinnous, and preferable, by the Consent both of Sense and Reason, to all other Divisions ever instituted. Those others, are the *Chromatic* and *Enharmonic Scales*, which, with the *Diatonic*, made the Three *Scales* or *Genera* of Melody of the Antients. See *Genera*: See also *Enharmonic* and *Chromatic*.

Office and Use of the Scale of Musick.

The Design of the *Scale* of Musick, is, To shew how a Voice may rise and fall, less than any harmonical Interval, and thereby move from the one Extreme of any Interval to the other, in the most agreeable Succession of Sounds. The *Scale* therefore, is a System, exhibiting the whole Principles of Musick; which are either harmonical Intervals (commonly called *Concords*) or *Concinnous Intervals*; the first are the essential Principles, the others, subservient to them, to make the greater Variety. See *Concord* and *Intervals*. Accordingly, in the *Scale*, we have all the Concords, with their concinnous Degrees, so placed, as to make the most perfect Succession of Sounds from any given Fundamental or Key, which is supposed to be represented by I. 'Tis not to be supposed, that the Voice is never to move up and down by any other more immediate Distances than those of the concinnous Degrees: For though that be the most usual Movement, yet to move by harmonical Distances, as Concords at once, is not excluded, but is even absolutely necessary. In effect, the Degrees were only invented for Variety sake, and that we might not always move up and down by harmonic Intervals, though those are the most perfect; the others deriving all their Agreeableness from the Subserviency to them. See *Diastem*. And that, besides the harmonical and concinnous Intervals, which are the immediate Principles of Musick, and are directly applied in Practice; there are other discord Relations, which happen unavoidably in Musick, in a kind of accidental and indirect Manner: For, in the Succession of the several Notes of the *Scale*, there are to be considered not only the Relations of those that succeed others immediately; but also of those betwixt which other Notes intervene. Now the immediate Succession may be conducted so, as to produce good Melody; and yet among the distant Notes there may be very gross Discords, that would not be allowed in immediate Succession, much less in Consonance. Thus in the first Series, or *Scale* above-delivered, though the Progression be melodious, as the Terms refer to one common Fundamental, yet are there several Discords among the mutual Relations of the Terms; *e.gr.* from 4th to 7th is 32:45, and from the greater 2d to the greater 6th is 27:40, and from the greater 2d to 4th is 27:32, which are all Discords; and the same will happen in the second Series. See *Discord*.

From what we have observed here, and under the Article *Key*, it appears, That the *Scale* supposes no determinate Pitch of Tune; but that being assign'd to any Key, it makes out the Tune of all the rest, with relation to it, shews what Notes can be naturally joyned to any Key, and thereby reaches the just and natural Limitations of Melody: And when the Song is arrived through several Keys, yet 'tis still the same natural *Scale*, only applied to different Fundamentals. If a Series of Sounds be fixed to the Relations of the *Scale*, 'twill be found exceedingly defective; but this Imperfection is not any Defect in the *Scale*, but follows accidentally from its being confined to this Condition, which is foreign to the Nature and Office of the *Scale* of Musick.

This is the Case in musical Instruments; and in this consists their great Deficiency. For, suppose a Series of Sounds, as those of an Organ or Harpsichord, fixed in the Order of this *Scale*, and the lowest taken at any Pitch or Tune; 'tis evident, 1°. that we can proceed from any Note, only by one particular Order of Degrees: Since from every Note of the *Scale* to its Octave, is contained a different Order of the Tones and Semi-tones. Hence, 2°. we cannot find any Interval required from any Note upwards or downwards; since the Intervals from every Note to every other, are also limited. And hence, 3°. a Song may be so contrived, that, beginning at a particular Note of the Instrument, all the Intervals, or other Notes, shall be found exactly on the Instrument or in the fixed Series; yet were the Song, though perfectly *Diatonic*, begun in any other Note, it would not proceed. In effect, 'tis demonstrable, there can be no such thing as a perfect *Scale* fixed on Instruments, *i.e.* no such *Scale* as from any Note upwards or downwards, shall contain any harmonical or concinnous Interval required. The only Remedy for this Defect of Instruments whose Notes are fixed, must be by inserting other Notes and Degrees betwixt those of the *Diatonic* Series. Hence some Authors speak of dividing the Octave into 16, 18, 20, 24, 26, 31, and other Number of Degrees; but 'tis easy to conceive, how hard it must be to perform on such an Instrument. The best on't is, we have a Remedy on easier Terms: For a *Scale* proceeding of Twelve Degrees, that is, Thirteen Notes, including the Extremes, to an Octave, makes our Instruments so perfect, that we have little Reason to complain. This, then, is the present *Scale* for Instruments, *viz.* Between the Extremes of every Tone of the natural *Scale* is put a Note, which divides it into two unequal Parts, called Semi-tones; whence the whole may be called the *Semitonic Scale*; as containing Twelve Semi-tones betwixt Thirteen Notes, within the Compass of an Octave. And to preserve the *Diatonic* Series distinct, these inserted Notes take either the Name of the natural Note next below, with the Mark # called a *Sharp*; or the Name of the natural Note next above, with this Mark ♭ called a *Flat*. See *Flat* and *Sharp*: See also *Semi-tone*.

For the *Scale* of *Semi-tones* See *Semitonic Scale*. For *Guido's Scale*, commonly called the *Gamut* See *Gamut*. For the *Scale* of the Antients, commonly called the *Diagram* See *Diagram*.

semitone

1728 CHAMBERS *Semi-tone*, in Music, one of the Degrees, or concinnous Intervals, of Concords: See *Degree*. There are three Degrees, or lesser Intervals, by which a Sound can move upwards and downwards successively from one Extreme of any Concord to the other, and yet produce true Melody; and, by means whereof, several Voices, and Instruments are capable of the necessary Variety in passing from Concord to Concord. These Degrees, are the greater and lesser Tone; and the *Semi-tone*. The *Ratio* of the First is 8:9; that of the Second 9:10. See *Tone*. The *Ratio* of the *Semi-tone* is 15:16. which Interval is called a Semi-tone, not that 'tis geometrically the Half of either of the Tones, for 'tis greater; but because it comes somewhat near it. 'Tis also call'd the *Natural Semi-tone*, and the *Greater Semi-tone*, because greater than the Part it leaves behind, or its Complement to a *Tone*, which is 15:16 in the *Less Tone*, and 128:135 in the Lesser. The *Semi-tone* is the Difference of the greater Third and Fourth, or of a Fifth, and lesser Sixth.

Every *Tone* of the Diatonic Scale is divided into a *Greater* and *Less*, or a *Natural and Artificial Semi-tone*. Mr. *Malcolm* observes, 'Twas very natural to think of a Division of each Tone, where 15:16 should be one Part in each Division, in regard this being an unavoidable and necessary Part of the Natural Scale, wou'd readily occur as a fit Degree, and the more, as 'tis not far from an exact *Half Tone*. In effect, the *Semi-tones* are so near equal, that, in Practice, at least, on most Instruments, they are accounted equal, so that no Distinction is made into *Greater* or *Less*. These *Semi-tones* are called *Fictitious Notes*, and, with respect to the Natural ones, are express'd by Characters called *Flats* and *Sharps*. See *Flat* and *Sharp*. Their Use is to Remedy the Defects of Instruments, which having their Sounds fixed, cannot be always made to answer to the Diatonic Scale: See *Scale*. By means of these we have a new Kind of Scale, called the *Semi-tonic-Scale*.

Semi-tonic Scale, or the Scale of *Semi-tones;* A Scale or System of Music, consisting of 12 Degrees, or 13 Notes, in the *Octave*; being an Improvement on the Natural or Diatonic Scale, by inserting between each two Notes thereof, another Note, which divides the Interval or Tone into two unequal Parts, called *Semi[-]tones*. See *Semi-tone*. The Use of this Scale is for Instruments that have fixed Sounds, as the Organ, Harpsichord, *&c.* which are exceedingly defective on the Foot of the *Natural*, or *Diatonic*, Scale. For the Degrees of the Scale being unequal, from every Note to its *Octave* there is a different Order of Degrees; so that from any Note we cannot find any Interval in a Series of fix'd Sounds: Which yet is necessary, that all the Notes of a Piece of Music carried through several Keys, may be found in their just Tune, or that the same Song may be begun indifferently at any Note, as may be necessary for accommodating some Instruments to others, or to the Human Voice, when they are to accompany each other in Unison.

The *Diatonic* Scale, beginning at the lowest Note, being first settled on an Instrument, and the Notes thereof distinguished by their Names *a. b. c. d. e. f. g*; the inserted Notes or *Semi-tones*, are called *Fictitious Notes*, and take the Name or Letter below with a # as *c* # called *c Sharp*; signifying, that it is a *Semi-tone* higher than the Sound of *c* in the natural Series, or this Mark ♭ (called a *Flat*) with the Name of the Note above, signifying it to be a *Semi-tone* lower. Now $\frac{15}{16}$ and $\frac{128}{135}$ being the two *Semi-tones* the greater *Tone* is divided into;

and $\frac{15}{16}$ and $\frac{24}{25}$, the *Semi-tones* the less *Tone* is divided into; the whole *Octave* will stand as in the following Scheme, where the *Ratio's* of each Term to the next, are wrote Fraction-wise between them below.

Scale of SEMI TONES

For the Names of the Intervals in this Scale it may be considered, that as the Notes added to the natural Scale are not design'd to alter the Species of Melody, but leave it still *Diatonic*, and only correct some Defects arising from something foreign to the Office of the Scale of Music, *viz.* the fixing and limiting the Sounds: We see the Reason why the Names of the *Natural* Scale are continued, only making a Distinction of each into a *Greater* and *Less*. Thus an Interval of one *Semi-tone* is called a *Lesser Second*; of two *Semi-tones*, a *Greater Second*; of three *Semi-tones*, a *Less Third*; of four, a *Greater Third*, &c.

A second Kind of *Semitonic Scale* we have from another Division of the *Octave* into *Semi-tone*; which is performed by taking an Harmonical Mean between the Extremes of the *Greater* and *Less Tone* of the Natural Scale, which divides it into two *Semi-tones* nearly equal: Thus the *Greater Tone* 8:9 is divided into 16:17, and 17:18; where 17 is an Arithmetical Division, the Numbers representing the Lengths of Chords; but if they represent the Vibrations, the Lengths of the Chords are reciprocal, *viz.* As 1:16: $\frac{8}{9}$, which puts the *Greater Semi-tone* $\frac{16}{17}$, next the lower Part of the *Tone*, and the Lesser $\frac{17}{18}$ next the Upper, which is the Property of the Harmonical Division. After the same Manner the *Lesser Tone* 9:10 is divided into the two *Semi-tones* 18:19 and 19:20, and the whole *Octave* stands thus:

[*c. c#. d. d# e. f........* etc.]

This Scale, Mr. *Salmon* tells us, in the *Philosoph. Transact.* he made an Experiment of, before the Royal Society, on Chords, exactly in these Proportions, which yielded a perfect Consort with other Instruments, touch'd by the best Hands. Mr. *Malcolm* adds, That having calculated the *Ratios* thereof, for his own Satisfaction, he found more of them false than in the preceding Scale; but their Errors were considerably less, which made Amends.

solfaing

1728 CHAMBERS *Sol-fa-ing*, in Music, the naming and pronouncing of the several Notes of a Song, by the Syllables *Sol, Fa, La, &c*, in learning to sing it. See *Note*.

Of the Seven Notes in the Scale, *ut, re, mi, fa, sol, la, si*; only Four are in Use among us, *viz. fa, sol, la, mi.* Their Office is principally in Singing: that by applying them to every Note of the Scale, it may not only be pronounced more easily; but chiefly, that by them, the Tones and Semi-tones of the natural Scale, may be better mark'd out and distinguish'd.

This Design is obtained by the Four Syllables, *fa, sol, la, mi*; thus, from *fa* to *sol* is a Tone; also from *sol* to *la*, and from *la* to *mi*, without distinguishing the greater or lesser Tone; but from *la* to *fa*, also from *mi* to *fa*, is a Semi-tone.

If, then, these by applied in this Order, *fa, sol, fa, sol, la, mi, fa, &c.* They express the Natural Series from *c*; and if that be to be repeated to a Second or Third Octave, we see by them how to express all the different Orders of Tones and Semi-tones in the Diatonic Scale; and still above *mi*, will stand *fa, sol, la*; and below it, the same reversed, *la, sol, fa*; And one *mi* is always distant from another by an Octave; which cannot be said of any of the rest because after *mi* ascending, comes always *fa, sol, la, fa*, which are repeated invertedly, descending.

To conceive the Use of this: it is to be remember'd, that the first Thing in teaching to sing, is to make one raise a Scale of Notes by Tones and Semi-tones to an Octave, and descend again by the same Notes, and then to rise and fall by greater Intervals, at a Leap, as a Third, Fourth and Fifth, &c. And to do all this, by beginning at Notes of different Pitch. Then, these Notes are represented by Lines and Spaces, to which those Syllables are applied, and the Learner taught to name each Line and Space, by its respective Syllable; which makes what we call *Sol-fa-ing*: The Use whereof is, that while they are learning to tune the Degrees and Intervals of Sound, express'd by Notes set on Lines and Spaces; or learning a Song, to which no Words are applied; they may do it the better, by means of an articulate Sound: but, chiefly, that by knowing the Degrees and Intervals express'd by these Syllables, they may more readily know the true Distance of Notes. See *Singing*.

Mr. *Malcolm* observes, that the Practice of *Sol-fa-ing*, common as it is, is very useless and insignificant, either as to the Understanding or Practising of Music; yet exceedingly perplexing: The various Application[s] of the several Names, according to the various Signatures of the Clef, are enough to perplex any Learner; There being no less than 72 various Ways of applying the Names *sol, fa, &c.* to the Lines and Spaces of a particular System. See *Scale*.

sound

1728 CHAMBERS *Sound*, in Music, the Quality and Distinction of the several Agitations of the Air, consider'd as their Disposition, Measure, *&c.* may make Music. See *Music*.

Sound is the Object of Music, which is nothing but the Art of applying *Sounds*, under such Circumstances of Tone and Tune, as to raise agreeable Sensations.

The principal Affection of *Sound*, whereby it becomes fitted to have this End; is that, whereby it is distinguished into *Acute* and *Grave*. See *Gravity, &c.*

This Difference depends on the Nature of the sonorous Body, the particular Figure and Quantity thereof; and even, in some Cases, on the Part of the Body where it is struck; and is that which constitutes what we call different Tones. See *Tone*.

The Cause of this Difference appears to be no other than the different Velocities of the Vibrations of the *sounding* Body. In effect, the Tone of a *Sound*, is found, by abundance of Experiments, to depend on the Nature of those Vibrations, whose Distances we can conceive no otherwise, than as having different Velocities: And since 'tis proved, That the small Vibrations of the same Chord, are all performed in equal Time; and that the Tone of a *Sound*, which continues for some Time after the Stroak, is the same from first to last: It follows, that the Tone is necessarily connected with a certain Quantity of Time in making each Vibration, or each Wave; or that a certain Number of Vibrations or Waves, accomplished in a given Time, constitute a certain and determinate Tone.

From this Principle, are all the Phænomena of Tune deduced. See *Tune*.

From the same Principle, arise what we call *Concords, &c.* which are nothing but the Results of frequent Unions and Coincidences of the Vibrations of two sonorous Bodies, and consequently of the Waves and undulating Motions of the Air, occasioned thereby. See *Concord*.

On the contrary, the Result of less frequent Coincidences of those Vibrations, is what we call a *Discord*. See *Discord*.

Another considerable Distinction of *Sounds*, with regard to Music, is that, whereby they are denominated *long* and *short*; not with regard to the sonorous Body's retaining a Motion once received, a longer or a less Time, though gradually growing weaker; but to the Continuation of the Impulse of the efficient Cause of the sonorous Body, for a *longer* or a *shorter* Time, as in the Notes of a Violin, *&c.* which are made longer or shorter, by Strokes of different Length or Quickness.

This Continuity, is, properly, a Succession of several *Sounds*, or the Effect of several distinct Strokes, or repeated Impulses on the sonorous Body, so quick, that we judge it one continued *Sound*; especially if it be continued in the same degree of Strength: And hence arises the Doctrine of *Measure* and *Time*. See *Time*.

Sounds, again, are distinguished, with regard to Music, into *Simple* and *Compound*; and that two Ways:

In the First, a *Sound* is said to be *Compound*, when a Number of successive Vibrations of the sonorous Body and the Air, come so far upon the Ear, that we judge them the same continued *Sound*; as in the Phænomenon of the Circle of Fire, caused by putting the fir'd End of a Stick in a quick, circular Motion; where, supposing the End of the Stick in any Point of the Circle, the Idea we receive of it there, continues till the Impression is renewed by a sudden Return.

A *simple Sound*, then, with regard to this Composition, should be the Effect of a single Vibration, or of so many Vibrations as are necessary to raise in us the Idea of *Sound*. In the Second Sense of Composition, a *simple Sound* is the Product of one Voice, or one Instrument, *&c.*

A *compound Sound*, consists of the *Sounds* of several distinct Voices or Instruments all united in the same individual Time and Measure of Duration, that is, all striking the Ear together, whatever their other Differences may be: But in this Sense, again, there is a two-fold Composition; a *Natural* and *Artificial* one.

The natural Composition, is that proceeding from the manifold Reflexions of the first *Sound* from adjacent Bodies, where the Reflexions are not so sudden, as to occasion Eccho's; but are all in the same Tune with the first Note. See *Resonance*.

The artificial Composition, which alone comes under the Musician[']s Province, is, that Mixture of several *Sounds*, which being made by Art, the Ingredient *Sounds* are separable, and distinguishable from one another. In this Sense, the distinct *Sounds* of several Voices or Instruments, or several Notes of the same Instrument, are called *Simple Sounds;* in contradistinction to the *Compound* ones, wherein, to answer the End of Music, the Simples must have such an Agreement in all relations, chiefly as to Acuteness and Gravity, as that the Ear may receive the Mixture with Pleasure. See *Composition*.

Another Distinction of *Sounds*, with regard to Music, is that, whereby they are said to be *smooth* and *even*, or *rough* and *harsh*, also *clear* and *hoarse*; the Cause of which Differences, depends on the Disposition and State of the sonorous Body, or the Circumstances of the Place; but the Ideas of the Differences must be sought from Observation.

Smooth and *rough Sounds* depend, principally, on the *sounding* Body; Of these we have a notable Instance in Strings that are uneven, and not of the same Dimension or Constitution throughout.

M. *Perrault*, to account for *Roughness* and *Smoothness*, maintains, there is no such thing as a simple *Sound;* but that the *Sound* of the same Chord or Bell, is a Compound of *Sounds* of the several Parts of it; so that where the Parts are homogeneous, and the Dimensions, or Figure uniform, there is always such a perfect Mixture and Union of all the *Sounds*, as makes one uniform and smooth *Sound*: Contrary Conditions, produce *Harshness*. In effect, a Likeness of Parts and Figure, makes an Uniformity of Vibrations, whereby a great Number of similar and coincident Motions conspire to fortify and improve each other, and unite, for the more effectual producing of the same Effect.

This Account he confirms, from the Phænomena of a Bell, which differs in Tone, according to the Part 'tis struck in; and yet strike it any where, there is a Motion over all the Parts. Hence, he considers the Bell as composed of an infinite Number of Rings, which, according to their different Dimensions, have different Tones; as Chords of different Lengths have; and when struck, the Vibrations of the Parts immediately struck, specify the Tone, being supported by a sufficient Number of Consonant Tones in other Parts. This must be allowed, that every Note of a string'd Instrument, is the Effect of several simple *Sounds*: For there is not only the *Sound* resulting from the Motion of the String; but that from the Motion of the Parts of the Instrument, which has a considerable Effect in the total *Sound*, as is evident from hence, that the same String on different Violins, *sounds* very differently.

But *Perrault* affirms the same of every String in itself, and without considering the Instrument. Every Part of the String, he says, has its particular Vibrations, different from the gross and sensible Vibrations of the whole; and these are the Causes of different Motions and *Sounds* in the Particles, which uniting, compose the whole *Sound* of the String, and make an uniform Composition, wherein the Tone of the particular Part struck, prevails; and all the others mix under a due Subordination with it, so as to make the Composition smooth and agreeable. If the Parts be unevenly, or irregularly constituted, the *Sound* is harsh; which is the Case in what we call *false Strings*, and various other Bodies; which, for this Reason, have no certain and distinct Tone; but a Composition of several Tones, which don't unite and mix, so as to have one predominant, to specify the total Tone.

As to *clear* and *hoarse Sounds*, they depend on Circumstances that are accidental to the sonorous Body: Thus a Voice or Instrument will be hollow and hoarse, if raised within an empty Hogshead, that yet is clear and bright out of it: The Effect is owing to the Mixture of other and different *Sounds*, raised by Reflexion, which corrupt and change the Species of the primitive *Sound*.

For *Sounds* to be fit to obtain the End of Music, they ought to be *smooth* and *clear*, especially the first; since without this, they cannot have one certain and discernable Tone, capable of being compared to others, in a certain relation of Acuteness, of which the Ear may judge; and of Consequence can be no Part of the Object of Music. Upon the whole, then, with Mr. *Malcolm*, we call that a *harmonic* or *musical Sound*, which being *clear* and *even*, is agreeable to the Ear, and gives a certain and discernable Tune; (hence called *tunable Sound*) which is the Subject of the whole Theory of Harmony. See *Harmony*.

string

1728 Chambers *String*, in Music. See *Chord*.

If two *Strings* or Chords of a musical Instrument only differ in Length; their Tones, that is, the Number of Vibrations they make in the same Time, are in an inverted *Ratio* of their Lengths.

If they only differ in Thickness, their Tones are in an inverted *Ratio* of their Diameters. As to the Tension of *Strings*, to measure it regularly, they must be conceived stretch'd or drawn by Weights; and then, *cæteris paribus*, the Tones of two *Strings* are in a direct *Ratio* of the Square Roots of the Weights which stretch them, that is, *e. gr.* the Tone of a *String* stretch'd by a Weight 4, is an Octave above the Tone of a *String* stretch'd by the Weight 1.

'Tis an Observation of an old standing, that if a Viol or Lute-*string* be touch'd with the Bow, or Hand, another *String*, on the same, or another Instrument, not far from it, if in Unison to it, or in Octave, or the like, will at the same Time tremble of its own accord. See *Unison*.

But it is now found, that not the whole of that other *String* doth thus tremble; but the several Parts, severally, according as they are Unisons to the whole, or the Parts of the *String* so struck. Thus supposing AB to be an upper Octave to *ac*, and therefore an Unison

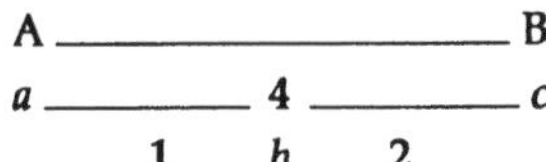

to each half of it stop'd at *b*.

If while *ab* is open, AB be struck, the two Halves of this other, that is *ab* and *bc* will both tremble; but the middle Point will be at rest; as will be easily perceiv'd, by wrapping a bit of Paper lightly about the *String ac*, and removing it successively from one End of the *String* to the other. In like manner, if AB were an upper Twelfth to *ac*, and, consequently, an Unison to its three Parts *a* 1, 1 2 and 2 *c*; if *ac* being open, AB be struck, its three Parts *a* 1, 1 2 and 2 *c* will severally tremble; but the Points 1 and 2 remain at Rest.

This, Dr. *Wallis* tells us, was first discover'd by Mr. *William Noble* of *Merton* College; and after him by Mr. *T. Pigot* of *Wadham* College, without knowing that Mr. *Noble* had observed it before. To which we may add, that M. *Sauveur*, long afterwards, proposed it in the *Royal Academy* at *Paris*, as his own Discovery, as 'tis like enough it might: But upon his being inform'd, by some of the Members then present, that Dr. *Wallis* had publish'd it before, he immediately resign'd all the Honour thereof.

system

1728 Chambers *System*, in Music, a compound Interval; or an Interval composed, or conceiv'd to be composed, of several lesser; such is the Octave, *&c*. See *Interval*.

The Word is borrowed from the Ancients, who call a simple Interval, *Diastem*, and a Compound one *System*.

As there is not any Interval in the Nature of Things; so we can conceive any given Interval, as composed of, or equal to the Sum of several others. This Division of Intervals, therefore, only relates to Practice; so that a *System* is properly an Interval, which is actually divided in Practice, and where, along with the Extremes, we conceive always some intermediate Terms. The Nature of a *System* will be very plain, by conceiving it an Interval, whose Terms are in Practice, taken either in immediate Succession; or the Sound is made to rise and fall, from the one to the other, by touching some intermediate Degrees; so that the whole is a *System* or Composition of all the Intervals, between one Extreme and the other. *Systems* of the same Magnitude, and consequently of the same Degree of Concord and Discord, may yet differ in respect of their Composition; as containing and being actually divided into more or fewer Intervals: And when they are equal in that respect, the Parts may differ in Magnitude. Lastly, when they consist of the same Parts, or lesser Intervals, they may differ as to the Order and Disposition thereof between the two Extremes.

There are several Distinctions of *Systems*; the most remarkable is, into *Concinnous* and *Inconcinnous*.

Concinnous Systems, are those consisting of such Parts, as are fit for Music, and those Parts, placed in such an Order between the Extremes, as that the Succession of Sounds, from one Extreme to the other, may have a good Effect. See *Concinnous*.

Inconcinnous Systems, are those, where the simple Intervals are *Inconcinnous*, or ill disposed betwixt the Extremes.

A *System*, again, is either *Particular* or *Universal*. An *universal System*, is that which contains all the particular *Systems* belonging to Music; and makes what the Ancients call the *Diagramma*, and we the *Scale of Music*. See *Scale*.

The Ancients also distinguish *Systems* into *Perfect* and *Imperfect*. The Disdiapason, or double Octave, was reckon'd the *perfect System*, because within its Extremes, are contained Examples of all the simple and original Concords, and in all the Variety of Order wherein their concinnous Part ought to be taken; which Variety constitutes what they call the *Species* or *Figures of Consonances*.

All the *Systems*, less than the *Disdiapason*, were reckoned *Imperfect*.

The double Octave was also called the *Systema Maximum*, and *Immutatum*; because they took it to be the greatest Extent or Difference of Time that we could go in making Melody; though some added a Fifth to it, for the greatest *System*: But the Diapason, or simple Octave, was reckon'd the most perfect, with respect to the Agreement of its Extremes; so that how many Octaves soever were put into the greatest *System*, they were all to be constituted or sub-divided the same Way as the First: So that when we know how the Octave is divided, we know the Nature of the *Diagramma* or *Scale*: The Varieties whereof, constituted the *Genera Melodiæ*, which were sub-divided into Species. See *Genera* and *Species*.

time

1728 CHAMBERS *Time*, in Music, is an Affection of Sound, whereby we denominate it *long* or *short*, with regard to its Continuity in the same Degree of Tune. See *Sound*.

Time and Tune are the great Properties of Sound, on whose Difference, or Proportions, Music depends: Each has has [sic] its several Charms; where the Time, or Duration of the Notes is equal, the Differences of Tune alone are capable to entertain us with endless Pleasure. See *Tune*.

And of the Power of *Time* alone, *i.e.* of the Pleasures arising from the various Measures of long and short, swift and slow; we have an Instance in the Drum, which has no Difference of Notes, as to Tune. See *Drum, Accent, &c.*

Time, in Music, is consider'd, either with respect to the absolute Duration of the Notes, *i.e.* the Duration consider'd in every Note by itself, and measured by some external Motion foreign to the Music; in respect to which, the Composition is said to be *quick*, or *slow*: or it is consider'd, with respect to the relative Quantity or Proportion of the Notes compared with one another. See *Note*.

The Signs or Characters by which the Time or Notes is represented, are shewn under the Article, *Characters in Music*; where the Names, Proportions, *&c.* are also express'd.

A Semi-breve, for Instance, is mark'd to be equal to two Minims, a Minim to two Crotchets, a Crotchet to two Quavers, so on, and still in a duplicate *Ratio, i.e.* in the *Ratio* of 2:1. Now, where the Notes respect each other, thus, *i.e.* where they are in this *Ratio*; the Music is said to be in *Duple*, i.e. *double* or *common Time*.

When the several Notes are Triple each other, or in the *Ratio* 3:1; that is, when the Semi-breve is equal to three Minims, the Minim to three Crotchets, *&c.* the Music is said to be *triple Time*.

Now, to render this Part as simple as possible, the Proportions already stated among the Notes, are fix'd and invariable; and to express the Proportion of 3:1, a Point (.) is added on the right Side [of] any Note, which is deem'd equivalent to Half of it; and by this means a pointed Semi-breve O· [sic] becomes equal to three Minims, *&c.* so of the rest.

From hence arise several other *Ratios* constituting new Kinds of triple Time; as 2:3 and 3:4, *&c.* but these Mr. *Malcolm* observes, are of no real Service, and are not perceived without a painful Attention. For the Proportions of the Times or Notes, to afford us Pleasure, must be such as are not difficultly perceiv'd; on which account, the only *Ratios* fit for Music, besides that of Equality, are the *Double* and *Triple*.

Common or duple Time, is of two Species; the First, when every Measure is equal to a Semi-breve, or its Value in any Combination of Notes of a lesser Quantity.

The Second, where every Bar is equal to a Minim, or its Value in lesser Notes. The Movements of this Kind of Measure are various; but there are Three common Distinctions; the first *slow*, signify'd at the beginning by the Mark C; the second *brisk*, signify'd by ₵; the third *very quick*, signify'd by Ɖ.

But what that slow, brisk and quick is, is very uncertain, and only to be learnt by Practice. The nearest Measure we know of, is to make a Quaver the Length of the Pulse of a good Watch; then, a Crotchet will be equal to two Pulses, a Minim to four, and the whole Measure or Semi-breve to eight. This may be reputed the Measure of *brisk Time*; for the *slow*, 'tis as long again, and the *quick*, only half as long.

The whole Measure, then, of common *Time*, is equal to a Semi-breve or a Minim: But these are variously subdivided into Notes of less Quantities. See *Measure*.

Now to keep the *Time* equal, we make use of a Motion of the Hand or Foot, thus: Knowing the true *Time* of a Crotchet, we shall suppose the Measure or Bar actually subdivided into four Crotchets for the first Species of common *Time*; then the Half Measure will be two Crotchets; therefore, the Hand or Foot being up, if we put it down with the very beginning of the first Note or Crotchet, and then raised with the Third; and then down to begin the next Measure: this is call'd *beating of Time*.

By Practice, we get a Habit of making this Motion very equal, and consequently of dividing the Measure or Bar into equal Parts, up and down; as also of taking all the Notes in the just Proportion, so as to begin and end them precisely with the beating. In the Measure of two Crotchets, we beat down the first, and the second up. Some call each Half of the Measure in common *Time, a Time*; and so they call this the Mode or Measure of *two Times*, or the *Dupla* Measure.

Again, some mark the Measure of two Crotchets with a 2 or $\frac{2}{4}$, signifying it to be equal to two Notes, whereof four make a Semi-breve; and some mark it $\frac{4}{8}$ for Quavers.

For Triple Time; see *Triple Time*.

transposition

1728 CHAMBERS *Transposition, in Music*, is a changing of the Notes of a Piece of Music. See *Note*.

Of this there are two Kinds; the first with respect to the *Clef*, the second with respect to the *Key*.

Transposition with respect to the Clef, consists in the changing of the Places or Seats of the Notes or Letters, amongst the Lines and Spaces; but so as that every Note is set at the same Letter. See *Clef*.

This is done either by removing the same Clef to another Line, or by using another Clef, but with the same Signature by reason the Piece is still in the same Key. See *Clef*.

The Practice is easy in either Case: In the first, you take the first Note at the same Distance above or below the *Clef-Note*, in its new Position as before; and all the rest of the Notes in the same Relations or Distances from one another; so that the Notes are all set on Lines and Spaces of the same Name.

In the second, or setting the Music to a different Clef, 'tis to be observed, the Places of the three Clef Notes are invariable in the Scale, and are to one another in these Relations, *viz.* the Mean a 5th above the Bass, and the Treble a 5th above the Mean. Now to *Transpose* to a new Clef, *e.gr.* from the Treble to the Mean; where-ever that new Clef is set, we suppose it the same individual Note, in the same Place of the Scale, as if that Piece were that Part in a Composition to which this new Clef is generally appropriated; that so it may direct to the same Notes we had before *Transposition*: Now, from the fix'd Relations of the three Clefs in the Scale, it will be easy to find the Seat of the first *transposed* Note; and then all the rest are to be set at the same mutual Distances they were at before. See *Scale*.

Suppose, *e.gr.* the first Note of a Song be *d*, a 6th above the Bass-clef; where-ever that Clef is placed, the first Note must be the greater 2d above it, because a greater 2d above the Mean is a greater 6th above the Bass-clef, the Relation of those two being a 5th.—So that the first Note will still be the same individual *d*.

The Use of this *Transposition* is, that if a Song being set with a certain Clef, in a certain Position, the Notes go far above or below the System of five Lines; they may, by the Change of the Place of the same Clef in the particular System, or by taking a new Clef, be brought more within the Compass of the Lines.

Transposition from one Key to another, is a changing of the Key; or a setting all the Notes of the Song at different Letters, and performing it, consequently, in different Notes upon an Instrument. See *Key*.

The Design hereof is, that a Song which being begun in one Note, is too high or low, or otherwise inconvenient for a certain Instrument; may be begun in another Note, and from that carried on in all its just Degrees and Intervals.

The Clef and its Position here remain the same; and the Change is of the Notes themselves, from one Letter, and its Line or Space, to another.

In the former *Transposition*, the Notes were express'd by the same Letters, but both removed to different Lines and Spaces: In this, the Letters were unmoved, and the Notes of the Song transferr'd to, or express'd by other Letters, and consequently set upon different Lines and Spaces, which, therefore, requires a different Signature of the Clef.

triple

1728 Chambers *Triple*, in Music, is one of the Species of Measure or Time. See *Time*.

Triple Time consists of many different Species; whereof there are in general four, each of which has its Varieties.—The common Name of *Triple* is taken hence, that the whole or half Measure is divisible into three equal Parts, and beat accordingly.

The first Species is call'd the *simple Triple*, whose Measure is equal either to three Semibreves, to three Minims, three Crotchets, three Quavers, or three Semiquavers; which are mark'd thus, $\frac{3}{1}$ or $\frac{3}{2}$, $\frac{3}{4}$, $\frac{3}{8}$, $\frac{3}{16}$; but the last is not much us'd, except in Church Music.

In all these, the Measure is divided into three equal Parts or Times, call'd thence *Triple Time*, or the Measure of *three Times*, whereof two are beat down, and the third up.

The second Species is the *mix'd Triple*: Its Measure is equal to six Crotchets, or six Quavers, or six Semiquavers, and accordingly mark'd $\frac{6}{4}$, or $\frac{6}{8}$, or $\frac{6}{16}$; but the last is seldom us'd.

Some Authors add other two, *viz.* six Semibreves, and six Minims, mark'd $\frac{6}{1}$ or $\frac{6}{2}$; but these are not in Use.

The Measure here is usually divided into two equal Parts or Times, whereof one is beat down, and one up; but it may also be divided into six Times, whereof the first two are beat down, and the third up; then the next two down, and the last up; *i.e.* each half of the Measure is beat like the *simple Triple*, (on which Account it may be call'd the *Compound Triple*); and because it may be thus divided either into two or six Times, (*i.e.* two *Triples*) 'tis call'd *mix'd*, and by some the *Measure of six Times*.

The third Species is the *Compound Triple*, consisting of nine Crotchets, or Quavers, or Semiquavers, mark'd $\frac{9}{4}$, $\frac{9}{8}$, $\frac{9}{16}$; the first and last are little us'd; some also add $\frac{9}{1}$, $\frac{9}{2}$, which are never us'd.

This Measure is divided either into three equal Parts or Times, whereof two are beat down, and one up; or each third Part may be divided into three Times, and beat like the simple *Triple*; on which Account it is call'd the *Measure of nine Times*.

The fourth Species is a Compound of the second Species, containing twelve Crotchets, or Quavers, or Semiquavers, mark'd $\frac{12}{4}$, $\frac{12}{8}$, $\frac{12}{16}$, to which some add $\frac{12}{1}$ and $\frac{12}{2}$, which are never us'd; nor are the first and third much us'd, especially the latter.

The Measure, here, may be divided into two Times, and beat one down, and one up; or each half may be divided, and beat as the second Species, either by two or three; in which Case it will make in all twelve Times, and hence is call'd *the Measure of twelve Times*.

The *French* and *Italian* Authors make a great many more Species and Divisions of *Triple* Time, unknown, or, at least, unregarded by our *English* Musicians, and therefore not so necessary to be dwelt upon here.

trumpet

1728 Chambers *Trumpet*, a musical Instrument, the most noble of all portable ones of the Wind Kind, us'd chiefly in War, among the Cavalry, to direct them in the Service. See *Music*.

'Tis usually made of Brass, sometimes of Silver, Iron, Tin, and Wood. *Moses*, we read, made two of Silver, to be us'd by the Priests, *Numb.* x. and *Solomon* made 200 like those of Moses, as we are inform'd by *Josephus*, lib. viii. which shews abundantly the Antiquity of that Instrument.

The Ancients had various Instruments of the *Trumpet* Kind; as the *Tubæ*, *Cornua*, and *Litui*; which see under their respective Articles.

The modern *Trumpet* consists of a Mouth-piece, near an Inch broad, tho' the Bottom be only one Third so much.—The Pieces which convey the Wind are call'd the *Branches*; the two Places where it is bent, *Potences*; and the Canal between the second Bend and the Extremity, the *Pavillion*; the Places where the Branches take asunder, or are solder'd, the *Knots*; which are five in Number, and cover the Joints.

When the Sound of the *Trumpet* is well manag'd, 'tis of a great Compass.—Indeed its Extent is not strictly determinable; since it reaches as high as the Strength of the Breath can force it.—A good Breath will carry it beyond four Octaves, which is the Limit of the usual Keys of Spinets and Organs.

In War there are eight principal Manners of sounding the *Trumpet*: The first, call'd the *Cavalquet*, us'd when an Army approaches a City, or passes thro' it in a March.—The second the *Boute-selle*, us'd when the Army is to decamp or march.—The third is when they sound to *Horse*, and then to the *Standard*.—The fourth is the *Charge*.—The fifth [is] the *Watch*.—The sixth is call'd the *double Cavalquet*.—The seventh the *Chamade*.—And the eighth the *Retreat*. Besides various Flourishes, Voluntaries, *&c.* used in Rejoycings.

There are also People who blow the *Trumpet* so softly, and draw so delicate a Sound from it, that it is used not only in Church Music, but even in Chamber Music: And 'tis on this Account that in the *Italian* and *German*

Music are frequently find Parts entitled *Tromba prima*, or I^a first *Trumpet*, Tromba II^a, *segonda*, III^a, *terza*, second, third *Trumpet*, *&c.* as being intended to be play'd with *Trumpets*.

There are two notable Defects in the *Trumpet*, observ'd by Mr. *Roberts*, in the *Philosophical Transactions* [1692];—The first is, that it will only perform certain Notes within its Compass, commonly call'd *Trumpet Notes*: The second, that four of the Notes it does perform, are out of Tune. See *Note*.

The same Defects are found in the *Trumpet Marine*; and the Reason is the same in both. See *Trumpet Marine*.

The Word *Trumpet* is form'd from the *French*, *Trompette*. *Menage* derives it from the *Greek*, στρόμβος, *turbo*, a Shell anciently used for a *Trumpet*. *Du Cange* derives it from the corrupt *Latin*, *Trumpa*, or the *Italian*, *Tromba*, or *Trombetta*; others from the *Celtic*, *Trompill*, which signifies the same Thing.

tune

1728 Chambers *Tune* or *Tone*, in Music, is that Property of Sounds whereby they come under the relation of *Acute* and *Grave* to one another. See *Gravity*, *&c.*

Though Gravity and Acuteness be mere Terms of Relation, yet the Ground of the Relation, the *Tune* of the Sound, is something absolute: Every Sound having its own proper *Tune*, which must be under some determinate Measure, in the Nature of the Thing.

The only Difference, then, between one *Tune* and another, is, in Degrees; which is naturally infinite, *i.e.* we conceive there is something positive in the Cause of Sound which is capable of less and more, and contains in it the Measure of the Degrees of *Tune*; and because we don't suppose a least or greatest Quantity of this, we conceive the Degrees depending on those Measures to be infinite. See *Sound*.

If two or more Sounds be compar'd together in this Relation, they are either equal or unequal in the Degree of *Tune*.—Such as are equal are call'd *Unisons*. See *Unison*.

The unequal constitute what we call an *Interval*, which is the Difference of *Tune* between two Sounds. See *Interval*.

Cause and Measure of Tune; or that whereon the Tune *of a Sound depends.*

Sonorous Bodies, we find, differ in *Tune*, 1^{0}. According to the different Kinds of Matter; thus the Sound of a Piece of Gold is much graver than that of a Piece of Silver of the same Shape and Dimensions; in which Case, the *Tones* are proportional to the Specific Gravitites.

2. According to the different Quantities of the same Matter in Bodies of the same Figure; as a solid Sphere of Brass, one Foot in Diameter, sounds acuter than a Sphere of Brass two Foot Diameter; in which Case the *Tones* are proportional to the Quantities of Matter.

Here, then, are different *Tunes* connected with different specific Gravitites, and different Quantities of Matter; yet cannot the different Degrees of Tune be referr'd to those Quantities, *&c.* as the immediate Cause. In Effect, the Measures of *Tune* are only to be sought in the Relations of the Motions that are the Cause of Sound, which are no where so discernable as in the Vibrations of Chords. See *Chord*.

Sounds, we know, are produc'd in Chords by their vibratory Motions; not, indeed, by those sensible Vibrations of the whole Chord, but by the insensible ones, which are influenc'd by the sensible, and, in all Probability, are proportional to them.—So that Sounds may be as justly measur'd in the latter, as they could be in the former, did they fall under our Senses: But even the sensible Vibrations are too small and quick to be immediately measur'd.—The only Resource we have, is to find what Proportion they have with some other Thing, which is effected by the different Tensions, or Thickness, or Lengths of Chords, which, in all other Respects, excepting some one of those mention'd, are the same. See *Vibration* [entry not reproduced].

Now, in the general, we find that in two Chords, all Things being equal, excepting the Tension, or the Thickness, or the Length, the *Tones* are different; there must therefore be a Difference in the Vibrations owing to those different Tensions, *&c.* which Difference can only be in the Velocity of the Courses and Recourses of the Chords, thro' the Spaces wherein they move to and again.—Now, upon examining the Proportion between that Velocity, and the Things just mention'd, whereon it depends, 'tis found to a Demonstration, that all the Vibrations of the same Chord are perform'd in equal Times.

Hence, as the *Tone* of a Sound depends on the Nature of those Vibrations whose Differences we can conceive no otherwise than as having different Velocities, and as the small Vibrations of the same Chord are all perform'd in equal Time; and as 'tis found true in Fact, that the Sound of any Body arising from one individual Stroke, tho' it grow gradually weaker, yet continues in the same *Tone* from first to last; it follows, that the *Tone* is necessarily connected with a certain Quantity of *Tune* in making every single Vibration; or that a certain Number of Vibrations, accomplish'd in a given Time, constitutes a certain and determinate *Tune*; for the frequenter those Vibrations are, the more acute is the *Tune*; and the slower and fewer they are in the same Space of Time, by so much the more grave is the *Tune*; so that any given Note of a *Tune*, is made by one certain Measure of Velocity of Vibrations, *i.e.* such a certain Number of Courses and Recourses of a Chord or String in such a certain Space of Time, constitutes a determinate *Tune*. See *Note*.

This Theory is strongly supported by our best and latest Writers on Music, Dr. *Holder*, Mr. *Malcolm*, &c. both by Reason and Experience.—Dr. *Wallis*, who owns it very reasonable, adds, that 'tis evident the Degrees of Acuteness are reciprocally as the Length of the Chords; tho', he says, he will not positively affirm that the Degrees of Acuteness answer the Number of Vibrations as their only true Cause: But his Diffidence arises hence, that he doubts whether the Thing have been sufficiently confirm'd by Experiment.—Indeed, whether the different Number of Vibrations in a given Tune is the true Cause on the Part of an Object, of our perceiving a Difference of *Tune*, is a Thing which we conceive does not come within the Reach of Experiment; 'tis sufficient the Hypothesis is reasonable. See *Concord, Harmony, &c.*

unison

1728 Chambers *Unison*, in Musick, is the Effect of two Sounds, which are equal in degree of Tune, or in point of Gravity and Acuteness. See *Tune*.

Or, *Unison* may be defined a Consonance of two Sounds, produced by two Bodies of the same Matter, Length, Thickness, Tension, equally struck, and at the same time; so that they yield the same Tone, or Note. See *Note*.

Or, it is the *Union* of two Sounds, so like each other, that the Ear perceiving no difference, receives them as one and the same Sound. See *Sound*.

What constitutes *Unisonance*, is the Equality of the Number of Vibrations of the two sonorous Bodies in equal Times: Where there is an Inequality in that respect, and of consequence an Inequality in degree of Time; the unequal Sounds constitute an *Interval*. See *Interval*, and *Vibration* [entry not reproduced].

Unison is the first and greatest of Concords; and the Foundation, or, as some call it, the *Mother* of all the rest: Yet some deny it to be any Concord at all; maintaining it to be only that in Sounds, which Unity is in Number. See *Unity* [entry not reproduced].

Others restrain the Word *Concord* to Intervals, and make it include a difference of Tune; but this is precarious: for as the Word *Concord* signifies an Agreement of Sounds, 'tis certainly applicable to *Unisons* in the first degree.

But tho *Unisonance*, or an Equality of Tune, makes the most perfect Agreement of Sound; it is not true that the nearer any two Sounds come to an Equality of Tune, they are the more agreeable.—The Mind is delighted with Variety; and the Reason of the Agreeableness or Disagreeableness of two Sounds, must be ascrib'd to some other Cause than the Equality or Inequality of the Number of their Vibrations. See *Concord*.

'Tis a fam'd Phænomenon in Musick, that an intense Sound being rais'd, either with the Voice or a sonorous Body, another sonorous Body near it, whose Tune is either *Unison* or Octave above that Sound, will sound its proper Note *Unison* or Octave to the given Note.—The Experiment is easily try'd by the Strings of two Instruments, or by a Voice and a Harpsichord, or a Bell, or even a drinking Glass.

This our Philosophers account for thus: One String being struck, and the Air put in Motion thereby; every other String within the reach of that Motion, will receive some Impression therefrom: But each String can only move with a determinate Velocity of Recourses, or Vibrations; and all *Unisons* proceed from equal or equidiurnal Vibrations; and other Concords from other Proportions. The *Unison* String, then, keeping equal pace with the sounding String, as having the same Measure of Vibrations, must have its Motion continued and still improv'd, till its Motion become sensible, and it give a distinct Sound. Other concording Strings have their Motions propagated in different Degrees, according to the frequency of the Coincidence of their Vibrations with those of the sounded String: The Octave, therefore, most sensibly; then the fifth: after which, the crossing of the Motions prevents any effect.

This they illustrate by the Pendulum; which being set a-moving, the Motion may be continu'd and augmented by making frequent, light, coincident Impulses; as blowing on it when the Vibration is just finish'd: But if it be touch'd by any cross or opposite Motion, and this, too, frequently; the Motion will be interrupted, and cease altogether.—So, of two *Unison* Strings, if the one be forcibly struck, it communicates Motion by the Air to the other: and being equidiurnal in their Vibrations, that is, finishing them precisely together, the Motion of that other will be improv'd and heighten'd, by the frequent Impulses receiv'd from the Vibrations of the first; because given precisely when that other has finish'd its Vibration, and is ready to return: But if the Vibrations of the Chords be unequal in Duration, there will be a crossing of Motions, less or more, according to the Proportion of the Inequality; by which the Motion of the untouch'd String will be so check'd, as never to be sensible. And this we find is the Case in all Consonances, except *Unison*, Octave, and the Fifth. See *Chord*.

voice

1728 CHAMBERS *Voice* .... The different Apertures of the Lips of the Glottis, then, produce all the different Tones in the six Parts of Musick, viz. *Bass, Common pitch, Tenor, Counter-tenor, Treble-Bass*, and *Treble*; and the Manner is thus:

The *Voice*, we have shewn, can only be form'd by the Glottis; but the Tones of the *Voice* are Modifications of the *Voice*; and can only be produced by the Modifications of the Glottis.—Now the Glottis is only capable of one Modification, which is, the mutual Approach or Recess of its Lips: 'Tis this, therefore, produces the different Tones.—Now that Modification includes two Circumstances: the first, and principal, is, that the Lips are stretch'd more and more, from the lowest Tone to the highest; the second is, that the more they are stretch'd, the nearer they approach.

From the first it follows, that their Vibrations will be so much the quicker, as they come nearer their highest Tone; and that the *Voice* will be just when the two Lips are equally stretch'd, and false when unequally; which agrees perfectly well with the Nature of String Instruments.

From the second it follows, that the higher the Tones are, the nearer will they approach each other; which agrees perfectly well with Wind Instruments, govern'd by Reeds, or Plugs.

The Degrees of Tension of the Lips, are the first and principal Cause of Tones; but their Differences are insensible.—The degrees of Approach, are only Consequences of that Tension; but their Differences are more easily assign'd.

To give a precise Idea of the thing, therefore, we had best keep to that; and say, that this Modification consists in a Tension, from whence results a very numerous Subdivision of a very small Interval; which yet, small as it is, is capable, physically speaking, of being subdivided infinitely. See *Divisibility* [entry not reproduced].

This Doctrine is confirm'd from the different Apertures found in dissecting Persons of different Ages of both Sexes.—The Aperture is less, and the exterior Canal always shallower in the Sex and Ages fittest to sing Treble.—Add, that the Reed of a Hautboy, separated from the Body of the Instrument, being a little press'd between the Lips, will yield a Tone somewhat higher than its natural one; and if press'd still more, will yield another still higher: And thus an able Musician may run successively thro' all the Tones and Semitones of an Octave.

'Tis different Apertures, then, that produce, or at least accompany different Tones, both in Natural Wind Instruments, and Artificial ones; and the Diminution of the Aperture, raises the Tones both of the Glottis and the Reed.

The Reason why lessening the Aperture heightens the Tone, is, that the Wind passes thro' it with the greater Velocity; and from the same Cause it is, that if any Reed, or Plug of an Instrument be too weakly blown, its Tone will be lower than ordinary.

Indeed, the Contractions and Dilations of the Glottis, must be infinitely delicate: By an exact Calculation of the ingenious Author abovemention'd [M. Dodart], it appears, that to perform all the Tones and Semitones of a common *Voice*, which is computed to reach 12 Tones to perform all the Particles and Subdivisions of those Tones, into Commas and other minuter tho still sensible Parts; to perform all the Shades, or the Differences in a Tone when sounded more or less strong, without changing the Tone: the little Diameter of the Glottis, which does not exceed $\frac{1}{10}$ of an Inch, but which varies within that Extent at every Change, must be actually divided into 9632 Parts; which Parts are yet very unequal, and therefore many of 'em much less than the $\frac{1}{963200}$ Part of an Inch.—A Delicacy scarce to be match'd by any thing but a good Ear, which has so just a Sense of Sounds, as, naked, to perceive Differences in all these Tones; even those whose Origin is much less than the 963200th Part of an Inch. See *Hearing* [entry not reproduced].

watch-work

1704 HARRIS *Watch-work* .... 2, As for *Chimes*, I need say nothing of the Lifting-pieces and Detents, to lock and unlock; nor of the Wheels to bridle the motion of the Barrel; only you are to observe, That the Barrel must be as long in turning round, as you are in Singing the Tune it is to Play.

As for the *Chime Barrel*, it may be made up of certain Bars that run athwart [sic] it, with a convenient number of Holes punched in them, to put in the Pins that are to draw each Hammer. By this means you may change the Tune, without changing the Barrel. Such is the *Royal-Exchange* Clock in *London*, and others. In this case, the Pins or Nuts which draw the Hammers, must hang down from the Bar, some more, some less, and some standing upright in the Bar; the reason whereof is, to Play the Time of the Tune rightly.

For the distance of each of these Bars may be a Semibrief, *&c.* of which hereafter.

But the usual way is, to have the Pins that draw the Hammers, fixed on the Barrel. For the placing of which Pins, you may proceed by the way of Changes on Bells, *viz.* 1, 2, 3, 4, *&c.* Or rather make use of the Musical Notes.

Where you must observe, what is the compass of your Tune, or how many Notes or Bells there are from the highest to the lowest; and accordingly, the Barrel must be divided from end to end.

Thus, in the following Examples, each of those Tunes are 8 Notes in compass; and accordingly, the Barrel is divided into 8 Parts. These Divisions are struck round the Barrel, opposite to which are the Hammer-tails.

I speak here, as if there was only one Hammer to each Bell, that you may more clearly apprehend what I am explaining. But when two Notes of the same Sound come together in a Tune, there must be two Hammers to that Bell, to Strike it. So that, if in all the Tunes you intend to Chime, of 8 Notes compass, there should happen to be such double Notes on every Bell, instead of 8, you must have 16 Hammers; and accordingly, you must divide your Barrel, and Strike 16 Strokes round it, opposite to each Hammer-tail.

Then you are to divide it, round about into as many Divisions, as there are Musical Bars, Semibriefs, Minums, *&c.* in your Tune.

Thus the 100th Psalm-tune hath 20 Semibriefs; and each Division of it is a Semibrief. The first Note of it also is a Semibrief, and therefore on the Chime Barrel must be a whole Division from 5 to 5, as you may understand plainly, if you conceive the Surface of a *Chime-Barrel* to be represented by the following Table, as if the Cylindrical Superficies of the Barrel were stretch'd out at length or extended on a Plain. And then such a Table so dotted or divided, if it were to be wrapped round the Barrel, would shew the Places where all the Pins are to stand in the Barrel: For the Dots running about the Table, are the Places of the Pins that Play the Tune.

The Notes of the 100 *Psalm.*

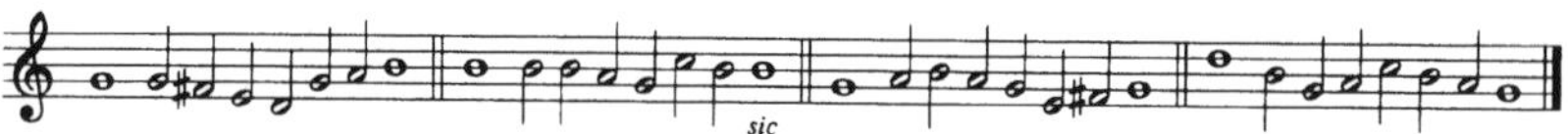

A Table for dividing the Chime - *Barrel of the* 100 *Psalm.*

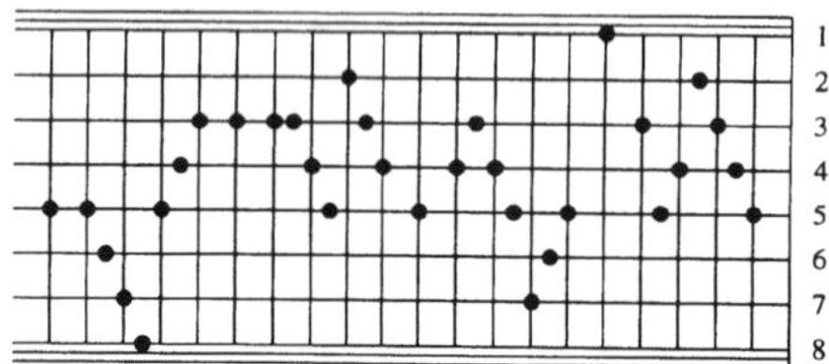

If you would have your Chimes compleat indeed, you ought to have a set of Bells to the Gamut Notes; so as that each Bell having the true Sound of *Sol, La, Mi, Fa,* you may Play any Tune with its Flats and Sharps; nay, you may by these means, Play both the Bass and Treble, with one Barrel.

And by setting the Names of your Bells at the Head of any Tune, you may easily transfer that Tune to your Chime Barrel, without any Skill in Musick. But observe, That each Line in the Musick is three Notes distant; that is, there is a Note between each Line, as well as upon it.

Bibliography

Primary sources (quoted)

Listed are all sources used in the preparation of the Dictionary. They consist of lexicographic works and theoretical writings on music, including treatises. Note that some modern editions of primary sources are listed where these have been consulted. The titles of manuscript items in the British Library generally follow those given in Hughes-Hughes, *Catalogue of Manuscript Music in the British Museum*, vol. III (London, Trustees of the British Museum, 1965), but may be abbreviated.

Agrippa, Henricus Cornelius. *Henrie Cornelius Agrippa, of the Vanitie and vncertaintie of Artes and Sciences: Englished by Ia. San. Gent.*, London, 1575.

Alsted, Johann Heinrich. *Templvm Mvsicvm: Or The Musical Synopsis, Of The Learned and Famous Johannes-Henricus-Alstedius, Being A Compendium of the Rudiments both of the Mathematical and Practical Part of Musick ... Faithfully translated out of Latin By John Birchensha*, London, 1664.

The Art of Mvsic collecit ovt of all Ancient Doctovris of Mvsic [by a Scotchman], after 1517, MS, BL Add. 4911.

A. B. *Synopsis of Vocal Musick: Containing The Rudiments of Singing Rightly any Harmonical Song*, London, 1680.

T. B. *The Compleat Musick-Master: Being Plain, Easie, and Familiar Rules for Singing, and Playing On the most useful Instruments now in Vogue, according to the Rudiments of Musick ... The third Edition, with Additions*, London, 1722.

Bailey, Nathan. *An Universal Etymological English Dictionary*, London, 1721; 3rd edition, London, 1726; 9th edition, London, 1740.

Dictionarium Britannicum: Or a more Compleat Universal Etymological English Dictionary Than any Extant, London, 1730; 2nd edition, London, 1736.

The Universal Etymological English Dictionary: Containing An Additional Collection of Words (not in the first Volume)...Vol. II, 3rd edition, London, 1737.

B[anister], J[ohn]. *The Most Pleasant Companion, Or Choice New Lessons For the Recorder or Flute...To which is added, plain and easie Rules and Instructions for young Beginners*, London, 1681.

Banner, Richard. *The Use and Antiquity of Musick in the Service of God. A Sermon Preach'd in the Cathedral-Church At Worcester*, Oxford, 1737.

Barley, William. *A new Booke of Tabliture, Containing sundrie easie and familiar Instructions, shewing howe to attaine to the knowledge, to guide and dispose thy hand to play on sundry Instruments, as the Lute, Orpharion, and Bandora*, London, 1596.

Bathe, William. *William Bathe. A Briefe Introduction To The True Art of Music*, ed. Cecil Hill, Colorado College Music Press, Critical Texts No. 10, Colorado Springs, Colorado, 1979.

A Briefe Introduction to the skill of Song, London, c. 1596.

Batman, Stephan, after Bartholomæus Anglicus. *Batman vppon Bartholome, His Booke De Proprietatibus Rerum*, London, 1582.

B[ayne], A[lexander]. *An Introduction To The Knowledge And Practice of the Thoro' Bass*, Edinburgh, 1717.

Bedford, Arthur. *The Excellency of Divine Musick: or a Sermon Preach'd at the Parish-Church of St. Michael's Crooked Lane*, London, [1733].

The Great Abuse of Musick, London, 1711.

The Temple Musick: Or, An Essay Concerning the Method of Singing The Psalms of David, London, 1706.

Blount, Thomas. *A World of Errors Discovered in the New World of Words, Or General English Dictionary*, [London], 1673.

Glossographia: or a dictionary interpreting all such hard words, London, 1656; 2nd edition, London, 1661; 3rd edition, London, 1670; 4th edition, London, 1674; 5th edition, London, 1681.

[?Brouncker, Lord]. *Renatvs Des-Cartes Excellent Compendium of Musick: with Necessary and Judicious Animadversions Thereupon. By a Person of Honovr*, London, 1653.

Bruce, Thomas. *The Common Tunes: Or, Scotland's Church Musick Made Plain*, Edinburgh, 1726.

Bullokar, John. *An English expositor: teaching the interpretation of the hardest words vsed in our Language*, London, 1616.

Burwell, Mary. Thurston Dart, 'Miss Mary Burwell's Instruction Book for the Lute', *The Galpin Society Journal*, 11 (May 1958), pp. 3–62.

Butler, Charles. *The Principles of Musik*, London, 1636.

Campion, Thomas. *A New Way of Making Fowre parts in Counter-point, by a most familiar, and infallible Rvle*, London, [1610].

Two Bookes of Ayres, London, [1610].

Cawdrey, Robert. *A Table Alphabeticall*, London, 1604; [2nd edition] by 'T. C.', London, 1609; 3rd edition, London, 1613; 4th edition, London, 1617.

Chambers, Ephraim. *Cyclopædia: Or, An Universal Dictionary Of Arts and Sciences*, London, 1728.

Church, John. *An Introduction to Psalmody*, London, 1723.

Cocker's English Dictionary, London, 1704.

Cockeram, Henry. *The English Dictionarie*, London, 1623.

Coles, Elisha. *An English Dictionary*, London, 1676.

The Compleat Instructor to the Flute, London, 1700.

Cooper, Thomas. *Thesavrvs lingvae romanæ & britannicæ*, London, 1565.

Cotgrave, Randle. *A dictionarie of the French and English tongves*, London, 1611.

[Davidson, Thomas]. *Cantus, Songs and Fancies. To Thre, Foure, or Five Partes, both apt for Voices and Viols. With a briefe introduction of Musick*, Aberdeen, 1662.

D[avis], J[ohn]. *Vocabolario Italiano & Inglese: A Dictionary, Italian and English. First Compiled by John Florio...By Gio. Torriano...Now Reprinted, Revised and Corrected, by J. D.*, London, 1688.

De La Fond, John Francis. *A New System of Music*, London, 1725.

Defoe, B. N. *A Compleat English Dictionary*, Westminster, 1735.

A Dictionarie French and English, [London], 1570/71.

Directions for Playing on the Flute With A Scale for Transposing any Piece of Musick to yͤ properest Keys for that Instrument, London, [after 1731].

Dowland, John. *The First Booke of Songes or Ayres of fowre partes with Tableture for the Lute*, [London], 1597.

Dowland, Robert. *Varietie of Lute-lessons*, London, 1610.

Dyche, Thomas and Pardon, William. *A New General English Dictionary; Peculiarly calculated for the Use and Improvement Of such as are unacquainted with the Learned Languages*, 2nd edition, London, 1737.

Elyot, Thomas. *Bibliotheca Eliotæ...The Dictionary of Syr T. E.*, London, 1538.

An Essay on Musick, wherein is contain'd the Principles of that Science, MS, Bodleian Rawlinson D. 751.

Florio, John. *A Worlde of Wordes, Or Most copious, and exact Dictionarie in Italian and English*, London, 1598.

Qveen Anna's New World of Words, or Dictionarie of the Italian and English tongues, London, 1611.

Fludd, Robert. *Utriusque Cosmi Maioris scilicet et Minoris Metaphysica, Physica atque Technica Historia*, Oppenheim, 1617–24.

Glossographia Anglicana Nova: Or, A Dictionary, Interpreting Such Hard Words of whatever language, as are at present used in the English Tongue, London, 1707.

Gorton, William. *Catechetical Questions in Musick, containing A Hundred and Seventy Questions, Fairly answered and made plain to the meanest Capacity*, London, 1704.

Greeting, Thomas. *The Pleasant Companion: Containing Variety of new Ayres and Pleasant Tunes for the Flagelet. To which is added Plain and Easie Instructions for Beginners*, 6th edition, London, 1683.

The Harpsicord Master Containing plain & easy Instructions for Learners on yͤ Spinnet or Harpsicord, written by yͤ late famous Mʳ. H Purcell at the request of a perticuler friend, & taken from his owne Manuscript, London, 1696, reproduced in *The Harpsicord Master. Book I*, ed. Christopher Hogwood, Oxford University Press, 1980.

Harris, John. *Lexicon Technicum: Or, An Universal English Dictionary of Arts and Sciences*, London, 1704.

Holborne, Anthony. *The Cittharn Schoole*, London, 1597.

Holder, William. *A Treatise of the Natural Grounds, and Principles of Harmony*, London, 1694.

A Treatise of the Natural Grounds, and Principles of Harmony...The whole being Revis'd, and Corrected, London, 1731.

Hollyband, Claudius [also known as Claude Desainliens]. *A Dictionarie French and English:*

Published for the benefite of the studious in that language, London, 1593.

Hotteterre Le Romain. *The Rudiments or Principles of the German Flute...faithfully translated into English*, London, [1729].

Howell, James. *A French-English Dictionary, Compil'd by Mr Randle Cotgrave: With Another in English and French. Whereunto are newly added the Animadversions and Supplements, &c. of James Howell*, London, 1650.

Huloet, Richard. *Abcedarivm Anglico Latinvm*, London, 1552.

Institutions of Musick Wherein are sett forth the Practicall Principles of Musical Composition in Two Parts, MS, appearing at rear of Library of Congress specimen of B[ayne], *An Introduction*, 1717.

Jackson, William. *A Preliminary Discourse To A Scheme, Demonstrating and Shewing The Perfection and Harmony of Sounds*, Westminster, 1726.

K[ersey], J[ohn]. *A New English Dictionary*, London, 1702; 3rd edition, London, 1731.

Dictionarium Anglo-Britannicum: Or, A General English Dictionary, London, 1708.

The New World Of Words: Or, Universal English Dictionary, 6th edition, London, 1706; 7th edition, London, 1720.

Lampe, John Frederick. *A Plain and Compendious Method Of Teaching Thorough Bass*, London, 1737.

The Art of Musick, London, 1740.

Le Roy, Adrien. *A Briefe and easye instrution to learne the tableture to conducte and dispose thy hande vnto the Lute englished by J Alford*, London, 1568.

Lenton, J. *The gentleman's diversion, or the violin explained*, London, 1683; or *The useful instructor of the violin*, 2nd edition, 1702 [presumed source, University of Wales College of Cardiff Music Library, M. C. 1. 90 (title page damaged)].

Letters addressed to Rev. William Holder, MS, BL Sloane 1388.

Locke, Matthew. *Melothesia: Or, Certain General Rules for Playing Upon A Continued-Bass*, London, 1673.

Mace, Thomas. *Musick's Monument; Or, A Remembrancer Of the Best Practical Musick, Both Divine, and Civil*, London, 1676.

Malcolm, Alexander. *A Treatise of Musick, Speculative, Practical, and Historical*, Edinburgh, 1721.

Matteis, Nicola. *The False Consonances of Musick (1682)*, ed. James Tyler, Monaco, Editions Chanterelle S.A., 1980.

Miege, Guy. *The great French Dictionary*, London, 1688.

Minsheu, John. *A dictionarie in Spanish and English, first published into the English tongue by Ric. Perciuale Gent. Now enlarged and amplified with many thousand woords, as by this marke * to each of them prefixed may appeere*, London, 1599.

Morley, Thomas. *A Plaine and Easie Introdvction to Practicall Mvsicke*, London, 1597.

Musical observations and experiments in musical sounds belonging to the Theoric part of music, MS, BL Harley 4160.

A New and Easie Method To Learn to Sing by Book, London, 1686.

Newton, John. *The English Academy: Or, A Brief Introduction to the Seven Liberal Arts*, London, 1677.

[North, Francis]. *A Philosophical Essay of Musick Directed to a Friend*, London, 1677.

North, Roger. An Essay of Musical Ayre, MS, BL Add. 32536.

Capt. Prencourts rules, MS, BL Add. 32549.

The Musicall Gramarian, MS, BL Add. 32533.

The Musicall Grammarian, MS, BL Add. 32537.

Roger North's 'Cursory Notes of Musicke' (c.1698–c.1703) A Physical, Psychological and Critical Theory, ed. Mary Chan and Jamie Kassler, Unisearch, University of New South Wales, 1986.

Roger North on Music. Being a Selection from his Essays written during the years c.1695–1728, ed. John Wilson, London, Novello, 1959.

Roger North's 'The Musicall Grammarian' 1728, ed. Mary Chan and Jamie Kassler, Cambridge University Press, 1990.

Short, Easy, & plaine rules to learne in a few days the principles of Musick, MS, BL Add. 32531.

The Theory of Sounds, MS, BL Add. 32534.

Theory of Sounds, MS, BL Add. 32535.

[Prendcourt's] The treatise of the Continued or thro-base, MS, BL Add. 32531.

[Prendcourt's] The Treatis of the Continued or Through Basse, MS, BL Add. 32549.

Untitled notebook, MS, after 1695, BL Add. 32532.

Ornithoparcus, Andreas. *Andreas Ornithoparcvs His Micrologvs, Or Introdvction: Containing the Art of Singing...[translated] By Iohn Dovland*, London, 1609.

Ortus Vocabulorum, Westminster, 1500.

Papers Relating to the Writings of John Birchensha, MS, BL Add. 4388.

The pathway to Musicke, London, 1596.

[Pepusch, John Christopher]. *A Short Explication Of Such Foreign Words, As are made Use of in Musick Books*, London, 1724.

A Short Treatise on Harmony, London, 1730.

A Treatise on Harmony...The Second Edition, London, 1731.

Perks, John. article 'Musick', *Lexicon Technicum* (ed. John Harris), 2nd edition, 1708–23, vol. II.

P[hillips], E[dward]. *The New World Of English Words: Or, A General Dictionary*, London, 1658; [2nd edition], London, 1662; 3rd edition, London, 1671; 4th edition, London, 1678; 5th edition, London, 1696.

Playford, John. *A breefe introduction to the skill of musick*, [London], 1654; *An Introduction To the Skill of Mvsick*, London, 1655; *A Brief Introduction To The Skill Of Musick*, [reissue of 4th edn] London, 1667; *An Introduction To The Skill of Musick...The Twelfth Edition. Corrected and Amended by Mr. Henry Purcell*, London, 1694; *An Introduction To The Skill of Musick*, 19th edn, London, 1730.

Musick's Delight on the Cithren, London, 1666.

Musicks Recreation: On The Lyra Viol, London, 1652; *Musick's Recreation on The Viol, Lyra-way*, 2nd edition, London, 1682.

The Practicall Theory of Musick—To perform Musick in perfect proportions, MS, BL Add. 4919.

The Praise Of Mvsicke, Oxford, 1586.

The praise of musicke, MS, BL 18. B. xix.

Preceptor for the Improved Octave Flageolet, London, [c.1710].

Prelleur, Pierre. *The Modern Musick-Master Or, The Universal Musician*, London, 1731.

[Purcell, Henry]. *A Choice Collection of Lessons for the Harpsichord or Spinnet...ye late M^r. Henry Purcell*, London, 1696.

Sonnata's of III Parts: Two Viollins And Basse: To the Organ or Harpsecord, London, 1683.

[Puttenham, George]. *The arte of English poesie*, London, 1589.

[Raguenet, François]. *A Comparison Between the French and Italian Musick And Opera's. Translated from the French; With some Remarks*, London, 1709.

Ravenscroft, Thomas. *A Briefe Discovrse Of the true (but neglected) vse of Charact'ring the Degrees*, London, 1614.

Ravenscrofts Treatise of Musick, MS, BL Add. 19758.

Rider, John. *Bibliotheca Scholastica*, Oxford, 1589.

[Riva, Giuseppe]. *Advice To The Composers And Performers of Vocal Musick. Translated from the Italian*, London, 1727.

Roberts, Francis. 'A Discourse concerning the Musical Notes of the Trumpet, and Trumpet-Marine, and of the defects of the same', *Philosophical Transactions of the Royal Society*, no. 195 (October, 1692), pp. 559–63.

Robinson, Daniel. *An essay upon vocal musick*, Nottingham, 1715.

Robinson, Thomas. *The Schoole of Mvsicke*, London, 1603.

Salmon, Thomas. *A Proposal To Perform Musick, In Perfect and Mathematical Proportions...With Large Remarks upon this whole Treatise, By the Reverend and Learned John Wallis*, London, 1688.

A Vindication Of An Essay To the Advancement of Musick, From Mr. Matthew Lock's Observations, London, 1672.

'The Theory of Musick reduced to Arithmetical and Geometrical Proportions', *Philosophical Transactions of the Royal Society*, no. 302 (1705 [no month given]), pp. 2072–7.

Simpson, Christopher. *The Division-Violist: Or An Introduction To the Playing upon a Grovnd*, London, 1659; *The Division-Viol, Or, The Art of Playing Ex tempore upon a Ground*, 2nd edition, London, 1665.

The Principles of Practical Mvsick Delivered In a Compendious, Easie, and New Method, London, 1665; *A Compendium of Practical Musick*, London, 1667.

Tans'ur, William. *A Compleat Melody: or, The Harmony of Sion*, 3rd edition, London, 1736.

Thomas, Thomas. *Dictionarivm Lingvae Latinae et Anglicanae*, London, 1587.

Thomas, William. *Principal rvles of the Italian grammer, with a Dictionary for the better understandyng of Boccacce, Petrarcha, and Dante*, London, 1550.

Torriano, Giovanni. *Vocabolario Italiano & Inglese, A dictionary Italian & English. Formerly Compiled by John Florio*, London, 1659.

Tractatus de Musicâ, MS, BL Add. 4923.

Treatise of the Thoro' Bass, MS, Yale Beinecke, Osborne Shelves, Music MS 3.

Tudway, Thomas. 'Thomas Tudway's History of Music', *Music in Eighteenth-Century England. Essays in Memory of Charles Cudworth*, ed. Christopher Hogwood and Richard Luckett, Cambridge University Press, 1983, pp. 22–46.

Turner, William. *Sound Anatomiz'd, in a Philosophical Essay on Musick*, London, 1724.

Various papers written in the autograph of Dr Christopher Pepusch, MS, BL Add. 29429.

Wallis, John. 'A Letter of Dr. John Wallis to Samuel Pepys Esquire, relating to some supposed Imperfections in an Organ', *Philosophical Transactions of the Royal Society* (1698 [no number or month given]), pp. 249–56.

'A Question in Musick lately proposed to Dr.

Wallis, concerning the Division of the Monochord, or Section of the Musical Canon: With his Answer to it', *Philosophical Transactions of the Royal Society*, no. 238 (March, 1698), pp. 80–4.

Weaver, John. *An Essay Towards an History of Dancing*, London, 1712.

Wither, George. *A Preparation to the Psalter*, [London], 1619.

Primary sources: sources consulted but not quoted

Listed are sources consulted but not quoted in the Dictionary because they were found to contain no usable information. The titles of manuscript items in the British Library generally follow those given in Hughes-Hughes, *Catalogue of Manuscript Music in the British Museum*, vol. III, (London, Trustees of the British Museum, 1965), but may be abbreviated.

Account of an echo, MS, BL Sloane 243.

Analogia inter Alphabetum Hebrajcum et Musicum, MS, BL Sloane 1326.

Apollo's Banquet: Containing Instructions, and Variety of New Tunes, Ayres, and several New Scotch Tunes For The Treble-Violin, 6th edition, [London], 1690.

Bacon, Francis. *Sylva sylvarum: or a naturall historie*, [London], 1626.

Bedford, Athur. Observations concerning Musicke made...1705 or –06 by...Reverend Mr. [Arthur] Bedford, MS, BL Add. 4917.

Bevin, Elway. *A Briefe and Short Instrvction of the Art of Mvsicke*, London, 1631.

The Bird Fancyer's Delight or Choice Observations, And Directions Concerning ye Teaching of all Sorts of Singing-birds, after ye Flagelet & Flute, London, 1717.

Blow, John. Rules for playing of a Through Bass, upon Organ & Harpsicon, MS, BL Add. 34072.

Browne, Richard. *Medicina Musica: Or, A Mechanical Essay on the Effects of Singing, Musick, and Dancing, on Human Bodies*, London, 1729.

Campion, Thomas. *Observations in the Art of English Poesie*, London, 1602.

[Chilmead, Edmund]. *De Musica Antiquâ Græcâ*, Oxford, 1672.

Coliere, Richard. *The Antiquity and Usefulness of Instrumental Musick in the Service of God. In a Sermon Preach'd at Isleworth, In the County of Middlesex*, London, 1738.

A Collection of Rules in Musicke from the Most Knowing Masters in that Science, with M[r.] Birchensha's 6: Rules of Composition; & his Enlargements there-on to the Right Hon[ble] William Lord Viscount Brounckor &c: Collected by Mee. Silas Domvill als Taylor, MS, BL Add. 4917.

The Compleat Tutor to the Hautboy, London, c.1715.

Coprario, John. Rules how to Compose, MS, Huntington Library San Marino, Facsimile edn by Manfred F. Bukofzer, Los Angeles, Ernest E. Gottlieb, 1952.

Coryate, Thomas. *Coryats crudities; hastily gobled up in five moneths travels*, London, 1610.

[Davidson, Thomas]. *Cantus, Songs and Fancies, To Three, Four, or Five Parts, Both apt for Voices and Viols. With a brief Introduction to Musick*, 2nd edition, Aberdeen, 1666.

Definitions of music, etc., in Latin, written in England in a sixteenth-century hand, MS, BL Sloane 1585.

Derham, William. 'Experiments and Observations on the Motion of Sound', *Philosophical Transactions of the Royal Society*, no. 26 (1708 [no month given]), pp. 380–95.

Dodwell, Henry. *A Treatise Concerning the Lawfulness of Instrumental Musick in Holy Offices*, London, 1700.

Dr. Blow's Rules for Composition, MS, BL Add. 30933.

Eccles, Solomon. *A Musick-Lector: Or, The Art of Musick (that is so much vindicated in Christendome) Discoursed of, by way of Dialogue between three men of several Judgments*, London, 1667.

An Essay tending to...a...conjecture att the Temperature and disposition, by the severall musicall modulations of the voyce in ordinary Speech and Discourse, MS, BL Sloane 3087.

Estwick, S[ampson]. *The Vsefulness of Church-Musick. A Sermon Preach'd at Christ-Chvrch, Novemb. 27. 1696. Upon Occasion of the Anniverary-Meeting of the Lovers of Musick, On St. Cœcilia's Day*, London, 1696.

Extracts from Elway Bevin's Introduction to the Art of Musick, 1631...apparently in the hand of Daniel Henstridge, MS, BL Add. 30933.

Extracts relating to music, taken apparently from translations by Portuguese Jesuits of compendia of the arts and sciences, MS, BL Eg. 2063.

Extracts relating to Welsh music, MS, BL Add. 14905.

Farmer, John. *Forty several ways of two parts in one*, London, 1591.

Finch, Edward. *Grammar for Through-Bass*, MS, Euing Collection, Glasgow University Library, R. d. 39.

The First Book of Apollo's Banquet: Containing Instructions, and Variety of New Tunes, Ayres, Jiggs, Minuets, and several New Scotch Tunes, for the Treble-Violin, 7th edition, [London], 1693.

Fragmentary notes, partly in shorthand, on the theory of music, MS BL Sloane 3888.

Fragments relating to music from a MS apparently written in England, MS, BL Royal Appendix 56.

Geminiani, Francesco. *The Art of Playing on the Violin*, London, [no date].

Rules For playing in a true Taste On The Violin[,] German Flute[,] Violoncello And Harpsicord, London, [c.1739].

General Rules for Playing on a Continued Bass, MS, BL Add. 31465.

Hall, Elias. *The Psalm-Singer's Compleat Companion*, London, 1708.

Hely, Benjamin. *The Compleat Violist*, London, [no date].

Hickman, Charles. *A Sermon Preached at St. Bride's Church, on St. Cæcilia's Day, Nov. 22. 1695. Being the Anniversary Feast of the Lovers of Musick*, London, 1696.

Hooke, Robert. A curious Dissertation concerning the Causes of the Power & Effects of Musick, MS, London Royal Society Cl. P. II. 31.

A Dissertation concerning the causes of the Power & Effects of Musick, MS, London Royal Society Cl. P. II. 32.

Hudgebut, John. *A Vade Mecum For the Lovers of Musick, Shewing the Excellency of the Rechorder: With some Rules and Directions for the same*, London, 1679.

Illustrations of prolation, written in England, MS, BL Royal Appendix 58.

Jacob, Hildebrand. *Of The Sister Arts; An Essay*, London, 1734.

Keller, Godfrey. *A Compleat Method For Attaining to Play a Thorough Bass, Upon Either Organ, Harpsicord, or Theorbo-Lute*, London, 1707.

Kersey, John. *Dictionarium Anglo-Britannicum: Or, A General English Dictionary*, 3rd edition, London, 1721.

Lawes, Henry. *Ayres and Dialogues For One, Two, and Three Voyces*, London, 1653.

A letter to a Friend in the Country, Concerning the Use of Instrumental Musick in the Worship of God, London, 1698.

Locke, Matthew. *Observations Upon A Late Book, Entituled, An Essay to the Advancement of Musick*, London, 1672.

The Present Practice of Musick Vindicated Against the Exceptions and New Way of Attaining Musick Lately Publish'd by Thomas Salmon, London, 1673.

Lodge, Thomas. *A Defence of Poetry, Music, and Stage-Plays, by Thomas Lodge*, Printed for the Shakespeare Society (publication no. 48), London, 1853.

'Μανουλ Βρυεννιου, αρμονικων [βιβλια γ]' ... Published, as far as fol. 87, by Dr John Wallis, [no date given], MS, BL Harley 5691.

Memoranda by an Englishman, MS, BL Sloane 2686.

Milbourne, Luke. *Psalmody Recommended in a Sermon Preach'd to the Company of Parish-Clerks, At St. Alban's Woodstreet, November 17. At St. Giles's in the Fields, November 22, 1712*, London, 1713.

A Musicall Banquet, Set forth in three choice Varieties of Musick, London, 1651.

Naish, Thomas. *A Sermon Preach'd at the Cathedral-Church of Sarum, Novemb. 22. 1700. Before a Society of Lovers of Musick*, London, 1701.

Narcissus, Lord Bishop. 'An introductory Essay to the doctrine of Sounds', *Philosophical Transactions of the Royal Society*, no. 156 (February, 1683/4), pp. 472–88.

Notes relating to music, apparently in the hand of Nathaniel Highmore, MS, BL Sloane 581.

Peacham, Henry. *The compleat gentleman*, London, 1622.

Portions of two treatises, of which the second at least is by Sim[on] Vych[an], MS, BL Add. 15046.

Rules; Or a Short and Compleat Method For attaining to Play a Thorough Bass upon the Harpsicord or Organ. By an Eminent Master, London, [no date].

(Rules) To sette a lute, MS, Cambridge, Trinity College MS O 2. 13 (cat. no. 1117), in J. Handschin, 'Aus der alten Musiktheorie', *Acta Musicologica*, 16–17 (1944–45), pp. 1–10, and Christopher Page, 'The 15th-Century Lute: New and Neglected Sources', *Early Music*, 9/1 (January 1981), pp. 11–21.

Salmon, Thomas. *An Essay To the Advancement of Musick*, London, 1672.

Two letters from Thomas Salmon to Sir Hans Sloane, MS, BL Sloane 4040.

Salter, Humphry. *The genteel companion; being exact directions for the recorder*, London, 1683.

Short Treatise in the hand of G. B. Fenoglio, MS, BL Add. 31613.

Simpson, Christopher. *A Compendium: Or, Introduction to Practical Music*, 8th edition, London, 1732.

The Division-Viol: Or, The Art of Playing Ex-tempore upon a Ground, 3rd edition, London, 1712.

South, Robert. *Musica Incantans, Sive Poema Exprimens Musicæ Vires, Juvenem in Insaniam adigentis, Et Musici inde Periculum*, Oxford, 1667.

The Sprightly Companion: Being A Collection of the best Foreign Marches, Now play'd in all Camps...Also Plain and Easy Directions for Playing on the Havtboy, London, 1695.

Stanesby, Thomas. *A new System of the Flute a'bec, or Common English Flute*, [1732?].

Stenhouse, Peter. *The right Use and Improvement of sensitive Pleasures, and more particularly of Musick. A Sermon Preach'd in the Cathedral Church of Gloucester*, London, 1728.

Talbot, James. James Talbot's manuscript (c.1680), Oxford, Christ Church Library, MS 1187, variously reproduced in *The Galpin Society Journal*, 1 (1948), pp. 9–26; 3 (1950), 27–45; 5 (1952), 44–7; 14 (1961), 52–68; 15 (1962), 60–9; 16 (1963), 63–72.

[Tate, Nahum]. *An Essay for Promoting of Psalmody*, London, 1710.

Taylor, Brook. 'De motu Nervi tensi', *Philosophical Transactions of the Royal Society* (1713 [no number or month given]), pp. 26–32.

To all true preachers (short treatise by Hugh Kinge in defence of music and dancing), MS, BL Harley 2019.

Tomlinson, Kellom. *The Art of Dancing Explained by Reading and Figures*, London, 1735.

Traité de La Musique Moderne...MDCCII, MS, BL Add. 4918.

Traité de l'Harmonie...MDCCXXXIII, MS, BL Add. 6137.

Transcript, said to have been made for Dr. Pepusch, MS, BL Add. 4912.

Transcripts by Dr. Pepusch of the musical portions of Tiberius, MS, BL Add. 4909.

Treatise in Welsh on the four kinds of music, MS, BL Add. 15038.

Treatises, or extracts from treatises, on music, in the hand of, and some of them probably compiled, if not written, by John Tucke, MS, BL Add. 10336.

Treatises, poems, and other fragments relating to music, MS, BL Sloane 1021.

[Vossius, Isaac]. *De Poematum Cantu et Viribus Rythmi*, Oxford, 1673.

Wallis, John. 'A Letter of Dr. John Wallis, to Mr. Andrew Fletcher; concerning the strange Effects reported of Musick in Former Times, beyond what is to be found in Later Ages', *Philosophical Transactions of the Royal Society*, no. 243 (August, 1698), pp. 297–303.

'Dr. Wallis's Letter to the Publisher, concerning a new Musical Discovery', *Philosophical Transactions of the Royal Society*, no. 134 (April, 1677), pp. 839–42.

Claudii Ptolemæi Harmonicorum Libri Tres, Oxford, 1682.

Operum Mathematicorum, Oxford, 1693–99.

Warren, Ambrose. *The Tonometer*, Westminster, 1725.

Webbe, William. *A discourse of English Poetrie*, London, 1586.

Yonge, Nicholas. *Musica Transalpina*, London, 1588.

Anthologies consulted

Smith, George Gregory (ed.). *Elizabethan Critical Essays*, 2 vols., Oxford, Clarendon Press, 1904.

Spingarn, J. E. (ed.). *Critical Essays of the Seventeenth Century*, 3 vols., Bloomington, Indiana University Press, 1963.

Strunk, Oliver (ed.). *Source Readings in Music History*, New York, Norton, 1950.

Secondary sources

Atcherson, Walter. 'Key and Mode in Seventeenth-Century Music Theory Books', *Journal of Music Theory*, 17/2 (Fall 1973), pp. 204–33.

'Symposium on Seventeenth-Century Music Theory: England', *Journal of Music Theory*, 16 (1972), pp. 6–15.

Bailey, Richard (ed.). *Dictionaries of English. Prospects for the Record of Our Language*, Ann Arbor, The University of Michigan Press, 1987.

Bately, Janet M.. 'Ray, Worlidge, and Kersey's Revision of The New World of English Words', *Anglia. Zeitschrift für Englische Philologie*, 85 (1967), pp. 1–14.

Brown, Howard Mayer and Sadie, Stanley (eds.). *Performance Practice. Music after 1600*, The New Grove Handbooks in Music, London, Macmillan Press, 1989.

Performance Practice. Music before 1600, The New Grove Handbooks in Music, London, Macmillan Press, 1989.

Burchfield, Robert (ed.). *Studies in Lexicography*, Oxford University Press, 1987.

Carter, Henry Holland. *A Dictionary of Middle English Musical Terms*, Indiana University Humanities Series 45, Bloomington, Indiana University Press, 1961, reprinted New York, Kraus Reprint Corporation, 1968.

Chenette, Louis Fred. 'Musick Theory in the British Isles during the Enlightenment', Ph.D. dissertation, Ohio State University, 1967.

Collison, Robert L. *A History of Foreign-Language Dictionaries*, London, Andre Deutsch, 1982.

Dictionaries of English and Foreign Languages. A Bibliographic Guide to both General and Technical

Dictionaries with Historical and Explanatory Notes and References, 2nd edition, New York, Hafner Publishing Company, 1971.

Encyclopaedias: Their History Through the Ages, 2nd edition, New York and London, Hafner Publishing Company, 1966.

Congleton, J. E., Gates, J. Edward, and Hobar, Donald. *Papers on Lexicography in Honor of Warren N. Cordell*, The Dictionary Society of North America, Indiana State University, 1979.

Cooper, Barry. 'Englische Musiktheorie im 17. und 18. Jahrhundert', *Geschichte der Musiktheorie*, vol. IX, Darmstadt, Wissenschaftliche Buchgesellschaft, 1986, pp. 141–329.

Coover, James B. 'Dictionaries and Encyclopedias of Music', *The New Grove Dictionary of Music and Musicians*, ed. Stanley Sadie, London, Macmillan, 1980, vol. V, pp. 432–6.

'Lacunae in Music Dictionaries and Encyclopedias' and 'A Non-Evaluative Checklist of Music Dictionaries and Encyclopedias', *Cum Notis Variorum*, 115, 116, 117 and 118 (Aug./Sep.–Dec. 1987), and 119, 120 and 121 (Jan./Feb.–Apr. 1988), occupying whole issues.

Music Lexicography, 3rd edition, Carlisle, Pennsylvania, Carlisle Books, 1971.

Dart, Thurston. 'Music and Musical Instruments in Cotgrave's *Dictionarie* (1611)', *The Galpin Society Journal*, 21 (1968), pp. 70–80.

Early English Books 1641–1700, 9 vols., Ann Arbor, Michigan, University Microfilms Incorporated, 1990.

Eggebrecht, Hans Heinrich (ed.). *Handwörterbuch der musikalischen Terminologie*, Wiesbaden, Franz Steiner Verlag, 1972–.

Görlach, Manfred. *Introduction to Early Modern English*, Cambridge University Press, 1991.

Hayashi, Tetsuro. *The Theory of English Lexicography 1530–1791*, Amsterdam Studies in the Theory and History of Linguistic Science, ed. E. F. K. Koerner, series III (Studies in the History of Linguistics), vol. xviii, Amsterdam, John Benjamins B.V., 1978.

Houle, George. *Meter in Music, 1600–1800. Performance, Perception, and Notation*, Bloomington, Indiana University Press, 1987.

Hughes-Hughes, Augustus. *Catalogue of Manuscript Music in the British Museum*, vol. III (Instrumental Music, Treatises, etc.), London, Trustees of the British Museum, 1965.

Humphries, Charles and Smith, William C. *Music Publishing in the British Isles*, second edition, Oxford, Basil Blackwell, 1970.

Kafker, Frank A. (ed.). *Notable Encyclopedias of the Seventeenth and Eighteenth Centuries: Nine Predecessors of the Encyclopédie*, Oxford, The Voltaire Foundation at the Taylor Institution, 1981.

Kassler, Jamie C. *The Science of Music in Britain, 1714–1830. A Catalogue of Writings, Lectures and Inventions*, 2 vols., New York and London, Garland Publishing, 1979.

Koopman, Ton. *Barok Muziek. Theorie en Praktijk*, Utrecht/Antwerp, Bohn Scheltema & Holkema, 1985.

The New Grove Dictionary of Music and Musicians, ed. Stanley Sadie, London, Macmillan, 1980.

The New Grove Dictionary of Musical Instruments, ed. Stanley Sadie, London, Macmillan, 1984.

Oliver, Alfred Richard. *The Encyclopedists as Critics of Music*, New York, Columbia University Press, 1947, and New York, AMS Press, 1966.

The Oxford English Dictionary, 2nd edition, Oxford, Clarendon Press, 1989.

Padelford, Frederick Morgan. *Old English Musical Terms*, Portland, Maine, Longwood Press, 1976 (first published Bonn, 1899).

Palisca, Claude V. *Humanism in Italian Renaissance Musical Thought*, New Haven and London, Yale University Press, 1985.

'Theory, theorists', *The New Grove Dictionary of Music and Musicians*, ed. Stanley Sadie, London, Macmillan, 1980, vol. xviii, pp. 741–62.

Pollard, A. W., and Redgrave, G. R. *A Short-Title Catalogue of Books Printed in England, Scotland, & Ireland And of English Books Printed Abroad 1475–1640*, 2nd edition, 2 vols., London, The Bibliographical Society, 1976–86.

Price, Curtis. *Henry Purcell and the London Stage*, Cambridge University Press, 1984.

Music in the Restoration Theatre. With a Catalogue of Instrumental Music in the Plays 1665–1713, Ann Arbor, UMI Research Press, 1979.

Riddell, James A. 'Attitudes Towards English Lexicography in the Seventeenth Century', *Papers on Lexicography in Honor of Warren N. Cordell*, ed. J. E. Congleton, J. Edward Gates and Donald Hobar, Indiana State University, The Dictionary Society of North America, 1979, pp. 83–91.

'The Reliability of Early English Dictionaries', *The Yearbook of English Studies*, 4 (1974), pp. 1–4.

Roche, Jerome and Elizabeth. *A Dictionary of Early Music, from the Troubadours to Monteverdi*, London, Faber, 1981.

Ruff, Lillian M. 'The 17th Century English Music Theorists', Ph.D. dissertation, University of Nottingham, 1962.

Schäffer, Jürgen. *Early Modern English Lexicography. Volume I. A Survey of Monolingual Printed Glossaries and Dictionaries 1475–1640*, Oxford University Press, 1989.

Smalley, Vera E. *The Sources of 'A Dictionarie of the French and English Tongues' by Randle Cotgrave (London, 1611). A Study in Renaissance Lexicography*, The Johns Hopkins Studies in Romance Literatures and Languages, extra vol. xxv, Baltimore, The Johns Hopkins Press, 1948.

Starnes, De Witt T. 'John Florio Reconsidered', *Texas Studies in Literature and Language*, 6/4 (1965), pp. 407–22.

Renaissance Dictionaries. English–Latin and Latin–English, Austin, University of Texas Press, 1954.

Starnes, De Witt T. and Noyes, Gertrude E. *The English Dictionary from Cawdrey to Johnson 1604–1755*, new edition with intro. and select bibliography by Gabriele Stein, Amsterdam and Philadelphia, John Benjamins, 1991.

Starnes, De Witt T. and Talbert, Ernest William. *Classical Myth and Legend in Renaissance Dictionaries. A Study of Renaissance Dictionaries in their Relation to the Classical Learning of Contemporary English Writers*, Chapel Hill, The University of North Carolina Press, 1955.

Stein, Gabriele. *The English Dictionary before Cawdrey*, Tübingen, Max Niemeyer Verlag, 1985.

Stephen, Leslie and Lee, Sidney (eds.). *The Dictionary of National Biography*, London, Oxford University Press, 1917 onwards, (reprint 1949–50).

Strahle, Graham. 'Fantasy and Music in Sixteenth and Seventeenth Century England', Ph.D. dissertation, University of Adelaide, 1987.

Tonelli, Giorgio. *A Short-Title List of Subject Dictionaries of the Sixteenth, Seventeenth and Eighteenth Centuries as Aids to the History of Ideas*, Warburg Institute Surveys, 4, Warburg Institute, University of London, 1971.

Warner, Thomas E. *An Annotated Bibliography of Woodwind Instruction Books, 1600–1830*, Detroit, Information Coordinators, Inc., 1967.

Wing, Donald. *Short-Title Catalogue of Books Printed in England, Scotland, Ireland, Wales, And British America And of English Books Printed in Other Countries 1641–1700*, 2nd edition, 3 vols., New York, Index Committee of the Modern Language Association of America, 1972–88.

Zimmerman, Franklin B. (intro. and glossary). *'An Introduction to the Skill of Musick' by John Playford: the Twelfth Edition Corrected and Amended by Henry Purcell*, New York, Da Capo Press, 1972.

Printed in Great Britain
by Amazon